T0180492

# Lecture Notes in Computer Science 9532

Commenced Publication in 1973
Founding and Former Series Editors:
Gerhard Goos, Juris Hartmanis, and Jan van Leeuwen

More information about this series at http://www.springer.com/series/7407

Guojun Wang · Albert Zomaya
Gregorio Martinez Perez · Kenli Li (Eds.)

# Algorithms and Architectures for Parallel Processing

ICA3PP International Workshops and Symposiums
Zhangjiajie, China, November 18–20, 2015
Proceedings

 Springer

*Editors*
Guojun Wang
Central South University
Changsha
China

Albert Zomaya
The University of Sydney
Sydney, NSW
Australia

Gregorio Martinez Perez
University of Murcia
Murcia
Spain

Kenli Li
Hunan University
Changsha
China

ISSN 0302-9743 ISSN 1611-3349 (electronic)
Lecture Notes in Computer Science
ISBN 978-3-319-27160-6 ISBN 978-3-319-27161-3 (eBook)
DOI 10.1007/978-3-319-27161-3

Library of Congress Control Number: 2015955380

LNCS Sublibrary: SL1 – Theoretical Computer Science and General Issues

Springer Cham Heidelberg New York Dordrecht London

Springer International Publishing AG Switzerland is part of Springer Science+Business Media
(www.springer.com)

# Welcome Message from the ICA3PP 2015 General Chairs

Welcome to the proceedings of the 15th International Conference on Algorithms and Architectures for Parallel Processing (ICA3PP 2015), which was organized by Central South University, Hunan University, National University of Defense Technology, and Jishou University.

It was our great pleasure to organize the ICA3PP 2015 conference in Zhangjiajie, China, during November 18–20, 2015. On behalf of the Organizing Committee of the conference, we would like to express our cordial gratitude to all participants who attended the conference.

ICA3PP 2015 was the 15th event in the series of conferences started in 1995 that is devoted to algorithms and architectures for parallel processing. ICA3PP is now recognized as the main regular event in the world that covers many dimensions of parallel algorithms and architectures, encompassing fundamental theoretical approaches, practical experimental projects, and commercial components and systems. The conference provides a forum for academics and practitioners from around the world to exchange ideas for improving the efficiency, performance, reliability, security, and interoperability of computing systems and applications.

ICA3PP 2015 attracted high-quality research papers highlighting the foundational work that strives to push beyond the limits of existing technologies, including experimental efforts, innovative systems, and investigations that identify weaknesses in existing parallel processing technology.

ICA3PP 2015 consisted of the main conference and six international symposia and workshops. Many individuals contributed to the success of the conference. We would like to express our special appreciation to Prof. Yang Xiang, Prof. Andrzej Goscinski, and Prof. Yi Pan, the Steering Committee chairs, for giving us the opportunity to host this prestigious conference and for their guidance with the conference organization. Special thanks to the program chairs, Prof. Albert Zomaya, Prof. Gregorio Martinez Perez, and Prof. Kenli Li, for their outstanding work on the technical program. Thanks also to the workshop chairs, Dr. Mianxiong Dong, Dr. Ryan K.L. Ko, and Dr. Md. Zakirul Alam Bhuiya, for their excellent work in organizing attractive symposia and workshops. Thanks also to the publicity chairs, Prof. Carlos Becker Westphall, Dr. Yulei Wu, Prof. Christian Callegari, Prof. Kuan-Ching Li, and Prof. James J. (Jong Hyuk) Park, for the great job in publicizing this event. We would like to give our thanks to all the members of the Organizing Committee and Program Committee as well as the external reviewers for their efforts and support. We would also like to give our thanks to the keynote speakers, Prof. John C.S. Lui, Prof. Jiannong Cao, Prof. Wanlei Zhou, and Prof. Hai Jin, for offering insightful and enlightening talks. Last but not least, we would like to thank all the authors who submitted their papers to the conference.

November 2015

Guojun Wang
Peter Mueller
Qingping Zhou

# Welcome Message from the ICA3PP 2015 Program Chairs

On behalf of the Program Committee of the 15th International Conference on Algorithms and Architectures for Parallel Processing (ICA3PP 2015), we would like to welcome you to join the conference held in Zhangjiajie, China, during November 18–20, 2015.

The ICA3PP conference aims at bringing together researchers and practitioners from both academia and industry who are working on algorithms and architectures for parallel processing. The conference features keynote speeches, panel discussions, technical presentations, symposiums, and workshops, where the technical presentations from both the research community and industry cover various aspects including fundamental theoretical approaches, practical experimental projects, and commercial components and systems. ICA3PP 2015 was the next event in a series of highly successful international conferences on algorithms and architectures for parallel processing, previously held as ICA3PP 2014 (Dalian, China, August 2014), ICA3PP 2013 (Vietri sul Mare, Italy, December 2013), ICA3PP 2012 (Fukuoka, Japan, September 2012), ICA3PP 2011 (Melbourne, Australia, October 2011), ICA3PP 2010 (Busan, Korea, May 2010), ICA3PP 2009 (Taipei, Taiwan, June 2009), ICA3PP 2008 (Cyprus, June 2008), ICA3PP 2007 (Hangzhou, China, June 2007), ICA3PP 2005 (Melbourne, Australia, October 2005), ICA3PP 2002 (Beijing, China, October 2002), ICA3PP2000 (Hong Kong, China, December 2000), ICA3PP 1997 (Melbourne, Australia, December 1997), ICA3PP 1996 (Singapore, June 1996), and ICA3PP 1995 (Brisbane, Australia, April 1995).

The ICA3PP 2015 conference collected research papers on related research issues from all around the world. This year we received 602 submissions for the main conference. All submissions received at least three reviews during a high-quality review process. According to the review results, 219 papers were selected for oral presentation at the conference, giving an acceptance rate of 36.4 %.

We would like to offer our gratitude to Prof. Yang Xiang and Prof. Andrzej Goscinski from Deakin University, Australia, and Prof. Yi Pan from Georgia State University, USA, the Steering Committee chairs. Our thanks also go to the general chairs, Prof. Guojun Wang from Central South University, China, Dr. Peter Mueller from IBM Zurich Research, Switzerland, and Prof. Qingping Zhou from Jishou University, China, for their great support and good suggestions for a successful the final program. Special thanks to the workshop chairs, Dr. Mianxiong Dong from Muroran Institute of Technology, Japan, and Dr. Ryan K.L. Ko from the University of Waikato, New Zealand, and Dr. Md. Zakirul Alam Bhuiyan from Temple University, USA. In particular, we would like to give our thanks to all researchers and practitioners who submitted their manuscripts, and to the Program Committee and the external reviewers who contributed their valuable time and expertise to provide professional reviews working under a very tight schedule. Moreover, we are very grateful to our keynote speakers who kindly accepted our invitation to give insightful and prospective talks.

Finally, we believe that the conference provided a very good opportunity for participants to learn from each other. We hope you enjoy the conference proceedings.

Albert Zomaya
Gregorio Martinez Perez
Kenli Li

# Welcome Message from the ICA3PP 2015 Workshop Chairs

Welcome to the proceedings of the 15th International Conference on Algorithms and Architectures for Parallel Processing (ICA3PP 2015) held in Zhangjiajie, China, during November 18–20, 2015. The program this year consisted of six symposiums/workshops covering a wide range of research topics on parallel processing technology:

(1) The 6th International Workshop on Trust, Security and Privacy for Big Data (TrustData 2015)
(2) The 5th International Symposium on Trust, Security and Privacy for Emerging Applications (TSP 2015)
(3) The Third International Workshop on Network Optimization and Performance Evaluation (NOPE 2015)
(4) The Second International Symposium on Sensor-Cloud Systems (SCS 2015)
(5) The Second International Workshop on Security and Privacy Protection in Computer and Network Systems (SPPCN 2015)
(6) The First International Symposium on Dependability in Sensor, Cloud, and Big Data Systems and Applications (DependSys 2015)

The aim of these symposiums/workshops is to provide a forum to bring together practitioners and researchers from academia and industry for discussion and presentations on the current research and future directions related to parallel processing technology. The themes and topics of these symposiums/workshops are a valuable complement to the overall scope of ICA3PP 2015 providing additional values and interests. We hope that all of the selected papers will have a good impact on future research in the respective field.

The ICA3PP 2015 workshops collected research papers on the related research issues from all around the world. This year we received 205 submissions for all workshops. All submissions received at least three reviews during a high-quality review process. According to the review results, 77 papers were selected for oral presentation at the conference, giving an acceptance rate of 37.6 %.

We offer our sincere gratitude to the workshop organizers for their hard work in designing the call for papers, assembling the Program Committee, managing the peer-review process for the selection of papers, and planning the workshop program. We are grateful to the workshop Program Committees, external reviewers, session chairs, contributing authors, and attendees. Our special thanks to the Organizing Committees of ICA3PP 2015 for their strong support, and especially to the program chairs, Prof. Albert Zomaya, Prof. Gregorio Martinez Perez, and Prof. Kenli Li, for their guidance.

Finally, we hope that you will find the proceedings interesting and stimulating.

Mianxiong Dong
Ryan K.L. Ko
Md. Zakirul Alam Bhuiyan

# Welcome Message from the TrustData 2015 Program Chairs

The 6th International Workshop on Trust, Security and Privacy for Big Data (TrustData 2015) was held in Zhangjiajie, China.

TrustData aims at bringing together people from both academia and industry to present their most recent work related to trust, security, and privacy issues in big data, and to exchange ideas and thoughts in order to identify emerging research topics and define the future of big data.

TrustData 2015 was the next event in a series of highly successful international workshops, previously held as TrustData 2014 (Dalian, China, March 2012) and TrustData 2013 (Zhangjiajie, China, November, 2013).

This international workshop collected research papers on the aforementioned research issues from all around the world. Each paper was reviewed by at least three experts in the field. We feel very proud of the high participation, and although it was difficult to collect the best papers from all the submissions received, we feel we managed to have an amazing conference that was enjoyed by all participants.

We would like to offer our gratitude to the general chairs, Dr. Qin Liu and Dr. Muhammad Bashir Abdullahi, for their excellent support and invaluable suggestions for a successful final program. In particular, we would like to thank all researchers and practitioners who submitted their manuscripts, and the Program Committee members and additional reviewers for their tremendous efforts and timely reviews.

We hope you enjoy the proceedings of TrustData 2015.

Keqin Li
Avinash Srinivasan

# Welcome Message from the TSP 2015 Program Chairs

On behalf of the Program Committee of the 5th International Symposium on Trust, Security and Privacy for Emerging Applications (TSP 2015), we would like to welcome you to the proceedings of the event, which was held in Zhangjiajie, China.

The symposium focuses on trust, security, and privacy issues in social networks, cloud computing, Internet of Things (IoT), wireless sensor networks, and other networking environments or system applications; it also provides a forum for presenting and discussing emerging ideas and trends in this highly challenging research area. The aim of this symposium is to provide a leading edge forum to foster interaction between researchers and developers with the trust, security, and privacy issues, and to give attendees an opportunity to network with experts in this area.

Following the success of TSP 2008 in Shanghai, China, during December 17–20, 2008, TSP 2009 in Macau SAR, China, during October 12–14, 2009, TSP 2010 in Bradford, UK, during June 29–July 1, 2010, and TSP 2013 in Zhangjiajie, China, during November 13–15, 2013, the 5th International Symposium on Trust, Security and Privacy for Emerging Applications (TSP 2015) was held in Zhangjiajie, China, during November 18–20, 2015, in conjunction with the 15th International Conference on Algorithms and Architectures for Parallel Processing (ICA3PP 2015).

The symposium collected research papers on the aforementioned research issues from all around the world. Each paper was reviewed by at least two experts in the field. We realized an amazing symposium that we hope was enjoyed by all the participants.

We would like to thank all researchers and practitioners who submitted their manuscripts, and the Program Committee members and additional reviewers for their tremendous efforts and timely reviews.

We hope you enjoy the proceedings of TSP 2015.

Imad Jawhar
Deqing Zou

# Welcome Message from the NOPE 2015 Program Chair

Welcome to the proceedings of the 2015 International Workshop on Network Optimization and Performance Evaluation (NOPE 2015) held in Zhangjiajie, China, during November 18–20, 2015.

Network optimization and performance evaluation is a topic that attracts much attention in network/Internet and distributed systems. Due to the recent advances in Internet-based applications as well as WLANs, wireless home networks, wireless sensor networks, wireless mesh networks, and cloud computing, we are witnessing a variety of new technologies. However, these systems and networks are becoming very large and complex, and consuming a great amount of energy at the same time. System optimization and performance evaluation remain to be resolved before these systems become a commodity.

On behalf of the Organizing Committee, we would like to take this opportunity to express our gratitude to all reviewers who worked hard to finish reviews on time. Thanks to the publicity chairs for their efforts and support. Thanks also to all authors for their great support and contribution to the event. We would like to give our special thanks to the Organizing Committee, colleagues, and friends who worked hard behind the scenes. Without their unfailing cooperation, hard work, and dedication, this event would not have been successfully organized.

We are grateful to everyone for participating in NOPE 2015.

Gaocai Wang

# Welcome Message from SCS 2015 Program Chairs

As the Program Chairs and on behalf of the Organizing Committee of the Second International Symposium on Sensor-Cloud Systems (SCS 2015), we would like to express our gratitude to all the participants who attended the symposium in Zhangjiajie, China, during November 18–20, 2015. This famous city is the location of China's first forest park (The Zhangjiajie National Forest Park) and a World Natural Heritage site (Wulingyuan Scenic Area).

The aim of SCS is to bring together researchers and practitioners working on sensor-cloud systems to present and discuss emerging ideas and trends in this highly challenging research field. It has attracted some high-quality research papers, which highlight the foundational work that strives to push beyond limits of existing technologies, including experimental efforts, innovative systems, and investigations that identify weaknesses in the existing technology services.

SCS 2015 was sponsored by the National Natural Science Foundation of China, Springer, the School of Information Science and Engineering at Central South University, and the School of Software at Central South University, and it was organized by Central South University, Hunan University, National University of Defense Technology, and Jishou University. SCS 2015 was held in conjunction with the 15th International Conference on Algorithms and Architectures for Parallel Processing (ICA3PP 2015), which highlights the latest research trends in various aspects of computer science and technology.

Many individuals contributed to the success of this international symposium. We would like to express our special appreciation to the general chairs of main conference, Prof. Guojun Wang, Prof. Peter Mueller, and Prof. Qingping Zhou, for giving us this opportunity to hold this symposium and for their guidance in the organization. Thanks also to the general chairs of this symposium, Prof. Jie Li and Prof. Dongqing Xie, for their excellent work in organizing the symposium. We would like to give our thanks to all the members of the Organizing Committee and Program Committee for their efforts and support.

Finally, we are grateful to the authors for submitting their fine work to SCS 2015 and all the participants for their attendance.

Xiaofei Xing
Md. Zakirul Alam Bhuiyan

# Welcome Message from the SPPCN 2015 Program Chairs

On behalf of the Program Committee of the Second International Workshop on Security and Privacy Protection in Computer and Network Systems (SPPCN 2015), we would like to welcome you to join the proceedings of the workshop, which was held in Zhangjiajie, China.

The workshop focuses on security and privacy protection in computer and network systems, such as authentication, access control, availability, integrity, privacy, confidentiality, dependability, and sustainability issues of computer and network systems. The aim of the workshop is to provide a leading-edge forum to foster interaction between researchers and developers working on security and privacy protection in computer and network systems, and to give attendees an opportunity to network with experts in this area.

SPPCN 2015 was the next event in a series of highly successful international conferences on security and privacy protection in computer and network systems, previously held as SPPCN 2014 (Dalian, China, December 2014). The workshop collected research papers on the above research issues from all around the world. Each paper was reviewed by at least two experts in the field.

We would like to offer our gratitude to the general chair, Prof. Jian Weng, for his excellent support and contribution to the success of the final program. In particular, we would like to thank all researchers and practitioners who submitted their manuscripts, and the Program Committee members and additional reviewers for their tremendous efforts and timely reviews.

We hope all of you enjoy the proceedings of SPPCN 2015.

Mianxiong Dong
Hua Guo
Tieming Cheng
Kaimin Wei

# Welcome Message from the DependSys 2015 Program Chairs

As the program chairs and on behalf of the Organizing Committee of the First International Symposium on Dependability in Sensor, Cloud, and Big Data Systems and Applications (DependSys2015), we would like to express our gratitude to all the participants attending the international symposium in Zhangjiajie, China, during November 18–20, 2015. This famous city is the location of China's first forest park (The Zhangjiajie National Forest Park) and a World Natural Heritage site (Wulingyuan Scenic Area).

DependSys is a timely event that brings together new ideas, techniques, and solutions for dependability and its issues in sensor, cloud, and big data systems and applications. As we are deep into the Information Age, we are witnessing the explosive growth of data available on the Internet. Human beings are producing quintillion bytes of data every day, which come from sensors, individual archives, social networks, Internet of Things, enterprises, and the Internet in all scales and formats. One of the most challenging issues we face is to achieve the designed system performance to an expected level, i.e., how to effectively provide dependability in sensor, cloud, and big data systems. These systems need to typically run continuously, which often tend to become inert, brittle, and vulnerable after a while.

This international symposium collected research papers on the aforementioned research issues from all around the world. Although it was the first event of DependSys, we received a large number of submissions in response to the call for papers. Each paper was reviewed by at least three experts in the field. After detailed discussions among the program chairs and general chairs, a set of quality papers was finally accepted. We are very proud of the high number of participations, and it was difficult to collect the best papers from all the submissions.

Many individuals contributed to the success of this high-caliber international symposium. We would like to express our special appreciation to the steering chairs, Prof. Jie Wu and Prof. Guojun Wang, for giving us the opportunity to hold this symposium and for their guidance in the symposium organization. In particular, we would like to give our thanks to the symposium chairs, Prof. Mohammed Atiquzzaman, Prof. Sheikh Iqbal Ahamed, and Dr. Md Zakirul Alam Bhuiyan, for their excellent support and invaluable suggestions for a successful final program. Thanks to all the Program Committee members and the additional reviewers for their tremendous efforts and timely reviews.

We hope you enjoy the proceedings of DependSys 2015.

Latifur Khan
Joarder Kamruzzaman
Al-Sakib Khan Pathan

# Organization

## ICA3PP 2015 Organizing and Program Committees

### General Chairs

| | |
|---|---|
| Guojun Wang | Central South University, China |
| Peter Mueller | IBM Zurich Research, Switzerland |
| Qingping Zhou | Jishou University, China |

### Program Chairs

| | |
|---|---|
| Albert Zomaya | University of Sydney, Australia |
| Gregorio Martinez Perez | University of Murcia, Spain |
| Kenli Li | Hunan University, China |

### Steering Chairs

| | |
|---|---|
| Andrzej Goscinski | Deakin University, Australia |
| Yi Pan | Georgia State University, USA |
| Yang Xiang | Deakin University, Australia |

### Workshop Chairs

| | |
|---|---|
| Mianxiong Dong | Muroran Institute of Technology, Japan |
| Ryan K.L. Ko | The University of Waikato, New Zealand |
| Md. Zakirul Alam Bhuiyan | Central South University, China |

### Publicity Chairs

| | |
|---|---|
| Carlos Becker Westphall | Federal University of Santa Catarina, Brazil |
| Yulei Wu | The University of Exeter, UK |
| Christian Callegari | University of Pisa, Italy |
| Kuan-Ching Li | Providence University, Taiwan |
| James J. (Jong Hyuk) Park | SeoulTech, Korea |

### Publication Chairs

| | |
|---|---|
| Jin Zheng | Central South University, China |
| Wenjun Jiang | Hunan University, China |

# Finance Chairs

Pin Liu                     Central South University, China
Wang Yang                   Central South University, China

# Local Arrangements Chairs

Fang Qi                     Central South University, China
Qin Liu                     Hunan University, China
Hongzhi Xu                  Jishou University, China

# Program Committee

# 1. Parallel and Distributed Architectures Track

## Chairs

Stefano Giordano            Italian National Interuniversity Consortium
                              for Telecommunications, Italy
Xiaofei Liao                Huazhong University of Science and Technology,
                              China
Haikun Liu                  Nanyang Technological University, Singapore

## TPC Members

Marco Aldinucci             Universitá degli Studi di Torino, Italy
Yungang Bao                 Chinese Academy of Sciences, China
Hui Chen                    Auburn University, USA
Vladimir Getov              University of Westminster, UK
Jie Jia                     Northeastern University, China
Yusen Li                    Nanyang Technological University, Singapore
Zengxiang Li                Agency for Science, Technology and Research,
                              Singapore
Xue Liu                     Northeastern University, China
Yongchao Liu                Georgia Institute of Technology, USA
Salvatore Orlando           Universitá Ca' Foscari Venezia, Italy
Nicola Tonellotto           ISTI-CNR, Italy
Zeke Wang                   Nanyang Technological University, Singapore
Quanqing Xu                 Agency for Science, Technology and Research
                              (A*STAR), Singapore
Ramin Yahyapour             University of Göttingen, Germany
Jidong Zhai                 Tsinghua University, China
Jianlong Zhong              GraphSQL Inc., USA
Andrei Tchernykh            CICESE Research Center, Ensenada, Baja California,
                              Mexico

## 2. Software Systems and Programming Track

**Chairs**

| | |
|---|---|
| Xinjun Mao | National University of Defense Technology, China |
| Sanaa Sharafeddine | Lebanese American University, Beirut, Lebanon |

**TPC Members**

| | |
|---|---|
| Surendra Byna | Lawrence Berkeley National Lab, USA |
| Yue-Shan Chang | National Taipei University, Taiwan |
| Massimo Coppola | ISTI-CNR, Italy |
| Marco Danelutto | University of Pisa, Italy |
| Jose Daniel Garcia | Carlos III of Madrid University, Spain |
| Peter Kilpatrick | Queen's University Belfast, UK |
| Soo-Kyun Kim | PaiChai University, Korea |
| Rajeev Raje | Indiana University-Purdue University Indianapolis, USA |
| Salvatore Ruggieri | University of Pisa, Italy |
| Subhash Saini | NASA, USA |
| Peter Strazdins | The Australian National University, Australia |
| Domenico Talia | University of Calabria, Italy |
| Hiroyuki Tomiyama | Ritsumeikan University, Japan |
| Canqun Yang | National University of Defense Technology, China |
| Daniel Andresen | Kansas State University, USA |
| Sven-Bodo Scholz | Heriot-Watt University, UK |
| Salvatore Venticinque | Second University of Naples, Italy |

## 3. Distributed and Network-Based Computing Track

**Chairs**

| | |
|---|---|
| Casimer DeCusatis | Marist College, USA |
| Qi Wang | University of the West of Scotland, UK |

**TPC Members**

| | |
|---|---|
| Justin Baijian | Purdue University, USA |
| Aparicio Carranza | City University of New York, USA |
| Tzung-Shi Chen | National University of Tainan, Taiwan |
| Ciprian Dobre | University Politehnica of Bucharest, Romania |
| Longxiang Gao | Deakin University, Australia |
| Ansgar Gerlicher | Stuttgart Media University, Germany |
| Harald Gjermundrod | University of Nicosia, Cyprus |
| Christos Grecos | Independent Imaging Consultant, UK |
| Jia Hu | Liverpool Hope University, UK |
| Baback Izadi | State University of New York at New Paltz, USA |
| Morihiro Kuga | Kumamoto University, Japan |
| Mikolaj Leszczuk | AGH University of Science and Technology, Poland |

| Paul Lu | University of Alberta, Canada |
| Chunbo Luo | University of the West of Scotland, UK |
| Ioannis Papapanagiotou | Purdue University, USA |
| Michael Hobbs | Deakin University, Australia |
| Cosimo Anglano | Università del Piemonte Orientale, Italy |
| Md. ObaidurRahman | Dhaka University of Engineering and Technology, Bangladesh |
| Aniello Castiglione | University of Salerno, Italy |
| Shuhong Chen | Hunan Institute of Engineering, China |

## 4. Big Data and Its Applications Track

### Chairs

| Jose M. Alcaraz Calero | University of the West of Scotland, UK |
| Shui Yu | Deakin University, Australia |

### TPC Members

| Alba Amato | Second University of Naples, Italy |
| Tania Cerquitelli | Politecnico di Torino, Italy |
| Zizhong (Jeffrey) Chen | University of California at Riverside, USA |
| Alfredo Cuzzocrea | University of Calabria, Italy |
| Saptarshi Debroy | University of Missouri-Columbia, USA |
| Yacine Djemaiel | Communication Networks and Security, Res. Lab, Tunisia |
| Shadi Ibrahim | Inria, France |
| Hongwei Li | UESTC, China |
| William Liu | Auckland University of Technology, New Zealand |
| Xiao Liu | East China Normal University, China |
| Karampelas Panagiotis | Hellenic Air Force Academy, Greece |
| Florin Pop | University Politehnica of Bucharest, Romania |
| Genoveva Vargas Solar | CNRS-LIG-LAFMIA, France |
| Chen Wang | CSIRO ICT Centre, Australia |
| Chao-Tung Yang | Tunghai University, Taiwan |
| Peng Zhang | Stony Brook University, USA |
| Ling Zhen | Southeast University, China |
| Roger Zimmermann | National University of Singapore, Singapore |
| Francesco Palmieri | University of Salerno, Italy |
| Rajiv Ranjan | CSIRO, Canberra, Australia |
| Felix Cuadrado | Queen Mary University of London, UK |
| Nilimesh Halder | The University of Western Australia, Australia |
| Kuan-Chou Lai | National Taichung University of Education, Taiwan |
| Jaafar Gaber | UTBM, France |
| Eunok Paek | Hanyang University, Korea |
| You-Chiun Wang | National Sun Yat-sen University, Taiwan |
| Ke Gu | Changsha University of Technology, China |

## 5. Parallel and Distributed Algorithms Track

**Chairs**

| | |
|---|---|
| Dimitris A. Pados | The State University of New York at Buffalo, USA |
| Baoliu Ye | Nanjing University, China |

**TPC Members**

| | |
|---|---|
| George Bosilca | University of Tennessee, USA |
| Massimo Cafaro | University of Salento, Italy |
| Stefania Colonnese | Universitá degli Studi di Roma La Sapienza, Italy |
| Raphael Couturier | University of Franche Comte, France |
| Gregoire Danoy | University of Luxembourg, Luxembourg |
| Franco Frattolillo | Universitá del Sannio, Italy |
| Che-Rung Lee | National Tsing Hua University, Taiwan |
| Laurent Lefevre | Inria, ENS-Lyon, University of Lyon, France |
| Amit Majumdar | San Diego Supercomputer Center, USA |
| Susumu Matsumae | Saga University, Japan |
| George N. Karystinos | Technical University of Crete, Greece |
| Dana Petcu | West University of Timisoara, Romania |
| Francoise Sailhan | CNAM, France |
| Uwe Tangen | Ruhr-Universität Bochum, Germany |
| Wei Xue | Tsinghua University, China |
| Kalyan S. Perumalla | Oak Ridge National Laboratory, USA |
| Morris Riedel | University of Iceland, Germany |
| Gianluigi Folino | ICAR-CNR, Italy |
| Joanna Kolodziej | Cracow University of Technology, Poland |
| Luc Bougé | ENS Rennes, France |
| Hirotaka Ono | Kyushu University, Japan |
| Tansel Ozyer | TOBB Economics and Technology University, Turkey |
| Daniel Grosu | Wayne State University, USA |
| Tian Wang | Huaqiao University, China |
| Sancheng Peng | Zhaoqing University, China |
| Fang Qi | Central South University, China |
| Zhe Tang | Central South University, China |
| Jin Zheng | Central South University, China |

## 6. Applications of Parallel and Distributed Computing Track

**Chairs**

| | |
|---|---|
| Yu Chen | Binghamton University, State University of New York, USA |
| Michal Wozniak | Wroclaw University of Technology, Poland |

**TPC Members**

| | |
|---|---|
| Jose Alfredo F. Costa | Universidade Federal do Rio Grande do Norte, Brazil |
| Robert Burduk | Wroclaw University of Technology, Poland |
| Boguslaw Cyganek | AGH University of Science and Technology, Poland |
| Paolo Gasti | New York Institute of Technology, USA |
| Manuel Grana | University of the Basque Country, Spain |
| Houcine Hassan | Universidad Politecnica de Valencia, Spain |
| Alvaro Herrero | Universidad de Burgos, Spain |
| Jin Kocsis | University of Akron, USA |
| Esmond Ng | Lawrence Berkeley National Lab, USA |
| Dragan Simic | University of Novi Sad, Serbia |
| Ching-Lung Su | National Yunlin University of Science and Technology, Taiwan |
| Tomoaki Tsumura | Nagoya Institute of Technology, Japan |
| Krzysztof Walkowiak | Wroclaw University of Technology, Poland |
| Zi-Ang (John) Zhang | Binghamton University-SUNY, USA |
| Yunhui Zheng | IBM Research, USA |
| Hsi-Ya Chang | National Center for High-Performance Computing, Taiwan |
| Chun-Yu Lin | HTC Corp., Taiwan |
| Nikzad Babaii Rizvandi | The University of Sydney, Australia |

# 7. Service Dependability and Security in Distributed and Parallel Systems Track

**Chairs**

| | |
|---|---|
| Antonio Ruiz Martinez | University of Murcia, Spain |
| Jun Zhang | Deakin University, Australia |

**TPC Members**

| | |
|---|---|
| Jorge Bernal Bernabe | University of Murcia, Spain |
| Roberto Di Pietro | Universitá di Roma Tre, Italy |
| Massimo Ficco | Second University of Naples (SUN), Italy |
| Yonggang Huang | Beijing Institute of Technology, China |
| Georgios Kambourakis | University of the Aegean, Greece |
| Muhammad Khurram Khan | King Saud University, Saudi Arabia |
| Liang Luo | Southwest University, China |
| Barbara Masucci | Universitá di Salerno, Italy |
| Juan M. Marin | University of Murcia, Spain |
| Sabu M. Thampi | Indian Institute of Information Technology and Management – Kerala (IIITM-K), India |
| Fernando Pereniguez-Garcia | Catholic University of Murcia, Spain |
| Yongli Ren | RMIT University, Australia |
| Yu Wang | Deakin University, Australia |
| Sheng Wen | Deakin University, Australia |

| | |
|---|---|
| Mazdak Zamani | Universiti Teknologi Malaysia, Malaysia |
| Susan K. Donohue | University of Virginia, USA |
| Oana Boncalo | University Politehnica Timisoara, Romania |
| K.P. Lam | University of Keele, UK |
| George Loukas | University of Greenwich, UK |
| Ugo Fiore | Federico II University, Italy |
| Christian Esposito | University of Salerno, Italy |
| Arcangelo Castiglione | University of Salerno, Italy |
| Edward Jung | Kennesaw State University, USA |
| Md. Zakirul Alam Bhuiyan | Central South University, China |
| Xiaofei Xing | Guangzhou University, China |
| Qin Liu | Hunan University, China |
| Wenjun Jiang | Hunan University, China |
| Gaocai Wang | Guangxi University, China |
| Kaimin Wei | Jinan University, China |

## 8. Web Services and Internet Computing Track

### Chairs

| | |
|---|---|
| Huansheng Ning | University of Science and Technology Beijing, China |
| Daqiang Zhang | Tongji University, China |

### TPC Members

| | |
|---|---|
| Jing Chen | National Cheng Kung University, Taiwan |
| Eugen Dedu | University of Franche-Comte, France |
| Sotirios G. Ziavras | NJIT, USA |
| Luis Javier Garcia Villalba | Universidad Complutense de Madrid (UCM), Spain |
| Jaime Lloret | Universidad Politecnica de Valencia, Spain |
| Wei Lu | Keene University, USA |
| Stefano Marrone | Second University of Naples, Italy |
| Alejandro Masrur | Chemnitz University of Technology, Germany |
| Seungmin (Charlie) Rho | Sungkyul University, Korea |
| Giandomenico Spezzano | ICAR-CNR, Italy |
| Jiafu Wan | South China University of Technology, China |
| Yunsheng Wang | Kettering University, USA |
| Martine Wedlake | IBM, USA |
| Chung Wei-Ho | Research Center for Information Technology Innovation in Academia Sinica, Taiwan |
| Xingquan (Hill) Zhu | Florida Atlantic University, USA |
| Nikos Dimitriou | National Center for Scientific Research Demokritos, Greece |
| Choi Jaeho | CBNU, Chonju, Korea |
| Shi-Jinn Horng | National Taiwan University of Science and Technology, Taiwan |

## 9. Performance Modeling and Evaluation Track

### Chairs

| | |
|---|---|
| Deze Zeng | China University of Geosciences, China |
| Bofeng Zhang | Shanghai University, China |

### TPC Members

| | |
|---|---|
| Ladjel Bellatreche | ENSMA, France |
| Xiaoju Dong | Shanghai Jiao Tong University, China |
| Christian Engelman | Oak Ridge National Lab, USA |
| Javier Garcia Blas | University Carlos III, Spain |
| Mauro Iacono | Second University of Naples, Italy |
| Zhiyang Li | Dalian Maritime University, China |
| Tomas Margalef | Universitat Autonoma de Barcelona, Spain |
| Francesco Moscato | Second University of Naples, Italy |
| Heng Qi | Dalian University of Technology, China |
| Bing Shi | Wuhan University of Technology, China |
| Magdalena Szmajduch | Cracow University of Technology, Poland |
| Qian Wang | Wuhan University, China |
| Zhibo Wang | Wuhan University, China |
| Weigang Wu | Sun Yat-sen University, China |
| David E. Singh | University Carlos III of Madrid, Spain |
| Edmund Lai | Massey University, New Zealand |
| Robert J. Latham | Argonne National Laboratory, USA |
| Zafeirios Papazachos | Queen's University of Belfast, UK |
| Novella Bartolini | Sapienza University of Rome, Italy |
| Takeshi Nanri | Kyushu University, Japan |
| Mais Nijim | Texas A&M University – Kingsville, USA |
| Salvador Petit | Universitat Politècnica de València, Spain |
| Daisuke Takahashi | University of Tsukuba, Japan |
| Cathryn Peoples | Ulster University, Northern Ireland, UK |
| Hamid Sarbazi-Azad | Sharif University of Technology and IPM, Iran |
| Md. Abdur Razzaque | University of Dhaka, Bangladesh |
| Angelo Brayner | University of Fortaleza, Brazil |
| Sushil Prasad | Georgia State University, USA |
| Danilo Ardagna | Politecnico di Milano, Italy |
| Sun-Yuan Hsieh | National Cheng Kung University, Taiwan |
| Li Chaoliang | Hunan University of Commerce, China |
| Yongming Xie | Hunan Normal University, China |
| Guojun Wang | Central South University, China |

## Secretariats

Zhe Tang                Central South University, China
Feng Wang               Central South University, China

## Webmaster

Xiangdong Lee           Central South University, China

# TrustData 2015 Organizing and Program Committees

## Steering Chairs

Guojun Wang      Central South University, China
Peter Mueller      IBM Zurich Research Laboratory, Switzerland

## General Chairs

Qin Liu      Hunan University, China
Muhammad Bashir      Federal University of Technology, Minna, Nigeria
  Abdullahi

## Program Chairs

Keqin Li      State University of New York at New Paltz, USA
Avinash Srinivasan      Temple University, USA

## Publicity Chairs

Shui Yu      Deakin University, Australia
Weirong Liu      Central South University, China

## Program Committee

| | |
|---|---|
| Andrei Tchernykh | CICESE Research Center, Mexico |
| Baoliu Ye | Nanjing University, China |
| Bimal Roy | Indian Statistical Institute, India |
| Chang-Ai Sun | University of Science and Technology, China |
| Chao Song | University of Electronic Science and Technology of China, China |
| Christian Callegari | The University of Pisa, Italy |
| Chunhua Su | Japan Advanced Institute of Science and Technology, Japan |
| Franco Chiaraluce | Polytechnical University of Marche (UVPM), Italy |
| Hai Jiang | Arkansas State University, USA |
| Horacio Gonzalez-Velez | National College of Ireland, Ireland |
| Imed Romdhani | Edinburgh Napier University, UK |
| Jianguo Yao | Shanghai Jiao Tong University, China |
| Joon S. Park | Syracuse University, USA |
| Kevin Chan | US Army Research Laboratory, USA |
| Lizhe Wang | Rochester Institute of Technology, USA |

# TSP 2015 Organizing and Program Committees

## Program Chairs

| | |
|---|---|
| Imad Jawhar | United Arab Emirates University, UAE |
| Deqing Zou | Huazhong University of Science of Technology |

## Program Committee Members

| | |
|---|---|
| Chao Song | University of Electronic Science and Technology, China |
| David Zheng | Frostburg State University, USA |
| Feng Li | Indiana University-Purdue University Indianapolis, USA |
| Haitao Lang | Beijing University of Chemical Technology, China |
| Huan Zhou | China Three Gorges University, China |
| Mingjun Xiao | University of Science and Technology of China, China |
| Mingwu Zhang | Hubei University of Technology, China |
| Shuhui Yang | Purdue University Calumet, USA |
| Xiaojun Hei | Huazhong University of Science and Technology, China |
| Xin Li | Nanjing University of Aeronautics and Astronautics, China |
| Xuanxia Yao | University of Science and Technology Beijing, China |
| Yaxiong Zhao | Google Inc., USA |
| Ying Dai | LinkedIn Corporation, USA |
| Yunsheng Wang | Kettering University, USA |
| Youwen Zhu | Nanjing University of Aeronautics and Astronautics, China |
| Yongming Xie | Changsha Medical University, China |

## Steering Committee

| | |
|---|---|
| Wenjun Jiang | Hunan University, China (Chair) |
| Laurence T. Yang | St. Francis Xavier University, Canada |
| Guojun Wang | Central South University, China |
| Minyi Guo | Shanghai Jiao Tong University, China |
| Jie Li | University of Tsukuba, Japan |
| Jianhua Ma | Hosei University, Japan |
| Peter Mueller | IBM Zurich Research Laboratory, Switzerland |
| Indrakshi Ray | Colorado State University, USA |

| Kouichi Sakurai | Kyushu University, Japan |
| Bhavani Thuraisingham | The University of Texas at Dallas, USA |
| Jie Wu | Temple University, USA |
| Yang Xiang | Deakin University, Australia |
| Kun Yang | University of Essex, UK |
| Wanlei Zhou | Deakin University, Australia |

## Web Chair

| Shan Peng | Central South University, China |

# NOPE 2015 Organizing and Program Committees

## Steering Committee Chairs

| | |
|---|---|
| Wei Li | Texas Southern University, USA |
| Taoshen Li | Guangxi University, China |

## Program Chair

| | |
|---|---|
| Gaocai Wang | Guangxi University, China |

## Program Committee Members

| | |
|---|---|
| Dieter Fiems | Ghent University, Belgium |
| Shuqiang Huang | Jinan University, China |
| Juan F. Perez | Imperial College London, UK |
| Haoqian Wang | Tsinghua University, China |
| Yitian Peng | Southeast University, China |
| Hongbin Chen | Guilin University of Electronic Technology, China |
| Jin Ye | Guangxi University, China |
| Junbin Liang | Hong Kong Polytechnic University, Hong Kong, SAR China |
| Xianfeng Liu | Hunan Normal University, China |
| Hao Zhang | Central South University, China |
| Chuyuan Wei | Beijing University of Civil Engineering and Architecture, China |
| Hongyun Xu | South China University of Technology, China |
| Zhefu Shi | University of Missouri, USA |
| Songfeng Lu | Huazhong University of Science and Technology, China |
| Yihui Deng | Jinan University, China |
| Lei Zhang | Beijing University of Civil Engineering and Architecture, China |
| Xiaoheng Deng | Central South University, China |
| Mingxing Luo | Southwest Jiaotong University, China |
| Bin Sun | Beijing University of Posts and Telecommunications, China |
| Zhiwei Wang | Nanjing University of Posts and Telecommunications, China |
| Yousheng Zhou | Chongqing University of Posts and Telecommunications, China |
| Daofeng Li | Guangxi University, China |

# SCS 2015 Organizing and Program Committees

## Steering Chairs

Jie Li      Tsukuba University, Japan
Dongqing Xie      Guangzhou University, China

## Program Chairs

Xiaofei Xing      Guangzhou University, China
Md. Zakirul Alam Bhuiyan      Central South University, China
     and Temple University, USA

## Program Committee Members

Marco Aiello      University of Groningen, The Netherlands
David Chadwick      University of Kent, UK
Aparicio Carranza      City University of New York, USA
Mooi Choo Chuah      Lehigh University, USA
Yueming Deng      Hunan Normal University, China
Christos Grecos      Independent Imaging Consultant, UK
Dritan Kaleshi      University of Bristol, UK
Donghyun Kim      North Carolina Central University, USA
Santosh Kumar      University of Memphis, USA
Muthoni Masinde      University of Nairobi, Kenya
Satyjayant Mishra      New Mexico State University, USA
Nam Nguyen      Towson University, USA
Jean-Marc Seigneur      University of Geneva, Switzerland
Hamid Sharif      University of Nebraska, USA
Sheng Wen      Deakin University, Australia

## Publicity Chairs

Zeyu Sun      Xi'an Jiaotong University, China
Yongming Xie      Hunan Normal University, China

# SPPCN 2015 Organizing and Program Committees

## General Chair

Jian Weng                 Jinan University, China

## Program Chairs

| | |
|---|---|
| Mianxiong Dong | Muroran Institute of Technology, Japan |
| Hua Guo | Beihang University, China |
| Tieming Chen | Zhejiang University of Technology, China |
| Kaimin Wei | Jinan University, China |

## Program Committee

| | |
|---|---|
| Fuchun Guo | University of Wollongong, Australia |
| Jianguang Han | Nanjing University of Finance and Economics, Nanjing, China |
| Debiao He | Wuhan University, China |
| Xinyi Huang | Fujian Normal University, China |
| Xuanya Li | Chinese Academy of Sciences, China |
| Fengyong Li | Shanghai University of Electric Power, China |
| Changlu Lin | Fujian Normal University, China |
| Chang Xu | Beijing Institute of Technology, China |
| Tao Xu | University of Jinan, China |
| Yanjiang Yang | I2R, Singapore |
| Yang Tian | Beihang University, China |
| Shengbao Wang | Hangzhou Normal University, China |
| Wei Wu | Fujian Normal University, China |
| Xiyong Zhang | Information Engineering University, China |
| Lei Zhao | Wuhan University, China |

# DependSys 2015 Organizing and Program Committees

## Steering Committee Chairs

| | |
|---|---|
| Jie Wu | Temple University, USA |
| Guojun Wang | Central South University, China |

## General Chairs

| | |
|---|---|
| Mohammed Atiquzzaman | University of Oklahoma, USA |
| Sheikh Iqbal Ahamed | Marquette University, USA |
| Md. Zakirul Alam Bhuiyan | Central South University, China and Temple University, USA |

## Program Chairs

| | |
|---|---|
| Latifur Khan | The University of Texas at Dallas, USA |
| Joarder Kamruzzaman | Federation University and Monash University, Australia |
| Al-Sakib Khan Pathan | International Islamic University Malaysia, Malaysia |

## Program Committee Members

| | |
|---|---|
| A.B.M Shawkat Ali | The University of Fiji, Fiji |
| A.B.M. Alim Al Islam | Bangladesh University of Engineering and Technology, Bangladesh |
| A. Sohel Ferdous | University of Western Australia, Australia |
| A.K.M. Najmul Islam | University of Turku, Finland |
| Abdul Azim Mohammad | Gyeongsang National University, South Korea |
| Abdur Rouf Mohammad | Dhaka University of Engineering and Technology, Bangladesh |
| Afrand Agah | West Chester University of Pennsylvania, USA |
| Andreas Pashalidis | Katholieke Universiteit Leuven – iMinds, Belgium |
| Asaduzzaman | Chittagong University of Engineering and Technology, Bangladesh |
| C. Chiu Tan | Temple University, USA |
| Changyu Dong | University of Strathclyde, UK |
| Dana Petcu | West University of Timisoara, Romania |
| Daqiang Zhang | Tongji University, China |
| Farzana Rahman | James Madison University, USA |
| Hugo Miranda | University of Lisbon, Portugal |
| Jaydip Sen | National Institute of Science and Technology, India |
| Jianfeng Yang | Wuhan University, China |
| Jinkyu Jeong | Sungkyunkwan University, South Korea |

| | |
|---|---|
| Kaoru Ota | Muroran Institute of Technology, Japan |
| Karampelas Panagiotis | Hellenic Air Force Academy, Greece |
| Lien-Wu Chen | Feng Chia University, Taiwan |
| Liu Jialin | Texas Tech University, USA |
| M.M.A. Hashem | Khulna University of Engineering and Technology, Bangladesh |
| M. Thampi Sabu | Indian Institute of Information Technology and Management, India |
| Mahbub Habib Sheikh | CASED/TU Darmstadt, Germany |
| Mahmuda Naznin | Bangladesh University of Engineering and Technology, Bangladesh |
| Mamoun Alazab | Australian National University, Australia |
| Manuel Mazzara | Innopolis University, Russia |
| Md. Abdur Razzaque | University of Dhaka, Bangladesh |
| Md. Arafatur Rahman | University Malaysia Pahang, Malaysia |
| Mohammad Asad Rehman Chaudhry | University of Toronto, Canada |
| Md. Obaidur Rahman | Dhaka University of Engineering and Technology, Bangladesh |
| Md. Rafiul Hassan | King Fahd University of Petroleum and Minerals, Saudi Arabia |
| Md. Saiful Azad | American International University, Bangladesh |
| Mehran Asadi | Lincoln University of Pennsylvania, USA |
| Mohamad Badra | Zayed University, UAE |
| Mohamed Guerroumi | University of Sciences and Technology Houari Boumediene, Algeria |
| Mohammad Asadul Hoque | East Tennessee State University, USA |
| Mohammad Mehedi Hassan | King Saud University, Saudi Arabia |
| Mohammad Shahriar Rahman | University of Asia Pacific, Bangladesh |
| Mohammed Shamsul Alam | International Islamic University Chittagong, Bangladesh |
| Morshed Chowdhury | Deakin University, Australia |
| Muhammad Mostafa Monowar | King AbdulAziz University, Saudi Arabia |
| N. Musau Felix | Kenyatta University, Kenya |
| Phan Cong | Vinh Nguyen Tat Thanh University, Vietnam |
| Qin Liu | Hunan University, China |
| Ragib Hasan | University of Alabama at Birmingham, USA |
| Raza Hasan | Middle East College, Oman |
| Reaz Ahmed | University of Waterloo, Canada |
| Risat Mahmud Pathan | Chalmers University of Technology, Sweden |
| S.M. Kamruzzaman | King Saud University, Saudi Arabia |
| Salvatore Distefano | Politecnico di Milano, Italy |
| Shan Lin | Stony Brook University, USA |
| Shao Jie Tang | University of Texas at Dallas, USA |
| Sheng Wen | Deakin University, Australia |

| | |
|---|---|
| Shigeng Zhang | Central South University, China |
| Sk. Md. Mizanur Rahman | King Saud University, Saudi Arabia |
| Subrota Mondal | Hong Kong University of Science and Technology, Hong Kong, SAR China |
| Syed Imran Ali | Middle East College, Oman |
| Tanveer Ahsan | International Islamic University Chittagong, Bangladesh |
| Tanzima Hashem | Bangladesh University of Engineering and Technology, Bangladesh |
| Tao Li | The Hong Kong Polytechnic University, Hong Kong, SAR China |
| Tarem Ahmed | BRAC University, Bangladesh |
| Tian Wang | Huaqiao University, China |
| Tzung-Shi Chen | National University of Tainan, Taiwan |
| Vaskar Raychoudhury | Indian Institute of Technology Roorkee, India |
| Wahid Khan | University of Saskatchewan, Canada |
| Weigang Li | University of Brasilia, Brazil |
| Weigang Wu | Sun Yat-sen University, China |
| William Liu | Auckland University of Technology, New Zealand |
| Xiaofei Xing | Guangzhou University, China |
| Xuefeng Liu | The Hong Kong Polytechnic University, Hong Kong, SAR China |
| Xuyun Zhang | University of Melbourne, Australia |
| Yacine Djemaiel | Communication Networks and Security, Res. Lab, Tunisia |
| Yifan Zhang | Binghamton University, USA |
| Yu Wang | Deakin University, Australia |

## Publication Chairs

| | |
|---|---|
| Jin Zheng | Central South University, China |
| Wenjun Jiang | Hunan University, China |

## Local Arrangements Chairs

| | |
|---|---|
| Fang Qi | Central South University, China |
| Qin Liu | Hunan University, China |
| Hongzhi Xu | Jishou University, China |

## Finance Chairs

| | |
|---|---|
| Pin Liu | Central South University, China |
| Wang Yang | Central South University, China |

## Web Chair

| | |
|---|---|
| Min Guo | Central South University, China |

# Contents

**The 6th International Workshop on Trust, Security and Privacy for Big Data (TrustData 2015)**

Nth-Order Multifunction Filter Employing Current Differencing Transconductance Amplifiers .................................. 3
    *Meili Cao, Haizhen He, Rongming Luo, and Lei Wen*

An Efficient Spatial Query Processing Algorithm in Multi-sink Directional Sensor Network ........................................... 13
    *Zheng Ma, Jin Zheng, Weijia Jia, and Guojun Wang*

An Improved Method for Reversible Data Hiding in Encrypted Image ...... 24
    *Yuling Liu and Zuhong Liu*

Study on Personalized Location Privacy Preservation Algorithms Based on Road Networks ........................................... 35
    *Hongyun Xu, Jun Yang, Yong Zhang, Mengzhen Xu, and Jiayi Gan*

A Hierarchical Identity-Based Signature from Composite Order Bilinear Groups ...................................................... 46
    *Peixin Chen, Xiaofeng Wang, and Jinshu Su*

STRATUS: Towards Returning Data Control to Cloud Users ........... 57
    *Ryan K.L. Ko, Giovanni Russello, Richard Nelson, Shaoning Pang,*
    *Aloysius Cheang, Gill Dobbie, Abdolhossein Sarrafzadeh,*
    *Sivadon Chaisiri, Muhammad Rizwan Asghar, and Geoffrey Holmes*

VSEP: A Distributed Algorithm for Graph Edge Partitioning ........... 71
    *Yu Zhang, Yanbing Liu, Jing Yu, Ping Liu, and Li Guo*

Scheduling Stochastic Tasks with Precedence Constrain on Cluster Systems with Heterogenous Communication Architecture ..................... 85
    *Qun Liao, Shuangshuang Jiang, Qiaoxiang Hei, Tao Li, and Yulu Yang*

An Output-Oriented Approach of Test Data Generation Based on Genetic Algorithm ................................................ 100
    *Weixiang Zhang, Bo Wei, and Huisen Du*

**The 5th International Symposium on Trust, Security and Privacy
for Emerging Applications (TSP-15)**

An Efficient Pre-filter to Accelerate Regular Expression Matching . . . . . . . .   111
   *Chengcheng Xu, Shuhui Chen, Xiaofeng Wang, and Jinshu Su*

A Hybrid Optimization Approach for Anonymizing Transactional Data . . . . .   120
   *Li-e Wang and Xianxian Li*

Program Obfuscator for Privacy-Carrying Unidirectional One-hop
Re-encryption . . . . . . . . . . . . . . . . . . . . . . . . . . . . . . . . . . . . . . . .   133
   *Mingwu Zhang, Biwen Chen, and Hua Shen*

Predicting Severity of Software Vulnerability Based on Grey System
Theory . . . . . . . . . . . . . . . . . . . . . . . . . . . . . . . . . . . . . . . . . . . . .   143
   *Jinkun Geng, Daren Ye, and Ping Luo*

Characterization of Android Applications with Root Exploit by Using Static
Feature Analysis . . . . . . . . . . . . . . . . . . . . . . . . . . . . . . . . . . . . . . .   153
   *Huikang Hao, Zhoujun Li, Yueying He, and Jinxin Ma*

LIP3: A Lightweighted Fine-Grained Privacy-Preserving Profile Matching
Mechanism for Mobile Social Networks in Proximity . . . . . . . . . . . . . . . .   166
   *Yufeng Wang, Xiaohong Chen, Qun Jin, and Jianhua Ma*

Context-Aware QoS Assurance for Smart Grid Big Data Processing
with Elastic Cloud Resource Reconfiguration . . . . . . . . . . . . . . . . . . . . .   177
   *Luyan Nie, Chuanzhi Xie, Yujun Yin, and Xin Li*

Continuous User Identity Verification for Trusted Operators in Control
Rooms . . . . . . . . . . . . . . . . . . . . . . . . . . . . . . . . . . . . . . . . . . . . . .   187
   *Enrico Schiavone, Andrea Ceccarelli, and Andrea Bondavalli*

Leakage-Resilient Anonymous Identity-Based Broadcast Encryption
in the Standard Model . . . . . . . . . . . . . . . . . . . . . . . . . . . . . . . . . . . .   201
   *Leyou Zhang, Zhuanning Wang, and Qing Wu*

Scheduling Resource of IaaS Clouds for Energy Saving Based
on Predicting the Overloading Status of Physical Machines . . . . . . . . . . . . .   211
   *Qingxin Xia, Yuqing Lan, and Limin Xiao*

Towards Mechanised Semantics of HPC: The BSP with Subgroup
Synchronisation Case . . . . . . . . . . . . . . . . . . . . . . . . . . . . . . . . . . . . .   222
   *Jean Fortin and Frédéric Gava*

Cloud Computing Threats and Provider Security Assessment . . . . . . . . . . . .   238
   *Huiming Yu, Ken Williams, and Xiaohong Yuan*

Collaborative Multiparty Association Rules Mining with Threshold
Homomorphic Encryption ................................. 251
 *Marcin Gorawski, Zacheusz Siedlecki, and Anna Gorawska*

An Illegal Indirect Access Prevention Method in Transparent Computing
System ................................................ 264
 *Wenjuan Tang, Yang Xu, Guojun Wang, and Yaoxue Zhang*

EPAMP: An Anonymous Multicast Protocol in Mobile Ad Hoc Networks... 276
 *Hongling Xiao, Hong Song, and Weiping Wang*

**The 3rd International Workshop on Network Optimization
and Performance Evaluation (NOPE 2015)**

Energy Saving Mechanism Analysis Based on Dynamic Resource Scaling
for Cloud Computing...................................... 293
 *Xiaojie Zhang, Nao Wang, Xin Zheng, Caocai Wang, and Dongmei Bin*

An Optimal Rate Adaptive Video Streaming Scheme to Improve QoE
of Dash ............................................... 302
 *Xiaolong Gong, Gaocai Wang, and Nao Wang*

Community-Based Energy-Aware Routing Protocol in Mobile Social
Networks............................................... 311
 *Dongmei Bin, Ying Peng, and Gaocai Wang*

Research of CMABC Algorithm in Intrusion Detection ............... 322
 *Ming Liu, Xiaoling Yang, Fanling Huang, and Yanming Fu*

A Parallel Tabu Search Algorithm with Solution Space Partition
for Cohesive Clustering Problems ........................... 333
 *Zheng Xu and Buyang Cao*

Symmetric Game for Distributed Estimation in Energy Harvesting Wireless
Sensor Networks with Selfish Sensors ........................ 344
 *Guiyun Liu, Jing Yao, Hongbin Chen, Han Zhang, and Dong Tang*

File Creation Optimization for Metadata-Intensive Application in File
Systems................................................ 353
 *Limin Xiao, Qiaoling Zhong, Zhisheng Huo, Ang Li, Li Ruan,
 Kelong Liu, Yuanyuan Zang, and Zheqi Lu*

A Sharing-Memory Based Ring Framework ...................... 364
 *Shicong Ma, Baosheng Wang, Xianming Gao, and Xiaozhe Zhang*

Streaming Computing Technology for Android Applications:
Design Model and Case Study .............................. 370
 *Binji Mo, Yang Xu, and Guojun Wang*

An Energy-Efficient Aggregation and Collection Algorithm
for Heterogeneous Wireless Sensor Network. . . . . . . . . . . . . . . . . . . . . . .    382
    *Lifang Liu, Xiaogang Qi, Gengzhong Zheng, and Mande Xie*

TDD-Based Massive MIMO Systems: Overview and Development . . . . . . . .    393
    *Ronghua Shi, Kun Tang, Jian Dong, Wentai Lei, Chunhua Peng,
    and Yunxiang Jiang*

**The 2nd International Symposium on Sensor-Cloud Systems (SCS 2015)**

A Hierarchical Shared Key Algorithm in Wireless Sensor Networks . . . . . . .    405
    *Zeyu Sun, Weiguo Wu, Xiaofei Xing, Chuanfeng Li, Yalin Nie,
    and Yangjie Cao*

Evaluation Model of the Cloud Systems Based on Queuing Petri Net . . . . . .    413
    *Yangjie Cao, Huimin Lu, Xiaodong Shi, and Pengsong Duan*

MTCPP: Multi-targets K-Coverage Preservation Protocol in Wireless
Sensor Networks. . . . . . . . . . . . . . . . . . . . . . . . . . . . . . . . . . . . . . . . .    424
    *Liu Yang*

**The 2nd Workshop on Security and Privacy Protection in Computer
and Network Systems (SPPCN 2015)**

Design Flaws in a Secure Medical Data Exchange Protocol Based on Cloud
Environments . . . . . . . . . . . . . . . . . . . . . . . . . . . . . . . . . . . . . . . . . . . .    435
    *Chun-Ta Li, Cheng-Chi Lee, Chun-Cheng Wang, Tzu-Hui Yang,
    and Song-Jhih Chen*

Privacy Preserving Personalization in Probabilistic Search . . . . . . . . . . . . . .    445
    *Rajeswary Ravi and Greeshma N. Gopal*

A Security-Critical Task Management Method for Distributed Real-Time
Systems . . . . . . . . . . . . . . . . . . . . . . . . . . . . . . . . . . . . . . . . . . . . . . . . .    454
    *Yang Yu, Qi Dong, Zhipeng Luo, Hao Chen, Jun Deng, and Wei Guan*

A Model of Dynamic Malware Analysis Based on VMI . . . . . . . . . . . . . . .    465
    *Chengye Li, Yangyue Xiang, and Jiangyong Shi*

Multiple Secret Sharing Using Natural Language Letter Based Visual
Cryptography Scheme . . . . . . . . . . . . . . . . . . . . . . . . . . . . . . . . . . . . . . .    476
    *Roshni Kadeparambil Raphel, H. Muhammed Ilyas,
    and Janu R. Panicker*

Reconstruction of Android Applications' Network Behavior Based
on Application Layer Traffic . . . . . . . . . . . . . . . . . . . . . . . . . . . . . . . . . .    487
    *Qun Li, Lei Zhang, Shifeng Hou, Zhenxiang Chen, and Hongbo Han*

Android Malware Network Behavior Analysis at HTTP Protocol Packet
Level. . . . . . . . . . . . . . . . . . . . . . . . . . . . . . . . . . . . . . . . . . . . . . . . . .        497
   *Shanshan Wang, Shifeng Hou, Lei Zhang, Zhenxiang Chen,*
   *and Hongbo Han*

Energy Efficient Encryption Scheme for Network-Coded Mobile Ad Hoc
Networks. . . . . . . . . . . . . . . . . . . . . . . . . . . . . . . . . . . . . . . . . . . . . . . .        508
   *Deepa S. Nair and H. Muhammed Ilyas*

**The 1st International Symposium on Dependability in Sensor, Cloud,
and Big Data Systems and Applications (DependSys 2015)**

Attribute-Based Ring Signcryption Scheme and Its Application in Wireless
Body Area Networks. . . . . . . . . . . . . . . . . . . . . . . . . . . . . . . . . . . . . . . .        521
   *Changji Wang and Jing Liu*

Dependable Cascading Target Tracking in Heterogeneous Mobile Camera
Sensor Networks. . . . . . . . . . . . . . . . . . . . . . . . . . . . . . . . . . . . . . . . . . . .        531
   *Zhen Peng, Tian Wang, Md Zakirul Alam Bhuiyan, Xiaoqiang Wu,*
   *and Guojun Wang*

A Web-Based Resource Management Platform for Transparent Computing. . .        541
   *Dacheng Wang, Hong Song, Yun Xu, Wenhao Zhang, and Jianxin Wang*

Architecture and Scheduling Method of Cloud Video Surveillance System
Based on IoT . . . . . . . . . . . . . . . . . . . . . . . . . . . . . . . . . . . . . . . . . . . . . .        551
   *Xia Wei, Wen-Xiang Li, Cong Ran, Chun-Chun Pi, Ya-Jie Ma,*
   *and Yu-Xia Sheng*

HiTrans: An FPGA-Based Gateway Design and Implementation in HPC
Environments . . . . . . . . . . . . . . . . . . . . . . . . . . . . . . . . . . . . . . . . . . . . .        561
   *Wei Shi, Gaofeng Lv, Zhigang Sun, and Zhenghu Gong*

Dealing with Reliable Event-Based Communications by Means of Layered
Multicast . . . . . . . . . . . . . . . . . . . . . . . . . . . . . . . . . . . . . . . . . . . . . . . . .        572
   *Christian Esposito, Aniello Castiglione, and Francesco Palmieri*

Scalable Network Intrusion Detection and Countermeasure Selection
in Virtual Network Systems . . . . . . . . . . . . . . . . . . . . . . . . . . . . . . . . . . .        582
   *Jin B. Hong, Chun-Jen Chung, Dijiang Huang, and Dong Seong Kim*

Removing Key Escrow from the LW-HIBE Scheme . . . . . . . . . . . . . . . . . .        593
   *Peixin Chen, Xiaofeng Wang, Baokang Zhao, Jinshu Su, and Ilsun You*

FASTDB: An Array Database System for Efficient Storing and Analyzing
Massive Scientific Data . . . . . . . . . . . . . . . . . . . . . . . . . . . . . . . . . . . . . .        606
   *Hui Li, Nengjun Qiu, Mei Chen, Hongyuan Li, Zhenyu Dai, Ming Zhu,*
   *and Menglin Huang*

An Effective Correlation-Aware VM Placement Scheme for SLA Violation
Reduction in Data Centers . . . . . . . . . . . . . . . . . . . . . . . . . . . . . . .     617
   *Sheng Xu, Binzhang Fu, Mingyu Chen, and Lixin Zhang*

Reliability-Aware Distributed Computing Scheduling Policy. . . . . . . . . . . .     627
   *Jemal Abawajy and Mohammad Mehedi Hassan*

An Escrow-Free Hierarchical Identity-Based Signature Model for Cloud
Storage . . . . . . . . . . . . . . . . . . . . . . . . . . . . . . . . . . . . . . . . .     633
   *Peixin Chen, Xiaofeng Wang, and Jinshu Su*

A Predictive Data Reliability Method for Wireless Sensor Network
Applications. . . . . . . . . . . . . . . . . . . . . . . . . . . . . . . . . . . . . . .     648
   *Adil Amjad Sheikh, Ahmed Lbath, Ehsan Ullah Warriach,*
   *and Emad Felemban*

A Cycle-Time-Analysis Model for Byzantine Fault Tolerance. . . . . . . . . . .     659
   *Liu Chen and Wei Zhou*

Resource Utilization Based Dynamic Pricing Approach on Cloud
Computing Application . . . . . . . . . . . . . . . . . . . . . . . . . . . . . . . . .     669
   *Adrian Johannes, Priyadarsi Nanda, and Xiangjian He*

Weight-Based Batch Rekeying Scheme for Dynamic Multi-privileged
Group Communications. . . . . . . . . . . . . . . . . . . . . . . . . . . . . . . . .     678
   *Wei Zhou, Yang Xu, Lijuan Yang, and Guojun Wang*

Application-Assisted Dynamic Attestation for JVM-Based Cloud . . . . . . . . .     691
   *Haihe Ba, Huaizhe Zhou, Zhiying Wang, Jiangchun Ren, Tie Hong,*
   *and Yiming Li*

New Escrow-Free Scheme for Hierarchical Identity-Based Encryption . . . . . .     701
   *Fang Qi, Xin Tang, and Quanyun Wei*

Neural Networks in Petrol Station Objects Calibration. . . . . . . . . . . . . . . .     714
   *Marcin Gorawski, Mirosław Skrzewski, Michał Gorawski,*
   *and Anna Gorawska*

A Dependable, Scalable, Distributed, Virtual Data Structure. . . . . . . . . . . .     724
   *Silvia Grampone, Witold Litwin, and Thomas SJ Schwarz*

Effect of Bias Temperature Instability on Soft Error Rate. . . . . . . . . . . . . .     736
   *Zhen Wang and Jianhui Jiang*

Security Modeling and Analysis of a SDN Based Web Service. . . . . . . . . . .     746
   *Taehoon Eom, Jin B. Hong, Jong Sou Park, and Dong Seong Kim*

Single Anchor Node Based Localization in Mobile Underwater Wireless
Sensor Networks.............................................. 757
   *Anjana P. Das and Sabu M. Thampi*

A Novel Bug Report Extraction Approach.......................... 771
   *Tao Lin, Jianhua Gao, Xue Fu, and Yan Lin*

ABR-Tree: An Efficient Distributed Multidimensional Indexing Approach
for Massive Data............................................. 781
   *Xin Zhou, Hui Li, Xiao Zhang, Shan Wang, Yanyu Ma, Keyan Liu,*
   *Ming Zhu, and Menglin Huang*

A Simple Local Search Algorithm for Minimizing Interference in Wireless
Sensor Networks............................................. 791
   *Zhihai Wang and Weidong Chen*

Unknown Bit Stream Protocol Message Discovery with Zero Knowledge.... 800
   *Fengli Zhang, Junjiao Zhang, and Hongchuan Zhou*

Distributed Authentication in the Cloud Computing Environment.......... 810
   *Yanzhu Liu, Zhi Li, and Yuxia Sun*

Influential Nuisance Factors on a Decision of Sufficient Testing.......... 819
   *Mahnaz Malekzadeh and Iain Bate*

Research of Improved Particle Swarm Optimization Based on Genetic
Algorithm for Hadoop Task Scheduling Problem ................... 829
   *Jun Xu and Yong Tang*

Acceleration of CFD Engineering Software on GPU and MIC ............ 835
   *Yang Liu and Liang Deng*

**Author Index** ............................................. 849

# The 6th International Workshop on Trust, Security and Privacy for Big Data (TrustData 2015)

# Nth-Order Multifunction Filter Employing Current Differencing Transconductance Amplifiers

Meili Cao, Haizhen He$^{(\boxtimes)}$, Rongming Luo, and Lei Wen

College of Information Science and Engineering,
Hunan University, Changsha 410082, China
{495643804,1213363756}@qq.com

**Abstract.** This paper presents a new nth-order current-mode multifunction filter based on current differencing transconductance amplifiers (CDTAs). The proposed circuit, which adopts $n$ current differencing transconductance amplifiers and $n$ grounded capacitors, can realize current responses of low-pass, band-pass and high-pass, without component-matching conditions and changing the topology. The filter also offers the features of low input and high output impedances and enjoys the simple configuration which is suitable for integrated circuit (IC) fabrication. The proposed third-order filter is simulated using PSPICE to confirm the presented theory, and the results have good agreement with the theoretical analysis. The influences of the CDTA non-idealities are also discussed.

**Keywords:** Active circuit · Current mode · CDTA · Nth-order filter · Analog integrated circuit

## 1 Introduction

In 2003, a current-mode 5-terminals active element, named current differencing transconductance amplifier (CDTA) [1] has been presented. This element seems to be a versatile component in the realization of a class of analog filters. It is really a current-mode element whose input and output signals are currents. In addition, it's converts currents into a pair of low-impedance inputs into a difference current, flowing from so-called z-terminal into an outside load. The z-terminal voltage is then converted into a couple of output currents into the x-terminals by internal operational transconductance amplifier (OTA) [2]. The current gain of the whole circuit will be given by the product of the outside z-terminal impedance and the OTA transconductance. That is why the CDTA is suitable especially for the synthesis of current-mode active filters. It should also be noted here that, the CDTA possesses an advantage of wider frequency bandwidth as compared to its close relative, the CDBA [3]. In addition, it can adjust the output current gain.

Considering these advantages of CDTA, over the last decade, many current-mode filters based on CDTAs have been presented in the literature [4–26]. However, these reported circuits suffer from one or more of the following weaknesses: (i) The above

© Springer International Publishing Switzerland 2015
G. Wang et al. (Eds.): ICA3PP 2015 Workshops, LNCS 9532, pp. 3–12, 2015.
DOI: 10.1007/978-3-319-27161-3_1

CDTA devices are mainly used for low-order filters design. (ii) These circuits not only have the complex structure, but also suffer from more than one passive component which is not suitable for integrated circuit (IC) fabrication and lead to relatively high power consumption. (iii) Few functions can be realized by these circuits. Generally, these circuits can only achieve high-pass, band-pass, low-pass, band-stop, and all-pass functions in one or two kinds.

In this paper, an nth-order current-mode analog filter based on CDTAs has been presented. The proposed circuit, which adopts $n$ CDTAs and $n$ grounded capacitors offers low-input impedance and high-output impedance and also free from matching constraints. The circuit uses only grounded capacitors and enjoys the simple configuration, which is especially interesting from the integrated circuit (IC) fabrication point of view. In addition, the proposed nth-order filter can realize multiple filter functions, such as low-pass (LP), high-pass (HP), band-pass (BP) simultaneously without changing the topology. Moreover, if necessary, through a rational combination of output current signals (HP, LP, BP), it is also easy to derive filter's band-stop, all-pass transfer functions. Non-ideal of the CDTA on the transfer function of the proposed filters are also analyzed.

The paper has the following structure: The circuit structure of the proposed current-mode nth-order universal filter is described in Sect. 2. Analysis of non-ideality characteristics is discussed in Sect. 3. PSPICE simulations are also organized in Sect. 4.

## 2   The Proposed Circuit

A CDTA whose electrical symbol and equivalent circuit are shown in Fig. 1, is a five-port versatile active device represented by the following equation:

$$V_p = V_n = 0, I_z = I_p - I_n, I_x+ = g_m V_Z, I_x- = -g_m V_z \tag{1}$$

In (1), $I_{X+}$, $I_{X-}$, $I_Z$ denotes the currents of the terminals $X_+$, $X_-$ and $Z$ of the CDTA, respectively. While $V_p$, $V_n$, $V_z$ denotes the voltages of the terminals p, n, and Z of the CDTA, respectively. Note that $g_m$ is a function of the bias current.

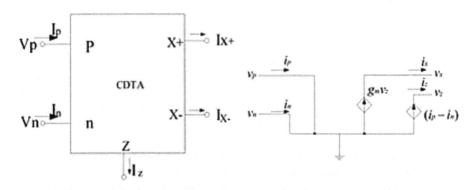

**Fig. 1.** Symbol and equivalent circuit of CDTA

Where $V_z = I_z \cdot Z_z$ and $Z_z$ is the external impedance connected to the z terminal of the CDTA. CDTA can be thought of as a combination of a current differencing unit followed by a dual-output operational transconductance amplifier, DO-OTA.

The CDTA is a versatile component in design of the current-mode filter circuits, especially for the design of high-order filters. The proposed current-mode nth-order multifunction filter based on CDTA is shown in Fig. 2. It is composed of $n$ CDTAs and $n$ grounded capacitors.

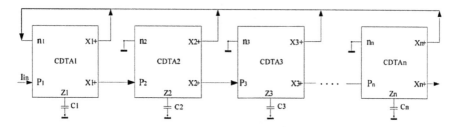

**Fig. 2.** Proposed nth-order current-mode filter

According to (1) and Fig. 2, by routine analysis, it is easy to get the circuit's currents constraint equations.

$$
\begin{cases}
I_{z1} = I_{p1} - I_{n1}, I_{p1} = I_{in} \\
I_{n1} = I_{x1} + I_{x2} + \ldots + I_{xn} \\
I_{x1} = I_{z1} \dfrac{g_{m1}}{SC_1} \\
I_{x2} = I_{z2} \dfrac{g_{m2}}{SC_2} = I_{x1} \dfrac{g_{m2}}{SC_2} \\
\ldots \\
I_{xn} = I_{zn} \dfrac{g_{mn}}{SC - n} = I_{x(n-1)} \dfrac{g_{mn}}{SC_n}
\end{cases}
\tag{2}
$$

Through synthesizing the above equations gives the following filter transfer functions (TFs):

$$
I_{z1} = \frac{S^n \tau_n}{\Delta S} I_{in}
\tag{3}
$$

Where

$$
\Delta S = S^n \tau_n + S^{n-1} g_{m1} \tau_{n-1} + \ldots + S\tau 1 \prod_{i=1}^{n-1} g_{mi} + \prod_{i=1}^{n} g_{mi}
\tag{4}
$$

$$\tau_n = \prod_{i=1}^{n} C_i, \tau_{n-1} = \prod_{i=2}^{n} C_i, \ldots, \tau_1 = C_n \qquad (5)$$

Corresponding output current can be given by

$$\frac{I_{xn}}{Iin} = \frac{\prod_{i=1}^{n} g_{mi}}{\Delta S} \qquad (6)$$

$$\frac{I_{z1}}{Iin} = \frac{S^n \tau_n}{\Delta S} \qquad (7)$$

$$\frac{I_{x1}}{I_{in}} = \frac{S^{n-1} \tau_{n-1} g_{m1}}{\Delta S} \qquad (8)$$

$$\frac{I_{x(n-1)}}{I_{in}} = \frac{S\tau 1 \prod_{i=1}^{n-1} g_{mi}}{\Delta S} \qquad (9)$$

Where the (6) ∼ (7) represent the output currents of low-pass, high-pass respectively; Moreover, (8) ∼ (9) in an arbitrary formula can achieve band-pass filter function. If add the type (6) and (9) can achieve the following filter transfer functions:

$$\frac{I_{z1} + I_{xn}}{I_{in}} = \frac{S^n \tau_n + \prod_{i=1}^{n} g_{mi}}{\Delta S} \qquad (10)$$

$$\frac{I_{z1} + I_{x1} + \ldots + I_{xn}}{I_{in}} = \frac{S^n \tau_n + S^{n-1} \tau_{n-1} g_{m1} + \ldots + S\tau 1 \prod_{i=1}^{n-1} g_{mi} + \prod_{i=1}^{n} g_{mi}}{\Delta S} \qquad (11)$$

Where, (10) ∼ (11) represent the output currents of band-stop and all-pass respectively; it may be stated here that the filter can be realized without any constraints on the component values, and it exhibits both low-input and high-output impedance characteristics, which will be more convenient in terms of cascading and connecting to other networks. These output current signals can also be used directly for supplying an independent load.

The proposed circuit adopts n CDTAs, n grounded capacitors and doesn't use any resistor, which avoid the influence of resistance on the bandwidth of circuit. Relative to the traditional CDTA-based filter, it also can achieve nth-order and even can realize all functions of high order filter.

A second-order filter (n = 2) is given as an example, which consists of two CDTAs, two grounded capacitors. The transfer function is obtained as

$$\frac{I_{x2}}{I_{in}} = \frac{g_{m1}g_{m2}}{S^2 C_2 C_1 + S C_2 g_{m1} + g_{m1}g_{m2}} \tag{12}$$

$$\frac{I_{z1}}{I_{in}} = \frac{S^2 C_1 C_2}{S^2 C_2 C_1 + S C_2 g_{m1} + g_{m1}g_{m2}} \tag{13}$$

Where (12) $\sim$ (13) present the proposed circuit operates as a second-order filter with low-pass and high-pass responses. In addition, a wide-band band-pass filter can also be realized by cascading the low-pass and high-pass filter directly. Note that it also without any condition or additional circuitry.

The corner frequency ($\omega_0$) and quality factor (Q) parameters of the filter are given as

$$\omega_0 = \sqrt{\frac{g_{m1}g_{m2}}{C_1 C_2}} \tag{14}$$

$$Q = \sqrt{\frac{C_1 g_{m2}}{C_2 g_{m1}}} \tag{15}$$

From (14) and (15) we can see that the parameter $\omega_0$ and Q can be adjusted independently. The $\omega_0$ can be adjusted by simultaneously changing $g_{m1}$ and $g_{m2}$ keeping $g_{m2}/g_{m1}$ constant while without disturbing Q. In the same way, we can adjust the parameter Q without disturbing $\omega_0$ by changing $g_{m2}$ and $g_{m1}$ simultaneously keeping $g_{m1}g_{m2}$ constant. Of course, to obtain this in practice, need exercise special care to provide it.

It is easy to know that the sensitivities of $\omega_0$ and Q in (14) and (15) are shown as follows:

$$S_{C_1}^{\omega_0} = S_{C_2}^{\omega_0} = S_{g_{m1}}^{Q} = S_{C_2}^{Q} = -\frac{1}{2} \tag{16}$$

$$S_{C_1}^{Q} = S_{g_{m1}}^{\omega_0} = S_{g_{m2}}^{\omega_0} = S_{g_{m2}}^{Q} = \frac{1}{2} \tag{17}$$

Consequently, all of the component sensitivities of $\omega_0$ and Q are less than unity in magnitudes.

## 3   Analysis of Non-Ideal Characteristics

In practice, the performance of the proposed circuits may deviate from the ideal by the non-ideal characteristic of the active device being used. For a complete analysis of the circuit, it is necessary to take into account the non-idealities of CDTA.

For the analysis of sensitivity, the CDTA's current and voltage characteristics can be described by the following equations.

$$I_z = \alpha_p I_p - \alpha_n I_n, I_x = \beta g_m V_z \tag{18}$$

Here $\varepsilon_p, \varepsilon_n$ and $\varepsilon_\beta$ denote current tracking errors, ideally equal to zero, and absolute values of all these terms are much less than unit value. All these gains ($\alpha p$, $\alpha n$ and $\beta$) slightly differ from their ideal values of unity by these tracking errors.

For the circuit, considering the aforementioned non-ideal effect, transfer function's denominator can be rewritten as follow:

$$\Delta S = S^n \tau_n + S^{n-1} \beta_1 g_{m1} \tau_{n-1} + \ldots + S\tau_1 \prod_{i=1}^{n-1} \beta_i g_{mi} + \prod_{i=1}^{n} \beta_i g_{mi} \tag{19}$$

$$\tau_n = \prod_{i=1}^{n} C_i, \tau_{n-1} = \prod_{i=2}^{n} C_i, \ldots, \tau_1 = C_n \tag{20}$$

For second-order filter, the non-ideal transfer function is given as

$$\frac{I_{x2}}{I_{in}} = \frac{\beta_1 \beta_2 g_{m1} g_{m2}}{S^2 C_2 C_1 + SC_2 \beta_1 g_{m1} + \beta_1 \beta_2 g_{m1} g_{m2}} \tag{21}$$

$$\frac{I_{z1}}{I_{in}} = \frac{S^2 C_1 C_2}{S^2 C_2 C_1 + SC_2 \beta_1 g_{m1} + \beta_1 \beta_2 g_{m1} g_{m2}} \tag{22}$$

Corresponding the corner frequency ($\omega_0$) and quality factor (Q) parameters of the filter can be given by

$$\omega_0 = \sqrt{\frac{\beta_1 \beta_2 g_{m1} g_{m2}}{C_1 C_2}} \tag{23}$$

$$Q = \sqrt{\frac{C_1 \beta_2 g_{m2}}{C_2 \beta_1 g_{m1}}} \tag{24}$$

From (23) and (24), the coefficient sensitivities of $S_{\beta_1}^{\omega_0}, S_{\beta_2}^{\omega_0}$ are 1/2. Meanwhile, the coefficient sensitivities of $S_{\beta_1}^{Q}, S_{\beta_2}^{Q}$ are -1/2, 1/2 respectively.

From the above calculations, it can be seen that all sensitivities are less than unity.

## 4   Simulation Results

In order to demonstrate the performance of the proposed circuit, a current-mode third-order filter according to the proposed circuit is simulated in PSPICE. The simulation program is created with TSMC 0.18um CMOS. The circuit of the third-order filter is simulated by using $\pm 1.5V$ power supplies, C1 = C2 = C3 = 1nF to obtain a LP, BP and HP responses with a pole natural frequency of fo = 1.59 MHz and a pole quality

**Table 1.** Comparison of the proposed high-order filter circuits based on CDTA

| References | [4] | [6] | [9] | [14] | [26] | This work |
|---|---|---|---|---|---|---|
| Implementation of the order | 8order | N order | N order | 4 order | 6 order | N order |
| Number of active elements | 7 | n | n | 5 | 6 | n |
| Number of capacitors | 8 | n | n | 5 | 6 | n |
| Number of resistors | 2 | 1 | 0 | 4 | 6 | 0 |
| Filter function | LP | LP | BP | BP | BP | LP,BP,HP |
| Power consumption | NA | 23 mw | 3.18 mw | NA | NA | 8 mw |
| Supply voltage | NA | NA | NA | ±1.25V | ±1.5V | ±1.5V |
| Frequency of filter example | 5.75 MHz | 1 MHz | 318 kHz | 1 MHz | 1 MHz | 1.59 MHz |

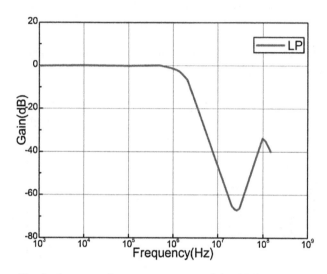

**Fig. 3.** Low-pass frequency responses of the third-order filter

factor of Q = 0.707. The simulation results are shown in Figs. 3, 4 and 5. It is noted that the results of circuit simulations are in agreement with the theory. The power consumption of the circuit in Fig. 2 is found approximately to be 8 mw.

The whole simulated performance of the circuit is shown in Table 1, and comparisons with previous published works are also included. The proposed devices are mainly used for low-order filters design and few functions can be realized. The proposed circuit, which adopts n current differencing transconductance amplifiers and n grounded capacitors, can realize low-pass, band-pass and high-pass filter responses simultaneously without to change the circuit structure. Also, the introduced filter employs only grounded capacitors as passive elements, and does not need passive element matching constraints thus it is ideal for IC realizations.

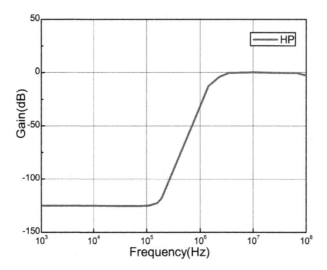

**Fig. 4.** High-pass frequency responses of the third-order filter

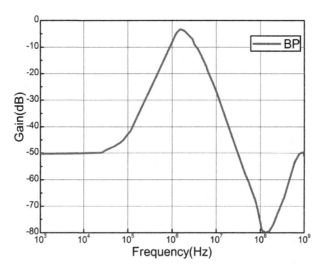

**Fig. 5.** Band-pass frequency responses of the third-order filter

## 5   Conclusion

In this paper, a high-order current-mode analog filter based on current differencing transconductance amplifiers is proposed. The proposed circuit, which adopts $n$ current differencing transconductance amplifiers and $n$ grounded capacitors, can realize low-pass, band-pass and high-pass filter responses simultaneously without to change the circuit structure. Also, the introduced filter is greatly reducing the power consumption, it is only

8 mw. PSPICE simulations for current-mode third-order filter based on this structure have also been conducted, and the results have good agreement with the theoretical analysis.

**Acknowledgments.** This work is supported by the Hunan Province natural science foundation of China [NO.14JJ7026] and the Open Fund Project of innovation platform in Hunan Universities [No.13K015], and the authors would like to thank the editors and anonymous reviewers for providing valuable comments which helped in improving the manuscript.

# References

1. Biolek, D.: CDTA—building block for current-mode analog signal processing. In: Proceedings of the European conference on circuit theory and design 2003, ECCTD 2003, pp. 397−400. Krakow (2003)
2. Deliyannis, T., Sun, Y., Fidler, J.: Continuous-Time Active Filter Design. CRC Press, USA (1999)
3. Acar, C., Ozoguz, S.: A new versatile building block: current differencing buffered amplifier suitable for analog signal processing filters. Microelectron 30, 157–160 (1999)
4. Uygur, A., Kuntman, H.: Seventh-order elliptic video filter with 0.1 dB pass band ripple employing CMOS CDTAs. AEU-Int. J. Electron. Commun. 61, 320–328 (2007)
5. Biolek, D., Biolková, V.: CDTA-C current-mode universal 2nd-order filter. In: Proceedings of the 5th WSEAS International Conference on Applied Informatics and Communications. World Scientific and Engineering Academy and Society (WSEAS), pp. 411–414 (2005)
6. Bekri A.T, Anday F.: Nth-order low-pass filter employing current differencing transconductance amplifiers (2005)
7. Dumawipata, T., Tangsrirat, W., Surakampontorn, W.: Current-mode universal filter with four inputs and one output using CDTAs. In: IEEE Asia Pacific Conference on Circuits and Systems, 2006, APCCAS 2006, pp. 892–895 (2006)
8. Tanjaroen, W., Dumawipata, T., Tangsrirat, W.: TISO cascadable current-mode multifunction filter employing current differencing transconductance amplifiers. In: IEEE International Joint Conference on SICE-ICASE, 2006, pp. 5703–5706 (2006)
9. Tangsrirat, W., Dumawipata, T., Surakampontorn, W.: Multiple-input single-output current-mode multifunction filter using current differencing transconductance amplifiers. AEU-Int. J. Electron. Commun. 61, 209–214 (2007)
10. Prasad, D., Bhaskar, D.R., Singh, A.K.: Universal current-mode biquad filter using dual output current differencing transconductance amplifier. AEU-Int. J. Electron. Commun. 63, 497–501 (2009)
11. Tanjaroen, W., Tangsrirat, W.: Current-mode second-order notch filter using CDTA-based allpass sections. In: 2008 SICE Annual Conference, IEEE, pp. 1143–1146 (2008)
12. Tangsrirat, W., Pukkalanun, T.: Structural generation of two integrator loop filters using CDTAs and grounded capacitors. Int. J. Circuit Theor. Appl. 39, 31–45 (2011)
13. Dumawipata, T., Tangsrirat, W., Surakampontorn, W.: Cascadable current-mode multifunction filter with two inputs and three outputs using CDTAs. In: 2007 6th International Conference on Information, Communications & Signal Processing, IEEE, pp. 1–4 (2007)
14. Dostal, T., Smejkal, V., Slezak, J.: Realization of arbitrary transfer current characteristic using transconductors CDTA. In: 2008 18th International Conference on Radioelektronika, IEEE, pp. 1–4 (2008)

15. Siripruchyanun, M., Jaikla, W.: Electronically controllable current-mode universal biquad filter using single DO-CCCDTA. Circuits Syst. Signal Process. **27**, 113–122 (2008)
16. Tanjaroen, W., Tangsrirat, W.: Current-mode second-order notch filter using CDTA-based allpass sections. In: 2008 SICE Annual Conference, IEEE, pp. 1143–1146 (2008)
17. Tanjaroen, W., Tangsrirat, W.: Resistorless current-mode first-order allpass filter using CDTAs. In: 5th International Conference on Electrical Engineering/Electronics, Computer, Telecommunications and Information Technology, ECTI-CON 2008, IEEE, pp. 721–724 (2008)
18. Tangsrirat, W., Pukkalanun, T., Surakampontorn, W.: Resistorless realization of current-mode first-order allpass filter using current differencing transconductance amplifiers. Microelectron. J. **41**, 178–183 (2010)
19. Prasad, D., Bhaskar, D.R., Singh, A.K.: Universal current-mode biquad filter using dual output current differencing transconductance amplifier. AEU-Int. J. Electron. Commun. **63**, 497–501 (2009)
20. Siripruchyanun, M., Jaikla, W.: CMOS current-controlled current differencing transconductance amplifier and applications to analog signal processing. AEU-Int. J. Electron. Commun. **62**, 277–287 (2008)
21. Kacar, F., Kuntman, H.H.: A new, improved CMOS realization of CDTA and its filter applications. Turkish J. Electr. Eng. Comput. Sci. **19**(4), 631–642 (2011)
22. Prasad, D., Bhaskar, D.R., Singh, A.K.: Multi-function biquad using single current differencing transconductance amplifier. Analog Integr. Circuits Signal Process. **61**, 309–313 (2009)
23. Biolek, D., Biolkova, V., Kolka, Z.: Current-mode biquad employing single CDTA. Indian J. Pure Appl. Phys. **47**, 535–537 (2009)
24. Kacar, F., Kuntman, H.: A new CMOS current differencing transconductance amplifier (CDTA) and its biquad filter application. In: EUROCON 2009, IEEE, pp. 189–196 (2009)
25. Tangsrirat, W., Pukkalanun, T.: Structural generation of two integrator loop filters using CDTAs and grounded capacitors. Int. J. Circuit Theor. Appl. **39**, 31–45 (2011)
26. Li, Y.: A modified CDTA (MCDTA) and its applications: designing current-mode sixth-order elliptic band-pass filter. Circuits Syst. Signal Process. **30**, 1383–1390 (2011)

# An Efficient Spatial Query Processing Algorithm in Multi-sink Directional Sensor Network

Zheng Ma[1,2], Jin Zheng[1], Weijia Jia[3], and Guojun Wang[1,4(✉)]

[1] School of Information Science and Engineering, Central South University,
Changsha 410083, Hunan, China
zhma@csu.edu.cn, zhengjin@mail.csu.edu.cn,
csgjwang@gmail.com
[2] School of Information Science and Engineering, Hunan University,
Changsha 410082, Hunan, China
[3] Department of Computer Science and Engineering, Shanghai Jiao Tong
University, Shanghai 200240, China
jia-wj@cs.sjtu.edu.cn
[4] School of Computer Science and Educational Software,
Guangzhou University, Guangzhou 510006, China

**Abstract.** In order to address the problem of energy- and time-efficient execution of spatial queries in directional sensor networks, an efficient hybrid spatial query processing algorithm called SQPDSN is proposed in this paper. In the majority of studies on query processing using wireless sensor networks, sensors are assumed to have an isotropic sensing and transmission model. However, in certain applications the sensors have directional sensing and directional transmission model. SQPDSN only requires each node within the query region send data message once which reduces the data messages. For achieving minimal energy consumption and minimal response time, our query processing model ensures that only the relevant nodes for the correct execution of a query are involved in the query execution. Each sector has a node which collects the sensory data in it, aggregates the data to derive partial query result and send it to the next sector. Compared with other techniques, the experimental results demonstrated an improvement of the proposed technique in terms of energy efficient query cover with lower communication cost.

**Keywords:** Multi-Sink wireless sensor networks · Directional transmission · Spatial query · Parallel processing

## 1 Introduction

In wireless sensor networks, senor nodes are deployed in a monitored region, which are capable of sensing, processing and storing environment information. It is used to query the data or events monitored or detected. A directional sensor network (DSN) is a collection of such directional sensor nodes spatially deployed in an ad hoc fashion that performs distributed sensing tasks in a collaborative manner. Unlike an omnidirectional

© Springer International Publishing Switzerland 2015
G. Wang et al. (Eds.): ICA3PP 2015 Workshops, LNCS 9532, pp. 13–23, 2015.
DOI: 10.1007/978-3-319-27161-3_2

sensor device, a directional one has limited range of communication and sensing capabilities as it can sense and communicate in only one direction or a certain angle.

The study of this paper is related to query-based routing protocol, so, next, we will introduce several routing protocols relevant to this paper. The tree-based approaches rely on network infrastructure (e.g., based on a spanning tree) for query propagation and processing. Such as, Tiny Aggregation (TAG) (Madden et al. 2002), the Dynamic Query-tree Energy Balancing (DQEB) (Yang et al. 2004) protocol, Gathering-Load-Balanced Tree Protocol (LBTP) (Chen et al. 2006), Semantic/Spatial correlation-aware tree (SCT) that exploits the correlation strategies was proposed by Zhu et al. (2008), the Workload-Aware Routing Tree (WART) algorithm (Andreou et al. 2011), the Energy-driven Tree Construction (ETC) algorithm (Andreou et al. 2011), and the Geometry-based Spatial Skyline Query (GSSky) (Zhang et al. 2014). These techniques rely on a network infrastructure for query propagation and processing. Some work (Tang and Xu 2006; Gnawali et al. 2009) aims to improve the query precision, besides extending the network lifetime. This centralized approach didn't generate an efficient query plan and resulted in high overhead as it requires that each node reports its metadata to the sink. Moreover the maintenance of such a network infrastructure (Chakraborty et al. 2011) is a major issue, especially when the sensor nodes failed.

The decentralized versions of spatial query execution programs are needed for sensor networks: by using a decentralized program instead of a centralized approach, it would be possible to contact only the relevant nodes for the execution of a spatial query, and hence the decentralized algorithms will incur less energy consumption (Demirbas and Ferhatosmanoglu 2003). It has been shown that, by avoiding the significant over-head of maintaining a network infrastructure, the decentralized spatial query processing techniques (Wu et al. 2007, 2008; Fu et al. 2007, 2010; Martina et al. 2014) outperform the infrastructure-based techniques. The performance (such as the query latency and the energy consumption) of itinerary-based spatial query processing techniques is dependent on the design of itineraries, such as Itinerary-Based KNN (IKNN), Density-aware Itinerary KNN query processing (DIKNN), Parallel Concentric-circle Itinerary-based KNN (PCIKNN), and Energy-Efficient and Fault Tolerant Spatial Query Processing (EEFT). With a long itinerary, long query latency and high energy consumption may be incurred due to a long itinerary traversal. On the other hand, allowing a query to run on an arbitrary number of short itineraries in parallel may result in significant collisions in the query dissemination phase.

In this paper we propose an efficient spatial query processing scheme (SQPDSN) by combining the strengths of both the infrastructure-based and the infrastructure-free query processing techniques to reduce communication collisions and alleviate the influence of nodes failure. Thus, our scheme can achieve energy-efficiency and time-efficiency.

The rest of the paper is organized as follows. We describe network model and assumptions in Sect. 2. In Sect. 3, the details of our propose SQPDSN system is presented. In Sect. 4, extensive experiments are conducted to evaluate the performance of the proposed algorithms, and we conclude our work in Sect. 5.

## 2  Network Model and Problem Definition

We consider a directional wireless sensor network, where sensor nodes are deployed in a two-dimensional space. Figure 1 is the example for architecture of WSN. In our assumptions, there are some pre-deployed sink nodes, which are powerful and location-aware. The sink nodes are not power constrained and stay on for the lifetime of the network. Thus, they do not have any effect on the power consumption characteristics of the network. Every sensor node can compute its sector ID according its own location and the location of every sink node via GPS or other localization techniques (Ma et al. 2011). By periodically exchanging beacon information with sensor nodes nearby, a sensor node maintains a list of neighbor nodes. Moreover, the sensed data are stored locally in sensor nodes.

We model the sector-based sensor network as a Graph $G = (C, S, E)$, where C is the set of sectors, S is the set of sinks, and E represents the implicit network edges of the sectors in C. $E = E_1 + E_2$, $E_1 \subseteq C \times C$, $E_2 \subseteq C \times S$. In E1, if sector i can directly communicate with sector j, $eij = 1$, otherwise, $eij = 0$. And, we assume that if $eij = 1$ then $eji = 1$. In E2, if sector i can directly communicate with sink j, then $eij = 1$, otherwise, $eij = 0$. And every sink can directly communicate with every sector. There are k sink nodes, n sensor nodes and m sectors in a network. $D(i)$ is the number of neighbor sector of sector i. $N(i)$ is the number of nodes in sector i. $\tau$ is the time for sensor node message transmission. $\sigma$ is the time for sensor node processing. In the real world, $\tau$ is much larger than $\sigma$, and $\sigma$ can be ignored.

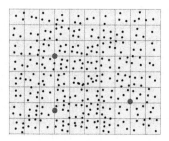

**Fig. 1.** Multi-sink directional sensor networks model

Each sensor has a unique sensing and communication model. These sensor nodes have a set of sensing and communication orientations or sectors. We can characterized a sensing or communication sector using the following attributes. Figure 2 is the sensing and communication model of a directional sensor node.

Rs is the maximum sensing radius and Rc is the maximum communication radius. $\theta s$ ($0 < \theta s < 2\pi$) is the maximum sensing angle and $\theta c$ ($0 < \theta s < 2\pi$) is the maximum communication angle. $\overrightarrow{Vs}$ is a directional vector that divides the sensing range into two equal parts, $\overrightarrow{Vc}$ is a directional vector that divides the communication range into two equal parts.

Figure 2 is the sensing and communication model of a directional sensor node.

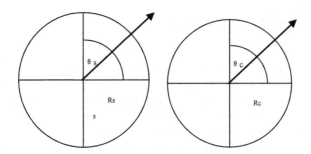

**Fig. 2.** Sensing and communication model of directional node

The spatial query SQL-based query language, which consists of a SELECT–FROM–WHERE clause, is commonly accepted and widely used in specifying queries for a sensor network. However, a sensor network has its own characteristics, and therefore extensions must be made to the basic SQL query. We provide some simple examples WSN query in the form of extended SQL: "*Select temp From sensors Where s.location is in R1 And Epoch Duration 20 s*" or "*Select average(temp) From sensors Where s.location is in R1 And Epoch Duration 20 s*". The former query requests the all temperature from all sensors inside the interest region, which is the row-data query. The latter one requests the average temperature from all sensors inside the interest region, which is the aggregated-data query. In this paper, we consider the latter kind.

Users of the system query the base station for data objects. For simplicity, we assume that each query asks for one data object acquired at a specific location area. We use query region to refer to the location specified in a query. A data object can be used to answer a query if the data object's spatial region covers the query region. The duration between the time the base station sending a query and the time the base station receiving the query answer is the query's response time.

Given a query Q over a sensor network, select an optimal set of sensors that satisfy the conditions of coverage as well as connectivity. The set of sensors are sufficient to answer the query such that (1) the sensing region of the selected set of sectors cover the entire geographical region of the query and (2) the selected set of sensors should form a logical routing topology for data gathering and transmission to the query source. In addition, (3) query processing except for time-constrained must incorporate energy awareness into the system to extend the lifetime of the sensor nodes and network by reducing the total energy consumption.

## 3   The SQPDSN Algorithm

In this section, we propose SQPDSN, a spatial query processing in directional sensor networks. The goal of SQPDSN is gathering regional aggregated values energy and time efficiently so that we can find some interest regions satisfying several conditions.

SQPDSN has two processing phases: the centralized initialization phase, the query dissemination and data collection phase, as in the prior work. In addition, SQPDSN employs several innovative ideas to improve the efficiency of spatial query result. Explicitly, the initial route, sector selection estimation, and the query dissemination are computed by the sink using its powerful capability and global knowledge. The route, the query dissemination, the data collection scheme are dynamically refined while the query is propagated using the local information. Moreover, to reduce redundant data transmission and improve the query accuracy, partial query results are collected at the some nodes and then sent back to the source node. The objective is to balance the energy consumption and time latency with the accuracy of query results constraint (Bai et al. 2012).

Next, we will elaborate the framework of SQPDSN. The framework of SQPDSN consists two phases: the centralized initialization phase, and the query dissemination and result back phase. In the former phase, the computation is done by sink nodes, and in the latter phase, the sensor nodes can obey the rule of the query processing and adjust according to the local information adaptively.

## 3.1   Centralized Initialization

The sink node acts as an initiator of the spatial query processing. The users register the spatial queries in one sink node. The sink node that received the query computes the cover sectors estimation, initial route, and the query dissemination and the data collection using the global information, which is based on the sector forest. The pseudo-code of sector forest construction is in Algorithm 1.

**Algorithm 1.** BFS Sector Forest Construction

**Input:** The wireless sensor networks graph $G$ and a user query $Q$

**Output:** The sector forest $F$

 Begin

   Initial step:

     Construct the set of object sectors $C'$, which cover the query region

     For every sector in $C'$, set $label$ =0

     Add sink nodes $s$ to $F$, every sink is the root of a tree $t$, the level of sink is 0. $\psi$ is the estimated time cost of the tree $t$. Set $\psi$=0

     Set $LEVEL = 0$

   Loop step:

     While a sector $label$ ==0 in $C'$ and new sector add in $F$ do

     For every sector $j$ which its level value equals $LEVEL$

       Add sector $i$ to $F$ and set its $level = LEVEL+1$ and $parent = j$ if it is not in $F$ and is the neighbour of the sector $j$. If $i \in C'$, then set its $label = 1$, set $flag = 1$ along the path from $i$ to the root until the flag value is 1 for any ancestral node of $i$

       End For

       $LEVEL = LEVEL+1$

     End while

   Critical Path Time Cost Estimation

   Find the highest tree $t$ in the $F$ which flag value is 1

     $\Psi = LEVEL * max(D(i)) * 2T$

   If value of the $\psi$ is larger than the epoch

     Then return to user

   Else send the query and the tree to the sink nodes.

 End

Algorithm 1 presents the main step of this procedure from the sink nodes to the leaf sectors. The first step calculates the sector sets which cover the query region based on the global information of sector Graph, and initializes the sector forest. The second step is loop step aiming that all the object sectors are added to the forest, if the Graph G is a fully connected graph. The last step estimated the time cost for the query. If the time cost is less than the epoch, then the query task will be parallelized to related sink nodes. Otherwise, it returns to the user that the epoch is not enough and gives the user the reasonable epoch.

After the sector forest being constructed, every related sink node will receive the query and related tree. It finds the shortest route to the query region and computes its object sectors collection path, then distributes it to the child sector based on the input. Also, the sink then schedules the last end time slots to result back for every sub tree to ensure accomplishing task in epoch duration. If the value of child's flag is 1, it shows the branch has the data query sector. The pseudo-code of the algorithm is as Algorithm 2.

During the initial phase, the sink is in charge of the computation using the known global information. It only consumes the sink node's energy. The time complexity of Algorithm 2 is $O(log\ m)$, where m is the number of sectors. And, the query task can be parallelized into some sub query tasks according to the query requirements, aim to reduce the query processing time and balance the energy cost in networks.

**Algorithm 2**. Initial query dissemination

A sink node receiving a query message from other sink node

**Input**:   Initial sink ID, tree of the current sink, the query

**Output**: Query messages (the initial query sector tree t, query id and information, last endtime e, sink ID)

Begin

  If flag $==0$ then return

    Set c value is the number of child sector node which flag is 1

     For Find child i of the root

      If flag $==1$

     Set endtime = endtime -c*$\tau$

       c--

    Then send the query message to the sector i

End

## 3.2    Query Dissemination and Result Back

In this section, we describe the process how to send the query and collect the data in a network. When a node in a sector receives the query from the upper level sector, it schedules the last end time slots to result back for every child sector whose flag is 1, to ensure accomplishing task in the epoch duration, and diffuses the query to the down sectors, then waits. And if it covers part of query region, it will collect the data in its sector, then waits to fuse the part query results from the down sectors. The proposed algorithms are as shown in Algorithms 3 and 4. The back path and collect sector set will be merged in the result back message. The dynamical information will be brought to the sink nodes at last, which is benefit for whole sector structure maintenance. But in this paper, this part of work will not be described.

**Algorithm 3.** The query dissemination

A node in sector i receiving a query message from a node in upper sector j

**Input**: Query message (the query sector tree t1, query id and information, last end time e, sink ID, initial sink ID)

**Output**: Sub query messages (the sub query sector tree, endtime, query id and information, sink ID, initial sink ID)

Begin

  If sector i is the leaf node of t1

    If covers part of query region

      Then collects the data in sector i, and sends fused the query result message to the upper sector j using certain sensing angle and sensing radius

     Else return

  If flag ==0 Then return

   Else Set parent = j for query id

    Set endtime = e for query id

    Set c value is the number of child sector node which flag is 1

For every child k of the root i

  If flag == 1 Set endtime = endtime -c*τ c--

  Then sends the sub query message to the sector k for query id using certain sensing angle and sensing radius

End For

If i covers part of query region

  Then collects the data in sector i and fuses query result for query id

End

In the query dissemination phase, only the query information and query route are sent to the down sector. Now we consider the computation complexity in the query dissemination phase. There are $m$ sectors in the query tree at most, and in each sector only one node transmits once. Therefore, it requires $m$ transmission for query dissemination. The depth of the query tree is $log(m)$, and the scheduling time for one level of the tree is $max(D(i))$, so the time of the query dissemination is $O((log\ m)*max(D(i)))$.

**Algorithm 4**. The query result back

A node in sector i receiving a result message from a node in down sector k

**Input:** Result message (query result, back path, collect sector sets, query id, sink ID)

**Output:** Fused result message (fused query result, back path, query id, sink ID)

Begin

  Fuses the query result, back path, and collect sets from sector k for query id

   If all child have been send result message or the time is ending

    Then sends fused the query result message to the upper sector j using certain sensing angle and sensing radius

   Else wait

End

In the query result back phase, only the query result and the back route are sent to the upper sector. The time of the result back is $O((log\ m)*max(D(i)))$, and it requires *m* result transmission too. So for a query, the cost of transmission is the $O(m + n)$, and the time cost is $O((\log m)*max(D(i)) + max(N(i)))$.

SQPDSN is an energy-balanced and delay-tolerated algorithm. During the initialization phase, the query has been partitioned so that multiple sinks can process it in parallel. There is no fixed head node for a sector, and every node is selected taking joint responsibility for query dissemination, data collection and query back (Wang et al. 2014). It can avoid that some nodes are dying fast in the hot space.

SQPDSN is fault tolerant due to several aspects. First, the sector structure in a wireless sensor networks will not be changed for a long time, so the sector query forest is stable. Second, node failure is masked without causing any update operation and structure change. For a dense sensor network, each sector contains several nodes and all nodes in the same sector share a common Sector ID. They can act on behalf of other nodes in the same sector. Third, SQPDSN can handle coverage holes nicely. Only if all the nodes inside a sector fail, a hole may be formed in SQPDSN. Even if the hole is formed, the node can re-route to the next sector to avoid the hole through local computation (Ma et al. 2011). Then it follows the query dissemination algorithm or data co0llection algorithm.

## 4  Performance Evaluation

The effects of node density and the size of the sensor network field (scalability) on query performance are investigated by changing the number nodes and/or the field size. And the proposed algorithm is evaluated by computer-based simulations compared with the GSSky, and EEFT based on the different density and different node failure rate. We compare these three algorithms in terms of lifetime, the average time cost, and accuracy rate.

The performance is evaluated based on NS2. The lifetime of network is the duration from the network initialization to the time 1/10 nodes are exhausted. The average time cost is the average time between the time a query is issued and the time the query result is returned to the sink node. The time unit is second. The accuracy rate is the ratio of the successful queries to the total queries. In our default settings, sink nodes and sensor nodes are static and location-aware. The max transmission range of sensor node is 10 units and the message delay for transmission is 30 ms. Every sensor node has the same initial energy, and energy consumption for message transmission is the same. In each round of the experiment, a series of queries are issued from randomly selected sink nodes in turn.

Table 1 shows the number of nodes on some size of sensor nodes to compare the proposed scheme with GSSky and EEFT. Every node has the same initial energy with the same max transmission range (10 units).

**Table 1.**  Network size and number of nodes for test

| Size of area(Unit) | Number of nodes | | | |
| --- | --- | --- | --- | --- |
| 225*225 | 1000 | 2000 | 3000 | 5000 |

Then, we investigate the impact of network density on the performance of the three examined algorithms. Figure 3 shows that the lifetime of network become longer when the network density increases in the three algorithms. Specifically SQPDSN has the longest life time. We can find that SQPDSN has the least latency for query and the highest accuracy in the three algorithms. In SQPDSN, the global information based on a sector is more stable, and thus the initial query plan is more proper. And SQPDSN decreases the number of messages for performing query dissemination in parallel, in order to save time. From the experimental results observed above, SQPDSN has the best performance under the experimental settings.

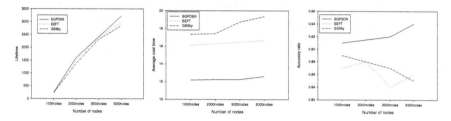

**Fig. 3.** Comparison with different density

Then, we investigate the impact of node failures on the performance of the three examined algorithms. The node failure rate of sensors unquestionably affects the performance of spatial query processing, especially to the infrastructure-based techniques. The network size is 225 * 225 units and the number of nodes is 3000. The node failure rate varies from 0 to 0.8. Performance study of these three algorithms is shown in Fig. 4. It shows that the life time of network becomes shorter when the node failure rate is increased in three algorithms. But SQPDSN has the longest life time among others because during the dissemination and result back phase, nodes can dynamically adjust the route to send the query and result. And the GSSky has the shortest life time. We can find that SQPDSN has the least latency for query and the accuracy is also highest in the three algorithms. The reason is that SQPDSN, which is not effected by nodes failure, is more fault tolerance.

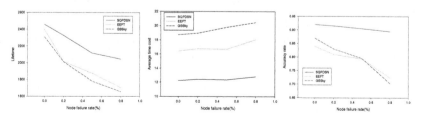

**Fig. 4.** Comparison with different node failure rate

# 5    Conclusion and Future Work

In this paper, we propose an efficient hybrid spatial query processing algorithm, SQPDSN, for spatial query processing in multi-sink directional sensor networks. This algorithm routes through the data query process and fully considers the characteristics of the data-query applications. The basic idea is to disseminate a query and collect data with pre-designed schedule and dynamic optimization. Initially, the SQPDSN is able to determine an optimal processing schedule for spatial query approximately using the backbone infrastructure. To deal with the node failure or local change during the query dissemination and data collection phase, we develop methods to bypass voids and to dynamically adjust the route. Experimental results show that SQPDSN significantly outperforms the existing query processing techniques in terms of energy consumption, query latency, query accuracy and scalability.

In future works, we intend to consider failures due to node mobility and also plan to extend for multiple queries other than snapshot queries. Finally, we intend to evaluate the proposed mechanism on a real test-bed.

# References

Andreou, P., Zeinalipour-Yazti, D., Pamboris, A., Chrysanthis, P.K., Samaras, G.: Optimized query routing trees for wireless sensor networks. Inf. Syst. **36**(2), 267–291 (2011)

Bai, S., Zhang, W., Xue, G., Tang, J., Wang, C.: DEAR: delay-bounded energy-constrained adaptive routing in wireless sensor networks. In: 2012 Proceedings of IEEE International Conference on Computer Communications (INFOCOM), pp. 1593–1601 (2012)

Chakraborty, S., Chakraborty, S., Nandi, S., Karmakar, S.: A tree-based local repairing approach for increasing lifetime of query driven WSN. In: Proceedings of 14th IEEE International Conference on Computational Science and Engineering (CSE), pp. 475–482 (2011)

Chen, T.-S., Tsai, H.-W., Chu, C.-P.: Gathering-load-balanced tree protocol for wireless sensor networks. Proc. IEEE Int. Conf. Sens. Netw. Ubiquit. Trust-Worthy Comput. **2**, 8–13 (2006)

Demirbas, M., Ferhatosmanoglu, H.: Peer-to-Peer spatial queries in sensor networks. In: Proceeding of the Third International Conference on Peer-to-Peer Computing (P2P), pp. 32–39 (2003)

Fu, T-Y., Peng, W-C., Lee, W-C.: Optimizing parallel itineraries for KNN query processing in wireless sensor networks. In: Proceedings of ACM Conference on Information and Knowledge Management (CIKM), pp. 391–400 (2007)

Gnawali, O., Fonseca, R., Jamieson, K., Moss, D., Levis, P.: Collection tree protocol. In: Proceedings of the 7th ACM Conference on Embedded Networked Sensor Systems (SenSys), pp. 1–14 (2009)

Ma, Z., Jia, W., Wang, G.: Routing with virtual region coordinates in wireless sensor networks. In: Proceedings of 10th IEEE International Conference on Trust, Security and Privacy in Computing and Communications (TrustCom), pp. 1657–1661 (2011)

Madden, S., Franklin, M.J., Hellerstein, J., Hong, W.: TAG: a tiny aggregation service for ad-hoc sensor networks. In: Proceedings of the Fifth Symposium on Operating Systems Design and Implementation (OSDI), pp. 131–146 (2002)

Pushpam, P., Felix, E.: Energy-efficient and fault tolerant spatial query processing in wireless sensor networks. Proc. Adv. Commun. Control Comput. Technol. (ICACCCT) **43**(5), 790–794 (2014)

Tang, X., Xu, J.: Extending network lifetime for precision-constrained data aggregation in wireless sensor networks. In: Proceedings of 25th IEEE International Conference on Computer Communications (INFOCOM), pp. 1–12 (2006)

Wang, G., Wang, T., Jia, W., Guo, M., Li, J.: Adaptive location updates for mobile sinks in wireless sensor networks. J. Supercomput. **47**(2), 127–145 (2009)

Wang, G., Bhuiyan, M.Z.A., Cao, J., Wu, J.: Detecting movements of a target using face tracking in wireless sensor networks. IEEE Trans. Parallel Distrib. Syst. **25**(4), 939–949 (2014)

Wu, S-H., Chuang, K-T., Chen, C-M., Chen, M-s.: DIKNN: an itinerary-based KNN query processing algorithm for mobile sensor networks. In: Proceedings of 23rd IEEE International Conference on Data Engineering (ICDE), pp. 456–457 (2007)

Wu, S.-H., Chuang, K.-T., Chen, C.-M., Chen, M-s: Toward the optimal itinerary-based KNN query processing in mobile sensor networks. IEEE Trans. Knowl. Data Eng. **20**(12), 1655–1668 (2008)

Yang, H., Ye, F., Sikdar, B.: A dynamic query-tree energy balancing protocol for sensor networks. Proc. Wireless Commun. Networking Conf. WCNC **3**, 1715–1720 (2004)

Zhang, L., Wang, Y., Song, B.: Geometry-based spatial skyline query in wireless sensor network. In: Proceedings of Web Information System and Application Conference, WISA, pp. 27–32 (2014)

Zhu, Y., Vedantham, R., Park, S.-J., Sivakumar, R.: A Scalable Correlation Aware Aggregation Strategy for Wireless Sensor Networks. Inf. Fusion **9**(3), 364–369 (2008)

# An Improved Method for Reversible Data Hiding in Encrypted Image

Yuling Liu[✉] and Zuhong Liu

College of Computer Science and Electronic Engineering,
Hunan University, Changsha 410082, Hunan, China
yuling_liu@126.com

**Abstract.** This paper proposes an improved method for reversible data hiding in encrypted image based on Zhang's algorithm when the embedding ratio is considered. A new fluctuation function is presented to evaluate the smoothness of image block. The fluctuation values of blocks are calculated, and then are sorted in ascending order. The blocks that the fluctuation values are smaller are selected to embed data. The number of blocks to be selected depends on the embedding ratio. Experimental results show that the new fluctuation function can give a better estimation, meanwhile the proposed method can achieve lower extracted-bit error rate than randomly selecting blocks in condition that the embedding ratio is considered.

**Keywords:** Encrypted image · Reversible information hiding · Fluctuation function · Data embedding ratio · Extracted-bit error rate

## 1 Introduction

Data hiding and encryption are two methods to protect data. However, in some cases we need to combine these two approaches. For example, in today's booming cloud technology, to ensure data privacy and security, the date should first be encrypted and then stored into the cloud and processed variously. The common data processing is mostly based on the plaintext, so the practical needs give birth to the research of data processing in encrypted domain. Recently, reversible data hiding in encrypted images has attracted much attention in application areas where privacy of the cover image is to be protected, especially in could environment.

Recent years, some reversible data hiding methods in encrypted image have been presented, and these methods can be mainly classified into two categories. The first is to find room for secret data after encrypting the image, referred as 'Vacating Room After Encryption'(VRAE). Methods in [1–10] follow this category. The second is to reversibly reserve required amount of space for secret data before encrypting the image. After encryption, data is hidden into the reserved space. This is referred as 'Reserving Room Before Encryption' (RRBE). Methods in [11, 12] follow this category.

In 2011, Zhang [2] proposed a very simple and practical algorithm for reversible data hiding in encrypted images which can be called LSB flipped method. This is a classical method that belongs to the 'VRAE' method. The encrypted images are divided into many blocks to embed data, and data is extracted and images are recovered

© Springer International Publishing Switzerland 2015
G. Wang et al. (Eds.): ICA3PP 2015 Workshops, LNCS 9532, pp. 24–34, 2015.
DOI: 10.1007/978-3-319-27161-3_3

according to the smoothness of image blocks. Later Hong et al. [3] improved the Zhang's algorithm and reduced the extracted-bit error rate by the use of a new fluctuation function and side match technique. Liao et al. [10] adopted a new improved fluctuation function based on the Zhang's algorithm. Although the above methods have some improvements comparing with the original methods, they still have some drawbacks. In fact, the data to be embedded into encrypted images is usually not much. Not all the blocks of image are used to embed data when the Zhang's method is adopted. So the data embedding ratio has practical meaning. The embedding ratio and how to further reduce the extracted-bit error rate based on the embedding ratio are what previous works neglect. Therefore, this paper proposes an algorithm based on the Zhang's method when data embedding ratio is considered. A new improved fluctuation function is used and the blocks of image are selected to embed data according to the correlation level of blocks. It can further reduce extracted-bit error rate by using these two methods based on the data embedding ratio. The rest of the paper is organized as follows. Section 2 briefly introduces the related works such as Zhang's, Hong's and Liao's method. The proposed method is described in Sect. 3. Experimental results and comparisons are presented in Sect. 4, and finally, we draw our conclusion in Sect. 5.

## 2 Related Work

The first reversible data hiding algorithm in encrypted image was proposed by Puech et al. [1], but the quality of image is poor after directly decryption. In 2011, Zhang proposed a simple and novel reversible data hiding algorithm in encrypted image by flipping LSB of the image pixels. Later Hong et al. and Liao et al. respectively proposed two improved methods.

In Zhang's algorithm, the content owner first uses the stream cipher to encrypt the original image by a bitwise exclusive-or operation. Then the encrypted images are divided into k non-overlapping blocks of size s × s. The pixels in each block are randomly classified into two sets $S_0$ and $S_1$ by using a data hiding key. For any image block, if the data to be embedded is 0, the 3 LSBs of pixels in $S_0$ are flipped. If the data to be embedded is 1, the 3 LSBs of pixels in $S_1$ are flipped. In this way, the data is embedded in encrypted image. Then the encrypted image that contains secret data is transferred to the receiver. The receiver decrypts the encrypted image directly according to the encryption key and partitions it into k non-overlapping blocks of size s × s. The pixels in each block are classified into two sets $S_0$ and $S_1$. For each block, 3 LSBs of pixels in $S_0$ and $S_1$ are flipped to form two new blocks denoted $H_0$ and $H_1$. Equation (1) is used to extract the hidden data.

$$f = \sum_{u=2}^{s-1}\sum_{v=2}^{s-1}\left|p_{u,v} - (p_{u-1,v}+p_{u+1,v}+p_{u,v-1}+p_{u,v+1})/4\right| \tag{1}$$

Apply Eq. (1) to estimate the fluctuation value of $H_0$ and $H_1$, and the results are denoted as $f_0$ and $f_1$. Because of spatial correlation in natural images, the fluctuation function of original block is generally lower than that of a seriously interfered version.

So if $f_0 < f_1$, regard $H_0$ as the original image block and let the extracted data be 0; if $f_0 > f_1$ regard $H_1$ as the original image block and let the extracted data be 1.

In Hong et al.'s method, a new improved fluctuation function was proposed, as the Eq. (2) shows

$$f = \sum_{u=1}^{s_2} \sum_{v=1}^{s_1-1} |p_{u,v} - p_{u,v+1}| + \sum_{u=1}^{s_2-1} \sum_{v=1}^{s_1} |p_{u,v} - p_{u+1,v}| \tag{2}$$

The new fluctuation function can judge the correlation more accurately and reduce the error rate more effectively by calculating the horizontal and vertical differences of pixels. Meanwhile, the side match technique was used to extract data and it can further reduce the extracted-bit error rate.

Liao et al. focused on the deficiency of fluctuation function with the Zhang's method, took all pixels of the block into consideration and divided the pixels of each block into three categories. The first category is the pixels with two adjacent pixels that use the Eq. (3) to calculate the fluctuation function values of pixels.

$$f = |p_{1,1} - (p_{1,2} + p_{2,1})/2| + |p_{1,s_2} - (p_{1,s_2-1} + p_{2,s_2})/2| + |p_{s_1,1} - (p_{s_1,2} + p_{s_1-1,1})/2| \\ + |p_{s_1,s_2} - (p_{s_1,s_2-1} + p_{s_1-1,s_2})/2| \tag{3}$$

The second category is the pixels with three adjacent pixels that use the Eq. (4) to calculate the fluctuation function values.

$$f = \sum_{u=2}^{s_1-1} \left( \left| p_{u,1} - \frac{p_{u-1,1} + p_{u+1,1} + p_{u,2}}{3} \right| + \left| p_{u,s_2} - \frac{p_{u-1,s_2} + p_{u+1,s_2} + p_{u,s_2-1}}{3} \right| \right) \\ + \sum_{v=2}^{s_2-1} \left( \left| p_{1,v} - \frac{p_{1,v-1} + p_{1,v+1} + p_{2,v}}{3} \right| + \left| p_{s_1,v} - \frac{p_{s_1,v-1} + p_{s_1,v+1} + p_{s_1-1,v}}{3} \right| \right) \tag{4}$$

The third category is the pixels with four adjacent pixels, which was considered in Zhang's algorithm and the fluctuation function is Eq. (1). Then, the fluctuation function values of the entire block are obtained by adding the fluctuation value of the above three kinds of pixels. Since this method takes the edge pixels of the block into account, the fluctuation function has a higher accuracy and can make the extracted-bit error rate lower. Although the data embedding ratio was considered in Liao's method [10], no steps have been taken to reduce the extracted-bit error rate based on the data embedding ratio.

## 3   Proposed Method

According to the Zhang's method and the following improved methods, it can be observed that the accuracy of fluctuation function is a key factor to reduce the extracted-bit error rate. Based on the previous methods, a new fluctuation function is adopted to evaluate the complexity of image blocks to obtain better estimation. Due to the presence of texture area in many images, extracted-bit error usually occurs in the complex area. This paper selects the blocks that don't belong to the texture area or the complex area to embed secret data when embedding ratio is considered.

## 3.1    The Selection of the Image Block

In fact, not all the blocks are used to embed data when the Zhang's method is adopted to hide data in encrypted image. Thus there is need to consider the data embedding ratio. Obviously it is not the best choice that the blocks are selected to embed data by sequentially or randomly. Especially if the error is mainly concentrated on some blocks, the sequential embedding may lead to larger extracted-bit error. Usually, the data extracted-bit error occurs in the texture area of image, and this area is often complex and has poor correlation. Therefore, we try to avoid selecting some blocks in the complex area.

In order to realize blind extraction, the 8-bit cover image I is shifted 3 bit to form a new image $I'$ by doing a right shift operation. Since $I'$ is constituted of the 5 MSBs of I, the smoothness of $I'$ can reflect the smoothness of I. Then $I'$ is divided into non-overlapping blocks of size s × s.

From the previous works, it can be found that the fluctuation function is very important. The accuracy of the fluctuation function decides the accuracy of data extraction. In this study, a new fluctuation function is used to calculate the fluctuation value, as shown in the Eq. (5). This new fluctuation function is similar to Hong's, but has more accuracy than Hong's fluctuation function according to empirical result, especially when the block size is small.

$$f = \sum_{u=1}^{s} \sum_{v=2}^{s-1} \left|2 * p_{u,v} - p_{u,v-1} - p_{u,v+1}\right| + \sum_{u=2}^{s-1} \sum_{v=1}^{s} \left|2 * p_{u,v} - p_{u-1,v} - p_{u+1,v}\right| \quad (5)$$

Then the fluctuation values of all blocks are calculated by using the new fluctuation function and sort them in an ascending order. Suppose that the size of $I'$ is M × N, then the number of blocks is $\lfloor M/s \rfloor \times \lfloor N/s \rfloor$; suppose that the embedding ratio is p, the $\lfloor M/s \rfloor \times \lfloor N/s \rfloor \times p$ blocks with the smaller fluctuation function value are selected to embed data. It can effectively avoid selecting complex blocks to embed data and then further reduce the extracted-bit error rate.

## 3.2    Procedures of the Proposed Method

(1)  Image Encryption

Let I be an 8-bit cover image of size M × N, $b_{i,j,k}$ represents the k-th bit($0 \leq k \leq 7$) of pixels at position (i,j). The content owners use an encryption key to generate a pseudo-random binary sequence and denote it as $r_{i,j,k}$. Then I is encrypted by performing a bitwise XOR operation with $r_{i,j,k}$.

$$B_{i,j,k} = b_{i,j,k} \oplus r_{i,j,k} \tag{6}$$

$B_{i,j,k}$ is concatenated orderly to obtain the encrypted image $I''$.

(2) Data embedding

Step 1: The data hider divides the encrypted image $I''$ into blocks of size s × s to get ⌊M/s⌋ × ⌊N/s⌋ blocks.

Step 2: For each block, pseudo-randomly divide the s × s pixels into two equal-sized sets $S_0$ and $S_1$ according to the data hiding key.

Step 3: Select the ⌊M/s⌋ × ⌊N/s⌋ × p blocks with the smaller fluctuation value to embed data according to the embedding ratio p.

Step 4: For each block, if the data to be embedded is 0, 3 LSBs of all pixels in $S_0$ are flipped;

$$B'_{i,j,k} = \overline{B_{i,j,k}}(i,j) \in S_0 \text{ and } k = 0,1,2 \tag{7}$$

If the data to be embedded is 1, 3 LSBs of all pixels in $S_1$ are flipped.

$$B'_{i,j,k} = \overline{B_{i,j,k}}(i,j) \in S_1 \text{ and } k = 0,1,2 \tag{8}$$

Repeat this process until all the data bits are embedded.

(3) Data extraction and image recovery

Step 1: The receiver uses the encryption key to generate a pseudo-random sequence $r_{i,j,k}$, then calculates the exclusive-or of the received data and $r_{i,j,k}$ to decrypt the image. If the 3 LSBs of the encrypted pixels are not flipped, directly decrypting can recover the original pixels. When 3 LSBs of the pixels are turned over, the decrypted LSBs are as following.

$$b'_{i,j,k} = r_{i,j,k} \oplus B'_{i,j,k} = r_{i,j,k} \oplus \overline{B_{i,j,k}} = r_{i,j,k} \oplus \overline{b_{i,j,k} \oplus r_{i,j,k}} = \overline{b_{i,j,k}}\, k = 0,1,2 \tag{9}$$

It is obvious that the decrypted 3 LSBs are flipped compared with the original 3 LSBs.

Step 2: After the image is decrypted, the receiver use the 5 MSBs of the decrypted image to form a new image $I'$. Calculate the fluctuation value of each block in image $I'$ and then sort them in an ascending order. Then select the ⌊M/s⌋ × ⌊N/s⌋ × p blocks with the smaller fluctuation function value to extract data depending on the embedding ratio p.

Step 3: For each of these blocks, respectively flip the 3 LSBs of pixels in $S_0$ and $S_1$ to form two new blocks, denote them as $H_0$ and $H_1$.

Step 4: Calculate the fluctuation values of $H_0$ and $H_1$ by using Eq. (5) and the results are denoted as $f_0$ and $f_1$. If $f_0 < f_1$, the embedded data is 0, and $H_0$ is the original block; If $f_0 > f_1$, the embedded data is 1, and $H_1$ is the original block. Repeat this process to obtain all the hidden data and recover the original image.

# 4   Experimental Results

In this section, some experimental results will be given to demonstrate the performance of the proposed method.

## 4.1   Evaluation of the Proposed Method

Image quality and extracted-bit error rate are two major issues in the area of reversible data hiding in encrypted images. For image quality, the peak signal-to-noise ratio (PSNR) of decrypted image is considered.

In this paper, some graylevel images of size 512 × 512 are used as the test images, including lena, man, plane, couple, tiffany, baboon as shown in Fig. 1. The PSNR value of the decrypted image in [2] is about 37.9 dB. When the data is embedded according to the embedded rate p, the PSNR of the decrypted image changes with the change of p.

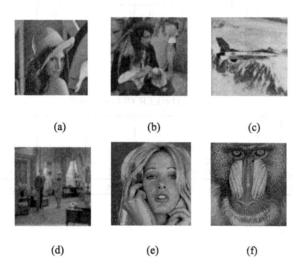

(a)                    (b)                    (c)

(d)                    (e)                    (f)

**Fig. 1.**  Six test images: (a) lena, (b) man, (c) plane, (d) couple, (e) tiffany, (f) baboon

Taking the Lena image as an example, Table 1 shows that the PSNR values of the decrypted image under different embedded ratio p. The PSNR value is about 37.9 dB and the smallest when p = 1. The larger the PSNR value is, the better the quality of decryption image is. Experimental results and theoretical data are consistent.

Extracted-bit error rate (EER) is also important to evaluate the effectiveness of the proposed method. The relationships of EER with respect to block sizes or data embedding ratio are analyzed in the following cases: the block size parameter $S \in \{4, 8, 12, 16, 20, 24, 28, 32, 36, 40\}$, the data embedding ratio $p \in \{0.5, 0.7, 0.9\}$. Tables 2, 3, 4, 5 and 6 respectively represent the results for the image lena, man, couple, tiffany and baboon. It can be observed that EER values are different for different embedding ratio and different size of block.

**Table 1.** PSNR values under different embedding ratio for lena

| p | 0.1 | 0.2 | 0.3 | 0.4 | 0.5 | 0.6 | 0.7 | 0.8 | 0.9 | 1.0 |
|---|---|---|---|---|---|---|---|---|---|---|
| PSNR(dB) | 47.98 | 44.97 | 43.24 | 41.99 | 41.02 | 40.23 | 39.56 | 38.97 | 38.45 | 37.94 |

**Table 2.** The EER (%) of lena

| s / p | 4 | 8 | 12 | 16 | 20 | 24 | 28 | 32 |
|---|---|---|---|---|---|---|---|---|
| 0.5 | 6.54 | 0.19 | 0 | 0 | 0 | 0 | 0 | 0 |
| 0.7 | 5.36 | 0.18 | 0 | 0 | 0 | 0 | 0 | 0 |
| 0.9 | 5.39 | 0.17 | 0 | 0 | 0 | 0 | 0 | 0 |

**Table 3.** The EER (%) of man

| s / p | 4 | 8 | 12 | 16 | 20 | 24 | 28 | 32 |
|---|---|---|---|---|---|---|---|---|
| 0.5 | 7.68 | 0.90 | 0.07 | 0.08 | 0 | 0 | 0 | 0 |
| 0.7 | 7.22 | 0.75 | 0.05 | 0.06 | 0 | 0 | 0 | 0 |
| 0.9 | 8.57 | 0.95 | 0.03 | 0 | 0 | 0 | 0 | 0 |

**Table 4.** The EER (%) of couple

| s / p | 4 | 8 | 12 | 16 | 20 | 24 | 28 | 32 |
|---|---|---|---|---|---|---|---|---|
| 0.5 | 6.32 | 0.10 | 0 | 0 | 0 | 0 | 0 | 0 |
| 0.7 | 6.56 | 0.17 | 0 | 0 | 0 | 0 | 0 | 0 |
| 0.9 | 7.80 | 0.46 | 0 | 0 | 0 | 0 | 0 | 0 |

**Table 5.** The EER (%) of tiffany

| p\s | 4 | 8 | 12 | 16 | 20 | 24 | 28 | 32 |
|---|---|---|---|---|---|---|---|---|
| 0.5 | 8.11 | 0.65 | 0.23 | 0 | 0 | 0 | 0 | 0 |
| 0.7 | 8.84 | 1.18 | 0.49 | 0.42 | 0.23 | 0 | 0 | 0 |
| 0.9 | 8.68 | 2.03 | 0.33 | 0.18 | 0 | 0 | 0 | 0 |

**Table 6.** The EER (%) of baboon

| p\s | 4 | 8 | 12 | 16 | 20 | 24 | 28 | 32 |
|---|---|---|---|---|---|---|---|---|
| 0.5 | 19.78 | 7.76 | 5.78 | 3.32 | 0.96 | 0.91 | 0.62 | 0 |
| 0.7 | 21.02 | 11.23 | 5.72 | 2.65 | 0.69 | 0.65 | 0.44 | 0 |
| 0.9 | 22.67 | 10.65 | 5.05 | 2.61 | 0.71 | 0.51 | 0.34 | 0 |

## 4.2 Comparisons of Performances

A new fluctuation function is used in this paper. To evaluate the performance of the new fluctuation function compared with other similar methods, six graylevel images of size $512 \times 512$ are selected as test images, including lena, man, plane, couple, tiffany, baboon. Experimental comparisons of fluctuation functions among the proposed method and other fluctuation functions in Zhang's [2], Hong's [3], Liao's [10] are shown in Fig. 2 when the embedding ratio $p = 1$ and the side match technique is used.

The experimental results show that the use of a new fluctuation function can further reduce the extracted-bit error rate, especially when the sizes of blocks are small. This indicates that the new fluctuation function has higher accuracy than the previous methods. When data is embedded based on the embedding ratio, the selected texture area blocks are becoming less. Additionally, using the new fluctuation function can further reduce the extracted-bit error rate. Taking the man and the couple as test images, the relationships of EER with respect to block sizes or data embedding ratio are analyzed. Compared with other methods, the proposed method can further reduce the EER value. Figure 3 shows the recovery results using Zhang's, Hong's, Liao's methods and the proposed method.

The results reveal that the proposed method can further reduce the extracted-bit error rate in the case that the embedding ratio is considered, especially when the size of block is small. For example, when $p = 0.5$ and $s = 4$, the extracted-bit error rate of the proposed method can be reduced by 20.25 % and 24.34 % with comparing with the Hong's and the Liao's methods for man image; the extracted-bit error rate of the proposed method can be reduced by 23.39 % and 40.55 % with comparing with the Hong's and the Liao's methods for couple image. Moreover, compared with Zhang's

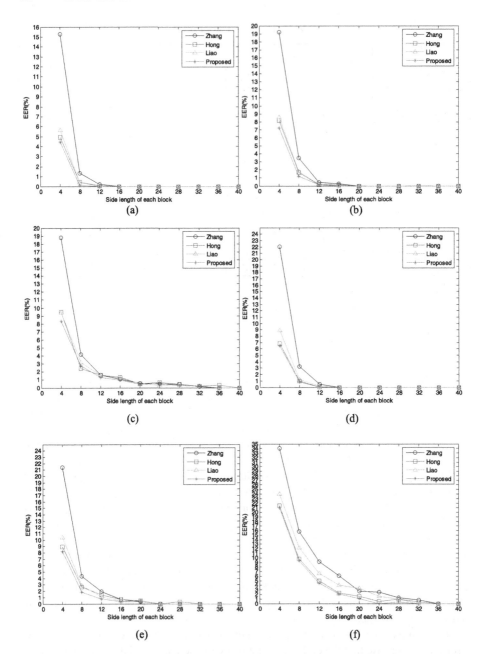

**Fig. 2.** comparisons of fluctuation function based on six images. (a) lena, (b) man, (c) plane, (d) couple, (e) tiffany, (f) baboon.

method, the proposed method has obvious advantages. It should be noted that the proposed method can obtain better results for some complex images. However, for some images which contain a large number of equal pixels, such as the MRI images,

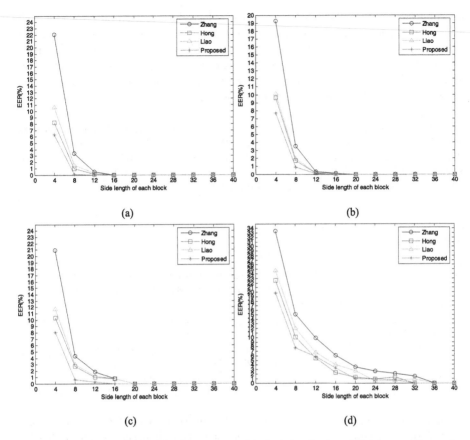

**Fig. 3.** Comparisons of EER(%) with respect to block sizes when p = 0.5 (a) man, (b) couple, (c) tiffany, (d) baboon.

cartoon images and other medical images, the results are not satisfying. It should also be noted that, because the encryption and decryption process in proposed method are similar to previous method, the security of these algorithms are only depending on the pseudo-random sequence, these methods have the same safety performance. The proposed method does not affect the confidentiality of the encrypted data.

## 5  Conclusions

In this paper, based on Zhang's method, we propose an improved algorithm for reversible data hiding in encrypted image when the embedding ratio is considered. A new fluctuation function is used, and then makes the estimation more precisely. The smoothness of each image block is calculated by using the new fluctuation function, and then the blocks are sorted in ascending order according to the fluctuation function value. We select some blocks with the smaller fluctuation function value that are smoother to embed data based on the embedding ratio. This way, we can avoid selecting the blocks with texture region and reduce the extracted-bit error rate. The experimental results show that the new fluctuation function is more precise and the proposed method can further reduce the extracted-bit error compared with other relevant methods when the embedding ratio is considered. In the future, we will go on improving the fluctuation function and improve the proposed method to use for the more smooth images, such as some MRI images and cartoon images.

**Acknowledgments.** This work was partially supported by National Natural Science Foundation of China (No. 61103215, 61232016, 61202439, 61202496, 61373132, 61303045, and 61373133), Hunan Provincial Natural Science Key Foundation of China (No. 13JJ2031), National Social Science Fund Projects (No.13CJY007), Youth Growth Plan of Hunan University, Ministry of Education, Humanities and Social Sciences Research Projects (No. 12YJAZH216).

# References

1. Puech, W., Chaumont, M., Strauss, O.: A reversible data hiding method for encrypted images security. In: Forensics, Steganography, and Watermarking of Multimedia Contents X, Proceedings of the SPIE, vol. 6819(2008)
2. Zhang, X.P.: Reversible data hiding in encrypted images. IEEE Signal Process. Lett. **18**(4), 255–258 (2011)
3. Hong, W., Chen, T., Wu, H.: An improved reversible data hiding in encrypted images using side match. IEEE Signal Process. Lett. **19**(4), 199–202 (2012)
4. Yu, J., Zhu, G., Li, X., Yang, J.: An improved algorithm for reversible data hiding in encrypted image. In: Shi, Y.Q., Kim, H.-J., Pérez-González, F. (eds.) IWDW 2012. LNCS, vol. 7809, pp. 384–394. Springer, Heidelberg (2013)
5. Hong, W., Chen, T.-S., Chen, J., Kao, Y.-H., Wu, H.-Y., Wu, M.-C.: Reversible data embedment for encrypted cartoon images using unbalanced bit flipping. In: Tan, Y., Shi, Y., Mo, H. (eds.) ICSI 2013, Part II. LNCS, vol. 7929, pp. 208–214. Springer, Heidelberg (2013)
6. Zhang, X.P.: Separable reversible data hiding in encrypted image. IEEE Trans. Inf. Forensics Secur. **7**(2), 826–832 (2012)
7. Zhang, X., Qin, C., Sun, G.: Reversible data hiding in encrypted images using pseudorandom sequence modulation. In: Shi, Y.Q., Kim, H.-J., Pérez-González, F. (eds.) IWDW 2012. LNCS, vol. 7809, pp. 358–367. Springer, Heidelberg (2013)
8. Kadam, P., Nawale, M.: Separable Reversible encrypted data hiding in encrypted image using AES algorithm and lossy technique. In: Proceeding of International Conference on Pattern Recognition, Informatics and Mobile Engineering, pp. 312–316(2013)
9. Zhang, X.P., Qian, Z.X., Feng, G.R., Ren, Y.L.: Efficient reversible data hiding in encrypted images. J. Vis. Commun. Image R **25**(2), 325–328 (2014)
10. Liao, X., Shu, C.W.: Reversible data hiding in encrypted images based on absolute mean difference of multiple neighboring pixels. J. Vis. Commun. Image R. **28**, 21–27 (2015)
11. Ma, K., Zhang, W.M., Zhao, X.F., Yu, N.H., Li, F.H.: Reversible data hiding in encrypted images by reserving room before encryption. J. IEEE Trans. Inf. Forensics Security **8**(3), 553–562 (2013)
12. Zhang, W.M., Ma, K.D., Yu, N.H.: Reversibility improved data hiding in encrypted images. J. Sig. Process. **94**, 118–127 (2014)

# Study on Personalized Location Privacy Preservation Algorithms Based on Road Networks

Hongyun Xu, Jun Yang, Yong Zhang$^{(\boxtimes)}$, Mengzhen Xu,
and Jiayi Gan

School of Computer Science and Engineering,
South China University of Technology, Guangzhou 510006, China
z.yoo@qq.com

**Abstract.** It is very important for LBS popularization and application to study personalized location privacy preservation algorithms based on road networks for the mobile users. This paper proposes the Prediction Group by L algorithm (i.e., PL) in which the road networks is represented as a weighted graph, and the value of the weight of each edge is equal to its selection rate; the edges of the graph are sorted by the depth-first search algorithm, and grouped by the privacy degree of user where the group is used as the anonymous edge set (i.e., AES) to realize the location privacy preservation. The experimental results show that PL has high success rate of privacy. Additionally, it is able to provide higher quality personalized location privacy preservation because the AES generated by this algorithm is more approached to the privacy requirements of users than some other typical algorithms.

**Keywords:** Road networks · Location privacy · K-anonymity · L-diversity · Location-based service

## 1 Introduction

With the popularization of smart phones and portable devices, location-based service (i.e., LBS) applications attract more and more users. Typical LBS applications include the nearest point of interest (POI) query, location-aware advertisement, and road navigation, etc.

However, if users want to obtain LBS, they have to send their private information (such as location, identity) to location server (i.e., LS), which is often untrusted and may reveal users' information, thus threatening user's privacy [1, 2]. Therefore, LBS applications should consider privacy preservation of user's information. In recent years, there have been lots of researches on how to preserve user's privacy information. So far, the mainstream methods on privacy preservation in LBS can be classified into two kinds.

The first one is based on Euclidean Space, which supposes that the user can move in a space without limit. This kind mainly uses K-anonymity [3, 4] and obfuscation region [5]. K-anonymity guarantees there are at least other K-1 users in the obfuscation region, and user's practical location will be replaced with the obfuscation region and

© Springer International Publishing Switzerland 2015
G. Wang et al. (Eds.): ICA3PP 2015 Workshops, LNCS 9532, pp. 35–45, 2015.
DOI: 10.1007/978-3-319-27161-3_4

sent to server. For personalized privacy preservation, this kind provides different degrees of privacy preservation [9, 10] by means of adjusting parameter K.

The second one is based on road networks, and it assumes that mobile user and query object are both located on practical roads. This kind [6–8] transforms the road network to graph, and uses K-anonymity and L-diversity [11] to implement privacy preservation, where L-diversity guarantees that there are at least L different physical locations in the obfuscation region. For personalized preservation, this kind completes the preservation by adjusting both parameters K and L of the obfuscation region.

The second one above can provide a higher practical value than the first one, since it considers the practical situations. Therefore we do some researches on the second method and propose a new personalized location privacy preservation algorithm. The main contributions of our paper are listed below:

- Based on the amount of mobile users on the road networks and the length of road sections, we define the road prosperous degree and selection rate, which are used for measuring probability of road section that users locates at.
- By using the analysis of Markov predicting method, we draw the conclusion that when mobile user is at the cross road, the larger selection rate of the road section is, the higher probability the user drives in.
- According to road selection rate and road prosperous degree, we propose a personalized location privacy preservation algorithm which satisfies both K-anonymity and L-diversity of user requirements.
- After lots of experiments and comparisons between our algorithm and some other typical algorithms, we make some analysis and draw a conclusion that our algorithm provides higher quality for personalized privacy preservation than other algorithms.

In Sect. 2 we summarize the related works; Sect. 3 introduces the road networks model, query model, system structure and attack model; Sect. 4 describes the algorithm in detail; Sect. 5 contains theory analysis and experiment analysis; and Sect. 6 is the conclusion of this paper.

## 2  Related Works

There have been many researches on the location privacy preservation problems based on road networks. Mouratidis et al. [7] propose using depth-first search algorithm (i.e., DFS algorithm) and breadth-first search algorithm (i.e., BFS algorithm). They use DFS or BFS to implement the process of linearization of road networks, and then generate the obfuscation region to implement the privacy preservation. However, this method doesn't consider L-diversity, which may have a hidden threat.

Wang et al. [6] propose a location privacy preservation algorithm called XStar. It represents the road section as a star in the intersection and it uses star and its neighbor stars to implement the anonymity. This algorithm considers both K-anonymity and L-diversity, however, its success rate is low.

Xue et al. [8] propose location privacy preservation method called anonymous Cycle and Forest (i.e., CCF). It transforms road networks to graph and uses BFS to find some satisfactory cycles or forests as an AES. However, if privacy degree of user is relatively low, the AES generated by this algorithm may contain more users and road sections than user's expectation, therefore it may result in low query quality.

To solve the above problems, we propose the concepts of road prosperous degree and selection rate in road networks, and design a personalized location privacy preservation algorithm which is based on road selection rate. Our algorithm, called Prediction Group by L algorithm, satisfies both user's K-anonymity and L-diversity.

## 3   System Models

This section introduces some system models, including the road networks model, the query model, system structure and attack model.

### 3.1   Road Networks Model

The road networks can be modeled as an undirected graph G = (V, E), where V represents nodes set, and E represents road sections set. The degree of nodes represents the amount of road sections which are connected with the intersections. As shown in Fig. 1, we can see that it can be represented as an undirected graph G = (V, E), and the nodes set V = {n1, n2, n3..., n13}, road sections set E = {n1n2, n2n3, n3n4, n3n12..., n12n13, n13n4}, the degree of node n3 is 4.

### 3.2   Query Model

We formulate the model Qu = {id, loc, req, K, L} as user's query model, where Qu represents a query from user u, and it is composed of user's identification information id, location information loc, query requirement req, location privacy requirements K and L. The parameters K and L represent K-anonymity and L-diversity respectively.

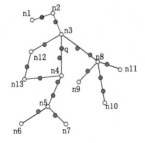

**Fig. 1.**  Road networks

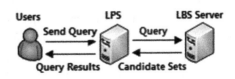

**Fig. 2.**  Central server structure

### 3.3  Location Privacy System Structure

We use Central Server Structure to preserve location privacy, as shown in Fig. 2, and we add a Location Privacy Server (i.e., LPS) in the middle. The main function of LPS is to receive query and generate AES according to parameters K, L and loc from Qu.

Suppose the AES is loc', the identification information of users in AES is id', combine loc', id' and req, LPS can get the new query Qu' = {id', loc', req}, then it sends Qu' to LBS server. Next LBS server returns the query results (called candidate set) to LPS, and then LPS filters the candidate sets and send the appropriate results to users.

### 3.4  Attack Model

The goal of attackers is to acquire users' privacy information from LPS. However, the ability of an attacker is related with his background and inference algorithms.

We suppose that the attacker knows the structure of road networks and the distribution of users in the networks. The attacker can take use of distribution to calculate the probability of each AES that the users locate at, and attack the users in the road section with higher probability since it has higher success rate.

Additionally, suppose attacker knows the AES of users, the topological graph of road networks, and the personalized privacy algorithm which is used to generate the AES. The attacker can implement location privacy preservation algorithm for each edge of AES and attack the users in the edge with higher probability.

## 4  Algorithm Design

This section introduces some related definitions and designs for the personalized location privacy preservation algorithm, Prediction Group by L.

### 4.1  Related Definitions

**Road Prosperous Degree.** It represents the amount of mobile users in a unit length of a road section. We use W to represent it. From the definition, we know if the road section has higher prosperous degree, then it has more mobile users in unit length of this road section.

As shown in Fig. 1, the red nodes represent mobile users, and we suppose the length of n3n8, n8n11, n8n10, n8n9 are all equal to 1. Then the road prosperous degrees of them are W(n3, n8) = 2, W(n8, n11) = 1, W(n8, n10) = 2, W(n8, n9) = 1 respectively.

**Selection Rate.** It defines the probability which road section the user will drive in and it is calculated by the ratio of the prosperous degree of a road section and the sum of all prosperous degrees of connected road sections. We use P to represent it. Usually it is used for the case when mobile user is in the cross road (like node n8 in Fig. 1), and it can infer most possible road section that user locates at.

As shown in Fig. 1, suppose the user locates at n8, then P(n3, n8) = W(n3, n8) /(W (n3, n8) + W(n8, n11) + W(n8, n10) + W(n8, n9)) = 1/3, in the same way, we can get that P(n8, n11) = 1/6, P(n8, n10) = 1/3, P(n8, n9) = 1/6, etc.

**Open Node [7].** It represents the node in the AES which satisfies that at least one road section connected with this node is not in the AES.

**KNN Query of Anonymous Edge Set [7].** It represents doing K-Nearest Neighbor query for the open node in the AES, namely, retrieves K objects that are nearest to the node, and query all the objects in the AES.

## 4.2   Prediction-Based Grouping Algorithm

### 4.2.1   Markov Prediction Analysis [12]

When the user drives in the intersection of the road networks, what is the characteristic of the next road section driving in? We use Markov Prediction method to make some analysis.

Markov Prediction method is to determine the future status according to the original probability and status transition probability of different status of an event. The probability of event transition is defined by Eq. (1), and we choose the biggest probability to determine the future status, namely choose the biggest one in P.

$$P = \begin{bmatrix} P11 & P12 & \ldots & P1n \\ P21 & P22 & \ldots & P2n \\ \ldots & \ldots & \ldots & \ldots \\ Pn1 & Pn2 & \ldots & Pnn \end{bmatrix} \tag{1}$$

Furthermore, we use selection rate as the transition probability of Markov Prediction method, which is used to predict the next road section that the mobile user will choose to drive in. And this analysis is based on the road networks of Oldenburg in Germany [13].

We set the number of mobile users N1 in the road networks to 6329 at time t1, and then use the biggest selection rate and the smallest selection rate as the prediction results of status transition probability; next we can get the result as Table 1 shown. In Table 1, the first column means in the next time t2, the number of users that appear in the predicted road section is N2; the second column means percentage of the users who are driving to the predicted road section. We use PS to represent it. The first row means the predicted result with the biggest selection rate; and the second row means that with the smallest selection rate. From Table 1, we can see that use bigger selection rate can have higher success rate than use smaller selection rate in predicting.

**Table 1.**  Results of Markov prediction

|  | N2 | PS |
|---|---|---|
| P set to largest | 2178 | 34.41 |
| P set to smallest | 696 | 11.00 |

From above all, we can see that the bigger the road selection rate is, the higher probability that the mobile user chooses this road section to drive in; otherwise, the lower probability that user choose this section to drive.

### 4.2.2 PL Algorithm

Prediction Group by L algorithm (i.e., PL), uses two privacy parameters, K-anonymity and L-diversity, to realize the personalized location privacy preservation of users. First it uses selection rate as the weight of road section, and depth-first search algorithm to traverse the road networks according to the value of weight, to get the linearized sequence. Next the algorithm groups the sequence according to user's personalized privacy parameters K and L, which makes the distribution of mobile users in different roads uniform. In this way, it can decrease the success rate of inference attack to weight of edges. The main steps of PL algorithm are shown in Algorithm 1.

**Algorithm 1.** Prediction Group by L Algorithm
Input: Road network G, the distribution of mobile users in G, the location information of user u, the requirement of privacy parameters K and L
Output: Anonymous edge set S
Step 1, calculate the prosperous degree and selection rate of each road section in G;
Step 2, use DFS algorithm to sort each road section in G, linearize G and get the linearized Array according to selection rate P. Obtain the index number IdL of Array where the user u locates in;
Step 3, group Array by user's requirement for L-diversity, and set the starting index number StartId = (IdL / L) * L and the ending index number EndId = (IdL / L) * L + L - 1 to S;
Step 4, calculate the number of mobile users in S, mark it as k';
Step 5, if k' < K, L adds 1, and jump to step 3;
Step 6, output S, end.

Here we give an example to show how to get the satisfied S. Suppose IdL = 27, L = 5, then StartId = (27 /5) * 5 = 25, EndId = (27 /5) * 5 + 5 - 1 = 29; calculate the users in S, if k' < K, L adds 1, and we get new StartId = (27 /6) * 6 = 24 and EndId = (27 /6) * 6 + 6 - 1 = 29. Repeat these steps, we can gradually increase the size of S and finally get the satisfied S.

## 5   Simulation Experiments and Analysis

This section compares and analyzes our algorithm and typical algorithms by experiments. The experiments are realized by Java, and the coding environment is Eclipse. The hardware environment is Intel(R) Pentium(R) 4 CPU 2.66 GHz, 1.49 GB internal memory. The operating system is Microsoft Windows XP SP3. The experiment platform uses the famous road networks generating platform [13], the Network-based Generator of Moving Objects (i.e., NGMO). It uses the map of Oldenburg in Germany to simulate experiments.

## 5.1    Parameters Setting

The parameters setting of experiments are shown in Table 2. The amount of nodes, edges and average length of edges represent the corresponding parts in the map, and the query amount represents the amount of queries that users send. User amount represents the amount of mobile users in the road network, and POI amount represents the total amount of POIs in the road network. Additionally, the value of K, L, the maximal L and kNN satisfy normal distribution.

**Table 2.** Simulation environment parameter table

| Item | Values | Item | Values |
|---|---|---|---|
| Nodes | 6105 | Minimal K | 3 |
| Total edges | 7035 | Average L | 5 |
| Average edges length | 184 | Minimal L | 3 |
| Query amount | 10000 | Maximal L | 20 |
| User amount | 17845 | kNN | 5 |
| Average K | 5 | POI | 4949 |

## 5.2    Algorithm Evaluation Target

In our paper we evaluate the algorithm in four aspects, namely the average information entropy, average anonymous edge set, average query cost and privacy success rate.

$$\text{Entropy} = -\sum_{l \in S} P(l)*\log(P(l)) \tag{2}$$

**Average Information Entropy.** It defined by Eq. (2) [6]. In Eq. (2) $P(l)$ represents the probability that user is in the road section $l$ of AES. When the amount of edges is steady, the more uniform of distribution of mobile users is, the larger the information entropy is, and lower the success rate of inference attack is.

**Average Size of Anonymous Edge Set.** It represents the amount of road sections in the AES, the smaller it is, the smaller the cost of network transition and query cost are. Thus the average size of AES can reflect the communication cost and query cost to some extent.

**Average Query Cost.** It can be evaluated by average query candidate set and average query time [8]. Average query candidate set is the average values of returned result sets that are received by LPS. Average query time is the average time of LBS server to complete the query.

**Privacy Success Rate.** It is the ratio of successful queries and the total queries [14], and success rate SR = Q_num' /Q_num, where Q_num is the amount of total queries, and Q_num' is the amount of successful queries in personalized location privacy preservation.

## 5.3    Analysis of Experiment Results

The experiments are mainly evaluated in average information entropy, average size of
AES, average query cost, average query time and anonymous success rate for XStar
[6], PL, CCF [8], BFS [7] and DFS algorithm [7]. For CCF, we only consider simple
road networks; for BFS and DFS, since they don't consider L, we only consider the
case when L takes mean value.

From Fig. 3(a) we can see that the average size of AES of PL, BFS and DFS are
similar, but XStar and CCF are higher. Since PL uses selection rate, the distribution of
users is uniform; for BFS and DFS, they don't have any redundant road sections.
For CCF and XStar, they use extra structures, which make the generated AES large.

From Fig. 3(b) we can see that the tendencies are similar. Since the user privacy
requirement can be satisfied easily, the influencing factor becomes L, and the tendencies become nearly linear growth. For CCF, it finds many cycles, thus needs more
edges when L is small.

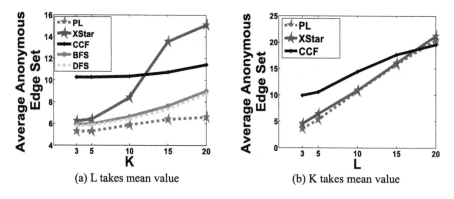

(a) L takes mean value                    (b) K takes mean value

**Fig. 3.**  The relation between average size of AES and privacy parameters

As Fig. 4(a) shows, the average information entropy for XStar and CCF are the best
since they have large AESs; PL has small anonymous set, but uses selection rate to
balance the distribution in the AES, thus the information entropy is relatively high.
For BFS and DFS, they don't consider the balance of distribution and this result in
lower information entropy.

From Fig. 4(b) we can see average information entropy is increasing gradually and
all of them are similar, since AESs are similar and have uniform distributions when K
is steady.

From Fig. 5 we can see that CCF is best for two conditions of average query
candidate set, and PL has larger candidate set than CCF, but smaller than XStar in some
cases. Since BFS and DFS have smaller AESs, the average size of query candidate set
is also small.

From Figs. 5 and 6, we can see the candidate set of CCF is small, but the average
query time is long, since the cycles in it are large and it has few open nodes in AES.
The average candidate set and average query cost of PL are larger than XStar and CCF

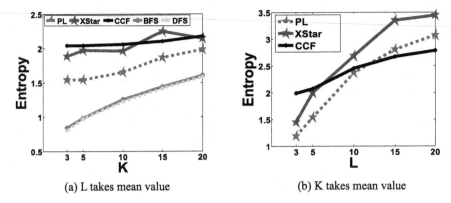

(a) L takes mean value                    (b) K takes mean value

**Fig. 4.** Relation between average information entropy and privacy parameters

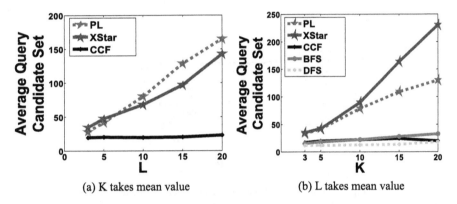

(a) K takes mean value                    (b) L takes mean value

**Fig. 5.** The relation between average query cost and K or L

when K takes mean value, because the connectivity of its AES becomes smaller and the amount of open nodes becomes larger with L increasing; when L takes mean value, PL is better since connectivity is steady and AES is smaller; for XStar, it has large AES which leads to large query candidate set and query time; for BFS and DFS, the small AESs and less open nodes lead to small average query candidate set, and also they have less query time since they have less open nodes.

From Fig. 7 we can see that with the increase of K, the success rate of XStar is apparently decreasing, since generated stars can bring redundant sections. The success rate of PL algorithm is steady and high since it considers both K-anonymity and L-diversity and avoids the shortage of redundant road sections; the success rate of PL can keep in 100 % since when L is steady and K is not large, we can always find satisfied AES, which means the query is successful. For CCF algorithm, the generated cycles have lots of road sections, which decreases success rate; for BFS and DFS algorithms, when the value of K is small, the amount of edges is smaller than L, thus they don't satisfy privacy degree,

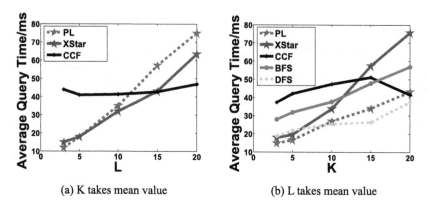

(a) K takes mean value          (b) L takes mean value

**Fig. 6.** The relation between average query time and K or L

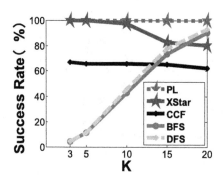

**Fig. 7.** The relation between privacy success rate and K

which leads to low success rate. From Fig. 7 we can see that the success rate of PL algorithm is higher than those in CCF, XStar, BFS and DFS.

## 6  Conclusions

Based on the practical road networks, we propose PL algorithm to implement the personalized location privacy preservation. When PL groups the users according to user's privacy parameters K and L, it considers the selection rate of road sections, which can satisfy K and L easily and lead to lower query cost. Additionally, it makes the distribution of users in each road section more uniform, which decreases the success rate of inference attack and increases the privacy degree. The experiment results show that PL can provide higher quality of service in personalized location privacy preservation than some typical algorithms like XStar and CCF algorithms.

**Acknowledgments.** This work was partially supported by the Natural Science Foundation of China (No. 61272403), by the Fundamental Research Funds for the Central Universities (No. 10561201474). We also appreciate Yaohui Zheng and Kai Tian for their kindly help of the experimental analysis and programming.

# References

1. Mokbel, M.F.: Privacy in location-based services: state-of -the-art and research directions. In: Proceedings of the 8th International Conference on Mobile Data Management, p. 228 (2007)
2. Pedreschi, D., Bonchi, F., Turini, F., Verykios, V.S., Atzori, M., Malin, B., Moelans, B., Saygin, Y.: Privacy protection: regulations and technologies, opportunities and threats. In: Giannotti, F., Pedreschi, D. (eds.) Mobility, Data Mining And Privacy, pp. 101–119. Springer, Berlin (2008)
3. Sweeney, L.: k-anonymity: a model for protecting privacy. Int. J. Uncertainty Fuzziness Knowl. Based Syst. **10**(5), 557–570 (2002)
4. Gruteser, M., Grunwald, D.: Anonymous usage of location- based services through spatial and temporal cloaking. In: Proceedings of the first International Conference on Mobile Systems, Applications, and Services. San Francisco, CA, USA, pp. 163–168 (2003)
5. Ardagna, C.A., Cremonini, M., Damiani, E., De Capitani di Vimercati, S., Samarati, P.: Location privacy protection through obfuscation-based techniques. In: Barker, S., Ahn, G.-J. (eds.) Data and Applications Security 2007. LNCS, vol. 4602, pp. 47–60. Springer, Heidelberg (2007)
6. Wang, T., Liu, L.: Privacy-aware mobile services over road networks. Proc. VLDB Endow. **2**(1), 1042–1053 (2009)
7. Mouratidis, K., Yiu, M.L.: Anonymous query processing in road networks. IEEE Trans. Knowl. Data Eng. TKDE **22**(1), 2–15 (2010)
8. Xue, J., Liu, X., Yang, X., et al.: A location privacy preserving approach on road networks. Chin. J. Comput. **34**(5), 865–878 (2011). (In Chinese)
9. Mokbel, M.F., Chow, C.Y., Aref, W.G.: The new casper: query processing for location services without compromising privacy. In: Proceedings of the 32nd International Conference on Very Large Data Bases, Seoul, Korea, pp. 763–774 (2006)
10. Hong-Yun, X., Jun, X., Gong, Y.-J., Meng-Zhen, X.: Algorithms to generate location privacy area based on location privacy protection with spatial cloaking. J. S. Chin. Univ. Technol. (Nat. Sci. Ed.) **42**(1), 97–103 (2014). (in Chinese)
11. Machanavajjhala, A., Gehrke, J., et al.: L-diversity: privacy beyond k-anonymity. In: Proceedings of 22nd International Conference on Data Engineering, Atlanta, Georgia, USA, pp. 24–36 (2006)
12. Baum, L.E., Petrie, T.: Statistical inference for probabilistic functions of finite state Markov chains. Ann. Math. Stat. **37**(6), 1554–1563 (1966)
13. Brinkhoff, T.: A framework for generating network-based moving objects. GeoInfomatica **6** (2), 153–180 (2002)
14. Pan, X., Xiao, Z., Meng, X.: Survey of location privacy-preserving. J. Front. Comput. Sci. Technol. **1**(3), 268–281 (2007). (In Chinese)

# A Hierarchical Identity-Based Signature from Composite Order Bilinear Groups

Peixin Chen[1]($^{(\boxtimes)}$), Xiaofeng Wang[1], and Jinshu Su[1,2]

[1] College of Computer, National University of Defense Technology,
Changsha 410073, China
{chenpeixin,xf_wang,sjs}@nudt.edu.cn
[2] National Key Laboratory for Parallel and Distributed Processing,
National University of Defense Technology, Changsha 410073, China

**Abstract.** Cloud storage has become one of the integral parts of online life. However, the cloud storage brings in new kinds of data security issues as well. Authentication framework for both users and services provides an efficient solution to the security and privacy problems of the cloud storage. In this paper we propose a Hierarchical Identity-Based Signature (HIBS) scheme using composite order bilinear groups. We present the methodology of dual system signature to prove that our scheme is secure against existential forgery on adaptively chosen message and identity attack under standard model. Our HIBS scheme shares the same system parameters with the hierarchical identity-based encryption (LW-HIBE) scheme by Lewko and Waters, and it is as efficient as the LW-HIBE. Combining our signature scheme with the LW-HIBE scheme yields a complete solution of an identity-based public key system, which can be utilized to build an authentication framework for cloud storage.

**Keywords:** Hierarchical identity-based signature · Dual system encryption · Composite order group · Bilinear map · Cloud storage

## 1 Introduction

As the network technology rapidly developing, cloud storage is becoming more and more convenient. Cloud storage service, such as Dropbox, Google drive, Apple iCloud drive, has become one of the integral parts of online life. People anywhere at anytime can access the data on cloud storage system in condition of the Internet connection. Besides the benefits, cloud storage also introduces security problem of user data. User has no ultimate control over the fate of their data without physically possession. Thus, traditional cryptographic primitives for the purpose of data security protection cannot be directly adopted [13]. Several works on securing the cloud storage with authentication framework have been presented [9,12,16]. Scholars have conceded that certificate-based authentication framework, such as SSL Authentication Protocol (SAP), is low efficient to be applied to the cloud storage [14,17]. Thus, Li et al. propose an identity-based authentication protocol for data protection in cloud computing [16]. Based on

© Springer International Publishing Switzerland 2015
G. Wang et al. (Eds.): ICA3PP 2015 Workshops, LNCS 9532, pp. 46–56, 2015.
DOI: 10.1007/978-3-319-27161-3_5

the Hierarchical Identity-based cryptography (HIBC) scheme, they achieve a certificate-free framework, which aligns well with demands of cloud computing. The IBC cryptosystem, consisting of Identity-Based Encryption (IBE) and Identity-Based Signature (IBS), is pioneered by Shamir in 1984 [18]. In the IBC, user identities, such as IP or e-mail addresses, are used as public key of uesr. And a trust party called Private Key Generator (PKG) is needed to generate private keys for users. Boneh and Franklin first propose a full functional system (BF-IBE) based on bilinear maps between groups [2]. Gentry and Silverberg introduce the idea of hierarchical IBE (HIBE) and propose the first scheme [10] to distribute the workload of PKG. Unlike the previous works that build (H)IBE and (H)IBS schemes from prime order groups, Lewko and Waters present an HIBE scheme from composite order groups [15]. They prove the full security of the scheme utilizing a methodology named dual encryption system [19].

Meanwhile, several bilinear map based IBS and HIBS schemes [4–8,11] have also been presented. Sharing the same system parameters with BF-IBE, Cha and Cheon present an identity-based signature scheme (CC-IBS) [7]. The BF-IBE and CC-IBS can be combined to provide a complete solution of an identity-based public key system. However, both of the schemes are proved security in random oracle model. Analogously, Chow et al. [8] present an HIBS scheme that shares the same system parameters with the BB-HIBE scheme [1]. However, their HIBS scheme is not efficient because both the key and signature scale linearly as identity depth increases. And it is also only secure in random oracle model. Constructing from composite order groups, Gerbush et al. propose two provably secure signature schemes. However, key generation algorithms in both the signature schemes use random output as public keys. That is, the signature schemes they proposed are not IBS schemes.

In this paper, we propose a hierarchical identity-based signature scheme from composite order bilinear groups and present formal security proofs utilizing the dual system signature methodology. To summarize, we make the following contributions:

1. We present an HIBS scheme from composite order bilinear groups, which shares the same parameters of LW-HIBE scheme [15].
2. We modify the dual system encryption and present a methodology named dual system signature to prove the security of the HIBS scheme. Utilizing the dual system signature, we prove that our HIBS scheme is secure against existential forgery on adaptively chosen message and identity attack under standard model.
3. Our scheme owns good performance features. That is, the private key becomes shorter as the depth of identity increases, and the size of signature is constant and short in our HIBS scheme.

## 2   Preliminaries

In this section, we review some background knowledge, including composite order bilinear group, the complexity assumptions used in our proof. We then introduce the methodology of the dual system encryption and present a modification that is referred to as dual system signature for our proof of HIBS scheme.

## 2.1   Composite Order Bilinear Groups

Composite order bilinear groups were first introduced by Boneh et al. [3]. Let $G$ and $G_T$ be multiplicative cyclic groups of order $N = p_1p_2p_3$ where $p_1$, $p_2$, $p_3$ are distinct primes, and $e : G \times G \to G_T$ be a bilinear map that has the following properties:

1. Bilinear: $\forall g, h \in G, a, b \in \mathbb{Z}_N, e(g^a, h^b) = e(g, h)^{ab}$
2. Non-degenerate: $\exists g \in G$, s.t. $e(g, g) \neq 1$
3. Computable: $\forall g, h \in G$, there is an efficient algorithm to compute $e(g, h)$.

The group $G$ is referred to as a composite order bilinear group if there exists such a group $G_T$ and map $e$. We use a group generator $\mathcal{G}$ with input $\tau$ to output a description of a bilinear group $G$. That is, input a security parameter $\tau \in \mathbb{Z}^+$, $\mathcal{G}$ outputs $(N = p_1p_2p_3, G, G_T, e)$.

Let $G_{p_1}$, $G_{p_2}$, and $G_{p_3}$ denote the subgroups of order $p_1$, $p_2$ and $p_3$ in $G$ respectively. Lewko and Waters illuminate that, when $h_i \in G_i$, and $h_j \in G_j$ for $i \neq j$, $e(h_i, h_j)$ is an identity element in $G_T$ [15]. Such property is referred to as orthogonality property of $G_{p_1}, G_{p_2}, G_{p_3}$.

## 2.2   Complexity Assumptions

We prove the security of our HIBS scheme based on same complexity assumptions as the LW-HIBE system [15] does. Let $\mathcal{G}$ be a group generator, $x \xleftarrow{R} G$ denote randomly choose an element $x$ from group $G$, and $G_{p_ip_j}$ denote subgroup of order $p_ip_j$ in $G$, these assumptions are defined as follows.

**Assumption 1.** Let $g \xleftarrow{R} G_{p_1}$, $X_3 \xleftarrow{R} G_{p_3}$, $T_1 \xleftarrow{R} G_{p_1p_2}$, $T_2 \xleftarrow{R} G_{p_1}$. And randomly choose $T \in \{T_1, T_2\}$. Given $\{\mathbb{G}, g, X_3, T\}$, no algorithm $\mathcal{A}$ can determine $T \in G_{p_1p_2}$ or $T \in G_{p_1}$ with more than a negligible advantage.

**Assumption 2.** Let $g, X_1 \xleftarrow{R} G_{p_1}$, $X_2, Y_2 \xleftarrow{R} G_{p_2}$, $X_3, Y_3 \xleftarrow{R} G_{p_3}$, $T_1 \xleftarrow{R} G$, $T_2 \xleftarrow{R} G_{p_1p_3}$. And randomly choose $T \in \{T_1, T_2\}$. Given $\{\mathbb{G}, g, X_1X_2, X_3, Y_2Y_3, T\}$, no algorithm $\mathcal{A}$ can determine $T \in G$ or $T \in G_{p_1p_3}$ with more than a negligible advantage.

## 2.3   Dual System Encryption and Dual System Signature

Dual system encryption is a scheme that can be used for proving security of encryption systems [19]. Two additional structures semi-functional key and semi-functional ciphertext are used. A normal key can be used to decrypt both normal and semi-functional ciphertexts. And a normal ciphertext can be decrypted by both normal and semi-functional keys. However, decrypting a semi-functional ciphertext with a semi-functional key will fall into fail.

Generally speaking, an attack game with an attacker and a challenger is used for proving the security of an encryption system. The encryption system is regarded as security if the attacker cannot win the game with a non-negligible advantage. Using the dual system encryption, a sequence of games are needed. Among the games, the first game is a real game and the others are modified games with the semi-functional keys and ciphertexts. To prove that an attacker cannot break the game, the challenger provides the last bogus game which is proved unbreakable to the attacker and proves that the attacker cannot distinguish one game from the other.

We modify the dual system encryption and present the methodology of dual system signature for proving security of signature systems. Analogous to the dual system encryption, the dual system signature also uses two additional structures and a sequence games to prove the signature system security. However, semi-functional signatures instead of semi-functional ciphertexts are used. A semi-functional key can be used to sign messages and a semi-functional signature can be verified by a corresponding identity. We will introduce the details of games and designing of semi-functional keys and semi-functional signatures in Sect. 4.2.

# 3   Overview of Hierarchical Identity-Based Signature Scheme

In this section, we briefly describe the generic construction of the hierarchical identity-based signature scheme. We then introduce the standard attack model for HIBS schemes that is firstly presented by Cha and Cheon [7].

## 3.1   Definitions

The hierarchical identity-based signature scheme consists of four algorithms: Setup, KeyGen, Sign and Verify.

**Setup.** The setup algorithm takes a security parameter as input and outputs the public parameters $Param$ and a PKG master key $MK$.

**KeyGen.** The key generation algorithm takes the PKG master key, multiple secret keys as well as an identity ID = $(ID_1, \ldots, ID_n)$ as input and output the private key.

**Sign.** The signing algorithm takes the public parameters $Param$, a message $M$, and a private key as input and outputs a signature $\sigma$.

**Verify.** The verification algorithm takes the public parameters $Param$, a signature $\sigma$, and a message $M$ as in put and check whether $\sigma$ is valid.

## 3.2   Security Model

The attack model for HIDS scheme derives from the existential forgery on adaptively chosen message attacks, which is the most general known notion of attack model of a non-ID-based signature scheme. The attack model is defined via the following game between an adversary $\mathcal{A}$ and a challenger $\mathcal{C}$.

**Setup Phase.** Challenger $\mathcal{C}$ runs setup algorithm of the scheme, and gives the resulting system parameters $Param$ to the attacker $\mathcal{A}$.

**Query Phase.** $\mathcal{A}$ issues the following queries as he wants:

– KeyGen query. Given an identity ID = $(ID_1, \ldots, ID_n)$, $\mathcal{C}$ returns the private key corresponding to ID which is obtained by running **KeyGen**.
– Signing query. Given an identity ID = $(ID_1, \ldots, ID_n)$, $\mathcal{C}$ returns a signature which is obtained by running **Sign**.

**Challenge Phase.** $\mathcal{A}$ outputs (ID, $m, \sigma$), where ID is an identity, $m$ is a message, and $\sigma$ is a signature, such that ID and (ID, $m$) are not equal to the inputs of any query to **KeyGen** and **Sign**, respectively. $\mathcal{A}$ wins the game if $\sigma$ is a valid signature of $m$ for ID.

**Definition 1.** *We say that the hierarchical identity based signature scheme is secure against existential forgery on adaptively chosen message and identity attacks if no polynomial time adversaries can achieve a non-negligible advantage in the security game.*

# 4   Our HIBS Scheme

In this section we propose our hierarchical identity-based signature scheme that is built on the composite order groups of order $N = p_1 p_2 p_3$ and identities in $\mathbb{Z}_N$. Based on the knowledge of dual system signature, we prove that our HIBS scheme is secure against existential forgery on adaptively chosen message attacks.

## 4.1   The Construction

The HIBS scheme consists of the following four algorithms:

**Setup.** The root PKG chooses a bilinear group $G$ of order $N = p_1 p_2 p_3$. Let $\ell$ denote the maximum depth of the HIBS, PKG randomly chooses $g, h, u_1, \ldots, u_\ell \in G_{p_1}, X_3 \in G_{p_3}$, and $\alpha \in \mathbb{Z}_N$, and publishes the public parameters $Param = \{N, g, h, u_1, \ldots, u_\ell, X_3, e(g, g)^\alpha\}$, and keep $\alpha$ as the PKG master key.

**KeyGen.** To generate a private key $d_{\text{ID}} = (K_1, K_2, E_{j+1}, \ldots, E_\ell)$ for identify ID=$(ID_1, \ldots, ID_j)$ $(j \leqslant \ell)$, the key generation algorithm of PKG picks a random $r \in \mathbb{Z}_N$, random elements $R_3, R'_3, R_{j+1}, \ldots, R_\ell$ of $G_{p_3}$, and outputs:

$$K_1 = g^r R_3, K_2 = g^\alpha \left( u_1^{ID_1} \cdots u_j^{ID_j} h \right)^r R'_3, E_{j+1} = u_{j+1}^r R_{j+1}, \ldots, E_\ell = u_\ell^r R_\ell.$$

Actually, the private key for ID can be generated just given a private key for $ID_{|j-1} = (ID_1, \ldots, ID_{j-1})$ as required. Let $(K_1', K_2', E_j', \ldots, E_\ell')$ be the private key for $ID_{|j-1}$. To generate the private key for ID, the algorithm picks $r' \in \mathbb{Z}_N$ and $\tilde{R}_3, \tilde{R}'_3, \tilde{R}_{j+1}, \ldots, \tilde{R}_\ell \in G_{p_3}$ randomly. The private key of ID can be computed as:

$$K_1 = K_1' g^{r'} \tilde{R}_3 = g^{r+r'} R_3 \tilde{R}_3,$$

$$K_2 = K_2' \left( u_1^{ID_1} \cdots u_{j-1}^{ID_{j-1}} h \right)^{r'} (E_j')^{ID_j} u_j^{r' ID_j} \tilde{R}'_3$$

$$= g^\alpha \left( u_1^{ID_1} \cdots u_j^{ID_j} h \right)^{r+r'} R_3' R_j^{ID_j} \tilde{R}'_3,$$

$E_{j+1} = E_{j+1}' u_{j+1}^{r'} \tilde{R}_{j+1} = u_{j+1}^{r+r'} R_{j+1} \tilde{R}_{j+1}, \ldots, E_\ell = E_\ell' u_\ell^{r'} \tilde{R}_\ell = u_\ell^{r+r'} R_\ell \tilde{R}_\ell.$
This private key is a properly private key for ID=$(ID_1, \ldots, ID_j)$. In contrast of the two private keys $d_{ID_{|j-1}}$ and $d_{ID}$, we can find that the private key becomes shorter as the depth of identity increases.

**Sign.** Given the message $M$ and a private key $d_{ID}$, the user sign the message with PKG parameters. It chooses $r' \in \mathbb{Z}_N$ and $\tilde{R}_3, \tilde{R}'_3 \in G_{p_3}$ randomly and generates the signature $\sigma = \{S_1, S_2\}$, where

$$S_1 = K_1 g^{r'} \tilde{R}_3, S_2 = K_2 \left( u_1^{ID_1} \cdots u_j^{ID_j} h \right)^{r'} E_{j+1}^M u_{j+1}^{r' M} \tilde{R}'_3.$$

The size of $\sigma$ is constant, without affecting by the length of identity.

**Verify.** To verify a signature $\sigma = (S_1, S_2)$ of a message $m$ for an identity ID, set $V_1 = u_1^{ID_1} \cdots u_j^{ID_j} u_{j+1}^M h$ and $V_2 = g$, and check whether

$$e(S_1, V_1)e(g, g)^\alpha = e(S_2, V_2).$$

If $\sigma = (S_1, S_2)$ is a valid signature of a message $m$ for an identity ID, then

$$S_1 = g^{(r+r')} R_3 \tilde{R}_3, S_2 = g^\alpha (u_1^{ID_1} \cdots u_j^{ID_j} u_{j+1}^M h)^{(r+r')} R_3' \tilde{R}'_3 R_{j+1}^M.$$

Thus

$$e(S_1, V_1)e(g, g)^\alpha = e(g^{(r+r')} R_3 \tilde{R}_3, u_1^{ID_1} \cdots u_j^{ID_j} u_{j+1}^M h)e(g, g)^\alpha$$

$$= e(g, (u_1^{ID_1} \cdots u_j^{ID_j} u_{j+1}^M h)^{(r+r')})e(g, g^\alpha)$$

$$= e(g, (u_1^{ID_1} \cdots u_j^{ID_j} u_{j+1}^M h)^{(r+r')} g^\alpha) = e(S_2, V_2).$$

Note that, some bilinear computation results in identities due to the orthogonality property of $G_{p_1}, G_{p_2}, G_{p_3}$, as described in Sect. 2.1. Take the bilinear map $e(R_3, u_1^{ID_1} \cdots u_j^{ID_j} u_{j+1}^M h)$ for example. There are $u_i, M \in G_{p_1}$ and $ID_i, h \in \mathbb{Z}_N$ for $i = 1, \ldots, j + 1$, such that $u_1^{ID_1} \cdots u_j^{ID_j} u_{j+1}^M h \in G_{p_1}$, and $R_3 \in G_{p_3}$. Thus the computation results in an identity of $G_T$.

## 4.2   Security Proofs

We prove full security of our HIBS scheme utilizing the dual system signature. As described above, the proof utilizes the semi-functional components and relies on a sequence of security games. The semi-functional key and signature designing, and the attack games are summarized as following.

- **Semi-functional Signature.** Let $\sigma = (S_1', S_2')$ denote the normal signature generated by the signing algorithm. Set $S_1 = S_1' g_2^x$, $S_2 = S_2' g_2^{x z_c}$, where $g_2$ is a generator of the subgroup $G_{p2}$, and $x, z_c \in \mathbb{Z}_N$ are chosen in random. $(S_1, S_2)$ is referred to as a semi-functional signature.
- **Semi-functional Key.** Let $(K_1', K_2', E_{j+1}', \ldots, E_\ell')$ denote the normal key generated by the key generation algorithm. Set $K_1 = K_1' g_2^\gamma$, $K_2 = K_2' g_2^{\gamma z_k}$, $E_{j+1} = E_{j+1}' g_2^{\gamma z_{j+1}}$, ..., $E_\ell = E_\ell' g_2^{\gamma z_\ell}$ where $g_2$ is a generator of the subgroup $G_{p2}$, and $\gamma, z_k, z_{j+1}, \ldots, z_\ell \in \mathbb{Z}_N$ are chosen in random. $(K_1, K_2)$ is referred to as a semi-functional key.
- **Game$_{Real}$.** It is the real security game described hereinabove.
- **Game$_{Restricted}$.** It is like Game$_{Real}$ except that the attacker cannot ask for keys for identities which are equal to the challenge identity modulo $p_2$.
- **Game$_k$.** It is like Game$_{Restricted}$, except that the signatures given to the attacker is semi-functional and the first $k$ keys are semi-functional. The rest of the keys are normal. Note that all the keys are normal and the signatures are semi-functional in Game$_0$.

**Lemma 1.** *Suppose there exists an algorithm $\mathcal{A}$ that can distinguish Game$_{Real}$ and Game$_{Restricted}$, then we can build an algorithm in breaking either Assumption 1 or Assumption 2.*

*Proof.* This proof is identical to the proof of *Lemma 5* in [15] since there is no difference for signature query between Game$_{Real}$ and Game$_{Restricted}$.

**Lemma 2.** *Suppose there exists an algorithm $\mathcal{A}$ that can distinguish Game$_0$ and Game$_{Restricted}$ with advantage $\varepsilon$. Then we can build an algorithm with same advantage $\varepsilon$ in breaking Assumption 1.*

*Proof.* $\mathcal{B}$ is given $g, X_3, T$. To simulate Game$_{Restricted}$ or Game$_0$ with $\mathcal{A}$, $\mathcal{B}$ first chooses random exponents $\alpha, a_1, \ldots, a_\ell, b \in \mathbb{Z}_N$ and sets $g = g, u_i = g^{a_i}$ for $i$ from 1 to $\ell$ and $h = g^b$. Parameters $\{N, g, h, u_1, \ldots, u_\ell, X_3, e(g,g)^\alpha\}$ are sent to $\mathcal{A}$. When $\mathcal{A}$ queries a key for identity $(ID_1, \ldots, ID_j)$, $\mathcal{B}$ chooses random exponents $r, t, w, v_{j_1}, \ldots, v_\ell \in \mathbb{Z}_N$ and returns key: $K_1 = g^r X_3^t$, $K_2 = g^\alpha (u_1^{ID_1} \cdots u_j^{ID_j} h)^r X_3^w$, $E_{j+1} = u_{j+1}^r X_3^{v_{j+1}}, \ldots, E_\ell = u_\ell^r X_3^{v_\ell}$. In signing query phase, $\mathcal{A}$ sends $\mathcal{B}$ a message $M^*$ and an identity $(ID_1^*, \ldots, ID_j^*)$. $\mathcal{B}$ forms signature: $S_1 = K_1 T \tilde{R}_3$, $S_2 = K_2 T^{a_1 ID_1^* + \cdots + a_j ID_j^* + b} E_{j+1}^{M^*} T^{a_{j+1} M^*} \tilde{R}_3'$.

- If $T \in G_{p_1 p_2}$, this is a semi-functional signature.
  Let $z_c = a_1 ID_1^* + \cdots + a_j ID_j^* + a_{j+1} M^* + b$. We notice that $T$ can be recorded

as $T = g^{r'}g_2^x$, where $r', x \in \mathbb{Z}_N$. Thus,

$$S_1 = K_1 g^{r'} g_2^x \tilde{R}_3 = K_1 g^{r'} \tilde{R}_3 g_2^x = S_1' g_2^x,$$
$$S_2 = K_2 (g^{r'} g_2^x)^{a_1 ID_1^* + \cdots + a_j ID_j^* + b} E_{j+1}^{M^*} (g^{r'} g_2^x)^{a_{j+1} M^*} \tilde{R'}_3$$
$$= K_2 g^{r'(a_1 ID_1^* + \cdots + a_j ID_j^* + b)} g_2^{x(z_c - a_{j+1} M^*)} E_{j+1}^{M^*} g^{r' a_{j+1} M^*} g_2^{x a_{j+1} M^*} \tilde{R'}_3$$
$$= K_2 (u_1^{ID_1^*} \cdots u_j^{ID_j^*} h)^{r'} E_{j+1}^{M^*} u_{j+1}^{r' M^*} \tilde{R'}_3 g_2^{x z_c} = S_2' g_2^{x z_c}.$$

- If $T \in G_{p_1}$, this is a normal signature. Denoting $T$ as $T = g^{r'}$, there are

$$S_1 = K_1 g^{r'} \tilde{R}_3,$$
$$S_2 = K_2 g^{r'(a_1 ID_1^* + \cdots + a_j ID_j^* + b)} E_{j+1}^{M^*} (g^{r'})^{a_{j+1} M^*} \tilde{R'}_3$$
$$= K_2 (u_1^{ID_1^*} \cdots u_j^{ID_j^*} h)^{r'} E_{j+1}^{M^*} u_{j+1}^{r' M^*} \tilde{R'}_3.$$

As supposed, $\mathcal{A}$ is able to distinguish the semi-functional and normal signature. Therefore, $\mathcal{B}$ can use the output of $\mathcal{A}$ to distinguish $T$. That is, it can break Assumption 1.

**Lemma 3.** *Suppose there exists an algorithm $\mathcal{A}$ that can distinguish $Game_{k-1}$ and $Game_k$ with advantage $\varepsilon$. Then we can build an algorithm with same advantage $\varepsilon$ in breaking Assumption 2.*

*Proof.* $\mathcal{B}$ is given $g, X_1 X_2, X_3, Y_2 Y_3, T$. To simulate $Game_{k-1}$ or $Game_k$ with $\mathcal{A}$, $\mathcal{B}$ first chooses random exponents $a_1, \ldots, a_\ell, b \in \mathbb{Z}_N$. and sets the public parameters as $g = g$, $u_1 = g^{a_1}$, $\ldots$, $u_\ell = g^{a_\ell}$, $h = g^b$, $e(g,g)^\alpha$, Parameters are sent to $\mathcal{A}$.
When $\mathcal{A}$ requests the $i^{th}$ key for identity $(ID_1, \ldots, ID_j)$.

- If $i < k$, $\mathcal{B}$ generates a semi-functional key. It chooses random exponents $r, z, t, z_{j+1}, \ldots, z_\ell \in \mathbb{Z}_N$ and sets:
  $K_1 = g^r (Y_2 Y_3)^t$, $K_2 = g^\alpha (u_1^{ID_1} \cdots u_j^{ID_j} h)^r (Y_2 Y_3)^z$,
  $E_{j+1} = u_{j+1}^r (Y_2 Y_3)^{z_{j+1}}, \ldots, E_\ell = u_\ell^r (Y_2 Y_3)^{z_\ell}$.
  Note that this is a properly distributed semi-functional key with $g_2^\gamma = Y_2^t$.
- If $i = k$, $\mathcal{B}$ lets $z_k = a_1 ID_1^* + \cdots + a_j ID_j^* + b$, chooses random exponents $w_k, w_{j+1}, \ldots, w_\ell \in \mathbb{Z}_N$, and sets:
  $K_1 = T, K_2 = g^\alpha T^{z_k} X_3^{w_k}, E_{j+1} = T^{a_{j+1}} X_3^{w_{j+1}}, \ldots, E_\ell = T^{a_\ell} X_3^{w_\ell}$.
  If $T \in G_{p_1 p_3}$, this is a normal key with $g^r$ equal to the $G_{p_1}$ part of $T$.
  If $T \in G$, this is a semi-functional key.
- If $i > k$, $\mathcal{B}$ generates normal keys by calling the usual key generation algorithm.

In signing query phase, $\mathcal{A}$ sends $\mathcal{B}$ a message $M^*$ and an identity $(ID_1^*, \ldots, ID_j^*)$. $\mathcal{B}$ forms signature:

$S_1 = K_1 X_1 X_2 \tilde{R}_3$,
$S_2 = K_2 (X_1 X_2)^{(a_1 ID_1^* + \cdots + a_j ID_j^* + b)} E_{j+1}^{M^*} (X_1 X_2)^{a_{j+1} M^*} \tilde{R'}_3$.
The signature $\sigma = (S_1, S_2)$ is a well-formed semi-functional signature since $X_1 X_2 \in G_{p_1 p_2}$. Details can be found in *Lemma 2*.

If $T \in G_{p_1p_3}$, then $\mathcal{B}$ has properly simulated $Game_{k-1}$ because the signatures as well as the first $k - 1$ keys are semi-functional, and the rest of the keys are normal. If $T \in G$, then $\mathcal{B}$ has properly simulated $Game_k$ because the signatures as well as the first $k$ keys are semi-functional, and the rest of the keys are normal. As supposed, $\mathcal{A}$ is able to distinguish $Game_{k-1}$ and $Game_k$. Therefore, $\mathcal{B}$ can use the output of $\mathcal{A}$ to distinguish between these possibilities for $T$. That is, it can break Assumption 2.

**Theorem 1.** *If Assumptions 1 and 2 hold, then our HIBS scheme is secure.*

*Proof.* If Assumptions 1 and 2 hold, $Game_{Real}$ is indistinguishable from $Game_q$ according to the *Lemmas* 1 to 3. $Game_q$ information-theoretically hiding all the queried value is the de facto game provided to the attacker. Therefore, the attacker can attain no advantage in breaking our HIBS scheme.

## 5     Performance

We compare the performance of our HIBS scheme with LW-HIBE in Tables 1 and 2. Each component of the schemes is a set of group elements and the number of the elements is referred to as the component size. The LW-HIBE and our HIBS scheme share the same private key form. Let $\ell$ denote the maximum depth of the HIBS (HIBE), $j$ denote the depth of the identity, the size of the private key is $\ell - j + 2$, i.e., it consists of $\ell - j + 2$ group elements. Table 1 shows that both the ciphertext in LW-HIBE and the signature in our HIBS have short and constant size.

Each algorithm of the two schemes may consists of three types of operations. Let $j$ denote the depth of identity, Table 2 shows the operation number for each algorithm. Assuming the pairing computation costs several times expensive than a point multiplication or an exponentiation, we can see that the verification is the most expensive while the signing is almost as efficient as the encryption.

**Table 1.** The size of components for LW-HIBE and our HIBS scheme.

| Components | Size (Number of group elements) |
|---|---|
| Private key | $\ell - j + 2$ |
| Ciphertext | 3 |
| Signature | 2 |

**Table 2.** The number of operations for LW-HIBE and our HIBS scheme.

| Algorithm | Bilinear map | Point multiplication | Exponentiation |
|---|---|---|---|
| Encrypt | 0 | $j+1$ | $j+3$ |
| Decrypt | 2 | 0 | 0 |
| Sign | 0 | $j + 7$ | $j + 4$ |
| Verify | 2 | $j + 2$ | $j + 2$ |

# 6 Conclusion

In this work, we present a hierarchical identity-based signature scheme from composite order bilinear groups. We modify the methodology of dual system encryption and present dual system signature to prove that our HIBS scheme is secure against existential forgery on adaptively chosen message and identity attacks. The proof is under the hardness assumptions of subgroups indistinguishable. Our scheme can share parameters with the LW-HIBE scheme. And it is as efficient as LW-HIBE. Combining the LW-HIBE and our HIBS scheme provides a practical complete solution of an identity-based public key system, which can be utilized to build an authentication framework for cloud storage.

# References

1. Boneh, D., Boyen, X.: Efficient selective-ID secure identity-based encryption without random oracles. In: Cachin, C., Camenisch, J.L. (eds.) EUROCRYPT 2004. LNCS, vol. 3027, pp. 223–238. Springer, Heidelberg (2004)
2. Boneh, D., Franklin, M.: Identity-based encryption from the weil pairing. In: Kilian, J. (ed.) CRYPTO 2001. LNCS, vol. 2139, pp. 213–221. Springer, Heidelberg (2001)
3. Boneh, D., Goh, E.-J., Nissim, K.: Evaluating 2-DNF formulas on ciphertexts. In: Kilian, J. (ed.) TCC 2005. LNCS, vol. 3378, pp. 325–341. Springer, Heidelberg (2005)
4. Boneh, D., Lynn, B., Shacham, H.: Short signatures from the weil pairing. In: Boyd, C. (ed.) ASIACRYPT 2001. LNCS, vol. 2248, pp. 514–532. Springer, Heidelberg (2001)
5. Camenisch, J.L., Lysyanskaya, A.: Signature schemes and anonymous credentials from bilinear maps. In: Franklin, M. (ed.) CRYPTO 2004. LNCS, vol. 3152, pp. 56–72. Springer, Heidelberg (2004)
6. Cheon, J.H., Kim, Y., Yoon, H., et al.: A new id-based signature with batch verification. IACR Cryptology ePrint Archive, 2004, p. 131 (2004)
7. Choon, J.C., Cheon, J.H.: An identity-based signature from gap diffie-hellman groups. In: Desmedt, Y.G. (ed.) PKC 2003. LNCS, vol. 2567, pp. 18–30. Springer, Heidelberg (2002)
8. Chow, S.S.M., Hui, L.C.K., Yiu, S.-M., Chow, K.P.: Secure hierarchical identity based signature and its application. In: López, J., Qing, S., Okamoto, E. (eds.) ICICS 2004. LNCS, vol. 3269, pp. 480–494. Springer, Heidelberg (2004)
9. Fu, S., Wang, D., Xu, M., Ren, J.: Cryptanalysis of remote data integrity checking protocol proposed by L. Chen for cloud storage. IEICE Trans. 97–A(1), 418–420 (2014). http://search.ieice.org/bin/summary.php?id=e97-a_1_418
10. Gentry, C., Silverberg, A.: Hierarchical ID-based cryptography. In: Zheng, Y. (ed.) ASIACRYPT 2002. LNCS, vol. 2501, pp. 548–566. Springer, Heidelberg (2002)
11. Gerbush, M., Lewko, A., O'Neill, A., Waters, B.: Dual form signatures: an approach for proving security from static assumptions. In: Wang, X., Sako, K. (eds.) ASIACRYPT 2012. LNCS, vol. 7658, pp. 25–42. Springer, Heidelberg (2012)
12. Huang, K., Xian, M., Fu, S., Liu, J.: Securing the cloud storage audit service: defending against frame and collude attacks of third party auditor. IET Commun. 8(12), 2106–2113 (2014). http://dx.doi.org/10.1049/ietcom.2013.0898

13. Juels, A., Kaliski Jr., B.S.: Pors: proofs of retrievability for large files. In: Proceedings of the 14th ACM conference on Computer and Communications Security, pp. 584–597. ACM (2007)
14. Kang, L., Zhang, X.: Identity-based authentication in cloud storage sharing. In: 2010 International Conference on Multimedia Information Networking and Security (MINES), pp. 851–855. IEEE (2010)
15. Lewko, A., Waters, B.: New techniques for dual system encryption and fully secure HIBE with short ciphertexts. In: Micciancio, D. (ed.) TCC 2010. LNCS, vol. 5978, pp. 455–479. Springer, Heidelberg (2010)
16. Li, H., Dai, Y., Tian, L., Yang, H.: Identity-based authentication for cloud computing. In: Jaatun, M.G., Zhao, G., Rong, C. (eds.) Cloud Computing. LNCS, vol. 5931, pp. 157–166. Springer, Heidelberg (2009)
17. Mao, W.: An identity-based non-interactive authentication framework for computational grids. Hewlett-Packard Laboratories, Technical report HPL-2004-96 (2004)
18. Shamir, A.: Identity-based cryptosystems and signature schemes. In: Blakely, G.R., Chaum, D. (eds.) CRYPTO 1984. LNCS, vol. 196, pp. 47–53. Springer, Heidelberg (1985)
19. Waters, B.: Dual system encryption: realizing fully secure IBE and HIBE under simple assumptions. In: Halevi, S. (ed.) CRYPTO 2009. LNCS, vol. 5677, pp. 619–636. Springer, Heidelberg (2009)

# STRATUS: Towards Returning Data Control to Cloud Users

Ryan K.L. Ko[1](✉), Giovanni Russello[2], Richard Nelson[1], Shaoning Pang[3], Aloysius Cheang[4], Gill Dobbie[2], Abdolhossein Sarrafzadeh[3], Sivadon Chaisiri[1], Muhammad Rizwan Asghar[2], and Geoffrey Holmes[1]

[1] University of Waikato, 3240 Hamilton, New Zealand
ryan@waikato.ac.nz
https://stratus.org.nz
[2] University of Auckland, 1142 Auckland, New Zealand
[3] Unitec Institute of Technology, 1025 Auckland, New Zealand
[4] Cloud Security Alliance (Asia Pacific), Singapore 247672, Singapore

**Abstract.** When we upload or create data into the cloud or the web, we immediately lose control of our data. Most of the time, we will not know where the data will be stored, or how many copies of our files are there. Worse, we are unable to know and stop malicious insiders from accessing the possibly sensitive data. Despite being transferred across and within clouds over encrypted channels, data often has to be decrypted within the database for it to be processed. Exposing the data at some point in the cloud to a few privileged users is undoubtedly a vendor-centric approach, and hinges on the trust relationships data owners have with their cloud service providers. A recent example of the abuse of the trust relationship is the high-profile Edward Snowden case. In this paper, we propose a user-centric approach which returns data control to the data owners – empowering users with data provenance, transparency and auditability, homomorphic encryption, situation awareness, revocation, attribution and data resilience. We also cover key elements of the concept of user data control. Finally, we introduce how we attempt to address these issues via the New Zealand Ministry of Business Innovation and Employment (MBIE)-funded STRATUS (Security Technologies Returning Accountability, Trust and User-centric Services in the Cloud) research project.

**Keywords:** Cloud security · Cloud computing · User data control · User-centric security · Data provenance · Homomorphic encryption · Situation awareness · Data resiliency

## 1 Rising Cyber Security Incidents: The Case for User Data Control

From the Apple iCloud celebrity nude photo leaks [1], to the abuse of children's photographs on social networking services (e.g. Flickr and Facebook) for use of

© Springer International Publishing Switzerland 2015
G. Wang et al. (Eds.): ICA3PP 2015 Workshops, LNCS 9532, pp. 57–70, 2015.
DOI: 10.1007/978-3-319-27161-3_6

explicit sites [2], to the recent adultery website Ashley Madison user information leak [3], we are regularly witnessing a serious problem: *the inability for data owners to help themselves in cyber security breeches situations.*

Underlying this problem, is a serious deficiency we are observing with the current state of the cyber security industry: *the inability for data owners to control their data.* When one gets compromised in a cyber security situation, one usually has no idea how to proceed to understand the situation, analyse the evidence and perhaps solve the situation (e.g. attribute and present compelling evidence against the perpetuator of the attack).

## 1.1 Lack of Ability Stemming from Lack of Data Control

Looking deeper into the gap of 'inability to help themselves', we notice the root of the issue is in the lack of control over the data they own, especially in the cloud or simply over the web. Sometimes, users do not even realise that their photographs taken from their mobile phone's camera are uploaded instantly onto public cloud storage, even though they may not have wanted those specific photos to go onto the cloud (despite agreeing to the terms and conditions of the application installation).

When we survey the landscape of cyber security tools, from the commonly known ones such as anti-malware and firewalls, to the sophisticated vulnerability scanners and penetration testing tools, none of them are built with the purpose of empowering the users to comprehensively help themselves in controlling their data's whereabouts and privacy in hacking incidents. There is no reversal or recourse.

## 1.2 Everyday Scenarios Demonstrating Users' Lack of Data Control

In 2010, a 27-year-old Google site reliability engineer was caught spying on teenagers on the GTalk service [4]. He abused his privileged administrator rights and was only found out after the parents of a teenager reported him. According to the Google, the extend of the damage or possible abuse is unknown, as there is no technology tracking the evolution of data from a data-centric point of view. There was also no technology which could alert the affected teenagers about the unauthorised access from the backend of the cloud service.

With no real accountability of administrators' rights over the access of clients' data, many more situations like these potentially happen on a daily basis in (both public and private) clouds utilised by businesses around the world. The sole reliance on the trust and reputation of a cloud service provider and their employees is neither a strong nor sustainable way forward for the cloud computing industry.

## 2   Elements of User Data Control and Related Work

Returning control of data to users is a 'holy grail' of cloud security research as it addresses trust tensions and accountability issues inherent in storing and processing of proprietary data in cloud environments.

Solving this 'holy grail' will also carve out a niche in security technologies around user control over their data through four proposed elements:

- **Element 1** – Transparency and auditability of data,
- **Element 2** – Privacy of data during processing and storing,
- **Element 3** – Detection and revocation of malicious actions, and
- **Element 4** – Resiliency and rapid recovery from untoward events.

Without all elements, the user cannot gain full control over their data, thus both technical and compliance aspects around these four elements will need to be addressed. We propose STRATUS (short for 'Security Technologies Returning Accountability, Trust and User-centric Services in the Cloud'), which will address the four elements, i.e. Research Aims (RAs), each focusing on one of these dimensions of user control of data. More details of STRATUS will be covered in Sect. 3 – Proposed Methodology. Before we delve into the STRATUS approach, we will need to understand in-depth, the elements of user data control in cloud environments. We will now provide a brief overview of the four main elements.

## 2.1 Element 1: Transparency and Auditability of Data Activities

Element 1 enables cloud users to trace and reconstruct data provenance, i.e. "what's happened to their data" behind the scenes. Technologies enabling cloud stakeholders to keep track of the provenance (i.e. derivation history) of their data will be built – enabling them to know if malicious insiders have accessed their data, or whether the users have leaked their important data to foreign systems.

Element 1 also covers the crucial governance aspects of cloud data and links technical implementations with auditing and compliance guidelines, standards, or regulations (e.g. CSA CCM [5], ISO27001 [6], PCI DSS [7]). From the global security perspective, Moreover, Element 1 addresses the difficulty in tracking criminals who use evasion and encryption techniques to mask their digital trails and activities.

## 2.2 Element 2: Protection of Privacy of Data During Processing and Storing

This Element addresses the issue of how users can ensure their data privacy in clouds, without compromising search, functionality or analytical capability. Currently, encrypted data cannot be processed or utilised meaningfully by computing systems. Element 2 aims to overcome this by enabling encrypted data to be utilised by cloud servers without revealing private data to the cloud system administrators – thereby preserving privacy of data without compromising the data utility.

## 2.3    Element 3: Immediate Detection and Revocation of Malicious Actions

This Element has three objectives:

1. Providing 'situational awareness' tools enabling cloud stakeholders to have real-time awareness of their data status.
2. New techniques that instantly reveal cloud software vulnerabilities and remedy them 'on the fly'. Current cloud technologies are protected by traditional but unsustainable methods (i.e. malware scanning using rule-based techniques).
3. Capabilities to attribute threat sources and revoke anomalous actions, i.e. achieving true control of one's data.

## 2.4    Element 4: Resiliency and Rapid Recovery from Untoward Events

Element 4's main objective is to enable rapid recovery from untoward incidents, malicious attacks and acts of nature. Due to a lack of work [8,9] devoted to defending business data from malicious attacks and from large scale disasters, the following techniques will be developed: (1) techniques building resiliency into services; (2) decentralised cloud storage, and (3) multi-cloud based disaster recovery techniques. Tools that can be used in clouds to protect the availability of data through a decentralised solution must be developed. The solution should enable back-ups to be automatically replicated at multiple independent sites in near real-time.

# 3    Proposed Methodology

As mentioned, the proposed STRATUS approach will be based on addressing the above four key elements of user data control in clouds. STRATUS will create a platform of novel user-centric cloud security technologies that can be used by New Zealand companies to differentiate their products and services in global markets.

Our over-arching research goal therefore is to create first-in-the-world to export cloud security technologies that enable users to be aware of, assess and manage security events themselves. The research programme to deliver this comprises four 'Research Aims' (RAs), which are listed below. Each RA comprises one to three projects, which represent more specific technology developments as follows:

## 3.1    RA1: Transparency and Auditability of Data Activities in Clouds

### Project 1: Tracking and Reconstruction of Data Provenance

**Aims** – This project enables cloud users to know data provenance, or "what has happened to their data" behind the scenes. Project 1 builds on Ko's research in cloud data provenance [10–14]. We will develop provenance tracking and reconstruction techniques to support data incident investigations. We will also build technologies that automate data-centric evidence acquisition and data forensics tasks required in RA3.

**Gaps & Scientific Principles Addressed** – The project addresses cloud data provenance and transparency of data activities. There is currently no elegant solution to this problem [10] due to the following challenging scientific problems. First, current cloud monitoring tools [15–17] (e.g. HyTrust [17]) only monitor utilisation and performance, and overlook data flow in clouds. Second, while most clouds adopt file-integrity checking systems (FICS) (e.g. Trip-Wire [18]) to detect file intrusions, they do not track the history of changes and only report the last change [19]. Third, existing data provenance techniques [10–12] are not user-centric but vendor-centric [20]. There is also an absence of real-time provenance and timeline reconstruction techniques to piece back data activities and threat sources.

**Methodology** – We will focus on investigating research questions and developing proofs-of-concept using continuous hypothesis testing [21] within the University of Waikato (UoW)'s Cloud8 (large-scale cloud test-bed): (1) redesigning cloud systems to embed provenance records in their metadata (2) design, patent and implement cloud data access protocols (3) building data-centric logging, provenance mining, and reconstruction mechanisms that collect provenance not only within, but also outside clouds. The inventions will be verified against our commercial collaborators. Then, they will be validated against real-life scenarios and infrastructures provided by commercial collaborators. Finally, we will create export advantages by building export-ready cloud data provenance services.

## Project 2: Data Governance and Accountability in Clouds

**Aims** – This project complements Projects 1 and 7, as it covers the cloud data governance and links technical implementations with auditing guidelines and compliance regulations. This builds on the experience of two existing CSA New Zealand Chapters research: (1) NZISM controls-mapping with unified security and governance controls (e.g. ISO 27001/2, COBIT, PCI-DSS, NIST800-53, BITS) (2) privacy requirements for data governance in New Zealand.

**Gaps & Scientific Principles Addressed** – This project primarily addresses the cross-border policy alignment and technology-to-policy alignment for innovations invented in the four RAs. The governance controls of cloud service providers do not support data sovereignty rights of cloud users [22–24]. Existing standards (ISO 27001, COBIT, ISO 38500, NIST 800-53, NZISM, PCI-DSS) do not offer controls that can accredit and audit cloud user cloud architecture for data governance. Governments have highlighted this pressing need in various documents [25,26].

**Methodology** – Comparative analyses of standards, legal controls and best practices will be conducted. Controls from our analysis will be documented according to the Deming (Plan-Do-Check-Act: PDCA) Cycle [27] as a first draft. Next, we will have two consultation rounds with industry (e.g. NZICT) and New Zealand Government (i.e. DIA, NZTE, ATEED). The unified framework draft will be accomplished. This draft will be sent to ISO committees, government and industry for review. The controls' validity will be tested by integration with software created by all RAs. Then, we will focus on publishing recommendations into international standardisation bodies (e.g. ISO, ITU-T). Finally, Cloud Security Alliance (CSA) (which is one of STRATUS research collaborators) will link up commercial collaborators to CSA corporate members, establishing a first-mover advantage and global market.

## 3.2   RA2: Protection of Privacy of Data During Processing and Storing

### Project 3: Secure Information Retrieval/Encrypted Search

**Aims** – This project will first provide data centre owners with new storage tools that allows search operations on encrypted data and provide stakeholders tools for statistical analysis and testing of cloud data while preserving privacy at a granular level. This project builds on the University of Auckland's current work [28]. We will combine previous results on proxy-encryption for simple search operations in a multiuser setting [29–31] with our latest work [28,32–38] supporting complex matching operations and indexing extensions.

**Gaps & Scientific Principles Addressed** – The main scientific principles addressed are cryptographic schemes which protect data confidentiality while supporting search operations on encrypted data. Current solutions either (1) support only simple queries based on equality matches (e.g. "Name = John") but not complex queries based on ranges (e.g. $18 < \mathrm{Age} < 65$), or (2) require users to share keys, complicating key management, i.e. requiring regular key regeneration. Related works have only partially solved these two issues. For example, single-user searchable encryption schemes [39–41] only work well for single users, while semi-fledged multi-user schemes [42–45] force other users to only perform 'read' operations if a user 'writes'. More recently, full-fledged multi-user schemes allow multiple users to 'write' and 'read' without sharing keys [29–31] but only support keyword-based searches. We aim to support both complex queries and do not require users to share keys.

**Methodology** – We will define security requirements, business cases, and create partial prototypes based on our previous research [28]. Next, we will deploy a fully working mechanism and study indexing techniques enabling lower latencies for data retrieval. Our commercial collaborators will provide requirements, business cases and access to dedicated hardware. Indexing will be integrated to the search mechanism; a tool which minimises data exposure while doing fast indexing will be implemented. Then, we will integrate and validate on thin-clients with constrained resources (e.g. battery), and implement client-side crypto schemes. Finally, search optimisation and parallel execution extensions will be built.

### Project 4: Efficient Privacy and Utility Preserving Encryption

**Aims** – This project attempts to achieve an efficient, practical method for a major scientific breakthrough: Gentry's fully homomorphic encryption (FHE) [46,47]. FHE allows computers to process data without the need to decrypt them, thereby solving all cloud data privacy concerns. However, FHE is currently inefficient and impractical ($\sim$ 15 mins/1 kilobyte) [47]. Therefore, there are opportunities to introduce innovation that gives New Zealand cloud providers a competitive advantage. We will focus on implementing practical homomorphic cryptographic mechanisms for supporting meaningful computation on encrypted data, e.g. statistical functions.

**Gaps & Scientific Principles Addressed** – FHE's drawback is that it requires huge ciphertext and cryptographic material that is not practical with today's computational power. Recently, small optimisations have been proposed [48,49]. Although these optimisations require smaller ciphertexts to work they are still far from being practical in a cloud environment serving large amount of users. Close to our approach is [47]. However, it is not ideal for corporates with numerous employees requiring access to the encrypted service. Pragmatically, our solutions will adopt partial homomorphic encryption (PHE), which supports a subset of well-defined operations. PHE is efficient in term of computation time. Furthermore, PHE can provide the same level of security as FHE. Our idea is that combining several PHE solutions supporting a range of operations can provide enough computation power to be used in several sectors including finance, healthcare and government. We will build from our previous work based on proxy encryption and Elgamal crypto blocks [29,32,33,38].

**Methodology** – We will define security and functional requirements with business requirements and study related cryptographic schemes. A prototype with different functions will be implemented, tested and evaluated. Then, the prototypes will be optimised and delivered as SaaS products. Next, we will implement the support of thin-clients and provide a platform for integrating different providers' services.

### 3.3 RA3. Awareness and Response to Anomalous Data Activities

### Project 5: Real-Time Situational Awareness

**Aims** – This project will draw from UoW's decade of machine learning (ML) experience (i.e. Weka [50]), and passive network measurement and anomaly detection expertise [51–54] to develop new techniques enabling cloud stakeholders with real-time situational awareness (SA) of their data. SA is a top priority in several defence organizations globally [55], as there is currently a lack of techniques for instant identification of trouble spots in the cloud [56]. We will apply ML techniques to develop actionable insights to improve SA.

**Gaps & Scientific Principles Addressed** – The ability to detect and report anomalous actions is the basis for notifying cloud stakeholders abnormal data provenance behaviour [57]. This permits active corrective actions rather than reactive. Cloud systems are also live and dynamic [10] – instances are live or shut down in ad hoc fashion. Therefore, accurately detecting and reporting abnormal behaviours from large-scale measurements with zero false positives is an open problem. SA needs to perform well with large data volumes, differentiate between harmless and malicious anomalies, and detect covert or stealthy information flows.

**Methodology** – Anomalous events will be identified and classified. Algorithms for effective detection over large datasets will also be developed. Next, the classifications and algorithms are combined to test against commercial collaborators and experimental findings from RA1. Finally, we will build export-ready cloud SA services integrated with the STRATUS platform.

## Project 6: Effective Cloud Vulnerability Scanning

**Aims** – This project will develop new techniques to instantly reveal and remediate from cloud security vulnerabilities. Virtualization in clouds increase scale and utilization of infrastructures but brings about new complexities and vulnerabilities. Currently, clouds are protected by traditional methods designed for single machines (i.e. malware scanning using rule-based techniques, firewalls); these are not sustainable. Our work builds on Ko's existing research on Cloud failures [58] and his collaborative research with Bell Labs on cloud reliability.

**Gaps & Scientific Principles Addressed** – This project will create a cloud vulnerability scanning kit which will enable security consultants, cloud service provider and cloud user (e.g. SaaS companies) to identify and recommend remedies for both software [59,60] and network vulnerabilities [61] efficiently. In the area of networks, work on addressing Internet Protocol version 6 (IPv6)-related vulnerabilties (e.g. firewalls deployed for IPv4 only, transiting from IPv4 to IPv6) are lacking. Existing work include the SecureCloud [62], RedShield [63], software fuzzers [59,60] and the THC IPv6 vulnerability scanning toolkit [61]. However, they are not ready for clouds' live and dynamic nature [11]. The main challenges stem from the widespread usage of virtualisation and software defined networks in clouds.

**Methodology** – We will automate fast and efficient malware analysis that traces back and attributes sources to empower law enforcement and prevent future outbreaks. Next, we will focus on classifying vulnerability types, and develop a suite of proofs-of-concept for each vulnerability type. Then, we will focus on tool productisation. Finally, we will build cloud vulnerability scanning suites for commercial collaborators.

## Project 7: Attribution and Revocation of Actions

**Aims** – This project builds on data from Projects 1, 2 and 5. Cloud stakeholders would have abilities to identify the actors or malware behind each cloud data anomaly, and revoke malicious actions, i.e. achieving true control of one's data. We will also develop the ability to cyber "fingerprint" attackers through identification and detection of their behaviours, and techniques. This automates repetitive tasks such as evidence collation, reducing workload of investigators.

**Gaps & Scientific Principles Addressed** – The principles addressed are identity management, access control [64–66], and revocation policies [67,68]. Related work such as sticky policies, EnCoRe and revocation schemes often run into scale and latency problems [67,69]. We aim to overcome these limitations to achieve near real-time control and policy implementation.

**Methodology** – We will focus on: (1) classification of identity types of all granularities within cloud systems, (2) development of access control policies which adhere to international auditing regulations identified by Project 2, and (3) building of proofs-of-concepts of attribution techniques. Our attribution techniques will be validated against our New Zealand commercial collaborators.

### 3.4    RA4. Resiliency and Recovery of Data

**Project 8: Rapid Disaster Recovery (DR) Infrastructure**

**Aims** – This project will develop capabilities for efficient data protection and rapid recovery from untoward incidents, malicious attacks and acts of nature. This project builds on prior work on decentralised network federation systems [70] at Unitec's Centre for Computational Intelligence for Cyber-Security.

**Gaps & Scientific Principles Addressed** – The project primarily addresses the challenge of business continuity via data resiliency and recovery mechanisms [8]. Applications must rapidly come back online after a failure occurs to minimise losses. Two existing mechanisms: (1) network reconfiguration [9,71,72], and (2) virtual machine migration or cloning [73] operate at service or platform layer but none connects DR to the infrastructure layer or consider geographic and network-topological locations. Citrix [73] and Pokharel et al. [74] considered secondary cloud infrastructures for disaster recovery but they require extra physical sites, i.e. higher costs. As such, we will (1) build resiliency into services (2) create decentralized cloud storage techniques and (3) create multi-cloud based disaster recovery techniques.

**Methodology** – We will build resilient services focusing on business continuity. Then, we will develop automated data distribution techniques that decentralises data storage and achieves cost reduction. Next, we will setup an industry-grade disaster recovery infrastructure, enable seamless integration of existing clouds as part of single wide-area resource leasing federation and a structured peer-to-peer routing method.

## 4    Opportunities for Cloud Security: A Technology Platform with Multiple Applications

STRATUS not only has the potential to achieve the elements of data control, but also establish, maintain and continually develop a wide portfolio of user-centric cloud security technologies.

Some examples include the development of user-centric data provenance tracking tools, which can inform the whereabouts of data to their owners. Other examples include a fully homomorphic range of cloud applications for the healthcare, banking and government sectors – reducing the reliance and risk trusting of cloud computing privileged system administrators.

The ability to know about users' data also empowers us with the potential ability to revoke and attribute malicious activities, giving full control of data to users.

This mix of user-centric cloud technologies, skills and resources will comprise the STRATUS platform. Our goal is for the combination of successful, real world 'proofs-of-concept' with supporting resources to ensure easy access for exporters and domestic users alike.

## 5  Concluding Remarks

In this position paper, we presented STRATUS, a New Zealand cyber security research project focusing on empowering users with control over their data in third party environments such as the cloud. We will create a platform of novel security tools, techniques and capabilities which return control of data to cloud computing users. Such innovations empowering users to have data control offer opportunities for companies across the cloud computing value system.

We proposed four elements of security technologies around user control over their data including (1) transparency and auditability of data, (2) privacy of data during processing and storing, (3) detection and revocation of malicious actions, and (4) resiliency and rapid recovery from untoward events. When all elements are addressed, we will return data control to users. It is our proposition that for the cloud to be a truly trustable service, cloud service providers must not be data owners but data processors.

**Acknowledgements.** This research is supported by STRATUS (Security Technologies Returning Accountability, Trust and User-Centric Services in the Cloud) (https:// stratus.org.nz), a science investment project funded by the New Zealand Ministry of Business, Innovation and Employment (MBIE).

## References

1. Goldman, D., Pagliery, J., Segall, L.: How celebrities' nude photos get leaked. CNN Money (2014). http://money.cnn.com/2014/09/01/technology/ celebrity-nude-photos/index.html?iid=EL. Accessed 7 September 2015
2. Quenqua, D.: Guardians of Their Smiles. The New York Times (2009). http:// www.nytimes.com/2009/10/25/fashion/25facebook.html. Accessed 7 September 2015
3. Isidore, C., Goldman, D.: Ashley Madison hackers post millions of customer names. CNN Money (2015). http://money.cnn.com/2015/08/18/technology/ashley-mad ison-data-dump/. Accessed 7 September 2015
4. Chen, A.: GCreep: Google Engineer Stalked Teens, Spied on Chats. GAWKER (2010). http://gawker.com/5637234/gcreep-google-engineer-stalked-teens-spied-on-chats. Accessed 7 September 2015
5. Cloud Controls Matrix v3.0 Info Sheet (2013). https://downloads.cloudsecurity alliance.org/initiatives/ccm/CCM_v3_Info_Sheet.pdf. Accessed 7 September 2015
6. Calder, A.: Information Security Based on ISO 27001/ISO 1779: A Management Guide. Van Haren Publishing, Zaltbommel (2006)
7. Morse, E.A., Raval, V.: PCI DSS: payment card industry data security standards in context. Comput. Law Secur. Rev. **24**(6), 540–554 (2008)

8. Alhazmi, O.H., Malaiya, Y.K.: Assessing disaster recovery alternatives: on-site, colocation or cloud. In: The IEEE 23rd International Symposium on Software Reliability Engineering Workshops (ISSREW), pp. 19–20 (2012)
9. Wood, T., Cecchet, E., Ramakrishnan, K.K., Shenoy, P., Van der Merwe, J., Venkataramani, A.: Disaster recovery as a cloud service: economic benefits & deployment challenges. In: Proceedings of the 2nd USENIX Conference on Hot Topics in Cloud Computing (HotCloud 2010), Berkeley, CA, USA (2010)
10. Ko, R.K.L., Jagadpramana, P., Mowbray, M.: TrustCloud - a framework for accountability and trust in cloud computing. In: IEEE 2nd Cloud Forum for Practitioners (ICFP 2011), pp. 1–5. IEEE, Washington DC (2011)
11. Ko, R.K.L., Kirchberg, M., Lee, B.S.: From system-centric to data-centric logging-Accountability, trust & security in cloud computing. In: Defense Science Research Conference and Expo (DSR), pp. 1–4 (2011)
12. Ko, R.K.L., Lee, B.S., Pearson, S.: Towards achieving accountability, auditability and trust in cloud computing. In: International Workshop on Cloud Computing: Architecture, Algorithms and Applications (CloudComp2011), pp. 5–18, Kochi, India (2011)
13. Tan, Y.S., Ko, R.K.L., Jagadpramana, P., et al.: Tracking of data leaving the cloud. In: IEEE 11th International Conference on Trust, Security and Privacy in Computing and Communications (TrustCom), pp. 137–144 (2012)
14. Zhang, O.Q., Ko, R.K.L., Kirchberg, M., Suen, C.H., Jagadpramana, P., Lee, B.S.: How to track your data: rule-based data provenance tracing algorithms. In: 2012 IEEE 11th International Conference on Trust, Security and Privacy in Computing and Communications (TrustCom), pp. 1429–1437 (2012)
15. RACKSPACE Cloud Monitoring (2015). http://www.rackspace.com/cloud/monitoring/. Accessed 7 September 2015
16. vRealize Hyperic (2015). http://www.vmware.com/products/vrealize-hyperic/. Accessed 7 September 2015
17. HyTrust Products (2015). http://www.hytrust.com/products/. Accessed 7 September 2015
18. Kim, G.H., Spafford, E.H.: Experiences with tripwire: using integrity checkers for intrusion detection. Purdue University Technical Reports (1994)
19. Ko, R.K.L., Jagadpramana, P., Lee, B.S.: Flogger: a file-centric logger for monitoring file access and transfers within cloud computing environments. In: 2011 IEEE 10th International Conference on Trust, Security and Privacy in Computing and Communications (TrustCom), pp. 765–771 (2011)
20. Ko R.K.L., Goh G., Mather T., Jaini S., Lim R.: Cloud Consumer Advocacy Questionnaire and Information Survey Results (CCAQIS) v1.0. Cloud Security Alliance (2011)
21. Popper, K.R.: The Logic of Scientific Discovery. Taylor and Francis Group, Routledge (1959)
22. American Bar Association.: Achieving Legal and Business Order in Cyberspace: A Report on Global Jurisdiction Issues Created by the Internet. The Business Lawyer, vol. 55, pp. 1801–1946 (2000)
23. Bradshaw, S., Millard, C., Walden, I.: Contracts for clouds: comparison and analysis of the terms and conditions of cloud computing services. Int. J. Law Inf. Technol. **19**, 187–223 (2011)
24. Hon, W.K., Millard, C., Walden, I.: Negotiating cloud contracts - looking at clouds from both sides Now. Queen Mary School of Law Legal Studies Research Paper (2012)

25. Regulation (EC) No 45/2001 of The European Parliament and of The Council. The European Parliament (2001)
26. Government of New Zealand. Summary Comparison with Overseas Jurisdictions (2010). http://www.consumeraffairs.govt.nz/legislation-policy/policy-reports-and-papers/discussion-papers/international-comparison-discussion-paper/part-2-summary-comparison-with-overseas-jurisdictions/. Accessed 7 September 2015
27. Susanto, H., Almunawar, M.N., Tuan, Y.C.: Information security management system standards: a comparative study of the big five (2011)
28. Eyers, D., Russello, G.: Toward unified and flexible security policies enforceable within the cloud. In: Dowling, J., Taïani, F. (eds.) DAIS 2013. LNCS, vol. 7891, pp. 181–186. Springer, Heidelberg (2013)
29. Dong, C., Russello, G., Dulay, N.: Shared and searchable encrypted data for untrusted servers. J. Comput. Secur. **19**, 367–397 (2011)
30. Russello, G., Dong, C., Dulay, N., Chaudron, M.R.V., van Steen, M.: Encrypted shared data spaces. In: Lea, D., Zavattaro, G. (eds.) COORDINATION 2008. LNCS, vol. 5052, pp. 264–279. Springer, Heidelberg (2008)
31. Russello, G., Dong, C., Dulay, N., Chaudron, M.R.V., van Steen, M.: Providing data confidentiality against malicious hosts in shared data spaces. Sci. Comput. Program. **75**, 426–439 (2010)
32. Asghar, M.R., Ion, M., Russello, G., Crispo, B.: ESPOON: enforcing encrypted security policies in outsourced environments. In: ARES (2011)
33. Asghar, M.R., Ion, M., Russello, G., Crispo, B.: Securing data provenance in the cloud. In: Camenisch, J., Kesdogan, D. (eds.) iNetSec 2011. LNCS, vol. 7039, pp. 145–160. Springer, Heidelberg (2012)
34. Ion, M., Russello, G., Crispo, B.: An implementation of event and filter confidentiality in pub/sub systems and its application to e-health. In: ACM Conference on Computer and Communications Security (2010)
35. Ion, M., Russello, G., Crispo, B.: Providing confidentiality in content-based publish/subscribe systems. In: SECRYPT (2010)
36. Ion, M., Russello, G., Crispo, B.: Supporting publication and subscription confidentiality in pub/sub networks. In: Jajodia, S., Zhou, J. (eds.) SecureComm 2010. LNICST, vol. 50, pp. 272–289. Springer, Heidelberg (2010)
37. Ion, M., Russello, G., Crispo, B.: Enforcing multi-user access policies to encrypted cloud databases. In: POLICY (2011)
38. Ion, M., Russello, G., Crispo, B.: Design and implementation of a confidentiality and access control solution for publish/subscribe systems. Comput. Netw. **56**, 2014–2037 (2012)
39. Bösch, C., Brinkman, R., Hartel, P., Jonker, W.: Conjunctive wildcard search over encrypted data. In: Jonker, W., Petković, M. (eds.) SDM 2011. LNCS, vol. 6933, pp. 114–127. Springer, Heidelberg (2011)
40. Popa, R.A., Redfield, C.M.S., Zeldovich N., Balakrishnan, H.: CryptDB: protecting confidentiality with encrypted query processing. In: SOSP (2011)
41. Song, D.X., Wagner, D., Perrig, A.: Practical techniques for searches on encrypted data. In: IEEE Symposium on Security and Privacy (2000)
42. Li, M., Yu, S., Cao, N., Lou, W.: Authorized private keyword search over encrypted data in cloud computing. In: 2011 31st International Conference on Distributed Computing Systems (ICDCS) (2011)
43. Rhee, H.S., Park, J.H., Susilo, W., Lee, D.H.: Trapdoor security in a searchable public-key encryption scheme with a designated tester. J. Syst. Softw. **83**, 763–771 (2010)

44. Yang, Y., Lu, H., Weng, J.: Multi-user private keyword search for cloud computing. In: 2011 IEEE Third International Conference on the Cloud Computing Technology and Science (CloudCom) (2011)
45. Zhu, B., Zhu, B., Ren, K.: PEKSrand: providing predicate privacy in public-key encryption with keyword search. In: ICC (2011)
46. Gentry, C.: A fully homomorphic encryption scheme. Stanford University (2009)
47. Naehrig M., Lauter K., Vaikuntanathan V.: Can homomorphic encryption be practical? In: Proceedings of the 3rd ACM Workshop on Cloud Computing Security Workshop, pp. 113–124 (2011)
48. Brakerski, Z., Gentry, C., Vaikuntanathan, V.: (Leveled) fully homomorphic encryption without bootstrapping. In: ITCS (2012)
49. Gentry, C., Halevi, S., Smart, N.P.: Fully homomorphic encryption with polylog overhead. In: Pointcheval, D., Johansson, T. (eds.) EUROCRYPT 2012. LNCS, vol. 7237, pp. 465–482. Springer, Heidelberg (2012)
50. Witten, I.H., Frank, E., Trig, L.E., Hall, M.A., Holmes, G., Cunningham, S.J.: Weka: practical machine learning tools and techniques with Java implementations (1999)
51. Nelson, R., Lawson, D., Lorier, P.: Analysis of long duration traces. ACM SIGCOMM Comput. Commun. Rev. **35**, 45–52 (2005)
52. Alcock, S., Nelson, R., Miles, D.: Investigating the impact of service provider NAT on residential broadband users (2010)
53. Lof, A., Nelson, R.: Comparing anomaly detection methods in computer networks. In: Fifth International Conference on Internet Monitoring and Protection (ICIMP), pp. 7–10 (2010)
54. Alcock, S., Lorier, P., Nelson, R.: Libtrace: a packet capture and analysis library. ACM SIGCOMM Comput. Commun. Rev. **42**, 42–48 (2012)
55. Cloud Security Alliance. The notorious nine: cloud computing top threats in 2013 (2013). https://cloudsecurityalliance.org/group/top-threats/. Accessed 7 September 2015
56. Krautheim, F.J.: Private virtual infrastructure for cloud computing. In: Proceedings of the 2009 Conference on Hot Topics in Cloud Computing (2009)
57. Dr Dobbs Journal. SIEM: A Market Snapshot (2007). http://www.drdobbs.com/siem-a-market-snapshot/197002909. Accessed 7 September 2015
58. Ko, R.K.L., Lee, S.S.G., Rajan, V.: Understanding cloud failures. IEEE Spectr. **49**(12), 84 (2013)
59. Sutton, M., Greene, A., Amini, P.: Fuzzing: Brute Force Vulnerability Discovery. Pearson Education, Upper Saddle River (2007)
60. Takanen, A., Demott, J.D., Miller, C.: Fuzzing for Software Security Testing and Quality Assurance. Artech House, Norwood (2008)
61. THC.org. THC-IPV6 (2015). http://www.thc.org/thc-ipv6/. Accessed 7 September 2015
62. Trend Micro. SecureCloud - Securing and Controlling Sensitive Data in the Cloud. SecureCloud (2015). http://www.trendmicro.com/us/enterprise/cloud-solutions/secure-cloud/index.html. Accessed 7 September 2015
63. Aura Information Security (2012). Aura RedShield (2015). https://auraredshield.com/. Accessed 7 September 2015
64. Bertino, E., Paci, F., Ferrini, R., Shang, N.: Privacy-preserving digital identity management for cloud computing. IEEE Data Eng. Bull. **32**, 21–27 (2009)
65. Gopalakrishnan, A.: Cloud computing identity management. SETLabs Briefings **7**, 45–54 (2009)

66. Celesti, A., Tusa, F., Villari, M., Puliafito, A.: Security and cloud computing: intercloud identity management infrastructure. In: The 19th IEEE International Workshop on Enabling Technologies: Infrastructures for Collaborative Enterprises (WETICE), pp. 263–265 (2010)

67. Agrafiotis, I., Creese, S., Goldsmith, M., Papanikolaou, N., Mont, M.C., Pearson, S.: Defining consent and revocation policies. In: Proceedings of 2010 IFIP/PrimeLife Summer School (2010)

68. Yu, S., Wang, C., Ren, K., Lou, W.: Attribute based data sharing with attribute revocation. In: Proceedings of the 5th ACM Symposium on Information, Computer and Communications Security, pp. 261–270 (2010)

69. Mont, M.C., Sharma, V., Pearson, S.: EnCoRe: dynamic consent, policy enforcement and accountable information sharing within and across organisations. Technical report, HP Laboratories HPL-2012-36 (2012)

70. Pang, S.: Research and development on decentralized analytical methods for network traffics with regional information. Unitec-NICT Research Center on Computational Intelligence for CyberSecurity (2012)

71. Pang, S., Ban, T., Kadobayashi, Y., Kasabov, N.: LDA merging and splitting with applications to multi-agent cooperative learning and system alteration. IEEE Trans. Syst. Man Cybern. Part B. **42**(2), 552–564 (2012)

72. Wood, T., Gerber, A., Ramakrishnan, K., Van der Merwe, J., Shenoy, P.: The case for enterprise ready virtual private clouds. In: Proceedings of the Usenix Workshop on Hot Topics in Cloud Computing (HotCloud), San Diego, CA, USA (2009)

73. Citrix Systems Inc., Business Continuity (2015). https://www.citrix.com/solutions/business-continuity/overview.html. Accessed 7 September 2015

74. Pokharel, M., Lee, S., Park, J.S.: Disaster recovery for system architecture using cloud computing. In: The 10th IEEE/IPSJ International Symposium on Applications and the Internet (SAINT), pp. 304–307 (2010)

# VSEP: A Distributed Algorithm for Graph Edge Partitioning

Yu Zhang[1,2(✉)], Yanbing Liu[1], Jing Yu[1], Ping Liu[1], and Li Guo[1]

[1] Institute of Information Engineering, Chinese Academy of Sciences,
Beijing 100093, China
{zhangyu,liuyanbing,yujing02,liuping,guoli}@iie.ac.cn
[2] University of Chinese Academy of Sciences, Beijing 100049, China

**Abstract.** With the exponential growth of graph structured data in recent years, parallel distributed techniques play an increasingly important role in processing large-scale graphs. Since strong connections exist between vertices in graph data, the high communication cost for transforming boundary data is unavoidable in the distributed techniques. How to partition a large graph into several partitions with low coupling and balanced scale becomes a critical problem. Most of research in the literature studies vertex partitioning methods, which leads us to reconsider an alternative approach for edge partitioning. In this paper, we propose a distributed algorithm for graph partition based on edge partitioning, named as VSEP. A novel vertex permutation method is used to partition the large graphs iteratively. Experimental results indicate that VSEP reduces the number of times vertices are cut by about $10\% \sim 20\%$ comparing with a state-of-the-art algorithm while retains the scale balance.

**Keywords:** Big graph · Edge partitioning · Distributed algorithm · Approximated algorithm · Graph engine

## 1 Introduction

In data analysis procedure, graph serves as an important role for representing or depicting the inner structure of big data, which is widely used in various domains, such as Internet, social network, recommendation system, etc. Numerous data analysis problems can be transformed to graph processing problems and solved by some basic graph algorithms. Since the scale of data increases exponentially in recent years, lots of graph processing problems need to be solved by distributed systems for graph analysis, such as Pregel [1], GraphLab [2], PowerGraph [3], GraphX [4], etc. In this case, original big graphs need to be partitioned into several subgraphs and processed respectively in different computing nodes of the distributed system. Compared with distributed systems for conventional data, the graph data processing requires frequent access to the neighboring vertices and edges of a certain vertex, which may be not stored in the same computing node with its neighboring information and cause high communication cost. Therefore,

© Springer International Publishing Switzerland 2015
G. Wang et al. (Eds.): ICA3PP 2015 Workshops, LNCS 9532, pp. 71–84, 2015.
DOI: 10.1007/978-3-319-27161-3_7

an ideal graph partition has to minimize the boundary vertices or edges that need to be cut and thus reduce the total communication cost. What's more, the load balance problem should also be taken into account.

As one of the most classic problem in graph theory, graph partitioning is proved to be NP-Complete [5]. Research in this field can be briefly classified into two categories: vertex partitioning and edge partitioning. Most of previous work focuses on the former approach. As shown in Fig. 1(a), vertex partitioning aims to partition vertices into different computing nodes with the constraint that each computing node contains similar number of vertices while shared edges among multiple computing nodes should be as less as possible. Though it has been studied for years, the performance of vertex partitioning in real-world application is not satisfied [6–8]. One primary reason is that the number of edges partitioned to different computing nodes differs greatly and thus cause unbalanced computing cost. Another reason is due to the fact that the number of edges in the real-world graphs is generally much larger than the number of vertices and lots of edges will be cut by the vertex partitioning approach, which leads to considerable communication cost.

Some research about edge partitioning has emerged in recent years [9–11]. As shown in Fig. 1(b), edge partitioning aims to partition edges into different computing nodes with the constraint that each computing node contains similar number of edges while shared vertices among multiple computing nodes should be as less as possible. [3,4,12] prove respectively from theory and practice aspects that edge partitioning results in better computing performance compared with vertex partitioning. Moreover, the edge partitioning approach is increasingly applied in the popular graph processing systems, including GraphLab, Power-Graph and GraphX. However, the current algorithms used in these systems are fairly simple, most of which rely on random partitioning mechanism. Though partitioning procedure is relatively fast in this way, it cannot guarantee the constraint of minimizing the number of times vertices are cut. So an effective and efficient edge partitioning algorithm for distributed graph systems has important influence for processing large-scale graphs.

(a)                              (b)

**Fig. 1.** Graph partitioning in tow ways: vertex partitioning and edge partitioning.

In this paper, we propose a parallel edge partitioning algorithm for distributed graph systems, named as VSEP (Vertex Swap and Edge Partitioning). VSEP applies heuristic method to compute edge partitioning iteratively. Two kinds of heuristic methods are proposed, namely VSEP-*square* and VSEP-*diagonal*. We compared our algorithm with a state-of-the-art algorithm, JA-BE-JA-VC [11]. Experimental results show that our VSEP-*diagonal* reduces the number of times vertices are cut by about $10\% \sim 20\%$ while retains the scale balance comparing with JA-BE-JA-VC.

The remaining of this paper is organized as follows. Section 2 introduces related work, including graph partitioning algorithms and distributed graph systems. In Sect. 3, we formally give the definition of graph partitioning problem and the formulation of optimization objective. The novel algorithm VSEP is introduced in detail in Sect. 4, including two heuristic methods VSEP-*square* and VSEP-*diagonal*. We conduct experimental studies in Sect. 5 and conclude this work in Sect. 6.

## 2   Related Work

Graph partitioning is one of the classic research fields about graph. Most of the current partition algorithms focus on vertex partitioning [13–20] while edge partitioning can be implemented by vertex partitioning through changing the original graph into a line graph. There are two major categories for vertex partitioning: (i) centralized algorithms, and (ii) distributed algorithms.

The centralized algorithms assume random access to the entire graph, and usually use Multilevel Graph Partitioning (MGP) [16] to gain better result. [17,20–22] combine MGP with several different heuristics to improve vertex partitioning. METIS [17] adds heuristics into the coarsening, partitioning, and uncoarsening phases. KAFFPA [20] exploits locality of graph based on flow and localized searches. Besides the effect of vertex partitioning, the partitioning speed is another aspect to be considered. Parallelization is a widely used technique to speed up the partitioning by some systems. PARMETIS [18] and KAFFPAE [23] are the parallel implement of METIS and KAFFPA.

Although the centralized algorithms can achieve fast and good min-cuts, their assumption of random access to the entire graph is not feasible for large graphs. The distributed algorithms which only require for direct neighbors or subset of vertices are much better for large graph partitioning. JA-BE-JA [13] is a fully distributed graph partitioning algorithm based on local search and simulated annealing techniques [24]. The algorithm is processed on each vertex independently which only access to direct neighbors and random vertices locally. [25] implements the adaptations of JA-BE-JA on Spark [26]. However, without global information, the distributed algorithms may produce partitions of drastically different sizes.

While edges are many orders of magnitude more than vertices, edge partitioning maybe more efficient than vertex partitioning. [9–11] are recent works for edge partitioning. SBV-Cut [9] proposes recursive application of structurally-balanced graph cuts based on a solution to identify a set of balanced vertices. DFEP [10] applies a market model to describe a distributed edge partitioning algorithm. In the market graph model, vertices represent the funding of buyers and vertices use their funding to buy edges. Initially, all partitions are given the same amount of vertices funding. Edge partitioning is progressed in iteration. In iteration, each partition tries to buy edges whose source or destination vertex is in the partition, and each edge will be sold to the highest offer which means the edge is divided to the partition. Moreover, there exists a coordinator to balance the size of each partition.

JA-BE-JA-VC [11] applies a local search algorithm into JA-BE-JA in each iteration. The authors proposed several heuristics to optimize the final partitioning and it can achieve the partitions of any required size. Their experiments indicate the algorithm outperforms DFEP and random partitioning.

## 3   Problem Statement

As used herein, a directed graph $G = (V, E)$ indicates a web graph, where $V$ represents the set of nodes and $E$ represents the set of edges in the graph. A $k$-way balanced edge partitioning divides the set of edges $E$ into $k$ subsets of equal size, where $k$ is an input parameter. Each partition also has a subset of vertices that hold at least one of the edges in that partition. However, vertices are not unique across partitions, that is, some vertices may appear in more than one partition, due to the distribution of their edges across several partitions. A good edge partitioning strives to minimize the number of vertices that belongs to more than one partition.

Formally, we use a function $P$ to label each edge with a number in $\{1,...,k\}$. The label $i = P(e)$ of an edge indicates that the edge belongs to partition $E_i$. $E_i$ needs to meet the following conditions:

$$\cup_{i=1}^{k} E_i = E \tag{1}$$

$$E_i \cap E_j = \emptyset, \forall i, j \in \{1, ..., k\} \tag{2}$$

If all the edges connecting to a vertex belong to the same partition, the vertex does not need to be cut. If all the edges connecting to the same vertices belong to $m(1 < m \leq k)$ partitions, the vertices need to be cut $m - 1$ times. We use $Count(v)$ to denote the number of different partitions that vertex $v$ is cut. The number of cut times of each vertex in the graph is defined as follows:

$$w(v) = Count(v) - 1, \forall v \in V \tag{3}$$

The sum of cut times of all the vertices in a graph, denoted by $W$, is calculated by the following formula:

$$W = \sum_{i=1}^{k} w(v_i), \forall v_i \in V \tag{4}$$

For various partitioning function, the value of $W$ will be different. Now we can formulate an optimization problem that is to find a partitioning function $P$ to get the minimumal $W$, and meet the following condition:

$$|E_i| = |E_j|, \forall i, j \in 1, ...k \tag{5}$$

Note, in all practical cases the conditions are relaxed, such that it requires partitions of approximately equal size. This is important, because the number of edges of the graph is not necessarily a multiple of $k$. Therefore, throughout this paper, we address the relaxed version of the problem.

# 4  Solution

## 4.1  Motivation

In practical applications, we use adjacency matrix or adjacency list to represent a graph. Figure 2 shows an adjacency matrix according to a graph. In the matrix, vertices in the $i$-th row or vertices in the $i$-th column represent the relations between vertex $v_i$ to all the other vertices in the graph. We use a square matrix $\{a_{i,j}\}$ containing 0s and 1s indicates the adjacency matrix. $a_{i,j}$ is 1 if there is an edge from $v_i$ to $v_j$, and 0 otherwise. Each edge in the graph can be uniquely mapped to one value 1 in the corresponding square matrix.

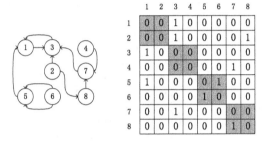

**Fig. 2.** Adjacency matrix to represent a graph.

Based on the edge partitioning approach, if two edges connect to the same vertex and are partitioned into two different partitions, the shared vertex will be cut once. As shown in Fig. 2, there are 4 shaded areas. The edges in different shaded areas do not have common vertices. Therefore, if we partition the edges in different shaded areas respectively into different partitions, no vertex will be cut. So we partition edges in graph according to the following steps.

(i) Divide vertices in graph into $k$ vertex sets sequentially, and each set corresponds to an edge partition.
(ii) Partition the edges whose two vertices belong to the same vertex set (in the shaded areas) into the edge partition according to the vertices set.
(iii) Partition the rest of edges into the edge partition according to any one of the two vertices linked to the edge.

From this process, we can find that if there were more edges whose two vertices belong to same vertices set the number of times vertices are cut would decrease and vice versa. Finally, the number of times vertices are cut is equal to the number of edges not in the shaded areas. So, it has become an effective way to reduce the number of times vertices are cut that how to divide vertices into $k$ sets to increase the number of 1s in the shaded areas.

## 4.2   Vertex Swap

For a graph, we label each vertex by an unique order number based on our proposed methods. Different methods lead to different locations of 1 s in adjacency matrix. Swapping order number of two vertices is a way to change the method. For example, in Fig. 3 we swap order number of vertex 2 and vertex 3. Correspondingly, the 2nd row in the adjacency matrix will be exchanged with the 3rd row. Simultaneously, the 2nd column in the adjacency matrix will be exchanged with the 3rd column. After swapping, the number of 1s in shaded area increases by 2. In this way, the number of times vertices are cut will decrease. So, effective swap will increase the number of 1s in shaded area and decrease the number of times vertices are cut.

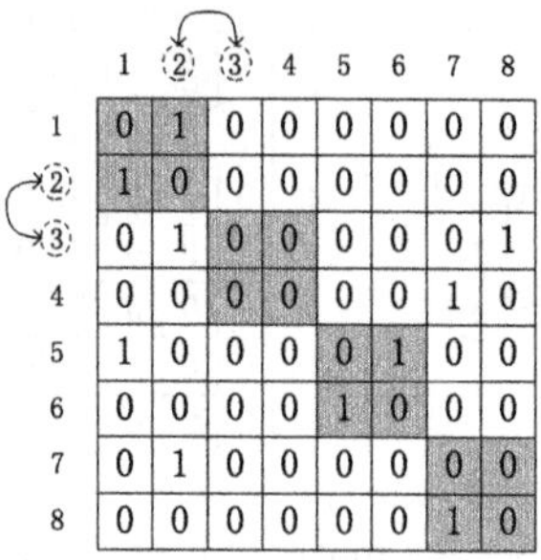

**Fig. 3.** Adjacency matrix with swapping order number of vertex 2 and vertex 3.

We define the area in the adjacency matrix as a target area which is shown as the shaded area in the Fig. 3. The target area, denoted by $T_{square}$, is a set of $a_{ij}$ in the matrix. We use the following formula to calculate $T_{square}$ where $k$ is the number of edge partitions:

$$s = \lceil \frac{|V|}{k} \rceil \tag{6}$$

$$T_{square} = \{a_{ij}\}, \forall i, j \in \{1, ..., k\}, \lfloor i/s \rfloor = \lfloor j/s \rfloor \tag{7}$$

We use $countones(T_{square})$ to count the number of 1s in $T_{square}$. For two vertices, we will swap the order number of them if $countones(T_{square})$ decreases. We call this heuristic $square$. According to this heuristic technique, we can select two vertices randomly and decide whether to swap them or not.

After several rounds of swapping, we partition the edges whose two vertices belong to same vertices set into the edge partition according to the vertices set and partition the rest of edges into the edge partition according to any one of the two vertices linked to the edge. We call this process as algorithm VSEP-$square$ which is shown in Algorithm 1, where $r$ indicates the number of iterations that can be set.

When swapping order number of two vertices, the elements in the corresponding two rows and two columns will be modified but the other elements

**Algorithm 1.** The VSEP-*square* algorithm.

---

**Input:** $V, E, r, k$
**Output:** $E_1, E_2, ..., E_k$

1: initialize $T_{square}$
2: **for** each $it$ in $1, ..., r$ **do**
3:     random select $v_i$ and $v_j$ from $V$
4:     $T'_{square} = \text{swap}(v_i, v_j)$ of $T_{square}$
5:     **if** countones($T'_{square}$) < countones($T_{square}$) **then**
6:         $T_{square} = T'_{square}$
7:     **end if**
8: **end for**
9: $E_1 = E_2 = ... = E_k = \emptyset$ and $s = \lceil \frac{|V|}{k} \rceil$
10: **for** each $e$ in $E$ **do**
11:     $i = $ order number of the start vertex of $e$
12:     $j = $ order number of the end vertex of $e$
13:     **if** $|E_{\lceil i/s \rceil}| < |E_{\lceil j/s \rceil}|$ **then**
14:         $E_{\lceil i/s \rceil}$ adds $e$
15:     **else**
16:         $E_{\lceil j/s \rceil}$ adds $e$
17:     **end if**
18: **end for**
19: **return** $E_1, E_2, ..., E_k$

---

will not. In practical applications, we just need to use an array to record the successful swap. At the beginning, the array is assigned to $1, ... |V|$ sequentially. When swapping, we just need to exchange two corresponding values in the array. So, this algorithm only need to access the graph without modification and only need to read/write the array.

This approach is very suitable for distributed parallel computing. In a distributed computing system like Spark and GraphLab, the approach uses one computing unit to create many pairs of difference vertices and distribute these pairs to other computing units to decide whether the pair of vertices should swap. And then the computing unit collects the results and modifies the array. Repeat this process if necessary.

### 4.3   Balanced Partitions

In VSEP-*square*, target area is $k$ equal-sized squares. This means every square corresponds to equal size of order number range of vertices. The prerequisite is every order number range of vertices contains equal size edges. It meets the requirements while the edge in graph distribute in balance. Otherwise it will lead to partitioning a large number of edges into one partition. So that although the number of times vertices are cut will decrease, the size of each partition differs greatly which does not meet the premise.

To solve this problem, we improve the *target area* into a zonal area along the diagonal in the matrix as shown in Fig. 4. The improved target area, denoted

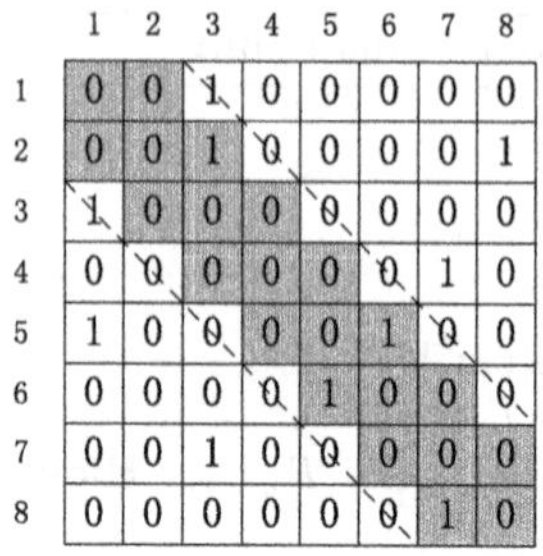

**Fig. 4.** The *target region* in adjacency matrix by *diagonal* heuristic.

by $T_{diagonal}$ is calculated by the following formula, where $b$ is the size of each partition:

$$b = \lfloor \sqrt{\lceil \frac{|V|}{k} \rceil} \rfloor \tag{8}$$

$$T_{diagonal} = \{a_{ij}\}, \forall i, j \in \{1, ...k\}, |i - j| \leq b \tag{9}$$

So we do not need to segment range of vertices into $k$ equal-sized partitions. We use $countones(T_{diagonal})$ to count the number of 1s in $T_{diagonal}$. For two vertices, we will swap the order number of them if $countones(T_{diagonal})$ decreases. After several swaps, we traverse the elements row by row in the adjacency matrix and add the edge corresponding to 1 into a partition until the size of this partition reaches $b$. Then we add the edges into another partition. Finally, we will get $k$ equal-sized partitions. We call this process as algorithm VSEP-*diagonal* which is shown in Algorithm 2.

## 5   Experiments

### 5.1   Metrics and Datasets

We measure the following three metrics to evaluate the quality of the partitioning:

(i) *Coefficient of Variation of Partition (CVP)*: this metric measures the degree of difference in sizes of partitions (in terms of the number of edges). The value is obtained by the Standard deviation divided by the average of the partitions. The higher value indicates greater difference between the different partitions of graph. When this value is 0, the size of different partitions is equal and achieve the best results.

(ii) *Vertex-cut-number*: this metric counts the number of vertices has to be cut. If a vertices is not cut, it only exists in one partition. This ensures that communication is not required and does not need extra storage space to store which partition the vertices belongs to. Therefore, the number of vertices to be cut fewer, the less additional storage space and the less communication is required.

**Algorithm 2.** The VSEP-*diagonal* algorithm.

**Input:** $V, E, r, k$
**Output:** $E_1, E_2, ..., E_k$

1: initialize $T_{diagonal}$
2: **for** each $it$ in $1, ..., r$ **do**
3:     random select $v_i$ and $v_j$ from $V$
4:     $T'_{diagonal} = \text{swap}(v_i, v_j)$ of $T_{diagonal}$
5:     **if** countones($T'_{diagonal}$) < countones($T_{diagonal}$) **then**
6:         $T_{diagonal} = T'_{diagonal}$
7:     **end if**
8: **end for**
9: $E_1 = E_2 = ... = E_k = \emptyset$ and $p = 0$ and $b = \lfloor \sqrt{\lceil \frac{|V|}{k} \rceil} \rfloor$
10: **for** each $i$ in $1, ..., k$ **do**
11:     **for** each $j$ in $1, ..., k$ **do**
12:         **if** there is an edge from $v_i$ to $v_j$ in $E$ **then**
13:             $e = $ the edge from $v_i$ to $v_j$ in $E$
14:             **if** the size of $E_p > b$ **then**
15:                 $p = p + 1$
16:             **end if**
17:             $E_p$ adds $e$
18:         **end if**
19:     **end for**
20: **end for**
21: **return** $E_1, E_2, ..., E_k$

(iii) *Vertex-cut-times*: this metric counts the number of times vertices are cut. That is, a vertex with one cut has replicas in two partitions, and a vertex with two cuts is replicated over three partitions. If a graph vertices are scattered over several partitions, every computation that involves a modification to a vertex, should be propagated to all the other replicas of that vertex, for the sake of consistency. Therefore, *Vertex-cut-times* directly affects the required communication cost of the partitioned graph.

We use four graphs of different nature and size for evaluating different algroithms. These graphs and some of their properties are listed in Table 1. Note, graphs Astroph and Email-Enron have power-law degree distribution.

**Table 1.** Description of testing practical graphs.

| Graphs | Nodes | Edges | Power-law | Source |
|---|---|---|---|---|
| Data | 2851 | 15093 | no | Walshwa Archive [27] |
| 4elt | 15606 | 45878 | no | Walshwa Archive [27] |
| Astroph | 18772 | 396160 | yes | Stanford Snap Datasets [28] |
| Email-Enron | 36692 | 367662 | yes | Stanford Snap Datasets [28] |

## 5.2   Comparisons with the State-of-the-Art Algorithm

We compare VSEP-square and VSEP-diagonal with the state-of-the-art algorithm JA-BE-JA-VC [11]. We configure JA-BE-JA-VC with parameter $T_0 = 2$ and $delta = 0.005$ as they set in the experiment in [11]. We configure VSEP-square and VSEP-diagonal with parameter $r = \lfloor |V|/2 \rfloor$ to iterate swap process $r$ times equaled to the half of vertex number in the graph. We use these three algorithms to partition the four real graphs into 2,4,8,16,32,64 partitions to measure the three metrics mentioned above.

Table 2 shows the $CVP$ of JA-BE-JA-VC and VSEP-*diagonal* over graphs. Table 3 shows the $CVP$ of VSEP-*square* over graphs. Since the limit size of edges in each partition is set in advance, the $CVP$ of JA-BE-JA-VC and VSEP-*diagonal* partition the graph equally as shown in Table 2. However, VSEP-*square* does not limit the size. This leads to that $CVP$ in Table 3 are greater than $CVP$ in Table 2 in the corresponding positions. For *Data* and *4elf* which are not power-law, $CVP$ of VSEP-*square* is slightly greater than the $CVP$ of JA-BE-JA-VC and VSEP-*diagonal*. For *Astroph* and *Emall-Enron* which are power-law, $CVP$ of square is highly greater than the $CVP$ of JA-BE-JA-VC and VSEP-*diagonal*. Because the edge distribution in power-law graphs is much more unbalance than no power-law graphs.

**Table 2.** $CVP$ of JA-BE-JA-VC and VSEP-*diagonal* over graphs with different number of partitions.

| Number of partitions | 2 | 4 | 8 | 16 | 32 | 64 |
|---|---|---|---|---|---|---|
| Data | 0.00 % | 0.02 % | 0.15 % | 0.31 % | 2.30 % | 4.63 % |
| 4elt | 0.00 % | 0.00 % | 0.03 % | 0.07 % | 0.69 % | 1.38 % |
| Astroph | 0.00 % | 0.00 % | 0.00 % | 0.00 % | 0.00 % | 0.00 % |
| Email-Enron | 0.00 % | 0.00 % | 0.00 % | 0.01 % | 0.15 % | 0.31 % |

**Table 3.** $CVP$ of VSEP-*square* over graphs with different number of partitions.

| Number of partitions | 2 | 4 | 8 | 16 | 32 | 64 |
|---|---|---|---|---|---|---|
| Data | 1.61 % | 2.37 % | 3.45 % | 5.20 % | 7.91 % | 10.71 % |
| 4elt | 0.12 % | 0.43 % | 0.65 % | 1.46 % | 2.79 % | 5.23 % |
| Astroph | 79.57 % | 81.46 % | 102.74 % | 110.67 % | 128.43 % | 146.30 % |
| Email-Enron | 87.70 % | 190.50 % | 302.51 % | 437.53 % | 510.06 % | 548.07 % |

Figure 5 shows the *Vertex-cut-number* of these three algorithms over graphs with different number of partitions. By the experimental results in Fig. 5, we found that the *Vertex-cut-number* of JA-BE-JA-VC is the most and VSEP-*square* is the least among all the algorithms in all cases. VSEP-*square*, compared with JA-BE-JA, reduces the *Vertex-cut-number* 36.82 % in *Data*, 17.81 % in *4elt*,

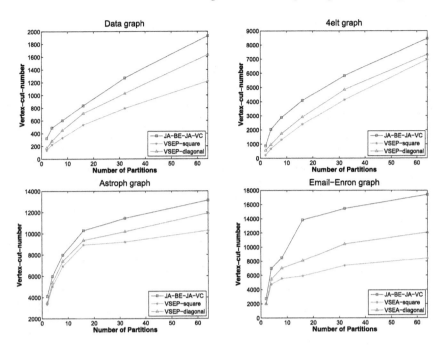

**Fig. 5.** Vertex-cut-number over graphs with different number of partitions.

21.55 % in *Astroph* and 51.50 % in *Emall-Enron* when $k$ is equal to 64. VSEP-*diagonal*, compared with JA-BE-JA-VC, reduces the *Vertex-cut-number* 15.38 % in *Data*, 13.45 % in *4elt*, 9.15 % in *Astroph* and 30.53 % in *Emall-Enron* when $k$ is equal to 64.

Figure 6 shows the *Vertex-cut-times* of these three algorithms over graphs with different number of partitions. By the experimental results in Fig. 5, we found that the *Vertex-cut-times* of JA-BE-JA-VC is the most and VSEP-*square* is the least among all the algorithms in all cases as the same result as above. VSEP-*square*, compared with JA-BE-JA-VC, reduces the *Vertex-cut-times* 45.60 % in *Data*, 30.13 % in *4elt*, 26.52 % in *Astroph* and 41.62 % in *Emall-Enron* when $k$ is equal to 64. VSEP-*diagonal*, compared with JA-BE-JA-VC, reduces the *Vertex-cut-times* 21.05 % in *Data*, 9.48 % in *4elt*, 13.94 % in *Astroph* and 26.26 % in *Emall-Enron* when $k$ is equal to 64.

Through all the above experiments, we can draw the following conclusions based on these datasets. VSEP-*square* achieves the best in *Vertex-cut-number* and *Vertex-cut-times*, but the worst in *CVP*. *CVP* of VSEP-*square* is close to the other algorithms over no power-law graph. Over power-law graph, *CVP* of VSEP-*square* is much worse than the others. *Vertex-cut-number* and *Vertex-cut-times* of VSEP-*diagonal* are better than JA-BE-JA-VC while these *CVP* of these two algorithms are equal.

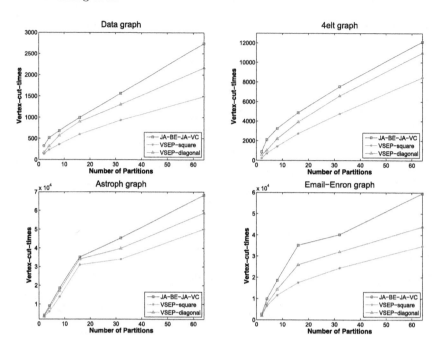

**Fig. 6.** Vertex-cut-times over graphs with different number of partitions.

## 6    Conclusion

We presented a parallel edge partitioning algorithm, named as VSEP (Vertex Swap and Edge Partitioning). This approach only needs to access the graph without modification by using an array to record the process of swapping. So it is very suitable for running on distributed computing system like Spark and GraphLab. VSEP uses two heuristic methods, VSEP-*square* and VSEP-*diagonal*, to compute edge partitioning iteratively. We compared our algorithm with JA-BE-JA-VC, a state-of-the-art algorithm. Experimental results show that our VSEP-*diagonal* reduces the number of vertex has to be cut by $9.15\% \sim 30.53\%$ and the number of vertex cut times by $9.48\% \sim 20.26\%$ while retains the scale balance comparing with JA-BE-JA-VC.

**Acknowledgment.** This research was supported by the National Natural Science Foundation of China (No. 61202477 and No. 61272427); the Strategic Priority Research Program of the Chinese Academy of Sciences (No. XDA06031000).

## References

1. Malewicz, G., Austern, M.H., Bik, A.J.C., et al.: Pregel: a system for large-scale graph processing. In: Proceedings of the 2010 ACM SIGMOD International Conference on Management of data, pp. 135–146. ACM (2010)

2. Low, Y., Gonzalez, J.E., Kyrola, A., et al.: Graphlab: a new framework for parallel machine learning (2014). arXiv preprint arXiv:1408.2041
3. Gonzalez, J.E., Low, Y., Gu, H., et al.: PowerGraph: distributed graph-parallel computation on natural graphs. In: OSDI, vol. 12(1), p. 2 (2012)
4. Xin, R.S., Gonzalez, J.E., Franklin, M.J., et al.: Graphx: a resilient distributed graph system on spark. In: First International Workshop on Graph Data Management Experiences and Systems, p. 2. ACM (2013)
5. Garey, M.R., Johnson, D.S., Stockmeyer, L.: Some simplified NP-complete graph problems. Theoret. Comput. Sci. 1(3), 237–267 (1976)
6. Abou-Rjeili, A., Karypis, G.: Multilevel algorithms for partitioning power-law graphs. In: 2006 20th International Parallel and Distributed Processing Symposium, IPDPS 2006, p. 10. IEEE (2006)
7. Lang, K.: Finding good nearly balanced cuts in power law graphs (2004). Preprint
8. Leskovec, J., Lang, K.J., Dasgupta, A., et al.: Community structure in large networks: natural cluster sizes and the absence of large well-defined clusters. Internet Math. 6(1), 29–123 (2009)
9. Kim, M., Candan, K.S.: SBV-Cut: vertex-cut based graph partitioning using structural balance vertices. Data Knowl. Eng. 72, 285–303 (2012)
10. Guerrieri, A., Montresor, A.: Distributed edge partitioning for graph processing (2014). arXiv preprint arXiv:1403.6270
11. Rahimian, F., Payberah, A.H., Girdzijauskas, S., Haridi, S.: Distributed vertex-cut partitioning. In: Magoutis, K., Pietzuch, P. (eds.) DAIS 2014. LNCS, vol. 8460, pp. 186–200. Springer, Heidelberg (2014)
12. Albert, R., Jeong, H., Barabsi, A.L.: Error and attack tolerance of complex networks. Nature 406(6794), 378–382 (2000)
13. Rahimian, F., Payberah, A.H., Girdzijauskas, S., et al.: Ja-be-ja: a distributed algorithm for balanced graph partitioning. In: 2013 IEEE 7th International Conference on Self-Adaptive and Self-Organizing Systems (SASO), pp. 51–60. IEEE (2013)
14. Baños, R., Gil, C., Ortega, J., Montoya, F.G.: Multilevel heuristic algorithm for graph partitioning. In: Raidl, G.R., et al. (eds.) EvoIASP 2003, EvoWorkshops 2003, EvoSTIM 2003, EvoROB/EvoRobot 2003, EvoCOP 2003, EvoBIO 2003, and EvoMUSART 2003. LNCS, vol. 2611, pp. 143–153. Springer, Heidelberg (2003)
15. Bui, T.N., Moon, B.R.: Genetic algorithm and graph partitioning. IEEE Trans. Comput. 45(7), 841–855 (1996)
16. Hendrickson, B., Leland, R.: A multi-level algorithm for partitioning graphs (1995)
17. Karypis, G., Kumar, V.: A fast and high quality multilevel scheme for partitioning irregular graphs. SIAM J. Sci. Comput. 20(1), 359–392 (1998)
18. Karypis, G., Kumar, V.: Parallel multilevel series k-way partitioning scheme for irregular graphs. SIAM Rev. 41(2), 278–300 (1999)
19. Walshaw, C., Cross, M.: Mesh partitioning: a multilevel balancing and refinement algorithm. SIAM J. Sci. Comput. 22(1), 63–80 (2000)
20. Sanders, P., Schulz, C.: Engineering multilevel graph partitioning algorithms. In: Demetrescu, C., Halldórsson, M.M. (eds.) ESA 2011. LNCS, vol. 6942, pp. 469–480. Springer, Heidelberg (2011)
21. Soper, A.J., Walshaw, C., Cross, M.: A combined evolutionary search and multilevel optimisation approach to graph-partitioning. J. Global Optim. 29(2), 225–241 (2004)
22. Chardaire, P., Barake, M., McKeown, G.P.: A PROBE-based heuristic for graph partitioning. IEEE Trans. Comput. 56(12), 1707–1720 (2007)
23. Sanders, P., Schulz, C.: Distributed evolutionary graph partitioning. In: ALENEX, pp. 16–29 (2012)

24. Talbi, E.G.: Metaheuristics: From Design to Implementation. Wiley, New York (2009)
25. Carlini, E., Dazzi, P., Esposito, A., Lulli, A., Ricci, L.: Balanced graph partitioning with apache spark. In: Žilinskas, J., et al. (eds.) Euro-Par 2014, Part I. LNCS, vol. 8805, pp. 129–140. Springer, Heidelberg (2014)
26. Zaharia, M., Chowdhury, M., Franklin, M.J., et al.: Spark: cluster computing with working sets. In: Proceedings of the 2nd USENIX Conference on Hot Topics in Cloud Computing, p. 10 (2010)
27. The graph partitioning archive. http://staffweb.cms.gre.ac.uk/~wc06/partition
28. Stanford large network dataset collection. http://snap.stanford.edu/data/index.html

# Scheduling Stochastic Tasks with Precedence Constrain on Cluster Systems with Heterogenous Communication Architecture

Qun Liao, Shuangshuang Jiang, Qiaoxiang Hei, Tao Li,
and Yulu Yang[✉]

College of Computer and Control Engineering,
Nankai University, Tianjin 300353, China
{liaoqun,highfly}@mail.nankai.edu.cn,
heiqiaoxiang@foxmail.com,
{litao,yangyl}@nankai.edu.cn

**Abstract.** Scheduling precedence constrained stochastic tasks on heterogenous cluster systems is an important issue which impact the performance of clusters significantly. Different with deterministic tasks, stochastic task model assumes that the workload of task and quantity of data transmission between tasks are stochastic variables, which is more realistic than other task models. Scheduling model and algorithms of precedence constrained stochastic tasks attract a large number of researchers' attention recently. An algorithm SDLS (Stochastic Dynamic Level Scheduling) has been proved performing well in scheduling stochastic tasks on heterogenous clusters. However, the assumption about communication time between tasks in SDLS is much simpler than its assumptions about task computing time, which makes it cannot depict the communication cost among heterogenous links well. In this paper, it is assumed that the quantity of data communication between tasks is a stochastic variable of normal distribution, instead of assuming communication time among heterogenous links a same stochastic variable immediately. Moreover, a modified scheduling model and algorithm SDLS-HC (Stochastic Dynamic Level Scheduling on Heterogenous Communication links) are proposed. Work in this paper focus on considering much more detailed communication cost in task scheduling based on SDLS. Evaluation on many random generated tasks experiments demonstrates that SDLS-HC achieves better performance than SDLS on cluster systems with heterogenous links.

**Keywords:** Stochastic tasks scheduling · Directed acyclic graph · Heterogenous clusters · Parallel and distributed processing · Distributed system

## 1 Introduction

Distributed computing is an important approach of high performance computing. A large number of clusters are widely used in areas of science computation, data mining, bioinformatics, and so on. Many parallel and distributed applications are

© Springer International Publishing Switzerland 2015
G. Wang et al. (Eds.): ICA3PP 2015 Workshops, LNCS 9532, pp. 85–99, 2015.
DOI: 10.1007/978-3-319-27161-3_8

deployed and executed as batches of tasks with precedence constrains on heterogenous cluster systems. Scheduling precedence constrained tasks is one of the key issues effecting performance of distributed systems significantly. Heterogeneity of clusters makes tasks scheduling much more complicated. Assigning tasks to adequate processors considering the heterogenous computing power and communication bandwidth is challenging.

Achieving optimal scheduling assignment is proved a NP-complete problem even in some simple cases [1]. However, many heuristic methods are invented to provide a feasible direction. Some categories of scheduling algorithms [2–15] are utilized in obtaining suboptimal solutions of problem of scheduling precedence constrained tasks on bounded heterogenous connected processors with acceptable computation complexity.

Most scheduling algorithms focus on scheduling tasks with deterministic workload of computation and communication, although workload of a task is always stochastic in many situations because of the complexity of code execution and variety of the input data [16]. Moreover, even if the workload is deterministic, it is difficult to estimate the accurate value of the workload which limited the performance of tasks scheduling algorithms. Therefore, scheduling stochastic tasks whose workloads of computation and communication are stochastic is regarded as an important technique to deal with randomness and uncertainty in many real-world distributed systems.

Some pioneering works have been studied in the area of stochastic tasks scheduling and some algorithms are proposed [17, 18]. Among these works, Li's paper [16] proposed a stochastic tasks scheduling model and SDLS algorithm. Li, et al. combine stochastic model and DLS [6] to deal with stochastic tasks whose workloads and communication time are assumed random variables. Some experiments have proved that SDLS algorithm obtains better performance than other competitors.

However, it is assumed that the communication time between two tasks is a random variable following normal distribution in [16], which is much simpler compared to the assumption about computation workload of a task given by Li. Assuming communication time a random variable ignoring the bandwidth of heterogenous link where the data pass through, which may limit the performance of SDLS in handling stochastic tasks on cluster systems with heterogenous communication architecture.

In this paper, an extension of work in [16] is proposed to take communication cost on heterogenous links for consideration. The scheduling model is modified to suit situations with heterogenous communication cost. A stochastic tasks scheduling algorithm SDLS-HC (Stochastic Dynamic Level Scheduling on Heterogenous Communication links) is proposed. Compared with SDLS through many random experiments on a simulation-based framework, SDLS-HC achieves better performance than SDLS.

## 2    Background and Related Works

Problems of scheduling tasks of a parallel application on bounded connected proces-sors have drawn a lot of researchers' attention for a long time. It is proved that these problems are NP-complete even in some simple cases [1]. However, many heuristics algorithms are invented to find acceptable suboptimal solutions. They can be summarized as mainly four categories: list scheduling [2–7], duplication based scheduling [8, 9], clustering based scheduling [10] and guided random search [11–15]. Among these algorithms, list scheduling, which maintain a sorted list ordered by priorities and select suitable processor for each task aiming to minimize a predefined cost function achieve wide popularity because they are able to provide good quality schedules at a much lower processing time in general.

Stochastic tasks scheduling problems have been studied since 1960 s, and some foundational findings were derived. The general bounds for many stochastic completion time scheduling problems have been proved by Möring et al. [19] and Scharbrodt et al. [20]. In most cases, the stochastic scheduling problem is represented by the notation of $Q|v \sim stoch,prec|E[C_{max}]$, where $E[C_{max}]$ refers to that the makespan is the key objective. Hagstrom [21] has shown that computing the probability distribution of the makespan is an NP-complete problem even for a simple class of stochastic scheduling problems with precedence constraints. Some methods to estimate the distributions of a task's execution time [22] and the makespan [17, 23] are proposed by some researchers.

Moreover, some algorithms to solve stochastic scheduling problems are proposed, such as SHEFT, Rob-HEFT and SDLS. Rob-HEFT is a heuristic algorithm based on HEFT proposed in [23], which is able to generate a set of solutions intended to have good performance for both makespan and standard deviation from a stochastic task graph. SHEFT and SDLS are proposed based on HEFT and DLS respectively in [18, 16]. These two algorithms incorporate the expected value and variance of sto-chastic processing and data transferring time into scheduling. It is proved that SDLS can obtains the best performance in these algorithms in scheduling stochastic tasks on heterogenous platform through many random experiments [16].

# 3    Stochastic Tasks Scheduling Problem

Stochastic tasks scheduling problem discussed in this paper aims to find efficient assignments of precedence constrained tasks with stochastic workloads to bounded processors with different power connected by heterogenous links.

## 3.1    Application Model

A parallel application is presented as a DAG (directed acyclic graph), $G = \{V,E\}$ in general. An example of application DAG discussed in this paper is presented in Fig. 1. Each node $v_i$ in set V presents a task of the parallel application G. The directed edge from node $v_i$ to $v_j$ is donated by $e_{ij}$, which means that the result of task $v_i$ is the input data of task $v_j$. Because of the dependence between $v_i$ and $v_j$, $v_i$ is called predecessor task of $v_j$, donated by $pred(v_j)$ and $v_j$ is $v_i$'s successor, donated by $succ(v_i)$. Any task may have more than one predecessors and successors. Any task $v_i$ can start to be executed as long as all its predecessors' result are recieved. If node $v_i$ has no predecessor, it is called an entry task, donated by $v_{entry}$. Moreover, $v_j$ is called exit task, donated by $v_{exit}$, if $v_j$ has no successors. DAGs with more than one entry or exit tasks can be transformed into DAGs with single entry or exit by adding a dummy predecessor to all entries or adding a dummy successor for all exits. Thus only DAGs with single entry and exit are discussed in this paper.

In addition, G is a weighted graph. Node $v_i$'s weight presents the workload of the task $v_i$, donated by $w_i$. And the data size of task $v_j$ received from $v_i$ is written as $w_{eij}$ which weights edge $e_{ij}$ correspondingly. Unlike deterministic tasks scheduling model, stochastic tasks scheduling model assumed that all the values of $w_i$ and $w_{eij}$ are stochastic variables following normal distributions. This assumption of has been justified by many real applications and adopted in many works [16, 18, 19, 28], which makes the analysis of many stochastic variables analytically tractable.

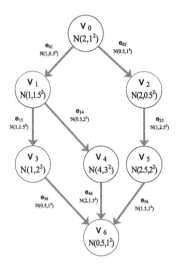

**Fig. 1.** An example of application DAG

## 3.2 Platform Model

The target computing platform is modeled as an arbitrary network of bounded heterogenous processors. There are n processors donated by $P_0$, $P_1$,...,$P_{n-1}$. The computation power of processor Pu is donated by $p_u$. $l_{uv}$ donates the link between processor $P_u$ and $P_v$. Matrixes $B = [b_{ij}]_{n \times n}$ and $L = [l_{ij}]_{n \times n}$ depict the bandwidths and latencies of all links of the platform respectively. And $b_{uv}$ and $l_{uv}$ present the bandwidth and latency of the communication link between $P_u$ and $P_v$. It is assumed that any communication link in the computing platform is bidirectional which means $l_{uv}$ and $l_{vu}$ have the same communication capabilities actually. In other word, matrixes $B$ and $L$ are both symmetric.

To depict the attributes of communication links, a linear-cost communication model is adopted in this paper. Thus the communication time to send a message of size X from $P_u$ to $P_v$ can be calculated as Eq. (1), supposing that $P_u$ and $P_v$ are different processors. Moreover, $b_{uu}$ is assigned infinite to present that every processor can fetch its local data immediately without any communication cost.

$$t_{comm} = \frac{X}{b_{uv}} + l_{uv} \qquad (1)$$

It is noteworthy that the full-overlap multi-port model [24, 25] is utilized in this paper. In this model, a processor can simultaneously receive data from more than one of its neighbors, perform some (independent) computation, and send data to more than one of its neighbors.

For the sake of simplicity, processor-task affinities are ignored; instead, it is as-sumed that only the number of floating point operations per second known as power of a processor determines the application execution speed. In addition, tasks execution cannot be preempted or interrupted. The time to complete execution of a task with workload w can be calculated as:

$$t_{comp} = \frac{w}{p_u} \qquad (2)$$

### 3.3 Scheduling Objective

As many other works, the scheduling model of stochastic tasks with precedence con-strain is defined as $Q|v \sim stoch.prec|E(C_{max})$ in this paper. $C_{max}$ donates the maximum of the earliest completion time of all tasks of application G. Different with determinis-tic scheduling model, $C_{max}$ is a stochastic variable instead of a common variable. A reasonable scheduling objective is to minimize the expectation of $C_{max}$ which is the objective of the scheduling problem discussed hereinafter.

## 4  Stochastic Tasks Scheduling Algrothm

### 4.1  Scheduling Attributes

A stochastic tasks scheduling algorithm SDLS-HC is proposed in this paper which explores scheduling stochastic tasks on cluster with heterogenous communication architecture based on SDLS algorithm. Before describe the detail of the scheduling algorithm proposed, some attributes have to be defined.

The earliest execution start time of task $v_i$ on processor $P_k$ is donated by $EST(v_i, P_k)$. It is naturally to assume that $EST(v_{entry})$ is zero. Any task $v_i$ will start execution on $P_k$ as long as all its input data are ready on $P_k$ and $P_k$ is available. It can be defined as:

$$EST(v_i, P_k) = MAX[DRT(v_i, P_k), EAT(P_k)] \qquad (3)$$

The time to get all $v_i$'s input data ready on $P_k$ is defined as $DRT(v_i,P_k)$. Task $v_i$ gets all its data ready as soon as finishing receiving data from all its predecessors. So DRT $(v_i,P_k)$ is calculated as:

$$DRT(v_i, P_k) = MAX\left[C(e_{ji})\right], v_j \in \text{pred}(v_i) \tag{4}$$

$C(e_{ij})$ donates the communication finish time of edge $e_{ij}$. And $\text{proc}(v_i)$ donates the processor task $v_i$ is executed on.

$$C(e_{ij}) = \begin{cases} C(v_i, \text{proc}(v_i)) + \frac{W_{e_{ij}}}{b_{ij}} + l_{ij}, i \neq j \\ C(v_i, \text{proc}(v_i)), i = j \end{cases} \tag{5}$$

$C(v_i,P_k)$ donates the earliest execution completion time of task $v_i$ on processor $P_k$ which is calculated as:

$$C(v_i, P_k) = EST(v_i, P_k) + ET(v_i, P_k) \tag{6}$$

$ET(v_i,P_k)$ donated the execution time of task $v_i$ on processor $P_k$ which can be calculated according to Eq. (2). $EAT(P_k)$ donates the earliest available time of processor $P_k$, it means all task assigned to $P_k$ have been finished at that time.

$$EAT(P_k) = MAX[C(v_i, P_k)] \tag{7}$$

In addition, the attribute $C_{max}$ can be calculates as:

$$C_{max} = C(v_{exit}, \text{proc}(v_{exit})) \tag{8}$$

An attribute, stochastic bottom level of task $v_i$, donated by sb_level($v_i$), introduced by SDLS algorithm is also utilized in SDLS-HC. sb_level($v_i$) is recursively defined as:

$$sb\_level(v_i) = MAX_{v_x \text{issucc}(v_i)}[\frac{W_{e_{ix}}}{\overline{b}} + \overline{l} + sb\_level(v_x)] + \frac{w(v_i)}{\overline{p}}] \tag{9}$$

As exit task $v_{exit}$ has no successor, so sb_level($v_{exit}$) can be calculated as:

$$sb\_level(v_{exit}) = \frac{w(v_{exit})}{\overline{p}} \tag{10}$$

sb_level($v_i$) describes task $v_i$'s expected time from $v_i$ start to the application completion. Intuitionisticly, if a task with big stochastic bottom level start earlier, the application could complete earlier. To make sb_level($v_i$) calculable before the task processor assignment is resolved, the average values of processors computation power, links bandwidths and latencies ($\overline{p}$, $\overline{b}$ and $\overline{l}$) are utilized in the definition of sb_level($v_i$) instead of some particular performance parameters. The definitions of the corresponding average values are presented as below.

$$\bar{p} = \frac{1}{n} \sum_{P_i \in P} p_i \tag{11}$$

$$\bar{b} = \frac{1}{n^2} \sum_{i \neq j, 0 \leq i < n, 0 \leq j < n} b_{ij} \tag{12}$$

$$\bar{l} = \frac{1}{n^2} \sum_{i \neq j} l_{ij} \tag{13}$$

### 4.2   Tasks Prioritizing Phase

As some other list scheduling algorithm, such as HEFT and SDLS, the scheduling algorithm SDLS-HC has two main phases: a tasks prioritizing phase for computing tasks priorities and a processor selection phase for scheduling tasks in order of their priorities and assigning each task to a best processor to minimize the application's completion time. As defined above, in this scheduling algorithm sb_level is computed recursively in tasks prioritizing phase.

**Algorithm 1**: Computing sb_level

---

**Input:** task DAG $G = \{V, E\}$

**Output:** the tasks' stochastic bottom levels
construct a list in reversed topological order donated
by *revTopList*;
compute *sb_level(v_{exit})* according to Eq.(9);
remove *v_{exit}* form *revTopList*;
**while** *revTopList* is not empty **do**
       remove the head of *revTopList* $v_x$;
       init *sb_level(v_x)* a stochastic variable N(0,0);
       **for** each $v_i$ who belongs to *succ(v_x)* **do**
            compute *sb_level(v_x)* according to Eq.(9);
       **end**
       compute $sb\_level(v_x) = sb\_level(v_x) + \dfrac{w(v_x)}{\bar{p}}$ ;

**end**

---

### 4.3  Processor Selection Phase

In processor selection phase task-processor assignments are determined considering the tasks' priorities and performance parameters of heterogenous platform. To indicate the impact of different processors' computation power, an attribute is defined as:

$$\Delta(v_i, P_k) = \frac{w(v_i)}{\overline{p}} - \frac{w(v_i)}{p_k} \tag{14}$$

A larger positive $\Delta(v_i, P_k)$ means that task $v_i$ will have a shorter execution time on processor $P_k$ while a lager negative one means the opposite. To determine which processor is suit the task to achieve scheduling objective, an attribute SDL is defined as:

$$SDL(v_i, P_k) = \text{sb\_level}(v_i) - EST(v_i, P_k) + \Delta(v_i, P_k) \tag{15}$$

According to SDL, a task with higher priority is scheduled with preference. For the processor selection part, a processor is preferred if a task will get earlier start time or sooner completion time. Detailed SDLS-HC algorithm is presented as Algorithm 2.

As stochastic variables are involved in tasks scheduling model some basic operation of stochastic variables are utilized in this paper. The result of summary of many stochastic variables of normal distribution is still a stochastic variable of normal distribution, as (16) presents. A stochastic variables of normal distribution multiple a rational number will get a stochastic variable as shown in (17).

$$X_i \sim N\left(\mu_i, \sigma^2\right), X = \sum_i X_i \Rightarrow X \sim N\left(\sum_i \mu_i, \sum_i \sigma_i^2\right) \tag{16}$$

$$X \sim N\left(\mu, \sigma^2\right), c \in \mathbb{R} \Rightarrow cX \sim N\left(c\mu, (c\sigma)^2\right) \tag{17}$$

It is worthwhile to note that the maximum of some stochastic variables of normal distribution is not a stochastic variables of normal distribution any longer. However, Clark equations [31, 32] providing an easy way to calculate approximation of maximum in recursive way, which is utilized in this paper to guarantee a feasible approach to conducting computation on the stochastic variables. Relevant equations and derivation can be found in some pioneering works [16, 26–28]. Moreover when comparison between two stochastic variables an operator $\prec$ is defined. Assume $X_1$ and $X_2$ are two stochastic variables of normal distribution, it is defined that $X_1 X_2$ if and only if $F(x_1) = F(x_2) = 0.9$ and $x_1 < x_2$, where 0.9 is a empiric parameter.

**Algorithm 2**: SDLS-HC Algorithm

---

**Input**: task DAG $G = \{V, E\}$

**Output**: A schedule $S = \{proc(v_i) | v_i \in V\}$

compute *sb_level* of each task $v_i$ according to **Algorithm 1**;
add $v_{entry}$ into a list of ready tasks *readyTaskList*;
**while** *readyTaskList* is not empty **do**
    init *MaxSDL* a stochastic variable N(0,0);
    init *selectedTask = null*;
    **for** each task $v_i$ in *readyTaskList* **do**
        **for** each $P_k$ in the cluster **do**
            compute $SDL(v_i, P_k)$ according to Eq. (15);
            **if** *MaxSDL* $\prec$ $SDL(v_i, P_k)$ **do**
                *MaxSDL = SDL($v_i, P_k$)*;
                *selectedTask = $v_i$*;
                $proc(v_i) = P_k$;
            **end**
        **end**
    **end**
    add *proc(selectedTask)* into $S$;
    remove *selectedTask* from *readyTaskList*;
    add unconstrained succ(*selectedTask*) into readyTaskList;
**end**

---

## 5  Performance Evaluation

In this section comparative evaluation of the performance of SDLS-HC and SDLS is presented. For this purpose, a simulation environment is developed, the target platform is deployed a cluster with 16 fully-connected processors at most, with their computation capacities in range from 1000 MPIS to 2000 MPIS and their communication bandwidths in range from 50 MB/s to 100 MB/s. The simulation-based experiments framework utilized in this paper first generates application DAGs randomly. Then, it executes the scheduling algorithms to obtain schedules as output. Finally, it computes the performance metrics based on the schedules. Some details about application graphs generator are discussed next. Some metrics for performance evaluation and parameters for graphs generation are presented, which is followed by experiment results and discussions.

### 5.1  Randomly Generated Application Graphs

In this paper, randomly generated application graphs are generated in performance evaluation experiments. The task workload and data transferring size are assumed to be normally distributed as many previous works [16, 18, 19, 28]. A sets of values to the parameters used by the random graph generator are assigned in the simulation-based framework utilized in this paper. For the generation of random graphs, which are commonly used to compare scheduling algorithms, five fundamental characteristics of a DAG are considered.

Size of a DAG: the number of stochastic tasks in an application DAG is n.

Height of a DAG: the height of a DAG is calculated as $\lceil \alpha \sqrt{n} \rceil$. N stochastic tasks are allocated in $\lceil \alpha \sqrt{n} \rceil$ levels randomly in graph generation. The number of tasks in each level of DAG ranges from 1 to $\lceil 2\sqrt{n} \rceil$.

Average out degree of node: average out degree of stochastic tasks of a DAG is d.

The minimum and maximum expected values $(T_{\mu_{min}}, T_{\mu_{max}})$ and variances $(T_{\sigma_{min}}, T_{\sigma_{max}})$ of task processing times: The expected value and variance of each task processing time on every processor are uniform random variables in the intervals $[T_{\mu_{min}}, T_{\mu_{max}}]$ and $[T_{\sigma_{min}}, T_{\sigma_{max}}]$ respectively. In the experiments of this paper, $T_{\mu_{min}} = 5, T_{\mu_{max}} = 10$ and $T_{\sigma_{min}} = 1, T_{\sigma_{max}} = 3$.

The computation communication ratio of an application DAG: The computation communication ratio is CCR. The minimum and maximum expected values and variances of communication times among tasks on each edge are obtained from multiplication of CCR and $(T_{\mu_{min}}, T_{\mu_{max}})$ and $(T_{\sigma_{min}}, T_{\sigma_{max}})$ respectively.

The different combinations of the above parameters are shown as Table 1. In our simulation experiments, for each combinations of the parameters 100 times of experiments are done to get the average makespan and speedup of SDLS and SDLSHC respectively.

**Table 1.** Parameters of DAGs generation

| Symbols | Parameters | Values |
|---------|-----------|--------|
| n | Size of DAG | [100, 200, 300] |
| α | Factor of the height of DAG | [0.3, 0.5, 1] |
| d | Average out degree of node | [2, 3, 4, 5] |
| CCR | computation communication ratio | [1 %, 5 %, 10 %] |
| P | Processor number of platform | [4, 8, 12, 16] |

## 5.2 Performance Metrics

The comparison of the algorithms is based on the following performance metrics.

Makespan: The makespan (or schedule length) is defined as the completion time of the exit task.

Speedup: The speedup is computed by dividing the sequential execution time (i.e., the cumulative execution time) by the parallel execution time (i.e., the makespan of the output schedule) [7, 16, 18] as shown in Eq. (18):

$$speedup = \frac{\sum\limits_{v_i \in V} ET(v_i)}{makespan} \tag{18}$$

$ET(v_i)$ donates the cumulative execution time of all tasks on a processor of the target platform to minimizing the cumulative execution time.

Difference of Speedup: the difference of speedup is defined as Eq. (19):

$$\Delta speedup = \frac{speedup_{SDLS-HC} - speedup_{SDLS}}{MAX(speedup_{SDLS-HC}, speedup_{SDLS})} \quad (19)$$

The subscript on the symbol $speedup_{SDLS-HC}$ indicates that the speedup is get from the experiments of SDLS-HC algorithm.

## 5.3   Results Discussion

Performance metrics are obtained from experiments with various parameters in Table 1 and analyzed below. All the results are depicted in Fig. 2, where each data points are the average of data collected from 100 experiments. The horizontal axis of Fig. 2 presents the number of times SDLS-HC get better performance than SDLS in 100 experiments, while the vertical one shows the average $\Delta speedup$. Data points obtained from experiments with different task number of application DAGs are depicted by different colored symbols.

Simulation results shows that SDLS-HC can get better performance in most experiments. The largest improvement is above 6 % and the biggest number of times getting better performance in 100 experiments is about 90. The main reason of the performance improvement is that consideration on communication cost on heterogeneous links helps to avoid large set of data transferring through links with small bandwidth, minimizing communication cost. Thought SDLS-HC reduces the communication time of data transferring, sometimes it won't lead to better speedup. First, actual communication cost deflect from its exception debases the performance of SDLS-HC. Additionally, in the situations where communication take too small percentage of overall cost SDLS-HC also performs approximately as or even worse than SDLS. It is also presented that results of experiments with different task numbers of application DAGs locate in similar tendency.

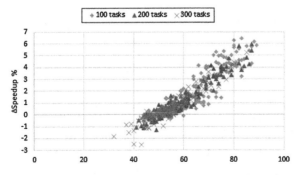

**Fig. 2.** Over all data points of $\Delta speedup$ in experiments

It is obvious that SDLS-HC get bigger performance improvement in experimrments with more processors as Fig. 3 depicted. Results of $\Delta speedup$ in experiments with different processors number is depicted in Fig. 3. Figure 3(a) shows all the results and the max, median and average value of performance improvements are presented in Fig. 3(b). The max value of $\Delta speedup$ achevies over 6 %, and 2.8 % more speedup on average in experiments with 16 processors. The comparison of makespan is shown in Fig. 3(c). Platforms with more processors keeps more heterogenous communication links in simulation, thus it is reasonable that consideration of communication cost on heterogenous communication links in scheduling obtians more porfit.

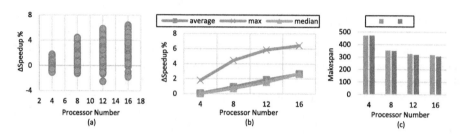

**Fig. 3.** Results of experiments with different processor number

Performance improvement varies in different CCR. It is obvious that SDLS-HC performs better when the communication cost takes bigger percentage of overall cost. Figure 4(a) shows all the results and the max, median and average value of perfor-mance improvements are presented in Fig. 4(b). The max value of $\Delta speedup$ achevies about 6 % when CCR is 0.05 or higher. The average and median value of $\Delta speedup$ swing around 2 % and 1 %. The comparison of makespan is shown in Fig. 4(c).

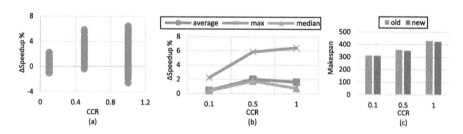

**Fig. 4.** Results of experiments with different CCR

Performance improvement in different average degree of DAG follows similar tendency above. DAGs with bigger average degree mean that the communication cost takes bigger percentage and the communication links between tasks are more com-plicated. Figure 5(a) shows all the results and the max, median and average value of performance improvements are presented in Fig. 5(b). The max value of $\Delta speedup$

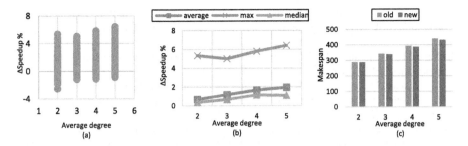

**Fig. 5.** Results of experiments with different average degree

increase to 6.3 % as the average degree of DAGs increase. The average value of $\Delta speedup$ increase to 2 %. The comparison of makespan is shown in Fig. 5(c).

Instinctively, the bigger percentage communication takes the more improvement can get via scheduling tasks with heavy data transferring to processors with wide bandwidth. However, experiments with DAGs whose CCR is 0.1 and average degree is 2 obtain bad performance, because the heavy communication costs concentrate upon small number of tasks when average degree is low. Though scheduling these tasks to processors with wide bandwidth optimizes communication cost, majority of tasks with light communication cost makes computation cost the main influencing factor of the scheduling performance. Trade-off between communication and computation cost may have higher risk to obtain bad performance than the original SDLS algorithm.

## 6   Conclusion

Scheduling stochastic tasks with precedence constrain on heterogenous cluster systems is studied in this paper. Differ from pervious works, communication cost on heterogenous links are considered in scheduling algorithm. In this paper a stochastic tasks DAG scheduling model which takes more complex communication cost into consideration is established exteding the shceduling approach in [16]. Moreover, based on SDLS a modified algorithm SDLS-HC is proposed to scheduling stochastic tasks to heterogenous processors in a heuristic method according to estimation both computation and communication cost on heterogenous processors and links. Because of diminishing heavy communication workloads to occur on links with small bandwidth, SDLS-HC obtains performance improvement comparing with SDLS. A batch of experiments on randomly-generated DAGs validate the performance improvement in this paper.

## References

1. Ullman, J.D.: NP-complete scheduling problems. J. Comput. Syst. Sci. **10**, 384–393 (1975)
2. Khan, M.A.: Scheduling for heterogeneous systems using constrained critical paths. Parallel Comput. **38**, 175–193 (2012)

3. Kwok, Y.-K., Ahmad, L.: Dynamic critical-path scheduling: an effective technique for allocating task graphs to multiprocessors. IEEE Trans. Parallel Distrib. Syst. **7**, 506–521 (1996)
4. Yang, T., Gerasoulis, A.: DSC: scheduling parallel tasks on an unbounded number of processors. IEEE Trans. Parallel Distrib. Syst. **5**, 951–967 (1994)
5. Liu, Z., Qin, T., Qu, W., Liu, W.: DAG cluster scheduling algorithm for grid computing. In: IEEE 14th International Conference on Computational Science and Engineering (CSE), pp. 632–636 (2011)
6. Sih, G.C., Lee, E.: A compile-time scheduling heuristic for interconnection-constrained heterogeneous processor architectures. IEEE Trans. Parallel Distrib. Syst. **4**, 175–187 (1993)
7. Topcuoglu, H., Hariri, S., Wu, M.-Y.: Performance-effective and low-complexity task scheduling for heterogeneous computing. IEEE Trans. Parallel Distrib. Syst. **13**, 260–274 (2002)
8. Bozdağ, D., Özgüner, F., Catalyurek, U.V.: Compaction of schedules and a two-stage approach for duplication-based dag scheduling. IEEE Trans. Parallel Distrib. Syst. **20**, 857–871 (2009)
9. Ranaweera, S., Agrawal, D.P.: A task duplication based scheduling algorithm for heterogeneous systems. In: Proceedings of 14th International Parallel and Distributed Processing Symposium, IPDPS 2000, pp. 445–450 (2000)
10. Cirou, B., Jeannot, E.: Triplet: a clustering scheduling algorithm for heterogeneous systems. In: 2001. International Conference on Parallel Processing Workshops, pp. 231–236 (2001)
11. Shroff, P., Watson, D.W., Flann, N.S., Freund, R.F.: Genetic simulated annealing for scheduling data-dependent tasks in heterogeneous environments. In: 5th Heterogeneous Computing Workshop (HCW 1996), pp. 98–117 (1996)
12. Singh, H.K., Youssef, A.: Mapping and scheduling heterogeneous task graphs using genetic algorithms. George Washington University (1995)
13. Wang, L., Siegel, H.J., Roychowdhury, V.P., Maciejewski, A.A.: Task matching and scheduling in heterogeneous computing environments using a genetic-algorithm-based approach. J. Parallel Distrib. Comput. **47**, 8–22 (1997)
14. Wong, Y.W., Goh, R.S.M., Kuo, S.-H., Low, M.Y.H.: A tabu search for the heterogeneous dag scheduling problem. In: 2009 15th International Conference on Parallel and Distributed Systems (ICPADS), pp. 663–670 (2009)
15. Fidanova, S.: Simulated annealing for grid scheduling problem. In: IEEE John Vincent Atanasoff 2006 International Symposium on Modern Computing, JVA 2006, pp. 41–45 (2006)
16. Li, K., Tang, X., Veeravalli, B., Li, K.: Scheduling precedence constrained stochastic tasks on heterogeneous cluster systems. IEEE Trans. Comput. **64**, 191–204 (2015)
17. Canon, L.-C., Jeannot, E.: Precise evaluation of the efficiency and the robustness of stochastic DAG schedules (2009)
18. Tang, X., Li, K., Liao, G., Fang, K., Wu, F.: A stochastic scheduling algorithm for precedence constrained tasks on Grid. Future Gener. Comput. Syst. **27**, 1083–1091 (2011)
19. Möhring, R.H., Schulz, A.S., Uetz, M.: Approximation in stochastic scheduling: the power of LP-based priority policies. J. ACM (JACM) **46**, 924–942 (1999)
20. Scharbrodt, M., Schickinger, T., Steger, A.: A new average case analysis for completion time scheduling. J. ACM (JACM) **53**, 121–146 (2006)
21. Hagstrom, J.N.: Comput. Complex. PERT Probl. Networks **18**, 139–147 (1988)
22. Dong, F., Luo, J., Song, A., Jin, J.: Resource load based stochastic DAGs scheduling mechanism for grid environment. In: 2010 12th IEEE International Conference on High Performance Computing and Communications (HPCC), pp. 197–204 (2010)

23. Canon, L.-C., Jeannot, E.: Evaluation and optimization of the robustness of dag schedules in heterogeneous environments. IEEE Trans. Parallel Distrib. Syst. **21**, 532–546 (2010)
24. Beaumont, O., Bonichon, N., Eyraud-Dubois, L.: Scheduling divisibleworkloads on heterogeneous platforms under bounded multi-port model. In: IEEE International Symposium on Parallel and Distributed Processing, IPDPS 2008, pp. 1–7 (2008)
25. Beaumont, O., Bonichon, N., Eyraud-Dubois, L., Uznanski, P., Agrawal, S.K.: Broadcasting on large scale heterogeneous platforms under the bounded multi-port model. IEEE Trans. Parallel Distrib. Syst. **25**, 2520–2528 (2014)
26. Clark, C.E.: The greatest of a finite set of random variables. Oper. Res. **9**, 145–162 (1961)
27. Letić, D., Jevtić, V.: The distribution of time for Clark's flow and risk assessment for the activities of pert network structure. Yugoslav J. Oper. Res. **19**, 195–207 (2009)
28. Sarin, S.C., Nagarajan, B., Liao, L.: Stochastic scheduling: expectation-variance analysis of a schedule, Cambridge University Press (2010)

# An Output-Oriented Approach of Test Data Generation Based on Genetic Algorithm

Weixiang Zhang$^{(\boxtimes)}$, Bo Wei, and Huisen Du

Beijing Institute of Tracking and Telecommunications Technology,
Beijing 100094, China
wxchung@msn.com

**Abstract.** Using genetic algorithm to transform test data generation problem into numerical optimization problem, evolution test is one of the hot topics in test data automatic generation. This paper proposed a software test data generation method based on evolution test, which was output-oriented and so suitable for black-box testing. The method transformed the coverage to software output domains into coverage to branches of pseudo-path by use of gray-box test technology. It defined a match function to describe the difference of the search trace to the aimed path, and then got its fitness function based on the match function. Some experimental results showed that the method implemented the coverage to software output domains, and was more efficient than random testing and manual testing.

**Keywords:** Software testing · Test data generation · Functional test · Genetic algorithm · Evolution test · Software engineering

## 1 Introduction

Software testing is one of the most important means to ensure software quality. Statistics show that software testing accounts more than 50 % of the total cost of software development in general [1]. With increasing software complexity, software testing is becoming more and more difficult and expensive. How to generate test data intelligently and automatically to improve the efficiency of software testing has becoming one of the most outstanding subjects [2].

Coverage to the software output domains test data is an important part of software testing design. In general, it is an essential test content especially in functional testing. Statistical results and causes analysis show that a large number of software failures occur on the border of software output domains, or when an output value appears in a special domain which normally is difficult to reach. Typically, coverage to all software output domains and test cases specially designed for domain boundaries, will achieve good effects. However, for a given output, automatically generate corresponding input test data just according to the software requirements specification is a difficult thing. This is one of the reasons why here are few studies.

At present, in functional test, due to the lack of formal specifications, test data generation is generally dependent on artificial selection. Exploratory testing [3] popular recently is indeed a typical manual testing. In structural testing, due to the limitations of

© Springer International Publishing Switzerland 2015
G. Wang et al. (Eds.): ICA3PP 2015 Workshops, LNCS 9532, pp. 100–108, 2015.
DOI: 10.1007/978-3-319-27161-3_9

symbolic execution and other automation technologies, software testers have to manually generate test data to cover some specific goals. Random testing can achieve a high degree of automation, but it will generate too much test data and these data cannot be guaranteed to cover the test objectives. It is why random testing is inefficient in troubleshooting [4].

Evolution test takes advantage of genetic algorithm to transform test data generation problem into numerical optimization problem, is one of the hot topics in test data automatic generation [4–6]. By simulating the process of biological evolution, genetic algorithm (GA) searches the optimal solution for the optimization problem. GA maintains a population of potential solutions; it randomly samples in the entire search space, and evaluates each sample in accordance with its fitness function. In the genetic algorithm, some operators such as selection, crossover and mutation are used, which constantly iterates (each iteration is equivalent to one cycle of biological evolution) to search for a global optimal solution, until the termination condition is met.

In evolution test, the search space of GA is the input domain of the software and the optimal solution is some test data to meet for the specified testing purposes. The search process can be automated, which is helpful to improve software test efficiency. Currently, GA is used widely in structural testing, taking coverage ability as optimization goal [7–10]. Researches on GA in functional testing are not very extensive. Existing methods include a method based on Z language specification [11] and the method based on pre/post-conditions [12]. Because of the high cost of formalization, these methods are difficult for large systems.

To this end, this paper proposed an output-oriented test data generation method suitable for functional testing. It used gray-box technology, transformed the coverage of software output domains into coverage to branches of pseudo-path, and then took use of ideas from structural testing. Some experimental results showed that the method was more efficient than random testing and manual testing.

## 2 Output-Oriented Functional Testing

### 2.1 Problem Formulation

From the view of whether concerns the internal structure of the software, software testing can be divided into black-box testing and white-box testing. Black-box testing, also known as functional testing, takes the tested software as a black box and uses only the relationship between software output and input to do testing. White-box testing, also known as structural testing, designs test cases by analyzing the internal structure of the tested software. Black-box and white-box testing have their advantages and disadvantages. Gray-box testing is a way between black-box and white-box testing, combining advantages of them, are often able to achieve better test results [13].

In gray-box testing [13], first, draw a functionality overview map based on the software requirements specification; then, based on understanding to the structure of software source code, refine and expand the map for advanced software design model named SHDM; finally, select some principles such as node coverage, edge coverage or path coverage to design test cases. So, we can use of gray-box technology to transform the coverage of software output domains into coverage to branches of pseudo-path.

In the evolution test of output domains coverage, the population are the set of test data, the individual is a test data, and test target is a specified pseudo-path (obtained through gray-box testing technique). The mission of GA is to optimize the population, based on the fitness function, to obtain a test data to perform the trace coverage test objectives.

The core issue here is how to construct an appropriate fitness function, to evaluate the merits of test data with respect to the test object.

## 2.2  Evaluation of Test Data

Without loss of generality, we assume the test object is a branch sequence named $aim = \langle b_1, b_2, \cdots, b_n \rangle$, the trace of a test data $data$ is $trace = \langle x_1, x_2, \cdots, x_m \rangle$, where $b_i (1 \leq i \leq n)$, $x_i (1 \leq i \leq m)$ is a branch. Compute their deviation by formula (1):

$$diff(aim, trace) = length(aim) - match(aim, trace) \tag{1}$$

Within, $length$ is named length function, $length(aim) = n$ denotes length of sequence $aim$; $match$ is named match function, $match(aim, trace)$ denotes the match degree between test data $data$ and aimed sequence $aim$.

The value of match function is in $[0, n]$. The larger value means a higher match degree and a smaller deviation $diff$; the smaller value means a lower match degree and a higher deviation $diff$. Defining properly the matching function can be reflected the quality of the test data to help evaluate the test data with respect to the test object.

## 2.3  Design of Match Function

For a test target $aim = \langle b_1, b_2, \cdots, b_n \rangle$ and a trace $trace = \langle x_1, x_2, \cdots, x_m \rangle$, calls a trace $\langle x_p, x_{p+1}, \cdots, x_q \rangle$ as a sub trace with power $(q - p + 1)$ of $trace = \langle x_1, x_2, \cdots, x_m \rangle$ corresponding to $aim = \langle b_1, b_2, \cdots, b_n \rangle$, if string $x_p x_{p+1} \cdots x_q$ is a sub string of $x_1 x_2 \cdots x_m$ and $x_p = b_1$.

Lets $\Theta = \{subtrace\}$ denote the set of all sub trace of $trace$ corresponding to $aim$, we define the match function of $trace$ corresponding to $aim$ as following formula (2):

$$match(aim, trace) = \begin{cases} \max_{subtrace \in \Theta} (length(subtrace)), if\ \Theta \neq \emptyset \\ 0, if\ \Theta = \emptyset \end{cases} \tag{2}$$

Obviously, the value of $match$ is in $[0, n]$. The larger the value, the higher the degree of matching.

For example, if $aim = \langle b_1, b_2, b_3 \rangle$, $trace_1 = \langle b_1, b_4, b_1, b_2, b_3 \rangle$ and $trace_2 = \langle b_1, b_4, b_1, b_2, b_5 \rangle$, then there are $match(aim, trace_1) = 3$ and $match(aim, trace_2) = 2$.

# 3 Test Data Generation Based on Genetic Algorithm

## 3.1 Process of Genetic Algorithm

In genetic algorithm (GA), each effective solution to the problem is called a "chromosome", with respect to each individual of population. A chromosome is a coded string using a specific encoding approach, and each unit of the coded string is called a "gene". By comparing the fitness values, GA distinguishes the pros and cons of chromosomes. The chromosome with larger fitness value is more outstanding.

In GA, fitness function is applied to compute the fitness value of corresponding chromosome; selection is used to choose some individual in accordance with certain rules, and form the parent population; crossover is applied to interchange part of genes of two individuals to generate their offspring chromosomes; mutation is used to change a few genes of selected chromosome to get a new one.

The main steps of GA include [15], as shown in Fig. 1:

STEP1.    To Initialize a population with $N$ chromosomes, get the genes of every chromosome in random manner and keep them inside the range of the problem definition. Denote the count of generation *Generation* and let *Generation* = 0.

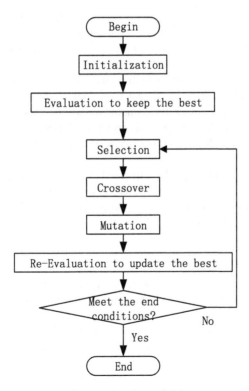

**Fig. 1.** Flowchart of GA

STEP2.  To evaluate each chromosome using fitness function, calculate the fitness value of every chromosome, save the best one whose fitness is largest and name it *Best*.

STEP3.  To do selection using of the manner such as Roulette wheel, generate the population with $N$ selected chromosomes.

STEP4.  To do crossover in accordance with the probability $p_c$. Each couple of selected chromosomes interchange some genes to generate their two offspring and replace themselves; other chromosomes retain in the population.

STEP5.  To do mutation in accordance with the probability $p_m$. Some new chromosomes are generated separately through altering a few genes of corresponding selected chromosome; other non-selected chromosomes retain in the population.

STEP6.  Re-evaluate each chromosome using the fitness function. If the largest fitness value in the new population is better than *Best*'s, replace *Best*.

STEP7.  Let *Generation* + +. If *Generation* exceeds the specified maximum generation or *Best* achieves the specified error requirement, end the algorithm; otherwise, goto STEP3.

## 3.2    Design of Representation

In order to facilitate genetic manipulation, the individual typically needs to be encoded into another representation (chromosomes). Coding strategy is designed largely dependent on the nature of the problem, common including binary coding, real coding, ordered string coding, etc. With binary coding, individual is represented as a binary bit string (vector), which is structurally similar to biological chromosome. It is helpful to use biological theory to explain the genetic algorithm, also makes easy genetic manipulation. With real coding, individuals represented as a real vector, the structure is easy to introduce relevant domain knowledge to increase the genetic algorithm search capabilities.

Since the test data can be generally expressed as a numeric vector, and therefore we have adopted a binary encoding in this paper. Real coding is also applicable actually. The scale of initial population affects to the search capability and operational efficiency of GA, so it usually range from 20 to 150.

## 3.3    Design of Fitness Function

Fitness function is used to calculate the fitness value of each chromosome and to guide the search direction of GA. So, it is the key part of genetic algorithm implementation. Generally, the fitness value is between 0 and 1. The individuals with larger value are more excellent, and have greater probability to evolve to the next generation.

Here, we adopt function $f$ as fitness function, as shown in formula (3):

$$f = \begin{cases} \frac{1}{diff}, & \text{if } diff \neq 0; \\ 0, & \text{if } diff < \varepsilon. \end{cases} \tag{3}$$

Where $\varepsilon > 0$ denotes a very small positive number, its value depends on the specific circumstances, as $10^{-5}$ for an example; *diff* is defined by formula (1).

### 3.4   Design of Other Operator

Roulette wheel selection is usually taken as the selection operator. For example, for a population with $k$ individuals, denotes $fitness_i$ for fitness of $i^{th}$ individual, the roulette wheel selection include 5 steps: first, calculate the fitness percent $fitness_i / \sum fitness_i$ which show the capability of each individual to yield offspring; second, sort the individuals by descending order of their fitness percent; third, for each individual, sum up all the fitness percent of individuals that are in ahead of it; then, select the first individual whose summed fitness is greater than the random number $r_s \in [0, 1]$; lastly, loop above steps until enough individuals is born. As can be seen, the individuals with greater fitness will have larger probability to be selected to produce the next generation, which is consistent with the principles of evolution. As needed, the policy of randomly selected may also be used.

Crossover generally uses single-point crossover, its probability values generally set at between 0.5 and 0.99. As needed, two-point crossover or three-point crossover may also be used.

Mutation changes some genes of the selected chromosome to generate a new individual. Mutation operators generally use random variation, mutation probability values are generally set between 0.001 to 0.1.

Note that if the target path is more difficult to hit, it is need to maintain a large selection pressure in order to accelerate the convergence speed of the genetic algorithm. In this case, we tend to use strategy with greater selective pressures such as roulette wheel selection, optimal survival, etc. Conversely, if the target path is easier to hit, we tends to use strategy with smaller pressures such as random selection [14].

## 4   Simulation Experiment

### 4.1   Test Objects

We choose three different types of C language program to verify the effectiveness of our method, are shown in Table 1.

### 4.2   Performance Indicators

We used the hit rate $p_{hit}$, the average number of evolution rounds $G_{hit}$ and the total numbers of test data *Total* as the performance indexes to check the performance of the proposed method.

Supposed that the total number of experiments is $C_0$, the number of successful experiments generated test data to meet the objectives is $C_{hit}$, population size is $N$, the biggest evolution round is $G_{max}$, the round of evolution obtained i-th satisfied test data is $G_{hit}^i$. The definitions of the hit rate $p_{hit}$, the average number of evolution rounds $G_{hit}$ and the total numbers of test data *Total* were given as follows:

**Table 1.** Description of tested softwares

| Name | Description | Inputs | Outputs |
|------|-------------|--------|---------|
| Triangle | To determine type of the triangle by analyzing its three sides length and their mutual relationship | Three sides: a, b, c | Scalene triangle, Equilateral triangle, Isosceles, Non-triangular. |
| PointCircle | To determine relative positional relationship of a given point and the circle by analyzing the center coordinates, radius and coordinates of the given point | Center coordinates: (x, y) Radius: r, Point coordinates: a, b | Within the circle, On the circle, Outside the circle |
| Equation | To judge the solutions number of equations $ax^2 + bx + c = 0$ by analyzing its parameters | Three parameters: a, b, c | None, One solution (two identical solution), Two different solution |

$$p_{hit} = \frac{C_{hit}}{C_0} \tag{4}$$

$$G_{hit} = \frac{\sum_{i=1}^{C_{hit}} G_{hit}^i}{C_{hit}} \tag{5}$$

$$Total = N \times (G_{hit} \times p_{hit} + G_{max} \times (1 - p_{hit})) \tag{6}$$

By definitions we can be seen: the higher the hit rate, the greater the probability of successful test data generation; the smaller the average number of evolution rounds, the algorithm converges faster; the smaller the total number of test data, the higher the efficiency of the algorithm. Note that complete hit herein referred to generate the desired test data set that coverage each output using at least one test data.

### 4.3    Results Analysis

The main purpose of the experiments is to use the hit rate and other indicators to examine the performance of the proposed method, and compare results with random tests. The main experimental procedure is as follows:

First, set strategies of evolution testing in the proposed method. For all the three tested software, used binary encoding, roulette wheel selection, random survival, single-point crossover and random mutation strategy. The basic strategies as shown in Table 2.

Then, for each of the tested software, configured the basic parameters of genetic algorithm such as the global population size and other parameters, the basic parameters shown in Table 3.

**Table 2.** Strategies of evolution testing

| Name | Configuration | Value |
|---|---|---|
| Representation | Binary encoding | Individual length: 20 |
| Selection | Roulette wheel selection | – |
| Survival | Random survival strategy | Survival probability $p_s = 0.95$ |
| Crossover | Single-point crossover | Crossover probability $p_c = 0.7$ |
| Mutation | Random mutation | Mutation probability $p_m = 0.02$ |

**Table 3.** Parameters of genetic algorithm

| Software | Population size | The biggest evolution round |
|---|---|---|
| Triangle | 40 | 50 |
| PointCircle | 50 | 50 |
| Equation | 40 | 50 |

Finally, for each tested software, conduct several experiments to statistics its hit rate $p_{hit}$, the average number of evolution rounds $G_{hit}$ and the total numbers of test data *Total* to compare with random testing (*N* groups in every round, $G_{hit}$ round in every experiment). As can be seen from Table 4, the proposed method of this paper has good advantages.

**Table 4.** Partial experimental results and comparison (15 experiments)

| Software | Output | Approach | $p_{hit}$ | $G_{hit}$ | *Total* |
|---|---|---|---|---|---|
| Triangle | Equilateral triangle | Proposed method | 0.867 | 34.31 | 1456 |
| | | Random | 0 | – | 30000 |
| | Isosceles triangle | Proposed method | 1.0 | 22.13 | 886 |
| | | Random | 0.2 | 26.67 | 27200 |
| PointCircle | On the circle | Proposed method | 0.8 | 39.58 | 1875 |
| | | Random | 0 | – | 30000 |
| Equation | Two identical solution | Proposed method | 1.0 | 18.33 | 734 |
| | | Random | 0.13 | 42.94 | 29453 |

# 5 Conclusion

Coverage to the software output domains is an important part of functional testing. However, since for a given output, to generate test data automatically according to the software requirements specification is a very difficult thing, there are very rare approaches with good operability to do it currently.

By transforming test data generation problem into numerical optimization problem, and taking the ability of coverage to program path as optimization goal, there are now some good researches on evolution test in structural testing.

This paper gave a new idea for solving the output domains coverage problem. By making use of gray-box technology, it transformed the coverage of software output domains into coverage to branches of pseudo-path. And then, made it to be feasible that those evolution testing methods in structural testing could be used in functional testing. Various experiments had shown that the proposed method in this paper was superior to random testing.

Next, we would experiment to compare the effects of different evolution testing methods in structural testing to obtain optimum method might be used to address specific output domains coverage issues of functional testing.

# References

1. Ammann, P., Offutt, J.: Introduction to Software Testing. Cambridge University Press, Cambridge (2008)
2. Patton, R.: Software Testing, 2nd edn. SAMS & Pearson Education, New York (2006)
3. Kaner, C., Bach, J.: The Nature of Exploratory Testing. http://www.testingeducation.org. 2004
4. Wegener, J., Sthamer, H., Baresel, A.: Application fields for evolutionary testing. In: European Software Testing Analysis & Review, Stockholm, Sweden, November 2001
5. Wegener, J.: Overview of Evolutionary Testing. In: IEEE Seminal Workshop, Toronto, Canada, p. 14, May 2001
6. Baresel, A., Binkley, D., Harman, M., Korel, B.: Evolutionary testing in the presence of loop-assigned flags: a testability transformation approach. In: International Symposium on Software Testing and Analysis, Boston, Massachusetts, pp. 108-118 (2004)
7. Jones, J.A., Harrold, M.J.: Test-suite reduction and prioritization for modified condition/decision coverage. IEEE Trans. Softw. Eng. 29(3), 195–209 (2003)
8. Jun-lin, Q.U.A.N., Lu, L.U.: Research test case suite minimization based on genetic algorithm. Comput. Eng. Appl. 45(19), 58–61 (2009)
9. Lin, J.C., Yeh, P.L.: Using genetic algorithms for test case generation in path testing. In: Proceedings of the Asian Test Symposium, pp. 241–246 (2000)
10. Jones, B.F., Sthamer, H.H., Eyres, D.E.: Automatic structural testing using genetic algorithms. Softw. Eng. J. 11(5), 299–306 (1996)
11. Baresel, A., Sthamer, H., Schmidt, M.: Fitness function design to improve evolutionary structural testing. In: Genetic and Evolutionary Computation Conference, New York, USA, pp. 1329–1336 (2002)
12. Wegener, J., Buhler, O.: Evaluation of different fitness functions for the evolutionary testing of an automatic parking system. In: The Genetic and Evolutionary Computation Conference, Seattle, Washington, pp. 1400–1412 (2002)
13. Weixiang, Z., Wenhong, L.: Application of grey-box testing method. J. Spacecr. TT&C Technol. 29(6), 86–89 (2010)
14. Shi, L., Baowen, X., Xie, X.: An Empirical Study of Configuration Strategies of Evolutionary Testing. Int. J. Comput. Sci. Netw. Secur. IJCSNS 6(1A), 44–49 (2006)
15. Zhang, W., Wei, B., Du, H.: Test case prioritization based on genetic algorithm and test-points coverage. In: Sun, X.-h., et al. (eds.) ICA3PP 2014, Part I. LNCS, vol. 8630, pp. 644–654. Springer, Heidelberg (2014)

# The 5th International Symposium on Trust, Security and Privacy for Emerging Applications (TSP-15)

# An Efficient Pre-filter to Accelerate Regular Expression Matching

Chengcheng Xu[1][✉], Shuhui Chen[1], Xiaofeng Wang[1], and Jinshu Su[1,2]

[1] College of Computer, National University of Defense Technology,
410073 Changsha, China
{xuchengcheng,shchen,xf_wang,sjs}@nudt.edu.cn
[2] National Key Laboratory for Parallel and Distributed Processing,
National University of Defense Technology, 410073 Changsha, China

**Abstract.** Regular expression matching is widely used in content-aware applications, such as NIDS and protocol identification. However, wire-speed processing for large scale patterns still remains a great challenge in practice. Considering low hit rates in NIDS, a compact and efficient pre-filter is firstly proposed to filter most normal traffics and leave few suspicious traffics for further pattern matching. Experiment results show that, the pre-filter achieves a big improvement in both space and time consumption with its compact and efficient structure.

**Keywords:** Regular expression matching · Pattern matching · Deep packet inspection · DPI · Pre-filter

## 1 Introduction

With the rapid growth in big data, massive network data needs to be captured and analyzed in real-time, which poses great challenges to traditional network security field, especially for Deep Packet Inspection (DPI) [7]. DPI requires to inspect the packet payload for further processing, which also needs real-time acquisition and analysis for massive network data. Currently, DPI is widely used in load balancing, traffic billing, Network Instruction Detection (NIDS) and protocol identification. The inspection process is to match the stream or packet payload with a set of pre-defined patterns, and the result indicates whether the stream satisfies some special features, such as a virus or an application-level protocol.

Regular expression is widely used in pattern matching scenarios for its powerful and flexible expression ability, for instance, the open source NIDS of Snort [3] and the Linux application protocol classifier [1] (L7-filter). Patterns are compiled to finite state machine (FSM) for automatic processing, and the matching process is represented with FSM state traversal which is driven by stream payload. Deterministic finite automata (DFA) and nondeterministic finite automata (NFA) are traditional FSMs which have opposite performance in memory occupancy and time consumption. NFA state number is linear with pattern length,

© Springer International Publishing Switzerland 2015
G. Wang et al. (Eds.): ICA3PP 2015 Workshops, LNCS 9532, pp. 111–119, 2015.
DOI: 10.1007/978-3-319-27161-3_10

while multiple potential states need to be traversed for an input symbol. On the contrary, only one DFA state needs to be accessed for each character, however, DFA may bring state explosion, which even makes it infeasible to construct an integrated DFA in many cases.

Current researches mainly exploit alternative FSMs for trade-off between FSM size and memory access requirements of per-character processing [5,6,10–12,14,15,17]. Despite of massive proposals, none of them has solved the problem satisfactorily, especially for large scale (namely hundreds to thousands) complex patterns. Yu [16] implemented popular solutions on GPU for large scale patterns, results showed that the highest performance is about 0.2 Gbps which is orders of magnitude lower than needed. In this work, we firstly propose a filtering mechanism to solve the contradiction between memory requirement and matching performance thoroughly.

## 2  Motivations

In matching process, for each input symbol, all current active states should be traversed to get the next active state set. As FSM is kept as state transition table (STT) in memories, time is mainly consumed for memory access. For large scale patterns, STT can only be deployed on high-latency global memories such as DDR SDRAM, resulting tens to hundreds cycles for per-character processing [8]. However, most streams cannot hit any of these patterns in applications such as NIDS and protocol identification. Thus, it's a huge waste to match all streams with whole STT in global memories.

In practice, most streams cannot match any pattern, and they are even not similar with these patterns especially for NIDS. Suppose a filtration process is carried out to trim the normal flows, then only the left small fraction of suspicious flows need to be matched with the whole STT. Based on this, if the pre-filter is compact enough to be deployed on fast on-chip memories, the performance of filtration process can be orders higher than that of whole pattern matching in global memories. Furthermore, if the pre-filter is accurate enough to trim an overwhelming majority of normal streams, the overall performance can be greatly improved. After filtration, the left suspicious streams should be matched with the whole pattern set deployed in high-latency global memories for further inspection and confirmation. In fact, each stream only needs to be matched with one or several patterns as the filtration process has indicated which rules the stream may belong to. Thus, there is no need to construct an integrated FSM for the whole pattern set. One FSM each pattern strategy is adopted to avoid state inflation brought by pattern interaction, and the strategy is definitely a practical method to solve state explosion. Figure 1 illustrates the matching process with Pre-filter. The patterns are compiled to an integrated FSM for filtration in front-end and separate FSMs for whole matching in back-end. Each stream should be matched with the Pre-filter FSM firstly, and only matched streams in front-end Pre-filter need to be sent to the corresponding back-end FSMs for further whole matching. As the back-end FSMs are deployed in large capacity memories where storage is not a problem, DFAs are employed for fast back-end matching.

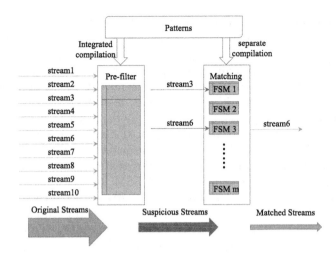

**Fig. 1.** Pattern matching process with Pre-filter

## 3 Pre-filter Design

To achieve the expected high throughput, the Pre-filter must be compact and accurate enough to filter most normal streams. Furthermore, to keep matching correctness, false positive can be eliminated by back-end traditional FSMs. While for false negative, the languages identified by the Pre-filter must be a superset of languages identified by the original pattern sets. For above purposes, we propose to construct a compact Pre-filter by extracting string segments from original regular patterns. The idea is motivated by observations that most streams are benign, and they are not even similar with malicious patterns, which means that they even don't contain the sub-strings in these patterns. By extracting string segments, a compact and efficient DFA-like automata can be constructed to filter most benign streams. The Pre-filter is composed of an improved AC [4] automaton and a state dependency table which records the order and dependencies among these extracted string segments. Traditional AC algorithm can only handle exact strings, with assistance of the state dependency table, the enhanced AC can deal with languages described by a fixed sequence of exact string segments.

For example, the integrated minimum DFA for pattern set of $regular[a - z]$ $\{10\}pattern. * set$ and $ab\backslash d + cd$ has 198 states,while the corresponding NFA has only 36 states. State explosion comes from dot-star and character class with length restriction. However, most normal streams even do not contain the ordered string segments in these patterns. A Pre-filter as shown in Fig. 2 where some transitions have been omitted for clarity, associated with the state dependency Table 1 can trim such normal streams. The dependency table is similar with tables in [9,13], while their target are solving all kinds of regular expressions which will have lots of limitations especially for overlaps. Our method has no such limitations, because our goal is filtration not matching. In Fig. 2, the original pattern $regular[a-z]\{10\}pattern.*set$ is split into segments of $regular$, $pattern$, $set$ which are matched simultaneously. A stream can pass through the Pre-filter for fully matching only when all these segments are matched in order, which is guaranteed by inquiring and updating the dependency status in Table 1. The match of any segment may trigger two actions, test and set operations. If the status label of the previous segment denoted by dependency state region is 0, which means the prior segment has not appeared, then no more operations will be taken. Else, the status label of the current segment will be set to 1. Further, if this segment is the last segment, a pre-filtration matching is hit and the stream will be sent to the corresponding back-end FSM for exact matching, as the stream 3 and stream 6 in Fig. 1. Finally, only stream 6 matches the original regular pattern 3. If a stream cannot hit any of these extracted patterns, it will never match the original patterns, as the other streams in Fig. 1, obviously there is no need to send these streams to back-end matching.

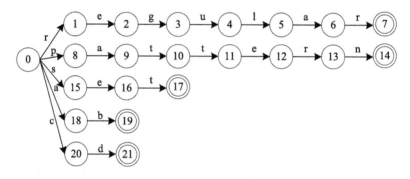

**Fig. 2.** FSM part of Pre-filter for patters $regular[a-z]\{10\}pattern.*set$ and $ab\backslash d+cd$

**Table 1.** The state dependency table for Pre-filter in Fig. 2

| State id | Status label | Dependency state | Matched rule |
|----------|--------------|------------------|--------------|
| 7        | 0/1          | -                | -            |
| 14       | 0/1          | 7                | -            |
| 17       | 0/1          | 14               | 1            |
| 19       | 0/1          | -                | -            |
| 21       | 0/1          | 19               | 2            |

Next, we will give some examples covering all possible situations to illustrate the matching process. For input sequence $regularabset$, state 7 is activated after processing $regular$, as state 7 is the last state of segment $regular$ and there is no dependency state for it, the status label of state 7 is set to 1. Then for input

$ab$, state 19 becomes the current active state, and just like state 7, there is no dependency state for state 19, thus its label is set to 1. Next for input *set*, state 17 will be activated, as it is the last state of segment *set*, its dependency state (state 14) should be checked for further operation. As the label of state 14 is 0, thus the label of state 17 cannot be set to 1 and no matching occurs for Pre-filtration even it has matched the last segment of the first pattern. For another input sequence $abefcd$, the input $ab$ will activate state 19 and set the corresponding label to 1. Then the following $e$ will make a transition to state 0, and $f$ will stay in state 0. Next, the input $cd$ will activate state 21, as the label of corresponding state 19 is set to 1, the label of state 21 will be set to 1 and a pre-filtration matching occurs. Then the whole sequence $abefcd$ will be sent to back-end FSM corresponding to the original pattern $ab\backslash d + cd$ for confirmation, obviously no matching occurs in the back-end FSM. While for another input sequence $ab123cd$, it can also pass through the pre-filtration as $abefcd$, and further it can make a full matching in the back-end FSM. In practice, the probabilities for above three situations are in a descending order, and most streams belong to the first situation. This distribution is very significant as we can trim most streams with a very compact and efficient FSM deployed in fast memories. In other words, a great improvement can be achieved with the Pre-filter mechanism.

## 4    Experiments

The experiments were conducted on an Intel Core i7 3770 platform (CPU: 3.40 GHz, L1 Cache: 32 KB, L2 Cache: 256 KB, L3 Cache: 8 MB) with 8 GB RAM and Linux system. We chose pcre-type rules from Snort pattern file back-door.rules and traces from DARPA [2] intrusion detection data sets. We compared the Pre-filter scheme with traditional NFA, DFA and state of the art Hybrid-FA [5] from FSM construction time, memory footprint and matching speed. Table 2 shows part of the state number statistics for different FSMs with increasing pattern scales. As memory footprint is nearly linear with state number, results in Table 2 can be regarded as memory consumption comparisons among these automatons. Despite of the back-end DFAs in Pre-filter, its size is orders lower than Hybrid-FA and DFA, and even comparable with traditional NFA. The main reasons are that separate compilation hinders the interactions among different rules and little explosion occurs in a single rule. Comparison between column 3 and column 7 also give a visual representation of how the pattern interaction can contribute to state explosion. Furthermore, compressing algorithms such as $D^2FA$ [11] can be employed in back-end standard DFAs to achieve more than 90 % space reduction.

The construction time of Pre-filter scheme consists of two parts: front-end filter compilation and back-end DFAs compilation. As the back-end DFAs can be compiled separately on parallel platforms, we only focus on the filter compilation time. Figure 3 shows construction time comparisons among these automatons, and DFA is omitted for clarity as it is orders higher than the others. Results show that construction time of both NFA and Pre-filter are linear with increasing

**Table 2.** State number statistics for different FSMs with increasing pattern scale

| No of rules | NFA size | DFA size | HFA | | Pre-filter | |
|---|---|---|---|---|---|---|
| | | | head size | tail size | front size | back size |
| 10 | 386 | 299 | 299 | 0 | 348 | 313 |
| 30 | 1151 | 13943 | 9101 | 41 | 952 | 1063 |
| 50 | 1811 | 120675 | 21492 | 109 | 1553 | 3863 |
| 100 | 3069 | >2M | 69218 | 371 | 2841 | 13180 |

pattern number. While, the construction time for Pre-filter is a little more than NFA as it needs additional time for AC determination and building state dependency table, but it is far more less than that of Hybrid-FA and DFA because no state explosion occurs in Pre-filter.

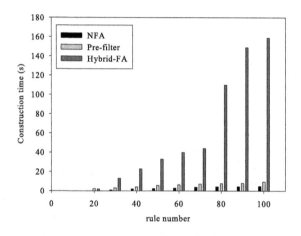

**Fig. 3.** Construction time comparison among NFA, Hybrid-FA and Pre-filter

The performance of Pre-filter highly depends on the filtration rate, if most streams need to be further processed in back-end DFAs, the overall throughput will drop rapidly. We employed four different DARPA files with average size of more than 300 MB to test the filtration effect, and results are presented in Fig. 4. All the traces achieve similar filtration ratios, and the filtration ratio declines with the increasing pattern set as streams filtered out by smaller filter may match with filter for larger rule set. Even with the declining trend, the filtration rate can still reach more than 95 % with 100 patterns, which contributes a lot to the overall high speed. Performance estimation is shown in Fig. 5, only part of DFA result is displayed as no DFA has been constructed for more than 70 rules in our platform. DFA and Hybrid-FA perform better when the pattern number is less than 20, it is because most transitions are accessed in the high-speed caches.

With the increase of pattern set, state explosion results in rapid speed decline for both DFA and Hybrid-FA. While for Pre-filter, the matching speed is insensitive to the pattern scale as the memory footprint for Pre-filter is linear with pattern size. As most streams have been filtered as shown in Fig. 4, matching speed for Pre-filter declines very slowly with the increasing patterns.

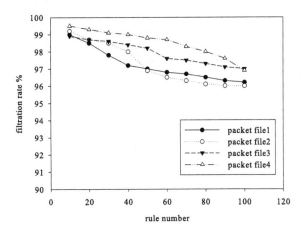

**Fig. 4.** Filtration rate statistics with different trace files and increasing pattern scale

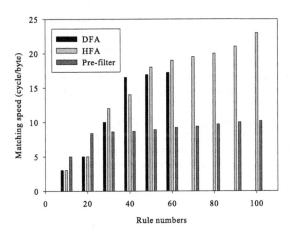

**Fig. 5.** Average cycles to process one input symbol

## 5    Conclusion

Considering that few streams can match the regular expression patterns in NIDS applications, we firstly proposed a Pre-filter matching mechanism which employs a compact and efficient filter to eliminate most benign streams and leaves the left suspicious streams for whole pattern matching. As the filter is compact enough to deployed in small fast memories, most streams can be processed efficiently. Further, benefiting from the high filtration rates in front-end, this method achieves high overall throughput as few streams need further whole matching. Compared with the state of art Hybrid-FA, our method performs better both in memory consumption and time complexity.

Future work will improve from the following aspects to achieve lower memory consumption and higher matching speed: (1) extending the front-end filter with multi-stride, (2) implementing the matching prototype with FPGA or ASIC, (3) employing compressing algorithms in back-end DFAs.

**Acknowledgements.** This work is sponsored by National Natural Science Foundation of China under Grant No. 61379148.

# References

1. Application layer packet classifier for linux (2009). http://l7-filter.sourceforge.net/
2. Darpa intrusion detection data sets (1999). http://www.ll.mit.edu/mission/communications/ist/corpora/ideval/data/index.html/
3. Snort v2.9 (2014). http://www.snort.org/
4. Aho, A.V., Corasick, M.J.: Efficient string matching: an aid to bibliographic search. Commun. ACM **18**(6), 333–340 (1975)
5. Becchi, M., Crowley, P.: A hybrid finite automaton for practical deep packet inspection. In: Proceedings of the 2007 ACM CoNEXT conference, p. 1. ACM (2007)
6. Becchi, M., Crowley, P.: A-dfa: a time-and space-efficient dfa compression algorithm for fast regular expression evaluation. ACM Trans. Archit. Code Optim. (TACO) **10**(1), 4 (2013)
7. Chen, C.P., Zhang, C.Y.: Data-intensive applications, challenges, techniques and technologies: a survey on big data. Inf. Sci. **275**, 314–347 (2014)
8. Chen, S., Lu, R.: A regular expression matching engine with hybrid memories. Comput. Stan. Interfaces **36**(5), 880–888 (2014)
9. Khalid, A., Sen, R., Chattopadhyay, A.: Si-dfa: Sub-expression integrated deterministic finite automata for deep packet inspection. In: 2013 IEEE 14th International Conference on High Performance Switching and Routing (HPSR), pp. 164–170. IEEE (2013)
10. Kumar, S., Chandrasekaran, B., Turner, J., Varghese, G.: Curing regular expressions matching algorithms from insomnia, amnesia, and acalculia. In: Proceedings of the 3rd ACM/IEEE Symposium on Architecture for Networking and Communications systems, pp. 155–164. ACM (2007)
11. Kumar, S., Dharmapurikar, S., Yu, F., Crowley, P., Turner, J.: Algorithms to accelerate multiple regular expressions matching for deep packet inspection. ACM SIGCOMM Comput. Commun. Rev. **36**(4), 339–350 (2006)
12. Smith, R., Estan, C., Jha, S., Kong, S.: Deflating the big bang: fast and scalable deep packet inspection with extended finite automata. ACM SIGCOMM Comput. Commun. Rev. **38**(4), 207–218 (2008)

13. Wang, K., Li, J.: Towards fast regular expression matching in practice. In: Proceedings of the ACM SIGCOMM 2013 Conference on SIGCOMM, pp. 531–532. ACM (2013)
14. Xu, Y., Jiang, J., Wei, R., Song, Y., Chao, H.J.: TFA: A tunable finite automaton for pattern matching in network intrusion detection systems (2014)
15. Yang, Y., Prasanna, V.K.: Space-time tradeoff in regular expression matching with semi-deterministic finite automata. In: 2011 IEEE Proceedings of INFOCOM, pp. 1853–1861. IEEE (2011)
16. Yu, X., Becchi, M.: Gpu acceleration of regular expression matching for large datasets: exploring the implementation space. In: Proceedings of the ACM International Conference on Computing Frontiers, p. 18. ACM (2013)
17. Zheng, K., Cai, Z., Zhang, X., Wang, Z., Yang, B.: Algorithms to speedup pattern matching for network intrusion detection systems. Comput. Commun. **62**, 47–58 (2015)

# A Hybrid Optimization Approach
# for Anonymizing Transactional Data

Li-e Wang[1,2] and Xianxian Li[1,2](✉)

[1] Guangxi Key Lab of Multi-source Information Mining and Security,
Guangxi Normal University, Guilin 541004, China
[2] College of Computer Science and Information Technology,
Guangxi Normal University, Guilin 541004, China
{wanglie,lixx}@gxnu.edu.cn

**Abstract.** Transactional data about individuals is increasingly being collected to support many important real-life applications ranging from healthcare to marketing. Thus, privacy issues in sharing transactional data among different parties have attracted considerable research interest in recent years. Due to the high-dimensionality and sparsity of transactional data, existing privacy-preserving techniques will incur excessive information loss. We propose a hybrid optimization approach for anonymizing transactional data through integrating different anonymous techniques. Experimental results verify that our approach significantly outperforms the current state-of-the-art algorithms in terms of data utility.

**Keywords:** Hybrid · Privacy protection · Bipartite graph · Data publishing

## 1 Introduction

Transactional data, containing information about individuals behaviors or activities, are increasingly used in applications, such as recommendation systems [1], e-commerce [2] and research purposes. Unfortunately, publishing transaction data in its original form may lead to privacy breaches since these data contain individuals private and sensitive information, which contains relational attributes and transaction attributes respectively. Thwarting item disclosure may additionally be needed [3,4]. Due to the high dimensionality and sparsity of transactional data, many methodologies have been proposed to protect the privacy of published transactional data including Generalization which operates by mapping original items to generalized items [4–8] and Suppression which removes items before releasing data [3], Bucketization which operates by separating sensitive items from the QID [9–11] and Perturbation which operates by adding or removing items from individuals transactions [12]. However, these privacy-preserving techniques mostly focus on anonymizing set-valued data only without concerning relational attributes.

© Springer International Publishing Switzerland 2015
G. Wang et al. (Eds.): ICA3PP 2015 Workshops, LNCS 9532, pp. 120–132, 2015.
DOI: 10.1007/978-3-319-27161-3_11

Actually, some applications may require analysis of relational attributes and transaction attributes together. For example, some studies may ask to count all customers above 30 years old who purchased products $a$ and $b$. Also, some may be interested in analyzing customer demographics and product information together. Purchase records are typical examples of transactional data. Lets take purchase records for example. Purchase records are comprised of transactions, which consist of relational attributes (e.g., attribute information of a customer, such as age, gender and zip code) and transaction attributes (e.g., the purchased products, a set of diseases). For details, see Fig. 1(a). So, a suitable approach to anonymize data having relational attributes and transaction attributes should be needed. Existing works [13, 14] proposed multi-dimensional $k$-anonymization of the whole attributes. There, the problem is that applying those anonymizations, in which they mainly use the approach of generalization to achieve anonymity, to datasets with multiple attributes will lose considerable amount of information.

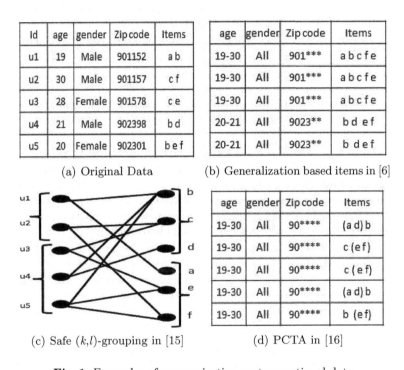

| Id | age | gender | Zip code | Items |
|----|-----|--------|----------|-------|
| u1 | 19 | Male | 901152 | a b |
| u2 | 30 | Male | 901157 | c f |
| u3 | 28 | Female | 901578 | c e |
| u4 | 21 | Male | 902398 | b d |
| u5 | 20 | Female | 902301 | b e f |

(a) Original Data

| age | gender | Zip code | Items |
|-----|--------|----------|-------|
| 19-30 | All | 901*** | a b c f e |
| 19-30 | All | 901*** | a b c f e |
| 19-30 | All | 901*** | a b c f e |
| 20-21 | All | 9023** | b d e f |
| 20-21 | All | 9023** | b d e f |

(b) Generalization based items in [6]

(c) Safe $(k,l)$-grouping in [15]

| age | gender | Zip code | Items |
|-----|--------|----------|-------|
| 19-30 | All | 90**** | (a d) b |
| 19-30 | All | 90**** | c (e f) |
| 19-30 | All | 90**** | c (e f) |
| 19-30 | All | 90**** | (a d) b |
| 19-30 | All | 90**** | b (e f) |

(d) PCTA in [16]

Fig. 1. Examples of anonymization on transactional data

**Example 1.** *Anonymization on Transactional Database.* Furthermore, we note that different applications (e.g. the personalized recommendation system and the mining of association rules) have different utility requirements. We will give an example to make the point clearer. As of now, most existing recommendation systems use user-based, item-based or collaborative approaches for helping users make decisions. They may require counting sales of products and analyzing customer demographics of products. Yet, another application of association rules are focusing on the relationship among products which are purchased by a customer or one type of customers. That is to say, different applications emphasize different aspects of data, such as statistical characteristics, relationships among products and so on. On the other hand, we notice that these existing anonymized techniques have their own advantages and shortcomings. For detailed explanations, see the Example 1.

As shown in Fig. 1(a), the original database has five transactions and six items. And three different approaches are used to anonymize the same transactional database. Figure 1(b) is 2-anonymous by employing generalization on itemset [6,9], Fig. 1(c) is 2-anonymous by employing a safe (2, 3)-grouping approach [15] and Fig. 1(d) is 2-anonymous by employing Privacy-constrained Clustering-based Transaction Data Anonymization (PCTA) [16]. We can see that Fig. 1(b), (c) and (d) satisfy 2-anonymous according to the model of $k$-anonymous, but the difference among the results of data utility on the three different published datasets is substantial. For example, a merchandising company wants to figure out what products the customers in particular age ranges prefer to buy. The approach of generalization based items in Fig. 1(b) can provide more information than Safe $(k,l)$-grouping and PCTA. However, a store wants to watch for the sale of products. The approach of safe $(k,l)$-grouping based on the bipartite graph in Fig. 1(c) can give an more accurate answer than Generalization and PCTA. The mining of association rules tends to employ the PCTA approach in Fig. 1(d).

Lots of research works has demonstrated that it needs to offer tradeoffs between privacy and utility for applications. Based on above analysis, it is quite clear that, different methods can preserve different aspects of data utility in spite of they all incur a large amount of information loss in terms of transaction attributes or associations among items. Existing methods, such as generalization, clustering, perturbing and suppression, are unable to accommodate specific utility requirements for different applications because they only consider a small number of transformations to anonymize data with multiple attributes. It may cause excessive information loss which would make data useless. Thus, this work proposes a hybrid approach that overcomes the deficiencies of aforementioned anonymized approach to satisfy different utility requirements.

**Contributions.** To overcome the problems mentioned above, we present a new framework which provides hybrid privacy preserving services based on the form of bipartite graphs via clustering and grouping. The anonymization version of data is presented as a partitioned bipartite graph and an association rules graph. In particular, we focus on different utility requirements of multiple applications. This is crucial difference between our approach and prior works. Note that it is not practical to adopting a single technique for preserving privacy for all different applications since they only consider a small number of transformations to anonymize data. For instance, the method introduced in [15] preserves the degree of nodes perfectly while the method introduced in [16] preserves more information in the mining of association rules. So we propose a hybrid optimization approach to satisfy different utility requirements by integrating different anonymous techniques.

In our framework, we present the anonymized data in a graph form which can handle high dimensional data well. Our approach adopts clustering to anonymize on relational attributes while employing grouping to perturb transaction attributes based on bipartite graphs. Since the approach of grouping items will incur information loss of association rules, we construct a graph of association rules as compensation to satisfy different utility requirements.

We devised an effective anonymization algorithm for generating safe groups which satisfy $k$-anonymous and $l$-diversity based on the graph of association rules. We evaluated its performance in real datasets, and experimental results confirm that our approach preserves better data utility to a degree not achieved through previous methods.

**Organization.** The rest of the paper is organized as follows: Sect. 2 introduces the graph model and utility metrics. Sections 3 and 4 describe our approach and algorithm description in detail. Section 5 demonstrates our approach through experimental study. Section 6 concludes the paper.

## 2    Preliminarties

### 2.1    Graph Model

In this paper, we focus on the problem of anonymizing transactional data and we use bipartite graphs $G = (V, W, E, Lv)$ to simply represent the original data where $V$ and $W$ denote the two types node sets and $E$ denotes the edge set. Each node in the graph has several labels, which represent the QID attributes of the node (such as age, gender and zip code except id). We use $Lv$ to represent the list of labels on nodes. We adopt a graph-based hybrid approach which combines different anonymous techniques to satisfy different utility requirements.

In our framework, we use a partitioned bipartite graph with labels to denote the anonymized graph which achieves anonymity through non-homogeneous generalization [17] and grouping. Meanwhile, we preserve association rules in a weighted graph form. Figure 2 shows a sample instantiation of the schema with Fig. 2(a) showing the original data and Fig. 2(b) showing the correlated bipartite graph with labels and Fig. 2(c) showing the correlated graph of association rules. Here the bipartite graph G in Fig. 2(a) and (b) consists of a set of customer nodes $V$ (such as $u1, u2, u3, \dots$) and a set of products nodes $W$ (such as $a, b, c, \dots$). An edge $((v \in V, w \in W))$ in $E$ indicates that the customer represented by node $v$ have bought the product represented by node $w$. In Fig. 2(b), a group is represented by a box and each node in the box belongs to the group.

A graph of association rules is shown in Fig. 2(c). Here the graph $G_w$ $(W, E)$ consists of $n = |W|$ nodes of products and a set of $|E|$ edges. An edge denotes the associations among products. And we use a tuple $e = (w1, w2)$ to denote an edge from $w1$ to $w2$. If such association incurs more than once, we use a weighted edge

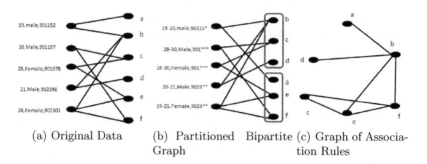

(a) Original Data          (b) Partitioned Bipartite    (c) Graph of Associa-
                               Graph                       tion Rules

**Fig. 2.** Examples of hybrid privacy protection

to present the duplicate associations. Each customer can buy different products in various combinations.

## 2.2 Utility Metrics

The goal of data publishing is to transform the data to generate a publishable version such that $(i)$ the $k$-anonymity privacy constraint is satisfied; and $(ii)$ utility is maximized. To capture data utility, popular measure include the normalized certainty penalty (NCP) [6,9], which is expressed as the weighted average of the information loss of all generalized items, and the utility loss ($UL$) [16,18], which we use to measure the information loss by generalization on relational attributes in this paper.

**Definition 1. Utility loss for non-homogeneous.** Given a node $v(l_1,\ldots,l_n)$ and the anonymized node $v'(l_1,\ldots,l_n)$ of $v$, the node set $V$ and its anonymized set $V'$, the cost of generalization node $v$ to $v'$ and the cost of generalization the whole node set $V$ to $V'$ are measured as follows respectively.

$$UL(v) = \sum_{i=1}^{n} \frac{|l'_i| - |l_i|}{n|V_i|}$$

$$UL(V) = \sum_{v \in V} \frac{UL(v)}{|V|}$$

where $|l_i|$ is the number of distinct values of attribute $i$ in $l_i$ and of attribute $i$ in $l_i^*$ ( $l_i^* < l_i$) in $V$. $|l_i|$ is the number of $l_i$ in $V$ and $n$ is the number of attribute in QID. $|V_i|$ is the number of distinct values of attribute $i$ in $V$. The utility loss of generalization a node $v$ is the weighted average of the utility loss of generalization all attributes of the node. And the utility loss of generalization the whole node set $V$ is the weighted average of the utility loss of generalization all nodes in the set $V$. The utility loss of a particular generalization ranges from 0 to 1 and can be easily measured. Obviously, the utility loss of non-homogeneous generalization is less than homogeneous generalization. It says that non-homogeneous generalization can preserve more data utility. Obviously, smaller values of $UL$ indicate less information loss.

On the other hand, information loss of transaction attributes we considering here is incurred by grouping an item to a group. That is, the information loss of transaction attributes is from disturbing a few associations among items. However, the graph of association rules we generated act as a compensation for the information loss which is incurred by grouping. So we omit the information loss of transaction attributes in the experimental section.

Furthermore, we also measure data utility through the quality of answering queries of aggregate analysis as previous work [15]. As defined in [15], we use the parameter of expected error $|\mu - Q|/Q$ to precisely evaluate utility, and the correct answer on original data is $Q$ and the expected answer on anonymized data is $\mu$ for each query. Smaller values of the expected error indicate better utility.

# 3    Achieving Anonymity Through Hybrid Anonymization

As stated above in Example 1, different applications have particular emphasis on different aspects, and different anonymized methods play a different role for preserving data utility. To maximize data utility, we propose a hybrid privacy-preserving approach for transactional data with relational and transaction attributes. The approach adopts non-homogeneous generalization and grouping to preserve the associations between customer nodes and product nodes to guarantee privacy. Meanwhile, we construct a graph of association rules to preserve the associations among products for improving data utility.

## 3.1    Generating a Graph of Association Rules

This work adopts a methodology of non-homogeneous generalization, which is introduced in [19] and developed in [17], to anonymize relational attributes. Non-homogeneous generalization can improve utility while maintaining an adequate level of privacy. Since non-homogeneous generalization has defined in [17], the details of how to achieve anonymity were omitted for brevity. Note that generalization will lose part of relationships among products, which are bought by a particular individual, since it is privacy. However, the relationships among products are very important for certain applications such as the mining of association rules and may endanger future data collection [20]. For satisfying different utility requirements, we construct a graph of association rules as a part of data publication. The following definition and example illustrates how to generate the graph of association rules.

**Definition 2. Graph of association rules.** Consider an original database with customer nodes set $V$ and items set $W$. A graph of association rules is a weighted graphs $G = (W, E)$. Any edge $a \rightarrow b \in E$ if and only if, $u \in V$ has bought both $a$ and $b$. An edge which has more than one occurrence is allowed and represented by weighted edges in graph $G$.

**Example 2.** *Constructing a Graph of Association Rules.* Figure 2(c) shows the graph being constructed for Fig. 1(a). The original database contains six items. In the graph, each node denotes an item and each edge denotes the association among items. For example, $u1$ has bought products $a$ and $b$, which mean that there is an association between items $a$ and $b$. Thus, they are represented by the edge $(a, b)$ in the graph of association rule. Also like that $u5$ has bought $b$, $e$ and $f$, which mean that there are associations among three items $b$, $e$ and $f$. Thus, it is represented by three edges $(b, e)$, $(b, f)$ and $(e, f)$, respectively. The assignment routine is called as Assignment edge. Moreover, we allow each association occurring more than once and use weighted edges to represent duplicate edges in the graph. In the process, we recursively invoke Assignment routine on each transaction until all transactions have been processed.

In the graph of association rules, it is easy to find maximum frequent patterns, which is a key problem in data mining research. We generate the graph of association rules as a part of data publication for preserving associations among product nodes, which is lost through grouping and generalization.

## 3.2   Grouping Based Association Rules

As mentioned above, we guarantee the privacy of relational attributes via generalization and preserve the relationships among products. In this section, we will devise a grouping approach which guarantees transaction attributes based on the association rules. For convenience, we define the relative notions listed below.

**Definition 3. $k$-anonymity of attributes.** A label of attributes is $k$-anonymous if and only if there is at least $k$ matched in the entire attribute set for each value.

**Definition 4. $k$-anonymity of itemset.** A set of items is $k$-anonymous if and only if the itemset contains at least $k$ individual items.

**Definition 5. $k$-anonymity in bipartite graph.** A bipartite graph is $k$-anonymous if and only if each label of all nodes attributes is $k$-anonymous and each itemset is $k$-anonymous in the graph.

Intuitively, a bipartite graph is $k$-anonymous if each node is indistinguishable from at least $k$-1 others. According to above definitions, we know whether a graph is $k$-anonymous depending on its label and its itemset. The problem of anonymization on relational attributes is addressed by non-homogeneous generalization. This section focus on addressing the privacy problem of transaction attributes by grouping items. For example, there is a 2-anonymous graph ($k$=2) in Fig. 2(b). The probability of an adversary associating a value of relational attributes, such as aged 20, to an individual in the graph is 1/2. And the probability of an adversary associating an item to a specific node in a group is 1/3. Thus, the bipartite graph satisfies 2-anonymous.

Our approach can be divided into three steps as follows. First, we sort product nodes by its degree in the graph of association rules. Second, we group product nodes based on the graph of association rules and try to find the maximal set of nodes that any edge is non-existent between them. That is, there is no association between the two nodes. So we can prevent the group against homogeneity attack. Let us take a concrete example as an illustration.

**Example 3.** *Anonymization on items through grouping based on association rules.*

Figure 3 illustrates step by step how the anonymized routine works by grouping nodes into 3-anonymous groups. The original database contains six items, as shown in Fig. 2(c). We prefer to choose the one with the biggest degree as a start point because the biggest degree means that fewer nodes are not associated to it.

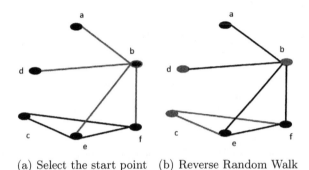

(a) Select the start point     (b) Reverse Random Walk

**Fig. 3.** Examples of grouping based on association rules

First, we create a new group $A$ containing $b$ alone, which is considered as a start point on account of its biggest degree 4. Then we walk to all of its neighbors $a$, $d$, $e$, $f$ and find the node $c$ which is not in the neighbor set (see Fig. 3(a)). So $c$ can add into group $A$. The Anonymize routine is called as reverse random walk. We will check the size of group $A$ after each walk and go on walking until $k$-anonymous is satisfied. $c$ is considered as a start point in the next walk since it has the second biggest degree in group $A$. And the next walk is from $c$ to $e$ and from $c$ to $f$. Then, we can place node $a$ and $d$ into group $A$ when the size of group do not exceed $k$. Due to the limitation of groups size, we choose $d$ into group $A$ randomly, as shown in Fig. 3(b). In the process, we recursively invoke Anonymize routine on each group by degree until all nodes have been processed. The output of the process is the sequence of groups which satisfy $k$-anonymous and $l$-diversity.

Toward different applications such as analyzing frequent pattern of products bought by customers in particular age ranges for recommendation system, counting the sale of products for commercial decisions, or finding maximum frequent patterns for mining association rules, our approach can provide an accurate answer than previous works. That is, our hybrid approach can protect privacy while satisfying different utility requirements.

# 4    Algorithm Description

In this section, we present a graph-based anonymization algorithm of grouping in our hybrid framework. The algorithm of non-homogeneous generalization was omitted for brevity, which attempts to solve the problem of anonymization on relational attributes. And we will explain the grouping algorithm to tackle the privacy problem of transaction attributes in detail.

---

**Algorithm 1.** *Grouping algorithm*

---

**Input:** $G$, $W$, $k$ //G is the graph of association rule
**Output:** *A k-anonymous grouping sequence GG.*
 1: candidate set $T \leftarrow \emptyset$, temp$\leftarrow \emptyset$, group sequence $GG \leftarrow \emptyset$.
 2: **for** each $w \in W$ **do**
 3:    select the node $v$ with the biggest degree in $W$;
 4:    create a new group $g = \{v\}$, $W = W - \{v\}$;
 5:    $T \leftarrow W$;
 6:    **for** each $w \in T$ **do**
 7:      **if** $\exists e(v, w) \in G$ **then**
 8:        $temp = temp \cup \{w\}$, $T = T - \{w\}$;
 9:      **end if**
10:    **end for**
11:    Sort candidate set $T$ by the degree in descending order;
12:    **for** each $w \in T$ **do**
13:      **if** $(|g|_{size} < k$ ) **then**
14:        $g = g \cup \{w\}$, $T = T - \{w\}$, $W = W - \{w\}$;
15:        $n$= next node in $T$;
16:        **while** $\exists e(w, n) \in G$ **do**
17:          $n$= next node in $T$;
18:        **end while**
19:        $w = n$;
20:      **else**
21:        $GG = GG \cup g$;
22:        break;
23:      **end if**
24:    **end for**
25: **end for**

---

The algorithm of how to generate a graph of association rules through grouping is shown in Algorithm 1. The inputs of the algorithm are the original product nodes list of $W$, its graph of association rules $G$ and the anonymous parameter $k$. The loop of lines 2–25 tries to find these product nodes that have no association. And the algorithm divides them into a $k$-anonymous group for resisting against homogeneity attacks. Line 3 selects the node having the biggest degree as a start point. Line 4 creates a new group $g$ containing $v$ alone, and deletes $v$ from $W$. The candidate set $T$ is set to the universal set $W$ in line 5. The loop of lines 6–10 tries to construct the candidate set which has no association with $v$. Line 11 sorts all nodes in candidate set $T$ by the degree in descending order. And we continue with sorted node sequence $T$ which can group nodes more effectively. The loop of lines 12–24 tries to generate a $k$-anonymous group for $v$ from its candidate set $T$. In detail, line 13 checks whether the size of group $g$ is more than $k$ or not. If the size of group $g$ is less than $k$, the algorithm will select a node $w$ having the second biggest degree from its candidate set $T$ and add $w$ into group $g$ and delete $w$ from $T$ in line 14. Then the algorithm tries the next node in $T$. If the size of group $g$ is larger than $k$, add $g$ into the partition sequence $GG$. And the process will create a new group and enter the next turn until all nodes in $W$ have been processed. In practice, a greedy algorithm is adopted to generate safe groups in our approach. Although this algorithm is possible to fail, it is easy to generate safe groupings and guarantee privacy on transaction attributes, since it is high-dimensional and sparse.

Differing from previous works, our hybrid framework integrating different anonymous techniques try to satisfy different utility requirements. In detail, we employ partitioning algorithm to achieve non-homogenous generalization for anonymizing on relational attributes while preserving the utility to the most degree. And we adopt grouping based on association rules for anonymizing on transaction attributes. Meanwhile, we also generate a graph of association rules which is non-trivial for improving data utility as a part of data publication. For the same privacy level, our approach preserves more useful information for satisfying different utility requirements via the combination of different anonymized techniques.

## 5   Experimental Study

### 5.1   Experimental Framework

In this section, we present an extensive empirical evaluation of our privacy-preserving approach. We evaluate its utility, compare it to competing techniques. All experiments for this paper are implemented in C++ and SQL Server 2008. We use DBLP, BMS-WebView-2(BMS2) and BMS-POS (POS), three vastly different datasets that have been used in evaluating previous works [9,10,15,16,18] for ensuring the fairness of comparative experiments. These datasets are widely used as benchmark datasets in the knowledge discovery community. Their characteristics are listed in Table 1. In our experiment, $L_v$ is synthetic data following the example of ADULT dataset since these datasets do not include relational attribute information.

We evaluate our approach as Hybrid against COAT [18], PCTA [16] and Safe $(k,l)$-grouping [15], in terms of data utility, under several different utility requirements. We compared the amount of data utility preserved by these methods by considering two utility measures: Utility Loss ($UL$) [16,18] and Expected Error ($ExpErr$) [15]. $UL$ captures the utility loss by non-homogeneous generalization on relational attributes. And $ExpErr$ captures the accuracy of query answering on anonymized data.

**Table 1.** Characteristics of the three datasets

| Dataset | #Trans | #Distinct items | # Max.trans.size | # Avg.trans.size |
|---------|--------|-----------------|------------------|------------------|
| DBLP | 216753 | 170371 | 71 | 5.4 |
| BMS-WebView-2 | 77370 | 3336 | 161 | 5.0 |
| BMS-POS | 306983 | 1177 | 5 | 2.65 |

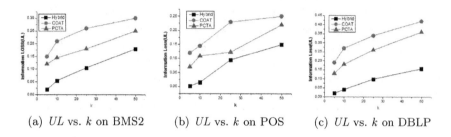

(a) *UL* vs. $k$ on BMS2    (b) *UL* vs. $k$ on POS    (c) *UL* vs. $k$ on DBLP

**Fig. 4.** Information loss on the three datasets

## 5.2  Experimental Results

Figure 4 plots the information loss under above approaches. Since Safe $(k,l)$-grouping is measured by aggregate query, we only compares the information loss of Hybrid to COAT and PCTA. As expected, increasing $k$ induced more information loss due to the utility/privacy tradeoff. Our hybrid approach outperform than other approaches in all the three datasets. This is because, as $k$ increases, the model of generalization in [16, 18] forces an increasingly large number of items to be generalized together, while our hybrid approach adopt grouping to perturb items instead of generalization. The impact of this generalization strategy on data utility was even more evident in the case of the DBLP dataset because of its big itemset, as shown in Fig. 4(c). This is expected, because generalization in [16, 18] will cause over-generalize when the size of itemset is "big", in which case substantial generalization is necessary. And our hybrid approach is stable than others.

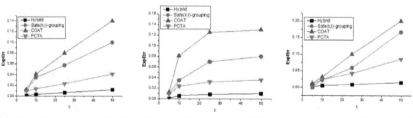

(a) *ExpErr* vs. $k$ on BMS2  (b) *ExpErr* vs. $k$ on POS  (c) *ExpErr* vs. $k$ on DBLP

**Fig. 5.** The expected error on the three datasets

Figure 5 reports how well anonymized data supports query answering using *ExpErr*. As expected, increasing $k$ induced more information loss because accurately answering queries involving many individuals is more difficult due to generalization. Observe that here, Hybrid are not raised obviously as $k$ increases. This is because non-homogeneous generalization does not incur too much information distortion or information loss with the increases of $k$ and the graph of association rules preserve the associations among items. So our approach can reduce information loss significantly for aggregate analysis. The quality of queries results shows that Hybrid proposed in this paper also consistently outperforms other approaches, using the expected error metric. Combined with the experimental results of Figs. 4 and 5, we can conclude that our hybrid approach can provide more accurate information for different applications than previous works employing the single anonymized technique.

# 6 Conclusion

In this paper, we introduced a hybrid optimization approach for anonymizing transactional data with relational and transaction attributes. To improve data utility, we anonymized relational attributes by adopting non-homogeneous generalization and anonymize transaction attributes via grouping based on the graph form. To satisfy different utility requirements, we constructed a graph of association rules as compensation to preserve the associations among items. Our experiment results demonstrated that our approach preserves data utility much better than previous works. The scalability of the proposed approach should be improved in our ongoing work.

**Acknowledgment.** The research is supported by the National Key Basic Research Program of China (973 Program, No. 2012CB326403), National Science Foundation of China (No. 61272535), Guangxi Bagui Scholar Teams for Innovation and Research Project, Guangxi Collaborative Innovation Center of Multi-source Information Integration and Intelligent Processing, Guangxi Natural Science Foundation (Nos. 2015GXNS FBA139246, 2013GXNSFBA019263, 2014GXNSF BA118288), Science and Technology Research Projects of Guangxi Higher Education (Nos. 2013YB029, 2015YB032), the Guangxi Science Research and Technology Development Project (No. 14124004-4-11) and Youth Scientific Research Foundation of Guangxi Normal University.

# References

1. Chang, C.C., Thompson, B., Wang, H.W., Yao, D.: Towards publishing recommendation data with predictive anonymization. In: Proceedings of the 5th ACM Symposium on Information, Computer and Communications Security, pp. 24–35. ACM (2010)
2. Zheng, Z., Kohavi, R., Mason, L.: Real world performance of association rule algorithms. In: Proceedings of the seventh ACM SIGKDD international conference on Knowledge discovery and data mining, pp. 401–406. ACM (2001)

3. Xu, Y., Wang, K., Fu, A.W.C., Yu, P.S.: Anonymizing transaction databases for publication. In: Proceedings of the 14th ACM SIGKDD International Conference on Knowledge Discovery and Data Mining, pp. 767–775. ACM (2008)
4. Terrovitis, M., Mamoulis, N., Kalnis, P.: Privacy-preserving anonymization of set-valued data. Proc. VLDB Endowment 1(1), 115–125 (2008)
5. Terrovitis, M., Mamoulis, N., Kalnis, P.: Local and global recoding methods for anonymizing set-valued data. VLDB J. Int. J. Very Large Data Bases 20(1), 83–106 (2011)
6. He, Y., Naughton, J.F.: Anonymization of set-valued data via top-down, local generalization. Proc. VLDB Endowment 2(1), 934–945 (2009)
7. Liu, J., Wang, K.: Anonymizing transaction data by integrating suppression and generalization. In: Zaki, M.J., Yu, J.X., Ravindran, B., Pudi, V. (eds.) PAKDD 2010, Part I. LNCS, vol. 6118, pp. 171–180. Springer, Heidelberg (2010)
8. Wang, L.E., Li, X.: A clustering-based bipartite graph privacy-preserving approach for sharing high-dimensional data. Int. J. Softw. Eng. Knowl. Eng. 24(07), 1091–1111 (2014)
9. Ghinita, G., Tao, Y., Kalnis, P.: On the anonymization of sparse high-dimensional data. In: 2008 IEEE 24th International Conference on Data Engineering. ICDE 2008, pp. 715–724. IEEE (2008)
10. Ghinita, G., Kalnis, P., Tao, Y.: Anonymous publication of sensitive transactional data. IEEE Trans. Knowl. Data Eng. 23(2), 161–174 (2011)
11. Wang, L., Li, X.: Personalized privacy protection for transactional data. In: Luo, X., Yu, J.X., Li, Z. (eds.) ADMA 2014. LNCS, vol. 8933, pp. 253–266. Springer, Heidelberg (2014)
12. Fung, B., Wang, K., Chen, R., Yu, P.S.: Privacy-preserving data publishing: a survey of recent developments. ACM Comput. Surv. (CSUR) 42(4), 14 (2010)
13. Poulis, G., Loukides, G., Gkoulalas-Divanis, A., Skiadopoulos, S.: Anonymizing data with relational and transaction attributes. In: Blockeel, H., Kersting, K., Nijssen, S., Železný, F. (eds.) ECML PKDD 2013, Part III. LNCS, vol. 8190, pp. 353–369. Springer, Heidelberg (2013)
14. Takahashi, T., Sobataka, K., Takenouchi, T., Toyoda, Y., Mori, T., Kohro, T.: Top-down itemset recoding for releasing private complex data. In: 2013 Eleventh Annual International Conference on Privacy, Security and Trust (PST), pp. 373–376. IEEE (2013)
15. Cormode, G., Srivastava, D., Yu, T., Zhang, Q.: Anonymizing bipartite graph data using safe groupings. Proc. VLDB Endowment 1(1), 833–844 (2008)
16. Gkoulalas-Divanis, A., Loukides, G.: Utility-guided clustering-based transaction data anonymization. Trans. Data Priv. 5(1), 223–251 (2012)
17. Wong, W.K., Mamoulis, N., Cheung, D.W.L.: Non-homogeneous generalization in privacy preserving data publishing. In: Proceedings of the 2010 ACM SIGMOD International Conference on Management of data, pp. 747–758. ACM (2010)
18. Loukides, G., Gkoulalas-Divanis, A., Malin, B.: Coat: constraint-based anonymization of transactions. Knowl. Inf. Syst. 28(2), 251–282 (2011)
19. Gionis, A., Mazza, A., Tassa, T.: k-anonymization revisited. In: 2008 IEEE 24th International Conference on Data Engineering. ICDE 2008, pp. 744–753. IEEE (2008)
20. Karr, A.F., Kohnen, C.N., Oganian, A., Reiter, J.P., Sanil, A.P.: A framework for evaluating the utility of data altered to protect confidentiality. Am. Stat. 60(3), 224–232 (2006)

# Program Obfuscator for Privacy-Carrying Unidirectional One-hop Re-encryption

Mingwu Zhang[1,2,3]($\boxtimes$), Biwen Chen[1], and Hua Shen[3]

[1] School of Computer, Hubei University of Technology, Wuhan 430068, China
[2] Fujian Provincial Key Laboratory of Network Security and Cryptology,
Fujian Normal University, Fuzhou 350007, China
[3] State Key Laboratory of Information Security,
Institute of Information Engineering, Chinese Academy of Sciences,
Beijing 100093, China
csmwzhang@gmail.com

**Abstract.** Program obfuscation is a cryptographic primitive that hides the secrets inside a program while preserving its functionality via so-called secure *virtual black-box* property. In this paper, we give the formal definition of one-hop and unidirectional re-encryption function, and also propose two kinds of encryption mechanisms to implicitly obtain the re-encryption functionality. We design an algorithm ReEncObf to implement a secure program obfuscator for the re-encryption function. The obfuscator can resist any attacker (even program executor) from the reversing engineering to obtain the sensitive information including both the secret key and the plaintext when running the obfuscated program.

**Keywords:** Obfuscation · Re-encryption · One hop · Average-case virtual black-box

## 1 Introduction

Taking an encrypted e-mail delegation as example: Suppose that *Alice* sends an encrypted e-mail to *Carol*, however, *Carol* is in vacation and cannot deal with the e-mail in that time. Then he delegates his secretary, *Bob*, to help deal with it. Traditionally, *Carol* had to provide his decryption key to Bob so that *Bob* can read the encrypted e-mail correctly. This is impractical since Carol's secret-key may associate with lots of business (not only for e-mail). Another naive way is to ask for a trusted server to implement the decrypt-then-encrypt [2,15,16]: Simply store Carol's secret key in the server, and the server decrypts the e-mail with Carol's secret key and then re-encrypt the e-mail with Bob's public key [1,2]. Obviously, in the mechanism the server must be fully trusted since it can gain the sensitive information of Carol's such as the secret key and the content of e-mail [1,2,5,6,11].

We now consider to design an algorithm ReEncObf to solve this (possible untrusted) problem: Before leaving for vacation, *Carol* deploys the algorithm

© Springer International Publishing Switzerland 2015
G. Wang et al. (Eds.): ICA3PP 2015 Workshops, LNCS 9532, pp. 133–142, 2015.
DOI: 10.1007/978-3-319-27161-3_12

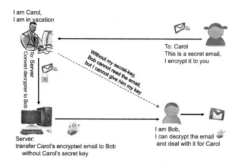

**Fig. 1.** Delegatable E-mail decryption with privacy-carrying

ReEncObf and some auxiliary information (implicit delegation key) to the campus server. For every encrypted e-mail, *Carol* re-sends to the server automatically, and the server executes uploaded ReEncObf program and sends the output to *Bob*. By this transformation, *Bob* can decrypt the encrypted e-mail with his own secret-key, without revealing the sensitive key of *Carol*'s. The model and deployment is described in Fig. 1.

In this scenario, we consider the issues: (1) Does the server gain any sensitive information about Carol? for example, secret key or cleartext of e-mail; (2) May *Bob* re-delegate the encrypted e-mail to another for decryption successfully? i.e., only one-hop. To respond these questions, we design a program obfuscator, namely ReEncObf, to implement the re-encryption functionality. That is, without revealing the sensitive information, the ReEncObf program/algorithm transforms a ciphertext encrypted under *Carol*'s public key into one that can be decrypted by *Bob*'s secret key.

An obfuscator is an algorithm, making computer programs *unintelligible* while preserving their *functionality*, to translate programs into functionally-equivalent similarly-sized circuits that are *hard to understand* [3,11], which can prevent the attacker from reversing engineering and thus have lots of appealing applications such as intellectual property protection for sensitive algorithms/softwares [3,12] and controlled delegation [4,8–10,14,17].

In the program obfuscator ReEncObf, the goal is to securely enable the re-encryption of e-mails from one key to another, without relying on trusted parties (i.e., the server is malicious). We also require that the re-encryption is unidirectional, i.e., the functionality of re-encryption can only translate the encrypted e-mail from Carol to Bob, but *must not* vice versa.

Actually, program obfuscation can hide the secrets inside a program while preserving its functionality via so-called *virtual black-box* property. More concretely, if a program can compute and implement from a function and it also be computed from an obfuscated input-output behavior of the program. That is, except the functionality preservation of the function, anything can be efficiently computed from the obfuscator given oracle access to the program.

In this work, we design a program obfuscator ReEncObf with the functionality of unidirectional re-encryption. The ReEncObf algorithm can perform the re-encryption only for one-hop, that is, the output of ReEncObf algorithm cannot be re-encrypted anymore, which has appealing application in secure e-mail delegation [15]. We propose two types of dual-state encryption schemes under an indicator $\beta$, namely scheme $\Pi_1$ and scheme $\Pi_2$, in which a level-2 ciphertext ($\beta = 1$) can be converted into a level-1 ciphertext ($\beta = 0$) under some auxiliary information. We provide the analysis of ReEncObf in functionality and computational efficiency, and also prove the virtual black-box property of security to achieve the practical program obfuscation without the leakage of secret key and plaintext when a malicious adversary runs the program.

## 2  Preliminaries

A function is *negligible* in $\lambda$ (denoted $\mathsf{neg}(\lambda)$) if it is smaller than the inverse of any polynomial, for all large enough value of $\lambda \in \mathbb{N}$. We use $\mathsf{PPT}$ to denote a probabilistic polynomial-time algorithm.

**Definition 1 (Obfuscator).** *A $\mathsf{PPT}$ algorithm $\mathcal{O}$ is called an obfuscator over a function family $\mathcal{F}$, if it holds the following properties:*

1. *(**Approximate Functionality**) For any $F \in \mathcal{F}$ and all inputs $x \in \{0,1\}^*$, $\Pr[\mathcal{O}_F(x) \neq F(x)]$ is negligible.*
2. *(**Polynomial Slowdown**) There is a polynomial $p$ such that, $\forall F \in \mathcal{F}$, $\mathcal{O}_F$ runs in time at most $p(T_F)$, where $T_F$ denote the worst-case running time.*
3. *(**Virtual Black-box**) For any $\mathsf{PPT}$ algorithm $\mathcal{A}$ and any polynomial $p$, there exists a $\mathsf{PPT}$ $\mathcal{S}$ such that for any function $F \in \mathcal{F}$ and sufficiently large $\lambda$,*

$$\left| \Pr_{\mathcal{A},\mathcal{O}}[b \leftarrow \mathcal{A}(\mathcal{O}_F) : b = 1] - \Pr_{\mathcal{S}}[b \leftarrow \mathcal{S}^F(1^{|F|}) : b = 1] \right| \leq 1/p(\cdot)$$

*where the probabilities are taken over the randomness of $\mathcal{A}$ and $\mathcal{S}$.*

*To avoid the worst-case impossibility of obfuscation as definition above, we consider the average-case virtual black-box such that the simulator can only simulate the output for a random function in the family. That is, for every polynomial size auxiliary $aux$, there exists a distinguisher $\mathcal{D}$,*

$$\left| \Pr_{\mathcal{A},\mathcal{O}}[F \leftarrow \mathcal{F}, \mathcal{D}^F(\mathcal{A}(\mathcal{O}_F, aux), aux) = 1] - \Pr_{\mathcal{S}}[F \leftarrow \mathcal{F}, \mathcal{D}^F(\mathcal{S}^F(1^{|F|}, aux), aux) = 1] \right|$$
$$\leq 1/p(\cdot)$$

## 3  Dual-State Encryptions and Re-encryption Function

At first we give an encryption scheme $\Pi$ (a variant in [1]), whose ciphertexts have two forms: level-1 ciphertext and level-2 ciphertext. We use a bit $\beta$ to specify the ciphertext form, *i.e.*, the ciphertext has level-1 form if $\beta = 0$ and the ciphertext has level-2 form if $\beta = 1$. The level-2 ciphertext is replayably secure against chosen-ciphertext attacks. A level-2 ciphertext can be converted into a level-1 one when obtaining some (auxiliary) information. Note that these two types of ciphertexts are in different in the form and length for different levels. Like in [13], in the system, we fist give the global parameters of bilinear group generator $\mathsf{BG}$, one-time signature scheme $\mathsf{SIG}$. Our scheme supports one hop transformation, *i.e.*, the level-1 ciphertext cannot be re-encrypted.

**Definition 2 (A Simple Dual-state Encryption Scheme).** *A dual-state encryption scheme* $\Pi_1 = (\mathsf{KeyGen}, \mathsf{Encrypt}, \mathsf{Decrypt})$ *is described as following algorithms:*

1. $\mathsf{KeyGen}(pp)$: *At random pick* $x \in \mathbf{Z}_p$ *and set the key pair* $(SK = x, PK = g^x)$.
2. $\mathsf{Encrypt}(PK, M, \beta)$: *If* $\beta = 1$, *at random select* $r \in \mathbf{Z}_p$, *and output the cipher-text* $CT = (\beta, PK^r, M \cdot Y^r)$ *where* $Y = e(g, g)$. *Otherwise, if* $\beta = 0$, *at random select* $r, t \in \mathbf{Z}_p$, *and output the ciphertext* $CT = (\beta, PK^{rt}, PK^t, g^{1/t}, M \cdot Y^r)$.
3. $\mathsf{Decrypt}(CT, SK, \beta)$: *If* $\beta = 1$, *parse* $CT = (\beta, C_0, C_3)$ *and* $SK = x$, *and output* $M \leftarrow C_3/e(C_0, g)^{1/x}$. *Otherwise if* $\beta = 0$, *parse* $CT = (\beta, C_0, C_1, C_2, C_3)$; *Check the equation* $e(C_1, C_2) = e(PK, g)$, *and output* $M \leftarrow C_3/e(C_0, C_2)^{1/SK}$ *if the test succeeds and output* $\perp$ *otherwise.*

We can convert a level-2 ciphertext $CT$ under public key $PK_2$ when $\beta = 1$ into a level-1 ciphertext under public key $PK_1$ in case $\beta = 0$. More concretely, the transformation is performed as:

1. At first produce a re-encryption key $R = PK_1^{1/SK_2} = g^{SK_1/SK_2}$;
2. At randomly choose $t \leftarrow \mathbf{Z}_p$, and compute $C_0 = C_0^t$, $C_1 = PK_1^t$, $C_2 = R^{1/t} = g^{SK_1/tSK_2}$;
3. Output the re-encryption ciphertext $CT = (0, C_0, C_1, C_2, C_3)$.

Clearly, it is easily to verify the correctness of the transformed ciphertext under public key $PK_1$.

Both the ciphertexts (*i.e.*, $\beta = 0$ and $\beta = 1$) satisfy the IND-CPA security. That is, given an encryption either message $M_0$ or $M_1$, the adversary cannot determine which one is the respective message. Furthermore, the ciphertext transformation is unidirectional when $\beta = 0$ (*i.e.*, cannot be re-encrypted). We give the security proof by the following theorem.

**Theorem 1.** *The dual-state encryption scheme* $\Pi_1$ *is semantically secure against chosen-plaintext attacks under the Decisional Bilinear Diffie-Hellman (DBDH) assumption and the 3-weak Decisional Bilinear Diffie-Hellman Inversion (3-wDBHI) assumption.*

**Proof.** We prove that if there exists an adversary algorithm $\mathcal{A}$ that can break the IND-CPA security of the scheme $\Pi_1$, then we can utilize the algorithm $\mathcal{A}$ to break the DBDH problem or 3-wDBHI problem. When $\beta = 1$, the ciphertext is $CT = (1, PK^r, M \cdot e(g, g)^r)$, which is a variant of ElGamal encryption in bilinear group [7] that is based on the Decisional Diffie-Hellman assumption. When $\beta = 0$, the ciphertext has the form $CT = (0, PK^{rt}, PK^t, g^{1/t}, M \cdot e(g, g)^r)$. Obviously, this type of ciphertext achieves the security of IND-CPA, since we can get the session key $e(g, g)^r$ by computing $e(PK^{rt}, g^{1/t})^{1/SK}$, which is similar to the decryption in case of $\beta = 1$.

We now give the IND-CCA secure construction of dual-state encryption, namely $\Pi_2$, which employs a one-time signature to guarantee the non-malleability of the message component. The detail scheme is described as follows:

1. KeyGen(pp): Each user at random picks $x_i \in \mathbf{Z}_p$ and sets the corresponding key pair as $(\mathsf{SK}_i, \mathsf{PK}_i) = (x_i, g^{x_i})$.
2. Encrypt(PK, $M, \beta$): On input a message $M \in \mathbf{G}_T$, $\beta \in \{0, 1\}$ and a public key $\mathsf{PK} = g^x$, the algorithm proceeds as follows:
   (a) Choose a one-time signature key pair $(ss, vk) \leftarrow \mathsf{SIG}.\mathcal{G}(\lambda)$.
   (b) At random $r \in \mathbf{Z}_p$, and compute $\overline{C}_0 = \mathsf{PK}^r$, $C_3 = M \cdot Y^r$, $C_4 = (vu^{vk})^r$.
   (c) If $\beta = 0$, then select $t \in \mathbf{Z}_p$, and compute $C_0 = \overline{C}_0^t$, $C_1 = \mathsf{PK}^t$, $C_2 = g^{1/t}$. Otherwise if $\beta = 1$, set $c_0 = \overline{C}_0$, $C_1 = \phi$, $C_2 = \phi$.
   (d) Generate a one-time signature $\sigma = \mathcal{S}(ss, (C_3, C_4))$ on components $(C_3, C_4)$.
   (e) Output the ciphertext $\mathsf{CT} = (\beta, vk, \sigma, C_0, C_1, C_2, C_3, C_4)$.
3. Decrypt(CT, SK, $\beta$): Let $\mathsf{CT} = (\beta, vk, \sigma, C_0, C_1, C_2, C_3, C_4)$ and $\mathsf{SK} = x$. The decryption algorithm proceeds as follows:
   (a) At first check the signature by verifying $\mathcal{V}(vk, \sigma, (C_3, C_4)) = 1$, and return $\perp$ if the verification fails.
   (b) If $\beta = 0$, verify the level-1 ciphertext by checking: $e(C_1, C_2) = e(\mathsf{PK}, g)$, $e(C_0, vu^{vk}) = e(C_4, C_1)$, and output the message $M \leftarrow C_3 \cdot e(C_0, C_2)^{-1/x}$ if the equations hold and return $\perp$ otherwise.
   (c) If $\beta = 1$, verify the level-2 ciphertext by checking $e(C_1, vu^{vk}) = e(\mathsf{PK}, C_4)$, and output $M \leftarrow C_3 \cdot e(C_0, g)^{-1/x}$ if the verification succeeds and output $\perp$ otherwise.

Fig. 2. Dual-state encryption scheme with CCA security

**Definition 3 (Dual-state Encryption Scheme with CCA Security).** *Let $\lambda$ be the system security parameter, and $\mathsf{BG}(\lambda)$ and $\mathsf{SIG}(\lambda) = (\mathcal{G}, \mathcal{S}, \mathcal{V})$ be the bilinear group generator and one-time signature under the security parameter $\lambda$, respectively. At first example an instance of bilinear group $(\mathbf{G}, \mathbf{G}_T, p) \leftarrow \mathsf{BG}(\lambda)$ with order $p$ s.t. $\log p \geq \lambda$, and then select $g, u, v \in \mathbf{G}$ and set the parameter $pp = (\mathbf{G}, \mathbf{G}_T, p, g, u, v, Y = e(g, g))$. A dual-state encryption scheme $\Pi = (\mathsf{KeyGen}, \mathsf{Encrypt}, \mathsf{Decrypt})$ is stated as the algorithms stated in Fig. 2.*

Actually, in scheme $\Pi_2$, the level-1 ciphertext (*i.e.*, $\beta = 0$) can be re-randomized by adding the random exponent in the corresponding components. That is, transform $(C_0, C_1, C_2)$ into $(C_0^{t'}, C_1^{t'}, C_2^{1/t'})$ for a randomly selected $t' \in \mathbf{Z}_p$. In this case, the verification computations of equations $e(C_1, C_2) = e(\mathsf{PK}, g)$ and $e(C_0, u^{vk}v) = e(C_4, C_1)$ still hold. The transformation of re-randomness can be performed publicly, and the procedure of a given level-1 ciphertext can be detectable.

**Lemma 1.** *The encryption scheme $\Pi$ is perfectly complete.*

**Proof.** If $\beta = 0$, the ciphertext is $\mathsf{CT} = (0, vk, \sigma, \mathcal{S}(vk, (C_3, C_4)), g^{xrt}, g^{xt}, g^{1/t}, M \cdot Y^r, (vu^{vk})^r)$. The decryption verification of level-1 ciphertext is: $e(C_1, C_2) = e(g^{xt}, g^{1/t}) = e(g^x, g) = e(\mathsf{PK}, g)$, and $e(C_0, vu^{vk}) = e(g^{xrt}, vu^{vk}) = e((vu^{vk})^r, g^{xt}) = e(C_4, C_1)$. The message is $C_3 e(C_0, C_2)^{1/x} = M \cdot Y^r e(g^{xrt}, g^{1/t})^{1/x} = M$.

For a level-2 ciphertext, *i.e.*, $\beta = 1$. In this case, $C_0 = \mathsf{PK}^r$, and thus the verification equation holds: $e(C_0, vu^{sk}) = e(\mathsf{PK}, (vu^{sk})^r) = (\mathsf{PK}, C_4)$. The message

$M$ in the ciphertext is extracted as: $C_3 e(C_0,g)^{-1/x}) = MY^r e(\mathrm{PK}^r,g)^{-1/x} = M e(g,g)^r e(g^{xr},g)^{-1/x} = M$.   □

*Remark.* In the level-2 ciphertext, the components $C_0, C_3$ and $C_4$ to guarantee that the encryption is semantically secure (*i.e.*, indistinguishable against chosen-plaintext attacks), and impose the one-time signature (*i.e.*, $vk$ and $C_4$) to ensure the IND-CCA security. Futhermore, in the level-1 ciphertext, we employ the component $C_0, C_1$ and $C_2$ to provide a knowledge proof that randomness $r$ is fully hidden in the ciphertext and cannot be extended, so as to guarantee the impossibility of re-encryption for any level-1 ciphertext, *i.e.*, the re-encryption is a one-hop scheme. We can define the key generation (access) circuit family as

$$\mathsf{Cir}_\lambda = \{C_{\mathrm{SK}_2,\mathrm{PK}_1} | (\mathrm{SK}_1, \mathrm{PK}_1) \leftarrow \mathsf{KeyGen}(\lambda), (\mathrm{SK}_2, \mathrm{PK}_2) \leftarrow \mathsf{KeyGen}(\lambda)\}$$

For a re-encryption scheme, an adversary cannot lean any information about the message corresponding to the ciphertext given the ciphertext CT and black-box access to a re-encryption circuit.

**Definition 4 (CCA-security with Oracle $C_{\mathrm{SK}_2,\mathrm{PK}_1}$).** *Let $\Pi_2 = (KeyGen, Encrypt, Decrypt)$ be a dual-state encryption scheme, and $\mathcal{A} = (\mathcal{A}_1, \mathcal{A}_2)$ be the PPT algorithm that the adversary makes. The scheme $\Pi_2$ is secure against chosen-ciphertext attacks under the circuit oracle $C_{\mathrm{SK}_2,\mathrm{PK}_1}$ if the advantage of $\mathcal{A}$ defined as below is negligible*

$$Adv_{\mathcal{A}}^{CCA}(\lambda) = \Big| \Pr[IND_{\mathcal{A}}(\lambda) = 0] - \Pr[IND_{\mathcal{A}}(\lambda) = 1] \Big|$$

*where the game $IND_{\mathcal{A}}(\lambda)$ is defined as follows:*
   $\underline{IND_{\mathcal{A}}(\lambda)}$

1. $(SK_1, PK_1) \leftarrow KeyGen(\cdot)$, $(SK_2, PK_2) \leftarrow KeyGen(\cdot)$
2. $(M_0, M_1, i, \beta, aux) \leftarrow \mathcal{A}_1^{C_{\mathrm{SK}_2,\mathrm{PK}_1}, \mathcal{O}_{Decrypt}(\cdot)}(\lambda)$ *s.t.* $M_0, M_1 \in \mathcal{M}$ *and* $|M_0| = |M_1|$
3. $CT \leftarrow Encrypt(PK_i, M_b, \beta)$
4. $b' \leftarrow \mathcal{A}_2^{C_{\mathrm{SK}_2,\mathrm{PK}_1}, \mathcal{O}_{Decrypt}(\cdot)}(CT, aux)$ *s.t.* $\mathcal{O}_{Decrypt}(\cdot) \neq \mathcal{O}_{Decrypt}(CT)$
5. *Output 1 if $b' = b$ and 0 otherwise.*

**Definition 5.** *A one-hop and unidirectional re-encryption is chosen-ciphertext secure (IND-CCA) at level-2 if the challenger is allowed to reveal the re-encryption auxiliary information to target user.*

**Theorem 2.** *Assuming the one-time signature Sig is strong unforgeable, the scheme as above is indistinguishably secure with access circuit oracle $C_{\mathrm{SK}_1,\mathrm{PK}_2}$ and decryption oracle $\mathcal{O}_{Decrypt}$ against replayable chosen-ciphertext attacks.*

In order to provide a secure re-encryption program executed by a (untrusted) program executor, we should ensure that the programm executor cannot gain any information about the sensitive information (*i.e.*, sensitive $\mathrm{SK}_1$ and program cleartext (reversed codes)). We define a function $F_{re}$ that implement a re-encryption scheme as follows:

---

**Algorithm ReEncObf**

**Input:** A circuit $C_{\mathrm{SK}_2,\mathrm{PK}_1} \in \mathsf{Cir}$.

**Init:**  1. Read $\mathrm{SK}_2 = x_2$ and $\mathrm{PK}_1 = g^{x_1}$ from the description of $C_{\mathrm{SK}_2,\mathrm{PK}_1}$.

   2. Calculate unidirectional key $R_{\mathrm{PK}_2 \to \mathrm{PK}_1} = \mathrm{PK}_1^{1/\mathrm{SK}_2} = g^{x_1/x_2}$.

**Obf:** Construct an obfuscated circuit $\mathcal{O}_{\mathrm{PK}_1,\mathrm{PK}_2,aux}$ as follows:

   1. Taking as a ciphertext $\mathtt{CT}_{\mathrm{PK}_2}(\cdot)$ and unidirectional key $R_{\mathrm{PK}_2 \to \mathrm{PK}_1}$ as inputs, parse $\mathtt{CT}_{\mathrm{PK}_2} = (1, vk, \sigma, C_0, \phi, \phi, C_3, C_4)$ and return $\bot$ if it is ill-form.

   2. Verify the signature by checking $\mathcal{V}(vk, \sigma, (C_3, C_4)) = 1$, and return $\bot$ if fail.

   3. Verify the equation $e(C_0, vu^{vk}) = e(\mathrm{PK}, C_4)$, and return $\bot$ if fail.

   4. At random select $t' \leftarrow \mathbf{Z}_p$, and calculate $C_0 = C_0^{t'}$, $C_1 = \mathrm{PK}_2^{t'}$ and $C_2 = \left(R_{\mathrm{PK}_2 \to \mathrm{PK}_1}\right)^{1/t'}$.

   5. Return $(0, vk, \sigma, C_0, C_1, C_2, C_3, C_4)$.

---

**Fig. 3.** Algorithm of ReEncObf

**Definition 6. *Re-encryption Function* $F_{re}$.** *A re-encryption function $F_{re}$ for the encryption $\Pi_2$ is defined as: on input a level-2 ciphertext, the re-encryption function $F_{re}$ decrypts the ciphertext and re-encrypts into a level-1 one.*

Actually, we can consider the function $F_{re}$ as a circuit. The basic functionality of $F_{re}$ is, when given a ciphertext created by Encrypt using $\mathrm{PK}_2$, a re-encryption circuit first decrypts the ciphertext using $\mathrm{SK}_2$ and then re-encrypts the message using $\mathrm{PK}_1$. A re-encryption obfuscation is also consider as a class of circuits that obtaining the same functionality of $\Pi_2$, without revealing the secret key $\mathrm{SK}_2$ and the message $M$ embedded in the ciphertext.

# 4 Obfuscator of Unidirectional One-hop Re-encryption Function

## 4.1 The Algorithm for One-hop Re-encryption Function

Let $(\mathrm{SK}_1, \mathrm{PK}_1) = (x_1, g^{x_1})$ and $(\mathrm{SK}_2, \mathrm{PK}_2) = (x_2, g^{x_2})$ be the key pairs of level-1 and level-2 respectively. From the description of re-encryption function $F_{re}$, we can extract a circuit family $\mathsf{Cir}_{(g^{x_2}, x_2, g^{x_1})}$ that the key values $(g^{x_2}, x_2, g^{x_1})$ can be read from the circuit description. We utilize an initiation box Init to describe this functionality (actually this Init algorithm performs only once before the obfuscated program was distributed). The algorithm of obfuscator ReEncObf is listed in Fig. 3.

## 4.2 Analysis

Obviously, the algorithm ReEncObf satisfies the functionality of re-encryption. That is, it implements the function of $F_{re}$. For the output of obfuscated ciphertext $(1, vk, \sigma, C_0, \cdots, C_4)$, it has identical distribution with the output of encryption under $\beta = 0$. From the analysis in Sect. 3, the level-2 ciphertext $\mathtt{CT}$ is a one-hop ciphertext and transferred level-1 ciphertext cannot be en-encrypted anymore. It cannot take as the input of algorithm ReEncObf to generate re-encryption output. This has an appealing application in delegated e-mail trans-action: One can authorize someone to read the encrypted e-mail but do not allow the delegatee to perform the re-delegation.

Moreover, the algorithm of obfuscator ReEncObf achieves an average-case secure obfuscator for the circuit family Cir. We now give the analysis and proof of computational slowdown in efficiency and average-case virtual black-box in preserving functionality.

**Lemma 2 (Computational Slowdown).** *The ReEncObf obfuscator satisfies polynomial slowdown property of a secure obfuscation.*

**Proof.** Polynomial slowdown is evident: Compared with the re-encryption scheme via decrypt-then-encrypt, it is easily to see that the obfuscator ReEncObf is efficient within the polynomial of the original scheme such that only calculates a few operations in group $\mathbf{G}$ and $\mathbf{G}_T$ (*i.e.*, exponentiations and bilinear maps in $\mathbf{G}$ and $\mathbf{G}_T$). Thus the obfuscator follows the computing efficiency requirement in polynomial slowdown. □

**Lemma 3 (Preserving Functionality).** *For any circuit $C_{SK_2,pk_1} \in$ Cir and let circuit $\mathcal{O}_{PK_1,PK_2,aux} \leftarrow ReEncObf$ be the output of obfuscation. For any possible input, the ReEncObf is an average-case secure obfuscator for the circuit family Cir from the identical distributions of $C_{SK_2,PK_1}$ and $\mathcal{O}_{PK_1,PK_2,aux}$.*

**Proof.** For a properly generated level-2 ciphertext of any message $M \in \mathcal{M}$, we observe that CT has the form

$$\mathsf{Encrypt}(\mathsf{PK}_2, M, 1) = (1, vk, \sigma, C_0, \phi, \phi, C_3, C_4)$$
$$= \big(1, vk, \mathcal{S}(ss, C_3, C_4), g^{x_2 r}, \phi, \phi, M \cdot e(g,g)^r, (vu^{vk})^r\big)$$

Since the components $C_3$ and $C_4$ are signed by one-time signature algorithm, and the verification equation for level-1 decryption ($\beta = 0$): $e(C_1, C_2) = e(\mathsf{PK}, g)$ and $e(C_0, vu^{vk}) = e(C_4, C_1)$, to ensure the non-malleability of the ciphertext and then achieves the CCA security.

When this level-2 ciphertext is fed into the obfuscator circuit $\mathcal{O}_{PK_1,PK_2,aux}$, the output has the form

$$\mathsf{Encrypt}(\mathsf{PK}_1, M, 0) = (1, vk, \sigma, C_0, C_1, C_2, C_3, C_4)$$
$$= \big(1, vk, \mathcal{S}(ss, C_3, C_4), g^{x_2 rtt'}, g^{x_2 tt'}, g^{\frac{x_1}{tt' x_2}}, M \cdot e(g,g)^r, (vu^{vk})^r\big)$$

for randomly selected $r, t, t' \leftarrow \mathbf{Z}_p$. Substituting $\bar{t} = tt'$, the level-1 ciphertext $\mathsf{Encrypt}(\mathsf{PK}_1, M, 0)$ can be rewritten as

$$\mathsf{Encrypt}(\mathsf{PK}_1, M, 0) = \big(1, vk, \mathcal{S}(ss, C_3, C_4), g^{x_2 r\bar{t}}, g^{x_2 \bar{t}}, g^{\frac{x_1}{x_2 \bar{t}}}, M \cdot e(g,g)^r, (vu^{vk})^r\big)$$

Obviously, the above distributions are identical. In order to obtain the property of virtual black-box, we should consider an adversary who outputs the code of the obfuscated circuit $\mathsf{Obf}(\mathsf{Cir})$, and thus we construct a simulator $\mathsf{Sim}^{\mathsf{Cir}}(\lambda, aux)$ to obtain a negligible advantage when the distinguisher $\mathcal{D}^{\mathsf{Cir}}$ takes as input the obfuscated circuit $\mathsf{Cir}$ and the auxiliary input $aux$. That is,

$$\left| \Pr[\mathcal{D}^{\mathsf{Cir}}(\mathsf{Obf}(\mathsf{Cir}), aux) = 1] - \Pr[\mathcal{D}^{\mathsf{Cir}}(\mathsf{Sim}^{|\mathsf{Cir}|}(\lambda, aux), aux) = 1] \right| \leq \mathsf{neg}(\lambda)$$

The simulator $\mathsf{Sim}$ explicitly does: $(i)$ Sample $R_{\mathsf{PK}_2 \to \mathsf{PK}_1}$ in $\mathsf{Init}$ algorithm, $(ii)$ Generate and output a circuit $\mathcal{O}'_{\mathsf{PK}_1, \mathsf{PK}_2, aux'}$ with the values $(\mathsf{PK}_1, \mathsf{PK}_2, R_{\mathsf{PK}_2 \to \mathsf{PK}_1})$ and, $(iii)$ Respond for the decryption query of obfuscated level-1 ciphertext. We devise two experiments $\mathsf{Nice}(\mathcal{D}^{\mathsf{Cir}}, aux)$ and $\mathsf{Junk}(\mathcal{D}^{\mathsf{Cir}}, aux)$ such that the outputs of $\mathcal{D}^{\mathsf{Cir}}(\mathsf{Obf}(\mathsf{Cir}), aux)$ and $\mathcal{D}^{\mathsf{Cir}}(\mathsf{Sim}^{|\mathsf{Cir}|}(\lambda, aux), aux)$ are distributed identically to $\mathsf{Nice}(\mathcal{D}^{\mathsf{Cir}}, aux)$ and $\mathsf{Junk}(\mathcal{D}^{\mathsf{Cir}}, aux)$, respectively (Fig. 4). We can prove that, in case the distinguisher $\mathcal{D}$ having oracle access to $C_{\mathsf{PK}_1, \mathsf{SK}_2}$ for the keys $\mathsf{PK}_1$ and $\mathsf{SK}_2$ are generated in the above experiments, both experiments have the identical distributed, and thus the distinguisher $\mathcal{D}$ obtaining the knowledge of the obfuscator circuit can be simulated with only knowledge of auxiliary input. i.e.,

| $\mathbf{Nice}(\mathcal{D}^{\mathsf{Cir}}, aux)$ | $\mathbf{Junk}(\mathcal{D}^{\mathsf{Cir}}, aux)$ |
|---|---|
| 1. $(\mathbf{G}, \mathbf{G}_T, e, p) \leftarrow \mathsf{BG}(\lambda)$ | 1. $(\mathbf{G}, \mathbf{G}_T, e, p) \leftarrow \mathsf{BG}(\lambda)$ |
| 2. $g \leftarrow \mathbf{G}$, $Y \leftarrow e(g, g)$ | 2. $g \leftarrow \mathbf{G}$, $Y \leftarrow e(g, g)$ |
| 3. $x_1, x_2 \leftarrow \mathbf{Z}_q$ | 3. $x_1, x_2 \leftarrow \mathbf{Z}_q$ |
| 4. $\mathsf{PK}_1 \leftarrow g^{x_1}$, $\mathsf{PK}_2 \leftarrow g^{x_2}$ | 4. $\mathsf{PK}_1 \leftarrow g^{x_1}$, $\mathsf{PK}_2 \leftarrow g^{x_2}$ |
| 5. $R_{\mathsf{PK}_2 \to \mathsf{PK}_1} \leftarrow g^{x_1/x_2}$ | 5. $R' \leftarrow \mathbf{G}$ |
| 6. $b \leftarrow \mathcal{D}^{\mathsf{Cir}}(\mathsf{PK}_1, \mathsf{PK}_2, R_{\mathsf{PK}_2 \to \mathsf{PK}_1}, aux)$ | 6. $b \leftarrow \mathcal{D}^{\mathsf{Cir}}(\mathsf{PK}_1, \mathsf{PK}_2, R', aux)$ |
| 7. Return $b$ | 7. Return $b$ |

**Fig. 4.** Simulated games

$$\left| \Pr[b \leftarrow \mathcal{D}^{\mathsf{Cir}}(Obf(\lambda, \mathsf{Cir}), aux) : b = 1] - \Pr[b \leftarrow \mathsf{Sim}^{|\mathsf{Cir}|}(\lambda, aux) : b = 1] \right| \leq \mathsf{neg}(\lambda)$$

This indicates that the obfuscator satisfies the average-case virtual black-box property. As the space limited, the detail proof refers to the full version.    □

## 5    Conclusion

We designed a program obfuscator algorithm to implement the secure cryptographic re-encryption function. The obfuscator can be distributed and executed in untrusted server, without concerning the sensitive information leakage issues such as re-encryption secret key being revealed and cleartext being recovered. The proposed obfuscator obtains the function properties of one-hop and unidirection, in which we employed two types of ciphertexts to avoid the possibility of multiple-hop and bidirectional re-encryption.

**Acknowledgements.** This work is supported by the National Natural Science Foundation of China under Grants 61370224 and 61502156, and the Open Fund Program for State Key Laboratory of Information Security of China under Grant 2014-04, and Fujian Provincial Key Laboratory of Network Security and Cryptology Research Fund (Fujian Normal University) under Grant 15006.

# References

1. Ateniese, G., Benson, K., Hohenberger, S.: Key-private proxy re-encryption. In: Fischlin, M. (ed.) CT-RSA 2009. LNCS, vol. 5473, pp. 279–294. Springer, Heidelberg (2009)
2. Ateniese, G., Fu, K., Green, M., Hohenberger, S.: Improved proxy re-encryption schemes with applications to secure distributed storage. ACM Trans. Inf. Syst. Secur. **9**(1), 1–30 (2006)
3. Balachandran, V., Emmanuel, S.: Software protection with obfuscation and encryption. In: Deng, R.H., Feng, T. (eds.) ISPEC 2013. LNCS, vol. 7863, pp. 309–320. Springer, Heidelberg (2013)
4. Barak, B., Goldreich, O., Impagliazzo, R., Rudich, S., Sahai, A., Vadhan, S.P., Yang, K.: On the (im)possibility of obfuscating programs. In: Kilian, J. (ed.) CRYPTO 2001. LNCS, vol. 2139, p. 1. Springer, Heidelberg (2001)
5. Chandran, N., Chase, M., Liu, F.-H., Nishimaki, R., Xagawa, K.: Re-encryption, functional re-encryption, and multi-hop re-encryption: a framework for achieving obfuscation-based security and instantiations from lattices. In: Krawczyk, H. (ed.) PKC 2014. LNCS, vol. 8383, pp. 95–112. Springer, Heidelberg (2014)
6. Cheng, R., Zhang, F.: Secure obfuscation of conditional re-encryption with keyword search. In: InCos 2013. IEEE (2013)
7. ElGamal, T.: A public-key cryptosystem and a signature scheme based on discrete logarithms. IEEE Trans. Inf. Theory **31**(4), 469–472 (1984)
8. Goldwasser, S., Rothblum, G.N.: On best-possible obfuscation. J. Crypt. **27**(3), 480–505 (2014)
9. Hada, S.: Zero-knowledge and code obfuscation. In: Okamoto, T. (ed.) ASIACRYPT 2000. LNCS, vol. 1976, pp. 443–457. Springer, Heidelberg (2000)
10. Hofheinz, D., Malone-Lee, J., Stam, M.: Obfuscation for cryptographic purposes. J. Crypt. **23**(1), 121–168 (2010)
11. Hohenberger, S., Rothblum, G.N., Shelat, A., Vaikuntanathan, V.: Securely obfuscating re-encryption. J. Cryptology **24**(4), 694–719 (2011)
12. Hohenberger, S., Sahai, A., Waters, B.: Replacing a random oracle: full domain hash from indistinguishability obfuscation. In: Nguyen, P.Q., Oswald, E. (eds.) EUROCRYPT 2014. LNCS, vol. 8441, pp. 201–220. Springer, Heidelberg (2014)
13. Libert, V., Vergnaud, S.: Unidirectional chosen-ciphertext secure proxy re-encryption. IEEE Trans. Inf. Theory **2011**, 1786–1802 (2011)
14. Sahai, A., Waters, B.: How to use indistinguishability obfuscation: deniable encryption, and more. In: STOC 2014, pp 475–484. ACM (2014)
15. Zhang, M., Takagi, T.: Efficient construction of anonymous multireceiver encryption protocols and their deployment in group email systems with privacy preservation. IEEE Syst. J. **7**(3), 410–419 (2013)
16. Zhang, M., Takashi, N., Yang, B., Takagi, T.: Anonymous encryption with partial order subset delegation and its application in privacy email system. IET Inf. Secur. **8**(4), 240–249 (2014)
17. Zimmerman, J.: How to obfuscate programs directly. In: Oswald, E., Fischlin, M. (eds.) EUROCRYPT 2015. LNCS, vol. 9057, pp. 439–467. Springer, Heidelberg (2015)

# Predicting Severity of Software Vulnerability Based on Grey System Theory

Jinkun Geng[1](✉), Daren Ye[1], and Ping Luo[2]

[1] School of Software, Beihang University, Beijing 100191, China
steam1994@163.com
[2] Key Laboratory for Information System Security, Ministry of Education, Tsinghua National Laboratory for Information Science and Technology (TNlist), School of Software, Tsinghua University, Beijing 100084, China
luop@mail.tsinghua.edu.cn

**Abstract.** Vulnerabilities usually represents the risk level of software, therefore, it is of high value to predict vulnerabilities so as to evaluate the security level of software. Current researches mainly focus on predicting the number of vulnerabilities or the occurrence time of vulnerabilities, however, to our best knowledge, there are no other researches focusing on the prediction of vulnerabilities' severity, which we think is an important aspect reflecting vulnerabilities and software security. To compensate for this deficiency, we propose a novel method based on grey system theory to predict the severity of vulnerabilities. The experiment is carried on the real data collected from CVE and proves the feasibility of our predicting method.

**Keywords:** Vulnerability · Software security · Severity · Prediction · Grey system theory

## 1 Introduction

With the fast progress of computer science and software engineering, software applications has been widely spread and applied in many fields. Meanwhile, software security is also gaining more and more attention [1–5]. As the main influence factor of software security and reliability, software vulnerabilities usually represent the risk level of software [7]. Therefore, it is of great value and practical use to make good predictions of software vulnerabilities for software evaluation.

Currently, many researches has shown great interest in software vulnerability prediction and several prediction models has been proposed [2, 8–14, 17, 20, 21]. Most of them just focus on predicting the number of vulnerabilities or the occurrence time of vulnerabilities. No one else seems to take the severity level of each vulnerabilities into consideration as far as we know. However, vulnerabilities differs in severity level actually. For example, some vulnerabilities are serious ones and might cause the corruption of the while software system once they occurred, while other vulnerabilities are less serious ones and might cause some damages but would not destroy the whole system. Considering this, we think it is unsuitable to ignore the severity of vulnerabilities or just

© Springer International Publishing Switzerland 2015
G. Wang et al. (Eds.): ICA3PP 2015 Workshops, LNCS 9532, pp. 143–152, 2015.
DOI: 10.1007/978-3-319-27161-3_13

regard the severity of each vulnerability as the same, which is the case in many current prediction models. To compensate for this deficiency, we intend to propose a novel method to predict the severity of vulnerabilities.

Among all predicting techniques, grey system theory, first proposed by Deng [6] in 1982, becomes a research interest recently because of its simplicity and accuracy [15, 16]. As an essential part of grey system theory, grey forecasting models has gained much attention due to their ability to characterize an unknown system by using small quantity of data points [19–24]. Vulnerability severity prediction can be regarded as a Grey system problem because various factors, such as the vulnerability's location, the software's popularity, and so on, combines to determine the severity of a vulnerability, but how these factors exactly affect the severity of vulnerability is hard to measure and has not been clearly known.

In this paper, we intend to solve the problem of predicting vulnerabilities' prediction based on Grey theory. A novel grey prediction model is proposed and via the proposed model we carried out our experiment with vulnerability data collected from Common Vulnerabilities and Exposures (CVE) [18]. The simulation experiment gains a good performance and proves the feasibility of our method.

The rest of the paper is organized as follows. Section 2 introduces the preliminaries of grey theory and proposes a novel grey prediction model for vulnerability severity prediction. Section 3 presents our simulation experiment and analyses the experiment result. Section 4 concludes the paper and talks about the future work directions.

## 2    Grey System Theory

Grey systems are defined as systems which lack concerned information, such as structure message, operation mechanism and behaviour document [6]. Grey means uncertain. The aim of Grey System Theory is to provide theory, techniques, notions and ideas for resolving (analysing) latent and intricate systems. Unlike traditional stochastic process, grey process tries to model with few data and turn the disorderly raw data into a more regular series by grey generating techniques for the benefit of modeling instead of modeling with original data.

As one main branch of Grey System Theory, Grey Prediction has been developed fast during past decades and applied in many fields such as energy, agriculture, economy, environment, and so on [15, 16, 19–23]. Among the family of grey prediction models, the GM(1,1) model is the most frequently used [19, 23]. Since first proposed by Deng, GM(1,1) has been studied deeply and many variants has been developed to improve its performance.

### 2.1    GM(1,1) Model

Let $X^{(0)}$ denote the original series (or raw series):

$$X^{(0)} = \left\{ x^{(0)}(1), x^{(0)}(2), \cdots, x^{(0)}(n) \right\},$$

where $x^{(0)}(i)$ is non-negative.

In order to reduce the noise and eliminate the disorderliness of the series data, GM(1,1) model converts the original data series into a monotonically increasing data series through accumulated generating operation (AGO). Through AGO, a new series $X^{(1)}$ is generated:

$$X^{(1)} = \left\{ x^{(1)}(1), x^{(1)}(2), \cdots, x^{(1)}(n) \right\},$$

where $x^{(1)}(k) = \sum_{i=1}^{k} x^{(0)}(i)$.

The new series $X^{(1)}$ is monotonic increase sequence and follows an approximate exponential law supposing the original series is smooth enough [6].

Based on $X^{(1)}$, we can get the its mean sequence:

$$Z^{(1)} = \left\{ z^{(1)}(2), z^{(1)}(3), \cdots, z^{(1)}(n) \right\},$$

where $z^{(1)}(k) = \theta x^{(1)}(k) + (1 - \theta) x^{(1)}(k - 1)$.

Traditionally, we set $\theta = 0.5$, then we get

$$z^{(1)}(k) = 0.5 x^{(1)}(k) + 0.5 x^{(1)}(k - 1).$$

The following equation

$$x^{(0)}(k) + a z^{(1)}(k) = b$$

is a differential model which is called GM(1,1) model since it is an one order equation with only one variable. (The one order and one variable grey model is abbreviated as GM(1,1)).

To build GM(1,1) model, only a few data are needed to distinguish it. To estimate the coefficients $a$ and $b$, least square method is adopted here.

Let's denote

$$B = \begin{bmatrix} -z^{(1)}(2) & 1 \\ -z^{(1)}(3) & 1 \\ \vdots & \vdots \\ -z^{(1)}(n) & 1 \end{bmatrix}, Y = \begin{bmatrix} x^{(0)}(2) \\ x^{(0)}(3) \\ \vdots \\ x^{(0)}(n) \end{bmatrix}, \beta = \begin{bmatrix} a \\ b \end{bmatrix},$$ then based on the principle of least

square method, we have

$$\beta = \left( B^T B \right)^{-1} B^T Y$$

Hence, using $a$ and $b$, we can construct the following response equation of GM(1,1) for future prediction:

$$x^{(1)}(k + 1) = \left( x^{(0)}(1) - \frac{b}{a} \right) e^{-ak} + \frac{b}{a}, k = 1, 2 \cdots, n - 1.$$

Thus the simulative value of $X^{(0)}$ can be calculated through

$$x^{(0)}(k+1) = x^{(1)}(k+1) - x^{(1)}(k).$$

## 2.2   Improvement of GM(1,1)

It has been admitted widely that GM(1,1) is an excellent prediction model for series data. However, GM(1,1) is sometimes too simple to deal with some complex sequence, especially the oscillatory sequence. Several researches has proved that GM(1,1) performs not so well in oscillatory sequence prediction [24–27].

Under the background of vulnerabilities' severity prediction, the severity of vulnerabilities is definitely an oscillatory sequence. Therefore, the classic GM(1,1) model may be not suitable. Improvement of the classic GM model are required to solve the problem.

The reason for the bad performance of GM(1,1) on oscillatory sequence is because the sequence data shows no monotony and is not smooth enough. Considering this, we intend to make some transformations of the sequence data before adopting GM(1,1) and recover it after the prediction.

For the original sequence data, we first make regularization of it. Let's again denote the original series (non-negative) as

$$X^{(0)} = \left\{ x^{(0)}(1), x^{(0)}(2), \cdots, x^{(0)}(n) \right\},$$

Suppose the largest data in the series is $x^{(0)}_{max}$, then we transform $X^{(0)}$ to $X^{(0)}_1$ by divide each data with $x^{(0)}_m$, that is

$$X^{(0)}_1 = \left\{ x^{(0)}_1(1), x^{(0)}_1(2), \cdots, x^{(0)}_1(n) \right\},$$

where $x^{(0)}_1(i) = \dfrac{x^{(0)}(i)}{x^{(0)}_{max}}$.

Obviously, $\forall x^{(0)}_1(i) \in X^{(0)}_1, x^{(0)}_1(i) \in [0, 1]$. We notice that

$$\sin(y) \in [0, 1], \text{ when } y \in \left[0, \frac{\pi}{2}\right].$$

Here we use the inverse function arcsin to make transformation of $X^{(0)}_1$ and get $X^{(0)}_2$, that is

$$X^{(0)}_2 = \left\{ x^{(0)}_2(1), x^{(0)}_2(2), \cdots, x^{(0)}_2(n) \right\},$$

where $x^{(0)}_2(i) = \arcsin\left(x^{(0)}_1(i)\right)$ and $x^{(0)}_2(i) \in \left[0, \frac{\pi}{2}\right]$.

To make a monotonic sequence, we again make transformation of $X^{(0)}_2$ and get $X^{(0)}_3$, that is

$$X_3^{(0)} = \left\{ x_3^{(0)}(1), x_3^{(0)}(2), \cdots, x_3^{(0)}(n) \right\},$$

where $x_3^{(0)}(i) = x_2^{(0)}(i) + i\pi$.

For two neighbor data in the sequence, we have

$$
\begin{aligned}
x_3^{(0)}(i+1) - x_3^{(0)}(i) &= \left( x_2^{(0)}(i+1) + (i+1)\pi \right) - \left( x_3^{(0)}(i) + i\pi \right) \\
&= \left( x_2^{(0)}(i+1) - x_3^{(0)}(i) \right) + ((i+1)\pi - i\pi) \\
&= \left( x_2^{(0)}(i+1) - x_3^{(0)}(i) \right) + \pi \\
&\quad \left( \because x_2^{(0)}(i+1) \in \left[0, \frac{\pi}{2}\right], x_2^{(0)}(i) \in \left[0, \frac{\pi}{2}\right], \therefore x_2^{(0)}(i+1) - x_3^{(0)}(i) \in \left[-\frac{\pi}{2}, \frac{\pi}{2}\right] \right) \\
&> 0
\end{aligned}
$$

$X_3^{(0)}$ serves as the final sequence data for prediction. With GM(1,1), we can obtain the predicted value $x_3^{(0)}(k+1)$.

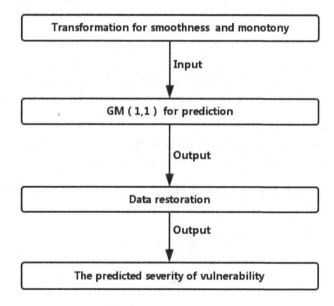

**Fig. 1.** Prediction process

Considering that

$$x_3^{(0)}(k+1) = x_2^{(0)}(k+1) + (k+1)\pi,$$

$$\left| \sin \left( x_2^{(0)}(k+1) + (k+1)\pi \right) \right| = \sin \left( x_2^{(0)}(k+1) \right),$$

$$x_1^{(0)}(k+1) = \sin\left(x_2^{(0)}(k+1)\right),$$

$$x^{(0)}(k+1) = x_1^{(0)}(k+1) \cdot x_{max}^{(0)}$$

we can restore the original data $x^{(0)}(k+1) = \left| x_{max}^{(0)} \cdot \sin\left(x_3^{(0)}(k+1)\right) \right|$.

The prediction process we adopted in this paper can be described as Fig. 1.

## 3  Experiment and Analysis

### 3.1  Data Source and Evaluation Metric

The experimental data comes from Common Vulnerabilities and Exposures (CVE) [18]. CVE provides a reference-method for publicly known information-security vulnerabilities and exposures. In CVE system, each vulnerability has been scored by experts based on its seriousness. The score ranges from 0.0 to 10.0 and the higher the score is, the more serious the vulnerability is. To validate our prediction method, we collect the vulnerability records of two software from CVE: Lynx, and Xpdf. The vulnerability data are arranged by their discovery date and construct sequences. Unlike some software like Firefox and Adobe Flash Player, and so on, which enjoy great popularity and possess rich vulnerability data. The two software are relatively less informative, which means that the vulnerability records of them are poor. Thus traditional statistical methods are not suitable since not enough data are available. On the contrary, grey models are better at dealing with this situation.

To measure the quality of the predicted result, Root Mean Square Error (RMSE) and Mean Relative Error (MRE) are adopted here to make evaluation.

**Define 1. (Root Mean Square Error, RMSE).**  Mean Relative Error is defined as

$$RMSE = \sqrt{\frac{1}{N}\sum_{i=1}^{n}\left(x_i - \widehat{x}_i\right)^2},$$

where $x_i$ is the real value of data and $\widehat{x}_i$ is the predicted value, $N$ represents the number of predicted data.

**Define 2. (Mean Relative Error, MRE).**  Mean Relative Error is defined as

$$MRE = \frac{1}{N}\sum_{i=1}^{n}\left|\frac{x_i - \widehat{x}_i}{x_i}\right| \times 100\,\%,$$

where $x_i$ is the real value of data and $\widehat{x}_i$ is the predicted value, $N$ represents the number of predicted data.

## 3.2   Result and Analysis

The experimental environment is: CPU Intel Core i5-2450 M; Basic Frequency 2.5 GHz; Memory 4 GB; Operating System Windows 7.

**Table 1.** Prediction result for Xpdf

| Real severity score | Predicted value by classical GM(1,1) | Predicted value by improved GM(1,1) |
|---|---|---|
| 7.5 | 11.3715 | 7.4941 |
| 7.5 | 8.7348 | 7.7784 |
| 2.1 | 6.8037 | 7.9503 |
| 5.1 | 2.8997 | 8.4105 |
| 7.5 | 2.8663 | 8.1657 |
| 7.0 | 6.6125 | 7.7566 |
| 7.5 | 10.4302 | 7.5168 |
| 7.5 | 8.5111 | 7.6946 |
| 7.6 | 7.5025 | 7.7963 |
| 6.8 | 7.8556 | 7.7712 |
| 6.8 | 6.8734 | 7.8710 |
| 8.7 | 6.4803 | 7.8939 |
| 6.9 | 8.4018 | 7.6993 |
| 5.9 | 7.8384 | 7.7817 |
| 8.3 | 6.0987 | 7.9628 |
| 9.3 | 6.8518 | 7.8218 |
| 6.8 | 10.4368 | 7.5412 |
| 6.8 | 8.4268 | 7.7603 |

The experimental platform is Matlab2013b.

In our experiment, the metabolism mechanism is adopted for the grey prediction model. More detailed explanation is as follows:

For the sequence $X^{(0)} = \{x^{(0)}(1), x^{(0)}(2), \cdots, x^{(0)}(n)\}$, the first 5 data $(x^{(0)}(1) \sim x^{(0)}(5))$ are used to predict the 6th data $(\hat{x}^{(0)}(6))$; then the next 5 data $(x^{(0)}(2) \sim x^{(0)}(6))$ are used to predict the 7th data $(\hat{x}^{(0)}(7))$., and so on.

The experiment result is shown in Tables 1 and 2. In the experiment, we also make a comparison of the improved GM(1,1) with the classical GM(1,1). The comparison is shown in Table 3.

**Table 2.** Prediction result for Lynx

| Real severity score | Predicted value by classical GM(1,1) | Predicted value by improved GM(1,1) |
|---|---|---|
| 5.0 | 4.1504 | 8.1111 |
| 7.5 | 5.0824 | 7.9825 |
| 7.5 | 6.1868 | 7.8256 |
| 7.5 | 9.1289 | 7.6215 |
| 7.6 | 8.8033 | 7.6758 |
| 10.0 | 7.6005 | 7.7972 |
| 4.6 | 10.3524 | 7.5579 |

**Table 3.** Comparison of evaluation results

| Evaluation metric | Xpdf | Lynx |
|---|---|---|
| RMSE (improved GM(1,1)) | 1.7802 | 1.8377 |
| RMSE (classical GM(1,1)) | 2.5110 | 2.7055 |
| MRE (improved GM(1,1)) | 27.79 % | 23.13 % |
| RMSE (classical GM(1,1)) | 37.96 % | 36.19 % |

From the comparison we can discover that the improved GM(1,1) with transformation gains a better performance both in RMSE and MRE than classical GM(1,1). Moreover, combined with Tables 1 and 2 we know that the RMSE and MRE are actually "pushed up" some extreme data. For example, the third vulnerability data of Xpdf is 2.1 and it is quite strange in the entire sequence, therefore it is understandable that the predicted result reaches a relative error of more than 200 % and just the special case elevate the two metrics. However, as we can see from Tables 1 and 2, the predicted value is quite close to the real value for most cases and the improved GM(1,1) model makes a better performance than the classical GM(1,1).

## 4    Conclusion and Future Directions

In this paper, we focus on the prediction of vulnerabilities' severity and propose a novel prediction method based on grey system theory. As far as we know, no other researchers has tried to solve the problem though the severity of vulnerabilities serves as an important aspect to reflect the characters of vulnerabilities and the prediction of it is also a valuable reference to evaluate the security level of the software. Unlike traditional statistical methods that require much history data for constructing prediction models, the GM(1,1) model in grey system theory can deal with the situation of poor information. Considering the oscillation of the sequence, we make transformation of the original data and recover the predicted result later. With the improved GM(1,1) model, we are able to get more accurate prediction results. The experiment is carried on the real vulnerability data collected from CVE and proves the feasibility of our method.

As for the future work, we think the following directions are worth further exploring:

(1) The prediction accuracy should be further improved, perhaps other grey models, such as discrete grey model (DGM), Verhulst model, perform better than GM(1,1). Further researches are required in this respect.
(2) Some other respects to describe vulnerabilities, such as the location of vulnerabilities, can also be predicted with grey system theory in our opinion. We will further study it in our future work.
(3) Comparisons between grey prediction methods and traditional statistical prediction methods are worth studying and it is important to make clear the application scope for different methods so that we can determine the most suitable method for prediction.

**Acknowledgments.** This paper is supported by Nuclear Takamoto Significant Special and National Development and Reform Commission Information Security Special.

# References

1. Nguyen, V.H., Tran, L.M.S.: Predicting vulnerable software components with dependency graphs. In: Proceedings of the 6th International Workshop on Security Measurements and Metrics, ser. MetriSec 2010, pp. 3:1–3:8. ACM, New York (2010). http://doi.acm.org/10.1145/1853919.1853923
2. Gürbüz, H.G., Er, N.P., Tekinerdogan, B.: Architecture framework for software safety. In: Amyot, D., Casas, P.F., Mussbacher, G. (eds.) SAM 2014. LNCS, vol. 8769, pp. 64–79. Springer, Heidelberg (2014)
3. Yafang, H., Yanzhao, L., Ping, L.: Ssrgm: software strong reliability growth model based on failure loss. In: 2012 Fifth International Symposium on Parallel Architectures, Algorithms and Programming (PAAP), pp. 255–261 (2012)
4. Yanzhao, L., Lei, Z., Ping, L., Yao, Y.: Research of trustworthy software system in the network. In: 2012 Fifth International Symposium on Parallel Architectures, Algorithms and Programming (PAAP), pp. 287–294 (2012)
5. Leveson, N.G.: Software safety: why, what, and how. ACM Comput. Surv. **18**(2), 125–163 (1986)
6. Deng, J.L.: Introduction to grey system theory. J. Grey Syst. **1**(1), 1–24 (1989)
7. Alhazmi, O.H., Malaiya, Y.K.: Quantitative vulnerability assessment of systems software. In: Proceedings of Annual Reliability and Maintainability Symposium, pp. 615–620 (2005)
8. Alhazmi, O., Malaiya, Y.: Prediction capabilities of vulnerability discovery models. In: Proceedings of the RAMS 2006, Annual Reliability and Maintainability Symposium, pp. 86–91 (2006)
9. Rahimi, S., Zargham, M.: Vulnerability scrying method for software vulnerability discovery prediction without a vulnerability database. IEEE Trans. Reliab. **62**(2), 395–407 (2013)
10. Shin, Y., Williams, L.: An empirical model to predict security vulnerabilities using code complexity metrics. In: Proceedings of ESEM 2008, pp. 315–317 (2008)

11. Scandariato, R., Walden, J., Hovsepyan, A., Joosen, W.: Predicting vulnerable software components via text mining. IEEE Trans. Softw. Eng. **40**(10), 1 (2014)
12. Shin, Y., Meneely, A., Williams, L., Osborne, J.A.: Evaluating complexity, code churn, and developer activity metrics as indicators of software vulnerabilities. IEEE Trans. Softw. Eng. **37**(6), 772–787 (2010)
13. Shin, Y., Williams, L.: Is complexity really the enemy of software security?. In: ACM Conference on Computer and Communications Security, pp. 47–50 (2008)
14. Rescorla, E.: Is finding security holes a good idea? IEEE Secur. Priv. Mag. **3**(1), 14–19 (2005)
15. Kayacan, E., Ulutas, B., Kaynak, O.: Grey system theory-based models in time series prediction. Expert Syst. Appl. **37**(2), 1784–1789 (2010)
16. Bauer, L., Garriss, S., McCune, J.M., Reiter, M.K., Rouse, J., Rutenbar, P.: Device-enabled authorization in the grey system. In: Zhou, J., López, J., Deng, R.H., Bao, F. (eds.) ISC 2005. LNCS, vol. 3650, pp. 431–445. Springer, Heidelberg (2005)
17. Shin, Y., Williams, L.: Can traditional fault prediction models be used for vulnerability prediction? Empirical Softw. Eng. **18**(1), 25–59 (2013)
18. Common Vulnerabilities and Exposures. http://cve.scap.org.cn/
19. Forecasting electricity demand using Grey-Markov model. In: 2008 International Conference on Machine Learning and Cybernetics, pp. 1244–1248. IEEE (2008)
20. Chen, C.I., Chen, H.L., Chen, S.P.: Forecasting of foreign exchange rates of Taiwan's major trading partners by novel nonlinear Grey Bernoulli model NGBM(1, 1). Commun. Nonlinear Sci. Numer. Simul. **13**(6), 1194–1204 (2008)
21. Rotchana, I., Salam, P.A., Kumar, S., et al.: Forecasting of municipal solid waste quantity in a developing country using multivariate grey models. Waste Manag. **39**, 3–14 (2015)
22. Hamzacebi, C., Es, H.A.: Forecasting the annual electricity consumption of Turkey using an optimized grey model. Energy **70**(3), 165–171 (2014). As the access to this document is restricted, you may want to look for a different version under "Related research" (further below) or for a different version of it
23. Xie, N.M., Liu, S.F., Yang, Y.J., et al.: On novel grey forecasting model based on non-homogeneous index sequence. Appl. Math. Model. **37**(7), 5059–5068.27 (2013)
24. Truong, D.Q., Ahn, K.K.: Wave prediction based on a modified grey model MGM(1,1) for real-time control of wave energy converters in irregular waves. Renew. Ener. **43**, 242–255 (2012)
25. Wang, Z.X., Dang, Y.G., Pei, L.L.: Modeling approach for oscillatory sequences based on GM(1,1) power model. Syst. Eng. Electron. **33**(11), 2440–2444 (2011). (In Chinese)
26. Wang, Z.X.: Grey forecasting method for small sample oscillating sequences based on Fourier series. Control Decis. **29**(2), 270–274 (2014). (In Chinese)
27. Wang, Z.X.: Oscillating GM(1,1) power model and its application. Control Decis. **28**, 1459–1464 (2013). (In Chinese)

# Characterization of Android Applications with Root Exploit by Using Static Feature Analysis

Huikang Hao[1]([⊠]), Zhoujun Li[1,2], Yueying He[3], and Jinxin Ma[4]

[1] School of Computer Science and Engineering, Beihang University,
Beijing 100191, China
{huikang329,lizj}@buaa.edu.cn
[2] Beijing Key Laboratory of Network Technology, Beihang University,
Beijing 100081, China
[3] National Computer Network Emergency Response Technical Team/Coordination
Center of China, Beijing 100029, China
[4] China Information Technology Security Evaluation Center,
Beijing 100085, China

**Abstract.** Recently, more and more rootkit tools are provided by some well-known vendors in the mainstream Android markets. Many people are willing to root their phones to uninstall pre-installed applications, flash third-party ROMs and so on. As it is reported, a significant proportion of Android phones are rooted at least one time. However, applications with root exploit bring critical security threat to users. When the phone is rooted, the permission system, which enforces access control to those privacy-related resources in Android phones, could be bypassed. Thus, the phone will be an easy point for malware to launch attacks. What's more, even the phone is unrooted, permission escalation attacks also can be carried out. Remarkably, an amount of sophisticated Android malware embeds root exploit payloads. Hence, root exploit always suggests high security risk. It is a pressing concern for researchers to characterize and detect applications with root exploit. In this paper, a novel method to extract key features of apps with root exploit is proposed. Contrary to existing works, contrasting the static features between applications with and without root exploit comprehensively are considered at the first time. We complete and evaluate the methodology on two clean apps and two malware dataset, comprising 52, 1859, 463 and 797 applications respectively. Our empirical results suggest the peculiar features can be obtained, which can capture the key differences between applications with and without root exploit to characterize Android root exploit applications.

**Keywords:** Android application · Root exploit · Static features · Apriori-based feature comparison · Feature combination · Characterization

© Springer International Publishing Switzerland 2015
G. Wang et al. (Eds.): ICA3PP 2015 Workshops, LNCS 9532, pp. 153–165, 2015.
DOI: 10.1007/978-3-319-27161-3_14

# 1    Introduction

Nowadays, mobile devices are reaching into almost every corner in our life rapidly. Due to the advanced smartphone operating system such as Android, IOS, we can enjoy feature-rich smartphones in which our security-sensitive information is stored, including contacts, photos and credentials. Among the mainstream mobile operating systems, Android dominates the mobile device market. As it is reported, more than 75 % shipments of smartphones run Android system in Q1 2015 [1]. The popularity of Android unsurprisingly draws malware authors' attentions, which results in the surge of Android malware. What's worse, an amount of sophisticated Android malware starts to launch attacks with root exploit. The utilization of root exploit technique makes that Android malware is more dangerous and difficult to detect.

One of the Android's most important security mechanisms against malware is permission control. Critical system resources are protected by permission mechanism so that any applications must explicitly declare what permissions they need to realize expected functions in the AndroidMeanifeast.xml file. When a user installs an app, a prompt will be raised to list all the critical permissions with its potential risky behaviors. The risk warning brings a binary choice for user to grant or reject these permissions that the application requires. Permission system ensures only the applications granted certain permissions can access corresponding resources. Otherwise, the resource access request would be rejected. To a large extent, we can say that the permissions that an app granted represent the app's capability to access system resources. As a result, permission system provides basic protections for the system resources of Android phones.

Android is a Linux-based platform. In the system design of Linux, users and groups are used to control access to the system's files, directories, and peripherals. The superuser (root) has complete access to the system resource and its configuration. An access to system resource with root privilege is almost unrestricted. Unprivileged users can use the *su* and *sudo* programs for controlled privilege escalation [2]. Nowadays, a variety of applications that provide one-click-root function emerge in every mainstream Android market. Many Android users utilize root exploit to customize their phones. Once a phone is rooted, its owner can remove the disliked pre-installed apps, customize personalized system, backup the phones, and flash third party ROMs. According to the report of NetQin [3], 23 % Android phones are rooted at least one time in China mainland by the first half of 2012. But it is important to note that root privilege brings serious security threats to users. First of all, the unrestricted resource access capability of root privilege makes it feasible that an application can access sensitive database files and hardware interfaces without corresponding permissions granted beforehand. That is to say, root exploit can disable the permission system. Faced with malware with root privilege, one of the Android security mechanisms, namely permission system, does not play any role. As a result, a lot of sophisticated malware samples launch attacks by using root exploit. As Yajin Zhou et al. revealed in [4], around one third (36.7 %) of the collected samples leverage root exploits to fully compromise the Android security. Moreover, for an once rooted phone, unrooting the phone will not prevent Android system from suffering security threat. Permission escalation attacks also can be carried out [5]. Hence, an application with root exploit always suggests high security risk to Android phone. To deal with this security threat, it is a pressing concern for users and researchers to characterize and detect applications with root exploit.

In this paper, a novel method to extract critical features of apps with root exploit is proposed, and these extracted features can be used to characterize root exploit effectively. We collect a relatively complete dataset of clean apps with root exploit payload and contrast the static features with other benign apps comprehensively. It is noted that the contrast is carried out in two groups: a clean app group and a malicious app group. Each group has one dataset with root exploit and one dataset without root exploit payloads. In each group, we calculate the difference values of feature items between two datasets. Note that, 11 static features which compromises *permission, API call, 4 components,.so file. native code, dynamic code, reflection code* and *obfuscation code* are involved in our method. After comparing feature individually, we filter the items whose difference value less than 0 for each feature. Thus the left items form the candidate itemset for each feature. Then, for the generation of feature combinations, we join all the candidate itemset as an joint itemset. Apriori-based algorithm is introduced on the itemset to generate the feature combinations. Eventually, based on the feature combinations generated from two groups, we contrast the two sets and authenticate mutually. Hence, the shared and consistent feature combinations in the two groups are selected as the output of our method. The contributions of our work can be summarized as follows:

- A novel method to extract the key and peculiar features of apps with root exploit is proposed and implemented in our paper. These features can be used to characterize Android applications with root exploit.
- To the best of our knowledge, it is the first attempt to explore the key features of root exploit by contrasting the static features between applications with root exploit and other apps.
- We collect a relatively complete dataset of clean apps with root exploit, covering 7 mainstream Android markets. It may be useful for further research.

The rest of the paper is organised as follows: In Sect. 2, we analysis the root exploit process and its security threat to the phone as background. Section 3 describes the experimental datasets that we collect for our research. We present our method for extracting key features of apps with root exploit in Sect. 4. The implementation and the obtained result are then reported in Sect. 5 along with a discussion of our findings. Related works are shown in Sect. 6 and finally we concluded the paper in Sect. 7.

## 2   Background

In this section, we study the processes and security threat of root exploit. The basic processes of root exploit are consistent generally, which determines the essential characteristics of root exploit. In addition, the root exploit disable permission system, which brings multiple risks for the phones.

## 2.1 Processes of Root Exploit

Since the heterogeneity of android os, a variety of rootkit tools are provided for users to root their phones. The processes of root exploit can be summarized as the following three steps: firstly, the applications called rootkit tools, exploit the Linux vulnerabilities to temporarily obtain root privilege. Up to now, the Linux vulnerabilities that have been exploited include *Gingerbreak, RageAgainstTheCage, ZergRush, Exploid, ASHMEM, Mempodroid, Levitator, Wunderbar, Zimperlich* and so on. Then, these applications place or replace a customized "su" binary file into */system/bin* or */system/xbin* directory. Finally, the root exploit payload sets the "su" file the *s* attribute that every user and role in the system can access it. Thus, the privilege escalation is completed and the system resource of system can be accessed with root privilege consistently.

## 2.2 Security Threat of Root Exploit

According to the Android core security design, the data and code execution of each application are isolated from each other by sandbox. The data and resource accesses are restricted strictly by the permission system. Because each Android application operates in a process sandbox, applications must explicitly share resources and data. The applications realize this by explicitly declaring permissions what they need for expected functions not provided by the basic sandbox. Thus, permission system, which is an access control mechanism, acts as the key system security mechanism in Android.

Android is a privilege-separated operating system, in which each application runs with a distinct system identity (Linux user ID and group ID) [6]. The Android system gives each app a distinct user ID(UID) at installation time and the ID cannot be changed all the time unless the app is removed. Generally, the UIDs of these user applications given by system are bigger than 10000. Thus, each app in Android system is isolated in its process space and regards as an unique Linux user. Unfortunately, when the phone is rooted, the UID of an app could be changed to 0, i.e. the root UID, which is able to match access control rule of all system resource almost.

The enforcement of permission system concentrates on two modules: Android system services and Linux kernel [7]. The two modules implement permission check on different levels, but they are all based on user and group mechanism in Linux access control.

**Android System Services.** The resources such as contacts and locations are protected by Android system services. For example, the location information is managed by *Location Manager Service*. When an app attempts to acquire these resources protected by system services, the service checks related permissions by invoking the general permission check interfaces(such as *check-Permission,checkCallingPermission,checkUriPermission etc.*) of *ActivityManagerService*. Then the check is redirected to *PackageManagerService*, which keeps a table that records the granted permissions for each application. The *PackageManagerService* returns the check result according to the records and the system services which protect resource judges to accept or deny the access of resource. The parameters of these APIs generally comprise PID(Process ID) and UID(User ID), which suggests the permissions are verified finally by matching user ID.

**Linux Kernel.** The permissions related to file system and hardware interface such as camera, bluetooth and network etc. are enforced in Linux kernel level. In Android, each kernel-protected system resource is tagged with corresponding kernel-enforced permission to protect. Then, the permission is assigned with a unique GID(Group ID) as indentifier. if an app requests the related permissions in the manifest, the app,i.e. the UID will become a member of the user group that is permitted to access the resources. Any app is checked to verify whether it has the corresponding GID before accessing the protected resources.

When the phone is rooted, an app can run with root UID 0, which can pass all the permission checks. By analysing the implementation of permission system, we demonstrate that root exploit disable the permission system fundamentally. Hence, root exploit brings critical threat to the Android security.

# 3   Experimental Dataset

In order to contrast the static features effectively, quite a number of applications embedded root exploit payloads and apps without root exploit are needed to collect respectively. In our research, we collect 4 data sets in total, i.e. a clean app set with root exploit payload, a clean data set including benign apps without root exploit and two malware datasets whose root exploit payloads are at least one and none individually. For convenience of description, we call above 4 data set as *clean root set, clean set, malicious root set* and *malicious set* successively. Clearly, the 4 data sets can be divided into two compared groups: a clean set group and a malicious set group.

The *clean root set* consists 52 benign apps with root exploit. We collect these apps from official Google Play and 6 third party Android markets, which cover the mainstream Android markets nowadays. When collecting this dataset, we notice that many apps are found to occur repeatedly and one developer may release new version of identical app with slight variation. To prevent identical apps from having a large impact on the result, we consolidate duplicate apps into single instance in the dataset. In *clean set*, there are 1859 benign applications that we collect from official Googel Play. These apps in *clean set* are widely distributed around all the 44 categories of Google Play. Note that all above two datasets are verified manually. We have sent original datasets with 60 and 1863 apps to VirusTotal [8] and collect the analysis result. According to the analysis result, we verify that whether the checked app embeds root exploit payload. Furthermore, the applications flagged as risky by at least 10 anti-virus products are removed and some applications about which VirusTotal has no information are also rejected. Eventually we collect 52 verified clean apps for *clean root set* and 1859 verified clean apps for our *clean set*. It is worth noting that 8 malware samples are found to masquerade as benign ones which claims to root users' phone in four third party markets(Yingyongbao, Anzhi, Mumayi, Anzhuo).

For our malware datasets, we used Zhou and Jiang's [4] collection of 1260 malicious applications, which comprises of 49 malware families. From the authors' analysis, among 1260 samples in the collection, 463 of them carry at least one root exploit payload. Here we collect these applications as *malicious root set*. The remainder 797 applications are well studied with no root exploit payload. Hence, we regard the 797 apps as our *malicious set*.

# 4  Method

To deal with the security threat, it is an urgent need to characterize and detect applications with root exploit. In order to extract key features of root exploit effectively, we propose a method to contrast the static features between apps with and without root exploit payload systematically. It should be clear that a complete static feature set is involved in our method, which compromises *permission, API call, 4 components,.so file. native code, dynamic code, reflection code* and *obfuscation code*. All above 11 individual features and feature combinations are considered to capture the characteristic of root exploit. Note that the clean set group and malicious set group are compared respectively by using the same procedures. The framework of our method is illustrated in Fig. 1 and the major processes of our method is outlined as follows.

**Individual Feature Comparison and Filtering.** In this process, 11 static features extracted from the 4 datasets are compared according to the two groups division. The purpose of this process is to obtain candidate features for further generation of feature combinations. For the feature comparison, we implement an analyzer based on Androguard [9] to extract and analyze all the 11 features. Androguard [9] is an open static analysis framework, which provides uncompress, decompilation and analysis of Android .apk file. All the feature items and its frequency can be obtained by our analyzer for further analysis.

Given $Dx$ is one of the input datasets which contains n applications. Then for a certain application in $Dx$, let $Si$ represent a feature of the application. Furthermore, we define $Si = \{A, B, C, \ldots\}$ as the set of possible items for a certain feature. Each item can be considered as a corresponding feature value as a feature. For example, permission CAMERA is an item of the feature "permission". In this process, we carry on feature comparison and filtering individually. For a feature $Si$, given one feature item $A$, we measure the importance of $A$ by utilizing the difference of frequency. We calculate the differences in the same group by $diff(A) = freq(A)_{root} - freq(A)$. Here *freq(A)root* refers to the frequency

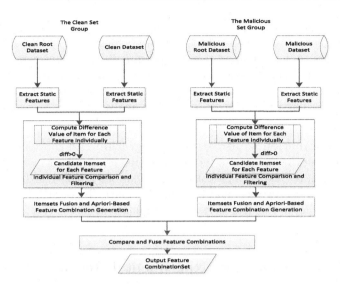

**Fig. 1.** The framework of our method

of item $A$ in the root dataset and $freq(A)$ is the frequency of $A$ in the dataset without root exploit.

If $diff(A) > \delta$, we add item $A$ to the candidate itemset $Fi$ for $Si$. Otherwise, the item $A$ will be discarded. Here, $\delta$ is a user-specified threshold value. In our research, we set the threshold $\delta$ 0 for capturing more feature items. After filtering the feature items, each feature has its corresponding itemset.

**Apriori-Based Feature Combination Generation.** In the former process, we obtain 11 candidate itemsets for 11 features individually. However, the behavior of applications is usually reflected in specific patterns and combinations of the extracted features. To this end, we define the joint set $F$ that comprises all the 11 candidate itemsets for all the extracted features

$$F := F_1 \cup F_2 \cup \ldots \cup F_{10} \cup F_{11}$$

Apriori algorithm [10] is an algorithm for frequent item set mining and association rule learning. Here we amend this algorithm to generate the feature combination patterns. *Support* is usually used as the measurement for the effectiveness of the item pattern. To put it simple, let $a, b \subseteq F$, then the frequency of the apps that contains feature items $a$ and $b$ simultaneously in the total dataset is just the support. Here, we define the difference value of the two sets' support in one group as the *support* of the joint candidate itemset. In the practise of the algorithm, we set $support >= \epsilon$ as a rule to pruning the candidate item set, where $\epsilon$ is a specific threshold. We start the feature combination generation by enumerating the single item in $F$ who matches pruning rule. Based on these single items, we add new items from $F$ one by one to test their *support*.

This joining operation is repeated continuously to increase the number of items until the *support* of the item set less than pre-defined $\epsilon$. In order to list all the possible feature combination, we take the pruning item set considerable and use frequent item set to generate new candidate item further. Finally, a set of feature combinations are formed for each comparing group. All the feature combinations are sorted according to its *support* for further analysis.

**Feature Combination Contrast and Integration.** All above two processes are conducted on the two group: the clean group and malicious group. After the previous procedures, two sets of feature combinations are obtained. As the final step, we contrast the two sets and authenticate mutually. Based on the result of comparison, we leave the shared feature combinations of the two groups as the outputs of our method.

# 5    Implementation and Experimental Result

## 5.1    Implementation

By using our approach, we complete a demo based on Androguard [9] in Python. As stated in pervious sections, 11 features in total is selected in our work as feature to describe applications behavior characteristic. Among them, *permission* and *API calls* are inspected by counting the feature names and their frequency. Here we focus *required permissions* and all the *API* decompiled from .apk file are considered. For the 4 app components, namely, *activity, service,content provider, broadcast receiver*, its numbers in each app are collected in a feature set. What's more,.so file are investigated with file name and file number. *native code, dynamic code, reflection code,obfuscation code* refer to whether applications have native code, dynamic code, reflection code and obfuscation code. We test apps with these features and compute their frequency.

For our implementation, Androguard-based module is used to extract static features. We amend Androguard [9] so that it can uncompress and decompile the .apk files to output all checked items of above 11 features. All these features are written in text file for further analysis. Then we complete analysis modules according to our algorithm in Python. Two scripts are coded to contrast individual features and generate feature combinations respectively. Note that, when we introduce our Apriori-Based feature combination generation algorithm, we set the threshold of *support* $\epsilon$ as 0.5, which is mainly to capture more effective feature combinations to distinguish root exploit.

## 5.2    Individual Feature Comparison

Our experiments are conducted on two dataset groups, which covers four datasets that are described exhaustively in Sect. 3. Then we show the results of individual feature comparison for the two groups separately.

**Table 1.** A list of top 15 required permissions ordered by difference value for the clean app group and malicious app group.

| The clean group comparison | | The malicious group comparison | |
|---|---|---|---|
| Permission | Difference value | Permission | Difference value |
| READ_PHONE_STATE | 0.5769 | CHANGE_WIFI_STATE | 0.6777 |
| GET_TASKS | 0.5385 | ACCESS_WIFI_STATE | 0.4048 |
| RECEIVE_BOOT_COMPLETED | 0.5192 | WRITE_EXTERNAL_STORAGE | 0.3613 |
| ACCESS_WIFI_STATE | 0.5192 | READ_EXTERNAL_STORAGE | 0.3117 |
| SYSTEM_ALERT_WINDOW | 0.4423 | ACCESS_LOCATION_EXTRA_COMMANDS | 0.3094 |
| WRITE_SETTINGS | 0.4230 | GET_TASKS | 0.1801 |
| WRITE_EXTERNAL_STORAGE | 0.4230 | ACCESS_NETWORK_STATE | 0.1340 |
| INSTALL_SHORTCUT | 0.4038 | INSTALL_PACKAGES | 0.1264 |
| KILL_BACKGROUND_PROCESSES | 0.3846 | ACCESS_FINE_LOCATION | 0.0891 |
| MOUNT_UNMOUNT_FILESYSTEMS | 0.3846 | RECEIVE_BOOT_COMPLETED | 0.0617 |
| ACCESS_MTK_MMHW | 0.3461 | CHANGE_CONFIGURATION | 0.0501 |
| CHANGE_WIFI_STATE | 0.3269 | READ_PHONE_STATE | 0.0267 |
| RESTART_PACKAGES | 0.3269 | ADD_SYSTEM_SERVICE | 0.0204 |
| READ_LOGS | 0.3077 | BROADCAST_STICKY | 0.0200 |
| GET_PACKAGE_SIZE | 0.2885 | MODIFY_AUDIO_SETTINGS | 0.0195 |

*Permission.* For the clean group, 112 permissions are involved in total. 45 permissions occurs in both the *clean root dataset* and *clean dataset*. 33 permissions are found only in the *clean root dataset*. The remainder 34 permissions are only required only by the applications in the *clean dataset*. For the malicious group, 64 permissions occur at all the time in both two datasets of the group. 16 and 35 permissions appear only in the *malicious root set* and *malicious set* respectively. In summary, there are 115 permissions for the malicious group. Note that, not all the permissions are Android-defined permissions. According to our filtering rules, 68 and 42 permissions are left to incorporate to candidate itemset of clean group and malicious group respectively. Table 1 lists the top 15 permissions ordered by difference value for the two groups.

According to the comparison results ordered by difference value, we observe that there are 20 shared permissions in the candidate itemsets for the two groups. Specially, among the top 15 required permissions in Table 1, 6 permissions, i.e. READ_PHONE_STATE, GET_TASKS, RECEIVE_BOOT_COMPLETED, ACCESS_WIFI_STATE, WRITE_EXTERNAL_STORAGE, CHANGE_WIFI_STATE, are common permissions.Permision READ_PHONE_STATE, GET_TASKS and RECEIVE_BOOT_COMPLETED are the top 3 for the clean group, while for the malicious group, thet are CHANGE_WIFI_STATE, ACCESS_WIFI_STATE, WRITE_EXTERNAL_STORAGE. We notice that READ_PHONE_STATE and RECEIVE_BOOT_COMPLETED are risky permissions significantly and requested widely in malicious data sets as reported in previous work [11], which results in that the two permissions don't have a particularly significant difference value as in the clean group. However, they are still important verifiable characteristic for root exploit. As literature [12] demonstrated the root exploit example, the rootkit tools collects information needed to exploit as the first step. So it is necessary to request READ_PHONE_STATE. Similarly, the rest 5 permissions are needed to complete basic processes for root exploit. Permission system is the key security design for Android. When a phone is not rooted, the system resources are restricted by permissions. Once an application attempts to root the phone, it should require a part of basic permissions for to complete root exploit. Meanwhile, a mass of permissions related to specific behaviors can be avoided.

*API Calls.* API calls are fine-grained descriptions of application behaviors. The so-called *Used Permissions* can be reflected by API calls. In our method, all the API calls that can be extracted from .apk file are involved. For the clean set group, 73886 APIs are extracted and 10472 API calls are common used by two datasets. Besides, 28678 API calls are unique ones that only appear in *clean root set.* For the malicious set group, 57779 API calls are the total number and 4687 API calls are common ones, 18000 API calls are found only in *malicious root set.* After sorting these API calls in accordance with difference values, we select 29792 and 21247 API calls whose values outnumber 0 to add into candidate itemsets for clean and malicious group respectively. Combining the comparison result of the two groups, we notice that third-party packages and correspond- ing APIs are widely used in applications with root exploit. For the clean group, packages *com.tencent.mm.sdk, com.umeng, com.zhiqupk.root, com.feiwo et.al.* are discovered in the *clean root set* exclusively. These third-party APIs are the key difference between apps with and without root exploit. Specially, among the top 10 APIs in the differen value order, 7 APIs are from the pack- age *com.tencent.mm.sdk.* Similarly, for the malicious group, the packages *com.google.update, com.keji, net.youmi.android* are viewed only in *malicious root set* and the packages *uk.co.lilhermit.android, com.adwo.adsdk, com.madhouse. android.ads, com.admogo.adapters, com.vpon.adon.android* are common API packages which can distinguish root exploit effectively.

*4 Components.* The 4 components reflect the structure of an application. We extract the number of certain component in an app as the feature item and compute its corresponding frequency among all the apps in the dataset. For the clean group, the total numbers of candidate items for *activity, content provider, service* and *broadcast receiver* are 20,5,13 and 12 respectively. On the other hand, the candidate item number of *activity, content provider, service* and *broadcast receiver* are 21,3,3 and 3 in the malicious group. The difference values of most the candidate items for the two groups doesn't exceed 0.1, while only the item "1" of *service* in the malicious group is 0.3014, which acts as the significant feature item.

*.so File.* The .so files are shared libraries (.so) in an Android application, which are usually under the dictionaries *lib/armeabi* and *assets.* Usually, the authors of applications dynamically load native code or author-specific code by introducing .so file. In our method, we compare the usage of .so files in two groups. For the clean set group, the type number of .so file in *clean root set* and *clean set* are 71 and 41 respectively. The candidate itemset has 71 files, in which *assets/libsecmain.x86.so, assets/libsecexe.x86.so, lib/armeabi/librgsdk.so* and the

file *lib/armeabi/libsmartutils.so* are the top 4 files whose difference values are surpass 0.10. For the malicious set group, the utilization of .so files of all the 463 apps in *malicious root set* converges on 14 types, while there are 37 types .so file in *malicious set*. As a result, 8 files are common in both two dataset and 13 files whose difference values are more than 0 are remainder as candidate items. Note that, the difference value of *lib/armeabi/libnative.so* file is 0.6160, which is much higher than other 12 files. The values of the rest ones in itemset are all less than 0.0205.

**Native Code, Dynamic Code, Reflection Code and Obfuscation Code.** For these 4 features, everyone has only one feature item, which refers to a certain application has native code, dynamic code, reflection code and obfuscation code or not. According to the calculation of the 4 feature item frequency, It is noticed easily that *native code* is a significant feature that differentiates applications with root exploit from others. *Dynamic code* feature is more frequent in applications without root exploit and *obfuscation code* feature has made no difference for our method. As for *reflection code* feature, it is not consistent in two groups. Finally, only *native code* feature item is left for the clean group and *native code,reflection code* are for malicious group.

### 5.3  Feature Combination Generation

After individual feature comparison, candidate itemsets for each feature are gained. Then, we unite these 11 candidate itemsets into a joint candidate set for the two groups.Thus 29982 feature items are included into the joint set of clean group and 21334 ones are in the joint set of malicious group. By introducing our Apriori-Based feature combination generation algorithm, a set of feature combinations are obtained and we display them in Table 2. All the supports of these feature combinations is over 0.5. We authenticate the result of two groups mutually and find out that the combination (READ_PHONE_STATE,ACCESS_WIFI_STATE,Native Code) and the combination (ACCESS_WIFI_STATE, CHANGE_WIFI_STATE, *lib/armeabi/libnative.so*,uk.co.lilhermit.android.core. Native,Native Code) are generally consistent. *ACCESS_WIFI_STATE* and *Native Code* are common features of two group and they can group together as a feature combination to be the output of our method. In addition, the peculiar feature items that only appears in the *clean root set* and *malicious root set* are collected as supplementary method, e.g. APIs in *com.tencent.mm.sdk.platformtools* are used only in *clean root set*, whose difference values doesn't surpass 0.5. But when an application uses these APIs, we justify the application has a higher possibility of embedding root exploit payloads.

## 6  Related Work

Note that some sophisticated malware samples launch attacks with root exploit, many techniques have been proposed as a part of malware detection technique. DroidRanger [13] implements dynamic execution monitoring that focuses on

**Table 2.** A set of feature combinations for the two groups.

|  | Feature combinations |
| --- | --- |
| Clean Group | (READ_PHONE_STATE,ACCESS_WIFI_STATE,Native Code), (READ_PHONE_STATE,GET_TASK,Native Code) (RECEIVE_BOOT_COMPLETED) |
| Malicious Group | (ACCESS_WIFI_STATE,CHANGE_WIFI_STATE,*lib/armeabi/ libnative.so*,uk.co.lilhermit.android.core.Native,Native Code), (CHANGE_WIFI_STATE,com.google.update.Dialog,com.google. update.UpdateService) |

system calls used by existing Android root exploits and/or made with the root privilege. In [14], in order to detect root exploit, the authors distill each known vulnerability into a corresponding static vulnerability-specific signature to capture its essential characteristics. Similarly, Rastogi et.al. [15] proposed the method based on vulnerability conditions, which can be considered as the signature.

Many tools and frameworks which are devoted exclusively to detect and prevent root exploit are also designed. Ho et. al. [16] propose PREC, a framework which can identify system calls from high-risk components and execute those system calls within isolated threads to detect and stop root exploit.In [17], a system that enables to extract and collect events related to root exploit is proposed, which can cope with root exploit effectively.

In summary, the methods proposed by the previous works mainly focus on two points. Many techniques [13,16,17] detect root exploits based on monitoring and searching for system calls and events related to known root exploit processes dynamically. Compared to these works, our method is implemented based on static feature analysis and we focus on the reflections of root exploit on Android code level, but not the system calls or events. On the other hand, such approaches [14,15] learn the well-studied root exploit vulnerabilities and extract the preconditions of them as signature for rule-matching. We observe that these methods are based on behaviors that will be exhibited when the vulnerability is being exploit. These works draw attentions to root exploit vulnerabilities, while our method inspects to search for essential features for root exploit on the .apk file level. Unlike the previous methods, our method provides a new angle to study the root exploit characterization and detection.

## 7   Conclusion

Root exploit brings a variety of security threats to the phones. Applications with root exploit always suggest high risk. To characterize and detect apps with root exploit, we propose a novel method to extract peculiar features of apps with root exploit. To the best of our knowledge, this work is the first one to focus on characterizing root exploit from the angle of static feature contrast. By applying our method, a set of key features and corresponding feature combinations are obtained to capture the key differences between applications with and without root exploit.

**Acknowledgements.** This work was supported in part by National High-tech R&D Program of China under grant No. 2015AA016004, NSFC under grants No. 61170189 and No. 61370126.

# References

1. IDC. http://www.idc.com/getdoc.jsp?containerId=prUS25282214
2. Users and Groups. https://wiki.archlinux.org/index.php/Users_and_groups#Group_management
3. NetQin: 2012 moblie phone security report (2012). http://cn.nq.com/neirong/2012shang.pdf
4. Zhou, Y., Jiang, X.: Dissecting android malware: characterization and evolution. In: S&P 2012, pp. 95–109. IEEE (2012)
5. Zhang, Z., Wang, Y., Jing, J., Wang, Q., Lei, L.: Once root always a threat: analyzing the security threats of android permission system. In: Susilo, W., Mu, Y. (eds.) ACISP 2014. LNCS, vol. 8544, pp. 354–369. Springer, Heidelberg (2014)
6. System Permission. http://developer.android.com/intl/zh-cn/guide/topics/security/permissions.html
7. Zhang, Y., Yang, M., Xu, B., Yang, Z., Gu, G., Ning, P., Wang, X.S., Zang, B.: Vetting undesirable behaviors in android apps with permission use analysis. In: CCS 2013, pp. 611–622 (2013)
8. VirusTotal. https://www.virustotal.com
9. Androguard. http://code.google.com/p/androguard
10. Apriori algorithm. https://en.wikipedia.org/wiki/Apriori_algorithm
11. Wang, W., Wang, X., Feng, D., Liu, J., Han, Z., Zhang, X.: Exploring permission-induced risk in android applications for malicious application detection. IEEE Trans. Inf. Forensics Secur. **9**(11), 1869–1882 (2014)
12. Lee, H.-T., Kim, D., Park, M., Cho, S.: Protecting data on android platform against privilege escalation attack. Int. J. Comput. Math. (ahead-of-print), 1–14 (2014)
13. Zhou, Y., Wang, Z., Zhou, W., Jiang, X.: Hey, you, get off of my market: Detecting malicious apps in official and alternative android markets. In: NDSS (2012)
14. Grace, M., Zhou, Y., Zhang, Q., Zou, S., Jiang, X.: Riskranker: scalable and accurate zero-day android malware detection. In: Proceedings of the 10th International Conference on Mobile Systems, Applications, and Services, pp. 281–294. ACM (2012)
15. Rastogi, V., Chen, Y., Enck, W.: Appsplayground: automatic security analysis of smartphone applications. In: Proceedings of the Third ACM Conference on Data and Application Security and Privacy, pp. 209–220. ACM (2013)
16. Ho, T.-H., Dean, D., Gu, X., Enck, W.: Prec: practical root exploit containment for android devices. In: Proceedings of the 4th ACM Conference on Data and Application Security and Privacy, pp. 187–198. ACM (2014)
17. Ham, Y.J., Choi, W.-B., Lee, H.-W.: Mobile root exploit detection based on system events extracted from android platform. In: SAM 2013, 1p. WorldComp (2013)

# LIP3: A Lightweighted Fine-Grained Privacy-Preserving Profile Matching Mechanism for Mobile Social Networks in Proximity

Yufeng Wang[1(✉)], Xiaohong Chen[1], Qun Jin[2], and Jianhua Ma[3]

[1] Nanjing University of Posts and Telecommunications,
Nanjing 210003, China
wfwang@njupt.edu.cn
[2] Waseda University, Saitama 359-1192, Japan
jin@waseda.jp
[3] Hosei University, Tokyo 184-8584, Japan
jianhua@hosei.ac.jp

**Abstract.** Recently, Device to Device (D2D) based mobile social networking in proximity (MSNP) has witnessed great development on smartphones, which enable actively/passively and continuously seek for relevant value in one's physical proximity, through direct communicating with other individuals within the communication range, without the support of centralized networking infrastructure. Specially, a user would like to find out and interact with some strangers with similar interest in vicinity through profile matching. However, in matching process, individuals always have to reveal their personal and private profiles to strangers, which conflicts with users' growing privacy concerns. To achieve privacy preserving profile matching (i.e., friend discovery), many schemes are proposed based on homomorphic and commutative encryption, which bring tremendous computation and communication overheads, and are not practical for the resource limited mobile devices in MSNP. In this paper we adapt Confusion Matrix Transformation (CMT) method to design a Lightweighted fine-grained Privacy-Preserving Profile matching mechanism, LIP3, which can not only efficiently realize privacy-preserving profile matching, but obtain the strict measurement of cosine similarity between individuals, while other existing CMT-based schemes can only roughly estimate the matching value.

**Keywords:** Mobile social networking in proximity (MSNP) · Privacy-Preserving · Profile matching · Confusion matrix transformation

## 1 Introduction

Today, modern mobile phones have the capability to detect proximity of other users and offer means to communicate and share data in ad-hoc way, with the people in the proximity, which naturally integrates those two trends: wireless opportunistic networking and decentralized online social networks, and leads to the great development

© Springer International Publishing Switzerland 2015
G. Wang et al. (Eds.): ICA3PP 2015 Workshops, LNCS 9532, pp. 166–176, 2015.
DOI: 10.1007/978-3-319-27161-3_15

and deployment of D2D based MSNP (Mobile social network in proximity), which is explicitly defined as: A wireless peer-to-peer (P2P) networking of spontaneously and opportunistically connected users (e.g., through the Bluetooth/WiFi interfaces on their mobile devices), exploits both geo-proximity and social interests as the primary filters in determining who is discoverable on the social network [1]. In contrast to traditional web-based online social networking, D2D based MSNP can enable more tangible face-to-face social interactions in public places such as parks, stadiums, and train stations, etc.

In MSNPs, individuals can maintain and store their sensitive data by themselves, which can alleviate the problem of big brother (privacy concern) in traditional MSN. This implies that the omniscient OSN provider that has become "a big brother", collects and stores all user's data (messages, profiles, location, relations, etc.), which may cause serious privacy concern, e.g., selling users' personal information, and targeted advertising, However, MSNP users still face growing privacy concerns.

Basically, the first step toward effective D2D based MSNP is for mobile users to choose whom to interact with. As an example, Alice wants to conduct a proximal talk with nearby passengers at the airport. Since she can simultaneously interact with only one or a few persons, it is crucial for her to select those who can lead to the most meaningful social interactions: The natural way is to select those whose social profiles most match hers. Widely known as profile matching, this method is rooted in the social fact that people normally prefer to socialize with others having similar interests or background over complete strangers.

A major challenge for profile matching is to ensure the privacy of personal profiles which often contain highly sensitive information related to gender, interests, political tendency, health conditions, and so on. This challenge necessitates private matching, in which two users compare personal profiles without disclosing them to each other. Generally, there are two mainstreams of approaches to solving the privacy-preserving profile-based friend matching problem. The first category is converted into Private Set Intersection or Private Set Intersection Cardinality, whereby two mutually mistrusting parties, each holding a private data set, jointly compute the intersection, or the intersection cardinality of the two sets without leaking any additional information to either party. These schemes could enable only coarse-grained private matching and are unable to further differentiate users with the same attribute(s). To solve this problem and thus further enhance the usability of MSNP, the second category includes fine-grained private matching mechanisms, which consider a user's profile as a vector with fine-grained attribute values, and measures the social similarity by private vector dot product [2].

Although, both kinds of approaches could effectively enforce privacy-preserving profile-matching among nearby users without the support of the trusted third party, they have the following disadvantage: Always rely on public-key cryptosystem and homomorphic encryption [3–6]. Usually, multiple rounds of interactions are required to perform the public key exchange and private matching between each pair of parties, which incurs high communication and computation costs to resource-limited mobile terminals in MSNP.

Based on non-homomorphic encryption-based privacy-preserving scalar product computation [7], an EWPM (Efficient Weight-based Private Matching) protocol was proposed to employ Confusion Matrix Transformation algorithm instead of computation-consuming homomorphic cryptographic system, to achieve the privacy preserving goal with a higher efficiency [8]. The main weakpoint in EWPM is that the inferred matching value doesn't have strict semantic meaning, and can only roughly represents the profile similarity among users. For example, in the following Subsect. 3.3, we give a special case, in which the obtained matching values by EWPM for two pairs of users are identical, but according to strict similarity metric (e.g., cosine similarity), those two matching values are not same.

Based on the above observation, this paper designs a Lightweighted fIne-grained Privacy-Preserving Profile matching mechanism for D2D based MSNP, LIP3, which, in comparison with the existing CMT schemes (e.g., EWPM), can provide strict and accurate profile matching value-cosine similarity result among individuals. The numerical results show that LIP3 can provide more accurate similarity measurement than EWPM, and bring no more computation and communication overheads.

The rest of this paper is organized as follows. Section 2 gives the system model of LIP3, and the adversary models dealt with in this paper. In Sect. 3, we describe the details of the proposed system, LIP3, and give an example to illustrate the advantage of LIP3 over EWPM. In Sect. 4, the security and complexity analysis are schematically provided. Finally, we briefly conclude this paper.

## 2   LIP3 System Model

### 2.1   System Architecture of LIP3

When people join MSNPs, they usually begin by creating a profile, and then interact with other users. The content of profile could be very broad, such as personal background, hobbies, contacts, places they have been to, etc. Privacy-preserving profile matching is a common and helpful way to make new friends with common interest or experience, find lost connections, or search for expert, without revealing participants' personal and private profiles.

Specifically, each user's interest profile is defined from a public attribute set consisting of $n$ attributes. The number of $n$ may range from several tens to several hundreds. Each attribute is associated with a user-specific integer value $i \in [1, l]$ (called as the weight of an attribute) indicating the corresponding user's association with this attribute. The higher the value of this attribute is, the more interest the user has in the attribute. Usually, letting $l$ equal 10 may be sufficient to differentiate user's interest level. Suppose two users Alice and Bob's interest sets are characterized as the following profile vectors $\vec{u}_A = (u_{A_1}, u_{A_2}, \ldots, u_{A_n})$ and $\vec{u}_B = (u_{B_1}, u_{B_2}, \cdots, u_{B_n})$, respectively. Each individual can modify her/his profile later on when needed. The most widely applied similarity metric to infer the matching value between individuals, say Alice and Bob, is cosine similarity:

$$similarity\,(A, B) = \frac{\vec{u}_A \cdot \vec{u}_B}{\|\vec{u}_A\| \cdot \|\vec{u}_B\|} = \frac{\sum_{i=1}^{l} u_{A_i} \cdot u_{B_i}}{\sqrt{\sum_{i=1}^{l} (u_{A_i})^2} \cdot \sqrt{\sum_{i=1}^{l} (u_{B_i})^2}} \tag{1}$$

Assume that Alice wants to find someone to chat, e.g., when waiting for the flight to depart. As the first step (Peer discovery), she broadcasts a chatting request via the MSNP application on her smartphone to discover proximate users of the same MSNP application. Suppose that she receives multiple responses including one from Bob who may also simultaneously respond to other persons. Due to time constraints or other reasons, both Alice and Bob can only interact with one stranger whose profile best matches hers or his. The next step (Profile Matching) is thus for Alice (or Bob) to compare her (or his) profile with those of others who responded to her (or whom he responded to). LIP3 will enable two users to measure the accurate similarity value between the above fine-grained privacy-preserving personal profiles using cosine similarity metrics.

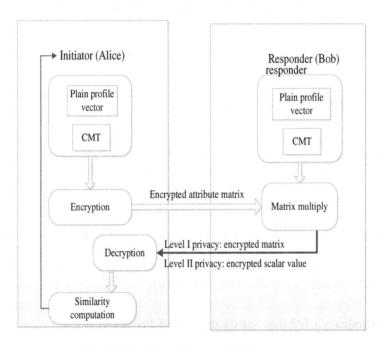

**Fig. 1.** System architecture of LIP3 scheme

Figure 1 illustrates the system architecture of the proposed privacy-preserving profile matching scheme LIP3, which is composed of two mobile users with specific interest profiles, and several component which facilitate the similarity calculation in LIP3 scheme.

The plain profile vectors in the initiator (say Alice) and responder (say Bob) are firstly transformed into corresponding attribute matrices through CMT, which can completely describe users' profiles. Then the initiator encrypts her attribute matrix and sends it to responder. The responder Bob will calculate the multiplication between the received encrypted matrix and the attribute matrix of herself. The obtained matrix (in Level I privacy) or the scalar value (in Level II privacy) will be sent to initiator who, then decrypts and obtains the cosine similarity between initiator and responder. Note that, in our proposal, the module of responder's profile vector should be explicitly sent to initiators.

## 2.2  Adversary Models

There exists attacks from outside adversaries, such as eavesdropping the wireless communication channel or modifying, replying and injecting the captured messages. We assume the users in our protocol are honest-but-curious (HBC), which means they will comply with the algorithmic procedure, but they are curious about other users and try to learn more information than allowed. Furthermore, some users may be inside attackers who monitor the matching process and obtain the intermediate results without complying the agreements. They try to infer users' profiles through these observations. Based on the adversary models, similar as [8], the following two privacy levels are defined.

- Level-I privacy: when LIP3 ends, both the initiator and responder learn nothing about each other's attribute, when they are HBC.
- Level-II privacy: when the LIP3 ends, both the initiator and responder learn nothing about each other's attribute, even when they are inside attackers.

# 3  The Detailed Procedure of LIP3

In our scheme, each individual, say Alice's profile vector is explicitly encoded into a profile matrix $A_{l \times n}$ whose elements depend on the individual's personal attributes and weights. This matrix can completely describe an user's profile, in which the row vectors indicate the weight of interest and column vectors mean the public attribute. Specifically, if the value of the $j$th attribute of Alice is set as $i$ ($i \in [1, l]$), then she sets $a_{ij} = 1$ and $a_{mj} = 0$ where $a_{mj} \in A_{l \times n}$, $m \neq i$.

A MSNP session involves two users and usually consists of three phases. First, two users need discover each other in the neighbor-discovery phase. Second, they need compare their personal profiles in the matching phase. Last, two matching users enter the interaction phase for real information exchange.

## 3.1  Preliminary LIP3 that Satisfy the Level-I Privacy

The main contribution of our paper is that LIP3 explicitly defines a weight matrix $W_{l \times l} = (w_{ij})_{l \times l}$ through which the accurate cosine similarity can be inferred, without revealing individuals' private profiles. Specifically, the element $w_{ij}$ is given as the Eq. (2).

$$\left(w_{ij}\right)_{l \times l} = i \cdot j \tag{2}$$

In LIP3, the initiator (Alice) and responder (Bob) respectively hold the attribute matrices $A_{l \times n}$ and $B_{l \times n}$, which are transformed from the both users' plain profile vectors. $p$ and $q$ are two large primes. $C_{l \times n}$ and $R_{l \times n}$ are two matrixes used for hiding personal information. The vector $\overrightarrow{k}$ is the secret key kept by initiator to decrypt the original results. The detailed procedure of LIP3 is given as follows.

- The initiator initializes her personal profile according to Algorithm 1, which can be run offline, and broadcasts her friend discovery request to others. When Algorithm 1 ends, the initiator keeps $\overrightarrow{k} = [k_1, k_2, \cdots, k_l]$, and $q$ secretly and sends $A^*_{l \times n}$ to the responder;
- After receiving $A^*_{l \times n}$, the responder computes $D_{l \times l} = (d_{ij})_{l \times l}$ according to Algorithm 2 and sends $D_{l \times l}$ to the initiator;
- The initiator operates the following steps: $T_{l \times l} = (t_{ij})_{l \times l} = (d_{ij} + k_i) mod \ q$. It is shown that the above constructed equation $T_{l \times l} = A_{l \times n} \times B^T_{l \times n}$. Moreover, let $T^*_{l \times l} = (t^*_{ij})_{l \times l}$, and $t^*_{ij} = \frac{t_{ij} - (t_{ij} mod \ p^2)}{p^2}$;
- The initiator considers the corresponding weights and computes:

$$H_{l \times l} = W_{l \times l} \cdot *T^*_{l \times l} = \begin{pmatrix} w_{11} \cdot t^*_{11} & \cdots & w_{1l} \cdot t^*_{1l} \\ \vdots & \ddots & \vdots \\ w_{l1} \cdot t^*_{l1} & \cdots & w_{ll} \cdot t^*_{ll} \end{pmatrix} \quad (3)$$

- in which the operator $\cdot *$ denote multiplying the corresponding elements of two matrices $W_{l \times l}$ and $T^*_{l \times l}$ to obtain the matrix $H_{l \times l}$.
- The initiator calculates the matching value $\tau = \sum_{i=1}^{l} \sum_{j=1}^{l} h_{ij}$, which equals the value $\overrightarrow{u}_A \cdot \overrightarrow{u}_B$, then the cosine similarity between two interacting individuals can be obtained.

The Algorithms 1 and 2 used in the LIP3 operation procedures are given as follows.

**Algorithm 1.** Initialization algorithm for private configuration

---

```
Input: Initiator's attribute matrix A_lxn;
Output: Encrypted matrix A*_lxn;
Choose two large primes p and q, where |p| = 256 and
q > (n + 1) · l² · p²;
Randomly generate two matrixes C_lxn and R_lxn, ∀c_ij ∈
C_lxn, ∀r_ij ∈ R_lxn, Σ_{i=1}^{l}(Σ_{j=1}^{n} c_ij) < (p − l · n), |r_ij · q| ≈ 1024;
∀a_ij ∈ A_lxn, ∀a*_ij ∈ A*_lxn, k_i ∈k⃗, the following procedure is done:
FOR (i=1; i ≤ l; i++) DO
    k_i = 0;
FOR (j=1; j ≤ n; j++) DO
IF a_ij = 1 THEN a*_ij = p + c_ij + r_ij · q;
ELSE      a*_ij = c_ij + r_ij · q;
ENDIF
k_i = k_i + r_ij · q − c_ij;
ENDFOR
ENDFOR
```

---

**Algorithm 2.** LIP3 for achieving the Level-I privacy

---

```
Input: A*ₗₓₙ, Bₗₓₙ;
Output: The cosine similarity between two individuals;
```
Compute $\boldsymbol{D}_{l \times l} = \left(t_{ij}\right)_{l \times l}$ through the following operations:
```
FOR (i =1; i ≤ l; i++) DO
    FOR (j=1; j ≤ l; j++) DO
```
$\qquad d_{ij} = 0;$
```
        FOR (m=1; m ≤ n; m++) DO
```
$\qquad\qquad$ **IF** $(b_{im} = 1)$ **THEN** $d_{ij} = d_{ij} + p \cdot a^*_{im};$
$\qquad$ **ELSE** $\quad d_{ij} = d_{ij} + a^*_{im};$
```
        ENDIF
        ENDFOR
    ENDFOR
ENDFOR
```
The responder sends computed $\boldsymbol{D}_{l \times l}$ and $\|\vec{v}\|$ to the initiator, according to the above equations (1), (2) and (3), the initiator computes $\tau$, then

$$similarity(A, B) = \frac{\tau}{\|\vec{u}_A\| \cdot \|\vec{u}_B\|}$$

---

## 3.2    Enhanced LIP3 Satisfying Level-II Privacy

Note that the above procedures can only satisfies the privacy level I. In order to resist the malicious users to achieve the Level-II privacy, instead of directly sending the matrix $\boldsymbol{D}_{l \times l}$ to initiator, the responder can send the scalar value $\sigma = \sum_{i=1}^{l}\sum_{j=1}^{l} t_{ij}$ to initiator, in which $\left(t_{ij}\right)_{l \times l} = \boldsymbol{D}_{l \times l} \cdot *W_{l \times l}$ is calculated based on Eq. (2). And then, on receiving the message $\sigma$, the initiator decrypts the matching value $\tau$ via the following operators:

$$\tau_1 = \left(\sigma + l\left(\sum_{i=1}^{l} k_i\right)\right) mod\ q; \quad \tau = \vec{u}_A \cdot \vec{u}_B = \frac{\tau_1 - (\tau_1 mod\ p^2)}{p^2}$$

Then the cosine similarity between Alice and Bob is following:

$$similarity(A, B) = \frac{\tau}{\left\|\vec{u}_A\right\| \cdot \left\|\vec{u}_B\right\|}$$

## 3.3    The Advantage of LIP3 over EWPM

We use a simple example to verify the correctness of our scheme. We assume three users Alice, Bob and Charles are within the communication range. The number of attributes n, is 3, and the maximal attribute value l, is 2. Suppose Alice is the initiator, with profile $\vec{u}_A = (1, 1, 2)$, translate to matrix is $A_{2\times3} = \begin{pmatrix} 1 & 1 & 0 \\ 0 & 0 & 1 \end{pmatrix}$, Bob and Charles are the responders and the profiles of Bob and Charles are $\vec{u}_B = (1, 1, 1)$, matrix $B_{2\times3} = \begin{pmatrix} 1 & 1 & 1 \\ 0 & 0 & 0 \end{pmatrix}$, $\vec{u}_c = (1, 2, 1)$ matrix $C_{2\times3} = \begin{pmatrix} 1 & 0 & 1 \\ 0 & 1 & 0 \end{pmatrix}$, respectively. Since the calculation process between Alice and Bob is similar to that of Alice and Charles, we just describe the process between Alice and Bob in detail, and give the matching value between Alice and Charles directly. Similarly as [8], we can get: $T^*_{2\times2} = \begin{pmatrix} 2 & 0 \\ 1 & 0 \end{pmatrix}$ which numerically equals the result as $A_{2\times3} \times B^T_{2\times3}$.

Then, according to Eq. (2), we obtain $W_{2\times2} = \begin{pmatrix} 1 & 2 \\ 2 & 4 \end{pmatrix}$, then $H_{l\times l} = W_{2\times2} \cdot$
$*T^*_{2\times2} = \begin{pmatrix} 2 & 0 \\ 2 & 0 \end{pmatrix}$ ; $\tau_{AB} = \sum_{i=1}^{l}\sum_{j=1}^{l} h_{ij} = 4$.

Note that, interestingly, the term $\tau$ equals the value of $\vec{u}_A \cdot \vec{u}_B$. Therefore, the similarity value between Alice and Bob is: $similarity(A, B) = \frac{\tau_{AB}}{\|\vec{u}_A\| \cdot \|\vec{u}_B\|} = \frac{4}{\sqrt{3} \times \sqrt{6}} = 0.943$.

Similarly, we can get the value $\tau_{AC} = 5$, and the similarity value between Alice and Charles is: $similarity(A, C) = \frac{\tau_{AC}}{\|\vec{u}_A\| \cdot \|\vec{u}_C\|} == \frac{5}{\sqrt{6} \times \sqrt{6}} = 0.833$.

Obviously, For initiator Alice, Bob is the better matching person than Charles.

However, using the protocol EWPM proposed in [8], We can only obtain $S_{AB} = 3$ (the matching value between Alice and Bob), and $S_{AC} = 3$ (the matching value between Alice and Charles). Those values neither have strict semantic meaning, nor distinguish whether Alice is more matching with Bob or Charles. Thus, LIP3 is obviously advantage over EWPM in terms of matching accuracy (measured with profile similarity).

## 4 Preliminary Performance Analysis

### 4.1 Security Analysis

① **Schematic Proof of Privacy Level I.** Depending on secure property of the confused matrix transformation, the correctness of the LIP3 is straightforward. However, in level I privacy, through $D_{l\times l}$, the initiator can obtain the $T_{l\times l}$ that numerically equals $A_{l\times n} \times B^T_{l\times n}$, and then it is possible for initiator to infer the responder's profile matrix $B$. However, as they are both HBC users, the initiator will not monitor the matching process and decrypt the intermediate results get the original results of $A_{l\times n} \times B^T_{l\times n}$, so she learns nothing about the responder other than the matching value. The privacy of the responder can be protected too.

**Table 1.** Complexity comparison among LIP3, EWPM and fine-grained privacy-preserving profile matching schemes

| Protocol | Offline Comp. | | Online Comp | | Comm. (in bits) | |
|---|---|---|---|---|---|---|
| | Initiator | Responder | Initiator | Responder | Initiator | Responder |
| Fine-grained | $2l \cdot n \cdot exp_1 + l \cdot n \cdot mul_2$ | – | $1 \cdot exp_2$ | $1 \cdot exp_1 + 1 \cdot exp_2 + n \cdot mul_2$ | $l \cdot n \cdot 2048$ | $1 \cdot 2048$ |
| EWPM Level-I | $2l \cdot n \cdot add + l \cdot n \cdot mul_1$ | – | $3l \cdot l \cdot add + 2l \cdot l \cdot mul_1$ | $l \cdot n \cdot add + l \cdot n \cdot mul_1$ | $(l \cdot n + 2) \cdot 1024$ | $l \cdot l \cdot 1024$ |
| EWPM Level-II | $2l \cdot n \cdot add + l \cdot n \cdot mul_1$ | – | $(l+2) \cdot add$ | $l \cdot n \cdot add + l \cdot n \cdot mul_1$ | $(l \cdot n + 2) \cdot 1024$ | $1 \cdot 1024$ |
| LIP3 Level-I | $2l \cdot n \cdot add + (l \cdot n + l \cdot l) \cdot mul_1$ | – | $3l \cdot l \cdot add + 2l \cdot l \cdot mul_1$ | $l \cdot n \cdot add + l \cdot n \cdot mul_1$ | $(l \cdot n + 2) \cdot 1024$ | $l \cdot l \cdot 1024$ |
| LIP3 Level-II | $2l \cdot n \cdot add + (l \cdot n + l \cdot l) \cdot mul_1$ | – | $(l+2) \cdot add$ | $l \cdot n \cdot add + l \cdot n \cdot mul_1$ | $(l \cdot n + 2) \cdot 1024$ | $1 \cdot 1024$ |

② **Schematic Proof of Privacy Level II.** The key point of proving the privacy level II of LIP3 lies in that: In level II, the responder only sends $\sigma$ instead of $D_{l \times l}$ to the initiator. Even the initiator Alice has $\overrightarrow{k}$ to get the original data, she has no way to learn the computation process. While the responder Bob knows the process, but he cannot obtain the $\overrightarrow{k}$. In this way, the users' privacy is protected from the internal attackers.

### 4.2   Complexity Analysis

Similar as EWPM [8], we can also use the offline, online computation cost as well as the communication overhead to measure the complexity of the proposed scheme LIP3. The computation cost is evaluated using the number of the multiplication and exponentiation operations, since these operations are always resource-consuming in mobile devices. The communication overhead is evaluated by counting the transmitting and receiving bits.

In our paper, h represents the hash function SHA-256, $exp_1$ means 1024-bit exponentiation operation, $exp_2$ means 2048-bit exponentiation operation, *add* indicates modular addition, and $mul_1$ and $mul_2$ mean 1024-bit and 2048-bit multiplication operation, respectively.

Assume that each user's interest profile has $n$ attributes, and the highest attribute value is $l$. Table 1 gives the corresponding complexities in the existing Fine-grained [4] scheme, EWPM [8], and our proposal LIP3. Note that LIP3 uses similar matching method as EWPM, so we compare the complexities of both Level-I and Level-II in those two schemes.

From Table 1, we can observe that, similar as EWPM, compared with Fine-grained scheme, LIP3 reduces computation and communication costs significantly. Specifically, in comparison EWPM, our scheme LIP3 only brings additional computation of the modules of the initiator's and responder's profile vectors, and additional transmission of a scalar value, which are all constant operations, independent of the parameters used in LIP3, e.g., the number of attributes $n$, and the maximal attribute value $l$. Those trivial additional overhead can be totally negligible.

## 5   Conclusion

In this paper, we propose an effective and secure CMT based privacy-preserving profile matching scheme for D2D based MSNP, LIP3, which can infer the accurate cosine similarity between two users by considering both the number of the common interests and the corresponding weights. In comparison with the existing CMT schemes (e.g., EWPM), LIP 3 can provide strict and accurate profile matching value, i.e., cosine similarity result, among individuals, without incurring extra computation and communication overhead. Therefore, LIP3 is suitable to be implemented by resource-constrained mobile devices, especially for various MSNP applications.

**Acknowledgments.** This work was supported by the NSFC 61171092, the JiangSu Educational Bureau Project under Grant 14KJA510004, and Prospective Research Project on Future Networks (JiangSu Future Networks Innovation Institute).

# References

1. Wang, Y.F., Vasilakos, A.V., Jin, Q., Ma, J.H.: Survey on mobile social networking in proximity (MSNP): approaches, challenges and architecture. ACM/Springer, Wirel. Netw. (WINET) **20**(6), 1295–1311 (2014)
2. Wang, Y.F., Xu J.: Overview on privacy-preserving profile-matching mechanisms in mobile social networks in proximity (MSNP). In: Proceedings of the 9th Asia Joint Conference on Information Security (AsiaJCIS) (2014)
3. Niu, B., Zhang, T., Zhu, X., et al.: Priority-Aware Private Matching Schemes for Proximity-based Mobile Social Networks, arXiv preprint arXiv: 1401.8064 (2014)
4. Zhang, R., Zhang, Y., Sun, J., et al.: Fine-grained private matching for proximity-based mobile social networking. In: Proceedings of the IEEE INFOCOM (2012)
5. Zhang, R., Zhang, J., Zhang, Y., et al.: Privacy-preserving profile matching for proximity-based mobile social networking. IEEE J. Selected Areas Commun. **31**(9), 656–668 (2013)
6. Zhu, H.J., Du, S.G., Li, M.Y., Gao, Z.Y.: Fairness-aware and privacy-preserving friend matching protocol in mobile social networks. IEEE Trans. Emerg. Topics Comput. **1**(1), 192–200 (2013)
7. Lu, R., Lin, X., Shen, X.: SPOC: a secure and privacy-preserving opportunistic computing framework for mobile-healthcare emergency. IEEE Trans. Parallel Distrib. Syst. **24**(3), 614–624 (2013)
8. Zhu, X.Y., Liu, J., Jiang, S.R., Chen, Z.B, Li, H., Efficient weight-based private matching for proximity-based mobile social networks. In: Proceedings of the IEEE ICC (2014)

# Context-Aware QoS Assurance for Smart Grid Big Data Processing with Elastic Cloud Resource Reconfiguration

Luyan Nie[1], Chuanzhi Xie[1], Yujun Yin[1], and Xin Li[2(✉)]

[1] NARI Group Corporation, Nanjing 211000, China
[2] College of Computer Science and Technology,
Nanjing University of Aeronautics and Astronautics, Nanjing 211106, China
lics@nuaa.edu.cn

**Abstract.** Smart grid is one of the most important area for big data applications, while the cloud-based platform is believed to be the deserved paradigm to conduct smart grid big data processing. Hence, elastic resource reconfiguration is a critical issue for smart grid big data application, since the widespread of data sources make the workload changing frequently. In this paper, we focus on the problem of context-aware QoS assurance for electric power application via elastic cloud resource reconfiguration, especially using the VM migration method. We present a framework of dynamical resource reconfiguration that characterize the major components needed for the QoS assurance during elastic resource reconfiguration. We take VM migration as the special concern, and discuss the major issues during VM migration procedure, and propose a VM migration mechanism for QoS assurance for application.

**Keywords:** Big data processing · Cloud data center · Context-aware · Elastic resource reconfiguration · Framework · QoS assurance · Smart grid

## 1 Introduction

Smart grid, which includes various computing technology, communication technology, and auto-control technology, is the future of electricity power industry [3,5]. Also, smart grid is one of the most important potential area for big data applications, since the widespread of electric power data and deployment of advanced sensing devices. It is believed that big data technology will be a powerful driving force for smart grid, and the cloud system becomes the deserved platform to conduct data analysis for smart grid big data [1,11].

Because of the decentrality of electric power facilities, the geo-distributed cloud data centers are necessary to deploy electrical applications, which is more than electric power data processing. Other electrical applications include collection information system, wide-area measurement system, all kinds of management system [13], scheduling system [7], and so on. In the virtualization-based

© Springer International Publishing Switzerland 2015
G. Wang et al. (Eds.): ICA3PP 2015 Workshops, LNCS 9532, pp. 177–186, 2015.
DOI: 10.1007/978-3-319-27161-3_16

cloud system, physical machine (PM) is partitioned into multiple logically isolation virtual machines (VMs), and VM is the basic unit for resource allocation
and resource sharing, and a set of VMs cooperate to conduct the application
tasks. Hence, all kinds of electrical applications (or services) are deployed on
VMs. Figure 1 shows the architecture of service provision with cloud infrastructure. The cloud data center provides computational resource and storage for
the VMs, and the resources are eventually utilized by applications for service
provision. Users can access the service from anywhere as long as the Internet is
accessible.

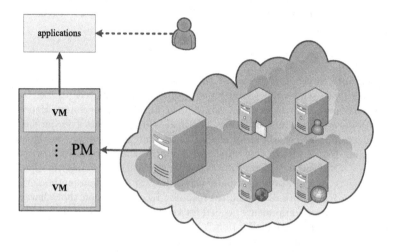

**Fig. 1.** The Architecture of service provision

For each application or service, there should be an SLA (Service Level Agreement) between cloud platform and application, which points out the QoS (Quality of Service) demands for each VM or service. Therefore, to guarantee the
QoS of application, sufficient cloud resources should be allocated to the relevant
VMs. However, application is evolving all the time and its resource requirement
is changing caused by the variation of user demands (workload). The VM that
host the application should adaptively update the occupied resource to synchronize the workload. Hence, it is necessary for the cloud data center to carry out
dynamical resource reconfiguration for the VMs to ensure QoS.

It is an important but complex issue to reschedule the resources dynamically
in cloud data centers. VM migration is an effective approach to achieve quickly
resource reconfiguration for VMs. At the same time, resource reconfiguration
may cause some negative impacts, some VMs benefit from the resource reconfiguration while some suffers. For example, VM migration will lead to service disruption for application that hosted on the VM to be migrated, it will also lead to
longer service response time. Therefore, an efficient VM resource reconfiguration
strategy is necessary to achieve efficient resource utilization while guaranteeing
the QoS for applications.

In this paper, we investigate the problem of adaptive cloud resource reconfiguration for QoS assurance for electrical application, especially for smart grid big data processing. We take into account various context of VM and cloud data center, and present a framework of resource reconfiguration. We take VM migration as the main approach, and propose a VM migration mechanism to determine how the migration procedure runs.

## 2  Background and Scenario

Given cloud data center with homogeneous PMs, we use *slot* to represent basic resource unit [9], which contains CPU, memory, disk, etc. For each VM, it occupies one or more *slots*. For all of the VMs, if their resource requirements are satisfied fully, then the current resource configuration is known as stable. Otherwise, there must exist resource conflict on some PM, resource conflict means that the sum of the resource requirements of the VMs that placed on the same PM exceeds the capacity of PM.

Stable resource configuration is the ideal state for cloud resource utilization. However, the application host on VM is evolving, and its resource requirements changes over time. Resource conflict may occur when more resources are required from the VMs, since the limitation of resource capacity of each PM. Hence, effectively dynamical resource reconfiguration should be conducted to eliminate the resource conflict and achieve a new stable resource configuration.

It should be aware that the resource reconfiguration is a costly process, e.g. service disruption, longer service response time, more energy consumption, network delay, etc. Therefore, the resource reconfiguration should be carried out as less as possible. However, improper resource reconfiguration will lead to new stable resource configuration for very short duration, and another resource reconfiguration must be carried out. So, a good resource reconfiguration should produce a longish duration of stable resource configuration. It is a complicated problem to execute resource reconfiguration due to the complexity of various resource demands from VMs. We present a framework to exhibit the global view of resource reconfiguration, as shown in Fig. 2. We interpret the components of the framework as follows:

- **Context.** Context indicates the feature of the VMs (application) and the cloud data center. Cloud data center architecture is one of the context information, which will be used to determine the communication cost between any two PMs in the data center. SLA and QoS are important information for dynamical resource reconfiguration, which will be taken into account when we decide which VM should be selected to reconfigure, since some VMs will be suffer during the resource reconfiguration. QoS indicates the priority of the VMs to enjoy more benefit.
- **Current Resource Configuration.** Current resource configuration refers to the current resource requirements of the VMs, and it is also the input of resource prediction model. The current resource configuration will be treated

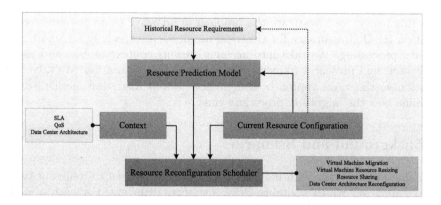

**Fig. 2.** The framework of dynamic resource reconfiguration

as historical data after resource reconfiguration, and also be used as input of resource prediction model.

- **Resource Prediction Model.** Resource prediction model predicts that the resource requirement for each VM. The predicted resource requirement will be used to guide how the resource reconfiguration executes. Historical resource requirements is one of the inputs of the model, it is very useful when the applications have periodic workloads, for example, periodic task processing for big data sets. Many prediction models have been proposed for various applications in cloud environment [2, 6].

- **Resource Reconfiguration Scheduler.** It is the core component of the framework for elastic resource reconfiguration. Resource reconfiguration scheduler conduct the adaptive resource reconfiguration procedure according to the reconfiguration principles. There could be various methods to achieve elastic resource reconfiguration. VM resource resizing is the simplest way to implement resource reconfiguration. However, the resource capacity of each PM is limited. It will be infeasible when the sum of the required resources of the VMs placed on the same PM are greater than the capacity of PM, which means the resource conflict occurs. Hence, resource sharing or VM migration will be adopted to mitigate the resource conflict. Resource sharing [8, 10] means that some VMs share the same resource slots, which is an effective method when the VMs have different resource utilization mode. Resource sharing cannot eliminate the resource conflict, especially when the VMs that placed on the same PM increase their resource requirements at the same period. VM migration an efficient method to eliminate the resource conflict of the VMs that placed on the same PM. But, VM migration is costly, since the migration is bandwidth-intensive and time-consuming. Data center architecture reconfiguration is another method to cope with the resource conflict, especially for eliminating the network bottleneck. However, data center architecture reconfiguration is really time-consuming, since it must be operated humanly, and it is a fallible procedure. Generally, VM migration is the most suitable method to conduct resource reconfiguration. We will take VM migration as the major method to conduct resource reconfiguration in this paper.

## 3    Virtual Machine Migration

To simplify the description of the VM migration, we introduce a formal definition of VM migration as follow.

**Definition 1** *[(**VM migration** $M(V_k, P_i, P_j)$)]. We define a VM migration M $(V_k, P_i, P_j)$ as that the VM $V_k$ is migrated from PM $P_i$ to PM $P_j$, and it can be simplified as $M(k, i, j)$.*

VM migration is one of the most important method to conduct cloud resource reconfiguration, which can achieve all kinds of goals. To gain better understand about the VM migration, we give an example in Fig. 3. In this figure, there are 3 homogeneous PMs and 6 VMs with different resource requirements. We can achieve various goals via different migrations. For example, VM migration $M(1, 1, 2)$ is an effective way to realize VM consolidation, which can increase the resource utilization and decrease the number of running PMs. This is because PM 1 will be idle via migration $M(1, 1, 2)$, and can be turned off or be switched into sleep mode. This is also an efficient way to achieve energy conservation for cloud data center. If the performance of VM is the major concern, load balancing is the straightforward target since the VMs hosted on the same PM will affect each other, and cannot realize fully performance isolation [4]. VM migration $M(4, 3, 1)$ can achieve load balancing in this example.

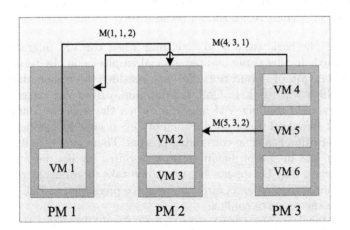

**Fig. 3.** An example of VM migration

Resource conflict is another reason that drives VM migration, which is also the major concern in this paper. For example, when VM 5 needs more resources, while PM 3 has no more available resources to be allocated. Hence, VM migration $M(5, 3, 2)$ is a feasible way to eliminate the resource conflict. However, it may be not the best choice to migrate VM 5 to PM 2, since if VM 2 or VM 3 need more resource, and another migration $M(2, 2, 1)$ or $M(3, 2, 1)$ is necessary to eliminate the resource conflict on PM 2. Here, we define the **VM migration wave** to characterize the phenomenon that one VM migration is caused by another VM migration between very short time duration. The new VM migration may be driven by resource conflict, VM consolidation, or load balancing. In this example, the continuous VM migration $M(5, 3, 2)$ and $M(2, 2, 1)$ is the VM migration wave. We will give more discussion about the case when VM 5 needs more resources.

- Though VM 4 maintains its resource requirement, the migration of VM 4 (e.g. $M(4, 3, 1)$) may be a better choice when VM 4 has little concern on the service disruption time, and has less size, while VM 5 has a strict demand on the service disruption constraint.
- The migration of VM 5 may be better before the resource conflict occurs, since the service disruption will be more serious during the resource conflict period. However, if the VM 6 finish its task and be removed from the PM when VM 5 requires more resources, it would be better to conduct the VM migration later than the resource conflict.

VM migration is a cost-consuming and time-consuming procedure, and it will cause service disruption of the application. Hence, the ideal VM migration should lead to a steady resource configuration state for longish time duration, but not for very short time. Therefore, we should avoid the VM migration wave during the resource reconfiguration procedure. From the example, we know that there are two important issues should be addressed:

- **Occasion**. The basic issue is to determine when the VM migration should be conducted. In this paper, we pay special emphasis on the target of guaranteeing the QoS of application. We just consider the reason that resource conflict, which will result in QoS deterioration, drives VM migration. Intuitively, we should conduct VM migration when the resource conflict occurs. However, it may lead to longer duration of QoS decline for application, since the VM migration is a time-consuming process. There may be still problem if we conduct VM migration before or after resource conflict, because the VM migration wave may be appear. So, we should take more consideration based on the resource requirements form the resource prediction model. The goal is to mitigate the resource conflict.
- **Object Selection**. This issue means that we should determine the VM to be migrated and the new destination PM. It contains two factors here, VM and PM, and this two factors cannot be considered independently. Intuitively, the VM that requires more resource should be selected and migrated. However, if the VM has larger size, it will cause longer service disruption, especially when the VM has more strict demands on QoS. Hence, it is necessary to take into

account to the QoS demands for the VMs when some VM need to be migrated. At the same time, the PM selection is also has significant impact on the VM migration, since inappropriate VM migration will lead to VM migration wave, which should be avoided. So, the context and current resource configuration should be taken into account when conduct the VM and PM selection.

## 4  VM Migration Mechanism

Here, we present a VM migration mechanism for QoS assurance resource reconfiguration. As mentioned above, there are two issues should be addressed when we adopt VM migration, the occasion and the participants. To clarify the description, we make the following settings:

- Time is divided into time-slots. The resource reconfiguration occurs at the beginning of each time-slot. It is easy to understand that the resource reconfiguration should not be operated continuous, since the resource reconfiguration is costly.
- The resource requirement of next time-slot for each VM can be given by the prediction model. For a practical resource prediction model, it is more like to predict the resource requirements of the next time-slot with high probability.
- Context of the VMs and the current resource configuration are given. For each VM, there exists SLA between the cloud provider and cloud user, hence, the context of the VMs is easy to know for the cloud data center. At the same time, it is easy to deploy resource monitors to collect the resource usage for each PM. So, the current resource configuration is easy to achieve.
- The architecture of cloud data center is known, which can define the communication cost and delay of VM migration between any two PMs.
- The VM migration cost is defined as proportional to the size of VM, i.e. the resource slots that the VM occupies. It is a widely used assumption in most related works, since the content in the memory is the major object to be migrated [12].

To define the resource configuration and the cost of VM migration quantitatively, we introduce some notations to represent resource requirements and QoS demands for VM. For VM $V_k$ (or just VM $k$), its resource requirement of the current time-slot is $\Theta_k$, and $\Omega_k$ indicates the actually resources that be allocated to VM $k$, i.e., VM $k$ occupies $\Omega_k$ slots. Let $\Lambda_k$ represent the resource requirement of VM $k$ at the next time-slot given by the resource prediction model. For each PM, let $C$ represent the capacity of PMs, i.e. every PM contains $C$ slots.

We aim to propose a feasible VM migration mechanism to optimize the QoS assurance for the application. To characterize the cost of resource conflict and VM migration, we introduce *penalty* functions for them.

- For the VM migration $M(k, i, j)$, its penalty function is defined as:

$$g(k, i, j) = \Theta_k \cdot w_{ij} \cdot r_k, \tag{1}$$

where $w_{ij}$ is the communication cost from PM $i$ to PM $j$, it can be the number of switches of the network link from PM $i$ to PM $j$ under the given data center architecture [9]. $r_k$ means the cost of service disruption of VM $k$, which indicates the *priority* determined by the QoS requirement of VM $k$. Less $r_k$ is more likely to be migrated.

– For the resource conflict appears on PM $i$, its penalty function is defined as:

$$f(i) = \sum_{k=1}^{n} (1 - \frac{\Omega_k}{\Theta_k}) \cdot r_k \cdot X_{ik}. \tag{2}$$

where $n$ is the number of VMs, and $X_{ik}$ is an indicator function:

$$X_{ik} = \begin{cases} 1, & \text{VM } V_k \text{ is hosted on PM } P_i; \\ 0, & \text{otherwise.} \end{cases} \tag{3}$$

We should be aware that the resource conflict will continue in the next time-slots, unless some VMs reduce their resource requirements and the resource conflict is eliminated.

Based on the above penalty functions, it is easy to make decision to maintain the the resource configuration or conduct resource reconfiguration via VM migration. If some VM will be migrated, we should decide where the VM be migrated to. To select the proper destination PM, we define a PM state $Q_i$ to indicate the probability that resource conflict will appear on PM $i$ at the next time-slot.

$$Q_i = \begin{cases} 0, & \text{if } \sum_{k=1}^{n} X_{ik} \cdot (\Lambda_k - \Theta_k) < C - \sum_{k=1}^{n} X_{ik} \cdot \Theta_k; \\ 1, & \text{if } \sum_{k=1}^{n} X_{ik} \cdot (\Lambda_k - \Theta_k) > C - \sum_{k=1}^{n} X_{ik} \cdot \Theta_k; \\ \dfrac{\sum_{k=1}^{n} X_{ik} \cdot (\Lambda_k - \Theta_k)}{C - \sum_{k=1}^{n} X_{ik} \cdot \Theta_k}, & \text{otherwise.} \end{cases} \tag{4}$$

Hence, we should select the PM with lowest resource conflict probability as the destination PM.

According to the above discussion, we can propose two basic principles for the resource reconfiguration:

– Prevention First. The resource reconfiguration (VM migration) should be conducted before the resource conflict, which is an efficient way to avoid VM migration wave. We can reduce the global penalty by pay less migration cost.
– Less Penalty. We should select the one with less penalty from the resource conflict and VM migration. It is easy to implement by comparing the two penalty functions.

Hence, we take the QoS demands as the major concern during resource reconfiguration. We present the basic procedure of the VM migration as follows:

- Locate the resource conflict. According to the current resource configuration and resource prediction model, it is easy to discover the PMs where the resource conflict will appear at the next time-slot.
- Choose less penalty. For the PM that will contain resource conflict, it is easy to make a decision to conduct VM migration or not according to penalty functions, Eqs. 1 and 2.
- Host selection. When some VM will be migrated, the most suitable destination PM is the one that will not trigger new VM migration, i.e. avoid the VM migration wave. It can be decided by the Eq. 4.

## 5 Conclusion

In this paper, we address the problem of context-aware QoS assurance for application via elastic cloud resource reconfiguration, especially using the VM migration method. We present a framework of dynamical resource reconfiguration that characterize the major components needed for the QoS assurance during elastic resource reconfiguration. We take VM migration as the special concern, and discuss the major issues during VM migration procedure, and propose a VM migration mechanism for QoS assurance for application.

**Acknowledgements.** We want to thanks the reviewers for insightful comments. Xin Li's work is supported in part by Project Funded by China Postdoctoral Science Foundation.

## References

1. Baek, J., Vu, Q.H., Liu, J.K., Huang, X., Xiang, Y.: A secure cloud computing based framework for big data information management of smart grid. IEEE Trans. Cloud Comput. **3**(2), 233–244 (2015)
2. Bennani, M.N., Menasce, D.A.: Resource allocation for autonomic data centers using analytic performance models. In: IEEE International Conference on Autonomic Computing, pp. 229–240 (2005)
3. Bera, S., Misra, S., Rodrigues, J.J.: Cloud computing applications for smart grid: a survey. IEEE Trans. Parallel Distrib. Syst. **26**(5), 1477–1494 (2015)
4. Cherkasova, L., Gardner, R.: Measuring CPU overhead for I/O processing in the XEN virtual machine monitor. In: USENIX Annual Technical Conference, pp. 387–390 (2005)
5. Hernandez, L., Baladron, C., Aguiar, J.M., Carro, B., Sanchez-Esguevillas, A.J., Lloret, J., Massana, J.: A survey on electric power demand forecasting: future trends in smart grids, microgrids and smart buildings. IEEE Commun. Surv. Tutorials **16**(3), 1460–1495 (2014)
6. Jung, G., Joshi, K.R., Hiltunen, M.A., Schlichting, R.D., Pu, C.: Generating adaptation policies for multi-tier applications in consolidated server environment. In: IEEE International Conference on Autonomic Computing, pp. 23–32 (2008)
7. Lin, Y.H., Tsai, M.S.: An advanced home energy management system facilitated by nonintrusive load monitoring with automated multiobjective power scheduling. IEEE Trans. Smart Grid **6**(4), 1839–1851 (2015)

8. Luo, Z., Qian, Z.: Burstiness-aware server consolidation via queuing theory app-roach in a computing cloud. In: IEEE International Parallel and Distributed Processing Symposium, pp. 332–341 (2013)
9. Meng, X., Pappas, V., Zhang, L.: Improving the scalability of data center networks with traffic-aware virtual machine placement. In: IEEE International Conference on Computer Communications, pp. 1154–1162 (2010)
10. Popa, L., Kumar, G., Chowdhury, M., Krishnamurthy, A., Ratnasamy, S., Stoica, I.: Faircloud: Sharing the network in cloud computing. In: ACM International Conference on the Applications, Technologies, Architectures, and Protocols for Computer Communication, pp. 187–198 (2012)
11. Simmhan, Y., Aman, S., Kumbhare, A., Liu, R., Stevens, S., Zhou, Q., Prasanna, V.: Cloud-based software platform for big data analytics in smart grids. Comput. Sci. Eng. **15**(4), 38–47 (2013)
12. Verma, A., Ahuja, P., Neogi, A.: pMapper: power and migration cost aware applica-tion placement in virtualized systems. In: Issarny, V., Schantz, R. (eds.) Middleware 2008. LNCS, vol. 5346, pp. 243–264. Springer, Heidelberg (2008)
13. Zhang, W., Xu, Y., Liu, W., Zang, C., Yu, H.: Distributed online optimal energy management for smart grids. IEEE Trans. Parallel Distrib. Syst. **11**(3), 717–727 (2015)

# Continuous User Identity Verification for Trusted Operators in Control Rooms

Enrico Schiavone$^{(\boxtimes)}$, Andrea Ceccarelli, and Andrea Bondavalli

Department of Mathematics and Informatics, University of Florence, 50134 Florence, Italy
{enrico.schiavone,andrea.ceccarelli,bondavalli}@unifi.it

**Abstract.** Human operators in control rooms are often responsible of issuing critical commands, and in charge of managing sensitive data. Insiders must be prevented to operate on the system: they may benefit of their position in the control room to fool colleagues, and gain access to machines or accounts. This paper proposes an authentication system for deterring and detecting malicious access to the workstations of control rooms. Specifically tailored for the operators in the control room of the crisis management system Secure!, the solution aims to guarantee authentication and non-repudiation of operators, reducing the risk that unauthorized personnel (including intruders) misuses a workstation. A continuous multi-biometric authentication mechanism is developed and applied in which biometric data is acquired transparently from the operator and verified continuously through time. This paper presents the authentication system design and prototype, its execution and experimental results.

**Keywords:** Biometrics · Verification · Trust · Security · Control rooms

## 1 Introduction

Secure user authentication is fundamental for several ICT (Information and Communication Technology) systems. User authentication systems are traditionally based on pairs of username and password and verify the identity of the user only at login phase. No checks are performed during working sessions, which are terminated by an explicit logout or expire after an idle activity period of the user. While this is often sufficient, it may not result enough against *insider attackers* [14, 18] in control rooms, where operators are using their workstation to access potentially sensitive data and to issue critical commands for the entire working session; the operators are directly responsible for such commands and for the data accessed, modified and deleted.

In this paper we consider the behavior and actions of the human operators working in the control room of the Secure! [1] *crisis management system*. Such operators are in charge of analysing and interpreting situations that describe the current status of an emergence. Using the information available, the operator from his workstation (mainly via text messages, using a keyboard) is able to command intervention teams on field, and to dispatch instructions to civilians in the target area.

More details regarding the objectives of the Secure! project and its resulting system are available in [1].

© Springer International Publishing Switzerland 2015
G. Wang et al. (Eds.): ICA3PP 2015 Workshops, LNCS 9532, pp. 187–200, 2015.
DOI: 10.1007/978-3-319-27161-3_17

It is required to protect the control rooms and its workstations from unauthorized people (*intruders*) and *insiders* that may want to acquire privacy-sensitive data, disrupt the crisis management operations, disseminate false information, or simply commit errors, which will be ascribed to the operator in charge of the workstation.

Consequently, in order to protect the workstations, we need to guarantee (i) *authenticity* of the commands/functions executed, meaning that commands that are transmitted and expected from an operator, are actually generated from him, and (ii) *non-repudiation* of the commands/functions executed, meaning that the worker which sends the commands from a workspace is known.

To timely detect misuses of computer resources and prevent that an unauthorized user maliciously replaces an authorized one, solutions based on *biometric continuous authentication* [2] are proposed in literature, turning user verification into a continuous process rather than a one time occurrence [3]. Additionally, to improve its security, biometrics authentication can rely on multiple biometric traits thus, being *multi-modal.* Finally, biometric data can be acquired *transparently* i.e., without explicitly notifying the user or requiring his/her interaction, aiming to improve service usability [5].

In this paper, we investigate a *continuous multi-modal biometric authentication* protocol for *transparent* verification of the operator identity in the Secure! control room, concretely presenting how to implement the approach on a real life case study. Starting from an analysis of solutions available in the state of the art, we tailored a solution that integrates face, fingerprint and keystroke recognitions. Face data is acquired using a camera, fingerprint data is acquired via a fingerprint sensor integrated in the mouse, and keystroke data is instead acquired via the keyboard.

The protocol removes the necessity of explicit interactions to prove the operator identity, and thanks to the multi-modality, it allows acquiring biometric data also when different operators are using the same workstation. For example, if more operators are in front of the camera thus in some cases compromising the face recognition, the legitimate operator can still use the fingerprint reader. Finally, authenticity and non-repudiation are guaranteed by the continuous authentication, which is intended to assure that the operator is within range of the workstation during its use.

The rest of the paper describes in Sect. 2 some of the available solution from the state of the art and the advancements of our work, in Sect. 3 the design of our tailored solution and in Sect. 4 the realization of our prototype. Results on its execution are reported in Sect. 5. Finally, conclusions are in Sect. 6.

## 2    Multi-modal Biometric Continuous Authentication

Biometrics refers to a measurement of physiological and/or behavioral characteristics of the human body; a biometric recognition system provides an automated method for confirming (*verification*) or determining (*identification*) the identity of an individual based on his characteristics [7]. Identity verification, which is the target of our work, consists of a one-to-one matching and occurs when an individual claims his identity. The system needs to compare the newly acquired biometric data and the previously enrolled digital representation of an individual's biometric characteristics, usually called templates. It is well-known that using multiple biometric characteristics combined with an appropriate rule, that is, providing a multi-modal biometric authentication, can yield a higher performance than using only one trait [15, 16].

Surveying the state of the art, a large number of studies can be identified regarding biometric continuous authentication. We review approaches on biometric authentication systems based on *multi-modality* and *continuous verification* where a *transparent* acquisition of biometric data is researched. Each of them could be used for our purpose but for each one we can find at least one reason that suggests the introduction of a new approach, ad-hoc for our requirements.

The work in [2] describes a multi-modal biometric passive continuous authentication system, combining face and fingerprint recognition to verify the physical presence of a user. The authors state that it introduces a significant overhead (between 26 % and 42 %) and the user's task are delayed; the reason is probably the bottleneck generated by a too frequent acquisition of the face (two times for each second) and fingerprint images (once per second).

The work in [3] proposes a multi-modal continuous biometric authentication system integrating information temporally as well as across multiple biometric modalities. The main idea of the method is based on the assumption that as time passes, the authentication system is less and less certain about the authentication score value. Experiments show that temporal information improves authentication accuracy. However, the acquisition of 15 images in less than a second suggests that the impact of this solution in terms of computational resource usage would be relevant, and seems legitimate to expect it would weigh down the system.

In [4] the objective is to investigate the opportunity of using a multimodal biometric system as input of a fuzzy controller for preventing user substitution after the initial authentication process. The chosen modalities are face and fingerprint. The role of the fuzzy controller is to request the fingerprint data only if the face recognition matching produces a trust level that is below a threshold. Nevertheless, we need a transparent acquisition of the traits and the explicit request of the fingerprint does not meet this requirement.

Finally, the work in [12, 13] proposes a continuous multi-modal sequential biometric authentication solution, where trust in the user is computed after each successful user identity verification and it is decreased as time passes without successful verifications. An authentication server is in charge of receiving biometric data, performs verifications and computes trust in the user. We adopt the trust formulation from [12, 13] because of its simplicity and easiness to adapt to different systems and sensors. Relevant tailoring w.r.t. [12, 13] was needed due to the different requirements of our system, in fact we are considering a control room with workstations and a defined set of sensors, selected on the basis of the usual actions of trained operators, rather than potentially any environment, kind of device, and user. For example, the operator is expected to have his hand on the mouse for most of the time, and this leads to introducing a fingerprint reader in the mouse. In addition, our system automatically grants access to all critical functions after login, while [12, 13] protects communication towards each specific service individually.

# 3    Our Approach to Continuous Authentication

The overall architecture of the biometric system is composed of the operators' workstations and the connected sensors required to acquire the biometric data. Biometric data are transmitted to an authentication system, which includes a database with the biometric templates of the operators.

## 3.1    The Protocol

In our protocol, the different biometric data are acquired continuously by the workstation, and the identity of the operator is verified; an estimation of the trust in the operator is then computed. Such trust is described as a value ranging through time in the interval [0; 1], and that decreases through time, at different rating speeds, depending on the action and behaviour of the operator (w.r.t. the available sensors). The trust value increases only when fresh biometric data is acquired and successfully verified. When such trust value is lower than a given threshold, the permissions of the operator are reduced thus limiting the possible actions that they can execute on the Secure! system until a new login is performed.

Considering the operator of the Secure! system and comparing a set of well-known biometric traits [6], we selected the following three traits for multimodal biometric authentication. First, fingerprints are acquired using a sensor integrated in the mouse [8] that will be described in Sect. 4, thus allowing fingerprint recognition. Second, facial images are acquired using a camera (a webcam) allowing face recognition. Third, keystroke data are acquired with keyboard allowing keystroke recognition. The objective is to combine the transparent and sequential acquisition of the above data to continuously assure trust in the operator.

The three above biometric traits have different levels of performance and measurability [6, 7] and complement each other. High measurability of facial images will help covering temporal gaps that could exist between two fingerprint acquisitions. Keystroke supports the other two traits despite its low performance. Especially keystroke can results useful when fingerprint acquisitions are missing e.g., because the operator is not touching the mouse: in fact, when the operators are typing on the keyboard, they are most likely unable to place their finger on the fingerprint reader.

Thus, we introduce a mechanism where (i) keystroke recognition on the text typed is executed in order to recognize the operator, and (ii) the usage of the keyboard is considered a justification for the absence of fingerprint acquisition. All these considerations will influence the computation of the trust in the operator.

In the rest of the paper, we present the implementation of the authentication system, where we choose three exemplary recognition algorithms, but we imagine that our method can work efficiently also with different face, fingerprint and keystroke recognition algorithms, and they can be changed if necessary.

The proposed continuous authentication protocol is shown in the sequence diagram of Fig. 1. It is based on three biometric subsystems, one for each trait, where each subsystem is composed of hw/sw elements necessary for the acquisition of biometric traits and for the verification process, including sensors and recognition algorithms.

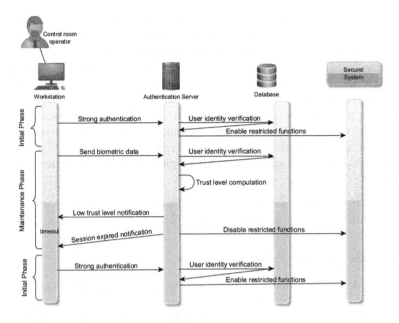

**Fig. 1.** Sequence diagram of the protocol

The protocol is divided in two phases: the initial phase and the maintenance phase.

**Initial Phase.** It is composed of the following steps:

- The user logs in to start a session that will also imply the possibility of using functionalities that need authentication. A strong authentication is here needed for login, with a one-time password (a password that is valid for only one login session or transaction) or by a successful biometric verification executed with all the three subsystems in a short time interval.
- Data are acquired by the workstation and transmitted to the authentication server.
- The authentication server uses the operator's templates contained in a biometric database and verifies his identity. In case of successful verification, the authentication server communicates to the Secure! system to establish a session and to allow all restricted functions expected for the operator's role. In addition, the authentication server computes and updates a trust level that decreases as time passes (trust computation is described in the next subsection); the session will expire when such level becomes lower than a threshold. The maintenance phase is started to compute a new trust level.

**Maintenance Phase.** The biometric continuous authentication protocol works as follows:

- The authentication server waits for fresh biometric data, from any of the three subsystems. No active participation of the operator is necessary, which only needs to use the mouse, the keyboard or to be positioned in front of the camera.

- When new biometric data is available for the different biometric subsystems, the authentication server verifies the identity claimed by the operator and, depending on the matching results of each subsystem, updates the trust level.
- When the trust level is close to the threshold, the authentication server sends a notification to the operator, to signal that in case biometric data is not transmitted, the session will expire soon.
- If the trust level is below the threshold, the authentication server communicates to the Secure! system to disable the restricted functions and notifies the operator that his session is expired. In this case, the operator can access only a set of non- restricted functions, i.e., functions with no or reduced criticality in terms of privacy and confidentiality.

The disabled functions will be available again only when the operator performs a strong authentication, restarting from the initial phase.

### 3.2    Internals: The Trust Level Computation

We now introduce some concepts useful to describe the algorithm for trust level computation, without the intent of being generic but focusing the discussion on the specificities of our system and the biometric traits used. A generic approach can be derived from the discussion below whenever needed.

Given the three unimodal biometric subsystems $S_1$ = fingerprint recognition, $S_2$ = face recognition, $S_3$ = keystroke recognition such that each one is able to decide independently if the user is genuine or not, we define $m(S_1)$, $m(S_2)$, $m(S_3)$ as the *trust in the subsystem* respectively $S_1$, $S_2$, $S_3$. The $m(S_1)$, $m(S_2)$, $m(S_3)$ are static values that lie in the interval [0,1]; the more trust we place in a subsystem, the higher its value.

We also define the trust level *trust(u, t)* that represents the trust put in the user $u$ at time $t$ by the authentication server. In other words, it corresponds to the probability that the operator $u$ is legitimate considering his behavior using the workstation. It takes into account the time from last acquisition of biometric data, and the combination of the individual decisions of the three subsystems $S_1, S_2, S_3$. Being considered as a probability, it is a value that lies the interval [0, 1].

Finally, we define a lower bound $trust_{min}$ corresponding to the minimum threshold of the trust level requested by the authentication system. If $trust(u, t) < trust_{min}$, the authentication server disables the restricted functions. If instead $trust(u, t) \geq trust_{min}$ the user is maintained authenticated and the access to all restricted functions is granted. To ease the readability of the notation, in the following the operator $u$ is often omitted.

The algorithm for the computation of the trust level is executed iteratively on the authentication server as explained in what follows. In the *initial phase*, at time $t_0$, the operator performs a strong authentication: if successful, the trust is set to $trust(t_0) = 1$.

The maintenance phase is here started. Each subsystem continuously tries to acquire, on the workstation, the biometric data of the operator and transmits them to the authentication server. The authentication server verifies the operator identity using all biometric data provided in a specific time interval; let us consider the time interval $[t_{i-1}; t_i]$ and consequently we reason for the status of the system at time instant $t_i$. We have the following options at $t_i$. In the first case, all the three biometric subsystems led to successful verification: the trust level is set to $trust(t_i) = 1$. In the second case, two of the three biometric subsystems led to successful verification. This means that one biometric subsystem could not acquire data or decided that the operator is not legitimate. The trust level is computed following (1):

$$trust\left(t_i\right) = m\left(S_{k1}\right) + \left(r \cdot m\left(S_{k2}\right)\right).$$ (1)

Where:

- $S_{k1}$ and $S_{k2}$ are the two subsystems, which correctly verified the identity of the operator, and $S_{k2}$ is the one with the lower performance;
- $r$ is a parameter that allows to weight $m(S_{k2})$ in order to have $trust(t_0)$ between 0 and 1.

For example, setting $r = 0.1$, $S_{k1} = 0.9$, $S_{k2} = 0.8$, $S_{k3} = 0.7$, we have the combinations reported in Table 1. The selection of these values can be conducted comparing the biometric traits, and from an analysis of their performance, i.e., in terms of number of false positives and false negatives produced by each. We found that these values can represent properly the accuracy of each subsystem, but other different values can be easily adopted, if necessary, following a similar approach. Until at least two subsystems do not decide that the user is legitimate in the same time interval, thus updating $trust(t_i)$ following Table 1, the trust level decreases and the session will expire when it is smaller than $trust_{min}$. If at $t_i$ at most one biometric verification is successful (e.g., for two biometric subsystems no biometric data is acquired, or verifications failed), the trust level $trust(t_i)$ is computed using the following.

**Table 1.** Example of the trust level computation

| Pair of biometric subsystems | Trust level computed as in Eq. (1) |
| --- | --- |
| $S_{k1}$, $S_{k2}$ | $0.9 + (0.1 \bullet 0.8) = 0.98$ |
| $S_{k1}$, $S_{k3}$ | $0.9 + (0.1 \bullet 0.7) = 0.97$ |
| $S_{k2}$, $S_{k3}$ | $0.8 + (0.1 \bullet 0.7) = 0.87$ |

Supposing we have $trust(t_{i-1})$ that is, the trust level computed at the previous iteration of the algorithm, we want to compute the new $trust(t_i)$, which will be smaller than $trust(t_{i-1})$. Therefore, at time $t_i$, the trust level is given by (2), [13]:

$$trust\left(t_i\right) = \frac{\left(-\arctan\left(\left(\Delta t_i - s\right) \cdot k\right) + \frac{\pi}{2}\right) \cdot trust(t_{i-1})}{-\arctan\left(-s \cdot k\right) + \frac{\pi}{2}}.$$ (2)

Where $\Delta t_i = t_i - t_{i-1}$, and parameters $k$ and $s$ are introduced to tune the decreasing function: $k$ affects the inclination towards the falling inflection point and $s$ allows anticipating or delaying the decay.

The selection of $k$ in particular affects the speed of the decrease of the trust level. We adopt three different values of $k$ in order to provide three different kinds of decrease, described below. A *fast* decrease ($k = 0.01$) is set when no verifications are successful or no biometric data is transmitted. In this case, the trust will rapidly decrease towards $trust_{min}$. An *average* decrease ($k = 0.001$) is set if only one verification is successful, for any biometric subsystem. Finally, a *slow* decrease ($k = 0.0008$) is set if face verification is successful and the usage of keyboard is detected, although data is not sufficient to perform keystroke recognition or keystroke recognition fails. This situation means that the Secure! operator is actually busy using the keyboard and he cannot send any fingerprint data, and that the amount of keys pressed is too low or too sparse to permit keystroke recognition. Thus, a small penalization is assigned to the trust in the operator, smoothly decreasing the trust level.

## 4    The Prototype

### 4.1    Hardware Prototype

Our prototype is composed of two PCs. On the client side, the workstation that we are using in our Secure! prototype is a Fujitsu Lifebook A-530 with an Intel® Pentium® P6200, 4 GB RAM, and running Windows 7, equipped with the following biometric sensors. For fingerprint acquisition, our choice is the SecuGen OptiMouse Plus mouse [8], which incorporates an optical fingerprint scanner at the place where a user would normally place their thumb. Such fingerprint scanner does not require active participation by the user, and therefore does not require that the operators periodically perform biometric-related tasks that are not part of their normal activities. For acquisition of the images for face recognition, we use the built-in camera of the workstation that can continuously capture images without the active cooperation of the user. For the acquisition of keyboard data, we collected them using the standard PS/2 keyboard integrated in the Fujitsu Lifebook. As authentication server, we are using an HP Pavilion Desktop PC500-420 nl with processor i5-4460S and 8 GB RAM which is in the same local network of the workstation.

### 4.2    Software Design

In this section, we describe our software implementation. All software we developed is implemented in Java. Client-server communication is based on RESTful web services, and developed using the Jersey framework, following the design specification of the Secure! project.

The workstation software is started by a *Client* object, which activates the methods of (i) *InvisibleFaceTracker*, (ii) *KeyListener* and (iii) *FingerPrintDetection*. Each class contains respectively: (i) an algorithm that, exploiting the camera, saves an image if (at least one) face is detected, (ii) a procedure that, exploiting the SecuGen OptiMouse Plus, cyclically detects and saves a fingerprint which, when available, is transmitted to Client, (iii) an algorithm that detects the pressing of the keys. At fixed time intervals, a text file is saved containing, for each row, the press and release times for each pressed key.

Such file is delivered to the authentication server. The *Client* is in charge of invoking the *UploadFileService* REST client to transmit via HTTP post the saved image, fingerprint and text file to the authentication server together with the client ID.

On the authentication server, the *TrustCalcService* guides the biometric verification, the calculation of the trust level, and the communication of session expiration to the Secure! system and to the workstation. The *TrustCalcService* class contains the RESTful web service that receives the transmitted biometric traits from the client, and a REST client to communicate the session expiration to the workstation. Getting the information from the client, the web service decides which methods of the *RecognitionHandler* class should be called to start the verification process. Each subsystem produces a decision about the legitimate of the user, as explained in Sect. 3. At fixed time intervals, the trust level is raised according to Table 1 or, if less than two traits are correctly verified, selecting the trust decaying function with the appropriate $k$ value as in Eq. (2).

However, for a final product realization, the implementation should integrate recognition algorithms with very high performance. Moreover, depending on the specific characteristics of the algorithms, the parameters and the time intervals have to be tuned properly.

### 4.3 Enabling Technologies

The SecuGen's FDx Software Developer Kit [8] provides low-level APIs for device initialization, fingerprint capture and matching functions. In the enrollment phase, templates are computed and stored in raw format.

We customized the face recognition software available in [10]; this is able to (i) analyze the frames captured via a camera, (ii) locate a face in the frames, and then ii) verify user's identity. When a face is present in front of the camera, the algorithm [10] detects its presence; in most of the cases, this happens within approximately 40 ms. Otherwise, if a face is not present, the algorithm takes up to 200 ms to ultimately notify that no face is present. The implementation available in [10] requested the installation and configuration of OpenCV [9], an open source library that includes several hundreds of computer vision algorithms, and of JavaCV, the related Java interface. Our customization of the software was necessary in order to (i) structure the implementation available in [10] in two client and a server sides, where the first is in charge of capturing images and deciding if a face is present, and the second performs verification, and (ii) make the acquisition of the biometric data transparent and automatic, removing the graphical interface and interactions of the user with the software. An enrollment phase is obviously required, in which the operator ID is associated to a set of face templates. The verification phase compares the selected face to the enrolled templates to produce a matching result.

Keystroke data acquisition relies on the library JNativeHook that provides keyboard (and mouse) listeners for Java. In particular, this library allows detecting keys press and release events and captures, in correspondence to those events, the time instant of the events. JNativeHook also permits to detect the keyboard usage (and the keys pressed), both if the user is typing in a specific text area or not: the cursor position is not relevant. This is consistent with our needs as we can capture keystroke data without being invasive for the activity of the control room operator.

Relying on such library, we realized the keystroke recognition in the *KeyAnalyzer* class, implementing the algorithm described in [11]. Such algorithm continuously collects the keystroke dynamics (the typed key and related pressing and release time) and applies a penalty/reward function on the dataset to measure the confidence that the user has not changed in the selected time interval. An enrollment session is required where the operator types several sentences, to create a biometric template based on the timing information for each typed key and key combination [11].

In our implementation of [11], when the keyboard is used with continuity i.e., there is evidence that someone is currently typing, we collect keystroke dynamics for a defined time interval and then we transmit all values to the authentication server. The selection of the time interval is critical because if the number of values collected is too low, verification will most likely fail: a short time interval would probably result ineffective for keystroke authentication following [11]. Moreover, a long time interval would imply a long wait before transmitting the values, thus risking that the session expires meanwhile. We evaluated that listening for up to 10 s of continuous typing was deemed sufficient to allow successful verification (we also remember that keystroke is the weakest of our biometric traits, and it is easily prone to false positives).

### 4.4　Availability, Security, Privacy and Performance

The Secure! system implements solutions for the overall availability of the system, the security and the privacy of the information managed, stored or exchanged, following a threat and risk analysis that was performed at the beginning of the project [14]. The mitigations identified for risks and threats, including time-related ones, also consider the workstations, the authentication server, and the related communication channels. Although such analysis and the Secure! architecture are not within the scope of this paper, we present considerations on availability, security, privacy and performance that we believe relevant.

Regarding availability, our authentication mechanism clearly requires that the authentication server and all communications channels in Fig. 1 are up and running. In case of unavailability of any of the above, the system administrator of the Secure! system is able to temporarily disable the continuous authentication, thus switching to a traditional password-based authentication approach. However, such alternative should be exploited only when needed and matched to immediate intervention for maintenance (strategies for rapid maintenance intervention are foreseen for the whole Secure! system).

Protection of the biometric data exchanged and stored, together with protection of the communication between the entities of Fig. 1 is mandatory. Briefly, the system in Fig. 1 represents a closed system, where all interacting entities are known, all communications are cabled, and no external machines are accepted. Communications are ciphered, and access to the entities is protected; solutions for the protection of data and communications are defined and applied to the whole Secure! system, as it manages several other sensitive and secure data, in addition to the biometric ones.

Privacy of data is fundamental in Secure! both for data related to crisis management and for data related to the continuous authentication, which describes the behaviour of the worker in the operating room. Although data management is part of the Secure!

architecture, it is worthy to discuss the authentication data. Such data is stored for a limited time (few days), and then removed, thus the system maintains only the recent history on the behaviour of the user. Access to such history is regulated by the procedures of the operating room and it is allowed only to investigate on suspected security breaches.

Regarding performance, the continuous authentication software executing on the workstation may potentially slow down the Secure! application used by the operator. We measured the overhead introduced on our prototype, resulting in approximately an increase of usage of 6 % for CPU and 2 % for RAM. Such overhead is limited and shall not affect the execution of the Secure! application. The authentication server is instead in charge of managing the biometric database and verifying the identities of the team of operators, thus it is subject to a relevant computational load especially for large teams. However, the authentication server is one of the (powerful) nodes of the Secure! framework, which has been built with scalability [17] in mind so that its nodes can be easily adapted to sustain high computational loads.

### 4.5  Usability

We comment on the impact of our authentication solution on the daily activities of the operator. The authentication solution and the values of its parameters were selected to achieve a compromise between security (a malicious operator is disconnected in at worst approximately 40 s, see Fig. 3) and usability (the worker maintains the session active, mostly thanks to the fingerprint reader in the mouse, which is used most of the time, and the face recognition). The experiments in Sect. 5, which adopt the configurations selected for Secure!, confirm that a worker is able to maintain the authentication until he voluntarily leaves the workstation. We are aware that usability studies in daily working sessions with multiple Secure! operators are required; this is the main objective of the ongoing experimentation of our solution.

## 5  Explanatory Results

We report on three typical scenarios where 10 runs have been performed using the prototype and the data for one case are plotted. The configurations selected for Secure! are the same as Sect. 3; trust threshold is set to $trust_{min} = 0.5$. The objectives of the three scenario analysis are respectively (i) verify that the operator working at a workstation is able to maintain authentication for a whole working session, (ii) verify that if the workstation is left unattended by the legitimate user, the trust will decay below the thresholds, (iii) verify the requirements on the environment, especially on illumination.

In the *first scenario,* an operator is in front of the client, working in an environment with good illumination. A working session of 50 min is performed: the operator does not leave the workstation, and alternates the usage of keyboard and mouse to perform his work. An extract showing the initial part of one run is shown in Fig. 2 to clarify the behavior of the protocol. At the beginning of the run (at second 13), a strong authentication is successfully performed providing in a time slot the three biometric traits (the time slot is set to 10 s): this means that the three biometric data should be provided and successfully verified in such interval. Note that additional delays due to transmission and processing time should always be taken into account. After the initial authentication, at time intervals of around 20 s, the authentication server verifies the biometric data. The first and second time intervals resulted in successfully performed verification for face and detection of the usage of keyboard (keyboard detection, or k.d., in Figs. 2 and 3), leading to a slow decrease of trust level with $k = 0.0008$. In the third time interval, only face is successfully verified, with no usage of keyboard detected. This leads to an average decrease of trust level, with $k$ set to 0,001. For clarity, this interval is also identified in Fig. 2 with the arrow with label "average". In the fifth time interval, at second 111 face and fingerprint subsystems successfully verify the operator identity, resulting in raising the trust level to 0,98 according to Table 1. Note that in Fig. 2 every time the operator is using the keyboard the trust level drops, in fact the usage of the keyboard was detected (keystroke detection), but keystroke recognition failed or was not performed due to insufficient data. Then the algorithm follows in a similar manner alternating different successful verifications in the time intervals for the whole duration of the experiment, with a predominance of face recognitions (the cases in which only one biometric trait is verified always refer to face). On the whole set of 10 runs, 1 facial image per second was acquired, and if face was detected, the algorithm processed the image. This resulted in an average of 5 missed face recognition per run (obviously, this is strictly dependent on the face recognition algorithm). Fingerprint lead only to an average of 2 mismatches out of approximately 200 checks per run, while keystroke lead to an average of 15 mismatches out of 24 attempts per run.

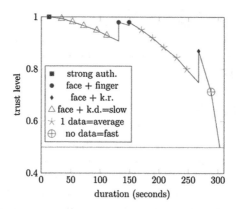

**Fig. 2.** Successful verifications: trust level is always above the threshold

The *second scenario* aims to show the possible behavior of the prototype when the operator leaves the workstation unattended, and consequently it is expected that the session will terminate due to failed biometric recognition or no acquisition of biometric data. In this experiment, we observe that ultimately the trust level decays below the threshold, resulting in session expiration. We show a sample run of the experiment in Fig. 3, as the others behave similarly. A strong authentication is initially performed with the same outcome as in the previous experiment. Then the trust level slowly decreases,

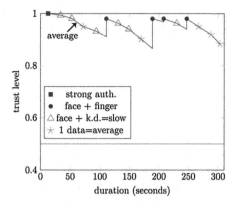

**Fig. 3.** Operator leaving the workstation unattended after a while.

given the recognition of face and the usage of keyboard, until second 131 in which the two biometric traits face and fingerprint are correctly acquired and verified. These are newly verified at second 149. Then the decay of the trust level is set to average because only the face is verified, until second 267 when the trust level is raised thanks to identity verification via face and keystroke recognition (e.g., the operator after reading some text was able to write an answer). The resulting trust is set to 0.87 following Table 1. At this point, no more biometric verification are successful, resulting in a fast decrease of the trust that leads to reaching the timeout in around 36 s. The threshold is ultimately reached at second 303. Such timeout is considered adequate for the purpose of Secure!, as in general this time is too short to have the operator leave the workstation unattended and execute commands or acquire data.

Finally, the last scenario is conducted in a room where the only source of lighting is a window placed behind the operator. The runs performed led to an unexpected termination of the session, because the facial recognition failed repeatedly leading to a decay of the trust thresholds. The implication is that it is required to set the control room environment appropriately in order to have our solution work properly.

## 6 Conclusions

This paper presented our realization of a continuous multi-modal biometric authentication system for the operator active in the Secure! control room. The protocol is able to transparently acquire face, fingerprint and keystroke traits to continuously verify the identity of the operator without his explicit involvement. The paper described the solution, its prototype realization and execution. Results show that, despite obvious limitations due to the necessity of continuously provide biometric data, when appropriately tailored for a working environment our solution allows maintaining the worker authenticated and improving system security.

As future work we are building and executing several test sessions with a larger number of different operators using Secure!, to investigate the tradeoff between security and usability for the different settings of the authentication system.

**Acknowledgments.** This work has been partially supported by the POR-CREO 2007-2013 Secure! project funded by the Tuscany Region, by the European FP7-IRSES project DEVASSES, and by the TENACE PRIN Project (n. 20103P34XC) funded by the Italian Ministry of Education, University and Research.

# References

1. Secure! Project. http://secure.eng.it
2. Kumar, S., Sim, T., Janakiraman, R., Zhang, S.: Using continuous biometric verification to protect interactive login sessions. In: 21st Annual Computer Security Applications Conference (ACSAC), pp. 441–450 (2005)
3. Altinok, A., Turk, M.: Temporal integration for continuous multimodal biometrics. In: Proceedings of the Workshop on Multimodal User Authentication (2003)
4. Azzini, A., Marrara, S., Sassi, R., Scotti, F.: A fuzzy approach to multimodal biometric continuous authentication. Fuzzy Optim. Decis. Making 7(3), 243–256 (2008)
5. Crawford, H., Renaud, K., Storer, T.: A framework for continuous, transparent mobile device authentication. Comput. Secur. 39, 127–136 (2013)
6. Jain, A.K., Ross, A., Prabhakar, S.: An introduction to biometric recognition. IEEE Trans. Circ. Syst. Video Technol. 14(1), 4–20 (2004)
7. Tripathi, K.P.: A comparative study of biometric technologies with reference to human interface. Int. J. Comput. Appl. 14(5), 10–15 (2011)
8. SecuGen OptiMouse Plus. http://www.secugen.com/products/po.htm
9. The OpenCV Reference Manual, Release 2.4.9.0 (2014)
10. Davison, A.: Killer Game Programming in Java. O'Reilly Media Inc., Sebastopol (2005)
11. Bours, P., Barghouthi, H.: Continuous authentication using biometric keystroke dynamics. In: The Norwegian Information Security Conference (NISK) (2009)
12. Ceccarelli, A., Bondavalli, A., Brancati, F., La Mattina, E.: Improving security of internet services through continuous and transparent user identity verification. In: IEEE 31st Symposium on Reliable Distributed Systems, (SRDS), pp. 201–206 (2012)
13. Ceccarelli, A., Montecchi, L., Brancati, F., Lollini, P., Marguglio, A., Bondavalli, A.: Continuous and transparent user identity verification for secure internet services. IEEE Trans. Dependable Secure Comput. 12(3), 270–283 (2015)
14. Nostro, N., Ceccarelli, A., Bondavalli, A., Brancati, F.: Insider threat assessment: a model-based methodology. Oper. Syst. Rev. (ACM) 48(2), 3–12 (2014)
15. Ross, A., Jain, A.K.: Information fusion in biometrics. Pattern Recogn. Lett. 24(13), 2115–2125 (2003)
16. Hong, L., Jain, A.K., Pankanti, S.: Can multibiometrics improve performance? Proc. AutoID 99, 59–64 (1999)
17. Montecchi, L., Nostro, N., Ceccarelli, A., Vella, G., Caruso, A., Bondavalli, A.: Model-based evaluation of scalability and security tradeoffs: a case study on a multi-service platform. In: Electronic Notes in Theoretical Computer Science, vol. 310, pp. 113–133 (2015)
18. Nostro, N., Ceccarelli, A., Bondavalli, A., Brancati, F.: A methodology and supporting techniques for the quantitative assessment of insider threats. In: Proceedings of the 2nd International Workshop on Dependability Issues in Cloud Computing (ACM), (3), pp. 1–6 (2013)

# Leakage-Resilient Anonymous Identity-Based Broadcast Encryption in the Standard Model

Leyou Zhang[1], Zhuanning Wang[1(✉)], and Qing Wu[2]

[1] Department of Mathematics, Xidian University, Xi'an 710071, China
lyzhang@mail.xidian.edu.cn, wuqingzly@163.com
[2] School of Automation, Xi'an University of Posts and Telecommunications,
Xi'an 710121, China

**Abstract.** Anonymous encryption has many applications in real life. But there are no efficient works with anonymous feature to be known in the identity-based broadcast encryption(IBBE) system. In addition, all existing IBBEs do not support leakage tolerance. In this paper, a new construction of anonymous identity-based broadcast encryption is proposed in the standard model. In the new construction, the ciphertexts and private keys are indistinguishable for the different receivers set. The proposed scheme has constant size ciphertexts and achieves adaptive security. In addition, the proposed scheme achieves leakage-resilient security. The security of the proposed scheme is reduced to some natural static assumptions in a composite group instead of other strong assumptions.

**Keywords:** IBBE · Leakage-resilient · Anonymous IBBE · Dual system encryption · Static assumptions

## 1 Introduction

Broadcast Encryption (BE) had been widely used in digital rights management applications such as pay-TV, multicast communication, and DVD content protection. Since the first scheme appeared in 1994 [1], many BE schemes have been proposed [2–5]. Identity-based encryption (IBE) was introduced by Shamir [6], where the recipient's identity could be used as a public key to encrypt a message. It does not need to distribute public key certificates and simplify many applications of public key encryption (PKE) [7–12].

Identity-based broadcast encryption(IBBE) [13–18] is a generalization of IBE. In an IBBE scheme, one public key can be used to encrypt a message to any possible group and any valid users in group can recover the message. In [13, 15], the proposed scheme was based on random oracles. In addition, the size of the ciphertexts grows linearly with the number of the users. The well known construction of IBBE was proposed by Delerablée [14]. This construction achieved constant size private keys and constant size ciphertexts. However the security of her main scheme achieved only selective-identity security(a weak security) and relied on the random oracles. In [17], two schemes with full security were proposed respectively. But they were impractical in real-life practice since their security relied on the complex assumptions which were

© Springer International Publishing Switzerland 2015
G. Wang et al. (Eds.): ICA3PP 2015 Workshops, LNCS 9532, pp. 201–210, 2015.
DOI: 10.1007/978-3-319-27161-3_18

dependent on the depth of users set and the number of queries made by an attacker. In addition, the work in [17] had the sublinear-size ciphertexts. Moreover, the authors in [17] used a sub-algorithm at the Encrypt phase to achieve full security which increased the computations cost. In [18], authors also proposed an anonymous broadcast encryption scheme. Recent works [19] were secure against quantum computer which incorporates the forward-security mechanism into broadcast encryption scheme from lattice.

*Our Method.* Recently, a new technique is applied to IBE. It is called Dual Encryption Technique. Waters [20] first proposed a broadcast encryption scheme based on this new technique. However, the proposed scheme is not based on identity and also inefficient since its cost of decryption is dependent on depth of users set. Based on this technique, two schemes are proposed in [21, 22] respectively. After, the proposed system [24] achieves adaptively secure with constant sized ciphertexts in the standard model. The size of the public key and the private keys are both linear in the maximum number of receivers. However, it is fully collusion-resistant and has stateless receivers.

However, the existing works are not anonymous. They can not protect the privacy of the receivers in the different subsets in $S$. Bellare et al. [25] treated firstly the notion of anonymity or key privacy for a cryptosystem. In this notion the ciphertexts of an encryption may not give any information on the key that was used to perform the encryption, in addition to the privacy of the message. Combining anonymity with identity-based encryption is a logical step. Anonymous identity-based cryptosystems can be used to construct Public key Encryption with Keyword Search (PEKS) schemes, which was observed by Boneh et al. [26]. Many schemes have appeared in this area [27, 28]. However, these techniques are not suit for the broadcast encryption system.

In these schemes, securities are guaranteed and achieved under some assumption that the secret key must be kept safely. If a single bit of these secrets is leaked, the security of these schemes may be lost. However, it is not easy to avoid all possible kinds of leakage, such as side-channel attacks. Side-channel attacks allow attackers to learn partial information about secrets by observing physical properties of a cryptographic execution such as timing, power usage, etc. [29, 30]. Recently, two leakage-resilient attribute-based encryption schemes [31], ciphertext-policy ABE (LR-CP-ABE) and key-policy ABE (LR-KP-ABE) are present. The schemes are proven to be adaptively leakage-resilient secure in the standard model under the static assumptions in composite order bilinear groups.

*Our Contributions.* According to the definition of anonymous IBE and leakage-resilient cryptosystem, we give the definition of the anonymous identity-based broadcast encryption with leakage-resilient. Then based on the dual system encryption, a concrete construction is proposed. The new scheme has constant size ciphertexts and achieves the adaptive security. The security of the new scheme is reduced to some static assumptions in the composite bilinear group.

# 2 Preliminaries

## 2.1 Anonymous IBBE

An identity-based broadcast encryption scheme (IBBE) with the security parameter and the maximal size $m$ of the target set is specified as follows.

**Setup**      Take as input the security parameter and output a master secret key and public key.

**Extract**      Take as input the master secret key and a user identity $ID$. Extract generates a user private key $d_{ID}$.

**Encrypt**      Take as input the public key and a set of included identities $S = \{ID_1, ..., ID_s\}$ with $s \leq m$, and output a pair $(Hdr, K)$. Then algorithm computes the encryption $C_M$ of $M$ under the symmetric key $K$ and broadcasts $(Hdr, S, C_M)$.

**Decrypt**      Take as input a subset $S$, an identity $ID_i$ and the corresponding private key, if $ID_i \in S$, the algorithm outputs $K$ which is then used to decrypt the broadcast body $C_M$ and recover $M$.

**Update**      Take as input the master secret key and update it.

## 2.2 Security Model

**Setup**      The challenger runs Setup to obtain a public key $PK$. He gives A the public key $PK$

**Query phase 1**      The adversary A adaptively issues queries $q_1, ..., q_{s0}$, where $q_i$ is one of the following:

- Extraction query $(ID_i)$: The challenger runs Extract on $ID_i$ and sends the resulting private key to the adversary.
- Leakage Oracle LO$(f, ID)$: On input $f \in$ F, it returns $f(msk, L_{ID}, mpk, ID)$.
- Update USK Oracle USO$(ID)$: This oracle is useful for schemes with probabilistic $ID$-based secret key generation, where a user of identity $ID$ may request for another $ID$-based secret key after obtained the first copy. It first checks the list $L_{ID}$ for the tuple in the form of $(sk_{ID}, ID, j)$ where $j$ is a positive integer. If there is no such tuple, $\bar{j}$ is set to 1. Otherwise, the maximum $j$ is retrieved and $\bar{j}$ is set to $(j + 1)$. Then, it runs $s\bar{k}_{ID} \leftarrow$ Ext$(msk, ID)$. It puts $(s\bar{k}_{ID}, ID, \bar{j})$ in the list $L_{ID}$ and returns $\bar{j}$. KEO, USO and LO can be queried for at most $q_e$, $q_u$ and $q_l$ times throughout this game respectively.

**Challenge**      When A decides that phase 1 is over, A outputs two same-length messages $(M_0 \ M_1)$ and two users set $(S_0^*, S_1^*)$ on which it wishes to be challenged. The challenger picks a random $b \in \{0, 1\}$ and sets the challenge ciphertext $C^* =$ Encrypt$(params, M_b, S_b^*)$. The challenger returns $C^*$ to A.

***Query Phase 2:***     The adversary continues to issue queries $q_{s0+1}, ..., q_t$, where $q_i$ is one of the following:

- Extraction query $(ID_i)$, as in phase 1 with the constraint that $ID_i \notin S_0^*, S_1^*$.

***Guess***     Finally, the adversary A outputs a guess $b' \in \{0, 1\}$ and wins the game if $b = b'$.

Let $t$ denote the total number of extraction queries during the game. The advantage of A in winning the game is defined as follows:

$$Adv_{IBBE}(t, m, A) = |2P(b = b') - 1|.$$

**Definition 1.** An anonymous identity-based broadcast encryption scheme(IBBE) is said to be $(t, m,)$-IND-ID-CPA secure if $Adv_{IBBE}(t, m, A)$ is negligible.

## 3   Our Construction

### 3.1   New Works

Let $G$ be cyclic group of order $N = p_1 p_2 p_3 p_4$ and $l$ denote the maximum number of the set of possible users. Our scheme works as follows.

***Setup***     To generate the system parameters, the PKG picks randomly $g_1, h_1, u_1, \cdots,$ $u_l \in G_{p_1}$, $g_3 \in G_{p_3}$, $g_4, h_4 \in G_{p_4}$, $\alpha_i \in Z_N, 1 \le i \le m$ and set $t = h_1$ where $m$ denote the secure parameter. The public parameters are defined as

$$PK = \{N, g_1, g_3, g_4, t, u_1, \cdots, u_l, v_i = e(g_1, g_1)^{\alpha_i}\},$$

the master key are defined as $g_1^{\alpha_j} R_{i,0}, R'_{i,0}, R_{i,1}, \cdots, R_{i,i-1}, R_{i,i+1}, \cdots, R_{i,k}$. Where elements $R_{i0}, R'_{i0}, R_{i1}, \cdots, R_{i(i-1)}, R_{i(i+1)}, \cdots, R_{ik} \in G_{p_3}$, $1 \le j \le m$.

***Extract***     Given the identity $ID_i \in S$ ($|S| = k \le l$), PKG selects randomly $r_i \in Z_N$. Then it computes private keys as follows:

$$d_{ID_i} = (d_{0j}, d', d_1, \cdots, d_{i-1}, d_{i+1}, \cdots, d_k)$$
$$= (g_1^{\alpha_j} R_{i0}(h_1 u_i^{ID_i})^{r_i}, g_1^{r_i} R'_{i0}, R_{i1} u_1^{r_i}, \cdots, u_{i-1}^{r_i} R_{i(i-1)}, u_{i+1}^{r_i} R_{i(i+1)}, \cdots, u_k^{r_i} R_{ik}), 1 \le j \le m$$

***Encrypt***     Without loss of generality, let $S = (ID_1, ID_2, \cdots, ID_k)$ denote the set of users with $k \le l$ and $M$ be the encrypted message. A broadcaster selects a random $s \in Z_N^*$ and $Z, Z' \in G_{p_4}$, computes

$$C = (C_0, Hdr) = (C_0, C_1, C_2)(\prod_{i=1}^{m} v_i)^s M, (t \prod_{i=1}^{k} u_i^{ID_i})^s Z, g_1^s Z').$$

***Decrypt***     Given the ciphertexts $C = (C_0, C_1, C_2)$, any user $ID_i \in S$ uses his/her private keys $d_{ID_i}$ to compute

$$M = C_0 \frac{e(C_1, d')}{e(\prod_{j=1}^{m} d_{0j}(\prod_{j=1, j\neq i}^{k} d_j^{ID_j}), C_2)}.$$

In order to show the correctness, the orthogonality property of $G_{p_i}(i = 1, \cdots, 4)$ will be used.

**Update**  Given the master key are set as $g_1^{\alpha_j} R_{i0}, R'_{i0}, R_{i1}, \cdots, R_{i(i-1)}, R_{i(i+1)}, \cdots, R_{ik}$. Then Choose randomly

$$T_{j0}, T'_{i0}, T_{i1}, \cdots, T_{i(i-1)}, T_{i(i+1)}, \cdots, T_{ik} \in G_{p_3} 1 \leq j \leq m,$$

and update master keys as $g_1^{\alpha_j} R_{i0} T_{j0}, R'_{i0} T'_{i0}, R_{i1} T_{i1}, \cdots, R_{i(i-1)} T_{i(i-1)}, R_{i(i+1)} T_{i(i+1)}, \cdots, R_{ik} T_{ik}$.

**Lemma [18].**  When $h_i \in G_{p_i}, h_j \in G_{p_j}$ for $i \neq j$, $e(h_i, h_j)$ is the identity element in $G_1$.

**Correctness**: By using Lemma 1, one can obtain

$$\frac{e(C_1^m, d')}{e(\prod_{j=1}^{m} d_{0j}(\prod_{j=1, j\neq i}^{k} d_j^{ID_j}), C_2)}$$

$$= \frac{e((t \prod_{i=1}^{k} u_i^{ID_i})^s Z, g_1^{r_i} R'_{i0})}{e(\prod_{j=1}^{m} g_1^{\alpha_j}(h_1 \prod_{i=1}^{k} u_i^{ID_i})^{r_i} R_{i0}^m (\prod_{j=1, j\neq i}^{k} R_{ij}^{ID_j}), g_1^s Z')}$$

$$= \frac{e((h_1 \prod_{i=1}^{k} u_i^{ID_i})^s, g^{r_i}) e(h_4^s, g^{r_i})}{e(\prod_{j=1}^{m} g_1^{\alpha_j}, g_1^s) e((h_1 \prod_{i=1}^{k} u_i^{ID_i})^{r_i}, g_1^s)}$$

$$\frac{e((t \prod_{i=1}^{k} u_i^{ID_i})^s, g^{r_i}) e((t \prod_{i=1}^{k} u_i^{ID_i})^s, R'_{io})}{e(R_{io}^m, g^s) e((\prod_{j=1, j\neq 1}^{k} R_{ij}^{ID_j}), g_1^s)} = \frac{1}{\prod_{j=1}^{m} v_j^s}.$$

## 3.2  Efficiency

The security of the proposed scheme is reduced to the static assumptions. In addition, our scheme achieves anonymous. Table 1 gives the comparisons with others.

In Table 1, *PK* and *pk* denote the public key and private key respectively. *Anony* is the anonymous feature. *LR* is Leakage-resilient. From Table 1, our scheme achieves only anonymous.

**Table 1.** Comparisons of efficiency

| Scheme | Hardness | PK size | pk size | Ciphertext size | Anony | LR |
|---|---|---|---|---|---|---|
| [16] | TBDHE | $O(\lambda)$ | $O(|S|)$ | $O(1)$ | NO | NO |
| [17] 1st | BDHE | $O(m)$ | $O(|S|)$ | $O(1)$ | NO | NO |
| [17] 2nd | BDHE | $O(m)$ | $O(1)$ | $O(1)$ | NO | NO |
| [17] 3rd | BDHE | $O(m)$ | $O(1)$ | Sublinear of $|S|$ | NO | NO |
| [22] | Static | $O(m)$ | $O(1)$ | $O(1)$ | NO | NO |
| [23] | Static | $O(m)$ | $O(|S|)$ | $O(1)$ | NO | NO |
| Ours | Static | $O(m)$ | $O(m)$ | $O(1)$ | YES | YES |

## 4 Security Analysis

In this section, we will prove the security of the proposed scheme. We will use some complex assumptions. These assumptions have been used in [20–23]. We first define semi-functional master keys, semi-functional keys and semi-functional ciphertexts. Let $g_2$ denote a generator of $G_{p_2}$.

**Semi-functional Master keys:** At first, a normal master key $g_1^{\alpha_l} R_{i0}, R'_{i0}, R_{i1}, \cdots,$ $R_{i(i-1)}, R_{i(i+1)}, \cdots, R_{ik}$ with $1 \leq l \leq m$ is given. Then some random elements $\gamma_{0l}, \gamma'_0, \gamma_j$ for $j = 1, \cdots, k$ and $j \neq i$ are chosen in $Z_N$. The semi-functional keys are set as follows.

$$g_1^{\alpha_l} R_{i0} g_2^{\gamma_{0l}}, R'_{i0} g_2^{\gamma'_0}, R_{i1} g_2^{\gamma_1}, \cdots, R_{i(i-1)} g_2^{\gamma_{i-1}}, R_{i(i+1)} g_2^{\gamma_{i+1}}, \cdots, R_{ik} g_2^{\gamma_k} s.$$

**Semi-functional Keys:** At first, a normal key $(\bar{d}_{0l}, \bar{d}', \bar{d}_1, \cdots, \bar{d}_{i-1}, \bar{d}_{i+1}, \cdots, \bar{d}_k)$ with $1 \leq l \leq m$ is obtained using the Extract algorithm. Then some random elements $\gamma_0, \gamma'_0, \gamma_j$ for $j = 1, \cdots, k$ and $j \neq i$ are chosen in $Z_N$. The semi-functional keys are set as follows.

$$d_{0l} = \bar{d}_{0l} g_2^{\gamma_0}, d' = \bar{d}' g_2^{\gamma'_0}, d_j = \bar{d}_j g_2^{\gamma_j}, j = 1, \cdots, k j \neq i.$$

When the semi-functional key is used to decrypt a semi-functional ciphertext, the decryption algorithm will compute the blinding factor multiplied by the additional term $e(g_2, g_2)^{x\gamma_0(\gamma'_0 - \gamma_c)}$. If $\gamma'_0 = \gamma_c$, decryption still work. In this case, the key is nominally semi-functional.

**Semi-functional Ciphertexts:** At first, a normal semi-functional ciphertext $(C'_0, C'_1, C'_2)$ is obtained using the Encrypt algorithm. Then two random elements $\lambda_1, \lambda_2$ are chosen in $Z_N$. The semi-functional ciphertexts are set as follows: $C_0 = C'_0$, $C_1 = C'_1 g_2^{\lambda_1 \lambda_2}, C_2 = C'_2 g_2^{\lambda_2}$.

We organize our proof as a sequence of games. We will show that each game is indistinguishable from the next (under three complexity assumptions). We first define the games as:

**Game$_{real}$:** This is a real IBBE security game. For $0 \leq i \leq q$, the Game$_i$ is defined as follows.

**Game$_i$:** Let $\Omega$ denote the set of private keys which the adversary queries during the games. This game is a real IBBE security game with the two exceptions: (1) The challenge ciphertext will be a semi-functional ciphertext on the challenge set $S^*$. (2) The first $i$ keys will be semi-functional private keys. The rest of keys in $\Omega$ will be normal.

Note: In game$_0$, the challenge ciphertext is semi-functional. In game$_q$, the challenge ciphertexts and all keys are semi-functional.

**Game$_{final'}$:** This game is same with game$_q$ except that the challenge ciphertext is a semi-functional encryption of random group element of $G_1$.

**Game$_{final}$:** This game is same with game$_{final'}$ except that the challenge ciphertext is a semi-functional encryption of random group element of $G_{p_1p_2p_4}$.

We will show that these games are indistinguishable in a set of Lemmas. Let $Adv_{game}A$ denote the advantage in the real game.

**Lemma 1.** Suppose that there exists an algorithm A such that $Adv_{game_{real}}A - Adv_{game_0}A = \varepsilon$. Then we can build an algorithm B with advantage $\varepsilon$ in breaking Assumption 1.

**Proof.** Our algorithm B begins by receiving

$$D = (N, G, G_1, e, g_1, g_3, g_4, A_1A_2, B_2B_3).$$

It works as follows:

**Setup.** B chooses random elements $\alpha_i, a_1, \cdots, a_l, b, c \in Z_N$ and sets

$$u_i = g^{a_i}, 1 \leq i \leq l, h_1 = g_1^b, h_4 = g_4^c.$$

It sends the public keys

$$PK = \{N, g_1, g_3, g_4, t = h_1h_4, u_1, \cdots, u_l, v_i = e(g_1, g_1)^{\alpha_i}\}$$

to A. Note that B knows the master keys at this phase.

**Query Phase 1.** The adversary A issues a private key query for identity $ID_i \in S$ ($|S| = k \leq l$). B answers as follows:

(1) If it is for Extract Oracle, B selects randomly $r, t_0, t_0', t_j, 1 \leq j \leq k, j \neq i$ in $Z_N$. Then it sets

$$d_{ID_i} = (d_0, d', d_1, \cdots, d_{i-1}, d_{i+1}, \cdots, d_k)$$
$$= (g^{\alpha_j}(h_1u_i^{ID_i})^r X_3^{t_0}, g^r X_3^{t_0'}, u_1^r X_3^{t_1}, \cdots, u_{i-1}^r X_3^{t_{i-1}}, \text{where} 1 \leq j \leq m.$$

It is a valid simulation to A.

(2) If it is for leakage oracle, it returns $f(msk, L_{ID}, mpk, ID)$ where $msk$ is semi-functional and for the last entry $(d_{ID}, ID, \cdot) \in L_{ID}$, $d_{ID}$ is semi-functional.

(3) If it is for UpdateUSK oracle, it puts a semi-functional key $d_{ID}$ into $L_{ID}$.

**Challenge.** The adversary A outputs two challenge message $M_0, M_1$ and the challenge sets $S_0^* = \{ID_{01}^*, \cdots, ID_{0k}^*\}, S_1^* = \{ID_{11}^*, \cdots, ID_{1k}^*\}$. Then the ciphertext $C = (C_0, C_1, C_2)$ is formed as

$$C_0 = \prod_{j=1}^{m} M_\gamma e(T, g_1)^{\alpha_j}.$$

**Query phase 2.** The adversary continues to issue queries $q_j$, where $q_i$ is the following:
- Extraction query $(ID_i)$, as in phase 1 with the constraint that $ID_i \notin S_0^*, S_1^*$.

**Guess.** Finally, the adversary A outputs a guess $\gamma' \in \{0, 1\}$ and wins the game if $\gamma' = \gamma$.

If $T \in G_{p_1 p_3}$, then $T$ can be written as $g_1^{s_1} g_3^{s_3}$ for random $s_1, s_3 \in Z_N$ and, $Z' = g_3^{s_3}$. In this case, $C = (C_0, C_1, C_2)$ is a normal ciphertext with $s = s_1$. If $T \in G_{p_1 p_2 p_3}$, then $T$ can be written as $g_1^{s_1} g_2^{s_2} g_3^{s_3}$ for random $s_1, s_2, s_3 \in Z_N$ and

$Z = g_3^{s_3 \sum_{i=1}^{k} a_i ID_{\gamma i}^* + b}$, $Z' = g_3^{s_3}$, $\lambda_1 = s_2, \lambda_2 = \sum_{i=1}^{k} a_i ID_{\gamma i}^* + b$. In this case, $C = (C_0, C_1, C_2)$ is a semi-functional ciphertext. Hence B can use A's guess to break Assumption 1 with advantage $\varepsilon$.

**Lemma 2.** Suppose that there exists an algorithm A that makes at most $q$ queries and such that $Adv_{game_{j-1}}A - Adv_{game_j}A = \varepsilon$ for $1 \le j \le q$. Then we can build an algorithm B with advantage $\varepsilon$ in breaking Assumption 1.

**Lemma 3.** Suppose that there exists an algorithm A that makes at most $q$ queries and such that $Adv_{game_q}A - Adv_{game_{final'}}A = \varepsilon$. Then we can build an algorithm B with advantage $\varepsilon$ in breaking Assumption 2.

**Lemma 4.** Suppose that there exists an algorithm A that makes at most $q$ queries and such that $Adv_{game_{final'}}A - Adv_{game_{final}}A = \varepsilon$. Then we can build an algorithm B with advantage $\varepsilon$ in breaking Assumption 3.

We adopt the same approach to prove the Lemmas 2, 3, and 4.

**Theorem 1.** If Assumptions 1, 2 and 3 hold, then our scheme is IND-ID-CPA secure.

**Proof.** If Assumptions 1, 2 and 3 hold, by the sequence of games and Lemma from 1 to 4, the adversary's advantage in the real game must be negligible. Hence our IBBE is IND-ID-CPA secure.

## 5   Conclusion

We propose a new IBBE with anonymous feature and leakage-resilient security. The scheme is constructed in a composite group. So it contains the desirable features such as short ciphertexts and achieving the adaptive security. The security of the new scheme is reduced to some general hardness assumptions instead of other strong assumptions.

**Acknowledgments.** This work is supported in part by the Nature Science Foundation of China under grant (61472307, 61100231, 61100165, 61402112), the Natural Science Basic Research Plan in Shaanxi Province of China (2012JQ8044, 2011JM8003, 2014JM8313) and the Fundamental Research Funds for the Central Universities of China.

# References

1. Fiat, A., Naor, M.: Broadcast encryption. In: Stinson, D.R. (ed.) CRYPTO 1993. LNCS, vol. 773, pp. 480–491. Springer, Heidelberg (1994)
2. Dodis, Y., Fazio, N.: Public key broadcast encryption for stateless receivers. In: Feigenbaum, J. (ed.) DRM 2002. LNCS, vol. 2696, pp. 61–80. Springer, Heidelberg (2003)
3. Dodis, Y., Fazio, N.: Public key broadcast encryption secure against adaptive chosen ciphertext attack. In: Desmedt, Y. (ed.) Public Key Cryptography. LNCS, vol. 2567, pp. 100–115. Springer-Verlag, Berlin (2003)
4. Boneh, D., Gentry, C., Waters, B.: Collusion resistant broadcast encryption with short ciphertexts and private keys. In: Shoup, V. (ed.) CRYPTO 2005. LNCS, vol. 3621, pp. 258–275. Springer, Heidelberg (2005)
5. Delerablée, C., Paillier, P., Pointcheval, D.: Fully collusion secure dynamic broadcast encryption with constant-size ciphertexts or decryption keys. In: Takagi, T., Okamoto, T., Okamoto, E., Okamoto, T. (eds.) Pairing 2007. LNCS, vol. 4575, pp. 39–59. Springer, Heidelberg (2007)
6. Shamir, A.: Identity-based cryptosystems and signature schemes. In: Blakely, G.R., Chaum, D. (eds.) CRYPTO 1984. LNCS, vol. 196, pp. 47–53. Springer, Heidelberg (1985)
7. Boneh, D., Franklin, M.: Identity-based encryption from the weil pairing. In: Kilian, J. (ed.) CRYPTO 2001. LNCS, vol. 2139, pp. 213–229. Springer, Heidelberg (2001)
8. Boneh, D., Boyen, X.: Efficient selective-ID secure identity-based encryption without random oracles. In: Cachin, C., Camenisch, J.L. (eds.) EUROCRYPT 2004. LNCS, vol. 3027, pp. 223–238. Springer, Heidelberg (2004)
9. Boneh, D., Katz, J.: Improved efficiency for CCA-secure cryptosystems built using identity-based encryption. In: Menezes, A. (ed.) CT-RSA 2005. LNCS, vol. 3376, pp. 87–103. Springer, Heidelberg (2005)
10. Boneh, D., Boyen, X., Goh, E.-J.: Hierarchical identity based encryption with constant size ciphertext. In: Cramer, R. (ed.) EUROCRYPT 2005. LNCS, vol. 3494, pp. 440–456. Springer, Heidelberg (2005)
11. Boneh, D., Boyen, X.: Secure identity based encryption without random oracles. In: Franklin, M. (ed.) CRYPTO 2004. LNCS, vol. 3152, pp. 443–459. Springer, Heidelberg (2004)
12. Gentry, C.: Practical identity-based encryption without random oracles. In: Vaudenay, S. (ed.) EUROCRYPT 2006. LNCS, vol. 4004, pp. 445–464. Springer, Heidelberg (2006)
13. Mu, Y., Susilo, W., Lin, Y.-X., Ruan, C.: Identity-based authenticated broadcast encryption and distributed authenticated encryption. In: Maher, M.J. (ed.) ASIAN 2004. LNCS, vol. 3321, pp. 169–181. Springer, Heidelberg (2004)
14. Delerablée, C.: Identity-based broadcast encryption with constant size ciphertexts and private keys. In: Kurosawa, K. (ed.) ASIACRYPT 2007. LNCS, vol. 4833, pp. 200–215. Springer, Heidelberg (2007)
15. Du, X., Wang, Y., Ge, J., et al.: An id-based broadcast encryption scheme for key distribution. IEEE Trans. Broadcast. **51**(2), 264–266 (2005)

16. Ren, Y.L., Gu, D.W.: Fully CCA2 secure identity based broadcast encryption without random oracles. Inf. Process. Lett. **109**, 527–533 (2009)
17. Gentry, C., Waters, B.: Adaptive security in broadcast encryption systems (with short ciphertexts). In: Joux, A. (ed.) EUROCRYPT 2009. LNCS, vol. 5479, pp. 171–188. Springer, Heidelberg (2009)
18. Libert, B., Paterson, K.G., Quaglia, E.A.: Anonymous Broadcast Encryption. Cryptology ePrint Archive Report 2011/475
19. Zhang, X., Wang, S., Zhang, W.: Forward-secure identity-based broadcast encryption scheme from lattice. Appl. Math. **9**(4), 1993–2000 (2015)
20. Waters, B.: Dual system encryption: realizing fully secure IBE and HIBE under simple assumptions. In: Halevi, S. (ed.) CRYPTO 2009. LNCS, vol. 5677, pp. 619–636. Springer, Heidelberg (2009)
21. Lewko, A., Waters, B.: New techniques for dual system encryption and fully secure HIBE with short ciphertexts. In: Micciancio, D. (ed.) TCC 2010. LNCS, vol. 5978, pp. 455–479. Springer, Heidelberg (2010)
22. Zhang, L., Hu, Y., Wu, Q.: Adaptively secure identity-based broadcast encryption with constant size private keys and ciphertexts from the subgroups. Math. Comput. Model. **55**, 12–18 (2012)
23. Zhang, L., Hu, Y., Wu, Q.: Fully secure identity-based broadcast encryption in the subgroups. China Commun. **8**(2), 152–158 (2011)
24. Kim, J., Susilo, W., Au, M.H., et al.: Adaptively secure identity-based broadcast encryption with a constant-sized ciphertext. IEEE Trans. Inf. Forensics Secur. **10**(3), 679–693 (2015)
25. Bellare, M., Boldyreva, A., Desai, A., Pointcheval, D.: Key-privacy in public-key encryption. In: Boyd, C. (ed.) ASIACRYPT 2001. LNCS, vol. 2248, pp. 566–582. Springer, Heidelberg (2001)
26. Boneh, D., Franklin, M.: Identity-based encryption from the weil pairing. In: Kilian, J. (ed.) CRYPTO 2001. LNCS, vol. 2139, pp. 213–229. Springer, Heidelberg (2001)
27. Seo, J.H., Kobayashi, T., Ohkubo, M., Suzuki, K.: Anonymous hierarchical identity-based encryption with constant size ciphertexts. In: Jarecki, S., Tsudik, G. (eds.) PKC 2009. LNCS, vol. 5443, pp. 215–234. Springer, Heidelberg (2009)
28. Zhang, L., Wu, Q., Hu, Y.: Adaptively Secure Identity-based Encryption in the Anonymous Communications. ICIC Express Letters **5**(9(A)), 3209–3216 (2011)
29. Kocher, P.C.: Timing attacks on implementations of Diffie-Hellman, RSA, DSS, and other systems. In: Advances in Cryptology –CRYPTO 1996, pp. 104–113 (1996)
30. Kocher, P.C., Jaffe, J., Jun, B.: Differential power analysis. In: Wiener, M. (ed.) CRYPTO 1999. LNCS, vol. 1666, pp. 388–397. Springer, Heidelberg (1999)
31. Zhang, M., Shi, W., Wang, C., Chen, Z., Mu, Y.: Leakage-resilient attribute-based encryption with fast decryption: models, analysis and constructions. In: Deng, R.H., Feng, T. (eds.) ISPEC 2013. LNCS, vol. 7863, pp. 75–90. Springer, Heidelberg (2013)

# Scheduling Resource of IaaS Clouds for Energy Saving Based on Predicting the Overloading Status of Physical Machines

Qingxin Xia$^{(\boxtimes)}$, Yuqing Lan, and Limin Xiao

School of Computer Science and Engineering, Beihang University,
Beijing 100191, China
{xiaqingxin,lanyuqing,xiaolm}@buaa.edu.cn

**Abstract.** Due to the wide applications of IaaS (Infrastructure as a Service), energy-saving technologies of IaaS clouds has attracted much attention. However, it is very difficult for IaaS cloud providers to guarantee both of energy saving and performance under the condition of satisfying SLA (Service Level Agreement). Recently, in researches of Iaas cloud resource scheduling strategies, it is focused that SLA violation or overloaded host can trigger migrations of virtual machines. However, it is a new difficulty to resource scheduling among the physical machines that high variable workloads have to be conducted. Therefore, in order to schedule resource optimally, we propose a novel status-prediction-based framework, which seamlessly integrates the virtual machine migration optimal time theorem and the status prediction model of physical machines based on the hidden Markov process. Further, we address a resource scheduling algorithm based on the status prediction model on physical machines. Finally, through real experimental scenarios, we verify the effectiveness of the virtual machine migration timing prediction and the resource scheduling algorithm.

**Keywords:** Prediction · IaaS · Hidden Markov Process · Energy saving

## 1 Introduction

In recent years, big data techniques have attracted much attention of the industrial and research communities [1,2]. The development and maturation of virtualization technology bring new ideas for the problem of high energy consumption of IaaS cloud platform. For example, the virtualization technology can concentrate multiple workloads on the same physical machine through migration of virtual machines to shut down the idle physical machines or switch them to sleep mode, so as to achieve the purpose of energy saving [3]. Moreover, it is a scientific problem when to do the virtual machine migration operation can cost the lowest energy consumption, which needs to give in-depth analysis of the virtual machine migration cost. Now, a few common examples will be given to explore the importance of virtual machine migration timing.

© Springer International Publishing Switzerland 2015
G. Wang et al. (Eds.): ICA3PP 2015 Workshops, LNCS 9532, pp. 211–221, 2015.
DOI: 10.1007/978-3-319-27161-3_19

Case 1: The migration of virtual machine occurs as soon as SLA violation is starting, which will not only affect the performance of the system and the users' feel, but also can not provide an optimal solution from the view of saving energy [4].

Case 2: The migration of virtual machine occurs as soon as the workload of physical machine exceeds the overloaded threshold set already [5]. So obviously, it is not an optimal scheme if using a fixed threshold. While the dynamic threshold adjustment [6], which often analyzes and adjusts the threshold according to the statistical analysis of historical data, can not reflect the real-time change characteristic of the system, which obtains nonideal results.

Both the virtual machine migration timings in cases 1 and 2 are not the optimal solution to the energy aware strategy. We try to find in which timing the virtual machine migration can save the most energy. We will provide the third case in the following:

Case 3: We predict the status of each physical machine at next time or during the next time interval according to the resource requirements. As the time took by virtual machine migration is known, we predict the time when the physical machine is overloading, then minus the time took by virtual machine migration to determine when the virtual machine starts to migrate. The solution above should be good, and the detail analysis will be presented in the following sections.

Based on the motivation above, we try to define the virtual machine migration time and provide the optimal migration time theorem firstly; Secondly, physical machine resource predicting model based on Hidden Markov process will be constructed, which can predict the overloading status of the physical machine in future time, with which the migration duration of virtual machines can be determined; Finally, we track the physical machine resource in one day through three real scenarios to verify the effect on virtual machine migration timing process caused by physical machine resource status predicting model based on Hidden Markov process.

## 2    The Cost Analysis of Virtual Machine Migration

$M$ virtual machines (VMs) are deployed on a physical machine (PM). First of all, making an assumption of the time, the total process is divided into $N$ intervals, with one second as each interval; Secondly, the energy consumption of PM was defined as $C_p t_p$, and $C_p$ is the energy consumption of PM in per unit time, while $t_p$ is the interval which PM experienced.

When the SLA violation occurs, resource providers will make the compensation $C_v t_v$, with $C_v$ as the energy costs in a unit of time due to SLA violation and $t_v$ as the time interval which SLA violation experienced. Then, we make the third assumption, $C_p = 1$, $C_v = s$, $(s \in \Re^+)$, so $C_p = 1$ and $C_v = 1$ are obtained. We define the time taken by migration as $T$, in the time $T$, another PM was needed as the PM of the migrating VMs, so the energy consumption in the migration process was $2C_p T$.

## 2.1 The Cost Function

According to the definitions of the problems mentioned above, we define the energy cost function $C(v, m)$, as shown in Eq. (1). Total energy cost includes the energy consumption caused by SLA violation, the physical machine and the migration operations. This energy cost function $C(v, m)$ are the three cases with parameters $v$ and $m$, in order to present the obvious description, $C_1$, $C_2$ and $C_3$ are used. $C_1$ represents the energy cost caused by the migration occurs before the violation of SLA, and the ending time of migration is earlier than the beginning time of SLA violation. According to the statement of the problem, $C_1$ does not violate SLA, in which the cost is due to the costs of the migration resulted in additional PM. $C_2$ represents the energy cost caused by the migration occurs before SLA violation, and SLA violation occurs at the end of migration.

$$C(v,m) = \begin{cases} (v-m)C_p & \text{if } m < v, v - m \geq T \\ (v-m)C_p + 2(m-v+T)C_p \\ +(m-v+T)C_v & \text{if } m \leq v, v - m < T \\ rC_p + (r-m+v)C_p + rC_v & \text{if } m > v \end{cases} \tag{1}$$

## 2.2 The Optimal Time of Virtual Machine Migration

Theorem 1 (The virtual machine migration optimal time theorem): In the off-line algorithm of virtual machine migration, the energy consumption cost by one virtual machine is $\frac{T}{s}$, with the necessary condition as $\frac{(v-m)}{T} = 1$.

Proof: According to the energy consumption cost function $C(v, m)$ shown in the Eq. (1), three parts will be used to prove it.

As $C(v, m)$ only has the relationship with the starting time of virtual machine migration $m$ and the starting time of SLA violation $v$, we give the definition: $(v - m) = aT(a \in \Re)$, then: $m = v - aT$, $a = \frac{v-m}{T}$. The detail proofs are as the three following steps:

(1) When $m < v, v - m \geq T$, so $a \geq 1$. Also $m = v - aT$, which will be drawn into the Eq. (1), then Eq. (2) will be obtained.

$$C_1(v, a) = (v - v + aT)C_p = aTC_p \tag{2}$$

(2) When $m \leq v, v - m < T$, $a \geq 0, a < 1$, so $0 \leq a < 1$. Then $m = v - aT$, which will be drawn into the Eq. (1), then Eq. (3) will be obtained.

$$\begin{aligned} C_2(v, a) &= (v - v + aT)C_p + 2(-aT + T)C_p + (-aT + T)C_v \\ &= T(2 - a)C_p + T(1 - a)C_v \end{aligned} \tag{3}$$

(3) When $m > v$, $a < 0$, which will be drawn into the Eq. (1), then Eq. (4) will be obtained.

$$\begin{aligned} C_3(v, m) &= rC_p + (r - m + v)C_p + rC_v \\ &= (2r - m + v)C_p + rC_v \end{aligned} \tag{4}$$

Here $r$ is the time interval from the starting time of SLA violation to the end of virtual machine migration, namely $r = m - v + T$. Then $m = v - aT$, so $r = T(1-a)$, which will be drawn into the Eq. (4), then Eq. (5) will be obtained.

$$
\begin{aligned}
C_3(v, a) &= (2T - 2aT - v + aT + v)C_p + T(1 - a)C_v \\
&= T(2 - a)C_p + T(1 - a)C_v \\
&= C_2(v, a)
\end{aligned}
\tag{5}
$$

Therefore, we obtain $C_3(v, a) = C_2(v, a)$, then we simplify this equation, eliminating one parameter $v$ further, a piecewise linear function about the parameter $a$ will be obtained, as is shown in Eq. (6).

$$
C(a) = \begin{cases} T(2 - a)C_p + T(1 - a)C_v & \text{if } a < 1 \\ aTC_p & \text{if } a \geq 1 \end{cases}
\tag{6}
$$

According to the definition, we draw $C_p = \frac{1}{s}$ and $C_v = 1$ into the Eq. (6), and Eq. (7) will be obtained.

$$
C(a) = \begin{cases} \frac{T(2-a)}{s} + T(1 - a) & \text{if } a < 1 \\ \frac{aT}{s} & \text{if } a \geq 1 \end{cases}
\tag{7}
$$

Therefore, we can easily obtain $Min\{C_a\} = \frac{T}{a}$, only when $a = 1$. So, the proof of virtual machine migration time theorem has been done.

# 3    The Predicting Model and Algorithm Implementation

## 3.1    The Predicting Model

The physical machine can be divided into three statuses: overload, underload and normal, which are not the sequence that can be observed, but a hidden status sequence known as the implicit status set. Below, we will analyze the observation status sequence. Taking the physical machine as the resource container of virtual machines, in the cloud environment, because of the performance, or for the consumption reasons, the migration of virtual machines will occur at some point between physical machines, during which three statuses of virtual machines will occur, including migrating in, out and none of them, and the three statuses appear according to IaaS cloud platform with different virtual machine scheduling strategies, that is to say it exists a certain probability distribution according to the operation status of the system, which will become the observation sequence in this paper.

Therefore, the IaaS cloud resource demand predicting model is a double stochastic process model, in which the status transition process is implicit, while the observable status stochastic process is a random function of implicit status conversion process, which is in line with constructing resource status prediction model based on the hidden Markov process.

The definition of the hidden Markov process model is described by a group of five parameters:

$$\lambda = (N, M, A, B, \pi) \tag{8}$$

Here: $N$ is a collection of physical machine's status, $M$ is a set of observations, $A$ is the probability matrix of status transition, $B$ is the probability distribution matrix of observations, $\pi$ is the probability distribution in initial status.

We have constructed the hidden Markov process model based on the physical machine and virtual machine resources of IaaS cloud platform, and our goal is to predict the resource demand, therefore, an algorithm is needed to drive our model. Below, a dynamic programming algorithm will be introduced $Viterbi$ algorithm, and a scene predicting process will be provided.

Hidden status set: $N = \{S_1, S_2, S_3\}$, in which, $S_1$ represents the $underload$ status of physical machine; $S_2$ represents the $normal$ status of physical machine; $S_3$ represents the $overload$ status of physical machine.

The obvious state set (the observation state set), $M = \{OUT, IN, NON\}$, in which, $OUT$ represents the state of virtual machine when "migrate out"; $IN$ represents the state of "migrate in"; $NON$ represents the state of "none of migrating out or in".

The initial status probability: $\pi = \pi_1, \pi_2, \pi_3$.

The hidden status transition probability: $A = (a_{ij})_{3\times 3}$ in which, represents the transfer probability from one status to another status.

The probability distribution of observation value: $B = b(M)$, $b(M)$ in which, is the probability distribution of element $M$.

### 3.2 The Algorithm Implementation

Now, we present a scenario of PM status prediction. PM $i$ is a status of moderate workload, which may have three kinds of status changing in the next point:

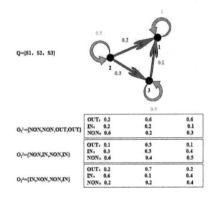

**Fig. 1.** HMM model status transition under moderate workloads

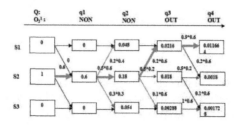

**Fig. 2.** The predicting Path of the safe status (Color figure online)

(1) Known: the status observation value set $O_2^1 = \{NON, NON, OUT, OUT\}$.
The initial status probability $\pi = \{0, 1, 0\}$, the status transition matrix $A$
and the probability distribution $B$ in the observation set are shown in Fig. 1.
In this scene, PM $i$ is in the moderate workload status, the status sequence
$q_1, q_2, q_3, q_4$ is: $S_2, S_2, S_1, S_1$, that is to say, when $t = 3$, the physical machine
will be in the *underload* status at next point. The calculation structure
diagram is shown in Fig. 3. The green arrow indicates the status sequence
path with maximum probability.

(2) Known: the status observation value set $O_2^2 = \{NON, IN, NON, IN\}$. The
initial status probability $\pi = \{0, 1, 0\}$, the status transition matrix $A$ and the
probability distribution $B$ in the observation set are shown in Fig. 1. Similarly, we can draw the conclusion as Fig. 2 followed. In this scene, PM $i$ is in a
moderate workload status, the status sequence $q_1, q_2, q_3, q_4$ is: $S_2, S_2, S_2, S_2$,
that is to say, when $t = 3$, the physical machine will be in the *safe* status at
next point. The calculation structure diagram is shown in Fig. 2. The green
arrow indicates the status sequence path with maximum probability.

(3) Known: the status observation value set $O_2^3 = \{IN, NON, NON, IN\}$. The
initial status probability $\pi = \{0, 1, 0\}$, the status transition matrix $A$ and
the probability distribution $B$ in the observation set are shown in Fig. 1.
Similarly, we can draw the conclusion as Fig. 4 followed. In this scene, PM $i$
is in a moderate load status, the status sequence $q_1, q_2, q_3, q_4$ is $S_2, S_3, S_3, S_3$:,
that is to say, when $t = 3$, the physical machine will be in the *overload* status
at next point. The calculation structure diagram is shown in Fig. 4. The green
arrow indicates the status sequence path with maximum probability.

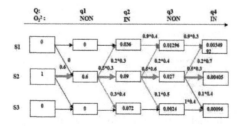

**Fig. 3.** The predicting Path of the underload status (Color figure online)

In Sect. 2.2, we presented an analysis of the optimal time theorem for virtual machine migration, and provided the proof. In Sect. 3, we constructed the prediction model of the physical machine resource status, with which the overloading time of the physical machine could be predicted. Based on the research of two sections, an energy aware virtual machine scheduling algorithm will be carried on. Now, The following is the process of *HMM-PSP* algorithm(energy aware VM scheduling algorithm of Physical machine Status Prediction based on Hidden Markov Model).

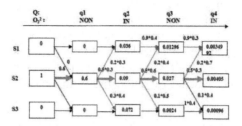

**Fig. 4.** The predicting Path of the overload status (Color figure online)

---

**Algorithm 1.** *HMM-PSP* Algorithm

---

**Input**: hostList, S1, S3
**Output**: vmMigrationList

1  for host in hostList do
2     while host.HMMmodel() = S3 do
3        overloadingHostList.add(host)
4  for host in overloadingHostList do
5     host.upThresh = getHMMupThresh()
6     host.lowThresh = getHMMlowThresh()
7     hUtil = host.getUtil()
8     while hUtil > host.upThresh ($\theta_2$) do
9        bestFitVm = findBestFitVm()
10    vmMigrationList.add(bestFitVm)
11    while hUtil < host.lowThresh ($\theta_1$) do
12       vmMigrationList.add(host.getVmList())
13 return vmMigrationList

---

# 4    Evaluation

## 4.1    Experimental Scenario

The hardware platform in real scene is the four physical nodes, of which two units are configured to AMD Opteron 2350 (2.0 GHz) quad core processor, 4 GB memory, the other two are configured to the Inter Core i7-5960 processor, 16 GB memory. All physical nodes run on the cloud platform software– OpenStack JUNO [7]. A disk array is connected with each node by optical fiber, which is as a shared storage of the cluster. The virtual machines used in the experiment were all cloned from the VM templates–Windows XP(SP3) and CentOS 7.0. All the virtual machines are configured to 1 vCPU, 1 GB memory, 1 virtual network card.

The physical machines, the virtual machines, the workload and some other environment configuration have been introduced in the part of experimental platform, in the description of experimental scenario, we define the workload input value as the normal distribution workload, the purpose of which is to observe the experimental results well, which will also not affect the general conclusion. The sampling interval of system is 5 min, the length is 1 day, which has been divided into 288 sampling time intervals, consistent with the sampling intervals of workloads. The experiments will be validated by comparisons of three scenarios as Fig. 5 followed.

Scenario A: Using the improved BFD algorithm [8], and the overloading detection method with 0.9 as the upper threshold.
Scenario B: Using the LF-MMT algorithm [9], and the dual threshold underloading and overloading detection method, with 0.9 as the upper threshold and 0.4 as the lower threshold.
Scenario C: Using the HMM-PSP algorithm, and the underloading and the overloading detection method with 0.9 as the upper threshold and 0.4 as the lower threshold as the same as Scenario B.

When we take the multidimensional vector BFD algorithm of workload characteristics classification, the initial fixed threshold is used.

## 4.2   Results Analysis

The experiment has experienced $15 \times 24$ h (15 days), with 5 min interval, starting from time t0 to the ending time t288. In this process, the CPU resource status changes of 4 physical machines and the migration steps of 100 virtual machines are all shown in Fig. 5. Now we present a brief introduction of the initial information in Fig. 5, $PMi = \{PM1, PM2, PM3, PM4\}$, $ti = \{t0, t1, ..., t288\}$, $v$ in $\langle v, u \rangle$ represents the number of virtual machines in the corresponding $PMi$, 'the red letter' represents the current CPU utilization in the corresponding $PMi$. 'Green arrow' represents the direction and time point of virtual machine migration between the physical machines.

In Fig. 6, it can be seen that the HMM-PSP algorithm presented in this paper has more advantages than the other two algorithms, the three aspects of the VM migration number, the average time of SLA violation (SLATAH) and the energy consumption three aspects are greatly reduced, the detail analysis the experiment is as follows:

(1) In the aspect of VM migration number: it has reduced 22.2 percents of the migration times per day in average than BFD algorithm, and 5.6 percents of

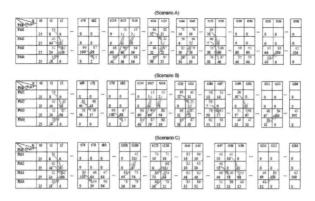

**Fig. 5.** PM's status transition and VM migration under Scenario A, B and C (Color figure online)

the migration times daily in average than LF-MMT algorithm, which illustrates that the HMM-PSP algorithm has greatly reduced the extra energy cost by VM migration consumption.

(2) In the aspect of the average time of SLA violation: it has reduced 29 times of the SLA violation time per day in average than BFD algorithm, and 20 times of the SLA violation time per day in average than LF-MMT algorithm, which illustrates that the HMM-PSP algorithm can provide more comfortable in the performance of system for users.

(3) In the aspect of energy consumption: it has reduced 92.6 percents of energy consumption per day in average than BFD algorithm, and 37.1 percents of energy consumption per day in average than LF-MMT algorithm, which illustrates that the HMM-PSP algorithm has greatly reduced the extra energy cost by VM migration consumption.

What's more, we can draw an important regular pattern about the HMM-PSP algorithm that it is a monotone decreasing trend which can be shown in the aspect of three metrics in Fig. 6.

## 5   Related Work

In the energy-saving field of IaaS cloud platform, the migration technology of overload detection is divided into two parts-static threshold and dynamic threshold. M. Bichler et al. [10] put forward a mathematical programming method to optimize the numbers of VMs that a PM can hold, which is insufficient that only the isomorphism of PM has been studied. Maurya et al. [11] proposed an adaptive threshold and double threshold method, using CloudSim simulation, proved to be more energy-saving compared with other dynamic strategies.

In the field of resource management based on resource prediction, Park, N. et al. [12] do the research on multi-tenant storage management through the

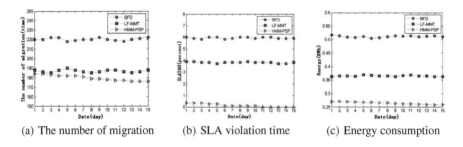

(a) The number of migration    (b) SLA violation time    (c) Energy consumption

**Fig. 6.** Running time vs Minimum Utility Threshold

performance prediction method. However, the research does not present energy saving from the perspective of further exploration. Chen L. et al. [13] summarize the overview of the bandwidth resource deployment in datacenters, which is a detailed analysis of the bandwidth resource prediction. Our work is to make resource predictions more concrete.

## 6    Conclusion

This study analyzes the cost of virtual machine migration, presents the virtual machine migration optimal time theorem and proves it further. According to the theorem, we must predict the occurrence time of overloading physical machine through using the Hidden Markov process to construct the status prediction model. In the real experiment, our HMM-PSP algorithm has obtained great results in the SLA violation and energy consumption through the comparisons of three algorithms.

**Acknowledgments.** This paper is respectively supported by National Natural Science Foundation of China under Grant No. 61232009 and No. 61370059, Beijing Natural Science Foundation under Grant No. 4152030, the Fundamental Research Funds for the Central Universities under Grant No. YWF-15-GJSYS-085, the Open Project Program of National Engineering Research Center for Science and Technology Resources Sharing Service.

## References

1. Tong, Y., Zhang, X., Chen, L.: Tracking frequent items over distributed probabilistic data. World Wide Web, pp. 1–26 (2015)
2. Tong, Y., Chen, L., She, J.: Mining frequent itemsets in correlated uncertain databases. J. Comput. Sci. Technol. **30**(4), 696–712 (2015)
3. Deore, S.S., Patil, A.N.: Energy-efficient job scheduling and allocation scheme for virtual machines in private clouds. Energy **5**(1), 56–60 (2013)
4. Kusic, D., Kephart, J.O., Hanson, J.E., Kandasamy, N., Jiang, G.: Power and performance management of virtualized computing environments via lookahead control. Cluster Comput. **12**(1), 1–15 (2009)

5. Vasi, N., Novakovi, D., Miucîn, S., et al.: Dejavu: accelerating resource allocation in virtualized environments. ACM SIGARCH Comput. Architect. News **40**(1), 423–436 (2012)
6. Huber, N., Brosig, F., Kounev, S.: Model-based self-adaptive resource allocation in virtualized environments. In: Proceedings of the 6th International Symposium on Software Engineering for Adaptive and Self-Managing Systems, pp. 90–99. ACM (2011)
7. Openstack: JUNO the tenth openstack release. http://www.openstack.org/software/juno/
8. Weisstein, E.W.: "bin-packing problem." from mathworld-a wolfram web resource. http://mathworld.wolfram.com/bin-packingprogram.html
9. Beloglazov, A., Buyya, R.: Optimal online deterministic algorithms and adaptive heuristics for energy and performance efficient dynamic consolidation of virtual machines in cloud data centers. Concurrency Comput. Pract. Exp. **24**(13), 1397–1420 (2012)
10. Speitkamp, B., Bichler, M.: A mathematical programming approach for server consolidation problems in virtualized data centers. IEEE Trans. Serv. Comput. **3**(4), 266–278 (2010)
11. Maurya, K., Sinha, R.: Energy conscious dynamic provisioning of virtual machines using adaptive migration thresholds in cloud data center. Int. J. Comput. Sci. Mob. Comput. 74–82 (2013)
12. Park, N., Ahmad, I., Lilja, D.J.: Romano: autonomous storage management using performance prediction in multi-tenant datacenters. In: SoCC (2012)
13. Chen, L., Li, B., Li, B.: Allocating bandwidth in datacenter networks: a survey. J. Comput. Sci. Technol. **29**(5), 910–917 (2014)

# Towards Mechanised Semantics of HPC: The BSP with Subgroup Synchronisation Case

Jean Fortin and Frédéric Gava$^{(\boxtimes)}$

LACL, University of Paris-East, Créteil, France
`frederic.gava@univ-paris-est.fr`

**Abstract.** The underlying objective of this article is to exhibit the problems that might be encountered when working on a mechanised semantics of an HPC language. We take for instance a language to program BSP algorithms with subgroup synchronisation *à la* MPI. We give two mechanised semantics using the COQ system and prove some common properties. By comparing the sizes of the semantics and proofs, we discuss about the potential scaling problems that would arise if we would like to extend this work to a mainstream language or adding more HPC routines.

**Keywords:** BSP · Mechanised semantics · Coq · Subgroup · MPI

## 1 Introduction

To design tools for the *correctness* of programs or having *certified compilers*, a classical step is to provide *operational semantics* of the language [8]. A recent approach is the use of theorem provers (*e.g.* COQ, http://coq.inria.fr/) for the development of *mechanised semantics* [8] and then formally prove their properties. In this paper, using COQ, we present some mechanised semantics for a core **B**ulk-**S**ynchronous **P**arallel [2] (BSP) language with *subgroup synchronisation*. The language is the one of our own tool for correctness of BSP programs called BSP-WHY [6]. Using subgroups allows synchronising only a part of the threads running on the processors and avoid *global barriers* of the whole distributed machine.

**Why BSP?** The BSP model is a *bridging model* between abstract execution and concrete HPC systems [2]. Its goal is to have *portable* programs with *scalable performance predictions*. BSP is thus especially suitable for HPC [2] as a wide range of *modern architectures* can be seen as BSP computers.

But for HPC, the common solution is using an MPI library. MPI in its entirety does not satisfy the BSP model. However, a large number of MPI programs use only *global operations* [4]. These can be viewed as BSP programs, if we allow BSP programs to synchronise over a subgroup of processes. In order to be able to study this kind of HPC programs, it is necessary to study their semantics.

**Why several semantics? What properties?** *Big-step* semantics are close to the *meaning* of program's execution [8] whereas *Small-step* ones describe more

G. Wang et al. (Eds.): ICA3PP 2015 Workshops, LNCS 9532, pp. 222–237, 2015.
DOI: 10.1007/978-3-319-27161-3_20

**Pure terms:**

$t_e$ ::= $cst \mid x \mid !x \mid \phi(t_e, \ldots, t_e)$

**Expressions:**

| | | |
|---|---|---|
| $e$ ::= | $t_e$ | term |
| | let $x = e$ in $e$ | declaration |
| | let $x = $ ref $e$ in $e$ | variable |
| | if $e$ then $e$ else $e$ | conditional |
| | loop $e$ | infinite loop |
| | raise $(E\ e)$ | exception |

| | |
|---|---|
| try $e$ with $E\ x \rightarrow e$ end | catch it |
| fun $x \rightarrow e$ | function |
| $x := e$ | assignment |
| $e\ e$ | application |
| bsp_push $c\ x$ | registering |
| bsp_pop $c\ x$ | deregistering |
| bsp_put $c\ e\ x\ y$ | DRMA writing |
| bsp_get $c\ e\ x\ y$ | DRMA reading |
| $\Omega\ e$ | Parameters |

**Fig. 1.** Syntax of BSP-WHY-ML

closely the *interleaving* of the parallel computations. And because some semantics allow proving some properties easier [8], if we want a *coherent work*, we must ensure that they are equivalent. For instance, *confluence* is easier to prove using a big-step semantics rather than using a small-step one [8]. Confluence is a property of sequential programming, but remains an objective [4] for HPC [3].

**Contribution.** In this work, using COQ, we give both big-step and small-step semantics. This allows us to give *mechanically* checked proofs of some usual properties that are desired for semantics, ensuring a better *confidence* in our definitions and *measuring the difficulty* for passing to a real HPC language.

## 2  A Language for BSP with Subgroups: BSP-WHY-ML

For sake of space, the BSP model and subgroup synchronisation are not describe in this paper but are fully available at: http://www.lacl.fr/gava/papers/icapp_2015.pdf.

The syntax (Fig. 1) of BSP-WHY-ML [6] is the one of WHY-ML [5]. We choose BSP routines that are close to the ones defined in most BSP libraries for both **B**ulk **M**essage **P**assing (BSMP) and **R**emote **M**emory **A**ccess (DRMA).

Programs contain *pure terms* ($t_e$, terms without possible of side effects) made of constants (integers, the empty value void, *etc.*), variables, dereferences (written $!x$) and application of function symbols $\phi$ (*e.g.* =, ≤, *etc.*) to pure terms. There is no constraint for $\phi$ except to be without side effect. The special constants **nprocs** (equal to **p**) and **pid** (with range $0, \ldots, \mathbf{p} - 1$) were also added. We have also introduced the two special function symbols bsp_nmsg($t$) and bsp_findmsg($t_1, t_2$): The former corresponds to the number of messages received from a processor id $t$ and the latter allows getting the $t_2$-th message from processor $t_1$ (PUB's "C routines" of the same names).

let, if, raise, try, fun statements are as usual in a ML-like language. ref $e$ introduces a new reference initialised with $e$ that could be modified using :=. loop $e$ is an infinite loop of body $e$. The *while* and *sequence* are not part of the core language, but can be easily defined from the *loop* and *let* instructions.

In the following, $c$ stands for a *communicator*: a subgroup of processors that have been registered to communicating and synchronising together. The four operations are the common BSP ones. More details are given in [6].

$\Omega$ defines the "parameters" of the semantics [6], that is routines for which we do not know the code (such as $\phi$). It is "user defined": Routines can be defined by the user depending on its library. For this work, we require that such routines are deterministic but it is not necessary for BSP-WHY-ML [6]. In this way, we abstract how creating/deleting the communicators (which are a little different in PUB and MPI) and how performing communication between processors and synchronising them, that is the routines that perform a barrier (what we call the SYNC effect throughout the paper [6], *routine that are marked to doing a barrier* and finishing the super-step). Throughout this paper, we illustrates $\Omega$ with bsp_sync($c$) and bsp_send $c\ x\ e$ that is sending value of $e$ to processor $x$.

# 3   Formal Operational Semantics

We now present the semantics and the key ideas of our COQ development. The full files are available at http://lacl.fr/gava/icap3pp2015_coq.tar.gz. We try giving some details on the relation between the formalization in COQ and the semantics rules at a paper-and-pencil level. The development also contains rules for managing exceptions that have not been presented here for simplifyng the presentation. It also contains the semantics for BSP programs without subgroups.

## 3.1   States and Environments of Execution

**Environment.** Values to be sent and distant reading/writing are stored in environments of communications as simple list of messages. Aside from the environment of variables (here noted $\mathcal{E}$, the usual map from variable's names to values), each processor have six additional components ($C^{\text{send}}$, $C^{\text{put}}$, $C^{\text{get}}$, $C^{\text{pop}}$, $C^{\text{push}}$, $\mathcal{R}$), one per operation that needs communications. Each operation adds a new value to be sent in one of these environments: *e.g.*, a distant writing adds the pair value to be written, to which remote variable, to $C^{\text{put}}$. $\mathcal{R}$ is the list of received messages. Routines of $\Omega$ can modify the environments as needed. For example, for a collective broadcasting, **p** messages should be added to $C^{\text{send}}$. With $s$, we denote for an environment. We note $s.\mathcal{X}$ the access to the component $\mathcal{X}$ of the environment $s$; $\oplus$ the update of a component without modifying other ones; and $\{x \mapsto v\} \in s.\mathcal{X}$ tests the presence of a variable $x$ (and its associated value $v$) in $s.\mathcal{X}$.

**Memory Model.** In the COQ development, the memory model is defined as a function from memory blocks (pointers) to values. All exchanged variables contain data of the generic type value, which represents any elementary type. A few special values are defined, such as void, true, false, *etc.* We represent variables, blocks and processor identifiers as positive numbers. The link between a variable

$$\frac{s, e \Downarrow^i s', v \quad \text{where } (s'', o) \text{ is defined by } \Omega(s', v)}{s, \Omega\, e \Downarrow^i s'', o}$$

$$\frac{}{s, pid \Downarrow^i s, i} \qquad \frac{}{s, nprocs \Downarrow^i s, \mathbf{p}}$$

$$\frac{s, e_1 \Downarrow^i s', v \qquad s'[x \leftarrow v], e_2 \Downarrow^i s'', o}{s, \mathtt{let}\ x = e_1\ \mathtt{in}\ e_2 \Downarrow^i s'', o} \qquad \frac{s, e_1 \Downarrow^i s', E(v)}{s, \mathtt{let}\ x = e_1\ \mathtt{in}\ e_2 \Downarrow^i s', E(v)}$$

$$\frac{s, e_1 \Downarrow^i s', \mathrm{SYNC}(C, e')}{s, \mathtt{let}\ x = e_1\ \mathtt{in}\ e_2 \Downarrow^i s', \mathrm{SYNC}(C, \mathtt{let}\ x = e'\ \mathtt{in}\ e_2)} \qquad \frac{s, e \Downarrow^i s', v}{s, x := e \Downarrow^i s'[x \leftarrow v], void}$$

$$\frac{s, e \Downarrow^i s', E(v)}{s, x := e \Downarrow^i s', E(v)} \qquad \frac{s, e \Downarrow^i s', \mathrm{SYNC}(C, e')}{s, x := e \Downarrow^i s', \mathrm{SYNC}(C, x := e')} \qquad \frac{s, e;\ \mathtt{loop}\ e \Downarrow^i s', o}{s, \mathtt{loop}\ e \Downarrow^i s', o}$$

**Fig. 2.** Big-step semantics: examples of local sequential operations

and its memory block is then stored as a part of the execution environment $\mathcal{E}$. The memory model allows DRMA routines to share blocks of memory as in C.

A subgroup is defined as a function from the processor identifiers to booleans. A communicator, however, cannot be simply seen as a subgroup, as it is possible that several communicators share the same subgroups. Instead, we define a communicator as a unique positive number, as we did for other identifiers. Environments are defined using record types, following the previous definitions.

## 3.2    Big-Step Semantics

A big-step semantics is a set of inductive rules. It allows to construct an evaluation tree of a code. If there is no rule to continue the construction, it is a faulty program (or there is a bug in the semantics). We need local rules to execute asynchronous computations and global rules for managing the whole distributed machine. BSP programs are SPMD (**S**ingle **P**rogram **M**ultiple **D**ata) so an expression $e$ is started $\mathbf{p}$ times. Different codes can be run by the processors (resp. the subgroups) using conditionals on the "id" of the processors (resp. subgroups). For example "**if** pid=0 **then** code1 **else** code2" for running "code1" only on processor 0.

**Local Rules.** We first define semantics inductive rules for the local execution, *i.e.* on a single processor. With $s, e \Downarrow^i s', v$, we denote for the local reduction rules of a state $(s, e)$ to another one, on a processor $i$: $s$ is the environment before the execution, $e$ is the code to be executed, $s'$ the environment after the execution and $v$ is the resulting value. It may also be worth mentioning that this being an inductive semantics, this relation is undefined for an infinite reduction.

In Fig. 2, we give some examples of the rules for local operations: *pid* gives the id of the processor; *nprocs* gives the number $\mathbf{p}$ of processor; loop is for infinite loops; **let** and := are with traditional rules. For each control instruction and operation, it is necessary to give several rules, depending on the result of the execution of the different sub-instructions: one when an execution leads to a synchronisation (when processors finish a super-step, that is SYNC effect), one for an exception $E(v)$, and one if it returns directly a value. In the first

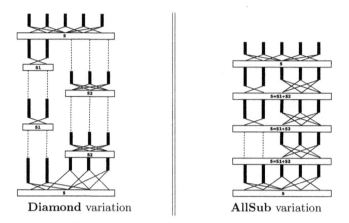

**Diamond** variation           **AllSub** variation

**Fig. 3.** Illustration of the two variations for the semantics of subgroups

case, we need to remember the instructions of the processor still to run. These intermediate synchronous configurations are noted $\text{SYNC}(C, e)$, if $e$ remains the code to be executed after a synchronisation on the communicator denoted by $C$. $(s, o)$ denotes a state where $o$ is an *outcome* that is a value $v$ or an exception $E(v)$ or a synchronous configuration $\text{SYNC}(C, e)$. $\Omega$ returns a state $s'', o$: a state with possibly a new environment and any outcome, depending of $\Omega$.

With subgroups, BSP routines are done in the scope of a communicator: every call takes an additional argument, the communicator, which describes the subset of processors in which the communications are done. For instance of an $\Omega$ rule, the one of "bsp_send" could manipulates $\mathcal{C}^{\text{send}}$ as follow:

$$\frac{s, e \Downarrow^i s', to \qquad to \in C \qquad \{x \mapsto v\} \in s'.\mathcal{E} \qquad s'' = s'.\mathcal{C}_C^{\text{send}} \oplus \{to, v\}}{s, \text{bsp\_send } C \; x \; e \Downarrow^i s'', \text{void}}$$

where "$C$" is a valid communicator in the environment. The message $v$ to processor "$to$" of the communicator $C$ is added to the queue of messages. Note that it is a typical case for the $\Omega$ rule: we return the empty value void and modify the environment. The rule for bsp_sync$(c)$ is simply:

$$\frac{s, e \Downarrow^i s', C}{s, \text{bsp\_sync } e \Downarrow^i s', \text{SYNC}(C, \text{void})}.$$

**Global Rules.** Compared to a common big-step semantics, the major changes are located within the distributed rules. Instead of having all the **p** processors synchronise and communicate together, it is now possible for a subgroup to synchronise together and make the needed communications. Several subgroups can also work independently from each other, and synchronise at the same time. There are two major variations in this situation: (1) All processors execute their code locally, until they reach a synchronisation state or they terminate; It is very close to the BSP execution without subgroups; We then execute all possible subgroup synchronisations, and then continue their computation; We call this variation **AllSub**; (2) Only one subgroup of processors execute their codes locally, until they reach a synchronisation; We execute the associated communications, then continue the computation; We call this variation **Diamond**.

With the subgroups, the BSP notion of *super-step* is less clearly defined, and the two variations could be seen as two different definitions of a super-step. Figure 3 illustrates them. Dotted lines are used when there is no evaluation for a group. In the **Diamond** variation we have also given only one possible interleave. In the **AllSub** variation, we can notice that the subgroup **s1** does nothing during the third super-step since subgroup **s2** has one more super-step.

There are *pros and cons* to both variations. In the **AllSub** variation, the rule is complex to write, even more so in COQ. However, it is perhaps the rule matching most closely the truly execution of a program where all processors compute in parallel. The **Diamond** definition is much easier to write and understand, but artificially gives priority to one subgroup over another one. This ordering of the subgroup executions leads to another issue: with this definition, the semantics loses its determinism, since when several subgroups are synchronising, it is possible to choose any subgroup to execute first.

We model this SPMD **p** times execution with global states that are **p**-vectors of states $(s_i, e_i)$: one pair (environment, expression) on each processor $i$. A terminated state is a **p**-vector of $(s_i, v_i)$. With $\Downarrow$, we denote this evaluation.

In Fig. 6 (page 14), we give 3 variations for the synchronisation rule. The first one is as it would be defined in a semantics without subgroup. The **AllComm** function models the exchanges of messages and thus specifies the order of the received messages depending on the parameter defined in $\Omega$: it modifies the environment of each processor $i$; it is "just" a reordering of the **p** environments.

The second rule $\Downarrow_{All}$ gives the **AllSub** variation where we first partition the set of processors in $k$ subsets that will synchronise, plus a subset $N$ of processors that do not synchronise. **AllCommSub** is then similar to **AllComm**. However, because there can be several subgroups synchronising, its exact definition is more complicated. It accepts as argument the set of communicators used in the synchronisation. In addition, it accepts as argument the array of the final values $v_i$ already reached in the super-step. For $i \in N$, the $i$-th processor terminates without synchronisation with the value $v_i$, so the $i$-th component of the result of **AllCommSub** will be the couple $(s'_i, v_i)$. For every set of processors matching a communicator $C_j$, all the communications corresponding to the communicator are done. Among the messages of these processors, the rule only considers the messages that were sent within the matching communicator.

The third rule $\Downarrow_{Diamond}$ corresponds to the **Diamond** variation. **CommDia** is similar to the **AllComm** function, with a few differences. It accepts a second argument (a communicator); it only modifies the environments of the processors in the range of the communicator; and among the messages of these processors, the rule only considers those that were sent within the matching communicator.

It is easy to see that even though this variation leads to non-determinism, it is still confluent. Because the only source of non-determinism is the communication rules, for which any matching communicator can be chosen. However, at any given point, the communications within two different communicators are independent, since each processor leads to a barrier in one communicator only.

Finally, for all the variations, the following rule terminates the execution:

$$\frac{\forall i \quad s_i, e_i \Downarrow^i s_i', v_i}{(s_0, e_0), \ldots (s_{\mathbf{p}-1}, e_{\mathbf{p}-1}) \Downarrow (s_0', v_0), \ldots (s_{\mathbf{p}-1}', v_{\mathbf{p}-1})}$$

that is all the processors compute their final value.

**Co-inductive Semantics Rules.** In addition to the standard inductive big-step semantics, it is often useful to define co-inductive (or infinite) semantics rules [8]. They allow characterising the behaviour of a program that runs indefinitely. Throughout this article, double horizontal lines in inference rules denote inference rules that are to be interpreted co-inductively; single horizontal lines denote the inductive interpretation. The co-inductive rules for the local control flow can easily be inferred from the regular big-step semantics rules. We give as an example one of the co-inductive rules for the "if" instruction:

$$\frac{s, e_1 \Downarrow^i s_1, \text{true} \qquad s_1, e_2 \Downarrow^i_\infty}{s, \text{if } e_1 \text{ then } e_2 \text{ else } e_3 \Downarrow^i_\infty}$$

The rule can be read as follow: "If $e_1$ evaluates to *true*, and if $e_2$ runs infinitely, then the program if $e_1$ then $e_2$ else $e_3$ will run infinitely". Local BSP operations (push, send, *etc.*) always terminate, so the co-inductive rules can also easily be inferred from the regular big-step semantics rules.

On the other hand, and more interestingly, we define the co-inductive global rules in Fig. 7 (page 14). The first rule states that if one of the processors runs infinitely, then the BSP program will run infinitely. In the other rules, it is said that if all the processors reach a synchronisation barrier, and if the program runs infinitely starting from the resulting state, then the BSP program runs infinitely. Note also that in both inductive and co-inductive semantics, if only one processor does not catch an exception before the barrier, the whole execution halts. We consider this case as a failure as there is no rule to evaluate "1+true".

**For the Coq Development.** For all the big-steps variations, there are two parts in the mechanical semantics. First, we define the local reduction rules, which represent the evaluation on a single processor, and then we give the global reduction rules. As is usual in COQ, the semantics rules are given as an inductive predicate — or co-inductive for infinite reductions. For the local reduction rules, eval_expr i.e. a e' o— defines the evaluation of the expression a in the environment e on the processor i (globally defined as the COQ's variable i:pid):

**Inductive** eval_expr: env → expr → env → outcome → **Prop** :=
| eval_Elet : ∀x a1 a2 e e' e'' v o, eval_expr e a1 e' (Outval v) →
                      eval_expr (update e' x v) a2 e'' o → eval_expr e (Elet x a1 a2) e'' o
| eval_Eraise : ∀a e e' v ex, eval_expr e a e' (Outval v) →
                          eval_expr e (Eraise ex a) e' (Outexn ex v)
| eval_Esync : ∀e, eval_expr e (Esync) e (Outsync sync Evoid)
| ...

The COQ definition of an outcome is as intended: there are 3 possible outcomes, either the computation returns a value Outval ($v$, case of the "let" rule), raises an exception Outexn ($E(v)$), or requests a barrier Outsync (SYNC($C, e$), case of a synchronous routine) with the code remaining to be executed.

The definition of the eval_expr predicate have several rules for each language instruction, depending on the kind of outcome obtained during the evaluation of the sub-expressions. There is typically one rule for a value outcome, one rule for an exception outcome and one rule for a synchronisation outcome. For each variation, we had two global rules, one for the communications and another one for ending the evaluation (similarly for the co-inductive semantics).

## 3.3   Small-Step Semantics

Small-step semantics specify the execution of a program, one step at a time. A set of rules is repeatedly applied on program states, until a final state is reached. If rules can be applied infinitely, it means the program diverges. If at one point in the execution there is no rule to apply, it is a faulty program.

In our BSP case, we will have two kinds of one-step reductions: (1) $\xrightarrow{i}$, for local reductions (on each processor $i$); (2) $\rightarrow$, for global reductions of the whole BSP machine. The full evaluation $\rightarrow^*$ of a program is the transitive and reflexive closure of $\rightarrow$. For diverging programs, we note the (co-inductive) reduction $\rightarrow_\infty$. Our semantics works as a set of rewriting rules. Despite misconceptions about the small-step semantics (they are easier to design [1,8] for concurrent codes), in our BSP case, the small-step semantics is harder to define than the big-step one.

**Problems.** As for big-steps, most of the rules are as usual. Synchronisation is the only problem. A naive solution would be to define a rule as:

$$\langle(s_0, \mathtt{bsp\_sync}; e_0), \ldots, (s_{p-1}, \mathtt{bsp\_sync}; e_{p-1})\rangle \rightarrow \langle(s_0', e_0), \ldots, (s_{p-1}', e_{p-1})\rangle$$

that is all processors are waiting for a synchronisation and then each of them executes what remains to be done. The problem with this rule is that it cannot evaluate a synchronisation inside a control structure *e.g.* if $b$ then bsp_sync else $e$: the rule only works for a sequence. Different solutions exist. First, adding specific rules for the synchronisation inside each control instruction; the drawback is that this implies too many rules. Second, using rules with "contexts" (a context is an expression with a hole, represented with a "_"): the bsp_sync instruction replaces the hole within a context on each processor; the drawback is that the rule for synchronisation becomes complicated to manage when using COQ. Third, in [10], the authors propose the rule "$s, \mathtt{bsp\_sync} \xrightarrow{i} s, Wait(skip)$" in addition to rules to propagate this waiting (as the ones of the big-step semantics) and the following rule: $\langle(s_0, Wait(e_0)), \ldots, (s_{p-1}, Wait(e_{p-1}))\rangle \rightarrow \langle(s_0, e_0), \ldots, (s_{p-1}, e_{p-1})\rangle$. But two subtleties persist: (1) the rule artificially adds a *skip* instruction that uselessly complicates the proofs; (2) in their work, "$(e_1; \mathtt{bsp\_sync}); e_2$" cannot be evaluated, only "$e_1; (\mathtt{bsp\_sync}; e_2)$" can. To remedy to the latter problem, in [7] (*without* subgroups), we choose to add the congruence (equivalence) "$(e_1; \mathtt{bsp\_sync}); e_2 \equiv e_1; (\mathtt{bsp\_sync}; e_2)$" but that also complicates the proofs.

$$s, \mathbf{\textit{nprocs}} \bullet \kappa \xrightarrow{i} s, \mathbf{p} \bullet \kappa$$

$$s, \mathbf{\textit{pid}} \bullet \kappa \xrightarrow{i} s, i \bullet \kappa$$

$$s, v \bullet (\texttt{let } x = \_ \texttt{ in } e_2) \bullet \kappa \xrightarrow{i} s[x \leftarrow v], e_2 \bullet \kappa$$

$$s, \texttt{let } x = e_1 \texttt{ in } e_2 \bullet \kappa \xrightarrow{i} s, e_1 \bullet (\texttt{let } x = \_ \texttt{ in } e_2) \bullet \kappa$$

$$s, x := e \bullet \kappa \xrightarrow{i} s, e \bullet (x := \_) \bullet \kappa$$

$$s, v \bullet (x := \_) \bullet \kappa \xrightarrow{i} s[x \leftarrow v], void \bullet \kappa$$

$$s, \texttt{loop } e \bullet \kappa \xrightarrow{i} s, e \bullet \texttt{loop } e \bullet \kappa$$

**Fig. 4.** Small-step semantics: example of local sequential operations

**Local Rules.** The solution we propose is the use of a "continuation semantics", in the spirit of the semantics described in [1]. This semantics mainly allows a uniform representation of states that facilitates the design of lemmas.

A local state is completed with a control stack $\kappa$. The terminated state is $(s, void \bullet \epsilon)$, the environment $s$ with the empty value and with an empty control stack. The control stack represents what has not been executed —where $\bullet$ is an associative operator. There are sequential control operators to handle local control flow. This is close to an abstract machine. In Fig. 4 we give some examples of local rules of control flow and in Fig. 5 for BSP operations ($\Omega$). For example, the rule for **nprocs** simply adds $\mathbf{p}$ in the stack. In the control stack we find expressions with holes. Each hole represents the sub-expression that is currently evaluated and is represented with a "_". Most instructions are dealt with by several rules. Generally, the first rule simply puts the instruction in the continuation stack, and sets the first basic element of the instruction to compute as the main program. Then, one or more rules will match the possible results of this execution, and perform the necessary operations for the control instruction. For instance, with the rule of the **let** statement, the **let** continuation is put in the control stack and $e_1$ is at the top of the stack. In a second rule, when $e_1$ has been evaluated, there is a value $v$ at the top of the control stack which is substituted in $s$ and the evaluation continues with the rest of the stack. A communication primitive consists of simply adding a new value in the environment. Synchronisation is just computing for which communicator $C$ we want to synchronise (SYNC($C$)) and waiting that a global rule performs the barrier. As in the big-step semantics, there is also no rule when one processor does not catch an exception.

**Global Rules.** As previously, global rules are mainly used to call local ones and $\mathbf{p}$ states have to be reduced. Figure 8 (page 18) gives those rules. First, the global reduction calls a local one. This represents a reduction by a single processor, which thus introduces an interleaving of computations. Communication and BSP synchronisation are done with the second rule: each processor $i$ of the communicator $C$ is in the case of a synchronous primitive (such as bsp_sync) with its control stack $\kappa_i$; that is noted $O_i$. As in the big-step semantics, **CommDia** computes the communication, and returns the new environments. Then what remains to be executed is only the control stacks since the synchronisation has been performed. Note that this semantics introduces an interleaving of local computations compared to the big-step one where all local computations are fully "running" in parallel in the different branches of the tree evaluation.

$$s, \Omega \; e \bullet \kappa \xrightarrow{i} s, e \bullet (\Omega \; \_) \bullet \kappa$$

$$s, v \bullet (\Omega \; \_) \bullet \kappa \xrightarrow{i} s', v' \bullet \kappa \quad \text{where } (s', v') \text{ is defined using } \Omega$$

Examples for **bsp_send** and **bsp_sync** routines:

$$s, \texttt{bsp\_send } C \; x \; e \bullet \kappa \xrightarrow{i} s, e \bullet (\texttt{bsp\_send } C \; x \; \_) \bullet \kappa$$

$$s, to \bullet (\texttt{bsp\_send } C \; x \; \_) \bullet \kappa \xrightarrow{i} s', \kappa \quad \text{if } to \in C \text{ and } s' = s.\mathcal{C}_{\mathcal{C}}^{\text{send}} \oplus \{to, x\}$$

$$s, (\texttt{bsp\_sync } e) \bullet \kappa \xrightarrow{i} s', e \bullet (\texttt{bsp\_sync } \_) \bullet \kappa$$

$$s', C \bullet (\texttt{bsp\_sync } \_) \bullet \kappa \xrightarrow{i} \texttt{SYNC}(C) \bullet \kappa$$

**Fig. 5.** Small-step semantics: example of $\Omega$ rules (**bsp_send** and **bsp_sync** routines)

**Co-inductive Semantics** $\to_{\infty}$. It is much easier to define. A program runs indefinitely if it has an infinite sequence of one-step reductions as in [8].

**For the Coq Development.** The small-step semantics use the same environments and memory model as the big-step ones. However, the semantics is significantly different. Since we chose to use continuations, we need to define them. For each statement in the language, zero, one, or several continuations will be defined, depending on the number of computations that are done sequentially in the statement. For instance, a "if" statement has one. The continuation stack is defined inductively, in a similar fashion as a list:

**Inductive** cont : **Type** :=
| Kempty: cont
| Klet: expr→ cont→ cont
| ...

**Kempty** is the empty continuation, and every other continuation is linked to a previous continuation. **Klet** is the continuation for the **let** statement (and there is one continuation case for each different statement of the language). As shown in Fig. 4, for the small-step rule of "let", we need the second expression $e_2$ of the **let** following the linked continuation and the hole (replacing $e_1$), hence the need of only one **expr** in the definition.

A major difference with the big-step semantics is the notion of program execution "state". For the big-step semantics, a state was simply the association of a program and an environment. In the small-step one, however, we define four kinds of states: (1) a "normal" state is similar to the notion of state in the big-step semantics; (2) result (terminated) states are the values returned when a computation is finished; (3) an Error state is characterised by an exception; (4) the synchronisation state is the result of a call to a synchronising parameter.

States are thus naturally defined as an inductive type, with four constructors:

**Inductive** state: **Type** :=
| State (a:expr)(e:env)(k:cont): state
| ResState (v:value)(e:env)(k:cont): state
| ErrState (ex:exn)(v:value)(e:env)(k:cont):state
| SyncState (c:comm)(e:env)(k:cont): state.

There is always a continuation in a state, even the empty one. A step is an inductive from states to states. The definition closely matches the rules of Fig. 4. The global reduction is defined on **p**-vector (each **p**-vector is a function from pids to local states). From there, the transitive closure **pstar** is defined in a standard manner.

# 4  Properties and Benchmarks

The mechanised semantics allowed us to prove a number of properties in COQ and we now discuss about the mentioned scaling problems if we want to extend our work to a mainstream language or adding more low-level routines.

## 4.1  Properties and Results

First of all, we defined two alternative variations for the big-steps semantics. One is the most direct translation of the BSP model, but is complex to write and to manipulate. The second one, shorter, but non-deterministic. We proved in COQ the following 3 lemmas, where $(s, e)$ denotes the **p** environments and expressions:

**Lemma 1.** *Without subgroup, the big-steps semantics is confluent that is:* $\forall e, s, s', s \approx s'$, *if* $(s, e) \Downarrow (s_1, v_1)$ *and* $(s', e) \Downarrow (s_2, v_2)$ *then* $(s_1, v_1) \equiv (s_2, v_2)$.

The proof is done by induction of the execution. Confluence makes also the hypothesis that all unknown operations of $\Omega$ are deterministic.

**Lemma 2.** *The **Diamond** semantics is confluent that is:* $\forall e, s, s'$, $s \approx s'$, *if* $(s, e) \Downarrow_{Diam} (s_1, v_1)$ *and* $(s', e) \Downarrow_{Diam} (s_2, v_2)$ *then* $(s_1, v_1) \equiv (s_2, v_2)$.

The proof is done using a special small-steps semantics where each step corresponds to a synchronisation of a subgroup. The interleaving of synchronisations holds a diamond property and the confluence follows.

**Lemma 3.** *Both semantics are equivalent that is:* $\forall e, s, s'$, $s \approx s'$, $(s, e) \Downarrow_{Diam}$ $(s_1, v_1)$ *if and only if* $(s', e) \Downarrow_{All} (s_2, v_2)$; *And* $(s_1, v_1) \approx (s_2, v_2)$.

The "only if" part is prove by an induction on the **Diamond** execution. For the "if" part, the proof is done by induction on the number $k$ of communicators used in a **AllSub** super-step: we can show that there is a **Diamond** derivation, formed by $k$ synchronisations, that simulates the **AllSub** synchronisation rule. Note that the proofs rely on a congruence $\approx$ over the states (values and environments): we need equivalence between **p** processors that can belong to different subgroups. This lemma justifies our choice of privileging the use of the **Diamond** rule.

We were able to prove some results linking the inductive and co-inductive semantics, both for big-steps and small-steps. And *with and without* subgroups:

**Lemma 4.** $\Downarrow$ *and* $\Downarrow_\infty$ *are mutually exclusive that is:* $\forall e, s$ *if* $(s, e) \Downarrow (s_1, v_1)$ *then* $\forall s', s \approx s'$, *then* $\neg((s', e) \Downarrow_\infty)$.

**Lemma 5.** $\rightarrow^*$ *and* $\rightarrow_\infty$ *are mutually exclusive that is* $\forall e, s$ *if* $(s, e) \rightarrow^* (s_1, v_1)$ *then* $\forall s', s \approx s'$, *then* $\neg((s', e) \rightarrow_\infty)$.

For both lemmas, proved by induction and co-induction on the evaluations and case analysis. Co-inductive semantics are also deterministic in the sense that the constructed infinite tree will always be the same. But as our semantics do not currently give the execution trace [8] of any routine (*e.g.*, the SYNC effect), this property is not relevant: we are not able to compare the infinite trees [8].

The small-steps semantics have fewer rules than the big-steps ones. But designing them is much harder. It is thus necessary to ensure that it is a valid semantics. We did it by proving its equivalence with the big-steps semantics.

**Lemma 6.** $\rightarrow^*$ *and* $\Downarrow$ *are equivalent.*

The proof has some common ground with classic big-steps to small-steps equivalences, with two difficulties: (1) The small-steps allows operations to execute on the different processors in any order, while the big-steps semantics fixes the order; (2) The continuations, coupled with the synchronisation, introduce the need for a notion of equivalence between a program and a continuation.

The first implication (big-steps to small-steps) is done by induction on the derivation of the big-steps execution. However, an induction directly on the stated theorem would not be enough, and we need to generalise the result by using a notion of equivalence between pairs of programs and continuations. This is because after a synchronisation, in the big-steps semantics, we still have a code to execute, while in the small-steps semantics it is a continuation.

For the second implication, we rely of the next lemma. Since the small-steps semantics is confluent, we can order the local executions in any order, in particular the order chosen with the big-steps semantics (execution on the first processor first until the synchronisation barrier, then the second, *etc.*). The proof is then done by induction on the derivation.

**Lemma 7.** $\rightarrow$ *is confluent.*

The small-steps semantics verifies the diamond property: if from one state two steps are possible, they can only be local executions on two different processors. Since the executions are independent within a super-step, we can reach a common state by executing the computations in any order. The confluence follows.

### 4.2   Benchmarks

As a measure of difficulty, we give the number of COQ code lines —without shared lemmas. We also count the number of lines to write the rules. This is not perfect but easy to count. We compare these numbers to two other developments: (1) our own version of WHY-ML, *i.e.* the sequential part of BSP-WHY-ML; (2) the certified C compiler 1.4 of [8] *without* the memory model. We get the following results:

| Language | Rules | Lemmas: | 1 | 2 | 3 | 4 | 5 | 6 | 7 | ALL |
|---|---|---|---|---|---|---|---|---|---|---|---|
| Our version of WHY-ML | 140 | | 40 | no sense | no sense | 23 | 10 | 90 | 26 | 670 |
| BSP-WHY-ML | 270 | | 130 | no sense | no sense | 66 | 22 | 350 | 100 | 1300 |
| BSP-WHY-ML (subgroups) | 320 | | no sense | 416 | 531 | 85 | 35 | 490 | 446 | 1500 |
| CompCert | 513 | | 1700 | no sense | no sense | 1200 | 100 | undef | 1800 | Big |

**BSP** without subgroup variation:

$$\dfrac{\forall i \quad s_i, e_i \Downarrow^i s_i', \text{SYNC}(e_i') \qquad \textbf{AllComm}\{(s_0', e_0'), \dots (s_{\mathbf{p}-1}', e_{\mathbf{p}-1}')\} \Downarrow (s_0'', v_0), \dots (s_{\mathbf{p}-1}'', v_{\mathbf{p}-1})}{(s_0, e_0), \dots (s_{\mathbf{p}-1}, e_{\mathbf{p}-1}) \Downarrow (s_0'', v_0), \dots (s_{\mathbf{p}-1}'', v_{\mathbf{p}-1})}$$

**AllSub** variation:

$$\dfrac{\{0, \dots, \mathbf{p}-1\} = N \oplus C_1 \oplus \cdots \oplus C_k \quad \forall i \in C_j \quad s_i, e_i \Downarrow^i s_i', \text{SYNC}(C_j, e_i') \qquad \forall i \in N \quad s_i, e_i \Downarrow^i s_i', v_i}{\textbf{AllCommSub}\{C_1 \dots C_k, v, (s_0', e_0'), \dots (s_{\mathbf{p}-1}', e_{\mathbf{p}-1}')\} \Downarrow_{All} (s_0'', v_0), \dots (s_{\mathbf{p}-1}'', v_{\mathbf{p}-1})}$$
$$\dfrac{}{(s_0, e_0), \dots (s_{\mathbf{p}-1}, e_{\mathbf{p}-1}) \Downarrow_{All} (s_0'', v_0), \dots (s_{\mathbf{p}-1}'', v_{\mathbf{p}-1})}$$

**Diamond** variation:

$$\dfrac{\exists C \ \forall i \in C \quad s_i, e_i \Downarrow^i s_i', \text{SYNC}(C, e_i') \qquad \textbf{CommDia}\{C, (s_0', e_0'), \dots (s_{\mathbf{p}-1}', e_{\mathbf{p}-1}')\} \Downarrow_{Diam} (s_0'', v_0), \dots (s_{\mathbf{p}-1}'', v_{\mathbf{p}-1})}{(s_0, e_0), \dots (s_{\mathbf{p}-1}, e_{\mathbf{p}-1}) \quad Diam \ (s_0'', v_0), \dots (s_{\mathbf{p}\ 1}'', v_{\mathbf{p}-1})}$$

**Fig. 6.** Big-step semantics: 3 variations for the synchronisation rule

One (at least) processor diverges:
$$\dfrac{\exists i \quad s_i, e_i \Downarrow_\infty^i}{\langle (s_0, e_0), \dots, (s_{\mathbf{p}-1}, e_{\mathbf{p}-1}) \rangle \Downarrow_\infty}$$

**BSP** without subgroup variation :
$$\dfrac{\forall i \quad s_i, e_i \Downarrow^i s_i', \text{SYNC}(e_i') \qquad \textbf{AllComm}\{\langle (s_0', e_0'), \dots, (s_{\mathbf{p}-1}', e_{\mathbf{p}-1}') \rangle\} \Downarrow_\infty}{\langle (s_0, e_0), \dots, (s_{\mathbf{p}-1}, e_{\mathbf{p}-1}) \rangle \Downarrow_\infty}$$

**Diamond** variation:
$$\dfrac{\exists C \ \forall i \in C \quad s_i, e_i \Downarrow^i s_i', \text{SYNC}(C, e_i') \qquad \textbf{CommDia}\{C, (s_0', e_0'), \dots (s_{\mathbf{p}-1}', e_{\mathbf{p}-1}')\} \Downarrow_\infty}{(s_0, e_0), \dots (s_{\mathbf{p}-1}, e_{\mathbf{p}-1}) \Downarrow_\infty}$$

**Fig. 7.** Global rules for the diverging big-step semantics

$$\dfrac{s_i, e_i \bullet \kappa_i \xrightarrow{i} s_i', e_i' \bullet \kappa_i'}{\langle (\dots, (s_i, e_i \bullet \kappa_i), \dots) \rangle \to \langle \dots, (s_i', e_i' \bullet \kappa_i'), \dots \rangle} \qquad \dfrac{\exists C \ \forall i \in C \quad O_i \equiv \text{SYNC}(C) \bullet \kappa_i}{\langle (s_0, O_0), \dots, (s_{\mathbf{p}-1}, O_{\mathbf{p}-1}) \rangle \to \textbf{CommDia}\{C, \langle (s_0, O_0), \dots, (s_{\mathbf{p}-1}, O_{\mathbf{p}-1}) \rangle\}}$$

**Fig. 8.** Small-step semantics: global reductions

Proving that the local (sequential) rules $\Downarrow^i$ are confluent (Lemma 1) takes approximately 40 lines and 130 lines with all the BSP rules. That indicates that the use of the BSP model involves a *4 times increase* in the size of the proof of confluence. And it is also 4 times bigger (416 lines) when introducing subgroups (Lemma 2). Proving the confluence with the small-step semantics takes approximately the same number of COQ lines (resp. 26, 100 and 446, Lemma 7) but the proofs are more *complicated* than just a structural induction of the big-step reduction. But once again, we find the 4 factors of work. We find that in our HPC case, using big-steps seems "better" for proving confluence. For CompCert, that is not visible, because it remains purely sequential.

Using big-step rules for *exclusivity* of finite and infinite *sequential* evaluations (Lemmas 4 and 5), few lines are needed; For BSP it is 3 times bigger. Using small-steps, the exclusivity is *simple* since it is mainly a difference between inductive and co-inductive rules. Adding BSP routines and subgroups does not change the proof really (10, 22, 3 lines, Lemma 5). This is because the proof is "generic" to any set of rules. But the exclusivity is longer to prove using big-step semantics (resp. 23, 66 and 85, Lemma 4). Mostly because, they are many cases even if most of them can be *automatically discharged*. This is also clearly visible for CompCert because there are many rules when using big-steps. Our rules are bigger in size due to the use of **p**-vector environments but remains few.

*We can deduce that for* HPC, *big-step semantics should be used for confluence whereas small-step ones should be used for exclusivity.*

For the equivalence of the semantics of sequential programs, 90 lines are needed. For BSP, it is *4 times bigger* and *5 times bigger using subgroups*. In conclusion, applying this work to the real-world semantics of CompCert, *unfortunately*, seems to be a *hard task*; It would roughly take at least 4 times longer and thus need the work of a team bigger than just two researchers.

As intended, the harder to define the semantics are, the harder the proofs are. There is a gap between our (sequential) core-language (140 lines) and CompCert (513 lines without counting their complex memory model). Adding the "simple" BSP routines increases by 4 the size of the COQ development. And adding another low-level routines will increase further the needed work. For a full HPC language such as C +MPI, it seems to be an *heavy work*. And finally, *how trust* a semantics with such a large number of complex rules? We can miss a specific case. Even by comparing the execution results of programs on truly computers with those of the semantic, some cases could be forgotten because we are not able to test all of them. The MPI reference manual (852 pages !) is not as accurate as the C one because it is hard to precisely define all the interactions of a routine with all others routines. It is thus hard (impossible?) to define what is *a valid behavior* or not.

# 5  Conclusion

**Summary of Contributions.** In this paper, we defined different *operational semantics*, in COQ, for a BSP kernel language with *subgroup synchronisation*. The semantics were proved *confluent* and *equivalent*. Confluence is an important property that makes easier code analysis and debugging. The big-step semantics uses different kinds of outputs to express the different situations of the program during its execution: exception, true value or synchronisation of a subgroup. The small-step semantics uses *novel continuations* to express more easily the synchronisation mechanism of the BSP model. The proofs were *mechanically* checked in COQ. The semantics can be used as a basis for verification tools of BSP, as well as for MPI algorithms relying on collective operations. Studying mechanical semantics in COQ of a core language allows also *measuring the difficulty* to move to a real-world HPC language such as C or JAVA adjoining BSP or MPI routines.

**Lessons Learned from this Work.** The authors know that this work does not introduce a new tool. But, this work is not only for proving the correctness of our tool and thus interesting for us only. The work is *relevant*, even for people that do not work in HPC computing, for two main reasons. First, it introduces "non-standard" mechanised semantics (the **p**-states and a specific continuation for synchronisation). Second, it measures the needed *scalability* for working on a more realistic HPC language. Our work indicates some categories of properties that are easier to be proved in each kind of semantics. In this way, users can select the appropriate semantics when proving properties.

A reader can think that the addition of subgroups to the semantics seems to require a rather limited effort and is just an incremental work of [7]. Global synchronisation is, of course, an important aspect of BSP programming, and subgroup synchronisation is just applying a similar synchronisation on only a particular subset of the running threads. The three following facts show that it is not true: (1) there is different possibilities of big-step rules (addresses non-trivial problems in modelling synchronisation); (2) the small-step semantics uses continuations (for both exceptions, not present in our previous works, and synchronisation); and (3) there is an increase of needed COQ lines for the typical lemmas. This is *not a good new* even if it was predictable. If we want to extend this work from the core-language of WHY to a *mainstream language*, there is a *big gap*. And the true problem comes mainly from the HPC routines. For BSP, about twenty primitives are necessary —even with the subgroups. For a bigger and more complicated library such as MPI, a hundred is required, thus 5 times more than BSP. This *terrible scaling* is measurable with our work: 4 times from sequential to BSP, 4 times again for adding subgroups, *etc.*; Thus at least a 20 times bigger work from a sequential C to C+MPI. That was not truly visible in [9] due to the use of abstract specifications. This kind of factors was also found in [8] for a sequential C semantics study. This raises the problem of confidence that can be given to a so big and complex semantics: *do they really reflect reality?*

# References

1. Appel, A.W., Blazy, S.: Separation logic for small-step CMINOR. In: Schneider, K., Brandt, J. (eds.) TPHOLs 2007. LNCS, vol. 4732, pp. 5–21. Springer, Heidelberg (2007)
2. Bisseling, R.H.: Parallel Scientific Computation. A structured approach using BSP and MPI. Oxford University Press, New York (2004)
3. Bocchino Jr., R.L., Adve, V.S., Snir, M.: Parallel programming must be deterministic by default. In: USENIX Conference on Hot Topics in Parallelism (2009)
4. Cappello, F., Guermouche, A., Snir, M.: On communication determinism in parallel HPC applications. In: Computer Communications and Networks (ICCCN), pp. 1–8. IEEE (2010)
5. Filliâtre, J.-C., Marché, C.: The why/krakatoa/caduceus platform for deductive program verification. In: Damm, W., Hermanns, H. (eds.) CAV 2007. LNCS, vol. 4590, pp. 173–177. Springer, Heidelberg (2007)
6. Fortin, J., Gava, F.: BSP-why: a tool for deductive verification of bsp algorithms with subgroup synchronization. J. Parallel Programm. 1–24 (2015)
7. Gava, F., Fortin, J.: Two formal semantics of a subset of the pub. In: Parallel, Distributed and Network-Based Processing (PDP). IEEE Press (2009)
8. Leroy, X.: Mechanized semantics with applications to program proof and compiler verification. In: Esparza, J., Spanfelner, B., Grumberg, O. (eds.) Logics and Languages for Reliability and Security. IOS Press, Amsterdam (2010)

9. Li, G., Palmer, R., Delisi, M., Gopalakrishnan, G., Kirby, R.M.: Formal specification of MPI 2.0: case study in specifying a practical concurrent programming API. Sci. Comput. Program. **76**(2), 65–81 (2011)

10. Tesson, J., Loulergue, F.: Formal semantics of DRMA-style programming in BSPlib. In: Wyrzykowski, R., Dongarra, J., Karczewski, K., Wasniewski, J. (eds.) PPAM 2007. LNCS, vol. 4967, pp. 1122–1129. Springer, Heidelberg (2008)

# Cloud Computing Threats and Provider Security Assessment

Huiming Yu[✉], Ken Williams, and Xiaohong Yuan

Department of Computer Science, North Carolina A&T State University, Greensboro, USA
{cshmyu,williams,xhyuan}@ncat.edu

**Abstract.** Cloud computing is an emerging technological paradigm that offers on-demand, scalable, resources and IT-based solutions without the need to invest in new infrastructure or train new personnel. Cloud computing has faced scrutiny regarding security risks involved with allowing sensitive data to be controlled and handled by third-party, off-site vendors. Many businesses with interest in using cloud services do not have a process to assess cloud providers security. In this paper we categorize cloud computing threats into external threats, guest-to-guest threats and cloud-to-guest threats; discuss the new version of the Consensus Assessments Initiative Questionnaire that was developed by the Cloud Security Alliance; propose a Fuzzy Likert Provider Security Measurement prototype that uses fuzzy logic, Likert scales and decision making technologies to assess the cloud service providers' security.

**Keywords:** Cloud computing security · Security assessment

## 1 Introduction

Cloud computing relies on sharing resources over a network. There are several kinds of models that are widely used. Infrastructure as a service is the basic model in which computing resources are owned and hosted by a service provider, and are offered to users on-demand. Platform as a service is the model in which cloud providers offer a computing platform including operating system, programming language execution environment, database and webserver. Users can develop and run their software solutions on the cloud platform instead of buying and managing the hardware and software. Software as a service is the model in which cloud providers manage the infrastructure and platform, and install the application software in the cloud. Users are provided access to application software and databases [6].

Cloud computing provides many benefits to government, academic, business and industries. It also brings various threats, risks and privacy issues to users. Except general external threats, cloud computing brings new threats such as guest to guest threats, cloud to guest threats and guest to cloud threats. Cloud computing security risks also involve allowing sensitive data to be controlled and handled by third-party, off-site, vendors whose datacenters may cross international boundaries [1]. The impacts of these threats can be very broad. Enhancing cloud computing security

© Springer International Publishing Switzerland 2015
G. Wang et al. (Eds.): ICA3PP 2015 Workshops, LNCS 9532, pp. 238–250, 2015.
DOI: 10.1007/978-3-319-27161-3_21

is critical. The cloud provider is responsible for managing the cloud so the client has uninterrupted and secure access to their data. These concerns over cloud security have become the primary roadblocks to the widespread adoption of cloud computing. Consequently, cloud service providers have been forced to provide evidence regarding the strength of their security controls. Organizations such as the Cloud Security Alliance, National Institute of Standards and Technology, Open Cloud Consortium, and Open Grid Forum have come together in order to promote, advance, and develop standardized best practices. One particularly worth noting is the Cloud Security Alliance, who in an effort to encourage transparency of cloud service providers (CSPs) security practices, launched the Security, Trust & Assurance Registry (STAR) initiative, which allows CSPs to use the Consensus Assessments Initiative Questionnaire (CAIQ) as an industry-accepted means of self-assessment (Cloud Security Alliance). STAR allows CSPs to upload their completed CAIQ documents into the STAR registry where prospective cloud clients have the ability to review responses submitted by CSPs and decide which CSP best meets their security expectations.

Fuzzy inference systems provide an ideal approach to integrating qualitative and quantitative data through its use of inference rules and its fuzzification process. The fuzzy logic approach is based on degrees of membership to a set. This can be compared to the more traditional binary set logic. This approach is an effective means to capturing the inexact nature of the real world by combining conventional mathematical logic with human-like decision making [10]. The idea of degrees of membership fits our problem well, in that, clients must decide to what degree does a CSPs response to each security question meet their expectations. When asking such a question, it is not likely the case that a CSP response will either completely meet expectations or not meet them at all. It is more likely that the CSP's suggested security controls will not meet, somewhat meet, meet, or exceed expectations. Likewise, choosing a CSP is not just a matter of investigating relevant numeric security metrics. Instead, there must be a concerted effort to balance careful evaluation of qualitative feedback from security professionals and any quantitative data. We propose a Fuzzy Likert Provider Security Measurement prototype that uses fuzzy logic, Likert scale and decision making technologies to assess the CSP security.

The remainder of this paper is organized as follows. In Sect. 2 cloud computing security related issues will be overviewed. In Sect. 3 assessing the providers security will be discussed. In Sect. 4 fuzzy logic and Likert scale related work will be discussed. In Sect. 5 Fuzzy Likert Provider Security Measurement Prototype will be presented. Conclusion and future work will be given in Sect. 6.

## 2    Cloud Computing Security

Cloud computing provides many benefits to government, academia, business and industries. It also brings various threats and privacy issues to users. We categorize these threats into external threats, guest to guest threats and cloud to guest threats, and discuss each of them.

## 2.1   Guest and Provider Sides of Cloud Computing

The guest is the end user who signs up with the company to use the cloud. The guest side of a cloud is what the client has access to when he/she creates an account. Depending on the cloud provider, the guest side may consist of storage of files, access to different virtual machines and any applications that are already stored on the cloud. Guests who are allowed to use the cloud are able to store, delete, and modify the information they provide on the cloud and run applications. For example the guest side can be the enterprise portion and the provider side is the service provider portion [5]. The guest side provides the end user with the ability to choose cloud services and environment such as operating system and applications they will use on the cloud. The guest side may consist of different users, laptops, tablets, cell phones, various computers and enterprise centers. An enterprise center can run business applications that include user data and an active directory. Business applications are the applications that the business has stored on the cloud for the users to have access to via the cloud. This is more cost efficient. The business does not have to install applications on every computer at the office. All applications will be used over the cloud so they can be used more efficiently. Since the applications are used on the cloud, the computer does not require many resources to keep the virtual machine running.

User data are the documents and other information that the guests have stored on the cloud and will be allowed access to when they sign into the cloud. Each guest will store his/her documents under a user directory. The user directory will be linked to the virtual machine they log into. Active directory is used for authenticating and authorizing all guests and computers within a network of the cloud that assigns and enforces security policies for all computers on that network. This is a very important function of cloud service providers, which ensures that guests can only access certain information depending on their privileges or credentials [5]. The enterprise center may consist of users at the enterprise office and remote users. Users at the enterprise office can use computers to gain access to the cloud. They need a valid username and password to sign into the cloud. These users have access to the cloud at any time and have the ability to store files and use the business applications. Remote users are the clients who will not be in the office but will still have access to the cloud in a remote location.

The provider side of a cloud is the service provider which may consist of application servers, service platforms, runtime environment and data centers [1], etc. One example of application server is WebSphere Application Server that is a Java EE, EJB supported technology based application platform. Users can build, deploy and manage robust, agile and reusable business applications and services of all types while reducing application infrastructure costs. There are multiple service platforms that perform management, engineering, inventory and repair functions for service providers and their networks. These support services are used when data in the datacenter might become corrupted. They provide support to get the datacenter up and running again so the customer will have access to their data. They consist of systems used to run business operations for customers, supporting processes of the cloud and product management. These services are used to create new functionality for the clients so using their cloud will be more convenient. There are more than one datacenters provided in case of an emergency so guests will always have access to their information on the cloud. It is the responsibility of the cloud service providers to manage those resources.

## 2.2    Threats

Cloud computing is based on network structures that are susceptible to network attacks [7, 8]. Due to the special characteristics of cloud computing new threats and exploits are being discovered regularly. In general, cloud computing threats can be categorized as external threats, guest to guest threats and cloud to guest threats.

- **External Threats.** External threats include computer and network attacks that can occur by using Internet. These threats can be SQL injection, Cross-site scripting, Denial of Service, Indirect Denial of Service, network sniffing, etc.

  SQL Injection is a way to bypass user authentication to gain access within the cloud. A hacker uses special characters for input in a log-in form that uses the SQL language to get access to data. One SQL injection example uses on a form that has username and password textboxes. The string of characters will bypass user authentication to the system and will log-in without entering in a valid username and password. This threat also exists with other internet websites that have basic user authentication.

  A different type of threat is a Denial of Service attack (DOS). A DOS attack is where a hacker exhausts a server's resources so no one else can use the services provided by the server. Exhausting a network's resources means that the hacker is doing something that will slow down the network so badly that no user will be able to log in, logout, load a webpage or make any requests to the server. One way this is achieved is by making an unlimited number of false requests to a server. The server wants to respond to the request the client made, but, since the client was not valid, it will wait to get confirmation from the client, and the server will end up slowing down. When all the resources on a network are exhausted, it makes the network unusable.

  An Indirect Denial of Service attack is another big threat to cloud computing. An Indirect Denial of Service attack occurs when a DOS attack denies more services than the hacker intended. Indirect Denial of Service works unintentionally because a hacker intends to deny the service of a specific aspect of a cloud but affects other aspects. Suppose a hacker wanted to stop users from logging into the cloud by sending false requests to slow down the network and increase the workload on the server. The hacker indirectly denies the service of users who also want to log out of the cloud and of users who want to upload or download from the cloud. The impacts depend on the level of sophistication of the cloud system. The cloud system notices the lack of availability, and may try to 'evacuate' the affected service instances to other servers. It results in additional workload for those other servers, and thus the DOS attack passes to another service type, and spreads throughout the whole computing cloud [8].

  Another type of external threat is network sniffing. A packet sniffer is intended to be used by a network or system administrator to monitor and troubleshoot network traffic. Using the information captured by the packet sniffer, an administrator can identify erroneous packets, use the data to pinpoint bottlenecks and help maintain efficient network data transmission. When packet sniffer is used by a hacker, an attack on the network can occur. A packet sniffer can capture sensitive data. Therefore, unencrypted data such as passwords and other web service related security configuration files can be intercepted. Some of these vulnerable files that are critical for web service are Universal Description Discovery and Integrity (UDDI), Simple Object Access Protocol (SOAP) and Web Service Description Language (WDSL) files. Network sniffing can capture packets sent to and from the cloud that can be stored in a file so later the hacker can decode those packets. The hacker can observe when users log in and out of the cloud to see patterns. They can capture any data that is not encrypted and use a user's credentials to sign into the cloud. The UDDI, SOAP and WSDL files can also assist the hacker with acquiring more information about the cloud's infrastructure.

- **Guest to Guest Threats.** A guest to guest threat is where a user of the cloud system attempts to attack another user on the cloud for malicious purposes. Guest to guest threats involve a user on the same cloud performing a malevolent attack against another user by sending a file that may contain a virus of some sort.

  One example is a cloud malware injection attack. Malware injection is a way to store malware onto another user's computer system, but in this case a cloud infrastructure. Malware may include spyware, which tries to steal user information, adware, which include programs that install or display advertisements, hijackers, which divert browsers to unsafe or other sites without permission, and many other kinds of software. Malware is dangerous because it can potentially damage or harm computer systems resulting in slow processor speeds, slow Internet connections, or identity theft of the user. Malware Injection aims to store some type of malicious software into another users' cloud space. It is achieved by storing a program on the cloud which other users will have access to. The program is disguised as a legitimate program but, when downloaded, it will store a user's username and password in some fashion. This type of cloud malware could serve any particular purpose the adversary is interested in, ranging from eavesdropping and data modifications to full functionality changes or blockings. The malware could possibly alter the sensitive data stored on the cloud or copy the data to a server without the user knowing. Malware Injection requires the adversary to create its own malicious service implementation or virtual machine instance and add it to the cloud system. The user has to trick the cloud system so that it treats the new service as one of the valid instances for the particular service attacked by the user. If the cloud does not check for viruses or malicious software before storing programs, the cloud is vulnerable to an attack [8].

  An additional type of threat is insecure or incomplete data deletion. Insecure data deletion occurs when unencrypted data was not deleted so other users can access it. The data is still present because there are multiple backups of the information that have not been deleted in different datacenters. If other users know the cloud infrastructure, they may be able to retrieve this data that could be a username, password, or credit card information. Incomplete data deletion means the cloud service provider did not correctly or accurately destroy the information the client requested to be deleted. This is also a threat to any operating system that may not delete sensitive data, that can possibly be restored by a different user who uses that system. With the cloud infrastructure, timely data deletion may also be very difficult because extra copies of data are available. Cloud computing has to be available to all its clients in real time which involves backups of their data that may be stored in different data-centers. When clients delete data, they have to delete all copies in every datacenter. If the data is not deleted correctly, then other users may gain access to that data.

"Mis-configuration may also contribute to the loss of data or allow a hacker to gain entry" [8]. The cloud infrastructure and the virtual machine that the client uses have to be up-to-date. Different cloud providers use different virtual machines to emulate many operating systems, so, if the operating system is an older one, it may be susceptible to this attack. It all depends on how the cloud is configured and how the operating system or virtual machine deletes its data.

- **Cloud to Guest Threats.** Cloud to guest threats could be the most malicious type of attack that can occur in the cloud infrastructure. A cloud with malicious software encapsulated within a virtual machine could bring down different virtual machines, making the cloud unstable. When a cloud service provider stores a virtual machine on the cloud, it is the cloud provider's responsibility to make sure it is scanned regularly to check for viruses and malware. If this is not done, a client can store malicious software. When that image is stored in the repository, other clients will be affected by it. While running, a susceptible virtual machine lowers the general security level of a virtual network of machines in the cloud. Running a malicious virtual machine is similar to moving the attacker's machine directly into the network. This is attained by bypassing any firewall or intrusion detection system and storing the virtual machine back on the cloud.

Another cloud to guest threat is the use of a Trojan horse. A Trojan horse is a malicious piece of software that can make copies of itself, steal information, or harm its host computer system. Virtual machine images also provide an easier way of developing and propagating Trojan horses. Using a virtual machine image as a carrier for the Trojan horse makes the attacker's job easier because the virtual machine image encapsulates all software dependencies of the Trojan horse. In other words, the dependency on the victim's software stack is eliminated. In essence, this can be a major problem seeing as, once the virtual machine image is infected with malicious software, other users who use the same image will also be affected. The cloud stores all these images in a repository, so, when other users download them, the Trojan horse can start to propagate. The cloud service provider is accountable for the virtual images they share with users. It is provider's duty to ensure the images stored in the repository do not contain any malicious software that can affect other users.

## 3  Assessing the Provider's Security

Cloud computing security concerns have become the primary roadblocks to the widespread adoption of cloud computing. Consequently, cloud service providers have been forced to provide evidence regarding the strength of their security controls. Organizations such as the Cloud Security Alliance, National Institute of Standards and Technology, Open Cloud Consortium, and Open Grid Forum have come together in order to promote, advance, and develop standardized best practices that address the cloud environment. The Cloud Security Alliance (CSA) has developed the Consensus Assessments Initiative Questionnaire (CAIQ), which has quickly become an industry-accepted way to document security controls found within cloud services [3]. The CSA CAIQ document provides prospective clients an in-depth look into the security controls of a given cloud service provider (CSP). One particularly worth noting is the Cloud Security Alliance, who in an effort to encourage transparency of CSPs security practices, launched the Security, Trust & Assurance Registry (STAR) initiative, which allows CSPs to use CAIQ as an industry-accepted means of self-assessment (Cloud Security Alliance). STAR allows CSPs to upload their completed CAIQ documents into the STAR registry where prospective cloud clients have the ability to review responses submitted by CSPs and decide which CSP best meets their security expectations.

The CSA is focused on providing industry-accepted ways to document what security controls exist in IaaS, PaaS, and SaaS offerings, providing security control transparency. The first Consensus Assessments Initiative Questionnaire was delivered in 2010. This questionnaire is available in spreadsheet format, and provides a set of questions a cloud consumer and cloud auditor may wish to ask of a cloud provider. It provides a series of "yes or no" control assertion questions which can then be tailored to suit each unique cloud customer's evidentiary requirements. This question set is meant to be a companion to the CSA Guidance and the CSA Cloud Controls Matrix, and these documents should be used together. The CSA released version 3.0.1 in 2014 [3].

However the assessment process is very complicated because it requires clients to examine hundreds of questions spanning different security control categories in CAIQ, answer yes/no followed by explanatory comments related to the corresponding question. How cloud consumers can objectively use the CAIQ to assess CSP security levels becomes an important and urgent problem.

## 4   Fuzzy Logic and Likert Scale Related Works

Supriya et al. used fuzzy logic to create a model for Trust Management which was used to estimate the trust value for a given CSP. The trust value could be used to help potential cloud clients make an informed choice when selecting an appropriate CSP [12]. Using fuzzy logic, a trust is calculated based on inference rules related to a CSP's agility, performance, and cost. Furthermore, Supriya et al point out that because CSPs offer multiple package deals, it is important for customers to be able to make decisions based on multiple criteria. The results of the study suggests that the fuzzy logic model based Trust Management system enables users to use varying criteria in order to determine their unique trust score. Arbabioon and Pilavari used fuzzy logic to assess user satisfaction of a given CSP [1]. Results showed that fuzzy logic can better assess user satisfaction than traditional numerical analysis because it considers overlap of a user's evaluations of the assessment categories. Furthermore, Arbabioon and Pilavari believe that the results can help CSPs perform gap analysis between current level and desired ones in order to identify obstacles within the organization that could negatively affect a user's evaluation of them.

Various studies have determined that the ambiguous nature of Likert scale responses can be made more reliable by evaluating responses using fuzzy logic. Hedayatpanah suggests that the evaluation of Likert scale responses over a fuzzy system has less ambiguity because fuzzy systems factor in the amount of overlap between integer scores [7]. Lee and Huang believe that this method of evaluation provides a more objective measure [10] because evaluations through fuzzy systems more precisely capture the extent of human emotion by providing a basis for a systematic way for the manipulation of vague and imprecise concepts [9]. The membership functions of a fuzzy system are able to overcome the implicit ambiguity of the Likert scale by including possible grey areas within the output space of possible solutions, which are used to calculate a final score. A study by Bharadwaj found that using a Fuzzy Likert System is statistically identical to a traditional ICF (International Classification of Functioning) model, which determines an individual's ability to take care of him or herself [2]. Rivera et al developed a tool to measure service provider's security [10].

As companies continue to contemplate migrating their assets to cloud based infrastructures, it is important that they have a reliable method for evaluating a prospective cloud provider's security posture. Davis' study indicates that 40% of those with interest in using cloud services do not have a process to assess cloud providers' security posture [4]. The Trust Management model designed by Supriya et al. does not account for cloud security issues. Furthermore, in Arbabioon and Pilavari's study, security is one of ten inputs used to determine the overall user satisfaction score for a CSP. Davis' study suggests that new tools are needed to help customers evaluate the level of security that CSPs can support. We propose a fuzzy Likert provider security measurement prototype that combines the qualitative data (CSP comments) and quantitative data (user-defined Likert scale evaluations of the comments), and uses fuzzy logic technology to calculate a Security Posture Score (SPS) so that potential cloud customers can make a better assessment about cloud providers security.

## 5  Fuzzy Likert Provider's Security Measurement Prototype

The CSA CAIQ document provides prospective clients an in-depth look into the security controls of a given CSP. This process requires clients to examine over one hundred questions spanning over different security control categories. In CAIQ version 1.0 the control categories include Compliance; Data Governance; Facility Security; Human Resources Security; Information Security; Legal; Operations Management; Release Management; Resiliency; Risk Management; and Security Architecture. The Cloud Security Alliance deleted some control categories in version 1.0 and add new control categories to the version 3.0.1. The version 3.0.1 control categories include Application & Interface Security; Audit Assurance & Compliance; Business Continuity Management & Operational resilience; Change Control & Configuration Management; Data Security & Information Lifecycle Management; Datacenter Security; Encryption & Key Management; Governance and Risk Management; Human Resource; Identity & Access Management; Infrastructure & Virtualization Security; Interoparability & Portability; Mobile Security; Security Incident Management, E-Discovery & Cloud Forencise;

Supply Chain Management, Transparency and Accountability; Threat and Vulnerability. CSP responses include yes/no answers followed by explanatory comments related to the corresponding question [4]. How can cloud consumers objectively use the CAIQ to assess CSP security levels? It is conceivable to believe that businesses will have their own unique way of performing this evaluation. However, when evaluating hundreds of questions for multiple CSP responses, it is likely that inconsistencies with scoring may arise, particularly when responses do not clearly belong to one of the evaluation choices: Does not meet, Below, Meets, Exceeds expectations. Will the evaluator round the score up or down? If there are multiple evaluators for the same set of responses, will evaluations be consistent? These questions lend themselves well to the idea that any evaluation based on human decisions must be able to handle the natural inconsistencies inherent to the human decision making process.

The Fuzzy Likert Provider's Security Measurement (FLPSM) prototype handles such grey areas by aggregating all the responses into one solution space from which the CSP Security Posture Score will be formulated. The FLPSM prototype calculates a Security Posture Score (SPS) based on client evaluations of the CSP responses to the CAIQ document and client-defined weights for each CAIQ category. Together, the CSA CAIQ and the FLPSM prototype can alleviate concerns regarding cloud computing security by providing a reliable security assessment tool.

The Fuzzy Likert Provider's Security Measurement prototype consists of three components that are Likert Scale, Sub-Fuzzy Inference System (SFIS) and Primary Fuzzy Inference System (PFIS). The FLPSM prototype diagram is shown in Fig. 1. Each CAIQ response will be scored on a scale of 0–3 in the Likert Scale component. In the Sub-Fuzzy Inference Systems (SFIS) all SFIS are used to calculate CAIQ category scores before the final SPS is calculated. In the Primary Fuzzy Inference System (PFIS) each of the individual CAIQ category scores are used as inputs into the PFIS in order to calculate the CSP's SPS.

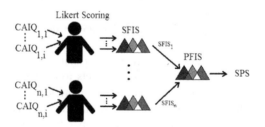

**Fig. 1.** FLPSM prototype diagram

## 5.1 Likert Scale

When implementing the FLPSM prototype the first step is to develop the Likert scale. The Likert scale is based on the questions: to what extent does the CSP response meet customers' expectations? The following is an example. The scale can include the following choices: 1→Does Not Meet Expectation; 2→Below Expectations; 3→Meets

Expectations; 4→Exceeds Expectations. Because Likert scales naturally inject ambiguity into the decision making process, it is important that these grey areas be considered in the evaluation process. To handle such situations, each evaluation is translated to a degree of membership as defined by membership functions and inference rules in separate fuzzy systems defined for each CAIQ category.

- *Sub-Fuzzy Inference System*
  The questions within each CAIQ category are evaluated over corresponding subfuzzy inference systems (SFIS) in order to determine a fuzzy category score (FCS). Using the Likert scale value, membership degrees for individual CAIQ responses are calculated using four triangular membership functions. The four membership functions define ranges for the Likert scale described above. For each SFIS, the number of inference rules is 4n, where n is the number of questions for that category. Each question is evaluated over the same set of inference rules. The inference rules are structured as follow:
  - If $R_n$ does not meet expectations, then $FCS_{cat}$ does not meet expectations.
  - If $R_n$ is below expectations, then $FCS_{cat}$ is below expectations.
  - If Rn meets expectations, then FCScat meets expectations.
  - If $R_n$ exceeds expectations, then $FCS_{cat}$ exceeds expectations.

Here, $R_n$ represents a CSP's response to the $n^{th}$ CAIQ question within a particular category. FCScat is the calculated fuzzy category2 score for the corresponding category. When client scores evaluated over each inference rule, the corresponding membership degree is used to define an output space from the output membership functions. In each SFIS, output membership functions are the same as input membership functions. The output space for each question is then aggregated into one combined output space to calculate the $FCS_{cat}$. For example, using Fig. 2(a) a user score for $R_1 = 2$ would yield, for each inference rule, membership degrees 0, 0, 1, 0, respectively.

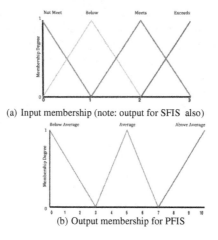

(a) Input membership (note: output for SFIS also)

(b) Output membership for PFIS

**Fig. 2.** Membership functions

## 5.2   Primary Fuzzy Inference System

Once the FCScat for each CAIQ category is calculated, they will become inputs for the PFIS. Input membership functions are the same as those created in the SFIS. Output membership functions, however, are different because the SPS is on a scale from 0–10. Therefore, the output membership function must reflect the desired output score range. The output membership function defines its output as fitting into the following categories: below average, average, above average. See Fig. 2(b). The area under these output curves is what will be aggregated in order to calculate the SPS.

*A. SPS calculation.*   Together, each component of the FLPSM prototype work to calculate a CSP security score, which is scaled from 0–10. The SPS calculation requires four steps.

Step 1. Evaluation of CAIQ responses: Client evaluates each of the CAIQ responses using the Likert scale. Each response is given a score between 0 and 4.
Step 2. FCScat calculations: Fuzzy category scores are calculated by evaluating each category's responses over its corresponding SFIS.
Step 3. Weight-defined PFIS: User-defined weights are assigned to each set of inference rules corresponding to specific categories.
Step 4. SPS calculation: Each FCScat will be evaluated over corresponding inference rules within the PFIS.
 - The final output space from which the SPS will be calculated is created by using the sum aggregation method. The area from each output curve is combined into a single output space from which the SPS will be determined.
 - The SPS is calculated by finding the centroid of this aggregated curve, using the following formula:

$$SPS = \frac{\int x \cdot \mu(x)\, dx}{\int \mu(x)\, dx}$$

Where x is a scaled score ranging from 1–10 that the SPS will be scaled to and $\mu(x)$ is the membership degree ranging from 0–1 for each input x.

The weighted-average SPS (WASPS) was calculated similarly in that individual category average scores were calculated first, followed by weights being used to calculate the final SPS. For each CAIQ category, the following formula was used to calculate an average category score (ACS):

$$ACS_i = \frac{\sum_{n-1}^{k} x_n}{k}$$

where k is the number of questions per category and $x_k$ is the client evaluated Likert value for the $k_{th}$ question for that category. After each ACS is calculated, the WASPS is found with the formula

$$WASPS = \frac{10 * \sum_{n=1}^{11} ACS_n * w}{33}$$

where $ACS_n$ is the ACS score for the $n^{th}$ category, as described previously and $w$ is the user defined weight of the category.

## 6   Conclusions and Future Work

Cloud computing has been widely used by individuals, academia, industry, government, etc. How to select a reliable and secure service provider is important. The Cloud Security Alliance's STAR initiative is a step in the right direction towards alleviating the concerns over cloud security.

We propose a Fuzzy Likert Provider Security Measurement prototype. Based on the CSA CAIQ this prototype integrates fuzzy logic and likert scale technologies with unique client's preferences to provide a reliable method to evaluate cloud computing provider's security. The FLPSM prototype can help bridge the gap between cloud opponents and advocates. Furthermore, CSPs can use FLPSM results as a means to facilitate quality improvements for those security control areas deemed unacceptable by clients. In the future we will implement this prototype for CAIQ version 3.0.1 and conduct experiments.

**Acknowledgments.** This work was partially supported by National Science Foundation under the award numbers CNS-0909980 and DUE-1129136.

## References

1. Arbabioon, P., Pilavari, N.: Fuzzy logic cloud computing user's satisfaction assessment methodology. Rev. Bus. Res. **11**, 151 (2011)
2. Bharadwaj, B.: Development of a fuzzy likert scale for the who ICF to include categorical definitions on the bases of a continuum. Master's thesis, Wayne State University (2007)
3. Cloud security alliance: consensus assessments initiative questionnaire v3.0.1. https://cloud securityalliance.org/download/consensus-assessments-initiative-questionnaire-v3-0-1/
4. Davis, M.: Cloud security: verify, don't trust, informationweek::report. http://reports. informationweek.com/abstract/5/8978/Cloud-Computing/Research-Cloud-Security-Verify-Don't-Trust.html
5. Decker, K.: What joni mitchell might say about cloud computing. http://decker.com/blog/ 2010/05/what-joni-mitchell-might-say-about-cloud-computing/
6. Gibson, J., Rondeau, R., Eveleigh, D., Qing, T.: Benefits and challenges of three cloud computing service models. In: Fourth International Conference on Computational Aspects of Social Networks (2012)
7. Hedayatpanah, A.: Fuzzy approach to likert spectrum in classified levels in surveying researches. J. Math. Comput. Sci. **2**, 394–401 (2011)
8. Jamil, D., Zaki, H.: Cloud computing security. Int. J. Eng. Sci. Technol. **3**(4), 3478–3483 (2011)
9. Lee, C.: Fuzzy logic in control systems: fuzzy logic controller. IEEE Trans. Syst. Man Cybern. **20**, 404–418 (1990)

10. Lee, Y., Huang, S.: A new fuzzy concept approach to kano's model. Expert Syst. Appl. **36**, 4479–4484 (2009)
11. Rivera, J., Yu, H., Williams, K., Zhan, J., Yuan, X.: Assessing the security posture of cloud service providers. In: International Conference on IS Management and Evaluation (2015)
12. Supriya, M., Venkataramana, L., Sangeeta, K., Patra, G.: Estimating trust value for cloud service providers using fuzzy logic. Int. J. Comput. Appl. **48**(19), 28–34 (2012)

# Collaborative Multiparty Association Rules Mining with Threshold Homomorphic Encryption

Marcin Gorawski$^{(\boxtimes)}$, Zacheusz Siedlecki, and Anna Gorawska

Institute of Computer Science, Faculty of Automation, Electronics,
and Computer Science, Silesian University of Technology, Akademicka 16,
44-100 Gliwice, Poland
{Marcin.Gorawski,Zacheusz.Siedlecki,Anna.Gorawska}@polsl.pl

**Abstract.** In this paper we introduce a new approach to multiparty association rules mining based on a polynomial representation of sets encrypted with a homomorphic threshold cryptosystem. We describe a homogeneous collaborative multiparty association rules mining protocol that is secure in a malicious model. Presented algorithm is designed to enhance security and privacy in distributed environments where a malicious adversary may deviate arbitrarily from the prescribed protocol as it attempts to compromise the privacy of the other parties' inputs or the correctness of the obtained result. To the best of our knowledge, the protocol presented in this paper is the first multiparty association rules mining protocol that is secure against malicious adversaries in distributed systems.

**Keywords:** Distributed data analytics · Association rules mining · Privacy preservation · Malicious model · Threshold encryption · Data mining

## 1 Introduction

Big data technologies may yield great results; however, with thousands of data points generated by people or machines every day many traditional means of privacy protection fail [37,45,49]. Anonymization of data is no longer sufficient, while relationships between collected records may lead to detecting individual's identity. Therefore, the privacy of information is one of the key issues that ought to be considered while extracting knowledge and distributed data analytics.

Most of the cryptographic work in privacy-preserving collaborative data mining has targeted the semi-honest threat model, which assumes that the parties correctly follow the protocol specification, yet may attempt to learn additional information by analysing the transcript of messages received during execution [17]. The assumption of the semi-honest adversary is usually unrealistic. In contrast, a malicious adversary may deviate arbitrarily from the prescribed protocol

© Springer International Publishing Switzerland 2015
G. Wang et al. (Eds.): ICA3PP 2015 Workshops, LNCS 9532, pp. 251–263, 2015.
DOI: 10.1007/978-3-319-27161-3_22

as it attempts to compromise the privacy of the other parties' inputs or the correctness of the result. Protocols that are secure in the malicious model provide a very strong security guarantee.

## 1.1  Related Works

There is a great interest in research on privacy-preserving data mining [2, 11, 32, 35]. Privacy-preserving algorithms have been proposed for different data mining applications, including clustering [25, 26, 41], association rules mining on randomized data [12, 38], association rules mining across multiple databases [20, 23, 28, 40, 48], Bayes classification [33, 42–44], decision trees on randomized data [2], frequent pattern mining [14], and collaborative filtering [4]. Additionally, several privacy-preserving solutions have been proposed for simple primitives that are very useful for designing privacy-preserving data mining algorithms [7]. These include computing scalar products [13, 16, 40, 46] and set operations [2, 10, 13, 24, 31]. The SMC (Secure Multiparty Computation) paradigm provides cryptographic solutions for privacy protection in any distributed computation [18, 47]. There are very few works describing data mining algorithms in the malicious model. The works most closely related to ours are [29, 31]. In [29] two-party secure protocols in the malicious model for equality, dot product and full-domain set operations are presented, while in [31] an Over-Threshold Set-Union Protocol secure in malicious model is described.

## 1.2  Our Contribution

The main goal was to enhance the process of knowledge discovery by increasing reliability and privacy in a distributed system that deals with the big data problem. Therefore, we have created a collaborative multiparty homogeneous association rules mining protocol that is secure against malicious adversaries. To the best of our knowledge, this is the first multiparty association rules mining protocol that is secure in the malicious threat model. We have created a new algorithm based on the initial FDM concept [6]. Unlike other secure multiparty association rules mining algorithms, we are not revealing globally non-supported *itemsets* to other parties. We introduce a new approach of finding the union of globally large *itemsets* in one step without revealing *itemsets* that are not supported globally. The *support count exchange* phase is realized using multiplication of encrypted polynomial representations of sets [13]. We have adopted this idea from the [31] and utilized it very specifically in our protocol. The association rule confidence is calculated using the additive homomorphism of the used encryption. Thanks to the additional properties of the encryption used, we are able to secure against malicious adversaries by use of zero-knowledge proofs.

## 2  Background

In this section, definitions and theorems that form the basis of our algorithm are introduced.

## 2.1   Globally and Locally Large Itemsets

We call a set of items *itemsets*. The support of an itemset $X$ is the fraction of records supporting $X$ with respect to the database. Itemsets with minimum support are called *large (or frequent) itemsets* [3].

Let us assume that a transaction database $T$ is horizontally partitioned [28] among $n \geq 3$ parties (namely $P_1, P_2, ..., P_n$). Each party has a private transaction database $T_1, T_2, ..., T_n$, where $T_i$ resides at party $P_i$. The itemset $X$ has the *local support count* at party $P_i$ of

$$sup_i(X) = \frac{\#\{r \in T_i \mid X \subseteq r\}}{\#T_i}. \tag{1}$$

Using values of $sup_i(X)$ for all $i$, we can calculate *global support count* $sup(X) = \sum_{i=1}^{n} sup_i(X)$. For a given minimum support threshold, $t$, $X$ is *globally large* if $sup(X) \geq t$; correspondingly, $X$ is *locally large* at site $P_i$ if $sup_i(X) \geq t$.

## 2.2   Privacy Preservation in the Homogeneous Collaborative Association Rules Mining

An *association rule* is an expression $X \Rightarrow Y$, where $X$ and $Y$ are sets of items. Given a database, $T$, $X \Rightarrow Y$ means that whenever a record contains $X$ then it also contains $Y$ with a certain confidence. The confidence is the percentage of records containing both $X$ and $Y$ with respect to the overall number of records containing $X$. The majority of association rules mining algorithms is based on the *Apriori* algorithm [3].

There have been two main approaches for privacy preservation in the multiparty association rules mining. One is a randomization approach [12,38] in which the privacy of data cannot always be fully preserved while achieving precise results [1,30]. The other is a cryptographic approach mostly using the SMC paradigm [7,47]. We focus on the SMC-based association rules mining algorithms on horizontally partitioned data in the cryptographic approach. This task is also known as a homogeneous collaborative association rules mining [23,28,50].

## 2.3   Homomorphic Threshold Public-Key Cryptosystem

Let $E(x)$ denote the encryption of a plaintext $x$ with a public key. The encryption algorithm $E$ is homomorphic if, given $E(x)$ and $E(y)$, one can obtain $E(x \perp y)$ without knowledge of the private key and without decrypting $x, y$ for some operation $\perp$.

**Threshold Decryption.** Given the common public key, the private key corresponding to the private public key has been divided into shares. The threshold decryption protocol outputs the random share of the decryption result along with the non-interactive zero-knowledge proof showing that the private key share is used correctly. These shares of the decryption result can be combined to calculate the final decryption result. Also, any single share of the private key cannot be used to decrypt the ciphertext alone.

## 2.4    Encrypted Polynomials

The polynomial ring, $R[x]$, consists of all polynomials with coefficients from $R$. For polynomial $f \in R[x]$, we represent its encryption, $E(f)$, as the ordered list of the encryptions of its coefficients under the additively homomorphic public-key cryptosystem $E(f[0]), ..., E(f[deg(f)])$ [31].

Let $f, g, p \in R[x]$ be polynomials such that $f(x) = \sum_{i=0}^{deg(f)} f[i]x^i$, $g(x) = \sum_{i=0}^{deg(g)} g[i]x^i$, and $p(x) = \sum_{i=0}^{deg(p)} p[i]x^i$. Using the homomorphic properties of the cryptosystem, we can calculate (without knowledge of the private key) product $p = f \times_h E(g)$ of an unencrypted polynomial, $f$, and an encrypted polynomial, $g$, by calculating the encryption of each coefficient:

$$E(p[i]) := (E(g[0]) \times_h E(f[i])) +_h (E(g[0]) \times_h E(f[i-1])) +_h ... +_h (E(g[i]) \times_h E(f[0])) \quad (2)$$

for $0 \le i \le deg(f) + deg(g) \wedge i > deg(f) \Rightarrow f[i] = 0 \wedge i > deg(g) \Rightarrow g[i] = 0$.

Given the encryption of polynomial, $f$, we can calculate the encryption of its derivative, $g := \frac{d}{dx}f$, by calculating the encryption of each coefficient, $E(g[i]) := (i+1) \times_h E(f[i+1])$ for $0 \le i \le deg(f) - 1$.

## 2.5    Polynomial Representation of Set of Itemsets

Let us denote the set of itemsets $X \in P$ of size $k$ for site $i$ as $S_{i(k)} = \{X\}$. We can create its representation $f \in R[x]$ as $f(x) = \prod_{X \in S_{i(k)}} \prod_{j=1}^{sup_i(X)} (x - X)$. The representation stores not only itemsets contained in the set, but also their supports. On the other hand, given a polynomial, $f \in R[x]$, we define the set of itemsets $S_{i(k)} = \{\{X\} \mid f(X) = 0 \wedge X \in P\}$. The itemset value is the root of the polynomial and the support of itemset is stored in the corresponding root multiplicity:

$$sup_i(X) = s \iff (x - X)^s \mid f \wedge (x - X)^{s+1} \nmid f. \quad (3)$$

## 2.6    Union Using Polynomial Multiplication

Let $f, g$ be polynomial representations of the sets of itemsets $S$ and $T$, respectively. We can compute the polynomial representation of their union with the additional property of evaluating a global support count of itemsets. We compute the polynomial representation of $S \cup T$ by calculating a product of their polynomial representation. The product $f \times g$ is a polynomial representation of $S \cup T$ because all elements that appear in either set $S$ or $T$ are preserved:

$$(f(x_1) = 0) \wedge (g(x_2) = 0) \Rightarrow ((f \times g)(x_1) = 0) \wedge ((f \times g)(x_2) = 0). \quad (4)$$

Additionally, as $f(x_1) = 0 \iff (x - x_1) \mid f$, the corresponding root multiplicity contains the sum of the support count for a given itemset:

$$(f(x_1) = 0) \wedge (g(x_1) = 0) \Rightarrow (x - x_1)^2 \mid (f \times g). \quad (5)$$

We will use this property to apply the support count threshold to the encrypted representation of set of items.

# 3 Multiparty Homogeneous Association Rules Mining Protocol THERM Secure Against Malicious Adversaries

The Threshold Homomorphic Encryption Rules Mining (THERM) protocol conducts association rules mining on a data set that consists of all the parties' private data without revealing private data sets to each other. First the globally large itemsets of given size and with support satisfying given threshold are generated. This is carried out iteratively like in the Apriori algorithm, but in the distributed secure manner: first the set of locally large itemsets is generated, then the union of globally large itemsets is determined. The union of globally large itemsets is determined in one step without revealing itemsets that are not supported globally. The support count exchange phase is realized using multiplication of encrypted polynomial representations of sets. Then from the set of globally large itemsets the set of association rules is generated. The association rule confidence is calculated using the additive homomorphism of the encryption used.

In the THERM protocol we have to consider $n \geq 2$ honest-but-curious parties (namely $P_1, P_2, ..., P_n$), where $g < n$ dishonestly collude. Each party $P_i$, has a private database $T_i$ from the horizontally partitioned transaction database $T = \bigcup_{i=1}^{n} T_i$. For the determination of the set of strong association rules minimal support threshold $t$ as well as minimal confidence threshold $c$ ought to be presented at the initial phase of the protocol. Apart from the previously mentioned parameters it is essential to supply:

- maximum itemset length $d$,
- fixed polynomials $F_0, ..., F_{d-1}$ of degree $0, ..., d-1$ respectively, which have no common factors or roots representing elements of domain $P$,
- public key for an additively homomorphic public-key cryptosystem,
- share of a corresponding secret key (divided into $n$ shares).

Moreover, the protocol requires introduction of variables as follows:

- $k$ - the itemset length,
- $S_{i(k)}$ - the set of candidate $k$-itemsets for party $P_i$,
- $LL_{i(k)}$ - the set of locally large $k$-itemsets for party $P_i$,
- $d$ - the count of locally large $k$-itemsets $d = \#LL_{i(k)}$,
- $L_{(k)}$ - the set of globally large $k$-itemsets,
- $C$ - the set of frequent association rules (with support satisfying $t$).

## 3.1 The THERM Protocol's Homomorphic Threshold Public-Key Cryptosystem

In this work we use an additively homomorphic public-key cryptosystem, so operation $\perp$ (defined in Sect. 2.3) is the addition of plaintexts. We require that the cryptosystem supports the following operations:

– Given ciphertexts $E(x)$ and $E(y)$ of any $x$ and $y$ from the plaintext domain, calculate ciphertext of their sum $E(x+y) := E(x) +_h E(y)$ without knowledge of the private key and plaintexts.
– Given a constant $a$ and the encryption $E(x)$ of $x$ from the plaintext domain, calculate ciphertext of $a \times x$ denoted $E(a \times x) := a \times_h E(x)$ without knowledge of the private key and the plaintext.

Additionally, we require that:

– Both operations described above cause output ciphertext re-randomization. The ciphertext is transformed so as to form an encryption of the same plaintext, under a different random value than the one originally used.
– The cryptosystem support secure (n, n)-threshold decryption. This means that the private key is shared by a group of $n$ parties, and decryption must be performed by all parties acting together.
– No PPT adversary can recover the sizes of the subfields of R with greater than negligible probability.
– It is possible to prove in zero-knowledge. that the party has followed the threshold decryption protocol correctly.
– It is possible to construct zero-knowledge proofs of plaintext knowledge.

### 3.2   Zero-Knowledge Proofs

We use non-interactive zero-knowledge protocols in the random oracle model to prove that the actions taken by the parties are correct without revealing any other information [8]:

– *Proof of plaintext knowledge* - a party, $P_i$, can compute the zero-knowledge proof $PPK(E(x))$ if he knows a plaintext, $x$.
– *Proof of correct decryption* - a party, $P_i$, can generate the non-interactive zero knowledge proof $POD(E(x), s_i)$ showing that it correctly used its private key to generate a random share of the decryption result, $s_i$.
– *Proof of correct multiplication* - a zero-knowledge proof of knowledge $ZKPK(f \mid p = f \times_h E(g))$ that the party knows a polynomial, $f$, such that encrypted polynomial $p = f \times_h E(g)$, given the encrypted polynomial $p$ and $E(g)$.

### 3.3   Adopted Over-Threshold Set-Union Protocol

We have adopted Over-Threshold Set-Union Protocol [31] to the THERM protocol in a very specific way to compute union of globally large itemsets in one step without revealing itemsets not supported globally. We are using the Over-Threshold Set-Union Protocol designed for multisets, but instead of multisets the input contains set of *itemsets*. Instead of multiplicity function we use *itemset* local support. In such a way we can compute union of itemsets with global support defined by a global support threshold.

# 4 Secure Union of Globally Large Itemsets in the THERM Protocol

In previous secure multiparty association rule mining protocols union of globally large *itemsets* was usually calculated in two steps. First the union of locally large *itemsets* was obtained then each of its elements' global support was tested against global support threshold. It originated from the initial FDM algorithm concept [6], which was also the basis for [39]. We present a new approach to finding the union of globally large *itemsets* in one step without revealing *itemsets* that are not supported globally.

## 4.1 Generating a Set of Locally Large Itemsets

In the first phase of the THERM protocol a set of candidate itemsets $S_{i(k)}$ is generated for each of the $n$ parties, $P_i$:

- if $k = 1$ then $S_{i(1)} \leftarrow \{\{X\} \mid X \in \bigcup T_i\}$ is a set of one-element candidate itemsets which consists of all elements of transactions in $T_i$
- else if $k > 1$ then

$$S_{i(k)} \leftarrow \{a \cup \{b\} \mid a \in LL_{i(k-1)} \cap L_{k-1} \wedge b \in \bigcup(LL_{i(k-1)} \cap L_{k-1})\} \quad (6)$$

is generated using *Apriori* property [3].

Then, for each party $P_i$, it generates sets $d = \#LL_{i(k)}$ and a set of locally large $k$-itemsets $LL_{i(k)} \leftarrow \{X \in S_{i(k)} \mid supp_i(X) \geq t\}$.

## 4.2 Secure Determination of the Union of Globally Large Itemsets

The set of large itemsets $L_{(k)}$ consists of all $k$-itemsets (itemsets of size $k$) that are globally supported. The set of locally large itemsets $LL_{i(k)} \subseteq S_{i(k)}$ consists of all k-itemsets supported locally at party $P_i$. We briefly describe concept of secure obtaining $L_{(k)}$ - details are given in Sect. 4. The concept was inspired by work [31].

For $1 \leq i \leq n$ each party $P_i$ creates polynomial representation $f_{i(k)}$ of set $LL_{i(k)}$ and encrypt it. Next, all parties using homomorphic properties of the cryptosystem obtain the encryption of polynomial $p = \prod_{i=1}^{n} f_{i(k)}$, the representation of $\bigcup_{i=1}^{n} LL_{i(k)}$. Since the multiplicity of roots of $f_{i(k)}$ equals local support count of corresponding itemset and $sup(X) = \sum_{i=1}^{n} sup_i(X)$ then multiplicity of roots of $p$ equals to global support count of the corresponding itemset. For given support threshold $t$ each party $P_i$ for $1 \leq i \leq c + 1$ chooses random polynomials $r_{i,0}, ..., r_{i,t-1}$, and calculates the encryption of the polynomial $\sum_{l=0}^{t-1} p^{(l)} \times F_l \times r_{i,l}$ for masking itemsets with support lower than threshold. Next all parties calculate the encryption of the polynomial $g_{(k)} = \sum_{l=0}^{t-1} p^{(l)} \times F_l \times (\sum_{i=0}^{c+1} r_{i,l})$ and perform a group threshold decryption to obtain its plaintext. The polynomial $g_{(k)}$ is the representation of a set of globally large itemsets

$L_{(k)} = \bigcup_{i=1}^{n} LL_{i(k)} \setminus \{X : supp(X) < t\}$. As at most $c$ parties may dishonestly collude, the polynomials $\sum_{i=0}^{c+1} r_{i,l}$ are known to no party and uniformly distributed. Next, each party $P_i$ for $1 \leq i \leq n$ for each its local large itemset chooses $b_{i,j} \leftarrow R$ for $1 \leq j \leq \#LL_{i(k)}$ and computes

$$u_{i,j} = b_{i,j} \times g_k((LL_{i(k)})_j) + (LL_{i(k)})_j. \tag{7}$$

Some of $u_{i,j}$ values will be uniformly distributed over $R$, but some of them are globally large itemsets:

$$u_{i,j} = (LL_{i(k)})_j \Rightarrow (LL_{i(k)})_j \in L_{(k)}. \tag{8}$$

Then the parties shuffle elements $u_{i,j}$ [5,9,15,27,34]. Each party learns all of the elements, but does not learn from which party set they came from. The set formed by those shuffled elements is $L_{(k)}$.

## 4.3   Finding Strong Association Rules

After determination of the globally large itemsets all parties are forced to find all non-empty subsets $a \in l \wedge a \neq \varnothing$ for each set $l \in L_{(k)}$. For each and every created subset, $a$, a rule of the form $a \Rightarrow (l \setminus a)$ is created. In consequence, the set of strong association rules is generated [3]:

$$C \leftarrow \{\{a \Rightarrow (l \setminus a)\} \mid l \in L_{(k)} \wedge a \in l \wedge a \neq \varnothing\} \tag{9}$$

Next, for each of $n$ parties, $P_i$, for each rule, $(X \Rightarrow Y) \in C$,

- send to all other players encryption of exceeding rule confidence [28] $E(supp_i(X \cup Y) - c \times supp_i(X))$ along with proof of plaintext knowledge $PPK(E(supp_i(X \cup Y) - c \times supp_i(X)))$
- verify all proofs of plaintext knowledge received from other parties
- use additive homomorphism property of the cryptosystem to calculate encryption of exceeding confidence $E(\sum_{m=1}^{n} (supp_m(X \cup Y) - c \times supp_m(X)))$.

All parties jointly decrypt each association rule exceeding confidence $e = \sum_{m=1}^{n} (supp_m(X \cup Y) - c \times supp_m(X))$ (sending and verifying $POD$ along with decryption shares).

For each association rule, the THERM protocol selects only rules with non-negative exceeding confidence and creates a set of strong association rules

$$R \leftarrow \{X \Rightarrow Y \mid (X \Rightarrow Y) \in C \wedge \sum_{m=1}^{n} (supp_m(X \cup Y) - c \times supp_m(X)) \geq 0\}. \tag{10}$$

## 5   The THERM Protocol Security

Assuming that the additively homomorphic threshold cryptosystem is semantically secure [19], that the specified zero-knowledge proofs and proofs of correct decryption cannot be forged, and that the shuffle protocol is secure, then no party or coalition of at most $g < n$ colluding parties can learn more than in the ideal model.

To find globally large itemsets of size $k$ and minimal support $t$, all parties evaluate and decrypt

$$\mu = \sum_{l=0}^{t-1} \lambda_{n(k)}^{(l)} \times F_l \times \left( \sum_{m=0}^{g+1} r_{m(k),l} \right). \tag{11}$$

As the maximum coalition size is smaller than $g+1$, the polynomials $\sum_{m=0}^{g+1} r_{m(k),l}$ $(0 \le l \le t-1)$ are distributed uniformly over all polynomials of approximate size $nk$ and all coefficients of $\lambda_{n(k)}^{(l)} \times F_l (0 \le l \le t-1)$ are in the set $R^* \cup \{0\}$. Thus $\mu = gcd(\lambda_{n(k)}^{(t-1)} \times F_{t-1}, \lambda_{n(k)}^{(t-2)} \times F_{t-2}, ..., \lambda_{n(k)} \times F_0) \times \vartheta$ , for some uniformly distributed polynomial $\vartheta$. As $\vartheta$ is uniformly distributed for any inputs, no party or coalition can learn more than $gcd(\lambda_{n(k)}^{(t-1)} \times F_{t-1}, \lambda_{n(k)}^{(t-2)} \times F_{t-2}, ..., \lambda_{n(k)} \times F_0)$. If $gcd(\lambda_{n(k)}, F_0, ..., F_{t-1}) = 1$ with overwhelming probability, then

$$gcd(\lambda_{n(k)}^{(t-1)} \times F_{t-1}, \lambda_{n(k)}^{(t-2)} \times F_{t-2}, ..., \lambda_{n(k)} \times F_0) = gcd(\lambda_{n(k)}^{(t-1)}, \lambda_{n(k)}^{(t-2)}, ..., \lambda_{n(k)}). \tag{12}$$

with overwhelming probability. Thus

$$\mu = gcd(\lambda_{n(k)}^{(t-1)}, \lambda_{n(k)}^{(t-2)}, ..., \lambda_{n(k)}) \times z, \tag{13}$$

where $z$ is a random polynomial of the appropriate size. As $z$ has only a polynomial number of roots, and with overwhelming probability any root of $z$ does not represent any element from $P$, $z$ is a polynomial representation of the empty set with overwhelming probability. The polynomial $gcd(\lambda_{n(k)}^{(t-1)}, \lambda_{n(k)}^{(t-2)}, ..., \lambda_{n(k)})$ has roots which are the itemsets with a global support count of at least $t$ (see Proof of Lemma 4 in [31]). The set of roots exactly represents the set of globally large itemsets of size $k$, and can thus be derived from the answer that would be returned by a Trusted Third Party (TTP). The protocol reveals the set of globally large itemsets of size $k$, exactly as TTP would do in the ideal model.

To calculate the exceeding association rule confidence, the additive homomorphism property of the cryptosystem is used, which is secure due to assumptions. Since the decrypted exceeding confidence $\sum_{m=1}^{n} (supp_m(X \cup Y) - c \times supp_m (X))$ contains the sum of exceeding local confidences, no party or coalition can learn local confidence values.

The following zero-knowledge proofs of knowledge were added to prevent malicious misbehaviour:

- choosing polynomial representation of sets of locally large itemsets $f_{i(k)}$ without knowledge of its roots representing itemsets,
- choosing $f_i$ such that it is not the product of linear factors,
- not performing the polynomial multiplication of $\lambda_{i-1(k)} \times f_{i(k)}$ correctly,
- not calculating $r_{i(k),l} \times \lambda_{n(k)}^{(l)}$ correctly,
- not evaluating the encrypted polynomial $\mu$ correctly,
- not performing threshold decryption correctly,
- not calculating encrypted elements $(V_{i(k)})_j$ correctly,
- sending encryption of exceeding rule confidence $E(supp_i(X \cup Y) - c \times supp_i(X))$ without knowledge of its value,
- not decrypting $\sum_{m=1}^n supp_m(X \cup Y) - c \times supp_m(X))$ correctly.

# 6   Conclusions and Implementation Perspectives

The presented THERM protocol is designed to enhance security and privacy in distributed environments [21] where a malicious adversary may attempt to abuse the data and compromise its privacy. Security, privacy and ethical issues ought to be address to protect vast amounts of data that mostly represents every single aspect of people life in great detail.

The security versus efficiency trade-off between the protocols that are secure in the semi-honest model and those that are secure in the malicious model is not clear in practice [29]. By using multiplication of encrypted polynomial representations of sets, we have improved the Secure Set Union method [7] commonly used in multiparty association rules mining algorithms.

Implementation is already at a very advanced stage. Enterprise Integration Patterns (EIP) were adopted for the implementation of the THERM algorithm. Data from various parties are transmitted as messages and processed by the system components. Technically the implementation of the THERM algorithm is written in Java based on Spring Framework Integration, which is the implementation of the EIP.

There is an ongoing work in incorporating this approach into a various of real-life applications. We are performing a detailed analysis of the corresponding costs affecting real system performance. For research purposes, the system using Paillier's cryptosystem [36] has been implemented in Java using the Spring Integration framework. Moreover, the issue of privacy preservation in distributed environments with big data will be addressed to industrial applications such as liquefied petroleum management and leakage detection systems [22]. Experimental studies and further results will be published in our subsequent works.

# References

1. Agrawal, D., Aggarwal, C.C.: On the design and quantification of privacy preserving data mining algorithms. In: Proceedings of the twentieth ACM SIGMOD-SIGACT-SIGART symposium on Principles of database systems, PODS 2001, pp. 247–255. ACM, New York, NY, USA (2001)

2. Agrawal, R., Evfimievski, A., Srikant, R.: Information sharing across private databases. In: Proceedings of the 2003 ACM SIGMOD International Conference on Management of Data, SIGMOD 2003, pp. 86–97. ACM Press, New York, NY, USA (2003)

3. Agrawal, R., Srikant, R.: Fast algorithms for mining association rules in large databases. In: Bocca, J.B., Jarke, M., Zaniolo, C. (eds.) Proceedings of 20th International Conference on Very Large Data Bases VLDB 1994, pp. 487–499. Morgan Kaufmann, Santiago de Chile, Chile, 12–15 September 1994

4. Canny, J.: Collaborative filtering with privacy. In: Proceedings of the 2002 IEEE Symposium on Security and Privacy, SP 2002, pp. 45–57. IEEE Computer Society, Washington, DC, USA (2002)

5. Chaum, D., Acm, C.O.T., Rivest, R., Chaum, D.L.: Untraceable electronic mail, return addresses, and digital pseudonyms. Commun. ACM **24**, 84–88 (1981)

6. Cheung, D.W., Han, J., Ng, V.T., Fu, A., Fu, Y.: A fast distributed algorithm for mining association rules. In: International Conference on Parallel and Distributed Information Systems, PDIS, pp. 31–42. IEEE Computer Society Technical Committee on Data Engineering, and ACM SIGMOD, Los Alamitos, CA, USA (1996)

7. Clifton, C., Kantarcioglu, M., Vaidya, J., Lin, X., Zhu, M.Y.: Tools for privacy preserving distributed data mining. ACM SIGKDD Explor. **4**, 28–34 (2003)

8. Cramer, R., Damgård, I.B., Nielsen, J.B.: Multiparty computation from threshold homomorphic encryption. In: Pfitzmann, B. (ed.) EUROCRYPT 2001. LNCS, vol. 2045, p. 280. Springer, Heidelberg (2001)

9. Desmedt, Y.G., Kurosawa, K.: How to break a practical MIX and design a new one. In: Preneel, B. (ed.) EUROCRYPT 2000. LNCS, vol. 1807, p. 557. Springer, Heidelberg (2000)

10. Emura, K., Miyaji, A., Rahman, M.S.: Efficient privacy-preserving data mining in malicious model. In: Cao, L., Feng, Y., Zhong, J. (eds.) ADMA 2010, Part I. LNCS, vol. 6440, pp. 370–382. Springer, Heidelberg (2010)

11. Estivill-Castro, V., Brankovic, L.: Data swapping: balancing privacy against precision in mining for logic rules. In: Mohania, M., Tjoa, A.M. (eds.) DaWaK 1999. LNCS, vol. 1676, pp. 389–398. Springer, Heidelberg (1999)

12. Evfimievski, A., Srikant, R., Agrawal, R., Gehrke, J.: Privacy preserving mining of association rules. In: Proceedings of the Eighth ACM SIGKDD International Conference on Knowledge Discovery and Data Mining, KDD 2002, pp. 217–228. ACM, New York, NY, USA (2002)

13. Freedman, M.J., Nissim, K., Pinkas, B.: Efficient private matching and set intersection. In: Cachin, C., Camenisch, J.L. (eds.) EUROCRYPT 2004. LNCS, vol. 3027, pp. 1–19. Springer, Heidelberg (2004)

14. Fu, A.W.-C., Wong, R.C.-W., Wang, K.: Privacy-preserving frequent pattern mining across private databases. In: Proceedings of the Fifth IEEE International Conference on Data Mining, ICDM 2005, pp. 613–616. IEEE Computer Society, Washington, DC, USA (2005)

15. Furukawa, J., Sako, K.: An efficient scheme for proving a shuffle. In: Kilian, J. (ed.) CRYPTO 2001. LNCS, vol. 2139, p. 368. Springer, Heidelberg (2001)

16. Goethals, B., Laur, S., Lipmaa, H., Mielikäinen, T.: On private scalar product computation for privacy-preserving data mining. In: Park, C., Chee, S. (eds.) ICISC 2004. LNCS, vol. 3506, pp. 104–120. Springer, Heidelberg (2005)

17. Goldreich, O.: Secure multi-party computation, manuscript (2002)

18. Goldreich, O., Micali, S., Wigderson, A.: How to play any mental game. In: Proceedings of the nineteenth annual ACM symposium on Theory of computing, STOC 1987, pp. 218–229. ACM, New York, NY, USA (1987)
19. Goldwasser, S., Micali, S.: Probabilistic encryption. J. Comput. Syst. Sci. **28**(2), 270–299 (1984)
20. Gorawski, M.: Advanced data warehouses. Studia Informatica, **30**(3B) (2009)
21. Gorawski, M., Bularz, J.: Distribution-based methods of preserving data privacy in distributed spatial data warehouse. IJBIDM **2**(4), 383–400 (2007)
22. Gorawski, M., Gorawska, A., Pasterak, K.: Liquefied petroleum storage and distribution problems and research thesis. In: Kozielski, S., Mrozek, D., Kasprowski, P., Mrozek, B.M., Kostrzewa, D. (eds.) BDAS 2015. Communications in Computer and Information Science, vol. 521, pp. 540–550. Springer, Heidelberg (2015)
23. Gorawski, M., Stachurski, K.: On efficiency and data privacy level of association rules mining algorithms within parallel spatial data warehouse. In: First International Conference on Availability, Reliability and Security, ARES 2006, pp. 936–943. IEEE Computer Society (2006)
24. Hazay, C., Nissim, K.: Efficient set operations in the presence of malicious adversaries. In: IACR PKC (2010)
25. Jagannathan, G., Pillaipakkamnatt, K., Wright, R.N.: A new privacy-preserving distributed K-clustering algorithm. In: SDM (2006)
26. Jagannathan, G., Wright, R.N.: Privacy-preserving distributed k-means clustering over arbitrarily partitioned data. In: Proceedings of the Eleventh ACM SIGKDD International Conference on Knowledge Discovery in Data Mining, KDD 2005, pp. 593–599. ACM, New York, NY, USA (2005)
27. Jakobsson, M.: A practical mix. In: Nyberg, K. (ed.) EUROCRYPT 1998. LNCS, vol. 1403, pp. 448–461. Springer, Heidelberg (1998)
28. Kantarcioglu, M., Clifton, C.: Privacy-preserving distributed mining of association rules on horizontally partitioned data. IEEE Trans. Knowl. Data Eng. **16**(9), 1026–1037 (2004)
29. Kantarcioglu, M., Kardes, O.: Privacy-preserving data mining in the malicious model. Int. J. Inf. Comput. Secur. **2**(4), 353–375 (2008)
30. Kargupta, H., Datta, S., Wang, Q., Sivakumar, K.: On the privacy preserving properties of random data perturbation techniques. In: Proceedings of the Third IEEE International Conference on Data Mining, ICDM 2003, p. 99. IEEE Computer Society, Washington, DC, USA (2003)
31. Kissner, L., Song, D.: Private and threshold set-intersection. Technical report CMU-CS-05-113, Carnegie Mellon University, February 2005
32. Lindell, Y., Pinkas, B.: Privacy preserving data mining. In: Bellare, M. (ed.) CRYPTO 2000. LNCS, vol. 1880, p. 36. Springer, Heidelberg (2000)
33. Meng, D., Sivakumar, K., Kargupta, H.: Privacy-sensitive bayesian network parameter learning. In: Proceedings of the Fourth IEEE International Conference on Data Mining, ICDM 2004, pp. 487–490. IEEE Computer Society, Washington, DC, USA (2004)
34. Neff, C.A.: A verifiable secret shuffle and its application to E-voting. pp. 116–125. ACM Press (2001)
35. O'Leary, D.E.: Some privacy issues in knowledge discovery: the OECD personal privacy guidelines. IEEE Expert: Intell. Syst. Appl. **10**(2), 48–52 (1995)
36. Paillier, P.: Public-key cryptosystems based on composite degree residuosity classes. In: Stern, J. (ed.) EUROCRYPT 1999. LNCS, vol. 1592, p. 223. Springer, Heidelberg (1999)

37. Perera, C., Ranjan, R., Wang, L., Khan, S.U., Zomaya, A.Y.: Big data privacy in the internet of things era. IT Prof. **17**(3), 32–39 (2015)
38. Rizvi, S.J., Haritsa, J.R.: Maintaining data privacy in association rule mining. In: Proceedings of the 28th international conference on Very Large Data Bases, VLDB 2002, pp. 682–693. VLDB Endowment (2002)
39. Tassa, T.: Secure mining of association rules in horizontally distributed databases. IEEE Trans. Knowl. Data Eng. **26**(4), 970–983 (2014)
40. Vaidya, J., Clifton, C.: Privacy preserving association rule mining in vertically partitioned data. In: Proceedings of the Eighth ACM SIGKDD International Conference on Knowledge Discovery and Data Mining, KDD 2002, pp. 639–644. ACM, New York, NY, USA (2002)
41. Vaidya, J., Clifton, C.: Privacy-preserving k-means clustering over vertically partitioned data. In: Proceedings of the Ninth ACM SIGKDD International Conference on Knowledge Discovery and Data Mining, KDD 2003 pp. 206–215. ACM, New York, NY, USA (2003)
42. Vaidya, J., Clifton, C.: Privacy preserving naive bayes classifier on vertically partitioned data. In: 2004 SIAM International Conference on Data Mining (2004)
43. Vaidya, J., Kantarcioglu, M., Clifton, C.: Privacy-preserving naive bayes classification. VLDB J. **17**(4), 879–898 (2008)
44. Wright, R., Yang, Z.: Privacy-preserving bayesian network structure computation on distributed heterogeneous data. In: Proceedings of the Tenth ACM SIGKDD International Conference on Knowledge Discovery and Data Mining, KDD 2004, pp. 713–718. ACM, New York, NY, USA (2004)
45. Xu, L., Jiang, C., Wang, J., Yuan, J., Ren, Y.: Information security in big data: privacy and data mining. IEEE Access **2**, 1149–1176 (2014)
46. Subramaniam, H., Wright, R.N., Yang, Z.: Experimental analysis of privacy-preserving statistics computation. In: Jonker, W., Petković, M. (eds.) SDM 2004. LNCS, vol. 3178, pp. 55–66. Springer, Heidelberg (2004)
47. Yao, A.C.: How to generate and exchange secrets. In: Proceedings of the 27th Annual Symposium on Foundations of Computer Science, pp. 162–167. IEEE Computer Society, Washington, DC, USA (1986)
48. Yi, X., Zhang, Y.: Privacy-preserving distributed association rule mining via semi-trusted mixer. Data Knowl. Eng. **63**(2), 550–567 (2007)
49. Yu, Y., Mu, Y., Ateniese, G.: Recent advances in security and privacy in big data. J. UCS **21**(3), 365–368 (2015)
50. Zhan, J., Matwin, S., Chang, L.: Privacy-preserving collaborative association rule mining. J. Netw. Comput. Appl. **30**(3), 1216–1227 (2007)

# An Illegal Indirect Access Prevention Method in Transparent Computing System

Wenjuan Tang, Yang Xu, Guojun Wang$^{(\boxtimes)}$, and Yaoxue Zhang

School of Information Science and Engineering,
Central South University, Changsha 410083, China
{wenjuantang,xuyangcsu,csgjwang,zyx}@csu.edu.cn

**Abstract.** Transparent computing is a novel network computing paradigm in which operating systems, applications, data, etc. are stored and managed on remote servers, and complex computing tasks are performed on local clients in real time. The unified and professional storage managements on servers make clients capable of owning an intrinsic advantage of storage security. However, due to runtime computing tasks of applications, protecting information flow security in end devices becomes important. In this paper, we propose a secure information flow model and design an information flow search algorithm based on Depth-first-search to prevent illegal access between files in transparent computing local environment. The main idea is to detect indirect access in information flow graph constructed with historic access records at first. Then compare the indirect access with previously designed white list to find out whether there are illegal behaviors. Intercepting access behavior is implemented by a special and secure file filter above file system at kernel level. Algorithm and security analysis show that our work can provide a secure information flow mechanism efficiently.

**Keywords:** Transparent computing · Information flow · Illegal access · File filter

## 1 Introduction

The rapid development of network communication and the diversification of terminal equipments bring along many novel different technologies, such as cloud computing, mobile internet, and big data, etc. But most of them fail to compatible different hardware and software, which bring some negative effects to user experience. Transparent computing [1, 2] is a novel network computing paradigm aiming to provide convenient cross-platform services for users. In this paradigm, operating systems (OSes), applications, data, etc. are stored and managed on remote servers and are streamed to end users on demand, which makes the clients owning intrinsic advantage of storage security. However, runtime computing tasks of applications makes it significant to protect information flow security in local system.

For example, there are applications APP_A and APP_B working at the same time in transparent computing system. APP_A has two permissions: getting geographical location information and writing information to local external storage, APP_B has two

G. Wang et al. (Eds.): ICA3PP 2015 Workshops, LNCS 9532, pp. 264–275, 2015.
DOI: 10.1007/978-3-319-27161-3_23

totally different permissions: reading information from local external storage and connecting to the internet. Thus if APP_B reads information from external storage after APP_A gets geographical location information and writes it to local external storage. Then, APP_B illegally 'steals' the user's location information and may send it to the internet. In this example, the APP_B illegally gets geographical location information in an indirect way and deliberately sends it to the internet, which results in information leakage problem.

Almost all information flow control strategies focus on providing security management for subjects at different security levels, but taking no account of restricting information flow between different processes at same security level. This means that the processes at same security level can communicate with each other by accessing to a same object like a file. Consequently, the process can get information that beyond its privilege with the help of other processes, which results in illegal information flow problem.

As a solution, we argue to propose a security method to prevent illegal information flow. The main idea is recording direct access operation of processes, using them to construct a sequential information flow graph, and detecting illegal indirect flow using information flow detection algorithm base on DFS. And intercepting direct access behavior can be realized by designing a special file filter above the file system in kernel level. More details will be discussed in later sections.

The rest of paper is organized as follows. In Sect. 2, we present related work. In Sect. 3, we give a brief introduction of file filter and the role it plays in our work. In Sect. 4, security model and algorithm is discussed. In Sect. 5, we present an implementation. In Sect. 6, we give algorithm and security analysis. Finally, we draw a conclusion and future work in Sect. 7.

## 2 Related Work

Access control is one of the powerful and generalized approaches of information resources protection. There are a few popular access control strategies, such as BLP model [3], which is one of the earliest and most popular multi-level security model, its main idea is that a subject can only read the object whose security level is not higher than the subject, and can only write the object whose security level is not lower than the subject. The BLP model is also used in network computing system. For example, Dai proposed a system-based privacy protection model based on the BLP model [4] for transparent computing system. Except the BLP model, there are many other access control models. Object-based Access Control Model [5] connects access control list with object or the attributes of object. Task-based Access Control Model [6] builds a security model from the task aspect. Role-based Access Control Model [7] distributes different permissions to different roles. And Action-based Access Control Model [8] introduces roles, temporal states and environmental states as security-relevant elements to information system. While all the access control models above focus on making rules for direct access to information or subjects and objects which have different security levels, they ignore the indirect access to information flow transferring between a few applications at same security level.

Information flow control model proposed by Denning [9] plays an equally important role in the field of information security as well as access control model. It is widely used in information systems with its primary contribution of data propagation tracking and limitation. Aeolus [10] designs an information flow control platform to build secure distributed applications, providing data confidentiality and integrity. Literatures [11–13] devote to enhancing information flow security from program language aspect. Literature [14] defends the applications against the deputy attacks through tracking the corresponding inter-process communication (IPC) between applications. TaintDroid [15] is a system-wide dynamic taint tracking and analysis system which is capable of simultaneously tracking multiple sources of sensitive data in Android system. The authors of literature [16] also discuss how to prevent illegal information flow based on role-based access control model.

We take some steps beyond the information flow control by enforcing security strategy that monitors and handles file operations at runtime at operating system kernel level. Compared with existing access control models and information flow control models, our method aims at detecting illegal indirect information flow between applications at same security level dynamically.

## 3 Preliminary

File system filter driver can intercept requests targeted at the file system or another file system filter driver. By intercepting the request before it reaches the intended target, the filter driver can extend or replace the functionality provided by the original target of the request. Thus developer can modify the filter driver to be equipped with functions of anti-virus [18], backup [19], encryption [20], security access control [21] etc..

In transparent computing systems [22], file filter is a file system agent that intercepts all file access requests and translates them into three virtual disks: mono disk, shadow disk and private disk. For Windows operating system, it is implemented as a file system driver sitting on top of the device driver chain for handling system operations. It intercepts the I/O request packet (IRP) from the built-in Windows I/O manager for redirection.

The level of file system filter driver in operating system is shown in Fig. 1. It locates upon file system driver, can acquire I/O request packet (IRP) from upper applications before they arrive at file system driver. There are a few kinds of operations in IRP, whose function codes are: IRP_MJ_CREATE (a create request), IRP_MJ_READ (a read request), IRP_MJ_WRITE (a write request), IRP_MJ_CLOSE (a close request), IRP_MJ_CLIEANUP (a cleanup request) etc..

We classify the operations above into two kinds of behavior: read and write. Apart from the read request and write request, the rest of IRP such as the create request, close request and clean up request do not generate information flow which transforms between process and file, therefore we only use filter driver to collect the IRP_MJ_READ and IRP_MJ_WRITE access information, and extract information of what process tries to read or write what file at what time. Thus we will get a series of operations, like "process $P_a$ tries to read $F_1$ at time $T_1$", and "process $P_a$ tries to write $F_2$ at time $T_2$" etc..

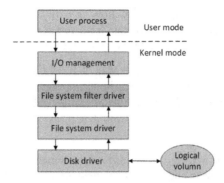

**Fig. 1.** File system filter driver

## 4  Security Model and Algorithm

In this section, we propose a secure information flow model to describe the unauthorized access problem, and design a search algorithm to find information flow based on DFS. Relatively, how to construct information flow graph with information access is presented.

Firstly, we make some definitions as follows.

*Definition 1. Process set P:* $\{p_1, p_2, \ldots, p_m\}$

*Definition 2. File set F:* $\{f_1, f_2, \ldots, f_n\}$

*Definition 3. Time set T:* $\{t_1, t_2, \ldots, t_n\}$, $t_i (1 \leq i \leq n)$ is the system time of the $i_{th}$ information access from process to file.

*Definition 4. Access information* $O:(p_i, f_j, t_k) = r/w$, process $p_i$ has a direct read or write access to $f_j$, specially, we use $O_c$ represent current information access.

*Definition 5. Information flow* $\varphi$: $(p_1, f_1, p_2, f_2, \ldots, f_t) \in (P \times F)$, is a union set of sequential information access, that means every later information access happens after the former one, and information begins from the former element then flows into the later one. Every two of adjacent elements do not belong to the same set like P or F (there is much excellent research work about Inter-Process Communication, which is shown in the related work, thus we only consider the operation of process access to file, leave out communication between processes).

*Definition 6. Information flow graph G:* G = < P, F, T >, P and F are the sets of vertexes, T is the weight of edge between P and F.

*Definition 7. Direct flow* →: a process access to a file directly. For example, $\varphi = (p_1, f_1)$ means there is a direct flow $p_1 \rightarrow f_1$. In the information flow graph, direct flow means there is a directed edge between file and process.

*Definition 8. Indirect flow* →~: a process access to a file through a few direct flow.

For example, there is an information flow $\varphi = (p_1, f_1, p_2, f_2)$, $p_1 \rightarrow_\sim f_2$ is an indirect flow. In G, there is not directed edge from vertex $p_1$ to vertex $f_2$ but they have directed connection through other vertexes.

*Definition 9. Security strategy* S: $\{\#p_i \rightarrow \#f_j, \#f_j \rightarrow \#p_i\}$, according to the access control matrix, if the value of element $A_{ij}$ in access control matrix is r, it means the flow from $p_i$ to $f_j$ is secure, we express this as $\#p_i \rightarrow \#f_j$; similarly, if the value of element $A_{ij}$ is w, it means the flow from $f_j$ to $p_i$ is secure, we express this as $\#f_j \rightarrow \#p_i$.

*Definition 10. Decision set*: D = {yes, no}, the element 'yes' means the current information access is allowed and added to the new information flow graph, 'no' means the current information access is forbidden.

*Definition 11. Security Character 1*: direct flow security. iff $\forall \rightarrow: (p_i, f_j) \in \varphi, \exists$ $\#p_i \rightarrow \#f_j$, and $\forall \rightarrow: (f_j, p_i) \in \varphi, \exists \#f_j \rightarrow \#p_i$.

*Definition 12. Security Character 2*: indirect flow security. iff $\forall \rightarrow_\sim: (p_i, \ldots, f_j) \in \varphi, \exists \#p_i \rightarrow \#f_j,$ : and $\forall \rightarrow_\sim: (f_j, \ldots, p_i) \in \varphi, \exists \#f_j \rightarrow \#p_i$

The secure information flow model is defined by M = < O, G, S, D >.

In this model, the input is the access information O, it will bring a direct flow and a few indirect flow to information system, the security strategy S will decide whether the flow is legal, then make a decision (yes or no) as an output. (see Fig. 2.)

The security requirements of the model are simply stated: the execution of a sequence of access operation cannot give rise to any information flow that violates the security strategy. That means the system must satisfy the aforementioned two security characters, direct flow security (security character 1) and indirect flow security (security character 2).

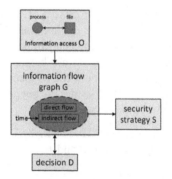

**Fig. 2.** Secure information flow model

## 4.1   Information Flow Graph Construction

The legal historic access records can be seen as a information flow graph, it is used to detect whether there are any illegal accesses for every current access information. We use a dot vertex to represent a process, and a square vertex to represent a file. Construction rules can be described as follows:

1. The initiate rule. The initiate information flow graph G = <P, F, T >, P = $\emptyset$, F = $\emptyset$, T = $\emptyset$.
2. Read rule. When access information is $(p_i, f_j, t_k) = r$, and it satisfies the security strategy for both the direct flow and indirect flow, add the G a directed edge from $f_j$ to $p_i$, whose weight is $t_k$
3. Write rule. When access information is $(p_i, f_j, t_k) = w$, and it satisfies the security strategy for direct flow and indirect flow, add the G a directed edge from $p_i$ to $f_j$, whose weight is $t_k$.

According to these construction rules, we take the following legal information access as case1.

$(p_1, f_1, t_1) = r$; $(p_1, f_2, t_2) = w$; $(p_1, f_3, t_3) = w$; $(p_2, f_3, t_4) = r$;
$(p_2, f_4, t_8] = r$; $(p_2, f_6, t_5) = w$; $(p_3, r_5, t_6) = r$; $(p_3, f_6, t_7) = w$;

$(t_1 < t_2 < t_3 < t_4 < t_5 < t_6 < t_7 < t_8)$, the symbol '<' means the time of left side happens before that of right side.

The G will be constructed like Fig. 3.

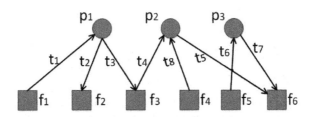

**Fig. 3.** Information flow graph

## 4.2   Algorithm Design for Indirect Information Flow Detection

Taking the case 1 for example, we suppose the current access information is $(p_4, f_6, t_9) = r$ $(t_8 < t_9)$, we must find if there is any indirect access path through the "bridge" of $f_6$.

The indirect flow is between all the pairs of nonadjacent vertexes in one certain information flow, thus the indirect flow occur if we find all the information flow ending up with current process $p_4$. According to the **Definition 5**, the information flow is a union set of sequential information access. And there is an edge between every information access, so information flow is a connected path in G only if the weight of edges in the path is in ascending order.

We use depth-first search algorithm to find all the connected paths that may flow the information to the current process $P_4$. The pseudo code is composed as follow:

```
Main:
1. G = null;
2. For information access (p, f, t) = r/w
       v=p;
       time=T;
       DFS(v, time)

DFS(v, time):
1. φ[] = {};
2. For each directed edge[w, v] Do:
     If weight[w, v] < time Then:
       φ[] ← DFS(w, weight[w, v]);
3. Return φ[];
```

We can detect two information flow ending up with process p4 with the above algorithm:

(1) $\varphi_1 = (f_5, p_3, f_6, p_4)$;
(2) $\varphi_2 = (f_1, p_1, f_3, p_2, f_6, p_4)$;

Especially, the sequence $(f_4, p_2, f_6, p_4)$ is not information flow as the sequence of edge weight $(t_8, t_5, t_9)$ is not in ascending order.

Thus, the indirect flow to file $f_5$, $f_1$ and $f_3$ has been detected:

$$f_5 \rightarrow \sim p_4, f_1 \rightarrow \sim p_4, f_3 \rightarrow \sim p_4$$

### 4.3    Optimization

Since the consumption of connected paths search algorithm in information flow graph will increase while historic records become larger, we present an optimization scheme by attaching file labels to reduce the length of information flow sequence when detecting indirect access.

Taking the information flow $\varphi_2 = (f_1, p_1, f_3, p_2, f_6, p_4)$ for example. Its former half flow $(f_1, p_1, f_3, p_2)$ has been found while dealing with the information access $(p_2, f_3, t_4) = r$, so it is totally resource waste to search this flow once again when the information access $(p_4, f_6, t_9) = r$ comes. Thus we propose to attach a former file label to the later file as optimization, then the $(f_3)$ will be updated as $(f_3 \cup f_1)$ after the information flow $(f_1, p_2, f_3, p_2)$ is found, and the information flow $\varphi_2 = (f_1, p_1, f_3, p_2, f_6, p_4)$ turns out to be $\varphi_2 = (f_3 \cup f_1, p_2, f_6, p_4)$ (see Fig. 4.)

After the optimization, the following theorem holds:

**Theorem.** The length of information flow sequence is no more than 5.

**Proof.** If the length of information flow sequence is more than 5, the information flow can be declared as: $\varphi = (\ldots, f_i, p_j, f_k, p_l, f_m, p_n)$,, but the inner information flow

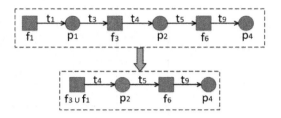

**Fig. 4.** Information flow search optimization

$(\ldots, f_i, p_j, f_k, p_l)$ has been found when dealing with the information access O: $(p_l, f_k, t_{lk}) = r$ undoubtedly, after that, $f_k$ will be $f_k \cup f_i$. Thus the information flow will be $\varphi = (f_k \cup f_i, p_l, f_m, p_n)$, i.e. the length of information flow sequence is less than 6.

The optimized pseudo code is composed as follow:

```
Main:
1. G = null;
2. For information access (p, f, t) = r/w
        v=p;
        time=T;
        DFS(v, time)
DFS(v, time):
1. If size(φ[])>= 5
        Return φ[];
2. Temp[] = {};
3. For each directed edge[w, v] Do:
        If weight[w, v]< time Then:
            Temp[] ← DFS(w, weight[w, v])
4. φ[] ← Temp[];
5. Return φ[];
```

After the optimization, this algorithm will have lower time complexity. More details will be discussed in the later section of performance analysis.

## 5   Implementation Scheme

### 5.1   White List

White list is an important reference object designed to stipulate what operation behaviors for files are legal or illegal. It is designed by developers in server, set rules for what processes have rights to read or write what files. In our work, white list is a comparison reference object setting rules for access to files. We design it using access matrix model which is invented by B. W. Lampson in 1969. The access matrix model is composed of a triple (S, O, A), S is a set of subjects, means a set of processes. O is a set of objects, means a set of files in this paper. And A represents access matrix, matrix

| Object\Subject | $f_1$ | $f_2$ | $f_3$ | $f_4$ | $f_5$ | $f_6$ | ... |
|---|---|---|---|---|---|---|---|
| $p_1$ | r | w | w | - | - | - | ... |
| $p_2$ | - | - | r | r | - | w | ... |
| $p_3$ | - | - | - | - | r | w | ... |
| $p_4$ | - | w | r | r | - | r | ... |
| ... | ... | ... | ... | ... | ... | ... | ... |

**Fig. 5.** Access control matrix

elements A[S, O] means the operation of subject S to object O. Usually, there are three kinds of operations, take the following matrix for example (see Fig. 5).

1. If process $p_i$ has a right to write file $f_j$, the element value of A[i][j] = w;
2. If process $p_i$ has a right to read file $f_j$, the element value of A[i][j] = r;
3. If process $p_i$ does not have a right to write nor to read file $f_j$, the element value of A [i][j] = -;

### 5.2    Function Module of File Filter

As described in Sect. 2, file filter intercepts IRP information and analyzes if there are illegal access behaviors according to the white list, then makes a decision about whether transferring the IRP to file system or not. In our implementation, we divide file filter to three sub-modules, including intercept module, analysis module, and decision module.

*Interception module:* It is an intrinsic function of the file system filter, which is used to intercept information access.

*Analysis module:* constructing information flow graph and analyzing information flow if it is illegal are the main function of this module.

*Decision module:* It passes the access request to the lower file system driver or returns the invalid signal to the upper level.

The procedure is as flow:

The first step, interception module intercepts the IRP information from I/O management, get and record the direct access operation extracted from IRP information in the form of information access $O : (p_i, f_j, t_k) = r/w$;

The second step, we detect the information flow and compare it with the security strategy. If it matches the security strategy, we pass "yes" signal down to decision module, else the signal is "no".

The third step, decision module passes IRP information down to file system driver if the signal is "yes", else returns invalid request signal to I/O management.

# 6 Algorithm and Security Analysis

## 6.1 Algorithm Analysis

Time analysis is a necessary step in algorithm design. Before optimization, time cost of information flow detection is O $(e_i)$ for current access request, $e_i$ is the number of edges in the current information flow graph, the growth of $e_i$ is proportional to the rise of number of access requests and the maximum $e_i$ is equal to the number of access requests (this case means every access request does not violate the two security strategies and can be added to the information flow graph), if there are m operations, the total time complexity is O $(m^2)$.

After algorithm optimization, time cost of information flow detection is O (n) for every access request, n is the number of nodes in the information flow graph (because the length of information flow sequence is no more than 5, so it can be seen as a constant number, so the time cost depends on the number of nodes in the graph G. If there are m access requests, the total time complexity is O (m × n). Obviously, the number of nodes in information flow graph is less than the number of edges, which is less than the number of access requests, thus n is less than m. So time complexity is reduced by optimization.

## 6.2 Security Analysis

The information flow graph is a dynamic graph, which transform from a state to another triggered by the decision made for current information access. The transformational rules are stated as follows:

$$G_0 = nul \tag{1}$$

$$G_{i+1} = G_i + O \tag{2}$$

$$O = \begin{cases} O_c, & d = yes \\ null, & d = no \end{cases} \tag{3}$$

$$d = \begin{cases} yes, character\ 1 \cap character\ 2 \\ no, else \end{cases} \tag{4}$$

According to rule (1), $G_0$ is null, so the initial graph is secure, thus the security proof of the system relies on proving the transformational rule (2) is secure.

**Proof.** If $G_{i+1} = G_i + O_c$, it means the graph is added by a new direct flow and a few indirect flows. Combining the rule (3) and rule (4), the system satisfy the two security characters, so the $G_{i+1}$ is also secure.

If $G_{i+1} = G_i$, it means the graph remain unchanged, so the $G_{i+1}$ is also secure.

In the above cases, the current information access $O_c : (p_4, f_6, t_9) = r$, we have detected one direct flow: $f_5 \rightarrow p_4$, and four indict flows: $f_5 \rightarrow_\sim p_4$, $f_4 \rightarrow_\sim p_4$, $f_1 \rightarrow_\sim p_4$, $f_3 \rightarrow_\sim p_4$, the indirect flows $f_5 \rightarrow_\sim p_4$ and $f_1 \rightarrow_\sim p_4$ fail to satisfy security strategy, then the decision module will set $d = no$, and return invalid signal. So the current information access will not be executed and the information flow graph will be kept unchanged and secure.

According to the analysis above, the system will not violate the security strategies, so the model is secure.

## 7  Conclusion and Future Work

Illegal resource access increases security risks such as information stealing, privacy leakage, etc. In this paper, we propose a novel security method to prevent illegal access to files in the transparent computing environment. Our main idea is detecting indirect file access based on DFS algorithm in information flow graph constructed with historic records in transparent client, then comparing the indirect access with preceding designed white list to find out whether there are illegal behaviors.

However, our present work is not perfect, it is a coarse-grained solution to illegal indirect access behavior, the process's reading and writing behaviors towards files do not mean the real information exchange between them. And as the access records grow, some files may not be accessed by any process which need to read or write them. We will address these challenges in our next work. Furthermore, we try to detect illicit processes by combining other malicious features with illegal indirect access to files, and extend this work to mobile environment.

**Acknowledgments.** This work is supported in part by the Joint Project of Central South University and Tencent Corporation under Grant Number 2014002H029, the Hunan Provincial Innovation Foundation for Postgraduate under Grant Number CX2015B047, the Hunan Provincial Education Department of China under grant number 2015C0589, the International Science & Technology Cooperation Program of China under Grant Number 2013DFB10070, and the China Hunan Provincial Science & Technology Program under Grant Number 2012GK4106.

## References

1. Zhang, Y.: Transparence computing: concept, architecture and example. Acta Electronica Sin. 32(12A), 169–173 (2004)
2. Zhang, Y., Zhou, Y.: Transparent computing: a new paradigm for pervasive computing. In: Ma, J., Jin, H., Yang, L.T., Tsai, J.J.-P. (eds.) UIC 2006. LNCS, vol. 4159, pp. 1–11. Springer, Heidelberg (2006)
3. Lapadula, L., Lapadula, L.J., Bell, D.E.: Secure computer systems: a mathematical model. Technical report 2547 (1996)
4. Xue, H., Dai, Y.: A privacy protection model for transparent computing system. Int. J. Cloud Comput. 1(4), 367–384 (2012)

5. Yang, Y., Ding, R., Min, Y.: Object-based access control model. Autom. Electr. Power Syst. **27**(7), 36–40 (2003)
6. Deng, J.B., Hong, F.: Task-based access control model. J. Softw. **14**(1), 76–82 (2003)
7. Ferraiolo, D., Kuhn, D.R., Chandramouli, R.: Role-based access control. Artech House (2003)
8. Li, F., Wang, W., Ma, J., Liang, X.: Action-based access control model and administration of actions. Acta Electronica Sin. **36**(10), 1881–1890 (2008)
9. Denning, D.E.: A lattice model of secure information flow. Commun. ACM **19**(5), 236–243 (1976)
10. Cheng, W., Ports, D.R., Schultz, D.A., Popic, V., Blankstein, A., Cowling, J.A., Curtis, D., Shrira, L., Liskov, B.: Abstractions for usable information flow control in aeolus. In: USENIX Annual Technical Conference, pp. 139–151 (2012)
11. Bichhawat, A., Rajani, V., Garg, D., Hammer, C.: Information flow control in WebKit's javascript bytecode. In: Abadi, M., Kremer, S. (eds.) POST 2014 (ETAPS 2014). LNCS, vol. 8414, pp. 159–178. Springer, Heidelberg (2014)
12. Hedin, D., Sabelfeld, A.: Information-flow security for a core of javascript. In: 25th IEEE Computer Security Foundations Symposium, pp. 3–18 (2012)
13. Hedin, D., Birgisson, A., Bello, L., Sabelfeld, A.: Jsflow: tracking information flow in javascript and its apis. In: Proceedings of the 29th Annual ACM Symposium on Applied Computing, pp. 1663–1671 (2014)
14. Dietz, M., Shekhar, S., Pisetsky, Y., Shu, A., Wallach, D.S.: Quire: lightweight provenance for smart phone operating systems. In: USENIX Security Symposium, p. 24 (2011)
15. Enck, W., Gilbert, P., Han, S., Tendulkar, V., Chun, B.G., Cox, L.P., Jung, J., McDaniel, P., Sheth, A.N.: Taintdroid: an information-flow tracking system for realtime privacy monitoring on smartphones. ACM Trans. Comput. Syst. **32**(2), 5 (2014)
16. Nakamura, S., Doulikun, D., Aikebaier, A., Enokido, T., Takizawa, M.: Role-based information flow control models. In: 28th IEEE International Conference on Advanced Information Networking and Applications, pp. 1140–1147 (2014)
17. Zhou, Y., Zhang, Y., Xie, Y., Zhang, H., Yang, L.T., Min, G.: Transcom: a virtual disk-based cloud computing platform for heterogeneous services. IEEE Trans. Netw. Serv. Manage. **11**(1), 46–59 (2014)
18. Chen, J., Jie, S., Zhang, X.: Implementation of virus prevention method based on file system filter driver. Comput. Technol. Dev. **23**(3), 143–146 (2013)
19. Qiu, S., Tang, G., Wang, Y.: Research of file backup method based on double cache and minifilter driver. In: 2015 International Conference on Advances in Mechanical Engineering and Industrial Informatics. Atlantis Press (2015)
20. Chen, J., Ye, J.: Research on the file encryption system based on minifilter driver. In: Long, S., Dhillon, B.S. (eds.) Proceedings of the 13th International Conference on Man-Machine-Environment System Engineering. Lecture Notes in Electrical Engineering, pp. 175–182. Springer, Heidelberg (2014)
21. Li, Z.: Research on the technology of dynamically access control based on file filter driver in windows system. Comput. Knowl. Technol. **8**(9), 2045–2047 (2012)
22. Zhang, Y., Zhou, Y.: TransOS: a transparent computing-based operating system for the cloud. Int. J. Cloud Comput. **1**(4), 287–301 (2012)

# EPAMP: An Anonymous Multicast Protocol in Mobile Ad Hoc Networks

Hongling Xiao[1], Hong Song[2($\boxtimes$)], and Weiping Wang[2]

[1] Information Network Center, The Second Xiangya Hospital,
Central South University, Changsha 410083, China
15957231@qq.com
[2] School of Information Science and Engineering,
Central South University, Changsha 410083, China
{songhong,wpwang}@csu.edu.cn

**Abstract.** We propose a new anonymous multicast protocol named Encryption and Pseudo-based Anonymous Multicast Protocol (EPAMP). EPAMP is an anonymous routing protocol based on MAODV in mobile ad hoc networks. It adopts the pseudonym mechanism to hide the senders identity, and uses encryption/decryption mechanism to thwart eavesdropping and intrusion attacks. It can ensure the anonymity of senders, receivers and the communication of neighboring nodes. Performance analysis and simulation results indicate that EPAMP can ensure anonymity performance, and effectively resist collusion attacks and predecessor attacks. It brings only slight transmission delay and decrease in packet transmission rate.

**Keywords:** Anonymous communication · EPAMP · Multicast · Pseudonym mechanism

## 1 Introduction

Secure communication and users privacy attract a lot of research attention in recent years. Forwarding mechanism is one of the key components to realize communication among nodes in mobile ad hoc networks (MANTEs) How to hide the communication location and communication relationship becomes one important issue in military and confidential communications. Due to the lack of predefined and opened system structure, the attackers are more likely to intercept the information and discover the real IP address, reveal the actual position and the communication relationship among communicating nodes in the network. Therefore, it is very important to study the anonymous communication mechanism in MANETs.

The demand of anonymity in mobile network includes [1,2] sender-receiver unlinkability, mutual authentication identity anonymity, location anonymity, and network topology and motion pattern anonymity. In the past several years, there are already many works on anonymous communication mechanisms in ad hoc

© Springer International Publishing Switzerland 2015
G. Wang et al. (Eds.): ICA3PP 2015 Workshops, LNCS 9532, pp. 276–289, 2015.
DOI: 10.1007/978-3-319-27161-3_24

network [3–13]. ANODR [3] uses the trap door and pseudonym strategy to hide the IP addresses of the source and the destination. ASR [1] encrypts the destination address by shared key between the destination and source node. In the data transmission stage, a node uses a shared confidential TAG authentication to determine whether the received packet is transmitted to it. If it is not for its own, a replacement strategy and XOR mechanism of random number would be used to fix the packet length in order to avoid the path tracking. The Mask protocol [4] assigns a series of conflict-free pseudonyms and corresponding key values for participating nodes through the trust authority server, and uses pairwise-anonymous authentication and confusion mechanism to achieve sender anonymity, receiver anonymity and position anonymity. The broadcast mechanism and onion communication has been used in SDAR protocol [5] to communicate between the sender and the receiver. All these anonymous mechanisms can solve the problem of anonymous communication to some extend in mobile ad hoc networks.

As multicast in ad hoc networks is used widely, more and more applications can be done better to complete the tasks by using multicast, such as disaster rescue and war in the communication command. Although there are some anonymous communication mechanisms using the feature of multicast in cable network, such as SAM [8] (Secure and Anonymous Multicast), Mapper [9], they are not suitable for large-scale dynamic networks for the sake of the low efficiency and scalability. Recent researches applied multicast anonymity technology to P2P networks. The M2 protocol [11] proposes a method that combines the forwarding paths of receivers in the same group. The MAM protocol [12] constructs an efficient multicast tree with bandwidth and/or delay. The BAM protocol [13] proposes a ring structure based on Bus. All these protocols use multicast mechanism to get mutual anonymity while decreasing the cost. However, because multicast in ad hoc networks have different features, these anonymous communication strategies proposed for cable networks are not suitable for ad hoc networks. There are some problems:

(1) The attacker can obtain the information of the multicast group and the sender by eavesdropping on the plaintext packets and tracking the transmission route of the packet.
(2) Some special tags of the same packet in the multicast protocol provide the clue for the attacker to find out the important member of the multicast system through reverse tracking.
(3) The global listeners can obtain multicast topology.
(4) The agent error will affect the entire network performance. In this paper, we propose a new pro anonymous multicast protocol based on MAODV, which is Encryption and Pseudo-based Anonymous Multicast Protocol (EPAMP). EPAMP adopts the pseudonym mechanism to hide the senders identity and uses encryption/decryption mechanism to thwart eavesdropping and intrusion attack. It can ensure the anonymity of senders, receivers and the communication of neighbor nodes.

The remainder of this paper is organized as follows. Section 2 presents the design of EPAMP. Section 3 analyzes the anonymity of EPAMP. Performance analysis and evaluation are presented in Sect. 4. We conclude the paper in Sect. 5.

## 2    Encryption and Pseudo-Based Anonymous Multicast Protocol (EPAMP)

The main idea of EPAMP is to use pseudonyms rather than real IP address to represent the nodes in the multicast tree for multicast communication process, and to use symmetric encryption method to communicate between the initiator and receiver for data communication process, with which sender anonymity and connection anonymity can be achieved. The whole process is divided into multicast data transmission and multicast tree maintenance. Every node saves the information of its own neighbor nodes in the same multicast tree. In order to finish the work of path establishment and data transmission, every node also creates a new routing table for saving the request information and a new multicast routing table for saving the related information of data forwarding.

### 2.1    Multicast Data Transmission

This process is mainly to build the path of the multicast group members and to transfer data along the path.

Step 1: The source node requests constructing path (Fig. 1).

The source node S, which wants to join the multicast group or which wants to send the data to the multicast group, will send routing request packet. The format of the RREQ packet is described as followed,

$$\{RREQ, rreqID, McastAddr, destSeq, srcpseudo, srcSeq, Hop\}$$

where rreqID in the packet is the sequence number, McastAddr represents the address of the terminal multicast group, destSeq is the latest sequence number received by the node, Srcpseudo is the nodes pseudonym generated by the hash function and its own IP address, and srcSeq is sequence number of the node and Hop is a random number. After sending out an RREQ request, the source node waits for the reply packet. If the source cannot receive the reply after several tries, it will announce itself as the leader of a new multicast group.

After receiving a RREQ request, intermediate node will judge out whether the multicast sequence number is greater than or equal to the multicast sequence number. If not, it generates its own pseudonyms and public-private key pair (PK, SK) and adds them into the routing table as following format.

(McastAddr, Mcastseq, LHCount, LcPseudo, PK, SK, NHPseudo, LPPseudo, lifetime)

The over record is used to save the information about multicast group, the intermediate node, the upstream node, the downstream node and their pseudonyms and etc. if (Hop-1)>0, then the node uses its own LcPseudo and

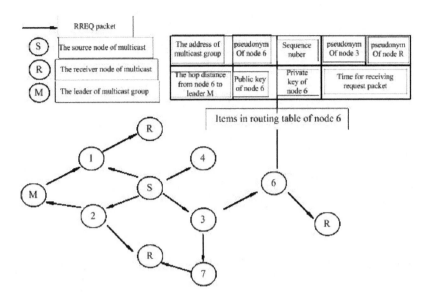

**Fig. 1.** Route request stage diagram

PK to replace srcPseudo and srcSeq of this packet and broadcast the modified packet.

Step 2: The destination replies the RREQ request. This process is shown in Fig. 2.

When the multicast member receives the request packet, it will reply the RREP packet to the source node by the original path if its multicast group sequence number is greater than or equal to the current serial number. The RREP packet is described as $\{RREP, Hop, McastAddr, destSeq, srcPseudo, PK, McastHop, leaderPseudo\}$.

The values of Hop and McastAddr come from the RREQ packet. destSeq is the current multicast group sequence number. srcPseudo is the node pseudonyms. PK is the public key in (PK, SK). McastHop is the number of hops from current node to the leader of multicast group and leaderPseudo is the leaders pseudonym.

After the intermediate node receives the RREP packet, it will check the routing table whether there is the same McastAddr and the same srcPseudo with which is in the RREP packet. If not, then the RREP packet is discarded. Otherwise, the intermediate node will record the information in RREP packet and generate a pair of public key and private key. Then After increase the value of hop and McastHop, the node modifies the value of PK and srcPseudo and forwards the RREP packert to next node in the reverse path. If the node receives several RREP packets, it will keep the information of the RREP packet with maximum sequence number or minimum Hop value.

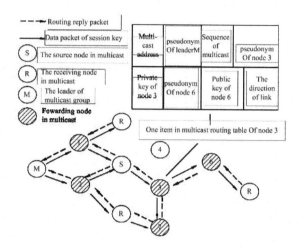

**Fig. 2.** The information which the node saves in the route response stage

Step 3: Path Activating. After waiting for a certain time, the source node chooses the path with the largest sequence number or the route with the minimum hops, and sends the MACT packet to activate the path. As shown in Fig. 3, the nodes m-1, m, and m+1 are three contiguous neighbor nodes in the path. When the source node S sends an MACT packet to the tree member node R it must finish the next five operations in turn.

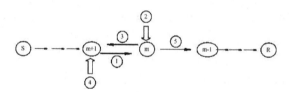

**Fig. 3.** The process of activating the route

Node m+1 sends a MACT message to node m. The message includes the pseudonym of node m+1 and node m, multicast group address, the pseudonym of the source node S, the session key of node m+1 and so on. All these information encrypts with the public key of node m.

After node m receives the MACT message, it lookups the item with the same pseudonym and decrypts the MACT package. Then it gets the session key of node m+1 and activates the path from node m+1 to node m.

After the path is activated, the node m sends to the node m+1 a data packet in which there are the session key of node m+1, node m-1 and node m.

After receiving the data packet, node m+1 records the session key and activates it.

Node m lookups the routing table and uses the pseudonym and public key of node m-1 to modify the MACT message. Then, MACT message is forwarded downward to the next node.

Step 4: Data transmission. After activating the transmission path, the source node can transmit data to the members of the group. The node who received data packets firstly checks whether there is an item with pseudonym srcPseudo in multicast routing table and whether the direction is in accordance with the tag. If its true, then the node can decrypt by the session key and replace srcPseudo with the pseudonym of the node, and encrypt McastAddr and load. At last, the node continually forwards the packet and repeats the process until the receiver gets the packet.

## 2.2   Multicast Tree Maintenance

The multicast tree maintenance process of EPAMP protocol is similar to that of MAODV. It uses encryption operation to enhance anonymity, and it includes four parts, which are pruning, splitting, merging, and repairing the link.

**(1) Pruning Multicast Tree.** The pruning process is taken place when a member node wants to leave the multicast group. The leaving node sends a MACT message with P tag and its own IP address. The upstream node that receiving this MACT message will decrypt it by corresponding session key and delete the information related to the leaving node. If the upstream node becomes a leaf node and it is not the member of the group, the process will be continued.

**(2) Repairing the Link.** When two nodes in the multicast tree are disconnected, the downstream node of the link will sends RREQ packet to repair the link. The destination IP address is set into multicast group address and the multicast group sequence number is the destination sequence number. The hops number of multicast group is set to the distance from the downstream node to the leader node. Only the member nodes of the multicast tree may be able to reply the RREQ packets. After repairing the multicast tree, the initiator node sends MACT message to update the downstream multicast tree.

If the upstream node of disconnected link is not the member node of multicast tree and it becomes a leaf node, then it sets the waiting time for pruning and does pruning operation after the time is past.

**(3) Splitting Multicast Tree.** If the disconnect network leads to failed repairing link, the initiator node will broadcast GRPH packet or MACT packet to split the original multicast tree into two sub-multicast tree? GRPH packet is sent out by the old multicast member, it contains the flag, update information of the leader, the hops number that GRPH packet has past, pseudonym of the leader, IP address of multicast group and the sequence number. All nodes who receive this GRPH message packet update their routing tables and multicast routing tables. MACT message with a G tag is sent out by the node who is not the member of multicast group. MACT message is used to inform the members updating. And the MACT message is forwarded by neighbor nodes and the forwarding process will not be ended until it reaches the multicast group member nodes.

**(4) Merging Multicast Tree.** If two multicast trees want to reconnect into a new multicast tree, the leader GL1 who has smaller group sequence number in two multicast trees will sent out the merging request. The leader GL2 with larger group sequence number becomes the leader of the new multicast tree. All members whose leader is GL1 request to join the new multicast tree by RREQ messages. After waiting for a period of time, the multicast tree with the leader GL1 select a forwarding path which distance is shortest to activate. As a result, the two multicast tree are merged into a new tree.

# 3    Anonymity Analysis of EPAMP

In order to understand EPAMP protocol, we use some attack models to analyze the anonymity of EPAMP protocol.

## 3.1    Eavesdropping Attack

EPAMP protocol uses pseudonym mechanism to achieve sender anonymity, receiver anonymity and the link of sender-receiver anonymity. And the eavesdropper cannot directly find out the real IP address of every node from the routing packets and data packets due to pseudonyms mechanism using in routing packets and data packets.

Moreover, in the stage of path initiating, multicast sender only broadcasts request with multicast address, while the receiver determines to reply the request only by multicast address and sequence number. So the attacker cant destroy data transmission, and cant trace the packet flag to find out the node who initiates the packet and the new leader after the initiating process is completed. The sender and the receiver are anonymous.

In the stage of path activating, the attacker cant distinguish the type of packets through eavesdropping because of the same format {$pseudonym$, $encryptioninformation$} of the MACT message and session key package. Also, the eavesdropper is unable to directly associate the path from the length or appearance of the packet because the public key and the session key are changed every time after forwarding. In data transmission stag, the eavesdropper cannot get the multicast group number and the serial number or the association path. And the session key exchange using public key encryption can prevent eavesdropper gets relevant information. Furthermore, the value of Hops in EPAMP is a random number and is changed during the transmission, which will prevent the eavesdropper inferring the possible position of the leader.

## 3.2  Surrounding Attack

When all neighbors of a node are compromised nodes, these compromised nodes can exchange their information to infer the common node and they can judge the type of the common node through their exchanging information because all messages must pass by these compromised nodes. If they find that the node has only output packets, they can infer that the surrounded node is source node immediately. We define this attack as Surrounding attack. Surrounding attack will destroy the source anonymity.

Assuming the area of the anonymous multicast network is l*w square meter, the range of the transmission is d meters, then the communication area occupied by each node Ai is pd2. At the same time, there are N nodes in the network, including C compromised nodes with the proportion of p. Let all nodes distribute uniformly within the anonymous multicast network, then we can calculate that the number of nodes M within the communication area of each node is

$$M = \frac{\pi d^2}{lw} N \tag{1}$$

Therefore, the number of neighbor nodes surrounded the source node in the communication range is (M-1). So the successful probability of surrounding attack is

$$P_I = \begin{cases} \left( \begin{matrix} Np \\ M-1 \end{matrix} \right) \Big/ \left( \begin{matrix} N \\ M-1 \end{matrix} \right) & p \geq \frac{M-1}{N} \\ 0 & p < \frac{M-1}{N} \end{cases} \tag{2}$$

Figure 4 shows the impact of surrounding attack with different p and M. In Fig. 4, the anonymous multicast network area is 1500 * 300 m2, there are 100 nodes and the proportion of p varies from 0.5 to 0.9. We test the variation of PI when the number of direct neighbors of each node M varies from 5 to 20.

From Fig. 4 we can conclude that the success probability PI of surrounding attack is increasing with the increasing proportion p of compromised attackers. The reason is that according to uniform distribution, the probability of attackers surrounding the node will be increased when the proportion of attackers increasing. Therefore, the possibility that all attackers are located in the communication range of the sender is also increased. But when the number of neighbors of the sender is increased, the probability of surrounding the sender will reduce as the proportion of the attacker is fixed.

In addition, Fig. 4 also shows that although the attackers increase the successful proportion of surrounding attack, the probability PI just increases a little. Even if the proportion of attackers p reaches 60 % and the number of neighbors M is 5, the successful probability PI of surrounding attack is only about 7.2 %.When the number of direct neighbors increases to 20, the successful probability PI of surrounding attack declines to 7.8208e-006. This result indicates that surrounding attack is almost impossible to succeed in the density of larger networks.

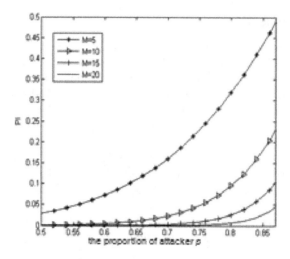

**Fig. 4.** PI with different p and M

## 3.3   Predecessor Attack

Predecessor attack is collaborated attack against anonymous protocols, in which
the attacker infer the possible sender by the sending times of each node after
tracking an identifiable stream of communications over a number of rounds (e.g.,
path reformations in Crowds) and simply logging any node which sends a message in each round.

In EPAMP protocol, every node records some information in a list, such as
the multicast address, neighbor nodes and leaders pseudonym. The attacker in
the forwarding path can get the content of packet according to the session keys
between upstream and downstream nodes. And it also can collaborate with other
attackers to determine whether they are located in the same multicast tree by
the multicast address and sequence number. Thus, the compromised attacker
can run a predecessor attack.

Suppose there are N nodes in the system, including C attackers, and the proportion of the attackers in the system is p. We also suppose that the probability
of successful attack is Pr.

From the structure of multicast tree in EPAMP protocol, we can learn that
the sender is only in the root node of the multicast tree. Therefore, any attacker
can determine that its direct predecessor is the sender only when it locates the
first position of the anonymous path. That is to say, when the attacker can
located in the first layer of multicast tree, it has the opportunity to infer the
sender. And when there is no attacker in the first layer of the tree, the predecessor
attack will not succeed. So if there are k nodes in the first layer of the multicast
tree, and the successful probability of predecessor attack Prl=k is:

$$\Pr\{l = k\} = 1 - \frac{\binom{N - pN - 1}{k}}{\binom{N}{k}} \tag{3}$$

Suppose there are M neighbors within the communication range of the sender, 1⩽M, then

$$\Pr = \sum_{m=1}^{M} \frac{1}{M} \Pr\{l = m\} = 1 - \frac{1}{M} \sum_{m=1}^{M} \frac{\binom{N - pN - 1}{m}}{\binom{N}{m}} \tag{4}$$

Suppose Ts is the number of observation rounds of the successful predecessor attack, that is to say, the predecessor attacker can infer the sender of the rerouting path with higher probability after reforming Ts rerouting paths. According to the lower bound of Chernoff in [14], the value of Ts is:

$$T_S \geq 8 \frac{M}{M - \sum_{m=1}^{M} \frac{\binom{N - pN - 1}{m}}{\binom{N}{m}}} \ln N \tag{5}$$

By the Formula (5) we can conclude that, the initiator will be inferred at least

$$\frac{1}{2} \left[ 1 - \frac{1}{M} \sum_{m=1}^{M} \frac{\binom{N - pN - 1}{m}}{\binom{N}{m}} \right] T \text{ times by the predecessor attacker with}$$

the probability $\frac{N-1}{N}$ among Ts rounds.

Figure 5 gives the relationship between Ts rounds and M direct neighbor nodes with different p in the anonymous multicast network. In Fig. 5, we suppose that there are N=100 nodes in the anonymous multicast network and the proportion p of attackers is varied from 10 % to 80 %. The situation of Ts varies with the proportion p when M is set to 5, 10, 15 and 20.

As shown in Fig. 5, with the increase of the direct neighbors number M of the sender, the rounds Ts which the successful predecessor attack requires is decreased. And Ts is also decreased with the increase of the proportion C/N. This is because the number of rerouting paths is decreased with less sender's direct neighbors and less times the attackers locating in first layer of multicast tree. When M is a certain value, the higher the proportion of the attacker, the probability of the attacker appearing in the first layer of multicast tree is higher. And the number of rounds Ts will be reduced.

Figure 5 also shows that even the proportion of attackers reaches 70 %and the number of direct neighbor nodes is 20, the rerouting rounds Ts for successful

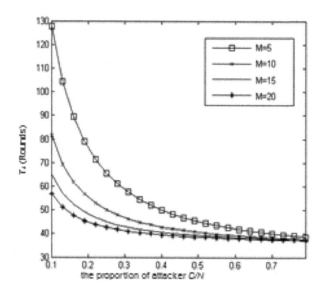

**Fig. 5.** Ts with different C/N and M

predecessor attack still needs about 40 rounds. That is to say, the predecessor attackers must try to compel the sender in protocol EPAMP to re-establish the forwarding path about 40 times in one data transmission process. Furthermore, the successful predecessor attacker can only get the nodes pseudonym through analyzing the content of data packet. Any captured nodes cannot give the information to determine whether its upstream node or its downstream node is leader or group member. The only thing that the predecessor attacker can do is to reduce the area of the senders location and it cant confirm the exact node, because the attacker is also surrounded by M-1 nodes.

## 4   Transmission Performance Analyses

We use NS2 to test the transmission costs of the EPAMP protocol. The area is set to 1500 * 300 m2 and there are 50 nodes in accordance with random distribution. The communication range of each node is 250 m and the wireless transmission rate is 2 Mbps. The movement model is random waypoint model with the maximum speed of 1 m/s, 5 m/s, 10 m/s, 25 m/s and 55 m/s, respectively. IEEE802.11 MAC protocol is used in MAC layer. The source node is randomly selected from 50 nodes. RC5 operation will need 20 ms and 930 ms is needed when the node using RSA algorithm to encryption/decryption. The cost of anonymity is measured by the data transfer rate and the transmission delay.

Figure 6 shows the effects of moving speed on transmission success rate. We can find that the transmission rate of two protocols will be declined along with the increasing node moving speed and the data successful transmission rate of EPAMP protocol is lower than that of MAODV. This is because EPAMP protocol will do encrypting and decrypting operations for each node. It requires more transmission time than that of MAODV. With the increase of the node moving speed, the number of failed links in unit time will increase, which will lead to higher probability of failure data packet transmission.

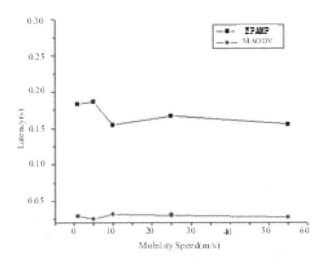

**Fig. 6.** Packet transmission ratio

Figure 7 shows the comparison of packet transmission delay of two protocols. The delay of the EPAMP protocol is larger than that of MAODV. Also the simulation results show that anonymous communication strategy based on encryption and decryption can receive good anonymity, but it is only applicable in wireless network of low mobility and low real-time requirements. When the node mobility rate is increased, the successful rate of data transmission is lower than that of MAODV, while the transmission delay is increased. This is because the encryption mechanism adopted in the EPAMP protocol, which will lead to decreased transmission performance. The reason for getting more anonymity with lower transmission performance mainly comes from two following parts:

First, In order to guarantee anonymity, we cancel the flags of routing request packet and reply packet in the design of data packets, so the attackers cant track the special flag. We also adopt multiple replying paths and activating process in merging multicast tree to avoid the attackers path tracing. But these measures will bring some time cost of nodes joining and multicast tree merging and path establishing.

Second, we use pseudonym mechanism instead of IP address to effectively hide the node address information. And session keys between two nodes and the public-private key pair (PK, SK) is used to encrypt/decrypt the content of transmission packet. Moreover, the relevant content in packet is modified by each

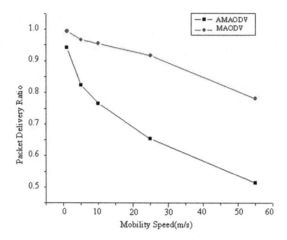

**Fig. 7.** The latency of packet transmission

intermediate node and is re-encrypted. At the same time, the intermediate node or receiver determines whether it is the receiver only relying on the pseudonym, which can guarantee not to disclose the relevant address information and to further enhance the anonymity.

Therefore, in order to minimize the cost of transmission and operation, (1) we just use pseudonyms to replace the IP addresses when broadcasting the request packets and reply packets because that transmitting plaintext can generate little impact on broadcasting speed; (2) When transmitting the controlling packet, we just use plaintext pseudonyms to decide whether it is the receiver, which can avoid lots of decrypting operations and can reduce the transmission time and computation cost; (3) During the data transmission process, all nodes in the path and their neighbor nodes use the same symmetry key to encrypt so that the data packet can send only once and can avoid energy wasting for many decrypting operations and repeatedly broadcasts. At the same time, the flag in data packet can also be used to avoid repeatedly broadcasting.

## 5  Conclusions

We have contributed a new anonymous multicast routing protocol EPAMP for providing anonymous multicast based on MAODV protocol. Anonymity analysis and transmission performance analysis results show that using pseudonym mechanism and encryption/decryption mechanism to implement anonymous multicast communication needs more transmission delay and brings lower data transmission rate, but it can effectively resist the collusion attack and the predecessor attack and it can increase the difficulty of destroying anonymous communication system and can effectively improve the anonymous performance.

**Acknowledgements.** This research was supported in part by the National Nature Science Foundation of China under Grant No. 61173169. The authors would like to thank the anonymous reviewers for their valuable comments.

# References

1. Zhu, B., Wna, Z., Kankanhalli, M.S., Deng, R.H.: Anonymous secure routing in mobile ad-hoc networks. In: The Proceedings of 29th Annual IEEE International Conference on Local Computer Networks, pp. 102–108. IEEE (2012)
2. Hong, X., Kong, J., Gerla, M.: Mobility changes anonymity: new passive threats in mobile ad hoc networks. Wirel. Commun. Mob. Comput. **6**(3), 281–293 (2012)
3. Kong, J., Hong, X., Gerla, M.: An identity-free and on demand routing scheme against anonymity threats in mobile ad-hoc networks. IEEE Trans. Mob. Comput. **6**(8), 888–902 (2007)
4. Zhang, Z., Liu, W., Fang, Y.: MASK: anonymous on-demand routing in mobile ad hoc networks. IEEE Trans. Wirel. Commun. **5**, 2376–2385 (2006)
5. Boukerche, A., El-Khatib, K., Xu, L., et al.: SDAR: a secure distributed anonymous routing protocol for wireless and mobile ad hoc networks. In: The Proceedings of the 29th Annual IEEE International Conference on Local Computer Networks, pp: 618–624 (2004)
6. Zhang, R., Zhang, Y., Fang, Y.: AOS: an anonymous overlay system for mobile ad hoc networks. Wirel. Netw. **17**(4), 843–859 (2011)
7. Zhang. P, Jiang. Y.X., Lin. C.: P-Coding: secure network coding against eavesdropping attacks, pp. 1–9. IEEE (2010)
8. Weiler, N.: Secure anonymous group infrastructure for common and future internet applications. In: The Proceedings of the 17th Annual Computer Security Applications Conference, New Orleans, Louisiana, pp. 401–410 (2001)
9. Bao-liu, Y., Tie-cheng, G., Min-qiang, W., et al.: Mapper: a multicast-based peer-to-peer file anonymous retrieval protocol. Acta Electronica Sinica **32**(5), 754–758 (2004)
10. Oliveira, L.B., Aranha, D.F., Gouva, C.P.L., et al.: TinyPBC: pairings for authenticated identity-based non-interactive key distribution in sensor networks. Comput. Commun. **34**(3), 485–493 (2010)
11. Perng, G., Reiter, M., Wang, C.: M2: multicasting mixes for efficient and anonymous communication. In: The Proceedings of 26th IEEE International Conference on Distributed Computing Systems, pp: 59–69 (2006)
12. Xiao, L., Liu, X., Gu, W., et al.: A design of overlay anonymous multicast protocol. In: The Proceedings of Parallel and Distributed Processing Symposium (IPDPS), pp. 1–10 (2006)
13. Wang, J., Niu, C., Shen, R.: Bus-based anonymous mulitcast in peer-to-peer overlay. In: The Proceedings of International Conference on Network and Parallel Computing - Workshops, Dalian, China, pp:148–151 (2007)
14. Wright, M., Adler, M., Levine, B., et al.: An analysis of the degradation of anonymous protocols. In: The Proceedings of Network and Distributed System Security Symposium, San Diego, California, pp. 34–43 (2002)

# The 3rd International Workshop on Network Optimization and Performance Evaluation (NOPE 2015)

# Energy Saving Mechanism Analysis Based on Dynamic Resource Scaling for Cloud Computing

Xiaojie Zhang[1], Nao Wang[2], Xin Zheng[1(✉)], Caocai Wang[2], and Dongmei Bin[2]

[1] Department Physics and Electronic Engineering,
Guangxi Normal University for Nationalities, Guangxi 532200, China
zhengxin_043@163.com
[2] School of Computer and Electronic Information,
Guangxi University, Guangxi 530004, China
{7482227,betty.bin}@qq.com, gcwang@gxu.edu.cn

**Abstract.** To solve the current high energy consumption problem in cloud computing, the paper proposes an energy saving strategy– Computing Resources Dynamic Power-aware (CRDP). For the case of multiple tasks on one server in cloud computing system, the strategy tries to set processor supply voltage to lower level when a task is finished and the computing resource it possesses is idle to reduce the energy consumption caused by computing resource idle. And the lowing of supply voltage is within left unfinished tasks response time constraint to ensure the system performance. Based on process analysis of executing tasks on a server, energy consumption model and performance model of system are built. Simulation results show that the CRDP can improve the energy efficiency while meeting the quality of service requirement.

**Keywords:** Cloud computing · Energy saving · Dynamic voltage frequency scaling · Energy efficiency analysis

## 1 Introduction

As a new computing mode, cloud computing garners a lot of attention since it is proposed. Nowadays themes about cloud computing have become significant research topics in academics. In industry, many large companies have built their own cloud computing platforms, such as IBM Blue cloud, Google cloud platform, Amazon EC2, Baidu cloud storage, and so on.

While developing rapidly, cloud computing bring many problems, one of which is high energy consumption. Statistics shows that electricity consumption of America datacenters in 2011 is 100 billion *Kw/h* and the total costs is 7.4 billion dollars. A report by Greenpeace shows that by 2020 main IT operators around the world will use about two trillions KW/h electricity consumption, exceeding the sum of France, Germany, Canada and Brazil. Therefore, the high energy consumption in cloud computing has become an urgent problem we have to solve.

© Springer International Publishing Switzerland 2015
G. Wang et al. (Eds.): ICA3PP 2015 Workshops, LNCS 9532, pp. 293–301, 2015.
DOI: 10.1007/978-3-319-27161-3_25

Dynamic Voltage Frequency Scaling (DVFS) is one of the main energy saving techniques in cloud computing environment, mainly to reduce executing power of servers. Executive energy consumption can be defined as the energy consumption generated by hardware when computer executing tasks. Power consumption of computer hardware to executing tasks is called executive power. In [26], Blume points out that in executing process of the same task the executive power changes with the run phase and executive feature of the task. For processors based on CMOS technique, the power consumption is dominated by dynamic power dissipation, and the dynamic power is squarely related to supply voltage.

In [27], the authors propose a scheduling heuristics to reduce energy consumption of parallel tasks in DVFS enabled clusters. They analyze the slack time for non-critical jobs, extend their execution time and reduce the energy consumption without increasing the task's execution time as a whole. In [28], based on the concept of slack sharing among processors, researchers propose two novel power-aware scheduling algorithms for task sets with and without precedence constraints executing on multi-processor systems. These scheduling techniques reclaim the time unused by a task to reduce the execution speed of future tasks, and thus reduce the total energy consumption of the system. In [31], for parallel tasks, researchers propose two energy-efficient scheduling algorithms-SSEF and EGSA to save energy in the environment of the computing resources supply voltage to be dynamically adjusted. While satisfying the sub-deadline distributed reasonably, which satisfying requirements of parallel tasks deadline, the two algorithms low the executive power of processor as much as possible to saving energy.

The above literature has considered the problem of reducing energy consumption from different aspects, but there is little research about how to reduce energy consumption caused by computing resource idle through lowing the supply voltage according to tasks executing and tasks request for computing resource in the environment of multiple tasks on one server. This paper focuses on reducing energy consumption by lowing processor voltage within left unfinished tasks response time constraint when a task is finished.

This paper is organized as follows. In Sect. 2, we give cloud computing model description, including task model and cloud computing model. In Sect. 3, we analyze the reason why servers in cloud computing system generate high energy consumption and propose an energy saving strategy based on DVFS. In Sect. 4, we analyze energy consumption and performance of cloud computing system. Then, we give simulation and analysis results in Sect. 5. Finally, we conclude our paper and give further research work in Sect. 6.

## 2 Cloud Computing System Model

### 2.1 Task Model in Cloud Computing System

Rapid development of cloud computing causes that its users are more and more and it has to execute a large number of tasks and data. For a single server in cloud computing system, there may be not one but several tasks running on it at the same time, and the tasks may belong to different users, or be a subtask of a parallel task, also can be a independent task. There, to simplify the research, we consider all tasks as independent homonymic tasks. In cloud computing system, the service different users request are various, leading that every task has different parameters, calculation amount and response time.

To define the cloud tasks, we use the tuple $(T, L, TR)$, where $T = \{t_i | 1 \leq i \leq m\}$ is the set of all tasks, $L = \{l_i | 1 \leq i \leq m\}$ is the set of calculation amount of all tasks and $RT = \{RT_i | 1 \leq i \leq m\}$ is the set of response time of all tasks request. Here, we can consider $T$ as the set of tasks running on one server in cloud computing system.

This paper mainly discusses tasks of CPU-intensive, in other words, the tasks in cloud computing system are all computing-intensive, and energy consumption of other components such as memory and I/O will be ignored.

## 2.2 Cloud Computing System Model

In general, cloud computing system is built on cheap large-scale server cluster. With good extendibility, cloud computing system can grow with size of users and applications. Cloud computing system contains lots of servers, and with virtualization and efficient management it uniformly manages the computing and storage resources of all servers.

We assume that the servers in cloud computing system all allow software to adjust frequency and voltage settings in tandem, and every server has several voltage modes. All voltage modes have different processor frequency or computing speed and executive power.

The cloud computing system can be defined as tuple $(S, M)$, where $S = \{s_j | 1 \leq j \leq n\}$ is the set of servers in cloud computing system and $M = \{m_j | 1 \leq j \leq n\}$ is the set of all the server voltage modes. Here, $m_j = \{(v_k, f_k, p_k) | 1 \leq k \leq z\}$ is the set of voltage modes of server $s_j$.

# 3 Energy Saving Strategy Based on DVFS

According to analysis above, a way to reduce the executive power of processor is to reduce the supply voltage. Therefore, using DVFS technique we can reduce executive power of processor while server is running through lowing processor supply voltage level according task implementation. But reducing of the supply voltage of processor will reduce the clock frequency, which can worsens performance of system and quality of service. So, when we design energy saving strategy using DVFS technique, we have to solve the problem of balancing reducing processor executive power and ensuring system quality of service.

For a server with multiple tasks running on it, as time goes on, there will be a task completed, and the processor resource it possessed will be idle, which can cause energy consumption. There, we can try to low the supply voltage level of processor to reduce the idle energy consumption. While we have to consider the server performance and quality of service, because lowing supply voltage level of processor will affect its computing speed which may influence the response time of other tasks. Therefore, when we low the processor supply voltage level we must firstly consider that the voltage lowing whether will affect response time of other tasks, if not we do it, otherwise don't.

According to analysis above, we design energy saving strategy Computing Resources Dynamic Power-aware (CRDP). The main idea of CRDP can be described as follow: defining a global variable $T_{left} = \{(t_i, l_i, RT_i) \mid 1 \le i \le m\}$ to store information of all unfinished tasks running on server $s_j$, like left calculation amount, left time, and so on; sorting all elements in voltage modes set $m_j$ of server $s_j$ by voltage $v_k$, we get ascending order $m_j$; iterating all unfinished tasks on server $s_j$ to add processor resource each task need to finish in time all up, then we get total processor resource $RC$ left unfinished tasks need; iterating $m_j$ to compare $RC$ to clock frequency of each level voltage, when getting a clock frequency less than $RC$ we break the iterating and update information of all unfinished tasks such as left calculation amount and left time. Pseudo code of the algorithm is described as follow:

```
Algorithm CRDP
1:   if T_left≠φ do
2:     for i=1 to m do
3:       RC=RC+ l_i/RT_i;
4:     end for
5:     for k=1 to z do
6:       if RC≤ m'_j.f_k do
7:           update T_left;
8:           break;
9:       end if
10:    end for
11: end if
```

Then, we analysis the time complexity of the energy saving algorithm. Steps from 2 to 4 add processor resource every task need to finish in the request response time all up. There are up to $m$ tasks, and the maximum executing time is $O(m)$. Steps from 5 to 10 iterate all voltage modes of the server processor and search the lowest voltage level which can match the request of all left tasks finishing in time. In the worst-case scenario, the executing time is $O(z)$. Taken together, the worst time complexity of the energy saving algorithm is $O(m) + O(z)$.

# 4 Analysis for Energy Consumption and Performance of Cloud Computing System

## 4.1 Analysis for Cloud Computing System Energy Consumption

As assuming above, all the tasks we discuss are cpu-intensive, and the energy consumption of the system mainly comes from tasks execution. To get the system energy consumption, we firstly analysis how a server executes tasks running on it.

When server $s_j$ has multiple tasks running on it, its current voltage mode is $m_1$; after $s_j$ running time $a_1$, a task $t_1$ finished, then the management component of system executes CRDP on server $s_j$, resetting the voltage mode as $m_2$ and setting left calculation amount and left time of all unfinished tasks. Next, the server keep on running; after $s_j$ running another time $a_2$, another task $t_2$ finished, then the management component of system executes CRDP on server $s_j$, resetting the voltage mode as $m_3$ and setting left calculation amount and left time of all unfinished tasks. Next, the server keeps on running; run the server like this, until all the tasks are finished. To be clear, $m_1$ is not the first one of all voltage modes of server $s_j$ but the first one as voltage mode changes with tasks executing, and $m_2$ is the second one. Likewise, $t_1$ is the first finished task and $t_2$ is the second finished task. Process of executing tasks on server $s_j$ can be figured out in Fig. 1.

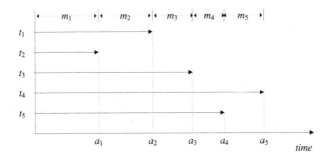

**Fig. 1.** The execution of tasks on server $s_j$

We can get the energy consumption of server $s_j$ from analysis above as Formula 1:

$$E_j = \sum_{i=1}^{m} m_j . p_i \cdot (a_i - a_{i-1}) \tag{1}$$

where, $a_0 = 0$ is the moment when server $s_j$ begins executing tasks. The total energy consumption of the whole cloud computing system is composed of energy consumption of each server, and then we have Formula 2:

$$E = \sum_{j=1}^{n} E_j = \sum_{j=1}^{n} \sum_{i=1}^{m} m_j . p_i \cdot (a_i - a_{i-1}) \tag{2}$$

### 4.2 Analysis for Cloud Computing System Performance

After users submit tasks to cloud computing system, they care a lot about response time of tasks. Therefore, we use system response time as the performance evaluation measure.

According to analysis of tasks executing process in last section, response time of server $s_j$ equals to the total executing time of $s_j$ from $s_j$ begins executing to all tasks on it are finished to the number of tasks ratio. We have Formula 3:

$$RT_j = a_m/m \tag{3}$$

Then we get the whole system response time as shown in Formula 4:

$$RT = \frac{\sum_{j=1}^{n} RT_j}{n} = \frac{\sum_{j=1}^{n} a_m/m}{n} \tag{4}$$

## 5  Simulation Results and Analysis

In this section, we simulate and analyze cloud computing system by using cloud computing simulation software CloudSim. By extending associated components of CloudSim, we apply energy saving strategy CRDP to cloud computing system to analyze energy saving efficiency of the strategy and its impact on system performance.

To analyze the effectiveness of strategy CRDP, we compare CRDP and energy saving algorithm Lowest-DVFS proposed in [4], from system performance to energy consumption. The main idea of algorithm Lowest-DVFS is that based on quantity of computing resources the tasks request, the manager of system set processor frequency to the lowest level within response time constraint. On the basis of analysis in last section, we compare two algorithms from total energy consumption to average response time.

To be clear, CRDP focuses on the situation one server running multiple tasks, if CRDP is effective on one server, it must be too effective when we apply it to cloud computing with multiple servers too. Easily to prove, we can just apply CRDP to each server. To simplify the simulation, we just set one datacenter in cloud computing system and one server in datacenter. Other parameters are set as follow: (1) number of tasks $m = 5$; (2) calculation amount $l_i$ of each task is randomly generated between 1000 and 6000; (3) response time is randomly generated between 5 and 40. Processor of server has 6 voltage modes, detailed parameters of processor are as shown in Table 1.

We carried out 20 experiments, and in each one we randomly generate 5 tasks. The results are shown in Figs. 2 and 3, respectively.

We can observe that in multiple experiments energy consumption of strategy CRDP is always lower than strategy Lowest-DVFS. The reason is that when a task is finished the computing resource it possesses will be idle, to reduce energy consumption caused by idle resource, CRDP can reset the voltage mode of processor and reasonably low voltage level based on total computing resources requested by all unfinished tasks. And strategy Lowest-DVFS just set the voltage mode lowest within response time constrain based on total computing resources all tasks request before processor executing tasks, but it can not reset processor voltage mode to lower level according to resources using, causing computing resources idle and idle energy consumption.

**Table 1.** The voltage model of processor on server

| Voltage ($v_k$) | Frequency ($f_k$) | Power ($p_k$) |
|---|---|---|
| 1.1 | 200 | 5.2 |
| 1.2 | 300 | 9.2 |
| 1.25 | 500 | 12.0 |
| 1.3 | 700 | 15.1 |
| 1.35 | 800 | 18.6 |
| 1.4 | 1000 | 25.0 |

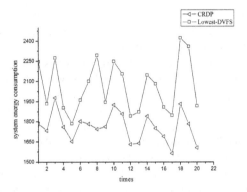

**Fig. 2.** The comparison of system total energy consumption

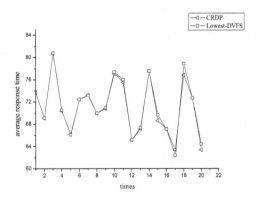

**Fig. 3.** The comparison of system average response time

Figure 3 shows the average response time of the system. We observe that average response time of system using strategy CRDP and system using strategy Lowest-DVFS is aligned. The reason is that when CRDP tries to low voltage level it considers the impact of lowing voltage level to system response time first. In other words, if lowing voltage level will affect response time of unfinished tasks, CRDP do not do it, otherwise don't. And strategy Lowest-DVFS sets processor frequency to the lowest level before processor executing tasks to reduce energy consumption, but it is also based on satisfying tasks finishing time, so it can ensure the response time of system.

Taken together, performance of strategy CRDP can be consistent with strategy Lowest-DVFS, while it will achieve better energy efficiency. So we achieve the researching goal.

## 6  Conclusions and Further Research Work

For the high energy consumption problem in cloud computing system, the paper analyzes the executive process of multiple tasks on one server, the reason of high energy consumption, and proposes an energy saving strategy-Computing Resources Dynamic Power-aware. Within left unfinished tasks response time constraint, the strategy tries to set processor voltage to lower level when a task is finished and the computing resource it possesses is idle to reduce the energy consumption caused by computing resource idle. Then the paper gives the energy consumption model and performance model. Simulation results show the effectiveness of the strategy.

The strategy is effective, but it has its own limitation-the tasks in cloud computing system are all got in advance, while tasks in real system arrive stochastically and continuously. For tasks arriving stochastically and continuously, how to low the supply voltage to reduce energy consumption of cloud computing system according to execution of tasks will be the research next step.

**Acknowledgments.** This research is supported in part by the National Natural Science Foundation of China under Grant Nos. 61562006, 61262003, in part by the Natural Science Foundation of Guangxi Province under Grant No. 2010GXNSFC013013.

## References

1. Kang, C., Zheng, W.: Cloud computing: system instances and current research. J. Softw. **20**(5), 1337–1348 (2009)
2. Mell, P., Grance, T.: NIST: the nist definition of cloud computing. Commun. ACM **53**(6), 50 (2011)
3. Ammbrust, M., Fox, A., Griffith, R., et al.: A view of cloud computing. Commun. ACM **53**(4), 50–58 (2010)
4. Zhang, G.: Cloud computing is a high energy consumption projects [EB/OL]. http://www.cstor.cn/textdetail.asp?id=1652
5. Williams, C.: What is a green data center? http://www.mnn.com/greentech/computers/stories/what-is-a-green-data-center
6. Berl, A., Gelenbe, E., Girolamo, M.D., et al.: Energy-efficient cloud computing. Comput. J. **53**(7), 1045–1051 (2010)

7. Lin, C., Tian, Y., Yao, M.: Green network and green evaluation: mechanism, modeling and evaluation. Chin. J. Comput. **34**(4), 593–612 (2011)
8. Baliga, J., Ayre, R.W.A., Hinton, K., et al.: Green cloud computing: balancing energy in processing, storage, and transport. Proc. IEEE **99**(1), 149–167 (2011)
9. Song, J., Li, T., Yan, Z., et al.: Energy-efficiency model and measuring approach for cloud computing. J. Softw. **23**(2), 200–214 (2012)
10. Zhang, X., He, Z., Li, C., et al.: Research on energy saving algorithm of datacenter in cloud computing system. Appl. Res. Comput. **30**(4), 961–964 (2013)
11. Wang, L., Laszewski, G.V., Dayal, J., et al.: Towards energy aware scheduling for precedence constrained parallel tasks in a cluster with DVFS. In: IEEE/ACM International Conference on Cluster, Cloud and Grid Computing, pp. 368–377. IEEE (2010)

# An Optimal Rate Adaptive Video Streaming Scheme to Improve QoE of Dash

Xiaolong Gong$^{(\boxtimes)}$, Gaocai Wang, and Nao Wang

School of Computer and Electronic Information,
Guangxi University, Nanning 530004, Guangxi, China
275070349@qq.com, {gcwang,wangzhuo}@gxu.edu.cn

**Abstract.** As the simplicity at the server side, HTTP-based adaptive streaming has become a popular choice for streaming contents to a wide range of user devices. In HTTP-based streaming systems, the server simply stores the video chunked into a series of small chunks coded in many different qualities and sizes, and leaves the decision of which chunk to download to the client for achieving a high quality experience. This decision making is a challenging task, especially in mobile environment due to unexpected changes in network bandwidth as the user moves through different regions. In this paper, we consider Markov Decision Process (MDP) to explore the optimum chunk selection strategy that maximizes streaming quality.

**Keywords:** HTTP dynamic streaming · Optimal decision choice · DASH · Markov model

## 1 Introduction

In the recent years, due to the prevalence of multimedia devices, multimedia streaming services have experienced rapid growth. For multimedia streaming service, various media protocols are available and can be classified into two main categories: push- and pull-based protocols. In push-based streaming, server maintains session state and pushes the video packets to the client. RTP (real-time transport protocol) or UDP (user datagram protocol) based RTSP (real time streaming protocol) is one of the most common push-based protocols. In pull-based streaming protocols, server response depends on the client's requests when the server is otherwise idle or blocked for that client and TCP based HTTP is a common protocol for pull-based media delivery [1].

Today, HTTP has becomes a main protocol for the multimedia streaming for some reasons. Any connected device supports HTTP and HTTP easily traverse firewall and NAT devices. Also, HTTP servers are more scalable than other streaming servers [2]. To guarantee the quality of multimedia streaming service over HTTP, HTTP based adaptive video bit rate control solutions such as smooth streaming, HTTP Live streaming, and HTTP Dynamic streaming have been developed [3]. In this trend, a new standard called DASH (dynamic adaptive streaming over HTTP) has been developed by MPEG and 3GPP to enable interoperability in the industry. DASH provides formats to enable efficient delivery of MPEG media over HTTP in adaptive, progressive download fashion.

© Springer International Publishing Switzerland 2015
G. Wang et al. (Eds.): ICA3PP 2015 Workshops, LNCS 9532, pp. 302–310, 2015.
DOI: 10.1007/978-3-319-27161-3_26

The key concept in DASH is to code the same video in multiple bit rates (qualities) and store each stream into a series of small video chunks of 2–4 s duration. A client simply downloads and plays a chunk of a given quality using the standard HTTP GET command used for fetching any other objects on the Web [4]. Since video has strict display deadlines for every frame, each chunk needs to be downloaded before its deadline to avoid the 'freezing' effect. It therefore becomes the responsibility of the client to dynamically select the 'right' quality of the next chunk to ensure a smooth video at the receiver with the highest possible quality and minimum number of quality switches from one chunk to the next. The DASH standard only specifies how the video chunks should be stored and what metadata about the chunks should be provided to a client. The actual streaming strategy, the client intelligence for selecting the right quality for each chunk in order to produce a high quality of experience (QoE) for the viewer is left to the developers [5].

In this paper, we deal with a case in which a user with mobile terminals downloads and plays a video stream. The user's goal is to minimize the total cost which includes his/her dissatisfaction due to playback disruptions and the monetary cost for downloading the video stream via wireless networks. The considered system can be modeled as a stochastic optimization problem as the underlying processes in it are not deterministic. Section 2 reviews the related research work. Section 3 describes the theory and the specific optimization problem. Section 4 shows simulation results and analysis. And conclude this paper and prospect the future work in Sect. 5.

## 2 Related Work

DASH has been a hot topic in recent years. There are many commercial products which have implemented DASH in different ways, such as Apple HTTP Live Streaming and Microsoft smooth streaming. Since the clients may have different available bandwidth and display size, each video will be encoded several times with different quality, bit rate and resolution. All the encoded videos will be chopped into small chunks and stored on the server, which can be a typical web server. These small chunks will be downloaded to the browsers' cache and played by the client (browser or browser plug-in). The video rate adaptation is performed at the client side, which is also called the pull-based approach. The client will determine the quality version of the requested video chunk according to its current available bandwidth, resolution and the number of buffered unwatched chunks [7]. After the current chunk is completely downloaded, the rate adaptation algorithm will be invoked again for the next chunk. Rate adaptation is one of the most important research issues for DASH. Akhshabi et al. [8] compared rate adaptation for three popular DASH clients: Netflix client [6], Microsoft smooth streaming [9], and Adobe OSMF [10]. The conclusion in [8] indicates that none of the DASH client-based rate adaptation is good enough, as they are either too aggressive or too conservative. Some clients even just jump between the highest bit rate and the lowest bit rate. Also, all of them have relatively long response time under network congestion level shift.

There exist several research works about rate adaptation for DASH, such as bandwidth-based rate adaptation schemes [10–12] and buffer-based rate adaptation schemes [13]. All these existing rate adaptation algorithms aim to either adapt a video bit rate to an available bandwidth so as to achieve high bandwidth utilization efficiency, or ensure a buffer in the client to provide a continuous video playback. However, due to the inherent bandwidth variations, there is a fundamental conflict between video bit rate smoothness and bandwidth utilization, and existing algorithms do not balance the needs for these two aspects well.

In order to optimize this rate adaptation process for video streaming over wireless links and take the video quality of service (QoS) requirements, the wireless channel profiles, and the wireless service costs of links in to considering [15–17], we formulate the video streaming process as a reinforcement learning task. For each step, we define a state to describe the current situation, such as the index of the requested chunks, the current available bandwidth and other system parameters. A finite state Markov Decision Process (MDP) can be modeled for this reinforcement learning task [18–22].

# 3 Theory Background and Problem Description

## 3.1 System Model

We consider how to use wireless access net-works for video streaming. As an example, 3G or WiFi access networks are considered. Since a wireless channel may suffer from time-varying fading, shadowing and interference, the available bandwidth of a wireless link may vary all the time [23–30]. In addition, different smart phones or tablets may have different screen size and resolution. Taking these two aspects into consideration, similar to Microsoft smooth streaming, the server should store several different with one-second duration [8]. We design a pull-based algorithm for video streaming. After initialization, the client first requests the video information which includes video resolutions, bit rates and qualities from the server through the WiFi or 3G links. The rate adaptation agent will request an appropriate quality version of video chunks based on the current buffer length and available bandwidth. Once the request decision is made, HTTP requests over WiFi or 3G will be issued to download the video chunks of chunk. This process will continue until the last chunks have been downloaded or the video has been terminated by the user. Take the limited computation capacity of mobile devices and the high variation of wireless access links into considering; we formulate the optimal rate adaptation problem as a finite Markov Decision Process, which can deal with the random network condition with a relatively simple approach that is feasible for mobile devices. For each video chunk, the client uses MDP to make a decision on which action to conduct given the current client state. There are four components for MDP, i.e., action, state, transition probability and reward. In the following, we define them one by one.

Actions: At each state, the decision taken is referred to as an action. For our adaptive HTTP streaming system, an action is basically a decision about the quality leave for the next chunk. If we have levels of video versions to choose from, then we have $N+1$ possible action. An action chosen at the current state will influence the transition probability of reaching to a specific state at the next step. The action set for a give state is $A(s) = \{A_i, A_w\}$, where $A_i$ $(i = 1, \ldots\ldots, N)$, means to request the next chunk whose quality is $i$ level and $A_w$ means to wait for a duration time.

States: we define steps $n$ as to download chunk $n$, so the total number of steps equals to the number of chunks. For each step $n$, we define the state as $s_n = \{L_n, \Delta L_n, v_n, \Delta v_n, b_{wn}, d_n\}$. $L_n$ Represents the number of queue length, with the range between 0 and represents $QL$ (the maximum buffer size). $\Delta L_n$ is the queue length variation after a new chunk has been retrieved. $v_n(\in\{1, 2, \ldots, N\})$ is the video quality version of the n-th chunk. $\Delta v_n$ Indicates the difference of video versions requested in consecutive steps, and a larger number represents a better-quality version. $b_{wn}$ means the available current bandwidth of the wireless channel (WiFi link or the 3G link). $d_n$ indicates the current requested chunks index. As the total number of video chunks is NT, $d_n$ is in the range of $[0, N_T]$.

Transition probabilities: According to the measurements or using the historical data, the Markov models for the channel can be obtained. With the wireless channel model, we can obtain the available bandwidth state transition probability. According to the Markov property, all states only depend on their immediately previous state. Given any state s and action a, the transition probability of the MDP can be derived as:

$$P(a, s, s') = p_{ss'}^a = \Pr\{s_{n+1} = s' | s_n = s, a_n = a\} \tag{1}$$

Indicating the probability of the transition from the state of $S_n$ to $S_{n+1}$ after taking action a when the system is in the state of $S_n$. To imitate the wireless link variation, we implement a bandwidth emulator which runs in the phone to control the raw data rates of the wireless channel links. As the wireless channel condition may change randomly, the finite-state Markov model has been widely used to describe the variation of wireless channel conditions, and thus it can also be used to describe the wireless link data rate variation for broadband wireless systems. We used a discrete-time four state Markov model to capture the variation of the available bandwidth, and the duration of the time step for the Markov model is constant.

Revenue function: The reward in MDP is the payoff obtained when a particular action is taken at a state, $R = R(s) + U(v) - C(x,v)$ where $R$ maps the state to a reward. $R(s)$ refers to the rewards associated with states. $U(v)$ means a reward for selecting a chunk in video version and $C(x,v)$ refers to a penalty for a change of quality level and we can assign different penalties for difference types of quality switches. So we can make a trade-off between average playback quality and playback smoothness that $U(v)$ refers to the user's satisfaction and $C(x,v)$ refers that frequent changes will affect the QoE of the video streaming.

Lastly, we could formulate the rate adaptation problem as an optimization problem. The objective is to find a strategy(s) for the action taken at a state s to maximize the reward received in the long run. The streaming policy $\pi$ is a mapping of possible action at each step. The long-term reward under policy $\pi$ can be computed as

$$V^\pi(s) = \sum_{s'} p_{ss'}^a [R + \gamma V^\pi(s')] \tag{2}$$

Where $\gamma$ is the discounting rate and $0 \leq \gamma \leq 1$. The optimal strategy policy $\pi^*(s)$ which can maximize the long-term reward is the goal of the reinforcement learning task of video streaming. And then our video streaming mission can be finally constructed as an optimization problem:

$$\pi^*(s) = \arg\max_{\pi} \sum_{s'} p_{ss'}^a [R + \gamma V^{\pi}(s')] \tag{3}$$

## 3.2 Dynamic Programming

Dynamic programming is an effective method to solve the MDP problem. In the case of the convergence of the algorithm, the value iteration can shorten the process of the strategy estimation. Every iteration scans each state one time. In the actual use of the process, we often set a threshold as the termination conditions, when the value change is very small, we can approximate the thought to obtain the optimal strategy. To solve the finite MDP problem, after finite iterations, value iteration algorithm can converge to the optimal strategy of $\pi$.

**Algorithm Value Iteration**

1: Initialize $V(s)=0$, for all state $s$
2: Repeat
3:    $\Delta \leftarrow 0$
4: For each $s \in S$ :
5:        $temp \leftarrow V(s)$
6:        $V(s) \leftarrow \max_a \sum_{s'} p_{ss'}^a \left[R^a + \gamma V^{\pi}\left(s'\right)\right]$
7:        $\Delta \leftarrow \max\left(\Delta, | temp - V(s) |\right)$
8: until $\Delta < \theta$ ($\theta$ express a number small enough)
9: Output a deterministic policy $\pi$, such that
10: $\pi^*\left(s\right) = \arg\max_{\pi} \sum_{s'} p_{ss'}^a \left[R + \gamma V^{\pi}\left(s'\right)\right]$

The outcome of the optimization is an optimal action for each given state. This set of actions is called the optimal strategy. Given an MDP strategy, an HTTP-streaming client can simply make the decision about the quality of the next chunk by first observing its current state, the quality of the last downloaded chunk, and then looking up a strategy table.

## 4  Simulation Results

In order to evaluate the performance, we implemented our proposed user optimal rate adaptation algorithm (UORA) on the DASH reference player, which is developed by DASH industry forum and compared it with Evensn's rate adaptation algorithm (KERA) in [14]. The buffer length $Q_L$ is set to 20 chunks for both algorithms, and the video configuration is shown in table. And Tables 1, 2 and 3 shows parameters of the Revenue function. To reduce the randomness, we run the experiments 20 times and calculate the average results.

**Table 1.** Rewards associated with states

| $s_t = s$ | $R(s)$ |
|---|---|
| $(*,*,*,*,*,N_T)$ | 0 |
| $(0,*,*,*,*,*)$ | $-Q_L + \Delta L$ |
| $(Q_L,*,*,*,*,*)$ | $-Q_L - \Delta L$ |
| $(*,\Delta L,*,\Delta v,*,*)$ | $\min(-|\Delta v|, -|\Delta L|)$ |

**Table 2.** Rewards associated with $U(v)$

| Video version($v$) | 1 | 2 | 3 |
|---|---|---|---|
| $u(v)$ | 5 | 10 | 20 |

To mimic the wireless link variation, we implement a bandwidth emulator which runs in a four-state Markov channel models to describe the variations of the wireless network links. The duration of the time step for our four-state Markov model is a constant of 2 s (equals to the time duration for one video chunks). A set of probability transition matrices was used. The matrices are list as:

$$\begin{pmatrix} 0.5 & 0.5 & 0 & 0 \\ 0.2 & 0.6 & 0.2 & 0 \\ 0 & 0.1 & 0.7 & 0.2 \\ 0 & 0 & 0.2 & 0.8 \end{pmatrix},$$

With the probability transition matrices, we can obtain the steady state probabilities and the available bandwidth setting is listed in Table 3.

**Table 3.** State probability and available bandwidth

| State | 1 | 2 | 3 | 4 |
|---|---|---|---|---|
| State probability | 0.08 | 0.20 | 0.36 | 0.36 |
| Bandwidth | 64 | 128 | 256 | 512 |

The experimental results are presented in Table 4. We compared the two algorithms in three aspects. First, we take the interruption radio (IR) which defined as the time of interruption occurred over all the video time. There can found that no interruption in UORA algorithm, as we made a negative reward to avoid interruption. For the KERA algorithm, nearly 19 % annoyed interruptions happened. The interruptions come from two aspects: imprecise estimation of available bandwidth and the insufficient consideration of the buffer status. Then, we looked for the difference of average playback quality (APQ) which explains the quality of video version. These two algorithms get similar data, to be a greedy algorithm; KERA tends to choose the higher possible quality version. While UORA algorithm would prefer to takes the future available bandwidth and buffer status into consideration, which makes it may not select the highest possible quality version in order to avoid interruption appear in the next some times. Commonly, a longer expected play length of video chunks leads to a smoother watching experience. So the play smoothness (PS) is measured by the expected run length and we have PS $= \sqrt{\sum_{r=1}^{N} (n_r)^2 / N}$. We define a consecutive play of video quality $i$ as one run. For the $r$-th run, $n_r$ is used to indicate the total number of chunks. The UORA algorithm can achieve a much higher PS than KERA. As the quality version change may bring a negative reward, UORA algorithm will try to maintain the video stay at the same quality, and KERA may changes the quality more frequently which may have a negative impact on smoothness for it is greedier.

**Table 4.** Experiment result

| Algorithm | IR | APQ | PS |
|-----------|------|------|-------|
| UORA | 0.00 | 1.93 | 15.36 |
| KERA | 0.19 | 1.97 | 4.56 |

It shows that the playback traces and buffer occupancy states of both algorithms in Fig. 1(a) and (b). The black rectangles represent the requested chunk quality version index, and the red curves represent the playback chunk index. Since the average bandwidths of wireless link cannot support stable highest quality version, so most time UORA algorithm request the second quality version video. To keep the playback smooth, UORA algorithm rarely changes the quality version. With the KERA algorithm, because it always selected the video version most close to the estimated available bandwidth according to the average download speed of the previous chunk, the video version was changed quite frequently in a dynamic environment. As KERA did not fully consider the buffer occupancy status, there are several times that the buffer was empty, and the interruptions occurred.

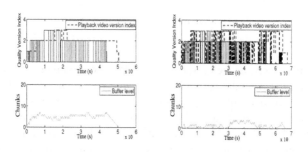

**Fig. 1.** (a) UORA algorithm (b) KERA algorithm (Color figure online)

# 5   Conclusion

In this paper, for DASH-based adaptive video streaming in wireless networks, we have formulated the rate adaptation problem as an MDP and used dynamic programming to solve the problem. Experiment results have shown that the proposed solution is feasible and substantially outperforms the one proposed by Evensen et al. [14]. There are several issues worth further investigation. How to reduce the complexity of the calculation and use multiple link network to improve the bandwidth need further investigation.

**Acknowledgments.** This research is supported in part by the National Natural Science Foundation of China under Grant Nos. 61562006, 61262003, in part by the Natural Science Foundation of Guangxi Province under Grant No. 2010GXNSFC013013.

# References

1. Stockhammer, T.: Dynamic adaptive streaming over http-standards and design principle. In: MMSys 2011 Proceedings of the 2nd Annual ACM Conference on Multimedia Systems, pp. 133–143. ACM, New York (2011)
2. Lian, C.-J., Chieng, S.-Y., Lin, C.-P.: Power-aware multimedia: concepts and design perspectives. IEEE Circ. Syst. Mag. **7**, 26–34 (2007). IEEE
3. Emrah, A., Mihaela, V.S.: Compression-aware energy optimization for video decoding systems with passive power. IEEE Trans. Circ. Syst. Video Technol. **18**, 1300–1306 (2008). IEEE
4. Lei, B., Jin, W., Zhang, H.: Optimization and implementation of AVS-M decoder on ARM. In: 4th International Conference on Image and Graphics, pp. 255–258. IEEE Press, Sichuan (2007)
5. Cheng, L., Bossi, S., Mohapatra, S., Zarki, M.E., Venkatasubramanian, N., Dutt, N.: Quality adapted backlight scaling (QABS) for video streaming to mobile handheld devices. In: Lorenz, P., Dini, P. (eds.) ICN 2005. LNCS, vol. 3420, pp. 662–671. Springer, Heidelberg (2005)
6. HTTP adaptive streaming in practice. http://web.cs.wpi.edu
7. Guo, Y., Hao, F., Varvello, M.: Unreeling netflix: understanding and improving multi-CDN movie delivery. In: 2012 Proceedings of the IEEE INFOCOM, Orlando, pp. 1620–1628 (2012)
8. Akhshabi, S., Begen, A.C., Dovrolis, C.: An experimental evaluation of rate-adaptation algorithms in adaptive streaming over HTTP. In: MMSys 2011 Proceedings of the 2nd Annual ACM Conference on Multimedia Systems, pp. 157–168. ACM, New York (2011)
9. IIS smooth streaming technical overview. http://www.microsoft.com
10. Open source media framework 1.6. http://www.osmf.org/
11. Liu, C., Bouazizi, I., Gabbouj, M.: Rate adaptation for adaptive HTTP streaming. In: MMSys 2011 Proceedings of the 2nd Annual ACM Conference on Multimedia Systems, pp. 169–174. ACM, New York (2011)
12. Wang, J., Zou, Z., Wen, J.: Bandwidth estimation and rate adaptation in HTTP streaming. In: International Conference on Computing, Networking and Communications, pp. 734–738. IEEE Press, HI (2012)

13. Cicco, L.D., Mascolo, S., Vittorio, P.: Feedback control for adaptive live video streaming. In: MMSys 2011 Proceedings of the 2nd Annual ACM Conference on Multimedia Systems, pp. 145–156. ACM, New York (2011)
14. Evensen, K., Kaspar, D., Griwodz, C., Halvorsen, P.: Improving the performance of quality-adaptive video streaming over multiple heterogeneous access networks. In: MMSys 2011 Proceedings of the 2nd Annual ACM Conference on Multimedia Systems, pp. 145–156. ACM, New York (2011)
15. Yu, W., Jin, X., Goto, S.: Temporal scalable decoding process with frame rate conversion method for surveillance video. In: Qiu, G., Lam, K.M., Kiya, H., Xue, X.-Y., Kuo, C.-C., Lew, M.S. (eds.) PCM 2010, Part II. LNCS, vol. 6298, pp. 297–308. Springer, Heidelberg (2010)
16. Konstantin, M., Emanuele, Q., Giaiiluca, G.: Adaptation algorithm for adaptive streaming over HTTP. In: IEEE 19th International Packet Video Workshop, pp. 173–178. IEEE Press, Munich (2012)
17. Evensen, K., Kaspar, D., Griwodz, C.: Improving the performance of quality-adaptive video streaming over multiple heterogeneous access networks. In: MMSys 2011 Proceedings of the 2nd Annual ACM Conference on Multimedia Systems, pp. 57–69. ACM, New York (2011)
18. Xiang, S., Cai, L., Pan, J.: Adaptive scalable video streaming in wireless networks. In: MMSys 2012 Proceedings of the 3rd Multimedia Systems Conference, pp. 167–172. ACM, New York (2012)
19. Xing, M., Xiang, S., Cai, L.: Rate adaptation strategy for video streaming over multiple wireless access networks. In: IEEE Global Communications Conference, pp. 5745–5750. IEEE Press, New York (2012)
20. Arash, A., Vincenzo, M.: A survey on opportunistic scheduling in wireless communications. IEEE Commun. Surv. Tutor. **15**, 1671–1688 (2012). IEEE Press, New York
21. Garcia, S.A., Serrano, P., Banchs, A.: Energy-efficient optimization for distributed opportunistic scheduling. IEEE Commun. Lett. **18**, 1083–1086 (2014). IEEE Press, New York
22. Pulakis, M.I., Panagopoulos, A.D., Constantinou, P.: Channel-aware opportunistic transmission scheduling for energy-efficient wireless links. IEEE Trans. Veh. Technol. **62**, 192–204 (2014). IEEE
23. Yan, Z., Zhang, Z., Jiang, H.: Optimal traffic scheduling in vehicular delay tolerant networks. IEEE Commun. Lett. **16**, 50–53 (2012). IEEE
24. Huang, L., Jiang, H., Zhang, Z.: Optimal traffic scheduling between roadside units in vehicular delay tolerant networks. IEEE Trans. Veh. Technol. **64**, 1079–1094 (2015). IEEE
25. Van Phan, C.: A game-theoretic framework for opportunistic transmission in wireless networks. In: 5th International Conference on Communications and Electronics, pp. 150–154. IEEE, Danang (2014)
26. Wang, W., Motani, M., Srinivasan, V.: Opportunistic energy-efficient contact probing in delay-tolerant applications. IEEE/ACM Trans. Netw. **17**, 1592–1605 (2009). IEEE
27. Zhou, H., Zhao, H., Chen, J.: Energy saving and network connectivity tradeoff in opportunistic mobile networks. In: 2012 IEEE Global Communications Conference, pp. 524–529. IEEE (2012)
28. Gao, W., Li, Q.: Wakeup scheduling for energy-efficient communication in opportunistic mobile networks. In: INFOCOM 2013 Proceedings, pp. 2058–2066. IEEE, Turin (2013)
29. Osama, A., Lutz, L.: Opportunistic energy efficient cooperative communication. IEEE Wirel. Commun. Lett. **1**, 412–415 (2012). IEEE
30. Zuo, J., Dong, C., Nguyen, H.V.: Cross-layer aided energy-efficient opportunistic routing in ad hoc networks. IEEE Trans. Commun. **62**(2), 522–535 (2014)

# Community-Based Energy-Aware Routing Protocol in Mobile Social Networks

Dongmei Bin$^{(\boxtimes)}$, Ying Peng, and Gaocai Wang

School of Computer and Electronic Information, Guangxi University,
Guangxi 530004, China
betty.bin@qq.com, 623833@qq.com, gcwang@gxu.edu.cn

**Abstract.** Mobile social network (MSN) with delay tolerant nature of intermittent network connectivity and the node behavior of the network has certain social characteristics, which is helpful to the data sharing and transmission between the nodes. At present, most social routing algorithms do not take into account the energy consumption of the nodes, and the energy consumption of the mobile nodes is not balanced, so the performance optimization can not be achieved. In this paper, we proposes the community-based energy-aware routing protocol——CBEAR, an MSN network dynamic partition into several different community, transferring and sharing news in the intra-community and inter-community, considering node energy consumption rate and the encounter probability between node and each community to make routing decisions, avoid some nodes' energy consumption is too fast problem, to realize load balance between nodes. By comparison with existing routing protocols through extensive simulations, the simulation study show that although the CBEAR protocol has some delay performance, it has achieved better performance in terms of data transmission success rate, protocol overhead ratio and energy balance.

**Keywords:** Mobile social network · Community · Energy awareness · Load balance · Routing protocol

## 1 Introduction

With the rapid development of mobile phones and other mobile intelligent devices, wireless network technology and 3G network, data sharing between the human carrier terminal has been developed rapidly, such as Bluetooth, WiFi, NFC and other wireless communication technology for the development of the mobile social networks in technology provides support and guarantee, their vigorous development for mobile access to social network future increase the motive force of the development [1]. Mobile Social Network (MSN), which has a certain social relationship, has gradually formed a mobile social network.

Compared with traditional DTN, nodes in mobile social networks to follow certain patterns of social behavior, such as carrying social relationship exists between the portable equipment and mobile network nodes with some regularity of these nodes have the social feature information can be used in auxiliary network data routing improves the routing efficiency [2].

© Springer International Publishing Switzerland 2015
G. Wang et al. (Eds.): ICA3PP 2015 Workshops, LNCS 9532, pp. 311–321, 2015.
DOI: 10.1007/978-3-319-27161-3_27

In this paper, we mainly study node energy consumption rate and the encounter probability between node and each community in mobile social networks. The remainder of this paper is organized as follows. Section 2 reviews the related research work. Section 3 describes the system model and community division. Section 4 presents community-based energy-aware routing protocol in mobile social network. Section 5 shows simulation results and analysis. And conclude this paper and prospect the future work in Sect. 6.

## 2   Related Work

In the mobile social network, there is generally no link between the end to end, the routing mode of "storage, carrying and forwarding" is usually used in the nodes, through the opportunity to pass the message. The research work includes three aspects: Based on the flood routing protocol, based on the prediction of routing protocols and based on the opportunity routing protocols.

Based on the flood routing protocol is used to copy the message, and put the multiple copies of the message into the network, and the spread of the whole network makes the message reach the destination node. In [3], the authors propose the Epidemic routing protocol, which relies on multiple copies, so that information can be reached through multiple paths. In [4], the authors present the spray and wait routing algorithm is a compromise between the node transmission performance and cost, resulting in better performance, good to reduce the consumption of network resources. Then proposed the spray and focus routing algorithm in [5], which is the further improvement of the algorithm in reference [4]. And a copy of the distribution has a great blindness, it will waste a certain number of copies, to some extent, reduce the transmission success rate, increasing the transmission delay.

Based on the prediction of routing protocols research, it is based on the contact between the nodes of the historical record and the prediction of the flow behavior. Such as in [6], the authors use mobile user trajectory regularity in delay tolerant networks, with the greatest probability of encounter, maximum average encounter probability and maximum initial encounter probability as relay selection mechanism, to improve the transfer rate, reduce transmission delay. In [7] the authors propose prophet routing protocol, the prophet is mainly use such as meeting record, delivery transfer records and other historical records, in order to estimate each node successful delivery of messages to the destination node probability.

Based on the opportunity routing protocols research, the workers mainly obtain network structure according to mobile social center, similar, community and connection strength of social contact metric, so we can use these attributes to carry out data transmission. A distributed optimal community awareness of opportunistic routing algorithm is proposed in paper [8], they introduced community home model reduce the time and space complexities of the algorithm, using the node arrived home community probability of obtaining community network diagram. In [9], the author proposed the SimBet routing protocol, when some nodes meet, the algorithm makes the nodes with the maximum efficiency value and in the opportunistic network, and the nodes can improve the routing performance by the combination of the intermediate centrality and the similarity. In [10], the author adds the concept of relationship strength on the basis of the algorithm, and proposes a SimBetTS algorithm.

In this paper, we focus on mobile social network nodes energy consumption problem of the news, we not only pay attention to improve information delivery success rate, but also to consider the energy consumption balance between mobile nodes. At present, most of the mobile social network opportunistic routing are not considered inter node energy consumption problem, in this paper, we propose the community-based energy-aware routing protocol (CBEAR) on the basis of social routing protocols, a mobile social network is divided into a number of communities and then, considering the encounter probability between the node and each community and energy consumption pattern.

# 3    System Model and Community

## 3.1    Network Model

In mobile social networks, each node has a certain social and regular movement, and it is not completely random. Network is composed of a large and small community; the number of communities is far less than the number of nodes. In the community, the nodes contact frequently, but the probability of the nodes in different communities is relatively low. Therefore, we consider that the nodes in the network can be divided into different communities according to the frequency of meeting. The mobile node transmits data by using the opportunity to route the "storage, carrying, forwarding" mode, and the communication between the mobile nodes is achieved by the opportunity of the mobile node. The network model is shown in Fig. 1.

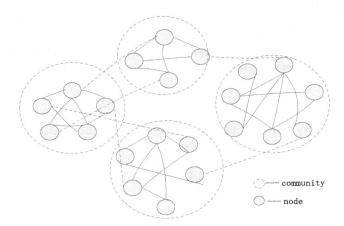

**Fig. 1.**  Network model

## 3.2  Community Concept

In this paper, we assumed that each node $v \in V$ only visits a few communities with close contact with their own most of the time, nodes with common interests and hobbies often visit with a community to form a community, In addition, if a node frequently visited several community, that it belongs to a number of communities. Specifically, the community is defined as follows:

**Definition 1.** Community. community $C$ is composed of a series of nodes that have a common interest.

**Definition 2.** Node feature model. The basic attribute of node $V_i$ in opportunistic networks is $(a_1, a_2, ..., a_n)$ vector, denoted as $V_i = (a_1, a_2, ..., a_n)$. Among $a_i$ is an attribute of node $V_i$. In this paper, the node is defined as a four tuple, that is to say, $V_i = (S_{id}, N_{buffer}, E_{energy}, C_{id})$. Among $S_{id}$ means that the node has a unique identifier, $N_{buffer}$ indicates the size of the node cache, $E_{energy}$ means the number of nodes energy, and $C_{id}$ indicates the number of nodes in the community.

In this paper, we assume that the source node know which communities that the destination node belongs to. This assumption is reasonable because the source generally knows some basic information about the destination in most message delivery tasks. In fact, the source node has many ways to know the basic information of the destination node. A similar assumption is also adopted in previous work [14].

## 3.3  Community Division

The mobile social network can be classified into a number of communities, community internal nodes connected between the relatively close, but between each community connection is relatively small. Therefore, we consider that the nodes in the network will be divided into different communities according to the probability of meeting.

**Definition 3.** Encounter probability. Refers to the number of encounters between nodes $i$ and $j$ within a given time, denoted as $M_{(i,j)}$, which indicates the degree of contact between nodes.

**Definition 4.** Probability threshold. Refers to the number of nodes $i$ and $j$ contact. When the node probability is greater than the given threshold (contact is assumed the number $M_{(i,j)} \geq 3$), nodes have the existence of edge, and otherwise, there is no edge. This would solve the network in the presence of weak connection problems.

According to node social connections and weights of the intensity change of social relations, the relation matrix is composed of all the nodes in the vector as input, simulating the real social scene, according to the strength of the social relationships between nodes, nodes are divided into different communities. 10 nodes are used for the classification of the community, the partition of the adjacent matrix A is listed as follow, the results of the community as shown in Fig. 2.

$$A = \begin{pmatrix} \infty & 3 & 5 & 0 & 0 & 1 & 2 & 0 & 0 & 1 \\ 3 & \infty & 4 & 0 & 0 & 0 & 0 & 1 & 0 & 0 \\ 5 & 4 & \infty & 0 & 1 & 0 & 0 & 0 & 0 & 1 \\ 0 & 0 & 0 & \infty & 6 & 4 & 0 & 1 & 0 & 0 \\ 0 & 0 & 1 & 6 & \infty & 3 & 5 & 0 & 0 & 0 \\ 1 & 0 & 0 & 4 & 3 & \infty & 7 & 1 & 0 & 0 \\ 2 & 0 & 0 & 0 & 5 & 7 & \infty & 0 & 0 & 1 \\ 0 & 4 & 0 & 1 & 0 & 1 & 0 & \infty & 5 & 6 \\ 0 & 0 & 0 & 0 & 0 & 0 & 0 & 5 & \infty & 2 \\ 1 & 0 & 1 & 0 & 0 & 0 & 1 & 6 & 2 & \infty \end{pmatrix} \tag{1}$$

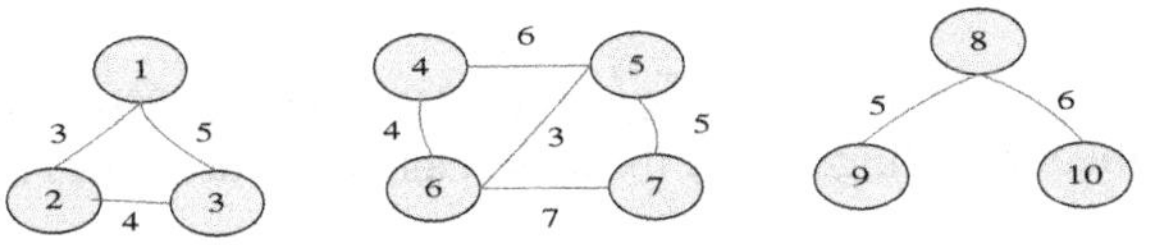

**Fig. 2.** Community division

# 4 Community-Based Energy-Aware Routing Protocol in Mobile Social Networks

## 4.1 Node Energy Flag

Because each mobile terminal battery power is limited, if the excessive consumption of energy of a mobile terminal will produce energy consumption is not fair, Therefore, energy aware content distribution to achieve load balancing. The energy of the nodes is very important for ensuring that the node can participate in the forwarding process of the message.

We can set up an energy flag to indicate whether the current node has enough energy to transmit messages. For each node in the community, an energy threshold is set as the threshold for the energy of the node to be used for message forwarding. Set up a flag bit S, marking whether a node has enough energy to participate in message forwarding.

$$S = \begin{cases} 1, & \text{if } E_{energy}(t) > threshold \\ 0, & \text{if } E_{energy}(t) < threshold \end{cases} \tag{2}$$

When $S = 1$ said node is used for message forwarding energy is sufficient, and when $S = 0$ said node is used for message forwarding energy is lower than the threshold value, then only accept the destination address is its own message. When the remaining energy of the node is reduced to 0, the node will be shut down and exit the network.

## 4.2 Energy Consumption of Nodes

For a community $C$, mobile terminal m energy consumption is defined as:

$$E_m = E_{m,B,r} + E_{m,j,r,C} + E_{m,i,t,C}$$
$$= y_{B,m} \cdot En_{m,B,r}(Ld) + \sum_{j=C,j\neq m} v_{j,m} \cdot En_{m,j,r}(Ld)$$
$$+ \sum_{i=C,i\neq m} v_{m,i} \cdot En_{m,i,t}(Ld) \tag{3}$$

The energy of each mobile terminal m within the community $C$ is $Er_m$, assuming that the remaining energy of the mobile terminal m is $Er_m$, then the energy of each mobile terminal $E_{energy}$:

$$E_{energy} = E_m + Er_m \tag{4}$$

The energy consumption speed is $E_m / Er_m$, the greater the energy consumption, the more important the forwarding task of the nodes, and the other nodes messages should be reduced.

For each node $m \in C$, the efficacy function is defined as follows:

$$Ut_m(C) = -\left(a_m \cdot E_m + \beta_m \cdot \frac{E_m}{Er_m}\right) \tag{5}$$

Among $\alpha_m \geq 0$ and $\beta_m \geq 0$ respectively show weight coefficient of energy consumption and energy consumption speed of the mobile terminal $m$, on behalf of its importance. $0 < E_m/Er_m \leq 1$, this means that the mobile terminal $m$ due to forwarding content must consume energy, but the consumption of energy $E_m$ can not exceed the remaining energy $Er_m$.

## 5   CBEAR Energy Aware Content Distribution Strategy

### 5.1   Intra-community Energy Aware Content Distribution Strategy

The information transmission in intra-community considers the maximum probability between node and each community and the energy consumption rate. Because of the nodes frequent move in intra-community, the chance of meeting between nodes is high, the method of limiting the number of copies of the message to achieve message forwarding. When the message is forwarded in intra-community, the first in the source node S generates a message M, but also generates L portion copies. When the probability value of the other nodes in intra-community to the destination node is high, the number of copies of the copy number is limited, and the consumption of the network bandwidth is reduced. When the maximum probability value of the node is greater than the threshold and has a high energy, we only forward to the maximum of the probability of the node.

In this paper, the intra-community transmission of messages within the meeting prediction probability is used to measure the reach ability between nodes forwarding the message, the greater the value, indicating that the messages among the nodes is transmitted to the target node is more likely. The probability of meeting is as follows:

$$P(i,j)_{new} = P(i,j)_{old} + (1 - P(i,j)_{old}) \times Er_m(j) / E_{energu}(j) \times P_{init} \tag{6}$$

$P_{int} \in [0, 1]$, indicating that the probability value of the node $i$ and $j$ first met. $Er_m(j)$ is the residual energy of the node $j$, $E_{energy}(j)$ is the initial energy of the node $j$.

The probability forecast is transmitted, and the transmission formula is as follows:

$$P(i,k)_{new} = P(i,k)_{old} + (1 - P(i,k)_{old}) \times P(i,j) \times P(i,k) \times Er_m(c) / E_{energu}(c) \times \beta \tag{7}$$

$\beta \in [0, 1]$ ,it is a constant, which is passed between nodes and node strength.

CBEAR routing algorithm not only considers the probability of meeting between nodes and communities, but also considers the node's energy constraint, and improves the overall performance of the network.

### 5.2   Inter-community Energy Aware Content Distribution Strategy

The frequency of communication is determined by the number of communication between two communities. Thus, this paper sets up the social relations between the community and the community as the social value of the two communities, as a standard for the inter-community message forwarding. Message transmission in the community, the message carries node meet no target community node, then it will be a message forwarding give social goal with maximum weight community as community relay nodes, we will these relay community active high degree of node as the center point of section. First select the center node of relay community as a passing messages among community intermediary message forward first to the central node, through the central node to forward information to the target community, by community message transmission mechanism, the message forwarding to the target community where the destination node.

**Definition 5.** Social weights. if the node $i$ of a community and node $j$ of another community contact, the social value plus 1, the value show the meeting time n in the time t between two communities.

## 6   Simulation Results and Analysis

In order to evaluate the performance of the above methods, we constructed *6000 m* *\*4000 m* square to simulate the network scenario. Set up 3 kinds of mobile nodes *A, B, C*, mobile nodes are randomly distributed in the scene area; the number of mobile nodes is 20, 60 and 100 respectively. Specific simulation parameters Table 1.

We will put forward in the paper based on community energy aware routing protocol CBEAR and PROPHET and EPIDEMIC were compared, mainly focuses on the comparison of three kinds of routing algorithms in data transmission success rate and average transmission delay, energy balance in the results (Fig. 3).

**Table 1.** Different parameter values used in simulation

| Parameter | Value |
| --- | --- |
| $E_{energy}$ | 800[J] |
| network scenario | $6000 \times 4000[m^2]$ |
| path attenuation index | 3 |
| A nodes speed | 20-60 km/h |
| B nodes speed | 15-35 km/h |
| C nodes speed | 2-6 km/h |
| node cache size | 20 MB |
| $p_{max}$ | 0.80 |
| $p_{min}$ | 0.40 |
| $P_{init}$ | 0.75 |
| $\beta$ | 0.45 |
| message copy number | 20 |
| message survival cycle | 1500 s |
| simulation time | 12 h |

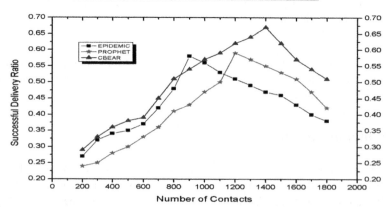

**Fig. 3.** Data transmission success rate of different contact times

## 6.1 Data Transmission Success Rate

We can see three routing protocols in the different number of contacts of transmission success rate, the algorithm CBEAR limit the weak link of message transmission, reduces the number of unnecessary forwarding and reduce the number of message copies. After the contact number is over 900 times, the success rate of EPIDEMIC algorithm is beginning to drop. This is because some nodes due to heavy load, node energy quickly reduced to 0, out of the network. The success rate of PROPHET algorithm is also beginning to drop, the same is due to the beginning of the node energy began to decrease to 0. And the CBEAR algorithm in the 1500 contact number of times after the start to decline, indicating that the CBEAR algorithm to use energy regulation to achieve the energy balance between the nodes. It can be seen that in the simulation of the middle and later stage, the advantages of the CBEAR algorithm is more obvious than the other two routing protocols.

## 6.2  Average Transmission Delay

EPIDEMIC algorithms due to the copy of the contagious diffusion leads to network congestion, so the time of the message in the relay node is longer, reducing the transmission speed of information, and the average transmission delay is increased. In the PROPHET algorithm, the probability of the target node encounter is small, and the transmission time of the weak link is increased by the message path hops. The algorithm CBEAR also considers the node energy consumption rate, when the node with high centrality but energy consumption is too fast, it will avoid the nodes, so the average number of hops is large, and the average transmission delay is relatively large, limiting the number of copies of the message, reducing the network overhead and congestion, thus balancing the average message delay. In the later stage of the simulation, the average transmission delay of the two protocols is gradually increased with the decrease of the node energy and the average transmission delay of 0 (Fig. 4).

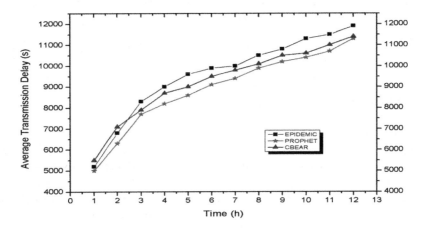

**Fig. 4.**  Average transmission delay of the three protocols

### 6.3  Routing Overhead Ratio

The routing overhead rate of the three algorithms is shown in Fig. 5, and the cost of the EPIDEMIC algorithm and PROPHET algorithm is relatively large. Epidemic algorithms because infections forwarding, resulting in a large number of copies of the message, making the message after the invalid relay times too much, and less successfully reached the destination of the message, so corresponding overhead ratio will be enormous. CBEAR algorithm can limit the number of copies and utilization of high mobility and high energy intermediate node forwarding, make the message more easily along the target node, and use the energy control mechanism to avoid the node energy over consumption and premature departure from network. Therefore, invalid number of messages relayed least, and managed to get into the destination of the message most, so protocol overhead ratio is the smallest.

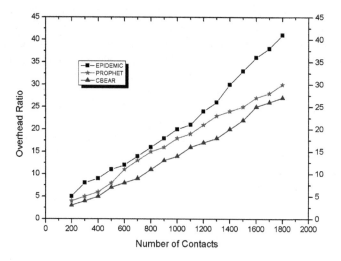

**Fig. 5.**  Routing overhead ratio of the three protocols

## 7  Conclusion

In this paper, we proposed based on community energy aware routing protocol in mobile social networks-CBEAR, dividing an MSN network dynamic partition into several different communities and between intra-community and inter-community transmission and sharing news, considering node energy consumption rate and the encounter proba-bility between node and each community, by the number of copies are restricted to routing decisions and avoid some nodes' energy consumption is too fast problem, to realize load balance between nodes. By comparison with existing routing protocols through extensive simulations, the simulation study show that although the CBEAR protocol has some delay performance, it has achieved better performance in terms of data transmission success rate, protocol overhead ratio and energy balance. There are several issues worth further investigation, such as community partition strategy relies on the server to meet data unified collection and control, node selfishness, this is we the next step research work.

**Acknowledgments.** This research is supported in part by the National Natural Science Foundation of China under Grant Nos. 61562006, 61262003, in part by the Natural Science Foundation of Guangxi Province under Grant No. 2010GXNSFC013013.

# References

1. Kayastha, N., Niyato, D., Wang, P., Hossain, E.: Applications, Architectures, and Protocol Design Issues for Mobile Social Networks: A Survey. Proc. IEEE **99**(12), 2130–2158 (2011)
2. Hui, P., Chaintreau, A., Scott, J., Gass, R., Diot, C.: Pocket Switched Networks and Human Mobility in Conference Environments. In: Proceedings of the 2005 ACM SIGCOMM Workshop on DTN, pp. 244–251. ACM, New York (2005)
3. Vahdat, A., Becker, D.: Epidemic Routing for Partially-Connected Ad Hoc Hetworks. Technique Report, Department of Computer Science, CS-(2000)-06, North Carolina, Duke University, Durham (2000)
4. Spyropoulos, T., Psounis, K., Raghavendra, C.S.: Spray and Wait: An Efficient Routing Scheme for Intermittently Connected Mobile Networks. In: Proceedings of ACM SIGCOMM 2005 Workshops: Conference on Computer Communications, pp. 252–259. ACM, New York (2005)
5. Spyropoulos, T., Psounis, K., Raghavendra, C.S.: Spray and Focus: Efficient Mobility-Assisted Routing for Heterogeneous and Correlated Mobility. In: Proceedings of the Fifth Annual IEEE International Conference on Pervasive Computing and Communications Workshops, pp. 79–85. IEEE, New York (2007)
6. Yuan, Q., Cardei, L., Wu, J.: An Efficient Prediction-Based Routing in Disruption-Tolerant Networks. In: IEEE Transactions on Parallel and Distributed System, vol. 23, no. 1, pp. 19–31. IEEE (2012)
7. Lindgren, A., Doria, A., Schelén, O.: Probabilistic routing in intermittently connected networks. In: Dini, P., Lorenz, P., de Souza, J.N. (eds.) SAPIR 2004. LNCS, vol. 3126, pp. 239–254. Springer, Heidelberg (2004)
8. Xiao, M., Wu, J., Huang, L.: Community-aware opportunistic routing in mobile social networks. IEEE Trans. Comput. **63**(7), 1682–1695 (2014)
9. Daly, E.M., Haahr, M.: Social network analysis for routing in disconnected delay-tolerant MANETs. In: MobiHoc 2007, pp. 32–40 (2007)
10. Daly, E.M., Haahr, M.: Social network analysis for information flow in disconnected delay-tolerant MANETs. IEEE Trans. Mobile Comput. **8**(5), 606–621 (2009). IEEE
11. Hui, P., Crowcroft, J., Yoneki, E.: BUBBLE rap: social-based forwarding in delay tolerant networks. IEEE Trans. Mobile Comput. **10**(11), 1576–1589 (2011). IEEE CS
12. Hui, P., Crowcroft, J.: How small labels create big improvements. In: Fifth Annual IEEE International Conference on Pervasive Computing and Communications Workshops, pp. 65–70. IEEE, New York (2007)
13. Duch, J., Arenas, A.: Community detection in complex networks using extremal optimization. Phys. Rev. E– Stat. Nonlin. Soft Matter Phys. **72**(2), 1–4 (2005)
14. Costa, P., Mascolo, C., Musolesi, M.: Socially-aware routing for publish subscribe in delay-tolerant mobile ad hoc networks. IEEE J. Sel. Areas Commun. **26**(5), 748–760 (2008)

# Research of CMABC Algorithm in Intrusion Detection

Ming Liu[1(✉)], Xiaoling Yang[1], Fanling Huang[2], and Yanming Fu[1]

[1] School of Computer and Electronic Information, Guangxi University,
Guangxi 530004, China
{744182326,1600665358,425454995}@qq.com
[2] School of Software, Tsinghua University, Beijing 100000, China
517190163@qq.com

**Abstract.** To the problem of the traditional parameters optimization algorithm may level into local optimal, a parameter optimization method crossover mutation artificial bee colony based on artificial bee colony algorithm is proposed to solve this problem and applied to intrusion detection. And introduced an improved artificial colony algorithm based on crossover mutation operator, the whole bee colony could be divided into two sub-populations according to the fitness value of colony and effectively avoid local optimum and enhance convergence speed, use standard test functions to verify the effectiveness of the algorithm. And the proposed algorithm's performance is tested by the KDD-99 datasets, the experimental results show that this method can effective improve the classification performance of intrusion detection.

**Keywords:** Intrusion detection · Support vector machine · Artificial bee colony · Crossover mutation

## 1 Introduction

Intrusion detection technology by collecting the key node computer network system information and analyze the behavior of the system security policy violations in a timely manner to respond [1]. As a method developed on the basis of a small sample of machine learning, Support Vector Machine (SVM) solve the small sample, nonlinear, high-dimensional problems through risk minimization principle, and can remain higher classification accuracy under priori knowledge insufficient, it is very suitable for network intrusion detection system.

The selection of penalty factor and kernel parameter in SVM classification algorithm directly affects the classification accuracy and its generalization performance. The traditional SVM parameter optimization algorithm for experienced method [2], genetic algorithm [3], and the gradient descent method, these traditional parameters optimization algorithm in the optimization process will be falling into local optimal problem in the optimization process, and can't establish an effective SVM optimal classification model.

Artificial bee colony, (ABC) algorithm is a new swarm intelligence optimization algorithm introduced by Karaboga in 2005 [4]. A number of experimental results show that the algorithm in solving optimization problems of parameters show some advantages, but for

G. Wang et al. (Eds.): ICA3PP 2015 Workshops, LNCS 9532, pp. 322–332, 2015.
DOI: 10.1007/978-3-319-27161-3_28

the unimodal problems slow convergence and multimodal function problems easy to fall into local optimal solution. In view of these problems, many scholars put forward some improved methods, Shi proposed hybrid optimization algorithm of PSO and ABC in 2010 [5], Zhu introducing a global optimal solution given in the GAB algorithm [6], in order to improve the convergence speed. These algorithms improve the convergence speed of the algorithm, but still fall into the optimal solution in different degrees, especially for multimodal optimization problems.

The study show that there is a multimodal function relationship between the SVM correct classification, penalty factor and kernel parameter [7]. In order to obtain the better parameters to improve the SVM classification performance, we use the thought of crossover and mutation in ABC algorithm to do further optimization, cross mutation operator is introduced into different subpopulations, improve the shortcomings of ABC algorithm early fall into the local optimum in multimodal optimization problems. Then, the ABC algorithm and improved ABC algorithm are applied to the SVM based on intrusion detection, and use the NSL-KDD [8] network intrusion detection data sets to test the effectiveness of the improved ABC algorithm.

## 2 Support Vector Machine

### 2.1 SVM

SVM is a linear machine learning method based on structural risk minimization of statistical learning theory of any priori knowledge. The main objective of SVM is to find the optimum hyper plane to separate the two classes. Given a training data set:

$$(x_1, y_1), \ldots, (x_n, y_n), x \in R^n, y \in \{+1, -1\}$$

Hyper plane is

$$(w \cdot x + b = 0) \tag{1}$$

To construct the optimal hyper plane, seeking maximum separation interval can be converted to the following optimization problem:

$$\varphi(w) = \frac{1}{2} \|w\|^2 + C \sum_{i=1}^{n} \xi_i \tag{2}$$

$$s.t. \quad y_i[(w \cdot x_i + b)] - 1 + \xi_i \geq 0 \quad i = 1, \cdots, n$$

Slack variable $\xi_i \geq 0$, $c \geq 0$ (constant), it determines the penalty for the wrong sample. Introducing LaGrange multiplier to convert it to a dual problem.

$$Q(\alpha) = \sum_{i=1}^{n} \alpha_i - \frac{1}{2} \sum_{i,j=1}^{n} \alpha_i \alpha_j y_i y_j K(x_i, x_j) \tag{3}$$

$$s.t \sum_{i=1}^{n} y_i \alpha_i = 0 \quad 0 \leq a_i \leq c, \quad i = 1, \ldots, n$$

By solving quadratic programming problem to obtain a final decision function:

$$f(x) = \text{sgn} \left\{ \sum_{i=1}^{n} a_i^* y_i k(x_i \cdot x) + b^* \right\}$$

(4)

### 2.2 Impacts of the Parameters

For the SVM based on RBF as the kernel function, the most important parameters that affect the performance of the SVM classification algorithm are the penalty factor $C$ and the kernel parameter $g$. Their selection directly affects the classification accuracy and the generalization performance of the support vector machines [9]. The penalty factor $C$ which can be used to balance the ratio of the SVM fiduciary range and empirical risk in the feature subspace. In the determining feature subspace, the smaller $C$ value represent the penalties on experience error is smaller, and resulting in greater error model training, experience risk value are greater, model predict the classification error rate is high, and appears "less learning" phenomenon.

Kernel parameters are closely related to kernel function. When the kernel function is determined, the mapping function and feature space are also determined. The selected of Kernel parameter $g$ will directly affect the kernel function characteristics, the distribution of sample data in high dimensional feature space complexity changes, that is the dimension of the feature space, improper $g$ is unable to ensure the structural risk minimization. It is a tunable parameter that controls the correlation among support vectors.

Therefore, in every feature subspace, there is a suitable penalty factor and kernel parameter make the generalization performance of SVM is best.

## 3   Support Vector Machine Parameter Optimization Model

### 3.1   Artificial Bee Colony Algorithm

The ABC algorithm is inspired by the intelligent foraging behavior of honey bees. In ABC algorithm, the swarm contains three groups of bees: exploit bees, onlooker bees and scout bees [10], they are according to different division of labor to complete the task. The number of exploit bees and onlooker bees each occupy half of the entire bees, each food source only allow a exploit bee to gather honey, when the food source of the nectar was collected, the corresponding exploit bees convert to scout bees. The onlooker bees to choose a new food source by observing the situation of each food source and repeat this process until the best food source is found.

In this algorithm, the solution for the optimize problem is given by the position of the food source. The honey amount of the food source corresponds to the quality (fitness) of that solution [11]. First, the algorithm initializes the food sources, randomly generated initial solution $(S_N)$, which is the number of exploit bees and food sources, each food source $x_i$ is a $D$ dimensional variable, $D$ represents the number of parameters need to optimize. Produce the initial source of food by using the following formula.

$$x_{ij} = x_{j\min} + rand\,(0,1)\left(x_{j\max} - x_{j\min}\right)\ i = 1, \ldots, S_N, j = 1, \ldots, D \qquad (5)$$

After initialization, it is begin to optimize the food source (solution), the optimization process of ABC algorithm consists of the following three stages: exploit stage, onlooker stage and scout stage [12].

Exploit stage: bees to exploit at the food source, and produce a disturbance near the food source (original solution), thereby generating a candidate food source position (candidate solutions), and the process is determined by the following formula:

$$v_{ij} = x_{ij} + \varphi_{ij}\left(x_{ij} - x_{kj}\right)\quad k \in \{1,2,\ldots S_N\}\quad j \in \{1,2,\ldots,D\}\quad k \neq i \qquad (6)$$

$x_i$ is the i-th food source, $x_k$ is a food source select randomly, $j$ is a randomly selected index, $\varphi_{ij}$ is a random number within the range $[-1,1]$. It can be seen that when the difference between $x_{ij}$ and $x_{kj}$ is reduced, namely two food source distance decreases, the disturbance to food source is reduce, and the bees search step is reduced until it convergence to the optimal solution.

Onlooker stage: to evaluate the candidate solutions of each food source generated by (6), the nectar amount of per new food source, which is the fitness of the solution. To calculate the probability of selecting every food source according to the fitness, and the formula is as follows:

$$P_i = \frac{fitness_i}{\sum\limits_{i=1}^{FN} fitness_i} \qquad (7)$$

*Fitness$_i$* is the fitness of the i-th food source, the greater of the $P_i$, it represents more nectar, and attracts more bees to gather honey.

In scout stage, after circulate exploit food source for many times, if exploit bees can no longer improve their solution and exceeds the preset threshold limit, then their solution is abandoned and they become scout bees. Scout bees will randomly select a new food source.

### 3.2 Crossover Mutation ABC(CMABC)

The basic ABC algorithm can only select one food source in the process of optimization, and only in one direction at the time of the update, which significantly limits the performance of the algorithm. In order to improve the optimization ability of ABC algorithm, we take the thinking of differential evolution algorithm, introduce crossover mutation and selection operator to enhance the ability of optimizing and application range [13], the crossover mutation operator is introduced into the ABC algorithm.

The CMABC algorithm is similar to the ABC algorithm, initialize and set parameters, and all the food sources are encoded by the decimal coding method. Then, after implement the stage of exploit and onlooker, the crossover mutation operator is introduced into the population to find the optimal solution.

1. According to the predefined population parameter $M$ to divide the whole population, the higher fitness value for outstanding population $P$, the rest of the relatively low fitness value of individual for population $Q$.
2. Randomly select two food source $x_1, x_2$ from outstanding populations and select food source $x'_1$ in the $Q$, for each of food source in population $P$ to precede mutation operation in accordance with the following formula:

$$v_i = x'_1 \varphi_1 + (x_1 - x_2)\varphi_2 \qquad x_1 \neq x_2 \neq x'_1 \tag{8}$$

$\varphi_1, \varphi_2$ are random number within the range $[-1,1]$. To compare the fitness value of $v_i$ and $x_i$, if the fitness of $v_i$ is better than that of $x_i$, use $v_i$ update $x_i$. Similarly, the rest of the food source using formula (9) to proceed the mutation operation, the $x_1$ randomly selected from the population P, $x'_1, x'_2$ from population $Q$.

$$v_i = x'_1 \varphi_1 + (x'_1 - x'_2)\varphi_2 \quad x'_1 \neq x'_2 \neq x_1 \tag{9}$$

To compare the fitness value of $v_i$ and $x_i$ again, if the fitness of $v_i$ is better than that of $x_i$, use $v_i$ update $x_i$, otherwise remain unchanged.

For the last scout stage, forsake the food source that have no exploit value, continue to look for a new food source.

The ABC algorithm introducing crossover operator, through the cross between the individuals in the parent population $Q$ and individuals in $P$ population, the multimodal optimization problems in the algorithm premature stagnation problem can be solved. Introducing the optimal individual in the population $P$ to the population $Q$ to cross can expand the diversity of population, and improve the ABC algorithm on the slow convergence of unimodal optimization problem.

### 3.3  SVM Parameter Selection Based on CMABC Algorithm

SVM algorithm parameters selection needs to be carried out in a large range, so the optimization process is very easy to fall into local optimum, crossover and mutation operator introduced into the CMABC algorithm, the parent population and poor fitness populations were crossed, can effectively solve the problem. In this paper, the CMABC algorithm is used to optimize the SVM algorithm of the two important parameters, the penalty factor $C$ and the kernel parameter $g$.

Step1. First, the relevant parameters are set up, the source of food is the number of bees $S_N$, the maximum number of food source cycle *limit*, and $N_{mc}$ is the number of termination cycle. Set the search scope of $C$ and g to improve the search efficiency.

Step2. The SVM parameters $C$ and $g$ are encoded by the real number, encoding of each solution are composed of a real vector, which is a possible optimization of the individual with $C$ and $g$. In the coding space, an initial group of individuals with $S_N$ is random generated.

Step3. According to the characteristics of SVM to set up the fitness function, and the goal of optimizing SVM and applied to the intrusion detection is to improve the classification accuracy. Fitness function:

$$V = V_{acc} \tag{10}$$

$V_{acc}$ is the classification accuracy.

Step4. Perform the stage of exploit and onlooker.

Step5. According to the fitness value and preset size to divide the population, the higher fitness value for outstanding population $P$, and the rest for population $Q$. All the food source process mutation operation according to the formulas (8) and (9), if the fitness of $v_i$ is better than that of $x_i$, use $v_i$ update $x_i$.

Step6. In the scout stage, eliminate the worthless food source and random generated new food source.

## 4   Simulation Experiment and Analysis

In this paper, four standard test functions are used to evaluate the performance of the CMABC algorithm and compare with the ABC algorithm. Experiment have two parts, the first part proved the effectiveness of CMABC algorithm; The CMABC algorithms used in intrusion detection based on the SVM parameter optimization in the second part, and make use of the intrusion detection evaluation index to evaluate the performance of CMABC-SVM.

The experiment used the Java language, Libsvm3.18 and Weka software to test and analysis.

### 4.1   SVM Parameter Selection Based on CMABC Algorithm

Three standard test functions are as follows:

(1)  Sphere unimodal function:

$$f_1(x) = \sum_{i=1}^{D} x_i^2 \tag{11}$$

where $-100 \le x_i \le 100$.

(2)  Rastrigin multimodal function

$$f_3(x) = \sum_{i=1}^{D} (x_i^2 - 10\cos(2\pi x_i) + 10) \tag{12}$$

where $-5.12 \le x_i \le 5.12$.

(3)  Griewank multimodal function

$$f_4(x) = \frac{1}{4000} \sum_{i=1}^{D} x_i^2 - \prod_{i=1}^{D} \cos\left[\frac{x_i}{\sqrt{i}}\right] + 1 \tag{13}$$

where $-600 \le x_i \le 600$.

The population parameter $M$ is set to 0.5, population size is 80, limit = Food-Number*D, the maximum iterations number $N_{mc} = 2000$, performance evaluation for two parts: (1) fixed dimension and iterations number, to evaluate convergence precision of algorithm; (2) to evaluate the iterations when algorithm achieves convergence precision.

**Convergence Precision of Fixed Iterations.** After the experiment run 30 times independent, we achieve the mean best fitness and standard deviation, the ideal result is 0. The experimental results for the candidate solutions D for 20 and 30 dimensions are shown in Tables 1 and 2.

**Table 1.** 20 dimensional optimization test results

| Function | Algorithm | Mean | Std |
|----------|-----------|------|-----|
| Sphere | ABC | 2.82081e-16 | 1.25638e-16 |
| | CMABC | 1.70907e-16 | 3.26864e-17 |
| Rastrigin | ABC | 0 | 6.30715e-13 |
| | CMABC | 0 | 0 |
| Griewank | ABC | 2.70154e-16 | 2.67812e-15 |
| | CMABC | 1.25825e-16 | 5.38039e-16 |

**Table 2.** 30 dimensional optimization test results

| Function | Algorithm | Mean | Std |
|----------|-----------|------|-----|
| Sphere | ABC | 1.46724e-15 | 8.81704e-15 |
| | CMABC | 4.36620e-16 | 6.52742e-16 |
| Rastrigin | ABC | 0 | 1.385591e-8 |
| | CMABC | 0 | 2.588355e-9 |
| Griewank | ABC | 8.43769e-15 | 5.58439e-15 |
| | CMABC | 5.35807e-16 | 6.20372e-16 |

From the experimental data, we can see that the improved CMABC algorithm is better than the ABC algorithm in the optimization performance. By introducing cross mutation operator, the ability of the population to find the optimal solution is improved, and avoid fall into the local optimal. Many experimental results show that the CMABC algorithm has good performance in both unimodal function and multimodal function. When the dimension increases, the search scope is enlarged, and the multimodal function will appear more local extreme points, and the optimization effect of the algorithm is better.

**Convergence Speed of Fixed Iterations.** Set the size of the population and the number of cycles are unchanged, when $D = 30$, the convergent tendency of the ABC algorithm and CMABC algorithm as shown in Figs. 1, 2 and 3.

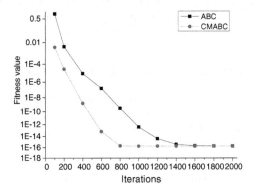

**Fig. 1.** Sphere function

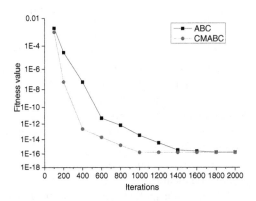

**Fig. 2.** Griewank function

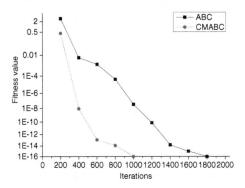

**Fig. 3.** Rastrigin function

From the figure above, we can see that the CMABC algorithm convergence speed is obviously superior to the ABC algorithm, Sphere and Griewank functions ultimately trend in 1e-16. To the Rastrigin function, CMABC algorithm converge to 0 after 1000 iterations. ABC algorithm converges to 0 after 1800 iterations. Through the cross between the parent population and the surplus population, the diversity of the population is enhanced, and the convergence speed of the algorithm is improved.

## 4.2    Application of CMABC Algorithm in Intrusion Detection

Experiment using intrusion detection standard data set KDD-99, the data set contains the training set and testing set, according to the proportion of each type, selected part of the data for experiment. The KDD-99 data set include normal data and abnormal data, the experimental data type distribution as shown in Table 3.

**Table 3.**  Experimental sample set

| Class | Normal | Abnormal | Totals |
|---|---|---|---|
| train set | 5600 | 1300 | 6900 |
| test set | 4600 | 1000 | 5600 |

At present, the evaluation standards of intrusion detection mainly include the attack detection rate, false alarm rate and accuracy [14].

Attack Detection Rate(ADR)-is the ratio between total numbers of attacks detected by the system to the total number of attacks present in the data set.

False Alarm Rate(FAR)-is the ratio between total number of misclassified instances to the total number of normal instances.

Accuracy-is the ratio between total numbers of correctly classified instances to the total number of samples from the data set.

The ABC and CMABC algorithm applied to intrusion detection based on SVM, after several comparative experiments, the population size of $S_N$ is set to 20, the limit is set to 50, terminate cycles of $N_{mc}$ is 100, SVM need to optimize two parameters, so the $D$ is 2, the search range of parameter set for the [0.01 1000]. Experimental results are shown in Table 4.

**Table 4.**  The detection performance of each data set

| Algorithm | ADR | FAR | Accuracy | C | g |
|---|---|---|---|---|---|
| ABC-SVM | 99.10 % | 0.03 % | 99.10 % | 256 | 0.05 |
| CMABC-SVM | 99.31 % | 0.01 % | 99.55 % | 300 | 0.09 |

From Table 4 can be seen that, by means of the ABC-SVM algorithm and CMABC-SVM algorithm to optimize the SVM parameters, the five data sets to compare, the latter is better than the former in detection performance, only the fifth data set is in high false alarm rate due to less sample data. By introducing cross mutation operator, the CMABC-SVM algorithm can make the individual trapped in local optimal out of bondage, and jump out of local optimal solution. The classification performance of SVM is improved by optimizing the parameters.

# 5 Conclusion

Based on the importance of SVM parameters to the SVM intrusion detection perform-ance, it is overcome the shortcomings of the traditional optimization algorithm to improve the performance of ABC algorithm, and through four standard test functions to verify the validity of the CMABC algorithm. On this basis, the paper puts forward the intrusion detection of SVM based on CMABC algorithm, to optimize the penalty factor C and kernel parameter g in SVM. The KDD-99 data set is used in simulation experiments, and the experiments result show that the CMABC-SVM algorithm can overcome the defects of the local optimum value, so that the detector can obtain higher detection rate, higher detection accuracy and lower false positive rate.

**Acknowledgments.** This research is supported in part by the National Natural Science Foundation of China under Grant Nos. 61262072.

# References

1. Bahri, E., Harbi, N., Huu, H.N.: A multiple classifier system using an adaptive strategy for intrusion detection. In: International Conference on Intelligent Computational Systems (ICICS), pp. 124–128 (2012)
2. Mao, Y., Zhou, X.-b., Pi, D.-y., et al.: Parameters selection in gene selection using Gaussian kernel support vector machines by genetic algorithm. J. Zhe Jiang Univ. Sci. **6**(10), 961–973 (2005)
3. Kumar, A.: Parameter optimization using genetic algorithm for support vector machine-based price-forecasting model in National electricity Market. IET Gener. Transm. Distrib. IET **4**(1), 36–49 (2010)
4. Karaboga, D.: An idea based on honey bee swarm for numerical optimization. Technical report-tr06, Erciyes university, engineering faculty, computer engineering department (2005)
5. Shi, X., Li, Y., Li, H., et al.: An integrated algorithm based on artificial bee colony and particle swarm optimization. In: Sixth International Conference on Natural Computation, ICNC, pp. 2586–2590 (2010)
6. Zhu, G., Kwong, S.: Gbest-guided artificial bee colony algorithm for numerical function optimization. Appl. Math. Comput. **217**(7), 3166–3173 (2010)
7. Unler, A., Murat, A., Chinnam, R.B.: mr 2 PSO: a maximum relevance minimum redundancy feature selection method based on swarm intelligence for support vector machine classification. Inf. Sci. **181**(20), 4625–4641 (2011)
8. KDD-99dataset for network-based intrusion detection systems. http://iscx.info/KDD-99
9. Drucker, H., Wu, D., Vipnik, V.N.: Support vector machines for spam categorization. IEEE Trans. Neural Netw. **10**(5), 1048–1054 (1999)
10. Karaboga, D., Ozturk, C.: A novel clustering approach: Artificial Bee Colony (ABC) algorithm. Appl. Soft Comput. **11**(1), 652–657 (2011)

11. Karaboga, D., Basturk, B.: A comparative study of artificial bee colony algorithm. Appl. Math. Comput. **214**(1), 108–132 (2009)
12. Qin, A.K., Suganthan, P.N.: Self-adaptive differential evolution algorithm for numerical optimization. In: The 2005 IEEE Congress on Evolutionary Computation, pp. 1785–1791. IEEE (2005)
13. Tinoco, J.C.V., Coello, C.A.: *hyp*DE: a hyper-heuristic based on differential evolution for solving constrained optimization problems. In: Schütze, O., Coello Coello, C.A., Tantar, A.-A., Tantar, E., Bouvry, P., Del Moral, P., Legrand, P. (eds.) EVOLVE - A Bridge Between Probability, Set Oriented Numerics, and Evolutionary Computation II. AISC, vol. 175, pp. 267–282. Springer, Heidelberg (2012)
14. Mezher, M.A., Abbod, M.F.: Genetic folding for solving multicast SVM problems. Applied Intelligence **41**(2), 464–472 (2014)

# A Parallel Tabu Search Algorithm
# with Solution Space Partition
# for Cohesive Clustering Problems

Zheng Xu[1(✉)] and Buyang Cao[1,2]

[1] School of Software Engineering, Tongji University, Shanghai 201804, China
`x.zheng91@gmail.com, caobuyang@tongji.edu.cn`
[2] China Intelligent Urbanization Co-Creation Center for High Density Region,
Tongji University, Shanghai 200092, China

**Abstract.** Clustering analysis plays an important role in a wide range of fields including data mining, pattern recognition, machine learning and many other areas. In this paper, we present a parallel tabu search algorithm for clustering problems. A permanent tabu list is proposed to partition the solution space for parallelization. Moreover, this permanent tabu list can also reduce the neighborhood space and constrain the election of candidates. The proposed approach is evaluated by clustering some specific dataset. And experimental results and speedups obtained show the efficiency of the parallel algorithm.

**Keywords:** Combinatorial optimization · Tabu search · Clustering analysis · Parallel tabu search · Parallel clustering · Solution space partition

## 1 Introduction

Clustering is essentially a multivariate statistical analysis method to find the logical or physical relationship between data. A clustering algorithm is commonly defined to consist of grouping a set of objects (based on a specific rule and the characteristics of the objects) in a manner that causes objects in the same group or cluster to be more similar (or closer) to each other than they are to objects in other groups or clusters [1]. In recent years, the clustering problem has been addressed in many contexts and by researchers in many disciplines [2–4]. This also reflects its broad appeal and usefulness as one of the steps in exploratory data analysis.

In the former research [5], Cao and Glover propose a tabu Search algorithm for a new problem class called cohesive clustering which arises in a variety of business applications. Regarding a parameterized variance component as an important part of the objective function, this algorithm generates higher quality solutions concerned with both compactness and similarity of clusters. The clustering model is originally conceived from the standpoint of generating solutions that provide a baseline to classify new elements, as where it is desired to assign new jobs to the proper job segments (on the cloud platform). Therefore, the goal of the algorithm is not to generate clusters rapidly but rather to create a judicious collection of clusters with the aim of using them multiple times over an extended horizon as a means for future classification.

© Springer International Publishing Switzerland 2015
G. Wang et al. (Eds.): ICA3PP 2015 Workshops, LNCS 9532, pp. 333–343, 2015.
DOI: 10.1007/978-3-319-27161-3_29

Since the first time Glove proposes Tabu Search (TS) [6], TS has obtained a lot of research achievements including parallel computing [7]. As a "higher level" heuristic procedure for solving optimization problems [8], TS offers a good framework for parallelism. In this context, a parallelism improve may handle the large scale data.

In this paper, as our main contribution, we propose a parallel tabu search algorithm for clustering. The general idea is that we partition the local sequential search heuristic used inside TS into several independent slave node by specific solution space. The slave nodes, performed in parallel, can process a complete search and generate clusters, without much loss of quality, while TS assures a high global quality of the solution. To the author's knowledge, a parallel TS based clustering algorithm and its implementation have not been reported in the literature.

In the next section, a brief review of the basic principles of TS for clustering is given. The parallelization of this algorithm is explained in Sect. 3, with emphasis on the solution space partition. Computational results are presented in Sect. 4. Finally, we offer our conclusions in Sect. 5.

## 2 Preliminaries

### 2.1 Problem Description

Generally, a clustering problem means classify a set of objects described by a number of attributes into a specific cluster such that objects in the same cluster present great homogeneity (based on a specific evaluation measure). In our study, it can be represented as follows:

Let $x(t)$ ($t = 1$ to $Nt$) and $C(s)$ ($s = 1$ to $Ns$) present the objects and clusters under consideration. $Nt$ identifies the number of such objects, while $Ns$ identifies the number of clusters. And let Score($t1$, $t2$) ($1 \leq t1$, $t2 \leq Nt$) denote the "score" that measures the desirability or undesirability of assigning $t1$ and $t2$ to the same cluster. The calibration of the values represented by Score($t1$, $t2$) is highly important. Different measures affect clustering results a lot. In our study, Euclidean distance is preferred:

$$\text{Score}(t_1, t_2) = \sqrt{\sum_{k=1}^{p} \left(x_{t1,k} - x_{t2,k}\right)^2} \tag{1}$$

This $x(t) = (x1,...,xp)$ represent a vector of p-attributes describing a specific type of the input object $x(t)$. To evaluate the clusters, we define some metric values of $C(s)$:

$$FullVal(s) = \frac{Val(s)}{NumLinks(s)} \tag{2}$$

We use Val(s) to present the "scores" produced by all the objects in cluster C(s). Considering cluster C(s) as a complete graph, whose number of objects we denote by n(s), NumLinks(s) is defines as the number of all the edges between each objects in C(s). Hence, here comes the first metric FullVal(s), means the average score on an edge, to evaluate the compactness of the cluster C(s).

However, to solve cohesive clustering problems, the variance of cluster C(s), FullVari(s), is proposed as another metric to evaluate both distributions and similarities [9] of objects in cluster C(s):

$$FullVari(s) = \frac{\sum\left(\left(Score(t_i, t_j) - FullVal(s)\right)^2 | t_i < t_j \& x(t_i), x(t_j) \in C(s)\right)}{NumLinks(s)} \quad (3)$$

Finally, this clustering problem turns to a mathematical optimization problem, find the minimum ObjVal after a special distribution of all the elements in each clusters:

$$ObjVal = \alpha \sum_{S=1}^{Ns} FullVal(s) + \beta \sum_{S=1}^{Ns} FullVari \quad (4)$$

This $\alpha$ and $\beta$ here in (4) present weights of the full value and variance, and provide flexibility to consider different balances between distributions and similarities of objects. Furthermore, a special setting, $\beta = 0$ may be in common use for a normal clustering problem.

## 2.2   Neighborhood Operation

TS is an iterative algorithm, which moves step by step from an initial feasible solution toward a solution S* that seeks to minimize ObjVal, at least approximately. We define the operations that move a selected objects x(t0) from the source cluster C(s0) to the target cluster C(sA) under the control of a tabu search process. And some values are defined to evaluate the move operation:

$$AddVal(t_0, s_A) = \sum(Score(t_0, t_A) | x(t_A) \in C(s_A)) \quad (5)$$

This AddVal(t0,sA) is the increased amount of the "Scores" in C(sA) caused by the move t0-> sA. Likewise, as Score(t0,t0) = 0, AddVal(t0,s0) means drop value actually. It indicates the decreased amount of the "Scores" in C(sA) caused by the move t0-> sA.
Then, we define the final metrics to evaluate a move operation:

$$MoveVal(t_0, s_A) = \alpha \times DelFullVal + \beta \times DelFullVari \quad (6)$$

Note MoveVal(t0, sA) here is actually the change in the objective function value ObjVal caused by the move t0-> sA. DelFullVal and DelFullVari means the varition of the average scores and the variance. Under a minimization objective, MoveVal(t0, sA) < 0 identifies an improving move while MoveVal(t0, sA) >= 0 identifies a non-improving move. The MoveVal may lead neighborhood search to optimal solution.

## 2.3    Basic Procedures

The key feature of TS is precisely to forbid moves that would bring the process back to one of the recently visited solutions in order to limit the risk of cycling. For doing this, the last moves and the reverse of the last moves are collected in tabu list of forbidden moves. And a special diversification phase is applied to help the algorithm generate better result. Algorithm 1 shows the overall TS algorithm for solving cohesive cluster problems (Bound, penalty and other strategies are not mentioned here, because they are not the focus of this paper).

```
Initialization:
    Construct an initial solution s;        // greedy strategy is applied here
    s* = s;                                 // s* = best solution so far
    iter = 0; improved=0 ;                  // iterations counter and last improved iter
    initialize related values;              //including TabuList, AddVal, MoveVal
While  iter < itermax  do
    If  (iter –improved)< NoImproveLimit  then
        iter++;
        Intensification:
            Find a best solution s' around s;
            // the minimal MoveVal leads to the s'
            If s' is better than s then improved=iter;
            If s' is better than s* then s*=s';
            s = s' ;
            update related values;
    Else
        Improved=iter;
        Diversification:
        Generate a new solution s' according to s;
        //randomly select objects in clusters whose size is larger than others
        //and move these objects to clusters whose size is smaller than others.
        s=s';
        recalculate related values;
End
```

The sequential version of the above algorithm was tested in [5]. Experimental results in [5] were shown that the clustering results were very high in accuracy.

## 3    Methodology

### 3.1    Solution Space Partition

In iterative search techniques, and in TS in particular, different types of parallelism may be distinguished [10]. We consider here a solution space partition method used for search-level parallelization. Different solution space are parallel occupied in independant searchs, which finally combine to find a global optimal solution.

For the solution space partition, we propose a permanent tabu list. Like moves in tabu list are forbidden in a TS move, objects in the permanent tabu list are forbidden to move in the entire TS process, even if the move satisfies the aspiration criteria. Based on this permanent tabu list, we can tie some objects to the clusters, which constrains the solution in specified solution space. Thus we propose a special parameter Gran, called the granularity in the following discussion, to evaluate the size of the permanent tabu list. Directly, the granularity here is the number of objects tied to one cluster. Algorithm 2 shows the procedures of the algorithm for generating initial solution with solution space partition method applied.

```
Construct Ns clusters each contains 2 objects;      //by Random Selection Method
Set the rest objects to a dummy cluster C(0);
Initialize MoveVal(t0,s);                           //x(t0) ∈C(0) & 1≤s≤Ns
i=0;                                                // a temp iterator
While I < Gran do
    i++;
    j=1;                                            // a temp iterator
    While j ≤ Ns do
        Find the minimal MoveVal( t* , j );         // x(t*) ∈C(0)
        Move x(t*) to C(j);
        j++;
    End
    Update MoveVal(t0,s);                           // x(t0) ∈C(0) & 1≤s≤Ns
End
ptList=∅ ;                                          //initialize the permanent tabu list
j=1;
While j ≤ Ns do
    Get all the objects ID t' in C(j);              //mark as permanent tabu
    ptList +=t';
End
Move the rest objects in C(0) to other clusters;   // by greedy strategy
//in the end, we get the initial solution
```

The initial solution affects the TS result a lot. And in the former experiments [5], we find that some part of the initial solution remains in the best solution we finally get. Besides, a number of different partition results will be applied in the parallel approach, a complete coverage of solution space can be assumed. Therefore, the parallel TS with solution space partition is supposed to be effective, which will be proved in Sect. 4.

### 3.2 Parallel Approach at Search-Level

Figure 1 shows the structure of the proposed approach that exploit parallelism at search-level.

In the beginning, a master node is activated to partition the solution space and generate initial solutions for slave nodes.

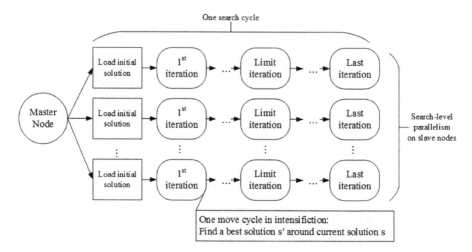

**Fig. 1.** The proposed parallel approach

At the search level, a number of parallel searches (based on the cores) are conducted where each search explores its own partitioned solution space. During the search process, each tabu search has an independent tabu list and a local best solution, which is the best solution the corresponding search has encountered so far. An iteration here equals an intensification move in sequential version in some degree.

To make the search more effective, we define a condition here: (iter–improved) < NoImproveLimit.

As stated in Algorithm 1, this condition means the last NoImproveLimit moves didn't generate a better solution. When the search first meet this condition, a special operation will be applied that release all the objects in permanent tabu list and set a very small value to NoImproveLimit. When the search meat this condition again, it will be shut down. This strategy can help find some apparent better solutions and end the search in short term.

Diversification phase in sequential version is removed here, because the parallel searches can also help escape the trap of local optimality and explore a new solution space. Once a search cycle is done, the result will be send to the master node. The master node will determine if another search is need and update the global optimal solution.

### 3.3 Candidate List

In a move cycle, the entire neighborhood is explored to find a best MoveVal, which indicates the best solution s'around the current solution s. The complexity of the neighborhood space ought to be approximate $O((Ns-1) \times Nt)$ since Nt objects can be moved to the other (Ns-1) clusters. With the solution space partition, Ns × Gran objects are permanent tabu, which reduce the complexity of the neighborhood space to $O(Ns-1) \times (Nt-Ns \times Gran))$. As the neighborhood is now much smaller, iterations are much faster to execute and the search procedure can examine the solution much more thoroughly in the given solution space. Even so, the number of moves, evaluated in a move cycle, is still huge. Thus it is worthwhile to identify candidate moves that potentially lead to good solutions.

As defined, MoveVal (6) consists of DelFullVal and DelFullVari. Therefore a complete computing of MoveVal is not necessary here, because it may cost too much. And DelFullVal is prefered, since the average compute is much faster. As for an object t0, DropVal is determined no matter which cluster it will be moved to. So, the *Min (DelFullValAdd(t0,sA)* | *sA ≠ s0)* determine the move t0-> sA* as a potentially positive candidate. DelFullValAdd(t0,sA) is defined as follows:

$$DelFullValAdd = \frac{Val(s_A) + AddVal(t_0, s_A)}{NumLinks(S_A) + n(S_A)} - FullVal(s_A) \qquad (7)$$

Now, in the move cycle, we explore the candidate list instead of the entire neighborhood space. This strategy reduces computational time apparently, because the complexity is finally reduced to $O(Nt\text{-}Ns \times Gran)$.

## 4  Experiments

To allocate computing resources more effectively to cover promising directions, a dynamic thread allocation technique is necessary. So we implement the parallel algorithm based on JAVA virtual machine (JVM). A number of threads (based on the number of cores) are generated in thread pool to handle slave nodes. The main thread with higher priority, as the master node, *wait()* when it's in idle period. And slaver thread will *notify()* the main thread when its own search cycle is done.

The computational environment for all experiments mentioned below is a desktop with Windows Server 2012 R2, Intel Xeon CPU E5-2630 @2.7 GHz, and 32 GB of RAM.

### 4.1  Accuracy and Speedup

**Scenario 1:** In this computational experiment, we created the corresponding datasets by generating points randomly distributed on a plane with some areas in high density. In order to determine and validate the accuracy of our parallel algorithm, we make a comparison with the former sequential algorithm and the famous K-means, which may be the most popular clustering algorithm.

Table 1 shows the computational results for this comparison. As the K-means algorithm do not consider a variance as an objective value, $\alpha$ and $\beta$ in objective function (4) are set to 1 and 0, respectively. Because of the random method is taken in the algorithms, the value and time cost shown in the table are the average value of several execution. Besides, TS is the former sequential algorithm, and PTS is the parallel tabu search algorithm we proposed above. The number of objects in the data file is presented by Nt, and the number of target clusters is presented by Ns.

**Table 1.** Results for comparison with K-means, TS and PTS

| No. | Nt | Ns | Time cost (mm:ss:ms) | | | Objective value | | |
|---|---|---|---|---|---|---|---|---|
| | | | K-means | TS | PTS | K-means | TS | PTS |
| 1 | 31 | 3 | 0:1:500 | 0:2:010 | 0:0:582 | 5.2410 | 5.2410 | 5.2410 |
| 2 | 200 | 4 | 0:1:533 | 0:2:140 | 0:2:684 | 256.2109 | 236.8732 | 248.9323 |
| 3 | 300 | 3 | 0:1:535 | 0:2:760 | 0:3:136 | 32.3792 | 31.9721 | 32.7564 |
| 4 | 400 | 8 | 0:1:558 | 0:2:295 | 0:3:277 | 268.6499 | 233.5477 | 280.4087 |
| 5 | 500 | 5 | 0:1:560 | 0:2:690 | 0:2:689 | 31.5286 | 31.6147 | 30.3130 |

From the computational results listed in Table 1, we are able to conclude that our PTS is an effective and accurate parallelism approach.

In the experiment No.1, because the dataset only contains 31 objects, the global optimal solution is easily obtained by all the three algorithm. But in the experiment No. 4, although PTS was executed several times, the results is not good. As the solution space partition begin with random selection, the randomness may be a limitation in our algorithm that the partitioned solution space may not cover the entire solution space.

**Scenario 2:** Likewise, to confirm the capability of solving cohesive clustering problems, we set $\alpha$ and $\beta$ in objective function 0.6 and 0.4, respectively. And experimental data is collected from a real cloud platform where data records need to be clustered or classified upon certain characteristics. Then we get another set of computational results in Table 2. CPT means compactness of clusters, i.e. $\sum_{S=1}^{Ns} FullVal(s)$, SV means similarity value, i.e. $\sum_{S=1}^{Ns} FullVari(s)$.

**Table 2.** Results for comparison between TS and PTS

| No. | Nt | Ns | Time cost | | CPT | | SV | |
|---|---|---|---|---|---|---|---|---|
| | | | TS | PTS | TS | PTS | TS | PTS |
| 6 | 400 | 3 | 0:12:681 | 0:25:999 | 184.021 | 182.934 | 4832.778 | 4725.547 |
| 7 | 500 | 3 | 0:41:231 | 0:33:273 | 31.2298 | 28.0785 | 75.6483 | 57.1873 |
| 8 | 600 | 4 | 0:42:567 | 0:33:759 | 1.1660 | 1.1669 | 6.9622 | 6.9626 |
| 9 | 700 | 4 | 1:1:231 | 0:44:054 | 1.8407 | 1.8984 | 16.0862 | 16.1256 |
| 10 | 800 | 4 | 1:27:696 | 0:52:231 | 1.1892 | 1.0151 | 6.9029 | 5.9780 |

The results show that, our parallel algorithm reduce the time cost apparently without much loss of quality, sometimes even better! Because a fixed *Gran* is applied, when the input dataset is small in experiment No. 6, a partitioned solution space constrains the search result and the algorithm need more searches to find the optimal solution. So the PTS may cost more time in this condition.

**Scenario 3:** Based upon the computational results, we can also conclude that our algorithm has the capability of detecting the patterns embedded in a dataset. For the data

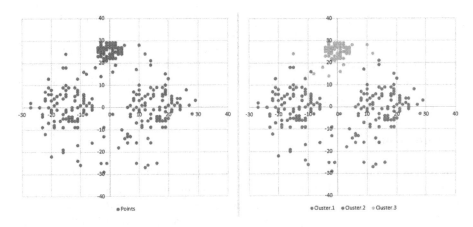

**Fig. 2.** Distribution of the data (left) and the clustering result (right)

in experiment No. 3 shown in Fig. 2 (left), the result depicted in the following picture Fig. 2 (right) confirms that our algorithm identifies the patterns properly in the dataset.

## 4.2 Scalability

This computational experiment employs the datasets based on a quantitative survey conducted on behalf of the Australian Charities and Not-for-profits Commission (ACNC) in 2013, publicly available online and maintained in [11]. And we slice the data into three problem size: 500, 1000, and 1500. The number of clusters is set to 7, $\alpha$ and $\beta$ is set to 0.6 and 0.4 respectively. For each size and configuration, the parallel algorithm has been tested with different numbers of processors. Figure 3 shows the

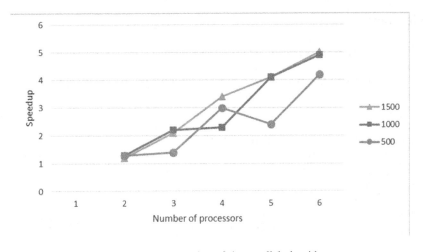

**Fig. 3.** Average speedup of the parallel algorithm

corresponding speedups, which are the ratios between the times required by the algorithm executed on one and p processors.

Because of the randomness and heuristic procedure, this algorithm is a nonlinear algorithm. So the speedup doesn't linearly increase with the number of processors increases. But the speedup still indicates this parallel tabu search algorithm is a useful and effective parallelism approach.

## 5   Conclusion

This paper presented an algorithm model based on tabu search for clustering problems. And a parallel tabu search algorithm for clustering problems is proposed and implemented on JVM. With a solution space partition, this algorithm can divide the solution space into several sub-space, which can speed up a search process apparently and lead to a much smaller neighborhood coordinated with the candidate list. Experiments on performance test show that this parallel approach can not only effectively reduce the time cost but also produce solution with high quality.

Limitation and future work:

- The solution space partition now is based on a greedy strategy with random selection method, which may not cover the global optimal solution. We can try to combine some advanced method to generate initial solution.
- The implementation of this parallel algorithm is based on multi-thread of JVM. A further study can lay emphasis upon some other parallel platform such as GPU based parallelism and Hadoop platform.

**Acknowledgments.** This research is partially supported by China Intelligent Urbanization Co-Creation Center for High Density Region (CIUC) under grant (No. 20140004).

## References

1. Jain, A.K., Murty, M.N., Flynn, P.J.: Data clustering: a review. ACM Comput. Surv. **31**(3), 264–323 (1999)
2. Han, J., Kamber, M.: Data Mining: Concepts and Techniques. Morgan Kaufmann, San Francisco (2011)
3. Vries, N.J., Reis, R., Moscato, P.: Clustering consumers based on trust, confidence and giving behaviour: data-driven model building for charitable involvement in the australian not-for-profit sector. PLoS ONE **10**(4), 1–28 (2015)
4. Hassan, D., Fahmy, H., Bahaa-ElDin, A.: RCA: efficient connected dominated clustering algorithm for mobile ad hoc networks. Comput. Netw. **2014**(75), 177–191 (2014)
5. Cao, B., Glover, F., Rego, C.: A tabu search algorithm for cohesive clustering problems. Jo. Heuristics **21**, 457–477 (2015)
6. Glover, F.: Tabu search-Part 1. Comput **1**, 190–200 (1989)
7. He, Y.: Research on tabu search with its parallelization. Chongqing China: Southwest University, IN, Chinese (2006)

8. Glover, F.: Tabu search: a tutorial. Pract. Math. Program. **20**(4), 74–94 (1990)
9. Linoff, G.S., Berry, M.J.: Data Mining Techniques, 3rd edn. Wiley Publishing Inc., Indianapolis (2011)
10. Fiechter, C.-N.: A parallel tabu search algorithm for large traveling salesman problems. Discrete Appl. Math. **51**, 243–267 (1992)
11. Office of the Australian Government. http://data.gov.au/dataset/trust-and-confidence

# Symmetric Game for Distributed Estimation in Energy Harvesting Wireless Sensor Networks with Selfish Sensors

Guiyun Liu[1(✉)], Jing Yao[1], Hongbin Chen[2], Han Zhang[3], and Dong Tang[1]

[1] School of Mechanical and Electric Engineering, Guangzhou University,
Guangzhou 510006, China
liugy@gzhu.edu.cn
[2] Key Laboratory of Cognitive Radio and Information Processing,
Guilin University of Electronic Technology, Ministry of Education,
Guilin 541004, China
[3] School of Physics and Telecommunications Engineering,
South China Normal University, Guangzhou 510006, China

**Abstract.** The power control problem for distributed estimation in energy-harvesting wireless sensor networks (EH-WSNs) poses a unique set of problems with the uncertain availability of resources. The fusion center (FC) usually is hard to predict the energy state of sensors that use ambient energy harvesting. Concerning the problem that existing decentralized power control schemes are not suitable in EH-WSHs, we propose a novel distributed symmetric game, which takes both energy harvesting and the characteristics of distributed estimation into account. And, each sensor makes decisions autonomously and is treated fairly. Then, some conclusions of Nash equilibriums (NEs) are introduced, and that can explain the trend observed in simulations. Finally, numerical results validate the effectiveness of the proposed symmetric game.

**Keywords:** Wireless sensor networks · Energy harvesting · Distributed estimation · Symmetric game

## 1 Introduction

It has been generally acknowledged that wireless sensor networks (WSNs) play a vital role in renovating our daily life style. WSNs have been used in lots of domain-specific applications, such as environmental monitoring, industrial monitoring, agriculture and home applications [1,2]. These applications have to adopt sophisticated data processing techniques and manage to achieve high-level tasks [3]. For example, WSNs are often deployed to monitor a toxic environment where toxic gases can not be smelled by humans. Within the WSNs, nodes measure the conditions of the toxic gases, aggregate, and transmit their observation values to a fusion center (FC). Meanwhile, because of the constrained resources (limited bandwidth, energy and computation capabilities), the above implementation is

© Springer International Publishing Switzerland 2015
G. Wang et al. (Eds.): ICA3PP 2015 Workshops, LNCS 9532, pp. 344–352, 2015.
DOI: 10.1007/978-3-319-27161-3_30

usually not a straightforward process and needs some necessary techniques. One of the important techniques is that nodes' observations are tactfully quantized before transmission [4]. The quantization becomes an integral part of the high-level estimation task.

Distributed estimation, as it is called, is to estimate a parameter of interest through a set of binary observations, as opposed to the straightforward estimation based on analog measurements. It is worth noting that distributed estimation is a general technology, which enables many potential applications, such as event detection, classification, and object tracking [5–8]. Previous work on distributed estimation for WSNs has been done in [4,6–8]. The distributed estimation problems under different topologies (the star, cluster-based and multihop topologies) for WSNs have been studied in [4,6–8]. When taking into account the strict bandwidth constraint, a general assumption of nodes with one-bit or $m$-bit quantizers is used. Meanwhile, techniques for optimizing the flow of quantized observations in WSNs also apply to deal with the energy-efficiency problem with small-size batteries, such as [9,10]. The proposed power optimization schemes of the data flow are obtained through solving Karush-Kuhn-Tucker (KKT) systems.

In this kind of applications, methods for deploying battery-operated wireless nodes pose a significant environmental risk with the disposal of large quantities of batteries. Meanwhile, the installation difficulty, maintenance cost and impossible replacement of batteries undermine these methods' technical advantages. Then the concept of energy harvesting comes in. Energy-harvesting technologies harvest energy from external sources, such as solar power, thermal energy, vibration, heat, and electromagnetic waves. It enables the realization of near perpetual WSNs and reduces the operation cost of WSNs [11]. After the method of energy harvesting is introduced, the technique of distributed estimation needs to be carefully redesigned subject to energy harvesting constraints.

For example, the distributed estimation in EH-WSNs has been analyzed [12] and its proposed utility maximization technique is effective based on the concave maximization method. However, it is assumed that the harvested energy is predictable. In [13], the maximum-likelihood estimator (MLE) is proposed to minimize total distortion subject to energy harvesting constraints and a particle-filtering based expectation-maximization (EM) algorithm is proposed to address the unknown nature of energy harvesting levels. Meanwhile, our prior work [14] considers a scenario in EH-WSNs, in which a extensive-form game of complete and perfect information is formulated. The extensive-form game proposes a novel distributed scheme instead of the former decentralized scheme [12]. It is noted that the game in [14] is extensive, which is suitable for the scenario of the adaptive distributed estimation [15].

In this paper, for the scenario of the fixed distributed estimation [9], we propose a simply symmetric game instead of the extensive game [14] to meet the given estimation performance requirement. Different from the decentralized method [12], our game-theoretic approach is distributed and each sensor makes decisions autonomously. It is noted that the scenario with digital forwarding schemes here is different from that with analog forwarding transmissions in [13]. And, the object is to obtain the equilibrium scheduling strategy, in which each sensor is treated fairly, instead of aiming for distortion minimization [13,16]. Our main contributions are shown as follows: (1) A symmetric game model for distributed estimation in EH-WSNs has been formulated; (2) Its strategy Nash equilibriums (NEs) have been proposed; (3) Some conclusions of NEs have been verified to be effective in simulations.

## 2 System Model

### 2.1 Distributed Estimation Problem

Let us consider a static WSN with $N$ sensors and a fusion center. This sensor network has been commonly used to observe a physical phenomenon (a scalar parameter), e.g., temperature and moisture of soil, toxicity of gas. The operation is known as distributed estimation. Due to stringent bandwidth and energy requirements imposed by sensors, distributed estimation is performed under the bandwidth constraint.

Let $x_t^k$, $t \in \mathbb{N}$, $k \in 1, ..., N$, denote the discrete-time noisy sample observed by the $k^{th}$ sensor at time $t$, given as

$$x_t^k = \theta + w_t^k, \tag{1}$$

where $\theta$ is a deterministic scalar parameter, and $w_t^k \sim N(0, \sigma^2)$ is a zero-mean additive white Gaussian noise (AWGN). Additionally, it is assumed that $\{w_t^k\}$ are independent and identically distributed (i.i.d.) across time, and independent and identically distributed across sensors.

It is assumed that the quantisation bit budget for each sensor is one bit per sample. Thus, we can generate a set of binary observations $\{b_t^k\}$ by

$$b_t^k = \begin{cases} 1, & x_t^k \in [\tau_k, +\infty), \\ 0, & \text{otherwise} \end{cases} \tag{2}$$

where $\tau_k$ is the quantisation threshold that determines the choice of binary observations $\{0, 1\}$. Without loss of generality, the same quantisation threshold $\tau$ is applied to all the sensors and all the time, i.e. $\tau_1 = \tau_2 = \cdots = \tau_N = \tau$. By assuming error-free communication among the FC and sensors, extensive related studies on distributed estimation problems have been introduced [9]. To obtain better estimation performance, the FC usually is required to have a priori knowledge of the sensors about the quantisation strategy and $w_t^k$.

The MLE and the CRLB can be obtained based on the set of binary samples $\{b_t^k\}$, given as

$$\hat{\theta}_{mle} = Q^{-1}(\frac{1}{N} \sum_{k=1}^{N} b_t^k) \tag{3}$$

and

$$CRLB(\theta) = \frac{1}{N} \frac{Q(\theta)(1 - Q(\theta))}{\dot{Q}(\theta)^2} \tag{4}$$

where $Q^{-1}(\cdot)$ denotes the inverse function of $Q(\cdot)$ and $\dot{Q}(\theta) = \frac{\partial Q(\theta)}{\partial \theta}$. It is noted that each $b_t^k$ is a Bernoulli random variable with parameter [4]

$$Q(\theta) := P_r(b_t^k = 1) = F(\tau - \theta) \qquad (5)$$

where $F(x)$ is the complementary cumulative distribution function of the zero mean, $\sigma^2$ variance Gaussian random variable $w(n)$. According to the formula (4), the CRLB varies inversely to its parameter $N$. Generally, the CRLB is improved if $N$ increases [4]. Thus, to meet the performance requirement, the minimum number of actual participating sensors $N_{min}$ is defined and $N_{min} \geq 1$. In other words, $N \geq N_{min}$ in (4) if the performance requirement is satisfied.

## 2.2 Energy Model

In this subsection, the energy model, including the energy income from energy harvesting and the energy usage in energy consumption, is discussed as shown in Fig. 1.

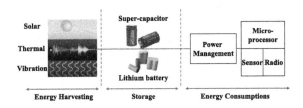

**Fig. 1.** The functional architecture of nodes in EH-WSN.

We consider static nodes equipped with solar-energy harvesters. The ideal capacitors are used to store the energy from solar-energy harvesters. It can store a limited amount of energy, does not have any inefficiency in charging and does not leak any energy over time. Meanwhile, the FC are powered by unconstrained power source.

Each day is considered as one cycle of the distributed estimation task. A typical solar model is adopted here. Each day is divided into $T$ slots. Let $\rho_{i,t}$ and $A_{i,t}$ denote the total amount of harvested energy and energy assumption for the sensor $i$ at slot $t$, $\{t = 1, 2, \cdots, T\}$. Let $B_{i,t}$ be the remaining energy of the sensor $i$ at slot $t$. Thus, $B_{i,t+1}$ can be depicted as

$$B_{i,t+1} = \max(B_{i,t} + \rho_{i,t} - A_{i,t}, 0) \qquad (6)$$

Meanwhile, for the sensor $i$ at slot $t$, $A_{i,t}$ should satisfy the following condition:

$$A_{i,t} \leq B_{i,t} + \rho_{i,t} \qquad (7)$$

It is noted that solar energy is dependent on sensors' solar cell size, its orientation to the sun, the temperature of the solar module, and seasonal characteristics, etc. It is assumed that the same amount of solar energy is harvested at any slot $t$ for all the sensor. We ignore the actual solar radiation deviation among sensors due to astronomical factors, such as the clouds. It is rational for a small-scale outdoor environment, because the sensors deployed in the WSN generally have almost the same solar radiation condition. Thus, for all the local sensor at slot $t$, we have

$$\rho_t = \rho_{1,t} = \rho_{2,t} = \cdots = \rho_{N,t} \tag{8}$$

The energy consumption for communication is only considered here. The radio hardware's energy dissipation is modeled as:

$$C_{i,t} = a \times E_{ele} \tag{9}$$

where $C_{i,t}$ and $a$ denote the energy dissipation for the sensor $i$ at slot $t$ and the number of bits, respectively. The electronics energy $E_{ele}$ denotes the energy consumption for transmitting one bit, including lots of factors such as modulation, coding, filtering, and spreading of signals.

It is assumed that all the sensors adopt the same power level of the transmission to guarantee the communication channels among sensors and the FC are error-free. Thus, the sensor's energy dissipation model is not associated with the distances between local sensors and the FC. Obviously, $a \in \{0, 1\}$. If the sensor $i$ at slot $t$ is scheduled to participate in the distributed estimation task, $a = 1$ and $A_{i,t} = C_{i,t} = E_{ele}$. Otherwise, $a = 0$ and $A_{i,t} = C_{i,t} = 0$.

## 2.3   Symmetrical Game Formulation

We formulate a symmetrical game to obtain the equilibrium scheduling strategy for the distributed estimation problem so that local nodes are satisfied with the given estimation performance.

The symmetrical game formulation for distributed estimation is as follows:

– Players: The players are selfish and rational sensors, the $N$ nodes participating in the estimation game. It is noted that only if any sensor $i$ at slot $t$ satisfies the condition (7), the sensor is one of the players. Thus, the number of the players changes over time. Note the number of all the players $N$ is required to be greater than or equal to 2, and is not the number of actual participating sensors (i.e., transmitting samples) in (4).
– Strategies: The pure strategy space includes two choices: transmitting its binary sample $b_t^k$ to the fusion center, denoted by the strategy 1 and not transmitting its sample, denoted by the strategy 0. Its strategy space is denoted as $S = \{1, 0\}$. Thus, it is noted that all players share the same available strategies. The vector profile of the players' strategies is denoted as $\mathbf{s} = \{s_1, s_2, \dots, s_N\}$ and $s_i \in S$ for the player $i$.
– Payoffs: Considering the performance requirement of the distributed estimation task, if $CRLB(\theta)$ in the formula (4) meets the requirement, the payoff for all the players adopting the strategy 1 is equal to $v - c$ and the payoff for all the players adopting the strategy 0 is equal to $v$. Otherwise, the payoff for

all the players adopting the strategy 1 is equal to $-c$ and the payoff for all the players adopting the strategy 0 is equal to 0. $v$ and $c$ denote the reward for successfully meeting the requirement and the cost of transmitting binary samples, respectively. It is assumed that $v$ is greater than $c$ and $c$ is positive. For example, the payoffs for the simple three-player distributed estimation game are shown in Fig. 2. Within the game, it is assumed that $CRLB(\theta)$ in the formula (4) meets the requirement if two of the three players choose the strategy 1. P1, P2 and P3 denotes the player 1, the player 2 and the player 3, respectively.

| P2＼P3 | 1 | 0 |
|---|---|---|
| 1 | (v−c, v−c, v−c) | (v−c, v−c, v) |
| 0 | (v−c, v, v−c) | (−c, 0, 0) |

P1=1

| P2＼P3 | 1 | 0 |
|---|---|---|
| 1 | (v, v−c, v−c) | (0, −c, 0) |
| 0 | (0, 0, −c) | (0, 0, 0) |

P1=0

**Fig. 2.** The payoffs for the simple three-player distributed estimation game.

The payoff function $U_{i,t}(\mathbf{s})$ for the player $i$ at slot $t$ is depicted as

$$U_{i,t}(\mathbf{s}) = \begin{cases} -c, & \text{if } s_{i,t} = 1 \text{ and } \sum_{i=1}^{N} s_{i,t} < N_{min}; \\ 0, & \text{if } s_{i,t} = 0 \text{ and } \sum_{i=1}^{N} s_{i,t} < N_{min}; \\ v - c, & \text{if } s_{i,t} = 1 \text{ and } \sum_{i=1}^{N} s_{i,t} \geq N_{min}; \\ v, & \text{if } s_{i,t} = 0 \text{ and } \sum_{i=1}^{N} s_{i,t} \geq N_{min}. \end{cases} \tag{10}$$

## 3   Solution Analysis: NEs

What actions will be chosen by the players in the symmetric game for distributed estimation? The choice is a Nash equilibrium (NE). It corresponds to a steady state $\mathbf{s}^*$ of the players' interaction with the property that no player $i$ can do better by choosing an action different from $\mathbf{s}_i^*$, given that every other player $j$ adheres to $\mathbf{s}_j^*$ [17].

In the following, some propositions of pure strategy NEs are introduced. These proofs are straightforward and omitted here.

**Proposition 1.** For the symmetric game for distributed estimation, the strategy $\mathbf{s}^* = \{1, 1, \ldots, 1\}$ is a NE if $N_{min} = N$, but not a NE if $N_{min} < N$.

**Proposition 2.** For the symmetric game for distributed estimation, the strategy $\mathbf{s}^* = \{s_i, s_{-i}\}$ with $s_i^* = 1$ and $s_{-i}^* = \mathbf{0}$ for every player $i$ is a NE, given that $N_{min} = 1$.

Moreover, another steady state in the symmetric game for distributed estimation is discussed. It is the stochastic instead of the purely deterministic state. In other words, it is assumed that the players are allowed to play mixed strategies. According to the above propositions, it is easily derived that there is at least a symmetric mixed strategy NE for the symmetric game for distributed estimation.

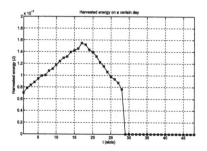

**Fig. 3.** Harvested energy on a certain day

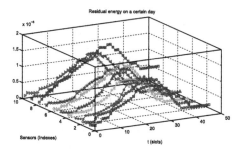

**Fig. 4.** Residual energy on a certain day

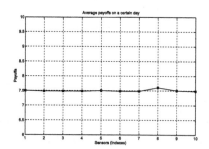

**Fig. 5.** Average payoffs on a certain day

## 4    Simulation Results

In the simulation, the EH-WSN with 10 selfish sensors are randomly deployed in a squared area of interest. Some energy parameters are set as $T = 48$, $E_{\text{elec}} = 100nJoules/bit$, the initial energy $\rho_{1,0} = \rho_{2,0} = \cdots = \rho_{10,0} = 10nJoules$, and $N_{min} = 6$. As shown in Fig. 3, the first slot $t = 1$ is defined from 5:00 to 5:30 AM and its level of harvested energy is low. Meanwhile, levels of harvested energy at the slots from $t = 14$ to $t = 21$ at noon are higher than that of previous and subsequent slots. It is noted that at night, the harvested energy is assumed to be $0 Joules$ for all the sensors. Additionally, the parameters of the symmetrical game are set as $v = 10$ and $c = 1$.

Considering the actual circumstances of the EH-WSN, according to the Eq. (7), the numbers of the players at slots are $\{0, 10, 10, 10, 10, 10, 10, 10,$ $10, 10, 10, 10, 10, 10, 10, 10, 10, 10, 10, 10, 10, 10, 10, 10, 10, 10, 10, 10, 10, 10,$ $10, 10, 10, 10, 10, 10, 10, 9, 7, 6, 4, 4, 4, 4, 4, 4, 4\}$. According to the Eq. (6), the residual energy of all the players is presented in Fig. 4. Clearly, the sensor 8 has more residual energy than others, while the residual energies of the rest other sensors are marginally the same. Additionally, the payoffs of all the players are shown in Fig. 5. It is noted that the payoff of the sensor 8 is higher than the other sensors, and the payoffs of the other sensors are the same.

## 5   Conclusions

In this paper, we focus on the communication and energy control problems for distributed estimation in EH-WSNs. A symmetric game is presented to solve the power control and communication problem for distributed estimation. Several propositions are proposed to determine the existence of NEs. Finally, simulation results show that the proposed symmetric game is efficient and all the selfish players are treated fairly.

**Acknowledgments.** This work was supported by National Natural Science Foundation, China (61403089, 61162008, 61002012, 61471176), Natural Science Foundation of Guangdong Province, China (S2013010016297), Foundation for Distinguished Young Talents in Higher Education of Guangdong, China (2013LYM_0068), Program for Guangzhou Municipal Colleges and Universities (1201431034), Guangdong Science & Technology Project (2013B0104) and Guangzhou Education Bureau Science and Technology Project (2012A082).

## References

1. Akyildiz, I., Su, W., Sankarsubramaniam, Y., Cayirci, E.: Wireless sensor networks: a survey. Comput. Netw. **38**, 393–422 (2012)
2. Alkhweldi, M.: Optimal observations transmission for distributed estimation under energy constraint. In: IEEE Symposium on Computational Intelligence for Communication Systems and Networks, pp. 1–6 (2014)
3. Guibas, L.J.: Sensing, tracking and reasoning with relations. IEEE Signal Process. Mag. **19**, 73–85 (2002)
4. Ribeiro, A., Giannakis, G.: Bandwidth-constrained distributed estimation for wireless sensor networks-Part I: gaussian case. IEEE Trans. Signal Process. **54**, 1131–1143 (2006)
5. Kumar, S., Zhao, F., Shepherd, D.: Collaborative signal and information processing in microsensor networks. IEEE Signal Process. Mag. **19**, 13–14 (2002)
6. Li, H., Fang, J.: Distributed adaptive quantization and estimation for wireless sensor networks. IEEE Signal Process. Lett. **14**, 669–672 (2007)

7. Liu, G., Xu, B., Chen, H.: Decentralized estimation over noisy channels in cluster-based wireless sensor networks. Int. J. Commun. Syst. **25**, 1313–1329 (2012)

8. Chen, H.: Performance-energy tradeoffs for decentralized estimation in a multihop sensor network. IEEE Sens. J. **10**, 1304–1310 (2010)

9. Xiao, J., Cui, S., Luo, Z., Goldsmith, A.: Power scheduling of universal decentralized estimation in sensor networks. IEEE Trans. Signal Process. **54**, 413–422 (2006)

10. Liu, G., Xu, B.: Energy-efficient scheduling of distributed estimation with convolutional coding and rate-compatible punctured convolutional coding. IET Commun. **5**, 1650–1660 (2011)

11. Tentzeris, M., Georgiadis, A., Roselli, L.: Energy harvesting and scavenging. Proc. IEEE **102**, 1644–1648 (2014)

12. Roseveare, N., Natarajan, B.: An alternative perspective on utility maximization in energy-harvesting wireless sensor networks. IEEE Trans. Veh. Technol. **63**, 344–356 (2014)

13. Hong Y.P.: Distributed estimation with analog forwarding in energy-harvesting wireless sensor networks. In: IEEE International Conference on Communication Systems, pp. 142–146 (2014)

14. Liu, H., Liu, G., Liu, Y., Mo, L., Chen, H.: Adaptive quantization for distributed estimation in energy-harvesting wireless sensor networks: a game-theoretic approach. Int. J. Distrib. Sens. Netw. **2014**, 1–9 (2014)

15. Liu, G., Xu, B., Chen, H., Zhang, C., Xiang, J., Zhou, C.: Adaptive quantization for distributed estimation in cluster-based wireless sensor networks. AEU - Int. J. Electron. Commun. **68**, 484–488 (2014)

16. Nourian, M., Dey, S., Ahlen, A.: Distortion minimization in multi-sensor estimation with energy harvesting. IEEE J. Sel. Areas Commun. **33**, 524–539 (2015). doi:10.1109/JSAC.2015.2391691

17. Drew, F., Jean, T.: Game Theory. MIT Press, Cambridge (1991)

# File Creation Optimization
# for Metadata-Intensive Application
# in File Systems

Limin Xiao[1,2], Qiaoling Zhong[1,2]($\boxtimes$), Zhisheng Huo[1,2], Ang Li[1,2], Li Ruan[1,2],
Kelong Liu[3], Yuanyuan Zang[3], and Zheqi Lu[3]

[1] State Key Laboratory of Software Development Environment,
Beihang University, Beijing, China
qiaoling.0605@163.com
[2] School of Computer Science and Engineering, Beihang University,
Beijing 100191, China
{xiaolm,ruanli}@buaa.edu.cn
[3] Space Star Technology Co., Ltd, Beijing 100086, China

**Abstract.** There are many steps among file creation, including creating
metadata files in metadata servers, creating data files in data servers, creating a directory entry and adding it in the parent directory. The above
steps are generic methods in distributed file system; however, it cannot
achieve good performance in the metadata-intensive application where
many clients create files at the same time, such as checkpointing, gene
biological computing, high energy physics experiments. In this article,
we present a method for file creation, called multi-stage file submission
for metadata, which is used to optimize file creation in the metadata-
intensive situation. This method is designed to make full use of the metadata servers' locality and decrease I/O operations. What we do is to make
some changes among file creation for metadata and metafile storage. The
procedure of file creation is based on Parallel Virtual File System version 2.8.2 (PVFS2) and we test the method in a simulation. The result
shows that the throughout reaches to 14.06 kops, contrast to the original
0.92 kops, in the situation of sixteen clients and eight metadata servers.
Of course, this method is used in metadata-intensive creation application.

**Keywords:** File system · File creation · Multi-stage file submission for
metadata · I/O locality · Throughout

## 1 Introduction

Nowadays demand for high I/O throughout for large scale storage system is con-
tinuing to be imperative [15]. Many previous researches focus on improving the
scale and performance on the data operations that read and write large amounts
of file data by striping data across many servers or disks [6,10]. Many distributed
file systems, such as PVFS2 [12], Lustre [10], Ceph [18], Hadoop Distributed File

© Springer International Publishing Switzerland 2015
G. Wang et al. (Eds.): ICA3PP 2015 Workshops, LNCS 9532, pp. 353–363, 2015.
DOI: 10.1007/978-3-319-27161-3_31

System (HDFS) [16], separate metadata from data and storage them on different servers, which are metadata servers and data servers. The operations of metadata are much more than data operation, such as file lookup, file creation and file search. There are many involved metadata operations among a file operation. Researches [7,8,14] show that metadata access and modification operation make up to about seventy percent of file system I/O operations. In large scale file system, we cannot get the expected performance through deploying more servers and adapting more sophisticated hardware for the metadata wall [1]. It's the key to make metadata effective accessed in the large file system.

The metadata access characteristic of scientific computing and business computing application is intensive. Checkpointing is indispensable fault tolerance tool, commonly used by high-throughput applications. Checkpoint is massively parallel application for thousands of computing nodes [3]. File creation is one kind of intensive-metadata access operation [13]. We must optimize file creation to meet the metadata-intensive situation.

In this article, we present our method to optimize file creation for metadata-intensive application, called multi-stage file submission for metadata. The rest of paper is the following. In Sect. 2, we analyze related work; In section Sect. 3, we present basic file creation procedure in distributed metadata file system. In Sect. 4, we would present our method to scale file creation performance, called multi-stage file creation, which would mainly contain file creation protocol and metadata storage method. In Sect. 5, we give our experiment result to give evidence of the performance. At last, we give our conclusion.

## 2   Releted Work

In distributed file system, file creation consists of interaction protocol and metadata storage. The file creation interaction protocol charges with the message passing or data flow between client and server in the procedure of file creation.

There are many steps to accomplish file creation, including creating data file, creating metadata file, and adding a directory entry in the parent directory. Devulapalli et al. [5] designed alternative method based on distributed metadata file creation protocol in PVFS2, which contains compound operation, handling selection strategies and leased handles, leading to decrease the interaction between metadata servers and data servers and hidden the delay of parallel operation. Carns et al. [4] also designed a method to avoid several clients to send many independent file creation requests to decrease overhead, which is based on collective communication protocol among servers, simplifying the file creation consistent problem and improving file creation performance. Yi et al. [20] proposed a new protocol, Cx, in which the affected servers Concurrently eXecute the sub-operations of a cross-server file operation, and respond immediately to a client. From the above descriptions, the current researches focus on eliminating metadata accessing bottleneck of single file creation. When multiple clients create files, they will contend system resources. This leads to locality miss and degrades performance.

When we talk about metadata storage, the current method is to optimize the data storage of metadata server to improve metadata write performance. Stender et al. [17] presented BabuDB, a database, which stores file system metadata relying on LSM-tree-like index structures, which offers better scalability and performance than equivalent ext4 and Berkeley DB-based metadata server implementations. Ali et al. [2] presented two metadata management schemes, both of which remove the need for a separate metadata server and replace it with object-based storage. All of above storage methods can be concluded to separate metadata and data for storage, leading the metadata access to be small I/O and discrete and influencing the metadata write performance.

In massive parallel file creation, the current file creation protocol cannot enough meet the locality in metadata-intensive situation, degrading write metadata performance, because of metadata access interleaving. The storage method of metadata separates different file metadata among different location. This makes the disk I/O scheduler choose the best storage location in massive file creation situation and issues many unordered metadata access requests.

## 3  Basic File Creation Protocol

Now we firstly introduce the architecture of distributed metadata file system, and then we give the detail of file creation of distributed file system. The following Fig. 1 shows the architecture of distributed metadata file system.

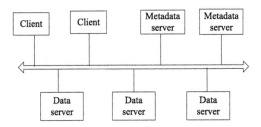

**Fig. 1.** Architecture of distributed file system

**Table 1.** Components of a file in distributed file system

| Entity | Description |
| --- | --- |
| Multiple data files | A large file consists of multiple data file |
| Metadata file | Owner, group, timestamp etc. |
| An entry in parent directory | Directory entry in parent directory |
| Additional attributes | A large file consists of multiple data file |

In distributed metadata file system, there are many components in a file, which is identified by a 64-bits long integer, called handle. Generally, a single file strips across several data servers and owns multiple entities on data servers and metadata servers. Table 1 shows components of a file in distributed metadata file system [12].

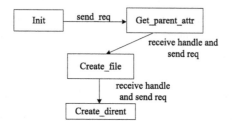

**Fig. 2.** File creation state machine on clients

In order to create a file, a client must get parent attribute to know the location of parent directory. A client can get the parent directory handle by lookup method, and then send a request to metadata servers to create a file. After creating a metafile, client sends request to metadata server and adds a directory entry in the parent directory. In the Fig. 2, we show the interaction between client and metadata servers.

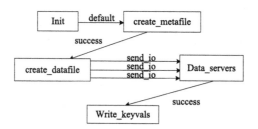

**Fig. 3.** File creation state machine on metadata servers

From the metadata server, if receiving a request from client, it starts to create a metafile and allocates a handle for this metafile. Then metadata server sends I/O requests to data servers to create data files for the metafile. At last, metadata server writes down the information of data files in the metafile (Fig. 3).

## 4    Design Alternatives

This section talks about our design method. There are several types of metadata access operation among file creation, including getting information of parent directory, file metadata creation, directory entry creation and adding it in parent directory. In massively parallel file creation situation, current file creation cannot take full advantage of the locality in the metadata servers, impacting the performance of metadata access. At the same time, there are many duplicated metadata access and discrete metadata operation. In order to obtain high performance, we must decrease duplicated metadata access and translate discrete metadata operation into serial metadata operation. Figure 4 shows the architecture of our method, called multi-stage file submission for metadata.

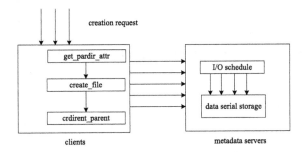

**Fig. 4.** Multi-stage file submission for metadata method

## 4.1 Client

In order to take advantage of the locality, we want to accommodate sub operations of file creation. The followings are the steps:

1. If a client sends a file creation request to server, a client must get enough information about the process to distinct different sub operation of file creation from different process.
2. In the client, we apply a monitor on file creation process, and then adjust file creation to adapt multi-stage file submission for metadata, separating file creation into multiple file creation sub operation. We set a timer on the sub operation queue, such as get_parentdir queue, create_file queue. Therefore, if a request is send from a client to servers, it would not be transmitted immediately, only after a time interval.
3. In the last, the processes in the clients add sub operation of file creation into the relative queue and wait the request to be completed.

Figure 5 shows how clients handle file creation. When a file creation request from a process send to metadata servers, it would be separated into several sub operations, which are added into relative queue, such as create_file queue, get_parentdir queue. In order to make use of the locality, we add a timer on the queue. After a time interval, a job request would be send to the metadata servers to get service. In this way, we expect to make use of the locality of metadata servers in massively parallel file creation application.

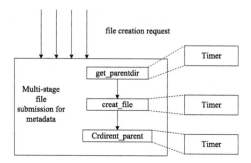

**Fig. 5.** Multi-stage files submission for metadata on clients

## 4.2 Metadata Servers

In the situation of metadata-intensive file creation, we adapt metadata I/O schedule algorithm and metadata storage to improve metadata write performance. The metadata I/O schedule algorithm is used to schedule the metadata I/O and aggregate the same directory file metadata creation requests into one request, and then only this one request would be send to underlying file system to complete file creation. The followings are the steps:

1. Based on the metadata request information, such as metadata file creation, metafile modification, etc., we build several queues about different metafile operation.
2. After receiving a metadata request from client, metadata server daemon process add it to the relative queue, such as creation queue. In our method, we add metafile creation requests in the same directory into the same creation queue.
3. On the metadata servers, we set a timer interval, which is as an aggregation time. At the expiration, the metafile creation requests are aggregated into one metafile creation request and send the underlying I/O operation.

Figures 6 and 7 show the procedure how metadata servers deal with file creation. Based on the metadata request information, we put metadata file creation request into creation queue and aggregate several file creation requests in the same directory into one file creation request after an aggregation time interval. In this way, we decrease the number of disk I/O, because the disk I/O is a key factor for improving performance.

## 5    Experiments and Results

In this section, we would present our experiment environment, including hardware, software and workload trace. After that, we present our result to get our expectation.

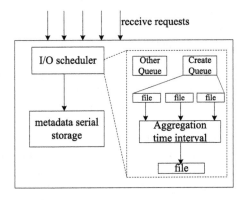

**Fig. 6.** Architecture of metadata servers on multi-stage files submission for metadata

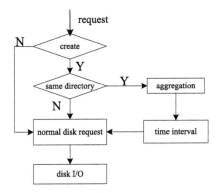

**Fig. 7.** Metadata servers file creation on multi-stages file submission for metadata

## 5.1 Experiment Environment

In our pass study, we has developed a simulation about distributed metadata file system, called DMFSsim [19], which is derived from PFSsim. PFSsim [9] is a simulation of PVFS2, which can effectively simulate the procedure of inter-action between clients and servers, including network simulation, and runs in the OMNet++, an open source simulation tool [11]. Because PFSsim cannot support multiple metadata servers, we have developed another simulation DMF-Ssim, which is proved to be high efficiency and useful. In our experiment, we use DMFSsim to test our method and represent the results. In DMFSsim, all the nodes are connected with a high speed network with the average latency of 0.2 ms and the bandwidth of 1 Gbps. We evaluated our design by running simulations on a server with AMD Quad-core processor, 8 GB RAM, and 1 TB Seagate 7200 RPM hardware driver.

## 5.2   Workload and Results

Because we want to prove our method would be effective, we take two steps to
verify our method.

Firstly, we show that only one client would run effectively after adapting this
method in distributed metadata file system. In the experiment, we simulate one
client and eight metadata servers. On the part of client, it runs a trace file to
simulate an application, which runs in distributed metadata file system. In this
simulation, we create a trace file, which stands for file creation workload in the
same directory and is created by a script. In the trace file, we suppose that a
client would create one thousand files continuously. At the same time, we set
several request intervals to make simulation more real.

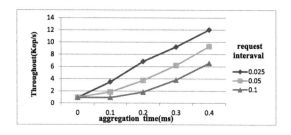

**Fig. 8.** Throughout for a client file creation

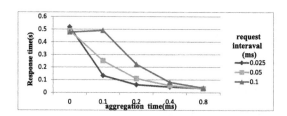

**Fig. 9.** Mean response time for a client file creation

The Figs. 8 and 9 show the file creation result for one client and eight metadata servers. From the above, if we handle file creation by the original method in
distributed metadata file system, the throughout is about 0.95 kops for different
request intervals. If a client send file creation by multi-stage file submission for
metadata and metadata servers aggregate several metadata files into one metadata file, the throughout increases. Increasing of aggregation time, the throughout increases. For example, if request interval is 0.1 ms and aggregation time is
0.4 ms, the throughout can get up to 6.57 kops, which about times six throughout of the original method. Even there are different request intervals, throughout
increases. The result shows that if there is less request interval, throughout can
get more improvement. At the same time, response time is important for client.

From the experiment result, it shows that the original response time is about 0.5 s. If request interval is 0.1 ms, the response time increases at first and then decreases with the aggregation time increasing. The response time can get up to 0.03 s when the aggregation time is 0.8 ms. Although there may be more time to pay on a file creation request, the mean response time can decrease for that metadata servers can take full advantage of the locality and decrease the number of I/O.

Secondly, in order to prove that we can scale to multiple clients, we simulate sixteen clients and eight metadata servers. In this situation, we also make every client create one thousand file in the same directory.

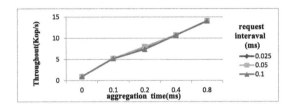

**Fig. 10.** Throughout for several clients files creation

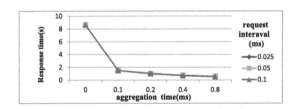

**Fig. 11.** Mean response time for several clients files creation

The Figs. 10 and 11 show the experiment result for sixteen clients and eight metadata servers. As expected, the throughout is about 0.92 kops in the old way. There will be an improvement for file creation by using multi-stage files submission for metadata method. No matter how long is the request interval, the throughout increases and even gets up to 14.06 kops with 0.8 ms aggregation time. At the same time, response time is also important for service. From the Fig. 11, the mean response time decreases. The mean response time is about 8.64 s when using the original method. By this method, the mean response time decreases to 0.52 s. Of course, we just test file creation operation for distributed metadata file system. The result shows that this method can scale to more clients, not only one client for distributed metadata servers.

## 6    Conclusion

In this paper, we firstly analyze the file creation protocol for distributed metadata file system, and then present our method, called multi-stage file submission for metadata. Of course, our method is just for intensive-metadata creation situation, which is more high performance. Because distributed metadata file system is more complex, we hope that this way could help distributed metadata file system design more useful for specific situation, especially for intensive-metadata creation.

**Acknowledgments.** The works described in this paper are supported by the fund of the State Key Laboratory of Software Development Environment under Grant No. SKLSDE-2014ZX-05, the National Natural Science Foundation of China under Grant No. 61370059 and No. 61232009, the Fundamental Research Funds for the Central Universities under Grant No.YWF-14-JSJXY-14, Beijing Natural Science Foundation under Grant No. 4122042, the Open Research Fund of The Academy of Satellite Application under grant NO. 2014-CXJJ-DSJ-04.

# References

1. Alam, S.R., El-Harake, H.N., Howard, K., Stringfellow, N., Verzelloni, F.: Parallel I/O and the metadata wall. In: Proceedings of the Sixth Workshop on Parallel Data Storage, pp. 13–18. ACM (2011)
2. Ali, N., Devulapalli, A., Dalessandro, D., Wyckoff, P., Sadayappan, P.: Revisiting the metadata architecture of parallel file systems. In: 3rd Petascale Data Storage Workshop, 2008. PDSW 2008, pp. 1–9. IEEE (2008)
3. Bent, J., Gibson, G., Grider, G., McClelland, B., Nowoczynski, P., Nunez, J., Polte, M., Wingate, M.: PLFS: a checkpoint filesystem for parallel applications. In: Proceedings of the Conference on High Performance Computing Networking, Storage and Analysis, p. 21. ACM (2009)
4. Carns, P.H., Settlemyer, B.W., Ligon III, W.B.: Using server-to-server communication in parallel file systems to simplify consistency and improve performance. In: Proceedings of the 2008 ACM/IEEE conference on Supercomputing, p. 6. IEEE Press (2008)
5. Devulapalli, A., Ohio, P.: File creation strategies in a distributed metadata file system. In: IEEE International Parallel and Distributed Processing Symposium, 2007, IPDPS 2007, pp. 1–10. IEEE (2007)
6. Ghemawat, S., Gobioff, H., Leung, S.T.: The google file system. ACM SIGOPS Oper. Syst. Rev. **37**, 29–43 (2003)
7. Gu, P., Wang, J., Zhu, Y., Jiang, H., Shang, P.: A novel weighted-graph-based grouping algorithm for metadata prefetching. IEEE Trans. Comput. **59**(1), 1–15 (2010)
8. Leung, A.W., Pasupathy, S., Goodson, G.R., Miller, E.L.: Measurement and analysis of large-scale network file system workloads. USENIX Ann. Tech. Conf. **1**(2), 5.2 (2008)
9. Liu, Y., Figueiredo, R., Clavijo, D., Xu, Y., Zhao, M.: Towards simulation of parallel file system scheduling algorithms with PFSSIM. In: Proceedings of the 7th IEEE International Workshop on Storage Network Architectures and Parallel I/O, May 2011
10. Lustre: Lustre. http://lustre.org/. Accessed 08 March 2015
11. OMNeT++: Omnet++ discrete event simulator - home. http://www.omnetpp.org/. Accessed 08 March 2015

12. ParallelVirtualFileSystemVersion2: Parallel virtual file system, version 2. http://www.pvfs.org/. Accessed 08 March 2015
13. Patil, S.V., Gibson, G.A., Lang, S., Polte, M.: Giga+: scalable directories for shared file systems. In: Proceedings of the 2nd International Workshop on Petascale Data Storage: Held in Conjunction with Supercomputing 2007, pp. 26–29. ACM (2007)
14. Roselli, D.S., Lorch, J.R., Anderson, T.E., et al.: A comparison of file system workloads. In: USENIX Annual Technical Conference, General Track, pp. 41–54 (2000)
15. Ross, R., Felix, E., Loewe, B., Ward, L., Nunez, J., Bent, J., Salmon, E., Grider, G.: High end computing revitalization task force (hecrtf), inter agency working group (heciwg) file systems and i/o research guidance workshop 2006 (2006)
16. Shvachko, K., Kuang, H., Radia, S., Chansler, R.: The hadoop distributed file system. In: 2010 IEEE 26th Symposium on Mass Storage Systems and Technologies (MSST), pp. 1–10. IEEE (2010)
17. Stender, J., Kolbeck, B., Hogqvist, M., Hupfeld, F.: BabuDB: fast and efficient file system metadata storage. In: 2010 International Workshop on Storage Network Architecture and Parallel I/Os (SNAPI), pp. 51–58. IEEE (2010)
18. Weil, S.A., Brandt, S.A., Miller, E.L., Long, D.D., Maltzahn, C.: Ceph: a scalable, high-performance distributed file system. In: Proceedings of the 7th Symposium on Operating Systems Design and Implementation, pp. 307–320. USENIX Association (2006)
19. Wu, Q.M., Xie, K., Zhu, M.F., Xiao, L.M., Ruan, L.: DMFSsim: a distributed metadata file system simulator. Trans. Tech. Publ. Appl. Mech. Mater. **241**, 1556–1561 (2013)
20. Yi, L., Shu, J., Ou, J., Zhao, Y.: Cx: concurrent execution for the cross-server operations in a distributed file system. In: 2012 IEEE International Conference on Cluster Computing (CLUSTER), pp. 99–107. IEEE (2012)

# A Sharing-Memory Based Ring Framework

Shicong Ma[✉], Baosheng Wang, Xianming Gao, and Xiaozhe Zhang

School of Computer, National University of Defense Technology,
Changsha 410073, China
msc91008@126.com

**Abstract.** A single-ring may become performance bottleneck for multi-consumer and multi-producer. Although multi-ring can solve above problems by allocating one ring for each task, it may decrease resource utilization. Thus, we put forward a sharing-memory based ring framework. It mainly consists of a series of small rings and a special mechanism: active-window. It uses active-window to translate task-speed into ring-speed, and to make ring-speed adapt to changes of task-speed by adjusting active-window, which can efficiently avoid performance bottleneck. At last, our experimental results show that big-ring is evidently better than single-ring at most times, and big-ring is better than multi-ring when task-speed exceeds one certain value.

**Keywords:** Multiple tasks · Single-ring · Multi-ring · Producer/consumer · Sharing-memory

## 1 Introduction

Software applications always adopt two ways to enhance their performance: first, applications are always divided into several sub-tasks, and these sub-tasks run together in pipeline with higher performance [1, 2]; second, applications has multiple copies of logical functions, and there copies run in parallel and independent [3–5]. Software applications can get high processing by using these above ways. Besides, tasks may communicate messages with others by using switching structure. Parts of tasks are regard as producers, which write messages into switching structure, and parts of tasks are regard as consumers, which are responsible for reading messages from switching structure. The switching structure mainly includes sharing-memory [6, 7] and crossbar [8] and so on. Software applications usually adopt sharing memory to achieve communication among tasks, instead using special hardware components. And ring is a typical sharing-memory, which is usually adopted in software system [9, 10]. For example, the switching structure between domain 0 and user domain uses ring to transmit messages.

Ring generally includes two types: single-ring and multi-ring. Single-ring only has one ring that including a large of storage units. And several tasks run in parallel and share the sole ring, in which they can write messages or read messages. Thus, single-ring may be adopted by developer when speed of each task is approximately equal. Multi-ring structure includes several rings, and each ring is allocated for one task. And each task only uses

G. Wang et al. (Eds.): ICA3PP 2015 Workshops, LNCS 9532, pp. 364–369, 2015.
DOI: 10.1007/978-3-319-27161-3_32

its ring to write or read messages. When each task varies in speed, developer should allocate a large of storage units for each ring. This way may result in low memory utilization.

Thus, we put forward a sharing-memory based ring. It includes a series of small rings, and each ring has a fixed of storage units, which is being occupied by sole task. Several tasks can write messages into it or read messages from it in parallel. And we introduce active-window to translate task-speed into ring-speed. And we prove that ring-speed can be dynamically adjusted by changing of active-window in processing of establishment of mathematic model. We further find that ring-interval can be used to adjust active-window. A dynamic adjustment mechanism of active-window is designed based on our mathematic model. At last, we make an experiment on three rings including single-ring, multi-ring, and big-ring, and further evaluate these three rings.

## 2  Related Works

It usually includes two types of ring structures adopted in multi-tasks including producers and consumers. Producers send messages to ring, and customers receive from ring. These two rings are single-ring and multi-ring as follows.

Several tasks equally share the same ring in single-ring. Several producers can write messages in parallel, and several customers can read messages in parallel. Each task has one ring used to write messages by producers and read messages by consumers, and each ring has a fixed ability in multi-ring.

Thus, we make lots of efforts to find a solution to ring structure for multi-task based on these two ring structures. We hope that several tasks should share the same ring, and differential speeds won't become performance bottleneck in our proposed scheme.

## 3  Big-Ring

### 3.1  System Overview

There are multiple tasks including a pair of one producer and one consumer, producer and consumer in one task need to communicate. So it's necessary to design a ring structure. However, current multi-ring including a series of rings to provide one ring for each task. Multi-ring may has a severe performance bottleneck when tasks vary in speed. Thus, we propose a new ring structure. It, compared with single-ring, also consists of multiple small rings, whose size is usually smaller than the size of rings in single-ring and in multi-ring. And it's different from multi-ring, because several tasks can share the same big-ring to complete write and read operations, as shown in Fig. 1.

It has two main features: first, it has a large of small rings; second, it has the conception of active-window to refer to available storage units in a single ring. They are presented as follows. There are a large numbers of rings, and each ring has a fixed amount of storage units that can be used by producers and consumers. Tasks write messages into one ring and read message from corresponding rings. However, each ring is being occupied by a single task. Namely, more than one task cannot share the same ring. If several tasks write messages into the same ring, some tasks have to stop their operations until

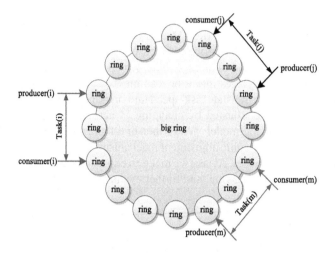

**Fig. 1.** Big-ring structure

there is free storage unit for them, which may make big-ring have more complex applications to solve above conflicts.

Except for a series of small rings, big-ring use active-window to solve conflict among tasks when speed of each task isn't the same. Active-window refers to available storage units for tasks, which is no higher than the size of a sing ring. For example, the size of ring is ten, and active-window is six, so tasks only use these six storage units to write or read messages, while the others are free. Besides, the maximum of active-window is equal to size of a single ring, and the minimum of active-window is one. When active-window is one, tasks just use one storage unit in one ring to write or read messages. At last, active-window is changing according to needs of each task.

Each task includes one producer and one consumer: producer is responsible for writing message into storage units in big-ring, and consumer aims to read messages from storage units in big-ring. Besides, each producer or consumer should use two pointers to point at storage unit in one ring. The two pointers are: (1) ring pointer, which refers to ring at which producer or consumer points, and (2) inter-ring pointer, which refers to storage unit at which producer or consumer points in one ring. Regardless of producers or consumers, they must use these two pointers to write or read messages. When one task continually writes messages, producer firstly writes messages in current ring until the amount of storage units occupied by messages in this ring exceeds a defined value, which is called as active-window.

From analysis of single-ring, tasks with the slowest speed are always performance bottleneck. Besides, task speed is always changing in processing of writing and reading messages, which also restricts overall performance of single-ring. Due to big-ring shared by several tasks, these two challenges also exist in big-ring: (1) task with slowest speed are usually performance bottleneck; (2) changing speed of each task may restrict overall performance. In big-ring, we mainly solve above two problems by using active-window. Active-window firstly translates task speed into ring-speed, so big-ring just solves tasks with slowest ring-speed. Besides, big-ring can adjust active-window to adapt to changing of task speed.

## 3.2   Ring-Speed

We use ring-speed to denote write/read speed of one task, which refers to how many rings producer (or consumer) can write (or read) in one second. It makes big-ring translate task-speed to ring-speed. Thus, we just find a solution to performance bottleneck that is resulted in by tasks with the slowest ring-speed.

Ring-speed is closely related with active-window. So it can change ring-speed by adjusting values of active-window. For example, if the actual task speed increases, big-ring can correspondingly increase values of active-window to keep ring-speed changeless; if the actual task speed decreases, it can keep ring-speed changeless by decreasing values of active-window. Thus, we can solve the first challenge by increasing or decreasing values of active-window. Big-ring can use active-window to keep ring-speed of each task changeless, so ring-speed of each task is approximately equal by adjusting active-window. Besides, active-window doesn't exceed the size of a single ring.

Ring-interval between two tasks, compared with interval between producer and consumer in one task, is related with one producer of one task and one consumer of one upstream task. When ring-interval is too high, the ring-speed of one task is lower than ring-speed of upstream task, and big-ring should try to reduce ring-interval to an appropriate value; otherwise, it may restricts speed of other downstream tasks. When ring-interval is too small, big-ring should increase ring-interval to an appropriate value; otherwise, it may restrict its speed, and reduce its producer speed.

## 3.3   Dynamic Adjustment Mechanism of Active-Window

Active-window determines how much storage units can be used to write and read messages, which can directly affect ring-speed of each task. So big-ring can dynamically adjust ring-speed by changing active-window. Besides, big-ring adjusts active-window based on ring-interval, which can finally control ring-speed of each task, as shown in Fig. 2.

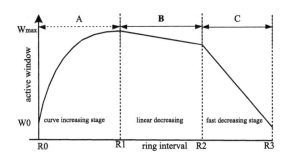

**Fig. 2.** Calculation function of active-window

It can be divided into three stages including curve increasing stage, fast decreasing stage and linear decreasing stage as follows. Curve increasing stage: when ring-interval is no higher than a definitive value, it continually increases with producer writing messages. Linear decreasing stage: when ring-interval is no higher than R3, and is higher than R2, it decreases with producer writing messages. Fast decreasing stage: when ring-interval is no higher than R2 and is higher than R1, it continually decreases with producer writing messages.

The calculation function of active-window is a core component, which directly ring-speed of each task. This calculation function includes three stages: curve increasing stage, fast decreasing stage and linear decreasing stage.

## 4    Experimental Results and Analysis

In this section, it aims to evaluate three rings including single-ring, multi-ring, and big-ring, and analyzes advantages and disadvantages of three rings, as shown in Fig. 3.

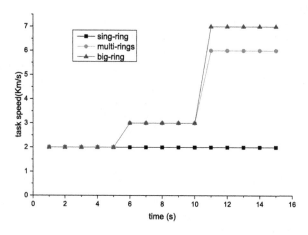

**Fig. 3.**    Task speed

From description of above experimental results, task speed in single-ring is only 2 km/s. So the performance of single-ring is determined by tasks with the slowest task speed. Task speed in multi-ring is equal to our wanted output during intervals between 0 s and 10 s; while the speed is only 6 km/s, which is slower than our input during intervals between 10 s and 15 s, because the maximum ability of a sing ring in multi-ring is only 6 km/s. Task speed in big-ring is totally equal to our input, because the maximum ability of is 12 km/s. Thus, big-ring is better than single-ring and multi-ring.

## 5    Conclusion and Future Works

Single-ring and multi-ring face with some challenges, such as performance bottleneck, and low memory-utilization. Thus, we propose a sharing-memory based ring framework, which allows multiple tasks to share the same big-ring in parallel. Besides, it can effectively solve performance bottleneck induced by tasks with the slowest speed and enhance overall performance. Our experimental results prove that dynamic adjustment mechanism of active-window can meet actual needs, and big-ring is better than the other rings including single-ring and multi-ring.

**Acknowledgments.** This work is supported by Program for National Basic Research Program of China (973 Program) 'Reconfigurable Network Emulation Testbed for Basic Network Communication', and research on XXX access authentication and authorization protocol standards.

# References

1. Kaashoek, F.: The click modular router. ACM Trans. Comput. Syst. **33**(5), 263–297 (2000)
2. Etsion, Y., Cabarcas, F., Rico, A., et al.: Task superscalar: an out-of-order task pipeline. In: Proceedings of the 2010 43rd Annual IEEE/ACM International Symposium on Microarchitecture, pp. 89–100. IEEE Computer Society Publications (2010)
3. Olivier, S.L., Prins, J.F.: Comparison of OpenMP 3.0 and other task parallel frameworks on unbalanced task graphs. Int. J. Parallel Program. **38**(5–6), 341–360 (2010)
4. Wang, B.: Task parallel scheduling over multi-core system. In: Jaatun, M.G., Zhao, G., Rong, C. (eds.) Cloud Computing. LNCS, vol. 5931, pp. 423–434. Springer, Heidelberg (2009)
5. Chakrabarti, S., Yelick, K., Demmel, J.: Models and scheduling algorithms for mixed data and task parallel programs. J. Parallel Distrib. Comput. **47**(2), 168–184 (1997)
6. Wu, J., Ding, L., Wang, Y., et al.: Identification and evaluation of sharing memory covert timing channel in Xen virtual machines. In: 2012 IEEE Fifth International Conference on Cloud Computing, pp. 283–291. IEEE (2011)
7. Li-Ping, M.A., Hai-Bo, G.E., Lei, O.Y.: A new design for multiprocessor parallel rapid communication based on sharing memory. Electron. Des. Eng. **7**, 020 (2011)
8. Krishna, P., Patel, N.S., Charny, A., et al.: On the speedup required for work-conserving crossbar switches. In: 1998 Sixth International Workshop on Quality of Service, (IWQoS 1998), pp. 225–234. IEEE (1998)
9. Lim, K.Y., Kumar, M., Das, S.K.: Message ring-based channel reallocation scheme for cellular networks. In: International Symposium on Parallel Architectures, Algorithms, and Networks, p. 426. IEEE Computer Society (1999)
10. Soundarabai, P.B., Thriveni, J., Manjunatha, H.C., Venugopal, K.R., Patnaik, L.M.: Message efficient ring leader election in distributed systems. In: Chaki, N., Meghanathan, N., Nagamalai, D. (eds.) Computer Networks and Communications (NetCom). LNEE, vol. 131, pp. 835–843. Springer, Heidelberg (2011)

# Streaming Computing Technology for Android Applications: Design Model and Case Study

Binji Mo[1], Yang Xu[1], and Guojun Wang[1,2(✉)]

[1] School of Information Science and Engineering,
Central South University, Changsha 410083, China
{csumbj,xuyangcsu}@csu.edu.cn, csgjwang@gmail.com
[2] School of Computer Science and Educational Software,
Guangzhou University, Guangzhou 510006, China

**Abstract.** Android is a mobile operating system released by Google on 2007, which has got strong support from major mobile phone manufacturers and became one of the most popular mobile operating systems quickly. However, the applications which increase explosively occupy a large amount of storage resources and make serious limitation on device's resources. Moreover, the frequent updating operation of the applications damages the user experience. We propose a new kind of mobile application model named Streaming Application Model based on the concept of Transparent Computing. By modularizing the ordinary application into some independent components and the devices load and launch the components dynamically, we can reduce the consumption of hardware resources and keep the users away from the complex and frequent application update processes, thus improving the user experience of Android devices.

**Keywords:** Transparent computing · Android · Streaming execution · Dynamic loading

## 1 Introduction

Benefiting from the strategy of open source and the strong ability of innovation, Android has become one of the most popular operating systems on mobile platform. While with the high-speed development of the mobile network, there are several shortages in Android system: Serious limitation in hardware resources, complex and frequent updating operation of the applications. With the explosive increase of mobile applications, it needs more and more storage resources to store the system and the applications which run on the system. Android doesn't provide incremental updating function for applications, it needs to download and reinstall the whole package when the application updates. In this paper we propose a new kind of mobile application model based the concept of "Transparent Computing (TC)". TC is a new kind of network computing concept: it separates the computing and storage resources by network and stores all the resources on the server. The Clients load and run the resources in the form of "stream" as they need [1–4]. This new kind of mobile application model is Streaming Application Model, the applications are modularized

G. Wang et al. (Eds.): ICA3PP 2015 Workshops, LNCS 9532, pp. 370–381, 2015.
DOI: 10.1007/978-3-319-27161-3_33

into some independent function components and stored on the server. Android device runs the application in a streaming way: the components of the applications are loaded and launched dynamically. Streaming Application Model can reduce the hardware resource consumption effectively, by modularizing a single Android application into independent components, the mobile devices can obtain the components dynamically as they need. Mobile devices automatically get the latest version of components after they are released to the server by developers and users don't need to update the application manually. Furthermore, mobile traffic is saved and the response speed of the Streaming Application is improved by a cache management mechanism which caches the high-frequency accessed components.

## 2  Related Work

There are three major kinds of application models for Android: Native App, Web App and Hybrid App. Native App, or local application, is the most popular application model which the executable file of the application is downloaded from App Store and ran in the local device. Native App owns the features of high image performance and offline running supporting, etc. But the explosive increase of mobile applications brings serious hardware resource limitation into the system, because it stored the whole package of the application on the device. Moreover, the complex and frequent application update process damage user experience. Web App bases on Web technology, it's applications are stored on the server in the form of Web pages, mobile devices parse and execute the application with the browser. But unlike traditional web page, Web App's interface and operation model fit on the phone's screen directly. The new generation of Web standard HTML5 brings several new features, such as multimedia supporting, Canvas, local storage. Making the applications which based on HTML5 can provide excellent user experience and some powerful features. But HTML5 is not used in the actual development on a large scale because of it's several serious security problems [5–7]. Hybrid App, namely mixed application, appears as a local application, but most of the internal logic components of it are implemented by Web technology. Hybrid App can call native API to complete the task while Web technology is insufficient. This kind of application is also known as Shell App, with a certain degree of cross-platform feature. The research on streaming computing technology in Android application layer is very limited. On PC operating systems such as Windows and Linux, the component technology and dynamic loading technology can use to realize the application streaming execution effectively, their technical scheme and theory can be a reference to the streaming execution technology in Android system. Component technology evolved from object-oriented technology, the so-called components are some reusable software units which developers can easily combine into a larger software program without considering the implementation details. It plays a very important role in improving the software reusability. There are three main kinds of standards in component technology: Microsoft's ActiveX/DCOM architecture, OMG's CORBA (Common Object Request Broker Architecture) and SUN's JavaBeans technology [10–14]. Dynamic Loading technique separates the code libraries from application. The target code is loaded from file system only when it was needed. The popular several kinds of technology which would be used to realize the runtime loading are: Dynamic Link Library (DLL) on Windows, the class loader mechanism provided by Java virtual machine. Embedding Web controls into the application is also another option, which writes the web page with dynamic Web page language such as JSP and PHP. But because of the inherent defects of Web standards, there are a number of problems in Web applications such as poor browsing experience, no offline running supporting and the limitation of local system function calls.

## 3    Streaming Application Model

### 3.1    Android System

Android is a mobile operating system based on the Linux kernel, was released by Google on November 5, 2007. Like many other operating systems, Android adopts the software stack architecture. As it is shown in Fig. 1, the Android system architecture is divided into four layers: Linux kernel, Libraries, Application framework and Applications. Android applications support modular programming. Each application consists of four types of components: Activity, Service, Content Provider and Broadcast Receiver. Activity is the main part of the application. Each Activity is a standard component, which provides specified function interface. The system initializes the Activity component and controls the life cycle of it by these interfaces.

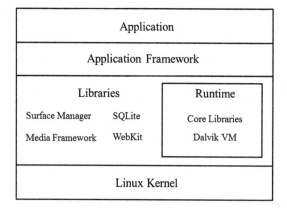

**Fig. 1.** Android system architecture.

Android system provides strict safety management mechanisms, mainly including: digital signature, security mechanism based on permissions and sandbox system. All of the installation package must be digitally signed when they are released. The digital signature is used to identify the application's developers and build the trust relationship between application and the system. Security mechanism based on permissions defines a set of system permissions to control the access for the system's key functions such as camera, location, internet, etc. Sandbox system requires the installation package (apk package) on the mobile device must be assigned with a unique Linux user ID (POSIX). Components of two different packages can't run in the same process. Each application runs in a single secure sandbox and can only get access to the resources of itself. The sandbox prevents other applications and the system from malicious application.

## 3.2 Streaming Application Model

In traditional application model just like Native App, the application is installed and launched on the local device. After development, the developer will pack the application into APK installation package and release to the app store. The users download the whole installation package from app store and install the package into device. Firstly, the system will verify the legitimacy of the package and only the legal application could be installed. Secondly, the system will copy the apk package into the system directory "/data/app", and create a new data directory for the application. Finally, the system will extract the dex file from the package and store it into the directory "/data/dalvik-cache". Because it needs to store the whole package on the local device, so the applications take up much of storage resources of Android devices. Streaming Application Model (SAM), which absorbs the thinking of "streaming execution" from Transparent Computing, modularizes the ordinary application into some independent components and stores them on the server. The android device will download the components from server and load them into the system only when it needs, thus executes the Android application dynamically in the form of "streaming block". SAM can reduce the storage resource consumption of android device effectively, by storing the applications in server and it is convenient for application updating. In another way, the application executes the executable file so it takes the full control of the device and plays higher performance of the device than Web App. SAM has the following features:

(1) **High performance:** As the same with the Native App, the Streaming Application execute local executable file and take the full control of hardware resource such as GPS, camera and so on. So it can provide better speed and performance, richer graphics and animation, and a better user experience than Web App.

(2) **Low consumption in storage resources:** Streaming Applications are stored on the server and downloaded by clients when they are needed and abandoned after use, would not reside on the device. That can remit the hardware resources limitation caused by the explosive growth of mobile applications.

(3) **Low cost in updating and deployment:** Streaming Applications don't need to be submitted to app store when deploying or updating. Users don't need to update them manually either. After the developers deployed the latest version of the applications to the server, user can always get access to them automatically.

(4) **New charging mode:** In the popular mobile environments such as Android and IOS platform, mobile applications are released through the App Store. A whole cost must be paid when the user first downloads the application, despite the frequency of utilization. SAM can achieve "on-demand fee" mode: user pay the

cost according to his demand of utilization, instead of paying the entire cost of the application at one time.

(5) **Higher security:** although android system provides a strict safety management mechanism, but still has place for the malicious software. For example, some malicious software injects malicious code into the application by decompilation, it's hard to distinguish them from original application. In SAM, the device runs the reliable components which are loaded from server dynamically.

# 4  Streaming Application Execution System

We design a Streaming Application Execution System to realize the Android application streaming execution, which is based on SAM. As is shown in Fig. 2, the system can be divided into the following three parts:

(1) **Client:** This system takes intelligent terminal equipment like Android mobile phone as client, which installs a lightweight SAEP and provides necessary interfaces for Streaming Application components. The clients get access to the remote servers and load certain components into local storage when needs them. Then it will hook up and launch the component with the execution platform according to the predetermined interface.

(2) **Network:** network connects the client and the server. Usually, the server is set up on the Internet and specified with an IP address and port number. Clients communicate with the server by accessing the server's IP address and port number after connecting to the Internet.

(3) **Server:** server is set up on the Internet to provide services for clients, such as user data maintaining, login validation and maintenance for the components and download service.

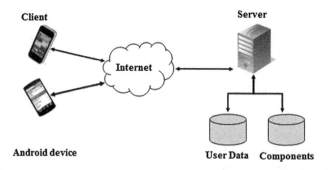

**Fig. 2.** Streaming application execution system.

## 4.1  Streaming Application Execution Platform

Base on Android programming model and the security mechanism, we build a Streaming Application Execution Platform (SAEP) within the Application layer of

Android system as client, to provide a running space for the components. The SAEP hooks up the components into the running space through the predetermined interface, and launches the application in the form of "stream". The modules of the client were shown in Fig. 3, the Application and Application Framework layer in the figure are Android System's original frameworks. The SAEP was built within Application layer to provide interface for upper Streaming Applications and lunches them dynamically after downloading. SAEP consists of three submodules: Downloading Module (DM), Cache Management Module (CMM) and Dynamic Loading Module (DLM). DM is responsible for download task of the platform. It can use a variety of file transfer protocols to download Streaming Applications components to the Android device. CMM is responsible for managing the Streaming Application files which were downloaded by the DM. Traditional cache replacement algorithm mainly use access frequency or the nearest access time of data blocks to determine whether they should be replaced, such as LRU and LFU algorithm. In our platform, LRU algorithm was used to manage the cache files. When the cached file reaches the expected maximum size, the least recently used data blocks would be replaced out of the cache. DLM is responsible for loading and launching the Streaming Application components dynamically. Android's code environment is Java, which is compiled to Java byte codes and then subsequently translated to different representation called dex files. When the component was launched in the platform, Dynamic Loading Module would read the Java byte codes and load the corresponding Java classes into the Java Virtual Machine with specific class loader provided by Android. The Java class loader is available from JDK1.0, which was used to read Java byte codes and load the corresponding Java classes into the Java Virtual Machine [8, 9].

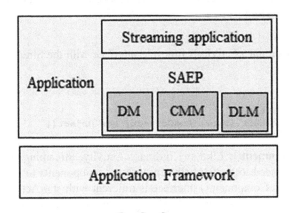

**Fig. 3.** Modules of client.

Figure 4 shows the process of launching a Streaming Application component on the platform: Firstly, the Downloading Module downloads the APK file of the component from server. Then a blank ContainerActivity component would be launched and passed some specific parameters. Finally, Dynamic Loading Module will load the Streaming Application into ContainerActivity with class loader and launch it.

The interface which the platform need to implement:

(1) **ContainerActivity:** ContainerActivity is a blank Activity, implements the LoadAPK() interface and lifecycle interface of the Activity. LoadAPK() interface is responsible for loading the Streaming Application component into ContainerActivity and launch it.

(2) **LoadAPK():** LoadAPK() is responsible for loading the corresponding streaming component class into ContainerActivity from the specified director:

```
LoadAPK:
  1. ClassLoader localClassLoader =
     ClassLoaer.getSystemClassLoader();
  2. DexClassLoader localDexClassLoader =
     new DexClassLoader(dexpath,dexoutputpath,
     null, localClassLoader);
  3. Class<?> localClass = localDexClassLoader.
     loadClass(activityname);
  4. Method localMethodSetActivity =
     localClass.getDeclaredMethod("setActivity",
     new Class[]{ Activity.class,
     Handler.class,Intent.class,String.class});
  5. Method method_onStart =
     localClass.getDeclaredMethod("onStart", new
     Class[]{});
```

Replace the ContainerActivity's lifecycle interface with the Streaming Application component:

```
onStart
  1. super.onStart();
  2. method_onStart.invoke(Loadobject, new Object[]
     {});
```

(3) **ChangeComponent():** Like any ordinary Activity, Streaming Application components also need to switch between different components to complete the execution. ChangeComponent() interface is different with startActivity() interface in the exsiting Android system, when a new component was started, the currently running component will be destroyed, no longer occupy system memory resources. And the new component runs in the environment of original component, so the system does not need to initialize running environment again for the new component. This kind of switching mode can significantly decrease the memory resource usage rate of mobile devices.

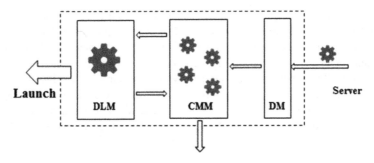

**Fig. 4.** The workflow of streaming application execution platform.

## 4.2 Streaming Application Component

Streaming Application components are some apk packages, each of them is a part of the application and perform specific task. The SAEP accomplish the execution of the application by loading the components into the running space one by one. The interface which the components need to implement:

(1) **SetActivity():** the first interface to be called when the component was launched, to pass some specific parameters such as Context, Intent and Handler into the component.
(2) **The Activity lifecycle interface:** As well as ordinary Activity, Streaming Application components also need to implement the lifecycle interface to complete the execution of the component.
(3) **LayoutCreate():** LayoutCreate() was used to create UI for the components. Ordinary Activity usually use XML layout files to create UI for the application, while Streaming Application components create UI with java code dynamically and efficiently.

## 4.3 Inter-module Communication

Streaming Application is composed of multiple components which are dynamically loaded into memory. Sometimes need to share data between these independent components and exchange information, this raises communication problem between components. In Android system, Intent is an effective tool for communication between the components within the same process. It describes the action, the operation data of the action and additional data of the application. Streaming Applications use Intend to transfer data and information between components. If the running component changes, an Intend would be passed into the new component, with some specific information and data.

## 4.4 Server

As shown in Fig. 5, the server is mainly responsible for providing service for the platform, such as handle the login request from client and components downloading. Users need to input the legitimate user name and password to login when they use the system. After the server receives the user's input, the information would be compared with the background database, only verified users can login the system. User will enter the SAEP after verification, and then he can select the desired components to load and launch them from the server dynamically. The clients communicate with server through HTTP communication protocol, which is one of the most widely used Internet network communication protocols. HTTP has features such as C/S mode, simple and quick, without connection status, etc. And we take Apache Tomcat as the server and MySQL as database.

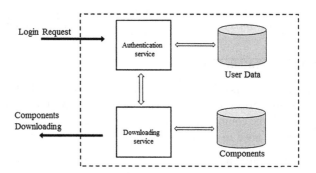

**Fig. 5.** Modules of server.

## 5   Experiment and Result Analysis

We develop a streaming health measurement system based on the Streaming Application Model, to provide services for measurements of a wide range of human physiological parameters such as blood pressure, blood oxygen, temperature, etc. The measurement functions of different physiological parameters are modularized into different components which were stored on the server as Streaming Application components. User can select measurement function component on-demand in the platform to load and launch them dynamically. The environment configuration of the system is as follows:

(1) **Client:** HUAWEI Y320-U01, Android 2.3.6, 3.64 GB in storage.
(2) **Network:** Wireless local area network, TL-WR842 N wireless router, the highest transmission rate is 300 Mbps.
(3) **Server:** ThinkPad T420, Intel i5 CPU, 4 GB in memory, Windows7 64 bit operation system.

Figure 6(a) is service selection page, Fig. 6(b) is blood pressure measurement page, Fig. 6(c) is blood oxygen measurement page. The workflow of the system: users enter the login page of client and input the correct user name and password to login, then connect the devices with the physiological parameters measurement front-end hardware and click on the icon to get access to the server for the latest version of the measurement component. After the measurement, the component will be abandoned automatically, instead of residing on the device to occupy the storage resources.

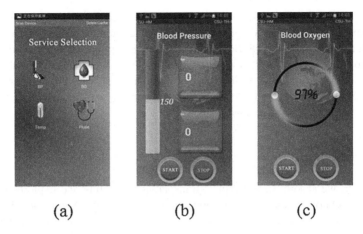

(a)                    (b)                    (c)

**Fig. 6.**  User interface of the streaming health measurement system

(1) **Startup time test:** In order to obtain the Android application startup time accurately, we launch the application with the ADB tools. The ADB (Android Debug Bridge) is a debugging tool provided by Android. Developers are able to manage the device or mobile phone simulator and execute shell command on the device with ADB tools. Through the Android shell commands we can start application and obtain startup time accurate to millisecond. Test result is shown in Table 1:

(2) **Storage usage test:** In order to verify the storage resource usage of Streaming Application Mode, we launch a certain number of Streaming Applications and ordinary applications to check the storage usage of each kind of application. The result of storage usage is shown in Table 2:

**Table 1.**  Result of startup time test.

|  | Average startup time of streaming application | Average startup time of ordinary application |
|---|---|---|
| First launch | 392 ms | 199 ms |
| Subsequent launch | 192 ms | 199 ms |

**Table 2.**  Result of storage usage test.

| Application numbers | 0 | 2 | 4 | 6 | 8 | 10 |
|---|---|---|---|---|---|---|
| Streaming application | 1.31 Mb | 1.31 Mb | 1.31 Mb | 1.31 Mb | 1.31 Mb | 1.31 Mb |
| Ordinary application | 0 Mb | 4.60 Mb | 9.22 Mb | 13.82 Mb | 18.32 Mb | 22.98 Mb |

The experiment has shown that the SAEP designed in this paper can effectively load and launch the Streaming Application component dynamically. Although component downloading would take some time, but the system can effectively reduce the download frequency of components with a caching mechanism, making the average startup time close to ordinary application. When a component needs to be updated, Users can automatically obtain the latest version of component if the component was released to the server, instead of update manually. As can be seen from Table 2, the storage resources of ordinary Android applications increase with the number linearly. While the SAM can launch a large number of components with smaller storage, reduce the occupancy rate of storage space effectively.

## 6    Conclusion

In this paper, we absorb the concept of transparent computing and explore streaming computing technology for Android application. A Streaming Application Execution Platform is developed and traditional Android application is divided into independent components which are stored on the server. Mobile devices load and launch the component dynamically with the SAEP and abandon them after execution. As a result, the limitation for the mobile device hardware can be reduced. Otherwise, mobile devices can automatically obtain and launch the latest version of Streaming Application components if the components on the server were updated. Tedious updating process was taken away for user. This system's cost is low but has a good user experience. In the future work, we will further optimize the interface of Streaming Application component, standardize the programming model, improve the execution efficiency for the platform and provide a better user experience.

**Acknowledgments.** This work is supported in part by the National Natural Science Foundation of China under Grant Numbers 61272151 and 61472451, the Joint Project of Central South University and Tencent under Grant Number 2014002H029, the Hunan Provincial Innovation Foundation for Postgraduate under grant number CX2015B047, the International Science & Technology Cooperation Program of China under Grant Number 2013DFB10070, the China Hunan Provincial Science & Technology Program under Grant Number 2012GK4106, and the "Mobile Health" Ministry of Education - China Mobile Joint Laboratory (MOE-DST No. [2012] 311).

## References

1. Zhang, Y., Zhou, Y.: Transparent computing: a new paradigm for pervasive computing. In: Ma, J., Jin, H., Yang, L.T., Tsai, J.J.-P. (eds.) UIC 2006. LNCS, vol. 4159, pp. 1–11. Springer, Heidelberg (2006)
2. Zhang, Y., Zhou, Y.: 4VP +: a novel meta OS approach for streaming programs in ubiquitous computing. In: Proceedings of the IEEE 21st International Conference on Advanced Information Networking and Applications (AINA 2007), Niagara Falls, Canada, pp. 394–403 (2007)
3. Yaoxue, Z., Zhou, Y.: Transparent computing: spatio-temporal extension on von neumann architecture for cloud services. Tsinghua Sci. Technol. **18**, 10–21 (2013)
4. Zhang, Y., Zhou, Y.: A cloud computing operating system TransOS: based on the design and implementation of transparent computing. Acta Electronica Sin. **39**(5), 985–990 (2011)

5. Andersson, K., Dan Johansson, J.: Mobile e-services using HTML5. In: Local Computer Networks Workshops, pp. 814–819 (2012)
6. Sun, S., Abbasi, A., Zhuge, J.: HTML 5 security research. Comput. Appl. Softw. **30**(03), 1–6 (2013)
7. Liu, H., Yang, G.: Research on HTML5-the next generation standard of Web development. Comput. Technol. Dev. **21**(08), 54–58 (2011)
8. Zuo, T., Zhu, Z., Hang, J.: The analysis of Java dynamic class loading. Comput. Sci. 32(04), 194–196 (2005)
9. Mariani, L., Pezzè, M.: A technique for verifying component-based software. Electron. Notes Theoret. Comput. Sci. **116**, 17–30 (2005)
10. Côté, D., StDenis, R.: Component-based method for the modeling and control of modular production systems. IEEE Trans. Control Syst. Technol. **21**, 1570–1585 (2013)
11. Li, Y., Yan, M.: The current situation and future of the software component technology. Comput. Eng. Appl. **39**(31), 86–93 (2003)
12. Sun, X., Zhuang, L., Liu, W.: An autonomous component customizable running support framework. J. Softw. **19**(06), 1340–1349 (2008)
13. Yan, M., Peng, X.: Permissions detection system based on Android security mechanism. Comput. Eng. Des. **3**, 22 (2013). Shanxi, Taiyuan University of Technology
14. Zhang, Y., Wang, K., Yang, H., Fang, Z., Wang, Z., Cao, C.: Android safety review. J. Comput. Res. Dev. **51**(7), 1385–1396 (2014)

# An Energy-Efficient Aggregation and Collection Algorithm for Heterogeneous Wireless Sensor Network

Lifang Liu[1], Xiaogang Qi[2(✉)], Gengzhong Zheng[3], and Mande Xie[4]

[1] School of Computer Science and Technology, Xidian University, Xi'an 710071, China
lfliu@xidian.edu.cn
[2] School of Mathematics and Statistics, Xidian University, Xi'an 710071, China
xgqi@xidian.edu.cn
[3] School of Computer Science and Engineering, Hanshan Normal University,
Chaozhou 521041, China
zgengz@126.com
[4] College of Computer and Information Engineering, Zhejiang Gongshang University,
Hangzhou 310018, China
mdxie@zjgsu.edu.cn

**Abstract.** This paper presents a virtual grid partition and optimal path selection-based data aggregation algorithm (GPOP). Virtual grid structure is a hierarchical network structure constructing based on the geographic location. Data aggregation is conducted in each virtual grid and aggregated packet is sent to base station through multi-hop path. When data forwards between two grids, the optimal transmission distance, the optimal transmission direction and the node residual energy is considered. Theoretical analysis and simulation results show that GPOP algorithm effectively reduces energy consumption of data forwarding to extend the network life time. Routing model also supports the data collection in heterogeneous wireless sensor networks and also meets a variety of test needs. In addition, a small part of Super Nodes arranged in the network can balance network load significantly.

**Keywords:** Wireless sensor networks (WSNs) · Virtual grid · Optimal routing path · Super nodes

## 1 Introduction

The fundamental task of wireless sensor networks is to gather data from all sensors to a distinguished SINK node [1]. In general, each intermediate node merges its received data with its own record according to some aggregation functions (e.g., taking the maximum or minimum of them) into a single packet with fixed size. This type of application is called data aggregation [2].

Early in 1970, Tobler's first law of geography was formulated to state that "Everything is related to everything else, but near things are more related than distant things" [3]. This statistical observation implies that data correlation increases with decreasing spatial separation. In WSNs, it is already noted that nearby sensor nodes monitoring an environmental feature (e.g., temperature or humidity) typically register similar values.

© Springer International Publishing Switzerland 2015
G. Wang et al. (Eds.): ICA3PP 2015 Workshops, LNCS 9532, pp. 382–392, 2015.
DOI: 10.1007/978-3-319-27161-3_34

This kind of data redundancy due to the spatial correlation between sensor observations inspires the research of in-network data aggregation.

In the in-network data aggregation process, according to the specific characteristics of the data, remove the redundancy of data and the amount of transmission data, which will significantly prolong the lifetime of the network. Clustering routing is suitable for data aggregation, because nodes in the same cluster with near space distance, monitoring data tend to have higher correlation. Cluster-based data aggregation protocol (such as LEACH [4], BCDCP [5], LEACH-M [6]) has aroused widespread concern. In these protocols, some nodes are selected as cluster head (CH). Cluster members send data to the cluster head which is responsible for data aggregation and then transmits aggregated data to the SINK node. However, cluster-based data aggregation protocol is also facing some challenges, such as cluster heads are unevenly distributed across the network, resulting network load is not balanced and the energy consumption of nodes with heavier load is fast, and this affects the network's lifetime.

Using geographic location information divided the network into single or multiple geographic grids, nodes according to the grid affiliation are organized into a certain group structure, on this basis, then the functions of the nodes are distinguished in order to achieve the hierarchical network structure and improve the performance of the network. The typical algorithms are GRID [7], GAF [8], EADA [9], the above three protocols are based on event-driven routing algorithm.

In this paper a data aggregation algorithm based on periodic data collection is proposed. In this algorithm, the network's coverage area is divided into many small square regions known as a grid. In each grid, selecting a node as the cluster head node and the other nodes are called ordinary nodes, thus balancing the cluster head distribution across the network. Ordinary nodes within the grids area are responsible for monitoring and reporting to the cluster head; cluster heads broadcast messages to the ordinary nodes, collect the monitoring data from ordinary nodes, and transmit aggregated data to SINK through multi-hop path. When select the next hop node, we consider the optimal transmission distance, the optimal transmission direction and the node residual energy. The GPOP algorithm has a wide range of applications, including industrial monitoring and control, environmental monitoring and precision agriculture, smart home furnishing, logistics management, military applications. For example, in a large substation, each transformer needs for real-time monitoring, so that each transformer can be regarded as a grid, arrangement of the sensors, the staff can monitor it beyond the distance. Each grid transmits aggregated packets to SINK node through multi-hop path, so the grid can be achieved in various different monitoring functions as needed, such as temperature, humidity, concentration. This routing protocol also supports for heterogeneous wireless sensor networks.

The main contributions of this paper are as follows:

(1) Using the grid partition method to divide wireless sensor networks into clusters, the algorithm will balance the distribution of cluster heads throughout network and satisfy a variety of practical monitoring needs.

(2) According to the energy consumption model [4], calculating the number of relay nodes arranged so that the total energy consumption is the minimum, while sending the information to a certain distance.

(3) Based on the optimal transmission distance, the optimal energy transfer direction and the remaining nodes, the next hop node is selected.

## 2   System Model

### 2.1   Relative Assumptions

(1) All nodes are no longer move after deployment;
(2) Nodes are divided into the common nodes and the super nodes, and all nodes cannot replenish their energy;
(3) Each node is equipped with GPS systems;
(4) Node communication radius is adjustable;
(5) SINK has two positions: at the network edge or at the network center.

### 2.2   Energy Consumption Model

Equations (1) and (2) are formulated the node to send messages and receive information of energy consumption model.

$$E_{Tx}(k,d) = E_{Tx-elec}(k) + E_{Tx-amp}(k,d)$$
$$E_{Tx}(k,d) = E_{elec} * k + \varepsilon_{amp} * k * d^2 \tag{1}$$

$$E_{Rx}(k) = E_{Rx-elec}(k)$$
$$E_{Rx}(k) = E_{elec} * k \tag{2}$$

where $E_{Tx}$ and $E_{Rx}$ express transmission circuit and receiver circuit energy consumption respectively. $\varepsilon_{amp}$ expresses energy consumption of space model amplifier. $k$ represents a data packet size. Using the parameters given in [4], we have

$$E_{Tx} = E_{Rx} = E_{elec} = 50\,nJ/bit, \quad \varepsilon_{amp} = 100\,pJ/bit/m^2$$

Taking the parameters into the formula (1), we have ($k$ takes 1)

$$E_{Tx}(1,d) = 50 \times 10^{-9} + 100 \times 10^{-12} d^2$$
$$= 5 \times 10^{-8} + 10^{-10} d^2 \tag{3}$$

Transmission distance of 1 bit data is $l$, when the relay node number is n (as shown in Fig. 1), the total transmission energy consumption E can be expressed as:

$$E = (n+1)E_{Tx} + nE_{Rx}$$
$$= (n+1)[E_{elec} + E_{amp}(\frac{l}{n+1})^2] + nE_{elec} \tag{4}$$
$$= (n+1) * 10^{-7} + 10^{-10} * l^2/(N+1)$$

**Fig. 1.** Data forwarding process.

From Eq. (4), to obtain the minimum total energy consumption $E$, $l$ and $n$ must satisfy $10^3 = (l/(n + 1))^2$, that is, when distance between nodes $d = l/(n + 1) = 31.6$, Energy utilization rate is relatively high, this distance can be used as the reference value of grid size.

## 2.3 Heterogeneity

Suppose the network is divided into $k \times k$ grids, SINK is arranged on the right side of the network as shown in Fig. 2. Aggregated data in the grids is sent to the SINK through relay nodes. For example, the sensing data of nodes in the first column will be aggregated into $k$ packets in each grid and these $k$ packets are sent to SINK through cluster head. Data in the respective sensing nodes within the grid aggregated total of $k$ packets passing through the cluster head to the SINK. Thus, nodes in second column will assume $k$ data packets forwarding task of nodes in first column, and so on, nodes in third column will assume $2k$ data packets forwarding task of nodes in the first two columns. Nodes in $k$th column will assume $(k - 1)k$ data packets forwarding task of nodes in the first $k$ column. So arranging some high-energy nodes in grids near SINK to balance load and prolong the network life time.

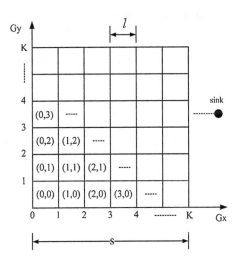

**Fig. 2.** Grid-based network model.

# 3    GPOP Protocol

## 3.1    Related Definitions

**Definition 1:**  Round is defined as the process of all nodes collect data one time and send to SINK.

**Definition 2:**  Network lifetime is defined as the lifetime of the first death node.

**Definition 3:**  Grid coordinates is defined as the logic coordinates of the virtual grid shown in Fig. 3, using a two topple to represent.

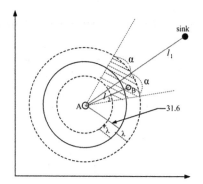

**Fig. 3.**    Relay node selection area of node A.

**Definition 4:**  $S_{candidate}$ is defined as the set of candidate relay nodes. Node in $S_{candidate}$ is responsible for forwarding packets to SINK to select the next hop node in this set.

**Definition 5:**  Super Node is defined as high energy node whose energy is twice times as large as ordinary node.

## 3.2    Algorithm Design

Suppose N nodes are randomly arranged in the $L * L$ square area, first the network is divided into $K * K$ grids, each grid can be regarded as a cluster. SINK node is arranged at the right side of the network as shown in Fig. 3. When the network layout is completed, SINK broadcasts its GPS location information, network coverage and grid side length $d = L/K$ to the whole network. When nodes receive the message, they will calculate their ownership of the grid coordinates (GX, GY) according to their GPS information (x, y).

$$\begin{cases} GX = \lfloor x/d \rfloor \\ GY = \lfloor y/d \rfloor \end{cases} \tag{5}$$

Before each round of algorithm iteration, each node need to determine its optimal next hop relay node set $S_{candidate}$. From Eq. (4), when the distance between nodes

$d = 31.6$, energy efficiency is the highest. Suppose the coordinate of node A is $(x_A, y_A)$, the coordinate of SINK is $(x_0, y_0)$, if node B $(x_B, y_B)$ becomes a candidate relay node of A, it should meet the following three conditions (as shaded area shown in Fig. 3).

- The Euclidean distance between node A and B should meet $d \in (30 - \lambda, 30 + \lambda)$, where $\lambda$ is the parameter.
- The angle between A → B (connection between A and B) and A → SINK should be less than $\alpha$, where $\alpha$ is the parameter.
- The distance between A and SINK should be less than the distance between B and SINK.

The slope of line between node A and SINK $k_1 = (x_A - x_0)/(y_A - y_0)$, The slope of line between node A and node B $k_2 = (x_A - x_B)/(y_A - y_B)$, so if B becomes candidate relay node of A, it should meet Eq. (6):

$$
\begin{cases}
30 - \lambda \le \sqrt{(x_A - x_B)^2 + (y_A - y_B)^2} \le 30 + \lambda \\
\left| \frac{k_1 - k_2}{1 + k_1 k_2} \right| \le \tan \alpha \\
\sqrt{(x_A - x_0)^2 + (y_A - y_0)^2} \le \sqrt{(x_B - x_0)^2 + (y_B - y_0)^2}
\end{cases} \tag{6}
$$

All the nodes satisfy the above conditions will be elected as candidate relay nodes of A, stored in $S_{candidate}$.

### 3.3   Algorithm Description

First, our proposed algorithm can the size of grids according to the actual needs. The network is divided into $K * K$ grids. Each grid selects cluster head according to the residual energy of the nodes. Each node within the grid starts to collect data and sends packet to the cluster head, cluster head conduct data aggregation, multiple data packets are aggregated into one.

After aggregating process of data is completed in each grid, cluster heads send the packets to SINK through multi-hop. Each node in its own set of candidate relay nodes $S_{candidate}$ selects one node with the largest residual energy as the next-hop node. There are two points to note. First, energy of SINK is assumed to be infinite, if the $S_{candidate}$ of a node has SINK, then the node sends packet directly to SINK. Second, if the $S_{candidate}$ of a node is an empty set, then this node adjusts its transmission power of and directly send packet to SINK.

## 4   Simulation and Experimental Performance Analysis

Our simulation environment is square area, the side length of which is 200 m. Simple averaging method adapts for data aggregation algorithm. The SINK node has center location of the network and edge location of the network respectively. No special instruction, we choose that value of parameter $\lambda$ and $\alpha$ are 12 and 20 respectively. Simulation parameter is the following Table 1.

**Table 1.** simulation parameters

| Parameter | Value |
|---|---|
| Length | 200 m |
| Node number | 300, 400 |
| Grid number | 9, 16, 25, 36 |
| BS position | (220, 100), (100, 100) |
| $E_{elec}(nJ/b)$ | 50 |
| $e_{fs}(pJ/b/m^2)$ | 100 |
| $E_{da}(nJ/b/m^2)$ | 5 |
| Data packet size (bits) | 1000 |
| Initial energy (J) | 2(4) |
| $\lambda$ | 8, 10, 12, 14, 16 |

## 4.1 Comparison and Analysis of Simulation Results

Figure 4(a) shows the number of different girds have impact on the lifetime of the network. When the network is divided into $3 \times 3$ grid, although the entire network in each round produce only nine aggregated data packets, cluster head makes a lot of data aggregation and ordinary nodes consume a large amount of energy by a long distance data transmission, which will result in short lifetime. When the network is divided into a greater number of grid, for instance, a $6 \times 6$ grid, in each round of data transmission across the network, a large number of aggregated data will produced, which will increase load of the node nearby the SINK node and not conducive to balance the load across the network. The blue histogram in Fig. 5 represents the network layout 300 nodes, while the red histogram represents the network layout 400 nodes. When the node density is higher, the number of candidate relay node will increase, the node may choose a path of small energy consumption in order to prolong lifetime of the network. Figure 6 shows lifetime of the network when the SINK node is located at the edge of the network. The lifetime decrease compared with Fig. 4(b), but the variation trend is similar to Fig. 4(a) in influence of the number of grids and node density. Form the above analysis, when nodes are deployed in $200 \times 200$ square region, and the entire network is divided into $4 \times 4$ grid, the lifetime is the longest.

The simulation results show that, the death of the nodes nearby SINK was significantly fast, which proved the network heterogeneous analysis. In the network, we arrange some high energy nodes close to the SINK, which can balance the network load and prolong the network life time. Table 2 demonstrates that, we arrange some Super Nodes in several grids near SINK, when the SINK is located in the edge of the network (220, 100). We should also ensure Super Nodes with a small number (accounted for about 10 % of the total number of nodes). For example, for grid number is 4 * 4 network,

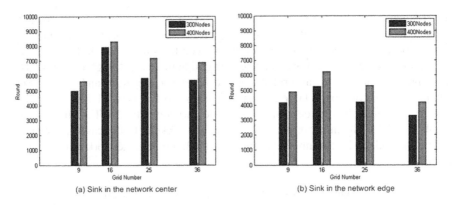

**Fig. 4.** The lifetime of the network with different number of grids.

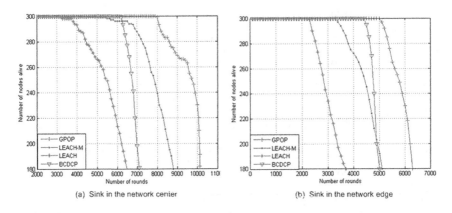

**Fig. 5.** The number of alive nodes change by rounds.

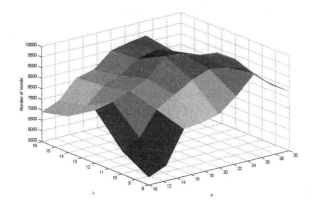

**Fig. 6.** Parameters α and λ influenceon the network life time.

we arrange nodes with initial energy 4 J in the grid coordinates (3, 1) and (3, 2). As you can see from Table 2, the network life time was improved significantly after decorate

Super Nodes. In Table 3, SINK is in network center. We arrange Super Nodes in the circular area with SINK as the center and of radius 40. Thus ensuring the number of Super Nodes account for about 1/8. As can be seen from the Table 3, the life time of network is also improved. However, when the grid number is 3 * 3, grid scale is larger, the number of nodes in one grid is overmuch, data aggregation and long distance communication consume a large amount of energy. So that network life time did not improve significantly after decorate Super nodes, wherever the SINK. When the Grid number is 6 * 6, the network produces more data packets. In the case of Table 1, if decorating nodes with the initial energy of 6 J, the life time of network can reach 9700 rounds.

**Table 2.** SINK at the network edge ($\lambda = 12, \alpha = 20$)

| Grid number | No super node (rounds) | Super node (rounds) | Improvement |
|---|---|---|---|
| 3 * 3 | **4180** | **5400** | 29.2 % |
| 4 * 4 | **5230** | **9140** | 74.8 % |
| 5 * 5 | **4200** | **8800** | 109.5 % |
| 6 * 6 | 3300 | 6500 | 97.0 % |

**Table 3.** SINK in the network center ($\lambda = 12, \alpha = 20$)

| Grid number | No super node (rounds) | Super node (rounds) | Improvement |
|---|---|---|---|
| 3 * 3 | **5000** | **5900** | 18.0 % |
| 4 * 4 | **7910** | **9780** | 23.6 % |
| 5 * 5 | **5840** | **10800** | 84.9 % |
| 6 * 6 | 5680 | 10400 | 83.1 % |

Figure 5(a) shows that the four algorithms' number of alive nodes changes by rounds. When the death number of nodes among the total numbers' 40 %, the simulation ends (where the GPOP algorithm $\lambda = 12, \alpha = 20$, grid number is 4 * 4). In Fig. 5(a), SINK is located at the center of the network. The life time of GPOP algorithm is much longer than other three algorithms. A comparison of GPOP performance to that of LEACH,LEACH-M and BCDCP shows that GPOP each provides improvements of up to 140 %, 70 % and 30 % in lifetime. That is because our proposed algorithm is based on mesh, which balanced the cluster size and cluster head distribution across the network. Forwarding data among the grids, we consider the optimal transmission path and the node residual energy. The death rate of GPOP node slows down gradually at first and then increases. This is because nodes near SINK assume the heavy task of forwarding packets, when a large number of nodes near SINK are dead, and nodes a little far away from SINK have to send packets by one hop. Long distance communication makes the dead speed of nodes increase rapidly. In Fig. 5(b), SINK is located at the edge of the network.

Figure 6 shows the influence of lifetime on parameter $\alpha$ and $\lambda$ (The SINK node is located at center of the network with supper energy). The smaller the value of parameter $\alpha$, the fewer element quantity of candidate set $S_{candidate}$ of each node is, which leads to frequently use the same node to transmit data and energy of this node will quickly pass away. However, the value of parameter $\alpha$ is larger, the lifetime of the network is longer, but when the lifetime increase to certain extent, forwarding data direction will change and then energy consumption will obviously increase, which leads to reduce lifetime. Performance of the network is the best when the value of parameter $\alpha$ and $\lambda$ are 12 and 20 respectively.

## 5  Conclusions

This paper presents a virtual grid partition and optimal path selection-based data aggregation algorithm (GPOP) for heterogeneous wireless sensor network. In our scheme, the network is divided into virtual grids, and each grid selects a cluster head by balancing cluster heads distribution across the network. By transmitting data between the grids considering the optimal transmission distance, the optimal transmission direction and the node residual energy, the energy consumption of data forwarding process is conserved. Simulation results show that, GPOP algorithm is superior to other clustering algorithms and significantly extends the network life time.

**Acknowledgments.** This work is partially supported by the Project of National Natural Science Foundation of China under Grants No. 71271165, 61373174 and 61572435, the Key Project of Natural Science Foundation of Shaanxi Province under Grants No. 2015JZ002 and 2015JM6311, the Project of the Guangxi Key Laboratory of Trusted Software under Grants No. kx201416, the Project of the High Level Talents in Colleges of Guangdong Province (Guangdong Finance Education [2013] No. 246), the Project of the Natural Science Foundation of Guangdong Province under Grants No. 2014A030307014, and the Central University Basic Scientific Research Funding (JB140712).

## References

1. Jiang, H., Jin, S., Wang, C.: Parameter-based data aggregation for statistical information extraction in wireless sensor networks. IEEE Trans. Veh. Technol. **59**(8), 3992–4001 (2010)
2. Bagaa, M., Challal, Y., Ksentini, A., Derhab, A., Badache, N.: Data aggregation scheduling algorithms in wireless sensor networks: solutions and challenges. IEEE Commun. Surv. Tutorials **16**(3), 1339–1368 (2014)
3. Tobler, W.R.: A computer movie simulating urban growth in the Detroit region. Econ. Geogr. **46**(2), 234–240 (1970)
4. Heinzelman, W., Chandrakasan, A., Balakrishnan, H.: Energy-efficient communication protocol for wireless microsensor networks. In: IEEE Proceedings of the Hawaii International Conference on System Science. Washington, pp. 300–304. IEEE Press (2000)
5. Muruganathan, S.D., Ma, D.C.F., Bhasin, R.I., et al.: A centralized energy-efficient routing protocol for wireless sensor networks. IEEE Radio Commun. **43**(3), 8–13 (2005)

6. Edward, J.: An energy efficient hierarchical clustering algorithm for wireless sensor network. In: Proceedings of the IEEE Wireless Communications and Networking Conference, pp. 1–8 (2003)

7. Liao, W.H., Tseng, Y.C., Sheu, A.P.: GRID: a fully location-aware routing protocol for mobile ad hoc networks. J. Telecommun. Syst. **18**(1), 37–60 (2001)

8. Xu, Y., Heidemann, J., Estrin, D.: Geography-informed energy conservation for ad hoc routing. In: Proceedings of the Seventh Annual ACM/IEEE International Conference on Mobile Computing and Networking (MobiComm), Rome, Italy, pp. 70–84 (2001)

9. Wang, N.C., Yeh, P.C., Huang, Y.F.: An energy-aware data aggregation scheme for grid-based wireless sensor networks. In: Proceedings of the 2007 International Conference on Wireless Communications and Mobile Computing, Honolulu, Hawaii, USA, pp. 87–492, 12–16 August 2007

# TDD-Based Massive MIMO Systems: Overview and Development

Ronghua Shi[1], Kun Tang[1], Jian Dong[1(✉)], Wentai Lei[1], Chunhua Peng[1], and Yunxiang Jiang[2]

[1] School of Information Science and Engineering, Central South University, Changsha 410083, China
{ShiRH,tangkun0213,dongjian,leiwentai,pengchunhua}@csu.edu.com
[2] Department of Electronic and Information Engineering, The Hong Kong Polytechnic University, Kowloon, Hong Kong
yunxiang.jiang@connect.polyu.hk

**Abstract.** With the increasing demands for high-speed data transmission and quality of service (QoS), massive multi-input multi-output (MIMO) is considered as a promising technology for next generation of mobile communications. This paper presents a comprehensive introduction of TDD-Based massive MIMO in the following three areas. The system models are analyzed firstly based on widely used multi-user massive MIMO networks. Then, the transceiver design of massive MIMO system is addressed, which includes the estimation of channel state information (CSI), signal detection and precoding schemes. At last, the detriment of pilot contamination and relative solutions are emphatically analyzed.

**Keywords:** Massive MIMO · Channel estimation · Signal detection · Precoding · Time-Division Duplexing (TDD) · Pilot contamination

## 1 Introduction

With the sustainable development of communication technologies, the traditional cellular mobile communication systems based on voice transmission are being replaced by high-speed Internet access broadband multi-media technologies. Higher channel capacity demands for the future wireless communications due to the scale of the network society will bring an exploding of mobile data traffic [1].

In order to achieve dramatic gains to solve above issues, the authors in [2, 3] propose massive MIMO systems for building a long-term network society. The massive MIMO systems deploy an antenna array at the base station (BS) which consists of a large number of antennas over active ten of terminals per unit area [4]. The massive MIMO systems have two basic advantages. The one is the channel vectors between the BS and terminals are asymptotically orthogonal. As a result, utilizing a simple linear processing at the BS, the unrelated thermal noise and fast fading can be eliminated. The other potential benefit is improvable spectral and energy efficiencies than conventional MIMO techniques.

Nevertheless, the massive MIMO systems have some drawbacks under certain circumstances. Pilot contamination would limit the performance of large array by

G. Wang et al. (Eds.): ICA3PP 2015 Workshops, LNCS 9532, pp. 393–402, 2015.
DOI: 10.1007/978-3-319-27161-3_35

reusing some pilot sequences in neighbor cells. The number of antennas cannot be arbitrary large due to the limited size of array and the influences from spatial correlation and mutual coupling.

Furthermore, the FDD mode is infeasible as the number of antennas at the BS goes to infinity because the time required to transmit the downlink pilot symbols is proportional and there is not enough coherence interval for data transmission [5, 6]. Hence, the massive MIMO systems are generally to operate in TDD mode.

In this paper, we analyze the massive MIMO channel models and topology in more details. Section 2 describes the propagation models of massive MIMO systems. Section 3 presents the channel estimation and signal detection in uplink and precoding for downlink in massive MIMO systems. Section 4 discusses the origin and jeopardy of pilot contamination in massive MIMO systems. Then, some relative solutions for pilot contamination are introduced. Finally, the development and challenges of massive MIMO is summarized in this article.

*Notation.* The transpose, conjugate and Hermitian transpose operators are denoted by $(\cdot)^T$, $(\cdot)^*$ and $(\cdot)^H$, respectively. The norm of a vector is denoted by $\|\cdot\|$.

## 2    Massive MIMO System Models and Performance Analysis

In this part, single-cell multi-user (SCMU) system is introduced in which one macro BS equipped with large number $n_{BS}$ antennas serves $K$ single-antenna users, shown in Fig. 1. Assuming that all transmission links are over flat-fading channel on a single frequency band and all transmissions are synchronously at transmitters.

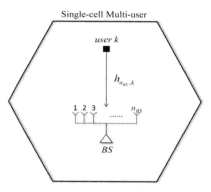

**Fig. 1.** One BS equipped with $n_{BS}$ antennas to serve $K$ single-antenna users.

In uplink transmission, the BS receives signals from $K$ single-antenna users can be expressed as

$$Y_{ul} = \sqrt{p_{ul}} H_{ul} X_{ul} + n_{ul}, \qquad (1)$$

where $p_{ul}$ denotes the uplink transmitted power, $X_{ul} \in C^{K \times 1}$ is the signal vector from the $K$ single-antenna users to BS, $n_{ul} \in C^{n_{BS} \times 1}$ is zero-mean noise vector with complex Gaussian distribution and identity covariance matrix, $H_{ul} \in C^{n_{BS} \times K}$ denotes the uplink channel matrix and perfect CSI is available at the BS, $n_{BS} >> K$. Assuming $h_{n,k}$ denotes the channel coefficient from the $k$-th user to the $n$-th antenna at the BS, which can be decomposed into a complex small-scale fading coefficient multiplying a large-scale fading coefficient [7], i.e.,

$$h_{n,k} = g_{n,k} d_{k,k}^{1/2}, n \in [1, \dots, n_{BS}], k \in [1, \dots, K]. \tag{2}$$

Therefore, the channel matrix can be rewritten as

$$H_{ul} = \begin{bmatrix} g_{1,1} & \cdots & g_{1,K} \\ \vdots & \ddots & \vdots \\ g_{n_{BS},1} & \cdots & g_{n_{BS},K} \end{bmatrix} \begin{bmatrix} d_{1,1} & \cdots & 0 \\ \vdots & \ddots & \vdots \\ 0 & \cdots & d_{K,K} \end{bmatrix}^{1/2} = G_{n,k} D_{k,k}^{1/2}. \tag{3}$$

By utilizing match filter (MF), the received signal $X_{ul}$ at the BS can be detected. The MF process at the BS is

$$H_{ul}^H Y_{ul} = H_{ul}^H (\sqrt{p_{ul}} H_{ul} X_{ul} + n_{ul}) \approx \sqrt{p_{ul}} D n_{BS} X_{ul} + H_{ul}^H n_{ul}. \tag{4}$$

As a result, the simple MF can separate the desired signals from different users and make the internal interference tends to be zero in massive MIMO system.

In downlink transmission, the received signal vector at the $k$ users is:

$$y_{dl\_k} = \sqrt{p_{dl\_k}} h_{dl\_k} \tilde{x}_{dl\_k} + n_{dl\_k}, \tag{5}$$

where $\tilde{x}_{dl\_k}$ is the precoding signal vector from BS to $k$-th user. By using maximal ratio combination (MRC), the precoding vector at the BS is given by

$$\tilde{x}_{dl\_k} \approx \frac{1}{\sqrt{n_{BS}}} g_{k,n_{BS}}^H x_{dl\_k}.$$

The (5) can be rewritten as

$$y_{dl\_k} \approx \sqrt{n_{BS} p_{dl\_k}} I_k d_{k,k}^{1/2} x_{dl\_k} + n_{dl}. \tag{6}$$

The Eq. (6) shows that the simple MRC precoding can also optimize the downlink transmission rate in massive MIMO system.

## 3 Transceivers Design

In this section, several relative issues on transceivers in massive MIMO systems are discussed, such as CSI acquisition and signal detection algorithms in the uplink and precoding schemes in the downlink, respectively.

### 3.1 CSI Acquisition

The CSI acquisition is important for data transmission because that uplink data decoding requires the BS known the uplink CSI, and downlink data precoding requires the BS known the downlink CSI [8]. However, the CSI cannot be wholly acquired at the BS in practical due to the internal interference and noise. In there, the literature [9] defined the formula for estimated CSI follow as

$$\tilde{h}(t) = G_{yh}^{H} G_{y}^{-1} y(t), \tag{7}$$

where $G_{yh} = SG_{h}$, $G_{y} = SG_{h}S^{H} + \sigma_{\omega}^{2}I$, $\tilde{h}(t)$ and $y(t)$ denote the estimated CSI and received signal vector at time $t$, respectively, $S$ is the pilot symbol matrix, $G_{h}$ is the full correlation matrix of the channel, $\sigma_{\omega}^{2}I$ is the correlation matrix of the noise vector.

### 3.2 Signal Detection Algorithm

Considering a SCMU-MIMO system for signal detection, where the BS estimates the signals of the $K$ users. For the linear detection, the approach is to use a matrix $W$, which is related with estimated channel coefficient, linearly combines the received signal $y_{ul\_k}$ to achieve detection. Three particular approaches are described as follows,

(1) MF method: $W_{MF} = \tilde{H}$, (2) Zero-forcing (ZF) method: $W_{ZF} = (\tilde{H}^{H}H)^{-1}\tilde{H}$, (3) Minimum Mean Square Error (MMSE) method: $W_{MMSE} = (\tilde{H}^{H}H + \frac{1}{p_{ul}}I_{n_{BS}})^{-1}\tilde{H}$.

Figure 2 depicts the ergodic achievable with MF and MMSE signal detection for large number of antennas in single-cell scenario. The simulation results show that the MMSE outperforms the MF and the ergodic achievable rate with P = N/3 is superior to P = N because the more inter-user interference. MMSE has a superior performance than MF when the number of antennas is approach to infinite. The performance of transmission in single-cell outperforms that in multi-cell due to the stronger inter-cell interference.

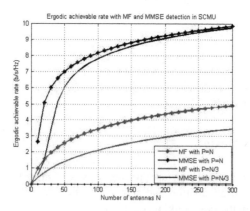

**Fig. 2.** Ergodic achievable rate with MF and MMSE signal detection in SCMU scenario when P = N and P = N/3, where N and P are the number of transmitter antenna and receiver antennas in SCMU scenario, respectively.

According to the simulation for bit error rate (BER) with MF, ZF and MMSE as a function of large number antennas and Quadrature Phase Shift Keying (QPSK) modulation demodulation in Fig. 3, the MF, ZF and MMSE have the similar BER at the lower SNR. With the increase of SNR, ZF outperforms MF since ZF can eliminate intra-cell interferences efficiently. An advantage of MF is easily implemented in a distributed manner MMSE has excelled in BER performance over ZF and MF consistently because the MMSE exploits receive correlation matrix or channel correlation matrix, which can provide an approximate optimization performance with low complexity.

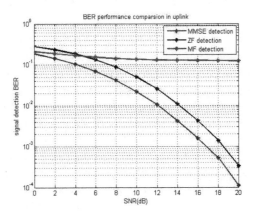

**Fig. 3.** BER performance comparison with MMSE, ZF and MF in signal detection.

When the number of BS antennas and users are approximately equal in massive MIMO system, non-linear detection methods such as generalized decision feedback equalizer (GDFE) [10, 11], random steps algorithm [12–14] and vertical Bell Laboratories Layered Space Time (V-BLAST) [15], can be used to detect signal in such scenarios [5].

### 3.3   Precoding Schemes in Downlink

In this section, several basic precoding schemes and their advantages are analyzed. Consider a multiuser massive MIMO model where the BS is equipped with $n_{BS}$ antennas and $K$ single antenna users, $n_{BS} >> K$. Assuming $R$ is the linear precoding at the BS, $\tilde{H}$ denotes the channel estimation from the uplink. Three simple linear precoding schemes can be considered as follows

(1)  MF procoding scheme

$$R_{MF} = \frac{1}{B_{MF}}(\tilde{H}^T)^H \sqrt{p_{dl}} = \frac{1}{B_{MF}}\tilde{H}^* \sqrt{p_{dl}},$$

where $B_{MF}$ is a scalar of Wiener Filter $B_{MF} = \sqrt{tr(A_{MF}A_{MF}^H)}$, $A_{MF} = \tilde{H}^*$.

(2)  ZF precoding scheme

$$R_{ZF} = \frac{1}{B_{ZF}}(\tilde{H}^*\tilde{H}^T)^{-1}\tilde{H}^*\sqrt{P_{dl}},$$

where $B_{ZF} = \sqrt{tr(A_{ZF}A_{ZF}^H)}$, $A_{ZF} = (\tilde{H}^*\tilde{H}^T)^{-1}\tilde{H}^*$.

(3)  MMSE precoding scheme

$$R_{MMSE} = \frac{1}{B_{MMSE}}(\tilde{H}^*\tilde{H}^T + \frac{K}{P_{dl}}I_K)^{-1}\tilde{H}^*\sqrt{P_{dl}},$$

where $B_{MMSE} = \sqrt{tr(A_{MMSE}A_{MMSE}^H)}$, $A_{MMSE} = (\tilde{H}^*\tilde{H}^T + \frac{K}{P_{dl}}I_K)^{-1}\tilde{H}^*$.

Intuitively, the construction of pseudo-inverse in ZF precoding is a computationally expensive workload that needs to obtain the inversion of estimated channel matrix. However, in massive MIMO systems, the $(\tilde{H}^*\tilde{H}^T)/n_{BS}$ tends to an identity matrix when $n_{BS}$ goes to infinity. Therefore, the complexity of ZF precoding is similar as the MF precoding [5]. In accordance with the analysis in [7], we assume that transmission condition and matrices used for detection and precoding are equal, hence, the precoding performance of MF, ZF and MMSE are coincident with detection in uplink. Simulation figures are omitted due to the limitation of space. According to calculating the transmission rate and BER, the MF has an excellent performance at low SNR than ZF; in the contrary, the ZF performs better at high SINR; the MMSE has the best performance over the whole SNR. Nevertheless, the processing of ZF cannot be implemented at each antenna because all the signal vectors have been processed at the BS [16].

Some non-linear precoding schemes such as dirty paper coding (DPC) [17], vector-perturbation (VP) technique [18] and Lattice-reduction-aided precoding [19] can improve the receiving performance when the number of antennas is not much larger than the users. In [17], the multi-user interference that is known non-casually at the BS can be completely removed by using DPC. The VP algorithm is a variation on channel inversion that regularizes the inverse and uses a sphere encoder to perturb the data to reduce the power of the transmitted signal, and it can achieve the near-optimal capacity in a rich scattering environment [18]. However, comparing with the linear precoding, the sphere encoder which needs to operate with matrix method has a quite higher complexity.

## 4    Pilot Contamination and Mitigation

### 4.1    Pilot Contamination

In multi-cellular system, when the antenna array at the BS correlates its received pilot signals with the pilot sequence associated with a particular terminal, it can obtain a channel estimation that is already contaminated by a linear combination of channels with other terminals which share the same pilot sequence [20, 21]. Downlink beamforming based on the contaminated channel estimate result can directly interfere with terminals that share the same pilot sequence.

We consider a multi-cell system with $S$ cells where BS is equipped with $n_{BS}$ antennas and $K$ single antenna users in each cell and $n_{BS} \gg K$. Assuming that all $S$ cells use the same set of $M$ pilot sequences, represented by the $\tau \times k$ orthogonal matrix $\theta = (\theta_1, \theta_2, \cdots, \theta_k)$, which satisfies $\theta^H \theta = \tau I$, $\tau$ denotes the length of pilot sequence and pilot transmission from different users is synchronized.

The received pilot signal matrix at the $i$-th BS is

$$y_i = \sqrt{p_{ul}} \sum_{s=1}^{S} H_{is}\theta^T + n_i, \tag{8}$$

where, $p_{ul}$ denotes the uplink transmission power, $H_{is} \in C^{n_{BS} \times k}$ denotes the channel matrix from all $K$ users in the $s$-th cell to the $i$-th BS, $n_i \in C^{n_{BS} \times \tau}$ denotes the noise.

To estimate channel, the received pilot signal vector multiplies the orthogonal matrix $\theta$

$$\tilde{H}_{ii} = \frac{1}{\tau\sqrt{p}}y_i\theta = H_{ii} + \sum_{s=1,s\neq i}^{S} H_{is} + \frac{n_i}{\tau\sqrt{p}}\theta, \tag{9}$$

where $\tilde{H}_{ii}$ is defined as estimated channel which is a linear combination of their inherent cell and users in other cells that using the same pilot sequence [22–24]. It is remarkable that pilot contamination produces a disastrous impact on channel estimation with the increasing number of cells.

Furthermore, the downlink transmission has also been affected caused by the contaminated channel estimation. In downlink, the BS beamforming signals are not only transferred to desired user but also sent to users in other cells who share the same pilot sequence.

### 4.2 Solutions for Pilot Contamination

#### 4.2.1 Protocol Design

From the (9), it reveals that the pilot contamination is produced dominating by the users in other cells that using the same pilot sequence synchronously. Thus, a based on adjustment of frame structure [23] is presented to mitigate the impact of pilot contamination. In [23], the author offers a method with shifted pilot locations in frames, which is to avoid overlapping in the process of pilot transmission. The basic scheme is in Fig. 4.

In Fig. 4, the users of cell group A sent pilot during interval time $\Gamma$ while the users in cell group B and C receiving precoding downlink signal from BS. The BS received pilots from the cell group A will avoid pilot contamination which from cell group B and C. The only interference comes from the downlink data transmitted by the BSs in cell group B and C and the users from inter-cell interference in group A.

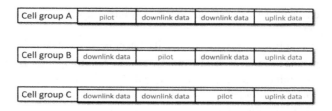

**Fig. 4.** Shift TDD transmission protocol

### 4.2.2 Precoding Scheme

By assigning the pilot sequences for transmission link does not completely remove the interference. The [24] proposes a new method to remove the interference caused by the pilot contamination, which called pilot contamination precoding (PCP). For this scheme, the authors assume that all signals are accessible to all base stations across the entire network and slow fading coefficients can be accurately estimated and make available to all base stations or alternatively to a network hub.

### 4.2.3 Blind Techniques

Another method based on the theory of large random matrices is proposed to solve the pilot contamination without need for pilot sequences to find the appropriate subspace [25]. The basic scheme is that the eigenvalue spectral of a large sample covariance matrix can be decomposed into disjoint bulks as the matrix size grows to large and facilities the column of channel coefficient corresponding to the eigenvalue of the covariance matrix of received vector to estimate CSI. For channel estimation, the multiplicative matrix ambiguity can be obtained by using a short pilot sequence that is assigned with pairwisely orthogonal in different cells.

## 5    Conclusion

In this article, we highlight the large potential of massive MIMO systems as a key technology in terms of enormous effects for future wireless communications. In order to take full advantages of massive MIMO, some extra works on simple and effective algorithms, hardware impairments, power optimization, antenna array design and field tests are need to research.

**Acknowledgments.** Work supported by the National Science Foundation of China under Grant 61201086 and Grant 61272495, in part by the Doctoral Fund of Ministry of Education of China under Grant 20110162120044, and in part by the Planned Science and Technology Project of Hunan Province under Grant 2014GK3022, Grant 2014FJ3044 and Grant 2012FJ3052, and General Project of Hunan Provincial Education Department under Grant 13C343, and Scientific Research Fund of Hunan Provincial Education Department under Grant 12A054.

# References

1. Marzetta, T.L.: Beyond LTE: hundreds of base station antennas! In: 2010 IEEE Communication Theory Workshop (2010)
2. Ngo, H.Q., Larsson, E.G., Marzetta, T.L.: Energy and spectral efficiency of very large multiuser MIMO systems. IEEE Trans. Commun. **61**(4), 1436–1449 (2013)
3. Ngo, H.Q., Larsson, E.G., Marzettat, T.L.: Uplink power efficiency of multiuser MIMO with very large antenna arrays. In: 2011 49th Annual Allerton Conference on Communication, Control, and Computing (Allerton) (2011)
4. Hoydis, J., ten Brink, S., Debbah, M.: Massive MIMO in the UL/DL of cellular networks: how many antennas do we need? IEEE J. Sel. Areas Commun. **31**(2), 160–171 (2013)
5. Vishwanath, S., Jindal, N., Goldsmith, A.: Duality, achievable rates, and sum-rate capacity of Gaussian MIMO broadcast channels. IEEE Trans. Inf. Theory **49**(10), 2658–2668 (2003)
6. Hoydis, J., et al.: Channel measurements for large antenna arrays. In: 2012 International Symposium on Wireless Communication Systems (ISWCS) (2012)
7. Hoydis, J., et al.: Making smart use of excess antennas: massive MIMO, small cells, and TDD. Bell Labs Tech. J. **18**(2), 5–21 (2013)
8. Ali Khan, M.H., et al.: A block diagonal jacket matrices for MIMO broadcast channels. In: 2013 IEEE International Symposium on Broadband Multimedia Systems and Broadcasting (BMSB) (2013)
9. Sarker, L., Abdul, M., Lee, M.H.: A fast channel estimation and the reduction of pilot contamination problem for massive MIMO based on a diagonal Jacket matrix. In: 2013 4th International Workshop on Fiber Optics in Access Network (FOAN) (2013)
10. Sun, Y.: Eliminating-highest-error and fastest-metric-descent criteria and iterative algorithms for bit-synchronous CDMA multiuser detection. In: 1998 IEEE International Conference on Communications, ICC 1998, Conference Record (1998)
11. Yi, S.: A family of linear complexity likelihood ascent search detectors for CDMA multiuser detection. In: 2000 IEEE Sixth International Symposium on Spread Spectrum Techniques and Applications (2000)
12. Datta, T., et al.: Random-restart reactive tabu search algorithm for detection in large-MIMO systems. IEEE Commun. Lett. **14**(12), 1107–1109 (2010)
13. Srinidhi, N., et al.: Layered tabu search algorithm for large-MIMO detection and a lower bound on ML performance. In: 2010 IEEE Global Telecommunications Conference (GLOBECOM 2010) (2010)
14. Alnajjar, K.A., Smith, P.J., Woodward, G.K.: Low complexity V-BLAST for massive MIMO. In: 2014 Australian Communications Theory Workshop (AusCTW) (2014)
15. Matsumoto, T., et al.: Experimental results between non-linear and linear precoding using multiuser MIMO testbed. In: 2013 IEEE 77th Vehicular Technology Conference (VTC Spring) (2013)
16. Windpassinger, C., Fischer, R.F.H., Huber, J.B.: Lattice-reduction-aided broadcast precoding. IEEE Trans. Commun. **52**(12), 2057–2060 (2004)
17. Shepard, C., Yu, H., Anand, N., Li, E., Marzetta, T.L., Yang, R., Zhong, L.: Argos: practical many-antenna base stations. In: ACM International Conference on Mobile Computing and Networking (MobiCom), Istanbul, Turkey (2012)
18. Shepard, C., Anand, N., Zhong, L.: Practical performance of MU-MIMO precoding in many-antenna base stations. In: Proceedings of the ACM CellNet Workshop (2013)
19. Studer, C., Larsson, E.G.: PAR-aware large-scale multi-user MIMO-OFDM downlink. IEEE J. Sel. Areas Commun. **31**(2), 303–313 (2013)

20. Jose, J., et al.: Pilot contamination problem in multi-cell TDD systems. In: 2009 IEEE International Symposium on Information Theory, ISIT 2009 (2009)
21. Krishnan, N., Yates, R.D., Mandayam, N.B.: Cellular systems with many antennas: Large system analysis under pilot contamination. In: 2012 50th Annual Allerton Conference on Communication, Control, and Computing (Allerton) (2012)
22. Gopalakrishnan, B., Jindal, N.: An analysis of pilot contamination on multi-user MIMO cellular systems with many antennas. In: 2011 IEEE 12th International Workshop on Signal Processing Advances in Wireless Communications (SPAWC) (2011)
23. Fernandez, F., Ashikhmin, A., Marzetta, T.: Interference reduction on cellular networks with large antenna arrays. In: Proceedings of the IEEE International Conference on Communications (ICC), Ottawa, ON, Canada (2012)
24. Ashikhmin, A., Marzetta, T.: Pilot contamination precoding in multi-cell large scale antenna systems. In: 2012 IEEE International Symposium on Information Theory Proceedings (ISIT) (2012)
25. Ngo, H.Q., Larsson, E.G.: EVD-based channel estimation in multicell multiuser MIMO systems with very large antenna arrays. In: 2012 IEEE International Conference on Acoustics, Speech and Signal Processing (ICASSP) (2012)

# The 2nd International Symposium on Sensor-Cloud Systems (SCS 2015)

# A Hierarchical Shared Key Algorithm in Wireless Sensor Networks

Zeyu Sun[1,2(✉)], Weiguo Wu[1], Xiaofei Xing[3], Chuanfeng Li[2],
Yalin Nie[2], and Yangjie Cao[4]

[1] Department of Computer Science and Technology, Xi'an Jiaotong University,
Xi'an 710049, China
lylgszy@163.com
[2] Computer and Information Engineering, Luoyang Institute of Science and Technology,
Luoyang 471023, China
[3] School of Computer Science and Educational Software, Guangzhou University,
Guangzhou 510006, China
[4] School of Software Technology, Zhengzhou University, Zhengzhou 450001, China

**Abstract.** Wireless sensor networks (WSNs) are often deployed in hostile environments, thus being subjected to great security risks. However, due to the influence of environment and dynamic topology, the communication radiuses of all nodes are not strictly consistent, which may cause different neighbor numbers and redundant neighbors for each central node. In this paper, we present a key agreement scheme without the trusted third parties by exploiting the special characteristics of Hopfield neural network: the two nodes converge in a steady state from their initial states respectively after iterating finite times, while maintaining the confidentiality of the key by quantifying the key to strings. Compared to existing solutions, the proposed method requires less memory and has lower communication overheads to key agreement.

**Keywords:** WSN · Shared key · Security · Authentication · Hierarchy

## 1 Introduction

In wireless sensor networks (WSNs) [1–3], sensors are deployed in an open environment which lacks infrastructure, the data is eavesdropped and even modified during transmissions and the measure to prevent eavesdropping is to construct a secure and authenticated link between two sensor nodes before communication, thus involving the key setup and distribution. So, the way how to achieve the shared key plays a very important role in establishing secure communications.

One challenge is that WSNs occurs with unidirectional links. A sensor network consists of a collection of wireless nodes; each node can communicate directly with other nodes within its transmission range. The data is forwarded from source node to sink node by neighbor sensors using multi-hop routing scheme. Hence, numerous protocols are proposed to discover neighbor (cluster) sensors, such as ReIn-ForM [4], LEACH [5, 6], GAF [7], Top-Disc [8]. All of them are assumed to be in the same communication

© Springer International Publishing Switzerland 2015
G. Wang et al. (Eds.): ICA3PP 2015 Workshops, LNCS 9532, pp. 405–412, 2015.
DOI: 10.1007/978-3-319-27161-3_36

ranges. However, the wireless communication range is actually related to its power, the more powerful a sensor is, the larger communication range it has. On one hand, the larger transmission radius involves a higher number of neighbors competing to access the medium; therefore each contract node has a longer contention delay for packet transmissions. On the other hand, smaller communication ranges involve fewer number of neighbors which are insufficient to maintain network connectivity.

## 2  Related Works

In 2003, Chang et al. proposed an anonymous auction protocol, they applied a simple method for ensuring anonymity of bidders, and it also provided some important properties of auction protocol [9]. However, Jiang et al. found there were still some weaknesses in the initial phase of Chang et al.'s protocol, so they improved it and proved its security in 2005 [10]. Because computation cost was not taken into account in their improvement, Chang et al. proposed the enhancement with the alias in their protocol and analyzed the computation cost in 2006 [11]. Another protocol which provided auction properties was proposed by Liaw et al. in 2006. By comparison with Hwang et al.'s protocol [12], they indicated that their protocol had strong security and was more efficient [13, 14]. By comparative analysis with those protocols, the proposed protocol showed good security and less computation cost.

For the above-mentioned disadvantages, Diffie-Hellman developed the acentric key agreement scheme based on the discrete logarithm problem (DLP), and the session key is established dynamically in a peer-to-peer manner without the TTP, but a drawback discovered by results in the man-in-middle attack when multiparty entities (malicious nodes) participate it. Recently, Mathur [15–17] has extracted a secret key from a wireless channel by exploiting special properties of the wireless channel [18], but the key establishment related to location is infeasible to node movement topology and too many redundant estimates incurs high levels of communication overheads to reduce the bit-error probability.

## 3  Network Model

We introduce our novel technique, a secure Multi-hop authentication scheme [19, 20], which consists of neighbor grouped discovery phase and packet verified phase. The core idea is hierarchical neighbors according to their communication range to the node and then Multi-hop authentication with keys derived from multiple low-overlap hash sub-chains. The network model is based on the following assumptions:

(1) Every node has the different transmission radius based on its power.
(2) The area of the network can be approximated as a square.
(3) Few nodes are mobile.

We combine our work with the principle of convergence in Hopfield neural network (HNN) [8] which is proposed by Hopfield. Different from forward neural network, it has feedback state from output layer to input layer and it converges in a steady state where data is stored in finite times, which is titled as associative memory [21], thus being used to solve optimization problems. HNN is divided into discrete and continue model according to its activation mode. The discrete model means that only one cell changes its state using signal function every time. In this paper we only consider discrete model [22], which is composed of $n$ cells interacting with each other, the cell is fed back $-1$ state when it is suppressed, and is fed back $+1$ state when it is activated, therefore n cells may have $N = 2n$ different states. The combination state set of n cells is denoted by the formula (1).

$$X_n = \left\{ (x_1 x_2 \ldots x_n) : x_i = -1 \text{ or } 1, \ i = 1, 2, 3 \ldots n \right\} \tag{1}$$

The output of each cell i is fed back to all other nodes $j$ ($j = 1, i - 1, i + 1, n$) through weights $w_{ij}$. Assuming the weights are symmetric, the interaction from the $j^{th}$ cell to the $i^{th}$ cell is $W_{ij}x_j$, so the total output result from the whole HNN to the $i^{th}$ cell is shown as formula (2)

$$Y_n = \sum_{j=1}^{N} W_{ij} x_j (t) \tag{2}$$

HNN runs automatically as follow: each cell is chosen with the $1/n$ probability at time t, if the total output results of the $i^{th}$ cell exceeds a threshold $\theta_i$ by inputting the cell state to a signal function that is given by formula (3) [23], the cell is active, denoted as $+1$; otherwise it is suppressed, denoted as $-1$.

$$x_j = sgn \left( \sum_{j=1}^{n} W_{ij} x_i - \theta_i \right) = \begin{cases} 1 & \text{active} \\ -1 & \text{suppressed} \end{cases} \tag{3}$$

So the state variation of every cell may lead a transformation from state set $X_n$ to $X_m$ according to formula (3). After iterating many times, HNN can converge in a steady state with minimum energy finally, which is computed as formula (4)

$$E = \frac{1}{2} \sum_{i=1}^{n} \sum_{j=1}^{n} W_{ij} x_i + \sum_{i=1}^{} \sum_{j=1}^{} \theta_i x_i \tag{4}$$

$$E(r) = k(2r)^n \tag{5}$$

$$T(e) = \frac{eR_{min}}{c} \tag{6}$$

$$e(R) = \left\lceil \frac{R}{R_{min}} \right\rceil \tag{7}$$

We conducted this study to develop a distributed grouping scheme which is similar to token-ring mode. A grouping $e(R)$ which a neighbor belongs to is defined by the formula (7), and the transmission time $T(e)$ of packet $p$ is defined by the formula (6) where independent variable $R$ is the real radio range of neighbor, the minimal radio range is denoted by $R_{min}$ and $c$ denotes the transmission speed [24].

The passed angle $\theta$ of query message for neighbor is derived by the formula (8). Where $n$ denotes hop number that message is passed with the query angle $\alpha_i$ is specified randomly by query node, where $i$ denotes query time, the incline angle $\beta$ can be calculated as formula (9), the process of neighbor discovery is illustrated in Fig. 1.

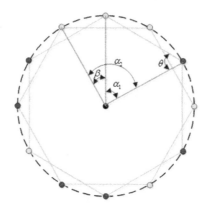

**Fig. 1.** Nodes at an angle of α1 degrees sends a query message

By the formula (7), and the transmission time $T(e)$ of packet $p$ is defined by the formula (6). Where independent variable $R$ is real radio range of neighbor, the minimal radio range is denoted by $R_{min}$ and $c$ denotes the transmission speed.

$$\theta = \frac{\pi}{2} + \alpha + (2n - 1)\beta \tag{8}$$

$$\sin \beta = \frac{1}{2e} \tag{9}$$

One nodes at an angle of $\alpha_1$ degrees sends a token message, which appends a radio range $R_i$, a time stamp TAP of current nodes, transmission time $T(e)$, minimum radio range $R_{min}$ and ID, When node A receives it, $T = TAP_A - TAP_o$ is computed in order to be compared with $T(e)$, if T is unequal to $T(e)$, the token message is forwarded at the angle of $\alpha_1$ degrees.

We assume that only one cell transfers to the next state through changing his weight every time, called serial model, and what is the next state of the cell is independent of its prior state in HNN. So the features possessed by the cell are coincident with Markov chain model, one cell's state is transformed from active to suppress or in reverse after importing the state to a signal function, while others' states keep original, so the probability of transferring to the next state is $1/n$, as shown in Fig. 2. Therefore, when it is activated enough times, it enters the reachable state finally, called associative state in HNNs. The matrix of transfer probability within one step is shown as the following formula.

$$P_{ij} = P\left\{X_j = p \mid X_i = q\right\} = \begin{cases} \sum\limits_{1 \le n}^{n} \dfrac{1}{n} & p \ne q \\ 1 - P_{ij} & p = q \end{cases} \tag{10}$$

$$n = \lceil log_2 N \rceil \wedge s = p \oplus q \tag{11}$$

We take the HNNs with four cells ($N = 16$) as an example to illuminate how one bit shared key is achieved. So each cell exists in possible sixteen different states, the combination state space of four cells is shown as the following formula:

$$X = \left\{X_0 = -1 - 1 - 1 - 1,\ X_1 = 1 - 1 - 1 - 1, \ldots,\ X_{15} = 1111\right\} \tag{12}$$

The threshold $t$ to guarantee key bit randomness is $-10$ and the threshold $\theta_n$ for HNN is shown as the following formula:

$$\theta = \left\{\theta_1, \theta_2, \theta_3, \theta_4\right\} = \left(\frac{1}{2}, \frac{1}{2}, -\frac{1}{2}, -\frac{1}{2}\right) \tag{13}$$

A and B randomly create an initial state XA and XB from X respectively, symmetrical matrix of weights WA and WB, for example Alice chooses X8 and Bob selects X14, WB is shown as the following formula, where $l/n$ denotes the proportion of weight.

$$W_B = \frac{l}{n}\begin{bmatrix} 1 & 1 & -1 & -1 \\ 1 & 1 & -1 & -1 \\ -1 & -1 & 1 & 1 \\ -1 & -1 & 1 & 1 \end{bmatrix} \tag{14}$$

A sends a target state T to Bob. After receiving it, B begins to transfer X14 as follow: shown as Fig. 3, while the fourth cell in B is selected, it is changed from active to suppress after importing the state to a signal function, but other three states keep original. So B achieves the state X6 from X14, the combination state transfer probability within one step is 1/4.

## 4  Performance Evaluations

Figure 2 shows that the network size N has little obvious impact on the memory space taken per node to establish keys in our scheme, but has a direct impact on the memory required in R-KPS—increasing the node number requires more memory space per node and decreasing the node number has the opposite effect. Moreover, the node of our scheme has less memory space than that of the R-KPS scheme, because the key is created dynamically and used until the current session is over, and then it is removed from the memory for the future session.

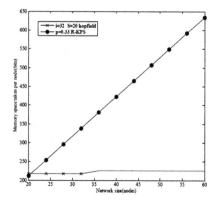

**Fig. 2.** The memory comparison with R-KPS and proposed scheme per node to get 32 bits key

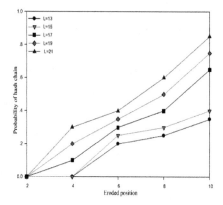

**Fig. 3.** The probability comparison of occurring at all layers

Figure 3 shows the probability comparison of hash chain corrosion occurrence and simultaneously any two sub-chains with an overlap of at all level chains with different chain length L, under the assumptions given $\alpha = 0.1$. It is believed that the security improvement in increase of chain length L outweighs the decrease of the eroded position d. Consequently, in order to keep the probabilities varying from 0.01 to 0.1, it would be best that the dereferencing of L is bigger than 20, based on the curve tendency of Fig. 3.

## 5   Conclusions

In this paper, we have introduced a key agreement scheme for secure communication between two participating entities. The essential idea is to combine key agreement with the principle of convergence in Hopfield neural network, while resisting the brute force attacks for the key by quantifying the key to i-bit strings. The key idea is hierarchical neighbors according to neighbors radio range to the node and authentication is to be achieved with keys derived from multiple low-overlap hash sub-chains, we employ torus topology similar to token-ring in neighbors group discovery phase and key redistributions phase to reduce the energy consumption and communication overheads, we further validated the eroded probability in Hash chains to alleviate jeopardy from internal attack launched by an adversary. We have also shown experiment results which shows that our technique requires less memory and has lower communication overheads than the existing schemes.

**Acknowledgement.** This work was supported in part by Projects (61170245, U1304603) supported by the National Natural Science Foundation of China; Project (2014B520099) supported by Henan Province Education Department Natural Science Foundation; Project (142102210471, 142102210063, 142102210568) supported by Natural Science and Technology Research of Foundation Project of Henan Province Department of Science; Projects (1401037A) supported by Natural Science and Technology Research of Foundation Project of Luoyang Department; the science and technology research project of education department of Henan Province (14A510009), the funding scheme for youth teacher of Henan Province (2012GGJS-191); China Postdoctoral Science Foundation under Grant (2014M562153), Projects (1201430560) supported by Guangzhou Education Bureau Science Foundation.

# References

1. Ang, G., Wei, W., Zhixiao, W., Yan, W.: A hierarchical authentication scheme for the different radio ranges sensor network. In: 2009 International conference on Computational Science and Engineering, pp. 494–501 (2009)
2. Hailun, T., Sanjay, J., Diet, O., John, Z., Vijay, S.: Secure multi-hop network programming with multiple one-way key chains. In: Proceeding of the First ACM Conference on Wireless Network Security, pp. 206–211 (2008)
3. Ang, G., Wei, W., Zhi, W.: Hopfield-association: establishing a shared key in the wireless sensor networks. In: 2010 Second International Conference on Networks Security, Wireless Communications and Trusted Computing, pp. 70–73 (2010)
4. Deng, J., Han, R., Mishra, S.: Defending against path-based dos attacks in wireless sensor networks. In: Proceedings of the 3rd ACM Workshop on Security of Ad Hoc and Sensor Networks, pp. 195–199 (2005)
5. Deb, B., Bhatnagar, S., Nath, B.: ReInForM:Reliable information forwarding using multiple paths in sensor networks. In: 28th Annual IEEE Conference on Local Computer Networks, pp. 350–354 (2003)
6. Heinzelman, W.R., Chandrakasan, A., Balarkrishnan, H.: An application-specific protocol architecture for wireless microsensor networks. IEEE Trans. Wirel. Commun. **1**(4), 36–49 (2002)
7. Chan, H., Perrig, A., Song, D.: Random Key predistribution schemes for sensor networks. In: IEEE Symposium on Security and Privacy, pp. 56–67 (2003)
8. Suhas, M., Wade, T., Narayan, M., Chunxuna, Y., Alex, R.: Radio-telepathy: extracting a secret key from an unauthenticated wireless channel. In: Proceedings of ACM MobiCom, pp. 236–242 (2008)
9. Chang, C.C., Chang, Y.F.: Efficient anonymous auction protocol with freewheeling bids. Comput. Secur. **22**(8), 728–734 (2003)
10. Jiang, R., Pan, L., Li, J.H.: An improvement on efficient anonymous auction protocols. Comput. Secur. **24**(2), 169–174 (2005)

11. Ye, F., Luo, H, Lu, S., Zhang, L.: Statistical route-filtering of injected false data in sensor networks. In: Proceeding IEEE INFOCOM, pp. 453–457 (2004)
12. Hwang, M.S., Lu, J.L., Lin, C.: Adding timestamps to the electronic auction protocol. Data Knowl. Eng. **40**(2), 155–162 (2002)
13. Horng, T.L., Wen, S.J., Chi, K.L.: An electronic online bidding auction protocol with both security and efficiency. Appl. Math. Comput. **174**(2), 1487–1497 (2006)
14. Neuman, B.C., Ts'o, T.: Kerberos: an authentication service for computer networks. IEEE Commun. **32**(9), 126–135 (1994)
15. Rivest, R.L., Shamir, A., Adleman, M.: A method for obtaining digital signatures and public-key cryptosystems. Commun. ACM **21**(2), 489–499 (1982)
16. Housley, R., Hoffman, P.: Internet X.509 pubic key infrastructure operational protocols: FTP and HTTP. IEEE Commun. 203–227 (1999)
17. Mathur, S., Trappe, W., Mandayam, N., Ye, C., Reznik, A.: Radio-telepathy: extracting a secret key from an unauthenticated wireless channel. In: Proceedings of ACM Mobicom 2008, pp. 522–530 (2008)
18. Xue, F., Kumar, P.R.: The number of neighbors needed for connectivity of wireless networks. Wirel. Netw. **10**(2), 1254–1263 (2002)
19. Perrig, A., Szewczyk, V., Wen, D.C., Tygar, J.D.: SPINS: security protocols for sensor networks. J. Wirel. Netw. **8**(5), 521–534 (2002)
20. Savo, G.G.: Optimal Transmission Radius in Sensor Networks. Advanced Wireless Sensor Network: 4G Technologies, pp. 568–571. Wiley, New York (2006)
21. Whit, D., Martin, H.: New directions in cryptography. IEEE Trans. Inf. Theor. **22**(6), 962–977 (2010)
22. Eschenauer, L., Gligor, V.D.: A key-management scheme for distributed sensor networks. In: Proceedings of ACM CCS 2002, pp. 520–523 (2002)
23. Xu, Y., Heidemann, E.J.: Geography-informed energy conservation for ad hoc routing. In: Proceedings of the 7th Annual International Conference on Mobile Computing and Networking, pp. 56–59 (2001)
24. Liming, S., Guiming, G.: A survey on energy efficient protocols for wireless. Commun. China Comput. Fed. (CCF) **7**(4), 13–16 (2002)

# Evaluation Model of the Cloud Systems Based on Queuing Petri Net

Yangjie Cao[1], Huimin Lu[2(✉)], Xiaodong Shi[3], and Pengsong Duan[1]

[1] School of Software Technology, Zhengzhou University, No. 97, Wenhua Rd.,
Jinshui 450000, Zhengzhou, People's Republic of China
`{caoyj,duanps}@zzu.edu.cn`
[2] School of Computer Science and Engineering, Changchun University of Technology,
No. 2055, Yanán Rd., Changchun 130012, People's Republic of China
`luhm.cc@gmail.com`
[3] School of E-Commerce and Logistics Management, Henan University
of Economics and Law, No. 80, Wenhua Road, Jinshui 450000, Zhengzhou,
People's Republic of China
`Shixd_hue1@163.com`

**Abstract.** Cloud system is difficult to be modeled and evaluated due to its large scale, complex structures, outstanding dynamics, and strong correlations among layers. Aiming to solve this problem, an evaluation model of cloud system is proposed based on queuing Petri net (QPNC). QPNC can effectively model and simulate complex cloud systems due to its strong capabilities of quantitative evaluation and behavioral description resulting from combining the theoretical characteristics of queuing theory and Petri net. On the basis of the model, we further improve the quantitative analysis and evaluation system of cloud system, and simulated a cloud system with dynamic service under a massively parallel environment. Experimental results show that QPNC is able to effectively reflect the architecture characteristics of various cloud system at the perspectives of performance, service, etc., and highly simulated various kinds of dynamic service behaviors of cloud systems.

**Keywords:** Cloud system · Queuing theory · Petri net · Queuing petri net · Evaluation model

## 1 Introduction

Cloud computing has rapidly developed in the fields such as government, economy and scientific research because of its advantages involving low cost, high expansibility, simplicity and so forth. Various cloud systems with different architectures, technologies and goals have appeared and show fast popularization and application.

It is one of the key factors for successfully implementing cloud computing to find out the ways for efficiently and accurately evaluating cloud architectures considering diverse cloud systems with miscellaneous technologies. Essentially, cloud computing is a kind of new service mode, in which, the service types and characteristics required

© Springer International Publishing Switzerland 2015
G. Wang et al. (Eds.): ICA3PP 2015 Workshops, LNCS 9532, pp. 413–423, 2015.
DOI: 10.1007/978-3-319-27161-3_37

by different service fields may significantly differ from each other. Therefore, it is difficult to obtain a kind of architecture or scheme of cloud computing which can provide optimal service and adaptability for all fields. Thus, it is more likely to result in problems such as high cost of cloud computing, low quality of services and waste of resources to deploy and construct cloud computing blindly in the absence of evaluation and prediction. Consequently, it fails to effectively satisfy practical service demands and performance requirements.

In order to evaluate cloud computing system, traditional evaluating techniques such as simulation systems (CloudSim, Emusim, koala, icancloud, *etc.*), prototype system and static mathematical model have been employed in many investigations. However, the characteristics such as huge public scale, complex structures, outstanding dynamics, and strong associations among layers may induce defects including poor capability of index quantification, high evaluation cost, low simulation degree, limited scale, *etc.* in practical evaluation process. Generally, the frequent lack of adequate theoretical support of simulating evaluation system makes it difficult to effectively simulate the new characteristics and details of features. Especially, the characteristics of cloud computing including large amount of users, complicated behaviors and dispersed distribution bring more difficulties to simulate cloud computing environments. Moreover, prototype system calls for high evaluation cost, and is difficult to be changed once achieved; therefore, it impedes the comparative evaluation on multiple architectures and platforms. As the scale and structure of cloud system are increasingly complex, the formalized model of the cloud system is increasingly huge and the complexity increases exponentially. Traditional methods based on mathematical derivation and theoretical explanation also fail to solve the problem of the explosive growths of data quantity, data amount and calculation amount existing in the analytical process of the formalized model of cloud systems. Stochastic queuing Petri net [1], as a kind of powerful graphics-oriented modeling language, not only can describe complex architectures of cloud computing, but also is able to dynamically analyze all kinds of behaviors of cloud computing system strongly. It inherits and develops the advantages of queuing network model and stochastic Petri net. Therefore, in addition to quantitatively modeling the operation performance of sources, it also can depict the dependency relationship among multilayered systems considering the characteristics of cloud system involving diverse application service, complex service behavior and superimposed hierarchical structures [2–4]. Therefore, Petri net is the first choice for system modeling because it is applicable for the evaluation and prediction of cloud computing both in terms of theoretical support and quantitative analysis.

According to the aforementioned problems, an evaluation model of cloud system on the basis of Petri net was proposed. Based on the system features of "Chinese cloud" of the *State Key Laboratory of High-end Server & Storage Technology*, a detailed and complete simulation modeling was performed on typical cloud architecture using this model by combining the characteristics of queuing Petri net theory. On the basis of this, the dynamic service performance provided by cloud computing was quantitatively analyzed. Experimental results revealed that the evaluation model was capable of reflecting the service characteristics and performance features of various kinds of cloud architectures. Meanwhile, the results of quantitative analysis were valuable references for promoting further development and application of cloud computing.

## 2    System Architectures of Typical Cloud

Figure 1 illustrates the basic working process, during which, cloud platform deals with user's tasks and works in accordance with the characteristics of the typical cloud system architecture. Dispatchers correspondingly distribute the works and tasks which reach the underlying resources. The obtainment of works and tasks by a computational node calls for a corresponding treatment, during which, the communication among computer nodes through the network is needed so as to interact computing information. Meanwhile, the computing nodes are also asked to communicate with storage nodes in order to fulfill the I/O operation of data, the communication of which can be accomplished through network or directly through SCSI, *etc*. The data of final results are returned to users via the network. Additionally, in some cases, the transfer operation of data among storage devices is conducted through the network as well.

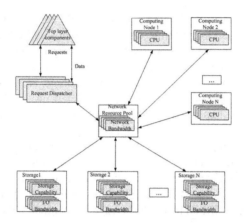

**Fig. 1.**  Basic working process of task processing on cloud platform.

Figure 2 shows the distributed system architecture, in which, virtual machines are placed on many computing nodes. Therefore, a computing resource pool is constituted, and represented and described using a computing subnet in the layered queuing networks. These peer-to-peer independent computing nodes are connected via the computing subnet. Meanwhile, all computing nodes possess their own incidental storage devices which are organized in a sharing form. The data are shared through the storage subnet which is used for the indication and description in the layered queuing Petri net. It is noteworthy that the storage and computing subnets are identical physically. Consequently, the competition of systems on network resources is induced, and expressed and illustrated using the network subnet in the layered queuing Petri net. Network resources may be the bottlenecks controlling the evaluation index such as performance and expansibility of distributed cloud system under high loads. Therefore, the competitive characteristics on network resources need to be reflected in subsequently layered queuing Petri net.

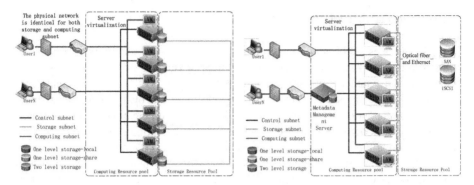

**Fig. 2.** Schematic diagram of the distributed architecture of cloud system.

**Fig. 3.** Schematic diagram of the centralized architecture of cloud system.

Figure 3 illustrates the centralized system architecture. As shown in the figure, virtual machines are laid on multiple computing nodes and therefore a computing resource pool is formed, which is denoted and expressed using a computing subnet in the layered queuing networks. There are one or several server nodes of metadata mainly providing metadata service on computing, storage, *etc.* in a centralized form. Metadata servers and computing nodes are connected through computing subnet. Therefore, the cloud system is required to obtain metadata information on computing and storage of virtual machine through metadata service in advance of providing various services of computing and data operation subsequently. In addition, the centralized architecture of cloud system also provides centralized storage service. By using optical fiber or ordinary Ethernet, the computing subnet is connected on storage pools such as SAN and ISCSI. The interconnection of storage devices and interaction of data are fulfilled using the storage subnet inside the storage pools, for example, SAN, NAS, iSCSI and so on.

The hybrid system architecture is plotted in Fig. 4. As shown, a computing resource pool of cloud system is composed by placing virtual machines on many computing nodes. It is characterized and described using the computing subnet in the layered queuing networks. The distributed, peer-to-peer independent computing nodes are connected through computing subnet. Meanwhile, each computing node possesses their own storage devices which preserve the data replica of current computing nodes rather than participating in the sharing among data. The sharing and transfer of data are accomplished through centralized storage service, and the computing subnet is connected on storage pools such as SAN and ISCSI using optical fiber or ordinary Ethernet. While, the interconnection of storage devices and interaction of data are fulfilled through the subnet of storage inside the storage pools (SAN, NAS, iSCSI, *etc.*). Physically, in the hybrid system architecture, the computing nodes of the computing subnet are distributed while the storage subnet is centralized. These results are expressed and demonstrated using computing subnet and storage subnet, respectively in the layered queuing networks.

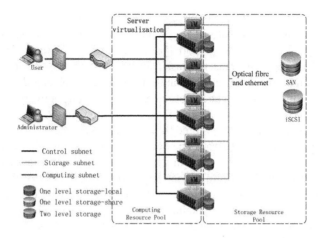

**Fig. 4.** Schematic diagram of the hybrid architecture of cloud system.

## 3    Evaluation Model of Cloud Architecture Queuing Petri Net

Based on the mentioned analysis on the characteristics of the alternative architecture scheme, the queuing Petri net models of distributed, centralized and hybrid architectures of cloud system are constructed. All architecture models of cloud system contain corresponding subnets of storage, network and computing and thus constitute the layered queuing Petri net model. The Petri net model of distributed cloud system is displayed in Fig. 5.

*Request* is a queue of the queuing and describes the work and task requests sent by users and upper components, in which, queuing time refers to the think time between works and tasks. The think time can be distributed exponentially according to practical system. *CPUresource* is a common position and mainly expresses the amount of computing resources. The resources quantity varies with the changes of the hardware devices, in which, Token quantity refers to the quantity of computing resources. *Snet_c* is a queuing subnet which depicts the tasks of cloud system queuing in computing subnet and performs relevant calculation of the tasks. *Snet_s* is a queuing subnet, describes the queuing of tasks in storage subnet and processes the tasks. *IOsource* is a common position which represents I/O source with the most of bandwidth resources. *Network* is a common position and depicts the network bandwidth resources in the current architecture of cloud system, in which, Token quantity represents the quantity of network resources. *Snet_n* is a queue of the queuing and refers to the transmission in a queue of the tasks in network subnet, in which, the network sources are competed by computing and storage subnets. *IOQ (remote)* refers to a queue of the queuing and indicates that the data request of the tasks reach remote storage devices, through which, the data are operated in a queue. The queues present that the tasks operate data in a queue on the remote storage devices, in which, corresponding parameters refer to the time and distribution of I/O processing. Concrete collocations are set based on simulations.

The main transitions in the model are expressed as follows. Tran 6 indicates that the tasks occur, enter into the virtual machine and conduct calculation. The trigger of this transition calls for corresponding support of computing resources, one of which is occupied by the tasks. Tran 3 illustrates that task data are not stored in local storage devices, triggers the transmission of the network data in next stage and obtains data from remote storage devices. This transition can be caused by corresponding network resources, one of which is occupied by the tasks. Meanwhile, this transition possesses weight of trigger. Tran 4 explains that task data are stored in the local storage devices and sources the operation of local data in next stage. The occurrence of this transition requires corresponding support of I/O resources, one of which is occupied by the tasks as well. This transition also shows the weight of trigger. Tran 10 demonstrates that the tasks reach remote storage devices and results in the operation of remote data in next stage. This transition can be induced by corresponding I/O resources, one of which is occupied by the tasks. The Petri net model of centralized architecture of cloud system is plotted in Fig. 6, in which, merely most important places and transitions which are different from those in Fig. 5 are listed.

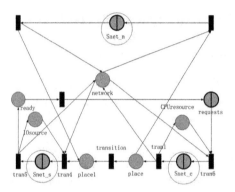
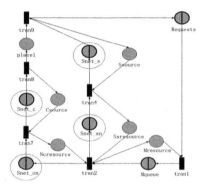

**Fig. 5.** Queuing Petri net model of distributed architecture of cloud system.

**Fig. 6.** Queuing Petri net model of centralized architecture of cloud system.

*Mresource* is a common position and refers to the metadata server resource of the centralized cloud system. The resource quantity determines the performance of the whole system to a great extent owing to the centralized resources. *Mqueue* is a queue of the queuing and describes the queue processing of the tasks on metadata server. It is required to firstly obtain corresponding virtual machine and data information through metadata server in the case of the arrival of new tasks. *Snet_sn* is a subnet of the queuing and indicates that the task transmits relevant data in storage subnet in a network queuing. *Msresource* is a common position and refers to the network resources of the storage subnet in the centralized cloud system. The application of a centralized storage results in the mutual independence of storage and computing subnets. *Snet_s* is a subnet of the queuing, describes the queue of data processing of tasks in storage subsystem and calls for the support of relevant storage resources. *Snet_cn* is also a subnet of the queuing and describes the computing operation of relevant tasks in network queuing in a computing subnet. *Snet_c* is a subnet of the queuing, depicts the task computing queuing of tasks in computing subsystem and requires the support of relevant computing resources. *Csource* is a common position, which illustrates the computing resources in current computing subsystem. The resource quantity is dynamically adjusted during simulation process. The transitions are not given in detail because they are similar to those corresponding to Fig. 5.

The Petri net model of centralized architecture of cloud system in Fig. 6 indicates that the metadata server resource in the queues of queuing (Mqueue) is the key resource in the whole architecture of cloud system. One task is required to obtain the information of computing and storage through metadata server in advance. In addition, the proportions of computing or storage resources needed by the same task are different in various types of applications. This is achieved by adjusting the Token quantity of Csource and Ssource in subsequent simulation experiments.

The Petri net model of hybrid architecture of cloud system in Fig. 7 presents that the hit rate of local replica of computing nodes is essential for improving the performance of the whole system. High hit rate of local replica can save the consumption of the network resource in resource pools and thus improves the performance of data operation.

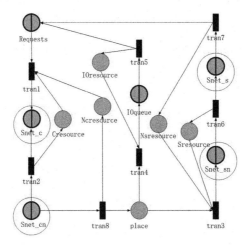

**Fig. 7.** Queuing Petri net model of the hybrid architecture of cloud system.

## 4 Analysis of Simulation Results

Currently, there are many kinds of software and tools used for the automatic calculation of mathematical models at home [5–8] and abroad [9–11]. According to the aforementioned characteristics of queuing Petri net, the QPME tool [12, 13] was adopted to simulate the layered queuing Petri net model of cloud system in this investigation. In this way, the concrete manifestations of evaluation indexes such as performance and expansibility under different system architectures and allocations were explored. Therefore, it offered helpful reference and advice for deploying and constructing cloud systems.

In order to evaluate the service characteristics and performances of cloud systems under different scales and loads, the load was further divided into 3 types by the model. X %: Y % refers to that the data of X % can be acquired through local storage system rather than the network in distributed or hybrid system architecture, while the data of Y % need to be read through the network. All data in centralized system architecture are obtained through the remote call of data network. Therefore, they are compute-intensive (Computing), data-intensive (Data), and calculation data balanced-type (Balance) architectures according to loads. The performances of the 3 types of cloud system architectures under different loads are displayed in Figs. 8, 9 and 10, respectively.

Figure 8 presents the changes of the task throughput in the distributed cloud system under different loads. Simulation results showed that the throughput of the whole system increased with the increase of loads. Simulated data also presented that as the range of the working set continuously increased, the data directly obtained through local storage device decreased because more data needed to be acquired from remote storage device via network transmission. All these increased the overall post-pone of the system and thus reduced the throughput. However, the network was the performance bottleneck of the whole cloud architecture and thus the throughput decreased rapidly as the data passing through the network constantly increased to approximate or exceed network process ability. As can be seen, the throughput of the state of 80 %: 20 % decreased by 36.9 % compared with that of the state of 20 %: 80 %.

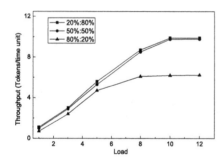 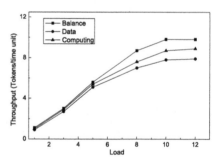

**Fig. 8.** Throughput of the distributed centralized architecture of cloud system under different loads.

**Fig. 9.** Throughput of the centralized architecture of cloud system under different loads.

Unlike the distributed architecture of cloud system, the simulation data in Fig. 9 indicated that the variations of application types resulted in unbalanced resources of the cloud system. The subsystem with inadequate resources was likely to be the performance bottleneck of the whole system, and thus reduced the throughput of the system. As shown, the throughput of the system in balanced type was 9.803. The final throughput was merely 7.894 in data-intensive application owing to the great control of storage performance showing a decrease of 19.5 % compared with the ideal balanced state. However, the cloud system presented an overall throughput of

8.88 which was between the former two ones under the compute-intensive application state. It was because that under this model, although the storage system was underutilized, the storage resources exerted more significant influence on the performance of the whole system than computing resources.

Figure 10 demonstrates the performance of hybrid architecture of cloud system. Simulation data showed that as the hit rate of local replica data decreased, the overall throughput of the system decreased gradually. However, the throughput was basically stable in case of the hit rate exceeding 8, during which, all data could not be acquired from local replica (0 %: 100 %). Finally, in case of the hit rate of the replica data exceeding 20 %, its increase insignificantly affected the increase of the overall throughput of the system.

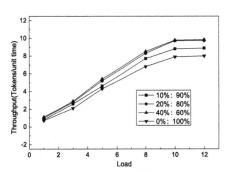

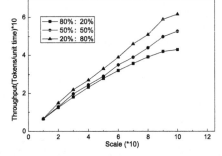

**Fig. 10.** Throughput of the hybrid architecture of cloud system under different loads.

**Fig. 11.** Throughput of the distributed architecture of cloud system under different scales.

The experimental results in Fig. 11 showed that the expansibility of the distributed cloud system was controlled by network resources. With the increase of the system scale, the entire performance of the cloud system continuously increased. As the scale expanded from 10 to 40, the throughput of the system increased from 6.51 to 23.24 showing a 3.56 times of increase and a basically linear expansion in the case of adequate network resources. However, as the scale enlarged, the network resources gradually became scarce, especially, when the resources quantity needed by the system approximated or reached the amount provided by the network resources, the cloud system presented a sharply declined expansibility. Furthermore, the simulation data also indicated that the smaller the proportion of obtaining remote data via network, the better the expansibility of the system and the more insignificant control of network resources in the distributed architecture of cloud system. It could be observed that the distributed architecture of cloud system could more favorably adapt to compute-type application or the applications with intensively distributed working set of the data instead of those applications with large data and large range of working sets.

# 5  Conclusions and Prospects

This study proposed an evaluation model of cloud systems based on the queuing Petri net and conducted layered modeling and evaluation on cloud systems. In addition to quantitatively modeling the operation performance of resources, this model could effectively depict the architecture characteristics of complicated and layered cloud system because of its inheritance and development of the advantages of queuing net model and stochastic Petri net. Research results indicated that this model was capable of accurately describing and analyzing the relationship among various layers and component models in cloud system owing to its favorable adaptability to the diversity and complexity of the cloud system. It effectively evaluated the performance of current typical cloud architecture by making full use of the advantages of queuing Petri net in terms of the capability of quantitative evaluation and behavioral description. Therefore, it offered the support of quantitative analysis and laid theoretical basis for deployment and on-line performance management of complex cloud systems.

**Acknowledgments.**  This work is partially supported by Natural Science Foundation of China under the grant No. U1304603, 11301488, the Natural Science Fund of Jilin Province under Grant No. 20130101055JC, the Jilin Development of Science and Technology Plan Projects under Grant No. 20150204005GX, the Significant Science and Technology Plan Project of Changchun under Grant No. 14KG082, the Industrial Technology Research and Development Special Project of Jilin Province under Grant No. 2011006-9. The authors also gratefully acknowledge the helpful comments and suggestions of the reviewers, which have improved the presentation.

# References

1. Marsan, M.A., Conte, G., Balbo, G.: A class of generalized stochastic Petri nets for the performance evaluation of multiprocessor systems. ACM Trans. Comput. Syst. **2**(2), 93–122 (1984)
2. Kounev, S., Non, R., Torres, J.: Autonomic QoS-aware resource management in grid computing using online performance models. In: Proceedings of 2nd International Conference Performance Evaluation Methodologies and Tools (VALUETooLS-2007), pp. 1–10. Nantes, France (2007)
3. Han, S.M., Hassan, M.M., Yoon, C.W., Huh, E.N.: Efficient service recommendation system for cloud computing market. In: Proceedings of 2nd International Conference on Interaction Sciences Information Technology, Culture and Human-ICIS 2009, pp. 839–845 (2009)
4. Wang, L., Ranjan, R., Chen, J.: Cloud Computing: Methodology, System and Applications, pp. 110–129. CRC Press, Boca Raton (2011)
5. Wu, S., Bai, X.: Interview on petri net analysis tool on internet. Comput. Sci. **23**(4), 27–30 (2006)
6. Lindeman, C.: DSPNexpress: a software package for the efficient solution of deterministic and stochastic Petri Nets. Perform. Eval. **22**, 3–21 (1995)
7. Henryk, A.: http://www.winpesim.de/index.html. Accessed 10 January 2014
8. Thurner, E.M.: TOMSPN: a tool for modeling with SPN. In: Proceedings on Computer System and Software Engineering, pp. 618–623 (1995)
9. Zeng, X., Xiang, H., Huang, F.: The design and implement of Petri net visibility tool. J. Huazhong Univ. Sci. Technol. (Nature) **30**(6), 43–45 (2002)

10. Zhang, J., Liu, Z., Li, H.: The study and development for Petri net graph modeling simulation system. J. Beijing Univ. Chem. Techn. (Nat. Sci. Ed.) **31**(2), 100–103 (2004)
11. Pan, X., Li, T., Liu, Q.: A design and implement of Petri net hierarchy model modeling tool. Comput. Appl. Softw. **25**(8), 33–35 (2008)
12. Kounev, S., Buchmann, A.: SimQPN - a tool and methodology for analyzing queuing Petri net models by means of simulation. Perform. Eval. **63**(4–5), 364–394 (2006)
13. Spinner, S., Kounev, S., Meier, P.: Stochastic modeling and analysis using QPME: queuing Petri net modeling environment v2.0. In: Proceedings of 33rd International Conference on Application and Theory of Petri Nets and Concurrency, vol. 73, no. 47, pp. 388–397 (2012)

# MTCPP: Multi-targets K-Coverage Preservation Protocol in Wireless Sensor Networks

Liu Yang[✉]

School of Information Management, Central China Normal University,
Wuhan 430079, China
Catyyyl@126.com

**Abstract.** In the process of coverage for multiple targets, the existence of a large number of redundant data decreases the effective coverage of monitoring area and increases the energy consumption of network. Therefore, this paper proposes a Multi-Targets K-Coverage Preservation Protocol (MTCPP). Firstly, the dependency of sensor nodes and target nodes is established by the network model, and the method of monitoring region coverage is given. Secondly, the network energy balance is achieved by using sensor node scheduling mechanism. Finally, the simulation experiments show the protocol can effectively reduce the number of active nodes and improve the network lifetime.

**Keywords:** Wireless Sensor Network (WSN) · Network life cycle · Coverage rate · Multi-targets · Preservation protocol

## 1   Introduction

With the advancement of science and technology, wireless sensor network technology has been developing by leaps and bounds [1–3], In engineering field, wireless sensor network is widely applied to many fields, etc. Take the military battlefield as an example, the multi-level(K)-covered sketch map is given, as shown in Fig. 1.

Covering quality and energy management are hot topics in wireless sensor network research, and each of them is a very important performance index in the structure of wireless sensor networks [4]. In general, sensor nodes are randomly deployed in the monitoring area. Because of the existence of randomness, there may be a large number of sensor nodes in the monitoring area. Since the notes are densely deployed, it is necessary to produce a large number of redundant nodes. The existence of redundant nodes will disturb communication channel, reduce the communication ability between the nodes, speed up the network energy consumption, and also inhibit network scalability.

© Springer International Publishing Switzerland 2015
G. Wang et al. (Eds.): ICA3PP 2015 Workshops, LNCS 9532, pp. 424–432, 2015.
DOI: 10.1007/978-3-319-27161-3_38

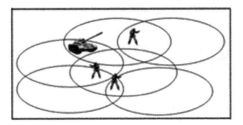

**Fig. 1.** K degree cover

# 2    Cover Qualities

In order to better study the coverage problem of wireless sensor network and the MTCPP algorithm, the following assumptions are made in this paper:

1. All sensor nodes have certain sense of perception and the range of sensing and communication is disc-shaped [12].
2. The sensing radius of sensor nodes is shorter than the length of the monitoring area.
3. The sensing radius of the sensor nodes is governed by the normal distribution.
4. All sensor nodes are randomly deployed in a square area, without consideration of the conditions for the existence of the boundary.

## 2.1    Basic Definitions

***Definitions 1:*** (K degree coverage) in the monitoring area, any target node is covered by K sensor nodes, which is called K degree coverage.

***Definitions 2:*** (coverage quality) in a two-dimensional plane, the ratio of the sensor nodes to the sensing area and the area of the monitoring area is called the coverage quality.

## 2.2    Coverage Quality

***Theorem 1:*** Set the arbitrary sensor node coverage rate as p. When it is K degree coverage, let K=2 and set m and n as the times that sensor nodes move. The probability of its occurrence is $p^2q^{n-2}$, the Conditional probability is $pq^{n-m-1}$ and the $q=^{1-p}$.

***Prove:*** Set X as the number of the first round moving and set Y as the number of the second round moving. According to the meaning of problems, in the first round of the m times, the target node is covered by sensor nodes. For the second gear, at the n time, target node has been covered twice and not covered n-2 times by sensor nodes. Therefore, the sensor nodes occurrence probability is:

$$P(X = m, Y = n) = p^2q^{n-2} \tag{1}$$

Joint probability for the first round and second round is:

$$P(X = m) = \sum_{n=m+1}^{\infty} P(X = m, Y = n) = \sum_{n=m+1}^{\infty} p^2 q^{n-2} = pq^{m-1} \tag{2}$$

$$P(X = m) = \sum_{n=m+1}^{\infty} P(X = m, Y = n) = \sum_{m=1}^{n-1} p^2 q^{n-2}$$
$$= (n-1)p^2 q^{n-2} \tag{3}$$

According to the multiplication formula of probability:

$$P(Y = n | X = m) = \frac{P(X = m, Y = n)}{P(X = m)}$$
$$= \frac{p^2 q^{n-2}}{pq^{m-1}} = pq^{n-m-1} \tag{4}$$

***Theorem 2:*** Set arbitrary sensor node coverage rate as p. For the two-dimensional plane, the coverage of any point is $P\ (nA) = 1 - (1 - p)^n$

***Prove:*** Mathematical induction method is used. In a two dimensional plane, any sensor nodes are not independent. According to the probability theory, when $K = 2$:

$$P(A + A) = p(A) + p(A) - p(A)p(A) = 1 - (1 - p)^2 \tag{5}$$

When $K = 3$, the joint coverage is

$$P(A + A + A) = p(A + A) + p(A) - p(A + A)p(A) \tag{6}$$

The formula (6) into the formula (5) can be obtained:

$$P(A + A + A) = 1 - (1 - p)^3 \tag{7}$$

When $K = i$, the formula (7) was:

$$P(nA) = 1 - (1 - p)^n \tag{8}$$

## 3    MTCPP Protocol

### 3.1    Energy Conversion

As for sensor nodes, the energy consumption is mainly existed in and communication module. When the data L bits are collected, the energy consumption of the perception module $E_R$ and the communication module $E_T$ are respectively:

$$E_T(l, d) = \begin{cases} lE_{T-elec} + l\varepsilon_{fs}d^2, & d < d_0 \\ lE_{T-elec} + l\varepsilon_{amp}d^4, & d \geq d_0 \end{cases} \tag{9}$$

Energy consumption model for receiving module is:

$$E_R(l) = E_{R-elec}(l) = lE_{elec} \tag{10}$$

Among them, l bit is the length of fixed transmission data; d stands for Euler distance between sensor nodes communication; $d_0$ is on behalf of the threshold value of sensor nodes communication distance or called proportional class. When the communication distance between sensor nodes is less than $d_0$, the energy attenuation exponent is 2. On the contrary, the attenuation exponent is 4.

*Definition 3:* (Optimal subset) Suppose Sensor nodes of wireless sensor network set is G. Within unit time, there exists a sensor node subset $G_1 \subset G$, making all the sensor nodes in $G_1$ completely cover the target set T. $G_1$ is called one of the G's optimal sub-sets.

*Definition 4:* (Energy attribute) W= {$w_1$, $w_2$, $w_3$ ..., $w_n$} is the initial energy collection of sensor nodes; W complies with W~N(($\mu$, $\sigma^2$) normal distribution; $w_i$ represents the initial energy of the sensor node $s_i$.

*Definition 5:* (the maximum distortion) in the premise of meeting a certain percentage of coverage, the maximum distortion is:

$$R(d((x_0, y_0), (u, v))) \le \sigma^2 - D/2 \tag{11}$$

$s_1(x, y)$ is the estimation value of the Euclidean distance between the sensor node and the target node, $s(x, y)$ is the mean value of measurement of the Euclidean distance of the sensor node and the target node.

## 3.2   MTCPP Algorithm

According to the basic idea of paper [11], the monitoring area is divided into several regions by means of the theory of clustering technique, and each cluster head node is responsible for managing and controlling the members of the cluster. In the initial stage of network operation, the cluster members first send the message "K-Coverage" to the cluster head node. For the first node of the cluster, firstly a list of KL is set up and stores the received message in the linked list. The received message contains many properties such as sensor node ID, node sensing range, energy attenuation, The list by the remaining energy of the nodes is sorted and ranked, and nodes in the chain are given certain weights. Then, find the list of all the data, and make a mark of meeting the coverage of the target node's sensor nodes. Finally, the "K-Notice" message is transmitted from the first node of the cluster to the qualified member, which is covered by the sensor nodes that meet the requirements.

### 3.3  MTCPP Algorithm Step

Step 1: Calculate the perceived intensity of the cluster members.
Step 2: Cluster member node sends "K-Coverage" to the cluster head node. After one or several unit time, the first node receives messages from all the nodes in the cluster.
Step 3: Cluster head node establishes a link list and stores the collection of information in the linked list. At the same time, the list is ranked according the energy size of the sensor nodes and a certain weight is given to a higher energy node.
Step 4: Find the sensor nodes that meet the requirements, and label them.
Step 5: If the target node is in a K degree, the cluster head will close Sensor nodes with weak perceived intensity by traversing the linked list.
Step 6: After the completion of the link list traversal, the cluster head node will schedule the optimal subset to complete the target node coverage process. Otherwise, the algorithm returns to the second step.

## 4  System Evaluations

In order to further verify the effectiveness and feasibility of the MTCPP algorithm, MATLAB7 is used as a simulation platform in this paper to conduct simulation experiment on MTCPP and paper [10] and paper [11] to give a variety of performance comparisons under different evaluation system.

The simulation parameters list is shown in Table 1.

**Table 1.** List of performance parameters

| Parameter | Value | Parameter | Value |
| --- | --- | --- | --- |
| Monitoring area III | 400*400 | $R_c$ | 20 $m$ |
| $R_s$ | 10 m | $E_{R\text{-elec}}$ | 50 J/b |
| Initial energy | 10 J | $E_{T\text{-elec}}$ | 50 J/b |
| Time | 600 s | $\varepsilon_{fs}$ | 10 (J/b)/m$^2$ |
| $e_{min}$ | 0.005 J | $\varepsilon_{amp}$ | 100 (J/b)/m$^2$ |

With the 400 * 400 m$^2$ as the simulation area, compare the number of sensor nodes and coverage change curve under different Sigma as shown in Fig. 2.

Figure 2 reflects the number of sensor nodes and coverage change curve under different Sigma. Due to the limit of $r_0 \geq 3.3\sigma$, the Sigma value is $\sigma = \{0, 1, 2, 3\}$, which can be seen in Fig. 2. In four different values of the sigma case, its coverage property is increasing. In the same coverage, the smaller the □ is, the more work nodes you need, and vice versa.

***Experiment:*** With the 400*400 m$^2$ as the simulation area, in the same, compare the proportion of the needed working nodes in the total number of nodes in different coverage, as is shown in Fig. 3.

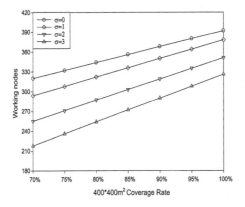

**Fig. 2.** Number of sensor nodes and coverage change curve under different Sigma

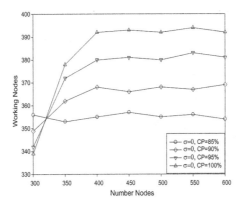

**Fig. 3.** σ = 0, sensor node number and node number of working curve

Figure 4 demonstrates in the same, the proportion of the needed working nodes in the total number of nodes in different coverage probability. In Figs. 3 and 4, at the initial time, the total numbers of sensor nodes are between 300 and 350 and the four curves rise faster. The main reason is that the needed is smaller and the number of sensors required is more. At this time it has not yet reached 99.9 % coverage. When more than 350, the 4 curves tend to be stable. In the same σ competed for the high coverage curve, more nodes are required. Therefore, the higher coverage curve is located at the top, and the lower coverage curve is located at the bottom. In Figs. 5 and 6, four curves basically tend to be stable, mainly worked as the reasons with respect to the two cases with large value. And the number of working nodes is maintained between 270 and 300 for lower coverage curves. The number of working nodes is maintained between 310 and 350 for higher coverage curves. That reflects the ECCA algorithm is extended in this paper. On the whole, the CP of Figs. 5 and 6 is higher than that of Figs. 3 and 4. For the same CP, needed working nodes of Figs. 5 and 6 are less than those of Figs. 3 and 4. This paper verifies the effectiveness of the ECCA algorithm.

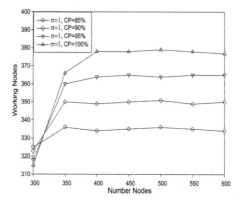

**Fig. 4.** σ = 1, sensor node number and node number of working curve

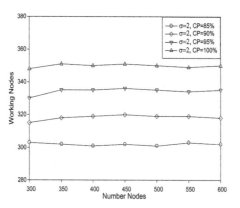

**Fig. 5.** σ = 2, sensor node number and node number of working curve

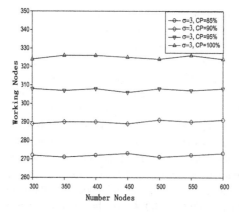

**Fig. 6.** σ = 3, sensor node number and node number of working curve

# 5  Conclusion

Firstly, the problems and shortcomings in the network coverage of wireless sensor are analyzed, on basis of which a multi-targets K coverage preservation protocol is presented in this paper. Secondly, the network model is established through the above analysis and the affiliation relationship between the sensor node and the target node is given. Then, the coverage rate and expected value of sensor nodes in the monitoring area are calculated and proved. At the same time, the solving process of the coverage rate of any node that is covered by the multi-sensor-nodes in the two-dimensional plane is given. In the node energy, the relationship between the communication distance and the maximum distortion is proved. This paper also presents the realization process of MTCPP protocol. Finally, the validity and feasibility of MTCPP protocol are verified by simulation experiments.

Later work mainly focuses on how to achieve effective coverage of the boundary of as well as the nonlinear coverage of the irregular monitoring area.

# References

1. Sun, Z.Y., Li, H., Chen, H., et al.: Optimization coverage of wireless sensor networks based on energy saving. Int. J. Future Gener. Commun. Netw. **7**, 35–48 (2014)
2. Tang, X.F., Guan, B.L., Ge, Q.B., Xu, X.L.: Multi-sensor quantized fusion tracking algorithm for non-cooperative target. Appl. Res. Comput. **31**, 2902–2906 (2014)
3. Sun, Z.Y., Ding, G.Q., Zhang, Y.S.: Based on energy efficiency optimized WSN coverage algorithm. Appl. Res. Comput. **28**, 2261–2263 (2011)
4. Liu, T., Peng, J., Yang, J.: Data delivery for heterogeneous delay tolerant mobile sensor networks based on forwarding probability. J. Softw. **24**, 215–229 (2013)
5. Meng, F.Z., Wang, H.Z., He, H.: Connected coverage protocol using cooperative sensing model for wireless sensor networks. Acta Electronica Sinica **39**, 772–779 (2011)
6. Hamid, M., Kaveh, M., Amir, M., et al.: Distributed deployment algorithms for improved coverage in a network of wireless mobile sensors. IEEE Trans. Ind. Inform. **10**, 163–174 (2014)
7. Mini, S., Siba, K., Samrat, L.: Sensor deployment and scheduling for target coverage problem in wireless sensor network. IEEE Sens. J. **14**, 636–644 (2014)
8. Zhao, C.J., Wu, H.R., Liu, Q., Zhu, L.: Optimization strategy on coverage control in wireless sensor network based on Voronoi. J. Commun. **34**, 115–122 (2013)
9. Du, J.Z., Wang, K., Liu, H., et al.: Maximizing the lifetime of K-discrete barrier coverage using mobile sensor. IEEE Sens. J. **13**, 4690–4701 (2013)
10. Sun, Z.Y., Wu, W.G., Wang, H.Z., et al.: A novel coverage algorithm based on event-probability-driven mechanism in wireless sensor network. EURASIP J. Wirel. Commun. Netw. **2014**, 1–17 (2014)
11. Xing, X.F., Wang, G.J., Li, J.: Polytype target coverage scheme for heterogeneous wireless sensor networks using linear programming. Wirel. Commun. Mob. Comput. **14**, 1397–1408 (2014)
12. Wang, Z.H., Meng, F.Z., Li, Z.Y.: Energy efficient coverage conserving protocol for wireless sensor networks. J. Softw. **21**, 3124–3137 (2010)
13. Teddy, M.C., Andrey, V.S.: A distributed self-deployment algorithm for the coverage of mobile wireless sensor networks. IEEE Commun. Lett. **13**, 877–879 (2009)

14. Hossain, A., Chakrabarti, S., Biswas, P.K.: Impact of sensing model on wireless sensor network coverage. IET Wirel. Sens. Syst. **2**, 272–281 (2012)
15. Yourim, Y., Yong, H.K.: An efficient genetic algorithm for maximum coverage deployment in wireless sensor network. IEEE Trans. Cybern. **45**, 1473–1483 (2013)
16. Sundhar, S., Manjunath, D., Srikamth, K., et al.: On the path coverage properties of random sensor networks. IEEE Trans. Mob. Comput. **6**, 1–13 (2007)
17. Mihaela, C., Jie, W.: Energy-efficient coverage problems in wireless ad-hoc sensor networks. Comput. Commun. **29**, 413–420 (2005)
18. Zhao, Q., Gurusamy, M.: Lifetime maximization for connected target coverage in wireless sensor networks. IEEE/ACM Trans. Netw. **16**, 1378–1391 (2008)
19. Jiang, H.B., Jin, S.D., Wang, C.G.: An energy-efficient framework for clustering-based data collection in wireless sensor network. IEEE Trans. Parallel Distrib. Syst. **22**, 1064–1071 (2011)
20. Zhu, J.M., Hu, X.D.: Improved algorithm for minimum data aggregation time problem in wireless sensor networks. J. Syst. Sci. Complex. **21**, 626–636 (2008). lay-Efficient Algorithm for Data Aggregation in Multihop Wireless Sensor Networks. IEEE Transaction on Parallel and Distributed Systems 22, 163–175 (2011)

# The 2nd Workshop on Security and Privacy Protection in Computer and Network Systems (SPPCN 2015)

# Design Flaws in a Secure Medical Data Exchange Protocol Based on Cloud Environments

Chun-Ta Li[3], Cheng-Chi Lee[1,2]([✉]), Chun-Cheng Wang[3],
Tzu-Hui Yang[3], and Song-Jhih Chen[3]

[1] Department of Library and Information Science, Fu Jen Catholic University,
510 Jhongjheng Road, New Taipei City 24205, Taiwan, ROC
cclee@mail.fju.edu.tw
[2] Department of Photonics and Communication Engineering, Asia University,
500 Lioufeng Road, Taichung City 41354, Taiwan, ROC
[3] Department of Information Management, Tainan University of Technology,
529 Zhongzheng Road, Tainan City 71002, Taiwan, ROC
th0040@mail.tut.edu.tw

**Abstract.** With the growing popularity of network technologies, cloud-based health care applications are becoming an essential part of telecare medical information systems have been widely studied in recent years. To protect patient privacy and restrict the access of precious services for legal privileged participants only, many secure medical data exchange protocols have been widely utilized for various service-oriented medical systems. In 2014, Chen et al. proposed a secure medical data exchange protocol based on cloud environments. They claimed that their protocol achieves better security as compared to those for other existing medical-oriented systems. However, in this paper, we found that Chen et al.'s data exchange protocol has two functional weaknesses such as (1) it fails to provide real-time monitoring service, (2) it has two design flaws in doctor treatment phase and is not easily reparable.

**Keywords:** Anonymity · Authentication · Body sensors · Cloud · Medical data · Mobile device · Security

## 1 Introduction

With the explosive growth of the Internet, the cloud based applications offer several benefits such as pay for use, rapid deployment, greater elasticity, remote sensing, data storage services [16], ubiquitous network access [13] and real time detection of patient health. Therefore, it is the first barrier for ensuring security of these various kinds of cloud service systems and the different security issues of cloud platform are discussed as follows [20, 24].

- Data security: Data security is one of the most critical requirements in any system and it is easily achieved in a standalone system. However, in cloud platform, the data is stored outside the user boundary, at the cloud vendor

© Springer International Publishing Switzerland 2015
G. Wang et al. (Eds.): ICA3PP 2015 Workshops, LNCS 9532, pp. 435–444, 2015.
DOI: 10.1007/978-3-319-27161-3_39

end and the data at rest in cloud vendor is not encrypted by default. Therefore malicious attackers may exploit weaknesses in the cloud platform to gain unauthorized access to data [6].

- Authentication and authorization: To prevent non-registered users' attempts of getting the serviceable resources maintained in cloud systems, authentication should be able to provide to verify the validity of the interacted actions. Moreover, authorization should be able to provide to verify whether certain participants are authorized to access cloud service data [11,15].
- Data privacy: Cloud platform involves the sharing or storage by users of their own data on cloud servers and it may operate and access by others through the Internet or other connections. As a result, cloud platform has significant implications for the data privacy of personal information as well as for the confidentiality of governmental and business information [12,14].
- Security threat: In cloud based environments, a malicious attacker can mount all possible attacks such as data interception, data modification at rest or in transit, privacy breach, entity impersonation, session hijacking and traffic flow analysis [2,10,21].

In order to protect the transmission of the sensitive medical data, there are several researches focused on security issues of medical system [1,5,7,9,15,17, 18,22,23,25]. In 2012, Wu et al. [23] proposed a secure authentication scheme for telecare medicine information systems, but He et al. [5] pointed out Wu et al.'s scheme cannot resist impersonation and insider attacks. He et al. further proposed a more secure authentication scheme for telecare medicine information systems, but Wei et al. [22] found He et al.'s cannot resist password guessing attacks. Wei et al. suggested an improved authentication scheme for telecare medicine information systems, but Zhu [25] pointed out Wei et al.'s improved scheme still existed password guessing attacks. In 2013, Jiang et al. [7] proposed an authentication scheme with privacy preserving for telecare medical information systems, but Kumari et al. [9] found their scheme existed stolen verifier attack, online password guessing attack and impersonation attacks. In the same year, Hao et al. [3] proposed a chaotic map based authentication scheme with user anonymity for telecare medicine information systems, but Jiang et al. [8] found that Hao et al.'s scheme existed stolen smart card attack and Jiang et al. introduced an improved version of Hao et al.'s authentication scheme. However, in 2014, Li et al. [15] discussed that Jiang et al.'s scheme still existed service misuse attacks for non-registered users and they further proposed an improved scheme to repair the security flaws found in Jiang et al.'s scheme. In the same year, Chen et al. [1] proposed a secure medical data exchange protocol based on cloud environment and asymmetric cryptosystem using bilinear pairings and timestamps and claimed that their communication protocol not only protects patient privacy but also prevents several kinds of security threats. However, in this paper, we found that Chen et al.'s protocol is unable to provide real-time monitoring service and patients cannot get treated proactively before their conditions worsen. Moreover, Chen et al.'s protocol cannot decrypt medical data during doctor treatment phase and cannot achieve non-repudiation evidence in doctor diagnosis.

The rest of this paper is organized as follows. In Sect. 2, we first describe the architecture of cloud-based medical treatment system, which will be helpful for better understanding. In Sect. 3, we provide overview of Chen et al.'s medical data exchange protocol in brief. In Sect. 4, we show three design flaws of Chen et al.'s protocol. We summarize our conclusions in Sect. 5.

## 2    The Architecture of Cloud-Based Medical Treatment System

In cloud-based medical treatment system, four roles participate in this system: the patient $(P)$, the healthcare center $(HC)$ the doctor $(D)$, and the cloud server $(C)$. Before accessing the system, every patient must register with the key generation center $(KGC)$ and $KGC$ will issue one pair of public key and private key for the patient. Then the patient $P$ can upload his/her personal health inspection reports to the cloud $C$. Moreover, $P$ can collect health personal items from body sensors and upload them to the cloud $C$. Once $P$ goes to the hospital for medical treatment, the doctor $D$ can download $P$'s personal health inspection reports and collected personal health items of the sensors from cloud $C$ and diagnose the symptoms via $P$'s authorization. As shown in [4], the format of patient's personal health inspection reports and collected personal health items of the sensors are shown in Tables 1 and 2, respectively. Figure 1 shows the entire architecture of cloud-based medical treatment system.

**Table 1.** The patient's personal health inspection items

| Item | Content |
|---|---|
| $ID$ | The patient's identity |
| $data_1$ | General inspection |
| $data_2$ | Electrocardiography |
| $data_3$ | Blood test |
| $data_4$ | X-ray |
| $data_5$ | Scopy exam |
| $data_6$ | Preventive medicine series |

**Step 1.** The patient $P$ goes to the healthcare center $HC$ to take a health inspection.

**Step 2.** The healthcare center $HC$ uploads $P$'s personal health inspection reports to $P$'s private cloud.

**Step 3.** The body sensors collect $P$'s personal health items and send them to $P$'s personal mobile device.

**Step 4.** The patient $P$ uses personal mobile device to upload $P$'s personal health items to his/her private cloud.

**Table 2.** The patient's collected health items of the body sensors

| Item | Content |
| --- | --- |
| $ID$ | The patient's identity |
| $BS\_data_1$ | Electrocardiography |
| $BS\_data_2$ | Electroencephalography |
| $BS\_data_3$ | Pulse oximetry |
| $BS\_data_4$ | Blood pressure |

**Step 5.** In the treatment time, the patient $P$ tells the doctor $D$ how to access the personal health items and health inspection reports in cloud. Then $D$ can download them from $P$'s private cloud.

**Step 6.** The doctor $D$ can diagnose the symptoms via $P$'s authorization and upload $P$'s treatment report to the cloud.

# 3    Review of Chen et al.'s Medical Data Exchange Protocol

In this section, we review the Chen et al.'s medical data exchange protocol [1] based on cloud environments. There are three phases involve in their protocol: health examination phase, patient uploads data phase and treatment phase. The notations used throughout this paper are summarized as follows:

- $ID_x$: The identity of entity $x$.
- $m_{HC}$: The patient's health inspection reports generated by the healthcare center.
- $m_{BS}$: The patient's health data collected by the body sensors.
- Response: The cloud's response message.
- Request: The doctor's request message.
- $Sig_x$: The signature of entity $x$.
- $e()$: The pairing function.
- $T_{xi}$: The $i$th timestamp generated by entity $x$.
- $\Delta T$: The valid transmission time interval.
- $E_k(M)$: Use the key $k$ to encrypt the message $M$.
- $D_k(M)$: Use the key $k$ to decrypt the message $M$.

## 3.1    Health Examination Phase

In this phase, the patient $P$ goes to the healthcare center $HC$ to take a health inspection and $HC$ uploads $P$'s health inspection report to the patient's private cloud $C$. The detailed steps are described as follows.

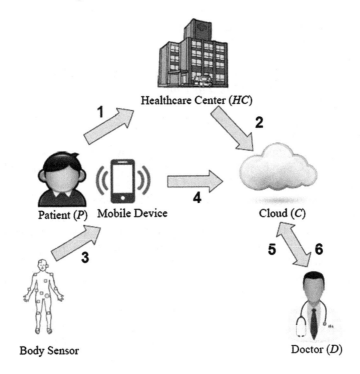

**Fig. 1.** The architecture of cloud-based medical treatment system

**Step 1.** $HC$ first encrypts $P$'s health inspection report and uses its private key $SK_{HC}$ to sign $P$'s health inspection, where $m_{HC} = (ID_P, data_1, data_2, ..., data_6, T_{HC})$, $C_P = E_{PK_P}(m_{HC})$ and $Sig_{HC} = E_{SK_{HC}}(ID_P, C_P)$. Then $HC$ chooses a random number $r_1$ and computes $s_1 = r_1 \cdot e(SK_{HC}, PK_C)$, $s_2 = r_1 \cdot PK_{HC}$, $C_1 = E_{PK_C}(s_1, s_2, T_{HC1})$ and the session key $key_{HC\_C} = H(s_1)$. And sends $C_1$ and $ID_{HC}$ to the cloud $C$.

**Step 2.** After receiving the messages from $HC$, $C$ reveals $(s_1, s_2, T_{HC1})$ by computing $D_{SK_C}(C_1)$. Then $C$ checks if the timestamp $T_{C1} - T_{HC1} \leq \Delta T$. If it holds, $C$ computes $s_1' = e(SK_C, s_2)$ and verifies if $s_1' = s_1$. If it holds, $C$ computes the session key $key_{HC\_C} = H(s_1')$ and $C_2 = E_{key_{HC\_C}}(\text{Response}, T_{C1})$ and sends $C_2$ to $HC$.

**Step 3.** After receiving $C_2$ from $C$, $HC$ reveals (Response, $T_{C1}$) by computing $D_{key_{HC\_C}}(C_2)$ and checks if the timestamp $T_{HC2} - T_{C1} \leq \Delta T$. If it holds, $HC$ computes $C_3 = E_{key_{HC\_C}}(ID_P, Sig_{HC}, C_P, T_{HC2})$ and sends it to $C$.

**Step 4.** After receiving $C_3$ from $HC$, $C$ reveals $(ID_P, Sig_{HC}, C_P, T_{HC2})$ by computing $D_{key_{HC\_C}}(C_3)$ and checks if the timestamp $T_{C2} - T_{HC2} \leq \Delta T$. If it holds, $C$ stores $Sig_{HC}$ and $C_P$.

### 3.2  Patient Uploads Data Phase

In this phase, the body sensors are embedded into the patient $P$'s body and $P$ uses the mobile device to collect the measured health items. Finally, $P$ can use the mobile device to transfer the measured health items to the cloud $C$. The detailed steps are described as follows.

**Step 1.** The body sensor collects the measured health information $m_{BS} = (ID_P, BS\_data_1, ..., BS\_data_6, T_{BS})$ and sends them to $P$'s mobile device via a secure channel.

**Step 2.** After receiving $m_{BS}$, $P$ computes $C_{BS} = E_{PK_P}(m_{BS})$ and stores $C_{BS}$ in the mobile device.

**Step 3.** $P$ chooses a random number $r_2$ and computes $s_3 = r_2 \cdot e(SK_P, PK_C)$, $s_4 = r_2 \cdot PK_P$, $C_4 = E_{PK_C}(s_3, s_4, T_{P1})$ and the session key $key_{P\_C} = H(s_3)$. And sends $C_4$ and $ID_P$ to the cloud $C$.

**Step 4.** After receiving the messages from $P$, $C$ reveals $(s_3, s_4, T_{P1})$ by computing $D_{SK_C}(C_4)$. Then $C$ checks if the timestamp $T_{C3} - T_{P1} \leq \Delta T$. If it holds, $C$ computes $s_3' = e(SK_C, s_4)$ and verifies if $s_3' = s_3$. If it holds, $C$ computes the session key $key_{P\_C} = H(s_3')$ and $C_5 = E_{key_{P\_C}}(\text{Response}, T_{C3})$ and sends $C_5$ to $P$.

**Step 5.** After receiving $C_5$ from $C$, $P$ reveals $(\text{Response}, T_{C3})$ by computing $D_{key_{P\_C}}(C_5)$ and checks if the timestamp $T_{P2} - T_{C3} \leq \Delta T$. If it holds, $P$ computes $C_6 = E_{key_{P\_C}}(C_{BS}, T_{P2})$ and sends it to $C$.

**Step 6.** After receiving $C_6$ from $P$, $C$ reveals $(C_{BS}, T_{P2})$ by computing $D_{key_{P\_C}}(C_6)$ and checks if the timestamp $T_{C4} - T_{P2} \leq \Delta T$. If it holds, $C$ stores $C_{BS}$.

## 3.3  Doctor Treatment Phase

In this phase, $P$ goes to the hospital and tells the doctor $D$ to download $P$'s health inspection reports and measured health items from the cloud $C$. Then $D$ can use these health information to diagnose $P$'s symptom via $P$'s authorization. The detailed steps are described as follows.

**Step 1.** $D$ chooses a random number $r_3$ and computes $s_5 = r_3 \cdot e(SK_D, PK_C)$, $s_6 = r_3 \cdot PK_D$, $C_7 = E_{PK_C}(s_5, s_6, T_{D1})$ and the session key $key_{D\_C} = H(s_5)$. And sends $C_7$ and $ID_D$ to the cloud $C$.

**Step 2.** After receiving the messages from $D$, $C$ reveals $(s_5, s_6, T_{D1})$ by computing $D_{SK_C}(C_7)$. Then $C$ checks if the timestamp $T_{C5} - T_{D1} \leq \Delta T$. If it holds, $C$ computes $s_5' = e(SK_C, s_6)$ and verifies if $s_5' = s_5$. If it holds, $C$ computes the session key $key_{D\_C} = H(s_5')$ and $C_8 = E_{key_{D\_C}}(\text{Response}, T_{C5})$ and sends $C_8$ to $D$.

**Step 3.** After receiving $C_8$ from $C$, $D$ reveals $(\text{Response}, T_{C5})$ by computing $D_{key_{D\_C}}(C_8)$ and checks if the timestamp $T_{D2} - T_{C5} \leq \Delta T$. If it holds, $D$ computes $C_9 = E_{key_{D\_C}}(\text{Request}, T_{D2})$ and sends it to $C$.

**Step 4.** After receiving $C_9$ from $D$, $C$ reveals $(\text{Request}, T_{D2})$ by computing $D_{key_{D\_C}}(C_9)$ and checks if the timestamp $T_{C6} - T_{D2} \leq \Delta T$. If it holds, $C$ computes $C_{10} = E_{key_{D\_C}}(C_P, C_{BS}, Sig_{HC}, T_{C6})$ and sends it to $D$.

**Step 5.** After receiving $C_{10}$ from $C$, $D$ reveals $(C_P, C_{BS}, Sig_{HC}, T_{C6})$ by computing $D_{key_{D\_C}}(C_{10})$ and checks if the timestamp $T_{D3} - T_{C6} \leq \Delta T$. If it holds, $D$ verifies the validity of health inspection reports by computing

$(ID_P, C_P) = D_{PK_{HC}}(Sig_{HC})$. If it holds, $D$ requests $P$ to use his/her private key to reveal health inspection reports and measured health items via $P$'s authorization and gets $m_{HC} = D_{SK_P}(C_P)$ and $m_{BS} = D_{SK_P}(C_{BS})$. Therefore, $D$ uses $m_{HC}$ and $m_{BS}$ to diagnose the symptom.

**Step 6.** After the treatment, $D$ uses the private key $SK_D$ to sign $P$'s health inspection reports and collected health items of the sensor, where $Sig_D = E_{SK_D}(C_P, C_{BS}, ID_P, ID_D, T_{D3})$ and $Treatment_{P\_D} = (Sig_D, C_P, C_{BS}, ID_P, ID_D, T_{D3})$. Finally, $D$ uploads $Treatment_{P\_D}$ to the cloud as the non-repudiation evidence.

## 4   Design Flaws in Chen et al.'s Medical Data Exchange Protocol

In this section, we demonstrate that Chen et al.'s medical data exchange protocol exposes the patient and the doctor to the flaw of private key reveal problem and is failing to provide real-time monitoring service and non-repudiation evidence in doctor diagnosis. The detailed descriptions of three design flaws are as follows.

### 4.1   Lack of Real-Time Monitoring Service

During the patient uploads data phase, the body sensors are embedded into patient's body and the patient can use the personal mobile device to transfer the collected health items to the cloud. Although patients can securely share the medical reports and health items to the doctors for diagnosing during the doctor treatment phase, for the critically ill and aged populations, Chen et al.'s cloud-based medical data exchange protocol is unable to provide real-time monitoring service.

Consider that an elderly patient $P$ lives independently at any location and sends the measured health items to a secure cloud-based platform where it is only stored and aggregated. However, if the elderly patient has an emergency accident and it is measured by his/her body sensors, the collected health items transmitted from $P$ to $C$ is helpless to cope with it. Therefore, a critical aspect that the secure medical data exchange platform needs to support real-time analytics with continuous remote monitoring on stream-oriented health items and the elderly patient can get treated proactively before his/her condition worsen. By leveraging cloud-based medical treatment systems, the health of patients can be monitored on a real-time basis, avoiding unnecessary doctor visits. This not only provides home care but also improves quality of life [19].

### 4.2   Impossibility of Decrypting Data During Doctor Treatment Phase

During the doctor treatment phase, the doctor $D$ will download the patient $P$'s health inspection reports $C_P$ and measured health items $C_{BS}$ from the cloud and $D$ will use these health information to diagnose $P$'s symptom via $P$'s authorization. Note that $C_P = E_{PK_P}(m_{HC})$, $C_{BS} = E_{PK_P}(m_{BS})$ and health data $(C_P, C_{BS})$ are downloaded and stored in $D$'s electronic devices or medical treatment systems. Clearly the data privacy of $C_P$ and $C_{BS}$ are securely protected by using $P$'s public key $PK_P$. Thus $D$ must request $P$ to use his/her private key $SK_P$ to reveal $m_{HC}$ and $m_{BS}$ via $P$'s authorization as follows:

$$m_{HC} = D_{SK_P}(C_P)$$
$$m_{BS} = D_{SK_P}(C_{BS})$$

However, the patient's private key $SK_P$ is securely stored in patient side and it is well-protected by $P$. Therefore, it is impossible for $P$ to share and expose his/her $SK_P$ to anyone including doctor $D$. In other words, in Chen et al.'s medical data exchange protocol, the doctor $D$ cannot successfully reveal $P$'s $m_{HC}$ and $m_{BS}$ during doctor treatment phase.

### 4.3    Lack of Non-repudiation Evidence in Doctor Diagnosis

In Step 6 of doctor treatment phase, the doctor will upload $Treatment_{P\_D}$ to the cloud as the non-repudiation evidence after the treatment. Note that $Treatment_{P\_D} = (Sig_D, C_P, C_{BS}, ID_P, ID_D, T_{D3})$ and $Sig_D = E_{SK_D}(C_P, C_{BS}, ID_P, ID_D, T_{D3})$. Clearly $Sig_D$ only means the doctor $D$ ever requested $P$'s $C_P$ and $C_{BS}$ without containing diagnose of $P$'s symptom. Therefore, Chen et al.'s protocol cannot provide non-repudiation evidence in doctor diagnosis.

In order to prevent above-mentioned weakness, we suggest doctor's diagnose of $P$'s symptom should be involved in $Sig_D = E_{SK_D}(C_P, C_{BS}, m_{DG}, ID_P, ID_D, T_{D3})$ during the doctor treatment phase, where $m_{DG}$ means doctor's diagnose of $P$'s symptom. Finally, $D$ uploads $Treatment_{P\_D} = (Sig_D, C_P, C_{BS}, m_{DG}, ID_P, ID_D, T_{D3})$ to the cloud as the non-repudiation evidence.

## 5    Conclusions

Medical data exchange with patient privacy and doctor treatment with non-repudiation are two important issues over cloud-based medical treatment systems. Recently, Chen et al. proposed a secure medical data exchange protocol with mutual authentication and key agreement based on asymmetric cryptosystem, pairing technology and timestamp for cloud environments. However, in this paper, we found that Chen et al.'s medical data exchange protocol is vulnerable to some design flaws for medical treatment systems. For the critically ill, their protocol cannot use the real-time information to provide timely care at an early stage. Moreover, by downloading the health data from cloud platforms, we found their protocol may fail to achieve non-repudiation evidence in doctor diagnosis and has the functional problem in doctor treatment phase. In the future, we plan to propose an improved version of their data exchange protocol and these design flaws should be considered for cloud-based medical treatment systems.

**Acknowledgements.** The authors would like to thank the anonymous reviewers for their valuable comments and suggestions. In addition, this research was partially supported by the Ministry of Science and Technology, Taiwan, R.O.C., under contract no.: MOST 104-2221-E-165-004 and MOST 104-3114-C-165-001-ES.

# References

1. Chen, C.L., Yang, T.T., Shih, T.F.: A secure medical data exchange protocol based on cloud environments. J. Med. Syst. **38**, 112 (2014)
2. Chung, P.S., Liu, C.W., Hwang, M.S.: A study of attribute-based proxy re-encryption scheme in cloud environments. Int. J. Netw. Secur. **16**(1), 1–13 (2014)
3. Hao, X., Wang, J., Yang, Q., Yan, X., Li, P.: A chaotic map-based authentication scheme for telecare medicine information systems. J. Med. Syst. **37**(2), 9919 (2013)
4. HAVO. http://www.hvc.com.tw/lang/HAVO-E/Home%20HAVO.html. Accessed 18 April 2015
5. He, D., Chen, J., Zhang, R.: A more secure authentication scheme for telecare medicine information systems. J. Med. Syst. **36**(3), 1989–1995 (2012)
6. Hsu, C., Zeng, B., Zhang, M.: A novel group key transfer for big data security. Appl. Math. Comput. **249**(15), 436–443 (2014)
7. Jiang, Q., Ma, J., Ma, Z., Li, G.: A privacy enhanced authentication scheme for telecare medical information systems. J. Med. Syst. **37**, 9897 (2013)
8. Jiang, Q., Ma, J., Lu, X., Tian, Y.: Robust chaotic map-based authentication and key agreement scheme with strong anonymity for telecare medicine information systems. J. Med. Syst. **38**(2), 12 (2014)
9. Kumari, S., Khan, M.K., Kumar, R.: Cryptanalysis and improvement of 'A privacy enhanced scheme for telecare medical information systems. J. Med. Syst. **37**, 9952 (2013)
10. Lee, C.C., Chung, P.S., Hwang, M.S.: A survey on attribute-based encryption schemes of access control in cloud environments. Int. J. Netw. Secur. **15**(4), 231–240 (2013)
11. Li, C.T., Hwang, M.S.: An efficient biometrics-based remote user authentication scheme using smart cards. J. Netw. Comput. Appl. **33**(1), 1–5 (2010)
12. Li, C.T., Lee, C.C., Weng, C.Y., Fan, C.I.: An extended multi-server-based user authentication and key agreement scheme with user anonymity. KSII Trans. Internet Inf. Syst. **7**(1), 119–131 (2013)
13. Li, C.T., Lee, C.C., Weng, C.Y.: An extended chaotic maps based user authentication and privacy preserving scheme against DoS attacks in pervasive and ubiquitous computing environments. Nonlinear Dyn. **74**(4), 1133–1143 (2013)
14. Li, C.T.: A new password authentication and user anonymity scheme based on elliptic curve cryptography and smart card. IET Inf. Secur. **7**(1), 3–10 (2013)
15. Li, C.T., Lee, C.C., Weng, C.Y.: A secure chaotic maps and smart cards based password authentication and key agreement scheme with user anonymity for telecare medicine information systems. J. Med. Syst. **38**(9), 1–11 (2014)
16. Li, C.T., Lee, C.W., Shen, J.J.: An extended chaotic maps based keyword search scheme over encrypted data resist outside and inside keyword guessing attacks in cloud storage services. Nonlinear Dyn. **80**(3), 1601–1611 (2015)
17. Li, C.T., Weng, C.Y., Lee, C.C.: A secure RFID tag authentication protocol with privacy preserving in telecare medicine information systems. J. Med. Syst. **39**(8), 1–8 (2015)

18. Li, C.T., Weng, C.Y., Lee, C.C., Wang, C.C.: Secure user authentication and user anonymity scheme based on quadratic residues for the integrated EPRIS. Procedia Comput. Sci. **52**, 21–28 (2015)
19. Khanna, A., Misra, P.: The Internet of things for medical devices - prospects, challenges and the way forward. Tata Consultancy Services. http://www.tcs.com/ SiteCollectionDocuments/White%20Papers/Internet-of-Things-Medical-Devices_ 0714-2.pdf. Accessed 18 April 2015
20. Subashini, S., Kavitha, V.: A survey on security issues in service delivery models of cloud computing. J. Netw. Comput. Appl. **34**(1), 1–11 (2011)
21. Wang, J., Yu, X., Zhao, M.: Fault-tolerant verifiable keyword symmetric searchable encryption in hybrid cloud. Int. J. Netw. Secur. **17**(4), 471–483 (2015)
22. Wei, J., Hu, X., Liu, W.: An improved authentication scheme for telecare medicine information systems. J. Med. Syst. **36**(6), 3597–3604 (2012)
23. Wu, Z.Y., Lee, Y.C., Lai, F., Lee, H.C., Chung, Y.: A secure authentication scheme for telecare medicine information systems. J. Med. Syst. **36**(3), 1529–1535 (2012)
24. Zissis, D., Lekkas, D.: Addressing cloud computing security issues. Future Gener. Comput. Syst. **28**(3), 583–592 (2012)
25. Zhu, Z.: An efficient authentication scheme for telecare medicine information systems. J. Med. Syst. **36**(6), 3833–3838 (2012)

# Privacy Preserving Personalization in Probabilistic Search

Rajeswary Ravi$^{(\boxtimes)}$ and Greeshma N. Gopal

College of Engineering, Cherthala, Pallippuram P.O,
Alappuzha 688541, Kerala, India
rrrrajeswary@gmail.com
http://www.cectl.ac.in/

**Abstract.** Nowadays users want to retrieve accurate and relevant information as fast as possible by preserving their privacy. The main challenge in ensuring privacy is to provide accurate results to user as well as to hide relevant information from external entities. To provide the security in information retrieval system the relevant information must be protected from external entities. The proposed mechanism named Privacy Preserving Probabilistic Search, provides the necessary privacy for a particular personalised search. The users profile helps to get essential input for personalized search. The main motivation for ontological query expansion is, to improve results by including terms that would lead to retrieving more relevant documents. In the proposed method, both the keyword and the entities interest are made hidden. An encrypted data scheme is used for uploading and retrieval of documents without loss of privacy. The probabilistic search ensure excellent result with high recall.

**Keywords:** Personalization · Privacy preserving · Probabilistic search

## 1 Introduction

Information retrieval is the science and art of locating and obtaining documents based on information needs expressed to a system in a query language. In probabilistic personalization of the search, it is needed to hide both keywords and the interests of user who is doing the search. To provide the privacy for user, a search mechanism is needed that to work over encrypted data. Traditionally database is protected by means of some kind of access control mechanism. Those mechanisms work fine under the assumption that database runs on a trusted server. To keep the data hidden from the non-authorized user, many of the publically available database systems offern the opportunity to encrypt records. However, none of those systems provide a way to efficiently query the encrypted records.

Search personalization typically involves the ranking of results for individual users based on modes of their interest. The privacy of user interset is provided by using an encryption schema, which enables the searching in an encrypted data. Three modules involved are data owner document upload module, server

© Springer International Publishing Switzerland 2015
G. Wang et al. (Eds.): ICA3PP 2015 Workshops, LNCS 9532, pp. 445–453, 2015.
DOI: 10.1007/978-3-319-27161-3_40

document upload module, user module. The three key problems that must be solved in any personalization approach are: representation, learning and ranking. Formalize these problems using probabilistic models for predicting the relevance a document to specific user with respect to a query.

## 2    Related Works

### 2.1    Data Retrieval Technique

Richard Brinkman [1] proposed Searching in encrypted data, when private information is stored in databases that are under the control of others. A typical way to protect the data, is to encrypt the data before storing it. To retrieve the data efficiently, a search mechanism is needed that still works over the encrypted data.

Privacy preserving search is very important for keep information retrieval. Many of the works are indicating the privacy for a particular user search on their own data. Or in some cases a trusted authority provide the privay. Ning Cao, Cong Wang, Li, Ming, Kui Ren and Wenjin Lou [3] indicating searching of Encrypted cloud data using Privacy-Preserving Multi-keyword Ranked Search (MRSE) method. In this method co-ordinate matching obtains the similarity between search query and data documents. Ning Cao, Cong Wang, Li, Ming, Kui Ren and Wenjing Lou [2] shows searching of cloud data using Secure Ranked Keyword Search method. The Order Preserving Mapping Technique is also used [2].

### 2.2    Personalized Search

Daw Xiaoding Song, Wagner, D., Perrig, A. [4] presented different techniques for searching the encrypted cloud data without any loss of data confidentiality using pseudo random function, Pseudo random generator and Sequential scan [5]. A cryptographic scheme overcomes the problem of searching the encrypted cloud data. In Automatic Identification of User Interest For Personalized Search [6] describes how a search engine can learn a users preference automatically based on her/his past click history and how it can use the user preference to personalize search results.

[7] Even though generic search engine concepts can be used to retrieve relevant information from the data store, proper privacy demands special attention in the case of probability based personalised search.

## 3    Proposed System

It is aimed to provide privacy to the user, with respect to the keyword and also the interests based on the profile. The searching takes place on encrypted data. With the known data from the profile of user, the search system helps to find more relevant informationpertaining to the user. Query is expanded based on the ontology of the keywords as well as interest. The ontology used here is WordNet. The expanded keywords are hashed to convert it to shorter fixed length data before sending it to the search system. For each user a key pair (public key, private key) is generated in the search system. When a request arrives from user then server send the public key of that particular user. By using public key the expanded and refined query keyword which is hashed is encrypted using the users public key, and send to the server. On reaching server the query list is decrypted by using private key of user. The further encryption is performed at server side which is required for the search over encrypted data. Server can store, search and retrieve information. Personalized search is a promising technique to improve retrieval effectiveness. User profile is updated during search. The probabilistic approach to information retrieval helps to retrieve relevent document. The proposed system consists of,

- Ontological query expansion
- Encryption schema
- Probabilistic search

### 3.1   Ontological Query Expansion

Here it is focused on using ontology for query expansion. Query expansion is the process of augmenting the users query with additional terms in order to improve result. The main motivation for query expansion is, needless to say, to improve results by including terms that would lead to retrieving more relevant documents. The ontology used is WordNet. Concepts in WordNet are called synsets; that is synonym sets. Usually in the context of WordNet concepts are referred to as senses. The terms describing each concept are the synonyms contained in the synset. For example the synset of bicycle is bicycle, bike,thus both terms are representing the same concept. The definition of a concept in WordNet is called gloss. There are two main strategies to find expansion terms: the first is to add related terms based on some automatic relatedness measure and the second is based on relevance feedback.

### 3.2   Encryption Schema

**Hashing.** A shorter length fixed value is generated for each ontologically expanded query keyword using hashing with SHA1 algorithm. SHA1 outputs a 160 bit digest of any sized file or input. This is followed by a public key encryption techniques and then later undergo encryption suggested by Richard Brinkman in his paper Searching In Encrypted Data.

**Encryption Schema.** The encryption is done on following stages to achieve privacy.

- Storage
- Search
- Retreival

**Storage.** When server gets information from data uploader, first of all server has to fragment the whole plaintext W into several fixed sized words $W_i[1]$. Each $W_i$ has length n. Server also generates encryption keys k' and k"(which are used for every word) and a sequence of reproducible random numbers $S_i$ using a pseudo-random bit generator. The server then calculates the following for each block $W_i$:

$W_i$ - plaintext block
k" - encryption key
$X_i = E_{k"}(W_i) = L_i$ , $R_i$ - encrypted text block
k' - key for f
$k_i = f_{k'}(L_i)$ - key for F
$S_i$ - random number i
$T_i = \langle S_i, Fk_i(S_i) \rangle$ - tuple used by search
$C_i = X_i \oplus T_i$ - value to be stored

Here E is a standard symmetric block cipher and f and F are pseudo- random functions:

E : $key_{64} \times int_n \rightarrow int_n$
f : $key_{64} \times int_{n-m} \rightarrow key_{64}$
F: $key_{64} \times int_{n-m} \rightarrow int_m$

The encrypted word $X_i$ has the same block length as $W_i$ (i.e. n).$L_i$has length n-m and $R_i$ has length m. The parameters n and m may be chosen freely. The value $C_i$ stored there.

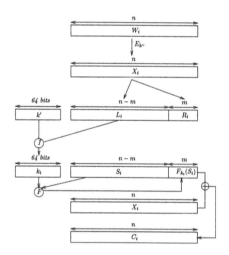

**Fig. 1.** Encryption schema

Figure 1 shows the flowchart of encryption schema. Figure 2 shows the sequence diagram of storage process. Here when user initiate the search query to server, server generate corresponding key pair value which includes public key $(P_{K_u})$ and private key $(P_{R_u})$. The public key will be send back to user. The onto-logically expanded query $(O_q)$ hashed before send to server. This expanded query encrypted with the public key of user $(P_{K_u})$ and send to server. Server decrypt the query using private key of user and gets hashed query. There is an encryption schema performed over this query. The encryption schema is shown in Fig. 1. For all keywords corresponding cipher text $(C_i)$ valure's are stored at database.

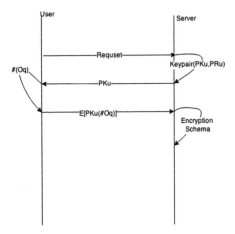

**Fig. 2.** The sequence diagram of storage

**Search.** The same storage encryption schema is performed during search. The following computation is done for each ciphertext block in the database $(C_P)$.

$$T_p = C_p \oplus X = \langle S_p, S'_P \rangle = \{\langle S_p, F_k(S_p)\rangle \text{ if } W_p = W_j, \text{ garbage otherwise if }$$
$S'_P = F_K(S_p)$ then return p, $C_p$.

With this even though particular cipher text block is identified in server side, actual the corresponding document index is made hidden to the server. Based on index number the document location is identified or its associated with a mathematical function. Here we have used the function f=3n+1. When there is a search, server identifies the index $C_i$ which is send to the user. The user computes the original index. From the index value user request for a set of block of indexes and document set. During search, for each keyword $X_i$ and FKi(Si) values are send to server side. All keywords are indexed as cipher text. Each cipher text is XOR with $X_i$. If the last 32 bit of XOR value is matching with FKi(Si), then the keyword is there. The corresponding index value is send back to user.

Figure 3: shows the sequence diagram of search. During the search process, the encryption schema at user will generate $X_i$ and FKi(Si). Both are send back to server. First $X_i$ value is XORed with each $C_i$ value corresponding to keyword and resulting $(T_p)$ value will be generated. Last 32 bit value of $(T_p)$ will be equated with FKi(Si). If these two values are equal the keyword is found.

**Retrieval.** All the documents are encrypted using AES algorithm, and store in the server side at the time of document storage. The encrypted AES document and the information of data owner are send back to user. With the handshake

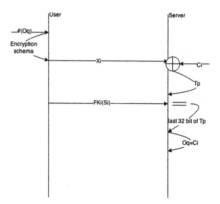

**Fig. 3.** The sequence diagram of search

of user and data owner, user gets the key for decrypt the document. In the following Fig. 4 it shows that a set of index value is requesting the user and the server sends the block of index value along with document list. All that documents are encrypted with AES algorithm. The user can fetch the relevant document by using probabilistic search. The user sends request for getting the key for encrypted document. With the handshake of data owner user gets the key to decrypt the document.

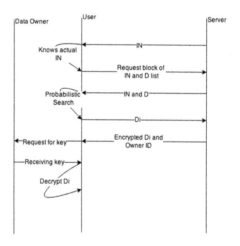

**Fig. 4.** The sequence diagram of retrieval

Figure 4: shows the sequence diagram of retrieval. Server send back the index number(IN)of matching keyword to user. By using the mathematical function user gets the actual index number(IN) and request the server for a block of index number along with document set(D). After recieving the list, the probabilistic search performed on the data obtained. Finally the relevant document is retrieved $D_i$. For getting the key of that document which is encrypted with the data owner, server also sent the id of data owner. With the handshake of data owner user can decrypt the document.

### 3.3 Probabilistic Search

In probabilistic model, its try to capture the information retrieval process from a probabilistic framework. The basic idea is to retrieve the documents according to the probability of the document being relevant.

– The Probabilistic Ranking Principle

Formally, given the document vector $\vec{d}$ and query vector $\vec{q}$, we rank the documents according to the probability of the document being relevant. Mathematically, the scoring function is given by,

$$P(R = 1| \vec{d}, \vec{q})$$

where $\vec{d}$ is the document vector, $\vec{q}$ is the query vector and R is the indicator random variable that takes value 1 if $\vec{d}$ is relevant w.r.t to $\vec{q}$ and 0 if, $\vec{d}$ is not-relevant w.r.t $\vec{q}$. One such probabilistic IR based algorithm is Okapi-BM25.

– Okapi-BM25

It is based on the probabilistic retrieval model that pays attention to the term frequencies and document length. Factor the term frequencies in each term, in that case. Given a query Q, containing keywords $q_1, ....., q_n$. the BM25 score of a document D is,

$$\text{score}(D, Q) = \sum_{i=1}^{n} IDF(q_i) \frac{f(q_i, D).(k_1+1)}{f(q_i, D) + k_1.(1 - b + b.\frac{|D|}{avgdl})}$$

where $f(q_i, D)$ is $q_i's$ term frequency in the document D, $|D|$ is the length of the document D in words, and avgdl is the average document length in the text collection from which documents are drawn. $k_1$ and b are free parameters, usually chosen, in absence of an advanced optimization, as $k_1 \epsilon [1.2, 2.0]$ and b = 0.75. $IDF(q_i)$ is the IDF (inverse document frequency) weight of the query term $q_i$. It is usually computed as: $IDF(q_i) = log\frac{N - n_q + 0.5}{n_q + 0.5}$.

## 4   Evaluation

A total of more than 1000 documents were taken for testing the results. The evaluation is done based on the parameters such as relevant documents, total retrieved document, retrieved relevant document, precision and recall. Values of these parameters are compared for different keywords like sports, states and network. This values are used for the evaluation of similarity based and probabilistic search. The values used for evaluation are given in Fig. 5.

Graphical representation of the evaluation based on values given in table are shown here. In Figs. 6 and 7, the performance graphs are shown for the

| Keywords | Model | Relevant documents | Total retrieved | Relevant retrieved | Precision | Recall |
|---|---|---|---|---|---|---|
| sports | Similarity | 108 | 84 | 63 | 0.75 | 0.58 |
| | Probabilistic | 108 | 98 | 89 | 0.90 | 0.82 |
| states | Similarity | 146 | 113 | 86 | 0.76 | 0.59 |
| | Probabilistic | 146 | 132 | 120 | 0.91 | 0.83 |
| network | Similarity | 120 | 92 | 71 | 0.77 | 0.59 |
| | Probabilistic | 120 | 109 | 99 | 0.91 | 0.83 |

**Fig. 5.** Comparison is done on similarity and probabilistic search

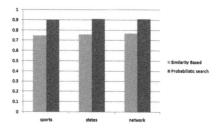

**Fig. 6.** Comparison with similarity and probabilstic search by precision

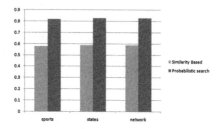

**Fig. 7.** Comparison with similarity and probabilstic search by recall

precision and recall value based on similarity and probabilistic search. Figure 6 shows the comparison with similarity based and probabilistic model by precision value. From the graph it is clear that precision values are greater in probabilistic model than similarity based for retrieval of relevant document. Figure 7 shows the comparison with similarity based and probabilistic model by recall value. From the graph it is clear that recall values of probabilistic model are greater than similarity based for relevant document retrieval.

## 5    Conclusion

The proposed method is a novel idea for preserving privacy during personalized search. Both keyword and user interest are protected while a user is doing the search. This technique generates a search mechanism over encrypted data. Privacy can be achieved by using this encryption schema. Personalized search helps to retrieve data more efficiently. This scheme greatly benefit to keep the ontological expansion of user query for searching. By using ontology based query expansion and probabilistic search recall value is improved.

# References

1. Brinkman, R.: Searching in encrypted data, pp. 14–17, June 2007
2. Wang, C., Cao, N., Li, J., Ren, K., Lou, W.: Secure Ranked Keyword Search over Encrypted Cloud Data. In: IEEE 30th International Conference on Distributed Computing Systems (ICDCS), pp. 253–262, July 2010
3. Cao, N., Wang, C., Li, M., Ren, K., Lou, W.: Privacy-preserving multi-keyword ranked search over encrypted cloud data. In: Proceedings of INFOCOM, pp. 829–837. IEEE, April 2011
4. Song, D.X., Wagner, D., Perrig, A.: Practical techniques for searches on encrypted data security and privacy. In: 2000 Proceedings of IEEE Symposium, pp. 44–55, May 2000
5. Shen, X., Tan, B., Zhai, C.: Privacy protection in personalized search. ACM SIGIR Forum **41**(1), 4–17 (2007)
6. Qiu, F., Cho, J.: Automatic Identification of User Interest For Personalized Search. In: Proceeding ACM, pp. 727–736 (2006)
7. Kumar, R., Sharan, A.: Personalized web search using browsing history and domain knowledge. In: 2014 International Conference on Issues and Challenges in Intelligent Computing Techniques (*ICICT*), pp. 493–497 (2014)

# A Security-Critical Task Management Method for Distributed Real-Time Systems

Yang Yu[1], Qi Dong[2(✉)], Zhipeng Luo[1], Hao Chen[1], Jun Deng[1], and Wei Guan[1]

[1] Academy of Engineering Physics, Mianyang 621900, China
fresh1985@qq.com
[2] School of Information and Software, University of Electronic Science
and Technology of China, Chengdu 611054, China
qidong92@163.com

**Abstract.** Security has become an important constraint in distributed real-time task system. For this paper, we give a security-critical distributed real-time task management model, then present a scheme for security-critical task management in the distributed real-time system, finally we propose an algorithm to solve the management problem in the distributed real-time system. We propose a security-critical distributed real-time task management model, and formulate the security-critical distributed real-time system task management issue into a shortest path problem. We solve the shortest path problem by using the improved Dijkstra algorithm. In addition, we validate the efficiency of the algorithm by simulation experiments.

**Keywords:** Security-critical · Distributed real-time system · Task management · Shortest path algorithm

## 1 Introduction

In recent years, with the rapid development of computer processing power, network bandwidth and storage capacity, distributed system has become the representative computing model for many scientific computing and commercial applications [1]. Similarly, a growing number of distributed systems are also applied to real-time computing [2]. Distributed real-time applications not only demand the distributed logic processing, but also require them to meet the real-time application response time limit. In addition, certain applications (such as industrial control, navigation, etc.) also have the security-critical real-time tasks. The realization of these real-time applications should address security-critical real-time task management problem.

With the research of distributed real-time systems attracting more attention and the gradually increasing of related research, there have been many achievement. Xie and Qin [3] have published many literatures on distributed real-time task management, and T. Xie has concluded a detailed study from energy and safety aspects of real-time tasks management problem [4, 5]. But they mainly discussed issues based on single or cluster and the studies did not extend to the distributed real-time systems. Distributed real-time systems face a number of factors such as issues, energy, security and other constraints.

© Springer International Publishing Switzerland 2015
G. Wang et al. (Eds.): ICA3PP 2015 Workshops, LNCS 9532, pp. 454–464, 2015.
DOI: 10.1007/978-3-319-27161-3_41

Although, management algorithm based on the distributed real-time systems has become one focus of computer, security-related key management algorithm research in the distributed real-time system is quite rare. In this paper, we will combine some security factors of distributed real-time applications to improve the management of security-critical distributed real-time system.

The rest of this paper is organized as follows. Security-critical distributed real-time task management model is presented in Sect. 2. In Sect. 3, we present the problem of the security-critical distributed real-time task management, and we put forward a solution that can solve the problem. Simulation results are discussed in Sect. 4, and Sect. 5 concludes the paper.

## 2 Security-Critical Distributed Real-Time Tasks Management Model

For the key task management in distributed real-time systems, in this paper we give a task management model in the distributed real-time system with the consideration of consideration of the security factors.

The distributed real-time system is quite complicated, Zhan Jinyu gave a simple model for mapping in [5] for this problem. In this paper, we consider one kind of simple distributed real-time system model and task. We use $T = \{T_i : i = 1, 2, \ldots, m\}$ to represent the set of distributed real-time tasks to be proceeded. And the real-time task model can be described as $T_i = (E, Sec, L, D, W)$, where $E$ is the execution time of real-time task, $Sec$ is on behalf of the security service, $L$ is on behalf of the security level of service, and $D$ is on behalf of the deadline time, $W$ is on behalf of amount of the task's data size (using KB as unit [2]). In addition, the tasks are non-periodic and non-preemptive, and they are independent of each other.

We use $DN = \{DNode_k : k = 1, 2, \ldots n\}$ to describe the distributed system. $DNode_k$ indicates the specific information of a distributed node. We divide the $n$ nodes $DN$ into $m$ groups as $PN = \{PN_i : i = 1, 2, \ldots m\}$, each group has varying amount of processing nodes $PN_i = \{PN_{ik} : k = 1, 2, \ldots h\}$. Actually, it is a directed acyclic graph. Real-time task scheduler firstly selects groups according to their priority, then selects a suitable processing node $PN_{ik}$ for processing operations [6] from each group.

Due to the need of considering a number of factors, especially safety and timeliness for the management of distributed real-time system, the key factor of the task $T_i$ will eventually be mapped to the selected node. We use $Node = (E, Sec, L, D, W)$ to represent a task that is mapped to the corresponding scheduled-node. $E$ represents the execution time of real-time task on each node, and $Sec$ is on behalf of the security service; $L$ is on behalf of the security level of service; $D$ is on behalf of the deadline; $W$ refers to the amount of data in each processing node. In the distributed real-time systems, there are a series of real-time instance set $TI = \{J_1, J_2, \ldots J_n\}$, the $J_i$ must be exceeded before $J_{i+1}$.

$E$ can be estimated under the processing capability of the distributed nodes. And the safety performance of real-time tasks is achieved by the overhead of systems. So when calculating the execution time of task, we should consider the security requirements and security benefits and the overhead that security requirements take. Figure 1 shows the task management model.

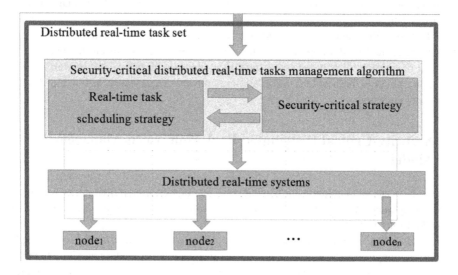

**Fig. 1.** Security-critical distributed real-time tasks management model

## 3   Security-Critical Distributed Real-Time Task Management Algorithm

The main goal of the management model raised in the previous section is to guarantee that the tasks can get the maximum security service assurance, under the circumstance that the tasks could meet the time constraints.

In this section, we will formulate the management goal and constraints. And we use the management model in previous section to solve the management problem by the improved Dijkstra algorithm. The algorithm is designed for Node-based model. The optimal path algorithm is to obtain the optimal management solution.

### 3.1   Problem Statement

Without loss of generality, we should guarantee the time limit of any management situation in the task set meet the tasks requirements, while achieving the security of the every task maximum. Here we ignore the impact of the CPU load on the risk, $\sigma$ represents the security risks of the distributed tasks set, formula was established to describe this relationship.

$$\sigma = \sum_{m=1}^{n} \frac{p}{p_m} SR(L) \tag{1}$$

According to the Sect. 2 model, we can dispatch formal description.

$$Schedule = \{PT_1, PT_2, \ldots PT_m\} \tag{2}$$

We use the $PT_i$ to represent the i-th task management in node $i$ $PT_i \rightarrow \{Node_{i1}\left(E_{i1}, Sec_{i1}, L_{i1}, D_{i1}\right), Node_{i2}\left(E_{i2}, Sec_{i2}, L_{i2}, D_{i2}\right), Node_{in}\left(E_{in}, Sec_{in}, L_{in}, D_{in}\right)$. It can therefore find a group $PNode$ group node, without loss of generality, we assume that this group of distributed nodes as $Node_{1i}, Node_{2j}, \ldots Node_{nk}$, which meet $1 \leq i \leq n$, and $1 \leq j \leq m, 1 \leq k \leq q$, while the real-time task set must satisfy the formulas 3, 4 and 5 three constraints.

$$E_{1i} + E_{2j} + \cdots + E_{nk} \leq E\,(System) \tag{3}$$

$$Sec_{1i} + Sec_{2j} + \cdots + Sec_{nk} \leq Sec\,(System) \tag{4}$$

$$D_{1i} + D_{2j} + \cdots + D_{nk} \leq D\,(System) \tag{5}$$

In this way, the problem is transformed into distributed nodes composed of a figure for the shortest path algorithm, as shown in Fig. 2.

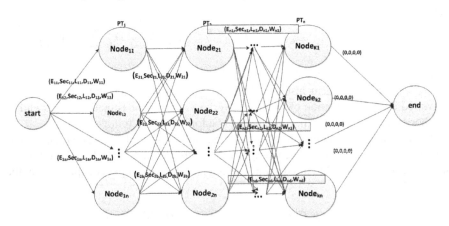

**Fig. 2.** Convert to a directed graph

Based on this, we make two definitions:
Definition 1: The connection of the $Node_{uv}$ and edges $Node_{ij}$ weights of the vertices defined as a sequence, as shown in Eq. 6 below.

$$w\left(Node_{uv}, Node_{ij}\right) = f\left(E_{ij}, Sec_{ij}, L_{ij}, D_{ij}, W_{ij}\right) \tag{6}$$

When we seek the shortest path, we have taken the arrangement of the weight, the balance of security, the additional overhead brought by security requirement in directed acyclic graph into account. So that we can balance the design of management performance parameters in the distributed real-time system.

In addition, we add two special vertices in the directed graph: the source vertex *start* and the purpose vertices *end* in a directed graph, the start of the source vertex is responsible for connecting the vertices of the first distributed nodes for a node $Node_{1i}$ $(1 \leq i \leq a)$, the weight of the edge could be seen in the formula 7 below.

$$w\left(start, Node_{1i}\right) = f\left(E_{1i}, Sec_{1i}, L_{1i}, D_{1i}, W_{1i}\right) \tag{7}$$

The final vertex *end* is responsible for connecting a vertex of the last set of nodes $Node_{nk}$ $(1 \leq k \leq d)$, the weight of the edges is $(0, 0, 0, 0, 0)$.

Definition 2: there is a path $p$ from $Node_{x+1j}$ to the starting point *start* crossing through the vertex $Node_{1k_1}$, $Node_{2k_2}$, ... $Node_{xk_x}$, $((k_1, k_2, ... k_x)$, are a, b, ..., m in the range of a value, the corresponding set of nodes in a group management node), the directed graph a path shown in Eq. 8.

$$p = \left(start, Node_{1k_1}, Node_{2k_2}, ... Node_{xk_x}\right) \tag{8}$$

The length of the path can be expressed as the expression 9.

$$wl\left(p:Node_{x+1,j} \rightarrow start\right) =$$
$$f\left(\sum_{i=1}^{x+1} E_{ik_i}, \sum_{i=1}^{x+1} Sec_{ik_i}, \sum_{i=1}^{x+1} L_{ik_i}, \sum_{i=1}^{x+1} D_{ik_i}, \sum_{i=1}^{x+1} W_{ik_i}\right) \tag{9}$$

In addition, the pre-vertex from $Node_{x+1j}$ to the starting point of start vertex is $\tau_{x+1j}$.

So, the security-critical distributed real-time system task scheduler question was converted into an evaluation of the source vertex start to the destination vertex end of the shortest path problem. This problem can be formalized as follows.

In distributed real-time system, schedulable node is described as an $m \times n$ matrix, the establishment of a band have the right value to the diagram $G(V, E)$ (where $V$ is the $m \times n$ matrix), the weights of edges in the graph with a five-tuple is expressed by the formula 10.

$$w\left(Core_{uv}, Core_{ij}\right) = f\left(E_{ij}, Sec_{ij}, L_{ij}, D_{ij}, W_{ij}\right) \tag{10}$$

The length of the path $p$ is the function value constituted by the performance parameters of the edge, and the relationship between the execution time is directly proportional to the amount of data, and it is proportional to the level required by the security service. We define the source vertex start to the purpose of the vertex end of the shortest path to meet the formula 11.

$$\tau(start, end) = \begin{cases} min\{|wl(p:start \rightarrow end)|\} \\ \infty, otherwise \end{cases} \tag{11}$$

The goal of the problem is to find such a vertex that from the starting point start to end of path $p$, the formula 12 was established.

$$wl(p:start \rightarrow end) = \tau(start, end) \tag{12}$$

## 3.2   Improved Dijkstra Algorithm

Dijkstra algorithm is a classical method of solving the diagram single-source shortest path problem. The algorithm requires a non-negative weight on the edges in the graph. It is shown in Fig. 2 that seeking the shortest path from the source vertex to the destination vertex by the improved algorithm. The path value from any vertex $Node_{xj}$ to the start vertex can defined by the formula 13.

$$wl\left(p{:}Node_{xj} \to start\right)$$
$$= f\left(\sum_{i=1}^{x} E_{ik_i}, \sum_{i=1}^{x} Sec_{ik_i}, \sum_{i=1}^{x} L_{ik_i}, \sum_{i=1}^{x} D_{ik_i}, \sum_{i=1}^{x} W_{ik_i}\right) \tag{13}$$

Each vertex may be in one of the following three states:

1. State 1: not updated, then the distance parameter is $(\infty, \infty, \infty, \infty, \infty)$;
2. State 2: updated, the distance parameter has been updated at least once;
3. State 3: terminated, the distance parameter is the optimal path value to the start vertex, and there is no need to be updated.

First of all, the source vertex of start is the terminated state, the distance parameter can be expressed as Eq. 14.

$$wl\left(p{:}start \to end\right) = (0,0,0,0,0) \tag{14}$$

Other vertex is not updated and the distance parameter is formula 15.

$$wl\left(p{:}Node_{xj} \to start\right) = (\infty, \infty, \infty, \infty, \infty) \tag{15}$$

Then, the start of the source vertex will update its adjacent vertices $(Node_{1k},$ $1 \leq k \leq a$, shown in Fig. 2), the distance parameters $\tau_{1k} = start$, the formula 16.

$$wl\left(p{:}Node_{1k} \to start\right) = wl\left(start, Node_{1k}\right) \tag{16}$$

Then these vertices move into State 2, and select a shortest path of vertices $wl\left(p{:}Node_{1k} \to start\right)$ in State 2, and so on, and then update its adjacent vertices from the parameters.

Ordinarily, when a vertex $Node_{xj}$ of the shortest path $wl\left(p{:}Node_{1k} \to start\right)$ in State 2 is transferred to the state 3, it will update the vertex $Node_{x+1,k}$ ($1 \leq k \leq m$). If distance parameter meets:

$$wl\left(p{:}Node_{x+1,k} \to start\right) > wl\left(p{:}Node_{xj} \to start\right) + w\left(Node_{xj}, Node_{x+1,k}\right),$$

Then we can get the formula 17.

$$wl\left(p{:}Node_{x+1,k} \to start\right) = wl\left(p{:}Node_{xj} \to start\right) + w\left(Node_{xj}, Node_{x+1,k}\right) \tag{17}$$

And there is $\tau_{x+1,k} = Node_{xj}$. Dijkstra algorithm will continuously update the status of the vertices in the graph, until the end of the purpose of vertices reach the end state. Then we can get a shortest path from start to end, and this path can be rigorously proved to be optimal by mathematic.

For solving the optimal path: the use of the improved Dijkstra algorithm need us to establish a directed graph, the vertices in the graph line corresponding to each node based on safety-critical distributed real-time systems. Each vertex with a five-dimensional parameter group said that the distance of the starting vertex start with the expression 18.

$$wl\left(p{:}Node_{xj} \rightarrow start\right)$$

$$= f\left(\sum_{i=1}^{x} E_{ik_i}, \sum_{i=1}^{x} Sec_{ik_i}, \sum_{i=1}^{x} L_{ik_i}, \sum_{i=1}^{x} D_{ik_i}, \sum_{i=1}^{x} W_{ik_i}\right) \tag{18}$$

We can obtain a recursive expression 19 according the model above.

$$wl\left(p{:}Node_{xi} \rightarrow start\right) = \min_{1 \leq k \leq m}\left\{wl\left(p{:}Node_{x-1,j} \rightarrow start\right) + wl\left(Node_{x-1,k}, Node_{xj}\right)\right\} \tag{19}$$

Then the establishment of an optimal path from the source vertex start to $Node_{xj}$ is completed.

## 4   Experimental Analysis

In this section, we simulate a distributed real-time task scheduler to evaluate the feasibility and effectiveness of the proposed task management model.

As we mention in Sect. 2, there are three kinds of security services we consider in this paper. We abbreviate the overhead of cryptographic security service as EO, the overhead of data integrity security service as IO, the overhead of certified security service Authentication as AO. And if the task need all the three security services, we use ALL as an abbreviation.

As we mainly consider the safety and timeliness of tasks in this paper, we assume that the data of all the tasks are in the same size, and the data size has no impact on the execution time of task. Table 1 lists the parameters of each node we simulated.

The goal of the task schedule simulation experiments is driving the distributed real-time task set to meet overall time requirement, and maximizing security requirements of the distributed real-time task set. In order to facilitate the data test, we simply the formula of path mapping, as it shows in formula 20.

$$w_{sec} = \lambda_1 \frac{f_1(k)}{f_{sec}(Sec)} + \lambda_2 f_e(E)\, \lambda_1 + \lambda_2 = 1,$$

$$\lambda_1 \in [0,1], \lambda_2 \in [0,1] \tag{20}$$

$f_1(k)$ is the scale factor of the time overhead for safe consumption, we agree the constant as 10 according to the time constant offered by tasks above. $f_{sec}(Sec)$ is the overhead of function of the level of security, and *Sec* represents the level of safety and security service. In order to simplify the experimental results, we assume that the three security service have the same overhead. $f_e(E)$ is the execution time of task or service time, and it is a static data in accordance with the agreement of the model. $\lambda_1$ and $\lambda_2$ is decided by the user to determine the scaling parameter of security overhead and time urgency in different level. Here, from the perspective of experimental simulation, we agreed to use: $\lambda_1 = \lambda_2 = \frac{1}{2}$.

We can map the got value to the nodes with the ignorance of message delivered overhead and use the value to represent the value of node path weights. And the weight value indicates the integrated value of security overhead and time constrains.

Table 1. Distributed nodes parameters table

| Node groups | Node ID | Execution times (ms) | Security service | Security service level | Deadline (ms) |
|---|---|---|---|---|---|
| $Node_1$ | $Node_{11}$ | 80 | ALL | 0.1 | 100 |
| | $Node_{12}$ | 110 | EO/IO | 0.2 | 200 |
| | $Node_{13}$ | 180 | ALL | 0.3 | 300 |
| $Node_2$ | $Node_{21}$ | 200 | EO/IO | 0.4 | 100 |
| | $Node_{22}$ | 150 | EO/AO | 0.2 | 200 |
| $Node_3$ | $Node_{31}$ | 160 | ALL | 0.3 | 400 |
| | $Node_{32}$ | 220 | ALL | 0.6 | 350 |
| | $Node_{33}$ | 350 | EO/IO | 0.7 | 400 |
| | $Node_{34}$ | 420 | IO/AO | 0.9 | 450 |
| $Node_4$ | $Node_{41}$ | 150 | ALL | 0.3 | 150 |
| | $Node_{42}$ | 180 | EO/IO | 0.4 | 200 |
| | $Node_{43}$ | 240 | ALL | 0.5 | 350 |

According to the simplified constraints of the security overhead and experimental data, we can roughly map the shortest path in Fig. 3.

Then we can run the management algorithm of the shortest path based on this directed graph. We can get the management node sequence diagram, where the solid black line is for management node sequence.

There are a number of factors for selection in the distributed real-time tasks, while the task itself has many constraints, and the choice of weight is of diversity. Although the shortest path algorithm can get the optimal path, the resultant management node sequence will be different due to different ways to calculate the weight and the task itself are different, such as energy consumption, security and other requirements (Fig. 4).

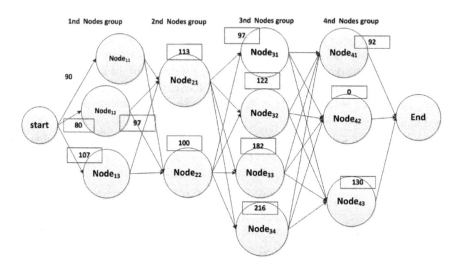

**Fig. 3.** The weight of the distributed nodes mapping

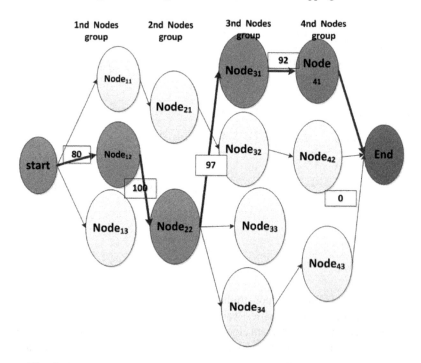

**Fig. 4.** Security-critical distributed real-time task management node sequence

In this paper we use a linked list to store the distributed node information, and then search for the solution. The time complexity of improved Dijkstra algorithm is $O\left(n^2\right)$. If you use the priority queue and the adjacency matrix to store node information, you can reduce the algorithm time complexity to $O(m + nlogn)$. From the simulation result we can see that the improved Dijkstra algorithm can largely guarantee the security of distributed real-time task set under the circumstance the time limit to meet the requirements. And achieving the purpose safety-critical distributed real-time task management basically.

## 5    Conclusion

In this paper, we have considered not only the real-time constraints, but also the security needs of the tasks during security-critical distributed real-time task management. We have resolved the security-critical distributed real-time task management problem using a weighted directed graph, and proposed an effective solution for the schedule of the distributed real-time tasks. This method guarantees the security needs of diverse real-time tasks. And it can be comprehensive evaluation system for real-time and safety, obtaining the optimal partition of the distributed real-time task management.

## References

1. Loyall, J., Schantz, R.: A distributed real-time embedded application for surveillance, detection, and tracking of time critical targets. In: Proceedings of the 11th IEEE Real-Time and Embedded Technology and Applications Symposium, pp. 88–97 (2005)
2. Xie, T., Qin, X.: Security-aware resource allocation for real-time parallel jobs on homogeneous and heterogeneous clusters. IEEE Trans. Parallel Distrib. Syst. **19**, 682–697 (2008)
3. Xie, T., Qin, X.: Performance evaluation of a new management algorithm for distributed systems with security heterogeneity. J. Parallel Distrib. Comput. **67**(10), 1067–1081 (2007)
4. Xie, T., Qin, X., Sung, A.: SAREC: a security-aware management strategy for real-time applications on clusters. In: Proceeding of ICPP 2005 Conference, Norway, pp. 5–12 (2005)
5. Huang, J., Wang, Y., Cao, F.: On developing distributed middleware services for QoS and criticality-based resource negotiation and adaptation. Real-Time Syst. **16**(2), 187–221 (2007)
6. Jinyu, Z., Guangze, X.: Optimal hardware/software co-synthesis for core-based SoC designs. J. Syst. Eng. Electron. **17**(2), 402–409 (2006)
7. Apvrille, A., Pourzandi, M.: XML distributed security policy for clusters. Comput. Secur. J. **23**(8), 649–658 (2007)
8. Azzedin, F., Maheswaran, M.: Towards trust-aware resource management in grid computing systems. In: Proceedings of the Second IEEE/ACM International Symposium on Cluster Computing and the Grid (2002)
9. Hou, C.-J., Shin, K.G.: Allocation of periodic task modules with precedence and deadline constraints in distributed real-time systems. IEEE Trans. Comput. **46**(12), 1338–1355 (2008)
10. Garey, M.R., Johnson, D.S.: Strong NP-completeness results: motivation, examples, and implications. J. Assoc. Comput. Mach. **25**(3), 499–508 (2008)
11. Houstis, C.E.: Module allocation of real-time applications for distributed systems. IEEE Trans. Softw. Eng. **16**(7), 699–709 (2007)
12. Tindell, K., Clark, J.: Holistic schedulability analysis for distributed hard real-time systems. Micro-processing Microprogramming **40**(20), 117–134 (2008)

13. Foster, I., Kesselman, C., Tsudik, G., Tuecke, S.: A security architecture for computational grids. In: Proceedings of the Fifth Conference on Computer and Communications Security San Francisco, CA, pp. 80–94 (2008)
14. Hong, K.S., Leung, J.Y.-T.: On-line management of real-time tasks. IEEE Trans. Comput. **41**(10), 1326–1331 (2008)
15. Goldberg, D.E.: Genetic Algorithms in Search, Optimization, and Machine Learning. Addison-Wesley, Reading (1989)

# A Model of Dynamic Malware Analysis Based on VMI

Chengye Li[✉], Yangyue Xiang, and Jiangyong Shi

National University of Defense Technology, Changsha 410073, China
{lichengye,yyx,shijiangyong}@nudt.edu.cn

**Abstract.** With the development of cloud computing technology, more and more malicious software attacks against virtual machines and virtualized environments have increased sharply. However, leading cloud security is particularly prominent. To solve this problem, we have designed a model to analyze the process of a virtual machine. The model is based on a virtual machine introspection technology, which can monitor the program running in the virtual machine. It combined with the characteristics of a plurality of open-source software, such as Drakvuf, Libvmi, Malheur. We have designed it with three parts, the preparing detected environment, capturing behavior and behavioral analysis. It can be used to capture the running process of malware, detect rootkit and analyze the sequence of system calls. Finally, the experiment result demonstrates the effectiveness and practicability of our proposed model.

**Keywords:** Virtual machine introspection · Malware analysis · System-call sequences · Cloud security · Rootkits

## 1  Introduction

Malware analysis refers to computer security researchers analyzed the malware in the operating system execution process, and its impact on operating system. Through malware behavior analysis, security researchers can identify specific steps to repair and protect the operating system.

Currently, malware analysis is essentially based on sandbox technology, which can extract malware behavior through its execution in an isolated virtual machine environment. Its typical applications include CWSandbox [1], Anubis [2] and Cuckoo [3], Cuckoo is based on virtual machine technology, combining with central control system, module design, and python features, which is already an automated malware behavior research environment. However, this sandbox is an independent operating environment. Although it ensures a safe working environment and reliability, the deployment is too complex to implement and protect the work environment.

Current cloud computing and virtualization technology develop rapidly, more and more application environment are proposed, their safety is more worthy of attention. In a virtualized environment, it has clear division level, especially Xen [4] based virtual machines are divided to different domains, we can use VMI (Virtual Machine Introspection) technology to extract rich information in a virtual machine to safeguard its security. Meanwhile, VMI mechanism is implemented in the VMM level, thereby it is

© Springer International Publishing Switzerland 2015
G. Wang et al. (Eds.): ICA3PP 2015 Workshops, LNCS 9532, pp. 465–475, 2015.
DOI: 10.1007/978-3-319-27161-3_42

not to be detected easily by malware, and have better concealment. VMI has been widely applied to the malware analysis [5], intrusion detection [6] and memory auditing [7].

Therefore, this article presents a model that based VMI for virtual environments malware behavior analysis. The rest of the paper is organized as follows. In Sect. 2, we discuss VMI technology and its application. In Sect. 3, we discuss design idea and implementation. In Sect. 4, we will talk experimental results and comparison with other model. In Section we give some conclusions on our model.

## 2   Related Works

To help better understand the following contents, it is beneficial for us to review the common architecture of virtual computer systems, especially some basic knowledge about the interactions between Guest OS and VMM.

Virtualization environment refers to a VMM logically divides a real physical machine into many virtual machines that can host operating systems. Each of these programs feels that it occupies the entire machine itself, that is to say, it has its own CPU, its own memory, its own I/O devices and so on.

Before the official presentation of the concept of VMI, its similar idea has been adopted in the research of computer system. In the early research of virtualization environment, which is usually deploy a monitoring program in a virtual machine. The program is used to monitor the software and process running in the virtual machine, while it simply likes a normal software. However, it is not reliable to install a virtual machine monitor directly inside the virtual machine, so that subsequent monitoring program will generate a form as a driver in a guest operating system. With the development of virtualization platform, there was implementation of a monitoring program in the VMM. VMI technology is completely deployed in the VMM, then we put forward the concept of Virtual Machine Introspection.

In the paper [8], it first proposed the concept VMI, then academic and technical communities was carried out extensive researches, which define VMI: the use of its internal state monitor virtual machine from an external method to analyze the software running in the virtual machine is running.

Lares [9], is a virtualization-based architecture designed to protect certain classes of security software that rely on the active monitoring of system events. A security application built on top of Lares should have the flexibility to place hooks in any location in the guest OS's kernel, at arbitrarily high abstraction levels.

Libvmi [10] library is implemented in C as a shared library. Because all Guest OS behaviors and internal state can be obtained within the VMM because it is the primary and direct hardware resources manager in the virtualized computing system. Figure 1 shows the overall software architecture.

Based on the Libvmi library, we can get the target Guest OS configuration. All operating systems have a few core data structures and global variables, through them plus the target Guest OS internal semantic knowledge, more useful and hidden information can be easily exploited and distilled.

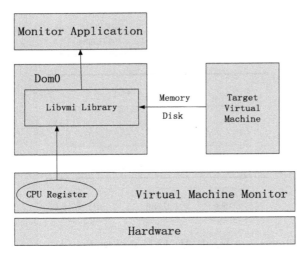

**Fig. 1.** The Libvmi architecture

We also can get the target Guest OS processes list that cannot be bypassed by the traditional techniques. At the same time, we also can get another view of the current processes in the target Guest OS utilizing its native tools, such as ps in Linux and tasklist in Windows or the like. Through the comparisons of the two view listings, it can derive whether the target Guest OS has hidden processes.

Drakvuf [11] is designed to minimize the resource requirements and to enable the fast deployment of virtual machines. It is built on the open-source Xen VMM and runs in the control domain (dom0) to make use of direct memory access (DMA) through the LibVMI.

## 3   Architecture

In order to introduce the design idea and performance of our model in detail, the first part is sample preparation which can add malicious software sample. The second part is behavior capture, by implementing VMI technology in VMM, we can capture system calls and API functions in virtual machine. The last part is behavior analysis, which is used to analyze the result of second part, discovering the presence of malware behavior.

### 3.1   Sample Preparation

In order to analyze the malware, we construct a malware execution environment in a virtual machine. By modifying the virtual machine disk information, we can inject malware samples to the malware execution environment. In order to avoid the use of the network during the sample injection while maintaining isolation of physical hosts and virtual machines. We use Guestfish [12] for malware sample injection, which is based on libguestfs. Meanwhile, it provides a API function copying the file to virtual machine.

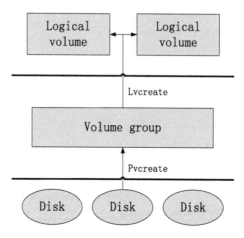

Fig. 2. The LVM architecture

The combination of LVM snapshot [13] and Xen disk memory mechanism is more suitable for fast backup and restore Xen virtual machine state. In this section we first look at LVM snapshot, Xen memory mechanism will be discussed in later section.

LVM is abbreviation of logical volume management, it is a disk partition management mechanism. LVM is a logical layer built on the hard disk partition to increase the flexibility of the disk partition management. LVM works between the disk partition and file system to shield the underlying disk partition for file system (Fig. 2).

Snapshot is a very useful feature offered by LVM. Its principle is to copy the original volume origin metadata to create a logical volume, and any data on the physical volume is not copied. Therefore, the creation process of LVM is in real-time. A snapshot is a special type of logical volumes, which contains the specified time to create complete data in the original logical volume, you can operate a snapshot without worrying about data changes so that the backup failed. LVM snapshots use a technique called "copy -on-write" technology to track and maintain data consistency. Its principle is very simple, that is to track changes in the block on the original volume, before the data is copied to the snapshot changes will set aside their own space (as the name suggests is called copy -on-write). When the time to read the snapshot, modified snapshot data is read from the reserved space, the unmodified data is redirected to the original volume up to read, and therefore between the snapshot of the file system with more than one device layer COW device.

### 3.2 Behavior Capture

Memory virtualization means, VMM by simulating memory so that the virtual machine operating system thinks its memory allocation results from the continuous memory address 0. In a non-virtualized environment, program when accessing memory design to virtual addresses into physical addresses process. In a virtualized environment, client physical address space, and memory virtualization is introduced through two NAT address space to support virtualization. That guest virtual address (GVA) is converted to guest physical address (GPA) firstly, and then converted to host physical address (HPA) [14].

Libvmi uses the Intel EPT [15] technology to virtualize the memory. EPT technology takes the EPT page table into the original CR3 page table to achieve another address mapping. CPU by querying the EPT page table, successive complete address translation, and finally obtain the physical address of the host. It is worth mentioning that, each time CPU querying EPT page table causes four times querying physical machine memory. Therefore, in order to achieve EPT technology, we must increase EPT-TLB to decrease the times of querying memory.

Based on memory virtualization, as long as we get the kernel base address of the virtual machine, it is easy to analyze the relative virtual address of the kernel structure and kernel functions. At first, we can get the operating state of OS kernel by means of analyzing the pdb kernel debugging file. Secondly we can use Rekall, which is a forensics tool, to get the running views of kernel functions. At runtime, FS and GS registers holds the kernel virtual address pointing_KPCR structure, the structure that holds a fixed RVA address, marking it as KiInitialPCR symbol. Finally, we only have to subtract the known RVA of the symbol from the address found in the vCPU register to obtain the kernel base address [16].

Considering the fact that a large number of malicious software also call user -level functions, so we should add sensitive functions of the user-level when extracting information to avoid some behavior of user-level functions. Most of the user-level functions are achieved by calling the dynamic link library functions, so we pay more attention to the functions in dll files, such as kernel32.dll, ws2_3.dll, wininet.dll and advapi32.dll.

Based on the capturing the kernel base address that we can get the distribution of kernel functions in memory. By #BP injected way [17] to monitor call of each kernel module and function, we can achieve the purpose of extracting malware behavior.

The injection mechanism relies on a series of events. When the virtual machine is created, our system will control the CR3 register, to capture file exchange events. Then walk through the kernel module that process loaded. If the kernel32.dll is loaded in the memory, it will be marked down and the virtual machine continues to execute until user-level code.

Hijacking mechanism occurs at the first instruction of user-level code, and locates the injection function of the position in the kernel32.dll. Then the process proceeds to hijack module, and save the hijack statement and RCX, RDX register into stack space. The return address is injected with a breakpoint at the end of the whole process execution to alert. Finally, the function will be injected into the RIP address register, then you can begin to analyze the work of the virtual machine (Fig. 3).

### 3.3 Behavior Analysis

The third part of this model is behavior analysis, which is used to analyze the behavior acquired in the second part. We adopted the clustering and classification analysis methods [18]. Classification is to classify the malware automatically among multiple

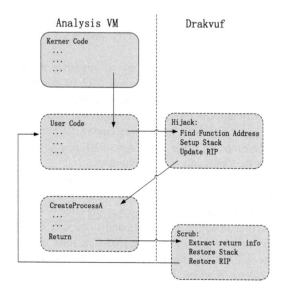

**Fig. 3.** Hijack the execution of malware sample

malwares, with the original cluster class (prototype) information as the basis of classification. Clustering is based on the original prototype extraction algorithm to re-extract and re-clustering the malware sample to generate new cluster classes. Before the samples analysis, we must use n-gram algorithm to generate high-dimensional vector space and extract the prototypes for cluster and classification.

Clustering for analysis of malware behavior has been proposed by Bailey and later refined by Bayer (Table 1).

**Table 1.** Clustering algorithm

| **Algorithm1** Clustering using prototypes |
| --- |
| 1: **for** $z, z0 \in prototypes$ **do** |
| 2: $distance[z, z0] \leftarrow \|\phi \hat{}(z) - \phi \hat{}(z0)\|$ |
| 3: **while** $\min(distance) < dc$ **do** |
| 4: merge clusters $z, z0$ with minimum $distance[z, z0]$ |
| 5: update $distance$ using complete linkage |
| 6: **for** $x \in reports$ **do** |
| 7: $z \leftarrow$ nearest prototype to $x$ |
| 8: assign $x$ to cluster of $z$ |
| 9: reject clusters with less than $m$ members |

Using each prototype as an individual cluster, the algorithm proceeds by iteratively determining and merging the nearest pair of clusters (line 4). This procedure terminates if the distance between the closest clusters is larger than the predefined parameter dc. To compute distances between clusters, the algorithm considers the maximum distance of their individual members—a standard technique of hierarchical clustering referred to as complete linkage.

The application of classification for the analysis of malware behavior has been studied by Lee and Mody and Rieck. In both approaches, behavior of unknown malware is classified to known classes of behavior, where the initial training data is labeled using anti-virus scanners (Table 2).

**Table 2.** Classification algorithm

| **Algorithm2** Classification using prototypes |
| --- |
| 1: **for** $x \in$ *reports* **do** |
| 2: $z \leftarrow$ nearest prototype to $x$ |
| 3: **if** $\|\phi\,\hat{}(z) - \phi\,\hat{}(x)\| > d_r$ **then** |
| 4: reject $x$ as unknown class |
| 5: **else** |
| 6: assign $x$ to cluster of $z$ |

For each report x, the algorithm determines the nearest prototype of the clusters in the training data (line 1–2). If the nearest prototype is within the radius dr, the report is assigned to the respective cluster, whereas otherwise it is rejected and held back for later incremental analysis (line 4–6).

## 4  Experimental Results

In order to evaluate the performance of our proposed model. The experiments were performed on Dell PowerEdge R730xd server, with Intel Xeon E5-2603 v3, 2 TB disk and 32 GB memory. The virtualization software is Xen 4.4.1.

The first experiment is used to evaluate clustering results of behavior analysis. To assess the performance of clustering, we employ the evaluation metrics of precision and recall. The precision P reflects how well individual clusters agree with malware classes and the recall R measures to what extent classes are scattered across clusters, as described in formula (1). Formally, we define precision and recall for a set of clusters C and a set of malware classes Y as [19]:

$$P = \frac{1}{n}\sum_{c \in C} \#c \text{ and } R = \frac{1}{n}\sum_{y \in Y} \#y. \tag{1}$$

where #c refers to the largest number of reports in cluster c sharing the same class and #y refers to the largest number of reports labelled y within one cluster. Consequently, the goal is to seek an analysis setup which maximizes precision and recall. An aggregated performance score is adopted for our evaluation, denoted as F-measure, which combines precision and recall. A perfect discovery of classes yields F = 1, while either a low precision or recall results in a lower F-measure.

$$F1 = \frac{2 \cdot P \cdot R}{P + R}.$$  (2)

Cuckoo is based on virtualization technology, using a central control system and module design, combining with the automation features of python, which is a quite automated malware behavior research environment. So the experiment used Cuckoo to compare with our model (Figs. 4 and 5).

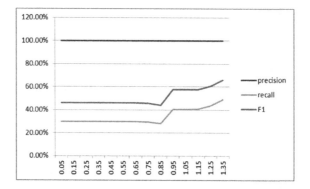

**Fig. 4.** The result of Cuckoo

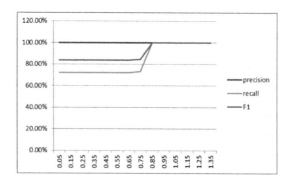

**Fig. 5.** The result of behavior analysis

Results for the evaluation of clustering are presented in above figures. F1-measure reflected the evaluation of clustering by balance the recall and precision, and better clustering effects comes with larger F1-measure. The abscissa represents the minimum distance between prototypes. It can be seen in Figure, the F1-measure is 65.8 %, when the minimum distance get the maximum value. While the F1-measure is 100 %, when the minimum distance is 0.85.

Our model can not only analyzes the malware but also detects the rootkit hidden in the OS kernel. The second experiment is used to check the result of rootkit detection. We get a rootkit sample thought the Internet.

Table 3 shows the results of two tools to extract the function calls of rootkit. Each tool has 3 min to monitor the virtual machine which is attacked by rootkit sample. Cuckoo can get the API function in user-level, while our model can get the kernel functions. The API functions Cuckoo get in 3 min is much too less than the kernel functions our model get, it is because rootkits usually modify internal kernel structures to hide their presence on a system. So it almost impossible for rootkit to call API functions.

**Table 3.** Function calls in rootkit

| Model | Function | Times |
|---|---|---|
| Our model | *ExAllocatePoolWithTag* | *52191* |
| | *NtClose* | 7059 |
| | *NtOpenProcess* | *6383* |
| | *NtQueryValueKey* | *3769* |
| | *NtCallbackReturn* | 2628 |
| | *NtOpenKeyEx* | *2328* |
| | *NtQueryInformationProcess* | *1865* |
| | *ExAllocatePoolWithQuotaTag* | *1724* |
| | *NtQueryInformationToken* | *1614* |
| | *NtAlpcSendWaitReceivePort* | *966* |
| Cuckoo | *NtReadVirtualMemory* | *3040* |
| | *RegOpenKeyExW* | 174 |
| | *RegCloseKey* | 157 |
| | *ZwMapViewOfSection* | 130 |
| | *LdrGetProcedureAddress* | 116 |
| | *RegQueryValueExW* | 105 |
| | *RegOpenKeyExA* | 71 |
| | *NtCreateSection* | 44 |
| | *LdrLoadDll* | 36 |
| | *DeviceIoControl* | 21 |

## 5 Conclusion

In this paper, we presented our model, a malware analysis model based on virtual machine introspection. Aiding by VMI, our model can monitor kernel functions and hijack the execution of malware in virtual machine and get its system calls as well as API functions sequence. Using machine learning algorithm which adopts the clustering and classification method enables our model to analyze malicious behavior in malware samples. We evaluated the model with two experiments showing its ability to get the function calls in the samples especially performed in system kernel. The first experiment shows the function calls sequence has a higher F1-measure and recall which reflects its better clustering effect and stronger malware analytical capacity. The second experiment shows its ability to detect rootkits hidden in the virtual machine which is not be achieved in other malware analysis tools. Our model needs to be improved in several aspects include the less system performance loss, better ways to trap memory accesses such as on a granularity without altering the memory contents and so on.

# References

1. Willems, G., Holz, T., Freiling, F.: Toward automated dynamic malware analysis using CWSandbox. IEEE Secur. Priv. **5**, 32–39 (2007)
2. Bayer, U., Moser, A., Kruegel, C., Kirda, E.: Dynamic analysis of malicious code. J. Comput. Virol. **2**, 67–77 (2006)
3. Cuckoobox. http://www.cuckoosandbox.org/
4. Xen. http://www.xenproject.org/
5. Jiang, X., Wang, X., Xu, D.: Stealthy malware detection through vmm-based out-of-the box semantic view reconstruction. In: Proceedings of the 14th ACM Conference on Computer and Communications Security, pp. 128–138 (2007)
6. Srivastava, A., Giffin, J.T.: Tamper-resistant, application-aware blocking of malicious network connections. In: Lippmann, R., Kirda, E., Trachtenberg, A. (eds.) RAID 2008. LNCS, vol. 5230, pp. 39–58. Springer, Heidelberg (2008)
7. Nance, K., Bishop, M., Hay, B.: Investigating the implications of virtual machine introspection for digital forensics. In: International Conference on Availability, Reliability and Security, ARES 2009, pp. 1024–1029 (2009)
8. Garfinkel, T., Rosenblum, M.: A virtual machine introspection based architecture for intrusion detection. In: Proceedings of the Network and Distributed Systems Security Symposium, pp. 191–206 (2003)
9. Payne, B.D., Carbone, M., Sharif, M., et al.: Lares: An architecture for secure active monitoring using virtualization. In: Proceedings of the 2008 IEEE Symposium on Security and Privacy, pp. 233–247. IEEE Computer Society (2008)
10. Xiong, H., Liu, Z., Xu, W., et al.: Libvmi: a library for bridging the semantic gap between guest OS and VMM. In: International Conference on Computer and Information Technology, pp. 549–556. IEEE (2012)
11. Lengyel, T.K., Maresca, S., Payne, B.D., et al.: Scalability, fidelity and stealth in the drakvuf dynamic malware analysis system. In: Proceedings of the 30th Annual Computer Security Applications Conference, pp. 386–395. ACM (2014)
12. Guestfish. http://libguestfs.org/guestfish.1.html
13. Payne, B.D.: Simplifying virtual machine introspection using libvmi. Sandia report (2012)
14. Intel Corporation Intel 64 and IA-32 architectures software developer's manual, volume 3B (2008)
15. Nakajima, J.: Intel virtualization technology roadmap and VT-d support in Xen (2006)
16. Okolica, J.S., Peterson, G.L.: Extracting forensic artifacts from windows o/s memory. Technical report, DTIC document (2011)

17. Deng, Z., Zhang, X., Xu, D.: Spider: stealthy binary program instrumentation and debugging via hardware virtualization. In: Proceedings of the 29th Annual Computer Security Applications Conference, ACSAC 2013, New York, NY, USA. ACM (2013)
18. Rieck, K., Trinius, P., Willems, C., Holz, T.: Automatic analysis of malware behavior using machine learning. J. Comput. Secur. **19**(4), 639–668 (2011)
19. Qiao, Y., Yang, Y., He, J., Tang, C., Liu, Z.: CBM: free, automatic malware analysis framework using API call sequences. In: Sun, F., Li, T., Li, H. (eds.) Knowledge Engineering and Management. AISC, vol. 214, pp. 225–236. Springer, Heidelberg (2014)

# Multiple Secret Sharing Using Natural Language Letter Based Visual Cryptography Scheme

Roshni Kadeparambil Raphel$^{(\boxtimes)}$, H. Muhammed Ilyas, and Janu R. Panicker

Computer Science & Engineering, College of Engineering Cherthala,
Alappuzha 688541, Kerala, India
roshnikraphel@gmail.com
http://www.cectl.ac.in

**Abstract.** Visual cryptography (VC) is a method used for encrypting visual informations in such a way that it can be easily decrypted by human visual system. Existing visual cryptographic schemes focuses only on using transparencies as shares and the shares appear as noise like pixels. These meaningless shares are not user friendly and create transmission risk problems. And schemes generating meaningful shares are limited to single secret sharing. This paper proposes a Letter-based Visual Cryptography Scheme (LVCS), which creates meaningful shares for sharing multiple secrets that can be used for both binary and grayscale images. In this method we use natural language letters for representing pixels of secret images. Here we are generating meaningful text files instead of share images. So here the text files contain meaningful data and an attacker will not recognize them as containing secrets. This method satisfies security conditions since the secret information can be reconstructed by any k shares but with less than k shares reveal nothing.

**Keywords:** Letter-based VCS · Multiple secrets · Meaningful share · Pixel expansion · Secret image

## 1 Introduction

With the advancement of technologies, transmission of information through the Internet has become more convenient. And the internet became the common medium for trasmitting various confidential informations such as military maps and secret keys. Attackers may make use of poor link over communication network to steal secret information that they need. So while sharing secret informations, security issues should be taken into consideration. To deal with the security problems of sharing secret images, various secret sharing methods have been developed.

Visual cryptography is introduced by Noar and Shamir [1] first in 1994. Visual cryptography (VC) is a method used for encrypting visual informations in such a way that it can be easily decrypted by human visual system that does not require a computer. Visual cryptography avoids complex computation at the time of decryption process, and the secret images can be decoded by simply

© Springer International Publishing Switzerland 2015
G. Wang et al. (Eds.): ICA3PP 2015 Workshops, LNCS 9532, pp. 476–486, 2015.
DOI: 10.1007/978-3-319-27161-3_43

stacking $n$ shares. This property makes visual cryptography more useful for the low computation load requirement.

Nowadays most of the personal datas are digitized, so more effort is required on data security. Protecting the data in a safe and secure way was always remains as a problem. Many attempts have been made to solve this problem within the cryptographic community. But all these conventional methods include complex algorithms and computations. But visual cryptography allows us to effectively and efficiently share secrets between a number of trusted parties since the decryption is as simple as superimposing shares.

Traditional VC mainly deals with a single binary secret image sharing between a number of participants, where the secret image is encoded into multiple shares and then decoded without any computation. This paper proposes a method for sharing multiple secrets with meaningful shares using letter based visual cryptography scheme.

The rest of this paper is organized as follows: In Sect. 2, we shall briefly review the concept of the different multiple secret sharing schemes. Motivation and design concepts are described in Sect. 3. In Sect. 4 we introduces the proposed encryption algorithms. Section 5 includes experimental results and analysis. Lastly, we conclude our work in Sect. 6.

## 2  Related Work

Visual cryptography provides a very powerful technique by which one secret can be distributed into two or more shares. Visual cryptography uses the idea of hiding secrets within images. These images are encoded into multiple shares and later decoded without any computation. In most of the visual cryptographic methods secret image is encrypted into n shares by by expanding each secret pixel into m subpixels. Pixel expansion results in large share size. Size reduced VCS were proposed in [2,3].

C.Yang proposed a probabilistic VCS(PVCS) method with nos pixel expansion [4]. Instead of expanding the pixel into m sub pixels, here only used one pixel to represent each pixel of secret image. All these methods genertes noisy shares as shown in Fig. 1, the noisy shares are easily attacked by hackers. Wen-Pinn Fang proposed a progressive VC with meaningful shares for single secret sharing in [5].

### 2.1  Multiple Secret Sharing

**Secret Sharing Based on Elliptic Curve Cryptography.** L. Pang et al. [6] proposed a new verifiable multi-secret sharing scheme based on an elliptic curve integrated encryption scheme (ECIES). In this method shares of each participant can be reused. Here even though $n$ pseudo shadows have been exposed among many co-operating participants, the real secret shadow is well protected by the properties of the two-variable one-way function. This method helps in cheater identification. But this method includes computations at time of secret reconstruction and also they have noisy shares.

Fig. 1. Shares and stacked result of (2,2)-PVCS

**Flip Visual Cryptography.** S.J. Lin et al. [7] proposed a flip visual cryptography (FVC) scheme with perfect security and no expansion of size. The proposed FVC scheme encodes two secret images into two dual purpose transparencies. Stacking the two transparencies can reveal one secret image. Flipping one of the two transparencies and then stacking with the other transparency can reveal the second secret image. Here there is no pixel expansion. But this scheme is also limited to two secret sharing and generate noisy shares.

**Secret Sharing Based on Master Key.** Jonathan Weir et al. [8], proposed a method based on master key where multiple secrets are taken into consideration. Here initially a master key is generated for all the secrets. Then merge these shares into a combined share, and adjust the master key and generate a new key. The secrets are revealed when the key is superimposed on the combined share in different locations.

**Secret Sharing Using Ring Shadow Image Technology.** Chen and Wu [9] proposed a (2,2) visual secret sharing scheme for two secret images. Here by simply stacking two share images the first secret image can be revealed. The second secret image is decoded by rotating first share image and then stacking with the other. The rotating angle can only be $90^o$, $180^o$ or $270^o$ that means the share images are in rectangular form.

To solve the problem of angle rotation of Chen and Wu's scheme, Hsu et al. [10] proposed another scheme to encode two secret images in two share images with random rotating angles. This scheme rolls up the share images in the form of rings so that the share images can be easily rotated at any random angle. But, here also the number of secret images remains limited.

J. Feng et al. [11] proposed a visual secret sharing scheme for hiding multiple secret images into two share images. The encryption process is based on a stacking relationship graph of secret pixels and a set of visual patterns which are defined according to this graph. Here the secret images can be obtained from the two share images at aliquot stacking angles.

**Secret Sharing Using Circle Shares.** To deal with the limitation of rotating angles Hsien-Chu Wu et al. [12] proposed an improved (2,2)-visual secret sharing scheme that uses circular shares. In this method two secret images can be embedded in the same shares. Stacking two shares reveals the first secret. After rotating one of the shares to a certain degree and stacking it with another share, the content of the second confidential message can be obtained. S. Shyu et al. [13], proposed a visual secret sharing scheme that encodes a set of $x \geq 2$ secrets into two circle shares and the $x$ secrets can be obtained one by one by stacking the first share and the rotated second shares with $x$ different rotation angles. But all these methods generate meaningless noisy shares.

**Secret Sharing Based on Cover Images.** Mustafa Ulutas, [14] presented a new scheme for hiding two halftone secret images into two meaningful shares created from halftone cover images. Meaningful shares are more desirable than noise-like meaningless shares because they look natural and do not attract attackers attention. But here the number of cover images increases with increase in number of secret images.

## 2.2 Comparison with the Traditional Scheme

Most of the traditional VCS mainly deals with a single binary secret image sharing between a number of participants, where the secret images are encoded into different noisy shares. These shares are not user friendly and also easily recognize them as containing secrets. And most of exisiting methods are limited to binary secret images sharing. This paper proposes a method for sharing multiple secrets with meaningful shares using letter based visual cryptography scheme. This scheme can be used for both binary and graysacle images. And as we are using text files this scheme is more secure than the traditional schemes.

## 3    Motivation and Design Concepts

So many methods are proposed for sharing multiple secrets using visual cryptography. But all these methods generate noisy shares and in most of these methods the amount of the confidential message is limited. Here we proposed a (k,n)LVCS method for sharing multiple secrets with meaningful shares.

Takizawa et al. [15] proposed methods which are based on Japanese letters for sharing secrets. The methods are based on the position of letters, but a single share contains only a single secret letter. At encoding phase, they divide the secret data into different shares with one letter of the secret and complete share generation by creating a meaningful sentence using the secret letter. For decoding the secret data, arrange all the shares vertically in order, and the secret can be revealed from a particular horizontal line. But theis method does not satisfy the threshold property of secret sharing.

Hsiao-Ching Lin et al. [16], presented a letter-based VCS (LVCS) where pixels are represented by letters for the share images. This paper solves the issues in Takizawa's scheme ([15]). Here instead of black and white pixels they used natural language letters. Also it shows the property of conventional VCS to use whiteness to distinguish black and white. In addition, it shows stacking security, where one cannot reveal any information with less than k shares. But this method is only for sharing single secrets and the shares contain random letters. The proposed method is based on this LVCS method.

## 4   Proposed System

In the proposed method each pixel is replaced by natural language letters(English). This uses the LVCS method specified in paper [16]. This method is based on the concept of superimposing more letters gain more darkness. Here in the reconstructed image black and white pixels are represented using overlapped and non-overlapped letters.

The Algorithm 1 specifies the steps included in the method for generating shares for sharing multiple binary secret images. Each share will have a size that can represent the pixels of $n$ secret images. We generate first share by choosing a meaningful paragraph and rearranging it according to the size of $n$ secret images. Now we have $share_1$ which contains a meaningful data. Figure 2 shows an example of $share_1$, it contains a meaningful passage. Then compare $share_1$ and secret images and copy the same letters from $share_1$ to $share_z$, where $2 \leq z \leq k$ based on the positions of white pixels in the secret images. Analyze and find out the blank positions of $share_z$ and then complete the share generation using Algorithm 2.

---

**Algorithm 1.** The proposed algorithm for binary images

---

**Input:** $n(w \times h)$ binary secret images $s_0, s_2...s_{n-1}$.
**Output:** $k$ shares with size $(w \times (h * n))$.
   Select a paragraph and rearrange it as $Share_1$ having size $(w \times (h * n))$;
   Here $0 \leq x \leq w - 1, 0 \leq y \leq h - 1$;
   $P_{x,y}$ = pixel at $x, y$ th position of secret images;
   **for** $z = 2$ to $k$ **do**
      **for** all $w \times h$ secret images $s_i$ i.e. $i = 0$ to $n - 1$ **do**
         **if** $P_{x,y}$ of $s_i$ is a white pixel(i.e. $= 0$) **then**
            Copy the same letter of $Share_1$ to $Share_z$ i.e. in $(x, (n * i) + y)$th position of $Share_z$;
         **else**
            Blank the specific position of $Share_z$ according to the black pixel of secret image;
         **end if**
      **end for**
   **end for**
   By using Algorthm2 pick up appropriate letters in blank positions and complete the generation of $k$ shares;
   Output $(share_1, share_2...share_k)$;

---

In Algorithm 2 we analyze the letters and blank positions in each share, say $share_z$ and find out the matching word having the highest probability based on the character positions from the word collections. If the predicted word is same as the word in the corresponding positions of $share_1$ to $share_{z-1}$ then fill the blank position with another matching word which having second highest probability. Similarly genarate $k$ shares. Here each share will have different letters for corresponding black pixels in secret images and same letters for white pixels. Now copy the contents of each share to text file. Here we are transmitting $k$ text files, which contains share data instead of share images. Since we are transmitting text files containing meaningful data an attacker was not able to recognize them as conatining secrets images.

At the receiver side these text files are converted into images. So the proposed scheme is more secure than the existing visual cryptographic schemes. Here in the reconstructed image black and white pixels are represented using overlapped and non-overlapped letters. There are 26 different letters are available in English language. Out of which we can form 325 combinations of two overlapped letters. The number of pixels used to represent two overlapped letters is always greater than the number of pixels used to represent a non-overlapped letter. So the overlapped letters are always darker than the non-overlapped letters. Here we used 13 point Arial typeface letters for share generation.

---

**Algorithm 2.** The proposed algorithm for share generation using word prediction

---

**Input:** ($share_1$ and $k - 1$ incomplete shares having size ($w \times (h * n)$)).
**Output:** $k$ meaningful shares with size ($w \times (h * n)$).
   for $z = 2$ to $k$ **do**
     **if** $(x, y)$th position of $share_z$ is blank **then**
       Predict the matching word based on the character positions from the word collections
       **if** Predicted word is same as the word in the corresponding positions of $share_1$ to $share_{z-1}$ **then**
         Fill the blank position with another matching word which having second highest probability;
       **else**
         Fill the blank position with predicted words;
       **end if**
     **end if**
   **end for**
   Output ($share_1, share_2...share_k$);

---

Since the proposed system using (k,n)LVCS (in [16]) it satisfies contrast and security conditions i.e. secret information can be reconstructed by any $k$ shares but nothing can be revealed with less than $k$ shares. Here we are using (k,n)LVCS based on (k,n)PVCS i.e. there is no pixel expansion. Here $OR(0 \mid q)$ and $OR(1 \mid q)$ denotes a set $n$ tuple letters which are used to represent white and black colors when stacking any $q$ shares out of $k$. Let A() be the probability of appearance of the the non-overlapped letters. The contrast condition and the security condition of (k,n)-LVCS are defined as follows:

$$A(OR(1 \mid q)) \leq (p_t - \alpha) \qquad (1)$$

$$A(OR(0 \mid q)) \geq (p_t) \qquad (2)$$

for $q = k$, where $p_t$ is a threshold probability and $\alpha$ is a relative difference.

$$A(OR(1 \mid q)) = A(OR(0 \mid q)) \qquad (3)$$

for $q \leq (k-1)$.

In equation (3), the probability of appearance is same in both cases i.e. no secret data can be revealed from $k-1$ shares. If $q \geq k$ then we will have more overlapped letters in the area of black pixels than the white pixel area. Since the number of pixels needed to represent two overlapped letters is always greater than the number of pixels needed to represent a single non-overlapped letter. So it is possible to visually decode the secret information through Human Visual System.

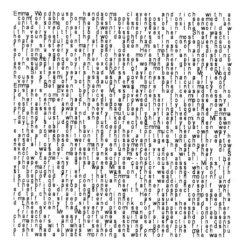

**Fig. 2.** Share1 of proposed LVCS

Algorithm 3 specifies the steps included in share generation for grayscale images. In the case of binary images each pixel value will be either 0 or 1 i.e. white or black and we use overlapped letters to represent black and non-overlapped letters to represent white. For grayscale images we have 256 possible pixel values. Here we define two threshold values $T_1$ and $T2$. Based on these threshold values we divide the pixel values of grayscale image into three sections i.e. first one is values less than $T_1$, second one is values between $T_1$ and $T2$ and third one is values greater than $T2$. In Algorithm 3 we described (3,4)-LVCS algorithm for grayscale images. Here we generate 4 shares out of which minimum 3 shares are needed for secret image reconstruction. Here also we generate first share by choosing a meaningful paragraph and rearranging it according to the size of $n$ secret images. Share generation process is same as that is used for binary images. And the detailed procedure is mentioned in Algorithm 3.

---

**Algorithm 3.** (3,4)-LVCS algorithm for grayscale images

---

**Input:** $n(w \times h)$ grayscale secret images $s_0, s_2...s_{n-1}$ and two threshold values $T_1$ and $T_2$.

**Output:** 4 shares with size $(w \times (h * n))$.

    Select a paragraph and rearrange it as $Share_1$ having size $(w \times (h * n))$;

    Here $0 \leq x \leq w - 1, 0 \leq y \leq h - 1$;

    $P_{x,y}$ = pixel at $x, y$ th position of secret images;

    **for** $share_2$ **do**

        **for** all $w \times h$ secret images $s_i$ i.e. $i = 0$ to $n - 1$ **do**

            **if** $T_1 \leq P_{x,y} \leq 255$ of $s_i$ **then**

                Copy the same letter of $Share_1$ to $Share_2$ i.e. in $(x, (n * i) + y)$th position of $Share_2$;

            **else**

                Blank the specific position of $Share_2$ according to the black pixel of secret image;

            **end if**

        **end for**

    **end for**

    **for** $share_z$ where $z = 3$ to 4 **do**

        **for** all $w \times h$ secret images $s_i$ i.e. $i = 0$ to $n - 1$ **do**

            **if** $T_2 \leq P_{x,y} \leq 255$ of $s_i$ **then**

                Copy the same letter of $Share_1$ to $Share_z$ i.e. in $(x, (n * i) + y)$th position of $Share_z$;

            **else**

                Blank the specific position of $Share_z$ according to the black pixel of secret image;

            **end if**

        **end for**

    **end for**

    By using Algorthm2 pick up appropriate letters in blank positions and complete the generation of 4 shares;

    Output $(share_1, share_2...share_4)$;

---

## 5   Experimental Results and Analysis

In the given experiment a (2,3)LVCS for binary images was implemented. Figure 3 shows the three secret images having size 50 × 50. Generte 3 text files containg shares based on Algorithms 1 and 2. At the recevier side convert text files into images. Here a single secret does not reveal any information about secrets.

484    R.K. Raphel et al.

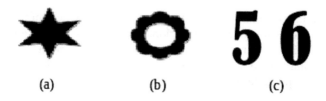

(a)              (b)              (c)

**Fig. 3.** (a) Secret 1, (b) Secret 2, (c) Secret 3

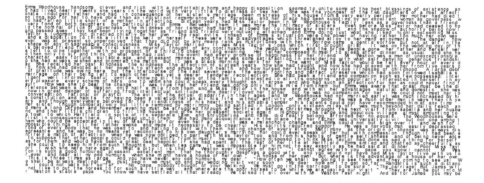

**Fig. 4.** $Share_1$

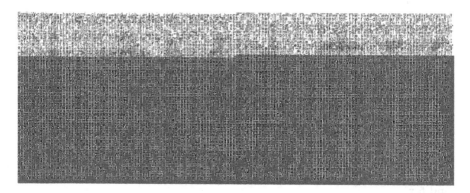

**Fig. 5.** $Share_1 + Share_2 + Share_3$

Figure 4 shows the meaningful $Share_1$. Here we need atleast 2 shares to reveal the complete secrets. Figure 5 shows the stacking of three shares $Share_1$, $Share_2$ and $Share_3$ which reveals the secret images.

In existing VCS a small error will create a wrong pixel in the shares. Since,in LVCS black pixels are represented by overlapped letters even if there is an error, this method have the highest probability to show the correct color.

**Security Analysis.** In the proposed method we are generting text files of each share images. Then these text files are transmitted to the receiver side. The size of these text files are always lesser than the share images and these text files reduce transmission risk problems. Even if these text files are disclosed by an attacker, he will not recognize them as containing secrets. At the receiver side the secret information can be reconstructed by any k shares but with less than k shares recevier may not able to reveal any information about the secret data. So all these prove that the proposed method is more secure than the exisiting visual cryptographic methods.

## 6  Conclusion

A novel (k,n)-LVCS for sharing multiple secrets that can be used for both binary and grayscale images is proposed in this paper. Conventional VCS focus on either sharing multiple secrets with noisy shares or generating meaningful shares for one secret image. Also existing LVCS method is only for sharing single binary secret image with random letter based shares. The proposed method increases the number of secrets and creates meaningful shares at the same time for both binary and grayscale images. Here in the reconstructed image black and white pixels are represented using overlapped and non-overlapped letters. Here the proposed method satisfies contrast and security conditions of LVCS. Since we are using meaningful shares, this scheme is more user friendly than existing schemes. Here we have only acceptable visual quality for reconstructed image. This method can be extended for obtaining better visual quality.

## References

1. Naor, M., Shamir, A.: Visual cryptography. In: Santis, A. (ed.) EUROCRYPT 1994. LNCS, vol. 950, pp. 1–12. Springer, Heidelberg (1995)
2. Thien, C., Lin, J.: Secret image sharing. Comput. Graph **26**, 765–770 (2002)
3. Wang, R., Su, C.: Secret image sharing with smaller shadow images. Pattern Recogn. Lett. **27**, 551–555 (2006)
4. Yang, C.: New visual secret sharing schemes using probabilistic method. Pattern Recogn. Lett. **25**, 481–494 (2004)
5. Fang, W.-P.: Friendly progressive visual secret sharing. Pattern Recogn. **41**, 1410–1414 (2008)
6. Pang, L., Li, H., Yao, Y., Wang, Y.: A Verifiable (t, n) multiple secret sharing scheme and its analyses. In: International Symposium on Electronic Commerce and Security (2008). 978-0-7695-3258-5/08
7. Lin, S.J., Chen, S.K., Lin, J.C.: Flip visual cryptography (fvc) with perfect security, conditionally-optimal contrast, and no expansion". J. Vis. Commun. Image Representation **21**, 900–916 (2010)
8. Weir, J., Yan, W.: Sharing Multiple Secrets Using Visual Cryptography. IEEE (2009). 78-1-4244-3828-0/09
9. Chen, L.H., Wu, C.C.: A study on visual cryptography, Master Thesis, National Chiao Tung University, Taiwan, ROC (1998)
10. Hsu, H.C., Chen, T.S., Lin, Y.H.: The ring shadow image technology of visual cryptography by applying diverse rotating angles to hide the secret sharing. In: Proceedings of the 2004 IEEE International Conference on Networking, Sensing & Control, Taipei, Taiwan, pp. 996–1001, March 2004

11. Feng, J., Wu, H., Tsai, C., Chang, Y., Chu, Y.: Visual secret sharing for multiple secrets. Pattern Recogn. **41**, 3572–3581 (2008)
12. Hsien-Chu, W., Chang, C.-C.: Sharing visual multi-secrets using circle shares. Comput. Stan. Interfaces **28**, 123–135 (2005)
13. Shyu, S., Huang, S., Lee, Y., Wang, R., Chen, K.: Sharing multiple secrets in visual cryptography. Pattern Recogn. **40**, 3633–3651 (2007)
14. Ulutas, M.: Meaningful Share Generation for Increased Number of Secrets in Visual Secret-Sharing Scheme, Hindawi Publishing Corporation, Mathematical Problems in Engineering, vol. 2010, Article ID 593236 (2010)
15. Takizawa, O., Yamamura, A., Makino, K.: Secret sharing scheme using natural language text. J. Nat. Inst. Inf. Commun. Technol. **52**, 173–183 (2005)
16. Lin, H.-C., Yang, C.-N., Laih, C.-S., Lin, H.-T.: Natural language letter based visual cryptography scheme. J. Vis. Commun. Image R **24**, 318–331 (2013)

# Reconstruction of Android Applications' Network Behavior Based on Application Layer Traffic

Qun Li[1], Lei Zhang[1]([✉]), Shifeng Hou[2], Zhenxiang Chen[1], and Hongbo Han[1]

[1] School of Information Science and Engineering, University of Jinan,
Jinan 250022, China
zhanglei@ujn.edu.cn
[2] Library of Rizhao Polytechnic, Rizhao 276826, China

**Abstract.** In recent years, a dramatic change was bring to us with the rapid development of intelligent terminal technology and the popularity of mobile services. Android platforms alone have produced staggering revenues, which has attracted cybercriminals and increased malware in Android markets at an alarming rate. However, the mobile phone network traffic is used to analyze malicious software recently, but this method lack of a visual way to understand network behavior of malware as well as without integrity explanation. In this paper, we introduced a method that can reconstructed the Android applications' network behavior based on application layer traffic. We reconstruct the application network behavior in two ways, namely, network behavior time sequence model and network connection behavior model, we can understand the network behavior of Android applications by the model we reconstructed, it provides the network interaction process integrity explanation and shows that malwares traffic include malicious traffic and normal traffic.

**Keywords:** Reconstruction · Android application · Network traffic · Malware · Detection

## 1 Introduction

With more than 1 billion of Android-activated devices reported on Sep 2013, mobile platforms have clearly become ubiquitous with trends showing such a pace is unlikely slowing down [1]. Smart phones have becomes a strong consumer personal mobile terminal which fuse the financial, interactive communications, personal business, commercial and entertainment services. Mobile devices and their application marketplaces drive the entire economy of the today's mobile landscape. Android platforms alone have produced staggering revenues, which has attracted cybercriminals and increased malware in Android markets at an alarming rate. Static detection and dynamic detection are the two most common methods that used to detect malicious software currently, however, the mobile phone network traffic is also used to identify malicious software recently.

© Springer International Publishing Switzerland 2015
G. Wang et al. (Eds.): ICA3PP 2015 Workshops, LNCS 9532, pp. 487–496, 2015.
DOI: 10.1007/978-3-319-27161-3_44

Static analysis has become very difficult with the development of code obfuscation technology and code encryption technology, dynamic behavior analysis make up for the disadvantage of static analysis commendably, meanwhile, this dynamic behavior analysis technology with the ability to discover some unknown malware. Dynamic behavior analysis depends on the dynamic behavior of malware reconstruction, reconstruction content contains the processes of files and creating process, the communication process between processes, etc. Reconstruction process requires shown the interaction of malware behavior in detail, so as to better understand the dynamic behavior of applications.

In this paper, we report our ongoing work collection and reconstruction of Android application network behaviors in detail, then employ active traffic generator and passive sniffers on the network to record all sent traffic and received traffic. We reconstruct the network behavior time sequence model and network connection behavior model so we can understand the network behavior of Android applications get through the model we reconstructed. This paper mainly makes the following contributions:

- Reconstruct network behavior time sequence model of application based on mobile application's network traffic.
- Reconstruct applications network connection behavior model based on mobile application's network traffic.

## 2  Methodology

In order to get Android application's network traffic and reconstruct a network behavior model of mobile application, we have designed a workable platform that generate traffic and collect traffic of application.

### 2.1  Preprocess Traffic

In order to reconstruct the network behavior directly, we have to preprocess traffic we captured from platform at first. Our approach of process is as follows: firstly, we read each data packet from every original traffic that we captured on the platform, then we do filtering operation to data packet according to the protocol type, and extracted packets belongs to the application layer protocol from the original traffic, finally the extracted packets can be used as the input data to reconstruct the network behavior directly.

For purpose of the result more accurate, our work joined the step that extracted pure malicious traffic. Firstly, we split every flow in network traffic according to the quintuple form (source IP, source port, destination IP, destination port and protocol). Secondly, we parsed the HTTP packets of each flow and extracted Host fields. Then we send this field to VirusTotal [8] to test. If the test result is abnormal, we can determine the flow as malicious traffic. Then we find the DNS packets which has the same field with Host field, then add the DNS packets and HTTP packets to our malicious traffic dataset. In this way we finally got our pure malicious traffic dataset.

## 2.2   Reconstruction Method

In this section, we provided two ways to reconstruct Android application network behavior, more details are illustrated as follows. In the model that we reconstructed, the circular represents source IP address, the square represents DNS server, the rectangle represents domain name server, the triangle represents other protocol type server, and the rhombus represents the resolved information returns by DNS server.

---

**Algorithm 1.** The network behavior time sequence model generation algorithm

---

**Input:** Preprocessed traffic.
**Output:** Network behavior time sequence model of Android applications network
  behavior.
  Extract the source IP address from the preprocessed traffic;
  **while** not at end of preprocessed traffic **do**
     Read the first package;
     **if** protocol type is DNS **then**
        Records the time of this packet and fill it into the column named Time;
        Records the domain name and filled domain name request into the square;
        Find the DNS protocol packets that returned, extracts the needed information
        into the column named Content;
     **else if** protocol type is HTTP **then**
        Use a rectangle to represents the domain name server;
        Records the time of this packet and fill it into the column named Time;
        Records HOST fieldand filled this filed into the column named Content;
     **else**
        Use a triangle to represent the package;
        Records the time of this packet and fill it into the column named Time;
        Records Info in the packet and fill it into the column named Content;
     **end if**
     Read next package;
  **end while**

---

The first approach to reconstruct Android application network behavior is reconstruct network behavior time sequence model, this method described the network behavior of applications in terms of the time. The steps to reconstruct the network behavior time sequence model as follows: First, get the source IP address from the preprocessed traffic, and then start reading each packet from preprocessed traffic. Second, analyzing the protocol type. Third, if it is DNS protocol, records the time of this packet and fill it into the column named Time, records the domain name and filled domain name request into DNS server, namely, the square, find the DNS protocol packets that returned, extracts the resolved IP address and the CNAME information then filled this information into the column named Content. Fourth, if it is HTTP protocol, then records the time of this packet and fill it into the column named Time, record HOST field in this packet and filled this filed into the column named Content. Fifth, in other

**Algorithm 2.** The application network connection behavior model generation algorithm

---

**Input:** Preprocessed traffic.
**Output:** Network connection behavior model of Android applications network behavior.
  Extract the source IP address from the preprocessed traffic;
  **while** not at end of preprocessed traffic **do**
    Read the first package;
    **if** protocol type is DNS **then**
      Fetch the domain name requested to resolve and fill it into the square;
      Extracts the resolved IP address and resolved the CNAME;
      IP address information and CNAME are written in different rhombus respectively;
      Connect the square with all rhombus;
      Connecting the circular and a square by a solid line;
    **else if** protocol type is HTTP **then**
      Use a rectangle to represents the domain name server;
      Extracted the HOST field and identify DNS servers that has same domain name with HOST field;
      Connect rectangle and the corresponding square with a dotted line;
      Connecting the circular and a rectangle by a solid line;
    **else**
      Use a triangle to represent packages;
      Extracted the contents of Info from the packet and fill in the triangle;
      Connecting the circular and a triangle by a solid line;
    **end if**
    Read next package;
  **end while**

---

cases, then records the time of this packet and fill it into the column named Time, records Info in the packet and fill it into the column named Content. More details are shown in Algorithm 1. The second approach to reconstruct Android application network behavior is reconstruct applications network connection behavior model, this method described the network behavior of applications in terms of the request times and the number of information that transferred. The steps to reconstruct the applications network connection behavior model as follows: First, get the source IP address from the perprocessed traffic, and then start reading each packet from preprocessed traffic. Second, analyzing the protocol type. Third, if it is DNS protocol, then fetch the domain name requested to resolve and fill it into the square, find the DNS protocol packets that returned and extracts the resolved IP address and resolved the CNAME information, then write IP address information and CNAME into different rhombus respectively, then connect the square with all rhombus, parse out the information as property node of DNS server, then connecting circular which represents the source IP address and a square by a solid line, then we set the solid line weights by the number of this domain requested. Fourth, if it is HTTP protocol, then extracted the HOST field and identify DNS packets that has same domain name with HOST field, connect rectangle and the corresponding square with a dotted line, then connecting circular which represents the source IP address and a rectangle by a solid line, after that set the solid line weights by the number of transmit HTTP packages. Fifth, in other cases, use a triangle to represent, extracted the contents of Info from the packet and fill in the triangle, then connecting circular which represents IP address and a triangle by a solid line. More details are shown in Algorithm 2.

# 3   Experiment and Analysis

In this chapter, we run a normal version and repackaged malicious version of the same Android application on the platform we designed, Figs. 1 and 2 are the screenshot of part of traffic that generated by normal application and malware respectively, Figs. 3 and 4 is the screenshot of preprocessed traffic.

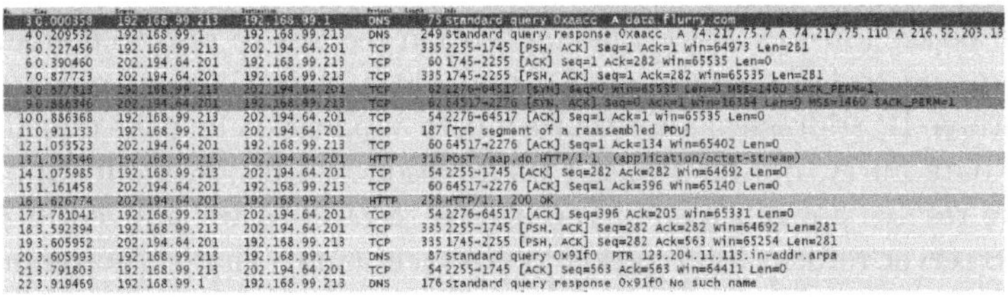

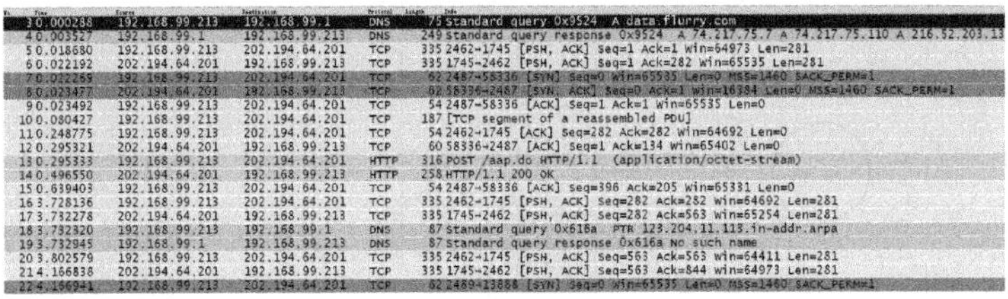

**Fig. 1.** Part of traffic that generated by normal application

**Fig. 2.** Part of traffic that generated by malware

Our experimental platform is Microsoft Windows 7 Ultimate (SP1) (64-bit) operating systems. In a software which named eclipse, we write a program to reconstruct model, and we get Figs. 5, 6, 7, 8 and 9 by calling Java graphics toolkit. Figures 5 and 6 is the network behavior time sequence model of normal application and malware respectively, put information about the server into a column named Server, meanwhile, put the time of each package about the server into a column named Time, then put the resolved information and domain name

| | | | | | |
|---|---|---|---|---|---|
| 3 0.000358 | 192.168.99.213 | 192.168.99.1 | DNS | 75 | standard query 0xaacc A data.flurry.com |
| 4 0.209532 | 192.168.99.1 | 192.168.99.213 | DNS | 249 | standard query response 0xaacc A 74.217.75.7 A 74.217.75.110 A 216.52.203.13 |
| 13 1.053546 | 192.168.99.213 | 202.194.64.201 | HTTP | 316 | POST /aap.do HTTP/1.1 (application/octet-stream) |
| 16 1.626774 | 202.194.64.201 | 192.168.99.213 | HTTP | 258 | HTTP/1.1 200 OK |
| 20 3.605993 | 192.168.99.213 | 192.168.99.1 | DNS | 87 | standard query 0x91f0 PTR 123.204.11.113.in-addr.arpa |
| 22 3.919469 | 192.168.99.1 | 192.168.99.213 | DNS | 176 | standard query response 0x91f0 No such name |

**Fig. 3.** Application layer traffic that generated by normal application

| | | | | | |
|---|---|---|---|---|---|
| 3 0.000288 | 192.168.99.213 | 192.168.99.1 | DNS | 75 | standard query 0x9524 A data.flurry.com |
| 4 0.003527 | 192.168.99.1 | 192.168.99.213 | DNS | 249 | standard query response 0x9524 A 74.217.75.7 A 74.217.75.110 A 216.52.203.13 |
| 13 0.295333 | 192.168.99.213 | 202.194.64.201 | HTTP | 316 | POST /aap.do HTTP/1.1 (application/octet-stream) |
| 14 0.496550 | 202.194.64.201 | 192.168.99.213 | HTTP | 258 | HTTP/1.1 200 OK |
| 18 3.732320 | 192.168.99.213 | 192.168.99.1 | DNS | 87 | standard query 0x616a PTR 123.204.11.113.in-addr.arpa |
| 19 3.732945 | 192.168.99.1 | 192.168.99.213 | DNS | 87 | standard query response 0x616a No such name |
| 129 264.579380 | 192.168.99.213 | 192.168.99.1 | DNS | 81 | standard query 0xa180 A security.ie.sogou.com |
| 130 264.581512 | 192.168.99.1 | 192.168.99.213 | DNS | 222 | standard query response 0xa180 CNAME security.sogou.com CNAME cnc.security.s |
| 142 264.588203 | 192.168.99.213 | 202.194.64.201 | HTTP | 745 | POST /q HTTP/1.1 (application/json) |
| 143 264.612619 | 202.194.64.201 | 192.168.99.213 | HTTP | 283 | HTTP/1.1 200 OK (image/gif) |
| 156 264.739709 | 192.168.99.213 | 202.194.64.201 | HTTP | 745 | POST /q HTTP/1.1 (application/json) |
| 157 264.763668 | 202.194.64.201 | 192.168.99.213 | HTTP | 283 | HTTP/1.1 200 OK (image/gif) |

**Fig. 4.** Application layer traffic that generated by malware

into a column named Content. Figures 7 and 9 are the network connection behavior model of normal application and malware respectively, Fig. 8 is the network connection behavior model of pure malicious traffic that we extracted from malware's traffic.

It can be seen in Fig. 5 that the application request to resolve domain name data.flurry.com to DNS server applied in 0.0004s, then DNS server returns the resolved three IP addresses, after that connect application and the domain name server of data.flurry.com for transfer information in 1.0535s, finally application request to resolve domain name in-addr.arpa to DNS server applied in 3.6060s, then DNS server returns information as No such name. That's the communicate process between application and network. So we can see that same application but with malicious code behavior of interacts with Internet by Fig. 6.

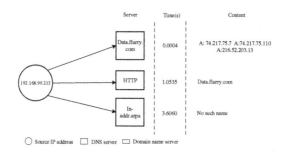

**Fig. 5.** The network behavior time sequence model of normal application

It can be seen in Fig. 7 that application request to resolve domain name data.flurry.com and in-addr.arpa to DNS server respectively, then DNS server returns the resolved three IP addresses about data.flurry.com but cannot resolve domain name in-addr.arpa, finally application communicates with domain name server of data.flurry.com. That's the communicate process between application

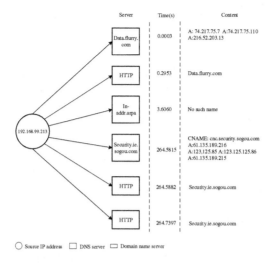

**Fig. 6.** The network behavior time sequence model of malware

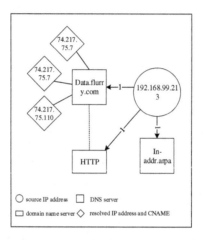

**Fig. 7.** Network connection behavior model of normal application

and network. So we can see that same application but with malicious code behavior of interacts with Internet by Fig. 9.

These model we reconstructed could provide the network interaction process integrity explanation on the behavior of Android applications. By observing Figs. 7, 8 and 9, it can be seen that difference between application and malware clearly and the malware network connection behavior model consist of application network connection behavior model and pure malicious traffic network connection behavior model, namely, it is provide proof for malwares traffic include malicious traffic and normal traffic. Maybe the network behavior model of application can be used to identify malicious software.

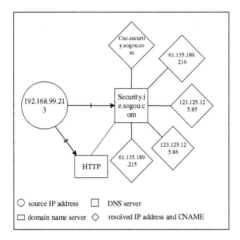

**Fig. 8.** Network connection behavior model of pure malicious traffic

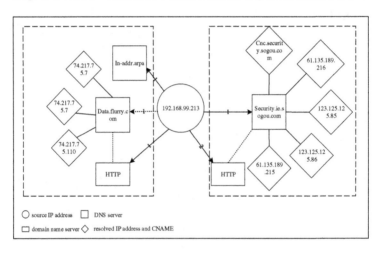

**Fig. 9.** Network connection behavior model of malware

## 4    Related Work

Only a small number of studies have focused on Android applications network behavior reconstruction. Conventional mobile terminal network behavior analysis confined to some statistical analysis of network characteristics [2], for example, access to the port, packet size, access time and other characteristics of the statistical analysis, but it did not characterize the interactions between a mobile network terminal and a remote server, such interactions is necessary for understanding the interaction between the mobile terminal and a remote malicious server, the lack of network behavior reconstruction in existing research, especially lack of the integrity explanation to network interaction process.

To better understand this slew of threats, Fattori et al. [9] presents CopperDroid, an automatic VMI-based dynamic analysis system to reconstruct the behavior of Android malware. Based on the key observation that all interesting behaviors are eventually expressed through system calls, CopperDroid presents a novel unified analysis able to capture both low-level OS specific and high-level Android-specific behaviors. To this end, CopperDroid presents an automatic system call centric analysis that faithfully reconstructs events of interests.

Zhou et al. [10] dissected the characterization and evolution of Android malwares. They had managed to collect more than 1,200 malware samples that covered the majority of existing Android malware families. In addition, they systematically characterized malware from various aspects, including their installation methods, activation mechanisms as well as the nature of carried malicious payloads.

Lee [3] introduce a malware activity detection mechanism, GMAD: Graph-based Malware Activity Detection that utilizes a sequence of DNS queries in order to achieve robustness against evasion techniques. To detect malicious domain names utilized to malware activities, GMAD applies domain name clustering using the graph structure and determines malicious clusters by referring to public blacklists. We reconstruct the network behavior time sequence model and network connection behavior model based on application layer (such as DNS protocol traffic, HTTP protocol traffic and SSL protocol traffic, etc.) traffic, so we can understand the network behavior of Android applications get through the model reconstructed, it provides the network interaction process integrity explanation.

## 5   Conclusion

In this paper, we provided an effective Android malware traffic generation and collection mechanism in the real Internet environment. Then we processing the traffic we captured from platform, it can be used as the input data to reconstruct the network behavior directly. After that we have reconstructed network behavior time sequence model of applications network behavior based on mobile application's network traffic and reconstruct applications network connection behavior model based on mobile application's network traffic, it provides the network interaction process integrity explanation and these models shows that malwares traffic include malicious traffic and normal traffic.

Therefore, in the future, we will also be use the model to identify malicious software over a network behavior model of application, it is effective to identifying malware by means of this model through comparing the normal network behavior model and malicious network behavior model in this paper. For instance, by observing Figs. 7, 8 and 9, we can see that difference between application and malware clearly. We will continue to do work in this area later and identify malicious software by the model we reconstructed.

**Acknowledgments.** This work was supported by the National Natural Science Foundation of China under Grants No. 61472164 and No. 61203105, the Natural Science Foundation of Shandong Province under Grants No. ZR2014JL042 and No. ZR2012FM010.

# References

1. King, R.: Google readies android 'kitkat' amid 1 billion device activations milestone, September 2013
2. Chen, Z., Han, H., Yan, Q., et al.: A first look at android malware traffic in first few minutes. In: International Conference on Trust, Security and Privacy in Computing and Communications, TrustCom 2015. IEEE (2015)
3. Lee, J., Lee, H.: GMAD: graph-based malware activity detection by DNS traffic analysis. Comput. Commun. **49**, 33–47 (2014)
4. Zheran Fang, Y.L., Han, W.: Permission based android security: Issues and countermeasures. Comput. Secur. **43**, 205–218 (2014)
5. Enck, W., Ongtang, M., McDaniel, P.: Understanding Android security. IEEE Security and Privacy Magazine (2009)
6. Android. http://developer.android.com/tools/help/monkeyrunner/uline_concepts.html
7. Yajin, Z., Xuxian, J.: Dissecting android malware: characterization and evolution. In: 2012 IEEE Symposium on Security and Privacy (SP), pp. 95–109. IEEE (2012)
8. VirusTotal. https://www.virustotal.com/
9. Fattori, A., Tam, K., Khan, S.J., Cavallaro, L., Reina, A.: On the Reconstruction of Android Malware Behaviors. This is pioneering work which uses Binder as a central component of an Android malware analysis system (2014). http://www.isg.rhul.ac.uk/sullivan/pubs/tr/MA-2014-01.pdf
10. Zhou, Y., Jiang, X.: Dissecting android malware: characterization and evolution. In: 2012 IEEE Symposium on IEEE Security and Privacy (SP), Conference Proceedings, pp. 95–109 (2012)
11. Falaki, H., Lymberopoulos, D., Mahajan, R., Kandula, S., Estrin, D.: A First look at traffic on smartphones. In: Proceedings of the 10th ACM SIGCOMM Conference on Internet Measurement, Conference Proceedings, pp. 281–287. ACM (2010)

# Android Malware Network Behavior Analysis at HTTP Protocol Packet Level

Shanshan Wang[1], Shifeng Hou[2], Lei Zhang[1]([✉]),
Zhenxiang Chen[1], and Hongbo Han[1]

[1] School of Information Science and Engineering,
University of Jinan, Jinan 250022, China
zhanglei@ujn.edu.cn
[2] Library of Rizhao Polytechnic, Rizhao 276826, China

**Abstract.** Smart phones, particularly the ones based on Android, have become the most popular devices. The surfing habits of users have been changed from the traditional PC terminal to mobile terminal officially. However, the mobile terminal application exposes more and more problems. Two common ways to analyze malware are source code analysis and dynamic behavior analysis. Researchers pay little attention to the network traffic generated by mobile terminal application. Nevertheless, shell technology makes source code analysis difficult while dynamic behavior analysis consumes too much resource. In fact, normal application and malware perform differently at the network level. We found that the features of HTTP packet are dramatically different in normal traffic and malicious traffic dataset. The application analysis from the perspective of network traffic can provide us a new way to detect malware.

**Keywords:** Android · Malware · Network traffic · Analyze · Detection

## 1 Introduction

The vigorous development of smart phones leads us to a new network area, where we have no time limitations, no space limitations and even no hardware limitations. A variety of smart devices and mobile applications flood every aspect of people's lives. But as former computer age, virus, Trojans and other security threats are also predictable. How to protect users' smart devices from invasion and protect users' privacy are more and more important.

Now there are two common mobile malware detection technologies: The one is statistic scanning technology. The other one is dynamic analysis technology. The main idea of statistic scanning is based on the known characteristics of the virus to match with the source code of the application. If the scanning results are consistent with a virus in some aspects, it is considered as a malware. If the result does not contain any virus' feature, it can be considered as a normal application. Dynamic analysis technology is according to the procedure of invoked method. The invoked methods mainly include unusual behavior of the operating system layer, accessing to sensitive data, calling to key system functions, etc.

© Springer International Publishing Switzerland 2015
G. Wang et al. (Eds.): ICA3PP 2015 Workshops, LNCS 9532, pp. 497–507, 2015.
DOI: 10.1007/978-3-319-27161-3_45

This approach requires massive calculation and mobile phones consume too much resource.

Generally speaking, no matter malwares or unwanted applications will affect the network behavior patterns. Just on the application layer of network can we find a number of different network traffic features. The innovations and contributions of this paper are as follows:

- An automatic network traffic generation and collection platform [1] was exploited. Through this platform we obtain abundant traffic data of normal Android applications and Android malwares.
- We analyzed the network traffic features of normal Android applications and Android malwares. In the process of features analysis and comparison, we concluded that there were a great differences between normal traffic and malicious traffic.

## 2   Related Work

Now a lot of network traffic analysis are aimed at computer terminals and pay little attention to the mobile terminals. But there are still some previous researches provide us with a lot of reference.

Zhou et al. [2] dissected the characterization and evolution of Android malwares. They had managed to collect more than 1,200 malware samples that covered the majority of existing Android malware families. In addition, they systematically characterized malware from various aspects, including their installation methods, activation mechanisms as well as the nature of carried malicious payloads. Cheng et al. [3] designed SmartSiren to collect the communication activity information from the smart phones. But it must run a agent on the smart phones. Hong et al. [4] made some summarizes about smart phone viruses characteristic and detection method comprehensively. They collected the flow of traffic and compared them to the fitting curve in real time. Tenenboim-Chekina et al. [5] described and analyzed a new type of malware which has the ability of self-updating. They also analyzed this malware based on network.

These prior works showed that malwares and normal applications have many different behaviors in many sides. This paper focuses on the network traffic features between malwares and normal applications. In fact we have found that on the network traffic layer the noramal traffic and malicious traffic have different traffic features. For instance, sending and receiving bytes, sending and receiving data, inner and outer time intervals. By comparison and analysis of the same feature in normal traffic and malicious traffic, we can better understand the network behavior patterns of malware. This approach provides a new idea for malware detection.

## 3   Methodology

Firstly, we obtained abundant normal Android applications and Android malwares (In this paper, we only focus on Android application. So for the sake of

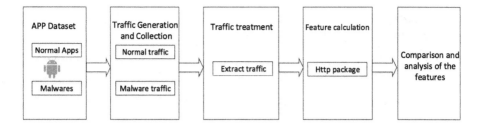

**Fig. 1.** Flow diagram of the mathodology

simplicity, in the following we called normal Android applictions as normal applications, the malicious Android applications as malwares). Secondly, we collected the network traffic generated by normal applications and malwares respectively using the traffic generation and collection platform. Thirdly, we calculated the same feature in normal traffic and malicious traffic dataset respectively. Fourthly, we compared these features and analyzed the reasons. Figure 1 is a flow diagram of our work. It can describe the work from an overall perspective.

### 3.1  Normal Application Dataset and Malware Dataset

In experiment, the normal application dataset is obtained from the Android market. We wrote a crawlers using the python language. The crawkers can realize downloading the applications to the PC from the Android market uninterruptedly. In order to make the result more accurate, four virus detection tools (kaspersky [6], avira, Lookout, AVG) concurrently were used to test the applications which we download from the Android market. That is to say, as for every application from the Android market was tested four times. The malious applications were filtered out. The applications whose four test results are benign were selected as our normal application dataset. 5666 applications are divided into 18 categories.

The malwares are obtained from Drebin project [4]. Additionally, it includes all samples from the Android Malware Genome Project [2]. We removed the ads applications out. The remaining 5560 malwares as our malware dataset.

### 3.2  Traffic Generation and Collection Platform

In order to get the network traffic which the experiment required. We utilize the traffic generation and collection platform to obtain traffic dataset. This platform is made up of four parts: foundation platform, traffic generator, traffic collector and network proxy/firewall.

The foundation platform consists of Android emulator (AVD) and Android debug bridge(ADB). This foundation platform provides a basic Android simulation environment and command line mode of interaction and it could realize some basic functionalities: creation, installation and operation. The traffic generator's

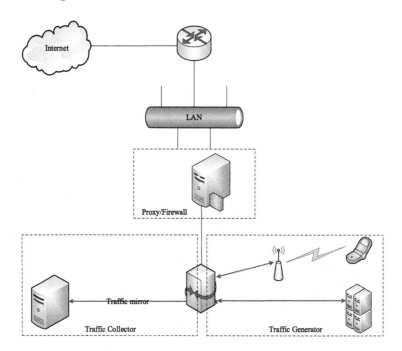

**Fig. 2.** Traffic generation and collection platform

task is to install and activate the normal applications and malwares to generate traffic. The traffic collector is designed to realize the function of capturing normal traffic and malicious traffic dataset. We utilize traffic mirror technology to mirror traffic data which pass through the gateway of server. The network proxy's/firewall's task is to mirror and control the attack behavior. Figure 2 is the structure diagram of traffic generation and collection platform.

### 3.3   Extracting Pure Malicious Traffic

The traffic generated by malware are not all malicious. So in order to make the result more accurate, our work joined the step that extracted pure malicious traffic. Firstly, we split every flow in network traffic according to the quintuple form (source IP, source port, destination IP, destination port and protocol). Secondly, we parsed the HTTP packets of each flow and extracted 'Host' fields and then these fields were sent to VirusTotal [7] to test. If the test result is abnormal, we can determine the flow as malicious flow. Then the flow was added to the malicious traffic as the malicious traffic dataset. In this way, finally we got our pure malicious traffic dataset. Table 1 lists the application dataset and network traffic dataset. The $ANumber$ represents application number while the $TNumber$ represents traffic number.

**Table 1.** The applcation dataset and network traffic dataset

| Normal applications | | | Malwares | | |
|---|---|---|---|---|---|
| Category | ANumber | TNumber | Family | ANumber | TNumber |
| Game | 1328 | 320 | FakeInstaller | 925 | 79 |
| Productivity | 581 | 350 | DroidKungfu | 667 | 193 |
| AntiVirus | 385 | 385 | Plankton | 625 | 475 |
| DailyLife | 385 | 350 | Opfake | 613 | 89 |
| Reading | 343 | 343 | GinMaster | 339 | 3 |
| NewsAndMagazine | 332 | 332 | BaseBridge | 330 | 220 |
| HealthAndFitness | 328 | 328 | Iconosys | 152 | 39 |
| Finance | 324 | 274 | Imlog | 52 | 12 |
| Education | 320 | 320 | FakeDoc | 132 | 119 |
| MediaAndVideo | 290 | 290 | Geinimi | 92 | 3 |
| Photography | 237 | 237 | Adrd | 91 | 13 |
| Input | 228 | 228 | Hamob | 124 | 12 |
| Social | 208 | 208 | ExplcitLinuxltoor | 70 | 2 |
| Communication | 116 | 116 | Glodream | 69 | 12 |
| TravelAndLocal | 103 | 103 | MobileTx | 69 | 46 |
| Personalization | 62 | 62 | FakeRun | 61 | 52 |
| Tools | 52 | 52 | SMSreg | 108 | 7 |
| Browser | 44 | 44 | Gappusin | 58 | 89 |

## 4  HTTP Packet Analysis

On the basis of above traffic dataset, we began our analysis. Our analysis are at the packet level. We counted the application layer protocol and found that: On the application layer, the number of HTTP protocol packets accounted for 71.69 % and the number of DNS protocols packet accounted for 28.25 %, while only 0.06 % is the SSL protocol packets. Moreover, the most common way to get users' information is through HTTP request. Users' private information were sent to the server and this paper mainly analyzes the features of HTTP packet.

First of all, different time or different applications may affect the result of the experiment. But we obtained normal traffic and malicious traffic under the same network environment. Moreover, we get a large number of traffic data, the result is relatively reliable.

### 4.1  The HTTP Packet Average Length

HTTP packet length occupies an important position in the analysis of network traffic. In general, for all kinds of malware traffic, the packet length is an important parameter. Especially in data loss and in theft behavior detection

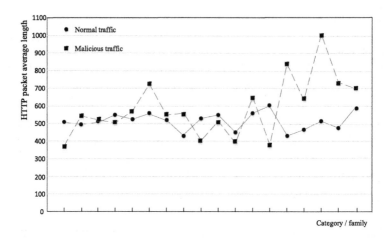

**Fig. 3.** HTTP packet average length in normal traffic and malicious traffic

technology, HTTP packet length plays an important role. So we calculated the HTTP packet length in normal traffic and in malicious traffic and then two sets of data were contrasted to looking for the rule.

For normal traffic dataset and malicious traffic dataset, the HTTP packet length were analyzed. Figure 3 is the HTTP packet average length in noraml traffic and in malicious traffic. The horizontal axis represents category name in normal traffic or family name in malicious traffic. The ordinate axis represents the HTTP packet average length of every category or every family.

From the comparison of HTTP packet average length in normal traffic and in malicious traffic. Several points were concluded.

- We calculated that the minimal HTTP packet average length is 433 bytes and the biggest HTTP packet average length is 604 bytes in normal traffic samples. while the minimal HTTP packet length is 369 bytes and the biggest HTTP packet length is 1038 bytes in malicious traffic samples.
- According to the formula of standard deviation we calculated that the standard deviation of the normal traffic samples is 50.3 and the standard deviation of malicious traffic samples is 173.5. Because the standard deviation can be used to measure the fluctuation magnitude of a batch of data. Under the condition of the same sample size, the bigger standard deviation shows the greater data volatility. The calculation results indicated that the HTTP packet length in normal traffic is more stable than in malicious traffic.

### 4.2   HTTP Packet Length Distribution

Figure 4 declares HTTP packet length distribution of normal traffic and malicious traffic. From this figure, we found the following points.

- No matter in normal traffic or in malicious traffic, the HTTP packet length distribution accords with normal distribution in general.

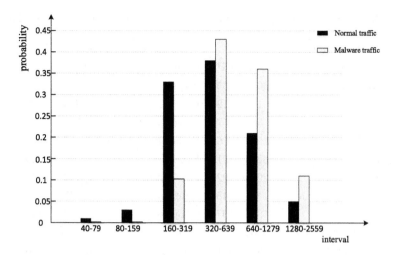

**Fig. 4.** HTTP packet length distribution in noraml traffic and malicious traffic dataset

- Both normal traffic and malicious traffic, most of data which the proportion of HTTP packet length fall in the interval of 320-619. Specific data of the proportion is 35 % in normal traffic and 43 % in malicious traffic dataset.
- The HTTP packet length is bigger in malicious traffic dataset than in normal traffic generally speaking. Such as HTTP packet length within the interval of 1280-2559, 640-1279, 320-639 accounted for 12 %, 35 %, 43 % in malicious traffic dataset while accounted for 5 %, 20 % and 5 % in normal traffic respectively.

### 4.3 HTTP Upload Packet Number and Download Packet Number

Table 2 shows HTTP upload and download packet number. For simplicity, the *DPN* is defined as HTTP download packet number and the *UPN* means HTTP upload packet number.

- Both normal traffic and malicious traffic dataset, the number of HTTP upload packet equals with the number of HTTP download packet generally speaking.
- As for normal traffic, In 11 samples (account for 61.1 %), the number of HTTP download packet is greater than the number of HTTP upload packet. There are 7 samples (account for 38.9 %) in which the number of HTTP download packet is less than the number of HTTP upload packet. For malicious traffic dataset, there are 3 samples (account for 16.7 %) in which the number of HTTP download packet is greater than the number of HTTP upload packet. There are 8 samples (account for 44.4 %) in which the number of HTTP download packet equals to the number of HTTP upload packet. In 11 samples (account for 38.9 %) the number of HTTP download packet is less than the number of HTTP upload packet.

**Table 2.** HTTP download packet and upload packet number in two traffic dataset

| Normal traffic dataset | | | Malicious traffic dataset | | |
|---|---|---|---|---|---|
| Category | DPN | UPN | Family | DPN | UPN |
| AntiVirus | 6675 | 5357 | Adrd | 13 | 13 |
| Browser | 124 | 123 | BaseBridge | 344 | 859 |
| Communication | 583 | 570 | DroidKungFu | 735 | 733 |
| DailyLife | 2980 | 2868 | ExploitLinuxlotoor | 8 | 8 |
| Education | 3222 | 3517 | FakeDoc | 469 | 469 |
| Finance | 2005 | 1929 | FakeInstaller | 142 | 142 |
| HealthAndFitness | 1484 | 1457 | FakeRun | 147 | 143 |
| Input | 1826 | 1974 | Gappusin | 197 | 199 |
| MediaAndVideo | 6602 | 6593 | Geinimi | 10 | 20 |
| NewsAndMagazines | 3353 | 3311 | GinMaster | 6 | 6 |
| Personalization | 747 | 933 | GlodDream | 13 | 13 |
| Photography | 1372 | 1399 | Hamob | 74 | 75 |
| Productivity | 2030 | 1976 | Iconosys | 40 | 40 |
| Reading | 6716 | 6680 | Imlog | 6 | 6 |
| Social | 4775 | 4505 | MobileTx | 472 | 464 |
| Tools | 372 | 380 | Opfake | 195 | 196 |
| TravelAndLocal | 2225 | 2479 | Plankton | 1931 | 2207 |
| Games | 3145 | 3200 | SMSreg | 10462 | 21997 |

After application installed successfully, many applications will load a lot of resources, so the HTTP download packet number is greater than the HTTP upload packet number. In the malicious traffic dataset, the majority of malware is activated [8] after restarting. The activated malwares' network behavior become more active. They not only need to load the application resources, but also need to receive and execute command from a remote server. At the same time, malwares upload a lot of user information to a remote server. So most of the HTTP download packet number is less than or equal to HTTP upload packet number in malicious traffic dataset.

### 4.4　HTTP Upload Bytes and Download Bytes

Table 3 describes HTTP download bytes and upload bytes of normal traffic and malicious traffic dataset. The *DBytes* is defined as HTTP download bytes and the *UBytes* means HTTP upload bytes. From Table 3 we can conclude several points.

**Table 3.** HTTP download bytes and upload bytes in two traffic dataset

| Normal traffic | | | Malicious traffic | | |
|---|---|---|---|---|---|
| Category | DBytes | UBytes | Family | DBytes | UBytes |
| AntiVirus | 4,314,141 | 1,767,586 | Adrd | 3445 | 6147 |
| Browser | 69,864 | 51,817 | BaseBridge | 182,665 | 459,353 |
| Communication | 366,386 | 217,205 | DroidKungFu | 419,541 | 348,344 |
| DailyLife | 1,840,103 | 1,405,723 | ExploitLinuxlotoor | 4332 | 3754 |
| Education | 1,914,591 | 1,651,154 | FakeDoc | 394,789 | 151,836 |
| Finance | 1,352,451 | 857,346 | FakeInstaller | 167,651 | 38,267 |
| HealthAndFitness | 923,474 | 601,519 | FakeRun | 61,312 | 96,120 |
| Input | 865,516 | 788,152 | Gappusin | 128,213 | 95,066 |
| MediaAndVideo | 3,584,366 | 3,450,731 | Geinimi | 4724 | 7519 |
| NewsAndMagazines | 2,237,195 | 1,443,726 | GinMaster | 3502 | 2648 |
| Personalization | 458,590 | 306,132 | GlodDream | 5768 | 4401 |
| Photography | 806,805 | 742,071 | Hamob | 52,298 | 46,343 |
| Productivity | 1,351,631 | 1,066,844 | Iconosys | 13,670 | 15,808 |
| Reading | 3,262,301 | 1,066,844 | Imlog | 4770 | 5196 |
| Social | 2,367,845 | 1,954,169 | MobileTx | 350,172 | 246,696 |
| Tools | 217,712 | 170,121 | Opfake | 287,074 | 118,935 |
| TravelAndLocal | 1,089,088 | 1,153,457 | Plankton | 1,405,248 | 1,628,966 |
| Games | 2,150,731 | 1,615,773 | SMSreg | 10,462 | 21,997 |

- For normal traffic, in all the samples, HTTP download bytes are bigger than HTTP upload bytes.
- For malicious traffic dataset, in 10 samples (account for 55.6 %), HTTP download bytes are bigger than HTTP upload bytes. In 8 samples (account for 44.4 %), HTTP download bytes are less than HTTP upload bytes.

In the first a few minutes many applications need to load the network resources they required. So the number of HTTP download bytes are larger in normal traffic. While for malicious applications, malware is activated and then a lot of malwares began to carry out illegal activities, such as stealing users' personal information and then uploading to remote server etc. So in some samples HTTP upload bytes are greater than download bytes.

## 5   Evaluation

We have analyzed several features of application-layer protocols. Because HTTP protocols account for a crucial part on application-layer, we focuses solely on HTTP protocol packet. The features we analyzed are HTTP packet average length, variance of HTTP packet length, distribution of HTTP packet length, radio of HTTP upload packet number and download packet number as well as radio of HTTP upload bytes and download bytes. We found every feature performs differently in normal traffic and malicious traffic. But we cant assert every feature can be used to detect malware. Moreover there are large numbers of traffic features, which we didnt analyze. Our next work is to analyze more traffic features and find some specific features which can recognized malware from normal applications.

## 6   Conclusion

In this paper, we get abundant traffic dataset. A lot of differences at HTTP package protocol level were present of normal traffic and malicious traffic. By analyzing the causes of these differences, we can better understand the network behavior of malicious software. From the aspect of network traffic, normal application and malwares have different features which lays the foundation for the next work. The next step of our work is to deeply analyze the features of traffic and then to detect malware. In this experiment, there are some different features, such as HTTP packet average length, the distribution of HTTP packet length, the number of HTTP upload packet and download packet etc. This paper provides a feasible method for malware detection. Namely, if a feature of network traffic performs great differently in noraml traffic and malicious traffic dataset and then they can be used to detect malwares.

**Acknowledgment.** This work was supported by the National Natural Science Foundation of China under Grants No. 61472164 and No. 61203105, the Natural Science Foundation of Shandong Province under Grants No. ZR2014JL042 and No. ZR2012FM010.

## References

1. Chen, Z., Han, H., et al.: A first look at android malicious traffic dataset in first few minutes. In: The 14th IEEE International Conference on Trust, Security and Privacy in Computing and Communications (2015)
2. Zhou, Y., Jiang, X.: Dissecting Android malware: characterization and evolution. In: 2012 IEEE Symposium on Security and Privacy (SP), Conference Proceedings, pp. 95–109. IEEE (2012)
3. Jerry, C., Wong Starsky, H.Y., Hao, Y., Songwu, L.: Smartsiren: Virus detection and alert for smartphones. In: Proceedings of the 5th International Conference on Mobile Systems, Applications and Services, pp. 258–271. ACM (2007)
4. Yunfeng, H., Chao, X., Dixin, S.: Research of smart phone malware detection based on anomaly data flow monitoring. Comput. Secur. 9(11–14) (2012)
5. Tenenboim-Chekina, L., Barad, O., Shabtai, A., Mimran, D., Shapira, B., Elovici, Y.: Detecting application update attack on mobile devices through network features. In: INFOCOM 2013 (2013)

6. Kaspersky. http://www.kaspersky.com.cn/
7. Virustotal. http://www.virustotal.com/
8. Shabtai, A., Tenenboim-Chekina, L., Mimran, D., Rokach, L., Shapira, B., Elovici, Y.: Mobile malware detection through analysis of deviations in application network behavior. Comput. Secur. **43**, 1–18 (2014)

# Energy Efficient Encryption Scheme
# for Network-Coded Mobile Ad Hoc Networks

Deepa S. Nair[✉] and H. Muhammed Ilyas

College of Engineering, Pallippuram P.O., Cherthala,
Alappuzha 688541, Kerala, India
d4deepanair@gmail.com
http://www.cectl.ac.in/

**Abstract.** A mobile ad hoc network (MANET) is a infrastructure-less network of mobile devices connected without any wires. Energy saving is an emerging issue in Mobile Ad Hoc Networks. Recent research works shows that network coding can help to reduce the energy consumption in MANETs by using less transmissions. Besides transmission cost, other main sources of energy consumption are data encryption or decryption process. Due to the dynamic nature of MANETs leads the networks more prone to various security threats. So the security needs are higher in MANETs in comparing with wired networks. Great security and authentication along with efficient power utilization and robustness are needed for the MANETs for successful transmission. Here proposes a new lightweight elliptic curve cryptography (ECC) based encryption scheme to provide confidentiality for MANETs in an energy-efficient way.

**Keywords:** Mobile Ad Hoc Networks · Energy saving · Network coding · Lightweight encryption · ECC

## 1  Introduction

Mobile Ad Hoc Networks (MANETs) are important wireless communication paradigms. The mobile and infrastructureless nature of MANETs makes them suitable for collecting emergency data in disastrous areas and performing mission-critical communication in battle fields. A critical issue in MANETs is how to reduce energy consumption and maintain a longer lifetime for mobile nodes. Several energy-efficient schemes are proposed to resolve this issue. Recent studies demonstrate that network coding can help achieve a lower energy consumption in MANETs. The energy saving comes from the fact that less transmissions are required when in-network nodes are enabled to encode packets.

Besides basic transmissions, energy consumption can also come from encryption and decryption operations at each node, as most MANETs need some level of protection on their content. This paper proposes a lightweight encryption scheme to fight against eavesdroppers in network-coded MANETs. Proposed encryption scheme which is lightweight in computation by leveraging

© Springer International Publishing Switzerland 2015
G. Wang et al. (Eds.): ICA3PP 2015 Workshops, LNCS 9532, pp. 508–517, 2015.
DOI: 10.1007/978-3-319-27161-3_46

network coding, which makes it very attractive in network-coded MANETs to further reduce energy consumption. Elliptic Curve Cryptography (ECC) based encryption scheme is proposed for network-coded MANETs. ECC takes less memory provides great security [7] and flawlessly suitable for low power devices like mobile nodes.

## 2    Related Works

MANETs authentication and encryption schemes should be lightweight and secure to provide a suitable environment for the nodes to communicate with each other in a safe community [3]. In order to enhance the network performance fast cryptographic operations has to be established.

### 2.1    P-Coding Scheme

P-Coding, a lightweight encryption scheme to provide confidentiality for network-coded MANETs in an energy- efficient way [1]. The basic idea of P-Coding is to let the source randomly permute the symbols of each packet (which is prefixed with its coding vector), before performing any network coding operations. Without any knowledge about the permutation, eavesdroppers cannot get any coding vectors for correct decoding, and thus cannot obtain any meaningful data from eavesdropping. P-Coding incurs minimal energy consumption compared to other encryption schemes. This new encryption scheme can fully exploit the security property of network coding. Since both coding vectors and message content are necessary for decoding, randomly mixing them will generate considerable confusion to the eavesdropping adversary. Here proposed P-Coding, a lightweight encryption scheme to fight against eavesdroppers in network-coded MANETs. Various parameters at the protocol level (such as cipher suites, authentication mechanisms, and transaction sizes, etc.) and the cryptographic algorithm level (cipher modes, strength) can have impact on the overall energy consumption for secure data transactions [3].

### 2.2    DSAB-Digital Signature (DSA) with Blowfish Algorithm

The dynamic feature of MANETs makes the networks vulnerable to different types of security attacks. So it is a great concern to provide security and authentication along with power utilization and robustness for the MANETs for successful transmission. Here introduced [5] novel hybrid security approach by using digital signature (DSA) with Blowfish algorithm (DSAB) and compared its performance with existing encryption techniques like AES, DES, etc. [8]. MANET is vulnerable to the malicious activities. Using a strong authentication algorithm along with an encryption technique can overcome the security problems. Therefore, here chosen DSA (Digital Signature Algorithm) for authentication purpose and Blowfish algorithm for encryption. Blowfish a symmetric key block cipher using 64 bits of data blocks and a variable size key maximum up to 448 bits [2]. It comprises of Feistel Network having 16 times iterative operations of a simple encryption function.

### 2.3  LEE: Light-Weight Energy-Efficient Encryption

Data confidentiality in wireless sensor networks is mainly achieved by using RC5 and Skipjack encryption algorithms. However, both algorithms have their own weaknesses, for example RC5 supports variable-bit rotations, which are computationally expensive and Skipjack uses a 80-bits key size, which leads to brute force attack. Here [6] introduces the design and implementation of a Light-weight Energy-Efficient Encryption Algorithm (LEE) that can be used in tiny constrained devices especially sensor nodes to provide security services (such as confidentiality) for the communications. This encryption algorithm does not allowed complicated operators or any s-Boxes. LEE was designed with as simple as possible computational operations in mind, suitable for sensor devices [6]. LEE is a 64-bit block Feistel Network with a 128-bit key and a suggested 32 rounds. Physical layer security has been considered to provide confidentiality against eavesdropping. Shift difference algorithm [4] has been proposed to transfer the data securely over the network.

## 3   Proposed System

In this system each mobile node uses elliptic curve cryptography based encryption to encrypt the packets and send it to other mobile nodes. ECC is a newer approach to public-key cryptography based on the algebraic structure of elliptic curves over finite fields. In ECC a 160 bits key, provides the same security as RSA 1024 bits key [8], thus lower computation power is required. The advantage of elliptic curve cryptosystems is the absence of sub exponential time algorithms, for attack. As ECC uses less key k size to provide more security, and for this advantage it is used to perform faster cryptographic operations. Key generation time is almost negligible compared to encryption/decryption time except when the file size is small in the ECC. The CPU execution time for ECC is shorter than the CPU execution time of the other algorithms [9].

### 3.1  Architecture

Initial part in case of encryption would be to establish the keys required while in case of data transmission it would include establishing a wireless connection.Then record the battery power and time at the mobile node. If the battery power of the node become low, then end the process. Otherwise nodes start the encryption or decryption process based ECC. After completing encryption/decryption process calculates the ramaining battery power. Then again continues this process upto minimum battery power. Figure 1 represents the mobile nodes with ECC encryption scheme.

Algorithm for message encoding and decoding are given below [10].

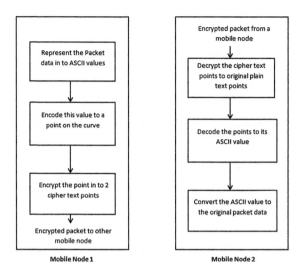

**Fig. 1.** ECC based Encryption and Decryption process in mobile nodes

### 3.2  Encryption Scheme

In public key cryptography each user or the device taking part in the communication generally have a pair of keys, a public key and a private key, and a set of operations associated with the keys to do the cryptographic operations. Only the particular user knows the private key where as the public key is distributed to all users taking part in the communication. In the case of elliptic curve cryptography Domain parameters are the constants. The domain parameters of elliptic curve are a sextuple [11]:

$$T = (P, a, b, G, n, h)$$

An elliptic curve over a field K is a curve defined by an equation of the form:

$$y^2 mod p = x^3 + a * x + b mod p$$

where a,b $\in$ K and $4 * a^3 + 27 * b^2 \neq 0$.

Each value of the a and b gives a different elliptic curve. All points (x, y) which satisfies the above equation plus a point at infinity lies on the elliptic curve. The public key is a point in the curve and the private key is a random number. The public key is obtained by multiplying the private key with the generator point G in the curve. The generator point G, the curve parameters a and b,n is the order of G, together with few more constants constitutes the domain parameter of ECC.

The basic EC operations are point addition and point doubling. Elliptic curve cryptographic primitives require scalar point multiplication [11]. Let us start with P($x_p, y_p$). To determine 2P, P is doubled. This should be an affine point on EC [7]. Use the following equation, which is a tangent to the curve at point P.

$$S = [(3x_p^2 + a)/2y_p]modp$$

Then 2P has affine coordinates $(x_r, y_r)$ given by:

$$x_r = (S^2 - 2x_p)modp$$
$$y_r = [S(x_p - x_r) - y_p]modp$$

Now to determine 3P, we use addition of points P and 2P, treating 2P=Q. Here P has coordinates $(x_p, y_p)$, Q=2P has coordinates $(x_q, y_q)$. Now the slope is:

$$S = [(y_q - y_p)/(x_q - x_p)]modp$$
$$P + Q = -R$$
$$x_r = (S^2 - x_p - x_q)modp$$
$$y_r = (S(x_p - x_r) - y_p]modp$$

---

**Algorithm 1.** Message Encoding[10]

---

1. Pick an elliptic curve $E_p(a, b)$
2. Let us say that E has N points on it
3. Let us say that alphabet consists of the digits 0,1,2,3,4,5,6,7,8,9 and the letters A,B,C,. . . , X,Y,Z coded as 10,11, . . . , 35
4. This converts message into a series of numbers between 0 and 35
5. Now choose an auxiliary base parameter, for example k = 20( both parties should agree upon this)
6. For each number mk (say), take x=mk + 1 and try to solve for y.
7. If it is not possible, then try x = mk +2 and then x = mk +3 until can solve for y.
8. In practice, find such a y before hit x = mk + k - 1. Then take the point (x,y). This now converts the number m into a point on the elliptic curve. In this way, the entire message becomes a sequence of points.

---

**Algorithm 2.** Message Decoding

---

Consider each point (x,y) and set m to be the greatest integer less than $(x - 1)/k$. Then the point (x,y) decodes as the symbol m.

---

**Key generation:** is an important part where have to generate both public key and private key. The sending node will be encrypting the message with receiving node's public key and the receiver node will decrypt its private key. For this select a number d within the range of n. Using the following equation, can generate the public key $P = d * G$.
d = The random number that should be select within the range of ( 1 to n-1 ). G is the point on the curve. P is the public key and d is the private key.

**Encryption:** Let m be the message for sending. First we represent this message on to an elliptic curve by converting it into a point. Consider m has the point M on the curve E. Randomly select k from [1 - (n-1)]. Two cipher texts will be generated let it be C1 and C2.

$$C1 = k * G$$
$$C2 = M + k * P$$

C1 and C2 will be send.

**Decryption:** Receiver node get back the message m that was send to it,

$$M = C2 - d * C1$$

M is the original message that have to get. Then

$$M = C2 - d * C1$$

M can be represented as $C2 - d * C1$
$C2 - d * C1 = (M + k * P) - d * (k * G)$ ( $C2 = M + k * P$ and $C1 = k * G$ )
$= M + k * d * G - d * k * G$ ( canceling out $k * d * G$ )
$= M$ ( Original Message )

## 4  Implementation

### 4.1  Generating Points on Elliptic Curve

To do operations with EC points in order to encrypt and decrypt, the points are to be generated first.The points are generating using given parameters a, b, and p of Elliptic Curve. Some of these points generated for the EC, $y^2 mod 751 = x^3 - 1x + 188 mod 751$ are shown below (Fig. 2).

When we plot these points using graph plotting algorithm, we get points symmetric to the elliptic curve according to the parameters.

### 4.2  Message Encoding and Decoding

Let us suppose a text message has to be encrypted, a user can encrypt the ASCII code of each and every printable character on the keyboard. All the points on the elliptic curve can be directly mapped to an ASCII value. Say the parameters of curve are: p=751,a=-1,b=188.

1. Say we have to send character 'b'.
2. 'b' is first encoded as number 11.
3. $x = mk + 1$ i.e. $11 * 20 + 1 = 221$ cannot solve it for a y such that $y^2 mod p = x^3 + a * x + b mod p$.
4. So go for $x = mk + 2$, $x = 222$, no y exists.
   $x = mk + 3$, $x = 223$, no y exists.
5. $x = mk + 4$ so $x = 224$ can solve it for y and $y = 248$.
6. Now the point (224,248) is point is encrypted and decrypted as a message.
7. To decode just compute $(x - 1)/k$ i.e. $(224 - 1)/20 = 223/20$ i.e. 11.15.
8. Return 11 as original plaintext(greatest integer less than $(x - 1)/k$, that is 11.
9. The number 11 is now decoded to character 'b'.

| | | | | | | | |
|---|---|---|---|---|---|---|---|
| (0,375) | (45,97) | (103,180) | (178,232) | (214,76) | (261,288) | (305,268) | (361,8) |
| (0,376) | (45,654) | (103,571) | (178,519) | (214,675) | (261,463) | (305,483) | (361,743) |
| (1,375) | (47,335) | (121,39) | (179,257) | (217,247) | (262,208) | (310,31) | (361,354) |
| (1,376) | (47,416) | (121,712) | (179,494) | (217,504) | (262,543) | (310,720) | (364,397) |
| (2,373) | (50,136) | (124,354) | (180,343) | (219,38) | (263,354) | (311,111) | (366,176) |
| (2,378) | (50,615) | (124,397) | (180,408) | (219,713) | (263,397) | (311,640) | (366,575) |
| (3,211) | (52,346) | (126,275) | (182,84) | (224,248) | (264,337) | (312,95) | (367,122) |
| (3,540) | (52,405) | (126,476) | (182,667) | (224,503) | (264,414) | (312,656) | (367,629) |
| (5,225) | (54,131) | (128,252) | (187,50) | (225,117) | (265,76) | (314,36) | (370,11) |
| (5,526) | (54,620) | (128,499) | (187,701) | (225,634) | (265,675) | (314,715) | (370,740) |
| (6,361) | (57,332) | (131,34) | (188,94) | (227,74) | (266,244) | (317,181) | (372,37) |
| (6,390) | (57,419) | (131,717) | (188,657) | (227,677) | (266,507) | (317,570) | (372,714) |
| (7,240) | (59,325) | (135,198) | (189,23) | (229,115) | (267,352) | (318,79) | (373,9) |
| (7,511) | (59,426) | (135,553) | (189,728) | (229,636) | (267,395) | (318,672) | (373,742) |
| (12,235) | (62,161) | (139,338) | (190,196) | (231,176) | (268,229) | (320,174) | (375,65) |
| (12,516) | (62,590) | (139,413) | (190,555) | (231,575) | (268,522) | (320,577) | (375,686) |
| (13,129) | (63,62) | (144,190) | (191,29) | (232,50) | (269,224) | (324,7) | (378,172) |
| (13,622) | (63,689) | (144,561) | (191,722) | (232,701) | (269,527) | (324,744) | (378,579) |
| (17,332) | (64,13) | (147,175) | (192,359) | (233,256) | (270,162) | (325,23) | (380,155) |
| (17,419) | (64,738) | (147,576) | (192,392) | (233,495) | (270,589) | (325,728) | (380,596) |
| (18,137) | (66,214) | (152,337) | (195,57) | (234,188) | (272,76) | (329,369) | (381,69) |
| (18,614) | (66,537) | (152,414) | (195,694) | (234,563) | (272,675) | (329,382) | (381,682) |
| (19,138) | (67,22) | (153,315) | (196,113) | (237,23) | (274,329) | (331,367) | (384,306) |
| (19,613) | (67,729) | (153,436) | (196,638) | (237,728) | (274,422) | (331,384) | (384,445) |
| (21,133) | (69,21) | (154,176) | (197,107) | (238,55) | (278,241) | (332,50) | (385,328) |
| (21,618) | (69,730) | (154,575) | (197,644) | (238,696) | (278,510) | (332,701) | (385,423) |
| (24,65) | (72,285) | (155,193) | (198,322) | (239,374) | (279,83) | (333,316) | (386,72) |
| (24,686) | (72,466) | (155,558) | (198,429) | (239,377) | (279,668) | (333,435) | (386,679) |
| (26,312) | (74,199) | (157,55) | (200,220) | (241,230) | (280,247) | (335,337) | (387,59) |
| (26,439) | (74,552) | (157,696) | (200,531) | (241,521) | (280,504) | (335,414) | (387,692) |
| (28,302) | (77,6) | (158,29) | (201,5) | (243,336) | (283,54) | (337,178) | (389,146) |
| (28,449) | (77,745) | (158,722) | (201,746) | (243,415) | (283,697) | (337,573) | (389,605) |
| (30,236) | (79,333) | (159,124) | (202,13) | (245,242) | (285,96) | (339,353) | (391,187) |
| (30,515) | (79,418) | (159,627) | (202,738) | (245,509) | (285,655) | (339,398) | (391,564) |
| (32,300) | (84,138) | (160,140) | (203,169) | (246,53) | (291,16) | (341,362) | (392,341) |
| (32,451) | (84,613) | (160,611) | (203,582) | (246,698) | (291,735) | (341,389) | (392,410) |
| (34,118) | (86,184) | (161,1) | (204,363) | (248,236) | (295,110) | (343,205) | (393,41) |
| (34,633) | (86,567) | (161,750) | (204,388) | (248,515) | (295,641) | (343,546) | (393,710) |
| (36,336) | (92,145) | (169,132) | (205,161) | (251,56) | (296,245) | (348,228) | (394,324) |
| (36,415) | (92,606) | (169,619) | (205,590) | (251,695) | (296,506) | (348,523) | (394,427) |
| (38,256) | (93,120) | (170,274) | (207,215) | (253,108) | (297,182) | (352,65) | (395,141) |
| (38,495) | (93,631) | (170,477) | (207,536) | (253,643) | (297,569) | (352,686) | (395,610) |
| (39,349) | (94,73) | (172,255) | (209,198) | (254,247) | (299,183) | (354,153) | (398,326) |
| (39,402) | (94,678) | (172,496) | (209,553) | (254,504) | (299,568) | (354,598) | (398,425) |
| (41,274) | (97,284) | (173,33) | (210,97) | (256,342) | (301,258) | (356,55) | (400,238) |
| (41,477) | (97,467) | (173,718) | (210,654) | (256,409) | (301,493) | (356,696) | (400,513) |
| (43,322) | (101,4) | (174,240) | (211,20) | (257,149) | (302,291) | (358,200) | (401,153) |
| (43,429) | (101,747) | (174,511) | (211,731) | (257,602) | (302,460) | (358,551) | (401,599) |
| (44,312) | (102,120) | (177,164) | (212,250) | (258,276) | (304,165) | (359,296) | (402,29) |
| (44,439) | (102,631) | (177,587) | (212,501) | (258,475) | (304,586) | (359,455) | (402,722) |

**Fig. 2.** Some generated points on EC

## 4.3    ECC Encryption

The base point G is selected as $(1,376)$. Base point implies that it has the smallest (x, y) co-ordinates which satisfy the EC. For example, encoded point $(224,248)$ for 'b' is used as message point M. The ECC method requires that we select a random integer k ($k < p$), which needs to be kept secret. Then kG is evaluated, by a series of additions and doublings. Suppose there are 2 mobile nodes 1 and 2, then mobile node 1 select the private key, called $d_1$, k can be generated by random number generators to give credibility.

For simplicity assume that k = 141, and $d_1 = 17$. The public key of mobile node 1 is evaluated by

$$P_1 = d_1 G$$
$$P_1 = 17 * (1, 376) = (522, 469)$$

Message Point for encrypting is $M = (224, 248)$. Two Cipher text points are formed.

$$C_1 = k * G = 141 * (1, 376) = (681, 312)$$
$$C_2 = M + k * P_1 = (224, 248) + 141 * (522, 469) = (279, 668)$$

These $C_1$ and $C_2$ are points on the elliptic curve and they send it to mobile node 2. Encrypted version of the message is: $((681,312),(279,668))$, where x1 = 681, y1 = 312, x2 = 279, y2 = 668.

**Table 1.** Encryption time comparison

| Message packets size in bytes | ECC (Time in ms) | Blow fish (Time in ms) |
|---|---|---|
| 2 | 11 | 28 |
| 4 | 18 | 30 |
| 6 | 21 | 32 |
| 8 | 26 | 34 |
| 10 | 34 | 36 |

### 4.4 ECC Decryption

For decrypting two cipher text points are obtained $C_1$ and $C_2$. Receiver node get back the message M by $C_2 - d_1 * C_1$.
So, $d_1 * C_1 = 17 * (681, 312) = (257, 149)$
$M = C_2 - d_1 * C_1 = (279, 668) - (257, 149) = (224, 248)$
This subtraction is another ECC procedure involving doubling and addition. But the only difference is that the negative term will have its y co-ordinate preceded by a minus sign. After decoding operation M is converted to 'b' (Table 1).

## 5 Experimental Results and Analysis

An elliptc curve was first defined and its points were calculated. Two mobile nodes were created and connection was established between them. The message to be send from one mobile node to the other is transformed into points on an elliptic curve. These points are encrypted using Elliptic curve cryptography. The mobile node receiving the encrypted points will decrypt them using the same. These decrypted points are decoded to get the original message. Encryption and decryption time were calculated for each mobile node. Execution time for encryption and decryption of each message point is calculated in mobile node. Execution time for different sized message packets were calculated and also compared it with blow fish encryption algorithm for MANETs. Tables and bar graphs showing the comparison results are given below. Less encryption time also means fewer CPU cycles, and less energy consumptions. So ECC consumes lesser energy in comparing with Blow fish (Tables 1 and 2).

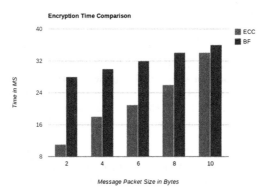

**Table 2.** Decryption time comparison

| Message packets size in bytes | ECC (Time in ms) | Blow fish (Time in ms) |
|---|---|---|
| 2 | 1 | 2 |
| 4 | 2 | 3 |
| 6 | 2 | 3 |
| 8 | 3 | 3 |
| 10 | 3 | 4 |

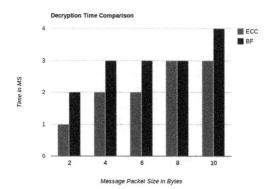

## 6    Conclusion and Future Work

A critical issue in MANETs is how to reduce energy consumption and maintain a longer life time for mobile nodes. Several energy-efficient schemes are proposed to resolve this issue. But most of them causes security issues. Besides basic transmissions, energy consumption can also come from encryption and decryption operations at each node. In order to avoid the energy consumption and security issues to the packets, a lightweight and highly secured ECC encryption scheme is proposed. Future work includes extending this application of ECC to other communication networks, e.g., vehicular ad hoc networks.

## References

1. Zhang, P., Lin, C., Jiang, Y., Fan, Y., Shen, X(.S).: A lightweight encryption scheme for network-coded mobile Ad Hoc networks. IEEE Trans. Parallel Distrib. Syst. **25**(9), 2211–2221 (2014)
2. Chehal, R., Singh, K., Singh, K.: Efficiency and security of data with symmetric encryption algorithms. Int. J. Adv. Res. Comput. Sci. Softw. Eng. **2**(8), 472–475 (2012)
3. Potlapally, N.R., Ravi, S., Raghunathan, A., Jha, N.K.: A study of the energy consumption characteristics of cryptographic algorithms and security protocols. IEEE Trans. Mob. Comput. **5**(2), 128–143 (2006)

4. Suhashini1, C., Sivakumar, S.: A secure approach with physical layer encryption in MANET. In: International Conference on Engineering Technology and Science (ICETS 2014), pp. 177–181, February 2014
5. Kumar, G., Saha, R., Kumar Rai, M.: DSAB A hybrid approach for providing security in MANET. Int. J. Inf. Secur. Sci., 82–87, July 2012
6. Komninos, N., Soroush, H., Salajegheh, M.: Algorithms & security group athens information technology. LEE: Light-Weight Energy-Efficient Encryption Algorithm for Sensor Networks, 1–6, January 2009
7. Ranaut, D., Lal, M.: A review on security issues and encryption algorithms in Mobile Ad-hoc Network. Int. J. Sci. Res. (IJSR), 146–148, March 2012
8. Kumar, A., Tyagi, S.S., Rana, M., Aggarwal, N., Bhadana, P.: A comparative study of public key cryptosystem based on ECC and RSA. Int. J. Comput. Sci. Eng. (IJCSE), 1904–1909, May 2011
9. Kofahi, N.A.: Yarmouk University Irbid, Jordan: "An empirical study to compare the performance of some symmetric and asymmetric ciphers". Int. J. Secur. Appl., 1–15 (2013)
10. Padma, B., Chandravathi, D., Prapoorna Roja, P.: Encoding And Decoding of a Message in the Implementation of Elliptic Curve Cryptography using Koblitzs Method. Int. J. Comput. Sci. Eng. $2(5)$, 1904–1907 (2010)
11. Anoop, M.S.: Elliptic Curve Cryptography An Implementation Guide, pp. 1–11

# The 1st International Symposium on Dependability in Sensor, Cloud, and Big Data Systems and Applications (DependSys 2015)

# Attribute-Based Ring Signcryption Scheme and Its Application in Wireless Body Area Networks

Changji Wang[1,2]([envelope]) and Jing Liu[1]

[1] School of Software, Yunnan University, Kunming 650500, China
wchangji@gmail.com
[2] Guangdong Key Laboratory of Information Security Technology,
Sun Yat-sen University, Guangzhou 510275, China

**Abstract.** Wireless body area network (WBAN) technology has attracted intensive attention from the academic and industrial research communities in recent years. For widespread deployment of WBANs, security and privacy must be addressed properly. In this paper, we introduce a new cryptographic primitive named key-policy attribute-based ring signcryption (KP-ABRSC) scheme, which is a combination of identity-based ring signature scheme and key-policy attribute-based encryption scheme. In KP-ABRSC, each signcrypted message is labeled by the sender with a set of descriptive attributes and a list of identities of potential senders, while an access structure is embedded in each user's private key by a trusted authority. We give formal syntax and security definitions for KP-ABRSC scheme and construct a KP-ABRSC scheme from bilinear pairings. The proposed KP-ABRSC scheme is proven to be indistinguishable against adaptive chosen plaintext attacks under the DBDH assumption and existentially unforgeable against adaptive chosen message and identity attacks under the CDH assumption. Finally, we present a cloud-based healthcare framework by exploiting our proposed KP-ABRSC scheme and WBANs, which can ensure data authenticity, confidentiality and non-repudiation, but also can offer participants privacy and fine-grained access control on encrypted medical data.

**Keywords:** Identity-based ring signature · Identity-based ring signcryption · Key-policy attribute-based encryption · Key-policy attribute-based ring signcryption · Wireless body area networks

## 1  Introduction

With the rapid development of wireless communication, low-power integrated circuits and physiological sensors, wireless body area networks (WBAN) technology has attracted intensive attention from the academic and industrial research communities in recent years [1–3].

Figure 1 illustrated a typical application of WBANs in the healthcare domain. The implanted intelligent physiological sensors in the human body will collect

© Springer International Publishing Switzerland 2015
G. Wang et al. (Eds.): ICA3PP 2015 Workshops, LNCS 9532, pp. 521–530, 2015.
DOI: 10.1007/978-3-319-27161-3_47

various vital signals in order to monitor the patient's health status no matter their location, and these collected signals will be transmitted wirelessly to a controller (a mobile computing device like a PDA or smart phone). The controller will transmit all information in real time or in non-real time to the third party remote server (e.g., health cloud server) to be stored, and these information will be shared by the patient's primary doctor, physicians and any other who needs to acquire the essential information for the patient's health.

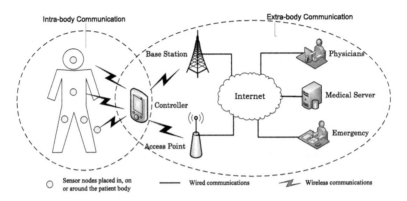

**Fig. 1.** Illustration of a typical WBAN.

Unlike conventional sensor networks, a WBAN deals with medical information, which has stringent requirements for security and privacy [4]. Zhang et al. [5] discussed the secure intra-body communication among sensor nodes, and proposed a key agreement scheme that allows neighboring nodes to share a common key generated by electrocardiogram signals. However, it is vulnerable to single node compromise attack. Malasri and Wang [6] discussed the secure extra-body communication between the controllers and the base station, and proposed a two-tier authentication scheme based on patient biometric and physiological data. They also proposed a key exchange protocol which allows base stations and controllers to securely derive symmetric keys without any prior shared secrets. To prevent both counterfeiting controllers and base stations, each controller needs to pre-configure with base stations' public keys and each base station needs to store controllers's biometric information. Hu et al. [7] proposed a fuzzy attribute-based signcryption scheme to provide security for patients in a WBAN. Unfortunately, it can not provide digital signature function in fact. Tan et al. [8] proposed a solution to share the sensitive patients' medical information among different medical operators by employing key-policy attribute-based encryption (KP-ABE) scheme. However, they did not consider data authenticity and unforgeability. Liu et al. [9] proposed two remote authentication protocols to enable remote WBAN users to anonymously enjoy healthcare service based on a certificateless signature scheme. However, they did not consider data confidentiality and access control for WBAN users.

In summary, existing solutions to provide security and privacy protection for WBAN in the literature are either unsafe or inefficient. In this paper, we first

introduce a new cryptographic primitive named key-policy attribute-based ring
signcryption (KP-ABRSC) by combining the notion of KP-ABE and identity-
based ring signature (IBRS), and give formal syntax and security definitions
for KP-ABRSC. Next, we construct a KP-ABRSC scheme from bilinear pairings, and prove the proposed scheme is indistinguishable against adaptively chosen plaintext attacks (IND-CPA) under the DBDH assumption, existentially
unforgeable against adaptively chosen message attacks and identity attacks
(EUF-CMIA) under the CDH assumption and strong anonymous. Finally, we
present a secure, privacy-protected and fine-grained access control framework
for WBANs by exploiting our proposed KP-ABRSC scheme.

## 2   Preliminaries

We denote by $x \xleftarrow{\$} \mathbf{S}$ the operation of picking an element $x$ uniformly at random
from the set $\mathbf{S}$. A bilinear group generator $\mathcal{G}$ is an algorithm that takes as input
a security parameter $\kappa$ and outputs a bilinear group $(q, \mathbf{G}_1, \mathbf{G}_T, \hat{e})$, where $\mathbf{G}_1$
and $\mathbf{G}_T$ are a cyclic additive group and a multiplicative group of prime order $q$,
and $\hat{e} \colon \mathbf{G}_1 \times \mathbf{G}_1 \to \mathbf{G}_T$ is a bilinear pairing with the following properties:

- Bilinearity: For $P, Q \xleftarrow{\$} \mathbf{G}$ and $a, b \xleftarrow{\$} \mathbf{Z}_q^*$, we have $\hat{e}([a]P, [b]Q) = \hat{e}(P, Q)^{ab}$.
- Non-degeneracy: There exists $P, Q \in \mathbf{G}$ such that $\hat{e}(P, Q) \neq 1$.
- Computability: There is an efficient algorithm to compute $\hat{e}(P, Q)$ for
  $P, Q \xleftarrow{\$} \mathbf{G}$.

**Definition 1.** *The Computational Diffie-Hellman (CDH) assumption in an
additive group $\mathbf{G}$ of prime $q$ order states that, given $\langle P, [a]P, [b]P \rangle$, it is computationally intractable to compute the value $[ab]P$, where $a, b \xleftarrow{\$} \mathbf{Z}_q^*$ and $P \xleftarrow{\$} \mathbf{G}$.*

**Definition 2.** *The Decisional Bilinear Diffie-Hellman (DBDH) assump-
tion in a prime order bilinear group $(q, \mathbf{G}, \mathbf{G}_T, \hat{e})$ states that, given
$\langle P, [a]P, [b]P, [c]P, \hat{e}(P, P)^z \rangle$, it is computationally intractable to determine
whether $\hat{e}(P, P)^z = \hat{e}(P, P)^{abc}$, where $a, b, c, z \xleftarrow{\$} \mathbf{Z}_q^*$ and $P \xleftarrow{\$} \mathbf{G}$.*

**Definition 3.** *Let $\mathbf{P} = \{\mathcal{P}_1, \mathcal{P}_2, \ldots, \mathcal{P}_n\}$ be a set of parties, and denote by $2^{\mathbf{P}}$ its
power set. A collection $\mathbb{A} \subseteq 2^{\mathbf{P}}$ is monotone if for every $\mathbf{B}$ and $\mathbf{C}$, if $\mathbf{B} \in \mathbb{A}$ and
$\mathbf{B} \subseteq \mathbf{C}$ then $\mathbf{C} \in \mathbb{A}$. An access structure (respectively, monotone access structure)
is a collection (respectively, monotone collection) $\mathbb{A}$ of non-empty subsets of $\mathbf{P}$,
i.e. $\mathbf{P} \setminus \emptyset$. The sets in $\mathbb{A}$ are called the authorized sets, and the sets not in $\mathbb{A}$ are
called the unauthorized sets [10].*

**Definition 4.** *A secret sharing scheme $\Pi$ for an access structure $\mathbb{A}$ over a set
of parties $\mathbf{P}$ is called linear over $\mathbf{Z}_q$ if*

- *The shares for each party form a vector over $\mathbf{Z}_q$.*
- *There exists a share-generating matrix $\mathbf{M}_{\ell \times n}$ for $\Pi$. Let $s \in \mathbf{Z}_q$ be the secret
  to be shared. For all $i = 1, 2, \ldots, \ell$, let the function $\rho$ defined the party labeling
  row $i$ of $\mathbf{M}_{\ell \times n}$ as $\rho(i)$, and define the column vector $\mathbf{v} = (s, r_2, \ldots, r_n)^{\top}$
  where $r_2, \ldots, r_n \xleftarrow{\$} \mathbf{Z}_q$, then $\boldsymbol{\alpha} = \mathbf{M}_{\ell \times n} \mathbf{v}$ is the vector of $\ell$ shares of the secret
  $s$ according to $\Pi$, and the share $\alpha_i = (\mathbf{M}_{\ell \times n} \mathbf{v})_i$ belongs to party $\rho(i)$.*

Beimel [11] showed that every linear secret sharing scheme (LSSS) according to the above definition enjoys linear reconstruction property: Suppose $\Pi$ is an LSSS for the access structure $\mathbb{A}$. Let $\mathbf{S} \in \mathbb{A}$ be any authorized set, and define $\mathbf{I} = \{i | \rho(i) \in \mathbf{S}\} \subset \{1, 2, \ldots, \ell\}$. There exist constants $\beta_i \in \mathbf{Z}_q$ for $i \in \mathbf{I}$, such that, if $\{\alpha_i\}$ are valid shares of any secret $s$ according to $\Pi$, then $\sum_{i \in \mathbf{I}} \alpha_i \beta_i = s$. These constants $\{\beta_i\}$ can be found in time polynomial in the size of $\mathbf{M}_{\ell \times n}$.

# 3  Syntax and Security Model for KP-ABRSC Scheme

A KP-ABRSC scheme consists of the following six polynomial-time algorithms:

- **Setup**: The probabilistic setup algorithm is run by a trusted private key generator (PKG). It takes as input a security parameter $\kappa$. It outputs the public system parameters $mpk$, and the master key $msk$ which is known only to the PKG.
- **IBKeyGen**: The probabilistic identity-based private key generation algorithm is run by the PKG. It takes as input $mpk$, $msk$, an identity $\mathsf{ID}_i$. It outputs the corresponding identity-based private key $sk_{\mathsf{ID}_i}$.
- **ABKeyGen**: The probabilistic attribute-based private key generation algorithm is run by the PKG. It takes as input $mpk$, $msk$, and an access structure $\mathbb{A}$ assigned to a user. It outputs an attribute private key $dk_{\mathbb{A}}$.
- **Signcrypt**: The probabilistic signcrypt algorithm is run by a signcrypting party. It takes as input $mpk$, a message $m$, an ad-hoc group of ring members $\mathbf{U} = \{\mathcal{U}_i\}_{i=1}^n$ with corresponding identities $\mathbf{ID} = \{\mathsf{ID}_i\}_{i=1}^n$, the signcrypting party's identity-based private key $sk_{\mathsf{ID}_s}$ with $\mathsf{ID}_s \in \mathbf{ID}$, and a set $\boldsymbol{\omega}$ of attributes. It outputs a signcrypted ciphertext $\mathsf{SC}$.
- **PubVerify**: The deterministic public verifiability algorithm is run by any outside receivers. It takes as input $mpk$, a signcrypted ciphertext $\mathsf{SC}$, the set $\mathbf{ID}$ of identities corresponding to the ring members $\mathbf{U}$, the set $\boldsymbol{\omega}$ of attributes. It outputs a bit $b$ which is 1 if the signcrypted ciphertext $\mathsf{SC}$ is generated by a certain member in the group $\mathbf{U}$, or 0 if the signcrypted ciphertext $\mathsf{C}$ is not generated by any member in the group $\mathbf{U}$.
- **UnSigncrypt**: The deterministic unsigncryption algorithm is run by a receiver. It takes as input $mpk$, a signcrypted ciphertext $\mathsf{SC}$, the set $\mathbf{ID}$ of identities corresponding to the ring members $\mathbf{U}$, the set $\boldsymbol{\omega}$ of attributes, the receiver's attribute-based private key $dk_{\mathbb{A}}$. It outputs the message $m$ if $\mathbb{A}(\boldsymbol{\omega}) = 1$ and $\mathsf{ID}_s \in \mathbf{ID}$. Otherwise it outputs $\perp$.

The set of algorithms must satisfy the following consistency requirement:

$$\mathbf{Setup}(1^\kappa) \to (mpk, msk), m \xleftarrow{\$} \{0,1\}^*, \mathsf{ID}_s \xleftarrow{\$} \mathbf{ID},$$
$$\mathbf{IBKeyGen}(mpk, msk, \mathsf{ID}_s) \to sk_{\mathsf{ID}_s}, \mathbf{ABKeyGen}(mpk, msk, \mathbb{A}) \to dk_{\mathbb{A}},$$
$$\text{If } \mathbb{A}(\boldsymbol{\omega}) = 1 \text{ and } \mathbf{SignCrypt}(mpk, \mathbf{ID}, sk_{\mathsf{ID}_s}, \boldsymbol{\omega}, m) \to \mathsf{SC},$$
$$\text{Then } \mathbf{UnSignCrypt}(mpk, dk_{\mathbb{A}}, \mathbf{ID}, \boldsymbol{\omega}, \mathsf{SC}) = m \text{ holds.}$$

We define IND-CPA secure for KP-ABRSC scheme in the selective-set model by the following game between an adversary $\mathcal{A}$ and a challenger $\mathcal{C}$.

- **Init:** $\mathcal{A}$ declares the set $\omega$ of challenged attributes.
- **Setup:** $\mathcal{C}$ runs the Setup algorithm, gives $mpk$ to $\mathcal{A}$, while keeps $msk$ secret.
- **Phase 1:** $\mathcal{A}$ is allowed to issue the following queries adaptively.
  - Singing private key queries on identity $\mathsf{ID}_i$. $\mathcal{C}$ runs **IBKeyGen**$(mpk, msk, \mathsf{ID}_i)$, and sends $sk_{\mathsf{ID}_i}$ back to $\mathcal{A}$.
  - Decrypting private key queries on access structures $\mathbb{A}_j$. If $\mathbb{A}_j(\omega) \neq 1$, then $\mathcal{C}$ runs **ABKeyGen**$(mpk, msk, \mathbb{A}_j)$, and sends $dk_{\mathbb{A}_j}$ back to $\mathcal{A}$. Otherwise, $\mathcal{C}$ rejects the request.
- **Challenge:** $\mathcal{A}$ submits two equal length messages $m_0$ and $m_1$, and a set of identities $\mathbf{ID}^* = \{\mathsf{ID}_i^*\}_{i=1}^n$ to $\mathcal{C}$. Then, $\mathcal{C}$ flips a random coin $b$, picks an identity $\mathsf{ID}_i^* \xleftarrow{\$} \mathbf{ID}^*$, runs **IBKeyGen**$(mpk, msk, \mathsf{ID}_i^*)$ and **Signcrypt**$(mpk, sk_{\mathsf{ID}_i^*}, \mathbf{ID}^*, \omega, m_b)$. Finally, $\mathcal{C}$ sends $\mathsf{SC}_i^*$ to $\mathcal{A}$.
- **Phase 2:** Phase 1 is repeated.
- **Guess:** $\mathcal{A}$ outputs a guess $b'$ of $b$.

The advantage of $\mathcal{A}$ in the above game is defined as $\mathrm{Adv}_{\mathcal{A}}(\kappa) = \Pr[b' = b] - \frac{1}{2}$.

**Definition 5.** *A KP-ABRSC scheme is said to be IND-CPA secure in the selective-set model if $Adv_{\mathcal{A}}(\kappa)$ is negligible in the security parameter $\kappa$.*

We define EUF-CMIA secure for KP-ABRSC scheme by the following game between an adversary $\mathcal{A}$ and a challenger $\mathcal{C}$.

- **Setup:** Same as in the above IND-CPA game.
- **Find:** $\mathcal{A}$ is allowed to issue the following queries adaptively.
  - Singing private key queries. Same as in the above IND-CPA game.
  - Decrypting private key queries. Same as in the above IND-CPA game.
  - Signcrypt queries on $\langle m, \mathbf{ID}, \omega \rangle$. $\mathcal{C}$ picks an identity $\mathsf{ID}_i \xleftarrow{\$} \mathbf{ID}$, runs **IBKeyGen**$(mpk, msk, \mathsf{ID}_i)$ and **Signcrypt**$(mpk, sk_{\mathsf{ID}_i}, \mathbf{ID}, \omega, m)$ in order. Finally, $\mathcal{C}$ sends $\mathsf{SC}_i$ back to $\mathcal{A}$.
- **Forgery:** $\mathcal{A}$ produces a new triple $\langle \mathsf{SC}^*, \omega^*, \mathbf{ID}^* \rangle$. The only restriction is that $\langle m, \mathbf{ID}^* \rangle$ does not appear in the set of previous Signcrypt queries during the Find stage and each of the signing private keys in $\mathbf{ID}^*$ is never returned by any IBKeyGen query.

$\mathcal{A}$ wins the game if **PubVerify**$(mpk, \mathbf{ID}^*, \omega^*, \mathsf{SC}^*) = 1$, and the advantage of $\mathcal{A}$ is defined as the probability that it wins.

**Definition 6.** *A KP-ABRSC scheme is said to be EUF-CMIA secure if no poly-nomially bounded adversary $\mathcal{A}$ has non-negligible advantage in the above game.*

**Definition 7.** *A KP-ABRSC scheme is strongly anonymous if for any sign-crypting party group $\mathbf{U}$ of $n_s$ members with identities $\mathbf{ID}$, any message $m$ and signcrypted ciphertext $\mathsf{SC}$, the probability to identify the actual signcrypting party is not better than a random guess, i.e., an adversary outputs the identity of actual signcrypting party with probability $1/n_s$ if he is not a member of $\mathbf{U}$, and with probability $1/(n_s - 1)$ if he is a member of $\mathbf{U}$.*

## 4  Our KP-ABRSC Construction

Our KP-ABRSC construction from bilinear pairings is described as follows.

- **Setup**: The PKG runs $\mathcal{G}(1^\kappa) \to \langle q, \mathbf{G}_1, \mathbf{G}_T, \hat{e} \rangle$, chooses $x, y \xleftarrow{\$} \mathbf{Z}_q^*$ and $t_i \xleftarrow{\$}$ $\mathbf{Z}_q^*$ for each attribute $\mathsf{atr}_i \in \Omega$, and two cryptographic hash functions $H_1 :$ $\{0,1\}^* \to \mathbf{G}_1$ and $H_2 : \{0,1\}^* \to \mathbf{Z}_q^*$. Then, the PKG computes $P_{pub} = [x]P$, $Y = \hat{e}(P, P)^y$ and $T_i = [t_i]P$ for $1 \leq i \leq |\Omega|$. Finally, the PKG sets $msk =$ $\langle t_1, \dots, t_{|\Omega|}, x, y \rangle$, and publishes $mpk = \langle \Omega, \{T_i\}_{i=1}^{|\Omega|}, P_{pub}, Y, H_1, H_2 \rangle$.
- **IBKeyGen**: Given an identity $\mathsf{ID}_i$, the PKG sets user's public key $Q_{\mathsf{ID}_i} =$ $H_1(\mathsf{ID}_i)$, and computes the corresponding signing private key $sk_{\mathsf{ID}_i} = [x]Q_{\mathsf{ID}_i}$, then sends $sk_{\mathsf{ID}_i}$ to the user via a secure channel.
- **ABKeyGen**: Given an LSSS access structure $\mathbb{A}$ described by $(\mathbf{M}_{\ell \times n}, \rho)$ that assigned to a user, the PKG chooses a vector $\boldsymbol{u} = (u_1, u_2, \dots, u_n)^\top \xleftarrow{\$} \mathbf{Z}_q^{*(n)}$ such that $\sum_{i=1}^n u_i = y$. For each row vector $\mathbf{M}_i$ of $\mathbf{M}_{\ell \times n}$, the PKG computes $\alpha_i = \mathbf{M}_i \cdot \boldsymbol{u}$ and $D_i = [\alpha_i/t_{\rho(i)}]P$. Finally, the PKG sends the decryption key associated to the access structure $dk_\mathbb{A} = \langle D_1, D_2, \dots, D_\ell \rangle$ to the user.
- **Signcrypt**: Let $\mathbf{U}$ be an ad-hoc group of $n$ members with identities $\mathbf{ID} =$ $\{\mathsf{ID}_i | 1 \leq i \leq n\}$ including the actual signcrypting party with identity $\mathsf{ID}_j$ where $1 \leq j \leq n$. To signcrypt a message $m \in \mathbf{G}_T$ on behalf of the group $\mathbf{U}$ under a set $\boldsymbol{\omega}$ of attributes, the signcrypting party performs as follows.
  - Choose $s \xleftarrow{\$} \mathbf{Z}_q^*$, compute $C' = m \cdot Y^s$ and $C_i = [s]T_i$ for all $\mathsf{atr}_i \in \boldsymbol{\omega}$.
  - For all $1 \leq i \neq j \leq n$, choose $R_i \xleftarrow{\$} \mathbf{G}_1$, compute $h_i = H_2(C'\|\boldsymbol{\omega}\|\mathbf{ID}\|R_i)$.
  - Compute $R_j = [s]Q_{\mathsf{ID}_j} - \sum_{i \neq j}(R_i + [h_i]Q_{\mathsf{ID}_i})$, $h_j = H_2(C'\|\boldsymbol{\omega}\|\mathbf{ID}\|R_j)$, $\sigma_1 = [h_j + s]sk_{\mathsf{ID}_j}$, $R = \sum_{i=1}^n R_i$ and $\sigma_2 = H_2(m\|R\|Y^s)$.
  - Output $\mathsf{SC} = \langle \boldsymbol{\omega}, \mathbf{ID}, C', \{C_i\}_{\mathsf{atr}_i \in \boldsymbol{\omega}}, \{R_i\}_{i=1}^n, \sigma_1, \sigma_2 \rangle$.
- **PubVerify**: Any receiver can check the validity of the signcrypted ciphertext $\mathsf{SC}$ against a set $\mathbf{ID}$ of identities as follows.
  - Compute $h_i = H_2(C'\|\boldsymbol{\omega}\|\mathbf{ID}\|R_i)$ for $1 \leq i \leq n$.
  - Check $\hat{e}(P_{pub}, \sum_{i=1}^n(R_i + [h_i]Q_{\mathsf{ID}_i})) = \hat{e}(P, \sigma_1)$. It outputs 1 if the equation holds, or 0 if the equation does not hold.
- **UnSigncrypt**: A receiver uses his decryption private key $dk_\mathbb{A}$ associated to the access structure $\mathbb{A}$ described by $(\mathbf{M}_{\ell \times n}, \rho)$ to recover and verify the signcrypted ciphertext $\mathsf{SC} = \langle \boldsymbol{\omega}, \mathbf{ID}, C', \{C_i\}_{\mathsf{atr}_i \in \boldsymbol{\omega}}, \{R_i\}_{i=1}^n, \sigma_1, \sigma_2 \rangle$ as follows.
  - Determine $\mathbb{A}(\boldsymbol{\omega}) = 1$. If not, the receiver rejects $\mathsf{SC}$.
  - Validate the signcrypted ciphertext $\mathsf{SC}$ as any receiver performs in the **PubVerify** algorithm.
  - Define $\mathbf{I} = \{i | \rho(i) \in \boldsymbol{\omega}\} \subset \{1, 2, \dots, \ell\}$. Let $\{\beta_i \in \mathbf{Z}_q\}$ be a set of constants such that if $\{\alpha_i\}$ are valid shares of $y$ according to $(\mathbf{M}_{\ell \times n}, \rho)$, then $\sum_{i \in \mathbf{I}} \alpha_i \beta_i = y$. The receiver computes $V = \prod_{\rho(i) \in \boldsymbol{\omega}} \hat{e}(D_i, C_{\rho(i)})^{\beta_i}$, $m' = C'/V$, and $R = \sum_{i=1}^n R_i$.
  - Check the equation $H_2(m'\|R\|V) = \sigma_2$. If it holds, the receiver accepts and outputs the message $m$. Otherwise, rejects and outputs $\perp$.

**Theorem 1.** *Our KP-ABRSC scheme satisfies consistency requirement.*

*Proof.* Consistency requirement can be verified as follows.

$$\hat{e}(P_{pub}, \sum_{i=1}^{n}(R_i + [h_i]Q_{ID_i})) = \hat{e}([x]P, \sum_{i=1,i\neq j}^{n}(R_i + [h_i]Q_{ID_i}) + R_j + [h_j]Q_{ID_j}) = \hat{e}(P,\sigma_1)$$

$$V = \prod_{\rho(i)\in\omega} \hat{e}(D_i, C_{\rho(i)})^{\beta_i} = \prod_{\rho(i)\in\omega} \hat{e}([\alpha_i/t_{\rho(i)}]P, [st_{\rho(i)}]P)^{\beta_i} = \hat{e}(P,P)^{sy}.$$

$$m' = C'/V = m \cdot Y^s/\hat{e}(P,P)^{sy} = m$$

**Theorem 2.** *Our KP-ABRSC scheme satisfies strong anonymity.*

*Proof.* Since $s \xleftarrow{\$} \mathbf{Z}_q^*$ and $R_i \xleftarrow{\$} \mathbf{G}_1$ for $1 \leq i \neq j \leq n$ are generated uniformly at random. All components of SC except $\sigma_1$ do not contain any identity information bound to them. Thus, we only need to check whether $\sigma_1 = [h_j + s]sk_{ID_j}$ will leak information about the actual signcrypting party.

According to $[s]Q_{ID_j} = R_j + \sum_{i\neq j}(R_i + [h_i]Q_{ID_i})$, anyone can compute $[s]Q_{ID_j}$ and tries to determine whether a user with identity $ID_k$ is the actual signcrypting party by verifying the following equation:

$$\hat{e}(R_k + \sum_{i\neq k}(R_i + [h_i]Q_{ID_i}), P_{pub}) \stackrel{?}{=} \hat{e}(\sigma_1, P)/\hat{e}([h_k]Q_{ID_k}, P_{pub}).$$

However, we can prove the above equation holds for all $1 \leq k \leq n_s$ as follows.

$$\hat{e}(R_k + \sum_{i\neq k}(R_i + [h_i]Q_{ID_i}), P_{pub}) = \hat{e}(\sum_{i\neq j}R_i + R_j + \sum_{i\neq k}[h_i]Q_{ID_i}, P_{pub})$$

$$= \hat{e}(\sum_{i\neq j}R_i + [s]Q_{ID_j} - \sum_{i\neq j}(R_i + [h_i]Q_{ID_i}) + \sum_{i\neq k}[h_i]Q_{ID_i}, P_{pub})$$

$$= \hat{e}([s]Q_{ID_j} - \sum_{i\neq j}[h_i]Q_{ID_i} + \sum_{i\neq k}[h_i]Q_{ID_i}, P_{pub}) = \hat{e}(\sigma_1, P)/\hat{e}([h_k]Q_{ID_k}, P_{pub})$$

Thus, even an adversary with unbounded computing power has no advantage in identifying the actual signcrypting party over random guessing.

**Theorem 3.** *Our KP-ABRSC scheme is IND-CPA secure in the selective-set model under the DBDH assumption.*

**Theorem 4.** *Our KP-ABRSC scheme is EUF-CMA secure in the adaptive model under the CDH assumption.*

Here we omit the proofs of Theorems 3 and 4 due to space limitation, and will give the security proofs in the extended version of the paper.

## 5    KP-ABRSC Application in WBANs

In this section, we present a secure, privacy-protected and fine-grained access control framework for WBANs by exploiting KP-ABRSC scheme. Figure 2 illustrates the proposed framework for WBANs, which involves five participants:

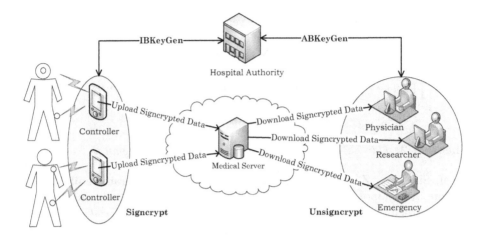

**Fig. 2.** Application of KP-ABRSC Scheme in WBANs

- One hospital authority (HA) who acts as the PKG. HA is responsible for generating system public parameters, issuing private keys for controllers based on their identities and private keys for medical personnel based on their assigned access structures.
- Multiple wearable or implanted sensors, which can sense and process vital signs or environmental parameters, and transfer the relevant data to the corresponding controller.
- Multiple controllers who aggregate information from sensors and ultimately convey the information about health status across existing networks to the medical server.
- One medical server who keeps electronic medical records of registered users and provides various services to the users and medical personnel.
- Multiple medical personnel (include doctors, nurses, researchers etc.) who may access the patients' medical information and provide medical services.

Sensors in and around the body collect the vital signals of the patient continuously and transmit the collected signals to the corresponding controller regularly. Each controller can be uniquely identified by the registered patient's identity who owns the controller. The controller aggregates the received signals and signcrypts the aggregated information $m$ as follows.

- Choose a group of identities $\mathbf{ID} = \{\mathsf{ID}_1, \mathsf{ID}_2, \ldots, \mathsf{ID}_n\}$ that includes the controller's own identity.
- Annotate $m$ with attributes $\boldsymbol{\omega}$ such as electrocardiogram (ECG), electroencephalography (EEG), pulse rate, temperature and so on.
- Run the Signcrypt algorithm to get the signcrypted ciphertext $\mathsf{SC}$ with the controller's private key, the aggregated information $m$, identities $\mathbf{ID}$ and attributes $\boldsymbol{\omega}$ as input.

The controller uploads $\mathsf{SC}$ with $\mathbf{ID}$ and $\boldsymbol{\omega}$ to the medical server. The medical server can verify $\mathsf{SC}$ by running the PubVerify algorithm. Since $\mathsf{SC}$ is actually

**Table 1.** Comparison of existing security schemes for WBANs

|  | Ours | [7] | [8] | [9] |
|---|---|---|---|---|
| Confidentiality | yes | yes | yes | yes |
| Authenticity | yes | yes | no | yes |
| Unforgeability | yes | yes | no | yes |
| Public Verifiability | yes | no | no | no |
| Fine-grained access Control | yes | no | yes | no |
| Untraceability for controller | yes | no | no | yes |
| Unlinkability for controller | yes | no | no | no |
| Untraceability for medical personnel | yes | yes | yes | no |
| Unlinkability for medical personnel | yes | yes | yes | no |

signed by the controller on the KP-ABE ciphertext using an identity-based ring signature scheme, data authenticity and unforgeability, anonymity for controller (includes untraceability and unlinkability) are achieved. Medical personnel can be identified by their own roles, and the HA issues private keys to medical personnel that associated with particular access structures by running the ABKeyGen algorithm. The private key would only open SC whose attributes satisfied the access policy associate with the private key. Since SC is actually encrypted by the controller using an KP-ABE scheme, data confidentiality, anonymity for medical personnel and fine-grained access control on encrypted medical data are achieved. Table 1 shows the comparison of our KP-ABRSC scheme with existing schemes in the literature that provides security and privacy protection for WBANs.

# 6    Conclusion

In this paper, we introduce a new cryptographic primitive called key-policy attribute-based ring signcryption scheme. The syntax, security definitions and a concrete key-policy attribute-based ring signcryption scheme are given. We also present a secure, privacy-protected and fine-grained access control framework for WBANs by exploiting our proposed scheme, which can not only ensure data authenticity, confidentiality and non-repudiation, but also can provide participants privacy and fine-grained access control on encrypted medical data.

**Acknowledgments.** This research is funded by National Natural Science Foundation of China (Grant No. 61173189), Foundation for Innovative Research Team of Yunnan University, Yunnan Province Software Engineering Key Laboratory Project (Grant No. 2015SE203).

# References

1. Chen, M., Gonzalez, S., Vasilakos, A., et al.: Body area networks: a survey. Mobile Netw. Appl. **16**(2), 171–193 (2011)
2. Cordeiro, C., Fantacci, R., Gupta, S., et al.: Body area networking: technology and applications. IEEE J. Selected Areas Commun. **27**(1), 1–4 (2009)
3. Kyung, S.K., Ullah, S., Ullah, N.: An Overview of IEEE 802.15.6 Standard. In: Proceedings of IEEE Symposium on Applied Sciences in Biomedical and Communication Technologies, pp. 1–6 (2010)
4. Li, M., Yu, S.C., Guttman, J.D., et al.: Secure Ad Hoc trust initialization and key management in wireless body area networks. ACM Trans. Sensor Netw. **9**(2), 1–35 (2013)
5. Zhang, Z.Y., Wang, H.G., Vasilakos, A.V., et al.: ECG-cryptography and authentication in body area networks. IEEE Trans. Inf. Technol. Biomed. **16**(6), 1070–1078 (2012)
6. Malasri, K., Wang, L.: Design and implementation of a secure wireless mote-based medical sensor network. Sensors **9**(8), 6273–6297 (2009)
7. Hu, C.Q., Zhang, N., Li, H.J., et al.: Body area network security: a fuzzy attribute-based signcryption scheme. IEEE J. Selected Areas Commun. **31**(9), 37–46 (2013)
8. Tan, Y.L., Goi, B., Komiya, R., et al.: Design and implementation of key-policy attribute-based encryption in body sensor network. Int. J. Cryptol. Res. **4**(1), 84–101 (2013)
9. Liu, J.W., Zhang, Z.H., Chen, X.F., et al.: Certificateless remote anonymous authentication schemes for wirelessbody area networks. IEEE Trans. Parallel Dist. Syst. **25**(2), 332–342 (2014)
10. Bethencourt, J., Sahai, A., Waters, B.: Ciphertext-policy attribute-based encryption. In: Proceedings of IEEE Symposium on Security and Privacy, pp. 321–334 (2007)
11. Beimel, A.: Secure schemes for secret sharing and key distribution. Ph.D. thesis, Israel Institute of Technology, Technion, Haifa, Israel (1996)

# Dependable Cascading Target Tracking in Heterogeneous Mobile Camera Sensor Networks

Zhen Peng[1], Tian Wang[1]($\boxtimes$), Md Zakirul Alam Bhuiyan[2], Xiaoqiang Wu[3], and Guojun Wang[4]

[1] College of Computer Science and Technology, Huaqiao University, Xiamen 361021, Fujian, China
wsnman@gmail.com
[2] Department of Computer and Information Sciences, Temple University, Philadelphia, PA 19122, USA
[3] Guangdong Electronics Industry Institute, Dongguan 523808, Guangdong, China
[4] School of Information Science and Engineering, Central South University, Changsha 410083, Hunan, China

**Abstract.** Recent years have witnessed the development of Camera Sensor Networks (CSNs), but most of existing researches are based on homogeneous CSNs, which are expensive for the transition from traditional Wireless Sensor Networks (WSNs). In this paper, we focus on the target tracking problem in Heterogeneous Mobile Camera Sensor Networks (HMCSNs) which consists of a large number of static common sensors and a small number of mobile camera sensors. The objective is to track the target dependably with maximized effective monitoring time and short moving distance. A novel tracking algorithm is proposed where multiple camera sensors cooperate with each other to track the target in a cascading scheme. It improves the effective monitoring time and shortens the moving distance of cameras. Moreover, the dependability is also improved even if the prediction about the target is not accurate. The effectiveness of the proposed algorithm is validated by simulation results, which show high monitoring ratio and comparatively short moving distance.

**Keywords:** Mobile camera sensor · Wireless sensor networks · Target tracking · Cascading · Dependability

## 1 Introduction

Camera Sensor Networks (CSNs) are made up of numerous sensors which are integrated with image cameras, embedded processors and wireless transceivers [1]. As a kind of derivative of Wireless Sensor Networks (WSNs), CSNs are characterized by their distinctive sensors which are equipped with cameras and hence are able to capture images of real-time scenes. With the significant ability of collecting visual

© Springer International Publishing Switzerland 2015
G. Wang et al. (Eds.): ICA3PP 2015 Workshops, LNCS 9532, pp. 531–540, 2015.
DOI: 10.1007/978-3-319-27161-3_48

information, CSNs have many promising applications derived from WSNs such as security and surveillance, traffic control, telepresence and so on [13]. Among them, Target tracking is a typical application of WSNs. For target tracking, a network needs to detect the movement trajectories of targets via activating nearby sensors [2]. As WSNs are comprised of abundant inexpensive sensors deployed in the area of interest, they are very suitable for tracking targets without high cost. Some popular applications scenarios for target tracking in WSNs include military surveillance, wildlife protection and so on.

In practice, CSNs are able to be used in target tracking applications [11]. Compared with common sensors, camera sensors can provide more comprehensive and accurate information about real-time situation. However, there are several problems for CSNs in target tracking. First, the deployment of CSNs is usually a high-cost project. Some widely used camera sensors, such as pan-tilt-zoom cameras, are very expensive combined with a control system. Second, blind spots are difficult to be avoided even in some well-designed systems of CSNs [4]. Information of real-time situation in blind spots is inevitably lost and becomes potential security threats.

Recently, development in electronic technology and image sensors makes it possible to deploy Mobile Camera Sensor Networks (MCSNs) [10]. A mobile camera sensor is able to move in the area of interest and takes pictures or live videos at the same time. The ability of mobility greatly expands MCSNs' application range [3]. Therefore, we consider target tracking problem in a Heterogeneous Mobile Camera Sensor Networks (HMCSNs) which are comprised of a few of mobile camera sensors and a lot of common static sensors. The use of mobile camera sensors can bring several benefits. First, HMCSNs are more economical because only a few of camera sensors are required to be introduced, which doesn't need a large number of investment for transition from existed WSNs. Second, HMCSNs have inherent high dependability for target tracking. As mobile cameras are able to move toward any corner of the area of interest, a large area can be monitored using only a few mobile sensors, and even blind spots can hardly exist. Third, the dependability of HMCSNs shows up in its fault tolerance as well. When failures occur in one sensor, such as exhaustion of energy or hardware fault, other mobile sensors are able to mitigate its adverse effects via their mobility.

In this paper, we study the target tracking problem based on HMCSNs. Multiple mobile camera sensors cooperate with each other to track the target in a cascading scheme. In consideration of dependability, those sensors will move to specified destinations with different priorities in case of changes in target's movement. A selected sensor will be responsible for tracking the target. In this way, tracking quality can be guaranteed and moving distance of mobile sensors can be reduced as well. The main contributions are listed as follows.

1. As far as we know, we are the first to propose the idea of HMCSNs for target tracking.
2. We design a cascading target tracking algorithm to maximize effective monitoring time and to reduce moving distance of mobile camera sensors.
3. We conduct extensive simulations, and the effectiveness of our proposed solution is validated.

The rest of this paper is organized as follows. Section 2 reviews related work. Section 3 introduces basic models and the problem description. Section 4 presents the dependable cascading tracking algorithm. In Sect. 5, simulation results are studied. Section 6 concludes this paper and discusses the future work.

## 2  Related Work

Recently, camera sensors emerged as a significant technology for target tracking. In [12], Liu et al. developed a nonlinear localization-oriented sensing model for camera sensors. Based on this model, they applied the sequential Monte Carlo (SMC) technique to estimate the brief state of the target location. In [15], Morye et al. considered the problem of using dynamic pan-tilt-zoom camera sensors to track mobile targets. They developed a solution to estimate the position of the target and obtain its images with vertical resolution. In [14], Ma et al. focused on the Minimum Camera Barrier Coverage Problem (MCBCP) in wireless camera sensor networks. An algorithm was proposed and proved to find a feasible solution for the MCBCP problem. In [18] and [6], researchers focused on techniques of image or video processing. In [18], Wang presented a cooperative multi-camera target tracking method, which was based on video background subtraction. In [6], focusing on reducing the amounts of image data for computation and communication, Fang et al. presented an energy-efficient method for distributed target tracking. In [8], Gao et al. proposed a hybrid localization system for moving target tracking, which is composed of a coarse-grained and a fine-grained localization system. However, all above solutions are based on static CSNs.

On the other hand, mobile tracking based on mobile sensors has been attracting more and more attention. As mobile sensors can follow targets and monitor them in a short distance, they are used to alleviate the problems in static sensor networks, such as unpredictable environments, sensor faults, etc. In [16], Tan et al. exploited mobile sensors to improve target detection performance. Those mobile sensors move toward a possible target with collaboration with static sensors to achieve required detection performance. In the research of Xu et al. [20], a mobile sensor controller uses measurement information from both the mobile target and the mobile sensor for estimating their locations. In our early research [17], we introduced a few of mobile sensors into traditional static sensor networks to continuously track targets. A solution of scheduling mobile sensors and static sensors in a reasonable awakening fashion is proposed. In these above solutions, all mobile sensors are common sensors that only measure scalar signals such as radio signal and sound signal.

Nowadays, mobile camera sensor networks, which combine CSNs and mobility together, have become a new tendency in target tracking application. In [9], Hu et al. studied the full view coverage problem for CSNs. They analyzed both the static and mobile camera sensor networks. Their work shows that mobility model can achieve higher percentage of full view coverage than stable one and can also decrease the sensing energy consumption. In [7], a visual servo controller was designed to control the pose of the camera to keep multiple objects in the field of view of a mobile camera. In [19], Wang et al. separated the tracking problem into two parts as the estimation of target position and the flocking control of multiple mobile camera sensors moving toward the estimated position. A distributed Kalman filter and a distributed flocking algorithm were developed. However, all these solutions are based on homogeneous CSNs.

**Fig. 1.** An illustration of mobile camera sensor's FOV

In this paper, we concentrate on the idea of using HMCSNs for target tracking. Based on the heterogeneous environment, we design an algorithm to dispatch mobile camera sensors to monitor the target in an established schedule with high tracking quality and low energy consumption.

## 3   Network Model and Tracking Problem

### 3.1   Network Model

In the network, mobile camera sensors and common static sensors are all randomly deployed in a 2-dimension area of interest. Static sensors can detect and find targets. We assume sensors can get the location of targets and their own positions according to existed localization methods [5]. For camera sensors, each of them has a field-of-view (FOV) region in the same shape, which is represented by a fan as shown in Fig. 1. The length of field is up to $d_{fov}$. Note that we do not consider the angle of view because a camera can rotate immediately in any direction. That is to say, when a target is detected by static sensors, camera sensors will adjust FOV to focus on the target immediately. Therefore, a target will be monitored when it is in the FOV region of any camera.

### 3.2   Problem Description

Consider $M$ mobile camera sensors and $N$ common static sensors deployed randomly in a $L \times L$ m$^2$ area of interest where $M \ll N$. A mobile sensor can move with a velocity $v_c$, which is upper bounded by $v_{cmax}$. A target, whose maximum speed is $v_{tmax}$, moves in a random pattern. That is, it moves in a random direction with speed $v_t$ for some time, pauses for a while, then moves in another random direction, and so forth. Once a target has been detected, camera

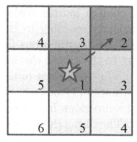 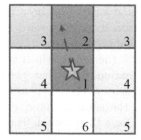 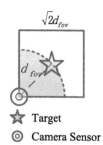

(a) Level-2 subregion is in the corner.  (b) Level-2 subregion is on the side.  (c) An illustration about the length of subregion.

**Fig. 2.** An illustration about the monitoring region and its 9 subregions.

sensors try to move to it in order to keep it being monitored. The total time when the target is under surveillance in FOV is called the effective monitoring time (EMT). Therefore, our objective is to maximize EMT with minimal moving distance of camera sensors.

## 4  Cascading Tracking Algorithm

In order to track the target effectively, we design a dependably cascading tracking algorithm. The basic idea is to schedule multiple camera sensors cooperatively. Once the target appears, a target-centered monitoring region is going to be set up around it within a certain range. This region is divided into 9 equal square subregions. According to predictions about the target's movement by static sensors, these 9 subregions are endowed with different priorities based on their positions. There are total 6 levels of priorities which are from level 1 to level 6 with decreasing importance. Among them, the subregion which contains the target is represented as level 1; the subregion which covers the target's moving direction is represented as level 2, and it is supposed to be in the corner or on the side of the monitoring region, which depends on the angle of moving direction of the target. Suppose

$$y = \theta_X \mod \pi/2 \tag{1}$$

where $\theta_X$ is the moving direction of the target and $\theta_X \in [0, 2\pi)$. Then, the position of level-2 subregion can be determined as follows:

$$\text{Level-2 subregion is} \begin{cases} \text{in the corner} & \text{if } y \in [\pi/8, 3\pi/8) \\ \text{on the side} & \text{if } y \in [0, \pi/8) \cup [3\pi/8, \pi/2). \end{cases} \tag{2}$$

The rest subregions are show in Fig. 2. The length of a subregion is supposed to be $\sqrt{2}d_{fov}$ so a target located in the center will be monitored by a camera sensor in any position of the subregion as shown in Fig. 2c. If the size of the area of interest is smaller than the whole monitoring region whose length is $3\sqrt{2}d_{fov}$, the number of subregions or their size can be adjusted correspondingly.

Once the monitoring region is set up, those mobile camera sensors within $3\sqrt{2}d_{fov}$ from the target begin to move toward this region. According to the priorities from high to low, subregions' centers are selected as destinations for those moving sensors. At first, the sensor which is closest to the target chooses level-1 subregion as the destination. After that, the sensor which is closest to the level-2 subregion among rest sensors chooses it as the destination. Other sensors choose their destinations in the same manner, until all subregions have been chosen or all moving sensors have their own destinations. The dispatching order is based on the consideration of dependability, as those subregions with higher probability to monitor the target will be under surveillance earlier. Therefore, the number of simultaneously moving sensors is no more than 9. Those sensors are able to ensure the quality of tracking even if the prediction is not exact. Moreover, preparing for potential transfer, the sensor in the level-2 subregion will further move toward the target in its region. During this period, the closest sensor to the target is responsible for tracking. The tracking sensor will follow the target with a separation distance $d_{fov}/2$. In consideration of energy saving, when the target is under surveillance, other mobile camera sensor will stop moving except the tracking one.

In order to track the target continuously, the monitoring region will be rebuilt when the target has moved out from level-1 subregion. Furthermore, when a sensor is closer to the target than the tracking sensor, it will take over the tracking task. This is called the cascading tracking, as the tracking task is transferring between sensors without losing the target. The whole procedure is shown in Algorithm 1. It can be analyzed that, the time complexity to set up monitoring region and to choose the tracking sensor is $O(n)$ as the tracking sensor is the closest one to the target. Therefore, the whole time complexity of the algorithm is $O(Tn)$, where $T$ is the time duration when target appears.

## 5   Experiments

In order to validate the effectiveness of our proposed algorithm, we conduct extensive simulations with NS-2 simulator. In the simulation scenario, sensors are randomly deployed in an area of interest which is $100 \times 100$ m$^2$. Some general parameters are listed in Table 1. In general case, there are 10 mobile camera sensors with the maximum velocity $v_{cmax}$ to be 1 m/s. The maximum velocity $v_{tmax}$ of the target is 3 m/s. And The length $d_{fov}$ of FOV for camera sensors is set to be 10 m.

For comparisons, there are two other target tracking algorithms being conducted. The first is direct tracking algorithm. In this algorithm, all mobile sensors within $3\sqrt{2}d_{fov}$ distance from the target will move to it directly for tracking, unless any of them can monitor the target. The second is static tracking algorithm with all camera sensors to be static. In this algorithm, camera sensors will wait for the target to be present within FOV of any of them. For the convenience of discussion, our proposed algorithm is referred to as *Cascade*, the direct tracking algorithm is referred to as *Direct*, and the static tracking algorithm is referred to as *Static*.

**Algorithm 1.** DependableTracking

**Input:** target's present location $X$, target's moving direction angle $\theta_X$, locations of mobile camera sensors $L_C$, monitoring region $G_C$;
**Output:** scheduling and moving process of mobile camera sensors;

1: **while** The target appears **do**
2:   **if** The target is not monitored by any camera sensor $\|$ The target has moved
3:   out the current level-1 subregion **then** /* Needs a new monitoring region. */
4:      Set up a new region $G_C$ with ceter $X$;
5:      Divided region $G_C$ into 9 equal square subregions with length $\sqrt{2}d_{fov}$;
6:      Sub-regions are endowed priorities shown in Fig. 2;
7:      Mobile sensors within $3\sqrt{2}d_{fov}$ range to center $X$ are selected into set $S$;
8:      **while** Set $S$ is not null &&There are empty subregions in region $G_C$ **do**
9:         Subregion $y :=$ the empty subregion with highest priority in region $G_C$;
10:        Sensor $i :=$ the closest sensor to subregion $y$ in set $S$;
11:        Sensor $i$ moves toward subregion $y$'s center; /* Subregion $y$ is not empty
12:        any more. */
13:        Sensor $i$ joins into set $R$;
14:        Sensor $i$ is removed from set $S$;
15:     **end while**
16:     The level-2 mobile sensor moves toward the target in its subregion;
17:     Sensor $k :=$ the closest sensor to the target;
18:  **end if**
19:  Sensor $j :=$ the closest sensor to the target in set $R$;
20:  **if** $j \neq k$ **then** $k := j$;
21:  **end if**
22:  Sensor $k$ follows the target for tracking with a separation distance $d_{fov}/2$;
23:  **if** The target is under surveillance by $k$ **then**
24:     For $\forall a \in \{x | x \in R, x \neq k\}$, sensor $a$ stops moving for saving energy;
25:  **end if**
26: **end while**

**Table 1.** Simulation parameters

| Parameters | Values |
|---|---|
| area size (m$^2$) | $100 \times 100$ |
| $N$—the number of common static sensors | 100 |
| $M$—the number of mobile camera sensors | 10 |
| $v_{cmax}$—the maximum velocity of cameras (m/s) | 1 |
| $v_{tmax}$—the maximal velocity of the target (m/s) | 3 |
| $d_{fov}$—the length of FOV for cameras (m) | 10 |

In simulations, these three algorithms are compared in *the effective monitoring ratio*. As mentioned in Sect. 3.1, a target will be monitored within FOV of any camera sensors, and the total time when the target is under surveillance is called the effective monitoring time (EMT). Therefore, the effective monitoring

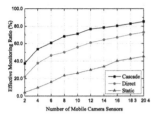
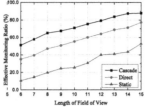
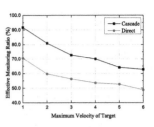

**Fig. 3.** Number of mobile sensors vs. effective monitoring ratio.

**Fig. 4.** Length of field of view vs. effective monitoring ratio.

**Fig. 5.** Target maximum velocity vs. effective monitoring ratio.

ratio is the result of EMT to simulation time. It reflects the quality of tracking since a higher ratio means the target is monitored in longer time in simulations.

In the first part, the variable factor is the number of mobile sensors that increased from 2 to 20. Figure 3 shows how the effective monitoring ratio was achieved by *Cascade*, *Direct* and *Static*, respectively. All results rose with the increase in the number of mobile sensors. Obviously, *Cascade* achieved the best performance among these three algorithms as its effective monitoring ratio is the highest all the time. Specifically, when there were 2 mobile sensors, the ratio achieved by *Cascade* outperformed that of *Direct* and *Static* by more than 70 % and 600 %, respectively; when the number was 20, *Cascade*'s performance was about 20 % and 90 % higher than that of *Direct* and *Static*, respectively. It can be seen that *Cascade* provides a more dependable tracking quality with scheduled moving behavior of sensors than that of *Direct*.

In the second part, the variable factor is the maximum velocity of the target that is from 1 m/s to 6 m/s. Since *Static* doesn't contain any mobile sensors and is not sensitive to target's velocity, it was not included in this simulation. Figure 5 shows how effective monitoring ratio of *Cascade* and *Direct* was influenced by the maximum velocity of the target, respectively. When the maximum velocity increased, performances of these two algorithms decreased more or less. The reason is that the faster the target moves, the harder for mobile camera sensors to follow or track it. Even so, the results show that *Cascade* performed better than *Direct* even when the maximum velocity of the target was up to 6 m/s, as its ratio outperformed that of *Direct* by 30 %.

In the third part, the variable factor is the length of FOV of camera sensors that increased from 6 to 15 m. Figure 4 shows how the performance of effective monitoring ratio was achieved by *Cascade*, *Direct* and *Static*, respectively. Once again, *Cascade* achieved the best performance among these three algorithms as its effective monitoring ratio was the highest all the time. Their performances were all improved with the increase in the length of FOV. Specifically, when the length of FOV was 6 m, the ratio achieved by *Cascade* outperformed that of *Direct* and *Static* by more than 40 % and 400 %, respectively; when the length was 15 m, *Cascade*'s performance was about 10 % and 70 % higher than that of *Direct* and *Static*, respectively. It can be seen that, with longer FOV, mobile sensors are able to monitor the target more easily.

## 6   Conclusion

Target tracking problem in Mobile Camera Sensor Networks (MCSNs) has been rarely discussed in existing literatures. In this paper, we consider the target tracking problem in Heterogeneous Mobile Camera Sensor Networks (HMCSNs). We propose a dependable cascading tracking algorithm in order to track the target with maximized effective monitoring time and short moving distance. Based on different priorities, mobile sensors will be assigned with different destinations which are related to target's location. On the one hand, these sensors are able to improve dependability by fulfilling the tracking task collaboratively. On the other hand, moving distance can be reduced since sensors will move to their specified positions for preparation instead of moving to the target directly. In simulation results, our proposed algorithm showed better performances in effective monitoring ratio than that of direct tracking algorithm and static tracking algorithm.

**Acknowledgments.** Above work is supported in part by grants from the National Natural Science Foundation (NSF) of China under grant No. 61572206, 61202468, 61272151, 61472451, and 61402543, the Natural Science Foundation of Fujian Province of China under grant No. 2014J01240, and the Guangdong Innovative Research Team Program under grant No. 201001D0104726115.

## References

1. Akyildiz, I.F., Melodia, T., Chowdhury, K.R.: A survey on wireless multimedia sensor networks. Comput. Netw. **51**(4), 921–960 (2007)
2. Bhuiyan, M., Wang, G., Vasilakos, A.: Local area prediction-based mobile target tracking in wireless sensor networks. IEEE Trans. Comput. **64**(7), 1968–1982 (2015)
3. Biswas, J., Veloso, M.: Depth camera based indoor mobile robot localization and navigation. In: IEEE International Conference on Robotics and Automation (ICRA), pp. 1697–1702. IEEE (2012)
4. Bouma, H., Baan, J., Landsmeer, S., Kruszynski, C., van Antwerpen, G., Dijk, J.: Real-time tracking and fast retrieval of persons in multiple surveillance cameras of a shopping mall. In: SPIE Defense, Security, and Sensing, pp. 87560A–87560A. International Society for Optics and Photonics (2013)
5. Chen, X., Edelstein, A., Li, Y., Coates, M., Rabbat, M., Men, A.: Sequential monte carlo for simultaneous passive device-free tracking and sensor localization using received signal strength measurements. In: 10th International Conference on Information Processing in Sensor Networks (IPSN), pp. 342–353. IEEE (2011)
6. Fang, W., Wang, D.H., Wang, Y.: Energy-efficient distributed target tracking in wireless video sensor networks. Int. J. Wireless Inf. Netw. **22**(2), 105–115 (2015)
7. Gans, N.R., Hu, G., Nagarajan, K., Dixon, W.E.: Keeping multiple moving targets in the field of view of a mobile camera. IEEE Trans. Robot. **27**(4), 822–828 (2011)

8. Gao, D., Zhu, W., Xu, X., Chao, H.C.: A hybrid localization and tracking system in camera sensor networks. Int. J. Commun. Syst. **27**(4), 606–622 (2014)
9. Hu, Y., Wang, X., Gan, X.: Critical sensing range for mobile heterogeneous camera sensor networks. In: IEEE INFOCOM, pp. 970–978. IEEE (2014)
10. Jiang, H., Xiao, Y., Zhang, Y., Wang, X., Tai, H.: Curve path detection of unstructured roads for the outdoor robot navigation. Math. Comput. Model. **58**(3), 536–544 (2013)
11. Kamal, A., Ding, C., Morye, A., Farrell, J., Roy-Chowdhury, A.K.: An overview of distributed tracking and control in camera networks. In: Wide Area Surveillance, pp. 207–234. Springer (2014)
12. Liu, L., Zhang, X., Ma, H.: Dynamic node collaboration for mobile target tracking in wireless camera sensor networks. In: IEEE INFOCOM, pp. 1188–1196. IEEE (2009)
13. Liu, X.: A survey on wireless camera sensor networks. In: Frontier and Future Development of Information Technology in Medicine and Education, pp. 1085–1094. Springer (2014)
14. Ma, H., Yang, M., Li, D., Hong, Y., Chen, W.: Minimum camera barrier coverage in wireless camera sensor networks. In: IEEE INFOCOM, pp. 217–225. IEEE (2012)
15. Morye, A., Ding, C., Song, B., Roy-Chowdhury, A., Farrell, J., et al.: Optimized imaging and target tracking within a distributed camera network. In: American Control Conference (ACC), 2011, pp. 474–480. IEEE (2011)
16. Tan, R., Xing, G., Wang, J., So, H.C.: Exploiting reactive mobility for collaborative target detection in wireless sensor networks. IEEE Trans. Mob. Comput. **9**(3), 317–332 (2010)
17. Wang, T., Peng, Z., Chen, Y., Cai, Y., Tian, H.: Continuous tracking for mobile targets with mobility nodes in wsns. In: International Conference on Smart Computing (SMARTCOMP), pp. 261–268. IEEE (2014)
18. Wang, Y., Wang, D., Fang, W.: Automatic node selection and target tracking in wireless camera sensor networks. Comput. Electr. Eng. **40**(2), 484–493 (2014)
19. Wang, Z., Gu, D.: Cooperative target tracking control of multiple robots. IEEE Trans. Ind. Electr. **59**(8), 3232–3240 (2012)
20. Xu, E., Ding, Z., Dasgupta, S.: Target tracking and mobile sensor navigation in wireless sensor networks. IEEE Trans. Mob. Comput. **12**(1), 177–186 (2013)

# A Web-Based Resource Management Platform for Transparent Computing

Dacheng Wang, Hong Song$^{(\boxtimes)}$, Yun Xu, Wenhao Zhang, and Jianxin Wang

School of Information Science and Engineering, Central South University,
Changsha 410083, China
{446757099,1260066581}@qq.com, {songhong,jxwang}@csu.edu.cn,
luferry@163.com

**Abstract.** Transparent Computing can separate the computing from storage, and split the software stack from the underlying hardware platform in order to solve the problems in Internet, such as users service selection, hardware platform updating and protecting data. As an important part of Transparent Computing, resource management must manage and monitor all kinds of resources effectively in transparent computing system, including the traditional OSes, applications and files/data which are used by different client terminals. In this paper, a Web-based Resource Management Platform for Transparent Computing (WRMP-TC) is designed and realized to provide an unified managing mode and monitoring mode for the servers and clients in Transparent Computing System. Experience result shows that WRMP-TC is effective and stable.

**Keywords:** WRMP-TC · Transparent computing · Resource management · State monitoring · Transparent terminals

## 1 Introduction

As a new computing paradigm first proposed by Zhang and Zhou in 2004, the transparent computing [1–3] is becoming a hot topic in compute science research. The core idea of transparent computing is to extend vonNeumanns architecture based on the stored program concept into networking environments spatio-temporally [4]. Users need to only care about the services they want and the quality of the service, but do not need to understand how the computer system realized. It includes four parts [6]. The first part is the separation of computation, storage, and management.and the second is enabling across-terminal and across-OS operations and enabling users to select the services they need. And instructions are exchanged in data streams or block scheduling between the network server and client terminal, and the super OS will conduct integrated management of all kinds of resources on the network. Finally, programs are dynamically scheduled to run on specific terminals or servers in a streaming way.

Based on the theory of transparent computing, a transparent computing architecture 4VP+ [5] is proposed and a paradigm TransCom [6] is developed. The paradigm treats the traditional OSes, applications and files/data as

© Springer International Publishing Switzerland 2015
G. Wang et al. (Eds.): ICA3PP 2015 Workshops, LNCS 9532, pp. 541–550, 2015.
DOI: 10.1007/978-3-319-27161-3_49

resources, and let them run on the same client terminal. It can reduce storage load and enhance the users' accessibility and security. Since there are various users use different terminals to access its own OSes, applications and files and data, the efficient management of terminals and servers, even resources must be treated at first. We must provide an efficient mechanism to manage the terminals/servers and resources so that the users can only care about the services that the transparent computing system can support while ignoring whether the services are cross-terminal or cross-OS.

Focus on this point, an implementation of Web-based Resource Management Platform for Transparent Computing is proposed in this paper, which is called WRMP-TC. The new WRMP-TC uses some new technologies, such as MVC framework, SSH protocol, Socket communication, to realized the management of users, servers and resources. And it can provide an convenient method to maintain and monitor the state of users and servers.

The rest of this paper is organized as follows. In Sect. 2, we discuss related work in the field. Section 3 presents the architecture of the transparent computing system and requirement of the resource management in transparent computing system. Section 4 describes the design and implementation of WRMP-TC. Practical results and the conclusion are given in Sect. 5.

## 2    Related Works

With the increasing popularity of transparent computing in recent years, more and more items of transparent computing are discussed by researchers. In the aspect of realization or implementation of transparent computing, 4VP+ [3] in LAN environments was implemented and the mechanism had promoted its industrialization and actual deployment. TransOS [6] as a paradigm of TC was conducted and was applied to tablet terminals and mobile phones, as well as mobile internet, home appliances and other devices. In [7], a virtual machine-based transparent computing system called MMNC-VX is implemented so that heterogeneous OSes can run unmodified on-demand in a transparent computing environment, but the performance has a big disparity compared with PC.

For network communication of transparent computing, an extended network-based client boot protocol ENCBP is proposed in [8] to boot multi-OS remotely by differentiating the kernel types of loaded OS. NSAP protocol is presented to allow users access remotely and retrieve from servers.With the new mechanism, the average system loading time of users is reduced about one third and the users experience on mobile transparent computing is improved effectively. The characteristics of TransComs real usage workload are analyzed in [9] by building a queuing model to locate the system bottlenecks. The results show that the disk is the primary bottleneck and the appropriate cache arrangement can significantly improve the capability of the TransCom server. For improving the security of transparent computing, the authors in [10] proposed a system-based privacy protection model for transparent computing systems. It is based on mandatory access control which can be proved to be safe.

Lots of data and files are distributed and dynamic and are saved in servers with the development of network and cloud computing. In cloud environment, existing related works on resource management are considered from the server terminal. But the methods of managing resources in cloud cannot be directly applied to transparent computing because there are not only resources stored in servers, but also servers and clients. The management system must construct the connections between clients/users with the resources in servers. Some researchers devote to providing effective methods to resource management. A remote resource management method (TMON) is proposed in [11], which includes the resource state of the devices and the state of applications. It consists of local monitoring facilities within the Xen hypervisor running on individual clients and a collective management component running on the server for monitoring and gathering information for hardware and software resources.

However, the above-mentioned solutions on resource management are not suitable and effective for transparent computing environment, for the special characters of resources are not taken into account, such as the attributes of resources and the relations of resources. There are physical resources (CPU, memory, storage, network elements, and so on) and logical resources (including operating system, network throughput/bandwidth, and so on) which must be managed efficiently, also there are states of users and servers which must be monitored timely. Therefore, this paper proposes a resource management system platform for transparent computing in order to schedule the resources effectively and promote the capability of transparent computing.

## 3    Transparent Computing System

This section provides a basic idea of transparent computing system and presents some requirements of resources management for transparent computing system.

### 3.1    Structure of Transparent Computing System

The transparent computing system consists of transparent clients, transparent servers and the resources which is used by users. Figure 1 shows the structure.

Transparent clients are used directly by users. Users can use their own terminals (such as PCs, mobile phones/platforms or so on) to access transparent server remotely and obtain the required services. The programs in transparent client are designed to be separated from the hardware platform of users and can be stored into the mobile storage device. It can start on any computers in Internet environment. Transparent servers are mainly responsible for the management of all storage resources, to provide users with the required data. Besides, it also sends data to transparent client by using flow block transmission protocols. And the storage servers are usually more than one in order to adopt to lots of users.

The resources in transparent computing system are including three parts:

The first is logical resources, such as the instants of operating systems, software, files and data. These logical resources are distributed in transparent servers and are needed by different transparent clients.

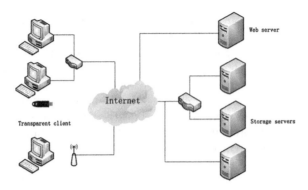

**Fig. 1.** Structure of transparent computing system

The second is Physical resources, such as CPU, memory, storage and the network throughput/bandwidth and so on. This physical resources are come from transparent clients and transparent servers. They can ensure the effective and correct use of transparent computing.

The third is Management information, such as the information of transparent clients and servers, the permissions information, logs and so on. The information is produced by management system when the transparent clients want to connect to transparent servers and to obtain the required services.

So it is vital to gather the overall resource information and manage all these resources in an efficient method.

### 3.2 Requirements for Resource Management in Transparent Computing System

Since the resource management is a core function for transparent computing system, there are some requirements.

First of all, the resource management platform can manage all of transparent clients, including authorization, management of client information, logging management, and etc. As there are multiple users, the platform must provide a method for new users to add or exist the usage of transparent computing system. And all these functions must be transparent and quickly for users.

Secondly, the platform can manage all of transparent servers. There will be more than one servers in transparent computing system and the images of OS instances and users resource are stored distributed in the transparent servers. The first thing that the platform should provide is monitoring the servers and getting the information of the servers, including the states of each server, the memory consumption of each server, the CPU utilization of each server, the throughput of each server and etc. Another thing that the platform should do is managing the resources dynamically which are existed in transparent servers to provide a on-time image file to the users.

And the platform can provide the connection of transparent clients and transparent servers on users demands. There are some users and several servers in transparent computing system. After each user logs in, the system must verify the identification of the user and select a proper server to provide the proper information to the user. Then by connecting with the proper server, the user can store his own data or files and use the part of servers disk as his own disk.

Then, the platform should provide a convenient mode for the administrator to maintain and to deal with the affairs or wrong operations which take place in transparent computing system and are harmful to the users using the services.

Finally, The platform should provide a flexible authority provisioning to different users and different resources. Different users and groups have different image files and private data. Some users may in the same group and they may share the same OS instance. Some users may use its own OS instance and private data. The flexible authority provisioning is needed to ensure the system performance in a desired pattern.

For the above requirements, WRMP-TC is designed and discussed in the following section.

## 4   The Design and Implementation of WRMP-TC

The components of WRMP-TC are shown in Fig. 2.

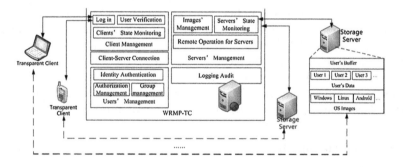

**Fig. 2.** Components of WRMP-TC

The management platform is mainly divided into five modules, and realizes the management of users, servers, clients in Transparent Computing system. At the same time, it provides logging audit. A friendly page is necessary for administrator to manage. The following part will introduce each module separately.

### 4.1   Users' Management

Transparent Computing system is used for multiple users, including the ordinary users and the administrator. Different users may be assigned different permissions. Meanwhile, some users may share the same image files or one OS instance. They may have the same operating permissions in transparent computing system. So in the WRMP-TC we introduce the concept of group.

The component of User' management includes some functions about users information and rights, such as registration, login-in, login-out, group management. Ordinary users can register new accounts. The account can not only be used to log in the platform, but also to use Transparent Computing system. Administrator can do operations of users and group, including adding, modifying, querying, deleting.

## 4.2   Clients' Management

The clients management is mainly designed to monitor the state of users terminal, including whether the terminal is online, the using operating system, and the online time.

Users use account and password to authenticate. After this, users can choose to use different operating system instance. Before making choices, the state of using operating system is no OS. When the user clicks into an operating system, the state will changes to the name of the OS instance, for example, win7. And when users are using any operating system, the platform judges that the user is online.

The principle of design: after users enter into operating system, the users terminal will send survival information to web server every 30 seconds. And the server will record the access time, and the current operating system.

When users shut down the operating system with normal procedures, it updates the users state as not online. But users terminal is easily influenced by power off, broken network and other external factors. So its full of uncertainly. At this time, the server is unable to know these exceptions that causes users abnormal exit. The platform checks the recently visit time in database every one minutes automatically. If the time exceeds two minutes than current time, its assumed that the users state is abnormal exit. This procedure is called Clients State Monitoring. Figure 3 shows the specific process of Clients State Monitoring.

## 4.3   Servers Management

The component of Servers Management has two functions, including Images Management, Remote Operations for Servers and Servers State Monitoring.

Images Management. The images are corresponding to the different operating systems. When users choose to use operating system, actually its the procedure that the terminal downloads image from storage server and then runs.

The platform stores the information of images, like images names, images locations, storage paths in database. When there is a users request, the platform is responsible to provide the images information, so user can download the right file. The images management is mainly contains adding and updating images information. Because there are many storage servers, so its complex for admin to add images by uploading. Therefore, the platform set a master server. The admin only upload the image to master server, then add images information to database by using the platform. Actually, in the background, the platform will step to the other servers. Like Fig. 4 shows. When synchronization is successful, the admin can look over the new images file, the ordinary users can use the new operating system as well.

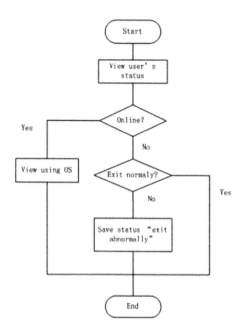

**Fig. 3.** Check out user status

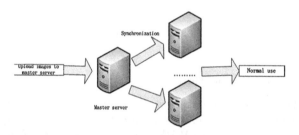

**Fig. 4.** Add images

Remote Operations for Servers. In this function module, we focus on the servers status, the usages of memory and CPU and some services status. So, the platform realizes the management of multiple servers by using web. The admin can view the state, execute some shell commands, view the usage of memory and CPU in different servers by browser. Considering different operations, the platform adopts two ways to achieve the management.

The operation on servers, like starting the service of MySQL. The principle is to connect to the server through SSH protocol, and execute some commands or shell scripts, then return results to the browser. Specific process is shown in Fig. 5.

Servers State Monitoring. When viewing the servers information, such as memory, CPU. The platform obtains the data in servers and uses the Socket programming to send information to the web servers and store in the database

**Fig. 5.** Start MySQL service

every 30 seconds. So when the administrator queries, the information are latest. Figure 6 shows the usage of servers disk.

**Fig. 6.** The usage of disk

## 4.4 Client-Server Connection

Before using the services in the transparent computing system, the user should construct the connection between a transparent client and a transparent server. The Client-Server Connection in WRMP-TC can provide the connection string to the user. It is implemented by two special servlet modules in control layer. The Client-Server Connection can produce two kinds of strings, including system string and user string. After the correct user logs in the system, the Client-Server Connection may feedback the particular system string and user string. The format of strings is described as following:

#@#@#@${requestScope.message}*@#&@#${Target.ip}*@#&@#${Target.target}*@#&@#${Target.name}*@#&#${Target.password}*@#&@#${requestScope.listSize}

In the format of the strings, #@#@#@$ is a fixed heading of system/user string. *@#&@#$ is a fixed division string. And others are variables to make up of the strings.

## 4.5 Logging Audit

The platform designs two kinds of logs, including users and administrators. The log about state of users terminal is to record the access time, exit time, whether the normal exit or not and the online time. It needs to use the monitoring condition of users terminal and save users behaviors and records to database.

The administrators log is to record the operation. The platform uses log4j component and change the configuration settings to generate the log to database.

## 5 Conclusions

The WRMP-TC platform has been implemented and applied in a transparent computing environment. All components are implemented with MVC structure. We use Java to realize the interface of WRMP-TC and C++ programming language to implement the monitoring procedures of clients and servers. In order to prevent the WRMP-TC from tampering or forging with the attackers, we use salt-hash technology and SQL injection prevention technology to enhance the security of WRMP-TC. The practical running results show that our WRMP-TC is capable of managing the transparent clients and servers, providing the proper and correct resource to the users on demand, and it is easy to access and convenient to operate. Besides, WRMP-TC ensures the normal operation of transparent computing and it has great significance in promoting transparent computing.

**Acknowledgments.** This research was supported by the International S&T Cooperation Program of China (ISTCP) under Grant no. 2013DFB10070 and the Strategic Emerging Industries I&A&R combined Innovation platform and capacity building program of Hunan under Grant no. 2012GK4106. The authors would like to thank the anonymous reviewers for their valuable comments.

## References

1. Zhang, Y.: Transparence computing: concept, architecture and example. Actaelectronica Sin. **32**(12A), 169–174 (2004)
2. Zhang, Y., Zhou, Y.: Transparent computing: a new paradigm for pervasive computing. In: Ma, J., Jin, H., Yang, L.T., Tsai, J.J.-P. (eds.) UIC 2006. LNCS, vol. 4159, pp. 1–11. Springer, Heidelberg (2006)
3. Zhang, Y., Zhou, Y.-Z.: 4VP+: a novel meta OS approach for streaming programs in ubiquitous computing. In: 21st International Conference on Advanced Information Networking and Applications(AINA), 21–23 May 2007, Niagara Falls, Canada, pp. 394–403. AINA (2007)
4. Zhang, Y., Yangb, L.T., Kuang, Y.Z.W.: Information security underlying transparent computing: impacts, visions and challenges. Web Intell. Agent Syst. **8**, 203–217 (2010)
5. Zhang, Y., Zhou, Y.: Transparent Computing: Concepts, Architecture, and Implementation, 1st edn. Gengage Learning Asia Ltd., Singapore (2009)
6. Zhang, Y., Zhou, Y.: TransOS: a transparent computing-based operating system for the cloud. Int. J. Cloud Comput. **1**(4), 287–301 (2012)
7. Guangbin, X., Yaoxue, Z., Yuezhi, Z., et al.: Design and implementation of a virtual machine-based transparent computing system. J. Tsinghua Univ. (Sci. & Tech.) **48**(10), 1675–1678 (2008)

8. Li, W., Guangbin, X.: ENCBP-an extended multi-OSs remote-booting method. J. Comput. Res. Dev. **46**(6), 905–912 (2009)
9. Gao, Y., Zhang, Y., Zhou, Y.: Performance analysis of virtual disk system for transparent computing. In: 2012 9th International Conference on Ubiquitous Intelligence and Computing and 9th International Conference on Autonomicand Trusted Computing, pp. 470–477 (2012)
10. Xue, H., Dai, Y.: A privacy protection model for transparent computing system. Int. J. Cloud Comput. **1**(4), 367–385 (2012)
11. Gao, Y., Zhang, Y., Zhou, Y.: A remote resource management method for transparent computing. In: 2012 International Conference on Computer Science and Information Processing, pp. 1378–1381 (2012)

# Architecture and Scheduling Method of Cloud Video Surveillance System Based on IoT

Xia Wei, Wen-Xiang Li$^{(\boxtimes)}$, Cong Ran, Chun-Chun Pi, Ya-Jie Ma,
and Yu-Xia Sheng

School of Information Science and Engineering, Wuhan University of Science
and Technology, Wuhan 430081, China
liwx2006@hotmail.com

**Abstract.** To realize conveniently deployed video surveillance applications, this paper designs a cloud service system employing ubiquitously available IoT nodes. Considering limited capacity of each IoT node, this paper first describes the system architecture and operation procedure for application requests, and introduces the design of scheduler's function and typical video processing algorithms. Further, for decreasing transmission conflicts among video/image processor nodes, this paper proposes a scheduling methods based on Genetic Algorithm to rationally utilize the cooperative IoT nodes. Simulation results show that, compared with common methods such as random scheduling and opportunity-balanced scheduling, this method yields much smaller processing delay and transmission delay, together with higher packet delivery ratio.

**Keywords:** Video surveillance · Internet of things · Cloud computing · Scheduling · Transmission conflicts · Video processing

## 1 Introduction

With rapid development of national economy and the breakthrough of information technology, the application of active video surveillance is becoming popular in various occasions (e.g., transportation, crucial department, community and temporary assembly). Users' demands for real-time, reliable and stable video services also propose such performance requirements as diversification and systematization of services, supported by improved capacities such as random deployment, high tolerance of load and intelligent processing.

Video surveillance system has made great progress in a short span of 20 years [1]. It has experienced the first generation of analog video surveillance system, the second generation of digital video surveillance system based on PC and multimedia card, and the IP-network-based third generation (IPVS). Currently, it is on the development of the fourth generation based on cloud computing [2]. Among the emerging new systems, the cloud video surveillance system based on Internet of things (IoT) has many advantages such as high utilization rate, large-data-volume support, strong scalability and low cost. For example, with a unified application platform among smart phones, one can get desired processing result for the target video from the help of others who are willing to

© Springer International Publishing Switzerland 2015
G. Wang et al. (Eds.): ICA3PP 2015 Workshops, LNCS 9532, pp. 551–560, 2015.
DOI: 10.1007/978-3-319-27161-3_50

share the idle capacities of their phones to collect and process the video. This method can effectively utilize available distributed physical resources of IoT nodes, and avoid expensive investment of physical servers in the cloud. Presently, there exist the following challenges in this field [3].

(1) Flash crowd phenomenon is prone to local or global transmission conflicts, and seriously deteriorates performance in terms of bit error rate, handoff efficiency, delay, and bandwidth stability. This further leads to such worse display effects as mosaic, jump screen and interruption.
(2) The increase of user's demands will bring higher costs for system deployment and operation. Therefore, it is necessary to rationally utilize IoT nodes of limited capacity for improving the performance and prolonging the lifetime of the system.

Currently there is some similar work [4–6] on implementing cloud video services based on IoT platform. However, the video processing functions in these works are simple and implemented individually without cooperation among IoT nodes. Considering the vast volume of video and image data, we design a unified cloud service platform for video surveillance, so that distributed portable IoT nodes can cooperatively handle these massive data. To handle the applications with composite steps for video and image processing, we develops an intelligent scheduling method for selecting proper cooperative processor nodes, so as to effectively utilize the IoT nodes with limited capacity. Specially, the scheduling method addresses how to avoid transmission conflicts in open wireless environment by time-disjoint allocation of resources.

The rest of this paper is organized as follows. Section 2 describes the system architecture and operation procedure. Section 3 illustrates the design of scheduler's key functions and typical video/image processing algorithms. Section 4 proposes the task scheduling method based on Genetic Algorithm. Section 5 performs simulation evaluation for relevant scheduling methods. At last, Sect. 6 gives the conclusion.

## 2 Architecture and Operation Procedure

The system architecture is shown in Fig. 1. The system consists of four types of entities. They are the scheduler that operates in the cloud's server and three types of mobile IoT nodes, including processor nodes, storage nodes and collector nodes. As registered physical resources of cloud, these nodes share their own information of capacity, functions and locations to the cloud, so the system can generate and publish virtualized logical functions. The operation procedure is as follows.

(1) The users specify the target and relevant parameters for video surveillance in task request. Scheduler receives task requests from different users, and sends out scheduling instructions to related processor nodes, storage nodes and collector nodes based on an optimal scheduling decision. The decision is based on the acquired states information of nodes, network and the tasks being processed.
(2) Collector nodes collect video data of the target location by scheduler's instruction, and send video data to the storage cloud. The selection of collector nodes depends on the position and direction of the monitored target.

(3) Storage nodes receive and keep video data from the collector nodes by the instruction of scheduler, and send video data to processing cloud as needed.

(4) processor nodes cooperatively complete the video processing steps by the instruction of scheduler, and then forward the results to the user. Due to the limitation of node's capability, each node can implement limited number of video processing functions or algorithms, such as modifying the video resolution and file format, and each function/algorithm corresponds to one processing step. For non-real-time applications, processor nodes retrieve data from the storage cloud. While, for real-time applications, processor nodes retrieve data from collector nodes directly.

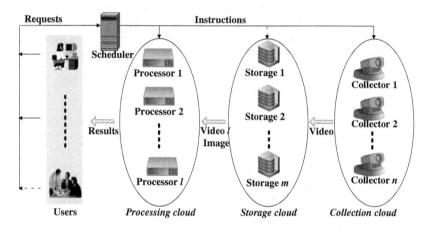

**Fig. 1.** Architecture of IoT cloud platform for video surveillance

Example scenarios of cooperative real-time processing for two different applications are shown in Fig. 2. The cloud system contains two collector nodes (Capt1 and Capt2) and four processor nodes (from Pr1 to Pr4). App1 (dotted frame) contains four processing steps, i.e., A1, A2, A3 and A4. And they are implemented in nodes Pr1, Pr2, Pr1 and Pr4 respectively. App2 (solid frame) contains three processing steps, i.e., A1, A5 and A6. And they are implemented in nodes Pr1, Pr2 and Pr3 respectively.

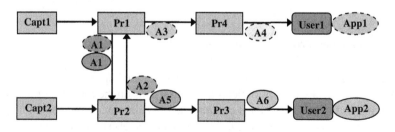

**Fig. 2.** Example of multiple tasks processing

# 3   Key Software Function Design

## 3.1   Scheduler

The scheduler model is shown in Fig. 3. The state information about energy consumption and resource utilization in IoT nodes and that about task processing (including progress and completion time) are sent to scheduler periodically for evaluation and reference. The scheduler receives user's request messages (including user's basic properties, current location and description of demand for video content) which arrive randomly, and divides each application request into several processing steps. After making decision, it generates the instructions for nodes with detailed designations of collector nodes, processor nodes, storage nodes, resource supply and the functions/algorithms for relevant steps. After processing, the results are sent to relevant users. There only exist control or state messages for scheduler, and it does not deal with the transmission of massive video data.

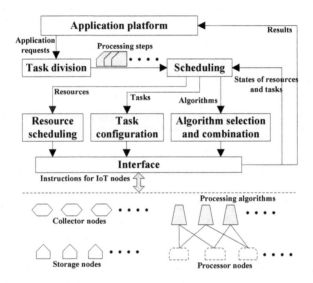

**Fig. 3.**  Scheduler function description

## 3.2   Typical Video Processing Algorithm

1)  Moving target detection based on adaptive background updating [7].
    Moving objects are mainly vehicles and pedestrians on the road. Interframe difference method is one of the most common methods in motion segmentation. In this method, the image's moving region is obtained by pixel-based interframe difference and threshold constraint for two or three adjacent interframes in a continuous image sequence. In sequence images, the difference between adjacent frames can be obtained by comparing the pixels. Detailed steps are as follows.

(1)  Rough classification of persons and vehicles by the width of the detected target.

$$f_w = \begin{cases} 1 & Width > T_w \\ 0 & else \end{cases} \tag{1}$$

$T_w$ is the width threshold. The target must be relatively large if target's width is greater than $T_w$. It could be a vehicle or a crowd. Otherwise, it is a small target, such as a person, a bicycle or a motorcycle.

(2)  Using morphological operators, i.e., Compactness and Aspect Ratio, to identify person and vehicle. Their definitions are as follows.

$$\begin{cases} Compactness = \frac{Area}{Perimeter^2} \\ Aspect\ Ratio = \frac{Height}{Width} \end{cases} \tag{2}$$

Among them, *Area* refers to the area of the target, *Perimeter* is the distance between two targets, and *Height* is the height of the target. The most obvious difference between crowd and vehicle is in *Compactness*. The *Compactness* of the crowd (typically 0.0144) is much smaller than that of a car (typically 0.0577). So we can distinguish the crowd from the vehicle by a linear partition function $G(Area, Compactness)$. The most obvious difference among person, bicycle and motorcycle is in *Aspect Ratio*. The *Aspect Ratio* of person is the largest with typical value 11.11, the next is bicycle with typical value 9.53, and the smallest is motorcycle with typical value 5.76. So we can distinguish the crowd with a linear partition function $H(Area, Aspect\ Ratio)$.

2)  Moving gesture tracking by particle filtering method [8].
Moving gesture tracking is to determine the position of human's hand for each frame of consecutive frames in real-time video sequence, and describes the moving trajectory information of human's hand. Common gesture tracking algorithm includes Calman prediction algorithm, particle filter algorithm, mean shift algorithm, etc. This paper adopts the particle filter algorithm. The detailed processing steps are as follows.

(1)  Select the target to be tracked;
(2)  Calculate the normalized color histogram of target area as the observation model, determine the number of particles and make initialization.
(3)  Calculate the color histogram of each particle and the Bhattacharyya Distance between each particle and the target, and then update the weight;
(4)  Discard the particles with smaller weight, and duplicate the particles with large weight;
(5)  The particle's weights stand for the probability of the gesture appearance in its center, and the center of the target gestures can be found by calculating the expectation of weights for all particles.

3)  Vehicle license plate recognition based on neural network.
One of the important application of BP (Back Propagation) network is pattern recognition. The task is to design and train a feasible and efficient BP network for

recognizing characters, letters and numbers in the vehicle license plate. After image preprocessing, it can send the final characteristic results of extracted characters into the BP network for training and recognition. Detailed training steps is shown in Fig. 4.

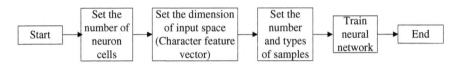

**Fig. 4.** Training process of character recognition based on neural network

## 4 Video Processor Scheduling Method

### 4.1 Scheduling Problem Description

Due to the limitation of capacity, each processor node can implement only a few different processing algorithms. However, each application may consist of several processing steps of specific sequence. So collaboration among several processor nodes is unavoidable and there are complex dependent relations among these nodes. It is necessary to set up optimization model to achieve the optimal scheduling of these resources [9]. The relevant issues to be considered are as follows.

(1) Selection of video collector. For real-time processing, there may be more than one collector that can monitor the target location, so we need to select the most suitable one according to processing process with considerations for such performance metrics as current load, transmission delay and energy consumption.

(2) Selection of video processor. There may have many processor nodes with proper algorithm that are suitable for a particular processing step. So we should select the most appropriate processor set for different applications according to the composition and relation of these processing steps and the location of users. Such issues as the structure of processing steps (including parallel, serial or hybrid), current load and processing delay should also be considered.

(3) Sorting method for tasks from different users on one video processor. Multiple tasks from different applications may be assigned to the same processor node. Considering the relation of all steps in an application, it is hard to describe the effects from different execution orders of these steps on the operation performance. So traditional shortest-delay-first strategy and priority-based strategy are no longer applicable, and we need a globally optimal or quasi-optimal scheme.

The elements [9] for scheduling problems modelling are as follows:

(1) Current load of each node;
(2) Processing delay of algorithms on each node and transmission delay of video/image data;
(3) The available functions or algorithms implemented on each node;

(4) Composition and relation of necessary processing steps and relevant data volumes to be processed for a specific application.

Based on these constraints, we allocate appropriate processor nodes to various processing steps in each decomposed application, so we can meet optimization objectives such as the minimizations of delay, cost and energy consumption.

### 4.2 Implementation of Scheduling Based on Genetic Algorithm

As a key optimization technique in modern intelligent computation, Genetic Algorithm [10] has no limit on derivation and function continuity, and can operate on the final results directly. With good self-adaptive capability for global optimization, it has been widely used in many fields such as combination optimization, machine learning, signal processing and adaptive control. The specific steps for processor nodes scheduling with Genetic Algorithm are as follows.

(1) Fitness function definition

Given $M$ processing steps from all decomposed applications, we get the time interval needed for algorithm execution $TE_i$ on the node and the time interval needed for data communication $TC_i$ between nodes during each processing step $ST_i$ ($1 \leq i \leq M$). The parameter $\alpha_k$ tries to decrease the transmission conflicts by time-disjoint allocation, and it is defined as the ratio of the sum of overlapped time durations to the sum of all time durations for all processing steps on node $k$. Obviously, the smaller $\alpha_k$ is, the less interference exists among these processing steps. So the fitness function for the objective of delay minimization is as follows.

$$F_{delay} = \frac{\sum_{k=1}^{N} \alpha_k}{\sum_{i=1}^{M} (TE_i + TC_i)} \tag{3}$$

In (3) $N$ is the total number of processing nodes in the cloud.

(2) Initial population generation

Each chromosome contains $M$ genes, and each gene corresponds to a processing step. The value of the gene is composed by the ID of assigned processor node, the starting time of processing and the starting time of transmission. We randomly generate $NT$ chromosomes as the initial population.

(3) Selection

Calculate the values of fitness function for each chromosome, and select $NT/2$ chromosomes with the highest values for the following steps.

(4) Crossover and mutation operation

Crossover is the most important searching operator in Genetic Algorithm. It imitates the process of gene recombination in the nature of sexual reproduction, and generates new individuals with better genetic. In this paper, we randomly match two chromosomes and select their starting gene for crossover randomly. Mutation can extend the searching scope and improve the diversity of population as algorithm converges. We select the gene for mutation randomly and replace its value with other possible value. This will generate $NT/2$ new chromosomes.

(5) Algorithm decision

When the number of the generations does not reach the threshold and the fitness function value is not convergent, we choose $N$ chromosomes with the highest fitness values as the new generation in all $3NT/2$ chromosomes, and return to step 3) for a new generation. Otherwise, we output the chromosome with the highest fitness value as the scheduling scheme and terminate the algorithm.

In addition, it is possible to define new fitness functions and execution mechanisms for different optimization objectives (including load balance and energy consumption minimization) according to specified performance requirement.

## 5   Performance Evaluation

We get the scheduling schemes for our Genetic Algorithm based optimal scheduling method (GAO), traditional random scheduling method (RAN) and opportunity-balanced scheduling method (BAL) [11, 12] by Matlab. The RAN method selects processor node randomly from the nodes with matching functions, and the BAL method selects processor node in turn from the nodes with matching function. Based on these scheduling schemes, we further make performance comparison among these three methods with simulation experiments in OMNet++.

The relevant parameters are specified as follows: Number of processor node is 20, and number of application types is 6 (including face recognition, vehicle traffic statistics, detection of lost things, video encoding, regional intrusion detection and moving object tracking). The number of processing steps in each application ranges from 3 to 5 with average value of 4. There are 12 processing functions in total. The number of implementation instances on all processor nodes for each algorithm ranges from 4 to 6 with average value of 5. So in average the number of algorithm instances on each processor node is $12*5/20 = 3$. The processing delay on processor node for data of 1 kbyte ranges from 0.5 s to 1.5 s with average value of 1 s, and the transmission delay for data of 1 kbyte ranges from 1 s to 3 s with average value of 2 s.

Based on above settings, we randomly construct 30 different cloud configuration scenarios, including the random designation locations and function deployment for all processor nodes. On the other hand, the transmission parameters are specified with default values in OMNet++. We get the average value of simulation results for these scenarios, so we can get objective and pervasive results. For convenience, we assign the load of each processor node as 0. Further we designate 10 task scenarios with increasing workload, and the number of applications in each task scenario increase from 5, 10, 15, … to 50.

The performance metrics are average overall processing delay and overall transmission delay for all application requests, together with average Packet Delivery Ratio (PDR) on all processor nodes. The results are shown in Figs. 5, 6 and 7.

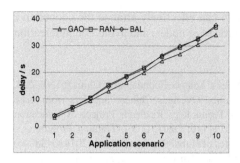

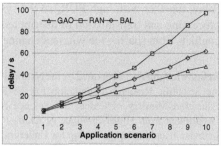

**Fig. 5.** Average overall processing delay    **Fig. 6.** Average overall transmission delay

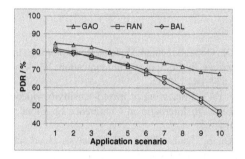

**Fig. 7.** Average packet delivery ratio

From these figures we can see, as the volume of data increases with different application scenarios, the delay of each strategy increases as expected. For processing delay, the results of RAN and BAL are similar, and are slightly larger than that of GAO. GAO yields the minimal transmission delay, and RAN yields the largest transmission delay. For task scenario of high workload, the transmission delay of RAN increases rapidly, and the reason is more frequent communication conflicts that lead to such behaviors as retransmission and channel back-off. However, GAO can effectively avoid such phenomena with mechanism of interference-less scheduling. In general, transmission delay is much larger than processing delay.

As for the average PDR, we observe that the PDRs of RAN and BAL decrease rapidly as application scenario changes. However, GAO achieves the highest PDR, and its PDR decreases slowly as application scenarios changes, for the obvious effect of intelligent scheduling.

## 6    Conclusions

The IoT based cloud video surveillance system and the scheduling method in this paper can be applied to scenarios of dynamical deployment with plenty of IoT devices. IoT nodes with different functions and roles can cooperatively handle a video processing request of several processing steps. Simulation results show that the scheduling method with time-disjoint resource allocation yields small processing delay and transmission delay, together with high PDR, so the system can effectively arrange the cooperative processing and transmission of distributed processor nodes, and avoid communication conflicts from sharing the wireless channel.

**Acknowledgment.** Supported by the National Natural Science Foundation of China (61501337), the Scientific Research Foundation for the Returned Overseas Chinese Scholars from State Education Ministry of China, the Science and Technology Research Project of Education Department from Hubei Province of China (Q20141110, D20151106), Training Programs of Innovation and Entrepreneurship for Undergraduates of Hubei Province, China (201410488046) and College Students' Renovation Foundation of Wuhan University of Science and Technology, China (14ZRA140).

# References

1. Aggarwal, V., Chen, X., Gopalakrishnan, V., Jana, R.: Exploiting virtualization for delivering cloud-based IPTV services. In: Computer Communications Workshops of IEEE INFOCOM, Shanghai, China, pp. 637–641 (2011)
2. Zhang, C.W., Chang, E.C.: Processing of mixed-sensitivity video surveillance streams on hybrid clouds. In: IEEE 7th International Conference on Cloud Computing, Anchorage, Alaska, pp. 9–16 (2014)
3. Luo, Y.Q., Dai, J., Qi, L.: Fault-tolerant video analysis cloud scheduling mechanism. In: International Conference on Virtual Reality and Visualization, Xi'an, China, pp. 119–126 (2013)
4. Rupanagudi, S.R., Ranjani, B.S., Nagaraj, P., et al.: A novel cloud computing based smart farming system for early detection of borer insects in tomatoes. In: International Conference on Communication, Information and Computing Technology, Mumbai, India, pp. 87–94 (2015)
5. Ali, A.M.M., Ahmad, N.M., Amin, A.H.M.: Cloudlet-based cyber foraging framework for distributed video surveillance provisioning. In: 4th World Congress on Information and Communication Technologies, Malacca, Malaysia, pp. 199–204 (2014)
6. Chien, S.-Y., Chan, W.-K., Tseng, Y.-H., et al.: Distributed computing in IoT: system-on-a-chip for smart cameras as an example. In: 20th Asia and South Pacific Design Automation Conference, Chiba/Tokyo, Japan, pp. 130–135 (2015)
7. Zhao, Y.H., Jiang, H., Zhou, K., et al.: Meeting service level agreement cost-effectively for video-on-demand applications in the cloud. In: IEEE INFOCOM, Toronto, Canada, pp. 298–306 (2014)
8. Aggarwal, V., Gopalakrishnan, V., Jana, R., et al.: Optimizing cloud resources for delivering IPTV services through virtualization. IEEE Trans. Multimedia **15**(4), 789–801 (2013)
9. Zhao, Z.: Scheduling policy analysis of cloud video service. In: IEEE GLOBECOM, Austin, Texas, pp. 1329–1335 (2014)
10. Faruk, G.: Process plan and part routing optimization in a dynamic flexible job shop scheduling environment: an optimization via simulation approach. Neural Comput. Appl. **23**(6), 1631–1641 (2013)
11. Ashraf, A., Jokhio, F., Deneke, T., et al.: Stream-based admission control and scheduling for video transcoding in cloud computing. In: 13th IEEE/ACM International Symposium on Cluster, Cloud and Grid Computing, Delft, Netherlands, pp. 482–489 (2013)
12. Bayyapu, K.R., Fischer, P.: Load scheduling in a cloud based massive video-storage environment. In: 16th International Symposium on Symbolic and Numeric Algorithms for Scientific Computing, Timisoara, Romania, pp. 349–356 (2014)

# HiTrans: An FPGA-Based Gateway Design and Implementation in HPC Environments

Wei Shi$^{(\boxtimes)}$, Gaofeng Lv, Zhigang Sun, and Zhenghu Gong

College of Computer, National University of Defense Technology,
410073 Changsha, China
shiwei0060@gmail.com, Gzh@nudt.edu.cn

**Abstract.** Infiniband and 10 Gbps Ethernet are two main high speed interconnect technologies adopted by High Performance Computing Environment, Ethernet is currently pervasively leveraged by storage devices while Infiniband is commonly used for high speed transmission among compute nodes, this distinction introduces interoperation between two heterogeneous networks which necessitate gateways, traditional software-based storage gateways show shortcomings in terms of high CPU utilization, long processing latency and poor performance, ASIC-based gateways overcome the above drawback but do not own enough programmability which enables flexible operations. This paper designs and implements an FPGA-based storage gateway called HiTrans to connect Infiniband and Ethernet in HPC environments based on EoIB technology, our main contributions focus on proposing the core processing procedure of HiTrans, and a static address mapping algorithm supporting fast protocol conversion between heterogeneous networks which boosts packet processing capability of storage gateway and reduces storage I/O latency. Experiment result has shown that performance of Hi-Trans can reach line-rate forwarding from Infiniband to Ethernet which is 3 times higher than traditional software-based implementation.

**Keywords:** High performance computing · FPGA · Storage gateway · Heterogeneous networks · Infiniband · Ethernet

## 1 Introduction

Constantly increasing computing power in HPC (High performance computing) systems induces more and more performance requirements of storage systems in terms of bandwidth and latency. AS parallel and distributed storage technology continues to develop and storage architecture such as NAS and SAN begin to be pervasively adopted, in order to improve storage capability, except for existing High-speed Transmit Network (HTN) used to connecting compute nodes, High-speed storage network (HSN) is gradually formed to provide rapid interconnection among compute nodes and storage nodes.

HTN characters with scalability, high bisectional bandwidth and low latency com-medications, typical switching technology includes InfiniBand [4], Ethernet and dedicated network such as HNR in MilkyWay-2 system are applicable to HTN [1]. HSN is not only sensitive to bandwidth and latency, but also requires direct connectivity to commercial storage servers and RAIDS, typical switching technologies applied in HSN are Infiniband and Ethernet.

© Springer International Publishing Switzerland 2015
G. Wang et al. (Eds.): ICA3PP 2015 Workshops, LNCS 9532, pp. 561–571, 2015.
DOI: 10.1007/978-3-319-27161-3_51

For performance/cost considerations, generally HTN and HSN adopt different switching technologies. In order to improve computing power, HTN deploys Infiniband or HNR, while Ethernet-based storage servers and RAIDs have lower prices and good compatibility, which makes it a more preferable option in HSN. As a result Ethernet Over X(X can be replaced with Infiniband or HNR) capsulation is pervasively adopted to interconnect HTN and HSN. Communication routine between HTN and HSN have to pass though storage gateways.

Storage gateways (SG) are elements of greatest importance for implementing heterogeneous network interoperation in HPC systems. Complementing scheduling policy and caching strategy on storage gateways will be of great significance for storage I/O performance to get a rise and QoS strategies to be fulfilled.

Current commercial storage gateways include ASIC-based Mellanox Gateway series products with Bridge-X or Switch-X chips incorporated [7, 8], which are able to implement protocol conversion between Ethernet and Infiniband at 10Gbps level, while they cannot provide necessary programmability to fulfill specific control requirements. For this reason IBM BlueGene/P and MilkyWay-2 system builds ION gateways upon commercial commodity servers which provides high programmability and are easy to scale to various control functionalities [1, 3], but performance stays low for protocol conversions are totally done by software [2].

Due to the above reasons, we propose a high performance FPGA-based storage gateway design called HiTrans, which provides a tradeoff between performance and flexibility, especially possibility for implementing queue scheduling and file caching.

This paper proposes HiTrans models as well as its core processing procedures, and provides static address mapping algorithm to accelerate protocol conversion. Prototype based on FPGA has been produced and performance has been given though experiment which is three times higher than traditional software-based ION gateways [2].

This paper is organized as follows: Chapter 2 introduces core function that storage gateway owns, Chapter 3 describes the key implementation of HiTrans—the static address mapping algorithm, Chapter 4 depicts the HiTrans prototype and performance experiment results, Chapter 5 discusses future work combining current software-defined storage technologies. Chapter 6 concludes this paper.

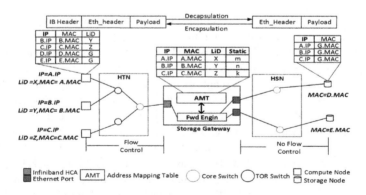

**Fig. 1.** Core function of HiTrans

## 2 Core Functions of HiTrans

### 2.1 Data Plane Functionality

In the scenario depicted in Fig. 1, compute nodes are named A, B, and C, storage nodes are named D and E, IP addresses and MAC addresses of compute nodes and storage nodes can be represent with NodeName.IP and NodeName.MAC, the InfiniBand link layer address—Lid are represented with x, y, z for node A, B and C, storage gateways are equipped with one 40 Gbps Infiniband HCA card and two 10 Gbps Ethernet NICs, IB address and Ethernet address of gateway is G and G.MAC. In compute nodes three tuple(<Dst_IP, NextHop_MAC, NextHop_Lid>) mapping relations are restored in a dedicated table, similarly in each storage node there exists a table which restores two tuple(<Dst_IP, NextHop_MAC>) mapping relations. Packets sent from storage nodes and destined for compute nodes only contain IP addresses of destinations, therefore it is necessary for gateway to establish and maintain a mapping table used for packet encapsulation to make address mapping for those packets in order to interconnect the heterogeneous networks. The above discussion can explain that the most important data plane functionality that storage gateway possesses is packet format conversion.

- Packet format conversion: As can be seen in Fig. 1 packets sent from compute nodes to storage nodes have different packet formats in HTN and HSN. In HTN an Infiniband header need to be encapsulated before an entire Ethernet packet, gateway performs decapsulation operation for these packets and puts the remain Ethernet packets into HSN. Conversely gateway needs to perform conversion and encapsulation operation for all packets sent from HSN to HTN, this operation needs three steps: step 1 is table lookup in AMT table using destination IP address to get destination MAC address and destination Lid address, step 2 is replacing destination MAC address with the destination MAC address in step 1, step 3 is to construct an InfiniBand header with the destination Lid in step 1 and make encapsulation to turn original Ethernets packet into Infiniband packets. After all three step are done, InfiniBand packets are sent to HTN though Infiniband HCA.

Gateway can also implement flow control and multicast management besides packet format conversion, which enables specific QoS policies conducted in storage gateway.

- Flow control: Under RC(Reliable Connection) mode Infiniband supports flow control functionality while Ethernet does not and can only rely on TCP layer to limit bandwidth of each connection, this divergence induces disadvantage effect that important features embodied in Infiniband HCA fails to work. Under this situation, storage gateway can help implement traffic shaping and multi-queue scheduling especially for packets sent to Ethernet.
- Multicast: Multicast is an important data transmission method in IP networks. For IO-intensive applications there are quite a lot of scenarios in which multicast is frequently leveraged, for example multiple replicas. Integrating multicast support into gateway data plane may greatly decrease workload in end hosts.

## 2.2    Control Plane Functionality

Corresponding to data plane functionalities, control plane functionalities in storage gateway will support AMT management, multicast management and multi-queue forwarding rule management.

- AMT management: AMT is a key data structure that packet format conversion needs, AMT management operation includes add/delete/query table entries, different address mapping methods need different AMT management functionality.
- Multicast group management: This incorporates Layer-2 multicast protocol implementation and multicast group management protocol support, which are responsible for dealing with group join/quit messages from end hosts and maintaining the state of multicast tree.
- Multi-queue forwarding rule management: Configuring queue rules for multi-queue is of most significance when conducting fine-granularity flow control. Queue rules may consist of the following type such as forwarding/caching, next hop routing selection and scheduled forwarding with specific bandwidth. Rules configurations could be controlled by outside hosts which requires gateway to offer corresponding functional unit.

Among all the features that storage gateway owns, packet format conversion is the most basic one and should be considered utmost important, for which this paper proposes a static address mapping algorithm to perform fast packet format conversion as depicted in the next chapter.

# 3    Address Mapping Mechanism

As a key component to satisfy interconnection requirements of heterogeneous networks, Address mapping algorithm relies on specific packet encapsulation format, typical formats include Ethernet over Infiniband and Infiniband over Ethernet. Taking EoIB as an example, each compute node equipped with an IB HCA possesses a virtual Ethernet interface, Ethernet packet will be encapsulated with an InfiniBand header before sent into HTN to make transmission in HTN possible, upon receiving these packets storage gateway performs decapsulation operation, restores Ethernet packets and then transmits them into HSN. When senders are storage hosts, Ethernet packets are transmitted to storage gateway directly, upon receiving these packets storage gateway encapsulate IB header to turn packets into Infiniband packets which will then be sent to HTN immediately. The following Table 1 shows the difference of EoIB and IBoE.

**Table 1.** Comparision of EoIB and IBoE

| Encapsulation format | End host encapsulation | Gateway address mapping |
|---|---|---|
| EoIB | Encapsulate Infiniband Header in front of Ethernet packet | Decapsulate/Encapsulate Infiniband header |
| IBoE | Encapsulate Ethernet Header in front of Infiniband packet | Decapsulate/Encapsulate Ethernet header |

Currently EoIB capsulation format is adopted by most hierarchical network interconnection systems, firstly, L2 network based on Ethernet rather than Infiniband is a mature technology which could be directly leveraged by EoIB, secondly, Infiniband is based upon centralized control, which will result in frequent communications among InfiniBand opensm and HSN hosts if IBoE is adopted. As a result IBoE will bring disadvantage effects such as higher processing complexity and workload for storage gateway.

The capsulation of IB header requires storage gateway to provide address mapping mechanism, the core function of this mechanism is to constructing AMT and provide corresponding table lookup algorithm. Each table entry in AMT includes three tuple <IP address, MAC address, Lid Address> mapping relationships of one compute node. Constructing AMT can be done by two different methods: static mapping and dynamic leaning.

Static mapping centralizes on opensm node in HTN, opensm node is a dedicated InfiniBand host which is responsible for assigning IP address, MAC address and Lid address for each compute node, one table entry is formed in opensm after one node is assigned. This kind of mapping relations are quite stable and storage gateway can make a local replica in its DRAM storage through deploying opensm agent inside which could be utilized to communicate with opensm. Algorithm 2.1 describe the pseudocode of static mapping.

Dynamic learning algorithm does not need opensm to bond the three-tuple addresses for each compute node. It is up to compute node itself to configure the three tuple address and incorporates them into broadcast packets. Packet classification unit in storage gateway needs to recognize these broadcast packets and extract the embodied three tuple addresses and store the mapping information as an AMT entry.

In Algorithm 2.1, CONP, ETHP and IBP are packets that storage gateway receives. CONP is the packet from opensm which carry along three tuple mapping information, ETHP represents Ethernet packets sent from HSN, IBP represents InfiniBand packets sent from HTN, packet_out refers to packets that have been encapsulated or decapsulated. Opensm is the centralized management host in InfiniBand network.

Static mapping algorithm avoids massive broadcast packets in HTN and it has low complexity which makes it easy for hardware to implement. Besides, large-capacity FPGA is equipped with enough DRAM storage unit to accommodate AMT in HPC systems. Taking MilkyWay-2 which has 16000 compute nodes as an example, the number of AMT table entry is 16 K, assuming that each entry possesses 128 Bytes memory space, the total DRAM space which AMT occupies will be only 2 MB. Duo to above reasons, HiTrans prefers static mapping algorithm to service address conversion.

## 4 Prototype Implementation and Performance Evaluation

We have already implemented a HiTran prototype which is based on EoIB capsulation format and static mapping algorithm. As depicted in Fig. 2, gateway has one InfiniBand HCA and one Ethernet NIC. The Green and the Red represents InfiniBand and Ethernet packet processing procedure respectively. Prototype implementation can be divided into four parts. Packet identification module is responsible for classifying

W. Shi et al.

---

### Algorithm 2.1 Packet Capsulation/Decapsulation Based on Static Mapping

---

**Input**: *Packet_in, opensm*

**Output**: *Packet_Out*

| | |
|---|---|
| 1. | If（*Packet_in* is CONP） |
| 2. | Three tuples =**Extract**(*Packet_in*) |
| 3. | **Store(Three tuples, AMT)** |
| 4. | **Endif** |
| 5. | **if (*Packet_in* is ETHP)** |
| 6. | DstIP=**Extract**(*Packet_in,ip*) |
| 7. | **If(TableLookUp(AMT,DstIP)=Success)** |
| 8. | Three tuples=**TableLookUp(AMT,DstIP)** |
| 9. | **Replace(*Packet_in*, Three tuples.MAC)** |
| 10. | **Construct(IB_hdr, Three tuples.LID)** |
| 11. | *Packet_out*=Encapsulate(*packet_in*, IBhdr) |
| 12. | **Transmit( *packet_out*, HTN)** |
| 13. | **Endif** |
| 14. | **If(TableLookUp(AMT,IP)=Failed)** |
| 15. | **Query(*opensm*, IP)** |
| 16. | Three tuples =**Extract(*opensm*.response)** |
| 17. | **If**(Three tuples=NULL) |
| 18. | **Drop(*Packet_in*)** |
| 19. | **Else** |
| 20. | **Store**(Three tuples,AMT) |
| 21. | **Goto** step 6 |
| 22. | **Endif** |
| 23. | **Endif** |
| 24. | **If** (Packet_in is IBP) |
| 25. | Packet_out=**Decapsulate** (packet_in, IBhdr) |
| 26. | **Transmit(** packet_out, HSN) |
| 27. | **Endif** |

packets of different types, for example packets from opensm are sent to address management module, and normal data plane packets are delivered to capsulation/decapsulation module. Capsulation/decapsulation module provides fast address conversion service in data plane. Address management module offers AMT storage and lookup service for capsulation/decapsulation module. Opensm agent module makes interactions with opensm to load and update AMT table.

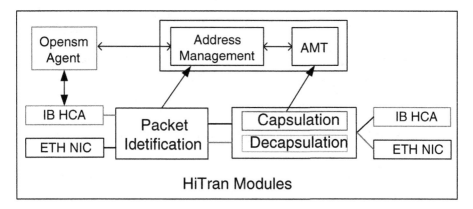

**Fig. 2.** HiTrans prototype implementation

The goal of performance evaluation is to examine bisectional packet processing capability of gateway, delegated by the TCP transmission bandwidth between compute nodes and storage nodes. Experiment environment consists of one FPGA-based storage gateway, one IBM storage server as storage node and one DELL server with two Intel Xeon E5 processors as compute node. We use a software tool called iperf to test TCP transmission speed between memories on endpoint nodes which avoids the interference of hard disk factors.

There are three parameters: thread number, TCP buffer size and packet length in this experiment. The first group of experiment adjusts thread number and TCP buffer size while keeping packet length maximum, the second group keep TCP buffer size steady while change the other two parameters. The experiment results can be observed in Figs. 3, 4, 5 and 6.

Figure 3 depicts TCP transmission performance from Ethernet to InfiniBand at packet length of 1500 Bytes, TCP transmission bandwidth increases linearly as TCP buffer size continues to grow if only one thread is created. However when thread number exceeds 2, TCP buffer size shows no obvious effect on TCP performance. Summit performance can be as high as 8.5 Gbps when buffer size is 1 MB and thread number is 8.

Figure 4 depicts TCP transmission performance from Ethernet to InfiniBand at packet length of 1500 Bytes, Summit performance (6.5 Gbps) can be reached when TCP buffer size is 256 KB and thread number is one, however, the increase of thread number does not bring performance boom.

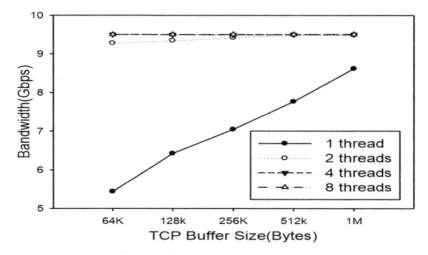

**Fig. 3.** TCP performance from InfiniBand to Ethernet at different window size

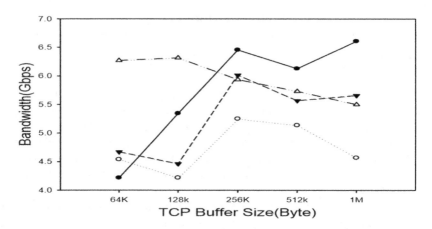

**Fig. 4.** TCP performance from Ethernet to InfiniBand at different window size

Figure 5 checks TCP performance from InfiniBand to Ethernet when thread number and packet length changes. End to end TCP Performance increases as thread number and packet length grows, summit performance (9.5 Gbps) can be reached when packet length is 1 KB and thread number is 8.

Figure 6 checks TCP performance from Ethernet to InfiniBand when thread number and packet length changes. The result is as similar as that in Fig. 5, and summit performance (9.5 Gbps) can be reached when packet length is 1 KB and thread number is 8.

The results of the experiment show that FPGA-based storage gateways are able to significantly improve bisectional transmission performance between hierarchical networks when compared with software-based ION nodes, it is worth noted that TCP

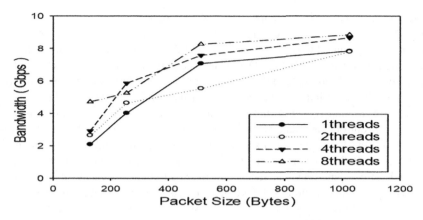

**Fig. 5.** TCP performance from InfiniBand to Ethernet at different pkt size

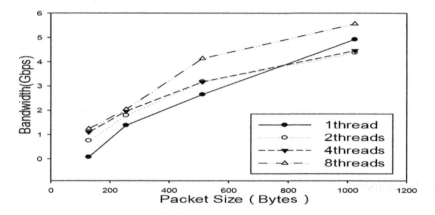

**Fig. 6.** TCP performance from Ethernet to InfiniBand at different pkt size

performance from InfiniBand to Ethernet has improved 3 times when ION is replaced by HiTrans. Besides, in most condition, transmission performance increases when thread number gains, indicating that HiTrans can avoid resource contention problem under heavy burden of concurrent IO flows, which IONs fail to tackle. As a result less HiTrans gateway nodes are required to provide identical bandwidth that current ION nodes are able to provide.

## 5  Future Work

As software-defined networking [6] technologies being put into practice in datacenter networks and cloud computing, more and more researches cast their attention on resolving QoS enforcing problems in large-scale distributed storage systems through software defined storage, in which IOflow [5] is the most typical one leveraged by Microsoft Azure datacenter.

IOflow architecture incorporates a centralized controller responsible for maintaining global topology such as routing information and network state such as link utilization rate, mapping between user policies and data plane rules, as well as real-time rule computation and distribution. Data plane is completely implemented on end hosts (compute node and storage node), any software layers on I/O request processing path can be regarded as an individual data plane which can implement QoS policies such as flow control, routing selection through creating queues and executing corresponding queue rules, controller and data plane interact with each other by calling specific API to complete feedback of flow/network state, queue management and rule distribution.

However, IOflow cannot scale to large-scale systems such as HPCs, tens of thousands of compute nodes in HPCs will overload controller easily. It is our future work to explore implementing software defined data plane on HiTrans, because typical HPCs has only hundreds of IONs, it can be assured that this software defined storage gateway architecture (SDHiTrans) can scale well even at systems as large as HPCs.

Controller can coexist with existing metadata server which is a key building block of parallel and distributed file systems, here file system state including server capacity and workload could be monitored by MDS-embodied controller, besides, controller may also communicate with SDHiTrans by connecting themselves to switches, controller will establish an individual queue for each storage flow inside SDHiTrans and compute queue rules according to user demand on bandwidth and latency. Key technologies of implementing basic software defined storage gateway will focus on translating user.

QoS request into parameters of hardware implemented flow control algorithm such as Deficit Round Robin and how to adjust queue rules according to real-time incoming flow bandwidth in each SDHiTrans.

# 6   Conclusion

This paper designs and verifies the first known FPGA-based storage gateway called HiTrans connecting hierarchical networks in HPC environments, together with its core processing unit and a practical algorithm to complement fast address conversion. Prototype tests illustrate that this prototype can realize 10Gbps line rate forwarding performance from InfiniBand to Ethernet which is three times higher than traditional software based ION, it is believed that HiTrans can effectively satisfy storage I/O demand that future HPC systems may eagerly require.

# References

1. Xu, W., Lu, Y., Li, Q., et al.: Hybrid hierarchy storage system in MilkyWay-2 supercomputer. Front. Comput. Sci. **8**(3), 367–377 (2014)
2. Vishwanath, V., Hereld, M., Iskra, K., et al.: Accelerating I/O forwarding in IBM blue Gene/P systems. In: 2010 International Conference for High Performance Computing, Networking, Storage and Analysis (SC), pp. 1–10. IEEE (2010)

3. Frings, W., Hennecke, M.: A system level view of Petascale I/O on IBM Blue Gene/P. Comput. Sci.-Res. Dev. **26**(3–4), 275–283 (2011)
4. InfiniBand Trade Association. InfiniBand Architecture Specification: Release 1.0. InfiniBand Trade Association (2000)
5. Thereska, E., Ballani, H., O'Shea, G., et al.: Ioflow: a software-defined storage architecture. In: Proceedings of the Twenty-Fourth ACM Symposium on Operating Systems Principles, pp. 182–196. ACM (2013)
6. McKeown, N.: Software-defined networking. INFOCOM Keynote Talk **17**(2), 30–32 (2009)
7. Mellanox. S X. 36-port 56 Gb/s InfiniBand Switch Systems
8. Saving, S.L.P.: Power Saving Features in Mellanox Products (2013)

# Dealing with Reliable Event-Based Communications by Means of Layered Multicast

Christian Esposito$^{(\boxtimes)}$, Aniello Castiglione, and Francesco Palmieri

Department of Computer Science, University of Salerno, 84084 Fisciano, SA, Italy
christian.esposito@unina.it, castiglione@ieee.org,
fpalmieri@unisa.it

**Abstract.** Nowadays, it is demanding to have multicast services able to jointly provide a high degree of reliability and good performances despite of failure occurrences. However, the current practice to tolerate failures in such services mainly consists in the adoption of retransmission-based methods, which obtain reliable multicast delivery with severe performance fluctuations and instability. An alternative solution is to apply coding to proactively recover the lost packets by reconstructing them from what has been received. Coding-based approaches achieve more predictable and stable performances, since the delivery time does not depend on the loss patterns imposed by network dynamics. However, they have been scarcely adopted within the context of large-scale multicast services due to important issues related to their tuning. In this paper we have gleaned from the experience of Layered Multicast, commonly applied to multimedia content delivery, and extended it to address the tunability problem of coding-based recovery approaches in large-scale multicast services.

**Keywords:** Event-based communications · Reliable multicasting · Forward error correction · Layered multicast · Loss tolerance

## 1 Introduction

Publish/subscribe services [1] are now considered as key technological solutions in several industrial projects aiming at realizing federated architectures over a Wide-Area Network (WAN). Due to the large scale of such systems, it is demanding that the federating middleware could exhibit good scalability guarantees, and publish/subscribe services are able to cope with such a demand due to their peculiarity of offering decoupled multicasting. However, several of these architectures exhibit other stringent non-functional requirements since they are used in critical scenarios, such as Air Traffic Management (ATM), monitoring of power grids, financial services and so on. Among these requirements, there is the need of achieving a data dissemination jointly able to tolerate any possible failures and to respect strict temporal constraints. The literature is rich of methods for guaranteeing reliability in publish/subscribe services [2]. The typical approach is to introduce temporal redundancy within the system by means

© Springer International Publishing Switzerland 2015
G. Wang et al. (Eds.): ICA3PP 2015 Workshops, LNCS 9532, pp. 572–581, 2015.
DOI: 10.1007/978-3-319-27161-3_52

of retransmissions: when a destination detects a packet loss (*e.g.*, it receives a packet with a sequence identifier different from the expected one) it asks for a retransmission. The strength of such retransmission-based approaches consists in guaranteeing that all the messages are delivered due to the closed control loop established among the destinations and the data source. However, such approaches suffer from (*i*) severe performance fluctuations in the communication latency, (*ii*) the influence of network dynamics on the number of retransmissions needed to successfully deliver an event (which makes latency unpredictable due to the high variability of network dynamics), and (*iii*) the incurrence of instability due to the possible saturation of queues for storing packets, which may be required for retransmission. In the current literature, a different approach to deal with communication losses is the one that adopts spatial redundancy, *i.e.*, additional information is sent along a notification so that eventual loss problem can be resolved without requiring retransmissions. Concrete examples are Forward Error Correction (FEC) [3] (where notifications to be distributed are encoded for generating additional information to be decoded for reconstructing lost packets) and Path Redundancy [4] (where several copies of the published notifications are disseminated along multiple available paths). The latter one is effective only if path diversity is guaranteed, *i.e.*, the multiple paths do not share any routing component, which is difficult to obtain over WANs [5]. On the other hand, FEC approaches have not found large adoption in large-scale settings due to some tuning issues. Typically, coding is performed at the source, and the applied redundancy degree is tailored on the worst loss rate experienced by one of the destinations. This may result not optimal and even dangerous for other destinations with lower loss rate and reduced capacity, so as to cause congestion phenomena. If such a rule is not followed and the redundancy degree is lower, then a subset of the destinations will experience losses and the achievable reliability degree is compromised.

The contribution of this paper is to resolve the issues related to the applicability of FEC to large scale settings by applying an approach theorized within the context of multimedia content delivery and called *Layered Multicast* [6]. Specifically, it consists in defining different layers with original data and coding data, so that a destination can join a particular set of layers in order to achieve the needed reliability based on the experienced network conditions. This allows us to optimize the applied redundancy degree at each destination without affecting the provided reliability guarantees.

## 2   Background and Related Work

As argued in [2], a series of failures can occur in large-scale settings. Several studies have demonstrated that WANs are affected by packet losses and link crashes. Nodes, on the other hand, can be also affected by aging phenomena or hardware malfunctioning that can cause crashes or hangs. A publish/subscribe service has to be equipped with proper methods to tolerate them and to guarantee the delivery of notifications to all interested destinations. Such methods are traditionally grouped into two main classes [2]: the one based on *Temporal Redundancy* and the one based on *Spatial Redundancy*. The former one makes use of retransmissions to recover lost messages and encompasses the widely-known Automatic Repeat reQuest (ARQ) technique [7]. However, such a solution suffers from serious scalability and reliability limitations due to the centralization of the recovery duties at the publisher side. To overcome such a drawback, retransmission-based approaches have evolved by performing recovery duties in a distributed manner, and an example is the Gossiping [8], where nodes in the overlay of the publish/subscribe service send to other randomly-chosen destinations a summary of the received messages, so as to detect misses and trigger retransmissions. A criticism is that the reliability is always obtained at the expenses of the achievable performance of the data dissemination protocol. A more practical solution to provide both reliability and timeliness is to proactively take reliability actions even if losses have not yet occurred by adopting spatial redundancy rather than the temporal one. Specifically, Forward Error Correction (FEC) is used so that the publisher forwards additional data and the destination can reconstruct the original data even in presence of losses. In fact, in [9], we have seen that the loss-affected delay (both the mean and the standard deviation) of FEC is closer to the failure-free delay, and we have not found the same dependency on network conditions as seen with respect to gossip. Although FEC is strongly adopted in services based on IP Multicast, in the overlay-based ones it has not found the same enthusiastic use. We can find two different ways to embody FEC techniques within an overlay [10]. On the one hand, we have End-to-End FEC, where the multicaster encodes the packets to be delivered through the overlay network, while all the destinations decode the received packets. This method is easy to implement, while it is strongly affected by an issue that we can refer as "the boat unbalanced by the heaviest" (BUH) problem. Specifically, FEC redundancy degree is usually decided by the encoder with respect to the loss pattern experienced along the path with the worst quality. So, if only few paths exhibit heavy losses, the multicaster has to generate a large number of repair packets, even if the rest of destinations does not need it. This overwhelming redundancy degree may overload the nodes that need less redundancy and/or cause serious congestion in portions of the network. On the other hand, we can have a Link-by-Link FEC, where every node in the overlay encodes and decodes the messages, in order to protect the delivery from losses. This method is more flexible since the redundancy degree is chosen only with respect to the quality of an overlay link, so as to resolve the BUH problem, but also causes strong performance degradations due to the continuous execution of the two operations at every node. Heterogenous network conditions are a key problem not only for coding-based approaches, but a well-known problem for multimedia content multicasting [11]. In this context, a solution has been proposed in [6] with the name of Layered Multicast: multimedia content is encoded by using a layered algorithm so that the result is a set of layers, each disseminated independently at a certain rate. A destination will subscribe to a certain number of layers, depending on the capacity of its link towards the sender, so that the obtained quality of reception is tailored on the link capacity and there is no occurrence of congestion phenomena within the network. This scheme is adaptive not only to static heterogeneity of the network, but also to dynamic variations of the network conditions due to a simple adaptation rule driven by the receiver: ($i$) if congestion occurs, a layer is dropped; and ($ii$) if there is spare capacity, a layer is added. The application of this solution has been mainly related to rate allocation. However, layered multicast can also be applied to realize adaptable loss tolerance by approaching the intrinsic issues of FEC for communications over WANs and to resolve BUH problem. In [12], authors introduce the concept of Layered FEC: not only multimedia content is structured in layers (*i.e.*, source layers), but also the parity information (*i.e.*, parity layers), and the destinations, depending on the experienced loss patterns, can subscribe to a certain number of parity layers so as to tolerate them, and such selection is completely based on a Markov decision process. Such a solution, however, has been poorly applied outside the field of multimedia multicasting, where the reliability guarantees are more relaxed. In fact, a multimedia application is not interested in receiving all the packets disseminated by the multicaster, but just the ones that imply a good video quality [13]. What in our opinion is missing in the literature is to apply this scheme for other applications rather than multimedia content multicasting, such as critical applications with more stringent reliability and timeliness requirements. Moreover, all previous works applied this scheme to multicast services implemented by means of IP Multicast, which is known to have several deployability and scalability limitations when used in large-scale settings [14].

## 3 Preliminaries

A loss pattern affecting the links in a large-scale network is completely characterized by *Packet Loss Rate* (PLR), which is the probability to lose a packet, and *Average Burst Length* (ABL), which is the mean length of consecutive lost packets. Such characteristics, namely $PLR_x$ and $ABL_x$, are continuously monitored by each node $x$ over the overlay link that connects itself with the parent, *e.g.*, using the approach in [15], and disseminated towards the other nodes of the same group at the beginning (*i.e.*, after the node joins the group) and whenever there is a change in their value. In particular, the model adopted in this work to characterize the lossy behavior of a given link is the *Gilbert-Elliott Model* [16,17], one of the most-commonly applied in performance evaluation studies due to its analytical simplicity and the good results it provides in practical applications on wired IP networks [18]. The Gilbert Model is a $1^{st}$ order Markov chain model characterized by two states: state "Good", with a state dependent error rate equal to $1 - K$, and state "Bad", with a state dependent error rate equal to $1 - H$. Typically, K is assumed equal to 1 so that the "Good" state implies that no losses are experienced, while in our model we have assumed that $1 - H$ is equal to $PLR$. There are four transition probabilities: (1) the probability to pass from state "Good" to state "Bad" is called $P$; (2) the probability to remain in state "Good" is (1 - P); (3) the probability to pass from state "Bad" to state

"Good" is called $Q$; and last (4) the probability to remain in state "Bad" is (1 - $Q$). Given $PLR$ and $ABL$, it is possible to compute $P$ and $Q$ as follows [19]:

$$P = \frac{PLR \cdot Q}{1 - PLR} \quad Q = ABL^{-1}. \tag{1}$$

We assume that $K = 1$ means that no packets are lost when the model is in the "Good" state, while $H = 0$ means that packets are lost when the model is in the "Bad" state. It is simple to notice that, given such a model, the average probability of losing a given packet is equal to $PLR$ only over time. In end-to-end FEC approaches, coding is applied by the root of the multicast tree so as to introduce a suitable redundancy needed to tolerate the lossy behavior of the overlay links. Specifically, the root segments a notification received from the publishers in a block or *dataword* of $K$ symbols, *i.e.*, a sequence of bits with a given length $L$. Then, it produces a block of $N$, with $N > K$, symbols called *codeword*, so that any subset of $K$ encoded symbols are enough to reconstruct the original $K$ symbols of the dataword. This is denoted as $(N, K)$ code and allows a destination to successfully receive a given message even if $N - K$ losses happen when the message has been exchanged over a channel. In the last, several coding techniques have been proposed, each with its pros and cons, and some of them have their use protected by patents. In this work, we have considered the well-known technique of the *Random Linear Coding* (RLC) [20], which has become popular due to its simple implementation, no patent fees and good performance. RLC computes the additional symbols, namely $s_{code}$, by using a linear combination of the $K$ symbols of the dataword, namely $s_{data}$:

$$s_{code,j} = \sum_{i=1}^{K} \omega_{j,i} \cdot s_{data,i} \quad j = 1, \cdots N - K \tag{2}$$

where $\omega_{j,i}$ is the weight of the *i-th* symbol in the dataword, namely $s_{data,i}$, of the *j-th* symbol in the codeword, namely $s_{code,j}$, randomly taken from a certain Galois Field with fixed element length equal to the length of the symbols, *i.e.*, $GF(2^L)$. In [21], it is shown that the suitable length for the Galois Field is 8, *i.e.*, $GF(2^8)$. This allows picking independent weights and having fast operations over the field. In order to have an optimal configuration of the redundancy applied by the root, it is crucial to know the mean number of losses, namely $L$, that the transmission of $N$ packets will experience along the tree so that the total number of the packets received by each node, namely $RP$, is equal to the number of needed packets $K$, which is also the number of the original packets passed to the root. In particular, we can assume that $N$ is the sum of $K$ and the number of the redundant packets originated by the root, *i.e.*, $R$. Therefore, we can formulate the tuning rule for configuring a FEC scheme as follows:

$$RP = K + R - L \geq K \rightarrow R - L \geq 0 \tag{3}$$

$L$ can be obtained from the second-order statistics, specifically variance, of the Gilbert-Elliott model, which are derived in [19] via generating functions, and is expressed as follows, when $K = 1$ and $H = 0$:

$$L = c_v(N) = \sqrt{\frac{Q}{N \cdot P} + \frac{2 \cdot P \cdot Q(1 - P - Q)}{N \cdot P^2 (P + Q)} \cdot (1 - \frac{1 - (1 - P - Q)^N}{N(P + Q)})}. \tag{4}$$

We can have a simpler form of Eq. 4. First of all, we can simplify it by limiting the values that $N$ can potentially assume. In this work, we are assuming as a workload the traffic profile consisting on the dissemination of events with a size of 27 KB, *i.e.*, 16 datagrams. Therefore $N$ cannot have a value lower than 16, which is the value of $K$. Moreover, $PLR$ and $ABL$ are known beforehand due to the monitoring activities that each node performs on the incoming links, so $P$ and $Q$ are constants in Eq. 4 and only N is the variable term. We can approximate the non-linear function in Eq. 4 by means of a second degree curve by using least-squares parabola [22]:

$$y = a + b \cdot x + c \cdot x^2. \tag{5}$$

where $x$ and $y$ represent, respectively, $N$ and $L$. The driving idea of the least-squares parabola is to minimize the distance between the function to approximate, *i.e.*, $c_v(N)$ in Eq. 4, and the approximation curve given by Eq. 5:

$$min \ \Pi = \sum_{i=0}^{R_{max}} [c_v(N_i) - (a + b \cdot N_i + c \cdot N_i^2)]^2 \tag{6}$$

where $N_i$ is equal to $K$ plus $i$ redundant packets originated by the root. Coefficient $a$, $b$ and $c$ are unknown, while $N_i$ and $c_v(N_i)$ are known, given $PLR$ and $ABL$. We have studied the accuracy of the approximation of Eq. 4 by means of a least-squares parabola by considering three different scenarios with proper values assigned to PLR and ABL: a first scenario with $PLR = 0.02$ and $ABL = 2$, a second scenario with $PLR = 0.05$ and $ABL = 2$, and a last, third, scenario with $PLR = 0.05$ and $ABL = 3$. In these cases, we obtained a mean error around 0.01. However, for high values of $N$, *i.e.*, greater than 36, we have that the approximation diverges from the curve of Eq. 4, and the approximation error overcomes the value of 0.01 with a growing quadratic trend. This leads to the consideration of limiting the use of the approximation to values of $N$ lower than 36, which means that the applicable redundancy should be lower than 20.

Given the approximation of $c_v(N)$ in Eq. 5, reduced as a function of only $R$ and not $N$ (so that it is simple to obtain the new coefficients $a'$, $b'$ and $c'$ from $a$, $b$, $c$ and $K$), we can write Eq. 3 as follows:

$$R - L \geq 0 \rightarrow R - (a' + b' \cdot R + c' \cdot R^2) \geq 0, \tag{7}$$

Resolving Eq. 7 allows us to compute the lower bound on $R$ so that losses can be tolerated within the multicast service. We consider only the first solution, which lies on the side of the parabola that intersects the curve of $c_v(N)$:

$$R \geq \frac{(b' - 1) + \sqrt{(1 - b')^2 - 4 \cdot a' \cdot c'}}{-2 \cdot c'}. \tag{8}$$

## 4   The Proposed Approach for Layered FEC

As above mentioned, Layered FEC consists in structuring the multicast communications within a given group in multiple layers. We assume that the layer

0 consists in the simple distribution of plain application data, while the other layers contain the redundant data obtained by encoding the application data. Each $i$-th layer is characterized by a given redundancy degree, indicated as $\rho_i$. At the beginning, when a node joins a multicast group, it is automatically registered to the layer 0; therefore, it receives no redundancy. In addition, it activates a proper daemon, called Monitor, that continuously monitors the flow of arriving messages so as to periodically determine the statics of the experienced loss pattern and the determine the behavior of the node. Specifically, two reconfiguration rules are applied by the Monitor to change the number of the registered FEC layers The first is the *Augmentation Rule*. At the expiration of a timer $\tau$, the Monitor returns the total number, namely $\nu$, of packets missing to complete the notifications published in the period $\tau$, when the node is registered to $\phi$ FEC layers (initially, $\phi$ is equal to 0). If such a number is greater than 0, then the node requires to join more additional $\phi'$ FEC layers, where $\sum_{i=\phi+1}^{\phi'} \rho_i \geq \nu$. The other one is the *Reduction Rule*. At the expiration of a timer $\tau$, the Monitor returns also an estimation of the experienced traffic waste, named as $\omega$. Specifically, if all the interested notifications have been delivered, the Monitor estimates how many packets with redundancy information related to such notifications have been discarded. This is a symptom that the node has joined a too high number of FEC layers, then it has to unregister to $\phi''$ FEC layers, where $\sum_{i=\phi''}^{\phi} \rho_i \geq \omega$. To realize this recovery strategy, we have adopted the tree construction approach from Scribe [23], a widely-known topic-based publish-subscribe service. We have extended such a tree construction and maintenance approach by allowing a node to register to different FEC layers after joining a multicast Tree, and to unregister from a certain number of FEC layers, if the reduction rule is verified. These modifications also imply a change in the way notifications are distributed in the multicast tree. Before the introduction of Layered FEC, when a node receives a notification, it would replicate and distribute it towards all of its children. With Layered FEC, the node will distinguish if the notification contains application data or encoded data. In the former case, it would follow the above mentioned behavior by passing the notification to all the children. In the latter case, the node will check the FEC layer associated to incoming notifications, and pass it only to the children in the list related to that layer. A key design choise for a Layered Multicast approach is the proper assignment of redundancy degree for each FEC layer. As pointed out in [24], using thinner FEC layers, *i.e.*, with $\rho_i$ for the $i$-th layer very small (*e.g.*, equal to 1 in the worst case), implies a fine-grain protection and an optimal calibration of the redundancy that each node could receive. However, this generally yields a remarkable overhead to manage the construction of several trees for the high number of layers present within the multicast solution. Therefore, the scheme used to assign a given redundancy degree to each FEC layer should realize a proper trade-off between the need of a fine-grain FEC calibration and a low number of layers that each node has to join. The possible scheme is the *Uniform Assignment*, where all the FEC layers share the same redundancy degree that is equal to the integer $\rho$, properly chosen by the system administrator within the set $\mathbb{Z}^+$ of the positive integer numbers.

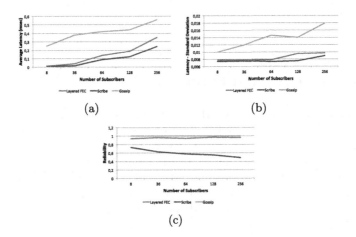

**Fig. 1.** Experiments results.

## 5   Experimental Evaluation

The scope of this section is to present a set of preliminary experimental results
to study the reliability and overhead (*i.e.*, the traffic generated by the approach
in terms of number of packets per link) of the proposed layered FEC. To achieve
this aim, we implemented our solution by using the OMNET++[1] simulator, and
decided to not use any real wide-area networks, such as PlanetLab, due to the
uncontrollable loss patterns that make the obtained results non reproducible [25].
The workload has been taken from the requirements of the SESAR project,
representative of a real critical large-scale system. Specifically, the exchanged
messages have a size of 23 KB, the publication rate is 1 message per second and
the total number of nodes is 256 (*i.e.*, the number of ATM entities involved in the
first phase of the SESAR project. The network behavior has 50 *ms* as link delay,
and 0.02 as PLR, based on a measurement campaign described in [25], with
message losses not independent. We have assumed that the coding and decoding
time are respectively equal to 5 *ms* and 10 *ms*. We have also considered the
block size equal to 1472 bytes, that is the size of MTU in Ethernet, so that a
single event is fragmented in 16 blocks. Finally, without loss of generality, we
considered a system with 1 publisher and 39 subscribers, all subscribed to the
same topic, *i.e.*, members of the same multicast tree. We have published 1000
events for each experiment, executed each experiment 3 times and reported the
average. We have compared our approach with the delivery quality achievable
with Scribe (with no reliability means) and with Scribe equipped with the Gossip
strategy. As it is possible to notice in Fig. 1(c), our approach and Gossip are able
to increase the reliability of the delivery protocol offered by Scribe, where Gossip
is more reliable due to its retransmission behavior. From the rest of Fig. 1(c),
we can notice that the higher reliability of the Gossip is obtained at the cost of

---

[1] www.omnetpp.org.

worse performances, as it has also been observed in [9], while our approach have performances comparable to the one of Scribe with no reliability.

# 6    Final Remarks and Future Work

In this paper, we have approached the issues limiting the applicability of coding-based approached to overlay reliable event-based multicasting. Our solutions consists in the application of Layered FEC so as to efficiently tune and manage the requited redundancy and cope with the failures affecting the event dissemination over large-scale networks. Our future work is to investigate on different assignment schemes (such as the one emulating the rate allocation in TCP and the one based on the well-known Fibonacci series), and how to combine our proposed Layered FEC with an ARQ scheme so as to achieve a better tuning of FEC and an increased reliability degree.

**Acknowledgment.** This work has been partially supported by the Italian Ministry of Research within PRIN project "GenData 2020" (2010RTFWBH).

# References

1. Eugster, P., Felber, P., Guerraoui, R., Kermarrec, A.-M.: The many faces of publish/subscribe. ACM Comput. Surv. **35**(2), 114–131 (2003)
2. Esposito, C., Cotroneo, D., Russo, S.: On reliability in publish/subscribe services. Comput. Netw. **57**(5), 1318–1343 (2013)
3. Rizzo, L.: Effective erasure codes for reliable computer communication protocols. ACM SIGCOMM Comput. Commun. Rev. **27**(2), 24–36 (1997)
4. Birrer, S., Bustamante, F.: A comparison of resilient overlay multicast approaches. IEEE J. Sel. Areas Commun. (JSAC) **25**(9), 1695–1705 (2007)
5. Han, J., Watson, D., Jahanian, F.: An experimental study of internet path diversity. IEEE Trans. Dependable Secure Comput. (TDSC) **3**(4), 273–288 (2006)
6. McCanne, S., Jacobson, V.: Receiver-driven layered multicast. ACM SIGCOMM Comput. Commun. Rev. **16**(4), 117–130 (1996)
7. Lin, S., Costello, D., Miller, M.: Automatic-repeat-request error-control schemes. IEEE Commun. Mag. **22**(12), 5–17 (1984)
8. Eugster, P.T., Guerraoui, R., Kermarrec, A.-M., Massoulié, L.: Epidemic information dissemination in distributed systems. IEEE Comput. **37**(5), 60–67 (2004)
9. Esposito, C., Platania, M., Beraldi, R.: Reliable and timely event notification for publish/subscribe services over the internet. IEEE/ACM Trans. Netw. **22**(1), 230–243 (2014)
10. Ghaderi, M., Towsley, D., Kurose, J.: Reliability gain of network coding in lossy wireless networks. In: Proceedings of the 27th Conference on Computer Communications (INFOCOM 08), pp. 2171–2179, April 2008
11. Lee, Y.-J., Atiquzzaman, M.: Optimal multicast loop algorithm for multimedia traffic distribution. In: Yang, L.T., Amamiya, M., Liu, Z., Guo, M., Rammig, F.J. (eds.) EUC 2005. LNCS, vol. 3824, pp. 1099–1106. Springer, Heidelberg (2005)

12. Chou, P., Mohr, A., Wang, A., Mehrotra, S.: FEC and pseudo-ARQ for receiver-driven layered multicast of audio and video. In: Proceedings of Data Compression Conference (DCC), pp. 440–449, March 2000

13. Bradai, A., Ahmed, T., Boutaba, R., Ahmed, R.: Efficient content delivery scheme for layered video streaming in large-scale networks. J. Netw. Comput. Appl. **45**, 1–14 (2014)

14. Diot, C., Levine, B., Lyles, B., Kassan, H., Balendiefen, D.: Deployment numbers for the IP multicast services and architecture. IEEE Netw. Spec. Number Multicasting **14**(1), 78–88 (2000)

15. Fragouli, C., Markopoulou, A.: A network coding approach to overlay network monitoring. In: Proceedings of the 43rd Allerton Conference on Communication, Control, and Computing, September 2005

16. Gilbert, E.: Capacity of a burst-noise channel. Bell Syst. Tech. J. **39**, 1253–1265 (1960)

17. Elliott, E.: Estimates of error rates for codes on burst-noise channels. Bell System Tech. J. **42**, 1977–1997 (1963)

18. Konrad, A., Zhao, B., Joseph, A.: Determining model accuracy of network traces. J. Comput. Syst. Sci. **72**(7), 1156–1171 (2006)

19. Hasslinger, G., Hohlfeld, O.: The Gilbert-Elliott model for packet loss in real time services in the internet. In: Proceedings of the 14th GI/ITG Conference on Measuring, Modelling and Evaluation of Computer and Communication Systems, pp. 1–15 (2008)

20. Ho, T., Medard, M., Koetter, R., Karger, D., Effros, M., Shi, J., Leong, B.: A random linear network coding approach to multicast. IEEE Trans. Inf. Theory **52**(10), 4413–4430 (2006)

21. Fragouli, C., Boudec, J.L., Widmer, J.: Network coding: an instant primer. ACM SIGCOMM Comput. Commun. Rev. **36**, 63–68 (2006)

22. Ahn, S., Rauh, W., Warnecke, H.-J.: Least-squares orthogonal distances fitting of circle, sphere, ellipse, hyperbola, and parabola. Pattern Recogn. **34**(12), 2283–2303 (2001)

23. Castro, M., Drushel, P., Kermarec, A., Rowstrom, A.: Scribe: a large-scale and decentralized application-level multicast infrastructure. IEEE J. Sel. Areas Commun. (JSAC) **20**(8), 1489–1499 (2004)

24. Tan, W.-T., Zakhor, A.: Video multicast using layered FEC and scalable compression. IEEE Trans. Circuits Syst. Video Technol. **11**(4), 373–386 (2001)

25. Esposito, C.: Data Distribution Service (DDS) Limitations for Data Dissemination w.r.t. Large-scale Complex Critical Infrastructures (LCCI), Mobilab Technical report, March 2011. (www.mobilab.unina.it)

# Scalable Network Intrusion Detection and Countermeasure Selection in Virtual Network Systems

Jin B. Hong[1]([✉]), Chun-Jen Chung[2], Dijiang Huang[2], and Dong Seong Kim[1]

[1] Department of Computer Science and Software Engineering,
University of Canterbury, Christchurch, New Zealand
jin.hong@pg.canterbury.ac.nz, dongseong.kim@canterbury.ac.nz
[2] Department of Computer Science, Arizona State University, Arizona, USA
{chun-jen.chung,dijiang}@asu.edu

**Abstract.** Security of virtual network systems, such as Cloud computing systems, is important to users and administrators. One of the major issues with Cloud security is detecting intrusions to provide time-efficient and cost-effective countermeasures. Cyber-attacks involve series of exploiting vulnerabilities in virtual machines, which could potentially cause a loss of credentials and disrupt services (e.g., privilege escalation attacks). Intrusion detection and countermeasure selection mechanisms are proposed to address the aforementioned issues, but existing solutions with traditional security models (e.g., Attack Graphs (AG)) do not scale well with a large number of hosts in the Cloud systems. Consequently, the model cannot provide a security solution in practical time. To address this problem, we incorporate a scalable security model named Hierarchical Attack Representation Model (HARM) in place of the AG to improve the scalability. By doing so, we can provide a security solution within a reasonable timeframe to mitigate cyber attacks. Further, we show the equivalent security analysis using the HARM and the AG, as well as to demonstrate how to transform the existing AG to the HARM.

**Keywords:** Attack graphs · Countermeasure selection · Intrusion detection · Network security · Scalability

## 1 Introduction

Adopting virtual network systems, such as the Cloud systems (i.e., Cloud), provides better service and resource utilizations for users, while the cost of operations for service providers is also reduced [9]. However, security is one of the major concerns for users to migrate to the Cloud [16]. Since virtual machines (VMs) can be controlled by the Cloud users rather than the network administrator (e.g., an Infrastructure-as-a-Service (IaaS) Cloud), addressing vulnerabilities of the Cloud system may not be feasible and also a possible violation of the *service-level agreement* (SLA). To address this problem, one approach is to prevent VMs

© Springer International Publishing Switzerland 2015
G. Wang et al. (Eds.): ICA3PP 2015 Workshops, LNCS 9532, pp. 582–592, 2015.
DOI: 10.1007/978-3-319-27161-3_53

being compromised and reused for cyber-attacks, by means of improving the intrusion detection (ID) [5,10,13,14,18–20,24]. Here, the ID identifies invalid access in the network (e.g., privilege escalation attacks). However, solely depending on the ID cannot provide a comprehensive security overview of the Cloud, as it is difficult to assess the potential attack scenarios of a cyber-attack.

To improve the security assessment and countermeasure selection based on the ID for the Cloud system, security models are incorporated into the framework [2,15,22]. For example, Chung et al. [2] incorporated an Attack Graph (AG) [17] in a defense-in-depth intrusion detection framework named *NICE*, which formulates effective countermeasures based on the security analysis of the AG when cyber-attacks are detected. The AG is a graphical security model that is capable of computing all possible attack scenarios and evaluate the security postures associated with them, which are used by security experts to enhance security. However, traditional security models, such as the AG, do not scale well when the size of the networked system becomes large [3,7]. On the other hand, Wang et al. [22] incorporated an Attack-Defense Tree (ADT) [6] to assess both attack and defense aspects of Cloud security. Tree-based security models such as ADTs can be generated automatically such as in [21], but the capability to adapt to dynamic changes of the Cloud in those security models are not well defined.

In this paper, we focus on improving the NICE framework by incorporating a scalable security model, namely the Hierarchical Attack Representation Models (HARMs) [4]. The HARM provides better scalability than the AG in various network environments [3], as well as an ability to adjust to changes when there are updates in the Cloud system [4]. First, we incorporate the HARMs into the NICE framework, and we demonstrate the computation of equivalent security metric values using the same methods described in the NICE framework (e.g., probability of an attack success [2]). Second, we describe how to transform an AG in the form of the HARMs. Third, we conduct security analysis of the Cloud with additional security metrics (e.g., probability, impact, risk, and Return-on-Investment). The contributions of this paper are as follows:

- Incorporate the HARMs into the NICE framework, and demonstrate an equivalent security analysis using the HARMs and the existing AG;
- Transform AG into HARM and HARM to AG;
- Conduct security analysis by utilizing various security metrics.

The rest of the paper is as organized as follows. The HARM is defined and incorporated into the Cloud security framework in Sect. 2. The security analysis with various security metrics is shown in Sect. 3, and we conclude our paper in Sect. 4.

## 2    A Scalable Security Model and a Cloud Security Framework

### 2.1    Cloud Security Framework

The abstract view of the NICE framework consists of three components; (i) the Cloud domain (CD), (ii) the attack analyzer (AA), and (iii) the network controller (NC) as shown in Fig. 1. The NICE-A (Network-based Intrusion Detection

584     J.B. Hong et al.

**Table 1.** Vulnerabilities in the example Cloud

| Host | Vulnerability | CVE ID | Base Score |
|------|---------------|--------|------------|
| VM hosts | LICQ BoF | CVE-2001-0439 | 0.75 |
| | ActiveX Stack BoF | CVE-2008-0015 | 0.93 |
| | GNU C Library loader flaw | CVE-2010-3847 | 0.69 |
| Admin Server | MS SMB service Stack BoF | CVE-2008-4050 | 0.93 |
| Gateway Server | OpenSSL predictable random var | CVE-2008-0166 | 0.78 |
| | Heap corruption in OpenSSH | CVE-2003-0693 | 1.00 |
| | Improper Cookie Handler OpenSSH | CVE-2007-4752 | 0.75 |
| Mail Server | Remote code in SMTP | CVE-2004-0840 | 1.00 |
| | Squid port scan | CVE-2001-1030 | 0.75 |
| Web Server | WebDAV vulnerability in IIS | CVE-2009-1535 | 0.76 |

System agent) and the VM Profiling components are merged as both of their tasks are operated in the CD. Each of the NICE framework component contains procedures (e.g., *IDS, Alert analyzer*) and modules (e.g., *Security Model, VMs Profile*), where procedures are depicted as boxes and modules as disks. The CD provides the AA with the events in the Cloud via the *IDS* and the *VM Profile*. The AA processes the information from the CD to generate a security model, which is then analyzed to formulate countermeasures. The NC deploys the countermeasure in the CD via the *Network Controller* and the *VM State Updater*.

The vulnerability information in the example virtualized system is shown in Table 1. The Base Score (BS) from the National Vulnerability Database (NVD) [11] will be used as the probability of vulnerability exploitation as described in [2]. Previously, the NICE framework incorporated an AG using the tool MulVAL [12], but there are limitations such as scalability and adaptability [3]. To cope with the dynamic nature and scalability of the Cloud, a HARM is used instead, where it is formally defined in [4].

## 2.2 Equivalent Security Analysis with an AG and a HARM

This section demonstrates the equivalence of the security analysis between the HARM and the AG. First, an example Cloud is used as shown in Fig. 2. The security information is gathered by the node controller (e.g., Xenserver [23]), network controller (e.g., OpenFlow [8]), and vulnerability scanners (e.g., NESSUS [1]) and databases (e.g., NVD [11]). Figures 3 and 4 show the AG and the HARM of the example Cloud respectively. Although the same information is stored, the structural properties are largely different (e.g., the number of edges, nodes, density etc.).

Using the vulnerability information from Table 1, we can compute the probabilities of attack success as follows:

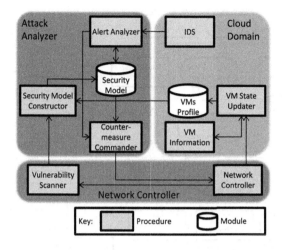

**Fig. 1.** An overview of the Cloud security framework

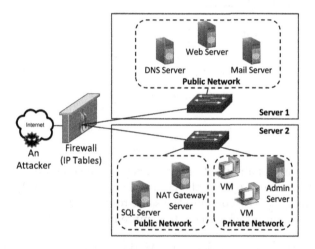

**Fig. 2.** An example Cloud

– The probability of attack success for any attack-step node $n$ in the AG with immediate predecessors set $W = parent(n)$,

$$Pr_{n|W} = 1 - \sum_{s \in W} (1 - Pr(s \mid W)) \tag{1}$$

For example, the probability of an attack success of compromising the guest privilege of the Admin Server is 0.525 as shown in Equation (2).

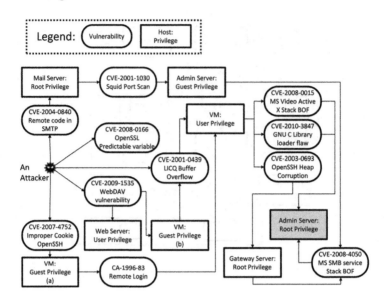

**Fig. 3.** The AG of the example Cloud

$$Pr_{Admin\_guest\_privilege} = 1 - \sum_{s \in W} Pr(s \mid W)$$
$$= 1 - (1 - 0.75 \times 0.7)$$
$$= 0.525$$
(2)

The condition probability of an attack success to compromise the root privilege of the Admin Server using the above calculation with an AG is 0.9366 [2]. Using the HARM, we can compute the same result as the following (in terms of the probability of an attack success to compromise):

1. gaining (a) the guest privilege of VM through OpenSSH improper cookie vulnerability in the NAT Gateway Server and then (b) the user privilege of the VM by remote login has the $Pr = 0.42$.
2. gaining (a) the guest privilege of VM through WebDAV vulnerability in the Web Server and then (b) the user privilege of the VM through by LICQ remote to user has the $Pr = 0.399$.
3. gaining the user privilege of the VM by LICQ buffer overflow has the $Pr = 0.525$.
4. Steps 1 to 3 result in gaining the user privilege of the VM with the $Pr = 0.8347$ (Step 1 or Step 2 or Step 3).
5. gaining the root privilege of the Gateway Server by OpenSSH heap corruption has the $Pr = 0.834$.
6. gaining the guest privilege of the Admin Server by the squid scan has the $Pr = 0.525$.

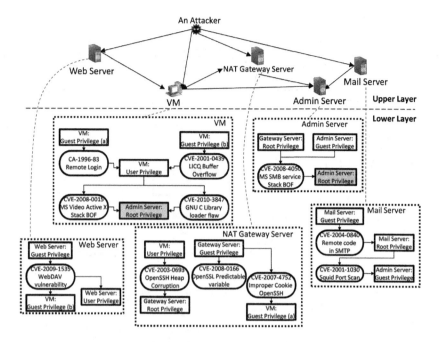

**Fig. 4.** The HARM of the example Cloud

7. with guest privilege of the Admin Server and the root privilege of the Gateway Server, gaining the root privilege of the Admin Server by MS SMB BoF has the $Pr = 0.333$.
8. gaining the root privilege of the Admin Server via ActiveX Stack BoF has the $Pr = 0.776$ and through GNU C library loader flaw has the $Pr = 576$.
9. combining the probability of gaining the root privilege of the Admin Server is 0.9366 (i.e., $1 - (1 - 0.766 \times 0.576 \times 0.333)$).

### 2.3   Transforming an AG to a HARM

The AG can be transformed into the HARM, as the structure of the HARM consists of those AG components in multiple layers. Steps are as follows:

1. The vulnerability information can be grouped based on the vulnerability scan results, as we already know which vulnerabilities belong to different hosts.
2. The upper layer HARM nodes (i.e., the hosts) are created and each vulnerability group is assigned to the belonging hosts.
3. based on the vulnerability connections in the AG, the upper layer HARM nodes establish connections between them.
4. separated vulnerability information is now only associated with its belonging host information in the upper layer.

For example, three vulnerabilities belongs to the NAT gateway server (i.e., CVE-2003-0693, CVE-2007-4752 and CVE-2008-0166). The CVE-2008-0166 and

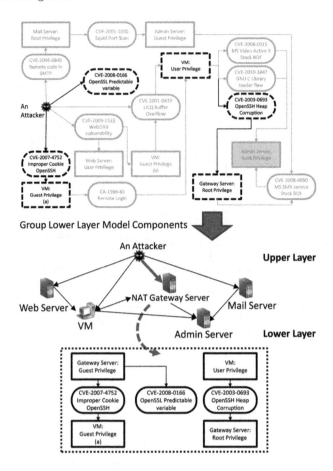

**Fig. 5.** Transforming an AG to a HARM

CVE-2007-4752 only require the guest privilege, whereCVE-2003-0693 requires the VM user privilege. Therefore, those vulnerabilities requiring different privileges can be separated but still under the same host (i.e., multiple entry and exit points in the lower layer model). Once, all lower layer vulnerability information is grouped, then the upper layer host can be connected based on the privilege requirements (e.g., Gateway root privilege is required to exploit vulnerability in the Admin Server, and the VM guest privilege is acquired exploiting the CVE-2007-4752, so the NAT gateway node connects to the VM and Admin Server nodes in the upper layer). These steps are shown in Fig. 5.

## 3    Security Analysis Using Various Security Metrics

In this section, we demonstrate the analysis process of the HARM with various security metrics. Similarly with the conditional probability calculation described

```
 1: procedure OPTIMAL_COUNTERMEASURE_SELECTION(HARM)
 2:    Let V be all HARM lower layer components
 3:    Let CM be all countermeasures
 4:    HARM.compute_probability
 5:    Let benefit[|V|, |CM|] = 0
 6:    Let ROI[|V|, |CM|] = 0
 7:    for all v ∈ V do
 8:       for all cm ∈ CM do
 9:          Pr_v = Pr_v × (1 − cm.effectiveness)
10:          HARM.compute_probability
11:          benefit[v, cm] = ΔPr(target_node)
12:          ROI[v, cm] = benefit[v,cm] / (cm.cost+cm.intrusiveness)
13:       end for
14:    end for
15:    return max(ROI[v, cm])
16: end procedure
```

**Fig. 6.** Pseudo code of LRAwFPC

**Table 2.** ROI of countermeasures applied in the example Cloud

|     | CVE-2008-4050 | CVE-2003-0693 | CVE-2008-0015 | CVE-2010-3847 |
|-----|---------------|---------------|---------------|---------------|
| CM1 | NA            | NA            | 5.03          | 1.97          |
| CM2 | 0.28          | 0.28          | 9.5           | 3.72          |
| CM3 | 0.15          | NA            | 8.94          | 3.5           |
| CM4 | 0.09          | 0.09          | 3.91          | 1.53          |

in Sect. 2.2, the cumulative probability of an attack success can be calculated using the Equation (3).

$$Pr_n = 1 - \sum_{s \in W} (1 - Pr(s)) \tag{3}$$

The benefit and return on investment (ROI) are calculated on the basis of four commonly used virtual networking based countermeasures; (a) CM1: Traffic isolation (intrusiveness: 4, cost: 2, effectiveness: 0.90), (b) CM2: Create filtering rules (intrusiveness: 1, cost: 2, effectiveness: 0.85), (c) CM3: MAC address change (intrusiveness: 2, cost: 1, effectiveness: 0.80), and (d) CM4: Network Reconfiguration (intrusiveness: 1, cost: 5, effectiveness: 0.70). The values of those countermeasures are randomly assigned to demonstrate the computations of the benefit and ROI. When a countermeasure is applied, the change in probability of an attack success measures the benefit of the countermeasure. In addition, the ROI measures the ratio between the benefit with cost and intrusiveness of the countermeasure. On the basis of ROI, the optimal countermeasure can be selected with the algorithm shown in Fig. 6 using the HARM.

For example, we assume that the attacker has gained the VM user privilege (i.e., the probability of attack success to compromise the VM user privilege equals to one). Then the model computes the possible attack paths from the given information. The attacker can exploit (i) CVE-2008-0015, or (ii) CVE-2010-3847, or (iii) compromise NAT gateway root privilege (CVE-2003-0693), admin server guest privilege via the mail server (CVE-2004-0840 and CVE-2001-1030) to exploit CVE-2008-4050 to compromise the admin server root privilege. At the current state without any countermeasures applied, the probability of an attack success to compromise the root privilege of the admin server is 0.912 (calculations omitted due to space limitations).

If we apply MAC address change to the admin server (i.e., CM3), then the probability of an attack success at the HARM lower layer node CVE-2008-4050 reduces from 0.071 to 0.014 (i.e., the original probability × (1 - the effectiveness of MAC address change) = 0.071 * (1-0.8) = 0.014). Then, final probability of an attack success becomes 0.906 as shown in Equation (4) (i.e., taking into account two other attack paths through exploiting CVE-2008-0015 or CVE-2010-3847). Hence, the benefit of applying the MAC address change to the admin server is 0.596 % (i.e., the change in probability), and the ROI is 0.1986. Table 2 shows the ROI of other example countermeasures applied. The optimal solution in the example is to apply CM2 on the VM host to mitigate attacks exploiting CVE-2008-0015 vulnerability.

$$
\begin{aligned}
Pr_{CM3} &= 1 - ((1 - Pr_{CVE-2008-4050}) \times (1 - Pr_{CVE-2008-0015}) \times \\
&\quad (1 - Pr_{CVE-2010-3847})) \\
&= 1 - ((1 - 0.014) \times (1 - 0.776) \times (1 - 0.576)) \\
&= 0.906
\end{aligned}
\tag{4}
$$

## 4   Conclusion

Various security frameworks are proposed to strengthen the security of the virtual network systems such as the Cloud. One of the major challenges of the Cloud security framework is to provide time-efficient and cost-effective countermeasures to mitigate cyber attacks, and previous work incorporated security models to address this problem. However, traditional security models do not scale for a large number of hosts in the Cloud, as well as not capable of dynamically adjusting to changes.

To address these problems, we incorporated a scalable security model named the HARM in the *NICE* Cloud security framework. First, we demonstrated the equivalent security analysis to an AG and second, we described methods to transform the existing AGs into the HARM. Lastly, we showed security analysis using various security metrics. In conclusion, this work provides a step closer towards scalable network intrusion detection and countermeasure selection in the virtual network systems.

**Acknowledgments.** This research was sponsored by NSF grant #1528099, and also supported by the NATO Science for Peace & Security Multi-Year Project (MD.SFPP 984425).

# References

1. Beale, J., Deraison, R., Meer, H., Temmingh, R., Walt, C.: The NESSUS Project. Syngress Publishing (2002). http://www.nessus.org
2. Chung, C., Khatkar, P., Xing, T., Lee, J., Huang, D.: NICE: network intrusion detection and countermeasure selection in virtual network systems. IEEE Trans. Dependable Secure Comput. **10**(4), 198–211 (2013)
3. Hong, J.B., Kim, D.S.: Performance analysis of scalable attack representation models. In: Janczewski, L.J., Wolfe, H.B., Shenoi, S. (eds.) SEC 2013. IFIP AICT, vol. 405, pp. 330–343. Springer, Heidelberg (2013)
4. Hong, J., Kim, D.: Scalable security models for assessing effectiveness of moving target defenses. In: Proceedings of the 44th Annual IEEE/IFIP International Conference on Dependable Systems and Networks (DSN 2014), pp. 515–526, June 2014
5. Khan, A., Kiah, M.M., Khan, S., Madani, S.: Towards secure mobile cloud computing: a survey. J. Future Gener. Comput. Syst. **29**(5), 1278–1299 (2013)
6. Kordy, B., Mauw, S., Radomirović, S., Schweitzer, P.: Foundations of attack–defense trees. In: Degano, P., Etalle, S., Guttman, J. (eds.) FAST 2010. LNCS, vol. 6561, pp. 80–95. Springer, Heidelberg (2011)
7. Lippmann, R., Ingols, K.: An Annotated Review of Past Papers on Attack Graphs. ESC-TR-2005-054 (2005)
8. McKeown, N., Anderson, T., Balakrishnan, H., Parulkar, G., Peterson, L., Rexford, J., Shenker, S., Turner, J.: OpenFlow: enabling innovation in campus networks. SIGCOMM Comput. Commun. Rev. **38**(2), 69–74 (2008)
9. Mell, P., Grance, T.: SP 800–145. The NIST Definition of Cloud Computing. Technical report, NIST, Gaithersburg, MD, United States (2011)
10. Modi, C., Patel, D., Borisaniya, B., Patel, H., Patel, A., Rajarajan, M.: A survey of intrusion detection techniques in Cloud. Netw. Comput. Appl. **36**(1), 42–57 (2013)
11. National Institute of Standards and Technology: National Vulnerability Database. https://nvd.nist.gov/
12. Ou, X., Govindavajhala, S.: MulVAL: a logic-based network security analyzer. In: Proceedings of the 14th USENIX Security Symposium (USENIX Security 2005), pp. 113–128 (2005)
13. Patel, A., Taghavi, M., Bakhtiyari, K., JúNior, J.C.: An intrusion detection and prevention system in cloud computing: a systematic review. J. Netw. Comput. Appl. **36**(1), 25–41 (2013)
14. Pham, C., Estrada, Z., Cao, P., Kalbarczyk, Z., Iyer, R.: Reliability and security monitoring of virtual machines using hardware architectural invariants. In: Proceedings of IEEE/IFIP International Conference on Dependable Systems and Networks (DSN 2014), pp. 13–24 (2014)
15. Poolsappasit, N., Kumar, V., Madria, S., Chellappan, S.: Challenges in secure sensor-cloud computing. In: Jonker, W., Petković, M. (eds.) SDM 2011. LNCS, vol. 6933, pp. 70–84. Springer, Heidelberg (2011)
16. Popovic, K., Hocenski, Z.: Cloud computing security issues and challenges. In: Proceedings of the 33rd International Convention on Information and Communication Technology, Electonics and Microelectronic (MIPRO 2010), pp. 344–349, May 2010

17. Sheyner, O., Haines, J., Jha, S., Lippmann, R., Wing, J.: Automated Generation and Analysis of Attack Graphs. Technical report, CMU (2002)
18. Subashini, S., Kavitha, V.: A survey on security issues in service delivery models of cloud computing. J. Netw. Comput. Appl. **34**(1), 1–11 (2011)
19. Vaquero, L., Rodero-Merino, L., Moran, D.: Locking the sky: a survey on IaaS cloud security. J. Comput. **91**(1), 93–118 (2011)
20. Vieira, K., Schulter, A., Westphall, C., Westphall, C.: Intrusion detection for grid and cloud computing. IT Prof. **12**(4), 38–43 (2010)
21. Vigo, R., Nielson, F., Nielson, H.: Automated Generation of Attack Trees. In: Proceedings of IEEE Computer Security Foundations Symposium (CSF 2014), pp. 337–350, July 2014
22. Wang, P., Lin, W., Kuo, P., Lin, H., Wang, T.: Threat risk analysis for cloud security based on attack-defense trees. In: Proceedings of the 8th International Conference on Computing Technology and Information Management (ICCM 2012), vol. 1, pp. 106–111, April 2012
23. Williams, D., Harland, J.: Virtualization with Xen(tm): Including XenEnterprise, XenServer, and XenExpress, 1st edn. Syngress Publishing, Rockland (2007)
24. Zhu, Y., Hu, H., Ahn, G., Huang, D., Wang, S.: Towards temporal access control in cloud computing. In: Proceedings of Annual IEEE International Conference on Computer Communications (INFOCOM 2012), pp. 2576–2580 (2012)

# Removing Key Escrow
# from the LW-HIBE Scheme

Peixin Chen[1]([✉]), Xiaofeng Wang[1], Baokang Zhao[1],
Jinshu Su[1,2], and Ilsun You[3]

[1] College of Computer, National University of Defense Technology,
410073 Changsha, China
{chenpeixin,xf_wang,bkzhao,sjs}@nudt.edu.cn
[2] National Key Laboratory for Parallel and Distributed Processing, National
University of Defense Technology, 410073 Changsha, China
[3] School of Information Science, Korean Bible University, Nowon District, Korea
isyou@bible.ac.kr

**Abstract.** Hierarchical Identity-Based Encryption (HIBE) provides an
efficient solution to the security problems existed in cloud storage. However, the key escrow problem, which is an inherent problem in HIBE,
primarily hinders the widespread adoption of the cryptographic scheme
in practice. To address the key escrow problem, this paper introduces
a provably-secure escrow-free model, which employs multiple Key Privacy Authorities (KPAs) to restrict the power of Public Key Generators
(PKGs) in HIBE scheme. We instantiate the model into an escrow-free
HIBE scheme that is referred to as the EF-LW-HIBE scheme, based
on the HIBE scheme introduced by Lewko and Waters. Utilizing the
Dual System Encryption methodology, we prove that our EF-LW-HIBE
scheme is IND-ID-CCA secure.

**Keywords:** Hierarchical identity-based encryption · Key escrow ·
IND-ID-CCA Security · Dual system encryption · Cloud storage

## 1 Introduction

Cloud storage is becoming increasingly popular with the rapidly network technology development. It does provide convenient and offer more flexibility to people
that one can access the data on cloud storage system via the Internet instead
of carrying around a physical storage. However, cloud storage has the potential
for security and compliance concerns. Many works on securing the cloud storage
have been presented [9,11,12,17,19]

Identity-Based Encryption (IBE) can be easily apply to the cloud storage.
IBE is a public key encryption scheme which allows a sender to encrypt message
for a receiver using the receiver's identity, such as IP address or email address,
as the public key [16]. Boneh and Franklin first formulate the concept of IBE
and propose a full functional scheme (BF-IBE) based on bilinear maps between

© Springer International Publishing Switzerland 2015
G. Wang et al. (Eds.): ICA3PP 2015 Workshops, LNCS 9532, pp. 593–605, 2015.
DOI: 10.1007/978-3-319-27161-3_54

groups [4]. The IBE scheme uses a trusted authority called Private Key Generator (PKG) to generate private key for users. In order to reduce the workload of the PKG, Gentry and Silverberg present the first construction of Hierarchical IBE (HIBE) with a root PKG and several domain PKGs in different levels [10]. To improve the efficient and security, a number HIBE schemes [1–3,7,15,18] have been presented.

Since the user private keys are generated by the PKGs, the construction of HIBE will inevitably lead to the key escrow problem. That is, the PKG knows all the private keys of its descendant and thus can unscrupulously decrypt the message intended for the users and maliciously make users' private keys public. Many prior works have been proposed to solve the problem [4,6,8,13,14]. One intuitional approach is to use distributed PKGs to reduce the power of single PKG. In the first IBE scheme, Bonech et al. apply the threshold method to suggest an $(n,t)$ distributed PKG mechanism [4]. They distribute the master key into $n$ parts that each PKG owns only one portion, and any more than $t+1$ PKGs can jointly compute a private key. However, they do not provide a formal security model and a proof. Kate and Goldberg present an efficient distributed PKGs model and construct the schemes for three well-known IBE schemes: BF-IBE, SK-IBE and $BB_1$-IBE [13]. However, the model cannot apply to the HIBE scheme and the presented schemes can only achieve security in the random oracle model. Other than the multiple PKGs mechanisms, Lee et al. present a key issuing model which introduced Key Privacy Authorities (KPAs) to protect the user private key privacy so that the PKG cannot obtain the complete information of the keys [14]. The idea of the multiple-KPAs model is inspired by the real word scenario such as elections, in which there is a single election administrator organizing the election procedures and multiple observers dispatched by major political parties to the voting office to prevent any illegal activity. Key escrow problem can be effectively reduced based on the assumption that at least one of the KPAs is honest. However, the key privacy service in their model needs to be sequential processed. Therefore, the multiple-KPAs model would introduce too high overhead to the basic HIBE scheme to make it practical. Moreover, the security of this key issuing mechanism has not been proved by formal approach. Because of the possibility of theoretically insecurity, this mechanism cannot be applied in practice. Cao et al. also use KPAs to achieve an escrow-free HIBE scheme (SA-HIBE) [6]. SA-HIBE avoids the inefficient sequential procedure in [14] and allows users to interact with KPAs synchronously. However, the scheme efficiency is still low because of the ciphertext and private keys, as well as the encryption and decryption time in SA-HIBE grow linearly in the depth of the hierarchy. And the scheme security is also proved in the random oracle model.

In this paper, we propose an efficient and provably-secure EF-LW-HIBE scheme, which is an escrow-free HIBE scheme based on the LW-HIBE. The EF-LW-HIBE scheme makes use of multiple KPAs to restrict the power of PKGs in HIBE so that the PKGs cannot obtain the full information of the private keys. On account of the synchronous key securing procedure with KPAs, our escrow-free model introduces acceptable cost to LW-HIBE. With the help of Dual System Encryption, we prove the full security of EF-LW-HIBE without random oracle model.

## 2   Preliminaries

### 2.1   Composite Order Bilinear Groups

Composite order bilinear groups were first introduced by Boneh et al. [5]. Let $p_1, p_2, p_3$ be distinct primes, and set $N = p_1 p_2 p_3$. For two multiplicative cyclic groups $G$ and $G_T$ of order $N$, we say a map $e : G \times G \to G_T$ is a bilinear map if it meets the following properties:

1. Bilinear: $\forall g, h \in G, a, b \in \mathbb{Z}_N, e(g^a, h^b) = e(g, h)^{ab}$
2. Non-degenerate: $\exists g \in G$, s.t. $e(g, g) \neq 1$
3. Computable: $\forall g, h \in G$, there is an efficient algorithm to compute $e(g, h)$.

Group $G$ is referred to as a composite order bilinear group. Let $G_{p_1}$, $G_{p_2}$, and $G_{p_3}$ denote the subgroups of order $p_1$, $p_2$ and $p_3$ in $G$ respectively. Lewko and Waters have illuminated that, when $h_i \in G_i$, and $h_j \in G_j$ for $i \neq j$, $e(h_i, h_j)$ is an identity element in $G_T$ [15]. Such property is referred to as *orthogonality property* of $G_{p_1}, G_{p_2}, G_{p_3}$.

### 2.2   Complexity Assumptions

We prove the security of EF-LW-HIBE scheme based on the same complexity assumptions as the LW-HIBE scheme [15] does. Let $G_{p_i p_j}$ denote subgroup of order $p_i p_j$ in $G$, the assumptions are defined as follows.

**Assumption 1.** Let $g, T_2$ be distinct random elements of $G_{p_1}$, $X_3$ be a random element of $G_{p_3}$ and $T_1$ be a random element of $G_{p_1 p_2}$. Randomly picking $T \in \{T_1, T_2\}$, we assume that given $g, X_3$, there is no probabilistic polynomial time $(PPT)$ algorithm $\mathcal{A}$ can determine $T \in G_{p_1 p_2}$ or $T \in G_{p_1}$ with negligible advantage.

**Assumption 2.** Let $g, X_1$ be distinct random elements of $G_{p_1}$, $X_2, Y_2$ be distinct random elements of $G_{p_2}$, $X_3, Y_3$ be distinct random elements of $G_{p_3}$, $T_1$ be a random element of $G$, and $T_2$ be a random element of $G_{p_1 p_3}$. Randomly picking $T \in \{T_1, T_2\}$, we assume that given $g, X_1 X_2, X_3, Y_2 Y_3$, there is no $PPT$ algorithm $\mathcal{A}$ can determine $T \in G$ or $T \in G_{p_1 p_3}$ with negligible advantage.

**Assumption 3.** Randomly pick $\alpha, s \in \mathbb{Z}_N$. Let $g$ be a random element of $G_{p_1}$, $X_2, Y_2, Z_2$ be distinct random elements of $G_{p_2}$, $X_3$ be a random element of $G_{p_3}$. Set $T_1 = e(g, g)^{\alpha s}$ and let $T_2$ be a random element of $G_T$. Randomly picking $T \in \{T_1, T_2\}$, we assume that given $g, g^\alpha X_2, X_3, g^s Y_2, Z_2$, there is no $PPT$ algorithm $\mathcal{A}$ can determine $T = e(g, g)^{\alpha s}$ or $T$ is a random element of $G_T$ with negligible advantage.

## 2.3  Dual System Encryption

Dual System Encryption is a scheme that is used for proving security of encryption schemes [18]. For proving, two additional structures called semi-functional key and semi-functional ciphertext are used. A semi-functional key is an efficient mathematical transformation of a normal key, and so as a semi-functional ciphertext. Suppose $CT_{normal}$ is a ciphertext with regard to normal key $K_{normal}$. Let $K_{semi}$ be a semi-functional key w.r.t. $K_{normal}$, and let $CT_{semi}$ be a semi-functional ciphertext w.r.t. $CT_{normal}$. The abilities of decryption between the key-ciphertext pairs are listed as in Table 1.

**Table 1.** Decryption ability between different types of keys and ciphertexts. $\sqrt{}$ means that a key $K_X$ with type $X$ is able to decrypt a ciphertext $CT_Y$ with type $Y$, $\times$ means that a key $K_X$ with type $X$ fail to decrypt a ciphertext $CT_Y$ with type $Y$.

| ciphertext \ key | $K_{normal}$ | $K_{semi}$ |
|---|---|---|
| $CT_{normal}$ | $\sqrt{}$ | $\sqrt{}$ |
| $CT_{semi}$ | $\sqrt{}$ | $\times$ |

In the formal security proof, an attack game with an attacker and a challenger is used for an encryption scheme. The encryption scheme is regarded as secure if the attacker cannot win the game with a non-negligible advantage. Using the Dual System Encryption, a sequence of games are needed. Among the games, the first game is a real game and the others are modified games with the semi-functional keys and semi-functional ciphertexts. To prove that an attacker cannot break the game, the challenger provides the last bogus game which is proved unbreakable to the attacker and proves that the attacker cannot distinguish one game from the others. We will introduce the details of games and designing of semi-functional keys and semi-functional ciphertexts in Sect. 4.2.

## 3  Overview of Escrow-Free HIBE

In this section, we firstly introduce the intuition of our solution to the key escrow problem of HIBE. Then, we briefly describe the components of our scheme. Finally, we present the full security definition by illuminating the IND-ID-CCA game for our escrow-free approach.

### 3.1  Intuition of Escrow-Free HIBE

The essence of key escrow problem is that the Private Key Generator (PKG) exclusive owns the scheme master key. In order to restrict the power of PKG, we divide the master key into a PKG master key and a set of secret keys.

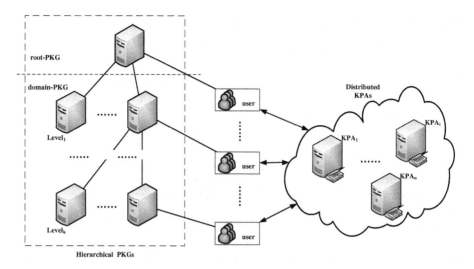

**Fig. 1.** The infrastructure of our escrow-free HIBE scheme.

We introduce multiple Key Privacy Authorities (KPAs) to keep the partial secret keys. A private key is jointly computed by the PKG and all the KPAs. Based on the assumption that at least one of the KPA is honest, we can keep the privacy of the private key. The infrastructure is showed as in Fig. 1. In our escrow-free HIBE scheme, each private key is generated by a domain PKG and the multiple KPAs. In order to reduce the authentication overhead caused by the KPAs, PKG can generate and assign the user a signature with regard to the its identity. The KPAs verify the signature so as to verify the user's identity.

### 3.2 Definitions

Our escrow-free hierarchical identity-based encryption scheme consists of four algorithms: Setup, KeyGen, Encrypt and Decrypt.

**Setup.** The setup algorithm comprises the PKG and KPAs setup stages.

- The PKG takes a security parameter as input and outputs the public parameters $Param_{PKG}$ and a PKG master key $MK$.
- $KPA_i$ then inputs $Param_{PKG}$ and outputs KPA parameter $Param_{KPA_i}$ as well as a secret key $SK_i$.

**KeyGen.** The key generation algorithm takes the PKG master key, multiple secret keys as well as an identity ID $= (ID_1, \ldots, ID_n)$ as input and output the user private key. It also consists of two stages:

- KeyIssue. With the identity, PKG launches the key issuing stage to generate a raw private key, and assigns it to the user.
- KeySec. After the KeyIssue stage, user synchronously asks for key securing from the KPAs and finally get the decrypt key $DK$.

**Encrypt.** The encryption algorithm takes the public parameters $Param_{PKG}$, KPA parameters $Param_{KPA_i}(i = 1, \dots n)$, a message $M$, and an identity as input and outputs a ciphertext $CT$.

**Decrypt.** The decryption algorithm takes the public parameters $Param_{PKG}$, KPA parameters $Param_{KPA_i}(i = 1, \dots n)$, a ciphertext $CT$, and a decrypt key $DK$ as input and outputs the message $M$.

### 3.3   Security Model

The full security model (IND-ID-CCA) for HIBE schemes is firstly suggested in [3]. We modify the model to present an IND-ID-CCA security for our escrow-free HIBE scheme, which is defined via the following game between an adversary $\mathcal{A}$ and a challenger $\mathcal{C}$.

**Setup.** $\mathcal{C}$ runs the PKG and KPA setup algorithms, and gives $\mathcal{A}$ the resulting scheme parameters $Param_{PKG}$ and $Param_{KPA_i}(i = 1, \dots n)$, keeping the PKG master key $MK$ and KPA secret keys $SK_i(i = 1, \dots n)$ to itself.

**Phase 1.** $\mathcal{A}$ issues private key queries and decryption queries.
For a private key query (ID), $\mathcal{C}$ runs the KeyGen algorithm and gives $\mathcal{A}$ the raw private key as well as the KPA key securing factors.
   For a decryption query (ID, $CT$), $\mathcal{C}$ runs the KeyGen algorithm to generate the private key of ID and decrypts the ciphertext $CT$ utilizing the private key.

**Challenge.** $\mathcal{A}$ gives $\mathcal{C}$ two messages $M_0$ and $M_1$, and a challenge identity ID $=$ $(ID_1, \dots, ID_n)$. The challenge identity must satisfy the property that no query identity in *Phase 1* is a prefix of it. And the challenge message must not be one of the messages of decryption queries. $\mathcal{C}$ randomly selects $\beta \in \{0,1\}$ and encrypts $M_\beta$ with the identity. It sends the ciphertext to $\mathcal{A}$.

**Phase 2.** This is the same as Phase 1 except that $\mathcal{A}$ cannot query the private key of the challenge identity and private keys of its ancestors.

**Guess.** $\mathcal{A}$ output a guess $\beta'$ for $\beta$. The advantage of $\mathcal{A}$ is defined to be $Pr[\beta' = \beta] - \frac{1}{2}$.

**Definition 1.** *We say that the escrow-free hierarchical identity based encryption is secure if no polynomial time adversaries can achieve a non-negligible advantage in the security game.*

## 4   EF-LW-HIBE Scheme

We build our escrow-free HIBE scheme based on the Lewko-Waters HIBE. Similar to the LW-HIBE, our construction uses composite order groups of order $N = p_1 p_2 p_3$ and identities in $\mathbb{Z}_N$. Based on the knowledge of Dual System Encryption, we prove that the EF-LW-HIBE scheme is IND-ID-CCA secure.

## 4.1 Construction

The EF-LW-HIBE consists of the following four algorithms:

**Setup.** The setup algorithm comprises the PKG setup and KPA setup stages.

- PKG Setup: The PKG chooses a bilinear group $G$ of order $N = p_1 p_2 p_3$. Let $l$ denote the maximum depth of the HIBE, PKG then randomly chooses $g, h, u_1, \ldots, u_l \in G_{p_1}, X_3 \in G_{p_3}$, and $\alpha_0 \in \mathbb{Z}_N$. PKG publishes the public parameters $Param_{PKG} = \{N, g, h, u_1, \ldots, u_l, X_3, e(g,g)^{\alpha_0}\}$, and keep $\alpha_0$ as the PKG master key.
- KPA$_i$ Setup: Each key privacy authority randomly chooses $\alpha_i \in \mathbb{Z}_N$. It takes the $Param_{PKG}$ and $\alpha_i$ as input and computes $e(g,g)^{\alpha_i}$. KPA$_i$ publishes parameter $Param_{KPA_i} = \{e(g,g)^{\alpha_i}\}$, and keeps $\alpha_i$ as KPA secret key.

**KeyGen($d_{\text{ID}_{|j-1}}$, ID).** The key generation algorithm comprises the key issuing stage by PKG and the key securing stage by KPAs.

- KeyIssue: To generate a private key $\nabla d_{\text{ID}} = (K_1, \nabla K_2, E_{j+1}, \ldots, E_l)$ for identify ID$=(ID_1, \ldots, ID_j)$ $(j \leqslant l)$, the key generation algorithm of PKG picks a random $r \in \mathbb{Z}_N$, random elements $R_3, R'_3, R_{j+1}, \ldots, R_l$ of $G_{p3}$, and outputs: $K_1 = g^r R_3$, $\nabla K_2 = g^{\alpha_0} \left( u_1^{ID_1} \cdots u_j^{ID_j} h \right)^r R'_3$, $E_{j+1} = u_{j+1}^r R_{j+1}$, $\ldots$, $E_l = u_l^r R_l$.

  We refer to the private key generated by KeyIssue algorithm as a raw private key. Actually, the raw private key for ID can be generated by just given a raw private key for ID$_{|j-1} = (ID_1, \ldots, ID_{j-1})$ as required. Let $(K'_1, \nabla K'_2, E'_j, \ldots, E'_l)$ be the raw private key for ID$_{|j-1}$. To generate the private key for ID, the algorithm picks $r' \in \mathbb{Z}_N$ and $\tilde{R}_3, \tilde{R}'_3, \tilde{R}_{j+1}, \ldots, \tilde{R}_l \in G_{p3}$ randomly. The raw private key of ID can be computed as:

$$K_1 = K'_1 g^{r'} \tilde{R}_3 = g^{r+r'} R_3 \tilde{R}_3, \quad \nabla K_2 = g^{\alpha_0} \left( u_1^{ID_1} \cdots u_j^{ID_j} h \right)^{r+r'} R'_3 R_j^{ID_j} \tilde{R}'_3$$

$$E_{j+1} = E'_{j+1} u_{j+1}^{r'} \tilde{R}_{j+1} = u_{j+1}^{r+r'} R_{j+1} \tilde{R}_{j+1}, \ldots, \quad E_l = E'_l u_l^{r'} \tilde{R}_l = u_l^{r+r'} R_l \tilde{R}_l.$$

This raw private key is a properly raw private key for ID$=(ID_1, \ldots, ID_j)$.
- KeySec: With the raw private key, user asks for key securing by the KPAs. Each KPA$_i$ randomly chooses $\hat{R}_i \in G_{p3}$ and compute the securing factor $g^{\alpha_i} \hat{R}_i$. User retrieves the securing factors from all the KPAs and compute a complete private key $d_{\text{ID}} = \{K_1, K_2, E_{j+1}, \ldots, E_l\}$, where

$$K_2 = \nabla K_2 g^{\alpha_1} \hat{R}_1 \cdots g^{\alpha_n} \hat{R}_n = g^{\sum_{i=0}^n \alpha_i} \left( u_1^{ID_1} \cdots u_j^{ID_j} h \right)^r R'_3 \prod_1^n \hat{R}_i$$

Note that, key securing of each KPA can be synchronously implemented.

**Encrypt($M, (ID_1, \ldots, ID_j)$).** Given the message $M$ and an identity, a user encrypt the message with PKG and KPA parameters. It chooses $s \in \mathbb{Z}_N$ randomly and generates the ciphertext $CT = \{C_0, C_1, C_2\}$. There are
$C_0 = M e(g,g)^{\sum_{i=0}^n \alpha_i s}$, $C_1 = \left( u_1^{ID_1} \cdots u_j^{ID_j} h \right)^s$, $C_2 = g^s$.

**Decrypt**$(d_{ID}, CT)$. The decryption algorithm can decrypt the message by computing the blinding factor:

$$\frac{e(K_2, C_2)}{e(K_1, C_1)} = \frac{e(g,g)^{\sum_{i=0}^{n} \alpha_i s} e(u_1^{ID_1} \cdots u_j^{ID_j} h, g)^{rs}}{e(g, u_1^{ID_1} \cdots u_j^{ID_j} h)^{rs}} = e(g,g)^{\sum_{i=0}^{n} \alpha_i s}.$$

Note that, some bilinear computation results in identities of $G_T$ due to the orthogonality property of $G_{p_1}, G_{p_2}, G_{p_3}$.

## 4.2   Security Proofs

We prove full security of EF-LW-HIBE utilizing the Dual System Encryption. As described above, the proof utilizes the semi-functional key and semi-functional ciphertext, and relies on a sequence of security games. We design the semi-functional key and ciphertext as follows.

- **Semi-functional Ciphertext.** Let $(C'_0, C'_1, C'_2)$ denote the normal ciphertext generated by the encryption algorithm. Set $C_0 = C'_0$, $C_1 = C'_1 g_2^{xz_c}$ and $C_2 = C'_2 g_2^x$, where $g_2$ is a generator of the subgroup $G_{p2}$, and $x, z_c \in \mathbb{Z}_N$ are chosen in random. $(C_0, C_1, C_2)$ is referred to as a semi-functional ciphertext.
- **Semi-functional Key.** Let $(K'_1, K'_2, E'_{j+1}, \ldots, E'_l)$ denote the normal key generated by the key generation algorithm. Set $K_1 = K'_1 g_2^\gamma$, $K_2 = K'_2 g_2^{\gamma z_k}$, $E_{j+1} = E'_{j+1} g_2^{\gamma z_{j+1}}$, $\ldots$, $E_l = E'_l g_2^{\gamma z_l}$ where $g_2$ is a generator of the subgroup $G_{p2}$, and $\gamma, z_k, z_{j+1}, \ldots, z_l \in \mathbb{Z}_N$ are chosen in random. $(K_1, K_2)$ is referred to as a semi-functional key.

To prove the security of our HIBE scheme, we introduce a series of indistinguishable games, illustrated as in Fig. 2. The left side of Fig. 2 are the lemmas that ensure the indistinguishability of each two attack games. We describe and prove the four lemmas as follows:

**Lemma 1.** *Suppose there exists an algorithm $\mathcal{A}$ that can distinguish $Game_{Real}$ and $Game_{Restricted}$ with advantage $\varepsilon$. Then we can build an algorithm with advantage $\geqslant \frac{\varepsilon}{2}$ in breaking either Assumption 1 or Assumption 2.*

*Proof.* Since we define the $Game_{Restricted}$ as [15] does, we can prove that the games $Game_{Real}$ and $Game_{Restricted}$ are indistinguishable following the same procedures. Details can be found in the proof of *Lemma 5* in [15].

**Lemma 2.** *Suppose there exists an algorithm $\mathcal{A}$ that can distinguish $Game_0$ and $Game_{Restricted}$ with advantage $\varepsilon$. Then we can build an algorithm with advantage $\varepsilon$ in breaking Assumption 1.*

*Proof.* $\mathcal{B}$ is given $g, X_3, T$. To simulate $Game_{Restricted}$ or $Game_0$ with $\mathcal{A}$, $\mathcal{B}$ first chooses random exponents $\alpha_0, a_1, \ldots, a_l, b \in \mathbb{Z}_N$ and sets $g = g$, $u_i = g^{a_i}$ for $i$ from 1 to $l$ and $h = g^b$. PKG parameters $\{N, g, h, u_1, \ldots, u_l, X_3, e(g,g)^{\alpha_0}\}$ and KPA parameters $\{e(g,g)^{\alpha_i}\}$ $(i = 1 \ldots n)$ are send to $\mathcal{A}$.

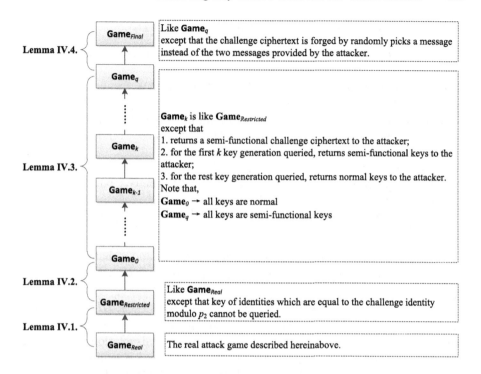

**Fig. 2.** A series of indistingusihable games. The indistinguishability between two games is ensured by a corresponding lemma. $q$ denotes the maximum number of key queries the attacker makes, and $p_2$ is one of the prime factor of the composite order.

When $\mathcal{A}$ queries a key for identity $(ID_1, \ldots, ID_j)$, $\mathcal{B}$ chooses random exponents $r, t, w, v_{j_1}, \ldots, v_l \in \mathbb{Z}_N$ and returns key: $K_1 = g^r X_3^t$,
$K_2 = g^{\sum_{i=0}^n \alpha_i} (u_1^{ID_1} \cdots u_j^{ID_j} h)^r X_3^w$, $E_{j+1} = u_{j+1}^r X_3^{v_{j+1}}, \ldots, E_l = u_l^r X_3^{v_l}$.

In challenge phase, $\mathcal{A}$ sends $\mathcal{B}$ two messages $M_0, M_1$ and a challenge identity $(ID_1^*, \ldots, ID_j^*)$. $\mathcal{B}$ randomly chooses $\beta \in \{0, 1\}$, and forms ciphertext:
$C_0 = M_\beta e(T, g)^{\sum_{i=0}^n \alpha_i}$, $C_1 = T^{a_1 ID_1^* + \cdots + a_j ID_j^* + b}$, $C_2 = T$.
If $T \in G_{p_1 p_2}$, then this is a semi-functional ciphertext with $z_c = a_1 ID_1^* + \cdots + a_j ID_j^* + b$. If $T \in G_{p_1}$, this is a normal ciphertext. As supposed, $\mathcal{A}$ is able to distinguish the semi-functional and normal ciphertext. Therefore, $\mathcal{B}$ can use the output of $\mathcal{A}$ to distinguish $T$. That is, it can break Assumption 1.

**Lemma 3.** *Suppose there exists an algorithm $\mathcal{A}$ that can distinguish $Game_{k-1}$ and $Game_k$ with advantage $\varepsilon$. Then we can build an algorithm with advantage $\varepsilon$ in breaking Assumption 2.*

*Proof.* $\mathcal{B}$ is given $g, X_1 X_2, X_3, Y_2 Y_3, T$. To simulate $Game_{k-1}$ or $Game_k$ with $\mathcal{A}$, $\mathcal{B}$ first chooses random exponents $a_1, \ldots, a_l, b \in \mathbb{Z}_N$. and sets the public parameters of PKG as $g = g, u_1 = g^{a_1}, \ldots, u_l = g^{a_l}, h = g^b, e(g, g)^{\alpha_0}$, public parameters of $KPA_i$ as $e(g, g)^{\alpha_i}$. Public parameters are sent to $\mathcal{A}$.

When $\mathcal{A}$ requests the $i^{th}$ key for identity $(ID_1, \ldots, ID_j)$.

- If $i < k$, $\mathcal{B}$ generates a semi-functional key. It chooses random exponents $r, z, t, z_{j+1}, \ldots, z_l \in \mathbb{Z}_N$ and sets:
$K_1 = g^r (Y_2 Y_3)^t$, $K_2 = g^{\sum_{i=0}^n \alpha_i} (u_1^{ID_1} \cdots u_j^{ID_j} h)^r (Y_2 Y_3)^z$,
$E_{j+1} = u_{j+1}^r (Y_2 Y_3)^{z_{j+1}}, \ldots, E_l = u_l^r (Y_2 Y_3)^{z_l}$.
Note that this is a properly distributed semi-functional key with $g_2^\gamma = Y_2^t$.
- If $i = k$, $\mathcal{B}$ lets $z_k = a_1 ID_1^* + \cdots + a_j ID_j^* + b$, chooses random exponents $w_k, w_{j+1}, \ldots, w_l \in \mathbb{Z}_N$, and sets:
$K_1 = T, K_2 = g^{\sum_{i=0}^n \alpha_i} T^{z_k} X_3^{w_k}$, $E_{j+1} = T^{a_{j+1}} X_3^{w_{j+1}}, \ldots, E_l = T^{a_l} X_3^{w_l}$.
If $T \in G_{p_1 p_3}$, this is a normal key with $g^r$ equal to the $G_{p_1}$ part of $T$.
If $T \in G$, this is a semi-functional key.
- If $i > k$, $\mathcal{B}$ generates normal keys by calling the usual key generation algorithm.

In challenge phase, $\mathcal{A}$ sends $\mathcal{B}$ two messages $M_0, M_1$ and a challenge identity $(ID_1^*, \ldots, ID_j^*)$. $\mathcal{B}$ randomly chooses $\beta \in \{0, 1\}$, and forms ciphertext:
$C_0 = M_\beta e(X_1 X_2, g)^\alpha$, $C_1 = (X_1 X_2)^{a_1 ID_1^* + \cdots + a_j ID_j^* + b}$, $C_2 = X_1 X_2$.

We notice that this sets $g^s = X_1$ and $z_c = a_1 ID_1^* + \cdots + a_j ID_j^* + b$. Since the $k^{th}$ key is not a prefix of the challenge key modulo $p_2$, $z_k$ and $z_c$ will seem randomly distributed to $\mathcal{A}$. Though it is hidden from $\mathcal{A}$, this relationship between $z_c$ and $z_k$ is crucial: if $\mathcal{B}$ attempts to test itself whether key $k$ is semi-functional by creating a semi-functional ciphertext for this identity and trying to decrypt, then decryption will work whether key $k$ is semi-functional or not, because $z_c = z_k$. In other words, the simulator can only create a nominally semi-functional key $k$. If $T \in G_{p_1 p_3}$, then $\mathcal{B}$ has properly simulated $Game_{k-1}$. If $T \in G$, then $\mathcal{B}$ has properly simulated $Game_k$. As supposed, $\mathcal{A}$ is able to distinguish $Game_{k-1}$ and $Game_k$. Therefore, $\mathcal{B}$ can use the output of $\mathcal{A}$ to distinguish between these possibilities for $T$. That is, it can break Assumption 2.

**Lemma 4.** *Suppose there exists an algorithm $\mathcal{A}$ that can distinguish $Game_q$ and $Game_{Final}$ with advantage $\varepsilon$. Then we can build an algorithm with advantage $\varepsilon$ in breaking Assumption 3.*

*Proof.* $\mathcal{B}$ is given $g, g^\alpha X_2, X_3, g^s Y_2, Z_2, T$. To simulate $Game_q$ or $Game_{Final}$ with $\mathcal{A}$, $\mathcal{B}$ first chooses random exponents $a_1, \ldots, a_l, b \in \mathbb{Z}_N$ and sets the public parameters of PKG as $g = g$, $u_1 = g^{a_1}$, $\ldots$, $u_l = g^{a_l}$, $h = g^b$, $e(g, g)^{\alpha_0} = e(g^{\alpha_0} X_2, g)$. It also randomly choose $\alpha_1, \ldots, \alpha_n \in \mathbb{Z}_N$ and sets public parameters of KPA$_i$ as $e(g, g)^{\alpha_i} = e(g^{\alpha_i} X_2, g)$. Public parameters are sent to $\mathcal{A}$.

When $\mathcal{A}$ requests key for identity $(ID_1, \ldots, ID_j)$, $\mathcal{B}$ chooses random exponents $c, r, t, w, z, z_{j+1}, \ldots, z_l, w_{j+1}, \ldots, w_l \in \mathbb{Z}_N$ and returns a semi-functional key: $K_1 = g^r Z_2^z X_3^t$, $K_2 = g^{\alpha_0} X_2 Z_2^c (u_1^{ID_1} \cdots u_j^{ID_j} h)^r X_3^w$,
$E_{j+1} = u_{j+1}^r Z_2^{z_{j+1}} X_3^{w_{j+1}}, \ldots, E_l = u_l^r Z_2^{z_l} X_3^{w_l}$.

Note that $\mathcal{B}$ returns a raw private key to $\mathcal{A}$, which is also a properly distributed semi-functional key. And $\mathcal{A}$ cannot distinguish it from the complete key. In challenge phase, $\mathcal{A}$ sends $\mathcal{B}$ two messages $M_0, M_1$ and a challenge identity $(ID_1^*, \ldots, ID_j^*)$. $\mathcal{B}$ chooses $\beta \in \{0, 1\}$ randomly, and forms ciphertext:

$C_0 = M_\beta T$, $C_1 = (g^s Y_2)^{a_1 ID_1^* + \cdots + a_j ID_j^* + b}$, $C_2 = g^s Y_2$.

This sets $z_c = a_1 ID_1^* + \cdots + a_j ID_j^* + b$. We notice that the value of $z_c$ only matters modulo $p_2$, whereas $u_1 = g^{a_1}, \ldots, u_l = g^{a_l}$, and $h = g^b$ are elements of $G_{p_1}$. So when $a_1, \ldots, a_l$ and $b$ are chosen randomly modulo $N$, there is no correlation between the values of $a_1, \ldots, a_l, b$ modulo $p_1$ and the value $z_c = a_1 ID_1^* + \cdots + a_j ID_j^* + b$ modulo $p_2$.

If $T = e(g,g)^{\alpha s}$, then this is a properly distributed semi-functional ciphertext with message $M_\beta$. If $T$ is a random element of $G_T$, then this is a semi-functional ciphertext with a random message. As supposed, $\mathcal{A}$ is able to distinguish these two kinds of ciphertext. Therefore, $\mathcal{B}$ can use the output of $\mathcal{A}$ to distinguish between these possibilities for $T$. That is, it can break Assumption 3.

**Theorem 1.** *If Assumptions 1, 2, and 3 hold, then our EF-LW-HIBE scheme is secure.*

*Proof.* If Assumptions 1, 2, and 3 hold, $Game_{Real}$ is indistinguishable from $Game_{Final}$ according to the *Lemma* 1 to 4. $Game_{Final}$ information-theoretically hiding the value of $\beta$ is the de facto game provided to the attacker. Therefore, the attacker can attain no advantage in breaking the EF-LW-HIBE scheme.

## 5 Conclusion

In this work, we introduced a provably-secure solution to the key escrow problem of PKGs in HIBE scheme. The main idea of the solution is to restrict the power of PKGs by employing multiple Key Privacy Authorities (KPAs) which partitions the main secret for generating private keys and each KPA obtains a portion of the secret. According to the idea, we presented the escrow-free HIBE scheme based on the LW-HIBE. We proved the full security of EF-LW-HIBE scheme, utilizing the methodology of Dual System Encryption. Although the PKG-KPAs model was instantiated into a specific scheme in this work, it can also be applied to other HIBE schemes.

**Acknowledgment.** This research is supported in part by the project of the National High Technology Research and Development Program of China(863 Program) No. 2011AA01A103; the program of Changjiang Scholars and Innovative Research Team in University (No. IRT1012); Science and Technology Innovative Research Team in Higher Educational Institutions of Hunan Province (network technology); and Hunan Province Natural Science Foundation of China (11JJ7003).

## References

1. Blazy, O., Kiltz, E., Pan, J.: (Hierarchical) identity-based encryption from affine message authentication. In: Garay, J.A., Gennaro, R. (eds.) CRYPTO 2014, Part I. LNCS, vol. 8616, pp. 408–425. Springer, Heidelberg (2014)

2. Boneh, D., Boyen, X.: Efficient selective-ID secure identity-based encryption without random oracles. In: Cachin, C., Camenisch, J.L. (eds.) EUROCRYPT 2004. LNCS, vol. 3027, pp. 223–238. Springer, Heidelberg (2004)

3. Boneh, D., Boyen, X., Goh, E.-J.: Hierarchical identity based encryption with constant size ciphertext. In: Cramer, R. (ed.) EUROCRYPT 2005. LNCS, vol. 3494, pp. 440–456. Springer, Heidelberg (2005)

4. Boneh, D., Franklin, M.: Identity-based encryption from the weil pairing. In: Kilian, J. (ed.) CRYPTO 2001. LNCS, vol. 2139, pp. 213–229. Springer, Heidelberg (2001)

5. Boneh, D., Goh, E.-J., Nissim, K.: Evaluating 2-DNF formulas on ciphertexts. In: Kilian, J. (ed.) TCC 2005. LNCS, vol. 3378, pp. 325–341. Springer, Heidelberg (2005)

6. Cao, D., Wang, X.F., Wang, F., Hu, Q.L., Su, J.S.: Sa-ibe: a secure and accountable identity-based encryption scheme. Dianzi Yu Xinxi Xuebao (J. Electron. Inf. Technol.) $33(12)$, 2922–2928 (2011)

7. Chen, J., Wee, H.: Fully, (almost) tightly secure IBE and dual system groups. In: Canetti, R., Garay, J.A. (eds.) CRYPTO 2013, Part II. LNCS, vol. 8043, pp. 435–460. Springer, Heidelberg (2013)

8. Chow, S.S.M.: Removing escrow from identity-based encryption. In: Jarecki, S., Tsudik, G. (eds.) PKC 2009. LNCS, vol. 5443, pp. 256–276. Springer, Heidelberg (2009)

9. Fu, S., Wang, D., Xu, M., Ren, J.: Cryptanalysis of remote data integrity checking protocol proposed by L. Chen for cloud storage. IEICE Trans. $97-A(1)$, 418–420 (2014). http://search.ieice.org/bin/summary.php?id=e97-a_1_418

10. Gentry, C., Silverberg, A.: Hierarchical ID-based cryptography. In: Zheng, Y. (ed.) ASIACRYPT 2002. LNCS, vol. 2501, pp. 548–566. Springer, Heidelberg (2002)

11. Huang, K., Xian, M., Fu, S., Liu, J.: Securing the cloud storage audit service: defending against frame and collude attacks of third party auditor. IET Commun. $8(12)$, 2106–2113 (2014). http://dx.doi.org/10.1049/iet-com.2013.0898

12. Kamara, S., Lauter, K.: Cryptographic cloud storage. In: Sion, R., Curtmola, R., Dietrich, S., Kiayias, A., Miret, J.M., Sako, K., Sebé, F. (eds.) RLCPS, WECSR, and WLC 2010. LNCS, vol. 6054, pp. 136–149. Springer, Heidelberg (2010)

13. Kate, A., Goldberg, I.: Distributed private-key generators for identity-based cryptography. In: Garay, J.A., De Prisco, R. (eds.) SCN 2010. LNCS, vol. 6280, pp. 436–453. Springer, Heidelberg (2010)

14. Lee, B., Boyd, C., Dawson, E., Kim, K., Yang, J., Yoo, S.: Secure key issuing in id-based cryptography. In: Proceedings of the Second Workshop on Australasian Information Security, Data Mining and Web Intelligence, and Software Internationalisation, vol. 32, pp. 69–74. Australian Computer Society, Inc. (2004)

15. Lewko, A., Waters, B.: New techniques for dual system encryption and fully secure HIBE with short ciphertexts. In: Micciancio, D. (ed.) TCC 2010. LNCS, vol. 5978, pp. 455–479. Springer, Heidelberg (2010)

16. Shamir, A.: Identity-based cryptosystems and signature schemes. In: Blakely, G.R., Chaum, D. (eds.) CRYPTO 1984. LNCS, vol. 196, pp. 47–53. Springer, Heidelberg (1985)

17. Wang, C., Chow, S.S., Wang, Q., Ren, K., Lou, W.: Privacy-preserving public auditing for secure cloud storage. IEEE Trans. Comput. $62(2)$, 362–375 (2013)

18. Waters, B.: Dual system encryption: realizing fully secure IBE and HIBE under simple assumptions. In: Halevi, S. (ed.) CRYPTO 2009. LNCS, vol. 5677, pp. 619–636. Springer, Heidelberg (2009)
19. Zeng, W., Zhao, Y., Ou, K., Song, W.: Research on cloud storage architecture and key technologies. In: Proceedings of the 2nd International Conference on Interaction Sciences: Information Technology, Culture and Human, pp. 1044–1048. ACM (2009)

# FASTDB: An Array Database System for Efficient Storing and Analyzing Massive Scientific Data

Hui Li[1,2(✉)], Nengjun Qiu[1,2], Mei Chen[1,2], Hongyuan Li[1,2], Zhenyu Dai[1,2], Ming Zhu[3], and Menglin Huang[3]

[1] Department of Computer Science,
Guizhou University, Guiyang 550025, China
{cse.HuiLi,gychm,cse.zydai}@gzu.edu.cn
[2] Guizhou Engineering Laboratory of ACMIS, Guiyang 550025, China
[3] National Astronomical Observatories,
Chinese Academy of Sciences, Beijing 100016, China
{mz,huangmenglin}@nao.cas.cn

**Abstract.** With the development of science and technology, the data size and complexity of scientific data are increased rapidly, which made efficient data storage and parallel analysis of scientific data become a big challenge. The previous techniques that combine the traditional relational database with analysis software tends cannot efficiently meet the performance requirement of large scale scientific data based analysis. In this paper, we present FASTDB, a distributed array database system that optimized for massive scientific data management and provide a share-nothing, parallel array processing analysis. In order to demonstrate the intrinsic performance characteristics of FASTDB, we applied it into the interactive analysis of data from astronomical surveys, and designed a series of experiments with scientific analysis tasks. According to the experimental results, we found FASTDB can be significantly fast than traditional database based SkyServer in many typical analytical scenarios.

**Keywords:** Scientific database system · Array database · Scientific analysis · Performance measurement · Massive data

## 1 Introduction

With the development of science and technology, the volume of scientific data approximately doubling every year. The relational database system have been widely used and proved its values in various areas. However, as the scientific data has the characteristic of high noise, massive computation and often prefer in array model in nature, RDBMS tends cannot to be the satisfactory solution to achieve scalable analysis and storage for data-intensive scientific areas [1, 2], e.g., astronomy survey like the Sloan Digital Sky Survey (SDSS) [3, 23], which aiming at creating a digital map of a big part of the universe by spectroscopic data. There are urgent needs to develop efficient and scalable array model based scientific database systems for scientific areas.

Given a concrete example, consider data from the five hundred meters Aperture Spherical radio Telescope (FAST) [4], the world's largest astronomical radio telescope.

© Springer International Publishing Switzerland 2015
G. Wang et al. (Eds.): ICA3PP 2015 Workshops, LNCS 9532, pp. 606–616, 2015.
DOI: 10.1007/978-3-319-27161-3_55

It can make the neutral hydrogen observation extends to the edge of the universe, make dark matter and dark energy observations, enable the arrive time precision of pulsar from the current 120 ns to 30 s and search for interstellar communication signal and extraterrestrial civilizations, etc. The data such as the strength of the radio celestial objects, spectrum and polarization data deriving from FAST has multidimensional characteristics that cannot matched to traditional relational database. For example, the process of cross-identification of multi-band radio data would merge multiple data sets, then it will become more complicated when it comes to the matrix inverse operation.

To meet the requirements of large-scale scientific data storage and analysis, the array model based database system have been proposed. It often provides with inherent support for multi-dimensional arrays and opt for the array as the first-class citizen and it is designed to be a share-nothing architecture [5–7].

In this paper, we present the analytical database system FASTDB [11], which builds on array model based SciDB engine [8–10] to provide a share-nothing, parallel processing and data management engine for needs of FAST [4]. In the internal of database engine layer, we hacked its implementation to enhanced SciDB's adaptive storage capability. Furthermore, we optimized its parallel loading capability and multiple join implementation, which can enable efficient complex astronomical data analysis such as cross-identification.

## 2   Related Work

In this decade [1, 2], there has been a trend to employ array model as the data schema to exploit large-scale scientific data management and analysis. SciDB [8–10] is an representative open source array database system proposed for management and analysis of scientific data. It is mainly developed Paradigm4 Inc [12]. It uses the array data model that like the array structure in mathematics, and it provide good support for multidimensional scientific data processing.

There several major technical featrues make SciDB engine is optimized to scientific areas by design. At first, there is no overwrite during the update. SciDB store different version of data and uses timestamp as the symbol of different historical data. At second, data compression algorithms are employed to save storage space. At third is Named Versions, in SciDB, changing the array will produce a new version of data. At fourth, it support the characteristic of data provenance, which can meet the need of data repeatability. The last is its capability for manage data uncertainty. Scientific data, especially the scenarios that data obtained by certain observational approaches, which often contain some inaccurate information. To solve this problem, SciDB's built-in mechanism allows data has error or approximation.

A typical SciDB array structure is illustrated as Fig. 1. Its basic unit is cell, each cell has the same value types. The value of cell can be one or more scalar value, also can be one or more array. Each dimension has contiguous integer values. SciDB uses the message mechanism for communication between nodes and uses array as the first-class citizen. Thus SciDB often to be efficient for processing large array data.

Generally, the operations scientist conducted over scientific data can be categorized into two types: data management and data analysis. The common data management task

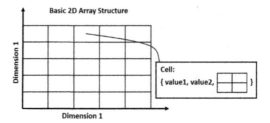

**Fig. 1.** Example of 2D array

of scientific data including the process of ingest, cook, group of raw data, etc. In scientific domain, scientist can obtain the value of the raw data through a series of processing, such as remove noise in the raw imagery, multiband fusion, cross-identification. The analysis of scientific data involves computing and statistics from the processed data, such as computing the distances to celestial objects.

In order to support efficient parallel query processing of large-scale astronomical celestial bodies, the university of Washington developed AscotDB system [13, 14] for large-scale astronomical data management and analysis. It take the SciDB cluster as the backend database engine and employ SciDB-Py package as system interface, which allow user to connect SciDB database using Python language.

Rasdaman (raster data manager) [15, 16] is an open source array database system originally developed by the Jacobs University Bremen and Rasdaman Inc [17]. It is fast and flexible, and have been successfully applied in geoscience and other scientific areas. MonetDB [18, 19] is another representative array-oriented database system. It is designed to provide high performance of the query support for large-scale scientific data, it can also be applied in analytical areas such as data mining, on-line analytical processing, text retrieval and multimedia retrieval.

Since MapReduce has been a trend for distributed processing, there also some analytical solution proposed for scientific data analysis by leverage the Hadoop system [20–22]. Howerver, since the complexity of analytics in scientific areas are go well beyond the MapReduce frameworks, and matching all the functionality delivered by array database like SciDB would require many Hadoop ecosystem components, including HDFS, PIG, HBase, Hive and analytical package like R, which will reslut the technical solution tends to be more complexity. Therefore, scientific data management and analysis community often prefere the array database system as their solution.

## 3   Overview of FASTDB

The FASTDB project is a collaboration of an inter-disciplinary team comprising astronomy and database researchers. The architecture of FASTDB is shown in Fig. 2. FASTDB is a share-noting distributed system for massive scientific data management and analytics. FASTDB integrates several pieces of technology: the system interface, the optimized SciDB engine for data storage and processing, a cluster monitor system and a front-end UI for interactive and exploratory data analysis. Since the FASTDB

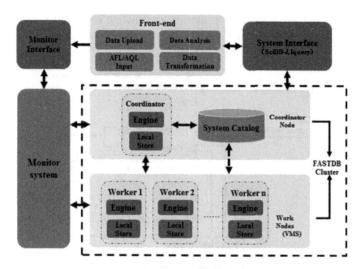

**Fig. 2.** Architecture of FASTDB

engine is implemented based on SciDB engine, we just present our enhancement and the difference of them, and ignore the rest of them which are identical.

**System Interface:** The system interface is the bridge between the interactive front-end and underlying database cluster, it is implement based on the command line interface Iquery and JDBC driver SciDB-J. In Iquery, both the functional-style array query language AFL and the SQL-like array query language AQL are can be used to interact with underlying database cluster. As to SciDB-J, we optimized its implementation to support error handling and enhanced its support for AFL.

**Interactive Front-end UI:** It provide the capability to visually interact and explore data. Since FASTDB is initiated for meet the needs of FAST [4], currently, all the functionality of the front-end are developed for astronomical data exploration like SkyServer [3, 23]. In the front-end of FASTDB, user can upload their own data into FASTDB cluster and then analyze it by either AFL/AQL statements or the built-in interactive visual explorative tools.

**Monitor:** The monitor subsystem consists of two components: agent and server. Each FASTDB node will be installed and configured the monitor agent. Via SNMP, the agent ends can collect various fine-grained system information of cluster server. The monitor server will analyzing the incoming monitoring data by preconfigured rules, and send out event alarms if necessary. All the monitored information, including the reports, static data and the configuration will be shown in a web based dashboard, which is convenient for users to know about the system information of the server.

**Parallel Data Loading:** FAST [4] will produce tens of data every day, which require FASTDB can load most of them into system for archive and further analysis. In order to achieve this goal, we optimization the implementation of SciDB's data load component as a new subsystem named FASTLoad. Its architecture is as Fig. 3.

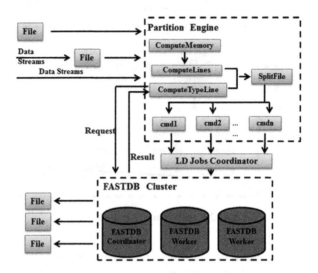

**Fig. 3.** Architecture of FASTLoad subsystem

When the FASTLoad system load data into system, the Partition Engine split the file into $n$ parts with specific sizes. $n$ is determined by the monitor (it know which FASTDB worker is busy) and FASTDB Coordinator, it means there will $n$ FASTDB worker. Then the task will scheduled by LD Jobs Coordinator to load the corresponding file later. Currently, we only use the simple FIFO strategy for job schedule in LD Jobs Coordinator. That means the loading order is same as the order of data file loading request received by the FASTDB Coordinator.

**Adaptive Chunk Determination:** Chunk is the basic storage unit of both SciDB and FASTDB. In SciDB and other array database systems, they primarily employ the fixed length strategy for chunk segmentation. If the length of the chunk is too big, it will increase the overhead of cell location during query analysis. On the contrary, it will make too many small chunks and increase the memory overhead. In the implementation of FASTDB, we developed an adaptive chunk length determination (CLD) algorithm to improve the performance of array database by reducing the number of track and prefetching technique when the data is read. Due to the space limitation, we don't present it in this paper, the detail of our CLD approach and its performance evaluation can be found in literature [11].

**Query Optimizer:** Database engine's optimizer aims produce better execution plan to achieve performance goal. As traditional database system, optimize the execution of join operators will also lead a performance improvement in SciDB or FASTDB. In the state-of-the-art SciDB 14.12 and the coming new edition, the join of SciDB is implement as a "cross-join" operator, and it only have several heuristic based rule for join optimization, which is far beyond the needs of produce good enough execution play for complex analytical task. In FASTDB, we developed an array statistics based cost-based optimization to solve this problem. Our evaluation in literature [11] proved that, towards the analytical task has multiple array joins, the execution plan produced by our optimization can reduce 40%–60% overheads than SciDB.

## 4  Design of Experimental Study

In order to characterize the performance between FASTDB the representative astronomical database system SkyServer [3], we designed a micro benchmark for performance evaluation. This benchmark are based on the real dataset of SDSS (Sloan Digital Sky Survey [24]), it consist of three types of astronomy analytical tasks from [25], which including 8 representative analytical queries:

Q1:  Find the Objects with movement speed equal to 1336, field equal to 11 from PhotoObj table of SDSS.

Q2:  Find the galaxies that its luminosity less than 22 and local extinction is greater than 0.175.

Q3:  Find galaxies in a given area of the sky, using a coordinate cut in the unit vector cx, cy and cz.

Q4:  Search for Cataclysmic variables and pre-CVs with white dwarfs and very late secondary from PhotoPrimary table.

Q5:  Find quasars from the Star table.

Q6:  It is a query with single Join and aims to find galaxies that are blended with a star and output the deblended galaxy magnitudes.

Q7:  Find all objects within 30 s one another that have very similar colors.

Q8:  Search for merging galaxy pairs, as the prescription in [25].

In above analytical tasks, Q1–Q5 is belong to the first type of task, which consist of several statements in the form of "SELECT * FROM * WHERE *". Q1 is to find objects in a particular field while Q2 is to find all galaxies with a special value of r and extinction_r. Q3, Q4, Q5 are to find the Objects in a given area of the sky. Q6 is belong to the second type task, which are composed by several statements in the form of "SELECT * FROM * JOIN * ON * WHERE *". The third type of task is consist of several statements in the form of "SELECT * FROM * AS * JOIN * ON * AS * JOIN * ON * (WHERE * AND *)", e.g., Q7 and Q8. Besides, we generated five scales of data sets from SDSS DR9 to use in our evaluation, their size are number of records are as Table 1.

Table 1.  Number of records in different datasets

| Data size | 1 GB | 10 GB | 20 GB | 50 GB | 100 GB |
|---|---|---|---|---|---|
| #Records | 80000 | 800000 | 1600000 | 4800000 | 8000000 |

## 5  Performance Evaluation and Discussion

### 5.1  Experimental Setup

In this section, we will compare FASTDB with traditional database based astronomic data analytical solution SkyServer. All of our evaluation are based on the real dataset of SDSS Data Release 9, which is an astronomy survey aiming at creating a digital map of a big part of the Universe, and it is about 12 terabytes of zipped data.

The experiments conduct on a cluster and each nodes have two Intel(R) Xeon(R) CPU E5-2620 @ 2.00 GHz processor, the operating system is CentOS 6.4 and Windows 2008 (SkyServer only can running on a Windows System). The Coordinator node has 40 GB main memory and 1 TB hard disk space, while each of 15 worker node has 8 GB main memory and 1 TB disk respectively. The backend Database engine of FASTDB and SkyServer is SciDB 14.3 and Microsoft SQL Server 2008 R2. During the evaluation, both system are use the default configuration.

### 5.2  Experimental Results and Analysis

In our evaluation, we measure the response time of FASTDB and SkyServer in different workload. Figure 4(a)–(h) illustrated their performance when they run aforementioned 8 queries over five different data set sizes. The x-axis denotes the data size, while y-axis measures the time to complete the analysis task. When FASTDB run the tasks of Q6, Q7 and Q8, since it consume too long time to complete the tasks than SkyServer, we just ignore the specific response time in corresponding figures.

As to Q1–Q5, FASTDB often to be better than SkyServer for its parallel processing capability. As to Q5–Q8, although Q5 and Q6, Q7, Q8 belong to different type of analytical tasks, they still have a common characteristic that they have at least one Join operation. Currently, the distributed scientific database like SciDB didn't have indexing mechanism and cannot support the Join operation very well. While the underlying database engine of SkyServer is SQL Server 2008, it has mature indexing capability which could enable high performance index join, it may become one of the major factor which significantly improved SkyServer's performance.

In our evaluation, since the data are uniformly distributed in all FASTDB Worker nodes, the Join operation need to manipulate all of the data in all worker nodes of FASTDB, thus the execution tends lead large network traffic. Additionally, FASTDB will compress data when store into the database engine, and the decompression overhead of large data size needed for the join query often to be very expensive, thus it may degrade the performance of join queries. Furthermore, the join operation needs a lot of computation in the coordinator node, thus FASTDB is relative easy to incur main memory bottleneck when the involved data size is large.

Let's take Q5 to characterize FASTDB's performance when it execute the first type of analytical tasks. As show in Fig. 4(e), when data sets become larger, we can know that the response time has rising in both two systems. Especially, on the 20 GB and 50 GB data sets, there is an obvious rising trend on SkyServer. Meanwhile, only a relative gradual growth trend is occurs on FASTDB due to it distributes the data to all

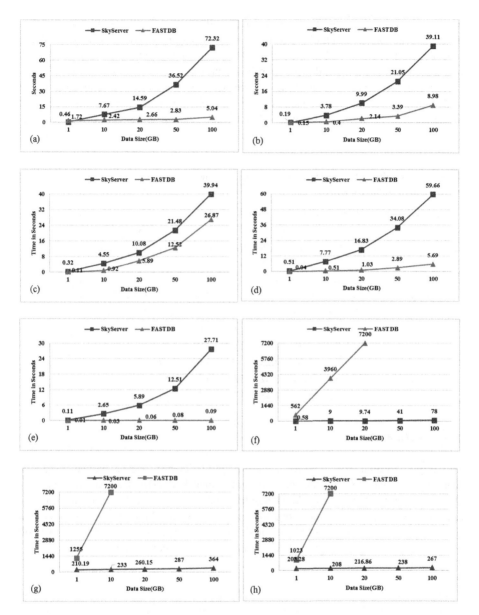

**Fig. 4.** Overall performance of FASTDB and SkyServer on different data sizes. (a)–(h) represent the Response Time of Q1–Q8.

of worker nodes by its chunking mechanism, which make each worker node can execute analysis tasks in parallel and results in the FASTDB based solution is about 10 to 30 times faster than SkyServer.

Besides evaluate the parallel processing capability of FASTDB, we also conduct a series of experiment to evaluate single node FASTDB with SkyServer. The results are tabulated in Table 2. As to Q1–Q5, FASTDB tends 2 times faster than SkyServer when data size equal or larger than 10 GB (the performance number are mark as bold), this is most benefit from FASTDB's array model for it can convenient to obtain data by dense packing, which make it tends to obtain better performance than relation model based system like SkyServer. As in cluster scenarios, when FASTDB running tasks which have Join operators, due to the lack of indexing capability, and other reasons mentioned in the analysis of Fig. 4, most of task Q6–Q8 are timeout in FASTDB.

**Table 2.** Overall performance of Single FASTDB node and SkyServer. " —" means the response time is more than 7200 s.

| System | Dataset | Query overheads (second) | | | | | | | |
|---|---|---|---|---|---|---|---|---|---|
| | | Q1 | Q2 | Q3 | Q4 | Q5 | Q6 | Q7 | Q8 |
| SkyServer | 1 GB | 0.46 | 0.19 | 0.32 | 0.51 | 0.11 | 0.58 | 210 | 203.3 |
| | 10 GB | 7.67 | 3.78 | 4.55 | 7.77 | 2.65 | 9.01 | 233 | 208 |
| | 20 GB | 14.59 | 9.99 | 10.08 | 16.83 | 5.89 | 9.74 | 260 | 216.86 |
| | 50 GB | 36.5 | 21.05 | 21.48 | 34.08 | 12.5 | 41 | 287 | 238 |
| | 100 GB | 72.32 | 39.11 | 39.94 | 59.66 | 27.71 | 78 | 364 | 267 |
| FASTDB | 1 GB | 0.76 | 0.72 | 0.65 | 0.99 | 0.89 | 1900 | — | — |
| | 10 GB | **1.02** | **1.94** | **2.89** | **3.96** | **2.26** | — | — | — |
| | 20 GB | **1.16** | **4.23** | **7.34** | **5.69** | **2.71** | — | — | — |
| | 50 GB | **1.36** | **8.02** | **15.56** | **10.21** | **3.85** | — | — | — |
| | 100 GB | **3.11** | **24.45** | **31.11** | **19.59** | **5.12** | — | — | — |

# 6   Conclusions

To storing and analyzing massive scientific data efficiently, we developed a scalable share-nothing parallel array database system named FASTDB. Benefit from its array model and optimization of backend SciDB database engine, it has been proved significantly better than traditional relation model based database system SkyServer in non-join analytical tasks in both single node and cluster scenarios. In the future, we will continually working on optimize FASTDB to make it achieve better scientific analysis with multiple joins capability.

**Acknowledgments.** This work was supported by the China Ministry of Science and Technology under the State Key Development Program for Basic Research (2012CB821800), Fund of National Natural Science Foundation of China (No. 61462012, 61562010, U1531246), Scientific Research Fund for talents recruiting of Guizhou University (No. 700246003301), Science and Technology Fund of Guizhou Province (No. J [2013]2099), High Tech. Project Fund of Guizhou Development and Reform Commission (No. [2013]2069), Industrial Research Projects of the Science and Technology Plan of Guizhou Province (No. GY[2014]3018) and The Major Applied Basic Research Program of Guizhou Province (No. JZ20142001, No. JZ20142001-05).

# References

1. Gray, J., Liu, D.T., DeWitt, D., Heber, G., Nieto-Santisteban, M., Szalay, A.S.: Scientific data management in the coming decade. MSR-TR-2005-10 (2005)
2. Hey, T., Tansley, S., Tolle, K.: The fourth paradigm: data-intensive scientific discoveries. Microsoft research, p. 10 (2009)
3. Gray, J., Szalay, A.S., Thakar, A.R., Kunszt, P.Z., Stoughton, C., Slutz, D., et al.: Data mining the SDSS SkyServer database. MSR-TR-2002-01 (2002)
4. Five-hundred-meter aperture spherical telescope. http://fast.bao.ac.cn/en/
5. Abadi, D.J., Madden, S.R., Ferreira, M.: Integrating compression and execution in column-oriented database systems. In: Proceedings of SIGMOD, pp. 671–682 (2006)
6. Soroush, E., Balazinska, M., Wang, D.: ArrayStore: a storage manager for complex parallel array processing. In: Proceedings of SIGMOD, pp. 253–264 (2011)
7. Seering, A., Cudre-Mauroux, P., Madden, S., Stonebraker, M.: Efficient versioning for scientific array databases. In: Proceedings of ICDE, pp. 1013–1024 (2012)
8. Cudre-Mauroux, P., Kimura, H., Kimura, H., Lim, K.-T., Rogers, J., Simakov, R., Soroush, E., et al.: A demonstration of SciDB: a science-oriented DBMS. In: Proceedings of VLDB, pp. 1534–1537 (2009)
9. Stonebraker, M., Becla, J., Dewitt, D., Lim, K.-T., Maier, D., Ratzesberger, O., Zdonik, S.: Requirements for science data bases and SciDB. In: Proceedings of CIDR (2009)
10. Brown, G.: Overview of SciDB: large scale array storage, processing and analysis. In: Proceedings of ICDE, pp. 963–968 (2010)
11. Hui, L., Nengjun, Q., Hongyuan, L., Mei, C., Min, Z., Menglin, H.: FASTDB: a array database system for efficient storing and analyzing massive scientific data. Technical report, GZU-ACMIS-TR-2014-07, pp. 1–104. (in Chinese)
12. Paradigm 4 Inc. http://www.paradigm4.com/
13. Marcos, D., Connolly, A.J., et al.: ASCOT: a collaborative platform for the virtual observatory. In: Proceedings of ADASS XXI, vol. 461, pp. 901–904 (2012)
14. Vanderplas, J., Soroush, E., Krughoff, S., Balazinska, M., Connolly, A.: Squeezing a big orange into little boxes: the AscotDB system for parallel processing of data on a sphere. IEEE Data Eng. Bull. **36**, 11–20 (2013)
15. Baumann, P., Dehmel, A., Furtado, P., Ritsch, R., Widmann, N.: The multidimensional database system RasDaMan. In: Proceedings of SIGMOD, pp. 575–576 (1998)
16. Baumann, P., Dumitru, A.M., Merticariu, V.: The array database that is not a database: file based array query answering in rasdaman. In: Nascimento, M.A., Sellis, T., Cheng, R., Sander, J., Zheng, Yu., Kriegel, H.-P., Renz, M., Sengstock, C. (eds.) SSTD 2013. LNCS, vol. 8098, pp. 478–483. Springer, Heidelberg (2013)
17. Rasdaman Inc. http://www.rasdaman.com/
18. Ivanova, M., Nes, N., Goncalves, R., Kersten, M.L.: MonetDB/SQL meets SkyServer: the challenges of a scientific database. In: Proceedings of SSDBM, pp. 7–13 (2007)
19. Kersten, L., Zhang, Y., Ivanova, M., Nes, N.: SciQL, a query language for science applications. In: Proceedings of Array Databases Workshop, pp. 1–12 (2011)
20. Xiangsheng, K.: Scientific data processing using MapReduce in cloud environments. J. Chem. Pharm. Res. **6**, 1270–1276 (2014)
21. Lai, W.K., Chen, Y.-U., Wu, T.-Y., Obaidat, M.: Towards a framework for large-scale multimedia data storage and processing on Hadoop platform. J. Supercomputing **68**, 488–507 (2014)

22. Buck, B., Watkins, N., LeFevre, J., et al.: SciHadoop: array-based query processing in Hadoop. In: Proceedings of International Conference for High Performance Computing, Networking, Storage and Analysis, pp. 66:1–66:11 (2011)
23. SkyServer. http://skyserver.sdss.org/
24. Data Release 9 of Sloan Digital Sky Survey. http://skyserver.sdss.org/dr9/en/
25. Typical astronomic queries. http://cas.sdss.org/dr9/en/help/docs/realquery.asp

# An Effective Correlation-Aware VM Placement Scheme for SLA Violation Reduction in Data Centers

Sheng Xu, Binzhang Fu$^{(\boxtimes)}$, Mingyu Chen, and Lixin Zhang

SKL Computer Architecture, ICT, CAS, University of Chinese Academy of Sciences, Beijing 100190, China
{xusheng01,fubinzhang,cmy,zhanglixin}@ict.ac.cn

**Abstract.** Correlation-aware virtual machine placement (CA-VMP) has been demonstrated as one of the most effective energy saving methodologies. Uncorrelated applications are placed together, which based on the off-peak values for application demand, can reduce the number of required servers significantly while meeting the requirements of service level agreement (SLA) at the same time. However, previous works using insufficient constraints for CA-VMP can't provide a good guarantee of SLA performance. In this paper, a detailed analysis is first conducted on the reasons of performance degradation of SLA. To optimize SLA performance, we present a set of placement constraints on the placement capacity of server. We proposed an optimal placement algorithm **SSP** to achieve a tradeoff between SLA performance and energy cost. According to the simulation experiment results, compared with existing correlation based placement methods, our proposed algorithm provides up to more than five times SLA performance improvement with negligible cost increase.

**Keywords:** Correlation-aware · SLA performance · Energy cost optimization

## 1 Introduction

Today, data center infrastructure providers are in an embarrassing position. On the one hand, the increasing demands of customers and applications require larger and larger data centers [1,7]. On the other hand, considering the high energy consumption of large-scale data centers, the low utilization causes a large amount of unnecessary OPEX. Literatures [2,12,13] have shown that the average utilization rate of data centers is between 10 %–50 % mainly due to the fact that many resources are wasted on reservation to meet the rarely happened peek demand of applications. In order to achieve energy savings without any significant SLA degradation, correlation of resource utilization patterns among applications are exploited in many works [6,9–11]. However, there are only two constraints considered in these existing works: (1) un-correlation and (2) sum of

© Springer International Publishing Switzerland 2015
G. Wang et al. (Eds.): ICA3PP 2015 Workshops, LNCS 9532, pp. 617–626, 2015.
DOI: 10.1007/978-3-319-27161-3_56

off-peak values of application's demands on a server can not exceed the physical capacity of server. As a result, such insufficient constraints for CA-VMP can't provide a guarantee for SLA performance.

The goal of this paper is to design an efficient CA-VMP scheme which could reduce SLA violation and keep energy cost at a low level. Therefore, we first analyze the reasons of causing SLA performance degradation and present several placement constraints for limiting the placement capacity of an server. We use the probability of demand congestion[1] as the metric of evaluating SLA performance. To guarantee SLA performance, we also set a probability threshold for each server. Experiment results show that our scheme achieves a good tradeoff between SLA performance and energy consumption. Increasing no more than 10 % servers, the SLA performance is improved by more than 5 times.

## 2    The Computational Models

***SLA Violation Probability:*** We have the following notations for the computation of SLA violation probability of server:

- $r_i$: The demand size of the application $i$ assigned to the server.
- $m$: The total number of applications whose VMs are placed on the server.
- $C$: Server physical capacity.
- $\alpha_{90th}$: The tail bound parameter.
- $PAR$: The peak to average ratio in resource demand.
- $\alpha_{mean}$: The inverse of $PAR$, $\alpha_{mean} = \frac{1}{PAR}$ and $\alpha_{mean} < \alpha_{90th}$.
- $C_i$: The maximum capacity that the server provides to the application $i$.

In order to calculate the probability of SLA violation, two assumptions are first given: (1) First, when one or several applications in the same server exceed their allocated resources at the same time, the others will be in a low level of resource demand. Here, we use average resource demands, $r_i \cdot \alpha^{mean}$, to represent these applications' demands. (2) Second, when an application exceeds its allocation, the size of the application demand follows uniform distribution. In other words, if $r_i \cdot \alpha^{90th} \leq c \leq r_i$, the probability of $r_i(x) > c$ can be calculated using $\int_c^{r_i} \frac{0.1}{r_i(1-\alpha^{90th})} dx$, where $r_i(x)$ represents the resource demand of the application $i$ at one moment.

The probability of SLA violation can be calculated by $Pr = Pr^{(1)} + \cdots + Pr^{(m)}$, where $Pr^{(k)}$ represents the probability of demand congestion caused by $k$ applications exceeding their allocation at the same time. These uncorrelated applications are individual in resource demands, so the probability of $k$ applications exceeding their allocation at the same time is $(10\%)^k$ [3]. When $k > 2$, the value of probability is less than 0.1 %. So, in this paper, we only consider the case of $k = 1, 2$. For $k = 1$, we have $C_i = C - \sum_{l=1, l \neq i}^m r_l \cdot \alpha^{mean}$ which is the maximum capacity provided for the application $i$. $Pr_i^{(1)}$ and $Pr_{i,j}^{(2)}$ can be calculated by using the following formulas:

---

[1] In this paper, the congestion probability of application demand is also called as the violation probability of SLA.

$$Pr_i^{(1)} = \begin{cases} 0, & \text{if } r_i \leq C_i; \\ \int_{C_i}^{r_i} \frac{0.1}{r_i(1-\alpha^{90th})} dx, & \text{else.} \end{cases}$$

$$Pr_{i,j}^{(2)} = \begin{cases} 0, & \text{if } r_i + r_j \leq C_{i,j}; \\ \int_{C_{i,j}}^{r_i} \int_{C_{i,j}-y}^{r_j} \frac{0.01}{r_i r_j (1-\alpha^{90th})^2} dx dy, & \text{else.} \end{cases}$$

Thus, the value of $Pr$ can be obtained by $Pr = \sum_{i=1}^{m} Pr_i^{(1)} + \sum_{i=1}^{m} \sum_{j=i+1}^{m} Pr_{i,j}^{(2)}$.

***Data Center Energy-cost:*** To calculate the energy-cost of data center, we use energy-cost model presented in [4], which is

$$\Psi(m) = \sum_{i=1}^{N} \phi_i \cdot \delta + m \cdot \rho \tag{1}$$

where $m$ is the number of required servers for the deployment of $N$ applications, and $\phi_i$ is the network cost caused by application $i$ in the final placement. Here, $\phi_i$ is determined by the number of servers that application $i$ has placed VMs on them. $\delta$ is the unit cost caused by one inter-server traffic link and $\rho$ is the unit cost of opening a new server. We use $\rho = \lambda \cdot \delta (\lambda > 1)$ to describe the relationship between $\rho$ and $\delta$, and $\lambda$ is the proportional coefficient.

## 3   Constraints and Scheme for CA-VMP

### 3.1   Placement Constraints for SLA Violation Reduction

*Constraint 1 (Server Constraint, **SC**):* The total number of VMs placed on a server can't exceed the physical capacity of server, which can be formalized as:

$$\sum_{i=1}^{m} (r_i \cdot \alpha^{90th}) \leq C \tag{2}$$

where $m$ represents the amount of applications whose VMs are placed on the server. In constraint 1, the sum of resource demands(VMs), according to *90 percentile* function, can't exceed the server physical capacity. From the inequality 2, the maximum number of VMs that a server can accommodate is $\lfloor C/\alpha^{90th} \rfloor$, so we have $\sum_{i=1}^{m} r_i \leq \lfloor C/\alpha^{90th} \rfloor$. If $m = 1$, we have $r_1 \leq \lfloor C/\alpha^{90th} \rfloor$. Thus, an application can place $\lfloor C/\alpha^{90th} \rfloor$ VMs to a server at most. It's clear that when $r_1 > C$, there is a high risk of SLA violation on the server.

*Constraint 2 (Application Constraint, **AC**):* The number of VMs of same application placed on a server can't exceed the server physical capacity.

$$max\{r_i \mid 1 \leq i \leq m\} \leq C \tag{3}$$

In constraint 2, if only one application is placed on the server, since the number of VMs is less than or equal to $C$, so the probability of SLA violation is

0 %. However, each server can accommodate $\lfloor C/\alpha^{90th} \rfloor$ VMs at most, so there are more than one application's VMs deployed on a server. If a server accommodates a number of VMs belonging to different applications, the resources that the server provides to an application are far less than the server physical capacity.

*Constraint 3 (Correlation Constraint, **CC**):* To further optimize SAL performance, we present a new constraint on the CA-VMP, which is shown in below:

$$max\{r_i \cdot (1 - \alpha^{mean})\} + \sum_{i=1}^{m}(r_i \cdot \alpha^{mean}) \leq C \tag{4}$$

According to the assumption 1, application's resource demands are divided into two parts: stable resource demand $r_i^s$ and variable resource demand $r_i^d$, which can be calculated by $r_i^s = r_i \cdot \alpha^{mean}$ and $r_i^d = r_i \cdot (1 - \alpha^{mean})$, respectively. The left side of the inequality 4 is divided into two parts: (1) $max\{r_i \cdot (1 - \alpha^{mean})\}$ represents the maximum value of variable resource demand for the server, and (2) $\sum_{i=1}^{m}(r_i \cdot \alpha^{mean})$ represents the sum of stable resource demand for the server. The variable resource demand cannot exceed the capacity provided by a server which can be calculated by $C - \sum_{i=1}^{m} r_i \cdot \alpha^{mean}$. Otherwise, there must be an SLA violation as the application's demand exceeds the maximum capacity that the server can provide for it. Here, the maximum capacity of the server provided for the application $i$ can be calculated by $C_i = C - \sum_{k=1,k\neq i}^{m} r_k \cdot \alpha^{mean}$.

## 3.2    Placement Constraint for Energy Cost Optimization

We use the server and network cost to represent the overall energy cost [4–6], as shown in formula 1. The server cost is proportional to the number of servers required. To minimize the number of required servers, each server should be packed based on the maximum capacity of servers. However, in CA-VMP, each application is sized by using off-peak function, the value obtained is far less than it's peak-utilization value, so there is always a high risk of SLA violation. Adding a constraint on the placement capacity of server, can greatly reduce the risk of SLA violation without increasing the number of servers required, but which may leads to a increase of network cost. This is because that when the value of placement constraint is far less than the server's physical capacity, the application are scattered into multiple servers. Therefore, in order to avoid excessive increase in network cost, the placement constraint should be as large as possible.

According to the inequality 2, the maximum number of VMs that a server can accommodate is $\lfloor C/\alpha^{90th} \rfloor$. We use $C/\alpha^{90th}$ to represent $\sum_{i=1}^{m} r_i$ for the inequality 4, and have

$$max\{r_i\} \leq C \cdot \frac{(\alpha^{90th} - \alpha^{mean})}{\alpha^{90th} \cdot (1 - \alpha^{mean})} \tag{5}$$

We use $\beta$ to represent $\frac{(\alpha^{90th} - \alpha^{mean})}{\alpha^{90th} \cdot (1 - \alpha^{mean})}$. The inequality 5 is written as $max\{r_i\} \leq C \cdot \beta$. Hence, the value of server placement constraint is determined by the factor $\beta$. $\beta$ is associated with two parameters:$\alpha^{90th}$ and $\alpha^{mean}$. As $0 < \alpha^{mean} < \alpha^{90th} < 1$, so we have $\beta < 1$.

# 4  Application Placement for Energy Cost Optimization

In order to optimize SLA performance, the placement constraint for the server is taken into account. Each server can host at most $C \cdot \beta$ VMs from an application. The energy cost consisted of server cost and network cost. The server cost is proportional to the number of required servers, while the network cost is affected by the number of provided servers. Generally, the network cost will be smaller when the more servers are available in the final placement. Therefore, the total energy cost should be determined by the number of provided servers, when the placement algorithm is determined. The energy-cost function is given by Eq. 1. When the value of $\lambda$ is determined, the Eq. 1 can be expressed as $\Psi(m) = \sum_{i=1}^{N} \phi_i + m \cdot \lambda$.

---

**Algorithm 1.** SSP: Sorting-based Split Placement.

---

**Input:**

   $m$ : the initialized number of empty servers; $S = \{s_1, \cdots, s_N\}$ refers to the remainder capacity of servers; $R = \{r_1, \cdots, r_N\}$ refers to the remainder number of required VMs; $C_s$ : the placement capacity constraint for servers.

**Output:**    the number of required servers and the final energy cost.

1: $Sort$(R);//Sorting the application according to the number of required VMs.
2: **while** $R \neq \emptyset$ **do**
3:   **if** there is at least one existing server satisfying the uncorrelation constraint with the $r_1$ in $R$, **then** placing $r_1$ on the server $s_i$, where $s_i$ is selected by best fit manner.
4:   **else** opening a new server for placing $r_1$ and adding 1 to $m$.
5:   **if** $r_1 = min\{r_1, s_i, C_s\}$ **then** $s_i \leftarrow s_i - r_1$ and remove $r_1$ from $R$.
6:   **else** $s_i \leftarrow s_i - min\{s_i, C_s\}$ and insert $r_1 - min\{s_i, C_s\}$ to the remaining set $R$ and preserve the descending order;
7:   **if** $s_i = 0$ **then** remove $s_i$ from $R$ ;
8:   **else** insert $s_i$ to the remaining set $S$.
9: **end while**
10: **return** $m$ and $\Psi(m)$;

---

We first consider an optimal placement algorithm here, motivated by the observation that the applications with more VMs may lead to higher network costs if they are scattered, as shown in Algorithm 1. The basic idea is to deploy the applications with more VMs first. Hence, we first order the applications in descending order of the number of required VMs. Each application is placed based on the best-fit decreasing strategy if the existing servers meeting uncorrelation constraint have sufficient resources to host the whole application. Otherwise, the server meeting uncorrelation constraints with the most available resources is selected to host as many VMs as possible. The remainder that can't be placed on the current server is reinserted to the remaining unplaced applications set, while preserving the descending order. If there is no server meeting uncorrelation constraint among existing servers, we should open a new server.

We then consider the number of required servers $m$. For given applications $N$, we assume that there are uncorrelation between all pairs of applications, the lower bound of $m$ can be calculated by $m_l = \lceil \sum_{i=1}^{N} R_i \cdot \alpha^{90th} / C \rceil$. On the contrary, if there are positive correlation between all pairs of applications, the upper bound of $m$ can be calculated by $m_u = \sum_{i=1}^{N} \lceil R_i / (C \cdot \beta) \rceil$. Obviously, the value of $m$ should be in between $m_l$ and $m_u$. To find the optimal value of $m$, we use the binary search based algorithm($BSBA$) as shown in [5].

## 5    Experimental Evaluation

### 5.1    Simulation Methodology

We implement a greedy based placement (GBP) algorithm [5] and take it as the baseline placement algorithm. In our simulations, we have performed three types of placement constraints: server constraint(**SC**) $\lfloor C / \alpha^{90th} \rfloor$, application constraint(**AC**) $C$ and correlation constraint(**CC**) $\lfloor C \cdot \beta \rfloor$ for the server placement capacity $C_s$. We use $sla_{th}$ to refer to the threshold of SLA violation probability, and make sure each time after an application is deployed, the demand congestion probability of server should not exceed the threshold $sla_{th}$.

SLA Constraint(**SLA**): $Pr < sla_{th}$

To investigate the effectiveness of the different constraints, we implemented six deployment algorithms which are described as follows:

**GBP:** The baseline algorithm for evaluating energy-cost savings.

**GBP+SC:** The baseline algorithm for evaluating SLA performance.

**GBP+AC:** The placement capacity of server is limited by **AC**.

**GBP+CC:** The placement capacity of server is limited by **CC**.

**GBP+CC+SLA:** The placement capacity of server is limited by both **CC** and **SLA**.

**SSP+CC+SLA:** Using the proposed algorithm of **SSP**, and the placement capacity of server is limited by both **CC** and **SLA**.

Table 1. The simulation experiment parameters

| Experimental scale: 1000 | Capacity of server $C^{max}$ : 8,**12**,16,20,24,28,32 |
|---|---|
| Correlation coefficient: $N(0, 1/4)$ | Peak to average ratio $PAR$ : 3,4,**5**,6,7,8,9,10 34.7 |
| SLA threshold $sla_th$: 2% | Tail bound parameter $\alpha^{90th}$: 0.3,0.4,**0.5**,0.6,0.7,0.8,0.9 |
| Cost ratio $\lambda$: 12 | Correlation threshold : −0.5,−0.25,**0**,0.25,0.5 |

Each run of the experiments was done 100 times, and the results are obtained by using the average of these experiments. There are 7 types of application' resource demands:5,8,13,16,20,26,35 [5]. Other experimental parameters are shown in Table 1. The bold parameters are used as default parameters.

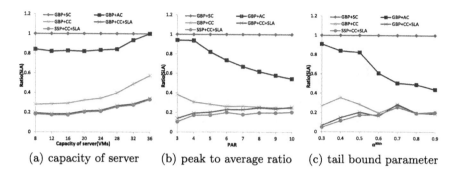

**Fig. 1.** The simulation results of SLA performance.

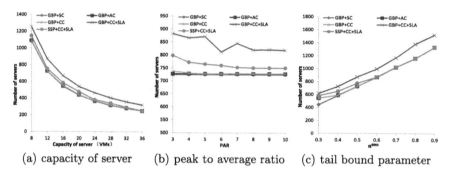

**Fig. 2.** The number of servers required.

## 5.2   Simulation Results

***The Effect of Different Parameters:*** Figures 1 and 2 show the simulation results of changing server capacity, peak to average ratio (PAR) and tail bound parameter from the five algorithms. The x-coordinate refers to the value of server capacity, PAR and tail bound parameter respectively. The y-coordinate of Fig. 1 refers to the ratio of the probability of SLA violation, given by the five algorithms, to the probability of SLA violation given by the baseline algorithm $GBP + SC$, while the y-coordinate of Fig. 2 refers to the number of servers required for the deployment of 1000 applications. As shown in Fig. 1, the value 1.0 refers to the result of using $GBP + SC$ placement algorithm. We got two conclusions: (1) By providing the constraint on the server placement capacity, we have achieved a great improvement in SLA performance; (2) Under the same placement constraint, $SSP$ matches or exceeds the performance of $GBP$. From the Fig. 2, we observed that $GBP + CC + SLA$ always require the most servers. This is because $GBP$ deploys applications randomly and thus the applications are placed dispersedly, which causes the difficult of finding a server satisfying the uncorrelation constraint from existing servers. In order to guarantee SLA performance, $GBP + CC + SLA$ requires more servers than $GBP + CC$.

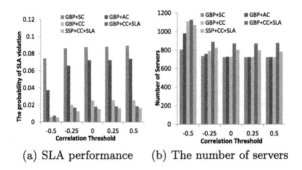

(a) SLA performance    (b) The number of servers

**Fig. 3.** The simulation results of changing correlation threshold.

Compared with $GBP + CC + SLA$, $SSP + CC + SLA$ can also provide a guarantee of SLA performance and requires the fewer number of servers.

***Correlation Threshold:*** The correlation coefficient of two applications follows the normal distribution $N(0, 1/4)$. Increasing the value of correlation threshold from $-0.5$ to $0.5$ ($-0.5, -0.25, 0, 0.25$ and $0.5$), the number of applications satisfying the uncorrelation constraint is increased from 23 to 977 (23,156,500,840 and 977).

Figure 3 shows the results of increasing the value of uncorrelation threshold. From the Fig. 3(a), we observe that the probability of SLA violation increases with the correlation threshold. This is because that the number of applications satisfying the uncorrelated constraint is increase with the increase of the correlation threshold, so most of servers are packed based on the maximum capacity of server and thus the high SLA violation. Furthermore, as shown in Fig. 3(b), when $Cor_{thr} = -0.25$, the number of uncorrelation applications for each application is 156, which takes up 15.6 % of total applications, the number of servers required has tended to a stable level. In worst case, $Cor_{thr} = -0.5$, there are little applications satisfying uncorrelation constraint, the number of required servers is increased from 800 to more than 1100 for $GBP + CC + SLA$. This result further proves that the scattered deployment of applications makes a difficult to find the server satisfying uncorrelation constraint. However, compared with the result of using peak-demand, which requires 1445 servers for 1000 applications, we have still obtained 23.8 % server savings.

***Communication Models:*** Two communication models are considered: centralized model and distributed model. The network cost is proportionate to the number of inter-server traffic links, so we use the number of links to define the energy-cost of network. Two types of network energy cost functions are introduced as shown below [5]:

Centralized Model Cost Function, **CCF**: $\phi_i = K_i - 1$.
Distributed Model Cost Function, **DCF**: $\phi_i = K_i(K_i - 1)/2$.
$K_i$ refers to the number of servers that the application $i$ has deployed on.

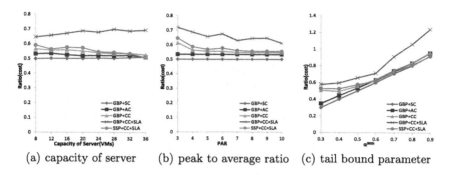

(a) capacity of server    (b) peak to average ratio    (c) tail bound parameter

**Fig. 4.** The simulation results of $CCF$ case.

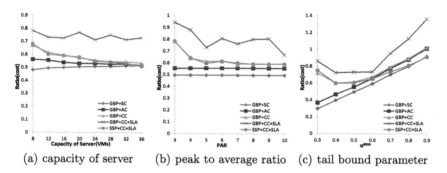

(a) capacity of server    (b) peak to average ratio    (c) tail bound parameter

**Fig. 5.** The simulation results of $DCF$ case.

Figures 4 and 5 show the simulation results of the energy-cost savings under the case of $CCF$ and $DCF$, respectively. The y-coordinate refers to the ratio of the energy-cost, given by the five algorithms, to the energy-cost given by the baseline algorithm $GBP$. The value of $\lambda$ is equal to 12. In terms of energy cost savings, $GBP + SC$ has the best performance, but which has the worst performance in term of the SLA violation. In contrast, $GBP + CC + SLA$ can provide a guarantee of SLA performance but which requires the more servers and hence leading to a high energy cost. To reduce energy cost and optimize SLA performance, we proposed $SSP + CC + SLA$ for the CA-VMP, which provides the better guarantee of SLA performance and requires the less servers, compared with $GBP + CC + SLA$. In summary, reducing the placement capacity of server, the energy cost becomes large. This is because applications are deployed on the more servers and thereby more network cost. For the same setting, case DCF has more energy cost than CCF. That is because there are more inter-server traffic links under DCF than CCF at the same placement. Furthermore, $SSP + CC + SLA$ has achieved the best tradeoff between SLA performance and energy cost. For example, compared with $GBP + SC$ which requires the fewest servers, $SSP + CC + SLA$ with an energy cost increase of less than 13 % in average have provided a guarantee of SLA performance for CA-VMP.

# 6 Conclusion

In this paper, we study the CA-VMP problem for SLA violation reduction and energy cost minimization. We first present a detailed analysis on the reasons of SLA performance degradation. Three types of placement constraints are discussed in our works for optimizing SLA performance. In order to reduce energy-cost and optimize SLA performance, we propose a novel placement algorithm *SSP*. To evaluate the performance of our proposed algorithm, theoretical analysis and extensive simulations are conducted. According to simulation experiment results, compared with existing CA-VMP methods, our proposed algorithm provides up to more than five times SLA performance improvement with negligible cost increase.

**Acknowledgments.** This work was partially supported by the Strategic Priority Research Program of the Chinese Academy of Sciences under Grant No. XDA06010401, by NSFC under Grant No. 61202056, No. 61331008 and No. 61221062, and by Huawei Research Programm YBCB2011030.

# References

1. Gao, P.X., et al.: It's not easy being green. In: SIGCOMM (2012)
2. Benson, T., et al.: Understanding data center traffic characteristics. In: WREN (2009)
3. Verma, A., et al.: Server workload analysis for power minimization using consolidation. In: Proceedings of the 2009 Conference on USENIX Annual Technical Conference (2009)
4. Meng, X., et al.: Improving the scalability of data center networks with traffic-aware virtual machine placement. In: INFOCOM (2010)
5. Li, X., et al.: Let's stay together: towards traffic aware virtual machine placement in data centers. In: INFOCOM 2014 (2014)
6. Zheng, K., et al.: Joint power optimization of data center network and servers with correlation analysis. In: INFOCOM (2014)
7. Verma, A., et al.: Virtual machine consolidation in the wild. In: Middleware 2014 (2014)
8. Halder, K., et al.: Risk aware provisioning and resource aggregation based consolidation of virtual machines. In: CLOUD 2012 (2012)
9. Meisner, D., et al.: Power management of online data-intensive services. In: SIGARCH 2011 (2011)
10. Wang, X., et al.: CARPO: correlation-aware power optimization in data center networks. In: INFOCOM (2012)
11. Kim, J., et al.: Correlation-aware virtual machine allocation for energyefficient datacenters. In: DATE 2013 (2013)
12. Verma, A., et al.: pMapper: power and migration cost aware application placement in virtualized systems. In: Middleware 2008
13. Meng, X., et al.: Efficient resource provisioning in compute clouds via vm multiplexing. In: The 7th International Conference on Autonomic Computing (2010)

# Reliability-Aware Distributed Computing Scheduling Policy

Jemal Abawajy[1]([✉]) and Mohammad Mehedi Hassan[2]

[1] Faculty of Science and Technology, School of Information Technology,
Deakin University, Geelong, Australia
jemal@deakin.edu.au
[2] Information Systems Department, College of Computer and Information Sciences,
King Saud University, Riyadh 11543, Saudi Arabia
mmhassan@ksu.edu.sa

**Abstract.** One of the primary issues associated with the efficient and effective utilization of distributed computing is resource management and scheduling. As distributed computing resource failure is a common occurrence, the issue of deploying support for integrated scheduling and fault-tolerant approaches becomes paramount importance. To this end, we propose a fault-tolerant dynamic scheduling policy that loosely couples dynamic job scheduling with job replication scheme such that jobs are efficiently and reliably executed. The novelty of the proposed algorithm is that it uses passive replication approach under high system load and active replication approach under low system loads. The switch between these two replication methods is also done dynamically and transparently. Performance evaluation of the proposed fault-tolerant scheduler and a comparison with similar fault-tolerant scheduling policy is presented and shown that the proposed policy performs better than the existing approach.

**Keywords:** Cloud computing · Job scheduling · Fault-tolerance · Replication · Performances

## 1 Introduction

Distributed computing such as Cloud computing systems can potentially furnish massively-integrated and virtually-shared computational and storage resources to solve their large-scale challenging applications. Due to the dynamic nature, complexity, and many uncertainties, distributed systems are highly susceptible to a variety of failures which make them less reliable [3, 4]. As a result, achieving large-scale computing in a seamless manner on distributed computing systems introduces not only the problem of efficient utilization and satisfactory response time but also the problem of fault-tolerance. As distributed computing are increasingly used for applications requiring high levels of performance and reliability [2], the ability to tolerate failures while effectively exploiting the distributed computing resources must be an integral part of distributed computing resource management systems.

In this paper, we address the problem of how to efficiently and reliably schedule applications in Cloud computing environments. It is known that resource failures can

© Springer International Publishing Switzerland 2015
G. Wang et al. (Eds.): ICA3PP 2015 Workshops, LNCS 9532, pp. 627–632, 2015.
DOI: 10.1007/978-3-319-27161-3_57

significantly affect scheduling performance [2]. However, research coverage of fault tolerant scheduling is limited as the primary goal for nearly all scheduling algorithms developed so far has been high performance by exploiting as much parallelism as possible. One of the reasons for this is that achieving integrated scheduling and fault-tolerance goal is a difficult proposition as the job scheduling and fault-tolerance are difficult problems to solve in their own right. As a result, there is a growing evidence that shows resource scheduling is key in achieving high reliability and performance in Cloud computing [2–4]. We propose a fault-tolerant dynamic scheduling policy that loosely couples dynamic job scheduling with job replication mechanism for efficiently and reliably executing parallel jobs. The novelty of the proposed algorithm is that it switches adaptively between using passive replication approach and active replication approach based on the system loads. Performance evaluation of the proposed fault-tolerant scheduling policy and a comparison with similar fault-tolerant scheduling policy is presented and shown that the proposed policy performs substantially better than the existing approach.

The rest of the paper is organized as follows. In Sect. 2, the background is discussed. Section 3 presents the proposed fault-tolerant scheduling policy. In Sect. 4, the performance analysis and results of the experiment are presented. Finally, the conclusion is presented in Sect. 5.

## 2   Background

Figure 1 shows a high level architecture of the Cloud computing system of interest. In this paper, we consider a Cloud computing ($G$) composed of m independent clusters, $G = \{S_1, S_2, \ldots, S_m\}$. Each cluster, $S_k \in G$, is composed of $P = \{P_1, P_2, \ldots, P_x\}$ hosts. The total processing capacity of the system is given as:

$$P = \sum_{i=1}^{|S|} \sum_{k=1}^{|P|} P_k \qquad (1)$$

Each host may fail with probability $f, 0 \leq f \leq 1$, and be repaired independently. In this paper, we assume that the core system architecture is designed around L-levels virtual hierarchy referred to as a cluster tree [8]. At the top of the cluster tree, there is a system scheduler while at the leaf level there is a local scheduler (LS) for each node. In between the system scheduler and the local schedulers, there exists a hierarchy of cluster schedulers (CS). Distributed computing environments are susceptible to a wide range of failures. We refer to all processors reachable from a given node in the cluster tree as its partition-reach. We associate a parameter called base load level (BLL) with each node in the cluster tree.

The execution environment manager (EM) maintains some state information for failure and recovery detections in Application Status Table (AST). It monitors applications at job-level and at task-level. At the time of job submission, the user specifies if fault-tolerance is required and if so the number of desired replicas. The same assumption is made in [8]. The input to the application replica manager algorithm is the job to be

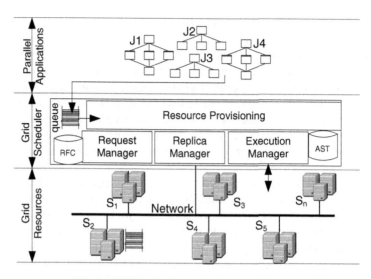

**Fig. 1.** High level cloud computing architecture

replicated (Ji) and the number of replicas (NR) to be created. The algorithm ensures that a job and its constituent task are replicated in a number of locations in the system. Jobs are replicated over clusters while tasks are replicated over processors. Specifically, when a job with fault-tolerance requirement arrives into the system, the replica manager algorithm undertakes the following steps: (1) create NR replicas of the job; (2) keep the replica and send the original job to a child that is alive and reachable; and (3) update the application status table (AST) to reflect where the job replicas are located. This process recursively follows down the cluster tree until we reach the lowest level cluster scheduler (LCS) at which point the replica placement process terminates.

The system receives $\mathcal{J} = \{J_1, J_2, \dots, J_n\}$ jobs for processing. Each job $J_i \in \mathcal{J}$ is defined by the following tuple:

$$J_i = < A_i, T_i, E_i, M_i, F_i, R_i > \tag{2}$$

The parameter $T_i$ denotes the set of tasks in job $J_i \in \mathcal{J}$ such that $J_i = \{T_1, T_2, \dots, T_k\}$. The parameters $A_i$, $E_i$ and $M_i$ are the arrival time, the service demand and the storage requirements respectively. Without loss of generality, we assume that all incoming jobs are submitted to the system scheduler where they are placed in the job wait queue until a placement decision is made. We assume that the user specifies if fault-tolerance is required ($F_i$) and the number of desired replicas ($R_i$) at the time of job submission [4].

## 3 Fault-Aware Resource Provisioning Policy

The proposed Dynamic Fault-Tolerant Scheduling (DFTS) algorithm uses the execution environment manager (EM), the replica manager (RM) and the job assignment to achieve fault-aware scheduling. The input to the application replica manager algorithm is the job to be replicated (Ji) and the number of replicas (NR) to be created. The algorithm ensures that a job and its constituent task are replicated in a number of locations in the cluster tree. Jobs are replicated over clusters while tasks are replicated over processors. Specifically, when a job with fault-tolerance requirement arrives into the system, the replica manager algorithm undertakes the following steps: (1) create NR replicas of the job; (2) keep the replica and send the original job to a child that is alive and reachable; and (3) update the application status table (AST) to reflect where the job replicas are located. This process recursively follows down the cluster tree until we reach the lowest level cluster scheduler (LCS) at which point the replica placement process terminates.

In DFTS, nodes in the system look for work when their load is below a given threshold (i.e., demand-driven). Specifically, whenever the *current load level* of a host falls below its base load level, the node sends a *Request for Computation (RFC)* message asking for $T_{req}$ units of computation to its parent. After sending RFC message to its parent, the node updates its *base load level* to ensure that it can have only one outstanding RFC at any given time. When a parent receives a RFC, if it has no job to send to the child, the new RFC is backlogged and processed when work becomes available. Otherwise, the RFC recursively ascends the cluster tree until the RFC reaches either the *system scheduler* or a node that has unassigned jobs. In the later case, a set of jobs/tasks are transferred down the hierarchy along the path the RFC has travelled. This amount is determined dynamically during parent and child negotiations and the number of unscheduled jobs. First, we determine an ideal number of jobs/tasks that can possible be sent to a child scheduler as follows:

$$T_{target} = \left\lceil \left( \frac{\wp_{child}}{\wp_{parent}} \right) \times \mathbb{N} \right\rceil \qquad (3)$$

where $\mathbb{N}$ denotes the number of unassigned jobs in the queue, $\wp_{child}$ is the partition reach of the child node and $\wp_{parent}$ is the parent partition reach. Once the target number of jobs is determined, the algorithm then considers the size of the RFC from the child as a hint to adjust the number of jobs that will actually be transferred down one level to the child as follows:

$$T_{target} = \begin{cases} min\left(T_{req}, |Queue|\right) & T_{req} > T_{target} \\ min\left(T_{req}, \wp_{child}\right) & Otherwise \end{cases} \qquad (4)$$

Finally, the algorithm selects jobs that have their replicas within the partition reach of the requesting schedulers. If there are no such jobs, then jobs belonging to the left sibling of the requesting node are searched. If this fails the jobs of the right sibling of the requesting node are selected. This process continues until the exact number of jobs to be sent to the requesting node is reached. After dispatching the jobs to a child, the parent informs the replica manager about the assignment and then updates the application status table (AST) to reflect the new assignment.

## 4   Performance Analysis

We used simulation to study the performance of fault-tolerant scheduling policies. We used the fault-tolerant scheduling algorithm (FTSA) [6] to compare the performance of the proposed scheduling policy. We modified the original FTSA policy to address the shortcomings we identified earlier. For example, to solve the race problem, we introduced a timer-based reservation scheme such that once a remote SM offers its resources to execute a job, it will not accept any request from another SM until such time that the SM that has reserved it releases it or the time expires or it completes the job assigned to it. The workload used is a synthetic matrix multiplication application characterized by an arrival time, service demand time in a dedicated environment, maximum parallelism, and size in Kbytes. This job model is common in many science and engineering applications. The cumulative service demand is generated using hyper-exponential distribution with mean 14.06 and the maximum parallelism is uniformly distributed over the range of 1 to 64 [5]. The default arrival coefficient of variation (CV) is fixed at 1 and the default service time CV is fixed at 3.5 as empirical observations at several super-computer centres indicated this to be a reasonable value [5]. In all experiments, we configured the system with two replicas. For validation, a batch strategy is used to compute confidence intervals (at least 30 batch runs were used for the results reported in this paper).

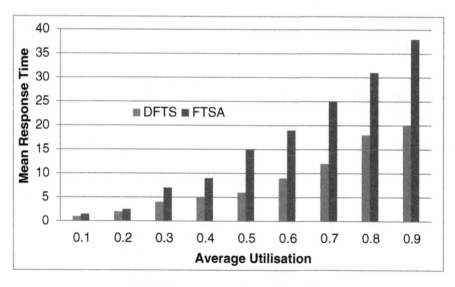

**Fig. 2.** Mean response time of the policies

Figure 2 shows the mean response time of the jobs under the FTSA and DFTS scheduling policies. In the experiment, selected nodes in a given cluster are made to fail at specific times. The objective of this experiment is to model transient failures. The nodes remain in failed state for a period of time and then become operational (i.e., repaired). We assume that the probability of multiple node failures in the same cluster at a given time interval is much smaller than the chance of a single node failure. From the data on the graphs, we observe that at low system load, DFTS is marginally better than FTSA policy. This is because of the fact that at this load level, there are many idle processors which means both FTSA and DFTS can schedule a job on several clusters and at least one of the replicas could finish without being interrupted by a node failure. However, as the load increases, performance of FTSA deteriorates. This can be explained by the fact that as load increases the number of idle processors decreases. As a result, finding $n$ idle clusters for FTSA to schedule jobs become harder. In contrast, DFTS uses demand-driven approach and multiple replicas of a job are only scheduled when there are ample free processors. For the workload type we studied, it seems that the DFTS approach is better than the active replication approach used in FTSA.

## 5    Conclusion and Future Directions

In this paper, we presented a fault-tolerant dynamic scheduling policy that loosely couples the dynamic job scheduling approach with the hybrid (i.e., passive and active replications) approach to schedule parallel jobs efficiently while at the same time providing fault-tolerance. The main advantage of the proposed approach is that fail-soft behavior (i.e., graceful degradation) is achieved in a user-transparent manner. Furthermore, being a dynamic algorithm estimations of execution or communication times are not required. An important characteristic of our algorithm is that it makes use of some local knowledge like faulty/intact or busy/idle states of nodes and about the execution location of jobs.

**Acknowledgement.**  This project was funded by the National Plan for Science, Technology and Innovation (MAARIFAH), King Abdulaziz City for Science and Technology, Kingdom of Saudi Arabia, Award Number (12-INF2885-02).

## References

1. Litke, A., Skoutas, D., Tserpes, K., Varvarigou, T.: Efficient task replication and management for adaptive fault tolerance in mobile grid environments. Future Gener. Comput. Syst. **23**(2), 163–178 (2007)
2. Javadi, B., Abawajy, J., Buyya, R.: Failure-aware resource provisioning for hybrid cloud infrastructure. J. Parallel Distrib. Comput. **72**(10), 1318–1331 (2012)
3. Javadi, B., Sinnott, R., Abawajy, J.: Scheduling of Scientific Workflows in Failure-Prone Hybrid Cloud Systems, Concurrency and Computation: Practice and Experience. Wiley, New York (2015)
4. Moon, Y.-H., Youn, C.-H.: Multihybrid job scheduling for fault-tolerant distributed computing in policy-constrained resource networks. Comput. Netw. **82**(8), 81–95 (2015)
5. Abawajy, J.H.: An efficient adaptive scheduling policy for high performance computing. Int. J. Future Gener. Comput. Syst. **22**(5), 364–370 (2008)
6. Weissman, J.B.: Fault-tolerant wide area parallel computation. In: Proceedings of IDDPS 2000 Workshops, pp. 1214–1225 (2000)

# An Escrow-Free Hierarchical Identity-Based Signature Model for Cloud Storage

Peixin Chen[1]([✉]), Xiaofeng Wang[1], and Jinshu Su[1,2]

[1] College of Computer, National University of Defense Technology,
Changsha 410073, China
{chenpeixin,xf_wang,sjs}@nudt.edu.cn
[2] National Key Laboratory for Parallel and Distributed Processing,
National University of Defense Technology, Changsha 410073, China

**Abstract.** Hierarchical identity-based cryptography is an efficient technology to address the security issues in cloud storage. However, the inherent key escrow problem primarily hinders the widespread adoption of this cryptosystem in practice. To address the key escrow problem, this paper proposes an escrow-free hierarchical identity-based signature model, in which a user signs messages with a user-selected secret and PKG signing factor apart from the private key. For proving the full security, we formulate three security games with respect to our signature model. We instantiate the escrow-free model into a specific scheme based on the SHER-IBS scheme and prove that our scheme is secure against adaptive chosen ID and message attacks.

**Keywords:** Cryptanalysis · Hierarchical identity-based signature · Key escrow · Bilinear pairing · CDH assumption

## 1 Introduction

Nowadays, cloud storage is becoming increasingly popular with the rapidly network technology development. Nevertheless, it raises a problem that user has no ultimate control over the fate of their data because data are outsourced to a remote server [14]. On the one hand, user authentication so as to limit the data access by unauthorized ones becomes a significant issue. And on the other hand, since data stored in cloud may be replaced by malicious or undesired copies, a user has a more pressing need to check the integrity of the data shared by others.

Digital signature scheme is the natural tool to provide user authentication and integrity verification. However, for traditional signing algorithms, such as RSA signing arithmetic, both user and storage service provider have to manage a great deal of public keys. Moreover, a trusted authority (a CA) is needed to issue certificates for verifying the authenticity of user public keys. Other than the RSA-like arithmetic that utilizes a random string as public key, Shamir pioneers a public-key cryptosystem called Identity-Based Signature (IBS) Scheme, allowing a user to sign messages with his private key while the signature is verified using the

© Springer International Publishing Switzerland 2015
G. Wang et al. (Eds.): ICA3PP 2015 Workshops, LNCS 9532, pp. 633–647, 2015.
DOI: 10.1007/978-3-319-27161-3_58

his identity as the public key [13]. Choon et al. propose the first practical IBS scheme that utilizes a Private Key Generator (PKG) to generate private key for users [4]. On this basis, Gentry et al. present the first Hierarchical IBS (HIBS) scheme, which greatly reduces the workload on PKG and improves the scalability [6]. Numerous HIBS schemes have been presented since then [2,5,7,12,17].

Since user private keys are generated by PKGs, deployment of HIBE scheme has inevitably to address the key escrow problem. Works on key escrow problem can be categorized into two types: IBC-applicable solutions [1,3,9,10,15] and IBS-applicable solutions [16,18].

**IBC-Applicable Solution.** This type of solutions can be apply to solve the key escrow problems in both the (H)IBE and (H)IBS schemes. Most of the solutions impose extra organizations to distribute the ability of PKG so that a single PKG is not able to generate and obtain user private keys. Boneh et al. first apply the threshold method to suggest an multi-PKG mechanism [1]. Kate and Goldberg improve their model and apply the model to three well-known IBE schemes [9]. Besides, some researchers introduce Key Privacy Authorities (KPAs) to restrict the power of PKG [3,10,15]. However, either the multi-PKG or PKG-KPAs models brings significant overhead because of the extra identity authentication and the more complicated key generating algorithms.

**IBS-Applicable Solution.** This type of solutions relies on the fact that the signer can attach extra information to the signature so that the message receivers can utilize the information along with the public key of the signer to verify the signature. Yuen et al. propose an escrow-free IBS model that each signer uses a public key and a secret key to sign messages [16]. Two signatures are generated and verified for one message. Besides, a judge and a Trusted Third Party are required in their model. Zhang et al. propose an escrow-free IBS scheme that unnecessarily depends on any judges [18]. The essence of their scheme is that a user-selected secret is added while generating the private key so that the PKG cannot obtain a complete key. However, either Yuen's model or Zhang's scheme is only for IBS schemes. Since each cryptosystem needs to be proved security utilizing formal mathematical methodology, it cannot directly extend a proved-secure IBS scheme to a secure HIBS scheme. To the best of our knowledge, no escrow-free HIBS scheme has been proposed.

In this paper, we propose an efficient model for addressing the key escrow problem in HIBS scheme, and instantiate the model into an proved secure escrow-free HIBS scheme, based on the SHER-IBS scheme. Our scheme utilizes a third party to blame the key abusing behavior of PKG. User can appeal to the party once he discovers signature with respect to his identity is bogus. Specifically, the main contributions of our paper are threefold.

1. We propose an escrow-free HIBS model. By modifying the signing and verification algorithms, our model can be apply to any primitive HIBS schemes to solve the key escrow problem.
2. We present three attack models consisting of existential-forgery, existential-key-abusing and existential-user-slander for the security proof of escrow-free (H)IBS schemes.

3. We instantiate our model into an HIBS scheme and prove that our HIBS scheme is full secure against adaptive chosen ID and message attacks under the simple CDH assumption.

The rest of this paper is organized as follows. We present the background and preliminary studies in Sect. 2. The idea of our escrow-free HIBS model is overviewed in Sect. 3. We present the construction and security proof of our HIBS scheme in Sect. 4. Our work is concluded in Sect. 5.

## 2    Preliminaries

In this section, we review some background knowledge, including the bilinear pairing and the complexity assumption used in our proof.

### 2.1    Bilinear Pairing

Let $G_1$ and $G_2$ be two cyclic multiplicative groups of the same order $p$. A map $e : G_1 \times G_1 \to G_2$ with following properties is referred to as a bilinear pairing:

1. Bilinear: $\forall u, v \in G_1, a, b \in \mathbb{Z}_N, e(u^a, v^b) = e(u, v)^{ab}$;
2. Non-degenerate: $\exists g \in G_1$, s.t. $e(g, g) \neq 1$, where 1 denotes the identity in $G_2$;
3. Computable: $\forall u, v \in G_1$, there is an efficient algorithm to compute $e(u, v)$.

### 2.2    Complexity Assumption

Our proofs are based on the following simple assumption.

**Definition 1 (CDH Assumption).** *Let $G$ be a cyclic multiplicative group generated by $g$ and $a, b \in \mathbb{Z}_p$. Given $g, g^a, g^b$, there is no probabilistic polynomial time algorithm $\mathcal{A}$ has a non-negligible advantage to compute the value $g^{ab}$.*

## 3    Overview of Our Escrow-Free HIBS Model

In this section, we introduce the intuition of our escrow-free solution, and briefly describe its construction. We then present the full security definition of escrow-free scheme by illuminating there attack games.

### 3.1    Intuition

In the HIBS scheme, a user private key is generated by a domain PKG. Therefore, either the domain PKG or the user can sign a message to obtain a valid signature. Since the signature verifier cannot determine the actual signer, two problems should be addressed in those primitive HIBS scheme: (1) *Key abusing problem.* A domain PKG is able to sign messages with the user keys generated by it without being detected; and (2) *User slandering problem.* The dishonest user is able to sign a message and slander that the PKG abuses its private key. That is, the undeniable property is missing in the primitive HIBS scheme.

For the key abusing problem, an intuitive solution is to limit the signing ability of the PKG. Therefore, we use a user-selected secret apart from the private key to generate the signature for a message. We also compute a user public parameter with the secret as input. The user sends the parameter along with the message and signature to the receivers. Signature verifying needs to take user parameter and signature as input. Since the PKG cannot obtain the user secret, it cannot generate a valid signature with respect to the user parameter. However, the PKG can generate a well-formed signature with a fake user parameter. Receiver will thereby accept the PKG generated signature-parameter pair. To solve such problem, we introduce an Arbitral Party (AP) to keep the users' public parameters. User publishes its user parameter, and attaches these same parameter to each signature. A receiver is not constrained to compare the user parameter attaching in the signature with the one publishing in the AP. Nevertheless, the PKG will be detected and blamed once it abuses a key to sign messages. Note that, an AP does not keep any confidential contents.

Since PKG is able to generate well-formed signatures with distinct user parameters, a user can slander the PKG by signing messages with randomly picked secret and sending the receiver a corresponding fake user parameter along with the signature. To solve this problem, we modify the signing algorithm so that the user can only generate well-formed signatures with regard to the parameter it published. After publishes the public parameter, user also needs to ask for a PKG signing factor from the root PKG. The root PKG computes the factor with the user parameter as well as the master secret as input and returns the factor to the user. User is desired to sign messages with the PKG signing factor.

Combining these two technologies, we can present a full secure escrow-free HIBS model. It can be applied to any HIBS schemes by modifying the signing and verifying algorithms.

### 3.2  Generic Construction

A primitive hierarchical identity-based signature scheme generally consists of four algorithms: Setup, KeyGen, Signing and Verification. To achieve the escrow-free property, we add Publish algorithm and Blame algorithm to our HIBS scheme. The generic construction of our HIBS scheme is as follows:

**Setup.** The setup algorithm takes a security parameter as input and outputs the HIBS public parameters.

**KeyGen.** The key generation algorithm takes a secret key and an identity ID as input and outputs a private key. More specifically, the root PKG takes the master secret as input and can generate private keys for any user. Each domain PKG takes its private key as input and generates keys for its descendant users.

**Publish.** The publish algorithm takes the user secret as input and outputs the user parameter. User uploads the parameter to the AP and get PKG signing factor from the root PKG.

**Signing.** The signing algorithm takes a message, a private key, as well as the user secret and PKG signing factor as input, and outputs a message signature.

**Verification.** The verification algorithm takes an identity ID, a message $m$ and a signature as input. If $\sigma$ is generated by singing $m$ with respect to ID, it outputs 1. Otherwise, it outputs 0. Note that, during this procedure, the receiver is not demanded to verify the user parameter carried along with the signature.

**Blame.** The algorithm takes a message-signature pair $\{m, \sigma\}$ and a user parameter as input. If $\sigma$ is generated by an honest signer with identity ID, it outputs 0. Otherwise, it outputs 1.

### 3.3  Security Model

We argue that an escrow-free hierarchical identity-based signature scheme with full security should be uncrackable against three attack games: *EF-ID-CMA*, *EKA-ID-CMA* and *EUS-ID-CMA*.

An attacker can break a signature scheme in four different level: a total break, universal forgery, selective forgery and existential forgery [8]. The existential forgery (*EF*) attack means that the attacker can forge a signature for at least one message. And a signature scheme is regarded as the most secure if it can resist the *EF* attack. We prove that our HIBS scheme is *EF* resistant against adaptive chosen ID and message attacks via the following game between an adversary $\mathcal{A}$ and a challenger $\mathcal{C}$.

- *Setup.* $\mathcal{C}$ runs the signature scheme setup algorithm to obtain the scheme parameters $Param$ and the master secret $MSK$. $Param$ is given to $\mathcal{A}$.
- *Query.* $\mathcal{A}$ is allowed to issue private key generating and signing queries.
  For a private key generating query with input $\{ID\}$, $\mathcal{C}$ runs the KeyGen algorithm and gives $\mathcal{A}$ the private key with regard to ID. $\mathcal{C}$ also gives the ID publish parameter $Param_{ID}$ to $\mathcal{A}$. However, the corresponding user secret is kept confidential.
  For a signing query with input $\{ID, m\}$, $\mathcal{C}$ runs the KeyGen algorithm if it does not obtain the private key $d_{ID}$ for ID. It then runs the Signing algorithm to sign the message $m$ with key $d_{ID}$ and user parameter $Param_{ID}$.
- *Challenge.* At the end of the game, $\mathcal{A}$ submits the challenge signature triple $\{ID^*, m^*, \sigma^*\}$. The triple should satisfy the condition that
  - $\mathcal{A}$ has never queried the key of $ID^*$
  - $\mathcal{A}$ has never queried the signature of $\{ID^*, m^*\}$

$\mathcal{A}$ wins the *EF-ID-CMA* game if and only if $\sigma^*$ can be correctly verified by the Verification algorithm.

**Definition 2 (*EF-ID-CMA* Security).** *We say that an HIBS scheme is secure if no probabilistic polynomial time (PPT) adversary $\mathcal{A}$ has a non-negligible advantage against the challenger $\mathcal{C}$ in the above EF-ID-CMA game. As shorthand, we say that the HIBS scheme is EF-ID-CMA secure.*

An escrow-free HIBS scheme should resist the vulnerability that the PKG abuses a user's private key to sign messages without being detected. Like the existential forgery attack, we define a strong attack model called existential key abusing (*EKA*) that an attacker can abuse at least one user's private key to sign at least one message. We prove that our HIBS scheme is *EKA* resistant against adaptive chosen ID and message attacks via the following game between an adversary $\mathcal{A}$ and a challenger $\mathcal{C}$.

- *Setup.* $\mathcal{C}$ runs the signature scheme setup algorithm to obtain the scheme parameters *Param* and the master secret *MSK*. *Param* is given to $\mathcal{A}$.
- *Query.* $\mathcal{A}$ is allowed to issue private key generating and signing queries. For a private key generating query with input {ID}, $\mathcal{C}$ runs the KeyGen algorithm and gives $\mathcal{A}$ the private key with regard to ID. $\mathcal{C}$ also gives the ID publish parameter $Param_{ID}$ to $\mathcal{A}$. However, the corresponding user secret is kept confidential.

  For a signing query with input {ID, $m$}, $\mathcal{C}$ runs the KeyGen algorithm if it does not obtain the private key $d_{ID}$ for ID. It then runs the Signing algorithm to sign the message $m$ with key $d_{ID}$ and user parameter $Param_{ID}$.
- *Challenge.* At the end of the game, $\mathcal{A}$ submits the challenge signature triple {ID*, $m^*$, $\sigma^*$}. The triple should satisfy the condition that
  - $\mathcal{A}$ has queried the key of ID* to obtain {$d_{ID^*}$, $Param_{ID^*}$}
  - $\mathcal{A}$ has queried a signature of {ID*, $m$} for at least one $m \neq m^*$

$\mathcal{A}$ wins the *EKA-ID-CMA* game if and only if

- $\sigma^*$ can be correctly verified by the Verification algorithm
- with input {ID*, $m$,* $\sigma^*$, $Param_{ID^*}$}, the Blame algorithm outputs 0

**Definition 3 (*EKA-ID-CMA* Security).** *We say that an HIBS scheme is secure if no PPT adversary $\mathcal{A}$ has a non-negligible advantage against the challenger $\mathcal{C}$ in the above* EKA-ID-CMA *game. As shorthand, we say that the HIBS scheme is* EKA-ID-CMA *secure.*

An escrow-free HIBS scheme should also resist the vulnerability that a dishonest user uses its private key to sign messages and denies by framing up the PKG. Like the existential forgery attack, we define a strong attack model called existential user slander (*EUS*) that an attacker can sign at least one message to successfully frame up the PKG. We prove that our HIBS scheme is *EUS* resistant against adaptive chosen ID and message attacks via the following game between an adversary $\mathcal{A}$ and a challenger $\mathcal{C}$.

- *Setup.* $\mathcal{C}$ runs the signature scheme setup algorithm to obtain the scheme parameters *Param* and the master secret *MSK*. *Param* is given to $\mathcal{A}$.
- *Query.* $\mathcal{A}$ is allowed to issue private key generating and signing queries. For a private key generating query with input {ID}, $\mathcal{C}$ runs the KeyGen algorithm and gives $\mathcal{A}$ the private key with regard to ID. $\mathcal{C}$ also gives the ID publish parameter $Param_{ID}$ as well as the corresponding user secret to $\mathcal{A}$.

For a signing query with input $\{ID, m\}$, $C$ runs the KeyGen algorithm if it does not obtain the private key $d_{ID}$ for ID. It then runs the Signing algorithm to sign the message $m$ with key $d_{ID}$ and user parameter $Param_{ID}$.

- *Challenge.* At the end of the game, $A$ submits the challenge signature triple $\{ID^*, m^*, \sigma^*\}$. The triple should satisfy the condition that
  - $A$ has queried the key of $ID^*$ to obtain $\{d_{ID^*}, Param_{ID^*}\}$
  - $A$ has never queried a signature of $\{ID^*, m^*\}$

$A$ wins the *EUS-ID-CMA* game if and only if

- $\sigma^*$ can be correctly verified by the Verification algorithm
- with input $\{ID^*, m,^* \sigma^*, Param_{ID^*}\}$, the Blame algorithm outputs 1

**Definition 4 (*EUS-ID-CMA* Security).** *We say that an HIBS scheme is secure if no PPT adversary $A$ has a non-negligible advantage against the challenger $C$ in the above EUS-ID-CMA game. As shorthand, we say that the HIBS scheme is EUS-ID-CMA secure.*

## 4 Our Hierarchical Identity-Based Signature Scheme

In this section, we first present the construction of our escrow-free HIBS scheme. Our HIBS scheme extends the SHER-IBS scheme [5]. We then prove the security of our scheme against there attacks.

### 4.1 Construction

Let $K$ be the security parameter given to the setup algorithm, and let $\mathcal{G}$ be a BDH parameter generator.

**Setup.** Given a security parameter, the PKG works as follows:

1. runs $\mathcal{G}$ on input $K$ to generate multiplicative groups $G_1, G_2$ of same prime order, and a bilinear pairing $\hat{e} : G_1 \times G_1 \rightarrow G_2$;
2. chooses random $\alpha \in \mathbb{Z}_p^*$ and two generators $g, g_2 \in G_1$, computes $g_1 = g^\alpha$;
3. randomly picks $h_1, \ldots, h_\ell \in G_1$;
4. chooses cryptographic hash functions $H_1 : \{0,1\}^* \times G_1 \rightarrow \mathbb{Z}_p^*$ and $H_2 : G_1 \times \{0,1\}^* \rightarrow G_1$;
5. publishes $Param = \{\hat{e}, g, g_1, g_2, h_1, \ldots, h_\ell, H_1, H_2\}$ as public parameters and keeps $MSK = g_2^\alpha$ as master secret.

**KeyGen.** For an input $ID = \{I_1, \ldots, I_k\}$, the $level_{k-1}$ domain PKG with private key $d_{ID_{|k-1}} = \{d'_0, \ldots, d'_{k-1}\}$ generates the key $d_{ID}$ as follows:

1. picks random $r_k \in \mathbb{Z}_p^*$;
2. set $d_{ID} = \{d'_0 F_k(I_k)^{r_k}, d'_1, \ldots, d'_{k-1}, g^{r_k}\}$, where $F_k(x) = g_1^x h_k$.

We refer to $g_2^\alpha$ as $d_{\mathrm{ID}_{|0}}$, and the user private key can be presented as $d_{\mathrm{ID}} = \{d_0, d_1, \ldots, d_k\} = \{g_2^\alpha \prod_{j=1}^k F_j(I_j)^{r_j}, g^{r_1}, \ldots, g^{r_k}\}$.

**Publish.** In this phase, user publishes a public parameter and gets PKG signing factor from the root PKG. It does the work as follows:

1. picks $s_{\mathrm{ID}} \in \mathbb{Z}_p^*$ as user secret and computes $g_{\mathrm{ID}} = g^{s_{\mathrm{ID}}}$;
2. publishes $g_{\mathrm{ID}}$ by submitting it to the AP;
3. sends $g_{\mathrm{ID}}$ to the root PKG, and gets $f^\alpha = H_2(g_{\mathrm{ID}}, \mathrm{ID})^\alpha$ computed by PKG.

**Signing.** To sign a message $m$ with respect to identity $\mathrm{ID} = \{I_1, \ldots, I_k\}$, user takes the private key $d_{\mathrm{ID}} = \{d_0, d_1, \ldots, d_k\}$, secret $s_{\mathrm{ID}}$ and PKG signing factor $f^\alpha$ as input, running the algorithm as follows:

1. picks a random $s \in \mathbb{Z}_p^*$ and computes $x = g_2^s$;
2. computes $h = H_1(m, x)$;
3. for $j = 1, \ldots, k$, computes $y_j = d_j^{s+h}$;
4. computes $f = H_2(g_{\mathrm{ID}}, \mathrm{ID})$;
5. computes $z = d_0^{s+h} f^{s_{\mathrm{ID}}} f^\alpha = d_0^{s+h} f^{s_{\mathrm{ID}} + \alpha}$;
6. sets signature as $\sigma = \{x, y_1, \ldots, y_k, z, g_{\mathrm{ID}}\}$.

**Verification.** To verify a signature $\sigma = \{x, y_1, \ldots, y_k, z, g_{\mathrm{ID}}\}$ on message $m$ with respect to identity $\mathrm{ID} = \{I_1, \ldots, I_k\}$, the algorithm works as follows:

1. computes $h = H_1(m, x)$ and $f = H_2(g_{\mathrm{ID}}, \mathrm{ID})$;
2. checks whether $\hat{e}(g, z) = \hat{e}(g_1, g_2^h x \prod_{j=1}^k y_j^{I_j}) \hat{e}(f, g_{\mathrm{ID}} g_1) \prod_{j=1}^k \hat{e}(y_j, h_j)$ holds. If so, outputs 1. Otherwise, outputs 0.

Actually, if the signature is valid, there is

$$\hat{e}(g, z) = \hat{e}(g, d_0^{s+h} f^{s_{\mathrm{ID}} + \alpha})$$

$$= \hat{e}(g, (g_2^\alpha \prod_{j=1}^k F_j(I_j)^{r_j})^{s+h}) \hat{e}(g, f^{s_{\mathrm{ID}}} f^\alpha)$$

$$= \hat{e}(g, g_2^{\alpha(s+h)}) \hat{e}(g, \prod_{j=1}^k g_1^{I_j r_j(s+h)} h_j^{r_j(s+h)}) \hat{e}(g^{s_{\mathrm{ID}}}, f) \hat{e}(g^\alpha, f)$$

$$= \hat{e}(g^\alpha, g_2^s g_2^h) \hat{e}(g, \prod_{j=1}^k g_1^{I_j r_j(s+h)}) \hat{e}(g, \prod_{j=1}^k h_j^{r_j(s+h)}) \hat{e}(f, g_{\mathrm{ID}} g_1)$$

$$= \hat{e}(g_1, x g_2^h) \hat{e}(f, g_{\mathrm{ID}} g_1) \hat{e}(\prod_{j=1}^k d_j^{I_j(s+h)}, g_1) \prod_{j=1}^k \hat{e}(d_j^{s+h}, h_j)$$

$$= \hat{e}(g_1, x g_2^h) \hat{e}(g_1, \prod_{j=1}^k y_j^{I_j}) \hat{e}(f, g_{\mathrm{ID}} g_1) \prod_{j=1}^k \hat{e}(y_j, h_j)$$

$$= \hat{e}(g_1, g_2^h x \prod_{j=1}^k y_j^{I_j}) \hat{e}(f, g_{\mathrm{ID}} g_1) \prod_{j=1}^k \hat{e}(y_j, h_j)$$

**Blame.** Given $\{\text{ID}, m, \sigma\}$, where $\sigma = \{x, y_1, \ldots, y_k, z, g_{\text{ID}}\}$, this algorithm requires the user parameter $g'_{\text{ID}}$ with respect to the identity ID from the AP. It outputs 1 if and only if $g_{\text{ID}} \neq g'_{\text{ID}}$ and 0 otherwise.

## 4.2   Security Proof

The security of our escrow-free HIBS scheme is proved according to the following Lemmas.

**Lemma 1.** *If there exists an EF-ID-CMA algorithm $\mathcal{A}$ that has non-negligible advantage against our HIBS scheme, then there is an EF-ID-CMA algorithm $\mathcal{B}$ that breaks the SHER-IBS scheme with the same advantage.*

*Proof.* We show how to construct algorithm $\mathcal{B}$ to win the *EF-ID-CMA* game against SHER-IBS scheme. $\mathcal{B}$ is given parameters of SHER-IBS scheme $parm = \{g, g_1, g_2, h_1, \ldots, h_\ell, H_1\}$, where $\hat{e} : G_1 \times G_1 \rightarrow G_2$ is a bilinear map, $g, g_2$ are generators of cyclic multiplicative group $G_1$, and $H_1$ is a hash function. As a simulator, $\mathcal{B}$ provides an *EF-ID-CMA* game to $\mathcal{A}$ and uses the final challenge information to break the SHER-IBS scheme.
$\mathcal{A}$ play the game as below:

**Setup.** $\mathcal{B}$ maintains hash oracles $H'_1 : \{0,1\} \times G_1 \rightarrow \mathbb{Z}_p^*$ and $H_2 : G_1 \times \{0,1\}^* \rightarrow G_1$. Parameters $param = \{g, g_1, g_2, h_1, \ldots, h_\ell, H'_1, H_2\}$ are sent to $\mathcal{A}$ as the parameters of our IBS scheme.

**Query.** $\mathcal{B}$ answers queries made by $\mathcal{A}$.

- *Hash queries.* For the $i^{th}$ queries with input $\text{ID}_i$ and corresponding $g_{\text{ID}_i}$, $\mathcal{B}$ randomly picks $t_i \in \mathbb{Z}_p^*$, and sets $H_2(g_{\text{ID}_i}, \text{ID}_i) = g^{t_i}$. For the $H'_1$ queries with input $\{m, x\}$, $\mathcal{B}$ firstly retrieve a correlative $f$. As aforementioned, hash value of $H'_1$ is queried while message signing is queried. Thus, $\mathcal{B}$ can always obtain an $f = H_2(g_{\text{ID}}, \text{ID})$ with respect to ID. $\mathcal{B}$ computes $x' = xf$ and queries $h = H_1(m, x')$ from SHER-IBS scheme. $h$ is returned as the value of $H'_1$.
- *Key queries.* $\mathcal{A}$ submits an identity ID. $\mathcal{B}$ maintains an ID-key list. If the queried key $d_{\text{ID}}$ is in the list, $\mathcal{B}$ returns $d_{\text{ID}}$ to $\mathcal{A}$. Otherwise, $\mathcal{B}$ takes ID as the input and queries $d_{\text{ID}}$ from SHER-IBS scheme. $\mathcal{B}$ also randomly picks $s_{\text{ID}} \in \mathbb{Z}_p^*$. It adds $(\text{ID}, d_{\text{ID}}, s_{\text{ID}})$ into the list and returns $d_{\text{ID}}$ to $\mathcal{A}$.
- *Signing queries.* $\mathcal{A}$ submits $\{\text{ID}, m\}$. If $\mathcal{B}$ does not have a private key $d_{\text{ID}}$ with respect to ID, it queries the private key from SHER-IBS scheme and picks a random $s_{\text{ID}} \in \mathbb{Z}_p^*$. $\mathcal{B}$ inputs $d_{\text{ID}}$ and $s_{\text{ID}}$ to sign message $m$ using the signing algorithm provided by SHER-IBS, and gets signature $\sigma = \{x, y_1, \ldots, y_k, z\}$. $\mathcal{B}$ invokes a hash query such that $f = H_2(g_{\text{ID}}, \text{ID}) = g^{t_i}$. It then computes $z' = zf^{s_{\text{ID}}+\alpha} = zg^{t_i s_{\text{ID}}} g_1^{t_i}$. $\mathcal{B}$ returns $\sigma' = \{x, y_1, \ldots, y_k, z', g^{s_{\text{ID}}}\}$ to $\mathcal{A}$.

**Challenge.** $\mathcal{A}$ finally outputs a triple $(\text{ID}^*, m^*, \sigma^*)$, where $\sigma^* = \{x^*, y_1^*, \ldots, y_k^*, z^*, g_{\text{ID}}^*\}$. Since $\mathcal{A}$ is able to win the *EF-ID-CMA* game with non-negligible advantage against our HIBS scheme as assumed, there is $\hat{e}(g, z^*) = \hat{e}(g_1, g_2^h x^*)$

$\prod_{j=1}^{k} y_j^{*I_j})\hat{e}(f, g_{\text{ID}}g_1)\prod_{j=1}^{k}\hat{e}(y_j^*, h_j)$, where $f = H_2(g_{\text{ID}}, \text{ID}) = g^{t_\gamma}$ and $h = H_1'(m, x^*) = H_1(m, x^*f)$.

Let $x' = x^*f$, $y_i' = y_i^*$ for $i = 1, \ldots, k$, and $z' = z^* g_{\text{ID}}^{-t_\gamma}$. To break the SHER-IBS scheme, $\mathcal{B}$ submits the challenge triple $(\text{ID}^*, m^*, \sigma')$, where $\sigma' = \{x', y_1', \ldots, y_k', z'\}$. Actually, we can get

$$\hat{e}(g, z') = \hat{e}(g, z^* g_{\text{ID}}^{-t_\gamma}) = \hat{e}(g, z^*)\hat{e}(g, g_{\text{ID}}^{-t_\gamma})$$

$$= \hat{e}(g_1, g_2^h x^* \prod_{j=1}^{k} y_j^{*I_j})\hat{e}(f, g_{\text{ID}}g_1)\left(\prod_{j=1}^{k}\hat{e}(y_j^*, h_j)\right)\hat{e}(g^{t_\gamma}, g_{\text{ID}})^{-1}$$

$$= \hat{e}(g_1, g_2^h x^* \prod_{j=1}^{k} y_j'^{I_j})\hat{e}(g_1, f)\prod_{j=1}^{k}\hat{e}(y_j', h_j)$$

$$= \hat{e}(g_1, g_2^h x^* f \prod_{j=1}^{k} y_j'^{I_j})\prod_{j=1}^{k}\hat{e}(y_j', h_j) = \hat{e}(g_1, g_2^h x' \prod_{j=1}^{k} y_j'^{I_j})\prod_{j=1}^{k}\hat{e}(y_j', h_j)$$

Therefore, $\mathcal{B}$ can breaks the SHER-IBS scheme with the same advantage as $\mathcal{A}$ breaks our HIBS scheme.

**Lemma 2.** *If there exists an algorithm for EF-ID-CMA against the SHER-IBS scheme, then CDH assumption can be broke within acceptable time.*

*Proof.* The lemma is proved by Sherman et al. in [5] (proof of *Theorem 1*).

**Lemma 3.** *If there exists an EKA-ID-CMA algorithm $\mathcal{A}$ that has non-negligible advantage against our HIBS scheme, then there is an algorithm $\mathcal{B}$ that breaks the CDH assumption.*

*Proof.* Supposing *EKA-ID-CMA* algorithm $\mathcal{A}$ can break our HIBS scheme, we show how to construct a PPT algorithm $\mathcal{B}$ to violate the CDH assumption. Let $q_1$ be the number of hash queries made by $\mathcal{A}$ to $H_1$, where $H_1$ is treated as a hash oracle. Note that each hash query to $H_1$ is corresponding to a singing query. Let $q_2$ be the number of distinct identities that appear in the signature query. Given $g, g^a, g^b$, $\mathcal{B}$ interacts with $\mathcal{A}$ as follows:

**Setup.** $\mathcal{B}$ generates $\hat{e} : G_1 \times G_1 \to G_2$ with $g$ as a generator of $G_1$. It randomly picks $\alpha, \alpha_1, \ldots, \alpha_\ell \in \mathbb{Z}_p^*$, $g_2 \in G_1$, and sets $g_1 = g^\alpha$, $h_j = g^{\alpha_j}$ for $j = 1, \ldots, \ell$. $\mathcal{B}$ also maintains hash oracles $H_1 : \{0,1\}^* \times G_1 \to \mathbb{Z}_p^*$ and $H_2 : G_1 \times \{0,1\}^* \to G_1$. Parameters $Param = \{\hat{e}, g, g_1, g_2, h_1, \ldots, h_\ell, H_1, H_2\}$ are sent to $\mathcal{A}$. $\mathcal{B}$ randomly picks three indexes $\hat{\gamma} \in \{1, \ldots, q_1\}$ and $\hat{\eta} \in \{1, \ldots, q_2\}$. $\mathcal{B}$ sets $g_{\text{ID}_{\hat{\eta}}} = g^b$.

**Query.** $\mathcal{A}$ submits KeyGen and Signing queries.

- *KeyGen queries.* $\mathcal{A}$ submits the $\eta^{th}$ key generation query with an identity $\text{ID} = \{I_1, \ldots, I_k\}$. If $\eta = \hat{\eta}$, $\mathcal{B}$ aborts. Otherwise, $\mathcal{B}$ maintains a ID-key list and generates a private key for $\mathcal{A}$:

- if $ID = \{I'_1, \ldots, I'_u\}$ with $d_{ID|u}$ is in the list such that $u < k$ and $I'_j = I_j$ for $j = 1, \ldots, u$, $\mathcal{B}$ randomly picks $r_{u+1}, \ldots, r_k \in \mathbb{Z}_p^*$ and sets $d_{ID} = \{d_0, \ldots, d_u, g^{r_{u+1}}, \ldots, g^{r_k}\}$;
- if $ID = \{I'_1, \ldots, I'_u\}$ with $d_{ID|u}$ is in the list such that $u \geqslant k$ and $I'_j = I_j$ for $j = 1, \ldots, k$, $\mathcal{B}$ sets $d_{ID} = \{d_0, \ldots, d_k\}$;
- otherwise, $\mathcal{B}$ randomly picks $r_1, \ldots, r_k \in \mathbb{Z}_p^*$ and sets
  $d_{ID} = \{g_2^\alpha \prod_{j=1}^k (g_1^{I_j} h_j)^{r_j}, g^{r_1}, \ldots, g^{r_k}\}$.
  $\mathcal{B}$ also randomly picks $s_{ID} \in \mathbb{Z}_p^*$. It stores $(ID, d_{ID}, s_{ID})$ into the list, and returns $d_{ID}$ as well as $g^{s_{ID}}$ to $\mathcal{A}$.

- *Signing queries.* $\mathcal{A}$ submits an identity $ID = \{I_1, \ldots, I_k\}$ and a message $m$. If $\mathcal{B}$ does not have a private key $d_{ID}$ with respect to $ID$, it generates the private key by implementing the algorithm in *KeyGen queries*. If $ID = ID_{\hat{\eta}}$ and $m = m_{\hat{\gamma}}$, $\mathcal{B}$ aborts. Otherwise, $\mathcal{B}$ replies the $\gamma^{th}$ signing query as below.
  - If $\gamma \neq \hat{\gamma}$, $\mathcal{B}$ randomly picks $r_\gamma \in \mathbb{Z}_p^*$ and sets $f = H_2(g_{ID}, ID) = g^{r_\gamma}$.
  - Otherwise, $\mathcal{B}$ sets $f = g^a$.
  $\mathcal{B}$ randomly picks $s \in \mathbb{Z}_p^*$, sets $x = g_2^s$, $h = H_1(m, x)$, $y_j = d_j^{s+h}(j = 1, \ldots, k)$, $z = d_0^{s+h} f^{s_{ID}+\alpha}$, and returns $\sigma = \{x, y_1, \ldots, y_k, z, g_{ID}\}$ to $\mathcal{A}$.

**Challenge.** With probability $\frac{(q_2-1)(q_1 q_2-1)}{q_1 q_2^2}$, $\mathcal{B}$ does not abort and $\mathcal{A}$ submits $(ID^*, m^*, \sigma^*)$ such that there exists a Signature Query of which the return values is $(ID^*, m, \sigma)$ and that $g^*_{ID} = g_{ID}$. Further, with probability at least $\frac{1}{q_1 q_2}$, $g_{ID} = g_{ID_{\hat{\eta}}}$ and $m^* = m_{\hat{\gamma}}$. Thus, there is

$$\hat{e}(g, z^*) = \hat{e}(g_1, g_2^h x^* \prod_{j=1}^k y_j^{*I_j}) \hat{e}(f, g_{ID} g_1) \prod_{j=1}^k \hat{e}(y_j^*, h_j)$$

$$= \hat{e}(g^\alpha, g_2^h x^* \prod_{j=1}^k y_j^{*I_j}) \hat{e}(f, g_{ID} g_1) \prod_{j=1}^k \hat{e}(y_j^*, g^{\alpha_j})$$

$$= \hat{e}(g, \left(g_2^h x^* \prod_{j=1}^k y_j^{*I_j}\right)^\alpha g^{ab} g^{a\alpha} \prod_{j=1}^k y_j^{*\alpha_j})$$

$$= \hat{e}(g, (g_2^h x^* g^a)^\alpha \left(\prod_{j=1}^k y_j^{*(\alpha I_j + \alpha_j)}\right) g^{ab})$$

So $\mathcal{B}$ gets $z^* = (g_2^h x^* g^a)^\alpha \left(\prod_{j=1}^k y_j^{*(\alpha I_j + \alpha_j)}\right) g^{ab}$, and computes $g^{ab} = \frac{z^*}{(g_2^h x^* g^a)^\alpha \prod_{j=1}^k y_j^{*(\alpha I_j + \alpha_j)}}$.

Therefore, PPT algorithm $\mathcal{B}$ can break the CDH assumption.

**Lemma 4.** *If there exists an EUS-ID-CMA algorithm $\mathcal{A}$ that has non-negligible advantage against our HIBS scheme, then there is an algorithm $\mathcal{B}$ that breaks the CDH assumption.*

*Proof.* Supposing *EUS-ID-CMA* algorithm $\mathcal{A}$ can break our HIBS scheme, we show how to construct a PPT algorithm $\mathcal{B}$ to violate the CDH assumption. Given $g, g^a, g^b$, $\mathcal{B}$ interacts with $\mathcal{A}$ in a selective identity game as follows:

**Setup.** $\mathcal{B}$ generates a bilinear map $\hat{e} : G_1 \times G_1 \to G_2$ with $g$ as a generator of $G_1$. It randomly picks $\alpha, \alpha_1, \ldots, \alpha_\ell \in \mathbb{Z}_p^*$, and sets $g_1 = g^a$, $g_2 = g^b$, $h_j = g^{\alpha_j}$ for $j = 1, \ldots, \ell$. Function $F_j : \mathbb{Z}_p \to G_1$ is defined as $F_j(x) = g_1^x h_j = g_1^x g^{\alpha_j}$. $\mathcal{B}$ also maintains hash oracles $H_1 : \{0,1\}^* \times G_1 \to \mathbb{Z}_p^*$ and $H_2 : G_1 \times \{0,1\}^* \to G_1$. Parameters $Param = \{\hat{e}, g, g_1, g_2, h_1, \ldots, h_\ell, H_1, H_2\}$ are sent to $\mathcal{A}$.

**Query.** $\mathcal{B}$ answers queries made by $\mathcal{A}$.

- *Hash queries.* $\mathcal{B}$ maintains lists $L_1$ and $L_2$ to store the answer of the $H_1$ oracle and $H_2$ oracle respectively.

  When $\mathcal{A}$ submits the $i^{th}$ $H_1$ hash query with input $\{m, x\}$, $\mathcal{B}$ checks the list $L_1$. If an entry is found, the same answer is returned to $\mathcal{A}$; otherwise, $\mathcal{B}$ randomly picks $h \in \mathbb{Z}_p^*$ and returns it to $\mathcal{A}$. $\mathcal{B}$ stores $\{m, x, h\}$ to the list $L_1$. When $\mathcal{A}$ submits the $i^{th}$ $H_2$ hash query with input $\{g_{\mathrm{ID}}, \mathrm{ID}\}$, $\mathcal{B}$ checks the list $L_2$. If an entry for the query is found, the same answer will be returned to $\mathcal{A}$; otherwise, $\mathcal{B}$ randomly picks $\beta_i \in \mathbb{Z}_p^*$ and sets $f = H_2(g_{\mathrm{ID}}, \mathrm{ID}) = g^{\beta_i}$. $\mathcal{B}$ stores $\{g_{\mathrm{ID}}, \mathrm{ID}, \beta_i\}$ to the list $L_2$.

- *KeyGen queries.* When $\mathcal{A}$ submits a private key query with input $\mathrm{ID} = \{I_1, \ldots, i_k\}$, $\mathcal{B}$ randomly picks $r_1, \ldots, r_k \in \mathbb{Z}_p^*$ and sets $d_0 = g_2^{\frac{-\alpha_k}{I_k}} \prod_{j=1}^k F_j$ $(I_j)^{r_j}$, $d_1 = g^{r_1}$, $\ldots, d_{k-1} = g^{r_{k-1}}$, $d_k = g_2^{\frac{-1}{I_k}} g^{r_k}$. Note that, there is $d_k = g_2^{\frac{-1}{I_k}} g^{r_k} = g^{\frac{-b}{I_k}} g^{r_k} = g^{r_k - \frac{b}{I_k}}$, $g_2^{\frac{-\alpha_k}{I_k}} F_k(I_k)^{r_k} = g_2^{\frac{-\alpha_k}{I_k}} (g_1^{I_k} g^{\alpha_k})^{r_k} = g_2^\alpha (g_1^{I_k}$ $g^{\alpha_k})^{r_k - \frac{b}{I_k}} = g_2^\alpha F_k(I_k)^{r_k - \frac{b}{I_k}}$. Thus we can get $d_0 = g_2^\alpha \left( \prod_{j=1}^{k-1} F_j(I_j)^{r_j} \right) F_k$ $(I_k)^{r_k - \frac{b}{I_k}}$, $d_1 = g^{r_1}, \ldots, d_{k-1} = g^{r_{k-1}}$, $d_k = g^{r_k - \frac{b}{I_k}}$, which is a well-formed private key.

  For each identity ID, $\mathcal{B}$ maintains a list $L_3$ to store the user key information. It randomly picks $s_{\mathrm{ID}} \in \mathbb{Z}_p^*$, and stores $(\mathrm{ID}, d_{\mathrm{ID}}, r_1, \ldots, r_k, s_{\mathrm{ID}})$ into the list $L_3$. Both the private key $d_{\mathrm{ID}}$ and user secret $s_{\mathrm{ID}}$ are returned to $\mathcal{A}$.

- *Signing queries.* When $\mathcal{A}$ submits a signing query with $\mathrm{ID} = \{I_1, \ldots, I_k\}$ and $m$ as input. If $\mathcal{B}$ does not have a private key $d_{\mathrm{ID}}$ with respect to ID, it generates the private key by implementing the algorithm in *KeyGen queries*. With key $d_{\mathrm{ID}}$ as well as $s_{\mathrm{ID}}$, $\mathcal{B}$ replies the signing query as below:
  - calculates $g_{\mathrm{ID}} = g^{s_{\mathrm{ID}}}$;
  - queries the hash oracle $H_2$ to obtain $\beta_i$ and sets $f = g^{\beta_i}$;
  - randomly picks $s \in \mathbb{Z}_p^*$, and sets $x = g_2^s$;
  - queries the hash oracle $H_1$ to obtain $h$ and sets $y_j = d_j^{s+h}$ for $j = 1, \ldots, k$;
  - sets $z = d_0^{s+h} f^{s_{\mathrm{ID}}+\alpha} = d_0^{s+h} g^{\beta_i(s_{\mathrm{ID}}+\alpha)} = d_0^{s+h} g_{\mathrm{ID}}^{\beta_i} g_1^{\beta_i}$.

  Signature $\sigma = \{x, y_1, \ldots, y_k, z, g_{\mathrm{ID}}\}$ is returned to $\mathcal{A}$.

**Challenge.** $\mathcal{A}$ finally outputs $(\mathrm{ID}^*, m^*, \sigma^*)$, where $\sigma^* = \{x^*, y_1^*, \ldots, y_k^*, z^*, g_{\mathrm{ID}}^*\}$ and the private key of $\mathrm{ID}^*$ has been queried during the *Query Phase*. $\mathcal{B}$ extracts the private key entry $(\mathrm{ID}^*, d_{\mathrm{ID}^*}, r_1, \ldots, r_k, s_{\mathrm{ID}'})$ from list $L_3$. Note that, since $\mathcal{A}$

can break our HIBS scheme against the *EUS-ID-CMA* game, there is $g'_{\text{ID}} \neq g^*_{\text{ID}}$, where $g'_{\text{ID}} = g^{s_{\text{ID'}}}$ is the extracted public secret of ID*.

Following the principle of forking lemma [11], $\mathcal{B}$ can replay $\mathcal{A}$ with the same random tape but different choices of $H_1$. It then obtains two valid signatures $(x^*, y_1^*, \ldots, y_k^*, z^*, g^*_{\text{ID}})$ and $(x^*, \bar{y}_1^*, \ldots, \bar{y}_k^*, \bar{z}^*, g^*_{\text{ID}})$ on message $m^*$ with respect to hash functions $H_1$ and $\bar{H}_1$ having different values $h \neq \bar{h}$ on $(m^*, x^*)$, respectively. For $j = 1, \ldots, k$, since $y_j^* = d_j^{s+h}$ and $\bar{y}_j^* = d_j^{s+\bar{h}}$, we can calculate $(y_j^*/\bar{y}_j^*) = d_j^{h-\bar{h}} = g^{r_j(h-\bar{h})}$. Thus, there is

$$\hat{e}(g, z^*)/\hat{e}(g, \bar{z}^*)$$

$$= \frac{\hat{e}(g_1, g_2^h x \prod_{j=1}^k y_j^{*I_j})\hat{e}(f, g^*_{\text{ID}}g_1)\prod_{j=1}^k \hat{e}(y_j^*, h_j)}{\hat{e}(g_1, g_2^{\bar{h}} x \prod_{j=1}^k \bar{y}_j^{*I_j})\hat{e}(f, g^*_{\text{ID}}g_1)\prod_{j=1}^k \hat{e}(\bar{y}_j^*, h_j)}$$

$$= \hat{e}(g_1, g_2^{h-\bar{h}} \prod_{j=1}^k d_j^{(h-\bar{h})I_j})\hat{e}(g, (g^*_{\text{ID}}g_1)^{\beta_u}(g^*_{\text{ID}}g_1)^{-\beta_v}) \prod_{j=1}^k \hat{e}(d_j^{h-\bar{h}}, g^{\alpha_j})$$

$$= \hat{e}(g, g^{ab(h-\bar{h})} \prod_{j=1}^k (g^{(h-\bar{h})r_j I_j})^a)\hat{e}(g, g^{*\beta_u}_{\text{ID}}g^{\bar{*}-\beta_v}_{\text{ID}}g_1^{\beta_u-\beta_v})\hat{e}(\prod_{j=1}^k g^{(h-\bar{h})\alpha_j r_j}, g)$$

$$= \hat{e}(g, g^{ab(h-\bar{h})}g^{*\beta_u}_{\text{ID}}g^{\bar{*}-\beta_v}_{\text{ID}}g^{a(\beta_u-\beta_v)} \prod_{j=1}^k (g^{aI_j}g^{\alpha_j})^{(h-\bar{h})r_j}) = \hat{e}(g, z^*\bar{z}^{*-1})$$

So $\mathcal{B}$ gets $z^*\bar{z}^{*-1} = g^{ab(h-\bar{h})}g^{*\beta_u}_{\text{ID}}g^{\bar{*}-\beta_v}_{\text{ID}}g^{a(\beta_u-\beta_v)} \cdot \prod_{j=1}^k (g^{aI_j}g^{\alpha_j})^{(h-\bar{h})r_j}$, and

computes $g^{ab} = \left( \dfrac{z^*(g^{\bar{*}}_{\text{ID}}g^a)^{\beta_v}}{\bar{z}^* \left( \prod_{j=1}^k (g^{aI_j}g^{\alpha_j})^{(h-\bar{h})r_j} \right)(g^{*}_{\text{ID}}g^a)^{\beta_u}} \right)^{1/(h-\bar{h})}$.

Therefore, PPT algorithm $\mathcal{B}$ can break the CDH assumption.

**Theorem 1.** *Our construction of HIBS scheme possesses EF-ID-CMA, EKA-ID-CMA and EUS-ID-CMA security under the CDH assumption in the random oracle model.*

*Proof.* Combining the proof of *Lemmas* 1 and 2, we can prove that if CDH assumption holds, our HIBS scheme is secure against *EF-ID-CMA*. Therefore, if CDH assumption holds, our HIBS scheme is secure against *EF-ID-CMA*, *EKA-ID-CMA* and *EUS-ID-CMA* attacks according to the *Lemmas* 1 to 4. Therefore, our escrow-free HIBS scheme is full secure.

## 5 Conclusion

In this work, we introduced a provably secure solution to the key escrow problem in HIBS scheme. The main idea of the escrow-free model lay on (1) imposing user-selected secret while signing message so as to restrict the PKGs' ability of generating an identical signature as user; and (2) introducing PKG signing factor to the signature so that the user could not generate well-formed signatures with different user parameter. According to the idea, we presented an escrow-free HIBS scheme based on the SHER-IBS scheme. We formulated *EF-ID-CMA*, *EKA-ID-CMA* and *EUS-ID-CMA* security model, following which an escrow-free scheme was regarded as full secure. Based on the CDH assumption, we proved the full security of our escrow-free HIBS scheme. Our scheme only introduced acceptable overhead to the SHER-IBS scheme and our escrow-free model was flexible and compatible to the primitive schemes. Although our escrow-free model was instantiated into a specific scheme in this work, it can be applied to any HIBS scheme without modifying the scheme's key generating algorithm.

# References

1. Boneh, D., Franklin, M.: Identity-based encryption from the Weil pairing. In: Kilian, J. (ed.) CRYPTO 2001. LNCS, vol. 2139, pp. 213–229. Springer, Heidelberg (2001)
2. Camenisch, J.L., Lysyanskaya, A.: Signature schemes and anonymous credentials from bilinear maps. In: Franklin, M. (ed.) CRYPTO 2004. LNCS, vol. 3152, pp. 56–72. Springer, Heidelberg (2004)
3. Cao, D., Wang, X.F., Wang, F., Hu, Q.L., Su, J.S.: SA-IBE: a secure and accountable identity-based encryption scheme. Dianzi Yu Xinxi Xuebao (J. Electron. Inf. Technol.) **33**(12), 2922–2928 (2011)
4. Choon, J.C., Cheon, J.H.: An identity-based signature from gap Diffie-Hellman groups. In: Desmedt, Y.G. (ed.) PKC 2003. LNCS, vol. 2567, pp. 18–30. Springer, Heidelberg (2002)
5. Chow, S.S.M., Hui, L.C.K., Yiu, S.-M., Chow, K.P.: Secure hierarchical identity based signature and its application. In: López, J., Qing, S., Okamoto, E. (eds.) ICICS 2004. LNCS, vol. 3269, pp. 480–494. Springer, Heidelberg (2004)
6. Gentry, C., Silverberg, A.: Hierarchical id-based cryptography. In: Zheng, Y. (ed.) ASIACRYPT 2002. LNCS, vol. 2501, pp. 548–566. Springer, Heidelberg (2002)
7. Gerbush, M., Lewko, A., O'Neill, A., Waters, B.: Dual form signatures: an approach for proving security from static assumptions. In: Wang, X., Sako, K. (eds.) ASIACRYPT 2012. LNCS, vol. 7658, pp. 25–42. Springer, Heidelberg (2012)
8. Goldwasser, S., Micali, S., Rivest, R.L.: A digital signature scheme secure against adaptive chosen-message attacks. SIAM J. Comput. **17**(2), 281–308 (1988)
9. Kate, A., Goldberg, I.: Distributed private-key generators for identity-based cryptography. In: Garay, J.A., De Prisco, R. (eds.) SCN 2010. LNCS, vol. 6280, pp. 436–453. Springer, Heidelberg (2010)
10. Lee, B., Boyd, C., Dawson, E., Kim, K., Yang, J., Yoo, S.: Secure key issuing in id-based cryptography. In: Proceedings of the Second Workshop on Australasian Information Security, Data Mining and Web Intelligence, and Software Internationalisation, vol. 32, pp. 69–74 (2004)
11. Pointcheval, D., Stern, J.: Security proofs for signature schemes. In: Maurer, U.M. (ed.) EUROCRYPT 1996. LNCS, vol. 1070, pp. 387–398. Springer, Heidelberg (1996)
12. Sahu, R.A., Padhye, S.: Provable secure identity-based multi-proxy signature scheme. Int. J. Commun Syst **28**(3), 497–512 (2015)
13. Shamir, A.: Identity-based cryptosystems and signature schemes. In: Blakely, G.R., Chaum, D. (eds.) CRYPTO 1984. LNCS, vol. 196, pp. 47–53. Springer, Heidelberg (1985)

14. Wang, C., Chow, S.S., Wang, Q., Ren, K., Lou, W.: Privacy-preserving public auditing for secure cloud storage. IEEE Trans. Comput. **62**(2), 362–375 (2013)

15. Wang, X., Chen, P., Zhou, H., Su, J.: T-hibe: a trustworthy and secure hierarchical identity-based encryption system. Chin. J. Electron. (in press, 2015)

16. Yuen, T.H., Susilo, W., Mu, Y.: How to construct identity-based signatures without the key escrow problem. Int. J. Inf. Secur. **9**(4), 297–311 (2010)

17. Zhang, X., Xu, C., Jin, C., Xie, R.: Efficient forward secure identity-based shorter signature from lattice. Comput. Electr. Eng. **40**(6), 1963–1971 (2014)

18. Zhang, Y., Liu, J.K., Huang, X., Au, M.H., Susilo, W.: Efficient escrow-free identity-based signature. In: Takagi, T., Wang, G., Qin, Z., Jiang, S., Yu, Y. (eds.) ProvSec 2012. LNCS, vol. 7496, pp. 161–174. Springer, Heidelberg (2012)

# A Predictive Data Reliability Method for Wireless Sensor Network Applications

Adil Amjad Sheikh[1,2], Ahmed Lbath[2], Ehsan Ullah Warriach[3]($\boxtimes$),
and Emad Felemban[3,4]

[1] Science and Technology Unit, Umm Al-Qura University,
Makkah, Saudi Arabia
[2] Department of Computer Science, LIG, University of Grenoble Alpes,
Grenoble, France
[3] Transportation and Crowd Management Center of Research Excellence,
Makkah, Saudi Arabia
warriach.ehsan@gmail.com
[4] College of Computer and Information Systems, Umm Al-Qura University,
Makkah, Saudi Arabia

**Abstract.** Wireless sensor networks consist of a large number of heterogeneous devices that communicate to collaboratively perform various tasks for users. Heterogeneous devices are deployed to sense the context of the environment. The context information is use to actuate various devices or services to support various activities of a user in a smart environment. Therefore, data correction is vital in managing issues arising from missing or corrupt contextual data due to system internal and external influences. We would like to investigate the machine learning techniques to ensure a complete and accurate sensor dataset for smart environment applications by runtime correcting missing or corrupt data due to sensor failures. We proposed a framework to correct dynamically sensory data. Specifically, we deal with the problems of faulty data (outliers, spikes, stuck-at, and noise), and missing information. Our proposed framework is able to learn temporal correlations in collected data from smart objects using Artificial Neural Network algorithm. We utilize the learned correlations to discover faulty data patterns to recover them, and imitate missing information. We implement the proposed data correction framework and test it on two real-world datasets collected from transportation domain (parking system, and road traffic).

**Keywords:** Data correction · Missing data · Prediction analysis · Reliable data · Wireless sensor networks · Artificial neural network · Time-series data analysis

## 1 Introduction

Wireless sensor networks (WSNs) consist of a large number of interconnected sensing devices, have been used to monitor probably very large, inaccessible

© Springer International Publishing Switzerland 2015
G. Wang et al. (Eds.): ICA3PP 2015 Workshops, LNCS 9532, pp. 648–658, 2015.
DOI: 10.1007/978-3-319-27161-3_59

and/or remote areas, such as smart buildings/offices, smart homes, health, and intelligent lighting applications. With the wide deployment of sensor networks in SEs it is not only possible to obtain a fine grain real-time information about the physical world but also to act upon this information. Unfortunately, data obtained from devices usually suffers from two problems: missing sensed data and outliers from malicious sensors. There are numerous factors that contribute to the existence of these problems such as packet loss and collisions, low battery, and memory levels, potential harsh environmental conditions, sensor aging, etc. The collected data is used to make certain application dependent actions. For a WSN application to infer an appropriate result, it is necessary that the data received is accurate, and complete. Subsequently, ensuring the reliability of the data in a sensor network is a challenging issue.

Let us consider a sensor network that monitors the temperature in an office environment by making new readings every few minutes. System knows beforehand the meaning of the measured data over this network during normal operation. Further, system can learn certain properties of the measured data over the time within the network, and measured data samples assumed to be impossible can be detected and corrected dynamically. This example illustrates how the meaning of the data, learned dynamically, can be used to test the validity of the samples within the network as they are recorded. The approach for data reliability that we propose in this paper will consider knowledge of any properties about the data source and will use them to perform data correction. We will exploit machine learning technique to learn knowledge dynamically from historical data. In this paper, we classify the sources of error into two types, transient and permanent, based on the effect they have on the sensor data. The method of data correction that we present here is designed to address the transient errors.

In this paper, we propose a novel approach to ensure the quality of collected data by exploiting the data features and temporal correlations between the data samples to correct faulty, and imitate missing sensory data samples. The early detection of faulty and missing data samples enables us not only to detect errors in sensor readings, but also to correct them proactively. The proposed approach is tested on two real-world datasets. The first dataset is collected from seven parking lots. The second dataset is collected from cameras, which are deployed at the road side to monitor the traffic. The real-time sensor data requires an innovative solutions to manage the collected data more efficiently. As data complexity grows, the quality assurance of data-driven applications become important. In this paper, the definition of reliable data, which means to ensure data are complete, correct, and useful. Data reliability means that data are reasonably complete and accurate. The quality, reliability, and timeliness of data obtained from sensor networks are extremely important since detrimental actions are usually taken based upon these sensed values. Specially, the cost of any faulty and missing data can be very significant since it is usually used for critical decisions or activation of actuators. In our proposed solution, we correct the faulty or imitate the missing data samples using the current and previous data samples within a certain defined period of time.

## 2   Related Work

Missing or faulty data detection is a very broad field and has been studied in the context of a large number of application domains where many detection methods have been applied according to the different data characteristics. Recently, there has been significant interest in predicting outliers in time series instead of detecting. Proactive approach itself bring the novelty into the state of the art solutions because application dependability will increase significantly. Abnormality and incompleteness of the data become an annoying issue for the real SE applications. Therefore, the question is, how to find faulty and missing date samples, and correct them proactively in sensor network systems to make SE application more reliable and reduce the manual interventions. A large number of solutions have been developed in various domains, where they are exploiting the spatial and temporal correlations among the different sensors [1,6,11] for data reduction and compression, and missing data treatment. However, these approaches require hardware redundancy in the system. Hardware redundancy uses an increased amount of resources such as redundant sensors, data acquisition channels/systems, inter-node communication, etc. to imitate the missing, and correct the faulty data samples [12]. It brings a lot of overhead in the system at the network level and also increase the consumption/usage of the computational resources. On the other hand, analytical approaches use mathematical models between measurements to predict a target sensor's values.

In [2], a data correction mechanism is presented for data streams based on the neural network and the k nearest neighbors algorithm in contrast to more extensive online model comparisons and selection. The proposed approach was tested on the electricity load data stream. A multiple linear Regression predicting method based on correlation analysis is proposed in [16], to correct the sensory data. The proposed method is tested on the data from the temperature sensor of real wireless sensor network monitoring system. A cloud-based Provenance Data Management System (ProvDMS) is presented in [3] to effectively collect and manage data while ensuring the datas accuracy and completeness from missing or corrupt data due to sensor failure, fouling, drifting, calibration error, or data logger failure. In [5,8], authors present a method for pre-processing the missing observed data by adopting the multiple imputation technique using the Adaptive Neuro-Fuzzy inference system. A hierarchical unsupervised fuzzy approach is presented in [10]. They used neural network to represent the data cluster prototypes and describe missing input patterns based on the network by using a spatial-temporal imputation technique. In [15], an approach is presented based on approximating the joint probability distribution over the sensors using undirected graphical models, ideally suited to exploit both the spatial correlations and the broadcast nature of communication. Most of these approaches follow the reactive approach, and based on spatial correlations, where redundant nodes are necessary. However, our proposed approach is proactively correct the faulty and missing data samples by exploiting only the temporal properties of sensed data at each individual node. It means our approach will add a little overhead on the system as compared to previous approaches in terms of computational requirements.

## 3   Proactive Data Correction Framework

We present an approach to dynamically infer temporal relationship between the sensory data not only to detect but also to proactively correct faulty and missing data samples. The temporal correlation means the temporal dependencies between the past readings of the same sensor node. It enables sensors to locally predict their current readings knowing both their own past readings and the learned data features. It means that sensors are aware of their context (history and the neighborhood). The basic idea of our proposed approach consists of using the properties of sensor data sources to correct faulty and missing data samples in the observed data.

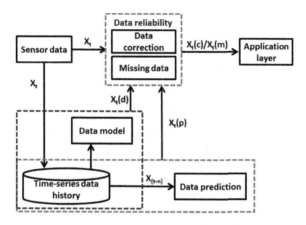

**Fig. 1.** Proactive data correction framework

The proposed framework consists of three mechanisms, namely, *data prediction model*, *contextual data model*, and *data correction* as shown in the Fig. 1. There is also one storage blocks, *time-series data history*, which keeps the time series data history. The data prediction is responsible to predict the value for incoming data samples based on the recent history of time-series data samples. The contextual data model is responsible to estimate/infer the value for incoming data samples based on the learned data model for that particular environmental entity. For example, the system can infer a data model based on the indoor temperature sensor values over a day. Finally, the basic aim of data correction mechanism is to correct the faulty value and imitate the missing values based on the input from data prediction and contextual data models. There are three inputs to our reliable data correction mechanism: the current sensor observations, learned contextual data model of every sensor, and predicted sensor value. The data correction algorithm can be placed at the sensor level or the base-station. We will study the tradeoffs and explicit computational requirements for each option.

## 4    Methodology

During the system normal operation, when a new sample of a sensor data $x_t$ is received, its predicted value $X_t(p)$ is computed by looking the past data in time window $X_{t-n}$ to predict the likelihood of the observed data being erroneous, where $n$ specify the length of past data samples for prediction, to make prediction for the next value $X_{n+1}$ at time $t + 1$. Additionally, contextual data model estimates the expected value $X_t(d)$. Later, the data correction mechanism uses $X_t(p)$ value and $X_t(d)$ values either to correct the faulty value or estimate the missing value at time $t$. Finally, the algorithm chooses the corrected or estimated value $X_t(c)/X_t(m)$ to forward the application layer, depending on the outcome of data correction. The difference between the $X_t(p)$ and $X_t(d)$ values and the observed value is used to detect whether the observation is correct or erroneous. The data correction algorithm makes use of the relationship between the missing data and other, known values within the dataset. We choose the machine learning technique to develop data prediction and contextual data models both offline and online.

The first step is to learn the data prediction models using the machine learning technique by analysis of the temporal properties of the source data. We will consider the prediction error, i.e., the difference between the observed data samples and predicted values as a performance metric, for the recently obtained samples. Second, we will use machine learning technique to infer the contextual data model using the context knowledge and real time data. This mechanism is responsible to provide an expected value $X_t(d)$ at time $t$ to data correction mechanism either to correct or estimate the faulty and missing data. Once a contextual data model is identified, it is used during normal operation of the system to estimate the vales for incoming data samples as shown in the Fig. 1. Finally, the optimal choice to take the decision for data correction would depend on various characteristics of the data source and the system: the level of randomness within the data, the stationarity properties of the generation process, the accuracy of the contextual data model, and the cost overhead.

## 5    Predictive Data Correction Model

Time series modeling is a dynamic research area which has attracted attentions of researchers community over last few decades. The main aim of time series modeling is to carefully collect and rigorously study the past observations of a time series to develop an appropriate model which describes the inherent structure of the series. This model is then used to generate future values for the series, i.e. to make predictions. It is obvious that a successful time series prediction depends on an appropriate model fitting. Various time series prediction models have been proposed in the literature [13]. A time series $S$ is a discrete function that represents real-valued measurements $s_t$ of an observable variable $S$ (resource attribute) at equal time intervals:

$$S = \{s_t : t \in T\}, T = \{1, 2, ....., n\} \qquad (1)$$

where $t$ represents the time elapsed. The variable $s_t$ is treated as a random variable. A time series containing records of a single variable is termed as univariate. But if records of more than one variable are considered, it is termed as multivariate. A time series can be continuous or discrete. The procedure of fitting a time series to a proper model is termed as time series analysis. It is often useful for future predictions. In time series analysis, past observations are collected and analyzed to develop a suitable mathematical model which captures the underlying data generating process for the series. The future events are then predicted using the model. One of the most popular and frequently used stochastic time series models is the artificial neural networks (ANNs). The most important feature of ANNs, when applied to time series analysis problems is their inherent capability of non-linear modeling, without any presumption about the statistical distribution followed by the observations [9].

## 5.1    ANN

An artificial neural network, usually called a neural network, is a mathematical model that is inspired by the structure and functional aspects of biological neural networks. We used ANNs to predict data with polynomial regression models. The purpose of using ANN is to predict the actual sensor measurements $x_{i,k}$ of a sensor node $i$ at time instant $k$ using the corrected measurements at each individual sensor. The intention is that each sensor learns a model function $f(.)$ that can be used for predicting its subsequent actual (error free) measurements through out the whole period of the experiment. ANN implements this in two phases, namely the training phase and the deployment phase. During the training phase, sensor measurements collected during the initial deployment period (training data set) are used to model the function $f(.)$. During the deployment phase, the trained model $f(.)$ is used to predict the subsequent actual sensor measurements $x_{i,k}$.

A typical simple ANN consists of three layers, namely, an input layer, a hidden layer, and an output layer. Each input node is connected to each hidden node by a connection weight (similar to coefficients in regression models). At each hidden node, a weighted linear combination of the inputs is summed to determine the net input to that node, which is compared with a threshold. When the threshold stimulus is achieved the node propagates further to the next layer in the network, otherwise it remains passive. Basically, learning or training in an ANN is the process of finding the values of these weights to solve problems presented to the network. The weights are determined iteratively, with the goal of minimizing error for all possible outputs [7]. The training procedure of ANN is composed of two processes. It involves feed forwarding the input data followed by back-propagation of error by adjusting weights to minimize the error on each training instance. A number of training algorithms have been proposed for finding ANN weights. Back-propagation is a popular method to find weights for multi-layer feed-forward networks and to minimize the prediction error [9]. Back propagation neural networks can be seen as a nonlinear regression. We use the Multi-Layer Perceptron (MLP) as a back propagation algorithm to learn an

ANN model [4,14]. The output of the model is computed using the following mathematical expression:

$$y_t = \alpha_0 + \sum_{j=1}^{q} \alpha_j g \left( \beta_{0j} + \sum_{i=1}^{p} \beta_{ij} y_{t-i} \right) + \epsilon_t, \forall t \tag{2}$$

where $y_{t-i}(i = 1, 2, ......, p)$ are the $p$ inputs and $y_t$ is the output. The integers $p, q$ are the number of input and hidden nodes respectively. $\alpha_j(j = 0, 1, ......, q)$ and $\beta_{ij}(i = 0, 1, 2, ....p; j = 0, 1, 2....q)$ are the connection weights and $\epsilon_t$ is the random shocks; $\alpha_0$ and $\beta_{0j}$ are the bias terms. Usually, the logistic sigmoid function $g(x) = \frac{1}{1+e^{-x}}$ is applied as the nonlinear activation function. Training a neural network is similar to fitting a regression model. It is performed by iteratively modifying weights such that outputs produced by the network will have a minimal amount of prediction error. For example, whenever the output is not close enough to the desired output, weights are modified to minimize the prediction error [4]. This difference is referred to as the prediction error of an ANN and is similar to the concept of minimizing the residuals in regression. The basic goal of MLP is to optimize the connection weights. The mean square error (MSE) is used to asses the performance of ANN prediction model.

$$MSE = \frac{1}{2} \sum_{i=1}^{n} \sum_{j=1}^{o} (x_{ij} - \hat{x}_{ij})^2 \tag{3}$$

where, $i$ refers to the instances within a set of $n$ instances, the $j$ denotes to the output unit, $x$ is the actual value, and $\hat{x}$ is the model predicted value.

## 6   Performance Evaluation

In this paper, we proposed a data correction framework to exploit the temporal relationship between the collected data. An observation window of size $n$ is used to predict each time-step within that window as if the data were faulty or missing.

### 6.1   Parking Dataset

To evaluate the performance and robustness of our proposed approach, we will use data collected from a parking system. A large number of sensor are deployed to monitor the existence of bicycles on each individual parking place in the parking lot. The data is collected from 1st October 2014 to 7th November 2014 at seven parking lots in Mitaka, Japan. The data was recorded at an interval of every 3 min and was collected during the opening hours of the bicycle parking. Each sensor measurement consists of 6 values, e.g., place (id of a parking lot), state (id corresponding to state), state (F(ull), C(rowded), V(can't), time stamp, capacity (the maximum number of bicycles parked in the parking lot), available

(the number of free spaces in the parking lot). Observation of the bicycle parking operation and a review of the collected data from the parking management
system indicated that data anomalies and outliers did exist in this data set.
Therefore, it is a reasonably representative sample of parking data that required
additional processing techniques to improve the quality of the data. The objectives of the analysis on this data were to identify and reveal the changing characteristic of time series collected data and the statistical properties of its outliers
to correct the faulty data, and imitate the missing sensory data values. Particularly, the parking lot 2 provides faulty data as shown in the Fig. 2. Therefore, we
choose the parking lot 2 collected sensory data for the experimental evaluation
of our proposed proactive data correction framework.

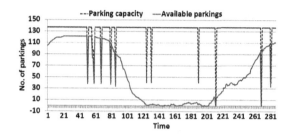

**Fig. 2.** Data from parking 2 (one day)

**Table 1.** Performance metrics for data correction model

| Performance metrics | Formula |
|---|---|
| Accuracy | $\frac{TP+TN}{TP+TN+FP+FN}$ |
| Precision | $\frac{TP}{TP+FP}$ |
| Recall | $\frac{TP}{TP+FN}$ |
| F-measure | $2 \cdot \frac{precision.recall}{precision+recall}$ |

## 6.2 Road Traffic Dataset

The *Masar* is an online platform for transportation analysis and visualization
which helps people to analyze road traffic and crowded area using different visualization techniques. Masar platform consist of two components. The first component of the platform is data collection, where heterogeneous sensors such as
mobile devices, wearable sensors, object detection using cameras, vehicle counting devices and some other sensor devices are used to sense the context of
given environment. The mobile devices are used to collect data using an android
application named *MapMyTrip*. Each measurement consists of the following values, e.g., such as location, speed, network and its type, signal strength, opera-
tor(mobile service provider), time stamp (of data collection & sending to server),

light sensor, accelerometer, gyroscope, magnetometer, device info (name, brand, model) and driver info (name, description of trip, age, ethnicity, driving). This collected data have been used for various applications in intelligent transportation systems. Most of these applications are very critical because the end-users have direct interaction with them. Therefore, it is necessary to have a complete data over time, which is accurate and complete. The data is collected during the Hajj 2014 in Mecca, Kingdom of Saudi Arabia. The data was recorded at an interval of every 1 min, and was collected during the day from 11:30 to 13:00. Figure 3 shows only the speed of vehicles. According to experimental setup and sample time, we must have 150 data samples in two and half hours. However, we collected 96 data samples out of 150 data samples. It clearly shows that a large number of data samples are missing.

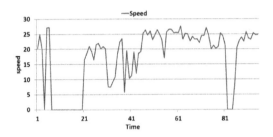

**Fig. 3.** Data from road traffic (two and half hour)

## 6.3   Performance Metrics

The goal of a data correction model is to predict sensor values and correct them accurately, efficiently and in a timely manner. An accurate data correction model would accomplish a one-to-one matching between predicted and true sensory values. We consider a number of performance metrics such as false positive, false negative, true positive, true negative, precision, recall, F-measure, and accuracy to evaluate the performance of data correction model.

Our aim is to implement the data correction model on a WSN platform. Therefore, the computational cost of the algorithm must be low. Furthermore, the data correction quality is an important factor, therefore, we considered true-positive and false-positive as important metrics to measure the performance of

**Table 2.** Performance of the data correction model

| Dataset | True positives | False positives | False negatives | Precision | Recall | Accuracy | F-measure |
|---------|----------------|-----------------|-----------------|-----------|--------|----------|-----------|
| Parking lot | 43 | 7 | 2 | 0.86 | 0.96 | 0.82 | 0.91 |
| Road traffic | 45 | 5 | 1 | 0.90 | 0.97 | 0.88 | 0.93 |

data correction models. We evaluate the performance of our predictive data correction model with two different real-world datasets. Table 2 summarizes the prediction performance of ANN algorithm. It shows that the proposed approach has promising results in terms of performance because it achieved high true-positive rate, and low false-positive rate.

## 7    Conclusions and Future Work

Data completeness, and accuracy are areas that must be addressed because of the large amounts of data will be generated from Internet of Things devices in the future. The result showed that our proposed solution effectively correct the missing or faulty data. We obtained these results using two different real-world datasets. In the future, our aim is to test the performance of proposed approach using more real-world datasets from various application domains. Moreover, we will compare the performance of the proposed approach with similar state of the art approaches [6, 11] studied during the literature study.

**Acknowledgments.** This work is funded by grant number NSTIP-10-INF1235-10 from the Long-Term National Plan for Science, Technology and Innovation (LT-NPSTI), the King Abdul-Aziz City for Science and Technology (KACST), Kingdom of Saudi Arabia. We thank the Science and Technology Unit at Umm A-Qura University, Makkah 21955, Saudi Arabia for their continued logistics support.

## References

1. Akyildiz, I.F., Vuran, M.C., Akan, O.B.: On exploiting spatial and temporal correlation in wireless sensor networks. In: Proceedings of WiOpt 2004: Modeling and Optimization in Mobile, Ad Hoc and Wireless Networks, pp. 71–80 (2004)
2. Bosnić, Z., Rodrigues, P.P., Kononenko, I., Gama, J.: Correcting streaming predictions of an electricity load forecast system using a prediction reliability estimate. In: Czachórski, T., Kozielski, S., Stańczyk, U. (eds.) Man-Machine Interactions 2. AISC, vol. 103, pp. 343–350. Springer, Heidelberg (2011)
3. Castello, C.C., Sanyal, J., Rossiter, J.S., Hensley, Z.P., New, J.R.: Sensor data management, validation, correction, and provenance for building technologies. In: Proceedings of the ASHRAE Annual Conference and ASHRAE Transactions (2014)
4. Fausett, L.V.: Fundamentals of Neural Networks: Architectures, Algorithms, and Applications, 1st edn. Prentice-Hall, Englewood Cliffs (1994)
5. Hocaoglu, F., Oysal, Y., Kurban, M.: Missing wind data forecasting with adaptive neuro-fuzzy inference system. Neural Comput. Appl. 18(3), 207–212 (2009)
6. Ji, Y., Tang, D., Guo, W., Blythe, P.T., Ren, G.: Detection of outliers in a time series of available parking spaces. Math. Prob. Eng. 12, 12 (2013)
7. Khashei, M., Bijari, M.: An artificial neural network (p,d,q) model for timeseries forecasting. Expert Syst. Appl. 37(1), 479–489 (2010)
8. Lei, K.S., Wan, F.: Pre-processing for missing data: a hybrid approach to air pollution prediction in Macau. In: IEEE International Conference on Automation and Logistics, pp. 418–422 (2010)

9. Li, J., Cheng, J., Shi, J., Huang, F.: Brief introduction of back propagation (BP) neural network algorithm and its improvement. In: Jin, D., Lin, S. (eds.) Advances in CSIE, Vol. 2. AISC, vol. 169, pp. 553–558. Springer, Heidelberg (2012)

10. Li, Y., Parker, L.: Classification with missing data in a wireless sensor network. In: 2008 IEEE Southeastcon, pp. 533–538 (2008)

11. Mukhopadhyay, S., Schurgers, C., Panigrahi, D., Dey, S.: Model-based techniques for data reliability in wireless sensor networks. IEEE Trans. Mobile Comput. **8**(4), 528–543 (2009)

12. Roshanzadeh, M., Saqaeeyan, S.: Error detection & correction in wireless sensor networks by using residue number systems. Int. J. Comput. Netw. Inf. Secur. **2**, 29–35 (2012)

13. Salfner, F., Lenk, M., Malek, M.: A survey of online failure prediction methods. ACM Comput. Surv. **42**(3), 10:1–10:42 (2010)

14. Serpen, G., Gao, Z.: Complexity analysis of multilayer perceptron neural network embedded into a wireless sensor network. Procedia Comput. Sci. **36**, 192–197 (2014)

15. Wang, L., Deshpande, A.: Predictive modeling-based data collection in wireless sensor networks. In: Verdone, R. (ed.) EWSN 2008. LNCS, vol. 4913, pp. 34–51. Springer, Heidelberg (2008)

16. Xiaozhen, Y., Hong, X., Tong, W.: A multiple linear regression data predicting method using correlation analysis for wireless sensor networks. In: 2011 Cross Strait Quad-Regional Radio Science and Wireless Technology Conference (CSQRWC), vol. 2, pp. 960–963 (2011)

# A Cycle-Time-Analysis Model for Byzantine Fault Tolerance

Liu Chen[1,2] and Wei Zhou[3(✉)]

[1] School of Physical Science and Technology, Central China Normal University,
Wuhan 430079, China
chenliu97@163.com
[2] School of Electrical and Information Engineering, Wuhan Institute of Technology,
Wuhan 430205, China
[3] School of Computer, Central China Normal University, Wuhan 430079, China
w.zhou@mail.ccnu.edu.cn

**Abstract.** Mission-critical services must be replicated in order to be available even if Byzantine faults happen. Castro and Liskov proposed a successful Byzantine fault tolerant protocol named CLBFT (Castro Liskov Byzantine Fault Tolerance), which overcame performance drawbacks of previous protocols. Other proposals extended CLBFT with further optimizations, but these protocols did not support asynchronous invocations from replicated calling services, thereby making these protocols unsuitable for nested computation model such as SOA (Service-Oriented Architecture). In this paper, we extend CLBFT to support asynchronous invocations, and we propose a window mechanism to support batch request and confirmation. A cycle-time-analysis model is proposed to analyze every stage of the protocol to measure performance improvements by window mechanism. Experimental results show effectiveness of proposed protocol.

**Keywords:** Replica · Byzantine fault tolerance · State machine replication · Window mechanism · Cycle time

## 1 Introduction

Fail-stop failures, such as host crashes, can be masked using redundant hosts. Achievement of Byzantine Fault Tolerance (BFT) requires more replicas than regular replication in fail-stop fault tolerance, since failures may be caused by malicious attacks and software bugs or hardware errors [1–3]. BFT requires a minimum of $3f + 1$ replicas to tolerate $f$ Byzantine faults [3].

For the sake of masking Byzantine faults, BFT protocols were proposed to tolerate up to f Byzantine faults [1–3]. The well-known CLBFT (Castro Liskov Byzantine Fault Tolerance) protocol proposed by Castro and Liskov was the first successful practical protocol. Some researchers proposed additional optimizations, reusing basic mechanisms of CLBFT [2].

WS-RM, an effective method to increase reliability of Web service interactions, had been widely supported by many commercial and open-source frameworks. However, WS-RM does not guarantee high availability of Web services [3].

© Springer International Publishing Switzerland 2015
G. Wang et al. (Eds.): ICA3PP 2015 Workshops, LNCS 9532, pp. 659–668, 2015.
DOI: 10.1007/978-3-319-27161-3_60

Zyzzyva is a protocol that uses speculation to reduce the cost of BFT replication [4]. In Zyzzyva, replicas reply to a client's request before running an expensive three-phase commits protocol to agree on the order of processed requests.

WS-FTM [5] is an implementation of the classic N-version model with Web services, which can easily be applied to systems with minimal changes.

Most protocols do not allow replicated called services (the services being called by others) to be accessed by replicated calling services (the services calling other services). Few protocols guarantee the safety and the liveness of replicated calling services if called services were compromised [6–8].

We propose N-CLBFT, a BFT that supports nested computation based on CLBFT to support nested computation such as SOA [9, 10]. We add pre-prepare stage, prepare stage and commit stage on the calling services to CLBFT [11–15]. In addition, a window mechanism supporting batch request and confirmation is used in N-CLBFT. A cycle-time-analysis model is proposed for the sake of analyzing every stage of the protocol and performance improvements by using window mechanism. We performed a Micro Benchmark to demonstrate the protocols effectiveness.

## 2    Overview of CLBFT

In CLBFT, the replicas move through a succession of configurations called views. In a view one replica is the primary and the others are backups. The client sends a request to all the replicas [16, 17]. The primary replica starts pre-prepare, prepare and commit stage after it received a request. The primary replica creates a view number to the request it received and broadcasts the request to other replicas in the pre-prepare stage. The replicas broadcast a prepare message to all the replicas to verify whether they all received the same request and sequence number from the primary replica to avoid primary replica being faulty or compromised. If a replica receive $2f$ prepare messages matching the pre-prepare message received from the primary, it broadcasts a commit message to all the replicas in the commit stage. When a replica gets commit messages from $2f + 1$ replicas, it executes the request and sends the result to the caller. If the called service receives $f + 1$ same replies, it accepts the reply. The three stages are shown in Fig. 1.

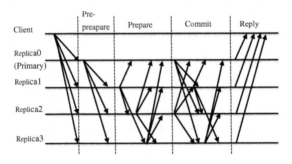

**Fig. 1.**   CLBFT stages

## 3    Introduction of Our Proposal

In this section we propose N-CLBFT, a BFT that supports nested computation based on CLBFT. The protocol contains two parts: a called service $t$ comprised of $n = 3f_t + 1$ replicas named $t_1, \ldots, t_n$, and a calling service $c$ comprised of $m = 3f_c + 1$ replicas named $c_1, \ldots, c_m$, where $f_t$ and $f_c$ are upper bounds of the number of faults tolerated by the target and calling services.

We illustrate the algorithm by tracing the execution of a request in normal case:

(1)    The current primary replica of $t$ waits for at least $f_c + 1$ matching requests.
(2)    The current primary replica of $t$ multicasts the request.
(3)    When a replica of $t$ reaches a receiving point, it starts a rcv-msg timer 1.
(4)    When the current primary replica of $t$ reaches a receiving point, it multicasts the message "CHECK-RECV (recpoint_id, primary_id)" to all replicas of $t$. Then the primary waits for $2f_t + 1$ replies from the replicas of $t$, including the primary itself. In N-CLBFT, we used a window mechanism to confirm the message in batch, which can effectively improve the throughout, as shown in Fig. 2.

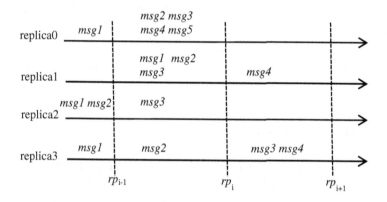

**Fig. 2.** Window mechanism

Receiving point is equidistant time point where replica checks if it receives new message. The time between two adjacent receive point is called Window.

In Fig. 2 there are four replicas (replica$_0$–replica$_3$) that can tolerate $f = 1$ fault. At the previous receive point $rp_{i-1}$, replica$_0$, replica$_2$, and replica$_3$ receive message $msg_1$, the new message $msg_1$ is confirmed. At the receiving point $rp_i$, the new message $msg_2$ and $msg_3$ are confirmed. Similarly, the new message $msg_4$ is confirmed at the receiving point $rp_{i+1}$.

(5)    When a replica of $t$ receives the "CHECK-RECV (recpoint_id, primary_id)" message, the replica verifies whether it has received a message with a sequential number larger than the number agreed upon at the last receiving point. If such a message exists, the replica sends a MODIFY message "MODIFY (recpoint_id,

seq_n, replica's id)" to the current primary replica of $t$, where seq_n is the largest sequence number among the messages received. If this message does not exist, the replica sends a "NO-MODIFY (recpoint_id, replica_id)" message to the current primary replica of $t$.

(6)    When the current primary replica of $t$ receives at least $2f_t + 1$ replies, it selects exactly $2f_t + 1$ replies randomly from all the replies and then determines which reply is majority: "MODIFY" or "NO-MODIFY." When MODIFY is major, the replica sets a valid sequence number seq_n (the r-f th largest sequence number in MODIFY messages), where $r$ is the number of "MODIFY" in the selected $2f_t + 1$ replies.

(7)    When a replica of $t$ receives a valid PRE_PREPARE message, the replica multi-casts PREPARE messages.

(8)    When a replica of $t$ receives identical $2f_t + 1$ valid PREPARE messages, it multi-casts COMMIT messages.

(9)    Using the local message queue, replicas of t de-queue messages, execute the request and send the results back to the current primary replica of $t$.

(10)   The current primary replica of $t$ collects $f_t + 1$ matching replies "REPLY (reply,t,r,v,seq)" and forwards the replies bundle (including all authenticators) to each $c$.

(11)   When replicas of $c$ receive the reply, the replica authenticates the reply bundle and forwards the reply to the current primary replica of $c$.

(12)   The current primary replica of $c$ utilizes CLBFT (step1–step11) in order to agree upon the reply.

## 4   Analysis Model for N-CLBFT

In this section, we propose an analysis model to analyze the cycle time of N-CLBFT. We track each stage of N-CLBFT. The following hypotheses are proposed:

- Processing times for a given message in calling services and called services are assumed to be identical.
- Replicas of calling services and called Services simultaneously begin each protocol cycle. Because of difference in waiting time in the replica queue, we use the following average waiting times.

The following paragraphs describe our predictive functions for each stage of the cycle time.

Step 1. Every replica of sends message $m^{c_i} = \langle REQUEST, o, x, t_{c_i}, c_i, v_p \rangle \mu_{c_i t_p}$ to primary replica $t_p$. Time $(T_1)$ in this stage includes time to encrypt the outgoing request message $T(encrypt_{req}^{c_k})$, waiting time of $m^{c_i}$ in the Output Queue: $T(avg\_outque)$, and latency of request message in the public network $T(transit_{req}^{wan})$.

Therefore, expected completion time $T_1$ is given by formula (1)

$$T_1 = T(transit_{req}^{wan}) + T(encrypt_{req}) + T(avg\_outque) \qquad (1)$$

Sub-tasks involved in calculating $T(encrypt_{req})$ included:

- The time using the hash function to calculate the digest of the request $T(digest_{req})$;
- The time that using the session key to encrypt the request message. $T(encrypt)_{req}^{ses}$ is given by formula (2)

$$T(encrypt_{req}) = T(digest_{req}) + T(encrypt_{req}^{ses}) \qquad (2)$$

Therefore, $T_1$ is given by the formula (3)

$$T_1 = T(transit_{req}^{wan}) + T(digest_{req}) + T(encrypt_{req}^{ses}) + T(avg\_outque) \qquad (3)$$

Step 2. Primary replica $t_p$ broadcasts the received request message to every replica. The time $(T_2)$ in this stage includes maximum time of $2f_c + 1$ $m^{c_i}$ waiting in the Input Queue of $t_p$, time needs to encrypts and verify $m^{c_i}$, time of $t_p$ to encrypt and obtain digests of the $3f_t$ request message, time of $3f_t$ request messages waiting in the Output Queue of $t_p$, and latency in the lan. Therefore, $T_2$ is given by formula (4):

$$\begin{aligned} T_2 = {} & T(decrypt_{req}^{t_p}) + T(transit_{req}^{lan}) + 3f_t \times (T(digest_{req}) \\ & + T(encrypt_{req}^{ses})) + (2f_c + 1) \times T(avg\_inque) \\ & + 3f_t \times T(avg\_outque) \end{aligned} \qquad (4)$$

$T(encrypt_{req}^{t_p})$ is given by formula (5):

$$T(encrypt_{req}^{t_p}) = (2f_c + 1) \times ((T(decrypt_{req}^{ses}) + T(verydig_{req}))) \qquad (5)$$

$T_2$ is given by formula (6):

$$\begin{aligned} T_2 = {} & 2f_c \times (T(decrypt_{req}^{ses}) + T(verydig_{req})) + T(transit_{req}^{lan}) \\ & + (2f_c + 1) \times T(avg\_inque) + (3f_t + 1) \times T(avg\_outque) \end{aligned} \qquad (6)$$

Step 3 (pre-prepare stage). Time $(T_3)$ in this stage includes waiting time of request message in the Input Queue; $t_k$ decrypt and verify the message sent by $t_p$; time of $t_k$ to encrypt and obtain the digest of the pre-prepare message; time of $3f_t$ pre-prepare message waiting in the Output Queue; latency of pre-prepare message in Lan. Therefore, $T_3$ is given by formula (7):

$$\begin{aligned} T_3 = {} & T(decrypt_{req}^{ses}) + T(verydig_{req}) + 3f_t \times (T(encrypt_{pre}^{ses}) \\ & + T(digest_{pre})) + T(transit_{pre}^{lan}) + 3f_t \times T(avg\_outque) \end{aligned} \qquad (7)$$

Step 4 (prepare stage). Time $(T_4)$ in this stage includes waiting time of pre-prepare message in Input Queue; time $t_k$ to decrypt and verify pre-prepare message; time of $t_k$ to encrypt and obtain the digest of the prepare message; time to prepare messages waiting in the Output Queue. Therefore, $T_4$ is given by formula (8):

$$T_4 = T(decrypt_{pre}^{t_k}) + T(encrypt_{prp}^{t_k}) + T(transit_{prp}^{lan})$$
$$+ 3f_t \times T(avg\_inque) + 3f_t \times T(avg\_outque) \tag{8}$$

$T\left(decrypt_{pre}\right)$ is given by formula (9):

$$T(decrypt_{pre}^{t_k}) = 3f_t \times (T(decrypt_{pre}^{ses}) + T(verydig_{pre})) \tag{9}$$

Therefore, $T_4$ is given by formula (10)

$$T_4 = 3f_t \times (T(decrypt_{pre}^{ses}) + T(verydig_{pre}) + T(encrypt_{prp}^{ses}) + T(digest_{prp}))$$
$$+ T(transit_{prp}^{lan}) + 3f_t \times T(avg\_inque) + 3f_t \times T(avg\_outque) \tag{10}$$

Step 5 (commit stage). Time $(T_5)$ in this stage is similar to the prepare stage; therefore, $T_5$ is given by the formula (11):

$$T_5 = T(decrypt_{prp}^{t_k}) + T(encrypt_{cmt}^{t_k}) + T(transit_{cmt}^{lan})$$
$$+ 3f_t \times T(avg\_inque) + 3f_t \times T(avg\_outque) \tag{11}$$

Step 6 (reply stage). Time $(T_6)$ in this stage is similar to the prepare stage; therefore, $T_6$ is given by formula (12):

$$T_6 = 3f \times (T(decrypt_{cmt}^{ses}) + T(verydig_{cmt})) + T(encrypt_{rep}^{ses})$$
$$+ T(digest_{rep}) + T(transit_{rep}^{lan}) + T(execute^{t_k})$$
$$+ 3f_t \times T(avg\_inque) + T(avg\_outque) \tag{12}$$

Step 7. Once the primary of $T(t_p)$ has received $f_t + 1$ reply messages to be verified, $t_p$ broadcasts the reply message to every replica of $c$. Therefore, $T_7$ is given by the formula (13):

$$T_7 = 2f_t \times (T(decrypt_{rep}^{ses}) + (3f_c + 1) \times (T(encrypt_{rep}^{ses}) + T(digest_{rep}))$$
$$+ T(transit_{rep}^{wan}) + T(verydig_{rep})) + 2f_t \times T(avg\_inque)$$
$$+ (3f_c + 1) \times T(avg\_outque) \tag{13}$$

Steps 8–13 mirror Steps 2–6. The entire request-reply stage $T$ is given by the formula (14):

$$T = 2T(transit_{req}^{wan}) + 9T(transit_{req}^{lan}) + T(execute^{t_k})$$
$$+ (9f_t + 15f_c + 4)T(digest_{req}) + (9f_t + 16f_c + 4)T(verydig_{req})$$
$$+ (11f_t + 12f_c + 6) \times T(avg\_inque) + (15f_t + 12f_c + 4) \times T(avg\_outque)$$
$$+ (9f_t + 15f_c + 4) \times T(encrypt_{req}^{ses}) + (11f_t + 13f_c + 5) \times T(decrypt_{req}^{ses})$$

$$(14)$$

## 5 Performance Evaluation

Micro benchmark was used for performance evaluation. We measured the cycle time between Calling and Called Services and the overhead of replicas.

### 5.1 Analysis of Cycle Time

In the first experiment, we measure the time required to complete each stage of cycle time between Calling and Called Services in which we use a configuration with four replicas. We use simple operations processed by called services with no significant cycle time.

Calling services conducted requests 1000 times in sequence, restarting the operation as soon as calling services received the reply to the previous invocation. In order to obtain the cycle time, we record the start time point and the time point when the reply for every request was received.

We select 100 requests (No. 200–No. 299) from 1000 requests to analyze. Cycle times are shown Figs. 3 and 4. Figure 3 shows the normal process of BFT without window mechanism, while Fig. 4 shows the process with window mechanism.

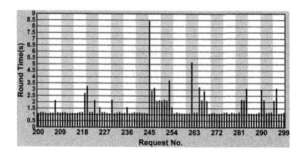

**Fig. 3.** Cycle time without window mechanism

As shown in Figs. 3 and 4, maximum cycle time is almost identical except for some noise point where the cycle time is particular high because of the latency of the network. Cycles of the noise are larger than normal cases due to network congestion. A comparison of Figs. 3 and 4 shows that the cycle time was much shorter when a window is used to verify requests in batch. When we use window mechanism in the BFT algorithm, there is approximately 50 % down in cycle time than CLBFT.

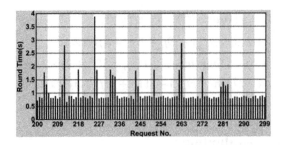

**Fig. 4.** Cycle time with window mechanism

## 5.2 Predicted Round Time Versus Actual Round Time

In order to predict the outcome of this experiment, we obtain measurements at each replica host and use average values for our prediction. Average measurements for all variables are shown in Table 1. Average results are based on 500 times tests.

**Table 1.** Variable VALUES

| Variable | Value |
|---|---|
| $f_c$ | {1,2,3,4,5,6,7,8,9,10} |
| $f_t$ | {1,2,3,4,5,6,7,8,9,10} |
| $execute^{t_k}$ | 0.033 s |
| $transit_{req}^{wan}$ | 0.0025 s |
| $transit_{req}^{lan}$ | 0.0025 s |
| $digest_{req}$ | 0.0069 s |
| $verydig_{req}$ | 0.0037 s |
| $encrypt_{req}^{ses}$ | 0.0052 s |
| $decrypt_{req}^{ses}$ | 0.0058 s |
| $avg\_inque$ | 0.0055 s |
| $avg\_outque$ | 0.0046 s |

From Figs. 5 and 6 we can see that the average cycle time with window and no window when configuration $f_c = f_t = f$ equals 1–10 and without window mechanism.

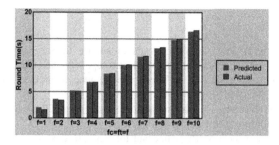

**Fig. 5.** Comparison of cycle time of predicted and actual without window mechanism

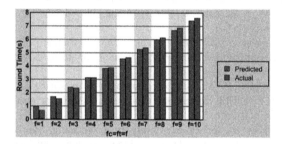

**Fig. 6.** Comparison of cycle time of predicted and actual with window mechanism

As shown in Figs. 5 and 6, predicted cycle times are greater than actual completion times. Differences between predicted and actual completion times are more pronounced for the $f_c = f_t = 1$ case compared to higher fault tolerance thresholds.

## 6    Conclusion

In this paper, we present a Byzantine fault tolerant protocol for nested computation. Most previous protocols did not support asynchronous invocations from replicated calling services, making these protocols unsuitable for nested computation such as SOA. We add agreement at the calling end to support nested computation and proposed a window mechanism to support batch request and confirmation. A cycle-time-analysis model is proposed to analyze every stage of the protocol in order to clarify performance improvements with window mechanism. We use a Micro benchmark test to measure the cycle time. By comparing CLBFT with N-CLBFT, we find there is significant decline in cycle time. The evaluation of cycle time shows that our proposal outperform CLBFT.

**Acknowledgments.** This research is supported in part by Research Project for Science and Technology of Hubei Provincial Department of Education, China under award B2015322, and by Youth Foundation of Wuhan Institute of Technology, China under award Q201407.

# References

1. Castro, M., Liskov, B.: Practical Byzantine fault tolerance. In: 3rd Symposium on Operating Systems Design and Implementation, New Orleans, pp. 173–186 (1999)
2. Lamport, L., Shostak, R., Pease, M.: The Byzantine generals problem. ACM Trans. Prog. Lang. Syst. **4**(3), 382–401 (1982)
3. Bilorusets, R.: Web services reliable messaging specification (2005). http://www.ibm.com/developerworks/library/specification/ws-rm
4. Kotla, R.: Zyzzyva: speculative Byzantine fault tolerance. In: 21st ACM SIGOPS Symposium on Operating Systems Principles, pp. 45–58(2007)
5. Wenbing Zhao, C.: BFT-WS: a Byzantine fault tolerance framework for web services. In: 11th International IEEE EDOC Conference Workshop, pp. 89–96 (2007)
6. Abd-El-Malek, M., et al.: Fault-scalable Byzantine fault tolerant Services. SIGOPS Oper. Syst. Rev. **39**, 59–74 (2005)
7. Merideth, M., Iyengar, A., Mikalsen, T., et al.: Thema: Byzantine-fault-tolerant middleware for web services applications. In: Proceedings of the IEEE Symposium on Reliable Distributed Systems, pp. 131–142 (2005)
8. Erradi, A., Maheshwari, P.: A broker-based approach for improving web services reliability. In: Proceedings of the IEEE International Conference on Web Services, Orlando, pp. 41–53 (2005)
9. Castro, M., Liskov, B.: Proactive recovery in a Byzantine fault-tolerant system. In: Symposium on Operating Systems Design and Implementation, pp. 287–301 (2000)
10. Wenbing, Z.: Byzantine fault tolerance for nondeterministic applications. In: Proceedings of the Third IEEE International Symposium on Dependable, Autonomic and Secure Computing, pp. 108–115. Loyola College Graduate Center, Columbia (2007)
11. Daniel, F. et al.: Benchmarking Of Web Services Platforms. In: International Conference on Web Information Systems and Technologies (WEBIST 2006), pp. 11–13, Setubal (April 2006)
12. TPC, 2008. TPC Benchmark App (Application Server) specification, version 1.3. Transaction Processing Performance Council. http://www.tpc.org/tpc_app/
13. Rodrigues, R., Castro, M., Liskov, B.: BASE: using abstraction to improve fault tolerance. In: Symposium on Operating Systems Principles, pp. 45–60 (2001)
14. Tadashi Araragi, C.: Byzantine fault tolerance for agent systems. In: Proceedings of the International Conference on Dependability of Computer Systems (2006)
15. Martin, J., Alvisi, L., Dahlin, M.: Minimal Byzantine Storage. In: 16th International Symposium on Distributed Computing Disc, pp. 311–325 (2002)
16. Paxson, V.: Bro: a system for detecting network intruders in real-time. Comput. Netw. **31**, 2435–2463 (1999)
17. de Sá, A.S., de Araújo Macêdo, R.J.: QoS self-configuring failure detectors for distributed systems. In: Eliassen, F., Kapitza, R. (eds.) DAIS 2010. LNCS, vol. 6115, pp. 126–140. Springer, Heidelberg (2010)

# Resource Utilization Based Dynamic Pricing Approach on Cloud Computing Application

Adrian Johannes[✉], Priyadarsi Nanda, and Xiangjian He

Faculty of Engineering and Information Technology, University of Technology Sydney,
Ultimo, NSW 2007, Australia
Adrian.Johannes@student.uts.edu.au,
{Priyadarsi.Nanda,Xiangjian.He}@uts.edu.au

**Abstract.** Utilizing cloud-based services, users are required to first specify their goal of using such cloud based applications and then obtain service compositions satisfying their specific needs from the cloud service providers. The process involves dynamic pricing schemes for service provisioning between themselves and their cloud service providers. As a result, it is quite challenging with existing supply and demand driven approaches to ensure true dynamic resource provisioning for users with critical applications. To address this problem, we propose a game theory approach based on fuzzy logic which is then used to ensure aspects of resource provisioning on cloud. In our approach, we perform a trade-off for resources between service provider, cloud resource provider and service user based on the user demand and avoid rejecting users to ensure reliable resource provisioning. Experimental results demonstrate that our proposed approach can improve resource utilization associated with users.

**Keywords:** Fuzzy logic · Game theory · Dynamic pricing · Resource provisioning · Cloud computing

## 1 Introduction

There have been a wide research interest amongst researchers from industry and academia involving cloud computing. Cloud technology has many important things to deliver for the future of computing and computing related applications. For example, cloud computing offers great opportunity to access medical information rapidly where both the health professionals and patients can obtain the information to fast track diagnosis and course of concerned treatments [1]. Users can access their information on cloud anywhere [2]. In cloud based model, there are three important things: availability of networks, distribution of resources and provision of on-demand services. Resources in cloud computing are delivered based on demand. Garg et al. [3] stated that cloud model is applied for utilizing service model and the existing tools by network if infrastructure, platform and software are provided as a service.

Dynamic pricing is the adjustment of price in order to meet consumer requirement for a given service. It consists of price dispersion and price discrimination [4]. Adopting a revenue management framework and analyzing market-driven dynamic pricing are

© Springer International Publishing Switzerland 2015
G. Wang et al. (Eds.): ICA3PP 2015 Workshops, LNCS 9532, pp. 669–677, 2015.
DOI: 10.1007/978-3-319-27161-3_61

implications for understanding market requirements for a service [5]. Kantere et al. [6] suggested optimal dynamic pricing in cloud cache and offered efficient querying on the back-end data. Some cloud computing providers adopt the utility computing model. They charge for resources based on usage.

In market competition, a provider has to determine establishing variable price spot position. In order to satisfy quality of service, developing economic model for service utilization and minimizing amount of resources wasted is highly required [7]. As cloud-based services become more abundant, resource provisioning becomes more challenging. Such resource provisioning problem has been studied by many researchers. Wei et al. [8] introduced new model by requesting the use of resources across a cloud-based network. In order to ensure resource provisioning that is not only available but also related to resource negotiation must be performed.

Users and providers have a link between theoretical and practical evaluation. By virtualisation, resources can be easily used in the form of service. Users consider different delivery models as and when required.

In this paper, we propose game theory approach based on fuzzy logic to ensure resource provisioning for cloud services. We adopt trade-off of resources between the service provider, cloud resource provider and service user based on demand to avoid rejecting users and to ensure resource provisioning. Experimental results show that our approach can improve utilization of resources and applicable for user requirements.

The major contributions of our research are threefold. First, we propose game theory based on fuzzy logic to ensure resource provisioning for cloud services. Second, we present a trade-off for resource negotiation between service provider, cloud resource provider and service user based on demand to avoid rejecting users and ensure proper resource provisioning. Third, experimental results show that our approach can improve utilization of resources.

The remainder of this paper is organized as follows: Sect. 2 reviews related work and analyses the research problem. In Sect. 3, we briefly present on fuzzy set and game theory. We propose fuzzy game theory approach and show the mathematical model. We experiment and evaluate our approach in Sect. 4. Finally, we conclude the paper with future work in Sect. 5.

## 2   Related Work and Problem Analysis

### 2.1   Related Work

Strategy for resource allocation enables provider and cloud resource provider to arrange their supplies and demands. When users send requests for cloud resources offered by provider, cloud resource provider process them to satisfy the user requirement if and only if required resource is available. As users depend on cloud providers to support their computing needs, they will involve detail quality of service to be sustained by their providers so as to meet their requirements. In cloud environment, [9] stated that provider and user have some advantages to develop cost-benefit model in decision-making. They create resource utilization and offer negotiation strategy for requesters.

Price competition has become a research topic in the context of demand-driven market in cloud computing involving dynamic pricing. The objectives of cloud dynamic pricing are optimizing the provision of cloud services. Selecting optimal price to obtain best service quality and develop game theory has been studied relating to finishing time and completing task [10].

Currently, researchers mainly focus on resource negotiation in cloud computing. Researchers in [11] presented negotiation between customer, broker agents and provider agents in cloud market. Also, found in [12] where, the authors used game theory to evaluate resource allocation in cloud computing. Li and Li [13] developed the model for user constraints, provider constraints and virtual machine constraints in relation to virtual machine. Yoo and Sim [14] developed a model to focus on agent-based multilateral price negotiation to improve two negotiation strategies: market driven agent model and concession making. Johannes et al. [15] designed cooperative model between resource on SaaS provider and SaaS user by fuzzy model.

## 2.2  Problem Analysis

As explained in Sect. 1, various service providers can exist in cloud service environment. Primarily, a negotiation strategy is based on the order of organizing resources between the cloud resource provider and user. In our approach, we attempt to consider utilization of resources where, users first need to obtain the resource from the provider. Resource consumption and processing resource request within a cloud provider is related to CPU, Memory and Bandwidth. In this problem, we design resource management based on the availability resources and negotiation mechanism related to peak time and non-peak time. We aim to solve resource negotiation among the cloud resource providers to ensure resource provisioning and avoid rejecting user for uncertainty demand. For this to happen, we decide resources at particular time based on a given user request. Provider sets the price by adjusting supply and user offers. It is important that the provider set the price before offering them to user. Existing model show the correlation between departure and arrival demand. With this pricing model, service provider will charge user based on the resources they use to complete their tasks [5].

Existing research on utilization of resources using cloud computing mainly focuses on cost and benefit model and developing negotiation strategy. They cannot be applied directly to our approach because the model only considers departure and arrival demand. Utilization of resources needs cooperation between user and provider to avoid rejecting user and ensure resource provisioning. A trade-off should be carried out between user and cloud resource provider using CPU, memory, bandwidth in normal, light and heavy demand.

Uncertainty problem is related to various cases and affected by input and output information. Uncertainty sources can be developed in mathematical model. In this research, we attempt to model resource utilization in uncertainty condition.

## 3    Fuzzy Game Theory Based Approach

### 3.1    Fuzzy Set

Zadeh [16] presented fuzzy set theory to build bargaining in mathematical model for uncertainties. This theory has been established and applied in many real applications in practice over the years. Fuzzy numbers are used to mathematically represent linguistic languages. A fuzzy subset $F$ in $G$ is characterized by its membership function $\mu_F(g)$. This function associates with every single element $g$ in $G$ in the interval $[0, 1]$.

### 3.2    Game Theory

Barron [17] mentioned that the theorem of von Neumann could be used to create formulation of game model which considers a saddle point. This is known as mixed strategies.

**Definition 1.** A mixed strategy is a vector $C = (c_1, \ldots, c_q)$ for Provider and $D = (d_1, \ldots, d_p)$ for User, where

$$c_z \geq 0, \sum_{z=1}^{q} c_z = 1 \, and \, d_j \geq 0, \sum_{j=1}^{p} d_j = 1 \tag{1}$$

The modules $c_z$ denote the probability that row z will be utilized by the provider, so $c_z$ = probability (provider utilizes row z), and $d_j$ the probability column j will be utilised by user, that is, $d_j$ = probability (user utilizes row j).

**Definition 2.** Given a selection of mixed strategy $C \in R_q$ for provider and $D \in R_p$ for user, selected freely the expected payoff to provider of the game is

$$G(C,D) = \sum_{z=1}^{q} \sum_{j=1}^{p} b_{zj} Prob \, (provider uses z and user uses j) \tag{2}$$

**Definition 3.** A saddle point is a pair $(C^*, D^*)$ of probability vectors $C^* \in R_q, D^* \in R_p$, which satisfies

$$G(C,D^*) \leq G(C^*,D^*) \leq G(C^*,D), \forall (C \in R_q, D \in R_p) \tag{3}$$

If provider utilizes a strategy other than $C^*$ but user still utilizes $D^*$, then it takes an expected-payoff. The same thing also holds for user. Hence, $(C^*, D^*)$ is equilibrium where provider ensures resource provisioning and avoids rejecting user.

### 3.3    Fuzzy Game Theory

Dhingra and Rao [18] stated that game theory helped in analyzing for conflict of interests which is necessary in selecting several strategies from a set existing strategies.

They applied the concepts of game theory and fuzzy set theory to produce a new optimization method.

We set up the mathematical model with the following parameters. These parameters contribute to resource negotiation in a typical user-provider relationship when user demand is satisfied by service provider. We assume a series of negotiation between the user and service provider before the final value is calculated:

- Parameter:

  $C^{cpu}$ = cpu speed of cloud provider
  $C^{ram}$ = capacity of memory of cloud provider
  $C^{net}$ = capacity of bandwidth of cloud provider
  $VM^{cpu}$ = cpu cloud resource required by a VM
  $VM^{ram}$ = memory cloud resource required by a VM
  $VM^{net}$ = bandwidth cloud resource required by a VM
  $P_{min}$ = Price minimum
  $P_{max}$ = Price maximum
  $T_{nt}$ = Non-peak time
  $T_{pt}$ = Peak time

- Type of user:

  H = Heavy User        L = Light User        N = Normal User

Determining membership function ($\mu$) for cpu, memory and bandwidth is related to capacity (C) and virtual machine (VM) and we create the model related to price minimum ($P_{min}$), price maximum ($P_{max}$), non-peak time ($T_{nt}$), and peak time ($T_{pt}$). In this problem, we consider three kinds of user. There are heavy user, light user and normal user. During negotiation, each user group attempts to maximize their utility and setting price and time based on user request.

Hence, following functions can be derived for negotiating, cloud resources using our model:

$$\mu\,(cpu) = \begin{cases} 1, C^{cpu} > VM^{cpu} \\ C^{cpu} - \sum_k VM^{cpu}, 0 \le C^{cpu} - VM^{cpu} \le 1 \\ 0, C^{cpu} < VM^{cpu} \end{cases} \tag{4}$$

Heavy user, with constraint 1, $C^{cpu} > VM^{cpu}$
Light user, with constraint $0 \le C^{cpu} - VM^{cpu} \le 1$
Normal user, with constraint 0, $C^{cpu} < VM^{cpu}$

$$\mu\,(ram) = \begin{cases} 1, C^{ram} > VM^{ram} \\ C^{ram} - \sum_k VM^{ram}, 0 \le C^{ram} - VM^{ram} \le 1 \\ 0, C^{ram} < VM^{ram} \end{cases} \tag{5}$$

Heavy user, with constraint 1, $C^{ram} > VM^{ram}$
Light user, with constraint $0 \leq C^{ram} - VM^{ram} \leq 1$
Normal user, with constraint 0, $C^{ram} < VM^{ram}$

$$\mu\,(net) = \begin{cases} 1, C^{net} > VM^{net} \\ C^{net} - \sum_k VM^{net}, 0 \leq C^{net} - VM^{net} \leq 1 \\ 0, C^{net} < VM^{net} \end{cases} \tag{6}$$

Heavy user, with constraint 1, $C^{net} > VM^{net}$
Light user, with constraint $0 \leq C^{net} - VM^{net} \leq 1$
Normal user, with constraint 0, $C^{net} < VM^{net}$

Now we define optimal fuzzy mixed strategies. $C$(D) is the set of fuzzy mixed strategies to be used by Provider (User). These could be finite, or some other infinite restricted set of fuzzy probabilities, and are not necessarily all possible fuzzy probability.

$$\bar{g}\,(\bar{d})_1 = min \left\{ \sum_{j=1}^{p} ((C^{cpu} - VM^{cpu}) + (C^{ram} - VM^{ram}) + (C^{net} - VM^{net})T_{nt}|P_{min} \right\} \tag{7}$$

The formulation represents the minimum value of cpu, memory and bandwidth to set price minimum and non-peak time.

$$\bar{g}\,(\bar{d})_2 = max \left\{ \sum_{j=1}^{p} ((C^{cpu} - VM^{cpu}) + (C^{ram} - VM^{ram}) + (C^{net} - VM^{net})T_{pt}|P_{max} \right\} \tag{8}$$

The formulation represents the maximum value of cpu, memory and bandwidth to set price maximum and peak time.

## 4    Experimental and Evaluation

The model is implemented in Matlab. We have demonstrated various parameter and resource utilization based on three types of users.

Figure 1 presents 729 rules of negotiation resources describing the negotiation process involving capacity, virtual machine, price and time and demonstrates impact on cpu, memory and bandwidth associated with resource utilization.

We consider cpu, memory and bandwidth as membership functions. The output from negotiation process (cpu normal, cpu light, cpu heavy, memory normal, memory light, memory heavy, bandwidth normal, bandwidth light and bandwidth heavy) involving user are presented in subsequent Figs. (2, 3, 4, 5, 6 and 7).

On Fig. 2, we present capacity, virtual machine and (cpu, memory and bandwidth) user. Virtual machine influence for cpu heavy user but capacity does not have any influence in this result. For bandwidth, all user influences virtual machine but capacity has little influence to ensure resource provisioning.

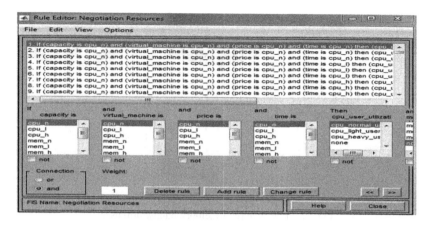

**Fig. 1.** Negotiation resources

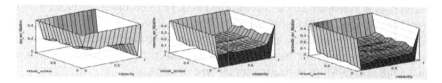

**Fig. 2.** Capacity-virtual machine (cpu-memory-bandwidth) user

**Fig. 3.** Capacity-price (cpu-memory-bandwidth) user

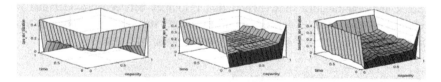

**Fig. 4.** Capacity-time (cpu-memory-bandwidth) user

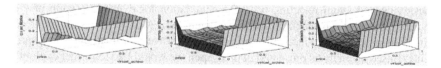

**Fig. 5.** Virtual machine-price (cpu-memory-bandwidth) user

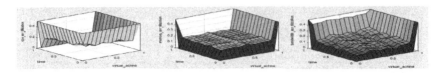

**Fig. 6.** Virtual machine-time (cpu-memory-bandwidth) user

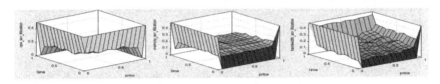

**Fig. 7.** Price-time (cpu-memory-bandwidth) user

On Fig. 3, we present capacity, price and (cpu, memory and bandwidth) user. Capacity does not have influence to cpu normal user. Price becomes one factor to ensure resource provisioning and impacts to bandwidth normal user.

On Fig. 4, we present capacity, time and (cpu, memory and bandwidth) user. Time influences to cpu normal user. Normal capacity and peak time impacts to ensure resource provisioning in bandwidth utilization for all type of users.

On Fig. 5, we present virtual machine, price and (cpu, memory and bandwidth) user. Minimum price and virtual machine influence resource provisioning in memory and bandwidth (light and heavy) user.

On Fig. 6, we present virtual machine, time and (cpu, memory and bandwidth) user. Time influences memory (normal and light) user and bandwidth (normal and light) user to ensure resource provisioning.

On Fig. 7, we present price, time and (cpu, memory and bandwidth) user. Price minimum and peak time influence memory and bandwidth user.

Overall, some negotiation offer resources are related to the parameter in capacity, virtual machine, price and time. The result represent the influence every parameter to resources and significantly show negotiation resources between provider and user. Accepting and rejecting user depends on the parameter support the resources. It means all parameters have impact to use resources based on the type of users.

## 5 Conclusion and Future Work

In this paper, we propose game theory based on fuzzy techniques to ensure resource provisioning and avoid rejecting user. By negotiation for dynamic pricing of cloud resources, providers can benefit from more efficient utilization of resources. We propose negotiation resources to reduce rejecting user and improve coordination resource provisioning. Based on analysis presented in this paper, we would like to further explore the next step to maximize revenue using dynamic pricing.

**Acknowledgments.** This work was supported by Directorate General of Higher Education, Ministry of Education and Culture (DIKTI), Republic of Indonesia, under PhD Scholarship Program.

# References

1. Lupse, O.S., Vida, M.M., Stoicu-Tivadar, L.: Cloud computing and interoperability in healthcare information systems. In: The First International Conference on Intelligent Systems and Applications, INTELLI, pp. 81–85 (2012)
2. Pandey, S., Voorsluys, W., Niu, S., Khandoker, A., Buyya, R.: An autonomic cloud environment for hosting ECG data analysis services. Future Gener. Comput. Syst. **28**, 147–154 (2012)
3. Garg, S.K., Versteeg, S., Buyya, R.: A framework for ranking of cloud computing services. Future Gener. Comput. Syst. **29**, 1012–1023 (2013)
4. Narahari, Y., Raju, C., Ravikumar, K., Shah, S.: Dynamic pricing models for electronic business. Sadhana (Acad. Proc. Eng. Sci.) **30**(2–3), 231–256 (2005)
5. Xu, H., Li, B.: Dynamic cloud pricing for revenue maximization. IEEE Trans. Cloud Comput. **1**, 2 (2013)
6. Kantere, V., Dash, D., Francois, G., Kyriakopoulou, S., Ailamaki, A.: Optimal service pricing for a cloud cache. IEEE Trans. Knowl. Data Eng. **23**, 1345–1358 (2011)
7. Pal, R., Hui, P.: Economic models for cloud service markets: pricing and capacity planning. Theor. Comput. Sci. **496**, 113–124 (2013)
8. Wei, G., Vasilakos, A.V., Zheng, Y., Xiong, N.: A game-theoretic method of fair resource allocation for cloud computing services. J. Supercomputing **54**, 252–269 (2010)
9. Dastjerdi, A.V., Buyya, R.: An autonomous reliability-aware negotiation strategy for cloud computing environments. In: 12th IEEE/ACM International Symposium on Cluster, Cloud and Grid Computing (CCGrid), pp. 284–291 (2012)
10. Feng, Y., Li, B.: Price competition in an oligopoly cloud market with multiple IaaS cloud providers. IEEE Trans. Comput. **63**(1), 59–73 (2013)
11. Sim, K.M.: Towards complex negotiation for cloud economy. In: Bellavista, P., Chang, R.-S., Chao, H.-C., Lin, S.-F., Sloot, P.M. (eds.) GPC 2010. LNCS, vol. 6104, pp. 395–406. Springer, Heidelberg (2010)
12. Teng, F., Magoulès, F.: A new game theoretical resource allocation algorithm for cloud computing. In: Bellavista, P., Chang, R.-S., Chao, H.-C., Lin, S.-F., Sloot, P.M. (eds.) GPC 2010. LNCS, vol. 6104, pp. 321–330. Springer, Heidelberg (2010)
13. Li, C., Li, L.: Resource allocation in cloud computing: model and algorithm. Int. J. Web Grid Serv. **9**, 193–211 (2013)
14. Yoo, D., Sim, K.M.: A multilateral negotiation model for cloud service market. In: Kim, T.-H., Yau, S.S., Gervasi, O., Kang, B.-H., Stoica, A., Ślęzak, D. (eds.) GDC and CA 2010. CCIS, vol. 121, pp. 54–63. Springer, Heidelberg (2010)
15. Johannes, A., Borhan, N., Ranjan, R., Liu, C., Chen, J.: A user demand uncertainty based approach for cloud resource management. In: IEEE 16th International Conference on Computational Science and Engineering (CSE), pp. 566–571 (2013)
16. Zadeh, L.A.: Fuzzy sets. Inf. Control **8**, 338–353 (1965)
17. Barron, E.N.: Game Theory: An Introduction, 2nd edn. Wiley, New York (2013)
18. Dhingra, A., Rao, S.: A cooperative fuzzy game theoretic approach to multiple objective design optimization. Eur. J. Oper. Res. **83**, 547–567 (1995)

# Weight-Based Batch Rekeying Scheme for Dynamic Multi-privileged Group Communications

Wei Zhou[1,2], Yang Xu[1], Lijuan Yang[1], and Guojun Wang[1,3(✉)]

[1] School of Information Science and Engineering, Central South University,
Changsha 410083, China
`polly_wei@163.com, xuyangcsu@gmail.com, ylj_csu@126.com,`
`csgjwang@csu.edu.cn`
[2] College of Information Science and Technology, Hunan Agricultural University,
Changsha 410128, China
[3] School of Computer Science and Educational Software, Guangzhou University,
Guangzhou 510006, China

**Abstract.** In multi-privileged group communications, the group users have different access privileges to multiple data resources. The influence on the system is different between the users when membership changes in the group. In batch rekeying, when the keys are not updated promptly, the more access privileges the users change, the more related resources are exposed to the malicious users. Unfortunately, in those existing batch rekeying schemes, the group users are treated equally. So in this paper, we propose a weight-based batch rekeying scheme for multi-privileged group communications to decrease the exposure of data resources in a batch. A weight is assigned for each membership change of the users. Then, rekeying is performed in batch when the sum of collected weights is larger than a predetermined threshold. In the operation of batch rekeying, a marking algorithm is devised to process a batch of joining/leaving/switching requests, and the related keys are updated according to the corresponding marks. We give some analysis on our scheme to show that our scheme can provide hierarchical access control, as well as backward security and weak forward security. It also shows that our scheme can save server cost substantially. At last, extensive simulation results show our scheme can improve the security to a certain extent.

**Keywords:** Multi-privileged group communications · Weight · Threshold · Batch rekeying · Security

## 1 Introduction

The increasing popularization of group-oriented applications, such as video conferencing, pay-per-view channels, and remote E-learning, triggers the secure need for its privacy, data integrity, and so on.

A practical solution to achieve secure group communications is to have a symmetric key to encrypt the data resources. In traditional single-privileged group communications, all members (also called users) in a group have the same access privileges. For protecting

© Springer International Publishing Switzerland 2015
G. Wang et al. (Eds.): ICA3PP 2015 Workshops, LNCS 9532, pp. 678–690, 2015.
DOI: 10.1007/978-3-319-27161-3_62

the data resources, a general group key is only shared by the group members. Group membership might be dynamic because the users join and leave the group frequently, so the group key needs to be updated and redistributed to all the authorized members securely when membership changes, in order to provide backward security (which ensures that the newly-joined user is unable to access the previous communications before joining the group) and forward security (which ensures that the departed user is unable to access the future communications after leaving the group) [1].

However, some group-based applications have multiple data resources, and members have different access privileges. So, multi-privileged groups come into existence, which brings new challenges to group key management. Group key management in the multi-privileged group communications should not only ensure that no users can access the data beyond their privileges but also be flexible enough to accommodate users' operations of joining, leaving and switching [2].

In multi-privileged group communications, one or more data resources to which the users subscribe can be encrypted by separate session keys (SKs). The SKs are usually refreshed immediately after each joining/leaving/switching request. It is called individual rekeying, in which the number of rekeying is directly proportional to the number of membership changes. So, the perfect and strong forward/backward security can be obtained in individual rekeying schemes. However, individual rekeying has two drawbacks: inefficiency and out-of-sync problem between keys and data [3]. Therefore, in order to alleviate these problems, batch rekeying is proposed, allowing several requests of membership changes to be handled simultaneously. Since the key server does not perform rekeying immediately, a departing member will remain in the group longer and a joining member has to wait longer to be accepted to the group. Due to such a delayed rekeying, batch rekeying causes security damage, and it can only achieve weak forward security. Therefore, batch rekeying can provide a trade-off between performance and security.

In some multi-privileged group-based applications as video on demand and online learning, the users can change their access privileges according to their willingness. The influence on system performance will vary between the different changes of access privileges of users. If the affected SKs are not rekeyed promptly when membership changes, the more access privileges the users change, the more related resources are exposed to the malicious users. Thus it brings more damages in security. Unfortunately, the existing batch rekeying methods [4, 5] treat all the users equally, which are inapplicable to the multi-privileged group communications. A large amount of the data resources would be exposed to the malicious users for a long time, which seriously declines the system security.

In this paper, we propose a weight-based batch rekeying for multi-privileged group communications. A weight is assigned for each membership change of the users. Then in a batching interval, the key server collects these weights of membership changes of users. Then rekeying is performed once the sum of collected weights is larger than a predetermined threshold $W$. In order to reduce the rekeying overhead, the integrated key model is reconstructed and a marking algorithm is devised to process a batch of joining/leaving/switching requests. We give the secure analysis on our scheme to show that our scheme can provide hierarchical access control, as well as backward security and weak forward security. The analysis results also show our scheme can save server cost substantially. At last, extensive simulation results show our scheme can reduce the duration that the data resources are exposed to the leaving/switching-out users, and therefore improve the security to a certain extent.

## 2 Related Work

In order to ensure strong forward/backward security, the keys should be rekeyed immediately after each joining, leaving, and switching request, which is called individual rekeying. Most of the schemes [2, 6] only consider the operations of individual rekeying. But this kind of approach has two drawbacks. First, it is relatively inefficient. Second, there is an out-of-sync problem between keys and data.

Batch rekeying in which the keys are updated after batch requests has been proposed to be applicable in reality. It can alleviate the drawbacks of individual rekeying. The keys are not updated immediately after each request, but after rekeying in each batch, the joining/switching-in users cannot access the previous communications before they join/switch in and the leaving/switching-out users cannot access the future communications after they leave/switch out, which can respectively obtain backward security and weak forward security. Therefore, batch rekeying provides a trade-off between performance and security. Many applications can accommodate this compromise, for example, multimedia application can allow the users to keep watching in the previous group for a time after the expiration.

Most of batch rekeying schemes are proposed for single-privileged group communications. The users are formed into a whole group to share the same data resources. Batch rekeying can be performed after a time period. In those key tree based schemes [3, 5, 7], the reallocation of the tree nodes to keep the tree balanced is their concern to reduce the rekeying overhead. Literature [8] defines hybrid protocols with the combination of individual rekeying and batch rekeying, where joins and leaves are performed in batch programmatically while evictions are performed immediately. A stochastic model for batch rekeying is presented in [9] by using queuing theory and used to deduce the relationship between the rekeying interval and the system parameters. The rekeying interval can be calculated quantitatively. In the above-mentioned schemes [3, 5, 7, 8], rekeying is performed after a fixed-length interval. In order to obtain the efficient group rekeying, the batch rekeying interval is dynamically configured in [9]. The total rekeying cost per unit time can be minimized. Batch rekeying also can be performed after a fixed number of requests of membership changes. A threshold-based scheme for periodic batch rekeying is proposed in [10]. The number of requests is accumulated in the key server, and when it is beyond a pre-determined threshold (which is the maximum number of request in each period), the rekeying will be performed.

In multi-privileged group communications, the batch rekeying will be handled with difficultly. Several batch rekeying schemes [4, 11] are proposed for multi-privileged group communications. Their proposals are based on the integrated graph, and focus on rekeying and the reconstruction of key graph. Batch rekeying is performed in IDHKGS [4] when a rekeying period expires. After the related keys are marked with different tags according to the joining/leaving/switching requests, some of them can be deduced by using agreed algorithms both on the key distribution center (KDC) and the users. KDC only needs to distribute those keys which cannot be deduced by the users. However, the addition and deletion of nodes in the integrated key graph are considered, but the reconstruction of service group subtrees is not. Therefore, the storage of keys increases to some extent.

Batch rekeying usually falls into two categories: rekeying after a time period [3–5, 7–9] or rekeying after a fixed number of requests [10]. The batch rekeying scheme [11] is proposed based on the integrated key graph combined with the above-mentioned two categories. Min($N$, $T$) policy is used in this scheme, where the batch rekeying process starts even before the rekeying interval $T$ expires or if a maximum of $N$ users are waiting to join/leave/switch. So, the users need not wait before the rekeying interval is reached. The reconstruction of binary trees of service groups is considered to reduce the key storages. However, the scheme fails to guarantee the forward security strictly.

## 3  System Description

We introduce the basic concepts which describe the group communications containing multiple data resources and users with different access privileges, and then introduce the application scenario and the key model, which are suitable for our proposed scheme.

### 3.1  System Description

Let $\{r_1, r_2, \ldots, r_M\}$ denote the set of data resources in the multi-privileged group communications, where $M$ is the total number of data resources. In this scenario, each data resource corresponds to a data stream that is transmitted in one multicast session.

In multi-privileged group communications, the users can be divided separately according to different dimensions. One data group (DG) contains the users which can access to a particular resource. It is clear that the DGs have overlapped membership because the users may subscribe to multiple resources. The users are also divided into non-overlapping service groups according to access privileges. One service group (SG) contains the users which are authorized to access the exactly same set of data resources. The DGs are denoted by $\{D_1, D_2, \ldots, D_M\}$. Users in the DG $D_m$ are authorized to obtain the data resource $r_m$. The SGs are denoted by $\{S_1, S_2, \ldots, S_I\}$, where $I$ is the total number of SGs. It is easy to prove that $I \leq 2^M - 1$. To make clear mathematical representations, $t_m^i$ is defined as:

$$t_m^i = \begin{cases} 1, & \text{the SG } S_i \text{ can access the resource } r_m \\ 0 & \text{otherwise} \end{cases} \tag{1}$$

for $i = 1, \ldots, I$ and $m = 1, \ldots, M$. In addition, we define a virtual SG, $S_0$, to represent the users which do not participate in any group communications. Clearly, $t_m^0 = 0$ for $m = 1, \ldots, M$.

### 3.2  Hierarchical Access Control in Multi-privileged Group Communications

In order to achieve hierarchical access control without redundant data transmission, it is necessary to encrypt different resources using separate keys. Thus, the users in each DG share a key, referred as the data group key. The data group key (also be called SK in this paper) of $D_m$, denote by $K_m^D$, is used to encrypt the data resource $r_m$. Obviously, the users in SG $S_i$ must possess $\{K_m^D, \forall m: t_m^i = 1\}$.

In the applications containing multiple SGs, the users not only join/leave the service, but also switch between SGs by subscribing to or dropping data resources. We note $S_i \rightarrow S_j$ to represent that a user switches from $S_i$ to $S_j$.

Hierarchical access control for multi-privileged group communications should achieve the forward and backward security. When a user switches from $S_i$ to $S_j$, it is necessary to guarantee (1) the forward security that the data group keys of $\{D_m, \forall m: t_m^i = 1 \text{ and } t_m^j = 0\}$ should be updated; and (2) the backward security that the data group keys of $\{D_m, \forall m: t_m^i = 0 \text{ and } t_m^j = 1\}$ should be updated.

### 3.3 Key Model

Multimedia application that distributes data in multi-layer format is a typical example for our proposed scheme. Suppose there are three data resources for different layer of the multimedia stream: low ($r_1$), medium ($r_2$) and high quality ($r_3$). The users subscribing to a certain layer can access the data resources of the current and the lower layers. Therefore, the users subscribing to low quality ($S_1$) can access $\{r_1\}$; the users subscribing to medium quality ($S_2$) can access $\{r_1, r_2\}$; and the users subscribing to high quality ($S_3$) can access $\{r_1, r_2, r_3\}$.

The users are organized through the hierarchy which we once proposed in [12] of Fig. 1 by three different SGs. A centralized key server is exploited to generate, distribute and manage keys. The key graph contains two parts, the SG subtrees and the DG subgraph. The SG subtrees are based on multiway trees (each node in SG subtrees has $d$ children nodes), and the DG subgraph is constructed by binary trees according to the partial-ordered relationship of SKs between the SGs to store all the SK nodes and the nodes between the root nodes of SG subtrees (but not involved in the DG subgraph) and the SK nodes in the key graph.

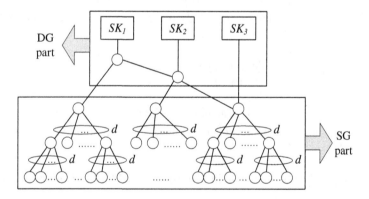

**Fig. 1.** The integrated key graph with multiway subtrees ($d$ is the degree of subtree)

In the key graph, each node is associated with a key. Each SK node is associated with the session key which encrypts the corresponding data resource. Each leaf node of SG subtrees is called user node, which is associated with a user's privacy key. The intermediate nodes are virtual nodes, which are not actual entities. They are associated with key encryption keys (KEKs) which are auxiliary keys to encrypt other keys. For ease of description, the keys in SG subtrees are called SG keys. Similarly, the keys in DG subgraph are called DG keys.

Each user holds a set of keys in the path from his user node to the accessible SK nodes related to required resources. When a user requests to join/leave the group or switch between some SGs, the keys he hold should be updated to obtain the forward/backward security.

## 4 The Weight-Based Batch Rekeying Scheme in Multi-privileged Groups

In this section, the weight-based batch rekeying scheme is proposed for dynamic multi-privileged group communications.

### 4.1 The Design of Weight Value

In our scheme, the users which change more access privileges have priority in starting the rekeying operation, which can improve the security to a certain extent.

A value of weight $w$ is assigned to each operation of membership change. When a user switches from $S_i$ to $S_j$, then $w$ is obtained as:

$$w\left(S_i \to S_j\right) = \left|\left\{K_m^D, \forall m:t_m^i = 1\right\} \Delta \{K_m^D, \forall m:t_m^j = 1\}\right| \tag{2}$$

That is to say, the weight $w$ of each user change is the number of the SKs which should be updated, and the value equals the sum of the number of SKs hold by $S_i$ and $S_j$ except for the shared keys between them.

Specifically, according to our application scenario, because the users with higher privileges can also access the lower-privileged data resources, $w$ is also computed as $w\left(S_i \to S_j\right) = \left|N_j^r - N_i^r\right|$, where $N_j^r$ and $N_i^r$ denote the number of accessed data resources by $S_i$ and $S_j$, separately.

### 4.2 Marking Algorithm

We present a marking algorithm for the key server to process a batch of requests.

In dynamic multi-privileged group communications, the switching rekey can be considered as the superposition of one leaving rekey and one joining rekey.

We use $J_i$ to denote the number of joins in $S_i$ in a batch, $L_i$ to denote the number of leaves from $S_i$ in a batch, $SL_i$ to denote the number of switches out from $S_i$ in a batch, and $SJ_i$ to denote the number of switches into $S_i$ in a batch. We assume that within a batch, each user requests to membership change only once.

Given a batch of requests, the main task for the key server is to identify which keys should be added, deleted, or updated. In individual rekeying, all the keys on the path from the request location to the accessible SKs have to be updated. When there are multiple requests, there are multiple paths. These paths form a subtree, called rekey subtree, which includes all the keys to be added or updated. The rekey subtree does not include individual keys.

The key server cannot control which users might leave, but it can control where to place the new/switching-in users in the integrated key graph. Thus, the key server should carefully place the new/switching-in users so that the number of updated keys is minimized.

When the user requests to join the group communication, he will be assigned to a certain SG according to his access privileges. Each SG subtree will be reconstructed after a rekeying interval.

For $SG_i$, if $J_i + SJ_i = L_i + SL_i$, the key server replaces leaving nodes (including the nodes of users in $S_i$ who leave the group communication and switch out from $S_i$) by joining nodes (including the nodes of users who join and switch into $S_i$), and mark all the nodes from the replacement locations to the accessible SKs UPDATE. If $J_i + SJ_i < L_i + SL_i$, the key server picks $J_i + SJ_i$ shallowest (smallest height) leaves out of the $L_i + SL_i$ leaves, replaces these $J_i + SJ_i$ leaves with the $J_i + SJ_i$ joins. All the nodes from the accessible SKs to the leaves and replacement locations are marked UPDATE or DELETE. Those leaving nodes without joining replacements are marked DELETE. A non-leaf node is marked DELETE if and only if all of its children are marked DELETE. If $J_i + SJ_i > L_i + SL_i$ and $L_i + SL_i = 0$, the key server finds a shallowest leaf node $v$, and then removes $v$ from the tree. A complete but not necessarily balanced tree, $\mathcal{F}$ is constructed, which has all the new/switching-in users and $v$ as leaf nodes. The remaining nodes of $\mathcal{F}$ are new keys. $\mathcal{F}$ is attached to the old location of $v$. All the internal nodes of $\mathcal{F}$ are marked NEW, and all the nodes from the accessible SKs to the parent of $v$'s old location UPDATE BY JOIN. If $J_i + SJ_i > L_i + SL_i$ and $L_i + SL_i > 0$, the key server replaces all leaves by joins, finds a shallowest leaf node, $v$, among the replacement locations, and remove $v$ from the tree. A complete tree $\mathcal{F}$ is constructed, which has the extra joins/switches (into $S_i$) and $v$ as leaf nodes. The root and intermediate nodes of $\mathcal{F}$ are new keys. Then, $\mathcal{F}$ is attached to the old location of $v$. Therefore, the key server marks all internal nodes of $\mathcal{F}$ NEW, all the keys from the old location of $v$ to the accessible SKs UPDATE BY JOIN, and all the keys from the replacement locations (except the old location of $v$) to the accessible SKs UPDATE.

### 4.3 Execution of Batch Rekeying

A user will join/leave the group communications or switch between some SGs due to the change of his access privileges. Each membership change of users is assigned a weight $w$ as the above-mentioned method in subsection 4.1. Then, the key server collects each weight of membership changes and computes the sum of them as $\sum_{k=1}^{n} w_k$. Here $n$ is the total number of requests of membership changes in each batch, and its value in each batch is not fixed. Note that the sum collected with some low weights may be not enough to trigger the batch rekeying. In order to avoid this case, another trigger policy that the rekeying interval $T$ is elapsed is introduced. Once the sum of weights is larger than a threshold value $W$ or the $T$ time is elapsed, whichever occurs first, the server starts the rekeying operation.

The key server reconstructs the integrated key graph and marks the affected nodes as the marking algorithm in subsection 4.2. The nodes marked DELETE are removed.

In each SG subtree, the keys of the nodes marked by UPDATE BY JOIN will be deduced like the joining operation, and the keys of those marked by UPDATE will be deduced like the leaving operation.

Because the keys in the DG part may be shared by several SGs, some DG keys will be affected by the reconstruction of those SGs. Then after the above-mentioned mark algorithm, some affected keys in the DG part should be marked many times. Notice that when a user switches between some SGs, the access privileges of those shared data resources between the SGs have not been changed, so the share SKs of those data resources should not be updated. For this purpose, each of the affected key nodes in the DG part is attached by a record of the identifications (IDs) of the switching users. The record includes the list of IDs of switching-in users and the list of IDs of switching-out users. If the two lists of user IDs are exactly matched, the key should not be updated because the access privileges of those switching users have not been changed. Then, as far as the other affected DG nodes are concerned, if a node is once marked by UPDATE no matter whether is marked by UPDATE BY JOIN or not, the key will be deduced like leaving operation, and if the node is marked only by UPDATE BY JOIN regardless of how many times to be marked, the corresponding key will be deduced like joining operation.

In joining operation, the keys affected by the joining/switching-in users can be deduced from the old keys by a one-way function like $k' = f(k)$. Here $k$ denotes a key and $k'$ denotes the updated version of $k$. The new version of the affected keys can be unicast to each of joining/switching-in users. In leaving operation, a certain secret $s$ can be randomly generated and efficiently distributed to the remaining users (except the leaving/switching-out users) in secure way. Then, the affected keys can be deduced by the one-way function with the old version of keys and the secret $s$ like $k' = f(k \oplus s)$.

## 5    Theoretical Analysis

### 5.1    Security Analysis

Individual rekeying provides perfect security that the keys can be updated every time a user joins/leaves the group or switches between the SGs. But in batch rekeying, all joining/leaving/switching requests received within a batch period are processed together at the same time.

In our scheme, the joining/switching-in users should wait a moment to be accepted. And then, the joining/switching-in users do not know the keys before they join/switch in, so they cannot know the previous group communications. Furthermore, although after the rekeying for each batch, the joining/switching-in users can obtain the new keys which are deduced from the previous ones by one-way function as $k' = f(k)$, it is infeasible for them to compute the previous keys from the new keys they hold because the one-way function is computationally irreversible in polynomial time. Therefore, backward security is maintained.

For those leaving/switching-out users in a batch, the key server will generate a secret $s$ and distribute it to the remaining users of the group via secure channels when rekeying for a batch. Then, the affected keys can be updated from those previous keys and the secret $s$ by the one-way function as $k' = f(k \oplus s)$. Therefore, although the malicious leaving/switching-out users know the previous keys and the one-way function $f$, they are still unable to get new keys without the secret $s$. But due to the delayed rekeying for leaving/switching-out users, those users can access the group communications until the leaving/switching-out requests are handled, so the forward security is violated to some extent until the batch rekeying starts. In this way, weak forward security is maintained.

Our scheme can provide hierarchical access control. The users can obtain the related keys according to their access privileges, so they cannot access those data resources beyond their privileges. When they change their access privileges, the corresponding keys are updated. And they cannot access the previous communications of those data resources before they join or the future communications after they leave because of backward security and weak forward security. Suppose that the adversaries can eavesdrop all the communication traffic. They cannot hold any keys and the secret $s$ because they do not belong to any service groups. So they are unable to obtain any keys of current group communications. Moreover, because the adversaries are unaware of previous keys and the secret $s$, they cannot deduce new keys.

Therefore, our scheme provides hierarchical access control and backward/weak forward security.

## 5.2 Analysis on Communication Cost

Batch rekeying techniques increase efficiency in number of required messages, thus it takes advantage of the possible overlap of new keys for multiple rekey requests and further reduces the possibility of generating new keys that will not be used.

In this paper, we exploit an analytical model of average number of keys which should be updated to analyze the communication cost of a level-homogeneous tree. In joining and switching (into a certain SG) scenarios, the current members in the group can generate new keys for themselves when some users join or switch into some SGs and the rekeying messages are unicast to each joining/switch-in user. But the rekeying operations in the leaving and switching out (from a certain SG) process are more complicated than those in the joining and switching (into an SG) process. Therefore, the leaving/switching-out scenario is focused in this subsection.

In the leaving/switching-out scenario, even though the number of leaving/switching-out group members is the same, the number of keys to be updated varies according to the positions of the leaving/switching-out group members in the integrated key graph. We exploit a probabilistic method to analyze the number of the updating keys. The number of updating keys is modeled into the number of non-full baskets when balls are picked out randomly from the same-sized fully occupied baskets, called the balls and baskets model [13]. In this model, the leaving/switching-out members correspond to the picked balls, and subtrees at each level correspond to the fully occupied baskets of the same size as that of the subtree at each level. Thus, the keys to be updated correspond to non-full baskets.

From the balls and basket model, the average number of updating keys in each SG, when $e$ members leave/switch out, can be obtained as follows:

$$m\left(ST, e\right) = \sum_{i=1}^{H} \sum_{k_i=b}^{B} Pr\left[n\left(e, N/\prod_{j=i}^{H} a_j, \prod_{j=i}^{H} a_j\right) = k_i\right] \cdot k_i \cdot \leq \left(a_i - 1\right) - e \tag{3}$$

where, $n(e, v, w)$ (or also $k_i$) is the number of non-full baskets when $e$ balls are picked out randomly from $v$ identical $w$-sized full baskets, and $b$ and $B$ are the minimum and maximum number of non-full baskets, respectively. $ST = ST\left(a_1, a_2, \dots, a_H\right)$ represents a homogeneous SG subtree which has $H$ levels and each node in the $i$th level has $a_i$ child nodes, thus there are $N = \prod a_i$ leaves (also called the user nodes) in the tree. In our scheme, each SG subtree is a multiway tree whose degree is $d$, so each node in SG subtree (except for leaves) has $d$ child nodes, i.e. $ST = ST\left(d, d, \dots, d\right)$.

$G_{SG}$ is a key graph which has $I$ level-homogeneous SG subtrees. For the DG part, the average number of updating keys is noted as $m(G_{DG}, e) = m_{DG}$ ($1 <= m_{DG} <= 2*I -1$). So, when $e$ members leave or switch from some SGs, the average number of updating keys is

$$m\left(G, e\right) = m\left(G_{SG}, e\right) + m\left(G_{DG}, e\right)$$
$$= \sum_{i=1}^{I}\left(\sum_{i=1}^{H}\sum_{k_i=b}^{B} Pr\left[n\left(e_l, d^{i-1}, d^{H-i}\right) = k_i\right] \cdot k_i \cdot \left(d - 1\right) - e_l\right) + m_{DG} \tag{4}$$

In a batch rekeying interval, the KDC cannot predict the exact number of leaving/switching group members. Thus, to calculate the average number of updating keys in the batch rekeying, the Poisson distribution is used for calculating the number of leaving/switching group members. Thus, the average number of keys in a batch rekeying interval $T_i$ is calculated as follows:

$$E_{\lambda, T_i}\left[m(G, q)\right] = \sum_{k=1}^{N} m(G, k) \cdot P_{\lambda, T_i}(q)$$
$$= \sum_{q=1}^{N}\left\{\sum_{l=1}^{I}\left(\sum_{i=1}^{H}\sum_{k_i=b}^{B} Pr\left[n\left(e_l, d^{i-1}, d^{H-i}\right) = k_i\right] \cdot k_i \cdot \left(d - 1\right) - e_l\right) + m_{DG}\right\} \cdot \frac{e^{-\frac{\lambda_L+\lambda_S}{2}} \cdot \left(\frac{\lambda_L+\lambda_S}{2} T_i\right)^q}{q!} \tag{5}$$

where $P_{\lambda, T_i}(q) = e^{-T_i}(T_i)^q/q!$, $\lambda_L$ and $\lambda_S$ are the leaving rate and switching rate of group members leave and switch out the group, and $q$ is the number of leaving and switching-out group members.

From the above analysis, although the BKTMG [11] scheme and our WBRS scheme are based on the integrated key graph [2], the degree of the SG subtrees in BKTMG is 2, and the degree of the SG subtrees in our scheme is set as $d > = 2$. So the height of SG subtrees will be larger than our scheme to accommodate the same number of users. Further, the average number of keys of a batch rekeying interval in BKTMG is larger than ours. Thus our scheme can reduce the cost of the key server substantially because the introduction of multiway subtrees can decrease the number of updated keys.

# 6  Simulation

Extensive simulations have been conducted to evaluate the performance metrics of the proposed scheme. In this section, we report simulation results of the security damage cost.

## 6.1  Simulation Setup

In our simulation, there are five data resources ($r_1$, $r_2$, $r_3$, $r_4$, and $r_5$) and five SGs ($S_1$, $S_2$, $S_3$, $S_4$, and $S_5$). The users in $S_1$, $S_2$, $S_3$, $S_4$, and $S_5$ can access $\{r_1\}$, $\{r_1, r_2\}$, $\{r_1, r_2, r_3\}$, $\{r_1, r_2, r_3, r_4\}$ and $\{r_1, r_2, r_3, r_4, r_5\}$ respectively. Suppose there are 500 users in the scenario. The users are randomly distributed in different SGs initially. The joining, leaving, and switching probability in a time unit is respectively set as 0.001, 0.001 and 0.1. In our scheme, the rekeying is performed in batch when the sum of weights is larger than $W$ or when the fixed interval $T$ is elapsed appears first. Here $T$ is set as 10 time units and $W$ is set as different values to measure the performance. Each case of our simulation runs for 1000 time units.

## 6.2  Simulation Results

When users leave or switch out from an SG, the data resources in the SG which they just leave or switch out can be accessed and will be exposed to the leaving/switching-out users until the end of the batch interval. The exposed data resources are our concern to measure the security of the proposed scheme.

We compared our WBRS scheme with BKTMG [11]. In BKTMG, the batch rekeying is performed after the number of requests is larger than $N$ or the fixed interval $T$ is elapsed.

Figure 2 shows the total number of the exposed data resources in a batch interval between BKTMG and our WBRS scheme. And Fig. 3 shows the duration of the exposed data resources in a batch interval. Because in our scheme, the larger the number of access privileges changed by users, the more quickly the rekeying is performed, and vice versa.

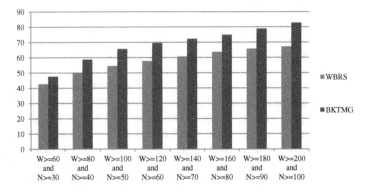

**Fig. 2.** The comparison of the number of the exposed data resources

So we can see that our scheme reduces the total number and the total duration of the data resources which are exposed to the leaving/switching-out users before performing the batch rekeying. So, our scheme can improve the security of batch rekeying to a certain extent.

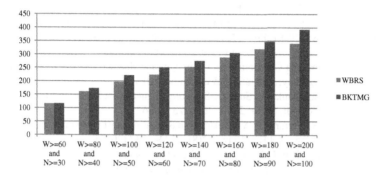

**Fig. 3.** The comparison of the duration of the exposed data resources

## 7    Conclusion

In this paper, a weight-based batch rekeying for multi-privileged group communications is proposed. In order to differentiate the influence on the system performance incurred by the membership changes of the users, we assign a weight to each membership change. When the users request to join/leave/switch, the weight of each membership change is collected. Once upon the sum of weights is larger than a pre-determined threshold $W$ or a pre-determined interval $T$ is elapsed, the key server starts to perform the rekeying operation. Thus the users with more privilege changes have prior to starting to update the related keys. In the rekeying operation, the integrated key is reconstructed to be balanced so that the rekeying overhead is reduced. The analysis shows that our scheme is better for batch rekeying, and achieves more security compared with other similar scheme.

**Acknowledgments.** This work is supported by the National Natural Science Foundation of China under grant numbers 61272151 and 61472451, the Youth Science Foundation of Hunan Agricultural University in China under grant number 14QN15, and the Central South University - Tencent Joint Project and the Hunan Provincial Innovation Foundation for Postgraduate under grant numbers CX2015B047.

## References

1. Rafaeli, S., Hutchison, D.: A survey of key management for secure group communication. ACM Comput. Surv. **35**(3), 309–329 (2003)
2. Sun, Y., Liu, K.J.R.: Scalable hierarchical access control in secure group communications. In: IEEE INFOCOM 2004, vol. 2, pp. 1296–1306. IEEE Press, Hong Kong (2004)

3. Li, X.S., Yang, Y.R., Gouda, M.G., Lam, S.S.: Batch rekeying for secure group communications. In: The 10th International Conference on World Wide Web, pp. 525–534, Hong Kong (2001). doi:10.1145/371920.372153

4. Wang, G., Ouyang, J., Chen, H., Guo, M.: Efficient group key management for multi-privileged groups. Comput. Commun. 30(11–12), 2497–2509 (2007)

5. Pegueroles, J., Rico-Novella, F.: Balanced batch LKH: new proposal, implementation and performance evaluation. In: 2003 IEEE Symposium on Computers and Communications (ISCC), pp. 815–828. IEEE Press, Turkey (2003). doi:10.1109/ISCC.2003.1214218

6. Gu, X., Wang, Y., Zhou, W.: A key tree merge algorithm in multi-privileged groups. In: 2013 IEEE 16th International Conference on Computational Science and Engineering, pp. 288–294. IEEE Press, Sydney, Australia 3–5 December 2013

7. Ng, W.H.D., Cruickshank, H., Sun, Z.: Scalable balanced batch rekeying for secure group communication. Comput. Secur. 25(4), 265–273 (2006)

8. Veltri, L., Cirani, S., Ferrari, G.: A novel batch-based group key management protocol applied to the internet of things. Ad Hoc Netw. 11(8), 2724–2737 (2013)

9. Li, G., Li, B., Du, T., Pan, J., Li, Y.: Batch rekeying model based on queuing theory in secure group communications. In: 2010 IEEE International Conference on Information Theory and Information Security (ICITIS), pp. 247–250. IEEE Press, Beijing, China. doi:10.1109/ICITIS.2010.5689453

10. Cho, J., Chen, I., Eltoweissy, M.: On optimal batch rekeying for secure group communications in wireless networks. Wireless Netw. 14, 915–927 (2008). doi:10.1007/s11276-007-0032-y

11. Muthulakshmi, A., Anitha, R.: Balanced key tree management for multi-privileged groups using (N, T) policy. Secur. Commun. Netw. 5(5), 545–555 (2012)

12. Xu, Y., Zhou, W., Wang, G.: Multiway tree-based group key management using Chinese remainder theorem for multi-privileged group communications. J. Appl. Sci. Eng. 17(1), 81–92 (2014)

13. Je, D., Lee, J., Park, Y., Seo, S.: Computation-and-storage-efficient key tree management protocol for secure multicast communications. Comput. Commun. 33, 136–148 (2010)

# Application-Assisted Dynamic Attestation for JVM-Based Cloud

Haihe Ba[(⊠)], Huaizhe Zhou, Zhiying Wang, Jiangchun Ren,
Tie Hong, and Yiming Li

College of Computer, National University of Defense Technology,
Changsha 410073, China
{haiheba,huaizhezhou,zywang,jcren,tiehong,yimingli}@nudt.edu.cn

**Abstract.** In the recent years, cloud computing has expanded rapidly and improved the working efficiency for a number of cloud users, however, a few enterprises hesitate to move to the cloud because of the runtime security challenges of applications although cloud vendors promise to provide a trustworthy execution platform. In this paper, we propose Trusted Cloud Root Broker to give robust trustworthy guarantees to those JVM-Based applications. The broker as the application-root of the trust is to make the evaluation of the runtime trustworthiness and support dynamic attestation about the integrity state of an application with the assistance of Java virtual machine. It could not just prove the authenticity but also offer the availability for these targeting applications. What is more, our broker has less performance overheads.

**Keywords:** Cloud computing · Java virtual machine · Dynamic attestation · Runtime trustworthiness

## 1 Introduction

Cloud computing has expanded rapidly as a promising technology in the recent years and has drastically altered most opinion about computing mode and application deployment. Cloud has been the center of attentions in governments, enterprises and academic institutes for its extraordinary characteristic, such as on-demand self-service, ubiquitous network access, rapid elasticity [7]. For the sake of efficiency and benefits, more and more enterprises move their services to the cloud [8].

Nevertheless, a number of organizations hesitate to embrace the cloud because of those open security issues. It even exacerbates security challenges and trust risks which restrict more users to further delegate their own services to the cloud [9,10]. Cloud Services may run buggy, malicious application codes or are improperly configured to raise runtime threats. Last but not least, organizations worry about whether cloud computing has supported more availability for the cloud applications even though suffering from malicious outside attacks.

For cloud providers' perspective, they are bound to provide best-quality services to attracting more users. Service providers are inclined to collaborate with

© Springer International Publishing Switzerland 2015
G. Wang et al. (Eds.): ICA3PP 2015 Workshops, LNCS 9532, pp. 691–700, 2015.
DOI: 10.1007/978-3-319-27161-3_63

good-reputation cloud providers. But some inherent features of the cloud leads that a few insiders and outsiders launch an attack to gain illegal income. In the paper we assume that the hardware infrastructures are in a good state. Cloud providers are always willingly responsible for the trustworthiness of the platform environment for the sake of their revenue. Whereas many a research [11,15] have been done to tackle trustworthy issues, yet most of them are concerned about the integrity of platform.Whereas attention has been paid more on applications to promote cloud services trustworthy.

In this paper, we propose a dynamic cloud attestation architecture to support runtime verification by exploiting applications semantics with the assistance of Java Virtual Machine (JVM). Targeting JVM-based applications doesn't limit its applicability at all, since these applications are basically ubiquitous [12]. We introduce trusted computing into Java virtual machine and build the application-root of trust for JVM-Based Cloud applications, called Trusted Cloud Root Broker (TCRB).

The significant contributions of our work are as follows:

- **Application-assisted Attestation.** We propose dynamic attestation for cloud computing with the assistance of applications that are running inside HotSpot VM. We utilize the serviceability of Java virtual machine for the proposed approach to gain the state of application services at the runtime.
- **Runtime-Integrity Verification.** The traditional measurement solutions always checks the loading-time integrity of the binaries [1], however, it does not reflect the dynamic features of targeting services. We build a runtime verification approach to deal with the dynamic issue of these applications.
- **Trustworthiness Estimate.** To effectively capture dynamic changes about the state of running applications and give an intuitive perception to cloud consumers, we employ CertainTrust [13] and CertainLogic [14] to do the evaluation of the trustworthiness of application.

The rest of this paper is organized as follows. Section 2 is a brief introduction about the related works. Section 3 is the primary motivation of our architecture and Sect. 4 present the architecture of trusted cloud root broker. Experiment evaluation is in the Sect. 5. At the end, we give our conclusion of this paper in the Sect. 6.

## 2   Related Work

A amount of research in the related area has been proposed, most of which are about the improvement of trusted computing in the system level and the trustworthiness enhancement for services in cloud platform.

Some prior works are presented to focus on the feasibility and usability of remote attestation. Sailer [1] has proposed IMA(TCG-based integrity measurement architecture) to check and verify the whole loaded executable contents, however, it is to approximate the integrity state when they are running and could not reflect the runtime behavior, needless to say, tackles those runtime threats. In view of the above exiting issues, Jaeger [2] introduces IMA-based PRIMA(Policy-Reduced Integrity Measurement Architecture), which uses CW-Lite model to enhance the capacity of SELinux to assure information flow integrity to resolve the challenges raised by wrong input data. Nonetheless, it does not still address the integrity issue about the code at the runtime, which means that it is incapable of capturing the running changes. DR@FT(dynamic remote attestation framework and tactics) is build by Xu [3] to improve the efficiency in the measurement about a targeting system on the basis of IMA [1] and PRIMA [2]. Nevertheless it is not suitable for the applications based on JVM, such as Java-based services, because these applications are the input data in its opinion.

Plenty of works have been done to address the issue about trustworthiness. Cloud-DLS is proposed by Wang [16] to use Bayesian cognitive model and social trust relationship to integrate existing DLS algorithms with the requirement of trust for cloud computing. It is assumed by Richardson [17] that those statements are independent for the purpose of addressing the trust source problem. But a web of trust is employed, which takes only single valued beliefs and trusts in consideration. Yet these researches do not make use of trusted computing to protect the integrity of services.

A few existing works are similar to our works. Semantic remote attestation [5] which is based on language-based virtual machines are proposed to certify various properties of code that is running inside the virtual machine, but this mechanism could not make sure the runtime integrity. Although JMF(Java Measurement Framework) [4] is capable of more sophisticatedly handling some security risks about process integrity for supporting runtime assurance, yet it is unable to ensure availability of the active service and reflect the dynamic nature using the trust theory.

## 3    Motivation

### 3.1    Threat Challenges

While cloud computing gains more and more popularity of institutional organization, yet numerous security threats occur in the cloud systems. Although a great deal of promising works [6,16] are proposed to overcome these security limitations, cloud applications have been still up against more and more serious challenges.

It is crucial to deal with a security challenge that the code is not running as the expectation of the cloud-user. This challenge results from either deliberate tamper or inaccurate operation. Plenty of prior researches [1,2] have been used to provide applications with the capability of trusted assurance, however, few of them treat JVM-based applications as the measurement target and only guarantee the integrity of the binary executable at the loading time.

It is possible for an adversary to rise more subtle attacks on the availability of business services, which will generate zero revenue for the unable to provide continuous services in the view of service providers. Consequently, service providers will be not confident in the relevant cloud providers and decline to work jointly next time.

## 3.2   Framework and Role

Owing to the diversity and complexity of cloud-based applications, we introduce
Trusted Cloud Root Broker(TCRB) as the application root of the trust. In this
paper, we assume that TCRB is trustworthy and JVM can run correctly at
the protection of PRIMA [2]. As depicted in Fig. 1, TCRB could obtain an
array of bytes about a class loaded into the virtual machine through Trusted
Class Loader(TCL) with the assistance of HotSpot VM. TCL make sure these
applications started as the expectation of cloud user, but it fails to determine
whether the applications can be always running correctly.

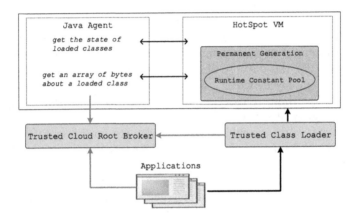

**Fig. 1.** A Framework of Application-Assisted Attestation for Cloud Applications

We design this framework to enable the collaboration between TCRB and a
verified application for the real runtime state from the target. It is essential to
tackle the issues from the diversity and complexity in the cloud platform. In the
framework, TCRB is a vital part in the dynamic attestation, which raises a measurement to the application in a periodic manner with the help of HotSpot$^{TM}$
attach mechanism.

When launch an attestation, TCRB drives HotSpot to execute Java Agent
in the target process. Java Agent gains the state of loaded classes. In general,
TCRB would designate certain class loaders, for instance, AppClassLoader or
other class loaders implemented by Tomcat. Then, it acquires an array of bytes
for the selective class respectively and sends to TCRB through interprocess communication. At the side of the broker, it would extract an array of bytes from
the constant pool and method when accepting a class. It enters a verification
stage to judge whether the target runs correctly.

## 4   Trusted Cloud Root Broker

Most of consumers feel so anxious for cloud computing because of trustworthiness issues of runtime execution environments. It seems to impede the adoption

of cloud computing and cause the recent development of the cloud to remain stagnant.

In spite of numerous solutions proposed to solve the existing threats about cloud, a majority of countermeasures are on the integrity of OS-based virtual machine. There is little concern about the trustworthiness in the application layer, which does not have a direct effectiveness and efficiency when confronted with those threats targeting cloud service.

### 4.1 Trusted Property

We present an application-root of trust inside the cloud platform to provide high assurance for top services. As consumers have misgivings about the cloud, building a cornerstone to instills trust is requisite. A safeguarding solution should be endowed with some trusted properties for the interest of cloud users.

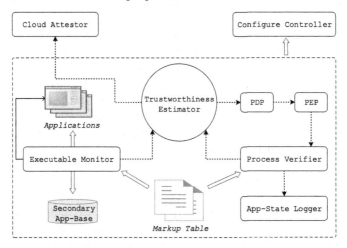

**Fig. 2.** A overview of Trusted Cloud Root Broker

- *Integrity.* It is deemed that the executables of an application could reflect logical behavior. To guarantee trustworthiness, to introduce a measurement to judge the integrity is imperative.
- *Authenticity.* Despite the executable integrity, it is not enough to support high-assurance. It requires to ensure process authenticity because malicious adversary could change a running application.
- *Availability.* A cloud service always demand more stronger capability of continuous business. How to guarantee available when being subjected to intentional attack remains to be resolved.

### 4.2 System Overview

We design TCRB to arm cloud application on account of those existing issues. It is presented to be the application-root of the trust with the trusted properties.

The architecture of TCRB is illustrated in Fig. 2, which is composed of eight core components and two auxiliary components.

- *Trustworthiness Estimator.* Since cloud applications are highly distributed, it is vital to enforce the evaluation of trustworthiness. Capturing dynamic changes in trust can represent the state of the target services. It not just gives an intuitive judgment but provides a reference criteria to adjust policy decisions.
- *Executable Monitor.* This component is responsible for monitoring the integrity of binary executables of a cloud application. It is in a fast-verification mode, which only ensure the integrity of the entire executable. A fine-grained approach targeting a class file is utilized to rapidly locate when detecting a malicious adversary.
- *Process Verifier.* Process verifier could enforce an attach mechanism to gain the runtime Constant-Pool and ByteCode with the assistance of HotSpot virtual machine. The verifier validates the authenticity of the critical parts to make an application run as the expectation of a cloud users.
- *App-State Logger.* To prove the trustworthiness of the current service, it is a need to not only make a verification for the process but also store the result. This component is utilized to log the state of a running application securely. On the other hand, it can also respond to the attest of the consumers after a consumer wants to look up the past verification information.
- *Policy Decision Point.* Depending upon measurement feedbacks from the process verifier, trustworthiness estimator could effectively capture the dynamic change in trust. According to the evaluation of the trustworthiness, PDP makes the corresponding decision to adjust the security policy.
- *Policy Enforcement Point.* With the guidance of PDP, PEP drives the Process Verifier to enforce the corresponding policy. In the case that multiple services are running in the same process and one of them turns out to be distrusted, PEP will direct the Process Verifier to only adjust the security policy of this service to make it more trustworthiness.
- *Cloud Attestor.* After enterprise users delegate application services to the cloud, they may be urgent to gain the runtime state. It is a need to bring remote attestation into the cloud platform. This component could accept an attestation request and then respond with an integrity proof. When cloud attestor catches a request, it will raise the verification of targeting process in which the application is running so as to make determination whether it runs correctly.
- *Configure Controller.* When introducing the trusted broker to give these applications the support of high assurance, it also brings some inevitable overheads into the cloud platform. To balance both system performance and security safeguard, we design the configure controller to make dynamic regulation of the capability of the broker.
- *Secondary App-Base.* We put this component into the TCRB in order to address the available issue when an application in the cloud environment sustains the malicious tampering intrude. In our application-root of the trust,

it is able to both resist an attack at the time of class-loading and prop up a perilous situation at the runtime. These secondary applications could be from those trusted cloud consumers or be backed up when they are proved to be trusted.

- *Markup Table.* This component is in charge of giving a reference criterion to the measurement procedure. In other words, it could provide supports for the Executable Monitor and Process Verifier. In this paper, we assume that Markup Table is enough trusted to complete the verification mission and don't take any malicious attack of this Markup Table into account.

### 4.3   Trustworthiness Estimate

Trust is a hypothesis about future behavior of current running application in the cloud computing platform. It is a significant aspect of decision making for the state of cloud applications. The trust ability of a cloud-application could be defined in a particular regard like integrity, authenticity or any property. The trustworthiness of an application service depends on the verification results of the TCRB, including both Executable Monitor and Process Verifier. We use the statements of these properties(integrity and authenticity) to present the verification results of the delegated service.

**Table 1.** The definition of these symbols (t, c, f)

| Symbol | Definition |
|---|---|
| $t \in [0,1]$ | average trusted value by the measurement |
| $c \in [0,1]$ | certainty associated with average trusted value |
| $f \in [0,1]$ | initial expected trusted value, set to 0.95 |

To effectively capture dynamic change in trust, we use CertainTrust [13] and CertainLogic [14] as the basic for the evaluation of the trustworthiness of an application. We define the trustworthiness value $T$ of a proposition in Eq. (1). Table 1 shows the definition of every symbol in Eq. (1). We choose a class of the targeting application as the object of the measurement. There are three types of the verification results, which are belief (b), disbelief (d) and uncertainty (u). Equations (2) and (3) show how to calculate the average trusted value t and the corresponding certainty c: $n_b$ means the number of those classes with belief; $n_d$ indicates the number of those classes with disbelief; $n_u$ expresses the number of those classes with uncertainty.

$$T = t * c + (1 - c) * f \tag{1}$$

$$t = \begin{cases} 0 & \text{if } n_b + n_d = 0 \\ \frac{n_b}{n_b + n_d} & \text{otherwise} \end{cases} \tag{2}$$

$$c = \frac{(n_b + n_d + n_u)(n_b + n_d)}{2 * n_u + (n_b + n_d + n_u)(n_b + n_d)} \tag{3}$$

We use propositional logic operators of AND ($\wedge$) in CertainLogic for the combination of these properties. The operator of AND allow the evaluation of an application under uncertainty. Because in our approach, the HotSpot would generate some classes to assist in the dynamic measurement, which are based on Java language and running in the same virtual machine with the application.

## 5  Evaluation

We design the experiments based on OpenJDK-6, which is an implementation of HotSpot virtual machine. It runs on Intel$^{\circledR}$ Core$^{TM}$ i3-2130 @3.4 GHz and Linux Mint 16 with the specification version 1.2 of the TPM chip. We build a set of experiments for the functional evaluation of our trusted broker. In addition, we run SPECjvm2008 benchmark to estimate the performance overheads.

Our trusted architecture could not only recognise those malicious attack at the binary executables of targeting applications in Table 2, but also prevent

**Table 2.** Functional Experiment for our broker

| No. | Test item |
| --- | --- |
| 1 | Add malicious codes into binary executables |
| 2 | Modify the execution logic of binary executables |
| 3 | Load unchartered application based on Java |
| 4 | Load malicious modified application services |
| 5 | Tamper with the runtime data of application process |
| 6 | Inject malicious codes in Java process |

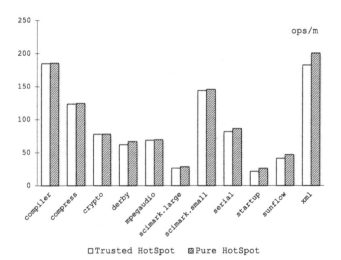

□ Trusted HotSpot    ⊠ Pure HotSpot

**Fig. 3.** Execution overheads for applications

those unchartered applications from loaded into the memory; What is more, it is also able to detect those runtime adversary to provide applications with high-assurance support.

In addition, our trusted broker has less overhead on the applications' execution. Figure 3 proves our conclusion that the benchmark *xml* has an approximate loss of 9 % at the worst situation and *mpegaudio* has a better loss of 1 %. The Trusted Cloud Root Broker could bring cloud-user stronger trustworthiness protection with the less overheads of the running application.

# 6    Conclusion

With the tremendous momentum, cloud computing develops rapidly in the government and enterprise organizations. Nevertheless, it also introduces a great many unchartered threats on which those traditional solutions have very little effectiveness and efficiency. It would result in fewer and fewer consumers to embrace the cloud although some are intent to delegate their own applications into the cloud computing platform.

To tackle these above security challenges, we propose the Trusted Cloud Root Broker to provide cloud users with dynamic attestation about the trustworthy proof of the targeting application. In this paper, the trusted broker could bridge the trust gap between service providers and cloud providers with the assistance of the high-level language virtual machine. TCRB is able to bring integrity, authenticity and availability property into the cloud execution environment to guarantee those application services running with a continued and expected state.

Future work occurs in some aspects. In this paper, we assume that TCRB is trusted and cloud-applications aren't trusted. Nonetheless, in fact TCRB may suffer from malicious adversaries and it need to be protected from them. We will bestow the capability of SELinux on the TCRB to become more trustworthy. On the other hand, we will improve the runtime verification approach rather than current periodic measurement so as to reduce the overheads and enhance the ability of the trusted broker.

**Acknowledgments.** The work is funded in part by the National Natural Science Foundation of China (No. 61303191). It is also supported by a grant from the National High Technology Research and Development Program of China (863 Program) (No. 2015AA016010).

# References

1. Sailer, R, Zhang, X, Jaeger, T, Van Doorn, L: Design and implementation of a TCG-based integrity measurement architecture. In: 13th USENIX Security Symposium, vol. 13, pp. 223–238 (2004)
2. Jaeger, T, Sailer, R, Shankar, U: PRIMA: policy-reduced integrity measurement architecture. In: SACMAT, pp. 19–28 (2006)

3. Xu, W., Zhang, X., Hu, H., et al.: Remote attestation with domain-based integrity model and policy analysis. IEEE Trans. Dependable Secure Comput. **9**(3), 429–442 (2012)
4. Thober, M, Pendergrass, J.A., Jurik, A.D: JMF: Java measurement framework: language-supported runtime integrity measurement. In: STC, pp. 21–32 (2012)
5. Haldar, V, Chandra, D, Franz, M: Semantic remote attestation- a virtual machine directed approach to trusted computing. In: VM 2004, vol. 3, pp. 3–15 (2004)
6. Podesser, S., Toegl, R.: A software architecture for introducing trust in Java-based clouds. In: Park, J.J., Lopez, J., Yeo, S.-S., Shon, T., Taniar, D. (eds.) STA 2011. CCIS, vol. 186, pp. 45–53. Springer, Heidelberg (2011)
7. Mell, P., Grance, T.: The NIST definition of cloud computing. Nat. Inst. Stand. Technol. **53**(6), 50 (2009)
8. Armbrust, M., Fox, A., Griffith, R., et al.: A view of cloud computing. Commun. ACM **53**(4), 50–58 (2010)
9. Zissis, D., Lekkas, D.: Addressing cloud computing security issues. Future Gener. Comput. Syst. **28**(3), 583–592 (2012)
10. Jensen, M, Schwenk, J, Gruschka, N, Iacono, L.L: On technical security issues in cloud computing. In: IEEE CLOUD, pp. 109–116 (2009)
11. Hofmann, O.S., Dunn, A.M., Kim, S, Roy, I, Witchel, E: Ensuring operating system kernel integrity with OSck. In: ASPLOS, pp. 279–290 (2011)
12. Learn About Java Technology. http://www.java.com/en/about/
13. Ries, S: Extending Bayesian trust models regarding context-dependence and user friendly representation. In: SAC, pp. 1294–1301 (2009)
14. Ries, S., Habib, S.M., Mühlhäuser, M., Varadharajan, V.: CertainLogic: a logic for modeling trust and uncertainty. In: McCune, J.M., Balacheff, B., Perrig, A., Sadeghi, A.-R., Sasse, A., Beres, Y. (eds.) Trust 2011. LNCS, vol. 6740, pp. 254–261. Springer, Heidelberg (2011)
15. Baumann, A, Peinado, M, Hunt, G: Shielding applications from an untrusted cloud with haven. In: OSDI, pp. 267–283 (2014)
16. Wang, W., Zeng, G., et al.: Cloud-DLS: dynamic trusted scheduling for cloud computing. Expert Syst. Appl. **39**(3), 2321–2329 (2012)
17. Richardson, M., Agrawal, R., Domingos, P.: Trust management for the semantic web. In: Fensel, D., Sycara, K., Mylopoulos, J. (eds.) ISWC 2003. LNCS, vol. 2870, pp. 351–368. Springer, Heidelberg (2003)

# New Escrow-Free Scheme for Hierarchical Identity-Based Encryption

Fang Qi, Xin Tang$^{(\boxtimes)}$, and Quanyun Wei

School of Information Science and Engineering, Central South University,
Changsha 410083, China
csuqifang@csu.edu.cn
{tangxcsu,wqycsu}@gmail.com

**Abstract.** Key escrow is an inherent problem in identity-based encryption (IBE) since it was first proposed by Shamir in 1984. We present a new scheme to remove key escrow from IBE and HIBE, based on the security notion of anonymous ciphertext indistinguishability against key generation center (ACI-KGC) proposed by Chow. In view of this, we first show how to equip a modified framework in (H)IBE system in ACI-KGC security. In the system architecture, the PKG and ICA cooperate an anonymous private key generation protocol such that the PKG can issue a private key to a user authenticated by ICA without knowing the list of users' identities. Next, we apply proposed scheme to hierarchical identity-based encryption (HIBE) system to ensure the high security and efficiency. It is worth noting that, our proposal focus on the mitigating the key escrow problem which has not been well-studied in HIBE, and do not change the fundamental structure of systems as well as keep the efficiency and security of HIBE.

**Keywords:** Key escrow · HIBE · ACI-KGC · PKG · ICA

## 1 Introduction

The concept of Identity-Based Encryption (IBE) was first proposed by Shamir [1] in 1984. However it took nearly two decades to put forward the practical and efficient IBE (BF-IBE) by Boneh and Franklin [2]. IBE is a public key encryption mechanism where the user's public key is an arbitrary string that related to the identity, and the private key is generated by a trusted authority called Private Key Generator (PKG) which holds a master secret key and generates all the private keys for entities in the system. The identity information such as user's name, address, email can be used as its public key, so that the sender doesn't need the recipient's certificate from traditional public key infrastructure (PKI). Therefore, IBE can eliminate the complexity of the certificates' distribution and management.

Nevertheless, the advantages is confronted with severe challenge which is known as the key escrow problem. In IBE systems, the private keys of all the

© Springer International Publishing Switzerland 2015
G. Wang et al. (Eds.): ICA3PP 2015 Workshops, LNCS 9532, pp. 701–713, 2015.
DOI: 10.1007/978-3-319-27161-3_64

users are generated by a trusted authority called private key generator (PKG) or key generation center (KGC). The PKG or KGC should be completely trusted and is free to engage in malicious activities without any risk of being confronted in a court of law, which is a great security threat to the application and implementation of IBE.

Since the traditional IBE systems only have a single PKG, they face two problems as follows: (a) the PKG takes time and cost to generate, transmit, update private keys in secure channel. Especially in a large network with multiple users, the PKG will become a performance bottleneck. (b) the PKG becomes the main target of attack. Since the PKG holds all the user's private key, once the PKG is attacked or captured, or the PKG becomes malicious, the users' private keys will be leaked.

In this case, hierarchical identity-based encryption (HIBE) was put forth [3]. HIBE is a generalization of IBE which reflects an organizational hierarchy and provides a more practical mechanism. It allows a root PKG to distribute the workload of private key issuing and identity authentication to lower-level PKGs. Generally, each layer has one PKG which has its own master secret key and is responsible for generating private keys for users in their domains in the next level. Besides the disclosure of a domain PKG's secret does not compromise the secrets of higher-level PKGs.

The focus of this paper is on the key escrow of HIBE. The practical application of HIBE make it attractive in the real world, especially in large companies or e-government systems where there are hierarchical administrative issues. Meanwhile, it makes a contribution to the secure cloud storage. Therefore, high secure scheme can guarantee the applications to be well implemented. A HIBE scheme with escrow-free for PKGs and less computing cost is proposed in this paper.

## 1.1 Attempts in Reducing Trust in the PKG

As the intrinsic defect of IBE, the key escrow is an important issue HIBE faces. If we cannot solve the problem of key escrow, it is hard to apply IBE as well as HIBE to large-scale application and implementation. Against this problem, many researchers have approached corresponding solutions to mitigate the key escrow problem.

*Distributed PKGs* [2] was initially proposed by Boneh and Franklin in 2001, where the master secret key is distributed to multiple PKGs or based on threshold PKGs, i.e. the master secret key is spilt to multiple PKGs. This solution comes at the cost of introducing much extra communication and infrastructure.

*Multiple trust authority* [4] was proposed by Chen et al. It similar to distributed PKGs, but these multiple PKGs each have their own master secret key instead of sharing the master secret key. The user authenticates its identity to these PKGs, the PKGs generate the part private keys using the own master secret key and send them to the user respectively. Then the user selects an arbitrary vector with n dimension and the element is 0 or 1, and make an operation with the received part private keys to compose its private key.

*Certificate based encryption* [5] was proposed by Gentry. There is an authentication center (CA) to authenticate the user's identity and the validity of the public key, and returns a public key certificate to the user. The user utilize the certificate and the private key calculated by PKG to compose its integrated private key. Consequently solve the problem of key escrow of PKG, but this solution bring extra computational complexity and loss the benefit of IBE because of the certification scheme.

*Certificateless public key cryptography (CL-PKC)* [6] was first proposed by Al-Riyami and Paterson. The user's private key is calculated with the part private key generated by PKG and user's own secret value, and the public key is calculated with the user's own secret value, identity and system parameters. Despite this solution can solve the key escrow problem for the KGC does not know the final private key, the sender cannot simply select the receiver's identity as the public key, accordingly the advantage of IBE has been weakened.

*Accountable IBE (A-IBE)* [7] was proposed by Goyal in 2007. The user's private key is generated together by the PKG and the user through a key generation protocol. The protocol ensures that the user can get its private key without leaking its identity to the PKG. If the PKG generate the user's private key maliciously, the user can prove the PKG fabricate the private key through a tracking algorithm, thus the PKG is discouraged from selling or leaking any user's secret key, but it is difficult for the user to get the fake private key generated by maliciously PKG.

*Anonymous IBE* [8] was proposed by Sui where the task of identity authentication and private key issuing is separated to the key generate center (KGC) and the local registration authority (LRA). However this anonymity guarantee just considers the outsider attackers, and the internal attackers are the most common sources of cracking attacks. Accordingly, Chow [9] proposed a new security notion ACI-KGC, means anonymous ciphertext indistinguishability against key generation center, to make sure KGC cannot decrypt if it does not know the intended recipient's identity of the ciphertext. In this scheme, the task of the identity authentication and private key issuing is also separated to two parties: an identity-certifying authority (ICA) and a KGC. ICA is responsible for authenticate user's identity by issuing certificate, KGC is responsible for verifying the certificate and still holds the master secrete key solely. Then KGC generates the private key with a complicated interactive protocol collaborating to an authenticated user without knowing the list of users' identities.

## 1.2 Organization

This paper is organized as follows. In Sect. 2, we formally define an HIBE system, give the complete security definition, describe the bilinear groups, and state our assumptions. In Sect. 3, we present our modified HIBE scheme with key-escrow free based on the approached schemes. We prove the security of scheme and analysis the efficiency in Sects. 4 and 5. In Sect. 6, we conclude and discuss open directions for further research.

## 2   Preliminaries

In this section, we give some definitions including hierarchical identity-based encryption, bilinear pairing and complexity assumptions, similar to those given in [3,10].

### 2.1   Hierarchical Identity-Based Encryption

In HIBE, the workload of private key generation of a single root KGC is delegated to many lower-level KGCs. HIBE was first introduced by Horwitz and Lynn [3] with a 2-level HIDE scheme. The first efficient construction for HIBE was proposed by Gentry and Silverberg [10] where security is based on the Bilinear Diffie-Hellman (BDH) assumption in the random oracle model. A subsequent construction was proposed by Boneh and Boyen [11] based on BDH where the secure without random oracles under a weaker selective-ID secure. Subsequently, a series of variants [12–15] have been proposed to achieve stronger notions of security in standard model and full model, i.e. IND-ID-CCA security.

The same as an IBE system, a HIBE is composed of four algorithms: *Setup, Extract, Encrypt, Decrypt*. In HIBE, entities including PKGs and users all have a unique position in the hierarchy, defined by their identities $ID_k = (I_1, I_2, \cdots I_k)$, which is vector of dimension $k$ representing an identity at level $k$ in the hierarchy. The entity's ancestors in the hierarchy tree are the root PKG and lower-level PKGs. The private key of $U_k$ (a certain user at level $k$) is generated by the upper level $PKG_{k-1}$. Generally, the four algorithms are as follows:

**Setup:** $(\lambda, l) \rightarrow (params, msk)$. The root PKG generates system public parameters $params$ and the master secret key $msk$ by inputting a security parameter $\lambda$ and the depth of hierarchy $l$. The system parameters include a description of the plaintext space $M$ and the ciphertext space $C$. Then lower-level entities must obtain the system parameters, and the lower-level PKGs select their own master secret key randomly used in issuing private key to its subordinate users.

**Extract:** $(ID_k, SK_{k-1}, msk, params) \rightarrow (SK_k)$. The $PKG_{k-1}$ takes $ID_k = (I_1, I_2, \cdots I_k)$ (the identity of a certain $U_k$) and the $SK_{k-1}$(the private key of $U_k$) as input, and outputs the private key $SK_k$ for the $U_k$.

**Encrypt:** $(m, ID_k, params) \rightarrow (c)$. A sender takes a message $m \in M$, the intended recipient's identity $ID_k$, and the public system parameters $params$ as input and outputs the ciphertext $c \in C$.

**Decrypt:** $(c, SK_k, params) \rightarrow (m)$. The recipient takes ciphertext $c \in C$, a private key generated by $PKG_{k-1}$, and the public system parameters $params$ as input, and outputs the message $m \in M$.

Encryption and decryption must satisfy the standard consistency constraint. The consistency requires that for any message decrypted as:

$$\forall m \in M : Decrypt(c, SK_k, params) \text{ where } c = Encrypt(m, ID_k, params)$$

## 2.2  Bilinear Groups Pairing

We let $G_1$ and $G_2$ are two cyclic groups of prime order $p$, $g$ be a generator of $G_1$. Let $e$ be a bilinear pairing, if $e : G_1 \times G_1 \to G_2$ is a map with the following properties.

- Bilinear: $\forall g_1, g_2 \in G_1$, $\forall a, b \in Z_p^*$, we have $e(ag_1, bg_2) = e(g_1, g_2)^{ab}$;
- Non-degeneracy: $e(g_1, g_2) \neq 1$.
- Computability: There is an efficient algorithm to compute $e(g_1, g_2)$ for any $g_1, g_2 \in G_1$.

## 2.3  Complexity Assumption

We review the bilinear Diffie-Heffman (BDH) assumption, which has been used to construct the first efficient HIBE scheme in GS-HIBE [10].

Let $G_1, G_2$ be two cyclic groups of prime order $q$, $e : G_1 \times G_1 \to G_2$ be an admissible bilinear map. And let $\{a, b, c\} \in Z_q$ be chosen at random, and $g$ be a generator of $G_1$. The BDH assumption introduced by BF-IBE [2] is that no probabilistic polynomial-time algorithm $\mathcal{B}$ can compute the $e(g, g)^{abc}$ from the tuple $(g, ag, bg, cg)$ with more than a negligible advantage $\varepsilon$. The advantage of $\mathcal{B}$ is:

$$|Pr[\mathcal{B}(g, ag, bg, cg) = e(g, g)^{abc}]| \geq \varepsilon$$

**Definition 1.** We say that the BDH assumption holds in G if no t-time algorithm has advantage at least $\varepsilon$ in solving the BDH problem in G.

## 2.4  ACI-KGC Security Definition

The security notion ACI-KGC was proposed in [9], this secure model provides an "embedded-identity encryption" oracle, which lets the adversary adaptively get many ciphertexts designated to the same unknown identity $ID^*$. If the KGC cannot distinguish the intended recipient in the ciphertext from the identity space, it can only decrypt the ciphertext by enumerating and generating all identity-based secret keys, which is very hard in polynomial time. Thus the notion of ACI-KGC depends on the number of random bits in the identity, we must ensure the anonymity of the key issuing procedure to protect the users identities and make the ACI-KGC meaningful, which is introduced in the sect. 3. In the definition of ACI-KGC, the adversary $\mathcal{A}$ making at most $q_E$ embedded-identity encryption oracle queries in time has advantage at most $\varepsilon$ in winning the game $Exp_{IBE, \mathcal{A}}^{aci-kgc}(\lambda)$ as follows.

**Setup:** $(\lambda) \to (param)$. The challenger $\mathcal{C}$ runs the *Setup* algorithm to obtain the public parameters *param*.

**KeyGen:** $('gen', param) \to (mpk, msk)$. The adversary $\mathcal{A}$ runs the KeyGen algorithm to generate the public secret key *mpk* and the master secret key *msk*. It gives *mpk* to the challenger and keeps the *msk* to itself.

**Query:** $\mathcal{A}^{enco_{(mpk,ID^*)}(m_i)} \rightarrow (m_0^*, m_1^*)$. $\mathcal{A}$ makes the $q_E$ times embedded-identity encryption oracle queries with message $m_i$ as input (for $i \in \{1, 2, \cdots q_E\}$), the algorithm $enco_{(mpk,ID^*)}(m_i)$ returns $Enc(mpk, ID^*, m_i)$ as the ciphertext based on a specific identity $ID^*$. Then $\mathcal{A}$ find two plaintext with equal length $m_0^*, m_1^*$, if $m_0^*, m_1^* \not\subset M$ or $|m_0^*| \neq |m_1^*|$ then return 0.

**Challenge:** $\mathcal{A}$ send $m_0^*, m_1^*$ to the challenger $\mathcal{C}$, $\mathcal{C}$ picks a random bit $b \in \{0, 1\}$ and returns the challenge ciphertext $C = Enc(mpk, ID^*, m_b^*)$ to $\mathcal{A}$.

**Guess:** $\mathcal{A}$ outputs a bit $b'$, if $b = b'$ return 1 (winning the game), else return 0. Where the advantage of $\mathcal{A}$ is defined as:

$$\left| \Pr[Exp_{IBE,\mathcal{A}}^{aci-kgc}(\lambda) = 1] - \frac{1}{2} \right|$$

It is similar to the traditional IND-ID-CPA security that the adversary has to distinguish between two messages from the challenge ciphertext.

**Definition 2.** An IBE scheme is $(t, q, \varepsilon)$ $ACI - KGC$ secure if all t-time algorithm adversaries making at most $q_E$ times embedded-identity encryption oracle queries that have advantage at most $\varepsilon$ in winning the game.

While it focus on the CPA security notion as above, it can consider stronger notion in the case that the KGC gains accesses to an embedded-identity decryption oracle, which is similar to CCA. Therefore, it can achieve the CPA security and CCA security simultaneously.

## 3    Constructions

We study the key escrow in hierarchical identity-based encryption scheme. Firstly, we present that how to equip an IBE system with modified structures in ACI-KGC security where append the identity authentication center (ICA). In the system architecture, the PKG and ICA cooperate with an anonymous key issuing (AKI) protocol so that the PKG can issue a private key to a user authenticated by ICA without knowing the list of users' identities. Then we construct the modified HIBE based on GS-HIBE [10], removing the escrow key by setting an ICA in each layer corresponding to the PKG. The proposed HIBE schemes keep the original performance and improve the security of the encryption systems, which has desirable application value.

### 3.1    Modified (H)IBE Structure with Escrow Free in ACI-KGC Security

To get ACI-KGC security, we are required to provide user-anonymity. Therefore, we utilize the anonymous key issuing (AKI) protocol. In the system architecture, it appends an honest third party ICA to keep the identities list of users and issue certificates. Thus, the duties of authentication and key issuing are separated to ICA and PKG. There are trust assumptions and requirements:

- The ICA does not collude with the KGC to ensure the KGC cannot get the identities lists easily and keep the secret key from ICA.
- The ICA would not impersonate any user.

We review AKI protocol in Chow's framework. It has to achieve two somewhat contradictory requirements simultaneously. The identity of a user should not be leaked, but a user must be authenticated to obtain the corresponding private key. This protocol functions in *Setup* and *Extract* algorithms from (H)IBE. For brevity, we only present the key extraction algorithm.

- The ICA probabilistically outputs the public/private key pair for certification $(pk_{cert}, sk_{cert})$.
- $SigCert(sk_{cert}, ID) \rightarrow (cert, aux)$. The ICA probabilistically outputs a certificate for identity ID and some auxiliary information $aux$.
- $ObtainKey(mpk, ID, cert, aux) \leftrightarrow IssueKey(sk, cert)$. A user and the KGC execute a private key generating protocol with the two interactive algorithms. The KGC gets the master secret key $msk$ and the certificate $cert$ as input, the user get the private key $sk$ as output.

In the above algorithm, firstly, the ICA issues a user a certificate on the identity with the master certifying key, where just utilizes a signature scheme. Then the user contact the KGC who issues a private key based on the certificate presented. For the user side, it needs to show this signature to the KGC without leaking the identity. For the KGC side, it authenticates the certificate and never gets to know the identity involved in the certificate, and generates the private key with the master secret key. To meet these security requirements, the user and the KGC engage in a secure two-party computational protocol [15], which may be cost-prohibitive. After obtaining the private key, users do not require any further interaction with these authorities for decryption. Thus the certificate is not used else in the system, i.e. the encryption itself is still purely ID-based.

Based on this structure, we present a modified scheme with higher efficiency and security. In our scheme, the ICA uses a similar implicit identity encapsulation method to both authenticate and conceal the user's identity in the issuing certificate. More specifically, the $SigCert$ is a signature and a commitment of an identity with computationally hiding. The ICA uses its private key to encrypt the user's identity to $ID^*$. Thus, the identity of user is concealed and embedded in the certificate. The KGC can compute the user's private key using the certificate with implicit identity $ID^*$, i.e. the KGC issues a private key with the $IssueKey(msk, cert(sk_{cert} \cdot ID))$. The $ID^*$ makes it sure that the KGC cannot learn anything about the real identity from the certificate because of the elliptic curve discrete logarithm problem. Therefore, for security protection of users, we only require a secure channel to ensure that users communicate anonymously, so the two interactive algorithms that execute a private key generating protocol between a user and the KGC is abrogated.

We give the general model used in traditional IBEs, Chow's IBE, and ours modified (H)IBE in Figs. 1 and 2. There is a remarkable difference between

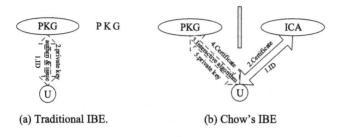

(a) Traditional IBE.              (b) Chow's IBE

**Fig. 1.** IBE system architecture.

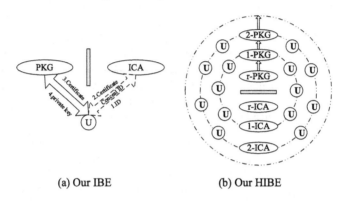

(a) Our IBE              (b) Our HIBE

**Fig. 2.** Modified (H)IBE system architecture.

Chow's and ours. Since our model let ICA conceal the users' identity by utilizing the certificate, and be a medium in the key generation, there have no extra interactive communication (*stage 3 in Fig. 1(b)*) between PKG issuing key and user obtaining key. Based on this model, we put modified AKI protocol in practice to make it ACI-KGC security. So we present a concrete modified HIBE based on GS-HIBE [10] in the following part.

## 3.2   Construction Based on GS-HIBE

GS-HIBE is the first efficient construction for HIBE was proposed by Gentry and Silverberg where security is based on the Bilinear Diffie-Hellman (BDH) assumption in the random oracle model. We describe our scheme in a format similar to that used in [2,11], which also has four algorithms: *Setup, Extract, Encrypt, Decrypt*.

**Setup:** Inputting a security parameter $\lambda$ and the depth of hierarchy $l$, let $G_1, G_2$ be a bilinear group of prime order $q$, and let $P_0$ be an arbitrary generator of $G_1$, and admissible pairing $e : G_1 \times G_1 \to G_2$. Outputting the system public parameters $params = \{G_1, G_2, e, P_0, n, H_1, H_2\}$. The $H_1 : \{0,1\}^* \to G_1$, $H_2 : G_2 \to \{0,1\}^n$ are two hash functions. The plaintext space is $M = \{0,1\}^n$, the ciphertext space is $C = G_1 \times \{0,1\}^n$.

Given the *params*, the root and lower-level PKGs as well as ICAs execute setup algorithm.

The root PKG picks a random $s_0^1 \in Z_q^*$ as its secret key, and set $P_{PKG} = s_0^1 P_0$ as its public key. The root ICA picks a random $s_0^2 \in Z_q^*$ as its secret key, and set $P_{ICA} = s_0^2 P_{PKG}$ as its public key.

The lower-level PKGs as $PKG_i$ each picks a random $s_i^1 \in Z_q^*$, the $i \in [1, l-1]$ component corresponds to the identity at level $i$. ICAs as $ICA_i$ each picks a random $s_i^2 \in Z_q^*$, and set $P_{ICA|i} = s_i^2 P_0$ as its public key. Then $PKG_i$ compute the $P_{PKG|i} = s_i^1 P_{ICA|i}$ as its public key. These secret keys are parts of master secret key for generating the users' private keys.

**Extract:** This algorithm utilizes the modified AKI protocol making ICA as a medium in the key generation. So it contains two stages to extract the user's private key.

*SigCert*: $U_k$ who is an entity at level $k$ with the identity $ID_k = (I_1, I_2, \cdots I_k)$ authenticates its identity to upper level $ICA_{k-1}$. $ICA_{k-1}$ creates the certificate on the $ID_k$ with a normal signature algorithm $sig(\cdot)$ as follows:

$$ICA_{k-1}: V_k \leftarrow sig(W_k), \ W_k \leftarrow s_{k-1}^2 Q_k, \ Q_k \leftarrow H_1(I_1, I_2 \cdots I_k)$$

$ICA_{k-1}$ maps the identity $ID_k$ to the bilinear group $G_1$, $Q_k \leftarrow H_1(I_1, I_2 \cdots I_k) \in G_1$, and encrypts $Q_k$ with its secret key $s_{k-1}^2$ as $W_k = s_{k-1}^2 Q_k$, and authenticates with a signature algorithm $sig(\cdot)$. Then $ICA_{k-1}$ sends the $(W_k, V_k)$ back to $U_k$.

*ObtainKey* $\leftrightarrow$ *IssueKey*: $U_k$ sends $(W_k, V_k)$ to upper level $PKG_{k-1}$ anonymously. $PKG_{k-1}$ verifies the $W_k \leftrightarrow veri(V_k)$ with the public key of $ICA_{k-1}$, if it is valid, $PKG_{k-1}$ generates the private key of $U_k$, $SK_k = SK_{k-1} + s_{k-1}^1 W_k = \sum_{i=1}^k s_{i-1}^1 W_i$. In particularly, the $W_k$ is an encrypted identity with the secret key of $ICA_{k-1}$, so $PKG_{k-1}$ could not learn about the user's real identity unless it have solved elliptic curve discrete logarithm problem.

**Encrypt:** To encrypt a message $m \in M$ under the recipient's public key as $Q_i = H_1(I_1, I_2 \cdots I_k) \in G_1 | 1 \le i \le k$, the sender picks a random $r \in Z_q^*$ as a session secret, and outputs ciphertext $c \in C$ as follows: $c = (U_0, U_2, ... U_k, V) = (rP_0, rQ_2, ... rQ_k, m \oplus H_2(g^r))$ where $g = e(Q_1, P_{ICA}) \in G_2$. Then sends $c$ to the recipient.

**Decrypt:** To decrypt the ciphertext $c = (U_0, U_2, ... U_k, V)$, the recipient outputs the plaintext $m \in M$ by using its private key $SK_k$ generated by PKG, system public parameters and the public keys of PKGs. The decryption as follows:

$$V \oplus H_2\left(\frac{e(U_0, SK_k)}{\prod_{i=2}^k e(P_{PKG \mid i-1}, U_i)}\right) = m \in M$$

Indeed, for a valid ciphertext, we have the consistency requirement as follows.

$$\frac{e(U_0, SK_k)}{\prod_{i=2}^{k} e(P_{PKG|i-1}, U_i)} = \frac{e(rP_0, \sum_{i=1}^{k} s_{i-1}^1 W_i)}{\prod_{i=2}^{k} e(s_{i-1}^1 P_{ICA|i-1}, rQ_i)}$$

$$= \frac{e(P_0, s_0^1 s_0^2 Q_1)^r e(P_0, s_1^1 s_1^2 Q_2)^r \dots e(P_0, s_{k-1}^1 s_{k-1}^2 Q_k)^r}{e(s_1^1 s_1^2 P_0, Q_2)^r e(s_2^1 s_2^2 P_0, Q_3)^r \dots e(s_{k-1}^1 s_{k-1}^2 P_0, Q_k)^r}$$

$$= e(P_0, s_0^1 s_0^2 Q_1)^r = e(Q_1, P_{ICA})^r = g^r$$

$$V \oplus H_2\left(\frac{e(U_0, SK_k)}{\prod_{i=2}^{k} e(P_{PKG|i-1}, U_i)}\right) = m \oplus H_2(g^r) \oplus H_2(g^r) = m$$

The above scheme we present do not change the fundamental structure of GS-HIBE.

## 4  Security Analysis

Our construction is based on ACI-KGC security model. As proved in [9], the scheme can still maintain the same level of security, such as the CPA or CCA security against the user (outsider adversary), and with the extra ACI-KGC protection. Since our scheme does not change the basic structure and encryption procedure of system, it does not affect the original security guarantees, i.e. IND-ID-CPA security. Therefore, we just give the security analysis in ACI-KGC, which mainly to the internal attackers.

**Theorem 1.** Suppose the BDH assumption holds in $G$, then the proposed scheme based on GS-HIBE is secure in ACI-KGC model.

**Proof:** Assume there is an adversary $\mathcal{A}$ breaks the ACI-KGC security of our scheme with advantage $\varepsilon$, we build an algorithm $\mathcal{B}$ that solves the BDH problem. Algorithm $\mathcal{B}$ works by interacting with $\mathcal{A}$ in a game as follows.

**Setup:** To generate the system parameters, algorithm $\mathcal{B}$ picks $g$ as generator of $G$ and sets $P_0 = g$, picks a random $s_i^2 \in Z_q^*$, and sets $P_{ICA|i} = s_i^2 P_0 = s_i^2 g$ as its public key, and selects two hash function: $H_1$, $H_2$. $\mathcal{B}$ returns the system parameters $\{g, P_{ICA}, e, n, H_1, H_2\}$ to $\mathcal{A}$.

**KeyGen:** $\mathcal{A}$ computes $P_{PKG} = s_0^1 P_0 = s_0^1 g$, which the master secret key $s_0^1$ is selected randomly and unknown to $\mathcal{B}$. Then computes the $P_{PKG|i} = s_i^1 P_{ICA|i}$ as public key. These secret keys are parts of master secret key for generating the users' private keys.

**Query:** $\mathcal{A}$ makes the $q_E$ times embedded-identity encryption oracle queries with message $m_i$ as input (for $i \in \{1, 2, q_E\}$). $\mathcal{B}$ responds to these queries based on the selected identity $ID_k^*$ with the ciphertext.

**Challenge:** When $\mathcal{A}$ decides the queries is over, it outputs two messages $\{m_0^*, m_1^*\}$ with the equal length which it wishes to be challenged. Algorithm

$\mathcal{B}$ picks a random bit $b \in \{0,1\}$ and a random $r \in Z_q^*$ to generate the ciphertext with the identity public key $Q_i^*$, and responds the ciphertext $c = (rP_0, rQ_2^*, ...rQ_k^*, m_b \oplus H_2(e(Q_1^*, P_{ICA})^r))$ to $\mathcal{A}$.

**Guess:** The adversary $\mathcal{A}$ outputs a guess $b' \in \{0,1\}$, if $b = b'$ then outputs 1, otherwise it output 0. The advantage $\mathcal{A}$ wins in this game is defined as:

$$\left| \Pr[b = b'] - \frac{1}{2} \right|$$

If $\mathcal{B}$ can solve BDH assumption with the non-negligible advantage $\varepsilon$, given the parameters $(g, P_{PKG}, P_{ICA}, Q_k, rg)$, $\mathcal{A}$ can compute the session key $e(Q_1, P_{ICA})^r$, which can compose the valid ciphertext, and win the challenge game. In addition, in the practical proposed scheme, PKG has no clue to distinguish the recipient's identity $ID_k$ for that ICA's certificate conceal the real identity through $W_k = s_{k-1}^2 Q_k$, Hence, the scheme is ACI-KGC-secure.

# 5  Performance Analysis

Researches on (H)IBE almost concentrate on the improvement of security and performance. In this section, we analyze the performance of our scheme in computation and communication cost with the related schemes. The computing cost is evaluated by the operation time of the multiplication and exponentiation based on the group, especially the bilinear paring (Table 1).

**Table 1.** Summary of notations

| Notation | Description |
|----------|-------------|
| $P$ | The operation time of bilinear pairing $e$ |
| $pA_i$ | The operation time of point addition based on $G_i$ |
| $sM_i$ | The operation time of scalar multiplication based on $G_i$ |
| $M_i$ | The operation time of multiplication based on $G_i$ |
| $E_i$ | The operation time of exponentiation based on $G_i$ |
| $h_1$ | The operation time of hash function $H_1 : \{0,1\}^* \to G_1$ |
| $h_2$ | The operation time of hash function $H_2 : G_2 \to \{0,1\}^n$ |
| $k$ | The level of the recipient in HIBE |

Table 2 makes a comparison between Chow's and ours based on the EF-IBE. Although the concrete schemes is not given in this paper, we can apply the key-escrow model to the EF-IBE. Our scheme is an improvement on the basis of Chow's. The main difference is on the Extract stage. We let the ICA issues each user a certificate not only to authenticate but also to conceal the user's identity. The certificate issued by the ICA will as a medium for KGC

**Table 2.** Performance analysis for chow's and ours based on BF-IBE

|  | Chow-BF-IBE | Our-BF-IBE |
|---|---|---|
| **Extract** | $1 \cdot sM_1 + 1 \cdot h_1 + 2 \cdot E_1 + 2 \cdot sM_1 + 3E + 4D$ | $2 \cdot sM_1 + 1 \cdot h_1$ |
| Encrypt | $1 \cdot P + 1 \cdot sM_1 + 1 \cdot E_2 + 1 \cdot h_2$ | $1 \cdot P + 1 \cdot sM_1 + 1 \cdot E_2 + 1 \cdot h_2$ |
| Decrypt | $1 \cdot P + 1 \cdot h_2$ | $1 \cdot P + 1 \cdot h_2$ |
| **Security** | *IND-ID-CPA* | *IND-ID-CPA* |
|  | *ICA-PKG* | *ICA-PKG* |

**Table 3.** Performance analysis for original and ours based on GS-HIBE

|  | Original-GS-HIBE | Our-GS-HIBE |
|---|---|---|
| **Extract** | $k \cdot pA_1 + k \cdot sM_1 + k \cdot h_1$ | $k \cdot pA_1 + 2k \cdot sM_1 + k \cdot h_1$ |
| Encrypt | $1 \cdot P + k \cdot sM_1 + k \cdot h_1 + 1 \cdot E_2 + 1 \cdot h_2$ | $1 \cdot P + k \cdot sM_1 + k \cdot h_1 + 1 \cdot E_2 + 1 \cdot h_2$ |
| Decrypt | $k \cdot P + (k-1) \cdot M_2 + 1 \cdot h_2$ | $k \cdot P + (k-1) \cdot M_2 + 1 \cdot h_2$ |
| **Security** | *IND-ID-CPA* | *IND-ID-CPA* |
|  |  | *ICA-PKG* |

to compute the user's private key. Compared with Chow's scheme, our scheme does not need the complicated interactive protocol between PKG and users. The protocol is time-consuming and resource-consuming, which need two-round scalar multiplication $sM_i$, two-round exponentiation $E_i$, three-round encryption $E$ and one-round decryption $D$ [16].

Table 3 makes a comparison between GS-HIBE and our modified GS-HIBE. Our scheme appends ICA to participate the generation of private keys. Compared with original GS-HIBE scheme, ours just increases double scalar multiplication in *Extract* stage, the remaining stages take the same cost. However our scheme can achieve the ICA-PKG security without affecting the original security guarantee.

# 6   Conclusion

We presented a new scheme to remove key escrow from HIBE in ACI-KGC security. This escrow-free method is different from previous approaches, and can solve the problem without much cost. Furthermore, our proposal is focus on escrow-free problem which has not been well-studied in HIBE at present. Through constructing modified HIBE based on the typical GS-HIBE without change of fundamental structure of systems, as well as keep the efficiency and security of HIBE, we believe that our method is adaptable and extendable to existing HIBEs. For HIBE is especially useful in large companies or e-government systems where there are hierarchical administrative issues, our further work is to apply the escrow-free method to practical applications such as privacy protection and access control with HIBE infrastructure.

**Acknowledgements.** This work is supported by the National Natural Science Foundation of China under Grant No. 61103035 and the Science and Technology Program of Hunan Province under Grant No. 2014GK3029.

# References

1. Shamir, A.: Identity-based cryptosystems and signature schemes. In: Blakely, G.R., Chaum, D. (eds.) CRYPTO 1984. LNCS, vol. 196, pp. 47–53. Springer, Heidelberg (1985)
2. Boneh, D., Franklin, M.: Identity-based encryption from the Weil pairing. In: Kilian, J. (ed.) CRYPTO 2001. LNCS, vol. 2139, p. 213. Springer, Heidelberg (2001)
3. Horwitz, J., Lynn, B.: Toward hierarchical identity-based encryption. In: Knudsen, L.R. (ed.) EUROCRYPT 2002. LNCS, vol. 2332, pp. 466–481. Springer, Heidelberg (2002)
4. Chen, L., Harrison, K., Soldera, D., Smart, N.P.: Applications of multiple trust authorities in pairing based cryptosystems. In: Davida, G.I., Frankel, Y., Rees, O. (eds.) InfraSec 2002. LNCS, vol. 2437, pp. 260–275. Springer, Heidelberg (2002)
5. Gentry, C.: Certificate-based encryption and the certificate revocation problem. In: Biham, E. (ed.) EUROCRYPT 2003. LNCS, vol. 2656, pp. 272–293. Springer, Heidelberg (2003)
6. Al-Riyami, S.S., Paterson, K.G.: Certificateless public key cryptography. In: Laih, C.-S. (ed.) ASIACRYPT 2003. LNCS, vol. 2894, pp. 452–473. Springer, Heidelberg (2003)
7. Goyal, V.: Reducing trust in the PKG in identity based cryptosystems. In: Menezes, A. (ed.) CRYPTO 2007. LNCS, vol. 4622, pp. 430–447. Springer, Heidelberg (2007)
8. Sui, A.f., Chow, S.S., Hui, L.C., Yiu, S.M., Chow, K.P., Tsang, W.W., Chong, C., Pun, K., Chan, H.: Separable and anonymous identity-based key issuing. In: Proceedings of 11th International Conference on Parallel and Distributed Systems, pp. 275–279. IEEE (2005)
9. Chow, S.S.M.: Removing escrow from identity-based encryption. In: Jarecki, S., Tsudik, G. (eds.) PKC 2009. LNCS, vol. 5443, pp. 256–276. Springer, Heidelberg (2009)
10. Gentry, C., Silverberg, A.: Hierarchical id-based cryptography. In: Zheng, Y. (ed.) ASIACRYPT 2002. LNCS, vol. 2501, pp. 548–566. Springer, Heidelberg (2002)
11. Boneh, D., Boyen, X.: Efficient selective-id secure identity-based encryption without random oracles. In: Cachin, C., Camenisch, J.L. (eds.) EUROCRYPT 2004. LNCS, vol. 3027, pp. 223–238. Springer, Heidelberg (2004)
12. Baek, J., Safavi-Naini, R., Susilo, W.: Efficient multi-receiver identity-based encryption and its application to broadcast encryption. In: Vaudenay, S. (ed.) PKC 2005. LNCS, vol. 3386, pp. 380–397. Springer, Heidelberg (2005)
13. Boneh, D., Boyen, X., Goh, E.-J.: Hierarchical identity based encryption with constant size ciphertext. In: Cramer, R. (ed.) EUROCRYPT 2005. LNCS, vol. 3494, pp. 440–456. Springer, Heidelberg (2005)
14. Waters, B.: Dual system encryption: realizing fully secure IBE and HIBE under simple assumptions. In: Halevi, S. (ed.) CRYPTO 2009. LNCS, vol. 5677, pp. 619–636. Springer, Heidelberg (2009)
15. Zhang, L., Wu, Q., Hu, Y.: Hierarchical identity-based encryption with constantsize private keys. ETRI J. **34**(1), 142–145 (2012)
16. Chase, M.: Efficient non-interactive zero-knowledge proofs for privacy applications. Ph.D. thesis, Brown University (2008)

# Neural Networks in Petrol Station Objects Calibration

Marcin Gorawski[1,2]([✉]), Mirosław Skrzewski[1], Michał Gorawski[3],
and Anna Gorawska[1,2]

[1] Faculty of Automation, Electronics, and Computer Science,
Institute of Computer Science, Silesian University of Technology,
Akademicka 16, 44-100 Gliwice, Poland
{marcin.gorawski,miroslaw.skrzewski,anna.gorawska}@polsl.pl
[2] Department of Data Spaces and Algorithms, AIUT Ltd., Wyczółkowskiego 113,
44-100 Gliwice, Poland
[3] Institute of Theoretical and Applied Informatics, Polish Academy of Sciences,
Bałtycka 5, 44-100 Gliwice, Poland
mgorawski@iitis.pl

**Abstract.** The fuel tank autocalibration problem is an important issue
in managing the amount of fuel stored in the tank. Current values are
calculated basing on fuel sold (going out through nozzles - dispensing)
and fuel pumped into the tank by a tanker (delivered). The difference
in these values may point to different reasons - leakage, theft, or other
errors. To pinpoint the cause it is important to rule out the case of wrong
tank calibration, hence the tank autocalibration method is required. In
this paper we present autocalibration method based on a neural networks
algorithm, along with method's drawbacks and an alternative calibration
method proposition.

**Keywords:** Autocalibration · Petrol tanks calibration · Neural networks · Leak detection · Inventory reconciliation

## 1   Introduction

To evaluate the petrol inventory in petrol stations, daily inventory records are
used. These records are needed to assess the current petrol level in tank and
quantity of sold and bought petrol. This whole process is called the reconciliation process, and it is a basic method of detecting any abnormalities in petrol
station operation, which can imply theft, leaks or technical problems with tank
or petrol pumps.

Problem of data reconciliation is well researched and defined [13–15]. The reconciliation process can be performed in different cycles - the granularity (month,
week, day or hour) is chosen basing on the needs of the specific case. The reconciliation process returns $Var$ – defined as a variance or an error (Eq. 1).

$$Var = V_s - V_p - V_d \tag{1}$$

© Springer International Publishing Switzerland 2015
G. Wang et al. (Eds.): ICA3PP 2015 Workshops, LNCS 9532, pp. 714–723, 2015.
DOI: 10.1007/978-3-319-27161-3_65

where:

- $V_s$ – volume of fuel sold
- $V_p$ – volume of fuel pumped out of the tank during sale
- $V_d$ – volume of delivered fuel, the amount of fuel added to the tank's volume

The variance is interpreted as follows:

$$\begin{cases} Var < 0 \text{ leak or theft} \\ Var = 0 \text{ perfect} \\ Var > 0 \text{ fluid surplus} \end{cases} \tag{2}$$

The variance represents a single error during specific time period; however, to perform a long term analysis the Cumulative Variance $(CV)$ is used. The $CV$ is a sum of variances during considered time period. The $CV$ at a time $i$ can be denoted as (Eq. 3):

$$CV_i = CV_{i-1} + Var_i \tag{3}$$

In ideal situation variance equals zero, which means that the balance between dispensed, delivered and stored fuel is correct so there are no losses or gains. As mentioned before, the reconciliation process gives an insight in any abnormal changes in fuel quantity. Differences in theoretical inventory and real inventory can be a warning on serious problems like fuel leaks or spills, which are environmentally dangerous [4,12]. Moreover, the problem may be caused by petrol theft, or that the petrol station infrastructure such as tanks, petrol pumps, and nozzles need maintenance.

Proper tank calibration gives also the exact data about the free space remaining in the tank and this allows for optimization of delivery process, refilling the tank in fully, not only partially. Because the storage, distribution, and management of fuel inventories are key issues in various industries, the proper tank calibration is a major problem in managing fuel tanks [5,8,16]. To exclude the petrol tank errors, the measurements of its condition should be precise and reliable. The tank calibration process may deliver this level of information assurance.

The proper tank calibration is a crucial problem in managing fuel tanks [3,5,8,16]. The difference in bought/sold amount of fuel can mean serious problems like theft (especially by petrol truck drivers during delivery) or leaks. The latter are very important considering ecological issues. Also proper tank calibration gives the information on the exact amount of fuel that can be poured into the tank during delivery. Such prognosis could optimize delivery rates so that the fuel level in the tank after delivery is maximum, instead of it being filled only partial. Taking these facts into consideration it is crucial to assure tank proper calibration and the quality and precision of measurements to make them trustworthy.

The storage, distribution, and management of fuel inventories is a crucial matter in various industry branches. Therefore this paper presents the autocalibration system, that automatically calibrates tanks, to assure that measured petrol tank levels are accurate. Works carried out in this area are the subject of a project founded by the Polish Council of the National Centre for Research and Development within the DEMONSTRATOR+ program [1].

## 2   Tank Calibration

The tank usually has a cylindrical shape with a circular section, which stores the fuel (liquid). The level of fluid in the tank is measured using the internal probe. The initial measurements contain only height of fuel, which is strictly connected to the particular tank. Having the reconciliation process performed on volumes of fuel, measured fluid height is calculated to actual fluid volume in the tank. The dependence between fluid height $(H)$ and fluid volume $(V)$ is not linear and depends on various factors (e.g. tank shape, probe setting, temperature, tank pitch). Because of potential changes in these factors, the dependence of $H$ and $V$ factors can be variable. Changes to the tank structure or position, partial malformations have a direct impact on the relation between height $H$ and volume $V$ for particular tank and as a result they may introduce changes to this relation only in some height ranges.

The problem is modelled using the neural network $N$ [6,7,9,11], which is trained using tank's calibration table $(CT)$. The calibration table represents relation between measured fuel height $H$ and corresponding volume $V$. Initially, the $CT$ table is created when the tank is emptied and it is being filled with precisely measured quantities of fuel e.g. 300 or 500 l of petrol. After pouring each portion of petrol to the tank, the probe height readouts are recorded with the corresponding total volume values giving real and current height - volume $(H-V)$ tank characteristics. After the petrol tank is filled to the certain height during petrol delivery, the petrol levels are diminishing respectfully to the sales quantity.

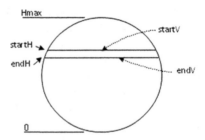

**Fig. 1.** Calculating quantity of sold petrol using the neural network

During normal working conditions the tank probe measures petrol level at the beginning of the sale $startH$ and at the end of the sale $endH$. At the same time the petrol pump registers quantity of sold petrol $V_s$. The neural network $N$ returns values $N(startH) = startV$ and $N(endH) = endV$, which are starting $startV$ and final volume of fluid in the tank $(endV)$. The difference is

$V_t = N(startH) - N(endH)$ (Fig. 1). The difference between $V_t$ and $V_s$ is denoted as $E_t$ – model's error for a given reconciliation interval (transaction).

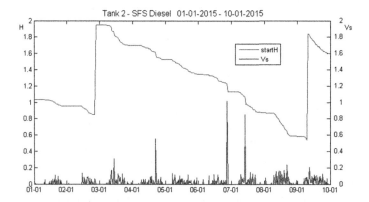

**Fig. 2.** Reconciliation intervals – a set of height changes in response to sold petrol volumes

Sequence of points in time, that correspond to fluid levels H after each performed dispensing transaction, creates a graphs representing process of emptying the tank. Together with $V_s$ values, these data are used to assess the quality of the $H - V$ characteristic of the neural network. The process of refilling the petrol tank (delivery) initializes next sequence of $H$ points representing record of next tank emptying processes (Fig. 2). Sequences of such records are used to train the network in order to minimize neural network error.

On the Fig. 3 the effect of neural networks processing is presented, i.e. the calibration curve.

The correct calibration curve is a crucial part of the whole reconciliation process. Errors in the calibration curve's shape can implicate errors in the reconciliation process. To minimize adverse effects of some random errors of neural networks utilization, proposed solution uses ensemble of 10 independent neural networks. Each of the separate networks is fed with the same training set, and the final result is an average value of all networks output in the ensemble.

## 3   Current Method Discussion

The current algorithm was implemented in the Matlab environment. The neural network input data are created basing on petrol tank data and contain:

- Output data from previous calibration (current neural network ensemble).
- Tables of a manual tank calibration, along with networks created on its basis that are not yet calibrated – used for comparison of current and future solutions.
- Set of height values $startH$ and $endH$.

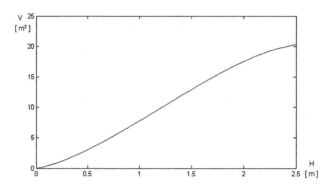

**Fig. 3.** Sample calibration curve

- Set of volumes values *startV* and *endV*, respectfully corresponding to heights *startH* and *endH*. Basing on these values and the current network, the fluid level change in petrol tank is calculated – the sale $V_s$ and delivery $V_d$. These values are compared with data from petrol pumps and nozzles and the errors $E_t$ are calculated for each reconciliation interval.
- Set of temperatures in the tank *startTemperature* and *endTemperature* for values *startH* and *endH*. These values are used for thermal tank compensation (rescaling results to selected reference temperature - the Temperature Model).

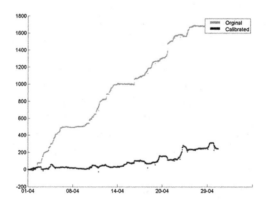

**Fig. 4.** Cumulative variance – an original (grey) and calibrated (black) [litres]

Using the current neural network, the data from a new data set are analysed and the MSEs (mean squared errors) are calculated. For a considered time interval, the data ranges of a length larger than minimal are marked, and the errors - differences between neural networks data and sales data in these ranges are checked to not exceed the threshold set by the user. The sets of data that meet these criteria are used as training sets.

Then, the neural network is fed with next training sets. The more sets are fed to the network the better the network results are (smaller errors) [2].

After the tank is calibrated basing on the best obtained network, the $CV$ errors are recalculated. To assess the neural network, the $CV$ graphs before and after calibration are compared (Fig. 4), and rating is calculated - the average weighted value of errors at certain tank height during tank working time period. Figure 4 shows two cumulative variances graphs. The upper curve (grey) is a result of the neural network calibration using the original calibration table. The lower curve (black) is a result of the calibration using new networks, fed with data from previous month. During this period, $300\,m^3$ of fuel were sold and total percentage error ($CV$ error/sold volume) were respectively 0.58 % (grey) and 0.08 % (black).

## 3.1  Problem of the Current Calibrating Solution

Currently proposed autocalibration method using neural networks ensemble improves the calibration of tanks in comparison to calibrating them using only the user given calibration curve. The process of the neural network learning is actually an algorithm which modifies the neural network to minimize errors for current data series. The *strengthening* of learning algorithm is minimal - to obtain more meaningful changes, many learning sets has to be processed. If the learning sets include only small part of tank height, the observed effect is local, outside of the considered fragment network errors can even increase - in conclusion obtained $CV$ graph is worse for the whole tank The user delivered CTs consider only the "working" part of the tank - during manual calibration the tank is not fully filled - the actual tank height is larger than the one given in CTs. Similarly the nominal tank volume can differ from its actual volume. For some tanks the lack of official CTs was solved by tanks working data. In effect the starting neural networks created from CT table can differ from actual tank H-V characteristics, and encumbered with starting error. Although the use of autocalibration methods has improved the network efficiency (in comparison with the use of CTs), the improvement is often only by a fraction of percent while sometimes the results might be even worse. There are still some emerging issues that can be a source of potential problems:

- The above shown method of networks efficiency assessment is not entirely fault-less. For some tanks, the networks taught with previously obtained data give smaller error values (CV graph); however, they are rejected because of larger rating values.
- For some cases the efficiency of network learning is neglectable - network in-creased its efficiency by a fraction of percent.
- Lack of access to source data – databases are placed inside users infrastructure (petrol station). The database should be duplicated, updated at least daily and available for access when calibration is necessary. Currently data

for calibration are incomplete, and because of "holes" in data the distortions are hard to pinpoint
- Lack of temporary database with repository of e.g. analysis results, methods comparison, hardware assessment.
- Change management process has to be addressed - information of all changes in user's hardware, algorithms, software has to be noted and available in calibration process.
- Neglecting errors and filtering them out causes the "holes" in data. Modifications of data structures in Matlab environment are quite difficult and time consuming. Data should be verified logically before processing e.g. deliveries and sales should be periodically balanced - if only sales data are taken into consideration it can lead to errors omitting and their accumulation.

## 3.2   New Calibration Methods

During research on above presented autocalibration methods and analysis of emerging problems an alternate autocalibration method was proposed. It is based on creating the neural network on data from theoretical tank model ($H - V$ dependence).

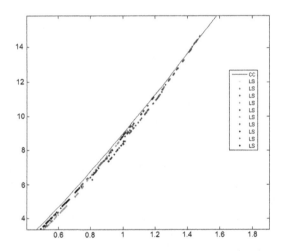

**Fig. 5.** Initial stage – comparison of learning sets $LS$ and the tank $H-V$ characteristics (magnified)

Initially the $H - V$ curve (calibration curve) is compared with collection of learning sets $LS$ points and model parameters ($H$ and $V$) are selected to match the slope of the learning sets. After selecting the initial tank parameters ($V$,$H$) tank model is assessed by calculating the $CV$ values. If the error grows the tank model parameters are changed ($Hmax$ or $Vmax$) until $CV$ graph is flat and almost equals zero. In many cases after the initial setup of tank parameter further learning is not necessary (rating 0.6 %–0.8 %). The further training of the network requires data sets with low error threshold (below 100 %) (Fig. 5).

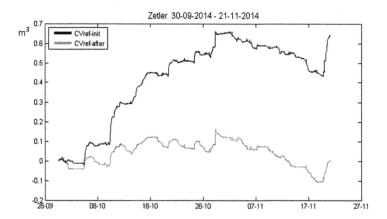

**Fig. 6.** CV curves obtained without neural network learning

After choosing the tank shape sometimes distortions appeared for extreme fluid levels (high and low). While there were small errors for middle values this can imply that the tanks shape is not a perfect cylinder e.g. more elliptic or flattened. This fact can be included by introducing more complex shapes of the theoretical tank. Below we present the effect of the new method that consists of two stages:

– choosing the theoretical model
– selecting the best obtainable model and neural network learning

Figure 7 shows the result of algorithm operation on exemplary tank Zetler_725 _ 2 with diesel stored. While magnified (Fig. 5), the lean of the learning sets are observed to be different than the tank $H - V$ curve and the initial $CV$ error increases by almost $0.7\,\mathrm{m}^3$.

To straighten out (moving up) the tank $H - V$ line, the model volume has to be increased along with the ellipse eccentricity. Basing on the theoretical model a new network and new learning sets are created. Then the tank is calculated with new characteristics of learning sets until adequate $CV$ error curve is obtained. In this case optimal model values are $V = 15.9$, $H = 1.9$, $m = 0.1$. Figure 6 shows the $CV$ curves without tank calibration (neural network learning). Figure 7 shows the rating graph. For heights $1.3\,\mathrm{m}$–$1.6\,\mathrm{m}$ a considerable error exists; however, overall rating (the mean value of the sum of the products of error for given height times the incidence of this height at the tank operation) equals $1.3717\,\%$, which can be further minimized with fixing the ellipse parameters.

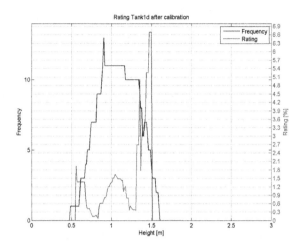

**Fig. 7.** Rating curves

## 4   Conclusions

In this paper the autocalibration of petrol tanks is presented. The adequately calibrated tank is needed to have a trustworthy data on actual petrol inventory, sales and deliveries. The proposed solution bases on the neural network ensemble, which considerably improves effect of the tank calibration comparing to the calibration based on the CT. While researching the original algorithm presented in Sect. 3, the number of issues were raised (Sect. 3.1).

Although the use of neural networks improves calibration correctness, there are some drawbacks that need to be addressed. While researching the original solution based on neural networks ensemble presented in Sect. 3, the number of issues were raised (Sect. 3.1). The alternative calibration solution was presented in Sect. 3.2. This calibration solution, is more intuitive than neural networks, and gives similar results in a faster and less complicated process. The simplification of calibration method improves further optimization and automation of the whole process. Future work will focus on improving the neural network algorithm, and researching alternative methods of calibration.

One of the issue raised in Sect. 3.1 concerned the data processing. In other works the authors research the architecture of a stream data warehouse that would significantly improve the processing of data and analysis performed in autocalibration system [5,10].

**Acknowledgments.** The project is founded by the Polish Council of the National Centre for Research and Development within the DEMONSTRATOR+ program.

# References

1. DEMONSTRATOR+ program, The Polish Council of the National Centre for Research and Development. http://www.ncbir.pl/en/domestic-programmes/demonstrator/
2. P. C. Stewart Ash. Measurement Accuracy And Sources Of Error In Tank Gauging. Class # 2270 (1990). http://help.intellisitesuite.com/Hydrocarbon/papers/2270.pdf
3. Du, Y.-G., Thibault, J., Hodouin, D.: Data reconciliation for simulated flotation process. Artif. Intell. Eng. **11**(4), 357–364 (1997)
4. Erkman, S.: Industrial Ecology: an Historical View. J. Clean. Prod. **5**(1), 1–10 (1997)
5. Gorawski, M., Gorawska, A., Pasterak, K.: Liquefied petroleum storage and distribution problems and research thesis. In: Kozielski, S.Ł., Mrozek, D., Kasprowski, P., Małysiak-Mrozek, B., Kostrzewa, D. (eds.) BDAS. CCIS, vol. 521, pp. 540–550. Springer International Publishing, Switzerland (2015)
6. Haykin, S.: Neural Networks: A Comprehensive Foundation, 2nd edn. Prentice Hall PTR, Upper Saddle River (1998)
7. Jovanović, R., Sretenović, A.A., Živković, B.D.: Ensemble of various neural networks for prediction of heating energy consumption. Energ. Build. **94**, 189–199 (2015)
8. Kato, T., Goto, Y., Nidaira, K.: Construction of Calibration Curve for Accountancy Tank, INMM in Japan (2008)
9. Kourentzes, N., Barrow, D.K., Crone, S.F.: Neural network ensemble operators for time series forecasting. Expert Syst. Appl. **41**(9), 4235–4244 (2014)
10. Kůrková, V.: Kolmogorov's theorem and multilayer neural networks. Neural Netw. **5**(3), 501–506 (1992)
11. Schmidhuber, J.: Deep learning in neural networks: an overview. Neural Netw. **61**, 85–117 (2015)
12. Sigut, M., Alayón, S., Hernández, E.: Applying pattern classification techniques to the early detection of fuel leaks in petrol stations. J. Clean. Prod. **80**, 262–270 (2014)
13. United States Environmental Protection Agency. Standard Test Procedures For Evaluating Leak Detection Methods: Statistical Inventory Reconciliation Methods. Final Report (1990)
14. United States Environmental Protection Agency. Introduction to Statistical Inventory Reconciliation For Underground Storage Tanks (1995). http://www.epa.gov/oust/pubs/sir.pdf
15. United States Environmental Protection Agency. Straight Talk on Tanks - Leak Detection Methods for Petroleum Underground Storage Tanks and Piping (2005)
16. Goto, Y., Kato, T., Nidaira, K.: Establishment of Accurate Calibration Curve For National Verification at a Large Scale Input Accountability Tank in RRP, IAEA-CN-184/61 (1995)

# A Dependable, Scalable, Distributed, Virtual Data Structure

Silvia Grampone[1], Witold Litwin[2], and Thomas SJ Schwarz[3]([✉])

[1] Universidad Católica del Uruguay, Montevideo, Uruguay
silviagrampone@gmail.com
[2] Université Paris Dauphine, Paris, France
Witold.Litwin@dauphine.fr
[3] Universidad Centroamericana, San Salvador, El Salvador
tschwarz@jesuits.org

**Abstract.** Cloud computing allows on-demand access to cheap computing resources. This capability can be used for solving problems autonomously by complete enumeration. We present here SDVRP a data structure based on range partitioning that allows to autonomously divide the computing tasks to as many nodes as are needed to meet a user-imposed dead-line (in the order of minutes) despite heterogeneity of nodes. The data structure monitors itself to deal with failures and changes in node capacities. We use simulation for a proof-of-concept of this data structure.

**Keywords:** Brute force calculations · Cloud · Data structure · Range partitioning · Scalable distributed data structures · Failure resilience

## 1 Introduction

Cloud computing has put inexpensive, massively distributed computing at the hands of the masses. If an organization can rent an almost unlimited amount of computing power in various clouds for short blocks of times (ten minutes), then we can use this enormous, temporary computing power to tackle classical optimization problems through complete enumeration, trading cheap on-demand computing power for the more sophisticated, classical algorithms [14]. Take as an example a database that needs to solve a knapsack problem with 50 variables. It took us 15.6 ms to solve a 15 variable knapsack problems on a single core by complete enumeration. The 50 variable problem would then take about 100 days on the single core, but if we can distribute the work over 15000 nodes, it would take less than 10 min. If Google Cloud would rent cores for 10 min only, it would cost $60.00.

We extend here this previous work by presenting a dependable version of a Scalable Distributed Virtual Data Structure (SDVDS), explained in Sect. 2, called Scalable Distributed Virtual Range Partitioning (SDVRP) (Sect. 3). In Sect. 4 we protect SDVRP against non-byzantine node failures that can upset

© Springer International Publishing Switzerland 2015
G. Wang et al. (Eds.): ICA3PP 2015 Workshops, LNCS 9532, pp. 724–735, 2015.
DOI: 10.1007/978-3-319-27161-3_66

the SDVRP's load distribution or overlook an optimal value if not dealt with. Section 5 evaluates failure resilience. Section 6 gives the related work and Sect. 7 concludes.

## 2   Scalable Distributed Virtual Data Structures

Scalable Distributed Virtual Data Structures (SDVDS) distribute the work involved of complete enumeration over a large number of nodes in a cloud. We envision them to be used in conjunction with databases and similar applications such as business intelligence decision tools. We now define a complete enumeration problem:

**Definition 1.** *A complete enumeration problem consists of a (record) range $I = \{N_0, N_{0+1}, \ldots N_l\} \subset \mathbb{N}$ and an objective function $\phi : I \longrightarrow \mathbb{R}$. A solution to a complete enumeration problem is a value $\iota \in I$ that maximizes $\phi$, i.e. $\phi(\iota) = \max(\{\phi(x) | x \in I\})$.*

An SDVDS solves a complete enumeration problem in phases. The user (application) generates a file scheme $S_F$ that describes $(I, \phi)$ and hands it to a coordinator node. The coordinator node is only used to begin the process and to communicate the result to the user application and thus does not constitute a bottleneck. In the *set-up* phase, the data structure allocates a sufficient number of nodes to guarantee finding a solution in a maximum time $T_{\max}$ specified by the user (application). Because of multi-tenancy, the speed at which nodes can evaluate $\phi$ is not constant. Each node therefore evaluates its capacity, the number of records it can evaluate and compares it with its load $L$, the number of records assigned to it for evaluation. If its capacity is smaller than its load, it reacts, often by recruiting another node to the data structure and then dividing its load with the other node. The set-up phase overlaps with the *scan* phase, where each node evaluates its assigned range of records $\subset I$. Each node also monitors its speed, since the node capacity might not remain constant. At the end of the scan phase, each node sends its value to a predecessor node, which in turn agglomerates the results send to it by selecting the $\iota \in I$ with maximum value $\phi(\iota)$. This *termination phase* finishes when the original node has processed the messages from all of its direct child nodes as well as its own set of records. We previously described the scan phase as having the nodes *materialize* the virtual records and scan them in order to provide the parallelism with Scalable Distributed Data Structures, but this relationship is not necessary in order to understand the basic functioning of the data structures [14]. Different data structures with different properties can be obtained by changing the way in which the record range is divided.

Any SDVDS definition consists of a definition of all the phases, but does not provide a description of the evaluation. An SDVDS is defined by (1) a node allocation process, usually through splitting; (2) an allocation of enumeration ranges to nodes; and (3) the set-up of a hierarchy for reporting the partial results and agglomerating them, and returning them to the user. The second

**Fig. 1.** A small SDVRP structure for the range of $0 \ldots 2^{16}$.

and the first step can usually be combined in a single step. An algorithm for an SDVDS consists of (1) a definition of the enumeration range $\subset \mathbb{N}$; (2) instance extraction, which is a method for creating an instance of a possible solution from an index within the range; and (3) an evaluation function.

For example, if we solve a 0–1 integer optimization problem with 40 variables, the range is $R = [0, 2^{40} - 1]$, the instance creation assigns to variable $x_i(n)$ the value of bit $i$ in a number $n \in R$, and the evaluation function ascertains first the truth of a conjunction of inequalities of form $\phi_j(x_1, \ldots, x_{40}) < m_j$ and then evaluates the optimization function.

## 3   SDVRP

Scalable Distributed Virtual Range Partitioning (SDVRP) is a SDVDS based on RP*, the scalable distributed data structure that provides range partitioning. It assigns contiguous sub-ranges of the record range to the nodes. Figure 1 gives a very small example. Each node maintains a left and a right neighbor. A node can move load to one of its neighbors while maintaining the contiguity of the range of records assigned to it. The data structure starts with a single node to which we assign the complete original range. After evaluating its capacity, the node (in all likelihood) decides that its capacity is not sufficient and splits. By local decisions only, the data structure acquires the nodes necessary to perform the enumeration phase within the user-set limit. At all times, the nodes are arranged in a linear list such that consecutive nodes have contiguous ranges of records to evaluate.

### 3.1   Node Allocation and Subrange Assignment

A node always splits if its load is larger than its capacity. The new node is randomly inserted to the left or to the right of the splitting node. The load is then equally divided between between the splitting and the new node. It takes maybe a second to ascertain the capacity of a node with reasonable accuracy.

Our simulation results in Sect. 5 show, this simple splitting mechanism can be easily improved by trying to use free capacity at a neighbor. In the improved splitting algorithm, a node that needs to split contacts one of its neighbors at random. If this neighbor has free capacity, it takes over part of the range of the splitting node to have its load equal its capacity. The splitting node then tries the same load shifting with the other neighbor. It is possible but unlikely that the splitting neighbor has reduced its load to zero, in which case it deallocates itself.

As always in distributed systems, the algorithm designer needs to prevent race condition. In our algorithm, a node only interacts with its direct neighbors. A node acquires a lock on its neighbor which cannot interact with its other neighbor until the first interaction has finished.

## 3.2 Result Agglomeration Hierarchy

All nodes but the original node (which becomes the coordinator node) are allocated by another node which becomes its parents. This generate a tree structure that becomes the agglomeration hierarchy. At the end of its scan phase, each node sends its result to its parent, which combines the results of its children with its own and sends the combined result to its parent. The coordinator node sends the result to the user application.

## 3.3 Fast Allocation

The allocation process of the node is not instantaneous. Each node uses a second or so to assess its own capacity and bases a decision on whether to split on the relation between assigned load and capacity. However, at the beginning of the allocation phase, it is clear that nodes will split. As a variant, we therefore propose *pre-splitting*. The coordinator node determines its load to capacity ratio and decides on a minimum number of nodes necessary. The minimum number is calculated using a safe, upper bound based on its capacity. Thus, if we use assume that node capacity is less than twice the capacity $C_0$ of the coordinator node, then the number $N$ of nodes needed depends on the total load $L$ by $N > L/(2C_0)$. Since setting up that many nodes in one step also takes time, the coordinator requests $M$ nodes and assigns to the them the enumeration range partitioned into $M$ pieces. Each of the $M$ nodes then allocates $N/M$ new nodes itself that become its children.

# 4 Providing Failure Tolerance

Cloud nodes are not meant to be very reliable. Instead, the application that uses cloud resources has the task to provide the failure tolerance it needs. Since cloud resources are commodities, the alternative would be a one-size-fits-all strategy that would not deliver for some applications or over-provision for other applications. According to Birman, it is even considered acceptable for a data center administrator to randomly shut down nodes in order to escape from an unstable situation [4].

Failure tolerance for distributed complete enumeration task is different than for many other applications. While an adversary might destroy a complete calculation by giving a false optimum and causing the other nodes to throw away their work, a byzantine malfunction for such a simple programming pattern is unlikely. If we can assume (as we argue that we can) that nodes do not create false results by either overlooking a local optimum or by reporting one where

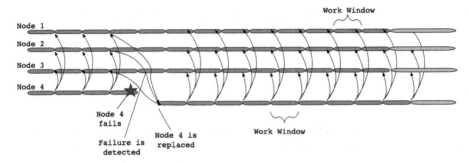

**Fig. 2.** A time line of the handling of a node failure. All nodes divide their work into work windows and send a resumé of their results to all other nodes in the group. The figure only shows the updates sent by Node 4. When Node 4 later fails, the failure of receiving the latest resumé or the lack of acknowledgment to resumés sent to Node 4 leads to a replacement of the node. The replacement node is brought up to the point of the last resumé of Node 4 so that the work of the first three work windows is not lost.

none exist, then the only thing that can go wrong is in the division of labor by the nodes. Complete enumeration is an "at least once" task. If the data structure assigns part of the range to two nodes (for example because it wrongly assumed that one has failed), then the only damage consists performing the same work twice and having to pay the rental costs of the superfluous node. The validity of the overall result is not affected.

Second, the result of a a partial enumeration can be resumed in very little space. If a node has scanned a subrange, the results of this scan can be subsumed in a description of the range scanned (usually the upper and the lower bound), and the pair $(\iota, \phi(\iota))$ consisting of the argument and best value seen so far. We call this the *resumé* of the partial evaluation at a node. Each resumé contains additionally information about the node such as the addresses of its neighbors and in case of the coordinator node, the address of the application. It functions essentially as execution checkpoints in languages such as Erlang or Scala.

In order to provide failure tolerance, we use the old idea of process groups [3] that has several processes in a distribute system monitor each other and provide solutions if one process has failed. In our setting, we divide the nodes into groups, which we call *buddy groups*. Buddy groups run a distributed membership and consensus protocol such as a version of Paxos or Raft [5,16,21]. We use the sending of resumés as a heart-beat.

In more detail, each node divides its work into work windows of about equal time (such as one minute). At the end of a work window, the node sends a resumé of its scan results up to now to all other nodes in the buddy group. Resumés should be small; in general, they will consist of the range scanned and the argument of the best result(s) seen in this range. If a resumé from another buddy group member does not arrive in time, then the membership protocol is triggered to ascertain whether the node has in fact failed. The buddy groups replaces a failed node with a new node requested from the cloud. The replacement node resumes the work of the failed work from the moment it sent its last resumé and does not start over, Fig. 2. Note that the resumé contains all the information needed by the replacement node.

Buddy group size is limited by the difficulties of running a membership protocol, since these protocols do not scale well, but they should not be so small that failure of all nodes in a buddy group in relatively short time is an event that is worth while to worry about. The splitting algorithm actually makes it unlikely that neighboring nodes are allocated immediately after the other, so that it is unlikely that neighboring nodes are physically located in the same server. We assume that buddy group sizes between four and seven provides the needed reliability without creating too much overhead.

Since our data structure is one-dimensional, forming groups is quite simple. A naïve solution would have the leftmost node starts a counting process that assigns the first $k$ nodes to the first group, the second $k$ neighbors to the second group, etc. and deals with a last group that is smaller than $k$ by merging it with the previous group. This nave algorithm is perfectly suited to small instances, but would take too long for a large data structure.

A more efficient algorithm generates buddy groups by local coagulation. After a node has finished the allocation phase, it becomes leader of a budding buddy-group. Each buddy group aims at having a membership between four and seven nodes. If it does not have the required number of nodes, the leader associates the group to one of its neighboring groups. If the resulting group has more than seven elements, it splits into two contiguous parts, each having at least four elements. This simple procedure works rapidly, guaranteeing that each group reaches the required amount of nodes in at most three join attempts. We avoid race conditions by locking leaders that are negotiating a merger.

## 5    Evaluation

### 5.1    Variability and Multi-Tenancy

We use simulation to evaluate the construction principles of SDVRP. First, we evaluated the effects of node capacity variation on node utilization. Node utilization (the ratio of total load divided over total capacity) measures the inefficiency of our work assignment algorithm. Given the nature of cloud computing, where resources are cheap, but are not free (as in P2P), we want utilizations over 50 %, but do not worry too much if they are not close to 100 %. We modeled variation in the capacity of a node by using the beta distribution with parameters $\alpha = 2$ and $\beta = 2$ to generate capacities distributed between $[0.5, 1.5]$, $[0.75, 1.25]$ and $[0.9, 1.1]$.

As Fig. 3 shows, the utilization oscillates between 0.5 and 1 with peaks where the initial load is close to a power of two. If there is no variation and all nodes have capacity exactly one, then the resulting utilization graph is a sawtooth graph. The utilization is one if the initial load is an integer power of two, and $1/2$ if the load is increased by an infinitesimal amount, since in this case all nodes have to split.

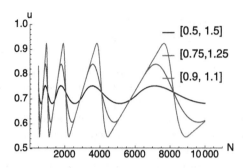

**Fig. 3.** Utilization u using the basic node splitting scheme depending on the load N

As the capacities vary more, the sawtooth curve flattens out, but oscillation in the utility still occurs. We observed the same behavior when we experimented with different beta distributions, even if the distributions were no longer symmetric, i.e. when the parameters $\alpha$ and $\beta$ of the curve were not equal.

If we used the more sophisticated splitting algorithm, we still observe oscillations with periods given by integer powers of two, but the behavior now is more involved, especially if we used smaller variations. In general, the more sophisticated splitting algorithm results in appreciable higher utilization.

We also compared the utilization with the one obtained after 90 % of the nodes change capacity and use the advanced algorithm to rebalance the load. The rebalancing is not entirely successful, but the difference is minute for the smaller variations in node capacity. Figure 4 gives our results. We used a light-gray fill to indicate the difference of the before and after values of the utilization. We can see that the difference becomes small as we move to systems with less variability, but the wave of changes that we introduced definitely lower the utilization, though not by much.

## 5.2   Reliability

An accurate, general failure model for nodes in a cloud data center does not exist. Two incidents show that cloud failures can be drastic and lead to complete outages. In 2011 an automatic misdiagnosis to a bad configuration resulted in a massive recovery effort for servers that had not failed [2]. Gmail suffered a massive service interruption in 2009 when routine maintenance resulted in a larger than expected change in the traffic load at some routers, who became overloaded and unresponsive [7].

Cloud outage based on hardware failure follow a Weibull distribution, but at the scale of minutes, failure rates are constant. In the absence of better information for modeling, we test our reliability scheme against two different scenarios. The first is a scenario where a large proportion of nodes suddenly becomes unavailable. The second scenario assumes independent failures at a given failure rate and models failures as a Poisson process. The truth is some combination of both scenarios and we need to test our scheme against both extremes. Finally,

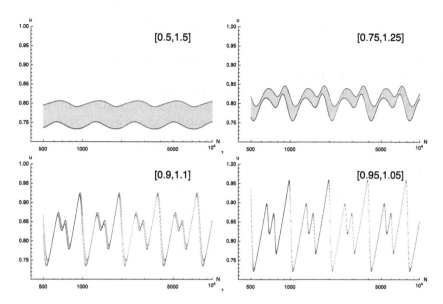

**Fig. 4.** Utilization u using the advanced node splitting scheme depending on initial load N. The upper graph shows the original utilization, the lower graph the utilization after 90 % of the nodes changed capacity. The node capacities vary between 0.5 and 1.5, 0.75 and 1.25, 0.9 and 1.1, and 0.95 and 1.05 respectively. The $x$-axis is logarithmic to bring out the oscillatory behavior.

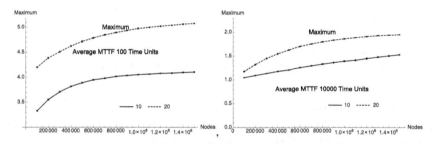

**Fig. 5.** Maximum number of restarts of a node's evaluation depending on the total number of nodes employed (x-axis). The failure rate during a time unit is a high 0.01 (left) and a more realistic 0.0001. If a time unit is a minute, this corresponds to a mean time to failure of less than two hours and 167 hrs. The calculation is slated to take 10 and 20, respectively, time units. We give error bars at the 99 % confidence level based on dividing the simulation runs into 20 batches.

a massive service disruption at the scale that were suffered by EC2 and Gmail is not controllable.

We first look at the effects of independent node failures. Typical maximum computation time is in the order of minutes or at most an hour, and at this scale, time between node failures can be assumed to be exponentially distributed.

We first determined the maximum number of restart that a single node would suffer in a system with $N$ nodes, Fig. 5. Our experiment assumed a high failure rate of 1 % per time unit. The total calculation is broken into ten and twenty work windows respectively. Each failure has to be discovered (usually at the end of the work window, unless we change the protocol to monitor nodes more aggressively) and the new node has to be allocated (and its load possibly partially distributed if its capacity is lower than its failed predecessor). Still, even at unrealistic node numbers of a million or more and a very high failure rate per time unit (corresponding in order of magnitude to a minute), the most the calculation is slowed down is by less than a fourth of the total time. Since a node suffers a double failure during its ten or twenty work windows only very rarely (or rather, the replacement node for a failed node suffers itself another failure during the rest of the work), we can allocate two instead of one replacement node to bring the maximum time to be spend for resuming work on a failed node to two work windows plus some allocation time.

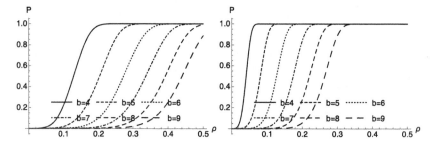

**Fig. 6.** Probability (P) that at least one buddy group has completely failed if a portion $\rho$ of the nodes in an ensemble with 10,000 (left) and 1,000,000 nodes (right) has failed.

We now consider the effects of a wave of node failures. We model this phenomenon by assuming the existence of a condition that will cause a portion $\rho$ of all nodes to fail during a work window. If there is a total of $N$ nodes and the buddy group size is $b$, then the probability that all $b$ members of a single group fail is $\rho^b$. The total number of groups is $N/b$, so that the probability that at least one group has failed is

$$1 - (1 - \rho^b)^{N/b}$$

This results in buddy group loss probabilities that quickly shift from almost zero to almost one, Fig. 6. The total number of nodes is – as has to be expected – very influential. For very large number of nodes, the structure does have a significant probability of loosing a complete buddy group with reasonable outage rates $\rho$. This will be noticed at the end of the calculation which will then be delayed by having to redo the work of the lost buddy group(s). The structure needs to be made more failure tolerant then. There are two possibilities. First, we can restart the work originally assigned to the lost group, but divide it over many more nodes in order to loose not that much time. The other possibility is to form buddy groups among buddy group leaders. Since buddy group leaders are replaced if they fail, a member of a higher level buddy group only vanishes if all its members in the lower level buddy group have disappeared during a working window, which happens at a rate of $\rho^b$.

# 6  Related Work

Complete enumeration has been a tool of desperation since the beginning of solving optimization problems on computers. Scalable Distributed Data Structures (SDDS) were developed in the nineties to marshal the resources of distributed systems (multicomputers) for databases supporting different modes of data access such as linear or extensible hashing [13,20] search trees [15], range queries [18], or R-trees [11]. Much research in SDDS was devoted to provide failure tolerance [17]. Scalable Distributed Virtual Data Structures apply these scans not to records generated by a user but to virtual records, generated directly from the record identifier [14].

P2P systems try to harvest the idle resources of computers connected to the Internet. Early work defined distributed hash tables (Chord, Pastry, Tapestry) to overcome the same scalability problems as SDDS in a more anarchic environment and resulted in mature, efficient structures such as Skip graphs [1] and the Willow DHT [24]. Key is a sophisticated metadata overlay such as SOMO [25]. The difference between our work and failure resilience for P2P systems is that P2P systems already use extensive replication to allow access to data and only need to react if failure rates are too high, whereas we need the results of the work assigned to all nodes.

Cloud computation targets a setting closer to the multicomputer environment envisioned for SDDS and many SDDS structures have come into their own, though not under their original name. Google's BigTable [6] is an SDDS based on range-partitioning, but with more functionality than RP∗ [19]. The same is true for MS Azure and MongoDB. Amazon's EC2 uses a distributed hash table called Dynamo [10]. VMWare's Gemfire provides its own hash scheme, etc. The novelty of our work lies in applying the scan functionality of SDDS to a completely different type of problem.

The idea of grouping processes in a distributed system into groups that monitor each other is fundamental and has become an accepted tool for reliability in distributed systems. While the use of replica and the topic of replica placement is important for P2P system, there seems to be very little literature on how to form small groups of peers. Slicing in P2P systems comes the nearest, but in general creates much larger groups [12].

Since our proposal is not using the cloud in a traditional way, previous work on cloud failure tolerance does not apply directly. For instance, Dai and colleagues note that grid users care about services that they are using instead of the resources and this is even more the case for cloud services. They therefore develop a holistic model for calculating the probability that a cloud service can successfully complete [8,9]. Similar models are given by Silva et al. and by Thanakornworakij [22,23].

# 7   Conclusion

We presented here a proof-of-concept for a Scalable Distributed Virtual Data Structure based on Range Partitioning that is failure tolerant. It assumes that cloud providers will eventually rent nodes for short times, controlling the demand by setting rental rates depending on the current demand. SDVDS are built on the principle of maximum autonomy. We applied this philosophy to the implementation of failure tolerance.

SDVDS extend the maximum size of optimization problems without the need to buy and administer special hardware. They will provide a very simple programming interface, as one only has to provide the evaluation function and define the enumeration space. The next step is the implementation.

## References

1. Aspnes, J., Shah, G.: Skip graphs. ACM Trans. Algorithms (TALG) **3**(4), 37 (2007)
2. Babcock, C.: Post Mortem: When Amazon's cloud turned on itself. Information Week 31 (2011). http://www.informationweek.com/cloud/infrastructure-as-a-service/post-mortem-when-amazons-cloud-turned-on-itself/d/d/-id/1097465
3. Birman, K.P.: The process group approach to reliable distributed computing. Commun. ACM **36**(12), 37–53 (1993)
4. Birman, K.P.: Guide to Reliable Distributed Systems: Building High-Assurance Applications and Cloud-Hosted Services. Springer, Heidelberg (2012)
5. Chandra, T.D., Griesemer, R., Redstone, J.: Paxos made live: an Engineering perspective. In: Proceedings of ACM Symposium on Principles of Distributed Computing, pp. 398–407 (2007)
6. Chang, F., et al.: Bigtable: a distributed storage system for structured data. ACM Trans. Comput. Syst. (TOCS) **26**(2), 4 (2008)
7. Claburn, T.: Gmail outage 'A big deal,' says Google. Information Week (2009). http://informationweek.com/applicaions/gmail-outage-a-big-deal-says-google/d/d-id/1082782
8. Dai, Y.S., Xie, M., Poh, K.L.: Reliability analysis of grid computing systems. In: Pacific Rim International Symposium on Dependable Computing, pp. 97–104 (2002)
9. Dai, Y.S., Yang, B., Dongarra, J., Zhang, G.: Cloud service reliability: modeling and analysis. In: Pacific Rim International Symposium on Dependable Computing (2009)
10. DeCandia, G., et al.: Dynamo: Amazon's highly available key-value store. ACM SIGOPS Operating Syst. Rev. **41**(6), 205–220 (2007). ACM
11. Du Mouza, C., Litwin, W., Rigaux, P.: SD-Rtree: a scalable distributed Rtree. In: IEEE International Conference on Data Engineering, pp. 296–305 (2007)
12. Fernández, A., Gramoli, V., Jiménez, E., Kermarrec, A.M., Rayna, M.: Distributed slicing in dynamic systems. In: International Conference Distributed Computing Systems, p. 66 (2007)
13. Hilford, V., Bastani, F.B., Cukic, B.: EH*-extendible hashing in a distributed environment. In: IEEE Computer Software and Applications Conference, pp. 217–222 (1997)

14. Jajodia, S., Litwin, W., Schwarz, T.: Scalable distributed virtual data structures. In: ASE International Conference on Big Data Science and Computing (2014)
15. Kröll, B., Widmayer, P.: Distributing a search tree among a growing number of processors. ACM SIGMOD Record **23**(2), 265–276 (1994)
16. Lamport, L.: Paxos made simple. ACM SIGACT News **32**(4), 18–25 (2001)
17. Litwin, W., Moussa, R., Schwarz, T.: LH*RS – a highly-available scalable distributed data structure. ACM Trans. Database Syst. (TODS) **30**(3), 769–811 (2005)
18. Litwin, W., Neimat, M.A.: k-RP*s: a scalable distributed data structure for high-performance multi-attribute access. In: International Conference on Parallel and Distributed Information Systems (1996)
19. Litwin, W., Neimat, M.A., Schneider, D.: RP*: a family of order preserving scalable distributed data structures. Very Large Databases **94**, 12–15 (1994)
20. Litwin, W., Yakouben, H., Schwarz, T.: LH* RS P2P: a scalable distributed data structure for P2P environment. In: International Conference on New Technologies in Distributed Systems. ACM (2008)
21. Ongaro, D., Ousterhout, J.: In search of an understandable consensus algorithm. In: Proceedings Usenix Annual Technical Conference (ATC) (2014)
22. Silva, B., Maciel, P., Tavares, E., Zimmermann, A.: Dependability models for designing disaster tolerant cloud computing systems. In: IEEE/IFIP International Conference on Dependable Systems and Networks (DSN), pp. 1–6 (2013)
23. Thanakornworakij, T., Nassar, R.F., Leangsuksun, C., Păun, M.: A reliability model for cloud computing for high performance computing applications. In: Caragiannis, I., Alexander, M., Badia, R.M., Cannataro, M., Costan, A., Danelutto, M., Desprez, F., Krammer, B., Sahuquillo, J., Scott, S.L., Weidendorfer, J. (eds.) Euro-Par Workshops 2012. LNCS, vol. 7640, pp. 474–483. Springer, Heidelberg (2013)
24. van Renesse, R., Bozdog, A.: Willow: DHT, aggregation, and publish/subscribe in one protocol. In: Voelker, G.M., Shenker, S. (eds.) IPTPS 2004. LNCS, vol. 3279, pp. 173–183. Springer, Heidelberg (2005)
25. Zhang, Z., Shi, S.-M., Zhu, J.: SOMO: Self-Organized Metadata Overlay for resource management in P2P DHT. In: Kaashoek, M.F., Stoica, I. (eds.) IPTPS 2003. LNCS, vol. 2735. Springer, Heidelberg (2003)

# Effect of Bias Temperature Instability on Soft Error Rate

Zhen Wang[1(✉)] and Jianhui Jiang[2]

[1] School of Computer Science and Technology, Shanghai University of Electric Power,
Shanghai 200090, China
wangzhenqq@hotmail.com
[2] School of Software Engineering, Tongji University, Shanghai 201804, China
jhjiang@tongji.edu.cn

**Abstract.** Aging and soft errors have become the two most critical reliability issues for nano-scaled CMOS designs. With the decreasing of device sizes the aging effect cannot be ignored during soft error rate (SER) estimation. In this paper, firstly the aging effect due to bias temperature instability (BTI) is analyzed on circuits using 32-nm CMOS technology for soft errors. Secondly, we derive an accurate SER estimation model which can incorporate BTI impact, including the negative BTI impact on PMOS and the positive BTI impact on NMOS. This model computes the failures in time (FIT) rate of sequential circuits. Experiments are carried on ISCAS89 circuits, and two findings are discovered: (1) for ten years simulation operating time, the maximum SER difference can go up to 12.5 % caused by BTI impact; (2) the BTI-aware SER grows quickly during the early operating time, and grows slowly in the later years.

**Keywords:** Aging · Positive bias temperature instability (PBTI) · Negative bias temperature instability (NBTI) · Critical charge · Soft error rate (SER)

## 1 Introduction

The continuous scaling of microelectronic technology enables system functionality and performance to keep on enhancing. Meanwhile, it also comes together with a reduction in ICs power supply and, consequently, noise margins, thus increasing significantly the susceptibility to soft errors (SEs) induced by atmospheric neutrons striking [1–3]. Particles strikes can cause errors either by striking state elements directly, or by striking combinational logic and propagating into downstream state elements. About the single event transients (SETs) affecting the combinational logic, there exists many studies devoted to the accurate modeling of transient faults [1, 2, 4, 5]. One SET occurring in an internal node of combinational circuits can cause a SE only when it propagates to the input of a sampling element during its setup and hold-time [3, 6, 7]. In [8], a comprehensive and accurate method computing soft error rate (SER) is proposed. It assesses the system-level FIT (failure-in-time, per $10^9$ h) rate caused by transient fault in individual logic gates and latches of a sequential circuit, which includes efficient methods to analysis soft errors of combinational logic addressing the logical, electrical and timing masks.

© Springer International Publishing Switzerland 2015
G. Wang et al. (Eds.): ICA3PP 2015 Workshops, LNCS 9532, pp. 736–745, 2015.
DOI: 10.1007/978-3-319-27161-3_67

Although many previous SER works considering process variation have reached high accuracy, the aging effect and its impact on circuit SER have not been thoroughly studied. The aging effect degrades the circuit and affects the device lifetime and performance significantly. Particularly bias temperature instability (BTI), including Negative BTI (NBTI) and positive BTI (PBTI), caused by both interface-state generation and charge trapping, has become the primary reliability concern for modern ICs [9, 10]. Since BTI affects the threshold voltage of devices [11, 12], it's necessary to consider this effect on SER.

Till now, to the best of our knowledge, there are only several researches work on this [13–18]. In [15], the research started to analyze the aging effect on combinational circuit SER, but no details were provided on how NBTI affects critical charge. In [13, 14], it described the critical charge variation under aging mechanism, while only focused on SRAM designs. The works in [12, 17] presented some preliminary analyses, showing NBTI impacted the critical charge of circuit nodes, and combined them to SER computation model. For comprehensive consideration, [18] also presented the critical charge of elementary gates with PBTI effect, while the SER computation was very complex.

In this paper, we first study the BTI effect on SER, second, an accurate and practicable FIT computation framework for sequential circuits considering both NBTI and PBTI is proposed.

The rest of paper is organized as following, in Sect. 2 we discuss the BTI effect on soft errors, and in Sect. 3 we derive the BTI-aware SER estimation model, then based on the experiments we analyze the experimental results in Sect. 4. At last we conclude this paper in Sect. 5.

## 2   BTI Effect on Soft Errors

In this section we firstly discuss the effect caused by BTI on transistor parameters, including change of threshold voltage $V_{th}$ and critical charge $Q_{crit}$ with different numbers of years; and secondly we point out how the BTI impacts the soft error susceptibility.

### 2.1   BTI-Induced Variation of Threshold Voltage and Critical Charge

BTI effects include NBTI and PBTI, which are observed in PMOS and NMOS transistors respectively. They cause performance degradation of MOS transistors when the transistors are in ON state (stress phase) at elevated temperatures. And when the MOS transistors are in OFF state (recovery phase), the BTI-induced degradation is partially recovered. During the stress phase, the traps generated at the Si-dielectric interface shield the applied gate voltage, which results in a threshold voltage increase. And the increase may reach 50 mV over 10 years [19].

The threshold voltage increase, denoted by $\Delta V_{th}$, is in direct proportion to the interface trap concentration $N_{IT}(t)$, i.e.

$$\Delta V_{th} = \frac{q(1+m)}{x} * N_{IT}(t) = k * N_{IT}(t) \tag{1}$$

Where the coefficient $k$ is used to distinguish between PBTI and NBTI effects on NMOS and PMOS transistors. In [20] it mentioned $k$ for PMOS transistors is bigger than that for NMOS transistors, therefore the NBTI effect is more severe than PBTI. The threshold voltage shift reduces the ability of a gate to maintain the correct voltage value on a node hit by an energetic particle, then it significantly degrades transistor performance.

The change of threshold voltage can lead to variation of critical charge of MOS transistors. In [18], HSPICE simulation was used to analyze how the BTI-caused N/ PMOS $\Delta V_{th}$ impacts $Q_{crit}$ of combinational circuits. The simulation was based on 32-nm technology with 1 V power supply, and carried out the conditions in both stress phase and recovery phase alternately. The simulated operating time was from 0 year to 10 years. For an example, Fig. 1 shows the simulation results obtained when two alpha particles, with the same energy, hit the same node within a NOT chain, at two different instants during circuit life time. Here, Fig. 1(b) denotes the scenario after 10 years of operating time, and Fig. 1(a) is at the beginning of the circuit lifetime. It's obvious that the glitch in (b) has higher amplitude than in (a). That's to say, the critical charge $Q_{crit}$ is considerably smaller after 10 years of circuit operation than at the beginning of circuit lifetime.

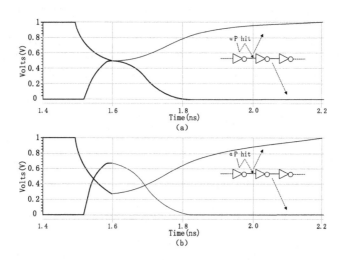

**Fig. 1.**  Simulation results for the case of an alpha particle hitting a node of a NOT chain

## 2.2   How the BTI Affect SER

As we all know, the soft error is caused by energetic particles striking on the node of the circuit. If the striking node is in combinational logic part, the SET occurs. Only when the collected charge reaches a critical value, i.e. $Q_{crit}$, which is high enough to make SET have an amplitude exceeding the fan-out gate logic threshold, an incorrect logic value can propagates. In combinational logic, the generated SET may propagate through the downstream logic and get captured by a sampling element, thus results in an SE.

Admittedly, if the particles strike on the sequential logic part, such as flip-flop or latches, single event upset (SEU) will occur, which may directly cause an SE.

Till now we can find the critical value $Q_{crit}$ is a clue for the relationship between BTI effect and SER estimation. With the operation time increases, BTI mechanism on N/PMOS makes the transistor $Q_{crit}$ decrease. Therefore for the circuits in same atmosphere, the particles with same energy would make the SET exceed the threshold easier, then the SER will increase. In the following section, we will analyze this effect in detail.

## 3 Consider BTI Impact on SER

In this section, we propose a framework to analyze SER based on BFIT method and consider the BTI effect during FIT computation for SE. Our discussion consists of three parts: first, the introduction of BFIT and the overall flow of SER analysis is presented; second, the extraction of BTI-aware computation model is derived; last, how to consider BTI effect during soft error FIT calculation is detailed.

### 3.1 BTI-Aware Soft Error FIT

BFIT [8] is an accurate methodology designed for analyzing the neutron FIT contribution of each combinational gate and latches in a sequential circuit, it can analyze SER in system-level by injecting fault in circuit-level. As known, when a particle strikes a combinational logic gate, a soft error will only occur when the resulting glitch is capturing by the downstream sequential elements. In BFIT, it simulated the neutron struck on the node in combinational circuit part, considering logical, electrical and timing masking during the model calculation. So this method is relatively comprehensive. Based on BFIT model, we make some modification to combine BTI effect, mainly including two aspects: (1) we derive new calculation model to take the $Q_{crit}$ as one of its parameters, hence take the $Q_{crit}$ variation caused by BTI into the soft error FIT calculation; (2) both PBTI effect on NMOS and NBTI effect on PMOS are considered to reflect the aging impact on SER.

### 3.2 Modified SER Computation Model

In BFIT method, the following formal model is used to compute the SER in the form of FIT.

$$FIT = avg\left(\frac{failures}{cycle}\right) * \frac{cycles}{10^9 hrs} = avg[\int_{q=0}^{\infty}\int_{t=0}^{t_{cycle}} R(q,t)N(q,t)dtdq] * \frac{cycles}{10^9 hrs} \qquad (2)$$

where the pair $(q, t)$ represents the magnitude of collected charge and the time within the clock cycle that the strike occurs. $R(q, t)$ represents the probability that a strike of exactly charge $q$ occurs at exactly time $t$ of the clock cycle. $N(q, t)$ is a Boolean function used to describe the outcome of each possible strike, and this function takes the value 1 to indicate the strikes latched in sequential elements, and 0 to indicate the glitch is not latched. Because only when the collected charge reaches or exceeds $Q_{crit}$, the strike can lead to bit error or state upset, that's to say, $N(q, t)$ will equal 0 if $q < Q_{crit}$, we can change the lower limit of the outer integration from $q = 0$ to $q = Q_{crit}$ in (2). Thus we get the modified FIT model, see (3).

$$FIT = avg[\int_{q=Q_{crit}}^{\infty} \int_{t=0}^{t_{cycle}} R(q, t) N(q, t) dt dq] * \frac{cycles}{10^9 hrs} \qquad (3)$$

And in [21], the numbers of strikes per second exceeding charge $q$ is given by (4).

$$R_q = F*A*K*exp(-q/Q_s) \qquad (4)$$

where $F$ is the neutron flux, $A$ is the sensitive drain diffusion area of the node collecting the charge, $K$ is a technology-independent fitting parameter and $Q_s$ is a technology-dependent fitting parameter representing charge collection efficiency. Because in [23] it is specified that $R(q, t)$ can be calculated by $dR(q)/dq * t_{step}$, where $t_{step}$ is the time step during the evaluating the integral numerically, we substitute $R(q)$ with (4) and can get

$$R(q, t) = F * A * K * exp\left(-\frac{q}{Q_s}\right) * \left(-\frac{1}{Q_s}\right) * t_{step} \qquad (5)$$

Before further derivation, we should note that the Boolean-valued function $N(q, t)$ is not an analytic formula, it is merely used to determine which $(q, t)$ pairs via some paths can lead to one or more latches capturing the glitch, and then chose them to be involved in the integral. For an example, $N(q, t)$ will equal 1 on the sensitized path, and if off the sensitized path, Eq. (3) is unnecessary to be computed. Based on this, when we substitute (5) into (3), we can get:

$$FIT = avg\left[F * A * K * \int_{q=Q_{crit}}^{\infty} exp\left(-\frac{q}{Q_s}\right) * \left(-\frac{1}{Q_s}\right) * \int_{t=0}^{t_{cycle}} t_{step} dt dq\right] * \frac{cycles}{10^9 hrs}$$
$$= avg\left[F * A * K * exp(-\frac{Q_{crit}}{Q_s})\right] * \frac{cycles}{10^9 hrs}. \qquad (6)$$

Till now, we finish the derivation and give the final modified SER model (6). According to Sect. 2.2, we know BTI mechanism can impact $Q_{crit}$ of transistors, so take the changed value of $Q_{crit}$ caused by BTI effect with different numbers of years and plug it into (6), we can calculate the corresponding FIT value.

### 3.3   Changed $Q_{crit}$ Under PBTI and NBTI

In [18], the $Q_{crit}$ variation has been evaluated by means of HSPICE simulations, which listed the critical charge values at the outputs of NOT, NAND and NOR gates with a variable number of inputs (up to four), for a circuit operating time up to 10 years. Table 1 is an example for NAND gates.

**Table 1.** Critical charge (fc) for 32-nm symmetric NAND gates with different inputs

| Operating time | 2 Inputs | | 3 Inputs | | 4 Inputs | |
|---|---|---|---|---|---|---|
| | NBTI | PBTI | NBTI | PBTI | NBTI | PBTI |
| 0 year | 5.13 | 5.13 | 3.97 | 3.97 | 3.60 | 3.60 |
| 1 year | 4.71 | 4.88 | 3.61 | 3.83 | 3.27 | 3.53 |
| 5 years | 4.40 | 4.75 | 3.42 | 3.73 | 3.10 | 3.44 |
| 10 years | 4.34 | 4.73 | 3.39 | 3.71 | 3.06 | 3.42 |

Based on the simulation data of [18], we analyze for every elementary gate, how to apply the $Q_{crit}$ value in the SER model of Eq. (6) under PBTI and NBTI effects, respectively. Since NBTI and PBTI are observed in PMOS and NMOS transistors respectively, we choose the $Q_{crit}$ value caused by NBTI when PMOS transistor is in ON state, and choose $Q_{crit}$ under PBTI effect when NMOS transistor is ON state. According to the circuit diagrams of NOT, NAND and NOR gates (In Fig. 2 the gates with 2 inputs are presented, for more inputs the diagrams are similar), we know when the gate output is signal 0, NMOS transistor will be ON state, then $Q_{crit}$ value under PBTI should be taken during the soft error FIT calculation; and when the gate output is signal 1, the $Q_{crit}$ value under NBTI should be chosen. Therefore, both NBTI and PBTI effect can be considered in SER estimation.

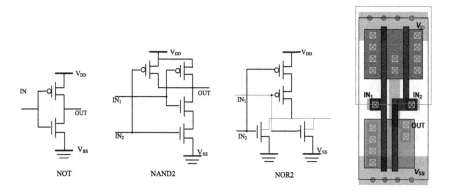

**Fig. 2.** The circuit diagram of NOT, NAND2, NOR2 gates and the layout of NAND2

About the term $A$ in (6), which denotes the critical area of the gate, i.e. the sensitive drain diffusion area of the node collecting the charge, we also research it according to the circuit diagrams, and put different value when the gate has different input logic. We make the assumption that stacked devices are all upsized according to the following rule: the double stacked devices are double wide; the triple stacked devices are triple wide, etc. When the pull-up network of the driver is ON, the critical area is the drain junction of the NMOS transistor(s) in the OFF-state connected to the output node of the gate. Similarly, when the pull-down is ON, the area of the drain junction of the PMOS transistor(s) in the OFF-state connected to the output node of the gate should be considered. $A$ is different when the gate has different input, for an example, in the NAND2 gate, the sensitized diffusion area of 10 ($IN_1$ is 1 and $IN_2$ is 0) state is double to that of 01 state (see NAND2 layout in Fig. 2).

## 4  Experimental Results

We implement the BTI-aware SER model using C++ on ISCAS89 benchmark circuits. In (6), we set the flux value $F$ as 56.5 neutrons$*m^{-2}s^{-1}$, corresponding to the rate of neutron flux at sea level [23], and the fitting parameter $K$ as $2.2*10^{-5}$ [21]. About the value of elementary gate critical charge $Q_{crit}$ which is affected by BTI mechanism, we refer to [18]. Since in [18], the elementary gates was implemented by 32-nm CMOS technology with 1 V power supply, for consistency we set parameters $Q_s$ and $A$ based on the same technology size and power supply. According to the technology-dependent estimates in [21] for the collection slope, we use $Q_s(NMOS) = 13fC$ and $Q_s(PMOS) = 6.2fC$. And we assume the unit area of $A$ is 32 nm*32 nm. As the program input, an important circuit modification is decomposing each non-inverting CMOS gate into inverting CMOS gates, so the recognized elementary gates includes NOT, NAND, NOR, ensuring a one-to-one correspondence between gates and hittable nodes.

**Table 2.**  Properties and BTI-aware SER of benchmark circuits

| Circuit | #Inputs | #Gates | #Latches | BTI-aware SER ($10^{-3}$FIT) | | | | SER increase rate (10y to 0y) |
|---------|---------|--------|----------|--------|--------|---------|----------|------|
| | | | | 0 year | 1 year | 5 years | 10 years | |
| s5378 | 214 | 3232 | 179 | 5.28 | 5.68 | 5.88 | 5.93 | 12.3 % |
| s9234 | 247 | 7230 | 228 | 20.89 | 22.25 | 22.98 | 23.13 | 10.7 % |
| s13207 | 700 | 10277 | 669 | 24.09 | 25.91 | 26.90 | 27.11 | 12.5 % |
| s15850 | 611 | 12712 | 597 | 43.44 | 46.63 | 48.42 | 48.81 | 12.4 % |
| s35932 | 1763 | 23012 | 1728 | 22.34 | 23.86 | 24.70 | 24.85 | 11.2 % |
| s38417 | 1664 | 28223 | 1636 | 99.07 | 105.48 | 109.28 | 110.07 | 11.1 % |
| s38584 | 1464 | 28854 | 1452 | 73.33 | 78.25 | 81.02 | 81.59 | 11.3 % |
| Average value | | | | 41.21 | 44.01 | 45.60 | 45.93 | 11.5 % |

The results for SER analysis on a variety of circuits are shown in Table 2 where column 5, 6, 7, 8 denote the measurements of SER under different years of the BTI effect. The results indicate that considering the BTI effect is important on accurate SER estimation, since the values of SER increase with the circuit age under the same technology size. The maximum statistical SER difference (0 year versus 10 years) can go up to 12.5 % on s13207. According to the average value in Table 2, we can find among different operating years the SER increases quickly after one year, and increases slowly from 5 years to 10 years, which is consistent with the tendency of transistor critical charge reduction.

Figure 3 displays the variation tendency of the seven circuits. It shows in different operating time, the SER relative values of the same group of circuits are consistent, which can verify correctness of our modified model in some degree. Generally, the SER is high when the circuit has big scale. We analyze the low FIT of s35932, and find that the NAND/NOR gates in this circuit only have 2 inputs, which is different from the other circuits which have many NAND/NOR gates with 3 and 4 inputs. The simpler circuit structure of s35932 brings high reliability for s35932. About s38584 has lower FIT than s38417, it is because there are less latches in s38584, while during FIT calculation the sensitized paths are traversed beginning from latches.

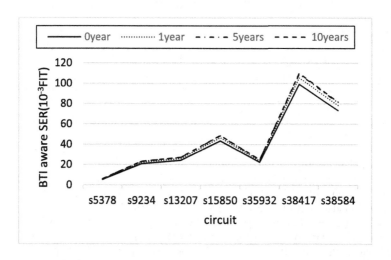

**Fig. 3.** Circuits BTI-aware SER in different operating years

# 5   Conclusion

Aging and soft errors have become the two most critical reliability issues for nano-scaled CMOS designs. In this work, we present that a new SER analysis framework that incorporates both NBTI and PBTI for the aging effect and particle strikes on PMOS and NMOS. We derive a $Q_{crit}$ dependent model of SER, and consider the impact of BTI degradation into the model. Experimental results show SERs will go up with years of aging effect, while during the increase of operating time the BTI effect becomes slower, so designers can take actions correspondingly.

**Acknowledgments.** This work is supported by National Natural Science Foundation of China (Grant No. 61432017) and the Excellent University Young Teachers Training Program of Shanghai Municipal Education Commission (No. ZZsdl15104).

# References

1. Seifert, N., Gill, B., Zia, V., Zhang, M., Ambrose, V.: On the scalability of redundancy based SER mitigation schemes. In: IEEE International Conference on Integrated Circuit Design and Technology, pp. 1–9. IEEE Press, Austin (2007)
2. Mavis, D.G., Eaton, P.H.: SEU and SET modeling and mitigation in deep submicron technologies. In: 45th Annual IEEE International Reliability Physics Symposium, pp. 293–305. IEEE Press, Phoenix (2007)
3. Baumann, R.C.: Radiation-induced soft errors in advanced semiconductor technologies. IEEE Trans. Device Mater. Reliab. **5**, 305–316 (2005)
4. Rossi, D., Cazeaux, J.M., Omana, M., Metra, C., Chatterjee, A.: Accurate linear model for SET critical charge estimation. IEEE Trans. Very Large Scale Integr. (VLSI) Syst. **17**, 1161–1166 (2009)
5. Cazeaux, J.M., Rossi, D., Omana, M., Chatterjee, A., Metra, C.: On-transistor level gate sizing for increased robustness to transient faults. In: 11th IEEE International On-Line Testing Symposium (IOLTS), pp. 23–28. IEEE Press, Saint Raphael (2005)
6. Rossi, D., Omana, M., Metra, C.: Transient fault and soft error on-die monitoring scheme. In: 25th IEEE International Symposium on DFT VLSI System, pp. 391–398. IEEE Press, Kyoto (2010)
7. Omana, M., Rossi, D., Metra, C.: High performance robust latches. IEEE Trans. Comput. **59**, 1455–1465 (2010)
8. Holcomb, D., Li, W., Seshia, S.A.: Design as you see FIT: system-level soft error analysis of sequential circuits. In: DATE 2009 the Conference on Design, Automation and Test in Europe, pp. 785–790. European Design and Automation Association, Leuven (2009)
9. Keane, J., Kim, T.-H., Kim, C.H.: An on-chip NBTI sensor for measuring PMOS threshold voltage degradation. IEEE Trans. VLSI Syst. **18**, 947–956 (2010)
10. Huard, V., Denais, M.: Hole trapping effect on methodology for DC and AC negative bias temperature instability measurements in PMOS transistors. In: 42nd Annual IEEE International Reliability Physics Symposium, pp. 40–45. IEEE Press, Crolles (2004)
11. Siddiqua, T., Gurumurthi, S., Stan, M.R.: Modeling and analyzing NBTI in the presence of process variation. In: International Symposium on Quality of Electronic Design (ISQED), pp. 1–8. IEEE Press, Santa Clara (2011)
12. Rossi, D., Omana, M., Metra, C., Paccagnella, A.: Impact of aging phenomena on soft error susceptibility. In: International Symposium on Defect and Fault Tolerance in VLSI and Nanotechnology Systems (DFT), pp. 18–24. IEEE Press, Vancouver (2011)
13. Bagatin, M., Gerardin, S., Paccagnella, A., Faccio, F.: Impact of NBTI aging on the single-event upset of SRAM cells. IEEE Trans. Nucl. Sci. **57**, 3245–3250 (2010)
14. Cannon, E.H., Osowski, A.K., Kanj, R., Reinhardt, D.D., Joshi, R.V.: The impact of aging effects and manufacturing variation on SRAM soft error rate. IEEE Trans. Device Mater. Rel. **8**, 145–152 (2008)
15. Ramakrishnan, K., Rajaraman, R., Suresh, S., Vijaykrishnan, N., Xie, Y., Irwin, M.J.: Variation impact on SER of combinational circuits. In: 8th International Symposium on Quality Electronic Design (ISQED), pp. 911–916. IEEE Press, Washington, DC (2007)

16. Harada, R., Mitsuyama, Y., Hashimoto, M., Onoye, T.: Impact of NBTI-induced pulse-width modulation on SET pulse-width measurement. IEEE Trans. Nucl. Sci. **60**, 2630–2634 (2013)
17. Lin, C.Y.H., Huang, R.H.-M., Wen, C.H.-P., Chang, A.C.-C.: Aging-aware statistical soft-error-rate analysis for nano-scaled CMOS designs. In: International Symposium on VLSI-DAT, pp. 1–4. IEEE Press, Hstinchu (2013)
18. Rossi, D., Omana, M., Metra, C., Paccagnella, A.: Impact of bias temperature instability on soft error susceptibility. IEEE Trans. VLSI Syst. **23**, 743–751 (2015)
19. Agarwal, M., et al.: Optimized circuit failure prediction for aging: practicality and promise. In: IEEE International Test Conference (ITC), pp. 1–10. IEEE Press, Santa Clara (2008)
20. Khan, S., Hamidioui, S., Kukner, H., Raghavan P., Catthoor, F.: BTI impact on logical gates in nano-scale CMOS technology. In: 15th IEEE International Symposium on Design and Diagnostics of Electronic Circuits and Systems (DDECS), pp. 348–353. IEEE Press, Tallinn (2012)
21. Hazucha, P., Svensson, C.: Impact of CMOS technology scaling on the atmospheric neutron soft error rate. IEEE Trans. Nuclear Sci. **47**, 2586–2594 (2000)
22. Berkeley FIT Estimation Tool (BFIT). http://www.eecs.berkeley.edu/~holcomb/BFIT.htm
23. Ziegler, J.: Terrestrial cosmic rays. IBM J. Res. Develop. **40**, 19–39 (1996)

# Security Modeling and Analysis
# of a SDN Based Web Service

Taehoon Eom[1]([✉]), Jin B. Hong[2], Jong Sou Park[1], and Dong Seong Kim[2]

[1] Department of Computer Engineering, Korea Aerospace University,
Seoul, South Korea
{eomth86,jspark}@kau.ac.kr
[2] Department of Computer Science and Software Engineering,
University of Canterbury, Christchurch, New Zealand
jin.hong@pg.canterbury.ac.nz, dongseong.kim@canterbury.ac.nz

**Abstract.** The introduction of a Software-Defined Network (SDN) provides a better functionality and usability over the traditionally static networks. The SDN separates controllers and networking peripherals onto the Control and Data Planes respectively. However, this separation creates new vulnerabilities between the planes. To address this problem, we propose to model and analyze the security of the SDN. Further, we propose a network reconfiguration technique to assess its effectiveness of minimizing the system risk. Our simulation results show that computing the optimal reconfiguration has an exponential time complexity, and there is also a trade-off between the system risk and the server delay.

**Keywords:** Attack Graphs · Attack modeling · Security models · Software defined networks · Security analysis

## 1 Introduction

Software Defined Networks (SDN) bring a lot of benefits. Users can control the network flow via the SDN easily than traditional networks. We can automate network tasks, control fine-details of network flows, and enforce security if necessary. For these advantages, many enterprises have been adopting the SDN, and a lot of research have been doing to improve various aspects of the SDN. However, the security of the SDN could hinder the usage of the SDN. Kreutz et al. [1] described threat vectors in a SDN. They listed the threat vectors into seven categories: (a) forged or faked traffic flows, (b) exploiting vulnerabilities in forwarding devices, (c) attacking SDN control communications, (d) exploiting vulnerabilities in SDN controllers, (e) trust issues between SDN controllers and apps, (f) exploiting vulnerabilities in the SDN admin station, and (g) trust issues between the Control and Data plane. The categories a, b, f and g also exist in traditional networks, but the categories c, d and e are specific to the SDN. For instance, a vulnerability in the SDN controller would increase the overall system risk from the security perspective. It is significant to analyze the security of a SDN under different threat vectors.

© Springer International Publishing Switzerland 2015
G. Wang et al. (Eds.): ICA3PP 2015 Workshops, LNCS 9532, pp. 746–756, 2015.
DOI: 10.1007/978-3-319-27161-3_68

One approach to assess the security of a SDN is to conduct security analysis on a real SDN environment. However, the approach requires extensive setup cost and time, which enforce restrictions on users. Another approach is to gather information of a SDN environment and construct a graphical security model. By using relevant security metrics for a SDN, we can concisely assess the security of a SDN. Moreover, the automation of security analysis using such a graphical security model can save time and cost, especially when the architecture of a SDN is complex. A graphical security models (including Attack Graphs (AGs) [2,3], Attack Trees [4], Attack Countermeasure Trees [5]) can represent all the possible paths from an attack to a target in the network. Various security analysis can be performed through the graphical security models in conjunction with security metrics [5,6]. To the best of our knowledge, there is no work to use a graphical security model to assess the security of a SDN. In this paper, we propose to use a formal security modeling technique to assess the security of a SDN. The main contributions of this paper are summarized as follows:

- Model and analyze the security of a SDN via a graphical security model (an AG);
- Compute the system risk associated with the SDN and apply reconfiguration of the network to minimize the overall system risk;
- Conduct simulations to assess the scalability and the trade-off between security and service of a SDN web service model.

The rest of the paper is organized as follows: Sect. 2 introduces a SDN architecture and its operations. Section 3 presents a graphical security model for a SDN based web service. Simulations and their results are presented in Sect. 4, and related work is given in Sect. 5. Finally, we conclude our paper in Sect. 6.

## 2   SDN Overview

### 2.1   A SDN Architecture

The architecture of an example SDN is shown in Fig. 1. It separates the SDN components onto two layers: (a) Data Plane, and (b) Control Plane. The SDN

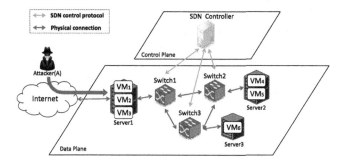

**Fig. 1.** A typical SDN architecture

controller is placed on the Control Plane, which controls how switches in the Data Plane are connected. The Data Plane contains those OpenFlow Switches and other networking devices (e.g., hubs, routers). The OpenFlow switches are specific for a SDN, where the hardware functions are to perform packet switching and the software functions are to communicate with the SDN controllers using the OpenFlow protocol to update their flow-tables and report any network errors.

We assume that there are three switches (i.e., OpenFlow Switches) and three server racks, where one switch is connected to one server rack each. All switches are connected to one another physically, as well as to the SDN controller. Server 1 is connected to the Internet, and Server 2 and Server 3 are internally connected only. We use one SDN controller for simplicity, but there can be multiple SDN controllers in the Control Plane. For each server, there may be one or two virtual machines (VMs), and the operating systems of those VMs are briefed in Table 1. We assume that $VM_4$ is the target of an attacker.

**Table 1.** Operation systems of VMs

| VM ID | OS | VM ID | OS |
|-------|-----|-------|-----|
| $VM_1$ | Windows 7 Service Pack 1 | $VM_4$ | Windows Server 2008 SP2 |
| $VM_2$ | Windows 7 Service Pack 1 | $VM_5$ | Redhat Enterprise Linux |
| $VM_3$ | Windows 7 Service Pack 1 | $VM_6$ | Windows Server 2008 SP2 |

Each OpenFlow switch has 12 physical ports, which are used to transfer data packets between the VMs or the other switches. However, the flow table is used to govern how packets are transferred through the SDN, where each switch maintains its own flow table controlled by the SDN controller. If the route of a packet cannot be determined by the flow table, then the switch requests the SDN controller for the routing information, or the packet can be dropped depending on the routing rules. In our example SDN, we set the routing rules to drop any packets unspecified in the flow table.

The flow table used in the example SDN is shown in Table 2. We only present the required information to construct a security model, but other flow table information can also be used if necessary. *SW Port* specifies the incoming traffic through the specified port. *VLAN ID* specifies the logical network ID. Even if the physical location of those switches in the same subnet, different *VLAN ID* specifies the different subnet and cannot communicate to one another. *Action* specifies how the packet of the given information is handled in the switches. *Priority* specifies how multiple packets in the queue are handled, with lower values are given a higher priority.

**Table 2.** Flow Table 3

| Switch | Match fields | | | | Action | Priority |
|---|---|---|---|---|---|---|
| | SW Port | Src IP | Dst IP | VLAN ID | | |
| SW1 | Port1 | 192.168.1.100 | 192.168.3.100 | 1 | Rewrite Dst IP to 192.168.2.100 and forward Port2 | 1 |
| | Port1 | 192.168.1.200 | 192.168.3.100 | 1 | Rewrite Dst IP to 192.168.2.200 and forward Port2 | 1 |
| | Port1 | 192.168.1.300 | 192.168.3.100 | 1 | Rewrite Dst IP to 192.168.2.200 and forward Port2 | 1 |
| | Port2 | * | * | 1 | Drop | 2 |
| | Port3 | * | * | 1 | Drop | 2 |
| SW2 | Port1 | 192.168.2.100 | 192.168.3.100 | 1 | Forward Port3 | 1 |
| | Port1 | 192.168.2.200 | 192.168.3.100 | 1 | Forward Port3 | 1 |
| | Port2 | 192.168.1.100 | * | 1 | Forward Port1 | 1 |
| | Port2 | 192.168.1.200 | * | 1 | Forward Port1 | 1 |
| | Port2 | 192.168.1.300 | * | 1 | Forward Port1 | 1 |
| | Port3 | * | * | 1 | Drop | 2 |
| SW3 | Port3 | 192.168.2.100 | 192.168.3.100 | 1 | Forward Port1 | 1 |
| | Port3 | 192.168.2.200 | 192.168.3.100 | 1 | Forward Port1 | 1 |
| | Port1 | * | * | 1 | Drop | 2 |

# 3   A Graphical Security Model for a SDN Based Web Service

We assume that VMs in the example SDN has one vulnerability each as shown in Table 3 for simplicity. Of course, more system vulnerabilities as we did in work [7] can be also modeled. We used the CVSS scores as the probability of an attack success, and the probability of an attack to all nodes in the SDN are equiprobable. The attack scenario is shown in Fig. 2, where the attacker is located outside of the network.

**Table 3.** Vulnerabilities of VMs

| VM ID | CVE ID | CVSS | Impact |
|---|---|---|---|
| $VM_1$ | CVE-2015-0096 | 9.3 | 10 |
| $VM_2$ | CVE-2015-0096 | 9.3 | 10 |
| $VM_3$ | CVE-2015-0096 | 9.3 | 10 |
| $VM_4$ | CVE-2015-2426 | 7.5 | 6.4 |
| $VM_5$ | CVE-2015-1211 | 9.3 | 10 |
| $VM_6$ | CVE-2015-2426 | 9.3 | 10 |

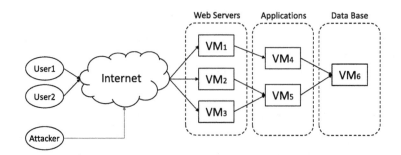

**Fig. 2.** An architecture and configuration of a SDN based web service

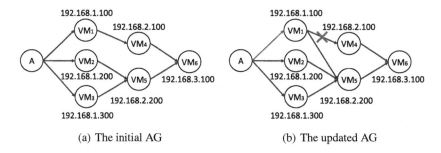

(a) The initial AG            (b) The updated AG

**Fig. 3.** The AGs before/after enforcing a new flow rule

We use an AG [2] to model the attack scenario shown in Fig. 2. Because we only assumed one vulnerability for each VM, the VM nodes in the AG represented the particular vulnerability described in Table 3. Figure 3(a) shows the AG of the example SDN. If we decided to update the SDN to prevent attacks through the $VM_4$, then one approach is to remove all the routing paths through $VM_4$ using the SDN controller to update the flow table (e.g., drop all packets from the source IP 192.168.1.100 on SW1 Port 1). Then, the AG is updated as shown in Fig. 3(b) accordingly.

## 3.1   System Risk Analysis

We conduct system risk analysis to assess the security of SDN. The algorithm 1 shows the process of computing all possible attack paths in the given SDN. The system risk is computed as the cumulative sum of risk associated with all possible attack paths. The risk associated with each node is calculated based on the CVSS score times the impact value as shown in Table 3.

## 3.2   System Delay Analysis

We use a deterministic performance values to demonstrate change in system delay. Of course more precise network measures can be used, but it is not needed

---

**Algorithm 1.** AG Security Analysis Algorithm

---

  **procedure** ANALYZEAG($AG_{SDN}, N_i, N_j$)
    lable $N_i$ as discovered
    $S.push(N_i)$
    if $N_i$ equals to $N_j$ then
      return $S$
    else
      for all $E$ from $N_i$ to $N_{next}$ in $AG.adjacentEdges(N_i)$ do
        if $N_{next}$ is not labeled as discovered then
          recursively call analyzeAG($AG_{SDN}, N_{next}, N_j$)
        end if
      end for
    end if
    $S.pop$
  end procedure

---

here as we are only demonstrating the computation of the trade-off between the system risk (as a security metric) and the system delay (as a performance metric). We assume that all web servers (i.e., $VM_1$, $VM_2$ and $VM_3$) require 2 s to process one user request, windows-based application server (i.e., $VM_4$) requires 1 s to process one web server request, linux-based application server (i.e., $VM_5$) requires 2 s to process one web server request, and the database server (i.e., $VM_6$) requires 1 s to process one application server request.

For example, the system risk associated with the initial state of the SDN (i.e., Fig. 3(a) is 74.7 and the processing time required to complete 100 jobs is 136 s, respectively. If we change the routing table of the SW1 to reconnect routing packets from $VM_4$ to $VM_5$ (i.e., Fig. 3(b)), then the system risk reduces to 70.2. However, because the processing time of $VM_5$ is greater than $VM_4$, the time required to process 100 jobs increases to 202 s. There are numerous network reconfiguration scenarios, but optimizing the trade-off between the system risk and the system delay is out of scope in this paper.

## 4    Simulation Results

We use a larger SDN as shown in Fig. 4 for our simulation experiments, and we show the trade-off between the system risk and the system delay. The Cloud system using the SDN can have more than 100 VMs hosted on the Data Plane. For our simulation, we assume that there are two Data Planes with one SDN controller for each Data Plane. An additional SDN controller for both Data Planes is placed for fault tolerance in case that any of those SDN controllers fail. The Data Plane 1 has 8 VMs, where $VM_1$ to $VM_3$ are connected to the Internet, $VM_7$ to $VM_{10}$ are VMs interconnected between the Data Planes, and $VM_{13}$ and $VM_{14}$ are connected to the database VM. Here, the attack scenario is for an attacker located outside of the network (i.e., the internet) to compromise the database VM by penetrating through the SDN.

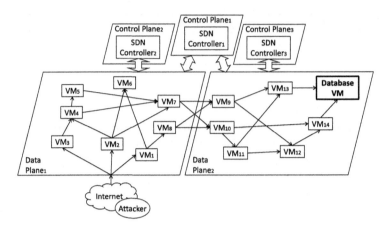

**Fig. 4.** A SDN configuration for simulation

The results on the trade-off between the system risk and the system delay in different network scenarios are depicted in Figs. 5 and 6 respectively. The network density indicates the number of connections between network nodes (i.e., VMs), where the network density value of one means that it is a fully connected network. Having a fixed number of network hosts and varying the network density by random connections, we can see the trade-off in Fig. 5. As the network density increases, the system risk also increases exponentially due to the increase in the number of possible attack paths. However, the system delay is reduced as there are more (packet) routing paths from users to the database VM, and the average number of hop lengths is reduced as more connections between VMs are established in the SDN. The result shows that the SDN with the network density value higher than 0.6 has approximately the same system delay, but the system risk continuously increases.

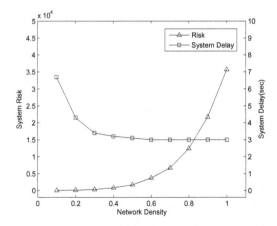

**Fig. 5.** Network density (10 nodes) vs. system risk and delay

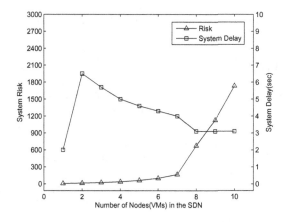

**Fig. 6.** Density 0.5 increasing the number of nodes vs risk and delay

We fixed the network density to 0.5 and experimented with a varying number of SDN nodes (i.e., VMs) as shown in Fig. 6. All VMs used in this simulation have the same job processing time. The result shows that the system risk increases exponentially with respect to the number of nodes in the SDN. Also, increasing the number of nodes decreases the system delay, as there are more connections established between the user and the database VM.

Our next experiment configured the SDN to minimize the system delay. Then, we made a single update in the SDN to reduce the system risk using a greedy algorithm. Each time when the update in the SDN reduced the system risk, the system delay also increased as shown in Fig. 7. This shows the trade-off between the system risk and the system delay, where they have a negative exponential relationship. Hence, it is possible with a given constraint (either the system risk or the system delay), we can optimize the system risk/delay by configuring the

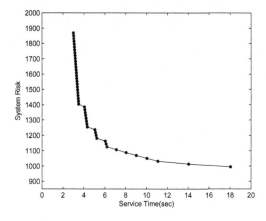

**Fig. 7.** The trade-off between the system risk and service delay

SDN on the basis of our analysis result, which can be performed in our future work in more detail.

## 5    Related Work

The previous work are mostly focused on the implementation of the SDN in different manners. For instance, the scalability of a network virtualization in the SDN is analyzed in [8,9], and different data forwarding algorithms for protection and restoration to improve the network resiliency against cyber-attacks and other component failures were proposed in [10]. Also, many others tackled various security issues of the SDN including the pros and cons of the SDN security [10], and designing a secure and dependable SDN control platform [1]. The work [11] dealt with network management challenges, as well as failures and recovery of single/multiple controllers [12–14]. A few work assessed SDN performance through experiments [15]. The dependability of SDN with respect to the number of network devices and hosts [16]. Furthermore, The works [17–20] made the security service for security issues in SDN. The paper [17] proposed security application to enhance security of OpenFlow Switch, and countermeasure methods against the Network Topology Poisoning Attacks was proposed in [18]. Also, the work [20] dealt with SYN Flooding Attack in the SDN environment. These papers dealt with the issue from OpenFlow Switch or SDN threat vector. Also, the work [21] carried out experiments to enhance security of the SDN control layer. To the best of our knowledge, there is no work to use a graphical security model to assess the security of a SDN. This work is the first work to use an AG to analysis the security of a SDN based web service and analyze the trade-off between the system risk and the delay.

## 6    Conclusion

Adopting the SDN allows users to better locate resources through the network by dynamically controlling how the network is configured. This improves the traditionally static networks with functionality and usability, but by separating the control from network peripherals create new vulnerabilities between SDN controllers and network components (e.g., VMs). To accurately assess the security of SDN, it is important to identify and analyze potential attack scenarios. In this paper, we used a security model to capture different attack paths that the attacker can exploit, and showed how a simple mitigation strategy of changing the routing path can minimize the system risk. Moreover, we have demonstrated a method to calculate the system risk to observe the trade-off between security and performance of the SDN. Our results have shown that we can optimize the security in respect to the performance of SDN with given system constraints.

## References

1. Kreutz, D., Ramos, F.M., Verissimo, P.: Towards secure and dependable software-defined networks. In: Proceedings of the Second ACM SIGCOMM Workshop Hot Topics on Software Defined Networking - HotSDN 2013, p. 55, August 2013

2. Sheyner, O., Haines, J., Jha, S., Lippmann, R., Wing, J.: Automated generation and analysis of attack graphs. Technical report, CMU (2002)
3. Ingols, K., Lippmann, R., Piwowarski, K.: Practical attack graph generation for network defense. In: Proceeding of the 22nd Annual Computer Security Applications Conference (ACSAC 2006), pp. 121–130 (2006)
4. Schneier, B.: Modeling security threats. Dr. Dobb's J. **24**(12), 21–29 (1999)
5. Roy, A., Kim, D., Trivedi, K.: Attack countermeasure trees (ACT): towards unifying the constructs of attack and defense trees. Secur. Commun. Netw. **5**(8), 929–943 (2012)
6. Manadhata, P., Wing, J.: An attack surface metric. IEEE Trans. Softw. Eng. **37**(3), 371–386 (2011)
7. Hong, J., Kim, D.: Scalable security models for assessing effectiveness of moving target defenses. In: Proceedings of the the 44th Annual IEEE/IFIP International Conference on Dependable Systems and Networks (DSN 2014), pp. 515–526, June 2014
8. Sezer, S., Scott-Hayward, S., Chouhan, P., Fraser, B., Lake, D., Finnegan, J., Viljoen, N., Miller, M., Rao, N.: Are we ready for SDN? implementation challenges for software-defined networks. IEEE Commun. Mag. **51**(7), 36–43 (2013)
9. Drutskoy, D., Keller, E., Rexford, J.: Scalable network virtualization in software-defined networks. IEEE Internet Comput. **17**(2), 20–27 (2013)
10. Vaghani, R., Lung, C.H.: A comparison of data forwarding schemes for network resiliency in software defined networking. Procedia Comput. Sci. **34**, 680–685 (2014)
11. Kuklinski, S.S., Chemouil, P.: Network management challenges in software-defined networks. IEICE Trans. Commun. **E97–B**(1), 2–9 (2014)
12. Li, H., Li, P., Guo, S., Nayak, A.: Byzantine-resilient secure software-defined networks with multiple controllers in cloud. IEEE Trans. Cloud Comput. **2**(4), 436–447 (2014)
13. van Adrichem, N.L., van Asten, B.J., Kuipers, F.A.: Fast recovery in software-defined networks. 2014 Third EuropeanWorkshop on Software Defined Networks, pp. 61–66. IEEE, September 2014
14. Yao, G., Bi, J., Guo, L.: On the cascading failures of multi-controllers in Software Defined Networks. In: 2013 21st IEEE International Conference on Network Protocols (ICNP), pp. 1–2. IEEE, October 2013
15. Gelberger, A., Yemini, N., Giladi, R.: Performance analysis of software-defined networking (SDN). In: 2013 IEEE 21st International Symposium on Modelling, Analysis and Simulation of Computer and Telecommunication Systems, pp. 389–393. IEEE, August 2013
16. Longo, F., Distefano, S., Bruneo, D., Scarpa, M.: Dependability modeling of software defined networking. Comput. Netw. **83**, 280–296 (2015)
17. Shin, S., Porras, P., Yegneswaran, V., Fong, M., Gu, G., Tyson, M.: FRESCO: Modular composable security services for software-defined networks. In: Proceedings of the 20th Annual Network and Distributed System Security Symposium (NDSS 2013), February 2013
18. Hong, S., Xu, L., Wang, H., Gu, G.: Poisoning network visibility in software-defined networks: new attacks and countermeasures. In: Proceedings of 2015 Annual Network and Distributed System Security Symposium (NDSS 2015), February 2015
19. Dhawan, M., Poddar, R., Mahajan, K., Mann, V.: SPHINX: detecting security attacks in software-defined networks. In: 22nd Annual Network and Distributed System Security Symposium, NDSS 2015, San Diego, California, USA, 8–11 February 2014 (2015)

20. Ambrosin, M., Conti, M., Gaspari, F.D., Poovendran, R.: LineSwitch: Efficiently Managing Switch Flow in Software-Defined Networking while Effectively Tackling DoS Attacks. CoRR abs/1502.02234 (2015)
21. Porras, P., Cheung, S., Fong, M., Skinner, K., Yegneswaran, V.: Securing the software-defined network control layer. In: Proceedings of the 2015 Network and Distributed System Security Symposium (NDSS), February 2015

# Single Anchor Node Based Localization in Mobile Underwater Wireless Sensor Networks

Anjana P. Das[1,2](✉) and Sabu M. Thampi[3]

[1] College of Engineering, Trivandrum 695016, India
anjanapdas@gmail.com
[2] LBS Centre for Science and Technology, Trivandrum 695001, India
[3] Indian Institute of Information Technology and Management-Kerala,
Trivandrum 695581, India
smthampi@ieee.org

**Abstract.** Underwater Sensor Networks (UWSN) provide a promising solution for aquatic applications. Localization in Mobile Underwater Sensor Networks is very challenging because of the harsh environmental characteristics and limitations of radio communication. Minimization of energy utilization is another critical issue in UWSN domain. Hence, networking protocols with least communication overhead are desirable. In this paper, we propose a single anchor node based localization scheme to minimize communication packets required for location estimation. A sensor node estimates its location using Time of Arrival and Angle of Arrival measurements. Location of mobile anchor nodes is updated periodically by adopting the mobility pattern of particles in ocean waves. We analyzed the performance of the scheme with real geographic coordinates of different locations in the Arabian ocean collected using Google Earth. Experimental results showed that the proposed method provided better performance for short range sensor nodes.

**Keywords:** Underwater sensor networks · Localization · Time of arrival · Angle of arrival · Equirectangular projection

## 1 Introduction

Underwater Sensor Networks(UWSN) have applications in various fields such as offshore surveillance, natural hazard detection, pollution monitoring, oceanographic data collection, oil field detection and so on. In mobile UWSN, sensor nodes can freely move with respect to the water wave motion in the deployed environment. Location tracking of a sensor node is one of the challenging issues because of the limitation of radio signaling and Global Positioning System(GPS) services in underwater environment. Sensed data with the exact location is highly desirable for correct interpretation of the environmental condition.

UWSNs are highly energy constraint since sensor nodes work on battery. Recharging or replacing of battery after deployment is very hard in the underwater domain [1,2]. Moreover, in mobile UWSN, the mobility pattern of a sensor

© Springer International Publishing Switzerland 2015
G. Wang et al. (Eds.): ICA3PP 2015 Workshops, LNCS 9532, pp. 757–770, 2015.
DOI: 10.1007/978-3-319-27161-3_69

node is hard to predict and model. The localization techniques for UWSN are categorized into two: *range based* and *range free* [6]. Range free provides course position estimates with hop count or continuity measures. Range based schemes require distance or angle measurement as input parameters to estimate the location of a sensor node and offer more accuracy than range free techniques. High localization accuracy is essential for applications such as target tracking. Most of the range based position tracking systems follow trilateration, triangulation and multilateration based localization schemes [4, 9, 12, 16]. In trilateration and multilateration techniques, the position of a sensor node is estimated with the help of Time of Arrival(TOA) or Angle of Arrival(AOA) measurement from three or more anchor nodes. In triangulation technique, the location of a sensor node is estimated by AOA measures from three anchor nodes. In all these cases, a sensor node receives and processes at least three packets from three anchor nodes for its location estimation. In the case of dense, large UWSNs, these type of location tracking systems generate high packet reception rate, which result in high energy consumption. Even though these methods provide better localization accuracy, the high communication overhead severely affects the network lifetime. Moreover, localization time plays an important role in time critical applications. Localization time is the time required for a sensor node to estimate its location. It is the summation of the packet transferring time, the time required for location computation and delay. As sensor nodes are mobile in UWSN domain, the estimated location of a sensor node would be different from the actual value if the localization procedure requires too long time. This high localization time significantly affects localization accuracy. As localization time has a linear variation with packet transfer rate, localization time increases with the number of supporting anchor nodes. Overall, communication overhead and computational complexity of localization system should be minimized for guaranteeing accurate location tracking and extended network lifetime.

In this paper, we proposed a localization scheme with single anchor node support (SAS). Location estimation of a sensor node requires only a single packet from an anchor node. TOA and AOA measurements are considered as input parameters. The location is estimated by projecting the geographical coordinates into a Cartesian plane using Equirectangular approximation. The network is enabled with mobile nodes by mapping the mobility pattern of particles in ocean waves. We simulated and tested the scheme with real geographic coordinate data of different locations in the Arabian ocean collected using Google Earth. Experimental results showed that SAS provided better performance for short range sensor nodes.

The rest of this paper is structured as follows. Section 2 summarizes the related works. Section 3 discusses the proposed localization scheme. Section 4 describes the experimental setup and results. Section 5 concludes the paper.

## 2   Related Work

As range free techniques provide course position estimates, we focus on range based schemes. Most localization techniques for Mobile UWSN work with the

**Table 1.** Range based mobile localization schemes

| Range based localization schemes | Number of supporting anchor nodes | Mechanism |
|---|---|---|
| Motion aware self localization [10] | No anchors | A node collects distance estimate between itself and neighbours |
| Collaborative localization [9] | More than one | Location of the profiler gives the prediction of future location of followers |
| Dive and Rise localization [4] | More than one | Bounding box and triangulation technique |
| Multi-stage localization [3] | 3 | Requires three non-coplanar anchor nodes |
| MobiL [12] | 3 | Trilateration, sensors predict its mobility pattern by observing neighbors |
| Multihops fitting approach [8] | 3 | Trilateration |
| SLMP [16] | More than one | Lateration |

support of anchor nodes. To improve the accuracy of localization procedure, the majority of schemes require multiple anchor support. A brief summary of localization methods proposed for mobile UWSN is included in Table 1. In [9], Erol et al. addressed a localization scheme with the aid of dive and rose underwater vehicles. In [10], Mirza et al. introduced a motion aware self-localization for UWSN, which is free from anchor nodes, but requires frequent messaging for distance estimation. Their extended work, collaborative localization [4] requires more than one anchor support. Erol et al. [3] introduced a multistage localization, in which location is estimated with the help of three non coplanar anchor nodes. And more, localization procedure creates high communication overhead in the network. Liu et al. [8] proposed a multihop fitting approach for node localization which follows trilateration. Ojha and Misra [12] introduced a trilateration based technique, in which sensors predict its mobility pattern by observing neighboring nodes. In [16], Zhou et al. addressed a scalable localization scheme with mobility prediction, which leads to efficient localization in large scale UWSN, but requires multiple anchor support. One solution for minimizing the communication overhead in UWSN is following a localization technique with least number of anchor support.

## 3  Proposed Localization Scheme

The network architecture of the proposed system consists of two types of network elements: *an anchor node* and *sensor nodes*. Anchor node(AN) is the gateway node floating on the water surface. It is attached to a GPS receiver and has acoustic and radio frequency transceivers. Sensor nodes(SN) are mobile sensors randomly deployed in underwater environment. AN is time synchronized with all sensor nodes. There is an underlying assumption that each SN is attached to a directional antenna to measure AOA. All SNs and AN are equipped with depth sensors. The network model of proposed UWSN is shown in Fig. 1.

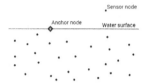

**Fig. 1.** UWSN model

AN periodically broadcasts its location information to the network. Once a sensor node senses a relevant environmental data, it accepts the packet transmitted by the AN. The received packet contains information about the location of anchor and time of transmission. Hence, the data available for the node of interest are:

– AN geographic coordinates $(\lambda_{AN}, \phi_{AN})$
– Time of transmission $(T_{Tr})$
– AOA $(\theta)$
– Depth measurement $(\delta)$
– Time of arrival $(T_{Arr})$

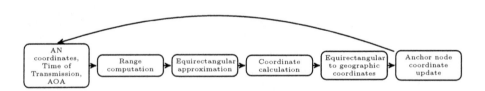

**Fig. 2.** SAS localization scheme

Figure 2 shows the data flow diagram of SAS localization scheme. The latitude $\lambda_{AN}$ and longitude $\phi_{AN}$, of anchor node is mapped to a Cartesian plane using Equirectangular projection. The coordinates of the sensor node are calculated using geometrical principles. In the next step, the Cartesian coordinates are transformed back to spherical coordinates. Periodically, the location of SN is updated with the mobility pattern of particles in an ocean wave until the data aggregation procedure ends. After a particular data aggregation process ends, the sensor node resets and enters in sleep mode. Hence, the localization procedure in SAS is accomplished in five steps: *range computation, transformation from Geographic coordinates to Cartesian coordinates, coordinate computation, transformation from Cartesian coordinates to Geographic coordinates* and *anchor node position update.*

### 3.1 Range Computation

Distance between the SN and AN is calculated using TOA measurement based on the assumption that both AN and SN are time synchronized. Let $T_{Arr}$ indicates time of arrival, $T_{Tr}$ denotes time of transmission and $S_{sound}$ denotes sound wave speed. The speed of sound signal in sea water depends on many factors such as water quality, pressure, temperature, and salinity. For a general noise free case, the speed of the sound wave is 1500m/s [1]. Range, $d_{computed}$ is calculated using Eq. (1).

$$d_{computed} = (T_{Arr} - T_{Tr}) \times S_{sound} \tag{1}$$

### 3.2 Transformation from Geographic Coordinates to Cartesian Coordinates

Spherical coordinates are projected into a two-dimensional Cartesian coordinate plane. After the critical review on various cylindrical projection techniques, Equirectangular transformation method [7] was chosen for projecting geographic coordinates into the Cartesian plane because of its computational efficiency. Let the geographic coordinates of Anchor node(AN)in earth surface be $(\lambda_{AN}, \phi_{AN})$, and then the corresponding Cartesian coordinates $(X_{AN}, Y_{AN})$ is computed using Eqs. (2) and (3).

$$X_{AN} = \lambda_{AN} \times cos(s) \tag{2}$$

$$Y_{AN} = \phi_{AN} \tag{3}$$

where $s =$ standard parallels (North and south of the equator where the scale of projection is true) and, $\lambda_{AN}$ and $\phi_{AN}$ are longitude and latitude respectively. The distance between AN and SN is transformed using Eq. (4).

$$d = d_{computed} \times cos(s) \tag{4}$$

### 3.3 Coordinate Computation

Projected geographic coordinates of AN are graphically visualized in Fig. 3. Assume that, SN is located at the origin of a Cartesian coordinate system. AN may be in any of the four quadrants. Suppose, AN is at the first quadrant. In Fig. 3, point B $(X_{AN}, Y_{AN})$ indicates the anchor node and A is the sensor node. Let the unknown coordinates of A be $(X_{SN}, Y_{SN})$. BE is the line normal to the x-axis from B $(X_{AN}, Y_{AN})$. The AOA measurement $\theta$, is projected as the angle between lines BA and AE. Transformed distance between SN and AN is d. The slope of the line joining points B$(X_{AN}, Y_{AN})$ and A$(X_{SN}, Y_{SN})$, m is given in Eq. (5).

$$m = tan(\theta) = \frac{Y_{AN} - Y_{SN}}{X_{AN} - X_{SN}} \tag{5}$$

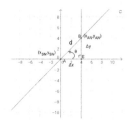

**Fig. 3.** Visualization of SN and AN in cartesian plane

Euclidean distance, D between $B(X_{AN}, Y_{AN})$ and $A(X_{SN}, Y_{SN})$ is

$$D = \sqrt{(X_{AN} - X_{SN})^2 + (Y_{AN} - Y_{SN})^2} \tag{6}$$

From Eqs. (5) and (6), the coordinates of SN are obtained as follows:

$$X_{SN} = X_{AN} - D \times cos(\theta) \tag{7}$$

$$Y_{SN} = Y_{AN} - D \times sin(\theta) \tag{8}$$

### 3.4  Transformation from Equirectangular to Geographic Coordinates

The computed Cartesian coordinates of SN is transformed back to the spherical coordinate system using Eqs. (9) and (10).

$$\lambda_{SN} = \frac{X_{SN}}{cos(s)} \tag{9}$$

$$\phi_{SN} = Y_{SN} \tag{10}$$

where $\lambda_{SN}$ and $\phi_{SN}$ are latitude and longitude of the sensor node in the geographical coordinate system.

### 3.5  Anchor Position Update

Since, UWSN domain is mobile, both sensor nodes and anchor is free to move along with the water current. These two types of nodes have mobility pattern of particles in an ocean wave. Movement of particles along with water wave depends on factors such as depth, wind speed, and activities of underwater animals and vehicles. Wave speed or celerity considerably varies with respect to depth. In deep water environment, water wave could not interfere with ocean bottom and hence waves are generated only because of wind and other turbulences. Particles in deep water wave follow a circular orbital motion as shown in Fig. 4(a). After half wavelength depth, the wave motion is negligible. The wave speed $V_{WAV}$, of a

**Algorithm 1.** SAS Localization algorithm

**Input**     : Anchor node coordinates($\lambda, \phi$)
              Transmission time(Tr)
              AOA meaurement(a0)
              Depth($\delta$)
**Output**  :Sensor node coordinates ($\lambda 0, \phi 0$)

1: Initialize $t_{count}$ as time counter.
2: Initialize $s$ as equirectangular transformation parameter.
3: Initialize $\lambda_{wav}$ as the wavelength of the ocean wave, $g$ as acceleration due to gravity and $S_{sound}$ as sound wave speed in underwater.
4: Compute range using Eqn(1)
5: Transform geographic coordinates into Cartesian coordinates using Eqn(2) to Eqn(4)
6: Calculate SN coordinates using Eqn(7) and Eqn(8)
7: Transform Equirectangular coordinates into geographic coordinates using Eqn(9) and Eqn(10)
8: Output the SN Latitude longitude pair ($\lambda_{SN}, \phi_{SN}$)
9: Change the indicator value of SN as AN
10: After $t_{count}$ expires update ($\lambda_{AN}, \phi_{AN}$)
11:      **If** (AN) **then**
12:          **If** (Deep water) **then**
13:              **If** ($\delta < \frac{\lambda_{wav}}{2}$) **then**
14:                  Calculate $V_{WAV}$ using Eqn(11)
15:                  Update latitude using Eqn(13) to Eqn(15)
16:              **Else** goto step 4
17:              **End if**
18:          **Else if** (Shallow water) **then**
19:              **If** $\delta < \frac{\lambda_{wav}}{20}$ **then**
20:                  Calculate $V_{WAV}$ using Eqn(12)
21:                  Update latitude using Eqn(13) to Eqn(15)
22:              **Else** goto step 4
23:              **End if**
24:          **Else** goto step 4
25:          **End if**
26:      **Else** goto step 4
27:      **End if**

typical deep ocean wave above half wavelength depth, depends on the wavelength of the water wave. $V_{WAV}$ is calculated using Eq. (11).

$$V_{WAV} = \sqrt{\frac{g\lambda_{WAV}}{2\pi}} \qquad (11)$$

where, g is the acceleration due to gravity and $\lambda_{WAV}$ is the wavelength of the water wave, which varies with the behavior of tides in the deployment domain. In the case of shallow water environment, there is negligible wave current below

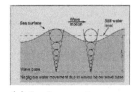
(a) In deep-water wave

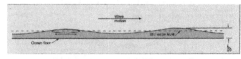
(b) In shallow-water wave

**Fig. 4.** Particle motion (picture taken from [14])

$\frac{1}{20}^{th}$ of wavelength depth. Particles follow an elliptical orbital motion, which is shown in Fig. 4(b). Speed of shallow water wave above $\frac{1}{20}^{th}$ of wavelength depth is influenced by both gravity and depth, which is calculated using Eq. (12).

$$V_{WAV} = \sqrt{g\delta} \tag{12}$$

where, g is acceleration due to gravity and $\delta$ is the water depth [14].

Once a sensor node estimates its location, it can act as an anchor node. Hence, the status of SN is changed to AN. The location of anchor node is predicted and periodically updated according to this mobility pattern. Since the particles follow circular motion, there would be negligible vertical variation in their position. Hence, we consider only horizontal displacement with respect to wave motion. The X coordinate and corresponding latitude is updated as follows:

$$x_{var} = t_{count} \times V_{wav} \tag{13}$$

$$X_{AN} = X_{AN} + x_{var} \tag{14}$$

$$\lambda_{AN} = \frac{X_{AN}}{cos(s)} \tag{15}$$

where $\lambda_{AN}$ is the updated latitude.

## 4    Experimental Results and Discussion

The performance of proposed localization technique was evaluated using MATLAB. Real geographic coordinates of different locations in the Arabian sea were collected using Google Earth for testing localization accuracy. Figure 5 shows the details of different locations chosen for testing. In Fig. 5(b), the central indicator is sensor node Z, which is located at (10.50672, 73.36807). All other indicators show anchors at different locations. Blue line is the reference line through SN. Anchors are located at $45°, 135°, 225°$, and $315°$ with the reference line and at different ranges. Table 2 lists out the geographic coordinates of anchor nodes and corresponding range from Z.

For testing the estimated location of sensor nodes, the following performance metrics were used.

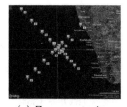

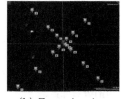

(a) Zoom out view          (b) Zoom in view

**Fig. 5.** Different locations in arabian sea collected using google earth for testing

**Table 2.** Geographic data collected using google earth

| Anchor node (AN) | AOA (Degree) | Latitude (Degree) | Longitude (Degree) | Range from Z (10.50672,73.36807) (Km) |
|---|---|---|---|---|
| H | 45 | 10.62282 | 73.4848 | 18.15 |
| I | 45 | 10.82791 | 73.70453 | 51.26 |
| J | 45 | 11.24845 | 74.14398 | 118.2 |
| K | 45 | 12.0823 | 75.03113 | 252.1 |
| L | 135 | 10.73618 | 73.14148 | 35.56 |
| M | 135 | 11.02747 | 72.82288 | 83.07 |
| N | 135 | 11.59843 | 72.25159 | 172 |
| O | 135 | 12.35073 | 71.49353 | 289.4 |
| P | 135 | 13.14368 | 70.72449 | 410.8 |
| Q | 225 | 10.34734 | 73.21838 | 24.13 |
| R | 225 | 10.15275 | 72.98767 | 57.28 |
| S | 225 | 9.589917 | 72.38342 | 148.4 |
| T | 225 | 8.971897 | 71.74622 | 246.4 |
| U | 225 | 8.418036 | 71.17493 | 334.4 |
| V | 315 | 10.42839 | 73.44635 | 12.21 |
| W | 315 | 10.26087 | 73.63312 | 39.85 |
| X | 315 | 9.774025 | 74.07806 | 112.6 |
| Y | 315 | 9.253936 | 74.60541 | 194.4 |

## 4.1 Latitude Error

Latitude error is the deviation of estimated SN's latitude values from the actual value [5]. Let $\lambda_{SN}^{R}$ and $\lambda_{SN}^{E}$ were the real and estimated latitude of sensor node respectively. Then the latitude error percentage $\lambda_{error}$, was calculated using Eq. (21).

$$\lambda_{error} = \frac{\Delta\lambda}{180} \times 100 \qquad (16)$$

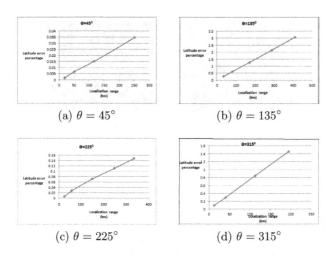

(a) $\theta = 45°$     (b) $\theta = 135°$

(c) $\theta = 225°$     (d) $\theta = 315°$

**Fig. 6.** Latitude error percentage with localization range for different AOA values

where, $\Delta\lambda = \lambda_{SN}^R - \lambda_{SN}^E$. Latitude error percentage with localization range for different AOA values were plotted (Fig. 6). Latitude error was accumulating when AN moves far away from SN. When range between SN and AN was below 50 Km, latitude error percentage was less than 0.1 for all corresponding AOA values. Accumulation of error was due to the noise factor affecting in range computation.

## 4.2   Longitude Error

Longitude error is the deviation between real and estimated SN's longitude values. Let $_{SN}^R$ and $\phi_{SN}^E$ were the real and estimated longitude of sensor node respectively. The longitude error percentage $\phi_{error}$ was calculated using Eq. (22).

$$\phi_{error} = \frac{\Delta\phi}{360} \times 100 \qquad (17)$$

where $\Delta\phi = \phi_{SN}^R - \phi_{SN}^E$. Longitude error percentage with localization range was plotted for different AOA values (Fig. 7). For localization range, up to 50 Km, estimated longitude values showed a very small deviation. Figure 9(a) shows the area graph of latitude error against longitude error of different test cases for anchor range up to 100 Km. Similarly, Fig. 9(b) shows area graph for anchor range beyond 100 Km. For anchor range up to 100 Km, the area was concentrated around the zero error value.

## 4.3   Localization Error

Localization error was calculated as the great circle distance between the real and estimated locations of sensor nodes.

Localization error=Great circle distance between$(\lambda_{SN}^R, \phi_{SN}^R)$ and $(\lambda_{SN}^E, \phi_{SN}^E)$

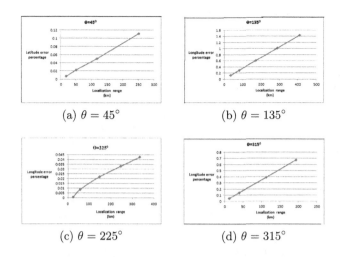

(a) $\theta = 45°$    (b) $\theta = 135°$

(c) $\theta = 225°$    (d) $\theta = 315°$

**Fig. 7.** Longitude error percentage with localization range for different AOA values

Great circle distance between two points on a sphere can be calculated using Haversine principle [15]. Hence, distance $d_{GC}$, between locations $(\lambda_{SN}^R, \phi_{SN}^R)$ and $(\lambda_{SN}^E, \phi_{SN}^E)$ was calculated using Haversine principle as follows:

$$P = sin^2(\frac{\Delta\lambda_{SN}}{2}) \tag{18}$$

$$H = P + cos(\lambda_{SN}^R) \times cos(\lambda_{SN}^E) \times sin^2(\frac{\Delta\phi_{SN}}{2}) \tag{19}$$

$$H1 = 2 \times atan2(\sqrt{H}, \sqrt{1-H}) \tag{20}$$

$$d_{GC} = R \times H1 \tag{21}$$

$$\Delta\phi_{SN} = \phi_{SN}^R - \phi_{SN}^E \tag{22}$$

where R is the radius of Earth, $\Delta\lambda_{SN} = \lambda_{SN}^R - \lambda_{SN}^E$ and $\Delta\phi_{SN} = \phi_{SN}^R - \phi_{SN}^E$. The localization error, which is the Haversine distance between real and estimated location in kilometer was plotted against localization range for different AOA values (Fig. 8). For short range anchors, localization error was very less.

### 4.4 Communication Cost

Communication cost was calculated as the number of packets required for a single sensor node to localize. Communication cost required for localization against the number of localized sensor nodes was analyzed. In Fig. 10, the communication cost for SAS was compared with Trilateration, Bilateration, and Triangulation. SAS requires only one packet from one anchor node for location estimation, whereas, in trilateration, TOA measurements from three anchor nodes are essential. Bilateration requires distance measurement and coordinate

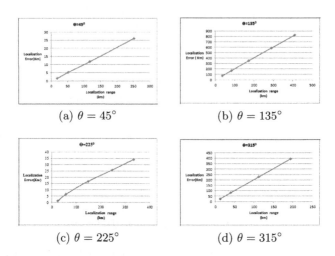

(a) $\theta = 45°$ 　　　　　　(b) $\theta = 135°$

(c) $\theta = 225°$ 　　　　　(d) $\theta = 315°$

**Fig. 8.** Localization error with localization range for different AOA values

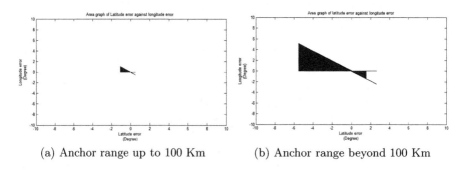

(a) Anchor range up to 100 Km 　　　(b) Anchor range beyond 100 Km

**Fig. 9.** Area graph of latitude error against longitude error of different test cases

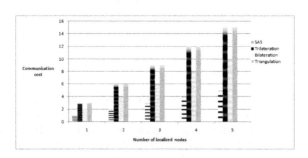

**Fig. 10.** Communication cost with number of localized nodes

information from two anchors. In the case of triangulation technique, location estimation is achieved with the help of AOA measurement from three anchor nodes [11]. The communication cost of SAS showed a lesser linear variation with respect to number of localized nodes compared with existing techniques. Hence, SAS can be applied as an energy efficient position tracking technique for medium range UWSNs.

Latitude error, longitude error, and localization error for different AOA values were analyzed for various localization ranges. Results indicated that the localization accuracy was declined with the increase in localization range. However, effect of direction of AN in localization accuracy is negligible. Since UWSN has acoustic communication channel, the maximum transmission range of the signal depends on the frequency of transmission and signal attenuation in water. Table 3 shows the bandwidth requirement of acoustic communication in underwater [13]. Bandwidth in the range of 6 to 10 KHz is practically reliable and offers transmission range from 1 to 10 Km. Very low bandwidth transmission is essential for transmission range greater than 100 Km. Hence, a medium bandwidth acoustic transmission provides maximum transmission range up to 10 Km. SAS offers good localization accuracy up to 50 km range. Hence, SAS is well appropriate for localization in small and medium range UWSNs. Moreover, SAS requires least communication cost when comparing with other existing techniques.

**Table 3.** Acoustic transmission in underwater

| Bandwidth (KHz) | Transmission range (Km) |
|---|---|
| less than one | 100 |
| 2 to 5 | 10-100 |
| 6 to 10 | 1-10 |
| 20 to 50 | 0.1-1 |
| Greater than 100 | less than 0.1 |

## 5  Conclusion and Future Work

Single anchor node based localization scheme was proposed and analyzed. It generates only minimum communication overhead in a network since a sensor node localizes itself by receiving a single packet from an anchor node. The proposed method is applicable for a UWSN domain, where both sensors and anchors are mobile. Even though all sensor nodes are required to be equipped with directional antennas to measure AOA, from the experimental results, it is clear that SAS is well suitable for small and medium area UWSNs. In future, we are planning to enhance SAS by integrating secure communication protocols.

**Acknowledgments.** The research was financially supported by Higher Education Department, Government of Kerala and the facilities are provided by College of Engineering, Trivandrum, India.

# References

1. Akyildiz, I.F., Pompili, D., Melodia, T.: Underwater acoustic sensor networks: research challenges. Ad Hoc Netw. **3**, 257–279 (2005)
2. Cui, J.H., Kong, J., Gerla, M., Zhou, S.: The challenges of building mobile underwater wireless networks for aquatic applications. IEEE Netw. **20**, 12–18 (2006)
3. Erol, M., Vieira, L.F., Caruso, A., Paparella, F., Gerla, M., Oktug, S.: Multi stage underwater sensor localization using mobile beacons. In: Second IEEE International Conference on Sensor Technologies and Applications, pp. 710–714. IEEE Press (2008)
4. Erol, M., Vieira, L.F., Gerla, M.: Localization with dive'n'rise (dnr) beacons for underwater acoustic sensor networks. In: Second ACM workshop on Underwater networks, pp. 97–100. ACM (2007)
5. Gomez, J.V., Sandnes, F.E., Fernandez, B.: Sunlight intensity based global positioning system for near-surface underwater sensors. Sensors **12**, 1930–1949 (2012)
6. Han, G., Jiang, J., Shu, L., Xu, Y., Wang, F.: Localization algorithms of underwater wireless sensor networks: a survey. Sensors **12**, 2026–2061 (2012)
7. Kennedy, M., Koop, S.: Understanding map projections. GIS by Environmental System Research Institute (1994)
8. Liu, L., Wu, J., Zhu, Z.: Multihops fitting approach for node localization in underwater wireless sensor networks. Int. J. Distrib. Sens. Netw. **2015**, 124 (2015)
9. Mirza, D., Schurgers, C.: Collaborative localization for fleets of underwater drifters. In: OCEANS, pp. 1–6. IEEE Press (2007)
10. Mirza, D., Schurgers, C.: Motion-aware self-localization for underwater networks. In: Third ACM International Workshop on Underwater Networks, pp. 51–58. ACM (2008)
11. Munoz, D., Lara, F.B., Vargas, C., Enriquez-Caldera, R.: Position Location Techniques and Applications. Academic Press, London (2009)
12. Ojha, T., Misra, S.: Mobil: A 3-dimensional localization scheme for mobile underwater sensor networks. In: IEEE National Conference on Communications, pp. 1–5. IEEE press (2013)
13. Kumar, R., Thakur, N., Thakur, V.: An overview of sonar and acoustic underwater communication. Int. J. Adv. Res. Electrical, Electronics and Instrumentation Engineering **2**, 1997–2003 (2013)
14. Thurman, H.V., Trujillo, A.P., Abel, D.C., McConnell, R.: Essentials of Oceanography. Prentice Hall, Englewood Cliffs (1999)
15. Veness, C.: Calculate distance and bearing between two latitude/longitude points using haversine formula in javascript (2015). http://www.movable-type.co.uk/scripts/latlong.html. Accessed 13 May 2015
16. Zhou, Z., Peng, Z., Cui, J.H., Shi, Z., Bagtzoglou, A.C.: Scalable localization with mobility prediction for underwater sensor networks. IEEE Trans. Mobile Comput. **10**, 335–348 (2011)

# A Novel Bug Report Extraction Approach

Tao Lin[1(✉)], Jianhua Gao[1], Xue Fu[1], and Yan Lin[2]

[1] Department of Computer Science and Technology, Shanghai Normal University,
Shanghai 200234, China
l.t@acm.org, jhgao@shnu.edu.cn, fuxuee@hotmail.com
[2] Department of Information Systems and Operations Management,
The University of Auckland, Auckland 92019, New Zealand
ylin688@aucklanduni.ac.nz

**Abstract.** There are more and more bug reports in software. Software companies and developers invest a large number of resources into the dramatic accumulation of reports. We introduce Bayes classifier into bug reports compression, which is the first effort in the literature. For this purpose, the vector space model as well as some conventional text mining values, such as tf-idf and chi-squared test, are designed to collect features for bug reports. The experiment proves that bug reports extraction by using Bayes classifier is outperformance to the method based on SVM through the evaluation of ROC and F-score.

**Keywords:** Bug report · Naïve Bayes classifier · Bug extraction · Tf-idf · Text mining

## 1 Introduction

The past decade witnessed a significant enhancement of software engineering. However, developers are increasingly bewildered by a great number of bug reports accumulated rapidly day by day. Admittedly, there are some excellent code management integrated development environments, such as Eclipse, and WingIDE. Besides some state of art tools can assist developers planning software projects, such as Microsoft Project, ProjectLibre and Openproj. On the other hand, it is obvious to note that there is little or no research on how to extract bug report to help developers as Table 1 shows.

Admittedly, there are many researchers have studied variety of documents summarization based on distinct methods. Goyal et al. investigated context-based extraction for general documents for improving traditional ways taking no consideration on contest [1]. There are a graph-based approach for documents similarity, and summarization introduced by Mills et al. [2].

As noted above, what is our motivation to research to extract bug report? Previously, there is little attention being paid on management of bug reports. Take waterfall model, one of primitive and key model in software engineering. The waterfall model divide a software entire life cycle into five main process, namely communication, planning, modeling, construction and deployment, of which construction chiefly focus on code and test. While test are concentration on unit testing, integration testing, system testing,

G. Wang et al. (Eds.): ICA3PP 2015 Workshops, LNCS 9532, pp. 771–780, 2015.
DOI: 10.1007/978-3-319-27161-3_70

and acceptance testing. As far as we are concerned, the whole software engineering pay little attention on bug reports management. There is a possible reason for maintenance being arduous is the lack of testing. To be precise, the short board on bug reports management in software engineering.

**Table 1.** Some tools to insist developers in variety of aspects in software engineering

| Aspects of software engineering | Assist tools |
| --- | --- |
| Code management | Eclipse, WingIDE |
| Planning project | Microsoft Project, ProjectLibre, Openproj |
| Bug reports extraction | ? |

Yet bug reports are increasingly stand a significant role in software engineering, in terms of assistance of software reuse, update, upgrade, etc. Bertram and Greenberg suggested that bug reports should be taken consideration on software team development [3]. Some researchers conducted investigation on which bug reports are more critical to the entire project, by this making determination to arrange the sequence of fixing bugs [4].

While there is no denying that software code has essential position in a project, it is not too much usefulness in future after the project. In contrast, bug reports can influence the future software development fundamentally, for example as reference and review. None the less, there are some side effects in modern software development on bug reports, mainly because there are too many reports to archive, even the project partici-pants can easily forget and ignore some important and major bug reports, let alone other managers not involve in the software project to arrange and trim the reports. Although some software companies demand that the developers summarize the bug reports just after fixing the bug. This is not an accept method for the following two reasons. To be admitted, most developers are good at fixing bugs, there are few developers can realize which bug reports are important in the future. The second reason is that developers do not have passion and responsibility to summary bug reports, due to company not always praising the task related to bug reports extraction.

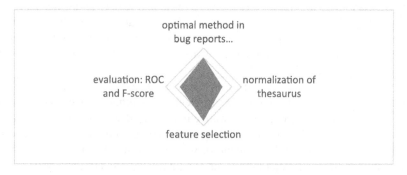

**Fig. 1.** Four contributions in our work

Therefore, it is urgent to research automatic archive methods on bug reports. It is wise to apply pattern reorganization approach to the area.

This paper makes four contribution as following Fig. 1.

According to our contributions, this paper mainly divided four sections:

In the first section, we briefly explain some core theory about naïve Bayes classier, and why this is optimal method to apply in the circumstance of bug reports.

In the second section, though we mainly focus on extractive approach, it is useful to process original bug report by abstractive approach, to be precise, we use a method of normalization of thesaurus.

In the third section, we want present the features in our classier, which is based on vector space model.

At last, we give an experiment and compute ROC curve and related evaluation values, such as precision, recall, F-score.

Though there are some work for document mining [5] and bug reports summarization based on support vector machine previously. This research maybe is the first time to extract bug reports by using Bayer classifier in the literature.

## 2    The Reason to Choose Naive Bayes Classifier

In machine learning, there are already a large number of classifiers, for instance, support vector machine and Logistic regression. In previous research, Rastkar et al. apply support vector machine methods to summary bug reports [6]. To be admitted, support vector machine method is an effective approach in many areas, such as geophysics analysis and face recognition. On the other hand, it is not a judicious and advisability way in bug report analysis for the following reasons. It is necessary to compute a great number of 'vectors' (word weight) in bug reports, by this, it is easily to depend on a tendency using a very high level vectors. Though it maybe increases the accuracy in training set, there is a marked plunge rate in test set. On the contrary to that, naïve Bayes classifier can avoid the problem of support vector machine by statistical method.

Therefore, how can we use naïve Bayes classier in bug report? Suppose the bug reports can be represented as $C_i = (C_1, C_2, C_3, \ldots, C_n)$. The attribute of bug reports, if have m attributes, can be noted as $a_i = (a_1, a_2, a_3, \ldots, a_m)$, besides the important and possessing profound historical significance bug reports are a subset of $a_i$. Therefore, the extraction of bug reports is a problem of posterior probability. By this we mean that according to Bayes formula, bug reports $a_i$ is part of $C_i$, if and only if

$$P\left(c_i | a_x\right) = p\left(c_i\right) \frac{p\left(a_x | c_i\right)}{p(a_x)} \tag{1}$$

$P(c_i)$ is the priori probability of one specific bug report?

One of significant rational to select naïve Bayes classifier is that it is simple and convenience to avoid the terminology of involving in specific software projects bug reports, in other words, naïve Bayes classifier can be generalized to more software projects.

## 3   Abstract Thesaurus

It is known to us all that one of inconvenience problems on natural language is that
English like most languages in the world being ambiguity. In this paper, for a better
result, firstly, we intend to eliminate the ambiguity by merge different thesaurus into
one. For the best consequence, we try to setup a merge Table 2.

**Table 2.**  Part of merge table to normalization of thesaurus

| Core word | Alternative word |
| --- | --- |
| Problem | Difficulty, drawback, issue |
| Fix | Tackle, arrange, solve |
| Good | Fine, ok, not bad |
| Suggestion | Proposal, proposition, submission, idea, recommendation |
| Agreement | Contract, arrangement, promise |

## 4   Bug Reports Features

One of the major task in this work is classification process, which includes word
segmentation, abstract thesaurus, feature selection, and vector space model as following
graph (Fig. 2).

In this section, we introduce vector space model firstly, then what we intend to
emphasize is feature selection, which is based on text mining methods, but maybe is the
first time use in bug reports extraction.

### 4.1   Vector Space Model

There are a large number of text mining methods in the literature, such as latent semantic
analysis, probabilistic latent semantic analysis, latent dirichlet allocation, and the correlated topic model [7]. None the less, it is vector space model suggested by Salton et al.,
one of the most popular and widely used, which is possible and optimal for preprocessing
of bug reports [8].

In vector space model, bug reports can be presented as vector. Every bug report can
be regarded as a two-valued feature vectors, as follows,

$$b = \{(t_1, w_1), (t_2, w_2), \dots, (t_n, w_n)\} \tag{2}$$

$t_i$ is the feature item, $w_i$ is the weight of corresponding $t_i$, and n is the length feature space.
In our work, the length feature space in bug reports is definite. Therefore, for the simplification of related work, the above formula can be simplified as

$$b = \{w_1, w_2, \dots, w_n\} \tag{3}$$

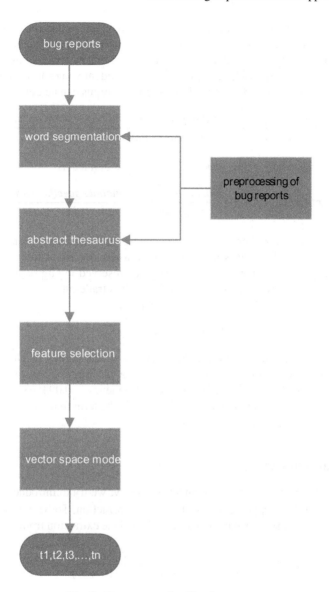

**Fig. 2.** Bug reports classification process

By this, it is convenient to get every bug report's vector space presentation by computing every items weight.

## 4.2   Term Frequency–Inverse Document Frequency

Though there are some extensive research on text feature extraction. As regards bug report, we mainly extract two main features. The first is key words, as we just put it in

Sect. 3. Then, it is obvious that the core words should be selected as features. While, we try to use some more objective methods. We compute term frequency–inverse document frequency (tf-idf), which is a value evaluate a word whether or not having key position in the total texts, and this value comprise two independent values term frequency and document frequency. Term frequency in bug reports corpus can be defined as

$$\text{term frequency} = \frac{\textit{specific word appeared in total bug reports corpus}}{\textit{total words in bug reports copus}} \tag{4}$$

Document frequency in bug reports corpus can be defined as

$$\text{document frequency} = \log \frac{\textit{number of reports include specific word}}{\textit{total number of reports in corpus}} \tag{5}$$

In our opinion, the higher document frequency, the more value in the specific bug reports. On the other hand, it is possible that the lower document frequency includes more information, in other words, it is should be preserved in bug reports extraction. Consequently, in regard of the above analysis, tf-idf is trade-off.

tf-idf is the multiple of tf and idf, in other words,

$$\text{tf} - \text{idf} = \text{tf*idf} \tag{6}$$

Therefore, for instance, there are 20458 words in the corpus in our experiment. 'Problem' appeared 73 times total. There are total 36 bug reports. And 'problem' appeared in 35 bug reports. Therefore, the term frequency is 0.003568, and document frequency is -0.02817. From above, we can compute the term frequency–inverse document frequency of 'problem' is $-1.005\,e^{-4}$.

### 4.3    Chi-Squared Test

Besides term frequency–inverse document frequency, we try to introduce chi-squared test ($\chi^2$ test) into bug reports core words features extraction. To be precise, $\chi^2$ test in debug reports show the relevance of one specific and the extraction from debug reports.

$$\chi^2\,(m, e) = \frac{T\,(AD - BC)^2}{(A + C)\,(B + D)\,(A + B)\,(C + D)} \tag{7}$$

T is the total bug reports in corpus. A is the number of extraction including specific word m. B is the number of exclude extraction including specific word m. C is the number of extraction not including specific word m. D is the number of exclude extraction not including specific word m. Obviously, $\chi^2\,(m, e) = 0$ when feature m and extraction are independent from each other. On the other hand, the larger $\chi^2\,(m, e)$, the more possibility including the word m in extraction. We use the 'problem' as example. We suppose every sentence as a dependent text. In the corpus as the experiment, there are total N = 2361 sentences in bug reports. There are 49 sentences including 'problem' (A = 59) in extraction. There are 24 sentences including 'problem' not in extraction (B = 14). There are

465 sentences in extraction, in which there are C = 406 sentences not including 'problem'. D equals 1882, which means there are 1882 sentences not including 'problem' not in extraction. Therefore the 'problem' of $\chi^2$ (m, e) = 66454.31.

In bug reports, $\chi^2$ test hold attention on the relation specific words between the extractions of bug reports.

### 4.4  Information Gain

The third indicator to determine a word whether or not being selected as core words is the value of information gain, which means the specific words have how much information quality.

$$IG(t) = -\sum_{i=1}^{2} p\left(c_i\right) * log_2 p\left(c_i\right) + p(t) \sum_{i=1}^{2} p\left(c_i|t\right) * log_2 p\left(c_i|t\right) + p(\bar{t}) \sum_{i=1}^{2} p\left(c_i|\bar{t}\right) * log_2 p\left(c_i|\bar{t}\right) \tag{8}$$

Information gain can note specific words bring how much information to the bug reports extraction. The more information, the more vital to the specific words in extraction. In bug reports extraction, information gain of every words is computed, throwing the words, which is lower the specific threshold. By this we mean that it is the words above the threshold can be regarded as features.

### 4.5  Sentence Complication

The other features is sentence complication. As we investigated, the higher complication sentence include much more crucial information than simple sentences, especially some sentences in the bug report only have one to three words, therefore, sentences bearing this characteristic should be excluded from the extraction. Take coups in our experiment for example. Some sentences, like 'Good point.', 'But go ahead', and 'How does it sound?' being little message, it is eligible not in extraction.

## 5  Experiment

In this paper, we use the Sarah Rastkar et al' bug report corpus.[1] One of a good reason to use this corps is that there is an annotation for this bug reports. By this we can train a naïve Bayes classifier based on Python Textblob.[2] It is the convention that we need to compute true positive rate and false positive rate to plot receiver operator characteristic curve, ROC and compute the Area-under-the-ROC curve, AUC.

---

[1] www.cs.ubc.ca/cs-research/software-practices-lab/projects/summarizing-software-artifacts, verified 2015/09/04.

[2] http://textblob.readthedocs.org/en/dev/, verified 2015/09/04.

## 6   Receiver Operator Characteristic Curve

First, we need to compute true positive rate.

$$\text{true positive rate} = \frac{bug\ sentences\ in\ classifier\ from\ annotation}{total\ sentences\ in\ annotation} \tag{9}$$

Then, we have to calculate false positive rate.

$$\text{false positive rate} = \frac{bug\ sentences\ in\ classifier\ not\ from\ annotation}{total\ sentences\ in\ bug\ report\ not\ in\ annotation} \tag{10}$$

At last, we can plot the ROC as shown in Fig. 3, and compute AUC.

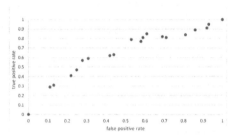

**Fig. 3.** ROC for Bayes classifiers

According to ROC, Area-under-the-ROC curve is 0.711, which is competitive to support vector machine, while Bayes classifier is much more less dimensionality

### 6.1   F-Score

We further analyses the effectiveness of our Bayer classifier by compute some standard value, namely, precision, recall, and F-score.

$$\text{precision} = \frac{bug\ sentences\ in\ classifier\ from\ annotation}{total\ senctences\ in\ classifier} = 0.61$$

$$\text{recall} = \frac{bug\ sentences\ in\ classifier\ from\ annotation}{total\ sentences\ in\ annotation} = 0.33$$

In fact, the value of recall equals true positive rate.

Because we cannot guarantee the two value both high, so it is common to use F-score to determine the quality of classifiers.

$$\text{F} - \text{score} = 2 * \frac{precision * recall}{precision + recall} = 0.43$$

There are some problem hard to solve to increase F-score value, for the inherent factors of natural language, such as the idea of modification, revocation. For example, one of developers in corpus said: "Once I started messing around with what is ticked, the problem went away." But later, he made supplementary: "Now I am also unable to reproduce it." These two examples are typical contradiction presentation in natural language. However, neither support vector machine classifier nor naïve Bayes classifier can make wise and right decision on this situation. As far as we are concerned, on the one hand, it is a necessity to conduct much more research on classifier. On the other hand, it is requisite that establish some essential standard in bug reports on the condition that not to confine developers creative idea and effective team cooperation.

## 7 Summary

Developers need excellent bug reports to enhance software development. However, there is little and no research in this area until now, except some complicated methods using support vector machine.

In this paper, may be initiated, we present a simple, but effective Bayes classifier, which is competitive to support vector machine classifier. One of main threats in this research is the corpus which we selected as experiment. To be precise, the corpus is not large enough, the annotation in the corpus is subjective, rather than objective. In other words, it is not easy to compare any bug reports classifier whether or not effectiveness in an objective standard. In the future work, it is one of our main target to setup a relative large enough software bug reports corpus. In addition, the bug reports in the corpus coming from Eclipse Platform, Gnome, Mozilla and KDE, which all are part of open-source software projects. By this we mean that we wonder how our classifier's effectiveness in commercial environment. However, this defect scarcely to solve straightforward, for almost all commercial software bug reports are confidential.

There are two main areas which need further research. The first is that we intend to design an automatic feature abstract classifier to eliminate thesaurus specifically for bug reports. Besides, there is possible more advantages if combining various classifiers to extract the bug reports, for instance, Bayes classifier and Decision Tree combination.

**Acknowledgments.** This work was supported by the National Science Foundation of China, No. 61073163, and Enterprise Innovation Special Fund of Shanghai Municipal Commisiion of Economy and Informatization, China, No. CXY-2013-88.

## References

1. Goyal, P., Behera, L., McGinnity, T.M.: A context-based word indexing model for document summarization. IEEE Trans. Knowl. Data Eng. **25**, 1693 (2013)
2. Mills, M.T., Bourbakis, N.G.: Graph-based methods for natural language processing and understanding—a survey and analysis. IEEE Trans. Syst. Man, Cybern. Syst. **44**, 59 (2014)
3. Bertram, D., Greenberg A.V.S.: Communication, collaboration, and bugs: the social nature of issue tracking in small, collocated teams. In: Proceedings of the ACM Conference on Computer Supported Cooperative Work (CSCW 2010), vol. 291 (2010)

4. Alenezi, M., Banitaan, S.: Bug reports prioritization: which features and classifier to use? In: 12th International Conference on Machine Learning and Applications (ICMLA), vol. 2, p. 112, Miami, FL (2013)
5. Kastner, C., Dreiling, A., Ostermann, K.: Variability mining: consistent semi-automatic detection of product-line features. IEEE Transactions on Software Engineering **40**, 67 (2014)
6. Rastkar S., Murphy G.C., Murray G.: Automatic Summarization of Bug Reports. IEEE Transactions on Software Engineering. 40. 366 (2014)
7. Sangno, L., Baker, J., Song, J., Wetherbe, J.C.: An empirical comparison of four text mining methods. In: 43rd Hawaii International Conference on System Sciences (HICSS), vol. 1, Honolulu, HI (2010)
8. Salton, G., Wong, A., Yang, C.S.: A vector space model for automatic indexing. Commun. ACM **18**, 613–614 (1975)

# ABR-Tree: An Efficient Distributed Multidimensional Indexing Approach for Massive Data

Xin Zhou[1], Hui Li[2(✉)], Xiao Zhang[1], Shan Wang[1], Yanyu Ma[3], Keyan Liu[3], Ming Zhu[4], and Menglin Huang[4]

[1] School of Infomation, Renmin University of China, Beijing 100872, China
{zhouxin,zhangxiao,swang}@ruc.edu.cn
[2] College of Computer Science and Technology, Guizhou University, Guiyang 550025, China
cse.HuiLi@gzu.edu.cn
[3] Nokia Solutions and Networks, Beijing 100016, China
{yanyu.ma,keyan.liu}@nsn.com
[4] National Astronomical Observatories, Chinese Academy of Sciences, Beijing 100012, China
{mz,huangmenglin}@nao.cas.cn

**Abstract.** In the big data era, there many application scenarios urgently need efficient distributed multidimensional indexing approach to accelerate the data analytics. To address this issue, in this paper, we propose ABR-Tree, a multidimensional distributed indexing approach. ABR-Tree consist of two components, the global append-efficient B + -Tree, and the local R*-Tree. Both of them are layered over the cloud database as the index and data store, which not only make ABR-Tree is easy to implement and inherently become a distributed cloud index, but also enable ABR-Tree can sustain high throughput workload and large data volumes, meanwhile, ensuring fault-tolerance, and high availability. We conducted extensive experiments over 1 TB real data set to evaluate its efficiency of processing multidimensional range queries, the results show that it is significantly fast than the existing representative distributed multidimensional cloud index method.

**Keywords:** Multidimensional index · Cloud index · Distributed index · HBase · Performance measurement · Massive data

## 1 Introduction

The need to store and manipulate large voluminous multidimensional data sets has emerged in many different application domains, such as geographic information system (GIS), mobile data management, computer vision, CAD/CAM and etc. Data in these applications are usually formulated as geometries that represent objects in two, three, or high dimensional spaces. These applications pose stringent requirements with respect to the storage and query operations that need to be supported. With the rapid data increasing in such applications, traditional data management tools have been insufficient for these multidimensional data processing and retrieval demands, the following location

© Springer International Publishing Switzerland 2015
G. Wang et al. (Eds.): ICA3PP 2015 Workshops, LNCS 9532, pp. 781–790, 2015.
DOI: 10.1007/978-3-319-27161-3_71

based services (LBS) showed that scalability becoming a crucial requirement which urgently needed by applications involved multidimensional data.

**Application:** Location based advertisements and coupon distribution. Consider a restaurant chain, such as McDonalds, running a promotional discount for the next hour to advertise a new snack and wants to disseminate coupons to attract customers who are currently near any of their restaurants spread throughout the country. An LBS provider issues multidimensional range queries to determine all users within 5 miles from any restaurant in the chain and delivers a coupon to their respecting devices. Another approach to run a similar campaign with a limited budget is to limit the coupons to only the 100 users nearest to a restaurant location. In this case, the LBS provider issues nearest neighbors queries to determine the users. In either case, considering a countrywide (or worldwide) presence of this restaurant chain, the amount of data analyzed by such queries is huge.

To solve the problems raised in application scenarios like aforementioned case, cloud computing and large scale data analytics technology is combined to solve these problems. Currently, most of those techniques are based on Distributed File Systems or Key-Value store system. In such system, data in storage systems are organized in the form of key-value pairs. Therefore, current large data storage systems, e.g., HBase, often only support key based search. When a query comes, result data are retrieved from DFS in accordance with contained keywords. Although many famous cloud systems use this information storage pattern, such as Google's GFS [1] and Hadoop's HDFS [2], they only provide services of key based queries for users. Therefore, users can only access information through "point query" which matches records to satisfy the verbal and/or numerical values, it's still far from enough to meet the requirement of scalable multidimensional data retrieval.

In order to provide scalable multidimensional query processing capability to users, researchers have proposed several techniques, such as MD-HBase [3], RT-CAN [4], EMINC [5] and so on [6–12]. In our study, we also devise and implements a multidimensional cloud index named ABR-Tree, which composed by a global AB-Tree (Append-efficient B-Tree) and multiple local R*-Tree. Both of the global and local index structure are layered over the cloud database as the underlying store, which not only make ABR-Tree is easy to implement and inherently become a distributed cloud index, but also enable ABR-Tree can sustain high throughput workload and large data volumes, meanwhile, ensuring fault-tolerance, and high availability. In our work, we implement prototype using the popular open-source cloud data store HBase [13].

The reset of this paper is organized as follows. Section 2 briefly introduces the related work of multidimensional cloud indexing approaches. Section 3 describe the details of how we design and implement ABR-Tree. Section 4 present our experimental evaluation of ABR-Tree. Finally, we draw the conclusion in Sect. 5.

## 2    Related Work

Multidimensional indexing and query processing over cloud system is still an emerging technology and there only several approaches proposed to meet the requirements. In this section, we will briefly describe several typical approaches.

MD-HBase is a representative technique to index large-scale multidimensional data stored in cloud data store system like HBase. In the MD-HBase paper, the authors propose Quad-Tree and KD-Tree with a novel longest common prefix naming schema for multidimensional indexing over HBase system, and the new system with multidimensional indexing capability is called MD-HBase. The architecture of MD-HBase is show as Fig. 1. In MD-HBase system, KD-Tree and Quad-Tree are layered on top of the HBase Key-Value store with minimum changes to the underlying store and negligible effect on the operation of the Key-value store. By using linearization techniques such as Z-ordering to transform multidimensional information into on dimensional space, the underlying Key-value store provides the ability to sustain a high insert throughput and large data volumes, while ensuring fault-tolerance and high availability. When implement MD-HBase, there are four storage models can be applied, they are table share model, table per bucket model, hybrid model and region per bucket model. The experimental results showed that the KD-Tree using table per bucket model often has best performance in both range query and kNN query processing.

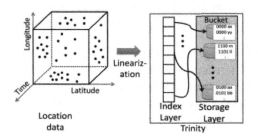

**Fig. 1.** Architecture of MD-HBase

RT-CAN is a state-of-the art distributed multidimensional indexing scheme, it target internet-scale applications with hundreds of users. RT-CAN integrates CAN-based routing protocol [15] and the R*-Tree based indexing scheme to support efficient multidimensional query processing in a Cloud system such as Amazon EC2 [14]. RT-CAN organizes storage and compute nodes into an overlay structure based on an extended CAN protocol, it is show as Fig. 2. In RT-CAN, it make a simple assumption that each compute node uses an R*-tree like global indexing structure to index the data that are locally stored. The global index in our system plays the role of an "overview" index, composed of R*-tree nodes from different servers.

RT-CAN is a typical peer-to-peer based distributed multidimensional indexing techniques (e.g., [4, 11, 12]). In this type of indexing scheme, communication overhead often tends to be excessive for routing query requests between computer nodes, which make the network latency is easy to be severely influences the performance of query processing. Furthermore, the peer-to-peer style distributed multidimensional index framework often to be hard to meet the frequent data insert, delete and update requirement due to the communication overhead incurred to synchronize the local index and global index is huge. However, in peer-to-peer system, accesses the local index in local disk is often faster than the master-slave style distributed index like EMINC [5].

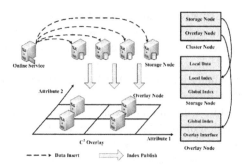

**Fig. 2.** Two types of Computer Nodes in RT-CAN

EMINC is a master-slave style distributed index which has two-layered indexes as well. It adopt R*-Tree as the global index which stored in master node, and each slave node indexes local data using KD-tree. A node cube stores the boundary information of each indexed dimension on each slave node. Each leaf node of the R*-Tree contains a node cube and one or more pointers that point to the slave nodes corresponding to its node cube.

The master-slave style distributed index architecture can locates the target computer node easily and heavily reduces communication overhead. Besides, the fault-tolerant ability of master-slave architecture is stronger than peer-to-peer system and its availability and security is better than peer-to-peer system as well. This is one of the major reason why we adopt master-slave architecture to design our ABR-Tree.

## 3    Design and Implementation of ABR-Tree

### 3.1    Overview of ABR-Tree

The proposed ABR-Tree is a multi-dimensional index schema based on master-slave distributed method. It has two levels. The top level is global index to index the ascending attributes using AB-Tree (Append-efficient B-Tree). The bottom level is local R*-Tree to index the rest attributes. ABR-Tree uses ascending attributes to partition all the data into many different intervals. Each interval will be map to one R*-Tree. In this paper, our ABR-Tree is implement by take HBase as the underlying index and data storage engine. The global AB-Tree is stored in one HBase table. Each R*-Tree also is storage in one HBase table. The implement processes of ABR-Tree are following: Use AB-Tree to index ascending attribute, such as time attribute. Partition all the data into different interval according to ascending attribute in AB-Tree. Build R*-Tree to index the rest attributes for each data in different interval.

From the implementation aspect, ABR-Tree is proposed by combine a global Append-efficient B + -Tree (AB-Tree) technique with multiple local R*-Tree index structures. In our implementation, both AB-Tree and R*-Tree index structures are implemented in HBase system by using table share model, it means either the global AB-Tree or multiple local R*-Tree index structures are represented as an HBase table.

The architecture of ABR-Tree is depicted in Fig. 3. As it shows, one of the major advantages of ABR-Tree is that it has good parallelism in nature when it answers queries: when a query processing request arrives, the global AB-Tree will first determine which local R*-Trees will involve in this query processing, then the corresponding local R*-Trees are employed to retrieval the result candidates in parallel and send them to the global query processer to merger them as the final query answers.

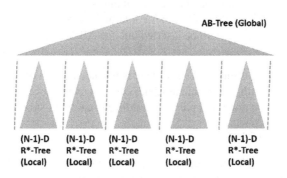

**Fig. 3.**   Architecture of ABR-Tree

## 3.2   Data Structure of AB-Tree

AB-Tree is evolved from the popular B + -Tree, it is a $d$-way tree with the aims of improving it to afford high speed of data insertion in continuous data incoming scenarios, whereas $d$ is the fanout of tree. From the data structure aspect, the AB-Tree can be divided into two separated parts, known as the left subtree and rightmost subtree. The left subtree of AB-Tree is nearly identical to conventional B + -Tree. The major differences between AB-Tree and B + -Tree are list as following:

First, there is no constraint that a node must have at least $d/2$ children as conventional B + -Tree. Second, there is no node splitting when a node gets full, and just by create a new node instead. Third, during the lifecycle of data, the index maintenance only needs to access the rightmost leaf.

Actually, in the proposed scenarios, only tuple append is occurred. At this moment, only the rightmost leaf is affected, and the corresponding pointer is updated, may be a new key-pointer pair is also added into the nodes of rightmost subtree. If the original leaf node is full, a new leaf node will be created to its right, and certain portions of key-pointer pair in the rightmost subtree of root need updates. If the worst case occurred, either a new node along the path from the root to the new leaf, or a new root has to be created.

The AB-Tree can be formally defined as follows:

(1)   As conventional B + -Tree, all internal nodes except the root have at most $d$ children, and at least two children.
(2)   The number of keys in each internal node is one less than the number of its children, and these keys partition the keys in the children to form a $d$-way search tree, this is also very similar to B + -Tree.

(3)  When the root is not a leaf, or the tree only has this root node, then the root has at most $d$ children, and at least two children.

(4)  For a tree with $n$ children ($n > 0$), and a height of $h$, each of the first $n$-1 children is the root of a subtree where it meet following constraints: all leaves in each subtree are on the same level, and all subtrees have a height of $h$-1. Meanwhile, each subtree's internal nodes have $d$-1 keys.

(5)  Toward the rightmost subtree of root node at the $n$-th child, it has a height of at least 1. When the height reaches $h$-1, and the internal nodes in each level are full, then the key of incoming data will be inserted into the AB-Tree and creates a new rightmost subtree.

Above five constraints ensure the AB-Tree is balanced for all of $n$-1 subtree of root node. When the data with monotonic attribute continuously arriving, it will grow until reaches the same height and maximal node loading as each left subtree of root node.

### 3.3  Data Insertion of AB-Tree

In the append-only application scenarios, the data insertion of AB-Tree turned into append of AB-Tree. In Figs. 4, 5, 6, and 7, we will illustrate how to insert continuous arriving data into an AB-Tree. It should be noted that, the key of the data is a monotonic attribute.

**Fig. 4.** Insert the data with key 1–7, a new root node created

In Fig. 4, four data tuples continuous arriving and their keys are 1, 2, 4, and 6. The insertion of them creates the root node of a new AB-Tree. Assume the fanout of index is 4, then the root node become full. When we insert the new data tuple with key 7 into the index, the root got split and produced two children. The newly inserted key not only becomes the only member of new root node, but also is the only entry of the rightmost subtree of root. This is a real case to show there no constraint to the number of entry in the rightmost leaf nodes.

In Fig. 5, we insert the continuous arrived data into the existing AB-Tree. The key of incoming data is ranging from 15 to 38, which make the index become full, and all the five subtrees of root are balanced in their paths.

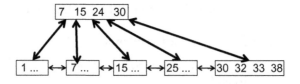

**Fig. 5.** Insert the data until key equal to 38

When we continue to insert the newly arrived data with key = 40, the root need split as in Fig. 6 and a rightmost leaf node and root node are created. In both nodes, the new key = 40 is the only member of entry. If we continue inserting the incoming keys from 42 to 45 into the index, it will turn into as shown in Fig. 7. To be noted that, when key = 45 is coming, a new rightmost leaf node and internode will be created, due to the old rightmost leaf node is full. Afterward, the key = 45 becomes the only entry of these newly created rightmost internal and leaf node, and all the two subtrees of root are balanced and have same height.

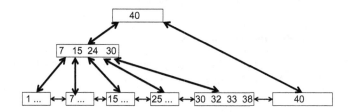

**Fig. 6.** Insert the data with key = 40 and created a new root node

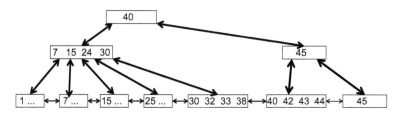

**Fig. 7.** Insert the data until key equal to 45 and created a new internal node

### 3.4   Search over ABR-Tree

The search over ABR-Tree is divide into two sub-tasks: the search over the global AB-Tree and the search over (multiple) local R*-Tree(s). The search for AB-Tree is very similar to that of B + -Tree since AB-Tree is actually a B + -Tree variant. All of the search are start from the root and end at the leaf node. Especially, the search for the newly arrived data always made through the path from the root to the rightmost leaf node by using two-way pointers which link to parent and children nodes. In ABR-Tree, the search over local R*-Tree is identical to conventional R*-Tree. Each local R*-Tree will return the local results to global query processor for final result combination. Due to the space limitation, we ignore the details of search algorithm and example illustration in this paper.

## 4   Performance Measurement

### 4.1   Experimental Setup

We evaluate our experiments in a cluster with 16 computer nodes. Each cluster node has 2 Intel E5645 2.4 GHz Xeon CPU, 48 GB main memory and 6 TB disk. All the cluster nodes are in the same rack, its network bandwidth is 1 Gbps/s. The OS of cluster nodes are RedHat 5.5. The storage layer of our multidimensional cloud index is based on HBase. We use the 1 TB Telematics real dataset from Nokia Solutions and Networks [16] for performance evaluation. The tuple of this data set is up to 2.5 billion, all of them are stored in HBase and randomly partitioned in 1030 regions. Each region is about 2.2 GB. Each record is about 450 Byte in local CSV file, and in average, it occupies 1044 Byte in HBase due to it will become key/value pairs inside HBase engine. Due to the space limitation, we only present the results of compare 3D ABR-Tree index with the representative distributed multidimensional indexing approach RT-CAN.

### 4.2   Experimental Results and Analysis

We first evaluate how the data size impact range query processing of ABR-Tree and the state-of-the-art RT-CAN in different selectivity. The results are depicted in Fig. 8.

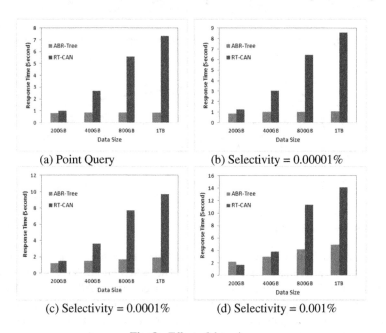

(a) Point Query                    (b) Selectivity = 0.00001%

(c) Selectivity = 0.0001%          (d) Selectivity = 0.001%

**Fig. 8.**   Effect of data size

From Fig. 8(a)–(d) we can know that: (1) ABR-Tree is superior to RT-CAN in nearly all scenarios, except in the case which illustrated in Fig. 8(d): when data size is 200 GB, and the selectivity of 3D range query is set as 0.0001 %. In this query case, about 25000 records will be returned by underlying HBase cluster as the final results, and ABR-Tree is slightly slower than RT-CAN, it consumed 2.185 s, while RT-CAN finished this query in 1.66 s. (2) When data size is equal to or larger than 400 GB, the performance of ABR-Tree can be 5 to 8 times faster than RT-CAN. This superiority is mostly benefit from ABR-Tree's parallelism during multiple local R*-Trees based query processing mechanism: the involved corresponding local R*-Trees will be employed to retrieval the result candidates in parallel and send them to the global query processer to merger them as the final query results.

In the second series of experiments in Fig. 9, we fix the data size and focus on illustrate how the selectivity impact the performance of 3D range query processing. Similar to the experimental results in Fig. 8, ABR-Tree is better than RT-CAN in nearly all the cases, except for the case we have discussed for Fig. 8.

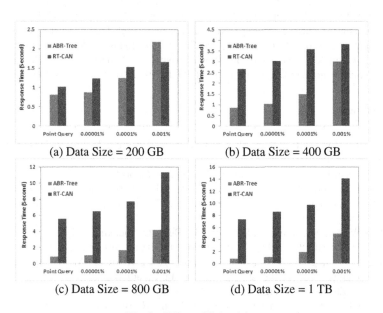

(a) Data Size = 200 GB          (b) Data Size = 400 GB

(c) Data Size = 800 GB          (d) Data Size = 1 TB

**Fig. 9.** Effect of Selectivity

From Fig. 9(a)–(d), we can clearly obtain that, during the query processing, both the overheads of ABR-Tree and RT-CAN are increased as the increase of selectivity. Furthermore, when the data size range from 800 GB to 1 TB and the selectivity is less than 0.001 %, the ABR-Tree based query processing often to be over 5 times faster than the RT-CAN based query processing. Especially, in the point query cases, the ABR-Tree based query processing can be over 8.5 times faster than RT-CAN.

## 5  Conclusions

In this paper, we developed ABR-Tree, a multidimensional cloud index approach, which combine a global AB-Tree (Append-efficient B + -Tree) with multiple local R*-Tree for efficient distributed multidimensional query processing. The design of ABR-Tree make it is easy to implement, meanwhile, has good parallelism in nature when it answers queries: the involved corresponding local R*-Trees will be employed to retrieval the result candidates in parallel and send them to the global query processer to merger them as the final query answers. Our evaluation over 1 TB real data set verified that, ABR-Tree is up to 8 times faster than the existing representative distributed multidimensional index method in nearly most scenarios.

**Acknowledgments.** This work was supported by the China Ministry of Science and Technology under the State Key Development Program for Basic Research (2012CB821800), Fund of National Natural Science Foundation of China (No. 61462012, 61562010, U1531246), Scientific Research Fund for talents recruiting of Guizhou University (No. 700246003301), Science and Technology Fund of Guizhou Province (No. J [2013]2099), High Tech. Project Fund of Guizhou Development and Reform Commission (No. [2013]2069), Industrial Research Projects of the Science and Technology Plan of Guizhou Province (No. GY[2014]3018) and The Major Applied Basic Research Program of Guizhou Province (NO. JZ20142001, NO. JZ20142001-05).

# References

1. Sanjay, G., Howard, G., Shun-Tak, L.: The Google file system. In: Proceedings of the SOSP 2003, pp. 29–43 (2003)
2. Hadoop Distributed File System. https://hadoop.apache.org/
3. Shoji, N., Sudipto, D., Divyakant, A., Amr, A.: MD-HBase: design and implementation of an elastic data infrastructure for cloud-scale location services. Distrib. Parallel Databases **31**(2), 289–319 (2013)
4. Jinbao, W., Sai, W., Hong, G., Jianzhong, L., Beng, O.: Indexing multi-dimensional data in a cloud system. In: Proceedings of the SIGMOD 2010, pp. 591–602 (2010)
5. Xiangyu, Z., Jing, A., Zhongyuan, W., Jiaheng, L., Xiaofeng, M.: An efficient multi-dimensional index for cloud data management. In: CloudDB 2009, pp. 17–24 (2009)
6. Zhou, X., Zhang, X., Wang, Y., Li, R., Wang, S.: Efficient distributed multi-dimensional index for big data management. In: Wang, J., Xiong, H., Ishikawa, Y., Xu, J., Zhou, J. (eds.) WAIM 2013. LNCS, vol. 7923, pp. 130–141. Springer, Heidelberg (2013)
7. Haojun, L., Jizhong, H., Jinyun, F.: Multi-dimensional Index on Hadoop Distributed File System. In: Proceedings of the NAS 2010, pp. 240–249 (2010)
8. Zou, Y., Liu, J., Wang, S., Zha, L., Xu, Z.: CCIndex: A complemental clustering index on distributed ordered tables for multi-dimensional range queries. In: Ding, C., Shao, Z., Zheng, R. (eds.) NPC 2010. LNCS, vol. 6289, pp. 247–261. Springer, Heidelberg (2010)
9. George, T., Dimitris, S., Timos, S.: Index-based query processing on distributed multidimensional data. GeoInformatica **17**(3), 489–519 (2013)
10. Beomseok, N., Alan, S.: Analyzing design choices for distributed multidimensional indexing. J. Supercomputing **59**(3), 1552–1576 (2012)
11. Andreas, P., Dimitrios, K.: A-Tree: distributed indexing of multidimensional data for cloud computing environments. In: Proceedings of the CloudCom 2011, pp. 407–414 (2011)
12. Xinfa, W., Kaoru, S.: DHR-Trees: A distributed multidimensional indexing structure for P2P systems. SCPE **8**(3), 291–300 (2007)
13. Apache HBase. http://hbase.apache.org/
14. Amazon Elastic Compute Cloud (Amazon EC2). https://aws.amazon.com/ec2/
15. Sylvia, R., Paul, F., Mark, Handley., Richard, K., Scott, S.: A scalable content-addressable network. In: Proceedings of the SIGCOMM 2001, pp.161–172 (2001)
16. Nokia Solutions and Networks. http://www.nsn.com

# A Simple Local Search Algorithm for Minimizing Interference in Wireless Sensor Networks

Zhihai Wang and Weidong Chen[✉]

School of Computer Science, South China Normal University,
Guangzhou 510631, China
chenwd2007@hotmail.com

**Abstract.** As one of fundamental issues in energy limited wireless sensor networks, the problem of minimizing the receiver interference of a wireless sensor network has been proved to be NP-hard, and effective algorithms need to be developed for practical applications. In this paper, a simple local search algorithm is proposed to tackle the problem. Beginning with a feasible solution generated randomly or yielded by a greedy method, the algorithm attempts to improve the initial solution by removing every node with maximum interference based on two simple strategies. Experimental results show that on random instances the algorithm effectively improves the solutions yielded by an existing greedy algorithm with time slightly longer than that of the greedy algorithm.

**Keywords:** Interference minimization · Local search · Topology control · Wireless sensor networks

## 1 Introduction

In recent years, wireless sensor networks have received enormous attentions due to their great potential use in many application scenarios such as battlefield, monitoring and surveillance, medical treatment, and city construction [3]. A set of mobile nodes deployed inside a region of interest make up a wireless sensor network, where each node is equipped with a wireless radio and a power source for communications. Due to power source constraints, it is necessary to conserve energy for extending the lifetime of the wireless sensor network. Reducing interference can be used for this purpose, and can be addressed through *the topology control method* which adjusts the transmission radii of nodes while preserving the network connectivity [6]. Two types of interference models have been proposed in the literature. One is called *the sender-centric model*, where interference refers to the edge interference. This model considers the interference from the sender rather than the receiver [2]. The other is called *the receiver-centric model*, where the interference on a node is the number of other nodes whose transmission ranges covers the node [8]. It is argued that the receiver-centric model is more rational to reflect the reality than the sender-centric one. Based on different optimization objectives and various connectivity requirements, several combinatorial optimization problems for minimizing the receiver interference in wireless sensor

© Springer International Publishing Switzerland 2015
G. Wang et al. (Eds.): ICA3PP 2015 Workshops, LNCS 9532, pp. 791–799, 2015.
DOI: 10.1007/978-3-319-27161-3_72

networks have been investigated through the topology control method [1]. Among these ones, the problem of minimizing the maximum interference while maintaining connectivity, **MMIP** for short, is one of the most well-known open algorithmic problems in wireless communications. The **MMIP** for a plane case has been proven to be NP-hard [5], while its computational complexity for a line case (i.e. *the high way model*) is still in the air [7]. The **MMIP** has an unusually complicated combinatorial structure so that some intuitions cannot always work in designing heuristics for tackling it [4]. Many previous topology control algorithms for the **MMIP** are based on *the nearest neighbor method*, which prefers to greedily establish a link between a node and one of its nearest neighbors [9]. But its performance is relatively poor in some cases such as exponential node chain networks. The most recent improved version of the greedy method, called *the best neighbor method*, works better in the conducted simulation experiments [10].

In this paper, in the framework of the topology control method, we propose a simple hill climbing algorithm to solve the **MMIP** in the two-dimensional case under the receiver-central model. Our algorithm is based on the previous best neighbor method, but can improve effectively the quality of initial solutions yielded by the greedy algorithm with time slightly longer than that of the greedy algorithm.

## 2     Problem Model and Existing Greedy Methods

### 2.1     Problem Model

A wireless sensor network in a plane is denoted by a set of nodes $V = \{1, 2,..., n\}$ which have coordinates $P = ((x_1, y_1), (x_2, y_2),..., (x_n, y_n))$ and transmission radii $r = (r_1, r_2, ..., r_n)$ so that $0 \leq r_i \leq R_i$ for each node $i \in V$, where $R = (R_1, R_2, ..., R_n)$ is the given transmission radius threshold vector. For any $i, j \in V$, if the transmission radius $r_i$ of node $i$ is not shorter than the Euclidean distance $d(i, j)$ between nodes $i$ and $j$, then node $i$ can send messages to node $j$. By saying nodes $i$ and $j$ can communicate we mean $r_i \geq d(i, j)$ and $r_j \geq d(i, j)$ since we consider here the scenario where a node needs receive an acknowledgement message when it sends a message to another node. Therefore, the communications among nodes of the wireless network can be modeled as an undirected graph $G_r = \langle V, E_r \rangle$, where $(i, j) \in E_r$ iff $r_i \geq d(i, j)$ and $r_j \geq d(i, j)$.

Given a transmission radius threshold vector $R = (R_1, R_2, ..., R_n)$, we call a transmission radius vector $r = (r_1, r_2, ..., r_n)$ a *transmission radius assignment* of the node set $V$ if $r$ satisfies $0 \leq r_i \leq R_i$ for each node $i \in V$. For a transmission radius assignment $r$, the graph $G_r = \langle V, E_r \rangle$, which is obviously a sub-graph of $G_R = \langle V, E_R \rangle$, is called the induced graph by $r$. Since the connectivity of a network is required for the purpose of communications, we always assume that $G_R = \langle V, E_R \rangle$ is a connected graph for the given transmission radius threshold vector $R = (R_1, R_2, ..., R_n)$.

The concepts of interference with regard to a given transmission radius assignment $r = (r_1, r_2,..., r_n)$ are described as follows. *The interference of node $v \in V$, denoted by $I_r(v)$, is the number of other nodes whose transmission ranges cover node $v$.* That is, $I_r(v) = |\{u \in V \backslash \{v\} | r_u \geq d(u, v)\}|$. *The interference of $r$, denoted by $I_r$, is the maximum interference among all nodes in $V$.* That is, $I_r = \textbf{max} \{I_r(v) | v \in V\}$.

**The Problem of Minimizing the Maximum Interference (MMIP):** *Given an n-node set $V = \{1,2,\ldots,n\}$ in a plane with coordinates $P = ((x_1, y_1), (x_2, y_2),\ldots, (x_n, y_n))$ and interference radius thresholds $R = (R_1, R_2, \ldots, R_n)$ satisfying $G_R = \langle V,E_R \rangle$ is connected, we are asked to find a transmission radius assignment $r = (r_1,r_2,\ldots,r_n)$ with minimum interference so that the induced graph $G_r = \langle V, E_r \rangle$ is connected.*

Given an instance of the **MMIP**, a transmission radius assignment $r = (r_1,r_2,\ldots,r_n)$ is called *a feasible solution* if its induced graph $G_r = \langle V, E_r \rangle$ is connected; a feasible solution $r = (r_1,r_2,\ldots,r_n)$ is optimal if it has the minimum interference among all feasible solutions. It is well-known that computing an optimal solution to an instance of the **MMIP** is NP-hard.

## 2.2    Two Existing Greedy Algorithms

We describe below two existing greedy methods, one called the nearest neighbor method [9] and the other one called the best neighbor method [10], which are closely related to our local search algorithm in Sect. 3. The intuition behind the nearest neighbor method is that a short transmission radius of a node implies a low interference it brings to other nodes. A simple algorithm based on the method for the **MMIP** (**NNA-MMIP** for short) works as follows [9]. At the beginning, it creates two node sets: $V_1 = \{v\}$ and $V_2 = V\backslash\{v\}$, where $v$ is a randomly chosen node. Then, it finds a node $p \in V_1$ and a node $q \in V_2$ such that they are closest among all pairs in $V_1 \times V_2$, establishes link $(p, q)$ by adjusting the transmission radii of $p$ and $q$, and moves node $q$ from $V_2$ to $V_1$. This implies node $q$ is connected to set $V_1$. Repeating the above operation until set $V_1$ contains all nodes in $V$.

In some special cases, the algorithm is counter-intuitive so that it shows a worst performance. Based on this observation, the recent best neighbor method captures the intuition of algorithm **NNA-MMIP** while avoiding some pathological cases [10]. A simple algorithm based on the best neighbor method (**BNA-MMIP** for short) works in a similar way to **NNA-MMIP** but prefers to those radius choices that cause the minimum increase in the interference of the current transmission radius assignment, and a tie during the process will be broken by **NNA-MMIP**.

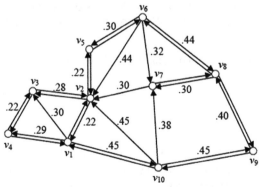

For the transmission radius assignment $r=R$, the interferences among nodes are hereinafter denoted by arcs. An arc from nodes $i$ to $j$ indicates that the transmission radius $r_i$ is not less than $d(i,j)$, the distance between nodes $i$ and $j$ labeled beside the arc. All nodes together with all bi-directed arcs form the induced graph $G_r$.

$R = (\ .45, .28, .28, .29, .30, .44, .30, .44, .45, .45\ )$

**Fig. 1.** An instance of the **MMIP**

One easily sees that each of algorithms **NNA-MMIP** and **BNA-MMIP** yields a feasible solution *r* in $O(n^2)$ time. The previous work has shown that **BNA-MMIP** has better performance with regard to solution quality than **NNA-MMIP** on random instances. An example instance is shown in Fig. 1, on which the results of these two algorithms are illustrated in Figs. 2 and 3.

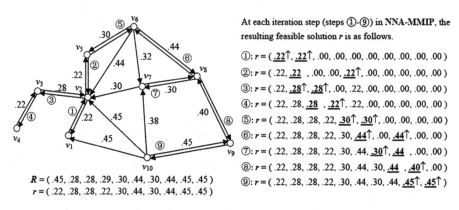

At each iteration step (steps ①-⑨) in NNA-MMIP, the resulting feasible solution *r* is as follows.

①: $r = (.\underline{22}\!\uparrow, .\underline{22}\!\uparrow, .00, .00, .00, .00, .00, .00, .00, .00)$

②: $r = (.22, .\underline{22}\ , .00, .00, .\underline{22}\!\uparrow, .00, .00, .00, .00, .00)$

③: $r = (.22, .\underline{28}\!\uparrow, .\underline{28}\!\uparrow, .00, .22, .00, .00, .00, .00, .00)$

④: $r = (.22, .28, .\underline{28}\ , .\underline{22}\!\uparrow, .22, .00, .00, .00, .00, .00)$

⑤: $r = (.22, .28, .28, .22, .\underline{30}\!\uparrow, .\underline{30}\!\uparrow, .00, .00, .00, .00)$

⑥: $r = (.22, .28, .28, .22, .30, .\underline{44}\!\uparrow, .00, .\underline{44}\!\uparrow, .00, .00)$

⑦: $r = (.22, .28, .28, .22, .30, .44, .\underline{30}\!\uparrow, .\underline{44}\ , .00, .00)$

⑧: $r = (.22, .28, .28, .22, .30, .44, .30, .\underline{44}\ , .\underline{40}\!\uparrow, .00)$

⑨: $r = (.22, .28, .28, .22, .30, .44, .30, .44, .\underline{45}\!\uparrow, .\underline{45}\!\uparrow)$

$R = (.45, .28, .28, .29, .30, .44, .30, .44, .45, .45)$
$r = (.22, .28, .28, .22, .30, .44, .30, .44, .45, .45)$

**Fig. 2.** The result of **NNA-MMIP** on the instance shown in Fig. 1, yielding interference 6

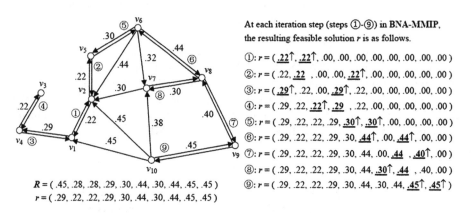

At each iteration step (steps ①-⑨) in BNA-MMIP, the resulting feasible solution *r* is as follows.

①: $r = (.\underline{22}\!\uparrow, .\underline{22}\!\uparrow, .00, .00, .00, .00, .00, .00, .00, .00)$

②: $r = (.22, .\underline{22}\ , .00, .00, .\underline{22}\!\uparrow, .00, .00, .00, .00, .00)$

③: $r = (.\underline{29}\!\uparrow, .22, .00, .\underline{29}\!\uparrow, .22, .00, .00, .00, .00, .00)$

④: $r = (.29, .22, .\underline{22}\!\uparrow, .\underline{29}\ , .22, .00, .00, .00, .00, .00)$

⑤: $r = (.29, .22, .22, .29, .\underline{30}\!\uparrow, .\underline{30}\!\uparrow, .00, .00, .00, .00)$

⑥: $r = (.29, .22, .22, .29, .30, .\underline{44}\!\uparrow, .00, .\underline{44}\!\uparrow, .00, .00)$

⑦: $r = (.29, .22, .22, .29, .30, .44, .00, .\underline{44}\ , .\underline{40}\!\uparrow, .00)$

⑧: $r = (.29, .22, .22, .29, .30, .44, .\underline{30}\!\uparrow, .\underline{44}\ , .40, .00)$

⑨: $r = (.29, .22, .22, .29, .30, .44, .30, .44, .\underline{45}\!\uparrow, .\underline{45}\!\uparrow)$

$R = (.45, .28, .28, .29, .30, .44, .30, .44, .45, .45)$
$r = (.29, .22, .22, .29, .30, .44, .30, .44, .45, .45)$

**Fig. 3.** The result of **BNA-MMIP** on the instance shown in Fig. 1, yielding interference 5

## 3    Local Search Algorithm

### 3.1    Basic Idea

Our local search algorithm begins with an initial feasible solution which is generated randomly or obtained by using a greedy algorithm. For the initial solution, the algorithm finds all nodes with maximum interference and attempts to reduce their interferences. Once the process of reducing interference is complete, an improved feasible solution is obtained, and the algorithm continues to work on the new solution. We take two strategies to reduce the interference of a node with maximum interference. We first define three node sets as follows.

$A_1(r) = \{v \in V \mid \text{node } v \text{ has the maximum interference for } r = (r_1, r_2, ..., r_n)\}$;

$A_2(r) = \{v \in V \mid \text{node } v \text{ has the second maximum interference for } r = (r_1, r_2, ..., r_n)\}$;

$B(r,v) = \{u \in V \mid \text{the interference of node } v \text{ can be decreased by reducing } r_u \text{ while maintaining the connectivity of the resulting induced graph}\}$.

For $v \in A_1(r)$, our strategies for reducing the interference of node $v$ are based on $B(r,v)$. If $B(r,v)$ is nonempty, we will apply *Strategy*1; otherwise apply *Strategy*2.

- **Case: $B(r,v) \neq \Phi$**

**Strategy1 (r, v)**

```
1. u ← a node in B(r,v) which has the maximum degree in the
induced graph after reducing its radius to the maximum value
less than d(u,v);
2. Reduce r_u to the maximum value less than d(u,v) and Update r.
```

We now turn to deal with the case of $B(r,v) = \Phi$, which implies that reducing the radius of any node $u$ that interferes node $v$ will incur a disconnected induced graph for the resulting $r$. Therefore, in order to preserve the connectivity of the induced graph, we must increase the radius of at least one node and in the meantime no new node with maximum interference is allowed to emerge for the purpose of improving the current solution. In order to facilitate the above process we will do a pretreatment that tries to decrease the interferences of some nodes with second maximum interference. The strategy is described as follows.

- **Case: $B(r,v) = \Phi$**

**Strategy2 (r, v)**

```
1. For each w∈A₂(r) Do
2.    If B(r,w)≠Φ Then
3.    { u ← a randomly chosen node in B(r,w);
4.       Reduce r_u to the maximum value less than d(u,w) and
Update r;}
5. For every node u which interferes node v Do
6. { Reduce r_u to the maximum value less than d(u,v) and obtain
all connected components G₁,...,Gₖ of the resulting induced graph
7.    If (G₁,...,Gₖ can be reconnected by BNA-MMIP and no new node
with maximum interference emerges) Then
8.       Update r and exit the loop;
9.    Else
10.      Retrieve r_u to its original value; }
```

Note that in **Strategy2** the pretreatment (Steps 1–4) sometimes is necessary because it can offer opportunities to decrease the number of nodes with maximum interference by increasing the radius of some other nodes. Figure 4 illustrates the use of **Strategy2**. The left of Fig. 4 gives the current feasible solution $r$ to an instance of the **MMIP**, where node $v_2$ has maximum interference 3 and node $v_5$ has second maximum interference 2. Applying **Strategy2**, we first do the pretreatment depicted in the middle of Fig. 4 to decrease the radius of node $v_2$ and thus reduce the interference of node $v_5$, and then increase the radius of $v_1$ and decrease the radius of node $v_4$. This results in an improved feasible solution $r$ with interference 2, shown on the right of Fig. 4.

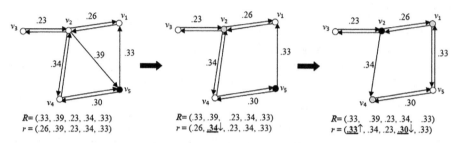

**Fig. 4.**  An illustration of applying **Strategy2**

## 3.2  Algorithm

Based on the above discussion, our local search algorithm can be described in a loop structure in which at each iteration step, it attempts to apply **Strategy1** or **Strategy2** to remove a node with maximum interference of the current feasible solution $r$. If it successes in removing all these nodes with maximum interference, it will continue this process for the resulting solution, until it fails and exits the loop.

**Alg.1. Local Search Algorithm (LSA-MMIP)**

**Input:** An $n$-node set $V=\{1,2,\ldots,n\}$ with coordinates and transmission radius thresholds $\mathbf{R}=(R_1,R_2,\ldots,R_n)$ satisfying $G_{\mathbf{R}}=\langle V, E_{\mathbf{R}}\rangle$ is connected.

**Output:** A feasible solution $\mathbf{r}=(r_1,r_2,\ldots,r_n)$ with a low interference.

1. Generate an initial feasible solution $\mathbf{r}=(r_1,r_2,\ldots,r_n)$;

2. **For** $v\in A_1(\mathbf{r})$ **Do**

3.     **If** $B(\mathbf{r},v)\neq\Phi$  **Then**

4.        Use **Strategy1**$(\mathbf{r},v)$;

5.     **Else**

6.     { Use **Strategy2**$(\mathbf{r},v)$;

7.        **If** $v\in A_1(\mathbf{r})$ **Then**

8.           Exit the loop; }

Figure 5 gives the result of **LSA-MMIP** on the instance shown in Fig. 1. On the left of Fig. 5 is the initial feasible solution $r$ yielded by **BNA-MMIP**, where node $v_2$ has maximum interference 5. Applying *Strategy2* to decrease the radius of node $v_6$ and increase the radius of $v_1$ results in an improved feasible solution $r$ with interference 4, shown on the right of Fig. 5. By contrast, the interference of the solution **NNA-MMIP** yields is 6 and the interference of the solution **BNA-MMIP** yields is 5.

**Theorem 1.** *Algorithm* **LSA-MMIP** *yields a feasible solution $r$ in $O(c \cdot I \cdot n^2)$ time for a wireless sensor network with n nodes, where c is the number of removed nodes with maximum interference, and I is the interference of the initial feasible solution.*

*Proof.* The correctness of the algorithm is clear since it always maintains a feasible solution during using *Strategy1* or *Strategy2*. Based on the loop structure, in order to obtain the time complexity, it suffices to show that removing a node with maximum interference requires time $O(I \cdot n^2)$. At each iteration step, when it uses *Strategy1* or *Strategy2* to deal with a node $v$ with maximum interference, it attempts to reduce the radius of a node which interferes node $v$ (the number of such nodes is at most $I$), and adjusts the radii of some other nodes to preserve the connectivity of the induced graph by using algorithm **BNA-MMIP**, which takes time $O(n^2)$. Since at most $I$ nodes may interfere node $v$, removing node $v$ takes time $O(I \cdot n^2)$. The proof is complete. ∎

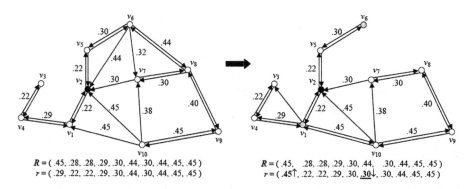

$R = (.45, .28, .28, .29, .30, .44, .30, .44, .45, .45)$
$r = (.29, .22, .22, .29, .30, .44, .30, .44, .45, .45)$

$R = (.45,\ .28, .28, .29, .30, .44,\ .30, .44, .45, .45)$
$r = (.45↑, .22, .22, .29, .30, \underline{.30↓}, .30, .44, .45, .45)$

**Fig. 5.** The result of algorithm **LSA-MMIP** on the instance shown in Fig. 1

## 4  Experiment

We evaluate below the performance of the proposed algorithm **LSA-MMIP** in terms of solution quality and running time by conducting simulation experiments to compare **LSA-MMIP** only with **BNA-MMIP** on randomly generated instances since the previous experiments have shown that **BNA-MMIP** outperforms **NNA-MMIP**.

Let $n$ be the number of nodes in an instance, $R$ be the transmission radius threshold vector (set to be the all-ones vector), and $d$ be the average degree of nodes in the induced graph $G_R = \langle V, E_R \rangle$, i.e., the edge density of graph $G_R$. Given $n$ and $d$, we randomly generate $n$ nodes in a $w \times w$ square as an instance for the pair $(n, d)$, where $d = n\pi/w^2$. These algorithms are programmed in C++ and the experiments are conducted on a PC with an intel i5 CPU of 2.5 GHz and 4 GB of RAM.

The experimental results are shown in Table 1 for those instances with node number $n = 500$. For given $n$ and $d$, $\bar{I}_i$ (Time, respectively) for every algorithm is the average of interferences (running times in milliseconds, respectively) given by the corresponding algorithm when run on 100 instances with node number $n$ and average degree $d$, and Top for every algorithm is the percent of the instances on which the corresponding algorithm gives the best interference result. Removed is the maximum number of removed nodes with maximum interference by LSA-MMIP on any instance. In algorithm LSA-MMIP, we use BNA-MMIP to generate the initial solution for every instance. From the table, one easily sees that LSA-MMIP outperforms on average BNA-MMIP with regard to solution quality on all these instances with time longer than the time of BNA-MMIP but less than Removed times that time.

**Table 1.** Experimental results of BNA-MMIP and LSA-MMIP on randomly generated instances with node number $n = 500$ and average degree $d \in \{10,20,40,60,80,100\}$

| $d$ | NBA-MMIP | | | LSA-MMIP | | | | |
|---|---|---|---|---|---|---|---|---|
| | $\bar{I}_1$ | Top | Time | $\bar{I}_2$ | Top | $(\bar{I}_1 - \bar{I}_2)/\bar{I}_1$ | Removed | Time |
| 10 | 4.98 | 28 % | 420 | 4.21 | 100 % | 12.9 % | 21 | 8713 |
| 20 | 4.96 | 25 % | 882 | 4.19 | 100 % | 13.2 % | 18 | 10401 |
| 40 | 4.91 | 27 % | 1155 | 4.17 | 100 % | 12.6 % | 15 | 10714 |
| 60 | 4.93 | 27 % | 1376 | 4.18 | 100 % | 12.8 % | 16 | 13437 |
| 80 | 4.94 | 35 % | 1389 | 4.26 | 100 % | 11.6 % | 17 | 16048 |
| 100 | 4.97 | 23 % | 1530 | 4.16 | 100 % | 16.3 % | 22 | 21356 |

## 5  Conclusion

In this paper, a simple local search algorithm has been proposed for finding a low interference connected topology for a sensor wireless network in a plane. Our algorithm begins with a feasible solution, and then improves the solution by reducing the interference of every node with maximum interference based on two simple strategies. These two strategies have good intuitions and put positive effects on reducing interference. The conducted simulation experiments have shown the local search algorithm is effective in terms of solution quality.

**Acknowledgments.** The research is supported by the National Natural Science Foundation of China (No. 61370003), and by the Scientific Research Foundation for the Returned Overseas Chinese Scholars, State Education Ministry.

# References

1. Bilò, D., Proietti, G.: On the complexity of minimizing interference in ad-hoc and sensor networks. Theoret. Comput. Sci. **402**(1), 43–55 (2008)
2. Burkhart, M., von Rickenbach, P., Wattenhofer, R., Zollinger, A.: Does topology control reduce interference? In: 5th ACM International Symposium on Mobile Ad-Hoc Networking and Computing, pp. 9–19. ACM, New York (2004)
3. Cardei, M., Wu, J.: Energy-efficient coverage problems in wireless ad-hoc sensor networks. Comput. Commun. **29**(4), 413–420 (2006)
4. Halldórsson, M.M., Tokuyama, T.: Minimizing interference of a wireless ad-hoc network in a plane. Theoret. Comput. Sci. **402**(1), 29–42 (2008)
5. Buchin, K.: Minimizing the maximum interference is hard. Arxiv: 0802.2134v1 (2008)
6. Santi, P.: Topology control in wireless ad hoc and sensor networks. ACM Comput. Surv. (CSUR) **37**(2), 164–194 (2005)
7. Tan, H., Lou, T., Wang, Y., Hua, Q.S., Lau, F.C.M.: Exact algorithms to minimize interference in wireless sensor networks. Theoret. Comput. Sci. **412**(50), 6913–6925 (2011)
8. von Rickenbach, P., Schmid, S., Wattenhofer, R., Zollinger, A.: A robust interference model for wireless ad-hoc networks. In: 19th International IEEE Parallel and Distributed Processing Symposium, pp. 239.1. IEEE CS, Washington, DC (2005)
9. von Rickenbach, P., Wattenhofer, R., Zollinger, A.: Algorithmic models of interference in wireless ad hoc and sensor networks. IEEE/ACM Trans. Netw. **17**(1), 172–185 (2009)
10. Zhang, X., Chen, W.: An effective algorithm for interference minimization in wireless sensor networks. In: Huang, D.-S., Bevilacqua, V., Premaratne, P. (eds.) ICIC 2014. LNCS, vol. 8588, pp. 572–581. Springer, Heidelberg (2014)

# Unknown Bit Stream Protocol Message Discovery with Zero Knowledge

Fengli Zhang, Junjiao Zhang$^{(\boxtimes)}$, and Hongchuan Zhou

School of Information and Software Engineering,
University of Electronic Science and Technology of China, Chengdu 610054, China
fzhang@uestc.edu.cn, {jjzhang0435,orange_3}@163.com

**Abstract.** Unknown protocol discovery has a great significance for the network management. However, discovering the unknown bit stream protocol with zero knowledge is very difficult. This paper proposes an unsupervised method which can automatically extract protocol features and discover protocols with zero knowledge. The method discovers protocols by frequent sequences and positions based on clustering and detects address fields based on similarity of the unit set in different positions. The experimental results show that the method accurately discovers unknown bit stream protocols with high precision and recall using the least number of features for the given target protocol messages such as ICMP and ARP. The detected address fields are also highly accurate.

**Keywords:** Frequent sequence · Frequent position · Address detection · Protocol discovery · Network security

## 1   Introduction

Nowadays, up to 40 % of Internet traffic belongs to the unknown applications [1], many of them ran by zombies and malicious communications which typically use proprietary protocols to intercept confidential data. The proprietary protocols usually have no public known specifications. To discover and prevent the unknown protocol is an important work to assess the security of network [2]. Zero knowledge means that we only know the protocol message composed of "0" and "1". Feature extraction [3] is an important work in the unknown protocol discovery. A lot of feature extraction technologies are mainly relying on manual operation previously. Unfortunately, as more and more zombies and malicious protocols appeared, manual works are very time consuming and difficult. Communication address is one of the most important features in protocol message. In order to improve the accuracy and effectiveness of network attacks, protocol address information plays a crucial role in the communication reconnaissance.

To address these issues, this paper proposes an unsupervised method to discovery unknown bit stream protocol with zero knowledge. The method firstly divides messages into several units and then filters out the frequent ones with Jaccard Index. Then splicing these frequent units into long frequent sequences

G. Wang et al. (Eds.): ICA3PP 2015 Workshops, LNCS 9532, pp. 800–809, 2015.
DOI: 10.1007/978-3-319-27161-3_73

and discovering frequent positions based on the statistics such as frequency. Discovering unknown bit stream protocol by these frequent sequences and positions based on clustering. The address detection algorithm adopts statistical method to find address fields based on calculating the similarity of the unit set in different positions. The experimental results show that the method is simple and effective. The rest of the paper proceeds as follows. In Sect. 2, we review related work. In Sect. 3, we provide the technical details of the methodology. In Sect. 4, we present implementation details and experimental results. Finally, we conclude the paper in Sect. 5.

## 2  Related Work

We divide our discussion of related work into two areas, namely feature extraction and protocol discovery. Extracting protocol feature indicates boundaries of protocol messages and contributes to discovering unknown protocols [4,5]. The n-gram approach has been widely used to extract feature in both text and binary protocols [6,7]. It uses a sliding window of size n bytes to break messages into equal-length sequences. It has a limitation that how to determine the suitable size of n-gram set. Zhang [8] proposed an approach to extract protocol feature, which breaks protocol payload into candidate words. It is difficult to select the appropriate numbers of candidate words. Communication address is one of the most important features of unknown protocol. Currently, there are few studies on detecting the address field in unknown protocol with zero knowledge.

The earliest research on protocol discovery is based on port number [9] managed by IANA [10]. But it is unreliable because in the unknown protocols the port number is unable to obtain with zero knowledge. Cui [11] proposed a system which reverse engineering the protocol message format from its network trace. It assumes the existence of some delimiters for dividing protocol formats into different sequences. The unknown protocols may not use delimiters and even if they use delimiters, such delimiters are unavailable to the public. Through summary and analysis of the existing technologies, the above methods cannot be used for unknown bit stream protocol discovery in the absence of prior knowledge. In this paper, we propose a method that can automatically extract protocol feature and discover protocol messages.

## 3  Protocol Discovery with Zero Knowledge

In this section, we present the discovery method of unknown bit stream protocol with zero knowledge. It consists of four components, namely data unit generator, frequent sequence and position extraction, protocol discovery and address detection. The overviews are described as follow.

### 3.1  Data Unit Generator

The content of protocol message has its own meaning according to the protocol format. However, in the process of communication, the bit stream messages are transmitted or received in the binary form of "0" and "1". It is very difficult to know the meaning of these binary sequences through observation. The research on bit stream protocol message is more complicated. We use the n-gram algorithm to break the messages into the specified units and then get the unit set $Unit = \{U_i : f_i\}$, where $U_i$ is the i-th unit and $f_i$ is the number of occurrences of the i-th unit. Jaccard Index is adopted to filter out the frequent units. We randomly divide protocol messages set into two groups $A = \{U1_i : f1_i\}$ and $B = \{U2_i : f2_i\}$. In order to adapt our method, the Jaccard Index is defined as follows (1). When the Jaccard index achieves the first maximum value, the corresponding threshold $\lambda$ is the filtering threshold. Then we can get the optimal frequent unit set $U = \{U_1, U_2, \cdots, U_m\}$ which is used to splice long frequent sequences in the next component.

Set $Unit(p_i) = \{U_1, U_2, \cdots, U_i\}$ is defined as union of the units where all of the units' position are $p_i$. The common unit set at position $p_i$ and $p_j$ is $Unit(p_i) \cap Unit(p_i) = \{U_1, U_2, \cdots, U_t, \cdots\}$. The unit $U_t$ appears in $Unit(p_i)$, also appears in $Unit(p_j)$. Set $Unit(U_i, p_i) = \{M_1, M_2, \cdots, M_n\}$ is defined as message union where unit $U_i$ appears in position $p_i$ in the messages. Similarity of the unit set in different positions is used to detect the address field. The similarity between two positions is defined as follows (2).

$$J(A, B) = \frac{\sum\limits_{i=1}^{n} f1_i * \sum\limits_{i=1}^{n} f2_i}{\sum\limits_{i=1}^{n} f1^2{}_i + \sum\limits_{i=1}^{n} f2^2{}_i - \sum\limits_{i=1}^{n} f1_i * \sum\limits_{i=1}^{n} f2_i} \tag{1}$$

$$Sim(p_i, p_j) = \frac{|Unit(p_i) \cap Unit(p_j)|}{|Unit(p_i)|} \tag{2}$$

### 3.2   Frequent Sequence and Position Extraction

Protocol keywords are subsequences in the protocol messages that can identify different messages. In this paper, the keywords combine frequent sequence and frequent positions together. The position of the sequence is the byte number from the header of the message. The keywords having the same sequence but different position are considered to be different. We splice the frequent units having adjacent position to get long frequent sequences as long as possible. Frequent sequence and position extraction is described in Algorithm 1. The threshold $Min\_pf$ and $Min\_sf$ are adopted to filter out frequent sequences set E and position set P. If the frequency of the sequence is 1 as well as its position's frequency also achieves 1, we refer to such sequence as public sequence.

### 3.3   Protocol Discovery

Each type of protocol messages follows a similar message format. This component clusters the same type of messages together based on keywords including frequent sequences and positions using k-means algorithm [12]. If the frequent sequence

**Algorithm 1.** Frequent Sequence and Position Extraction

**Input:** Message set $M = \{M_1, M_2, \cdots, M_n\}$. Frequent unit set $U = \{U_1, U_2, \cdots, U_m\}$. Threshold $Min\_pf$ and $Min\_sf$.

**Output:** Frequent Sequence set $F = \{p_i : sequence_i\}$.

**Step1:** Choose message $M_1 \in M$. Then locate the frequent units $U_i$ in this message.

**Step2:** If one unit is followed by another, splice them together to get a long sequence as long as possible and get the long sequences position and offset.

**Step3:** Choose another message $M_2 \in M$. Operate on the message just like Step 1 and Step 2. If the long sequences obtained in Step 3 have different positions with the corresponding ones in $M_2$, we divide them into several ones.

**Step4:** Repeat Step1, Step2 and Step3 until all of the messages in message set M are chose.

**Step5:** Collect all the long sequences with their position and offset. Calculate each positions frequency in the long sequences set. The position less than $Min\_pf$ should be removed. Get the frequent position set P.

**Step6:** At each position in the frequent position set, remove the sequence whose length is less than one byte in addition to the ones whose frequency is 1. According to approximate sequence matching method, merge two sub-sequences at the same position. Then remove the sequence whose frequency is less than $Min\_sf$. Get the frequent sequences set E.

**Step7:** Extracting the frequent sequences in E at each position in P. Then get $F = \{p_i : sequence_i\}$.

appears in the position corresponding to the message, the value of this position is set to 1, otherwise is 0. Then the similar messages are grouped into a cluster. This component enables our method to distinguish among messages belonging to the same protocol.

### 3.4   Address Detection

The address field format of unknown bit stream protocol is not unified and there is no characteristic. In the LAN environment, MAC address are relatively single. The MAC address may be frequent sequence. However, the address sequences are not necessarily frequent, such as IP address. It is of great difficulty to detect the address field of bit stream protocol with zero knowledge. In order to further understand the unknown protocol, we put forward an algorithm to detect address fields. The algorithm mainly includes the following steps: dividing messages into units, getting the candidate address and then getting the address set through splicing. We define pTopRate as the similarity of $Unit\,(p_i)$ and $Unit\,(p_j)$. The process of address detection is described in Algorithm 2.

## 4   Experiments and Evaluations

### 4.1   Data Set Description

In our experiments, the data comes from the DARPA (Defense Advanced Research Projects Agency) to insure the unbiased results. The data set contains different

**Algorithm 2.** The Address Detection Algorithm

---

**Input:** Message Set $M = \{M_1, M_2, \cdots, M_n\}$, pTopRate
**Output:** Address set $A = \{(p_i\, p_{i+1} \cdots, p_j\, p_{j+1} \cdots)\}$.
1: All messages in the Message Set are numbered and divided into byte units with position $P_i$
2: **for** each $M_i \in M$ **do**
3:     Calculate $Unit\,(p_i) = \{U_1, U_2, \cdots, U_r\}$, $Sum_i = Unit\,(p_i)\,.size()$
4:     Calculate $Unit\,(U_r, p_i) = \{M_1, M_2, \cdots, M_n\}$
5: **end for**
6: **for** i=0, $i < Unit\,(p_i)\,.size()$, i++ **do**
7:     **for** j=0, $j < Unit\,(p_j)\,.size()$, j++ **do**
8:         **if** $U_i$ equals $U_j$ **then**
9:             **if** $Unit\,(U_i, p_i) \cap Unit\left(U_j, p_j\right) == \Phi$ **then**
10:                 Count++; break;
11:             **end if**
12:         **end if**
13:     **end for**
14: **end for**
15: **if** $(Count/\,Sum_i \geq \text{pTopRate})\&\&(Count/\,Sum_j \geq \text{pTopRate})$ **then**
16:     $A.add(p_i, p_j)$
17: **end if**
18: **for** each $(p_i, p_j), (p_{i+1}, p_{j+1}) \in A$ **do**
19:     **if** $p_i$ isfollowedby $p_{i+1}$ and $p_j$ isfollowedby $p_{j+1}$ **then**
20:         splice $p_i$ and $p_{i+1}$, $p_j$ and $p_{j+1}$ as long as possible to get the address $A = \{(p_i\, p_{i+1} \cdots, p_j\, p_{j+1} \cdots)\}$.
21:     **end if**
22: **end for**

---

types of ARP and ICMP messages. We process the data set in the form of binary considered to be unknown. Due to the limited experimental conditions, we only conducted the experiment in bytes. However, the method can be extended to other cases.

## 4.2    Evaluation Metrics

We define two evaluation metrics to evaluate the experimental results: precision and recall. This paper also defines three sets as follows. True Positives: the set of messages X where each one message can be discovered by our method. False Positives: the set of not messages X where each one can be discovered by our method. False Negatives: the set of messages X where each one cannot be discovered by our method. Next, the following two metrics are defined to quantitatively evaluate the effectiveness of our method.

$$precision = \frac{|True Positives|}{|True Positives| + |False Positives|} \tag{3}$$

$$recall = \frac{|True Positives|}{|True Positives| + |False Negatives|} \tag{4}$$

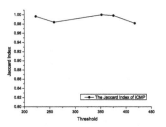 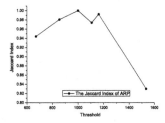

(a) The Jaccard Index of ICMP.        (b) The Jaccard Index of ARP.

**Fig. 1.** The Jaccard Index.

### 4.3    Experimental Results

In our experiment, the bit stream protocol messages are firstly broken into several units by n-gram algorithm. Then we filter out the frequent units with Jaccard Index. We first conduct an experiment in ICMP and ARP messages to discuss how to select the frequent units. We choose the most suitable length of units that a single binary byte according to the n-gram algorithm in our method. Figure 1 shows the relationship between Jaccard Index and frequency threshold. We observe that when the Jaccard index achieves the first maximum value, the threshold of frequent units $\lambda = 350$ for ICMP in Fig. 1(a) and $\lambda = 1000$ for ARP Fig. 1(b). Frequent units of ICMP messages are "00", "41", "10", "01", "45", "ac", "08", "03", "46", "7b", "33" and "38". For ARP messages, the frequent units are "08", "06", "00", "01", "04", "ac" and "10".

**Frequent Sequence and Position Extraction.** Next, the frequent units are spliced to get long frequent sequences. Taking into account the impact of frequent sequences position on the accuracy of bit stream protocol discovery, it is also of great importance to discover the frequent position set. Based on the frequent sequences and positions set, we can efficiently discover protocol messages. The threshold of frequency $Min\_pf$ is 0.5 and $Min\_sf$ is 0.1. Tables 1 and 2 present the details of ICMP and ARP protocols frequent sequences and positions. The frequent positions are in descending order by the frequency. We observe that the frequency at positions (12), (16), (20), (23) and (34) in Table 1 and (12), (28) and (38) in Table 2 all achieve 1. The sequences whose frequency achieves to 1 at these positions are public sequences. It means that the public sequences appear in each message with a fixed position and offset. These public sequences must be the keywords of protocol.

**Protocol Discovery.** Taking advantage of these frequent positions and frequent sequences in Tables 1 and 2 as identifying attributes to discover unknown bit stream protocols based on clustering. The public sequences appear in each message which cannot discover different messages. We conduct the experiment based on frequent sequences and positions whose frequency has not achieves 1.

**Table 1.** The details of ICMP protocols frequent sequence and position.

| Position | Frequency | Sequence | Position | Frequency | Sequence |
|---|---|---|---|---|---|
| (12) | 1 | 080045 | (16) | 1 | 00 |
| (20) | 1 | 0000 | (23) | 1 | 01 |
| (34) | 0.998 | 0800 | (34) | 0.998 | 0000 |
| (34) | 0.998 | 0303 | (38) | 0.978 | 00000000450000 |
| (38) | 0.978 | 000000000000000000000 0000000000000000000000 | (6) | 0.851 | 0010 |
| (0) | 0.841 | 0010 | (30) | 0.653 | ac10 |
| (54) | 0.620 | ac10 | (72) | 0.610 | 00100001000000000000 |
| (85) | 0.566 | 41414141414141414141 41414141414141414141 41414141414141410000 | (118) | 0.566 | 0001 |

**Table 2.** The details of ARP protocols frequent sequence and position.

| Position | Frequency | Sequence | Position | Frequency | Sequence |
|---|---|---|---|---|---|
| (12) | 1 | 080600010800060400 | (38) | 1 | ac10 |
| (28) | 1 | ac10 | (22) | 0.850 | 0800 |
| (22) | 0.850 | 0010 | (32) | 0.789 | 000000000000ac10 |
| (32) | 0.789 | 0010 | (6) | 0.700 | 0800 |
| (6) | 0.700 | 0010 | (0) | 0.665 | 0800 |
| (0) | 0.665 | 0010 | (0) | 0.665 | 0000 |
| (21) | 0.5 | 01 | | | |

Figures 2 and 3 show the average precision and recall of different types of messages for varying position of frequent sequences for ICMP and ARP. In Fig. 2, the frequent sequences at position (34) discover the ICMP messages with 100 % average precision and recall. They must be the keywords of ICMP messages. However, the frequent sequences at other position, such as position (0) has low average precision and recall. In Fig. 3, only just the sequence "01" at position 21 byte discovers ARP messages with 100 % average precision and recall. It is keywords of ARP messages. Figure 4 shows the plot of both precision and recall for varying frequent sequences' positions for ICMP error messages. For all of the positions, the precision is 100 % and the recall rate is more than 90 %. We can conclude that the frequent sequences at position (38), (54), (72), (85) and (118) can effectively discover error message. By the experiment, it can be seen that combining frequent sequences and position can accurately discover protocol messages using the least number of keywords with zero knowledge. Within the scope of the current research, we have not yet find the discovery method of unknown protocol based on zero knowledge. This method performs significantly faster and efficient.

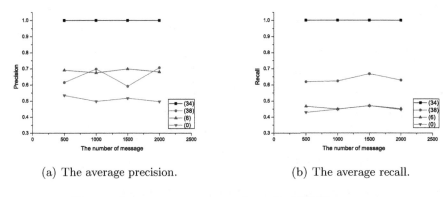

(a) The average precision.                    (b) The average recall.

**Fig. 2.** The average precision and recall of ICMP message.

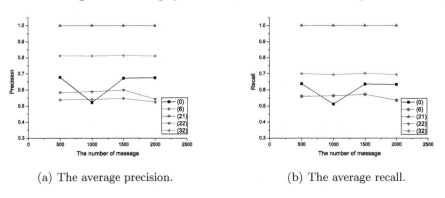

(a) The average precision.                    (b) The average recall.

**Fig. 3.** The average precision and recall of ARP message.

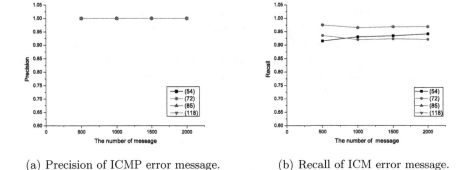

(a) Precision of ICMP error message.          (b) Recall of ICM error message.

**Fig. 4.** The Recognition Rate of ICMP error message.

**Address Detection.** The ICMP and ARP messages are adopted in the address detection experiment. We present the address result for varying values of pTo-pRate for protocol messages. In the experiment, we ranges of pTopRate $\in$ $\{0.4, 0.5\}$. In Fig. 5, when pTopRate $= 0.5$, all of the address fields are discovered

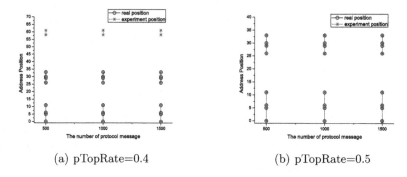

(a) pTopRate=0.4                    (b) pTopRate=0.5

**Fig. 5.** The address detection result of ICMP.

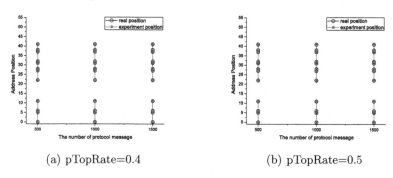

(a) pTopRate=0.4                    (b) pTopRate=0.5

**Fig. 6.** The address detection result of ARP.

correctly for ICMP. The discovered address fields are respectively from 0 to 5 byte, from 6 to 11 byte, from 26 to 29 byte and from 30 to 33 byte. Figure 6 shows all of the address positions discovered for ARP. The discovered address fields are respectively from 0 to 5 byte, from 6 to 11 byte, from 22 to 27 byte, from 28 to 31 byte, from 32 to 37 byte and from 38 to 41 byte. No matter whether the address fields are frequent or not, the proposed method can accurately detect address fields of protocol messages with zero knowledge.

## 5    Conclusions

In this paper, we propose an unsupervised method that can automatically extract unknown protocol's keywords, address fields and discover unknown bit stream protocol messages with zero knowledge. It solves the issue that the size of units set for splicing frequent sequences with Jaccard Index. The protocol's keywords extracted in our method combine frequent sequence and frequent position together which makes the unknown protocol discovery method more accurately and efficiently. The address detection algorithm adopts statistical method to find address fields based on calculating the similarity of the unit set in different positions. The verification experiments show that the results are accurately for ICMP and ARP protocol messages. It is of great significance for the work of unknown bit stream protocol discovery and address detection with zero knowledge. We are working towards extending our method to speculating the semantic relationships between the frequent sequences and positions and inferring the format of protocol messages.

**Acknowledgment.** This work is supported by National Natural Science Foundation of China (Grant No. U1230106; 61472064), Science and Technology Development Foundation of Chinese Academy of Engineering Physics (2012A0403021), Technology projects in Sichuan Province (2014GZ0109, 2015KZ002, 2015JY0178).

# References

1. I. netflow statistics. http://netflow.internet2.edu
2. Caballero, J., et al.: Dispatcher: enabling active botnet infiltration using automatic protocol reverse-engineering. In: ACM CCS (2009)
3. Merwe, J.V.D., Caceres, R., Chu, Y.H., et al.: mmdump: a tool for monitoring internet multimedia traffic. ACM SIGCOMM Comput. Commun. Rev. **30**(5), 48–59 (2005)
4. Long, W., Xin, Y., Yang Y.: An application-level signatures extracting algorithm based on offset constraint. In: International Symposium on Intelligent Information Technology Application Workshops: IITAW 2008. IEEE (2008)
5. Wang, Y., Zhang, N., Wu, Y., Su, B.: Protocol specification inference based on keywords identification. In: Motoda, H., Wu, Z., Cao, L., Zaiane, O., Yao, M., Wang, W. (eds.) ADMA 2013, Part II. LNCS, vol. 8347, pp. 443–454. Springer, Heidelberg (2013)
6. Jamdagni, A., Tan, Z., He, X., Nanda, P., Liu, R.P.: RePIDS: a multitier real-time payload-based intrusion detection system. Comput. Netw. **57**(3), 811–824 (2013)
7. Wang, Y., Zhang, Z., Yao, D.D., Qu, B., Guo, L.: Inferring protocol state machine from network traces: a probabilistic approach. In: Lopez, J., Tsudik, G. (eds.) ACNS 2011. LNCS, vol. 6715, pp. 1–18. Springer, Heidelberg (2011)
8. Zhang, Z., Zhang, Z., Lee, P.P.C., et al.: Toward unsupervised protocol feature word extraction. IEEE J. Sel. Areas Commun. **32**(10), 1894–1906 (2014)
9. Cai, X., Zhang, R., Wang, B.: Machine learning and keyword-matching integrated protocol identification. In: 3rd IEEE International Conference on Broadband Network and Multimedia Technology (IC-BNMT 2010). IEEE (2010)
10. IANA. www.iana.org/assignments/portnumbers
11. Cui, W., Kannan, J., Wang, H.J.: Discoverer: automatic protocol reverse engineering from network traces. In: SS 2007: Proceedings of 16th USENIX Security Symposium on USENIX Security Symposium (2007)
12. Macqueen, J., et al.: Some methods for classification and analysis of multivariate observations. In: Proceedings of the Fifth Berkeley Symposium on Mathematical Statistics and Probability (1967)

# Distributed Authentication in the Cloud Computing Environment

Yanzhu Liu, Zhi Li$^{(\boxtimes)}$, and Yuxia Sun

School of Computer and Communication Engineering,
University of Science and Technology, Beijing 100083, China
liuyanzhu213@163.com

**Abstract.** The cloud computing is considered as the next-generation of IT technology that can provide various elastic and scalable IT services in pay-as-you-go. This technology has been used by worldwide companies to improve their business performance. Therefore, authentication of both clients and services is a significant issue for the trust and security of the cloud computing. At present, to protect the security of the cloud, many ideas have been proposed. In this paper, we present DSA protocol concentrated on authentication of clients. It is an improved protocol based on Kerberos, which prevents password guessing attack by using dynamic session key. We also solved the problem of service availability by introducing two additional messages in the scheme.

**Keywords:** Cloud computing · Distributed authentication · Password guessing attack · Kerberos · Ticket

## 1 Introduction

With the development of Internet technology, the number of Internet users and data has increased dramatically. The existing computer systems and network resources cannot meet users' requirements. Integration and optimization of the resource have become the inevitable trend of the future development of network. Conveniently, the concept of cloud computing is proposed, the lives of people quietly entered the era of cloud [1–3]. In cloud computing, all kinds of information are within reach and resources service can be used on-demand, anywhere, at any time [4].

Cloud computing became popular in 2007, to which the first entry in the English Wikipedia from March 3, 2007 attests, which, again significantly, contained a reference to utility computing [5]. Cloud computing is a new computing model based on distributed system, parallel computing and grid computing [6]. It is a new sharing infrastructure, which provides users with data storage, and network services in a large distributed environment [7]. Based on the technology of Internet and distributed computing, by integrating computing, storage and bandwidth resources into a resource pool, cloud computing provides users services in a dynamic and on-demand way [8, 9]. This new computing model has brought a dramatic change for the IT industry.

According to IDC's report, by 2016, 40 percent of enterprises will make proof of independent security testing a precondition for using any type of cloud service. At year-end 2016, more than 50 percent of Global 1,000 companies will have stored

© Springer International Publishing Switzerland 2015
G. Wang et al. (Eds.): ICA3PP 2015 Workshops, LNCS 9532, pp. 810–818, 2015.
DOI: 10.1007/978-3-319-27161-3_74

customer-sensitive data in the public cloud [10]. Due to the huge advantage of cloud computing, majority of companies have a great enthusiasm on cloud computing services. However, one after another accidents not only cause irreparable loss for users, but also hinder the development of cloud computing industry. The first is emergence of Amazon cloud computing server that interrupts the services [11]. Soon, Google leaked the users' personal information [12]. Then, Sony PlayStation Service network was hacked, about 77 million users' personal information were stolen [13]. Right now, with more and more personal and corporate information being stored in the cloud, users may have worried about the safety of personal information. Hence, the security has become an important issue in the field of cloud computing.

To ensure the security of resources and services has become the main goal, while the core of security mechanism is the authentication. Authentication protocol can ensure a real and secure communications, prevent the identity of the participants, and also prevent illegal tampering and other malicious attacks. At present, many companies use Kerberos to authenticate users, who need to pass the Kerberos authentication for each application. However, there are some limitations in the Kerberos authentication, and the authentication security has room for improvement. In view of the potential threat of session key in the process of client and application server communication, this paper proposes an extensible authentication model DSA. By adding a nonvolatile memory to store key chain in the client and the application server, it can guarantee to avoid password guessing attack to some degree.

## 2   Related Work

Kerberos is an authentication mechanism that can be used to authenticate user in the cloud computing environment. By using Kerberos authentication protocol, a user can authenticate itself to multiple application servers with the tickets distributed by Kerberos authentication center during a certain period. Many schemes have been proposed to prevent vulnerabilities and threats in Kerberos authentication protocol. Figure 1 shows the basic Kerberos architecture.

Al-Janabi et al. [14] implemented public-key cryptography extension specifications to the traditional Kerberos standard which incorporated public-key infrastructure (PKI) into the scope of underlying systems trusted by Kerberos. In [15], a model of Kerberos Protocol Version 4 was verified to find problems with respect to the replay attack. The presence of Intruder in the system was considered and the possible replay attack between various entities was also found out. Dua et al. [16] used triple password scheme to prevent replay attack and password guessing attack. In their research, Authentication Server stored three passwords. Authentication Server sends two passwords which were encrypted with the secret key shared between Authentication server and Ticket Granting server to Ticket Granting Server. Similarly Ticket Granting Server sends one password to Application Server. Meanwhile service granting ticket was transferred to users by encrypting it with the password that TGS had just received from AS which help to prevent replay attack. In [17], the process of Kerberos authentication protocol was analyzed. The dynamic password was used to improve the encryption security during the process of interaction between the client and Kerberos key distribution center. By using Diffie-Hellman key, algorithm passwords were securely exchanged. Du et al. [18] presented to use dynamic password and one-time public key to improve the Kerberos protocol. The security of the session key and the password were considered. It made the protocol to improve the aspects of the resisting password guessing attack and replay attack. For mobile agent environment, Kandil and Atwan [19] introduced novel efficient and light security framework based on Kerberos system. By using 2-layer software that accomplishes the work of the hardware component, the framework could reduce the usual overhead resulting inside the Kerberos system.

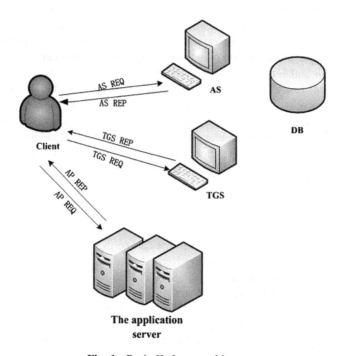

**Fig. 1.** Basic Kerberos architecture

In this paper, a formal model of DSA using a non-volatile memory is presented. The full schema of protocol dialogue is presented in next section and formal modeling of its operation will be modeled in future sections.

## 3   The Design of DSA Protocol

In this part, we propose a distributed service authentication (DSA) protocol in cloud. The protocol could realize authentication before client apply for services in the cloud.

## 3.1    System Model

The model is divided into three parts: client, application server and authentication server.

1. **The client.** The client has two main functions. Firstly, it listens the registration from client. Secondly, client can send requests to KDC, receive the feedback information and store them.
2. **The application server.** The main function of the application server is to monitor the request service from client and provide the service to client. Agent A would provide client with index of servers.
3. **The authentication server.** The authentication server has two key functions. First, it could monitor the requests of AS and TGS, meanwhile monitor the registration information from the client. Second, it could modify the information for registered client and authorize the client. The core algorithm of authentication service is AS authentication algorithm and TGS authentication algorithm.

## 3.2    The Procession of Authentication

The DSA model involves the following terms:

1. Client, can be the running processes or the ordinary users.
2. Server, application server. An entity provides service to the users.
3. TGS (Ticket Granting Server), issuing a ticket to the server. The users can show their identity by using the ticket to the application server.
4. AS (Authentication Server), an authentication server. Issue ticket to the users, by which the users can use to show their identity to TGS.
5. TGT (Ticket with Granting Ticket), client uses TGT issued by AS to prove its identity to TGS.
6. ST (Service Ticket), client use ST which is issued by TGS to prove its identity.

Now we will introduce DSA protocol from four aspects: request the ticket-granting ticket $TGT$, request the service-granting ticket $ST$, request the service index from agent and request the service from application server.

The procession of authentication of DSA protocol is shown in Fig. 2. The relevant symbols are shown in Table 1.

**Table 1.**  Key notations

| Notation | Explanation | Notation | Explanation |
|----------|-------------|----------|-------------|
| $ID_C$ | Identity of client C | $K_{C,A}$ | Key between client C and agent A |
| $T_{S1}$ | Timestamp | $AD_A$ | Network address of agent A |
| $P_C$ | Password of client C | $TGT$ | Ticket generated by AS |
| $TL_C$ | Trust level of client C | $ST$ | Ticket generated by TGS |

*(Continued)*

**Table 1.** (*Continued*)

| Notation | Explanation | Notation | Explanation |
|---|---|---|---|
| $K_{C,AS}$ | Password between client C and AS | $K_{A,TGS}$ | Session key between TGS and agent A |
| $AD_C$ | Network address of client C | $T_{S4}$ | Timestamp |
| $AD_{TGS}$ | Network address of Ticket server | $T_{S5}$ | Timestamp in $Auth_{C2}$ |
| $K_{TGS,AS}$ | Key between TGS and AS | $TGT$ | A ticket provided by AS |
| $Lifetime_1$ | Survival time of message m1 | $S_{List}$ | A service lists provided by agent A. |
| $Lifetime_3$ | Survival time of $ST$ | $T_{S6}$ | Timestamp |
| $Lifetime_2$ | Survival time of $TGT$ | $T_{S7}$ | Timestamp |
| $K_i$ | Session key between application server S and client C. | $S_c$ | The service selected by client C. |
| $T_{S2}$ | Timestamp | $SC_{List}$ | A server lists selected by client C. |
| $T_{S3}$ | The generation time of $Auth_{C1}$ | $T_{S8}$ | Timestamp |
| $Auth_{C1}$ | Client generate identification code to verify $TGT$ | $seq$ | Record the rank of message between server S and client C. |
| $K_{C,TGS}$ | Session key between TGS and client C | $R_{ES}$ | Service response from application server S. |

1. Request the ticket-granting ticket *TGT*

   ① m1: C→AS=[$ID_C$ ‖ $T_{S1}$ ‖ $Lifetime_1$];
   ② m2: AS→SH=[$ID_C$];
   ③ m3: SH→AS=[$P_C$ ‖ $AD_C$ ‖ $TL_C$];
   ④ m4: AS → C=E ($K_{C,AS}$ ‖[$Ticket_{C,TGS}$ ‖ $AD_{TGS}$ ‖ $T_{S2}$ ‖ $Lifetime_2$ ‖ $TGT$]);

   $$TGT = E\ (K_{TGS,AS}\|[Ticket_{C,TGS}\,\|\,ID_C\,\|\,AD_C\,\|\,AD_{TGS}\,\|\,T_{S2}\,\|\,Lifetime_2\,\|\,TL_C])$$

   In this part, the client C requests a ticket-granting ticket by sending its identity and password to the AS, indicating a request to use the TGS service. $K_{C,TGS}$ is the session key between client C and TGS.

2. Request the service-granting ticket *ST*

   ① m5: C→TGS=[$TGT\|Auth_{C1}$];
   ② m6: TGS→C=E ($Ticket_{C,TGS}$ ‖[ $K_{C,A}\|AD_A\|T_{S4}\| ST$])
   $Auth_{C1}$=E ($Ticket_{C,TGS}$ ‖[$ID_C\|AD_C\|T_{S3}$]),

   $$ST = E\ (K_{A,TGS}\,\|[\,K_{C,A}\,\|\,ID_C\,\|\,AD_C\,\|\,AD_A\,\|\,T_{S4}\,\|\,Lifetime_3\,\|\,TL_C]).$$

   Before the client C accesses to the service of server S, the first check is to have a service-granting ticket *ST*. If not, the client C should send a request message m5 to TGS for authorization.

3. Request the service index from agent A

&#9312;m7: C→A=[$ST \| Auth_{C2}$];
&#9313;m8: A→C=E ($K_{C,A} \| [T_{S6} \| S_{List}]$);
&#9314;m9: C→A=E ($K_{C,A} \| [S_c \| T_{S7}]$);
&#9315;m10: A→C=E($K_{C,A} \| [T_{S8} \| SC_{List}]$);

$$Auth_{C2} = E (K_{C,A} \| [[ID_C \| AD_C \| T_{S5} \| Lifetime_3]]).$$

Before the client C requests a service from application server, it must obtain a list of authorized services available from the agent A at first. Then, agent A decrypts the message m9 and sends back to the service index to the client C, according to the information selected by the client.

4. Request the service from application server

&#9312;m11: C→S=E ($K_i \| [ID_C \| S_c]$);
&#9313;m12: S→C=E ($K_{i+1} \| [R_{ES}]$).

When client C requests the service, it sends the message m11 to the corresponding application server S, which will provide the client with the corresponding service. In massage m11 and m12, we use $K_i$ as the session key between client C and Server S. When client C sends seq = i request message with $K_i$ encrypted to server S and server S uses $K_i$ to decrypt it, then server S uses $K_{i+1}$ to encrypt the message and the client C uses $K_{i+1}$ to decrypt the response message. In the way, $K_{i+1}$ will be a new session key

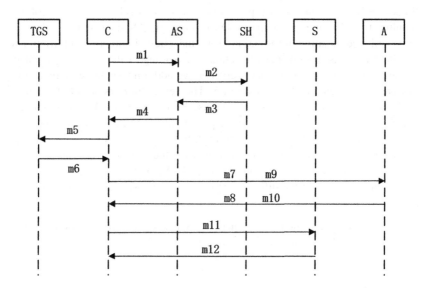

**Fig. 2.** Authentication process of DSA

in next request. In this paper, we apply the dynamic session key to increase the difficulty of password guessing attack and improve the security of the protocol.

## 4    Performance Analysis

In this part, we will compare the performance of DSA with Kerberos protocol and analyzed its security performance. The result shows that DSA authentication protocol can increase the ability to resist password guessing attack.

1. Service availability analysis

   The tickets of DSA protocol is an improvement of Kerberos. Kerberos need 6 messages and DSA protocol has 12 messages. In the six additional messages, two of them are used to access the service, these two messages solved the problem of service availability in Kerberos protocol.

2. Efficiency analysis

   Kerberos use a database to store all passwords and identities of users. Different from Kerberos, we use a non-volatile file to store the key in this scheme. Therefore, the DSA is more secure and efficient.

   DSA protocol uses a ticket data structure in the process of authentication. It can safely send the result of authentication and session key to the application server and can be reused in its lifetime. At the same time, it reduces the using frequency of password and the workload of the AS server. Therefore, DSA protocol could reduce overhead and improve the efficiency of authentication.

3. Security analysis

   For the security of DSA protocol, we mainly analyze password guessing attack. Since Kerberos cannot resist password guessing attack, DSA protocol uses a monitor to solve the problem. In DSA protocol, AS does not get the client's password and position information from the client indirectly, but from client's monitor which is responsible for validation. Aiming at the potential threat in the session key between client C and server S, we add a non-volatile memory to store key chain between client C and server S. The key chain $K_i$ is used to take the place of $Ticket_{C,S}$ to encrypt the message. We use $K_i$ as the session key between client C and Server S. When client C sends seq = i request message with $K_i$ encrypted to server S and server S uses $K_i$ to decrypt it, then server S uses $K_{i+1}$ to encrypt the message and the client C uses $K_{i+1}$ to decrypt the response message. In the way, $K_{i+1}$ will be a new session key in next request. We use the dynamic session key in the scheme to increase the difficulty of password guessing attacks and improve the security of the protocol.

   We also compared the performance of DSA with Kerberos (versions 4 and 5) in other aspects. The results are shown in Table 2 as follows.

**Table 2.** Performance comparison

| Items | Kerberos V4 | Kerberos V5 | DSA |
|---|---|---|---|
| Single sign-on | Yes | Yes | Yes |
| Resistance of password guessing attack | No | No | Yes |
| Database used for storing key | Yes | Yes | No |
| Service registration | No | No | Yes |
| Symmetric key | Yes | Yes | Yes |
| Dependence of operating system | Yes | Yes | No |
| Mutual authentication between entities | No | Yes | Yes |
| Access authorization | No | No | Yes |
| Resistance of denial of service attack | No | No | No |

## 5 Conclusion

In cloud computing environment, security is essential in all aspects of fields. Authentication and authorization is the first step for users to enjoy the service of cloud. Kerberos provides a third party authentication, by which client can authenticate itself to multiple servers using its password. However, it is not feasible when facing password guessing attack. With respect to the problems existing in Kerberos, this paper puts forward a distributed authentication (DSA) protocol in the cloud. The system could realize authentication when the client apply for services in the cloud. We apply a dynamic session key into the protocol, which increases the difficulty of the password guessing attack and improves the security of the protocol. Then we also compared DSA with Kerberos in efficiency and security. The result shows DSA protocol improved the performance of Kerberos. In protocol of DSA, the application server is available and the capacity of resistance password guessing attack is enhanced. In the future, we will further study the resistance in replay attack of Kerberos.

## References

1. Armbrust, M., Fox, A., Griffith, R., et al.: A view of cloud computing. Commun. ACM **53**(4), 50–58 (2010)
2. Marinos, A., Briscoe, G.: Community cloud computing. In: Jaatun, M.G., Zhao, G., Rong, C. (eds.) Cloud Computing. LNCS, vol. 5931, pp. 472–484. Springer, Heidelberg (2009)
3. Velte, T., Velte, A., Elsenpeter, R.: Cloud Computing, a Practical Approach. McGraw-Hill, Inc., New York (2009)
4. Qian, L., Luo, Z., Du, Y., Guo, L.: Cloud computing: an overview. In: Jaatun, M.G., Zhao, G., Rong, C. (eds.) Cloud Computing. LNCS, vol. 5931, pp. 626–631. Springer, Heidelberg (2009)
5. Boss, G., Malladi, P., Quan, D., et al.: Cloud computing. IBM white paper, vol. 1 (2007)
6. Wei, L., Zhu, H., Cao, Z., et al.: Security and privacy for storage and computation in cloud computing. Inf. Sci. **258**, 371–386 (2014)
7. Feng, D.G., Zhang, M., Zhang, Y., et al.: Study on cloud computing security. J. Softw. **22**(1), 71–83 (2011)

8. So, K.: Cloud computing security issues and challenges. Int. J. Comput. Netw. **3**(5), 1–9 (2011)
9. Sabahi, F.: Cloud computing security threats and responses. In: 2011 IEEE 3rd International Conference on Communication Software and Networks (ICCSN), pp. 245–249. IEEE (2011)
10. Talon, C., Insights, I.D.C.E.: The impact of cloud computing on the development of intelligent buildings. CABA Intell. Integr. Build. Counc. (IIBC), pp. 1–29 (2013)
11. Zunnurhain, K., Vrbsky, S.: Security attacks and solutions in clouds. In: Proceedings of the 1st International Conference on Cloud Computing, pp. 145–156 (2010)
12. Malandrino, D., Petta, A., Scarano, V., et al.: Privacy awareness about information leakage: who knows what about me?. In: Proceedings of the 12th ACM Workshop on Workshop on Privacy in the Electronic Society, pp. 279–284. ACM (2013)
13. Quinn, B., Arthur, C.: PlayStation network hackers access data of 77 million users. Guardian (2011)
14. Al-Janabi, S.T.F., Rasheed, M.A.: Public-key cryptography enabled Kerberos authentication. In: Developments in E-systems Engineering (DeSE), pp. 209–214. IEEE (2011)
15. Mundra, P., Shukla, S., Sharma, M., et al.: Modeling and verification of Kerberos protocol using symbolic model verifier. In: 2011 International Conference on Communication Systems and Network Technologies (CSNT), pp. 651–654. IEEE (2011)
16. Dua, G., Gautam, N., Sharma, D., et al.: Replay attack prevention in Kerberos authentication protocol using triple password. Int. J. Comput. Netw. Commun. **5**(2), 59 (2013)
17. Wang, C., Feng, C.: Security analysis and improvement for Kerberos based on dynamic password and Diffie-Hellman algorithm. In: 2013 Fourth International Conference on Emerging Intelligent Data and Web Technologies (EIDWT), pp. 256–260. IEEE (2013)
18. Du, Y., Ning, H., Yang, P., et al.: Improvement of Kerberos protocol based on dynamic password and "One-time public key". In: 2014 10th International Conference on Natural Computation (ICNC), pp. 1020–1025. IEEE (2014)
19. Kandil, H., Atwan, A.: Mobile agents' authentication using a proposed light Kerberos system. In: 2014 9th International Conference on Informatics and Systems (INFOS), pp. CNs-39–CNs-45. IEEE (2014)

# Influential Nuisance Factors on a Decision of Sufficient Testing

Mahnaz Malekzadeh[1]([⊠]) and Iain Bate[1,2]

[1] Mälardalen Real-Time Research Centre, Mälardalen University,
72123 Västerås, Sweden
`mahnaz.malekzadeh@mdh.se`
[2] Department of Computer Science, University of York, York YO105DD, UK
`iain.bate@york.ac.uk`

**Abstract.** Testing of safety-critical embedded systems is an important and costly endeavor. To date work has been mainly focusing on the design and application of diverse testing strategies. However, they have left an open research issue of when to stop testing a system. In our previous work, we proposed a convergence algorithm that informs the tester when the current testing strategy does not seem to be revealing new insight into the worst-case timing properties of system tasks, hence, should be stopped. This algorithm was shown to be successful while being applied across task sets having similar characteristics. For the convergence algorithm to become *robust*, it is important that it holds even if the task set characteristics here called *nuisance factors*, vary. Generally speaking, there might be either the main factors under analysis, called *design factors*, or nuisance factors that influence the performance of a process or system. Nuisance factors are not typically of interest in the context of the analysis. However, they vary from system to system and may have large effects on the performance, hence, being very important to be accounted for. Consequently, the current paper looks into a set of nuisance factors that affect our proposed convergence algorithm performance. More specifically, it is interested in situations when the convergence algorithm performance significantly degrades influencing its reliability. The work systematically analyzes each nuisance factor effect using a well-known statistical method, further, derives the most influential factors.

**Keywords:** Testin · Safety · ALARP · Nuisance factor · Real-time system · ANOVA · Analysis of variance

## 1 Introduction

Testing is an important part of the development and certification process in safety-critical systems in which failure can lead to catastrophic damage to people or environment. However, it is also one of the most expensive parts. Therefore, testers have to determine whether there is any benefit in running the current testing strategy further. Currently, this is at best a qualitative decision. Such a

© Springer International Publishing Switzerland 2015
G. Wang et al. (Eds.): ICA3PP 2015 Workshops, LNCS 9532, pp. 819–828, 2015.
DOI: 10.1007/978-3-319-27161-3_75

decision also plays an important role in the *As Low As Reasonably Practicable (ALARP)* principle which is an underpinning concept in most safety standards. According to the ALARP principle, risk-tolerability depends on practicability of further risk-reduction which is a cost-benefit analysis, i.e., it must be feasible to demonstrate that the cost of reducing the risk further would outweigh the benefit gained. We addressed this decision challenge quantitatively in our previous work [1] for the important problem of testing the Worst-Case Response Time (WCRT) of Real-Time Systems (RTS) [2] in which the correctness of the software not only depends on the functional correctness but also on the timely delivery of the computational results. In [1], We proposed a convergence algorithm based on the ALARP principle to decide when to stop testing the RTS as it was unlikely that significant new information would be obtained. The algorithm checked whether the *High WaterMark (HWM)*, which represents the *Maximum Observed Response Time (MORT)* during testing, is increasing at a sufficiently fast rate as well as the distribution of response times is varying significantly.

Our convergence algorithm got a set of design factors which were initially tuned using limited trial and improvement experiments. Further in [3], we used the *Design of Experiments (DOE)* approach to tune the design factors such that a better decision of when to stop testing is made and the analysis itself is more scalable. The experimental results showed that the tuning did improve the algorithm performance and scalability.

The convergence algorithm, so far, has been evaluated with task sets having similar characteristic. However, to have a robust algorithm, it is important that it holds when the task set characteristics change, i.e., in the presence of nuisance factors. A nuisance factor may be sometimes *unknown* and *uncontrolled*, i.e., we do not know that it exists and is even changing during the experiments. Such a nuisance factor may affect the process output. A design technique called *randomization* is used which helps averaging out the nuisance factor effect. However, there is a potentially serious problem with randomized experiment if the nuisance factor *significantly* affects the process output. To cut off the nuisance factor effect, firstly, the nuisance factor with large effect on the output has to be identified which helps to systematically control the nuisance source of variability. Secondly, when the nuisance factor becomes *known* and *controllable*, we can eliminate its effect using appropriate design techniques which, in effect, leads to robustness to conditions that can not be easily controlled.

The contributions of this paper are to address the concern raised by the presence of nuisance factors for our convergence algorithm and are as follows.

- To propose a set of nuisance factors to find out whether they have any significant effect on the convergence algorithm performance, also called *response*. The intuition behind choosing each factor is its effect on the worst-case timing properties of the task set.
- To systematically analyze the effect of each nuisance factor through *analysis of variance (ANOVA)* to see whether the factor does in fact influence the algorithm response and to eventually identify the most influential nuisance factors.

– To take the first step towards robust design of the algorithm by identifying under what conditions the algorithm response significantly degrades which also relates to the reliability, i.e., the likelihood of the algorithm failure in the presence of a nuisance factor. Robust design of the algorithm, further, tries to reduce the failure.

The remainder of this paper is structured as follows. Section 2 describes the background of the work. The convergence algorithm, system model and simulation environment in which we run our experiments are stated in Sect. 3. Section 4 includes the problem statement and the ANOVA approach for identifying the nuisance factors followed by the experimental results in Sect. 5. Section 6 finally states the conclusions and future work.

## 2    Background

This section describes the worst-case timing properties of real-time systems, the problems associated with the traditional timing analysis techniques and in what sense our algorithm tries to tackle those problems, followed by a related work. Safety-critical embedded systems are expected to work properly under extreme and uncontrollable conditions which significantly raises the requirements on their dependability and reliability. They also have real-time characteristics need to be fulfilled as part of the safety requirements which makes the worst-case timing analysis an important and necessary task. The traditional Response-Time Analysis (RTA) [4] techniques, however, are incapable of capturing features inhabiting complex real-time systems, thus, resulting in inaccurate WCRT analysis. They also depend on the exact *Worst-Case Execution Time (WCET)* of each task which itself is hard to be gained due to the advanced hardware features, temporal and execution dependencies between tasks [5], et cetera. Our convergence algorithm looks into the MORT of the tasks during testing and their distributions using HWM and a statistical test respectively such that it depends neither on an abstract system model nor the exact WCET estimation which also makes it suitable for real systems.

To the best of our knowledge there is no similar work on making a decision of sufficient testing, e.g., the authors in [6] look into the HWM and the distributions of the WCET in multi-path, therefore realistic programs, to estimate the WCET. They collect execution times by running the program under analysis and pick the HWM within randomly formed blocks of data, then, examine whether the HWMs matches one of the *Extreme Value Theory (EVT)* [7] distributions. They compare two successive distributions to see whether they have converged, thus, no more observations need to be collected. They estimate the WCET using the resulted EVT distribution. Although we use HWM and the worst-case timing distributions similar to theirs, our convergence algorithm, firstly, applies the HWM on the MORTs as it is a relatively cheap test. Then, it looks into the MORT distributions to see whether they are getting converged rather than the WCET distributions. Eventually, our goal is to derive a stopping point for testing rather than WCET estimation in [6].

## 3   Convergence Algorithm

Our proposed convergence algorithm in [1] decides when to stop testing the
RTS as no significant new information will be determined without clairvoyance.
The system model assumed and the task set simulator used by the convergence
algorithm are as follows.

- *System Model* comprises a set of applications. Each application consists of
  tasks which are assigned unique priorities according to some policy. Each
  *periodic* task $\tau_i$ gives rise to an infinite sequence of invocations separated by
  a period $T_i$. $T_i$ represents the minimum time between successive invocations.
  A task performs an amount of computation bounded by $C_i$ during each invocation which has to be completed by its deadline $D_i$. The time difference
  between completion and release time of a task is called its *response time*.
- *Task Set Simulator* generates testing data that allows a ground truth to be
  established and careful control of the task set characteristics, including complexity. Two ground truths are available for comparison: static analysis which
  in this particular situation gives an exact safe result [8], and a HWM but
  with significantly longer simulation. Longer simulation is possible due to the
  nature of the simulator, however, such increased testing would be prohibitively
  expensive in a real system. The simulator generates a set of preemptive tasks
  with no overheads and the following characteristics.
  - Total utilisation of the task set which falls within the range [80 %, 100 %].
  - Each task utilisation $U_i$ which is generated using the *UUniFast* algorithm
    [9] to generate random tasks with uniform distributions.
  - Each task $i$ execution time (depicted by $C_i$) which is set using the following
    equation.

$$C_i = U_i T_i \tag{1}$$

The simulation duration is set to $10^{13}$ when the MORTs of the tasks within
a set of 10 fall within 5 % of the last MORT observed during the whole simulation. All timings are in microseconds.

Algorithm 1 presents the convergence algorithm having the following design
factors: $\alpha$, $\lambda$, $i$, $\delta$ and *NumSet*. The response times of a task set and the proposed
*Stopping Point (SP)* by the convergence algorithm form the input and the output
of the algorithm respectively. The factor *NumSet* defines how many data sets
of the MORT distributions to be generated. The factor $\lambda$ defines the number of
bins and is to assort response times into equally-sized bins, each of size *BinSize*,
to foil the outliers effect and to improve scalability, i.e., instead of saving every
single response time, the frequencies of the response times falling in the range
[s, s + BinSize] are recorded.

For each task, the algorithm takes two overlapping distributions depicted by
$X$ and $Y$ such that $Y$ is a superset of $X$ (Line 7), i.e., to gradually examine
testing data for convergence. The algorithm, firstly, checks whether the HWM
is increasing (Line 9) and if it has not been increased for $i$ successive analysis
iterations (Line 14). If the HWM is passed, the algorithm checks whether the

distribution models of response times are being refined using the *Kullback-Leibler DIVergence (KLDIV)* test [10]. Otherwise, the HWM test is reset (Line 10). The criterion for the *KL DIV* test being passed is that the test result falls below the $\delta$ threshold (Line 17). The algorithm stops further analysis provided that both the HWM and KL DIV tests are passed, otherwise, the HWM test is reset (Line 25) and further datasets would be analysed (Line 27). *SPMORT* in Line 19 and 31 corresponds to the MORT value, observed for each task, when the algorithm stops. It is worth highlighting that the higher priority tasks in the task set tend to converge sooner than the lower priority tasks. However, the algorithm stops only if the latest task within the task set converges (Line 32, 33).

---

**Algorithm 1.** The *Convergence Algorithm*

```
   Input: ResponseTimes
   Output: AlgorithmStoppingPoint
 1  BinSize ← MaxPeriod/λ;
 2  foreach Task ∈ {TaskSet} do
 3      X = 1;
 4      Y = 1;
 5      OldMORT = 0;
 6      while Y <= NumSet do
 7          Y ← α * X;
 8          CurrentMORT = Maximum(ResponseTimes ∈ Y);
 9          if (CurrentMORT > OldMORT) then
10              HWMCounter ← 0;
11          end
12          else if (CurrentMORT <= OldMORT) then
13              HWMCounter ← HWMCounter + 1;
14              if (HWMCounter >= i);
15              then
16                  run KL DIV test;
17                  if (KLDIV <= δ);
18                  then
19                      save task testing time and MORT when the algorithm passes both tests:
                        Task(TestingTime, SPMORT);
20                      break;
21                  end
22              end
23          end
24          else
25              HWMCounter ← 0;
26          end
27          X ← X + 1;
28          OldMORT ← CurrentMORT;
29      end
30  end
31  foreach Point ∈ {TaskSet(TestingTime, SPMORT)} do
32      LatestConvergence ← Maximum(TestingTime);
33      Return Task(LatestConvergence, MORT at LatestConvergence);
34  end
```

---

## 4  Approach and Problem Formulation

For any testing strategy to be valid for a range of systems, it needs a clear understanding of what parameters of the system could make it invalid. These parameters are called nuisance factors. The nuisance factors, in our case, relate to those factors seem to be influential on the MORT based on the scheduling theory. More specifically, we focus on the factors which lead to more complex timing behaviour of the task set while they are being changed. We limit this work to the following nuisance factors: *Period, Offset, Number of tasks, Harmonic vs. nonharmonic* periods where the latest corresponds to the way task period is generated. Harmonic period requires that every task period evenly divides every longer period which is not the case for nonharmonic period.

## 4.1   The ANOVA Approach

As stated earlier, we use the ANOVA method to identify a set of nuisance factors which are the most influential on the convergence algorithm response. The ANOVA method determines whether any of the nuisance factors contributes to the variability transmitted to the response, further, decides which set of factors are significant at a given confidence level. In particular, we are interested in the *p-value* [11] which, in statistics, is a function of the observed sample results used for testing a statistical hypothesis. Before the test, a threshold value is chosen and is called the significance level of the test, traditionally 5 % or 1 % [1]. If the *p-values* are equal to or smaller than the significance level, then, it suggests that the observed data are inconsistent with the assumption of the null hypothesis correctness, thus, that hypothesis has to be rejected. In our approach, the null hypothesis suggests that the nuisance factor under analysis has no effect on the convergence algorithm response, thus, the *p-value* smaller than the significance level suggests that the null hypothesis must be rejected and eventually, derives a set of influential nuisance factors.

As the response times distributions being used in our analysis do not follow a normal distribution, the parametric ANOVA, which assumes normal distributions of data, should be replaced. Hence, we use the non-parametric analysis of variance test, called *Kruskal Wallis* test that does not depend on such an assumption. In the rest of the paper, however, we use the term ANOVA for simplicity.

## 4.2   Problem Formulation to Identify Nuisance Factors

We observe and analyze the effect of each nuisance factor through a set of response metrics. The response metrics relate to the algorithm performance and are defined such that the smaller values indicate better performance is achieved. They also form our ANOVA approach inputs and are as follows.

- $M_{achieve}$: Closeness of the algorithm SPMORT to the LM while LM corresponds to the last MORT observed during simulation assuming that virtually infinite test data resources are available.

    SPMORT has to be reasonably close to LM when the algorithm stops, thus, the smaller $M_{achieve}$, the better performance is gained.

$$M_{achieve} = \frac{LM - SPMORT}{LM} \qquad (2)$$

Ideally, LM has to be equal to WCRT from static analysis. However, in practice, it is not scalable especially for a low priority task. It is also less important as we want to make an ALARP decision.

- $M_{cost}$: The cost of testing in terms of the time that has been spent to generate and to analyse testing data. Similar to $M_{achieve}$, smaller values of $M_{cost}$ indicate better performance.

$$M_{cost} = \frac{TestingTimeatSP}{TestingTimeatLM} \qquad (3)$$

**Table 1.** Phase1 - ANOVA results

| Metrics | $M_{achieve}$ | $M_{cost}$ |
|---|---|---|
| Period | 0.5057 | 0.2288 |
| Harmonic vs. nonharmonic | 0.0002 | 0.7455 |
| Offset | 0.0242 | 0.0139 |
| Number of tasks | 2.9186E-10 | 0.8237 |

**Table 2.** Test power & sample size

| Nuisance Factors | Test Power | Sample Size |
|---|---|---|
| Harmonic vs. nonharmonic | 15 % | 265 |
| Number of tasks | 86 % | 27 |

# 5  Experimental Results

This section presents the experiments and ANOVA results to identify which nuisance factors are the most influential on the convergence algorithm performance. The task set simulator described in Sect. 3 is used in the experiments.

The ANOVA test is run at two phases: Phase 1 and Phase 2. Phase 1 includes 20 experiments, called *sample size*, for each level of the potential nuisance factor under analysis and it is called a *low resolution* phase as allows us to identify the most influential nuisance factors at relatively low cost. Phase 2, here called *high resolution* phase, includes the influential nuisance factors identified in Phase 1, however, with bigger sample size. The sample size is determined such that at least 90 % power would be associated with the ANOVA test. The potential nuisance factors are analyzed at the following levels.

- Period is analyzed in overlapping ranges each starts at 50000 and ends in the following upper bounds: {200000, 400000, 600000, 800000}.
- Harmonic vs. nonharmonic period includes task sets of the same characteristics except the way periods are generated.
- Offset is analyzed in overlapping ranges starting at 10000 and ending at upper bounds as follows: {50000, 100000, 200000, 300000}. The analysis also includes a level with no offset.
- Number of tasks includes experiments of {10, 30, 50} tasks within each task set.

The ANOVA results from Phase 1 are shown in Table 1. We are interested in *p-values* smaller than 0.05 that show the corresponding nuisance factor is significant on the observed response with 95 % confidence. Based on the achieved *p-values*, the nuisance factors {Harmonic vs. nonharmonic, Offset, Number of tasks} are the most influential on at least one of the response metrics. For scalability reason, the set {Harmonic vs. nonharmonic, Number of tasks} is chosen to be analyzed further at the high resolution phase as they are associated with much smaller *p-values* rather than the offset, i.e., they are much more significant.

The box plots in Fig. 1 show the algorithm performance in Phase 1 for the most infuential nuisance factors including Harmonic vs. nonharmonic period and Number of tasks. In each box plot, the *central box* represents the central 50 % of the data with lower and upper boundary lines are at the 25 %, 75 % quantile of the data respectively. The central line indicates the median of the data and the two vertical lines extending from the central box indicating the remaining data outside the central box that are not regarded as outliers. The + sign presents outliers. In both figures the horizontal axis shows the nuisance factor levels while the vertical axis presents the response metrics values for the whole sample size. As stated earlier, smaller values of $M_{achieve}$ and $M_{cost}$ indicate that the algorithm performance has been improved, i.e., when $M_{achieve}$ and $M_{cost}$ decrease it implies that the algorithm stops closer to the last MORT and is spending less effort to propose when to stop testing respectively. It can be seen that for both factors $M_{achieve}$ significantly degrades, i.e., becomes larger as the task sets get more complex timing behaviour while $M_{cost}$ does not change very much. For example, $M_{achieve}$ for nonharmonic periods is 2.3 times more than harmonic periods while $M_{cost}$ difference is 1.1 times. Also, for the task sets of size 50, $M_{achieve}$ is 4.5 times more than task sets of size 10 whereas $M_{cost}$ does not significantly differ (1.1 times).

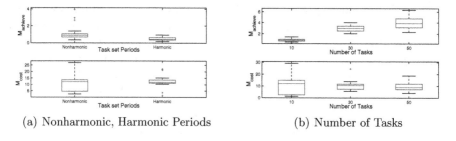

(a) Nonharmonic, Harmonic Periods          (b) Number of Tasks

**Fig. 1.** Algorithm performance

The results also imply that the reliability of the algorithm decreases either when we introduce nonharmonic periods to the system or increase the number of tasks which would also help to investigate the algorithm failure modes. To evaluate the algorithm performance, we introduce a quantified MORT called *ALARP MORT (AM)* relying on the ALARP principle. Ideal is that the algorithm stops later than AM but not far from it, i.e., by stopping too soon before AM, the MORT value at SP becomes far from the LM and by stopping too late after AM, it may result in higher cost without gaining useful new findings as it has already fallen within the ALARP region. In this paper, the MORT values within 5 % of the LM defines the ALARP region.

In order to proceed with the high resolution phase, firstly, we calculate the ANOVA test power achieved by sample size 20 in Phase 1 for each influential nuisance factor and the corresponding response metrics which includes the set {Harmonic vs. non-harmonic, Number of tasks} and response metric $M_{achieve}$ respectively. Secondly, we calculate the sample size of the high resolution phase such that 90 % power of the ANOVA test would be achieved. Table 2 shows that for both nuisance factors the test power achieved by sample size 20 is less then 90 %. Then, the required sample size is calculated, shown in column 3, such that at least 90 % power would be associated with the ANOVA test in Phase 2.

Phase 2 includes 265 and 27 experiments for harmonic vs. nonharmonic periods and number of tasks respectively to achieve the ANOVA results with 90 % power. Table 3 shows the results from Phase 2 which conform to Phase 1, i.e., both nuisance factors are influential on $M_{achieve}$, however, with much smaller $p$-values rather than Phase 1. $M_{cost}$ also shows to be affected in Phase 2 for harmonic vs. nonharmonic factor, i.e., the test gets more powerful to identify the transmitted variability as the sample size is significantly increased.

**Table 3.** Phase 2 - ANOVA results

| Metrics | $M_{achieve}$ | $M_{cost}$ |
|---|---|---|
| Harmonic vs. nonharmonic | **1.6954E-27** | *0.0039* |
| Number of tasks | **4.7434E-12** | 0.1158 |

## 6    Conclusions and Future Work

Testing as an important part of the development and certification process is very expensive. Therefore, it is extremely important to determine when to stop testing. Our previous work, firstly, proposed a convergence algorithm to make a quantified ALARP judgement of when sufficient testing has been done. Secondly, the algorithm was tuned based on the DOE approach to improve its performance and scalability. This paper focuses on the nuisance factors that vary from system to system and may affect the performance of the convergence algorithm. The reason is that there will be a huge bias in the experimental analysis caused by the nuisance factors if they significantly influence the algorithm response. So, it is very important that they are identified and their effect is controlled early on in the experiments. This paper proposes a set of nuisance factors, derived from system task set characteristics, that may potentially affect the convergence algorithm. Then, it systematically identifies whether the nuisance factors, in fact, influence the algorithm response.

This work also forms a stepping stone towards our future work. The future work, firstly, is around stress testing the algorithm based on the algorithm failure modes identified in this work, i.e., it uses the nuisance factor levels where the algorithm response significantly degrades. Secondly, it tries to remove the effect of the nuisance factors by robust design of the algorithm.

**Acknowledgement.** We acknowledge the Swedish Foundation for Strategic Research (SSF) SYNOPSIS Project for supporting this work.

## References

1. Malekzadeh, M., Bate, I.: Making an ALARP decision of sufficient testing. In: IEEE International Symposium on High-Assurance Systems Engineering, pp. 57–64 (2014)

2. Kopetz, H.: Real-Time Systems: Design Principles for Distributed Embedded Applications, 2nd edn. Kluwer Academic Publishers, Norwell (1997)
3. Malekzadeh, M., Bate, I., Punnekkat, S.: Using design of experiments to optimise a decision of sufficient testing. In: Euromicro Conference series on Software Engineering and Advanced Applications (2015)
4. Audsley, N.C., Burns, A., Davis, R.I., Tindell, K., Wellings, A.J.: Fixed priority pre-emptive scheduling: an historical perspective. Real-Time Syst. 8(2–3), 173–198 (1995)
5. Wilhelm, R., et al.: The worst-case execution-time problem-overview of methods and survey of tools. ACM Trans. Embed. Comput. Syst. (TECS) 7(3), 1–53 (2008)
6. Cucu-Grosjean, L., et al.: Measurement-based probabilistic timing analysis for multi-path programs. In: Proceedings of the Euromicro Conference on Real-Time Systems, pp. 91–101 (2012)
7. Gumbel, E.: Dover Books on Mathematics. Statistics of Extremes. Dover Publications, Mineola (2004)
8. Bate, I., Burns, A.: An integrated approach to scheduling in safety-critical embedded control systems. Real-Time Syst. J. 25(1), 5–37 (2003)
9. Bini, E., Buttazzo, G.C.: Measuring the performance of schedulability tests. Real-Time Syst. 30(1–2), 129–154 (2005)
10. Kullback, S., Leibler, R.A.: On information and sufficiency. Ann. Math. Stat. (AMS) 22(1), 79–86 (1951)
11. Box, G., Hunter, J., Hunter, W.: Statistics for Experimenters: Design, Innovation, and Discovery. Wiley Series in Probability and Statistics. Wiley-Interscience, New York (2005)

# Research of Improved Particle Swarm Optimization Based on Genetic Algorithm for Hadoop Task Scheduling Problem

Jun Xu[1,2(✉)] and Yong Tang[1]

[1] College of Computer, South China Normal University, Guangzhou 510631, Guangdong, China
xujun3447@163.com, ytang@scnu.edu.cn
[2] ATM Research Institute, GRGBanking, Guangzhou 510663, Guangdong, China

**Abstract.** Scheduling is NP-hard problem in Hadoop, because scheduling algorithm must use available resources to complete assignments in the shortest time. This paper proposes an improved Genetic-Particle Swarm Optimization (IG-PSO) algorithm to solve scheduling problems. Traditional PSO algorithm is easy to fall into local optimum solution, so novel improved Genetic-Particle Swarm Optimization (IG-PSO) algorithm introduced GA's mutation and crossover to overcome the shortcoming and increase the ability of global optimization. Compared with traditional PSO and GA, the experiment simulation shows that IG-PSO algorithm can escape from local optimal solution and find a better global optimal solution. Because the position of PSO particle falls into local optimal solution, GA uses mutation and crossover to diversify particles, which make the particle escape out of local optima.

**Keywords:** Hadoop · Genetic algorithm · Particle swarm optimization · Mapreduce

## 1 Introduction

When Cloud Computing emerges for internet businesses, many computing frameworks are proposed for the huge data store and highly parallel computing needs. These computing frameworks can provide a variety of on-demand services according to different requirements of users. Cloud computing [1] is a widely accepted solution that provides on-demand storage capacity and computing power for different users. There are three types of cloud system services: IaaS, PaaS and SaaS. IaaS. Infrastructure as a Service (IaaS) is to provide users with computing resources. Platform as a Service (PaaS) provides only the operating system and the basic platform of services. Last but not least, Software as a Service (SaaS) [2] is the top of the service, which provides users with a particular application.

In this framework, you can perform MapReduce applications [3, 4]. Two type's tasks of MapReduce are Map and Reduce. Due to the characteristics of MapReduce application model, it is very suitable for execution in the cloud. However MapReduce applications are difficult to schedule, they not only need location data, and also we need to consider the

© Springer International Publishing Switzerland 2015
G. Wang et al. (Eds.): ICA3PP 2015 Workshops, LNCS 9532, pp. 829–834, 2015.
DOI: 10.1007/978-3-319-27161-3_76

dependencies between tasks. So scheduling is a hot issue in a distributed computing research. In cloud computing, an important stage is scheduling in the MapReduce application. Task scheduling problems are of paramount importance which relate to the efficiency of whole cloud computing facilities. In this paper, for the goals of maximizing their utilization while minimizing the total task execution time, we propose an improved Genetic -Particle Swarm Optimization (IG-PSO) algorithm for task level scheduling in Hadoop MapReduce [5].

## 2   Task Scheduling Optimization Problem of Hadoop

For convenience of description, firstly we do mathematical modeling of Map/Reduce task scheduling. For a certain period of time, hypothesis that S tasks are firstly set up and wait for scheduling, there are N processing nodes for tasks, task j need computing power $T_j$, the computing capacity $R_i$ per unit time of i processing node, maximum processing task parallel number $Maxp_j$. How to make n tasks are assigned to M processing nodes, so that total task completion time is the shortest? As the objective function:

$$F = \min \sum_{j=1}^{s} \sum_{i=1}^{n} \frac{W_{j,i} T_j}{R_i} \tag{1}$$

In the formula, $W_{j,i}$: task j Occupation processing node i computing resources, the symbolic value is 1; otherwise, the value is 0.

Constraint: the processing task number of node j cannot exceed maximum parallel processing task number, i.e.

$$s.t. \sum_{j=1}^{s} W_{j,i} \leq M_i \tag{2}$$

## 3   Algorithm Description

Genetic Algorithm (GA) is a heuristic algorithm in a continuous spatial domain [6, 7]. In the GA, each decision variable is a real number on its chromosome representation (individual). As with any other evolutionary algorithm, GA initial population is randomly generated and evaluated. In the selection phase, three parent base vectors are selected for mutation and crossover operator, and then determine which passed on as a new population of individuals. Genetic Algorithm includes three core operators, as follow:

Mutation: according to the following expression, for each individual i-th iteration, each $x_j^i$ does mutation operation, to give the corresponding individual variation $y_j^{i+1}$:

$$y_j^{i+1} = x_a^i + R(x_b^i - x_c^i) \tag{3}$$

Where: $a, b, c \in \{1, \dots, N_P\}$ and $a \neq b \neq c \neq j$; $x_j^i$ as the base vector generation; scaling factor R is random control parameter between $[0, 2]$.

Cross: according to the following formula, the individual vector $x_j^i$ and variation individual $y_j^{i+1}$ do vector cross operates, to give individual $v_j^{i+1}$:

$$v_j^{i+1} = \begin{cases} y_{j,t}^{i+1}, if \ (rand\,(t) \leq C_R) & or \qquad t = q \\ x_j^i & otherwise \end{cases} \tag{4}$$

Where: $rant(x)$ is a random number in the range $[0, 1]$ uniformly distributed; $C_R$ usually choose crossover probability $[0, 1]$ helps algorithm escape from the local minim.

Selection: select the operation compares $V_j^{i+1}$ and $x_j^i$ individual's objective function value, the better individual is the next generation's individual.

$$x_j^{i+1} = \begin{cases} v_j^{i+1}, if \quad f(v_j^{i+1}) < f(x_j^i) \\ x_j^i \qquad otherwise \end{cases} \tag{5}$$

The key operator of Genetic Algorithm (GA) is mutation in a successful search for the optimal solution. Algorithms mutation operator is to find a better solution in maintaining the basic features of its parent. Crossover retains beneficial characteristics of candidate solutions and eliminates the bad parts.

The main advantages of PSO algorithm [8–10] is its simplicity and speed. However PSO algorithm lacks a solid mathematical foundation and easily converge local optima. To overcome these problems, IG-PSO algorithm integrates the respective advantages of PSO and GA. In this paper, we attempt to introduce GA mutation and crossover operators to quickly find the best solution in the PSO algorithm.

Here is the entire IG-PSO algorithm specific step:

(1) Initialing randomly population;
(2) Evaluating the objective function value of population according to the formula (1);
(3) Repeating iterations plus 1;
(4) Updating location speed: calculate the particle's new position and speed according to the formulas (6) and (7);

$$X_i(t + 1) = X_i(t) + V_i(t + 1) \tag{6}$$

$$V_i(t + 1) = W \cdot V_i(t) + (r_1 \cdot cons_1) \cdot [XP_i - X_i(t)] \\ + (r_2 \cdot cons_2) \cdot [XG - X_i(t)] \tag{7}$$

(5) Mutating: do mutation and crossover operation according to the formulas (3) and (4);
(6) Selecting: select the next generation's individual according to the Eq. (5);
(7) Ordering: calculate the fitness value of particles and sort;

(8) Updating: update the optimal value by comparing local optimum with global optimum;

(9) Determining the termination condition is satisfied. If it is satisfied and output the optimal solution, otherwise proceed to (3) to (9) step.

## 4   Simulation Experiment and Result Analysis

The simulation is implemented on a Hadoop cluster. The experimental results include convergence performance, resource utilization and optimization capabilities. The algorithm is executed on a Hadoop cluster, in which a computer can act as the NameNode and JobTracker, the other three acts as DataNode and TaskTracker. All cluster nodes have the same configuration on Hadoop2.0, which includes CPU 2.0 GHz, RAM 2048 MB and Hard Disk 50 GB. The results were classified in the following areas:

### 4.1   IG-PSO's Convergence Speed

Suppose that there are 30 missions and four processors. It is seen from Fig. 1 that compared with PSO and GA, the IG-PSO can get better objective function value, indicating that IG-PSO algorithm has faster convergence.

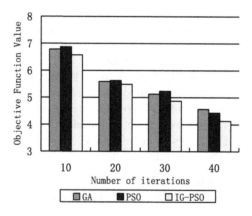

**Fig. 1.** Comparison of algorithm convergence performance

### 4.2   IG-PSO Task Completion Time

Figure 2 illustrates that IG-PSO can be faster out of local optima by taking into mutation and crossover operations with the iterative times increasing in three algorithms. Compared with PSO and GA, IG-PSO considers local and global scope of the solution space, and also adding a random sampling so that the IG-PSO has a stronger global optimization capability.

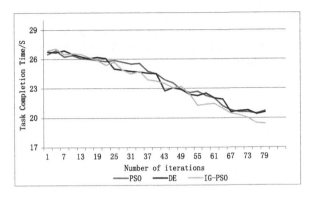

**Fig. 2.** Comparison of task completion time

## 5   Conclusions

In this paper, it is observed that IG-PSO algorithm can better escape from local optimal solution, and find a better global optimal solution. Novel algorithm uses GA mutation and crossover to diversify particles so that the algorithm can escape out of local optima. The experimental results show that the IG-PSO algorithm has better convergence and optimization capability than traditional PSO and GA, and can make use of shared resources.

## References

1. Luis, M.V., Luis, R.-M., Juan, C., Maik, L.: A break in the clouds: towards a cloud GA finition. SIGCOMM Comput. Commun. Rev. **39**(1), 50–55 (2008)
2. Michael, A., Armando, F., Rean, G., et al.: A view of cloud computing. Commun. ACM. **53**(4), 50–58 (2010)
3. Dean, J., Ghemawat, S., et al.: MapReduce: simplified data processing on large clusters. In: Sixth Symposium on Operating System Design and Implementation, San Francisco, pp. 1–13 (2004)
4. Ali, M.M., Fatti, L.P.: A differential free point generation scheme in the differential evolution algorithm. J. Global Optim. **35**, 551–572 (2006). MapReduce. Morgan and Claypool Publishers, 2010
5. Chaobo, H., Yong, T., Zhenxiong, Y., Kai, Z., Guohua, C.: SRSH: a social recommender system based on Hadoop. Int. J. Multimedia Ubiquit. Eng. **9**(6), 141–152 (2014)
6. Aluffi-Pentini, F., Parisi, V., Zirilli, F.: Global optimization and stochastic differential equations. J. Optim. Theor. Appl. **47**(1), 1–16 (1985)
7. Wang, G.Z., Salles, M.V., Sowell, B., Wang, X., Cao, T., Gamers, A.: Behavioral simulations in MapReduce. In: PVLDB2010, Singapore, pp. 952–963 (2010)
8. Kennedy, J., Eberhart, R.C.: Particle swarm optimization. In: Proceedings of IEEE International Conference on Neural Networks, pp. 1942–1948 (1995)

9. Clerc, M., Kennedy, J.: The particle swarm explosion, stability, and convergence in a multidimensional complex space. IEEE Trans. Evol. Comput. **6**(1), 58–73 (2002)
10. Rui, Z., Kalivarapu, V., Winer, E., Olive, J., Bhattacharya, S.: Particle swarm optimization-based source seeking. IEEE Trans. Autom. Sci. Eng. **12**(3), 865–875 (2015)

# Acceleration of CFD Engineering Software on GPU and MIC

Yang Liu[1]([✉]) and Liang Deng[2]

[1] State Key Laboratory of Aerodynamics,
China Aerodynamics Research and Development Center, Mianyang 621000, China
public@skla.cardc.cn
[2] Computational Aerodynamics Institute,
China Aerodynamics Research and Development Center, Mianyang 621000, China
cai@cardc.cn

**Abstract.** CartSolver is widely used three dimensional Euler solver software for Cartesian grids. In this paper, we use the latest many-core accelerators such as NVIDIA Fermi C2050, NVIDIA Kepler K20 and Intel MIC to do the acceleration, and achieve expected speedup over the serial solver. On the GPU platform, two versions of accelerated CartSolver are implemented and optimized. For MIC, we employ various optimization methods in order to achieve the best performance by an open source performance analysis tool. The differences in architecture and programming model between GPU and MIC are also discussed. In the experiments, the correctness and accuracy of the solvers is validated, and the great effect of optimization methods is also proved. Finally, a new criterion for measuring the workload is proposed, and several recommendations on selecting suitable accelerators for CFD engineering software are given on the base of the comparison of the criteria.

**Keywords:** CFD · Engineering software · GPU · MIC

## 1 Introduction

Recently, the heterogeneous many-core processors, such as Graphic Processing Unit (GPU) and Many Integrated Core (MIC) [9], are attracting more and more attention in High Performance Computing (HPC). Adopting these processors to achieve performance acceleration is regarded as an important technical innovation. With the growing development of many-core technology, the heterogeneous architecture is gradually turning to the main stream of the high-end supercomputers, such as TianHe-1A [4], Titan [6], TianHe-2 [7], etc. Compared with the homogeneous architecture which the traditional parallel computer systems employs, the heterogeneous architecture is now widely used and provides a great opportunity to the large-scale scientific and engineering computing.

To meet the increasing requirement of the market for graphic display, GPU has become the high-parallelism, many-core processing units, which has powerful processing capacity to adapt to the general computing. Take the GPU

© Springer International Publishing Switzerland 2015
G. Wang et al. (Eds.): ICA3PP 2015 Workshops, LNCS 9532, pp. 835–848, 2015.
DOI: 10.1007/978-3-319-27161-3_77

used in this paper, NVIDIA Tesla K20, for example. With 13 arrays of Streaming Multi-processors (SM), 2496 CUDA cores in total, the core frequency of 706 MHz and the bit wide of 320-bit, this GPU has much more advantage than CPU in the floating-point performance. The GPU general computing product, Compute Unified Device Architecture (CUDA), which was launched by NVIDIA Corporation in 2007, has changed the situation in which traditional GPUs were hard to be used for general computing. With the improvement of the hardware and the development tools and environment, GPU is widely used in the HPC area, such as computational fluid dynamics (CFD). More and more researchers and engineers attempt to shift their applications of numerical computing to this heterogeneous platform, and manage to make a satisfying acceleration. Dual-SPHysics [17] test their code on GTX 480, GTX680, Tesla K20 and GTX Titan to accelerate smoothes particle hydrodynamics which is to solve free-surface flow problems. OP2 domain-specific high-level framework [18] adopts Tesla K20 to make an acceleration of full-scale industrial CFD application, Hydra, which is used for the design of turbo machinery at Rolls Royce plc. Reference [19] introduces CUDA and OpenACC into existing CFD software for a 3-D Cartesian grid, and compares the workload of the performance optimization of those two versions. Reference [21] uses a quad-GPU platform to implement a Navier-Stokes solver for incompressible flows, and make an achievement of a two orders of magnitude speedup. With the help of GPU, other authors [1–3] also improve the performance in this area, which proves the powerful ability of GPU for CFD.

As a new type of accelerating component for many-core computing, Intel MIC features wide vector processing units and large thread parallelism. With 50+ processor cores which are connected by a high performance on-die bidirectional interconnect [9], the Intel Xeon Phi coprocessor is born for the large-scale parallel computing. Including a 512 bit wide vector processor unit (VPU), each processor core is a fully functional, in-order X86 core, supporting hardware multi-thread and up to four threads concurrent execution. This advanced architecture helps MIC performing be noticeable in the HPC area. TianHe-2, which is ranking No.1 on the Top500 list of supercomputers, is exactly a heterogeneous cluster system which combines Ivy Bridge-E Xeon host processors with Xeon Phi coprocessors. Though MIC and relative products come out not long, some researches into CFD parallel algorithm on MIC architecture have been done and relative CFD applications have been accelerated by MIC. Reference [12] takes advantage of the wide vector to optimize a molecular dynamics procedure and achieves a speedup of 7x. Note that it is very important to fully use the Single Instruction Multiple Data (SIMD) instructions to greatly improve the performance of the large-scale scientific computing. Reference [13] aims at the 3-D Euler equation and realizes the effective parallel computing in GPU and MIC. The optimization strategies, like SIMD for MIC and shared memory for GPU are adopted. Based on the two platforms, it is shown that GPU performs better than MIC. Reference [16] does the research into parallel computing and optimization for typical implicit CFD method on GPU and MIC. It compares these two platforms from the aspects of hardware and software, and gives the learning curves for programming by experience. Reference [8] makes a cluster-level tuning of a shallow water equation on MIC, and achieve a 90 % efficiency of parallelism. Others [22–24] also do much work on MIC-based CFD parallel algorithms and applications.

It is important to note that, however, the performance of GPU and MIC in the CFD applications which adopt the typical implicit scheme, like Lower-Upper Symmetric Gauss-Seidel (LU-SGS), is not as good as expected. None of those accelerators and coprocessors play a good role in data dependent computing, which is also the rival to the parallel computing. GPU and MIC are suitable for the data-parallel computing, and they are especially designed for the explicit scheme, like Runge-Kutta, and the half-implicit scheme, like Alternating Direction Implicit (ADI) [16]. Even so, the complex hardware structure and programming environment of the heterogeneous many-core architecture brings many practical difficulties and challenges for the CFD applications.

In this paper, based on the features of many-core architecture, we introduce GPU and MIC into 3-D Euler solver software for Cartesian grids, CartSolver [5]. Three versions of accelerated CartSolver are implemented and optimized. We analyze the growing GPU architectures and compare them with MIC by listing their speedup over a serial single-threaded Intel i7 CPU solver. The workload for accelerating the application is also compared. The speedup acquired is promising for CFD software of great engineering significance, and the comparison of the workload has more positive impact on the acceleration work for CFD applications in the future.

The rest of the paper is organized as follows. The CartSolver is described in Sect. 2. In Sect. 3, we introduce GPU and MIC into the Euler equation which employs an explicit scheme, and implement three versions of accelerated Cart-Solver. The results are reported from the contrast experiments In Sect. 4, and the conclusion is drawn in Sect. 5.

## 2   The CartSolver Software

This Euler solver software comprises of two applications, the CartSolver itself and the CartGrid, an automatic grid generating application based on adaptive Cartesian Grid. The introduction to CartSolver and its control equations are given below.

### 2.1   Introduction to CartSolver

CartSolver aims at solving Euler equations based on adaptive Cartesian grid. Coded by C++ Builder 6.0 and run under Windows, this software is very easy to use. The executable file CartSolver.exe runs the GUI shown in Fig. 1, and it triggers the actual computing application, Solver.exe, when the user starts to solve the flow field.

CartSolver features fast, convenient and batch processing. This software automatically generates the adaptive Cartesian grids and converges quickly in the computing process. It outputs the data which is needed by post-process softwares, and connects with CAD directly. Batch processing of multiple mach numbers, multiple angles of sideslip and multiple angles of attack is also equipped.

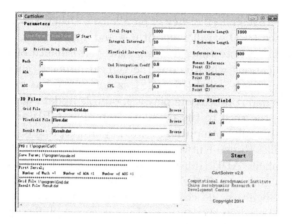

**Fig. 1.** CartSolver GUI.

CartSolver can perform plan design, aerodynamic analysis and multiple bodies separation. With this software, a large number of plans for aircraft design can be fast filtered, the whole aerodynamic features of the complex bodies can be computed, and the simulation of the multiple bodies separation of automatic positions and automatic grid update can be realized. Extensive calculations have been done for practical flow fields of fighter, missile and store separation. This software for engineering applications is applied in the numerical simulation of the complex bodies in the subsonic, transonic and supersonic flow.

### 2.2 Schemes and Methods

For the Cartesian grids, CartSolver uses a 4-stage Runge-Kutta scheme which is evolved from the widely used Jameson-Schmitt-Turkel [10] method. This scheme bases on the cell-center method, and has a widespread use in lots of applications with structured/unstructured grid.

The Runge-Kutta scheme is a typical explicit scheme which has a significant weakness. That is, the maximal time step allowed is small because of the stability limitation. To solve this problem, CartSolver adopts the local time step to accelerate the convergence.

## 3 Acceleration for CartSolver

As mentioned above, the Runge-Kutta scheme adopted in CartSolver is an explicit scheme which is born for data-parallel computing. In this section, we introduce GPU and MIC into CartSolver and expect an acceptable speedup. Three versions of accelerated CartSolver, PGI-based, CUDA-based and MIC-based, are implemented as follows.

### 3.1 Implementation by PGI Accelerator

Under GPU+CPU heterogeneous architecture, the fastest way to develop GPU-based CartSolver is to use The Portland Group (a.k.a. PGI) Accelerator with

OpenACC [20] directives. With OpenACC, an accelerator programming standard, programmers can easily take advantage of the power of the GPU accelerators. To enable the codes to run on the GPU device, we just simply add OpenACC directives, like *#pragma acc region*, ahead of the loop code, without modification to the source code itself. Those directives indicate the work region of the accelerators, and the PGI Accelerator compilers will automatically analyze the region and data that is used in that region. The codes are split by the compilers into two parts as specified by *#pragma*, one for host CPU and the other for the accelerator device. The compilers also use parallel cores, capabilities of hardware threading and SIMD vector to generate an optimized mapping of loops automatically.

With these directives, we easily make an acceleration over the original programs. However, the speedup is not as satisfied as we expected. Though there are more directives provided by the PGI Accelerator to enable us to control over the mapping of loops and the allocation of the memory in fine grain, we still need to comprehend the PGI Accelerator programming model in deep. That goes against our original intention to develop a GPU-based CartSolver in short time, and the optimization does not work well neither. To fully extract the hardware resources of GPU accelerators, we turn to CUDA for help.

### 3.2  CUDA Implementation of CartSolver

Programming with CUDA, unlike the one with PGI Accelerator, needs us to control the details in both the CFD solver itself and the CUDA programming model. First of all, which part of the codes that can be accelerated should be detected. A CFD solver usually comprises of three parts, pre-process, flow field computing and post-process, and normally, the pre-process and post-process cannot be parallelized. Therefore, the input and output of the data, convergence control and post-process are taken charge by the CPU, and the GPU focuses on the part of data-intensive parallel computing.

It is more tedious and time-consuming to accelerate a loop by CUDA. The __global__ declaration is used to distinguish the code for the CUDA kernel, and a new <<<...>>> execution configuration syntax is to invoke the CUDA threads to execute that kernel in parallel. The Single-Instruction Multiple-Thread (SIMT) architecture that CUDA adopts is much different from the CPUs. It allows the multiprocessor creates, manages, schedules, and executes threads in groups [15]. Thus in CUDA, unlike OpenMP, massive threads have to be executed concurrently to help GPU to hide the latency of the memory access to improve the computing efficiency.

In the original code of the CartSolver, the computing for the faces and cells of the Cartesian grid is mixed in the same loops, and this blocks us to achieve data parallelism. In CUDA-based CartSolver, we separate the loops into the face computing and the cell computing. One single loop is responsible for only one task, either face computing or cell computing. In the loop, one thread is in charge of one face or cell, and this thread mapping improves the computing efficiency by forcing the threads in the thread blocks to execute concurrently.

To take advantage of the latest Kepler architecture, which is adopted by Tesla K20, we use Dynamic Parallelism in this version of CUDA-based CartSolver to reduce the workload of coding. In traditional mode, such as Fermi architecture, every operation of GPU needs CPU to take part in. Dynamic Parallelism changes this situation, and GPU will dynamically update the threads while receiving the data. As the kernel is enabled to load the workload independently, this technique allows the programs running on the GPU directly.

To optimize the acceleration, Visual Profiler [14] is used to detect the key part of the CUDA program. To identify the optimization opportunities, this graphical profiling tool, launched by NVIDIA, includes an automated analysis engine, and displays a timeline of the CUDA applications activity of CPU and GPU. Profiling the solver with this tool, we find the reason why some function takes almost half of the whole time lies in that some data is not accessed coalesced. Such data is accessed many times in this program, and the performance is significantly reduced. The shared memory is employed to solve this problem. We store the data that are frequently accessed in the shared memory and it is coalesced accessed without multiple memory addressing. The greatly reduced total time demonstrates the effect of this optimization method.

The data transfer between the GPU and CPU is another performance bottleneck, because the GPU bandwidth is far more than the one of the PCI-E bus that connects the GPU and CPU. So, the data transfer between the host memory and global memory is requested to be minimized as much as possible. Unfortunately, CartSolver needs to present some aerodynamic coefficients on the interface to verify the convergence in real time, and a frequent data transfer from the global memory to the host memory is unavoidable. To solve this problem, zero-copy is used. GPU threads can directly access the host memory and avoid allocating the global memory.

Maximize register use, reducing the conditional branches, etc., are also worthy optimization methods to try and of benefit to the performance.

### 3.3    MIC Implementation of CartSolver

The major difference between MIC and GPU lies in the arithmetic unit and the thread model. MIC is based on many-core architecture, that is, it owns dozens of heavyweight cores. These cores are complete processor cores which are derived from Intel Pentium 4 CPU. Though the number of cores is much smaller than the one in Kepler, they are very powerful in performance and function. Consequently, MIC is capable of coarse-grained parallelism by heavyweight cores and fine-grained parallelism by instructions. By contrast, the massive lightweight cores in GPU architecture rely on fine-grained parallelism to show their high performance.

Another difference between the two is the program tuning. Based on traditional CPU and X86 instruction sets, MIC can inherit the original programming model, and make us easily code and optimize. As for GPU, its novel architecture burdens us with considerations for more details. Nevertheless, programmers can control the CUDA code deeply while the tuning for the MIC code only counts on digging the instruction-level parallelism.

To transfer CartSolver to the MIC platform, MIC provides kinds of programming models. Among them, the simplest way is to use OpenMP to parallelize the original serial codes and add the compiler option -mmic. Like PGI Accelerator with OpenACC, it seems very easy to accelerate the application by MIC, but the speedup turns out not satisfied. To dig the bottle-neck of the performance, an open source performance analysis tool, LIKWID [11] (Like I Knew What Im Doing), is used to help us to inquire the architecture information, memory usage, CPU performance counters, etc. This lightweight tool, developed by University Erlangen, features easy-to-use, portability and extendibility. With LIKWID, we can display and toggle the pre-fetch state of the hardware units on X86 processors by *likwid-features*, show the topology structure of the hardware threads and cache by *likwid-topology* to guide the locality, collect kinds of hardware indexes by *likwid-perfctr* to find the performance hotspot, and bind the threads and cores by *likwid-pin* to avoid the automatic deployment.

By LIKWID, we find that the first version of MIC-based CartSolver does not take advantage of the biggest feature, the wide vector. In this instruction level, there are two options to vectorization, the automatic vectorization and SIMD instruction optimization. The former is to check the vectorization report and insert the directives into the codes which are apt to be vectorized. For those that inclines to resist the vectorization, SIMD instructions are preferred. There has always been a performance problem in the automatic vectorization by the compiler, so the latter option, to manually rewrite the code, is necessary. Fortunately, we manage to vectorize the key computing codes and improves the speedup.

To improve the usage of the hardware resource of Intel Xeon Phi, MIC-based CartSolver tries best to abide the coarse-grained parallel principle. Cache blocking strategy is also adopted to ease the memory wall and it can improve the cache usage by maximizing data reuse. Another optimization method used is the Huge Page, which makes Translation Lookaside Buffer (TLB) map larger area of the virtual memory and the miss rate is reduced accordingly.

## 4    Experiments and Results

In this section, a number of experiments are conducted to evaluate the three versions of accelerated CartSolver. We firstly adopt a simple ball model to validate the correctness and accuracy, then compare the speedup for a real complex model, and finally discuss the workload to guide the future acceleration for CFD applications. Here, for simplicity, CPU-based is the original CartSolver executed serially, PGI-Fermi is the solver implemented by the PGI Accelerator under the Fermi architecture, PGI-Kepler is the PGI version under the Kepler architecture, CUDA-Fermi indicates CUDA-based under Fermi [19], CUDA-Kepler is the CUDA-based under Kepler, and MIC-based is the one for MIC implementation of CartSolver. The results in the following tables are all average values from multiple experiments.

### 4.1  Computer Configurations

The computer configurations for these experiments are shown in Table 1.

**Table 1.** Computer Configurations

| Device | Configuration |
|---|---|
| CPU | Intel Core i7 CPU 950 |
| Memory | 4 GB (2 x 2 GB DDR3) |
| GPU | NVIDIA Tesla C2050; |
| | NVIDIA Tesla K20; |
| Operating System | Windows XP SP3 |
| C++ | Visual Studio 2010, compile optimize option -O3 |
| CUDA | Version 5.0 |
| MIC | Intel Xeon Phi |

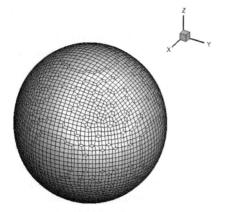

**Fig. 2.** The Cartesian grid of the ball model.

**Fig. 3.** The Mach number distribution of Mach 0.2 flow around the ball.

### 4.2  Compute Model

Figure 2 shows the Cartesian grid of the simple ball model.

### 4.3  Correctness and Accuracy Validation

The Mach number distribution of Mach 0.2 flow around the ball is shown in Fig. 3. The normal force (CN) values which are computed by different versions of solvers are compared in Fig. 4. The six convergence curves almost overlap each other, which means the output by the accelerated solvers all keeps very close to the standard result which is output by the CPU-based in single float precision.

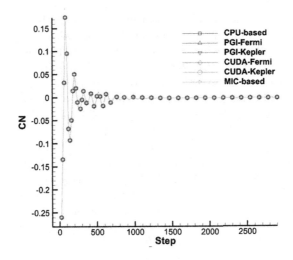

**Fig. 4.** Comparison of CN convergence curves.

**Table 2.** Speedup contrast of the ball model

| Solver | Running time (s) | Speedup |
|---|---|---|
| CPU-based | 1199.3 | 1.0 |
| PGI-Fermi | 497.63 | 2.41 |
| PGI-Kepler | 367.66 | 3.26 |
| CUDA-Fermi | 160.76 | 7.46 |
| CUDA-Kepler | 118.89 | 10.08 |
| MIC-based | 134.25 | 8.93 |

**Table 3.** Speedup contrast of the real model

| Solver | Running time (s) | Speedup |
|---|---|---|
| CPU-based | 9859.7 | 1.0 |
| PGI-Fermi | 3520.6 | 2.80 |
| PGI-Kepler | 2629.2 | 3.75 |
| CUDA-Fermi | 1156.15 | 8.53 |
| CUDA-Kepler | 770.13 | 12.80 |
| MIC-based | 962.67 | 10.25 |

## 4.4 Speedup Comparison

Table 2 gives the comparison of the speedup of all versions for the ball model. The speedup here, which is the final result after full optimization, equals dividing the running time of the CPU-based solver by the running time of the corresponding solver. As we can see, though the PGI version is fast to develop, its speedup is less than the half of the others. It is also seen that CUDA in the latest architecture performs better than MIC. The contrast between CUDA-Fermi and CUDA-Kepler confirms the advance of the Kepler architecture.

For a real model, we use a complex body which is much larger than the simple model. The comparison of the speedup, shown in Table 3, also proves the performance of the accelerators. The 12.80x with CUDA and 10.25x with MIC is satisfied and of great engineering significance. Meanwhile, as all the speedup for the real model are larger than the corresponding one for the ball model, the scalability of the parallel algorithm for the accelerators is proved.

For the real model, deeper researches are done into the optimizations.

Figure 5 illustrates the effect of the optimization methods in CUDA programming. CUDA-no-Op, which is the accelerated version without any optimization, barely achieves a 8.29x speedup over the CPU-based. The fast increment from 8.29 to 12.15 shows that, the shared memory which is used in *CUDA-SharedMem*, makes a great effect in the optimization. Such a progress benefits from the performance profiling by Visual Profiler. The speedup rises slowly after zero-copy is applied in *CUDA-ZeroCpy* and other optimization methods added in *CUDA-full-Op* turn out not good enough for this solver, neither.

A similar experiment is conducted to confirm the effect of the optimizations on MIC. In Fig. 6, a 3.41x speedup is achieved via *MIC-Omp* immediately the original code is parallelized by OpenMP. The *MIC-Vec* with vectorization makes a big step for the speedup. This indicates that, to get a better speedup on MIC, the wide vector should be made good use of. We can also see that, cache blocking and Huge Page are very important to MIC optimization, because the speedup increases 50 % after they are used in *MIC-full-Op*.

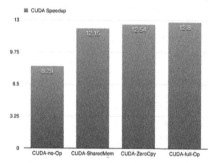
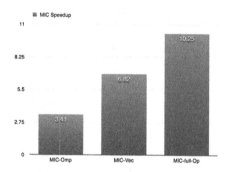

**Fig. 5.** Speedup contrast of the CUDA optimizations.

**Fig. 6.** Speedup contrast of the MIC optimizations.

### 4.5   Workload Comparison

Though the CUDA-based CartSolver obtains the largest speedup, the time cost in this implementation also rank the first. Thus, several criteria are used to compare the workload among the versions.

The first one is the ratio of line of code (LoC) changed, which equals dividing the number of the lines of the codes added or modified in the accelerated version by the total number of the lines of the original CPU-based codes. As illustrated in Fig. 7, for the 6000+ lines of the key codes for CFD flow field computing, the change of 35.2 % codes for CUDA-Fermi seems not very easy to finish. Though the new feature Dynamic Parallelism is adopted in CUDA-Kepler to reduce the workload, the ratio, 28.7 %, is far beyond the one of PGI-based and MIC-based. Here, as the codes for the PGI-Fermi and PGI-Kepler are the same, PGI-based is on behalf of these two.

Compared with PGI-based, MIC-based seems to gain a satisfying speedup without much code rewrite. However, in fact, many optimization methods, like vectorization, cache blocking, Huge Page, etc., are under consideration, and this version of CartSolver is also time-consuming work. Therefore, another criterion for the workload is the time cost. It is clearly seen in Fig. 8 that, the long time MIC-based takes, which is even more than CUDA-Kepler does, restore the difficulty of the optimizations on MIC. Note that, though the speedup is not good enough, such a fast solution to speed up the solver in only 10 and a half hours by PGI Accelerator is very attractive. This implies that, with acceptable speedup, PGI Accelerator can be adopted for fast development or program validation in the future development of GPU-based software. The long time bar in Fig. 8 demonstrates CUDA-based versions, including CUDA-Fermi and Cuda-Kepler, time-consuming work again.

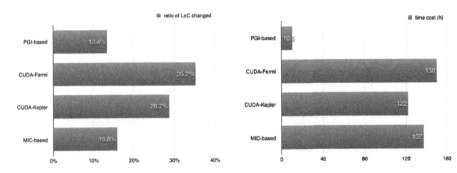

**Fig. 7.** The ratio of line of code changed for the solvers.

**Fig. 8.** The contrast of the time cost of speeding up the solver.

As mentioned above, to compare the ratio or the time alone does not properly reflect the real workload. To combine the two criteria, we define a new criterion, Workload per Speedup (WPS), in Eq. 5.

$$WPS = \frac{Ratio_{LoC} \times CostTime}{Speedup} \qquad (1)$$

Here, $Ratio_{LoC}$ indicates the ratio of LoC changed, CostTime indicates the time cost for acceleration and Speedup is the speedup achieved. This criterion measures how much workload needs to be paid when we want to get a 1x speedup. The larger WPS is, the more work is to be done.

This criterion compared in Fig. 9 reflects not only the workload of coding but also the time spent for the whole conversion process. As the difference between PGI-Fermi and PGI-Kepler only lies in the GPU used, we use PGI-Keplers speedup to compute PGI-based WPS. The value of 0.38 proves the simplicity and rapidity of the PGI Accelerator again. Note that the speedup of PGI-based may not be unacceptable, then the overworked CUDA-based or MIC-based has to be carried out.

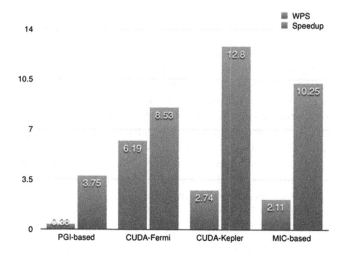

**Fig. 9.** The Workload per Speedup of the solver acceleration.

**Table 4.** Speedup Contrast of Other Real Models

| Solver | Speedup | | | |
|---|---|---|---|---|
|  | Model A | Model B | Model C | Model D |
| PGI-based | 3.75 | 3.22 | 4.78 | 2.63 |
| CUDA-based | 12.80 | 13.67 | 17.86 | 12.04 |
| MIC-based | 10.25 | 10.18 | 14.53 | 8.30 |

It can be seen in Fig. 9 that, though the speedup of CUDA-Kepler is larger than the one of MIC-based, the WPS values trend the same. Far below the 6.19 of CUDA-Fermi, the WPS value of CUDA-Kepler is still a little larger than the one of MIC-based. Taken together, the workload for CUDA-Kepler and MIC-based is close.

Generally speaking, for this kind of CFD software which uses explicit schemes, recommendations are given as follows:

- If a small speedup is acceptable, PGI Accelerator is the first choice for the fast development.
- For a larger speedup, CUDA-based and MIC-based has to be optimized both. It is time-consuming, but turns out worthwhile.
- The speedup results of other real models presented in Table 4 expose one fact, that CUDA-based CartSolver under the Kepler architecture always runs the fastest.

In contrast to the previous work, the speedup achieved may not be good enough. However, the solver implemented aims at 3-D Euler equations, and the compute model is complex. As it is used for practical applications and encapsulated in mature software, that speedup is promising and of great engineering significance.

## 5 Conclusions

In this paper, three versions of CartSolver, PGI-based, CUDA-based and MIC-based are implemented and optimized. The differences between the architectures of GPU and MIC are discussed and the expected speedup is achieved by adopting many optimization methods. Based on the experimental results, we propose WPS criterion to measure the workload and recommend selecting suitable accelerators for the development on different purposes.

In future, we are working on applying accelerators and coprocessors to the practical CFD engineering software. The CFD parallel computing under many-core heterogeneous architecture is also going to be further explored.

## References

1. Antoniou, A.S., Karantasis, K.I., Polychronopoulos, E.D.: Acceleration of a finite difference weno scheme for large-scale simulations on many-core architectures. In: Proceedings of the 48th AIAA Aerospace Sciences Meeting Including the New Horizons Forum and Aerospace Exposition, AIAA-2010-525. (2010)
2. Bader, M., Bungartz, H.J., Mudigere, D., Narasimhan, S., Narayanan, B.: Fast GPGPU Data Rearrangement Kernels using CUDA. Technical report arXiv:1011.3583 (2010)
3. Liu, Y., Liu, Y.C., Wang, F., Bai, H.L.: A GPU-based CFD Solver. In: Transaction of Nanjing University of Aeronautica & Astronautica, vol. 30(S), pp. 101–106 (2013)
4. Yang, X.J., Liao, X.K., Lu, K., et al.: The TianHe-1A supercomputer: its hardware and software. J. Comput. Sci. Technol. **26**(3), 344–351 (2011)
5. Xiao, H.S., Chen, Z.B., Liu, G., Jiang, X.: Applicarions of 3-D adaptive Cartesian grid algorithm based on the Euler equations. Acta Aerodyn. Sin. **21**(2), 202–210 (2003)
6. Levesque, J.M.: Application development for titan - a multi-petaflop hybrid-multicore MPP system. In: High Performance Computing, Networking, Storage and Analysis (SCC), 2012 SC Companion, pp. 1731–1821. IEEE (2012)
7. Gibbs, P.E.: Supercomputers, artificial intelligence & brain power. Prespacetime J. **4**(7), 725–728 (2013)
8. Vladimirov, A., Addison, C.: Cluster-level tuning of a shallow water equation solver on the Intel MIC architecture. Eprint Arxiv: 1408 (2014)
9. Intel Corporation: Intel Xeon Phi Coprocessor System Software Developers Guide. SKU: 328207–001EN (2012)
10. Jameson, A., Schmitt, W., Turkel, E.: Numerical Solutions of the Euler Equations by Finite Volume Methods using Runge-Kutta Time-Stepping Schemes. AIAA Paper 81–1259 (1981)
11. Treibig, J., Hager, G., Wellein, G.: LIKWID: Lightweight Performance Tools. In: Bischof, C., Hegering, H.-G., Nagel, W.E., Wittum, G. (eds.) Competence in High Performance Computing (CiHPC) 2010, pp. 165–175. Springer, New York (2012)

12. Jarvis, S.A.: Exploring SIMD for molecular dynamics, using intel xeon processors and intel xeon phi coprocessors. In: IEEE 27th International Symposium on Parallel & Distributed Processing (IPDPS), pp. 1085–1097. IEEE (2013)
13. Aoki, T.: Application Performances on Many-core Processors Xeon Phi versus Kepler GPU. Tokyo Institute of Technology, pp. 1–10 (2013)
14. NVIDIA Corporation: CUDA Profiler User Guide, v5.0. (2012)
15. NVIDIA Corporation: NVIDIA CUDA C Programming Guide, v5.0 (2012)
16. Deng, L.: Many-core Parallel Computing for Typical Implicit CFD Methods. National University of Defense Technology (2013)
17. Crespo, A.J.C., Domnguez, J.M., Rogers, B.D., et al.: DualSPHysics: open-source parallel CFD solver based on Smoothed Particle Hydrodynamics (SPH). Compu. Phy. Commun. **187**, 204–216 (2015)
18. Reguly, I.Z., Mudalige, G.R., Bertolli, C., et al.: Acceleration of a Full-scale Industrial CFD Application with OP2. eprint arXiv: 1403.7209 (2014)
19. Liu, Y., Pang, Y.F., Chen, B., Xiao, H.S., Bai, H.L.: CUDA implementation of a euler solver for cartesian grid. In: IEEE 10th International Conference on High Performance Computing and Communications, pp. 1308–1314. IEEE (2013)
20. The Portland Group: PGI Accelerator Programming Model for Fortran & C, v1.3 (2010)
21. Thibault J.C., Senocak, I.: CUDA implementation of a navier- stokes solver on multi-GPU desktop platforms for incompressible flows. In: Proccedings of the 47th AIAA Aerospace Sciences Meeting, AAIA-2009-758 (2009)
22. Che, Y.: Microarchitectural performance comparison of Intel Knights Corner and Intel Sandy Bridge with CFD applications. J. Supercomput. **70**(1), 321–348 (2014)
23. Li, Y., Che, Y., Wang, Z.: Performance evaluation and scalability analysis of NPB-MZ on intel xeon phi coprocessor. In: Xu, W., Xiao, L., Zhang, C., Li, J., Yu, L. (eds.) NCCET 2013. CCIS, vol. 396, pp. 143–152. Springer, Heidelberg (2013)
24. Che, Y., Zhang, L., Wang, Y., Xu, C., Liu, W., Cheng, X.: Performance optimization of a CFD application on intel multicore and manycore architectures. In: Wu, J., Chen, H., Wang, X. (eds.) ACA 2014. CCIS, vol. 451, pp. 83–97. Springer, Heidelberg (2014)

# Author Index

Abawajy, Jemal  627
Asghar, Muhammad Rizwan  57

Ba, Haihe  691
Bate, Iain  819
Bhuiyan, Md Zakirul Alam  531
Bin, Dongmei  293, 311
Bondavalli, Andrea  187

Cao, Buyang  333
Cao, Meili  3
Cao, Yangjie  405, 413
Castiglione, Aniello  572
Ceccarelli, Andrea  187
Chaisiri, Sivadon  57
Cheang, Aloysius  57
Chen, Biwen  133
Chen, Hao  454
Chen, Hongbin  344
Chen, Liu  659
Chen, Mei  606
Chen, Mingyu  617
Chen, Peixin  46, 593, 633
Chen, Shuhui  111
Chen, Song-Jhih  435
Chen, Weidong  791
Chen, Xiaohong  166
Chen, Zhenxiang  487, 497
Chung, Chun-Jen  582

Dai, Zhenyu  606
Das, Anjana P.  757
Deng, Jun  454
Deng, Liang  835
Dobbie, Gill  57
Dong, Jian  393
Dong, Qi  454
Du, Huisen  100
Duan, Pengsong  413

Eom, Taehoon  746
Esposito, Christian  572

Felemban, Emad  648
Fortin, Jean  222
Fu, Binzhang  617
Fu, Xue  771
Fu, Yanming  322

Gan, Jiayi  35
Gao, Jianhua  771
Gao, Xianming  364
Gava, Frédéric  222
Geng, Jinkun  143
Gong, Xiaolong  302
Gong, Zhenghu  561
Gopal, Greeshma N.  445
Gorawska, Anna  251, 714
Gorawski, Marcin  251, 714
Gorawski, Michał  714
Grampone, Silvia  724
Guan, Wei  454
Guo, Li  71

Han, Hongbo  487, 497
Hao, Huikang  153
Hassan, Mohammad Mehedi  627
He, Haizhen  3
He, Xiangjian  669
He, Yueying  153
Hei, Qiaoxiang  85
Holmes, Geoffrey  57
Hong, Jin B.  582, 746
Hong, Tie  691
Hou, Shifeng  487, 497
Huang, Dijiang  582
Huang, Fanling  322
Huang, Menglin  606, 781
Huo, Zhisheng  353

Ilyas, H. Muhammed  476, 508

Jia, Weijia  13
Jiang, Jianhui  736
Jiang, Shuangshuang  85

Jiang, Yunxiang 393
Jin, Qun 166
Johannes, Adrian 669

Kim, Dong Seong 582, 746
Ko, Ryan K.L. 57

Lan, Yuqing 211
Lbath, Ahmed 648
Lee, Cheng-Chi 435
Lei, Wentai 393
Li, Ang 353
Li, Chengye 465
Li, Chuanfeng 405
Li, Chun-Ta 435
Li, Hongyuan 606
Li, Hui 606, 781
Li, Qun 487
Li, Tao 85
Li, Wen-Xiang 551
Li, Xianxian 120
Li, Xin 177
Li, Yiming 691
Li, Zhi 810
Li, Zhoujun 153
Liao, Qun 85
Lin, Tao 771
Lin, Yan 771
Litwin, Witold 724
Liu, Guiyun 344
Liu, Jing 521
Liu, Kelong 353
Liu, Keyan 781
Liu, Lifang 382
Liu, Ming 322
Liu, Ping 71
Liu, Yanbing 71
Liu, Yang 835
Liu, Yanzhu 810
Liu, Yuling 24
Liu, Zuhong 24
Lu, Huimin 413
Lu, Zheqi 353
Luo, Ping 143
Luo, Rongming 3
Luo, Zhipeng 454
Lv, Gaofeng 561

Ma, Jianhua 166
Ma, Jinxin 153

Ma, Shicong 364
Ma, Ya-Jie 551
Ma, Yanyu 781
Ma, Zheng 13
Malekzadeh, Mahnaz 819
Mo, Binji 370

Nair, Deepa S. 508
Nanda, Priyadarsi 669
Nelson, Richard 57
Nie, Luyan 177
Nie, Yalin 405

Palmieri, Francesco 572
Pang, Shaoning 57
Panicker, Janu R. 476
Park, Jong Sou 746
Peng, Chunhua 393
Peng, Ying 311
Peng, Zhen 531
Pi, Chun-Chun 551

Qi, Fang 701
Qi, Xiaogang 382
Qiu, Nengjun 606

Ran, Cong 551
Raphel, Roshni Kadeparambil 476
Ravi, Rajeswary 445
Ren, Jiangchun 691
Ruan, Li 353
Russello, Giovanni 57

Sarrafzadeh, Abdolhossein 57
Schiavone, Enrico 187
Schwarz, Thomas SJ 724
Sheikh, Adil Amjad 648
Shen, Hua 133
Sheng, Yu-Xia 551
Shi, Jiangyong 465
Shi, Ronghua 393
Shi, Wei 561
Shi, Xiaodong 413
Siedlecki, Zacheusz 251
Skrzewski, Mirosław 714
Song, Hong 276, 541
Su, Jinshu 46, 111, 593, 633
Sun, Yuxia 810
Sun, Zeyu 405
Sun, Zhigang 561

Tang, Dong   344
Tang, Kun   393
Tang, Wenjuan   264
Tang, Xin   701
Tang, Yong   829
Thampi, Sabu M.   757

Wang, Baosheng   364
Wang, Caocai   293
Wang, Changji   521
Wang, Chun-Cheng   435
Wang, Dacheng   541
Wang, Gaocai   302, 311
Wang, Guojun   13, 264, 370, 531, 678
Wang, Jianxin   541
Wang, Li-e   120
Wang, Nao   293, 302
Wang, Shan   781
Wang, Shanshan   497
Wang, Tian   531
Wang, Weiping   276
Wang, Xiaofeng   46, 111, 593, 633
Wang, Yufeng   166
Wang, Zhen   736
Wang, Zhihai   791
Wang, Zhiying   691
Wang, Zhuanning   201
Warriach, Ehsan Ullah   648
Wei, Bo   100
Wei, Quanyun   701
Wei, Xia   551
Wen, Lei   3
Williams, Ken   238
Wu, Qing   201
Wu, Weiguo   405
Wu, Xiaoqiang   531

Xia, Qingxin   211
Xiang, Yangyue   465
Xiao, Hongling   276
Xiao, Limin   211, 353
Xie, Chuanzhi   177
Xie, Mande   382
Xing, Xiaofei   405
Xu, Chengcheng   111
Xu, Hongyun   35
Xu, Jun   829

Xu, Mengzhen   35
Xu, Sheng   617
Xu, Yang   264, 370, 678
Xu, Yun   541
Xu, Zheng   333

Yang, Jun   35
Yang, Lijuan   678
Yang, Liu   424
Yang, Tzu-Hui   435
Yang, Xiaoling   322
Yang, Yulu   85
Yao, Jing   344
Ye, Daren   143
Yin, Yujun   177
You, Ilsun   593
Yu, Huiming   238
Yu, Jing   71
Yu, Yang   454
Yuan, Xiaohong   238

Zang, Yuanyuan   353
Zhang, Fengli   800
Zhang, Han   344
Zhang, Junjiao   800
Zhang, Lei   487, 497
Zhang, Leyou   201
Zhang, Lixin   617
Zhang, Mingwu   133
Zhang, Weixiang   100
Zhang, Wenhao   541
Zhang, Xiao   781
Zhang, Xiaojie   293
Zhang, Xiaozhe   364
Zhang, Yaoxue   264
Zhang, Yong   35
Zhang, Yu   71
Zhao, Baokang   593
Zheng, Gengzhong   382
Zheng, Jin   13
Zheng, Xin   293
Zhong, Qiaoling   353
Zhou, Hongchuan   800
Zhou, Huaizhe   691
Zhou, Wei   659, 678
Zhou, Xin   781
Zhu, Ming   606, 781